ENCYCLOPEDIA
OF THE
STRANGE,
MYSTICAL, &
UNEXPLAINED

Titles of Similar Interest from Random House Value Publishing, Inc.

Astrological Secrets for the New Millennium

Encyclopedia of Unsolved Mysteries

Elvis Speaks from the Beyond and other Celebrity Ghost Stories

History of Magic and the Occult

Mysteries and Monsters of the Sea

Psychic Pets and Spirit Animals

Reincarnation and Your Past Memories

Strange But True

A Treasury of Superstitions

ENCYCLOPEDIA
OF THE
STRANGE, MYSTICAL, & UNEXPLAINED

Rosemary Ellen Guiley

Introduction by
Marion Zimmer Bradley

Gramercy Books
New York

This 2001 edition is published by Gramercy Books™, an imprint of Random House Value Publishing, Inc. 280 Park Avenue, New York, N.Y. 10017 by arrangement with Visionary Living, Inc.

Gramercy Books™ and design are trademarks of Random House Value Publishing, Inc.

Printed and bound in the United States of America.

(Previously published as Harper's Encyclopedia of Mystical and Paranormal Experience)

Random House
New York • Toronto • London • Sydney • Auckland
http://www.randomhouse.com/

Library of Congress Cataloging-in-Publication Data

Guiley, Rosemary.
    [Harper's encyclopedia of mystical & paranormal experience]
    Encyclopdia of the strange, mystical, and unexplained / Rosemary Ellen Guiley ; foreword by Marion Zimmer Bradley.
        p. cm.
    Originally published: Harper's encyclopedia of mystical & paranormal experience. 1st ed. San Francisco : HarperSanFrancisco, c1991.
    Includes bibliographical references.
    ISBN 0-517-16278-4 (hardcover)
        1. Occultism--Encyclopedias. 2. Parapsychology--Encyclopedias. 3. Supernatural--Encyclopedias. I. Title.

BF1407 .G85 2001
133'.03 2 21
                                                                                    2001023879

9 8 7 6 5 4 3 2 1

Illustration credits:
Page 86: From *The Chakras and the Human Energy Fields* by Shafica Kangulla, M.D. and Dora Van Gelder Kunz. Reprinted by permission of the Theosophical Publishing House. Page 121: Photo by Leon Isaacs. Courtesy The White Eagle Lodge. Page 133: Photos by Bonnie Sue. Used with permission. Page 186: Photo by Bonnie Sue. Courtesy the Foundation for Research on the Nature of Man. Page 352: Photo by Bonnie Sue. Courtesy Craig Junjulas. Page 490: Photo by Norman Seef. Courtesy Concept: Synergy. Page 525: Photo by Nandlal Ramyda, United Nations. Courtesy Dr. Erlendur Haraldsson. Page 602: Photo by Bonnie Sue. Reprinted by permission of Morgan Press Inc., 145 Palisades Street, Dobbs Ferry, NY 10522. Cards © Morgan Press.

For
James G. Matlock

Contents

Foreword

When I was first asked to write a foreword for this encyclopedia, I wasn't exactly enthusiastic. Reading an unbound manuscript almost ten inches tall is a bit of an ordeal. At least it takes a considerable stretch of the imagination to imagine what the final printed and bound volume will be like.

However, I remembered Rosemary's *The Encyclopedia of Witches and Witchcraft,* which adorns my own coffee table. I thought it an excellent book and quite worthy, so I agreed.

Among the virtual flood of books on the occult with which bookstores have been cluttered of late, this book stands out. I find it hard to imagine a better book for browsing or one that is likely to give the neophyte more comprehensive information on the subject. Even the person who is well informed is likely to find out *something* he or she didn't already know. And, after all, for what other purpose is an encyclopedia intended?

The classic book review, "This tells me more about penguins than I care to know," has always been a pitfall of encyclopedists. This is not the case with *Encyclopedia of the Strange, Mystical, and Unexplained.* Of course, it does not cover absolutely everything. No human work can do that. But, by and large, it informs readers about anything they're likely to want to know without boring them with irrelevant material.

I cannot tell you whether you are going to want to put this book on your coffee table, because interior decoration is not within my field of expertise, no matter how loosely that subject is defined. What I can say is that it's certainly good reading. It ought to be fun for the casual browser as well as the serious seeker of information, and it's likely to turn the former into the latter.

One of things I like most to do is start out in a book like this almost anywhere, find something so fascinating that one thing simply leads to another, and before you know it you've read the whole thing through.

Especially in these troubled times, we need information, and we need it badly. In fact, acquiring information can be the substitute for all those things to which we're supposed to "just say no." I sincerely believe that one of the things we can put in the place of any socially disapproved behavior is the gathering of information, one of the more satisfying things anyone can do.

And so publishing an encyclopedia in this day and age can contribute to one of the major spiritual challenges of our time. I don't know whether that's what Rosemary Ellen Guiley or her publishers first set out to do. But whether they know it or not, that's what they've done. And for that, I salute them.

Marion Zimmer Bradley

Preface

This book is a result of my personal odyssey into "alternate realities," which began years ago. As anyone else who has undertaken such a quest also knows, the subjects are many and the literature vast. Reading to find answers raises more questions in the process.

Early on in this quest, I began to wish for a handy reference—something that would provide a quick grasp of subjects and concepts that were new to me. I envisioned a book that would both satisfy an immediate need to know and stimulate deeper inquiries into subjects of particular interest. Looking around, I didn't find anything quite like what I had in mind. Years passed and eventually a series of synchronicities opened up an opportunity for me to materialize my own wish.

This encyclopedia is intended for the layperson who is curious about a good many topics that fall under the "alternate realities" umbrella. I use the term "alternate realities" for want of a better one. "Occult" is too limited and, for many, a tainted term; "supernatural" has its limitations as well. "New Age" came and, thankfully, went. Unfortunately, there is no broad, definitive term to describe the range of subjects that pique one's curiosity on a spiritual quest. "Alternate realities" suggests the worlds that open up through many paths of inquiry.

It was not difficult to decide what to include in the book. Rather, it was difficult to decide what to leave out. The book gives preference to subject over person. While it does include a number of biographies of people of historical note and popular interest, biographies were limited in favor of phenomena, disciplines, systems, philosophies, traditions, and concepts. The emphasis throughout is on experience. That emphasis, I believe, will be particularly helpful to those readers who are trying to understand and come to terms with unusual experiences they have had themselves. Some of my own experiences have become part of the research.

The book is not meant to be definitive, but a reflection of evolving thought. The reader will find that a good many of the subjects offer widely disparate theories and points of view. I have attempted to give objective overviews. Admittedly, I am not a skeptic, though I seek to be open-minded and consider all possible sides and arguments. The sources listed at the end of every entry will open additional doors for the reader who wishes to explore a topic further. Due to space limitations, and because sources are listed throughout, there is no bibliography at the end of the book. Sources include approximately 1,100 books and several hundred periodical articles.

My own interests have always been eclectic, which I believe is typical of the interests of many others. Consequently, I have sought to include a range of subjects under one cover. One scientist I interviewed expressed his unhappiness that parapsychology would be included with such topics as Tarot and channeling. Why shouldn't one have diverse interests? Casting a wide net is part of the discovery process. When a spiritual quest begins, one wishes to learn about a good many things. Only when one is informed can one make decisions about what to accept and what to reject. I hope that the reader who picks up this book because of an interest in one topic will in turn be introduced to something new.

Acknowledgments

I am deeply grateful to the many people who provided material, art, or critiques that helped the realization of this book. I would like to give special thanks to: Joanne P. Austin and Margaret Guiley, Seattle, and Don Wigal, Ph.D., and Bruce S. Trachtenberg, New York, for their meticulous help in the research and compilation of many entries; James G. Matlock, New York, parapsychologist and anthropologist, for his review of a substantial portion of this book, and for his comments and suggestions, which were of great help to me; Elda Hartley, founder of Hartley Films, Cos Cob, Connecticut, for providing me numerous photos taken during her many years as film chronicler of spiritual quests; and photographer Bonnie Sue, Somers, New York, for providing numerous photos as well. Special thanks also to Dorothy Kroll and Patricia Godfrey, New Jersey, for their help in research.

I also would like to thank the following individuals and organizations for their assistance: Reneé Haynes, past president of the Society for Psychical Research, London; the staff of the American Society for Psychical Research, New York; Eileen Coly, president of the Parapsychology Foundation, New York; author Tom Perrott, president of The Ghost Club, London; Susan Jion Postal, Zen priest, Meeting House Zen Group, Rye, New York; Tinley Nyandak, information officer of the Office of Tibet, New York; Celia Regan, public information officer of Sarah Lawrence College, Bronxville, New York; author Peter Russell, London; Thomas Berry, director of the Riverdale Center of Religious Research, Bronx, New York; Charles Honorton, director of the former Psychophysical Research Laboratories, Princeton, New Jersey; Peter M. Rojcewicz, assistant professor of folklore and humanities at the Juilliard School, New York; author David Spangler, Seattle; author and spiritual teacher Ram Dass; Colum Hayward, executive director of The White Eagle Publishing Trust, New Liss and London, England; Sir George Trevelyan, founder of the Wrekin Trust, West Malvern, England; the Krishnamurti Society of America, Ojai, California; author Dick Sutphen; the Sun Bear Tribe, Spokane, Washington; the Fifth Epochal Fellowship (formerly the Urantia Brotherhood), Chicago; and psychic and author Craig Junjulas, New Rochelle, New York.

Finally, I would like to thank my editor at HarperSanFrancisco, Mark D. Salzwedel, for shepherding this book through a lengthy and at times complicated creation process, and for providing me with guidance and numerous research materials.

Harper's Encyclopedia of Mystical & Paranormal Experience

A

A Course in Miracles

A self-study spiritual development course that was channeled through an atheist over a seven-year period, from 1965 to 1972. *A Course in Miracles* is a three-volume work comprising over 1,100 pages: a 622-page *Text,* which lays the theoretical foundation; a 478-page *Workbook for Students,* which includes 365 lessons, one for each day; and an 87-page *Manual for Teachers.*

Though written in Christian terminology for a contemporary audience, the material espouses no single religion, but has a broad mystical foundation of eternal truths. It is closely related to the Hindu Vedas. The *Course* is Zen-like in its approach to "holy instants," moment-to-moment experiences of truth achieved through love, forgiveness, and atonement. Like mainstream Christianity it denies reincarnation.

The basic message of the *Course* is that all human beings share a oneness of love and the capacity for compassion, forgiveness, and peace. It instructs in ageless lessons, such as love thy neighbor, love thyself, and forgive and forget. It stresses that rather than trying to reform the world, one must change oneself and one's view of the world. It defines miracles as shifts in perception that remove the blocks to one's awareness of love's presence, which are inherent in human-

kind. The opposite of love is not hate but fear.

The *Course* does not claim to be the only path to enlightenment. The *Manual* states that "Christ takes many forms with different names until their oneness can be recognized."

The *Course* was dictated by a clear inner voice to Helen Cohen Schucman, a psychologist at Presbyterian Hospital in New York and an assistant professor of psychology at Columbia University's College of Physicians and Surgeons. Schucman was born in the early 1900s to a Jewish family, but later became an atheist. For years she had experienced visions she called "mental pictures," which came to her like black-and-white still photographs. In the 1960s the visions began to appear in color and motion, and in meaningful sequences. The same changes occurred in her dreams. Schucman kept hearing a silent inner voice, which she called simply the "Voice." She feared she was going insane.

At the same time, she was undergoing stress at work. Schucman shared her visions and fears with William Thetford, her supervisor, who thought she might be having psychic experiences.

In September 1965 she felt she was about to begin something very unusual. A month later the Voice began dictating the *Course* with the opening words, "This is a course in miracles. Please take notes."

Frightened, Schucman wanted nothing to do with the Voice, but felt compelled to continue. She took the dictation in shorthand from the Voice almost daily, sometimes several times a day. It always resumed dictation precisely where it had left off, no matter how much time elapsed between sessions. Courteously, it never intruded during her work or social activities. The Voice never identified itself. It was clear but silent. Schucman never entered a trance or wrote automatically.

Schucman shared the material with Thetford. He encouraged her to continue, though the experiences greatly upset her.

Some of the material was dictated in prose, some was dictated in blank verse or iambic pentameter. Occasionally, Schucman was tempted to change the words that were dictated, but always restored them to their original dictation. Until almost the end of the project, she was fearful of the content of the material, and repeatedly expressed no interest in reading what the Voice had given her.

Beginning in 1971 Schucman and Thetford arranged the *Text* into chapters and subsections. By September 1972 the *Manual* was finished, completing the entire work. The Voice predicted that a woman would come along who would know what to do with it.

That woman was Judith R. Skutch, president of the Foundation for ParaSensory Investigation. In 1975 she met Thetford and Schucman, who gave her a copy of the *Course*. Skutch and her husband, Robert, changed the name of their foundation to the Foundation for Inner Peace. In 1976 they dedicated it to publishing and distributing the *Course*. Information spread solely through word-of-mouth. Schucman and Thetford chose to remain anonymous, but acted as advisers to the Foundation. Study groups, independent of the foundation, have been started around the world.

The Voice continued to speak to Schucman, who wrote down a collection of poems. According to her wishes, her name was not revealed until after her death in February 1981. The Foundation for Inner Peace published her poems as *The Gifts of God*. See **Channeling**.

Sources: A Course in Miracles: Manual for Teachers. Tiburon, CA: Foundation for Inner Peace, 1975; "Interview: Judith R. Skutch." *New Realities* 1, no. 1 (1977): 17–25; Robert Skutch. *Journey without Distance: The Story behind a Course in Miracles*. Berkeley, CA: Celestial Arts, 1984; Robert Skutch. "The Incredible Untold Story Behind *A Course in Miracles*." *New Realities* 6, no. 1 (July/August 1984): 17–27; Brian Van der Horst. "Simple, Dumb, Boring Truths and *A Course in Miracles*." *New Realities* 1, no. 1 (1977): 8–15+; Brian Van der Horst. "Miracles Come of Age." *New Realities* 3, no. 1 (August 1979): 48–55.

Acupressure

See **Bodywork**.

Acupuncture

See **Bodywork**.

Age of Aquarius

A supposed two-thousand-year-long era of enlightenment, joy, accomplishment, intellect, brotherly peace, and closeness to God, heralded by the entry of the sun into the zodiac sign of Aquarius.

Astrologers disagree on the exact start of the Age of Aquarius. Dates range from 1904 to 2160; the latter was arrived at in calculations made by the Hermetic Order of the Golden Dawn. The disparities in dates are due to the backward drift of the vernal equinox through the zodiac. The vernal equinox takes 25,920 years to make a complete cycle through the zodiac, but a gradual slipping creates a retrograde of one zodiac sign approximately every 2,160 years. Some astrologers take this slippage into account, others do not. American medium Edgar Cayce, called by some "the Prophet of the New Age," said the Age of Aquarius and its preceding age, the Age of Pisces, overlap and that the transition could not be fully understood until the beginning of the twenty-first century. The Age of Pisces is supposed to be characterized by disillusionment and skepticism. The transition to Aquarius allegedly will bring ferment and change in social behavior and institutions. Aquarius is ruled by two planets: Saturn, symbol of time, endurance, tests, and tasks; and Uranus, symbol of the new, revolutionary, strange, and bizarre. The 2160 starting date for the Age of Aquarius approximately coincides with various predictions of cataclysms, war, and a shift of the North Pole in the closing years of the twentieth century, followed by a two-thousand-year era of peace, tranquility, and brotherhood. See **Nostradamus; Revelation, Book of.** The term "Age of Aquarius" was popular during the 1960s, which saw a great deal of societal change and upheaval and interest in spiritual exploration. The Great Conjunction of the sun, moon, Venus, Mars, Mercury, Jupiter, and Saturn in Aquarius on February 5, 1962, was said by astrologers to be a significant influence on quickening the transition to the new era. The term "Age of Aquarius" has been supplanted by "New Age." See **Harmonic Convergence; New Age.**

Sources: "Astrology and the New Cult of the Occult." *Time* (March 21, 1969): 47–56; Mary Ellen Carter. *Edgar Cayce on Prophecy.* New York: Warner, 1968; Grace Cooke. *The Illumined Ones.* New Lands, England: White Eagle Publishing Trust, 1966; Jean-Charles de Fontbrune. *Nostradamus: Countdown to Apocalypse.* New York: Holt, Rinehart and Winston, 1980; Doreen Valiente. *Witchcraft for To-morrow.* Custer, WA: Phoenix Publishing, 1978.

Aikido

See **Martial arts.**

Akasha (akasa)

In Hinduism and Buddhism, the all-pervasive life principle or all-pervasive space of the universe. *Akasha* is the Sanskrit term for "all-pervasive space."

In Hinduism the akasha is seen as the substance ether, the fifth and subtlest element. The akasha permeates everything in the universe and is the vehicle for all life and sound. In the practice of yoga, the akasha is one of three universal principles, along with *prana* ("breath of life") and "creative mind," which form a trinity of sources of magical and psychic power, and are immanent in all things from the mineral kingdom on up, throughout the universe. From the akasha comes will, which enables all manner of feats to be accomplished.

In Buddhism the akasha is not ether but space, of which there are two kinds. One is space limited by the material and associated with the *skandas* or "aggregates," which form the personality: physical form, sensation, perception, mental formations, and consciousness. The second is space that is unlimited, beyond all description, unbound by the material yet the container for all things material.

A concept of the akasha was introduced to the West in the early twentieth century by Madame Helena P. Blavatsky, mystic and founder of the Theosophical Society. Blavatsky likened the akasha to other interpretations of the universal life force, such as the "sidereal light" of the Rosicrucians, the "astral light" of French occultist Eliphas Levi, and the "Odic force" of German physicist Baron Karl von Reichenbach. It also is seen as an equivalent of the Hebrew *ruah,* the wind, breath, air in motion, or moving spirit.

According to Blavatsky the akasha forms the *anima mundi* (the world soul, which allows divine thought to manifest in matter) and constitutes the soul and astral spirit of humankind. It produces mesmeric, magnetic operations of nature. See **Akashic Records; Universal life force.**

Sources: H. P. Blavatsky. *Isis Unveiled: A Master Key to the Mysteries of Ancient and Modern Science and Theology.* London and Benares: The Theosophical Publishing Society, 1910; H. P. Blavatsky. *The Secret Doctrine.* 1888. Pasadena, CA: Theosophical University Press, 1977; Joseph Campbell. *The Masks of God.* Vol. 4, *Oriental Mythology.* New York: Viking Penguin, 1962; *The Encyclopedia of Eastern Philosophy and Religion.* Boston: Shambhala, 1989; C. W. Leadbeater. *The Chakras.* Wheaton, IL: Theosophical Publishing House, 1927; Ormond McGill. *The Mysticism and Magic of India.* Cranbury, NJ: A. S. Barnes & Co., 1977.

Akashic Records

In Theosophy the master records of everything that has ever occurred since the beginning of the universe. The records are said to exist as impressions in the astral plane, and provide a dossier of sorts for souls who wish to examine their spiritual progress through many lifetimes.

The term "Akashic" comes from the Sanskrit word *akasha,* defined as either the fundamental etheric substance in the universe or all-pervasive space. According to Theosophy the akasha is an eternal record of the vibrations of every action, thought, emotion, light, and sound.

Some psychics say they consult the Askashic Records either through clairvoyance or out-of-body travel, to receive information about past history or lives. The process is variously described as tuning into an astral television set, or tuning into a radio broadcast, or visiting an enormous library and looking up information in books. Some say they encoun-

ter spirit guides, who assist them in locating information.

American medium Edgar Cayce often consulted the Akashic Records to look into past lives to find reasons for health, personal, and marital problems in the current lives of clients. Cayce alternately called the Akashic Records the "Universal Memory of Nature" and the "Book of Life."

In *Edgar Cayce on Reincarnation,* by Noel Langley, Cayce describes an apparent out-of-body trip to the Akashic Records to get information about a client. Cayce said he felt himself leave his body and travel in a narrow, straight shaft of light. On both sides of the shaft was fog or smoke, and shadowy beings who tried to distract him from his mission. Some pleaded for him to help them, but he kept to the light. As he continued on, the beings took on more distinct form and bothered him less. Eventually, they quit trying to distract him and seemed to help him on, then ignored him altogether. Finally, he arrived at a hill, where he saw a mount and a great temple. Inside was a large room like a library, filled with books of people's lives. All he had to do was pull down the book he wanted. See **Cayce, Edgar.**

Philosopher Rudolf Steiner delved into the Akashic Records, which he called the Akashic Chronicle, to produce his detailed descriptions of the mythical, lost civilizations of Atlantis and Lemuria.

According to Cayce and other psychics, the Akashic Records travel on waves of light, and anyone can gain access to them with proper psychic training and attunement. See **Akasha.**

Sources: Richard Cavendish, ed. *The Encyclopedia of the Unexplained.* New York: McGraw-Hill, 1974; *Individual Reference File of Extracts from the Edgar Cayce Readings.* Virginia Beach, VA: Edgar Cayce Foundation, 1976; Noel Langley. *Edgar Cayce on Reincarnation.* New York: Castle Books, 1967; Robert A. McDermott, ed.

and intro. *The Essential Steiner*. San Francisco: Harper & Row, 1984; Joan Windsor. *The Inner Eye: Your Dreams Can Make You Psychic*. Englewood Cliffs, NJ: Prentice-Hall, 1985.

Alchemy

Literally, an ancient art of transmutation and the precursor of modern chemistry and metallurgy. Symbolically, a mystical art for the transformation of consciousness.

Current Western interest in alchemy is due largely to psychiatrist Carl G. Jung, who saw it as having a spiritual dimension as well as a physical one: The true purpose of the art is the psychological and spiritual transformation of the alchemist.

Alchemy is called a "spagyric" art, from the Greek terms for "to tear" and "to bring together." As a mystical art, it draws on various spiritual traditions, including the Hermetica, Gnosticism, Islam, the Kabbalah, Taoism, and yoga. Western and Eastern alchemical arts have developed differently.

Alchemists at work

(From Philip Ulstadt's De Secretis Naturae, 1544)

Western Alchemy

Western alchemy draws on the Hermetic tradition, Greco-Egyptian esoteric teachings. According to legend the founder is Hermes Trismegistus, a form of the Egyptian and Greek gods of magic and wisdom, Thoth and Hermes, respectively. See **Hermetica.** In the late centuries B.C. and early centuries A.D., the Egyptians combined metallurgy with Hermetic philosophy and ideas drawn from Western mysteries, Neoplatonism, gnosticism, and Christianity. The Egyptians developed one of the basic fundamentals of alchemy: that the world was created by divine force out of a chaotic mass called *prima materia,* or "first matter." Thus in alchemy all things can be reduced to first matter through *solve et coagula,* "dissolve and combine," and transmuted to something more desirable. Specifically, alchemists sought to transmute through joining opposites.

By the fourth century A.D., alchemy had assumed its historical form and essentially replaced the disintegrating mysteries. It spread throughout Europe beginning in the twelfth century, a product of the Muslim occupation of Spain. It was a highly respected science, practiced by adepts who wrote their treatises and manuals in deliberately obscure language. The term "gibberish" is derived from a medieval alchemist named Jabir ibn Hayyan, generally known as Geber (c. 721–815), whose writings were largely unintelligible.

Alchemy was at its peak from the late Middle Ages through the Renaissance. Alchemists sought the elusive "philosopher's stone," or lapis, a mysterious substance believed to enable the transmutation of base metals into silver or gold. The philosopher's stone also served as the "elixir of life," a means to immortality. While most attempts at metals transmutations were failures, some alchemists claimed to succeed. Nicholas Flamel, one of the great alchemists of the fourteenth century, is said to have achieved the transmutation of mercury into silver or gold on three occasions.

The writings and drawings produced by the alchemists tend to be obscure and difficult to understand. The alchemists based their study primarily upon direct, personal revelation through visions and dreams. The alchemists did not describe their work in direct terms, but wrote and drew in symbols intended only for the comprehension of other adepts. They varied in their use of terminology.

According to early alchemy, all things have a hermaphroditic composition of two substances: sulfur, which represents the soul and the fiery male principle; and mercury, which represents spirit and the watery female principle. Later European alchemy added a third ingredient, salt, which corresponds to body. The transmutation process involves separating these three essentials and recombining them into a different form. The process must be done according to astrological auspices.

As a continuation of the mysteries, alchemy may essentially have been a euphemism for the sacred service of cocreation, made possible by immortalization, a status that had been achieved through initiation into the mysteries.

The hermaphroditic nature of alchemy was often expressed in erotic art, though there is no evidence that actual sexual rites were practiced.

Medieval and Renaissance alchemists were responsible for many discoveries important in metallurgy, chemistry, and medicines. See **Paracelsus.** However, in the early nineteenth century, alchemy was discredited by the discoveries of oxygen and the composition of water. Alchemy was reduced to the level of pseudoscience and superstition and was replaced by physics.

Interest in alchemy remained low key until about the second half of the twentieth century, when a revival of interest began taking hold in the West. Alchemy schools were founded to teach the ancient art, resulting in spagyric products for cosmetics, herbal medicines, beverages and wines, perfumes, and so on.

Eastern Alchemy

Alchemy was highly developed in ancient China. It was an oral tradition until c. A.D. 320, when the classic alchemical text, *Nei P'ien,* was written by Ko Hung. The immortality sought by the Chinese was not an extension of earthly years; they sought instead to attain a state of timelessness spent with the Immortals, in which one had supernormal powers. To this end ancient Chinese alchemy focused on various elixirs, which were purified by combining ingredients and repeatedly heating them in various vessels.

The alchemical process is analogous to Taoist meditation, in which *ch'i,* the universal life force, is created and purified in the body. *Ch'i* is created when the nutritious elements of food are combined with secretions from glands and organs. This forms blood and sexual energy (*ching*). Heat in the form of breath transforms the sexual energy to *ch'i,* which circulates up and down psychic channels along the spine, from the crown to the abdomen, somewhat akin to the *kundalini* energy of yoga. The *ch'i* passes through twelve psychic centers located along the channels. After many cycles the *ch'i* becomes refined. It reaches the crown in a highly concentrated state, where it can be manipulated or else sent back down to the abdomen. The *ch'i* can be stored for future use.

In India alchemy traces its roots to earlier than 1000 B.C. in the development of Ayurvedic ("the wisdom of life") medicine, where it continues to play a role today. Indian alchemy is a union of male (Shiva) and female (Parvati) principles; the result is *jivan,* an enlightened being.

In both Hindu and Chinese traditions, one may also achieve immortality through Tantric, yoga. Prolonged abstinence or coitus without ejaculation is believed to intensify the life force (*prana* or *ch'i*) and produce physiological changes.

Jung and Alchemy

Carl G. Jung's interest in alchemy grew out of his intense interest in Gnosticism, and his desire, as early as 1912, to find a link between it and the processes of the collective unconscious that would pave the way for the reentry of the Gnostics' *sophia* (wisdom) into modern culture. He found such a link in alchemy, which he saw as analogous to individuation, the process of becoming whole.

Jung had many significant dreams during his life, and in 1926 he had one in which he was a seventeenth-century alchemist who was creating a great alchemical work. The dream proved to be prophetic, for Jung made alchemy a focus of much of his work. Inspired by that and other alchemical dreams, Jung collected a vast body of works on alchemy and immersed himself in study of the subject.

His research was greatly influenced by *The Secret of the Golden Flower,* a Chinese mystical and alchemical tract discovered by Jung's friend Richard Wilhelm, and given him by Wilhelm in 1928 for comment. *The Secret of the Golden Flower* revealed to Jung the bridge between Gnosticism and the psychology of the unconscious. In comparing the Chinese tract with Latin alchemical works,

Jung found that the alchemy systems of both East and West essentially dealt with transformation of the soul.

Jung was amazed to notice that many of his patients—men and women of both European and American backgrounds—produced in their dreams and fantasies symbols that were similar or identical to those in myth, fairy tales, the mystery cults, and alchemical works. This insight led him to develop his ideas about the collective unconscious, a repository of primeval images and patterns of behavior shared by humankind.

Jung's first important words on alchemy were a lecture on alchemical symbolism in dreams, entitled "Dream Symbols and the Individuation Process," delivered in 1935 at Villa Eranos on Lake Maggiore in southern Switzerland. A year later, also at Eranos, he lectured on "The Idea of Redemption in Alchemy." His first book on the subject was *Psychology and Alchemy* (1944). *Aion, Alchemical Studies,* and *Mysterium Coniunctionis* also deal with alchemy. Jung's knowledge of alchemy is exemplified throughout all of his later writings.

Jung saw alchemy as a spiritual process of redemption involving the union and transformation of *Lumen Dei,* the light of the Godhead, and *Lumen Naturae,* the light of nature. The alchemists' experimental procedure of solve et coagula symbolized the "death" and "rebirth" of the substances they used. Alchemists were part of the process, and transmuted their own consciousness into a higher state through symbolic death and rebirth.

According to Jung the early Christian alchemists used the philosopher's stone as a symbol of Christ. Thus, in its highest mystical sense, alchemy represents the transformation of consciousness to love, personified by the hermaphrodite, the union of male-female opposites (physicality and spirituality) who are joined into a whole. See **Collective un-**

conscious; Gnosticism; Jung, Carl Gustav.

Sources: Richard Cavendish, ed. *The Encyclopedia of the Unexplained.* New York: McGraw-Hill, 1974; Martin Ebon, ed. *The Signet Handbook of Parapsychology.* New York: New American Library, 1978; Manly P. Hall. *The Secret Teachings of All Ages.* 1928. Los Angeles: The Philosophic Research Society, 1977; M. Esther Harding. *Psychic Energy: Its Source and Its Transformation.* Princeton: Princeton University Press, 1973; Stephan A. Hoeller. "C. G. Jung and the Alchemical Revival." *Gnosis* 8 (Summer 1988): 34–39; Stephan A. Hoeller. *The Gnostic Jung and the Seven Sermons to the Dead.* Wheaton, IL: Theosophical Publishing House, 1982; C. G. Jung. *Memories, Dreams, Reflections.* Recorded and edited by Aniela Jaffe. New York: Random House, 1961; C. G. Jung. *Psychology and Alchemy.* Rev. ed. Princeton: Princeton University Press, 1968; C. G. Jung. *The Practice of Psychotherapy.* 2d ed. Princeton: Princeton University Press, 1966; C. G. Jung. *Aion.* 2d ed. Princeton: Princeton University Press, 1968; C. G. Jung. *Mysterium Coniunctionis.* 2d ed. Princeton: Princeton University Press, 1970; John Lash. "Parting of the Ways." *Gnosis* 8 (Summer 1988): 22–26; Da Liu. *T'ai Chi Ch'uan and Meditation.* New York: Schocken Books, 1986; Jim Melodini. "The Age of Gold." *Gnosis* 8 (Summer 1988): 8–10; Hans Nintzel. "Alchemy Is Alive and Well." *Gnosis* 8 (Summer 1988): 11–15; Peter O'Connor. *Understanding Jung, Understanding Yourself.* New York and Mahwah, NJ: Paulist Press, 1985; Andrew Samuels, Bani Shorter, and Fred Plaut. *A Critical Dictionary of Jungian Analysis.* London: Routledge & Kegan Paul, 1986; Elemire Zolla. "Alchemy Out of India." *Gnosis* 8 (Summer 1988): 48–49.

Alexander Technique

See **Bodywork.**

Alpert, Richard

See **Ram Dass.**

Altered states of consciousness

Any of a variety of states characterized by a radical shift in the pattern of consciousness from one's "normal" waking state. The term "altered states of consciousness" (ASCs) was coined by parapsychologist Charles T. Tart. ASCs have been shown to be of some benefit in psi functioning, but have been difficult to study scientifically because of their subjective and internal nature. There is no universal "normal" state of consciousness from which to begin a study, though there are probably biological limitations to the possible range. The highest ASCs are mystical states of consciousness.

States of consciousness—ordinary and altered—take place in four levels of brain-wave activity: beta, alpha, theta, and delta. The beta level is complete, waking consciousness, with brain waves ranging from 14 to 27 cycles per second. Approximately 75 percent of the waking consciousness is consumed with monitoring physical functions. The alpha level is characterized by brain waves of 8 to 13 cycles per second. In the alpha state material from the subconscious is accessible. The brain is in this state during light hypnosis, meditation, biofeedback, daydreaming, and the hypnagogic and hypnapompic states just prior to and after sleep. In the theta level, brain waves range from 4 to 8 cycles per second. Theta is the equivalent of light sleep, a state of unconsciousness in which one is unaware of what is going on around one. Some people are able to drop into the theta level in biofeedback and meditation. The delta level is deep sleep, with brain waves ranging from 0 to 4 cycles per second.

Numerous ASCs can be differentiated, including: (1) dreaming, with periods of rapid eye movement (REM) and absence of "slow" brain waves; (2) sleeping, with "slow" brain waves and absence of REM; (3) hypnagogic, between wakefulness and sleep; (4) hypnapompic, between sleep and wakefulness; (5) hyperalert, or prolonged and increased vigilance induced by intense concentration or drugs; (6) lethargic, which includes depression, fatigue, and so on; (7) rapture, or overpowering positive emotion; (8) hysteria, or overpowering negative emotion; (9) fragmentation; (10) regressive, as in age regression induced by hypnosis; (11) meditative, characterized by continuous alpha waves, lack of visual imagery, and minimal mental activity; (12) trance, characterized by absence of continuous alpha waves; (13) reverie, which occurs during trance and with REM; (14) daydreaming; (15) internal scanning, or awareness of bodily feelings on a nonreflective level; (16) stupor; (17) coma; (18) stored memory, in which information must be recalled by conscious effort; (19) expanded consciousness, such as peak and mystical experiences; and (20) shamanic consciousness, an altered but lucid state in which a shaman accesses the underworld or the celestial world. See **Shamanism.**

ASCs can occur spontaneously, or can be induced through disciplines such as yoga, Zen, and other forms of meditation; prayer; and various occult and magical techniques. They also can be induced through dancing, chanting, intoxication, self-inflicted pain, sensory deprivation, sensory overload, sleep deprivation, progressive relaxation, hypnosis, fatigue, malnutrition, fasting and diet, physical and psychological trauma, birthing, staring, sex, and psychotic episodes.

ASCs and Psi

In laboratory tests since the early 1950s, ASC-inductive techniques, such as relaxation, sensory deprivation, ganzfeld stimulation, hypnosis, and meditation, have been shown to enhance psi functioning, especially in forced-choice extrasensory perception (ESP) tests, and also in free-response tests and psychokinesis (PK) tests. The most frequently used induction techniques are progressive relaxation and ganzfeld stimulation. See **Ganzfeld stimulation.** Drugs, especially psychedelics, are avoided because they are too disorienting. See **Drugs in mystical and psychic experiences.** Induced ASCs remove distractions from the conscious mind, and might serve to bolster the confidence and expectations of the test subject. The influence of suggestion, either deliberate or implicit, also must be considered, for suggestion alone can positively affect test results.

Not all parapsychologists agree on the value of ASCs in psi testing. Remote viewing (seeing a distant site or object by clairvoyance or visiting a distant site by out-of-body travel) produces equally good results in "normal" consciousness, for example. Some factors are unpredictable, such as the individual reactions to an ASC, and the potential for bad experiences among some individuals.

ASCs as a State-Specific Science

Orthodox science largely rejects the experiences and knowledge gained from ASCs, many of which are intensely spiritual in nature. Most ASCs have no physical phenomena and thus are epiphenomena, to which science gives little value. Furthermore, they are highly subjective and resist laboratory controls. However, in the mid-1970s Tart introduced the terms "discrete states of consciousness" and "altered states of consciousness," referring to recognizable patterns that are maintained despite variations in particulars.

Scientific research has been effective in the areas of dreams, meditation, biofeedback, and some intoxicated and drug-induced states. Transpersonal psychology has focused on the therapeutic benefits of ASCs, especially the higher mystical states. See **Biofeedback; Dreams;**

Meditation; Mystical experiences; Sheep/goat effect; Psychology.

Sources: Hoyt L. Edge, Robert L. Morris, John Palmer, and Joseph H. Rush. *Foundations of Parapsychology*. Boston: Routledge & Kegan Paul, 1986; Philip Goldberg. *The Intuitive Edge*. Wellingborough, Northamptonshire, England: Turnstone, 1985; Charles T. Tart, ed. *Altered States of Consciousness: A Book of Readings*. New York: John Wiley & Sons, 1969; Charles T. Tart, ed. *Transpersonal Psychologies*. San Francisco: Harper & Row, 1975; Charles T. Tart. *States of Consciousness*. New York: E. P. Dutton, 1975; John White, ed. *The Highest State of Consciousness*. Garden City, NY: Anchor Books/Doubleday, 1972; Benjamin B. Wolman, ed. *Handbook of Parapsychology*. New York: Van Nostrand Reinhold, 1977.

Alternative religious movements

Various churches, sects, and cults that are outside mainstream, conventional religions. In the West alternative religious movements have been on the rise since the early nineteenth century, and seem to have experienced significant growth since the 1970s; many are identified with the New Age movement. Most groups are small and sincere in pursuing their individual visions, but some cults have been accused of abusing and manipulating members.

There are various definitions of alternative religious movements. Social scientists divide them into three groups: churches, sects, and cults. Churches are large denominations that fit within the prevailing culture; sects are groups that have broken away from denominations, such as Quakers, Jehovah's Witnesses, and so on; and cults are groups that follow structures alien to the prevailing environment.

The term "cult" is subject to differing definitions. As alien and transplanted religions, Hinduism and Buddhism technically are cults in the West, and Christianity is a cult in the East. Some conservative Christians define cult as any religious group that is non-Christian. "Cult" also has become a pejorative term. Cults usually are identified as groups having a charismatic leader, which is characteristic of any emergent religion, including Christianity.

Alternative religious movements have existed throughout history. In the West they have arisen out of paganism, Christianity, and Western occultism, and have also been imported from the East. In the present day numerous Eastern religious groups have taken root and flourished in the West. Some of these groups exist primarily to serve the ethnic communities of immigrants, and have attracted the intellectual and religious interest of occidentals. Other groups have been established primarily to spread their teachings to Westerners. The common themes of Eastern religious groups include pantheistic universalism; a sense of the divine within; the goal of uniting with the inner divine through meditation or mystical experience; a cosmos that is an infinite, nondualistic, conscious, and transpersonal Reality, which is the divine that dwells within and is the true nature of all things; and karma and reincarnation.

The religions and philosophies of East and West have cross-fertilized each other since ancient times. Major influences on modern alternative movements date to the influence of Confucian philosophy on the Enlightenment, as well as on some of the founding fathers of America, including Benjamin Franklin. In the nineteenth century the Transcendentalists were influenced by Hinduism. Transcendentalism and Theosophy brought Eastern concepts to the West. They combined with other movements such as mental healing, Spiritualism, and a revival of occultism, and in turn influenced the formation of various alternative religious movements, whose numbers grew significantly after World War II. In the 1970s, following the social and political unrest of the 1960s, alternative religious movements increased. In America the lifting of strict immigration quotas for Asians also influenced this proliferation.

The number of alternative religious groups is unknown. Estimates vary greatly because of the different definitions applied. J. Gordon Melton, a scholar of alternative religions, estimates that in the United States there are five hundred to six hundred stable, nontraditional religious groups with a total of approximately 150,000 to 200,000 members, and that more than one hundred of the groups are ethnic and oriented to communities of immigrants. Various anticultists claim that thousands of cults, mostly destructive, exist; however, there is no evidence to support the claim. Membership figures do not include the unknown thousands who sample alternative religious movements but do not join.

Alternative religious movements appeal primarily to single, young, upper-middle class, urban adults, though the total audience is broader. In the United States, approximately 50 percent are Protestant, 25 percent are Catholic, and 25 percent are Jewish. With the exception of the Jews, who are over-represented in alternative religious groups, the figures are representative of the general religious population mix. More than 90 percent of those who become members of an alternative group leave within a few years — most within two — and either return to their original religion or follow no religion at all. The overwhelming majority of those who leave do so of their own volition. Only a very small minority must be deprogrammed.

Space considerations preclude a discussion of all of the alternative religious movements. The following groups, however, have received a great deal of attention and have at various times been the targets of anticult organizations.

International Society of Krishna Consciousness (ISKON)

A conservative form of Hinduism based on Bhakti (devotional) Yoga, ISKON was founded in America in 1965 by A. C. Bhaktivedanta Swami Prabhupada (born Abhay Charan De) of Calcutta, India. ISKON is the latest revival of a movement started in the sixteenth century by a Bengali saint, Chaitanya Mahaprabhu (1486–1534?). At age twenty-one, Chaitanya began chanting the name of Krishna, and attracted a following. Swami Prabhupada (1896–1977) became a follower of one of the revivalist movements, the Gaudiya Mission, and in 1933 was charged by its leader, Bhakti Siddhanta, with carrying Krishna Consciousness to the West. Prabhupada did little until 1965, when the United States lifted restrictions on Asian immigration. By that time Prabhupada was seventy. He came to New York and quickly built up a following. By 1970 ISKON was spread throughout the United States and to Europe, England, Australia, Canada, and Japan.

Devotees of ISKON are called the Hare Krishnas for their incessant chanting of the Hare Krishna mantra (see **Mantra**), which they believe will raise their consciousness to a state of bliss. Krishna is considered the Personality of the Godhead. Knowledge of the Vedic literature, especially the *Bhagavad-Gita,* is stressed, although all great scriptures are held to contain the Absolute Truth.

Devotees adopt clothing associated with the devotional life in India and follow a semimonastic life. They are vegetarians. They gained public attention for their chanting in the street and soliciting of funds in airports, practices that have become restricted. International headquarters are in West Bengal, India; American headquarters are in Los Angeles, California.

The Church Universal and Triumphant (Summit Lighthouse)

Founded by Mark L. and Elizabeth Clare Prophet, the Church Universal and Triumphant is often confused with a similar group, the "I AM" Religious Activity, with which it has never been affiliated. Both are centered on the Messengership of the Ascended Masters.

In 1958 Mark L. Prophet was anointed a new Messenger of the Masters by the Ascended Master El Morya, and began to give lectures based on the dictations he received. Several years later he married Elizabeth Clare Wulf, who subsequently was anointed a Messenger. When El Morya announced the Keepers of the Flame Fraternity, the Prophets formed Summit Lighthouse as a vehicle for their work. In 1973 Mark Prophet died of a stroke, and Elizabeth assumed full leadership. Mark is believed to dictate teachings to her. In 1974 the Church Universal and Triumphant was incorporated and Summit Lighthouse was made its publishing arm. The organization includes the Montessori International educational system, founded in 1970, and owns various properties, including a 33,000-acre ranch near Livingston, Montana, which supports a commune.

The church holds that God exists in the soul of each individual as the "I AM" Presence. Union with this presence is accomplished by raising the energy of the feminine principle and wedding the soul to the universal Christ consciousness. Doctrines include reincarnation and the law of karma.

The Montana ranch features a shelter, which members intend to use in the event of nuclear war, predicted at least twice by Prophet. In 1989 Prophet's second husband, Ed Francis, was charged with illegally purchasing semiautomatic weapons, ammunition, and handguns. Other weapons at the ranch were confiscated. In March 1990 several thousand followers purchased places in the shelter, some paying as much as $6,000, because Prophet warned of imminent nuclear war.

Divine Light Mission

Short-lived in the United States but successful elsewhere, the Divine Light Mission began informally in India in 1930 under the leadership of Sri Hans Maharaj Ji, a disciple of the Sant Mat tradition. In 1960 he founded the Divine Light Mission. He died in 1966 and was succeeded by his eight-year-old son, Prem Pal Singh Rawat, who was directed to do so by a divine voice. He took the title Maharaj Ji. The boy had been recognized as an adept and initiated at age six.

The Divine Light Mission acquired American followers in India, some of whom became initiates, or "premies," and invited the boy wonder to the United States. The Maharaj Ji arrived in 1971 at age thirteen, intending to spread the Divine Light Mission throughout the West, despite opposition from his mother. Tens of thousands flocked to him, but by 1973 the American drive was in trouble. A "Millennium 73" event held at the Houston Astrodome to announce the beginning of one thousand years of peace and prosperity was a huge flop. The Maharaj Ji's marriage in 1974 to his twenty-four-year-old secretary, whom he declared an incarnation of the goddess Dulga, added to the decline. In India his family ousted him from control of the Mission, and in 1975 he returned there to sue them. He won control of the Mission everywhere but in India.

A small following continues in the United States. The Maharaj Ji has been more successful converting followers in

South America, Southeast Asia, and the South Pacific.

Rajneesh Foundation International

The Bhagwan ("godman") Shree Rajneesh, born a Jain in India in 1931, proved to be one of the more controversial gurus to set up shop in the West. He claimed to have his first experience of *samadhi* (enlightenment) when he was seven; in 1953, while a student at the University of Saugar, he experienced a spiritual death and rebirth. In 1966 he became a full-time spiritual leader, espousing nontraditional teachings that became known as Rajneeshism, a synthesis of major religions and humanistic psychology. He was discovered by Westerners in Bombay in 1970. In 1974 he founded the Rajneesh Foundation (later the Rajneesh Foundation International) and established an ashram at Poona.

In 1981 Rajneesh came to the United States, where he purchased a 64,000-acre ranch near Antelope, Oregon; in 1982 it was incorporated as Rajneeshpuram. His followers were at constant odds with the residents of Antelope, especially when Rajneesh hosted seven thousand followers at a summer festival. In a 1982 election, devotees took control of the Antelope government. Efforts to deport Rajneesh failed, for he had been adopted in 1936 by an Indian who became a US citizen in 1973 — the father of his secretary, Ma Anand Sheela. Despite Rajneesh's blatant materialism, most notably a fleet of nearly one hundred Rolls Royces (gifts from his followers), his devotees increased across the country.

In 1985, in a storm of controversy that involved charges of attempted poisoning of a number of people, Ma Anand Sheela resigned, and Rajneesh denounced her and accused her of crimes against him and the movement. He then denounced Rajneeshism, which he said she had created. Within weeks he was indicted on charges of immigration fraud. He left Oregon and was arrested in North Carolina. In a plea bargain he confessed to two felonies and agreed to pay a $40,000 fine and leave the United States. He returned to India. Rajneeshpuram was closed and the property sold, which effectively ended the movement in the United States, but not in other countries. Rajneesh died of heart failure at age fifty-eight on January 19, 1990 in Poona, India.

Unification Church

The Unification Church, the target of the most anticult activity in the United States, was founded in 1954 in North Korea by the Reverend Sun Myung Moon (born Young Myung Moon in 1920). Moon was ten when his parents converted to Presbyterianism, and was sixteen when he had a vision of Jesus, who anointed him to fulfill Jesus' unfinished mission. According to Moon, in order to restore the world from the Fall, a messiah is required who conquers sin and manifests God's masculine nature, and marries a woman who manifests God's feminine nature. By not marrying and having children, Jesus offers only spiritual salvation but not physical salvation.

In Japan during World War II, Moon had another spiritual experience in which he entered the spirit world and engaged in winning combat over satanic forces. He then changed his name to Sun Myung Moon, which means "Shining Sun and Moon."

The Holy Spirit Association for the Unification of World Christianity, as the Unification Church officially is known, grew slowly after its founding in 1954, and was expanded to Japan in 1958. In 1960 Moon married his second wife, who bore twelve children by 1981. At that point Moon called himself "Lord of the Second Advent" and said he had completed Jesus' mission.

The church was imported to the United States by three Korean missionaries in 1959. Moon visited the United States in the 1960s—on one visit, the control of the medium Arthur Ford called him a New Age teacher/revealer—and in 1972 received a revelation to move to the United States. From 1972 to 1976 the church grew rapidly. Its goal is to evangelize the world according to the views of Moon. Initiates align themselves with the messiah by a period of sacrifice and celibacy, following which the Moons, known as the True Parents, select spouses and officiate at their wedding ceremonies. They conducted mass weddings in 1982.

To further its objectives and still critics, the church engages in a wide range of charitable, educational, political, ecumenical, and media enterprises that employ many nonchurch staff. Its most visible enterprise is the *Washington Times* daily newspaper in Washington, DC, the former *Washington Star*.

In 1982 Moon was convicted on charges of income tax evasion for interest income earned on a savings account in his name. He spent thirteen months in jail in 1984 and 1985, which ironically garnered him new supporters. Outside of the United States, the church is strongest in Japan and North Korea. A Unification Theological Seminary in Tarrytown, New York, trains church leaders.

Religious Groups and Violence

Many alternative religious groups are the targets of much opposition from established elements in society, chiefly churches that feel threatened and families that feel their children have been stolen. Alternative groups are charged with brainwashing, sexual perversion, violence, crime, and heresy. Antagonism was particularly high during cult scares in the 1960s and 1970s and was directed chiefly at groups with communal life-styles, such as ISKON, the Unification Church, and The Way International.

Some groups have been involved in incidents of violence or crime. The most notable example is Jim Jones's People's Temple, whose members, including Jones himself, committed murder and mass suicide at their compound in Guyana in 1979. However, incidents demonstrating threats to the established order have been isolated, and have been exaggerated by anticultists. More often than not, the alternative groups are the victims, rather than the perpetrators, of violence and persecution.

Many religious groups that are now well established in society were once persecuted in much the same manner. In the early nineteenth century in the United States, for example, Catholics were the targets of some of the severest persecutions in the history of the nation; they were accused by Protestants of deception and coercion, sexual perversion, murder, political subversion, and financial exploitation. Christian Scientists, Mormons, and Seventh Day Adventists have similarly been harassed. Quakers once were hung by the colonial Calvinists (who themselves came to America to escape persecution in England), and were sentenced to death for refusing to serve in the military. Undoubtedly, some of the alternative groups now perceived as threats will in the future achieve a more accepted status. See **Charismatic renewal; Church of All Worlds; Church of Christ, Scientist; Church of Jesus Christ of Latter-day Saints, the; Church of Scientology; ECKANKAR; "I AM" Religious Activity, the; Neo-paganism; New Age; Shakers; Society of Friends; Witchcraft.**

Sources: David G. Bromley and Anson D. Shupe, Jr. *Strange Gods: The Great American Cult Scare*. Boston: Beacon Press, 1981; Robert S. Ellwood, ed. *Eastern Spirituality in America*. New York: Paulist Press, 1987; Rev. James J. Lebar. *Cults, Sects, and the New Age*. Huntington, IN:

Our Sunday Visitor, 1989; J. Gordon Melton. *Encyclopedic Handbook of Cults in America.* New York: Garland Publishing, 1986.

American Society for Psychical Research (ASPR)

Organization founded in late 1884 in Boston under the auspices of the Society for Psychical Research (SPR) of England, and dedicated to the advancement of psychical research (now called parapsychology). The society became formally active in 1885; astronomer Simon Newcomb was elected the first president. Other major figures in the formation of the society were English physicist Sir William Barrett, and Harvard philosopher William James.

The early ASPR operated independently of the SPR, but organized itself along the same lines, with investigative committees to research and collect data on thought transference, telepathy, hypnosis, apparitions, mediumship, and other phenomena. Its membership included many scientists who considered psychical research of secondary interest. As a result, in 1889, less than five years after founding, the society was forced for financial reasons to dissolve and reorganize as the American Branch of the SPR. Richard Hodgson, a member of the SPR, moved to America and directed the branch's activities until his death in 1905.

In 1906 the American Branch was dissolved and the ASPR reestablished itself as an independent organization with headquarters in New York City. James H. Hyslop served as secretary until his death in 1920; most of the new leadership was comprised not of scientists, but of other professionals who had an avocational interest in psychical research and Spiritualism. During this period the ASPR suffered from a shortage of funds and did a modest amount of collective research. Hyslop was more interested in publishing, and devoted a great deal of time to fund-raising.

Following Hyslop's death the ASPR went through a strained and divisive period in which many members were extremely dissatisfied with the leadership's neglect of experimental parapsychology in favor of mediumship and seance phenomena. The division was exacerbated by a controversy over a fraudulent medium known as "Margery" (Mina Stinson Crandon) of Boston, to whom the ASPR devoted much attention and money. In 1925 a group of academically oriented opponents of Margery split off and formed the Boston Society for Psychic Research, which did little but publish. In the 1941 ASPR elections, a "palace revolution" occurred and the key Margery supporters were voted out of office. The ASPR terminated official involvement with Margery, who died later the same year. The Boston group returned to the fold.

Under the presidency of Hyslop's son, George Hyslop, and the leadership provided by eminent psychologist Gardner Murphy, who became chairman of the Research Committee, the society reinstated research as its primary function. Prior to the "palace revolution," the ASPR had been run to appeal to the lay public, not academics or scientists. The first sign of a change in this orientation occurred in 1938, when Murphy conducted the first systematic ESP experiments under the auspices of the ASPR, using American parapsychologist J. B. Rhine's ESP cards. Under the new administration, the organization returned fully to a scientific purpose. It benefited from the experimental work of Rhine, who saw parapsychology as an emerging scientific discipline, and from the academic approach of Murphy, who sought to integrate the paranormal with psychology and philosophy. Murphy's stature as a psychologist—he served for a time as president of the American Psychological

Association—did attract Rhine, Margaret Mead, Henry James (son of William James), and other luminaries to the board of directors. However, he did not achieve the great integration he desired.

From the 1940s until 1971, eight years before his death, Murphy served as key leader of the ASPR; he served as president from 1962 to 1971. In 1948 a "Medical Section" was established to research the integration of psychiatry and depth psychology to the paranormal; one outgrowth was the dream research of Montague Ullman and others. See **Dreams.** The Medical Section ceased operation in the 1950s, when a key member of the group, Jule Eisenbud, left New York for Denver.

In the mid-1950s Murphy directed ASPR attention to spontaneous psi, which he thought would yield more information on the nature of psi than did laboratory experiments. He encouraged research on creativity, altered states and psi, meditation and transpersonal factors of psi, deathbed observations, and survival after death. Laboratory equipment to induce altered states was purchased in the 1960s. See **Altered states of consciousness; Deathbed visions; Meditation.**

Membership and lecture attendance began to increase in the 1940s, and reached a peak in the 1960s and 1970s, fueled in part by the counterculture's interest in the paranormal. Liberals, however, were squeezed out by conservatives, and membership and interest then began to decline. Without Murphy factions again developed in the ASPR, between "reductionists," those who sought to define all phenomena as either ESP, PK, or chance, and more liberal researchers interested in out-of-body experiences, near-death experiences, behavioral medicine, dreams, and reincarnation. The ASPR has sought a balance of interests.

Scientific articles are published in a quarterly *Journal*, while informal articles appear in a quarterly *ASPR Newsletter.* The ASPR maintains one of the most comprehensive parapsychology libraries in the world, and offers symposia and lectures. Membership is international. See **James, William; Parapsychology; Society for Psychical Research (SPR).**

Sources: Roger I. Anderson. "The Life and Work of James H. Hyslop." *The Journal of the American Society for Psychical Research* 79 (April 1985): 167–200; Nandor Fodor. *An Encyclopedia of Psychic Science.* 1933. Secaucus, NJ: Citadel Press, 1966; James G. Matlock. "The ASPR in 1888." *ASPR Newsletter* 14, no. 3 (July 1988): 23; James G. Matlock. "The ASPR in 1913." *ASPR Newsletter* 14, no. 4 (October 1988): 29; James G. Matlock. "The ASPR in 1938." *ASPR Newsletter* 15, no. 1 (Winter 1989): 8; Seymour H. Mauskopf. "The History of the American Society for Psychical Research: An Interpretation." *The Journal of the American Society for Psychical Research* 83, no. 1 (January 1989): 7–32; Karlis Osis. "The American Society for Psychical Research 1941–1985: A Personal View." *The Journal of the American Society for Psychical Research* 79, no. 4 (October 1985): 501–29.

Amulet

Object, inscription, drawing, or symbol believed to be imbued with a supernormal or magical power to protect against disease, evil spirits, the evil eye, bewitchment, infertility, impotence, bad luck, and a host of misfortunes and calamities.

In their simplest form, amulets are natural objects that have an eye-catching color, an unusual shape—such as a holed stone—or are rare, such as a four-leaf clover or double walnut. Ancient civilizations, in their efforts to control spirits and the forces of nature, made amulets from a variety of materials. The practice continues universally in modern times.

The term "amulet" is derived either from the Latin *amuletum,* or the Old Latin *amoletum,* for "means of defense."

Amulets customarily are worn on the body, especially around the neck, in the form of jewelry or a charm, which is a magical phrase, rhyme, or prayer inscribed on paper, parchment, or an object. Amulets also are commonly worn as rings. Some amulets are designs, symbols, or inscriptions engraved on the doors or posts of homes, buildings, holy places, and tombs.

Virtually anything can become an amulet, depending on beliefs and resources. Among the most common are gems and semiprecious stones (see **Crystals**) fashioned into jewelry, statues of deities, or statues of animals associated with certain powers and properties. Eyes also are common; perhaps the best-known eye amulet is the Eye of Horus of ancient Egypt, which guarded health and protected against evil spirits. The Egyptians also used frog amulets against infertility, and scarab beetle amulets to guard the soul for resurrection after death and protect it against sorcery. Mummies have been found wearing pectoral necklaces containing scarabs and the Eye of Horus.

Vegetable amulets, including berries, fruits, nuts, plants, wood, and leaves, are very common in many parts of the world. The use of garlic as an amulet against evil, most notably vampires, may be traced to the ancient Romans, who used it against witches. Peach wood and stones are considered strong amulets against evil spirits in China.

Certain metals are believed to have amuletic properties. Iron universally is believed to keep away demons and witches. In India rings made of copper, silver, gold, and iron are worn to protect against sorcery. Elsewhere, iron horseshoes hung over the doorways of stables and homes keep out witches and evil spirits. Bells made of silver or iron will drive away the same. Amethyst pendants set in silver and worn on silver chains are believed to protect wearers from negative energy.

Written amulets also have been common since ancient times. The Romans had formulae for preventing various diseases. The ancient Hebrews believed in the protective powers of the names of angels and of God, and in the written word of scriptures. Written amulets are worn about the neck, hung over doors and beds, or carried in cases, boxes, and bags. The cylindrical mezuzah is one example of this type of amulet. Originally intended to protect against demons, it was later given religious significance with biblical inscriptions about monotheism. The mezuzah continues to be worn as a pendant and hung on the doorjambs of Jewish homes.

Other types of written amulets include spells, words of power, secret symbols and signs, religious phrases and scripture, and legends. In magic, magic circles are inscribed with amuletic symbols and words and names of power, which help protect the magician from harm by the spirits summoned in ritual. See **Magic; Talisman.**

Sources: Francis Barrett. *The Magus.* 1801. Reprint. Secaucus, NJ: Citadel Press, 1967; E. A. Wallis Budge. *Amulets and Superstitions.* 1930. New York: Dover Publications, 1978; Richard Cavendish. *The Black Arts.* New York: Perigee Books, 1967; Emile Grillot de Givry. *Witchcraft, Magic and Alchemy.* New York: Houghton Mifflin, 1931; Maria Leach, ed., and Jerome Fried, assoc. ed. *Funk and Wagnalls Standard Dictionary of Folklore, Mythology, and Legend.* San Francisco: Harper & Row, 1979.

Ancient astronauts, theory of

Popular but unsubstantiated theory, which holds that extraterrestrial beings visited ancient Earth, mated with human beings, and taught them advanced science, technology, and mystical wisdom.

Myths and legends of advanced beings, angels, or gods who come down from the sky have existed the world over since ancient times. The ancient astronauts theory holds that these accounts may be based on actual events. Erich Von Däniken, a German author, helped to popularize the theory in the early 1970s. In *Chariots of the Gods?* (1971), Von Däniken suggested that the mysteries of various ancient pictographs, sculptures, sites, myths, and legends could be explained as efforts by ancient peoples to depict how extraterrestrials and their spacecrafts appeared and how the aliens communicated with human beings. The theory also was offered as explanation for stupendous physical feats accomplished by ancient peoples, such as the construction of the pyramids in Egypt and Stonehenge in England, and the legendary but unproven civilizations of Atlantis and Lemuria.

Scholars dismiss the ancient astronauts theory as fantasy, yet some circumstances raise questions about its plausibility. The Dogon of Africa, for example, possess unusual knowledge about the star Sirius and still practice rituals based on a Sirian cosmology. Ancient drawings and artworks portraying alien gods who came down from the sky still exist in various parts of the world. For example, cave drawings in France, South America, and Africa depict men in spacesuit-type attire, including antennae-like spirals on their headgear. The figures in the "Spacemen of Val Camonica" drawings in Italy have geometrical symbols in their hands and wear headgear resembling modern space helmets.

The ancient astronauts theory proposes that the extraterrestrials who visited Earth long ago continue to monitor the progress of the human race. See **Atlantis; Extraterrestrial encounters; Lemuria; Nazca lines.**

Sources: Charles Berlitz. *Mysteries from Forgotten Worlds.* New York: Dell, 1972; Peter Kolosimo. *Not of This World.* Secaucus, NJ: University Books, 1971; Eric Norman. *Gods and Devils from Outer Space.* New York: Lancer Books, 1973; Robert K. G. Temple. *The Sirius Mystery.* Rochester, VT: Destiny Books, 1987; Erich Von Däniken. *Chariots of the Gods?* New York: Bantam Books, 1971; Erich Von Däniken. *Gods from Outer Space.* New York: Bantam Books, 1972; Erich Von Däniken. *The Gold of the Gods.* New York: Bantam Books, 1974; Erich Von Däniken. *Miracles of the Gods.* New York: Dell, 1976; Clifford Wilson. *Crash Go the Chariots.* New York: Lancer Books, 1972.

Andrews, Lynn V.

American author whose popular books describe her initiatory shamanistic experiences with various tribal medicine women. Lynn V. Andrews says the purpose of her books is to help restore the balance between male and female power, and to heal Mother Earth. Inevitably, she has been compared to Carlos Castaneda, author of books describing his personal experiences as apprentice to Yaqui sorcerers.

Andrews grew up in the Seattle, Washington, area. At age fifteen she moved to Los Angeles, California, where she enrolled in a Catholic girls' school through college. After graduating from college, she worked for a brief time as a stockbroker until she married. She became an accomplished equestrian and an avid art collector, and lived in Beverly Hills.

Her shamanistic journeys reportedly began in 1974, during a traumatic period following her divorce. According to Andrews she saw, or thought she saw, an intriguing Native American basket in a photography exhibit in Los Angeles. Though no one else recalled seeing the basket, Andrews tracked it down to Agnes Whistling Elk, a Cree medicine woman of Manitoba, Canada. Andrews traveled to Manitoba, where she met Agnes Whistling Elk and her colleague, the blind Ruby Plenty Chiefs. She learned that she had been brought there by a vision. The basket, a sacred marriage basket, could not be purchased, but had to be won. It was in the possession of Red Dog, a white man turned sorcerer, who had once been an apprentice of Agnes Whistling Elk. He had sought out Agnes to restore the female balance in his own consciousness, but had attempted to steal all the power for himself and had been dismissed. He had stolen the female power in the form of the basket.

Andrews became an apprentice to the medicine women and was the first white person to join the Sisterhood of the Shields, a secret society of forty-four shamanesses from various tribal cultures who had dedicated themselves to preserving their shamanic traditions. Agnes told Andrews she was to be a bridge between the tribal and industrialized cultures, and was to write about her experiences. Andrews retrieved the sacred basket from Red Dog, who then became her lifelong enemy, and went on to other initiations. She chronicled these adventures in four bestselling books: *Medicine Woman* (1981), *Flight of the Seventh Moon: The Teaching of the Shields* (1984), *Jaguar Woman: And the Wisdom of the Butterfly Tree* (1985), and *Star Woman: We Are Made from Stars and to the Stars We Must Return* (1986). She explored the culture of aboriginal shamanesses in *Crystal Woman: The Sisters of the Dreamtime* (1987), Nepalese female adepts in *Windhorse Woman* (1989), and medieval wise women in *The Women of Wyrrd* (1990).

Andrews's work has drawn criticism from some Native Americans who feel she has misrepresented Native American spirituality, citing factual inaccuracies of geography, rites, and language. Andrews has stated she changed certain names and facts to protect the identity of her teachers, and that she described her experiences as they happened. She is not teaching or practicing Native American

(Courtesy Baker Winokur Ryder)

Lynn V. Andrews

tradition, she says, but is providing information to help reinstate "the feminine consciousness."

Andrews, like Castaneda, has been charged by some with fictionalizing her accounts. She has denied those allegations. In addition to writing, she has given shamanic initiatory seminars. Andrews lives in Beverly Hills, California, and writes at her studio in Santa Fe, New Mexico. See **Castaneda, Carlos.**

Sources: Jonathan Adolph and Richard Smoley. "Beverly Hills Shaman." *New Age* (March/April 1989): 22–26+; Lynn V. Andrews. *Medicine Woman.* San Francisco: Harper & Row, 1981; Lynn V. Andrews. *Flight of the Seventh Moon: The Teaching of the Shields.* San Francisco: Harper & Row, 1984; Lynn V. Andrews. *Jaguar Woman: And the Wisdom of the Butterfly Tree.* San Francisco: Harper & Row, 1985; Lynn V. Andrews. *Star Woman: We Are Made from Stars and to the Stars We Must Return.* New York: Warner Books, 1986; Bob Groves. "Mainstream Mysticism: Author Takes Her New Age Act on the Road." *Los Angeles Herald Examiner* (September 1, 1988): B1+; Beth Ann Krier. "The Medicine Woman of Beverly Hills."

Los Angeles Times (November 23, 1987): part 5, 1+; Rose Marie Staubs. "Andrews's Sisters." *Omni* (October 1987): 28; "The Beverly Hills Medicine Woman: An *EWJ* Interview with Lynn Andrews." *East West Journal* (June 1984): 30–35.

Angel

An immortal being who lives in the spirit world and serves as an intermediary between God and humanity. The word "angel" is derived from the Greek *angelos* and the Latin *angelus,* which mean "messenger." In religion angels belong to the class of beings known as demons; they may be either friendly or hostile to humankind. In art angels are depicted with wings and halos.

Angelology was developed in ancient Persia, and was absorbed into Judaism and Christianity. According to the Babylonian Talmud, all beings are led and protected by angels, who connect the earth to God.

The ancient Hebrews applied the term *malakh* (angel) to anyone who carried God's message in the world, including people. In Genesis 18 three men, or angels, appear to Abraham to predict the birth of Isaac. Later angels became spirit beings, serving God in heaven and coming to earth upon his instructions. Some angels evolved into guardian angels, such as Michael, the guardian of Israel.

The legions of angels are ranked in hierarchies. The highest in Judaism and Christianity are the seven archangels, each of whom is assigned to one of the seven spheres of heaven: Gabriel, Raphael, Michael, Uriel, Jophiel, Zadkiel, and Samael (Satan). When Lucifer was cast out of heaven by God, his angels fell with him. Theodore of Mopsuetia, an early Christian father, said these angels were not demons, but men who submitted to Lucifer and became his instruments, spreading vice, heresy, lies, profane learning, and all manner of ills throughout the world.

Lesser-ranked angels are the cherubim, seraphim, and various virtues, among many others. Catholics and some Protestants believe every person has a guardian angel. See **Spirit guide.**

In the mystical Jewish Kabbalah, an archangel is assigned to each emanation on the Tree of Life: Metatron for Kether, Ratziel for Chokmah, Tzaphiel for Binah, Tzadqiel for Chesed, Khameal for Geburah, Raphael for Tipareth, Haniel for Netzach, Michael for Hod, Gabriel for Yesod, and Sandalphon for Malkuth. The ancient Hebrews believed Metatron also served as a heavenly scribe, recording the good deeds of Israel.

Islam has four archangels, Azrael, Israfil, Gabriel, and Michael.

The Gnostics, who were influenced by Persian traditions, emphasized angelic hierarchies as well, and believed that angels lived in a world of mystical light between the mundane world and the Transcendent Causeless Cause.

Until about the eighteenth century, angels played roles in everyday life. Magicians conjured angelic and demonic spirits to effect their spells and do their bidding. Visions of angels were often reported as portents. Wizards, wise women, and witches credited angels with effecting cures. Angels were blamed for plagues, and were believed to intercede in the affairs of humankind. The Age of Enlightenment, with its emphasis on science and intellectual thought, relegated angels to the realm of poetry and romantic fancy.

The eighteenth-century Swedish mystic Emanuel Swedenborg claimed to commune with angels in his mystical trances. He said all angels once lived as men and women. As angels they are forms of affection and thought, the recipients of love and wisdom. The Lord appears as the sun above them.

Occultist and philosopher Rudolf Steiner conceived of a complex society of angels and spirits, the result of his own visionary experiences. Angels, in his unique system, exist on the first level of consciousness above humankind; above them, in ascending order of levels, are Archangels, Archai (Original Forces), Exusiai (Revelations or Powers), Dynameis (Mights), Kyriotetes (Dominions), Thrones, Cherubim, and Seraphim. Beyond the Seraphim is the Godhead. Each level of being has higher and broader responsibilities in terms of spiritual evolution, beginning with archangels, some of whom are responsible for leading races or nations.

In 1924 Geoffrey Hodson, a clairvoyant and Theosophist, was contacted by an angel named Bethelda, who transmitted to him ideas and information that Hodson turned into five books, the best known of which is *The Brotherhood of Angels and Men* (1927). Hodson envisioned humankind and angels as two branches in the family of God, who need to work more closely together for the spiritual benefit of humans.

According to Hodson the angelic host is arranged in divisions: Angels of Power, who teach humankind how to release spiritual energy; Angels of Healing; Guardian Angels of the Home, who protect the hearth against danger, disease, and ill fortune; Building Angels, who perfect and inspire in the worlds of thought, feeling, and flesh; Angels of Nature, the elemental spirits; Angels of Music; and Angels of Beauty and Art. Hodson prescribed rituals of invocation and prayer that would bring humans closer to angels.

People continue to experience angelic visions today, as they have throughout history. Often the appearance of a brilliant, loving being of light is interpreted within the context of the individual's religious beliefs. According to research of near-death experiences, the most common element is the appearance of an angelic being to guide the dying across the threshold of death. Communication is done by telepathy. On rare oc-

Angel announcing the birth of Christ (Luke 2:10–11)

casions the angel may be visible to people who are near the dying one.

In New Age occult and religious beliefs, angels have made a comeback in popularity. They are portrayed in karmic aspects of astrology, channeled, meditated upon, and said to exist in spirit realms. Angelic forces are invoked in magic rituals in various magical systems and witchcraft. The popular view holds that angels are benevolent beings and are different from demons, who are malevolent beings. See **Demon; Encounter phenomena; Nature spirits; Near-death experience (NDE).**

Sources: Francis Barrett. *The Magus.* 1801. Reprint. Secaucus, NJ: Citadel Press, 1967; Jean Danielou, S.J. *The Bible and the Liturgy.* Ann Arbor, MI: Servant Books, 1956; Jacques de Marquette. *Introduction to Comparative Mysticism.* New York: Philosophical Library, 1949; Vergilius Ferm. *The Encyclopedia of Religion.* Secaucus, NJ: Poplar Books, 1955; Geoffrey Hodson. *The Brotherhood of Angels and Men.* 1927. Wheaton, IL: Theosophical Publishing House, 1982; Raymond A. Moody, Jr., M.D. *Life After Life.* New

York: Bantam Books, 1975; Gershom Scholem. *Kabbalah*. New York: New American Library, 1974; Rudolf Steiner. *The Influence of Spiritual Beings Upon Man*. Spring Valley, NY: Anthroposophic Press, 1961; Emanuel Swedenborg. *Divine Providence*. 1764. New York: Swedenborg Foundation, 1972; Keith Thomas. *Religion and the Decline of Magic*. New York: Charles Scribner's Sons, 1971; Leo Trepp. *Judaism: Development and Life*. Belmont, CA: Dickenson Publishing, 1966.

Animal psi (also Anpsi)

The apparent ability of animals to experience clairvoyance, precognition, telepathy, and psychokinesis (PK). It is not known conclusively that animals possess psi, though many owners of pets are certain they do. Scientific evidence suggests that if psi exists, it probably does so in both humans and animals.

If animal psi exists, it most likely occurs in all species. In this discussion the term "animal psi" is all-inclusive. Some individual pets seem to be especially gifted. Animal lovers suggest that psi-gifted pets are those most loved by their owners, and that love nourishes psi.

Some reports of animal psi would be quite remarkable if demonstrated by human psychics. Missie, an allegedly clairvoyant Boston terrier, reportedly gave the correct number of barks to predict the victors of presidential elections, the number of delays in the launching of *Gemini 12*, the end of a New York subway strike, and the winner of the 1966 World Series. Similarly, various horses have been said to have psychic powers, and have tapped out messages with their hooves or by picking out alphabet blocks. In some cases, however, it has been shown that the animals were in fact responding to subtle body language and physical cues from their owners. See **Horse.**

Information about animal psi is largely anecdotal. The experimental evidence for animal psi is weak but encouraging. Generally, animals do not test well for psi, and it is often difficult to determine if the human experimenter unconsciously uses psi to influence the results of a test. See **Experimenter effect.** Psi tests are also complicated by differences in physical sense characteristics of various species. The rattlesnake, for example, has sensors behind its nostrils to help it detect the slightest changes in temperature. Most animal psi tests in the laboratory are done with cats and rodents, which are among the easiest and most convenient animals with which to work.

American parapsychologist J. B. Rhine pursued animal psi tests at Duke University. From five hundred unsolicited stories reported by animal owners, Rhine found five basic types of animal psi: the ability to sense impending danger; the ability to sense at a distance the death of, or harm to, a beloved human or fellow animal; the ability to sense the impending return of a master; the ability to find the way home; and the ability to "psi trail."

The Ability to Sense Impending Danger

Some animals seem to have precognitive awareness of natural disasters, or doom for their loved ones or themselves. They also appear to know telepathically when their loved ones are in danger.

Animals have been reported to act strangely before various types of catastrophes, such as avalanches, cyclones, volcanic eruptions, fires, and bombings. In parts of China, animals are considered to be potential predictors of earthquakes. Hours before the 1963 earthquake in Skopje, Yugoslavia, animals in the zoo became restless and agitated, pacing back and forth in their cages and charging the bars. Some scientists say that these animals are not picking up information psychically, but are reacting to subtle changes in the natural environment, such as changes in air pressure and tremors in the Earth, which are too slight to be noticed by humans. That theory, however, does not satisfactorily explain many incidents.

During the Battle of Britain in World War II, some people watched cat behavior as a predictor of bombings. If the hair on a cat's back stood up and the animal ran for cover into a shelter, people took shelter as well.

A study at the University of Waterloo in Ontario, Canada, suggested that rats have a sense of their own impending doom. Researchers J. G. Craig and W. C. Treurniet released rats at one corner of a reference grid and recorded their activity. Some time later half of the group was randomly selected to be killed. A subsequent analysis of the slain rats' movements on the grid indicated that they had been more active than the rats who were spared.

Many psychics like to have animals accompany them when they are investigating apparitions and haunted houses, because animals are assumed to be more sensitive to ghosts and spirits. Many dogs and cats have been known to visibly react in fear when placed in a suspected haunted house. One of the functions of the witch's animal "familiar" is to sense the presence of unwanted or evil energy.

Various laboratory tests have been done on animals to see if their precognition of impending harm to themselves causes them to use PK to avert the harm. Researcher Helmut Schmidt exposed both brine shrimp and cockroaches to electric shock determined by a random number generator. The shrimp received fewer shocks than would be expected by chance, but the cockroaches were shocked more, perhaps indicating psi missing. See **Psi hitting and psi missing.** The tests were inconclusive. Schmidt could not replicate the results with the shrimp, and his dislike for cockroaches may have influenced those tests. See **Experimenter effect.**

The Ability to Sense at a Distance the Death of, or Harm to, a Loved One

Many reports exist of animals knowing that a master or companion animal is about to be harmed or is being harmed. Abraham Lincoln's dog reportedly began to howl and run around the White House shortly before Lincoln was assassinated. A veterinarian reported that a dog in his care while its owners were vacationing howled for the entire hour that the owners were stranded in a flash flood. When Lord Carnarvon, sponsor of the expedition that discovered King Tutankhamen's tomb, died in Cairo, his dog in England died at about the same hour.

Animals also seem to sense danger to loved ones who are related to their owners. A Great Dane sensed that his master's visiting sister had been killed while on a day trip. The dog's response was to gather the sister's personal belongings together, lie down on the floor, and whimper. On three different occasions packs of mice were seen abandoning a New York City townhouse a few days before the death of the house's owner.

Laboratory experiments also have suggested that animals experience physiological reactions when they psychically receive this type of information from distant people or animals. A boxer attached to an electrocardiograph had a violent heartbeat when his mistress in another room was suddenly threatened by an abusive stranger. Soviet researchers tested a mother rabbit and her reactions when her babies were in danger at a distance. The mother's brain was implanted with electrodes and monitored in a laboratory on shore, while her babies were taken out beneath the sea in a submarine. As each baby was killed, the mother's brain indicated a strong reaction.

The Ability to Sense the Impending Return of a Master

Animals will anticipate the return of a loved one from a short or long trip by sitting near the door or gate until the person's arrival. A Vietnam soldier coming home unexpectedly, and planning to surprise his family, was preempted by his dog, which had gathered the soldier's personal items and piled them by the door several hours before his arrival.

The Ability to Find the Way Home

Many animals exhibit remarkable abilities to find their way home through unfamiliar territory and without any discernible assistance or means. Scientists who have studied the homing and migratory instincts of birds have put forth theories that birds take cues from the position of the sun in the sky, or are sensitive to the Earth's magnetic field. In the 1950s American parapsychologist Gaither Pratt did extensive tests with homing pigeons. A pigeon's orientation within seconds of flight suggested to him that psi was a factor. His tests, however, were inconclusive.

The Ability to "Psi Trail"

Psi trailing is the ability of an animal that is separated from its owner to find its way over long distances to be reunited. Animal enthusiasts see it as a manifestation of the animal's great love and devotion. Researchers Vincent and Margaret Gaddis theorize that animals follow a "directional beam of love, a magnet of the heart."

In a laboratory setting at Duke University, parapsychologist Karlis Osis attempted to will cats to follow a certain direction. The higher number of correct choices was made by those cats with which he had developed a special rapport.

Animals in Out-of-Body Experience Tests

In the 1970s a group of researchers used animals as detectors in out-of-body experiments (OBE). A human subject, Keith Harary, projected himself out-of-body and visited the animals to see if they would react to his invisible presence. Poor results were obtained with rodents and a snake, but statistically significant results were obtained with a seven-week-old kitten that had demonstrated an immediate and strong rapport with Harary. During the tests Harary "visited" the kitten in a certain corner of the animal's box and comforted it. Consistently, the kitten was active except during Harary's OBE periods, when it became very quiet. Another test to determine the kitten's response to direction and distance of Harary's OBE yielded poor results. However, critics contend various factors could have interfered with the procedure. Compare with **Plants, psychism of.**

Sources: J. Allen Boone. *Kinship with All Life.* New York: Harper & Row, 1954; Hoyt L. Edge, Robert L. Morris, John Palmer, and Joseph H. Rush. *Foundations of Parapsychology.* Boston: Routledge & Kegan Paul, 1986; Jurgen Keil, ed. *Gaither Pratt: A Life for Parapsychology.* Jefferson, NC: McFarland, 1979; Robert L. Morris, Stuart B. Harary, Joseph Janis, John Hartwell, and W. G. Roll. "Studies of Communication During Out-of-Body Experiences." *Journal of the American Society for Psychical Research* 71, no. 1 (January 1978): 1–21; Sheila Ostrander and Lynn Schroeder. *Psychic Discoveries Behind the Iron Curtain.* Englewood Cliffs, NJ: Prentice-Hall, 1970; Rene Peoch. "Chicken Imprinting and the Tychoscope, an Anpsi Experiment." *Journal of the Society for Psychical Research* 55, no. 810 (January 1988): 1–9; D. Scott Rogo. *Psychic Breakthroughs Today.* Wellingborough, Northamptonshire, England: The Aquarian Press, 1987; Bill Schul. *The Psychic Power of Animals.* New York: Fawcett Gold Medal, 1977; Benjamin B. Wolman, ed. *Handbook of Parapsychology.* New York: Van Nostrand Reinhold, 1977; Joseph Edward Wydler. *Psychic Pets: The Secret World of Animals.* New York: Stonehill Publishing, 1978.

Anthroposophy

See **Steiner, Rudolf.**

Apocalypse, Book of the

See **Revelation, Book of.**

Apparition

The supernormal manifestation of people, animals, objects, and spirits. Most apparitions are of living people or animals who are too distant to be perceived by normal senses. Apparitions of the dead are also called ghosts. Despite extensive study since the late nineteenth century, science still knows little about the nature of apparitions.

Characteristics

Most apparition experiences feature noises, unusual smells, extreme cold, and the displacement of objects. Other phenomena include visual images, tactile sensations, voices, the apparent psychokinetic movement of objects, and so on. Visual images are seen in only a small percentage of reported cases.

A study of apparitions published in 1956 by American psychical researcher Hornell Hart and collaborators showed no significant differences between characteristics of apparitions of the living and of the dead. Some apparitions seem corporeal, while others are luminous, transparent, or ill-defined. Apparitions move through solid matter and appear and disappear abruptly. They can cast shadows and be reflected in mirrors. Some have

(Photo by Bonnie Sue.)

A possible apparition captured on film. Apparition was not visible when photographer took picture inside the Duomo church in Parma, Italy.

jerky and limited movements, while others are lifelike in movement and speech.

Apparitions invariably are clothed. Ghosts appear in period costume, and apparitions of the living appear in clothing worn at the moment.

More than 80 percent of the apparitions cases that have been studied manifest for a reason, such as to communicate a crisis or death, provide a warning, comfort the grieving, or convey needed information. Some haunting apparitions seem to appear in places where emotional events have occurred, such as murders or battles, while other hauntings seem to be aimless.

Apparitions can be divided into at least seven types:

1. Crisis apparitions: usually visual images, which appear in waking visions or dreams at a moment of crisis, such as to communicate dying or death. Typically, but not always, they appear to individuals who have

close emotional ties to the agent (the person who is the source of the apparition).

2. Apparitions of the dead: manifestations of the deceased, usually within a short time after death, to comfort the grieving or to communicate information, conclude unfinished business, or announce a role as guardian spirit.

3. Collective apparitions: manifestations of either the living or dead that occur simultaneously to multiple witnesses. Approximately one-third of reported apparitions are witnessed collectively.

4. Reciprocal apparitions: apparitions of the living in which both agent and percipient (the person who perceives the apparition), separated by distance, experience each other simultaneously. A possible explanation is that the agent has a strong desire or impulse to see the percipient and unconsciously projects out-of-body. See **Out-of-body experience (OBE).**

5. Veridical apparitions: apparitions that can be corroborated by fact. Veridical apparitions are of most value and interest to parapsychologists.

6. Deathbed apparitions: visual images of divine beings, religious figures, luminosities, and dead loved ones that are reported by the dying in the last moments of life. See **Deathbed visions.**

7. Apparitions in cases suggestive of reincarnation: "announcing dreams," in which the deceased appears in a dream to a member of the family into which it will be born. Such dreams occur frequently among the Tlingit and other Native Northwest American tribes, and in Turkey, Burma, and Thailand. See **Reincarnation.**

Systematic studies of apparitions were inaugurated in the late nineteenth century by the Society for Psychical Research (SPR), London. Founding members Edmund Gurney, Frederic W. H. Myers, and Frank Podmore questioned 5,700 people about apparitions of the living and published their findings in *Phantasms of the Living* (1886). In 1889 a Census of Hallucinations was undertaken by Henry and Eleanor Sidgwick, Alice Johnson Myers, A. T. Myers, and Podmore. They polled 17,000 people, of whom 1,684 (9.9 percent) reported having apparitional experiences of either the living or the dead. Some experiences were witnessed collectively.

The methodology for the census would not meet modern research standards. The number of 17,000 questionnaires was arbitrary, and there was no method to the distribution of forms. Most likely, many went to friends and acquaintances of the surveyors. The survey asked only one question: whether respondents had ever had an impression of a being or person, or had heard a voice, not of natural cause.

Of the 1,684 affirmative replies, approximately six hundred seemed to have natural explanations and were ruled out. There were about eighty cases of crisis apparitions seen within twelve hours before or after someone's death; only thirty-two of these were cases in which the percipient had no prior knowledge that the agent was ill or dying. However, even this small number was statistically significant when compared to the mortality tables of England.

A similar census was done in France, Germany, and the United States. It polled 27,329 people, of whom 11.96 percent reported apparitional experiences.

By the 1980s polls in the United States conducted by the University of Chicago's National Opinion Research Council (NORC) showed a dramatic increase in reported apparitions of the dead: 42 percent of the adult population, and 67 percent of widows, reported experiences, perhaps due in part to changing public attitudes toward acknowledging paranormal experiences. Of these 78 percent involved visual images, 50 percent noises and voices, 21 percent tactile sensations, 32 percent sensation of a presence, and 18 percent communication with the apparition. Forty-six percent experienced a combination of phenomena.

Theories about Apparitions

Numerous theories have been put forth, but none satisfactorily explains all types of apparitions. Both Gurney and Myers believed apparitions were mental hallucinations. Gurney proposed they were produced by telepathy from the dead to the living. In collective cases he said that a single percipient received the telepathy and in turn telepathically transmitted the hallucination to other witnesses. That theory, however, cannot explain why witnesses in a collective case notice different details. Myers, who believed in survival after death, began to doubt the telepathic theory as early as 1885. In *Human Personality and the Survival of Bodily Death* (1903), he proposed that apparitions had a "phantasmogenic center," a locus of energies that could be perceived by the most psychically sensitive people.

He conceived of a "subliminal consciousness" as the basis from which consciousness springs, and which survives the body after death. He theorized that the subliminal consciousness was receptive to extrasensory input.

An elaborate theory of "idea-patterns" was proposed by English researcher G. N. M. Tyrrell in *Apparitions* (1943; 1953). Like Gurney, Tyrrell believed that apparitions were hallucinations on the part of a percipient based on information received from the agent through ESP. The hallucination was created in a two-part drama. First, a part of the unconscious called the "Producer" received the information via ESP. Then, a "Stage Carpenter" produced the drama—with the required props, such as clothing and objects—in visions, dreams, or hallucinations.

Other theories propose that apparitions are:

- astral or etheric bodies of the agents
- an amalgam of personality patterns, which in the case of hauntings are trapped in a psychic ether or psi field
- recordings or imprints of vibrations impressed upon some sort of psychic ether, which play back to sensitive individuals
- personae or vehicles through which the "I-thinking consciousness" takes on a personality, perhaps not fully conscious, as well as temporarily visible form
- projections of the human unconscious, a manifestation of an unacknowledged need, unresolved guilt, or embodiment of a wish
- projections of will and concentration (see **Thought-form**)
- true spirits of the dead
- localized phenomena with their own physicality, directed by an intelligence or personality. No conclusive evidence has been found to indicate whether apparitions are animated by personalities, however.

The ability to have hallucinatory experiences may be a function of personality. In his examination of hallucinatory cases, researcher Andrew MacKenzie found that about one-third of the cases occurred just before or after sleep (see **Hypnagogic/hypnapompic states**), or when the percipient was awakened at night. Other experiences took place when the witness was in a state of relaxation, doing routine work in the home, or concentrating on some activity such as reading a book. With the external world shut out, the subconscious was able to release impressions, which sometimes took the form of an apparition. See **Haunting; Poltergeist.**

Sources: Loyd Auerbach. *ESP, Hauntings and Poltergeists: A Parapsychologist's Handbook.* New York: Warner, 1986; Richard Cavendish. *The Encyclopedia of the Unexplained.* New York: McGraw-Hill, 1967; Tracy Cochran. "The Real Ghost Busters." *Omni* 10, no. 11 (August 1988): 35–36+; Charles Emmons. *Chinese Ghosts and ESP.* Metuchen, NJ: Scarecrow Press, 1982; Andrew Greeley. "Mysticism Goes Mainstream." *American Health* (January/ February 1987): 47–55; Celia Green and Charles McCreery. *Apparitions.* London: Hamish Hamilton, 1975; Edmund Gurney, F. W. H. Myers, and Frank Podmore. *Phantasms of the Living.* 1886. London: Kegan Paul, Trench, Trubner & Co., Ltd., 1918; Hornell Hart. "Six Theories about Apparitions." *Proceedings of the Society for Psychical Research* 50, (May 1956): 153–236; Hornell Hart. *The Enigma of Survival.* Springfield, IL: Charles C. Thomas, 1959; Hornell Hart and Ella B. Hart. "Visions and Apparitions Collectively and Reciprocally Perceived." *Proceedings of the Society for Psychical Research* 41, part 130 (1932–33): 205–49; Renee Haynes. "What Do You Mean by a Ghost?" *Parapsychology Review* 17, no. 4: 9–12; Ake Hultkranz. *The Religions of the American Indians.* 1967. Berkeley: University of California Press, 1979; Andrew MacKenzie. *Hauntings and Apparitions.* London: William Heinemann Ltd., 1982; Elizabeth E. McAdams and Raymond Bayless. *The Case for Life after Death.* Chicago: Nelson-Hall, 1981; Edgar D. Mitchell. *Psychic Exploration: A Challenge for Science.* Edited by John White. New York: Paragon Books, 1974; Frederic W. H. Myers. *Human Personality and Its Survival of Bodily Death.* Vols. 1 and 2. 1903. New ed. New York: Longmans, Green & Co., 1954; Karlis Osis. "Apparitions Old and New." In K. Ramakrishna Rao, ed. *Case Studies in Parapsychology.* Jefferson, NC: McFarland & Co., 1986; Ian Stevenson. "The Contribution of Apparitions to the Evidence for Survival." *The Journal of the American Society for Psychical Research* 76, no. 4 (October 1982): 341–56; Keith Thomas. *Religion and the Decline of Magic.* New York: Charles Scribner's Sons, 1971; G. N. M. Tyrrell. *Apparitions.* 1943. Rev. 1953. London: The Society for Psychical Research, 1973; Peter Underwood. *The Ghost Hunter's Guide.* Poole, Dorset, England: Blandford Press, 1986.

Applied psi

An offshoot of parapsychology that assumes the existence of psychic abilities and seeks ways to apply them to mainstream life. The field also is called "applied parapsychology" and "psionics." The latter term was created in the early 1980s by American parapsychologist Jeffrey Mishlove, who borrowed it from science fiction literature.

Applied psi has existed since ancient times in so-called "primitive" cultures, in which shamans, medicine men, and sorcerers for centuries have used psychic powers to heal, control weather, ensure successful hunts and fecund marriages, and cast and lift spells. It continues to be used in present times, in its broadest sense, whenever anyone acts on intuition to make decisions.

Some experimental studies relevant to applied psi development, such as studies of mesmeric phenomena, date back to the eighteenth century. But as psychical research in general advanced, applied psi languished as a discipline until the twentieth century. In 1962 the Newark College of Engineering in New Jersey became one of the first engineering centers in the United States to explore the psi faculty in people. Researchers studied successful business executives, and found that most company presidents not only believe in psi, but use it daily in their jobs in the form of intuition, hunches, and gut instinct. Test results did not prove that precognition, the ability to see the future, was related to profit-making, but did demonstrate that the probability of a company being run by a superior profit-maker is enhanced with the choice of a person who scores well in precognition.

In the early 1980s Mishlove urged parapsychologists to look beyond laboratory experiments that seek to prove the existence of psi. He said that the existence of psi should be assumed, and research should focus on ways to apply it in social, business, industrial, and scientific activities. He accurately predicted that as the existence of psi became more accepted, scientists would spend less time convincing skeptics of the validity of research and devote more attention to the applications of research.

By 1984 applied psi had become an informal part of at least twenty-eight fields: archaeology, agriculture and pest control, animal training and interspecies communication, contests and gambling, creativity, education and training, entertainment, environmental improvement, executive decision making, finding lost objects, future forecasting, geological exploration, historical investigation, investigative journalism, medicine and dentistry, military intelligence, personnel management, police work, psychotherapy and counseling, safety inspection, scientific discovery, social control, and weather prediction control. However, the subjective and erratic nature of psi make it an unreliable tool.

Some experiments have raised interesting questions as to how effective applied psi can be used in financial investing. It is not uncommon for people to place a bet or make an investment based on a hunch, dream, or intuitive feeling. In 1937 British psychic researcher Dame Edith Lyttleton published *Some Cases of Prediction*. In many of these cases people had placed winning bets on horse races based on precognitive dreams and clairaudient voices. In the 1960s experiments showed the success of applied psi in roulette. In 1982 Delphi Associates in San Francisco, California, used a psychic to predict fluctuations in the silver market, which netted a reported $100,000 in profits. The predictions were made by psychic Keith Harary over a nine-week period. Harary did not predict actual price changes, but was asked to describe an object that was to be placed in his hands the following week. The objects were coded according to movements in the market. The money was invested by a group of investors participating in the experiment.

Another experiment, conducted by the *St. Louis Business Journal* in 1982, compared the investment results of a group of nineteen experienced brokers and a St. Louis, Missouri, psychic, Bevy Jaegers. Each participant picked five stocks. The stocks picked by the brokers fell in value, while Jaegers's stocks rose 17.4 percent.

Despite such successes a more widespread use of applied psi in the stock market apparently would backfire. If all investors could predict the market, the dynamic processes of the market itself would negate the intuition because there would be no price that balanced the buyers and sellers. See **Psychic archaeology; Psychic criminology; Psychotronics.**

Sources: Douglas Dean and John Mihalasky, and Sheila Ostrander and Lynn Schroeder. *Executive ESP.* Englewood Cliffs, NJ: Prentice-Hall, 1974; Jeffrey Mishlove and William H. Kautz. "An Emerging New Discipline!" *Applied Psi* 1, no. 1 (March/April 1982): 1; Jeffrey Mishlove. *Psi Development Systems.* Jefferson, NC: McFarland & Co., 1983; Jeffrey Mishlove. "Psionics: The Practical Application of Psi." *Applied Psi* 3, no. 3 (Fall 1984): 10–14, 16; Marshall Pease. "Intuition and the Stock Market." *Applied Psi* 3, no. 3 (Fall 1984): 7–9+ ; D. Scott Rogo. *Psychic Breakthroughs Today.* Wellingborough, Northamptonshire, England: The Aquarian Press, 1987.

Apport

An object certain mediums and adepts claim to materialize from thin air or transport through solid matter. Apports also are a phenomenon of poltergeist cases.

Most apports are small objects, such as candy, coins, feathers, pebbles, rings, or vials of perfume. Some are large and quite unusual, such as flowers, books, serving dishes, and live animals, fish, and birds. During the height of Spiritualism, apports were commonplace at seances. The live dove was a favorite. Madame d'Esperance produced impressive live and rooted flowers. William Stainton Moses produced showers of tiny semiprecious and precious stones. Some mediums were exposed as frauds in producing their apports, which they hid on their persons or in the room prior to the seance. Seances almost always were conducted in the dark, making trickery easy.

Mediums usually said their apports were brought to a seance as gifts from the spirits. Other theories proposed that the medium pulled objects from other dimensions through sheer willpower and some sort of psychic magnetism, or that the medium somehow took existing objects in other locations, disintegrated them, then transported and reassembled them.

The Sufis, the mystical adepts of Islam, and Hindu swamis and holy men are renowned for the apports they produce, including food, precious jewelry, religious objects, and *vibuti* (holy ash). Like mediums, some adepts have been detected using sleight of hand; but others, such as Sai Baba of India, have never been exposed as frauds. Sai Baba's apports include vibuti, sweets, entire banquets of hot food, business cards, jewelry, religious statuettes, and many other objects. Most are produced within his closed fist, while others are pulled out of sand on the ground. Food is produced in dishes. See Materialization; Poltergeist; Sai Baba; Teleportation.

Sources: Slater Brown. *The Heyday of Spiritualism.* New York: Hawthorn Books, 1970; Alfred Douglas. *Extrasensory Powers: A Century of Psychical Research.* London: Victor Gollancz Ltd., 1976; Nandor Fodor. *An Encyclopedia of Psychic Science.* 1933. Secaucus, NJ: Citadel Press, 1966; Erlendur Haraldsson. *Modern Miracles: An Investigative Report on Psychic Phenomena Associated with Sathya Sai Baba.* New York: Fawcett Columbine, 1987; Edgar D. Mitchell. *Psychic Exploration: A Challenge for Science.* Edited by John White. New York: Paragon Books, 1974; Benjamin B. Wolman, ed. *Handbook of Parapsychology.* New York: Van Nostrand Reinhold, 1977.

Archetypes

The contents of the collective unconscious as universal primordial images passed down from an ancestral past that includes not only early humankind but humankind's prehuman and animal ancestors. Archetypes are not part of conscious thought, but are predispositions toward certain behaviors—patterns of psychological performance linked to instinct—such as fear of the dark or the maternal instinct, which become filled out and modified through individual experience.

Psychiatrist Carl G. Jung developed, but did not originate, the concept of archetypes; they have existed universally for thousands of years in mythologies and in the motifs of fairy tales and folktales. The Greek philosopher Heraclitus was the first to view the psyche as the archetypal first principle. The idea of archetypes was articulated by Plato in his Theory of Forms, which holds that the essence of a thing or concept is its underlying form or idea. See **Plato.** The term "archetype" occurs in the writing of Philo Judaeus, Irenaeus, and Dionysius the Areopagite. The concept, but not the term, is found in the writings of St. Augustine.

Jung first wrote of primordial images in the unconscious of his patients in 1912. He first used the term "archetype" in 1919, in order to distinguish between the archetype itself and the archetypal image, which is perceived on a conscious level.

According to Jung archetypes are unlimited in number. They are created by the repetition of situations and experiences engraved upon the psychic constitution. They are not, however, forms of images filled with content, but forms without content. When a situation occurs that corresponds to an archetype, it becomes activated and a compulsiveness appears. God, birth, death, rebirth, power, magic, the sun, the moon, the wind, animals, and the elements are archetypes; as are traits embodied in the Hero, the Sage, the Judge, the Child, the Trickster, and the Earth Mother. Associations, symbols, situations, and processes are archetypes. Their role in the personality changes as an individual grows and encounters new situations. Archetypes communicate with the conscious, and one may achieve insight into the self by attempting to identify and pay attention to archetypal forces in one's life. Archetypes, said Jung, are psychic forces that demand to be taken seriously; if neglected they can cause neurotic and even psychotic disorders.

Jung identified four major archetypes as playing significant roles in human personality and behavior:

1. The persona. The public mask or "outward face," as Jung termed it, behind which a person lives in accordance with the expectations of society. Individuals have a collection of masks to meet various social situations.
2. The shadow. The inferior, other side of a person, which exists in the personal unconscious. The shadow is uncivilized and desires to do that which is not allowed by the persona. It remains primitive throughout life, and often appears in dreams as an unlikable, crude person of the same sex as the dreamer. The shadow is despised and rejected; the most difficult aspect of psychotherapy is getting the patient to face his or her own shadow.
3. The anima and animus. The female and male sides of the psyche, respectively. Every person has qualities of both sexes, which enables a full range of expressions. The anima and animus are projected first onto mother and father, then onto others. The anima and animus often are underdeveloped due to Western cultural conditioning, which discourages in children behavior associated with the opposite sex.
4. The self. The central archetype of the collective unconsciousness, and the organizing principle of the personality. It exists apart from the ego, which is the center of the conscious mind. The self unites the conscious and unconscious, and fosters an awareness of the interpenetration of all life and energies in the cosmos. It usually emerges in middle age, after sufficient development of the personality through individuation (the Hero's journey). Jung appreciated the paths to realization of self through Eastern religions and meditation, but said greater emphasis should be placed on knowledge of self, which may be obtained through dreams.

Jung said the existence of archetypes can be proved through dreams, the primary source; and through "active imagination," or fantasies produced by deliberate concentration. He said other sources of archetypal material are found in the delusions of paranoiacs, the fantasies of trance states, and the dreams of early childhood, from ages three to five.

Jung himself had an encounter with archetypes and the collective unconscious between the ages of three and four, when he dreamed of a dark opening in the Earth and of pagan god symbols. The dream had a profound impact on him, and he was unable to speak of it until he was sixty-five; he believed it was evidence of the collective unconscious. As a boy he began to feel that he had two separate personalities: one who was his normal self, and a second, archetypal personality who was much older, lived outside of time, and personified all the experiences of human life. As he grew older the second personality, whom he named Philemon, increased in dominance and was in conflict with his first personality.

Jung devoted a great deal of study to archetypes. Over the years he modified his concept of them but never offered a definitive definition. In 1946 he put forward the idea of the psychoid unconscious, which gave rise to the psychoid archetype. The psychoid unconscious refers to a most fundamental level of the unconscious, which cannot be accessed by the conscious, and which has properties in common with the organic world. It is formed of, and bridges, two worlds; it is both psychological and physiological, material and nonmaterial. Thus a psychoid archetype expresses a psychic/organic link: the psychic in the process of becoming material.

Jung's critics contended archetypes were "inherited representations" and superstition, to which Jung replied that if that were the case, then archetypes would be readily understood when they appear in the consciousness. In fact, he said, people are often mystified by archetypes, especially when they appear as unknown symbols in dreams.

Archetypes are central to Jungian psychotherapy in the process of individuation, a person becoming whole. Arche-

typal symbols in dreams reveal progress, or lack of it, in the process. By understanding them, the individual discovers what needs to be done to move forward. Interpretations of archetypes have been applied to diverse fields besides psychology, such as women's studies, mythologies, the healing professions, and the Tarot.

In transpersonal psychology archetypes emerge in certain transpersonal experiences, such as psychedelic therapy, in which they reflect the material world or have an existence of their own. In past-life regression therapy, past-life images are seen by some therapists as archetypes and not necessarily as real past-life material. See **Collective unconscious; Dreams; Jung, Carl Gustav; Mythology; Past-life therapy; Psychology; Symbols; Tarot.**

Sources: Joseph Campbell. *The Hero with a Thousand Faces.* 1949. New York: World Publishing, 1970; Joseph Campbell, ed. *The Mystic Vision: Papers from the Eranos Yearbooks.* Vol. 6. Princeton: Bollingen/Princeton University Press, 1968; Frieda Fordham. *An Introduction to Jung's Psychology.* 3d ed. Harmondsworth, England: Penguin Books, 1966; Stanislav Grof. *Beyond the Brain: Birth, Death, and Transcendence in Psychotherapy.* Albany, NY: State University of New York, 1985; Calvin S. Hall and Vernon A. Nordby. *A Primer on Jungian Psychology.* New York: New American Library, 1973; C. G. Jung. *The Archetypes and the Collective Unconscious.* 2d ed. Bollingen Series 20. Princeton: Princeton University Press, 1968; Carl G. Jung, ed. *Man and His Symbols.* 1964. New York: Anchor Press/Doubleday, 1988; C. G. Jung. "Commentary." *The Secret of the Golden Flower.* Translated and explained by Richard Wilhelm. Rev. ed. New York: Harcourt Brace Jovanovich, 1962; C. G. Jung. *Psychological Reflections.* 1945. Rev. 1949. Bollingen Series 31. New York: Pantheon Books, 1953; Carol Pearson. *The Hero Within: Six Archetypes We Live By.* San Francisco: Harper & Row, 1986; Andrew Samuels, Bani Shorter, and Fred Plaut. *A Critical Dictionary of Jungian Analysis*. London: Routledge & Kegan Paul, 1986; Roger Woolger. *Other Lives, Other Selves*. Garden City, NY: Doubleday, 1987.

Arigo

See **Psychic surgery.**

Artificial elemental

See **Thought-form.**

Ashram

A Sanskrit term for a retreat or center of spiritual study. Spending time at an ashram is believed to quicken one's progress in spiritual development. A Spartan daily discipline is usually followed. This may include yoga; a vegetarian diet (perhaps served in only one meal per day); sleeping on a mat on the floor; long periods of meditation, contemplation, and silence; work duties; and studying spiritual teachings under the tutelage of a guru.

Ashrams may admit outsiders into long- or short-term residencies. Permanent residents at some may hold outside jobs in the local community. In India most ashrams attract more Westerners than Indians and other Easterners; even so, many have few inhabitants. Westerners seek out ashrams to find spiritual fulfillment they feel is lacking in Western culture and religion. Young Indians, on the other hand, look to the West for a better, albeit material, way of life. One exception to the low residencies is Sathya Sai Baba's ashram, Prashanti Nilayam ("Abode of Great Peace") in Puttaparti, India, where thousands gather to be near Sai Baba. The emphasis at Prashanti Nilayam is on short meditation, devotion, purity in daily life, social and welfare work, and the singing of *bhajans,* or ancient religious songs. See **Guru; Sai Baba.**

Sources: Ram Dass. *Journey of Awakening: A Meditator's Guidebook.* New York: Bantam Books, 1978; Erlendur Haraldsson. *Modern Miracles: An Investigative Report on Psychic Phenomena Associated with Sathya Sai Baba.* New York: Fawcett Columbine, 1987; Stephen R. Wilson. "It's Therapeutic to Live in an Ashram." *Perspective* 9, no. 3 (October 1987): 2.

Assagioli, Roberto

See **Psychology.**

Association for Research and Enlightenment (ARE)

A nonprofit foundation established in 1931 by American medium Edgar Cayce and a group of associates in Virginia Beach, Virginia, to pursue work and education in spiritual healing, psychic development, reincarnation studies, holistic health care, and meditation instruction. The activities and teachings of the ARE are based on Cayce's philosophy and his thousands of trance readings. Membership is open to the public.

In 1928, prior to establishing the ARE, Cayce set up a hospital and university in Virginia Beach. In his dreams and trance readings, he had been directed to move from Dayton, Ohio, to Virginia Beach and establish a great learning institution. The institution foundered in the Depression and had to be closed in 1931. Urged by many to continue their work, Cayce and his associates regrouped and formed a new association, the ARE, the same year. The name was suggested by Dr. Manning Brown.

The ARE regained the hospital in 1956. In 1975 the ARE constructed a library/conference center, which receives more than 40,000 visitors and conference-goers a year. The library has one of the largest parapsychological and metaphysical collections in the world, with more than 55,000 volumes and 30,000 Cayce readings. In 1985 Atlantic University reopened.

One of the foundation's major concerns is health, and the treatment of diseases and illnesses in accordance with Cayce's diagnoses and remedies. More than half of his trance readings concerned physical conditions. The ARE maintains close ties with doctors who believe in Cayce's healing concepts. In 1970 the ARE established a medical clinic in Phoenix, Arizona, where patients are treated in accordance with Cayce's readings.

The ARE also publishes a wide range of materials, hosts seminars, and helps organize small study groups. See **Cayce, Edgar.**

Sources: Association for Research and Enlightenment; Mary Ellen Carter. *Edgar Cayce on Prophecy.* New York: Warner, 1968; Hans Holzer. *Beyond Medicine: The Facts about Unorthodox Treatments and Psychic Healing.* Rev. ed. New York: Ballantine Books, 1987; Thomas Sugrue. *There Is a River: The Story of Edgar Cayce.* Rev. ed. Virginia Beach, VA: ARE Press, 1973.

Astral body

See **Aura; Out-of-body experience (OBE).**

Astral projection

See **Out-of-body experience (OBE).**

Astrology

An ancient system of divination using the positions of the planets, moon, and stars. According to astrology the celestial bodies exert forces and exhibit personalities that influence people and events below. These influences may be determined by mapping positions in the sky at various times.

The origins of astrology may date to fifty thousand years ago, when Cro-Magnon people read patterns of stars in the sky and marked seasons by notching bones. It was not until about 3000 B.C. that astrology was developed into a system, first by the Chaldeans, who gazed at the heavens from their ziggurats, a type of staired tower.

The Babylonians also practiced astrology. Scholars disagree over whether the Chaldeans or the Babylonians formalized the zodiac, c. 3000 B.C. The zodiac is a band of twelve constellations through which the sun, moon, and planets appear to journey. The band is the ecliptic, the middle of which is the plane of the Earth's orbit around the sun. The term "zodiac" ("circus of animals") was coined later by the Greeks.

The ancients used the movements of planetary bodies through the zodiac to forecast auspicious times for matters of state and war, and to predict weather and natural disasters. Two types of astrology evolved: horary, which determines auspicious times for action; and mundane, which predicts disasters and other great happenings and is concerned with countries, races, and groups of people.

Around the fifth century B.C., the Chaldeans observed relationships between the positions of planets at the time of birth and a person's subsequent destiny. Gradually, the horoscope, or birth chart, was born, to be fully developed later by the Greeks. This third type of astrology, natal, has proved to be the most enduringly popular.

The ancient Chinese, c. 2000 B.C., also practiced astrology. The emperor was considered the high priest of the heavens and made sacrifices to the stars to stay in harmony with them. The four corners of the emperor's palace represented the cardinal points in space, the equinoxes and solstices, and he and his family moved from one corner to another as the seasons changed.

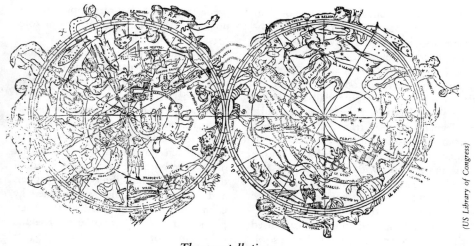

The constellations

The ancient Indians, Maya, Egyptians, and Tibetans also used various forms of astrology.

Typically, early astrology was the province of royalty. Around 600 B.C. to 500 B.C., the ancient Greeks assimilated Chaldean astrology and made it available to the masses. Pythagoras, Plato, and Aristotle were among the many great thinkers who accepted the influence, but not the rule, of the stars upon life on Earth. The Greeks believed that astrology could reveal favorable and unfavorable times for taking certain actions, but could not guarantee success.

The Romans learned astrology from Greek slaves c. 250 B.C.–244 B.C., contributing the names of the planets still used today. Astrologer fortune-tellers, many of them fraudulent, became so popular that they were driven out by decree in 139 B.C. by Cornelius Hispallus. They infiltrated society and reestablished themselves among all classes of society. Augustus was the first Roman emperor to become a believer in astrology.

Circa A.D. 140–200 the most important book in the history of Western astrology was written by Ptolemy, Greco-Egyptian astronomer who devised the Earth-centered Ptolemaic system of the universe. His *Tetrabiblios* (*Four Books on the Influence of the Stars*) created the foundation upon which astrology still rests.

In A.D. 333 Emperor Constantine, a Christian convert, condemned astrology as a "demonic" practice. Later St. Augustine also denounced it.

While astrology withered in the West, it continued to flourish in the East and the Islamic world. Avicenna, the tenth-century Persian alchemist and philosopher, refuted it, but it remained entrenched in royal courts and society.

Beginning in about the twelfth century, Arab astrology found its way back into the West through Spanish Kabbalists. By the time of the Renaissance, virtually all great scientists, alchemists, astronomers, physicians, and philosophers studied and accepted astrology. Paracelsus related it to alchemy and medicine, advising that no prescriptions be given without consulting the heavens. Astrology was taught in universities and was tolerated by the church.

With the development of science in the seventeenth century, astrology once again became relegated to superstition and the occult, but never fell out of public favor. Today it is followed by celebrities and the rich and powerful as well as the general public.

Psychiatrist Carl G. Jung sometimes consulted the horoscopes of his patients to search for inner potentials and latent problems. He believed that astrology, like alchemy, sprang from the collective unconscious—that it was a symbolic language of psychological processes, uniting the inner world with the outer. He also said that astrology is synchronistic: whatever is born or done has the quality of that moment in time.

In the East modern astrology is used chiefly for divination. In the West astrology has been used increasingly in alternative forms of counseling and therapy.

Natal Astrology

The horoscope—a Greek term meaning "I look at the hour"—predicts the general course of a person's character and destiny throughout life based on the positions of the planets at the exact time and place of birth. The oldest surviving horoscope is Babylonian, c. 410 B.C.; another found in Uruk, Chaldea (now Iraq), dates to 263 B.C.

The most important factor in a horoscope is the sun sign, the constellation of the zodiac occupied by the sun at the time of birth. The sun sign indicates overall personality traits.

Next in importance is the rising sign, or ascendant, which reveals character, abilities, the manner of self-expression, and one's early environment. The horoscope is divided into twelve houses, each of which influences a different facet of one's life. The houses are, in order, personality, finances, communication, early home, children, health and service, marriage, philosophy, profession, friends, and karma.

The horoscope ideally is a guide to opportunities and potential problems, not predestination. "The stars impel, they do not compel," is a slogan among astrologers.

Astrology often has been discredited in scientific tests, but has found support in the controversial research of French psychologist Michel Gauquelin. In 1949 Gauquelin began tests to disprove astrology, and succeeded to a great degree. However, he examined the horoscopes of 576 French physicians and found that more were born within the two hours of the rise and culmination of Mars, Jupiter, and Saturn than could be explained by chance. He then found that sports champions tended to be born after the rise and culmination of Mars.

His findings, which became known as "the Mars effect," were replicated by other researchers. The ensuing protest in the scientific community helped to form the Committee for the Scientific Investigation of Claims of the Paranormal (CSICOP), in Buffalo, New York, an organization of skeptics and debunkers. A scandal ensued when CSICOP attempted to disprove Gauquelin's work in 1981, and was accused by a former member of falsifying data. See **Committee for the Scientific Investigation of Claims of the Paranormal (CSICOP)**.

Gauquelin subsequently found the Mars effect among superachievers in other professions. He concluded that this does not demonstrate that planets and stars directly influence a person, but that a sort of cosmic biology is at work, including genetic heredity. He observed, as did French astrologer Paul Choisnard at the turn of the twentieth century, that children often are born with the same sun, moon, or rising sign as a parent. The effect is doubled if both parents share the same attributes. Furthermore, Gauquelin theorized that the unborn child may be reacting to cosmic influences when it chooses the moment of birth. The influences are negated, however, by Caesarian birth and artificially induced labor.

Sources: Jean Avery. *Astrology and Your Past Lives.* New York: Fireside/Simon & Schuster, 1987; "Astrology and the New Cult of the Occult." *Time* (March 21, 1969): 47–56; Bob Brier. *Ancient Egyptian Magic.* New York: Quill/Morrow, 1981; Richard Cavendish. *The Black Arts.* New York: Perigee Books, 1967; Michel Gauquelin. *Birth-Times.* New York: Hill and Wang, 1983; Michel Gauquelin. *Dreams and Illusions of Astrology.* Buffalo, NY: Prometheus Books, 1979; Linda Goodman. *Linda Goodman's Sun Signs.* New York: Bantam Books, 1971; Linda Goodman. *Linda Goodman's Love Signs.* New York: Fawcett Columbine, 1978; Alice O. Howell. *Jungian Symbolism in Astrology.* Wheaton, IL: Quest Books, The Theosophical Publishing House, 1987; *Into the Unknown.* Pleasantville, NY: Reader's Digest, 1981; I. W. Kelly. "Astrology Cosmobiology, and Humanistic Astrology." In *Philosophy of Science and the Occult.* Edited by Patrick Grim. Albany, NY: State University of New York Press, 1982; Warren Kenton. *Astrology: The Celestial Mirror.* New York: Avon, 1974; Michael Loewe and Carmen Blacker. *Oracles and Divination.* Boulder: Shambhala, 1981; Ellen Conroy McCaffery. *An Astrological Key to Biblical Symbolism.* New York: Samuel Weiser, 1975; Dennis Rawlins. "sTARBABY." *Fate* 34, no. 10, issue 379 (October 1981): 67–98; D. Scott Rogo. *Psychic Breakthroughs Today.* Wellingborough, Northamptonshire, England: The Aquarian Press, 1987; Dane Rudhyar. *The Astrology of Personality.* 2d ed. Garden City, NY: Doubleday, 1970; Frances Sakoian and Louis S. Acker. *The Astrologer's Handbook.* New York: Harper & Row, 1973; Barrett Seaman. "Good Heavens!" *Time* 131, no. 20 (May 16, 1988): 25; Paramahansa Yogananda. *Autobiography of a Yogi.* Los Angeles: Self-Realization Fellowship, 1946.

Atlantis

Fabled island-continent of ancient times that allegedly sank beneath the sea in a cataclysm. Numerous legends exist about the Atlanteans and their highly advanced civilization, and how they destroyed their land through their misuse of power. At least forty-five locations around the globe have been proposed as sites of the lost continent, but no proof has ever been found of its existence.

The story of Atlantis was first recorded by Plato c. 350 B.C. in *Dialogues,* specifically *Timaeus* and *Critias.* Plato, who said the story was told to Solon by a learned priest of Egypt, sited the island in the Atlantic Ocean behind the Strait of Gibraltar, or "the Pillars of Heracles." He said the island was larger than Libya and Asia Minor combined, and could be reached by travelers from other islands. The mighty Atlanteans had an ideal government and an advanced culture of wealth and technology. They ruled Africa from the border of Egypt and Europe to Tuscany, and sought to expand their rule throughout the Mediterranean.

Plato said the Atlanteans invaded Athens circa 9600 B.C. and a great war was fought. Despite their prowess the Atlanteans were defeated by the Atheneans. Their opulence, materialism, and aggression angered Zeus, who punished them by causing great earthquakes and floods that overwhelmed the continent and in one night caused it to sink beneath the sea. The story bears similarities to a legend of the Egyptian Middle Kingdom (2000 B.C.–1750 B.C.) and to a story in the *Mahabharata* of India.

Aristotle, Pliny, and Strabo thought the Atlantis story was Plato's illusion, and attempted to debunk it. Arab geographers kept the story alive, and as late as the Middle Ages it was believed that Atlantis had been a real place.

In 1882 US Congressman Ignatius Donnelly reignited popular interest in Atlantis with his controversial book, *Atlantis: The Antediluvian World.* Donnelly proposed that Atlantis must have been located in the middle of the Atlantic Ocean to serve as a bridge and source of culture to other areas around the globe. Studying the achievements of cultures around the world, particularly Egypt and Central and South America, he concluded that if similar cultures arose in such widely diverse geographic locations, they probably had a common source.

Numerous other theories have since been put forth. Madame Helena P. Blavatsky, mystic and cofounder of Theosophy, believed the Atlanteans were psychically developed descendants from another legendary lost continent, Lemuria, and were the Fourth Root Race of all humans. She claimed to have learned this from *The Book of Dyzan,* an alleged Atlantean work that survived the destruction and was kept in Tibet. Blavatsky said Atlantis was located in the North Atlantic Ocean, and was formed from surviving and coalescing chunks of Lemuria. She described the Atlanteans as twenty-seven-foot-high giants who built huge cities and erected twenty-seven-foot-high statues. Atlantis did not sink because of the depravity of its inhabitants, she said, but because it is the natural fate of every continent to be born, grow old, and die.

Around the turn of the twentieth century, occultist and philosopher Rudolf Steiner, claiming access to the Akashic Records, also said Atlanteans were descendants of Lemurians. They possessed incredible memories and thought in images, but were weak in logical reasoning. Their memory power enabled them to control the life force and to extract energy from plant stuffs. They rode about in powered vehicles that floated a short distance above the ground. He also claimed that unlike the Lemurians, who communicated by telepathy, the Atlanteans needed verbal communication, and developed the first language.

Lewis Spence, who founded and edited *The Atlantis Quarterly,* a journal reporting on Atlantean and occult studies, examined archaeological, anthropological, and geological evidence and folklore.

In *The History of Atlantis* (1926), Spence concluded that Atlantis existed on both sides of the Atlantic and was the means of dissemination of culture from East to West.

American medium Edgar Cayce sited Atlantis at Bimini, one of the Bahama Islands off the coast of Florida. In his trance "life readings" of sixteen hundred people, Cayce identified seven hundred as reincarnated Atlanteans. Cayce said the Atlanteans had misused crystals, their ancient power sources used to generate power for electricity and transportation, and to rejuvenate living tissues, including the brain; thus the rulers were able to control the populace. Through materialism, self-indulgence, and irresponsible use of the forces of nature, the Atlanteans eventually destroyed their continent. Many escaped to other lands. In subsequent reincarnations the Atlanteans still exhibited the same potentially destructive traits, Cayce said. He predicted in 1940 that portions of Atlantis would rise from the sea in the Bahamas during 1968 and 1969. No land mass arose, but apparent undersea ruins were discovered in 1968 off the coast of North Bimini, which some believed fulfilled his prediction.

Charles Berlitz, author of *Atlantis, the Eighth Continent* (1984), notes that the lands surrounding the north Atlantic Ocean bear similarities to the names given by ancient peoples to a legendary island continent with a variation of the name "Atlantis." The Atlanteans also have been linked to the Titans of Greek myth, the first race of beings on earth, who came from the sea and possessed the power to create thunderbolts, earthquakes, and terrestrial disturbances. See **Bermuda Triangle; Lemuria.**

Sources: Charles Berlitz. *Atlantis, the Eighth Continent.* New York: G. P. Putnam's Sons, 1984; H. P. Blavatsky. *The Secret Doctrine.* Abridged ed. by Katherine Hillard. New York: Quarterly Book Dept.,

1907; Edgar Cayce. *Edgar Cayce on Atlantis.* New York: Warner Books, 1968; James Churchward. *The Children of Mu.* New York: Ives Washburn, 1931; Ignatius Donnelly. *Atlantis: The Antediluvian World.* 1882. New York: Gramercy Publishing, 1985; *Into the Unknown.* Pleasantville, NY: The Reader's Digest Association, 1981; Ruth Montgomery with Joanne Garland. *Ruth Montgomery: Herald of the New Age.* New York: Doubleday/Dolphin, 1987; Lewis Spence. *The History of Atlantis.* 1926. Reissue. Secaucus, NJ: The Citadel Press, 1968; Rudolf Steiner. *Cosmic Memory.* San Francisco: Harper & Row, 1959; Immanuel Velikovsky. *Worlds in Collision.* Garden City, NY: Doubleday, 1950; Jennifer Westwood, ed. *The Atlas of Mysterious Places.* New York: Weidenfeld & Nicholson, 1987.

Attitudinal healing

See **Behavioral medicine.**

Augustine, St. (354–430)

One of the greatest fathers and doctors of the Christian church, whose philosophical and theological thought influenced Christianity for at least a thousand years. Augustine is not to be confused with St. Augustine of Canterbury, who died in 604.

He was born Aurelius Augustinus on November 13, 354, in Tagaste, in North Africa near Hippo; it is now Souk-Aras, Algeria. His mother, St. Monica, was a Christian and his father, a Roman official, was a pagan. He was raised a Christian. In 370, Augustine intended to become a lawyer and went to the university at Carthage to study rhetoric. He excelled in his studies. He took a mistress, who bore him a son, Adeodatus, his only child, in 372. The relationship lasted for fifteen years, until Augustine sent her away.

For a number of years Augustine believed in Manichaeism, a dualistic sect of Persian and Christian ideas. However, while teaching rhetoric in Milan, he discovered and was greatly influenced by the writings of Plotinus and other Neoplatonists, and decided to return to Christianity. St. Ambrose baptized him in Milan in 387. In 391 he was ordained a priest, and in 396 was named Bishop of Hippo. He remained in Hippo for the rest of his life. He vigorously defended Catholicism against various heresies, stating that pagan religion and magic were inventions of the Devil to tempt people away from Christianity. He said that error had no rights; therefore, heretics had no rights. Augustine witnessed pagan attacks on the Roman empire, including the Vandals' fourteen-month siege of Hippo beginning in May 430. In August, the third month, Augustine fell ill with fever. He died on August 28.

Roman Catholic religious orders and congregations called Augustinians trace a spiritual lineage to Augustine, but date their actual origins only from the tenth and later centuries. The young Martin Luther (1483–1546) was an Augustinian.

Augustine's *Confessions* (397–401), *On the Trinity* (400–416), and *City of God* (413–426) are his greatest writings; all helped define Christianity against pseudo-Christian sects of his and future ages. The first of these major works is one of the truly great autobiographies, but it is also a presentation of the writer's mystical experiences during his spiritual struggles to accept Christianity. However, it is not a mystical work in the sense of a contemplative introspection or poetic reflection; rather it is an expression of what has been called Augustine's "mysticism of action."

It is in his later works that Augustine became more philosophically theological. His references to mystical experience appear in *Confessions* and in *City of God.* In the latter he said of experiences of the supernatural:

> *When . . . we hear with the inner ear some part of the speech of God, we approximate to the angels. But in this work I need not labour to give an account of the ways in which God speaks. For either the unchangeable Truth speaks directly to the mind of the rational creature in some indescribable way, or speaks through the changeable creature, either presenting spiritual images to our spirit, or bodily voices to our bodily sense. (XVI, ch. 5)*

Augustine usually is acknowledged to be second only to St. Paul in influence on Christianity. His writings established the theological foundation for medieval Christianity, and much later influenced the dualistic philosophy of René Descartes.

Augustine's patriarchal and dualistic outlook has been criticized by some, most notably Matthew Fox, the leading spokesperson for creation-centered spirituality. According to Fox Augustine's influence, his preoccupation with personal guilt and salvation, and his promotion of introspective conscience, account to a large degree for the devaluation of the female principle and the loss of a living cosmology symbolized by the "Cosmic Christ." See **Creation spirituality.**

Sources: John Ferguson. *An Illustrated Encyclopedia of Mysticism and the Mystery Religions.* New York: Seabury Press, 1976; Vergilius Ferm, ed. *The Encyclopedia of Religion.* Secaucus, NJ: Poplar Books, 1955; F. C. Happold. *Mysticism: A Study and an Anthology.* Rev. ed. Harmondsworth, Middlesex, England: Penguin Books, 1970; Robert Maynard Hutchins, ed. *Great Books of the Western World.* Chicago: Encyclopaedia Britannica, 1952; Louis Kronenberger, ed. *Atlantic Brief Lives.* Boston: Little, Brown, 1971; Jeffrey B. Russell. *A History of Witchcraft.* London: Thames and Hudson, 1980; William J. Simpson. *St. Augustine's Conversion: An Outline of His Development to the Time of His Ordination.* New York: Macmillan, 1930; Michael Walsh, ed. *Butler's Lives of the Saints.* Concise ed. San Francisco: Harper & Row, 1985.

Aura

An envelope of vital energy, which apparently radiates from everything in nature: minerals, plants, animals, and humans. The aura is not visible to normal vision, but may be seen by clairvoyance as a halo of light. Then it often appears as a multicolored mist that fades off into space with no definite boundary, and having sparks, rays, and streamers.

Much of what is purported to be known about the aura is based on occultism and clairvoyance; no scientific evidence has been found to prove its existence. The body does have a magnetic field—a biofield, as it is called—but it is far too weak to account for a light-emitting aura. Even if the field were many times stronger, it still would be insufficient to emit light. It has been theorized that the aura might actually be a form of light vibrating at frequencies beyond the normal range of vision, caused by some yet-to-be-discovered light-emitting diodes embedded in living organisms. Another theory suggests that clairvoyants who say they see the aura may in fact see the magnetic field, which may register as light, perhaps because of some sort of sensitive magnetic detector in the brain.

The emanation of vital energy from life forms has been believed since ancient times, and appears in the writings and art of Egypt, India, Greece, and Rome. In the sixteenth century Paracelsus was one of the first Western scholars to expound upon the astral body, which he described as a "fiery globe." In the eighteenth century the clairvoyant Emanuel Swedenborg said in his *Spiritual Diary* that "there is a spiritual sphere surrounding every one, as well as a natural and corporal one." Scientific study of the aura began in the late eighteenth century, when Franz Anton Mesmer put forth the theory of "animal magnetism," an electromagnetic force that could be transmitted from one person to another and effect healing. In 1845 Baron Karl von Reichenbach, a German chemist, announced the discovery of the "odic force" energy. Reichenbach's clairvoyant test subjects sat in darkened rooms and saw flame-like energy radiating from fingertips, animals, plants, magnets, and certain crystals. The subjects described seeing flames of red, orange, green, and violet, which alternately appeared and disappeared; a violet-red, which disappeared in a smoke-like vapor; and intermingled sparks and stars among all colors.

Shortly before World War I, Dr. Walter J. Kilner, who was in charge of electrotherapy at St. Thomas's Hospital in London, discovered that an apparent human aura could be made visible if viewed through an apparatus containing a 'coal-tar dye called dicyanin, which made ultraviolet light visible.

Kilner saw the aura as a faint haze, which sometimes could be separated into two or three portions. It enveloped the whole body. Men in good health all showed the same aura characteristics. Women, however, varied. In childhood their auras appeared the same as males, but by adulthood were more developed and more refined in texture, Kilner said.

Kilner divided the aura into three parts: (1) the etheric double, a transparent dark space, narrow and often obliterated by the second band; (2) the inner aura, fairly constant in size and the densest portion; and (3) the outer aura, inconstant in size, which often appears blended into the inner aura. He also observed rays emanating from the body in healthy people. Kilner noticed that the aura reflected the state of health, and by 1919 formulated a method of auric diagnosis of illness. In some cases the aura was affected only locally, while in other illnesses the entire aura was affected; as the patient recovered, so did the aura. Kilner also noticed that weak, depleted auras suck off the auric energy of healthy, vigorous auras around them.

Kilner published his early research in *The Human Aura* in 1911. It was greeted with a great deal of skepticism, but he continued his experiments, attracting the interest of Sir Oliver Lodge. Kilner's work was interrupted by World War I. He published a revised edition of his book in 1920, which was sympathetically reviewed. He died on June 23, 1920.

In 1939 Semyon Davidovich Kirlian, a Russian electrician, began work that led to the development of techniques purported to record the aura on film. Kirlian photography, as it is called, remains controversial. See **Kirlian photography.**

Clairvoyants see the aura as emanating from and interpenetrating the human body. Health and emotion show in various colors, energy patterns or breaks, and clear and cloudy spots. Physical health seems related to the part of the aura that is closest to the body, often called the vital body or etheric body. Clairvoyant healers say that illness manifests first in the etheric body, sometimes months or years before its physical symptoms manifest. Medium Eileen J. Garrett said she could always see a misty energy field around every plant, animal, and person, which changed according to mood and health. From childhood Edgar Cayce saw colored fields around people, which he learned indicated their health, state of mind, and spiritual development.

With the exception of the etheric body, which appears to directly affect health, the composition of the aura is the subject of conflicting opinions. No two clairvoyants see exactly the same aura. Some say they see the entire aura, divided into different layers or bodies, while others say they see only parts of the aura. Some of the different bodies said to exist are:

1. Etheric, penetrated by chakras, or energy vortexes, which enable the universal life force to enter and nourish the organism. There are seven major chakras.
2. Astral or emotional, the seat of emotions and the vehicle for consciousness in out-of-body and near-death experiences. The astral body is said to be a nonsolid duplicate of the physical body, and to have its own seven primary chakras, which are separate from those of the etheric body.
3. Mental body, the seat of thought and intellect.
4. Causal body, the closest to the Higher Self.
5. Spiritual body.

Interpretations of the colors seen in the aura vary considerably. It appears that the aura fluctuates constantly, and that various colors reflect the fluctuations. However, clairvoyants seem to have their own scales for the meanings of the colors: what red means to one will mean something else to another. Colors, perhaps, should not be taken at a face value, but interpreted according to individual imagery systems. See **Imagery**.

Some psychics use the aura as a psychic screen for the projection of information concerning the past, present, and future. Much as a psychometrist handles an object to receive information from its "vibrations," an aura reader perceives images and symbols within the aura. See **Psychic reading.** See also **Bodywork; Chakras; Halo; Healing, faith and psychic; Out-of-body experience (OBE); Near-death experience (NDE); Universal life force.**

Sources: Oscar Bagnall. *The Properties of the Human Aura.* 1937. Rev. ed. New York: University Books, 1970; Robert O. Becker, M.D., and Gary Selden. *The Body Electric: Electromagnetism and the Foundation of Life.* New York: William Morrow, 1985; Arthur Ford in collaboration with Marguerite Harmon Bro. *Nothing So Strange: The Autobiography of Arthur Ford.* New York: Harper & Brothers, 1958; Richard Gerber. *Vibrational Medicine.* Santa Fe: Bear & Co., 1988; Shafica Karagulla, M.D., and Dora van Gelder Kunz. *The Chakras and the Human Energy Fields.* Wheaton, IL: Theosophical Publishing House, 1989; Walter J. Kilner. *The Human Aura.* 1920. Rev. ed. New Hyde Park, NY: University Books, 1965; C. W. Leadbeater. *The Chakras.* Wheaton, IL: Theosophical Publishing House, 1927; C. W. Leadbeater, *Man Visible and Invisible.* 1925. Abridged ed. Wheaton, IL: Theosophical Publishing House, 1987; Sheila Ostrander and Lynn Schroeder. *Psychic Discoveries Behind the Iron Curtain.* Englewood Cliffs, NJ: Prentice-Hall, 1970; L. J. G. Ouseley. *The Science of the Aura.* Romford, Essex, England: L. N. Fowler & Co., 1949; Nicholas Regush. *The Human Aura.* New York: Berkely Books, 1974; Joe H. Slate. *Psychic Phenomena: New Principles, Techniques, and Applications.* Jefferson, NC: McFarland, 1988.

Aurobindo, Sri (1872–1950)

One of India's greatest yogis. A one-time political activist for the independence of India, Sri Aurobindo experienced cosmic consciousness and turned his endeavors to transforming humanity. He developed Integral Yoga, a synthesis of yogic traditions adapted for modern times. He is the namesake of Auroville, the "first planetary city," in India. The object of his philosophy is the spiritualization of the natural world. While other yogic disciplines seek to escape the world through nirvana, Sri Aurobindo sought to embody God in everyday life.

Sri (an honorific) Aurobindo was born on August 15, 1872, to an illustrious family. His father, Dr. Krishna Dhan Ghose, was a popular surgeon, and his maternal grandfather was Rajnarayan Bose, a leader of the Indian Renaissance.

His original name was Aravinda Ackroyd, but he dropped Ackroyd during his school years in England.

From his early childhood Aurobindo had an inkling of the great destiny that lay before him, and which steadily unfolded: He had been sent to earth by God with the power to raise the consciousness of humankind to its next evolutionary level of Supermind. He was exposed to both Western and Eastern thought. From ages five to seven, he was raised and taught by Irish nuns in Darjeeling, and then was sent to England for his education. He spent fourteen years in England, during which time he was schooled in St. Paul's School in London and at King's College in Cambridge. At Cambridge he gave speeches advocating the political emancipation of India.

Despite his stance on independence, he received a civil service appointment in Baroda State, and in 1893 returned to India. Disembarking from his ship at Bombay, he experienced a profound calm that lasted for months, a harbinger of his own rising spiritual consciousness. He entered the employ of the Maharaja of Baroda, and served first as professor and then as vice-principal of Baroda College. Between 1898 and 1899 he began work on *Savriti: A Legend and a Symbol,* a poem about the spiritual ascent and transformation of the physical world. It reached 23,000 lines in length, and he revised it continually until immediately before his death.

While at Baroda he developed an interest in yoga, and began practicing *pranayama,* or breath control, which enabled him to write poetry at prodigious speed. Vishnu Bhaskar Lele, a Maharashtrian yogi, instructed him in communing with the Divine, which was seated within the heart.

From 1900 to 1908 Sri Aurobindo was a leading political activist for the freedom of India. As early as 1905 he identified what he called his three madnesses: He was destined to work for God;

he sought a direct realization of God; and he regarded India as the Mother, the embodiment of *shakti,* divine creativity. He vowed he would fight for the Mother not with the sword or gun but with the power of knowledge.

He was arrested on August 16, 1907, on charges of sedition, and was released on bail. On May 2, 1908, he was arrested again and charged with conspiracy against the British government. He spent a year in jail at Alipore awaiting trial, including several months in solitary confinement. During his jail term his first great spiritual breakthrough occurred. He meditated on the *Bhagavad-Gita,* felt the presence of Krishna, and read and was inspired by the writings of Vivekananda, the leading disciple of Ramakrishna. His experiences culminated in the realization of cosmic consciousness.

Sri Aurobindo was acquitted at his trial in 1909. A year later, following divine guidance, he withdrew from active politics and went to Pondicherry to practice yoga and to concentrate on the elevation of Indian consciousness through spiritual forces. He was by now less interested in the political independence of India than in its spiritual liberation. He said that India was the guardian of a body of spiritual knowledge and experience, the living reality of which had been lost under "the stress of alien impacts." The spirit of this dharma had to be revitalized and breathed into the fabric of India's society.

In 1910 Sri Aurobindo met Paul Richards, a French diplomat who described him as one of the greatest of divine men in Asia. Four years later, on March 29, 1914, Sri Aurobindo met Richards' wife, Mira, thirty-six, a long-time spiritual seeker, who saw in him Krishna. Sri Aurobindo recognized in her the Mother, the embodiment of shakti. The Richards' departed for Japan in 1915, and in 1920 Mira Richards returned to Pondicherry to begin a spiritual collaboration with Sri

Aurobindo. She became known as "the Mother."

Sri Aurobindo's philosophy grew out of his own spiritual experience. He saw the evolution of earth in three distinct stages: Matter, Life, and Mind. Mind can only evolve so far, and then must transform into a higher principle. Beyond Mind is Spirit, the Divine Consciousness, organized as Truth-Consciousness or the Supermind. In between the human mind and Supermind are other planes of consciousness, including the Overmind. According to Sri Aurobindo, it is possible, through rigorous spiritual discipline (yoga), to have the Supermind descend to the human mind, where its full power can begin to work in nature: Thus the natural world becomes spiritualized.

The ascent from mental to supramental consciousness occurs in what Sri Aurobindo called the Triple Transformation: First one undergoes a spiritual change and recognizes the Divine within; then a higher light descends, expanding consciousness to embrace the Divine in the All; finally comes the transmutation of ascent to Supermind and descent of the supramental consciousness into one's entire being and nature.

For Sri Aurobindo the first stage in the Triple Transformation occurred in the Alipore jail. The second stage occurred on November 26, 1926, Sri Aurobindo's "Day of *Siddhi*" (day of spiritual victory), when the Overmind descended into him. Sri Aurobindo retired into concentrated yoga. The Mother took charge of his small number of disciples and established an ashram.

For the next twenty-four years, Sri Aurobindo practiced his yoga and wrote, producing thirty volumes of writings and correspondence. His Integral Yoga is a synthesis of several other forms, chiefly, Jhana, Karma, Bhakti, and Tantra Yogas and the yoga of self-perfection. While other forms of yoga are named according to their objective and methods aimed at liberating one part of being, Integral Yoga is aimed at the liberation and perfection of the whole being, and takes up all of nature for the process of transformation. The object is not liberation of the individual (*mukti*) but fulfillment (*sampatti*) of the Will of God in Creation. In developing Integral Yoga, Sri Aurobindo drew on his interpretation of the *Gita*. Also central to his system is the concept of the Mother (shakti) as the focus for transformation. One must surrender completely to the will and power of shakti.

An ashram school was started in 1942. In 1950 Sri Aurobindo suffered from kidney illness. Prior to his death on December 5, 1950, he predicted that the Supermind would descend through the Mother. After death his body was placed on view for five days and then buried on the ashram grounds.

On February 26, 1956, the Mother announced that the Supermind had descended through her, and would "enter into a phase of realizing power in 1967." As part of that phase, she founded Auroville on February 29, 1968, near the Bay of Bengal. A community guided by Sri Aurobindo's teachings, Auroville is recognized by India as an independent city state. Its charter states that it belongs to nobody in particular, but to humanity as a whole. It is intended to be a place of unending education, the bridge between past and future, and "a site of material and spiritual researches for a living embodiment of an actual Human Unity," according to the charter. Automobiles are prohibited. Crops are grown organically. Aurovillians "must be a willing conservator of the Divine Consciousness," and are expected not to use alcohol, tobacco, or drugs, or engage in extramarital sex.

A great central city was planned, anchored by the Matrimandir, a giant sphere put in place in 1971.

The Mother died on November 17, 1973, of heart failure in her room at the

Sri Aurobindo Ashram in Pondicherry. Following her death, internal and financial problems arose at Auroville. The government of India sent in an administrator who remains to the present. The envisioned construction is not completed.

Sri Aurobindo was adamant that no religion, sect, or school of followers grow up around his philosophy, because that would surely be the death of it. Religions had failed, he said, because of their dogmas, rites, and institutional forms. In 1957 the Mother stated that the Supermind would usher in a new world in which there would be no religions or gods, only the expression of Divine Unity in all life. See **Yoga.**

Sources: Robert McDermott, ed. and new afterword. *The Essential Aurobindo*. Great Barrington, MA: Inner Traditions/Lindisfarne Press, 1987; M. P. Pandit. *Sri Aurobindo and His Yoga*. Wilmot, WI: Lotus Light Publications, 1987; John White, ed. *What Is Enlightenment? Exploring the Goal of the Spiritual Path*. Los Angeles: Jeremy P. Tarcher, 1984.

Automatic writing

The act of writing while in a dissociated or altered state of consciousness. Automatic writing sometimes produces astounding results that seem to be beyond the ordinary knowledge or ability of the writer. Many occultists say automatic writing is the product of communication with a discarnate being; psychical researchers generally believe it comes from the writer's own subconscious mind, or perhaps from information obtained through extrasensory perception (ESP).

Automatic writing is the most common form of automatism, or unconscious muscular movement often attributed to supernatural guidance. See **Automatism.** Most automatic writers want either to communicate with the dead or to contact a highly evolved discarnate being who will dispense wisdom.

In some cases automatic writing happens involuntarily, as in the case of Anna Windsor. In 1860 Windsor, a hysteric who suffered fits of delirium, began automatic writing with her right hand, which she derisively called "Stump." Stump had a personality of its own, writing out verses and prose while her left hand did other things.

The writer usually is unaware of what is being written. Some people experience a tingling sensation in the arms or hands. Typically, automatic writing is far more rapid than normal writing; as a consequence many words are joined together. The script is larger and more expansive than the writer's own script, and in some cases has duplicated the handwriting of the deceased person who has been contacted. Automatic writers also produce mirror script and write backwards, sometimes starting at the bottom right corner and working up to the top left.

Automatic writing was used a great deal during the height of Spiritualism, when mediums found it to be a better means of communicating with the dead than the laborious methods of rapping or the planchette (the precursor of the Ouija).

In the 1850s Judge John Worth Edmonds, an American Spiritualist, claimed to receive written messages from the sixteenth-century English philosopher Francis Bacon and the eighteenth-century Swedish mystic Emanuel Swedenborg, or "Sweedenborg," as the spirit signed his name. Though the messages were uniformly bland, pompous, and lacking the personalities of the deceased, Edmonds's writings stimulated a small boom in automatic writing by others. One result was a 150,000-word book credited to John Quincy Adams, who allegedly communicated to Josiah Brigham through a medium, Joseph D. Siles. Siles's automatic handwriting was virtually identical to the shaky script of Adams in his later years. The book comprised twelve messages from Adams, dealing with his arrival in heaven and his reception by such luminaries as Napoleon and Christ himself, who assembled his twelve apostles to honor Adams.

From the mid-nineteenth century and early decades of the twentieth century, many people attempted automatic writing as a way to communicate with dead friends and relatives. Numerous literary works were produced through automatic writing from unknown discarnates who suddenly announced their appearance. See **Worth, Patience.**

Before his death in 1901, British psychical researcher Frederic W. H. Myers studied at least fifty cases of automatic writing, most of which he considered uninteresting and lacking proof of spirit communications. One of the more interesting cases was a person who used two planchettes to write different messages simultaneously, a feat Myers felt would be virtually impossible to fake. See **Planchette.**

Philosopher and psychologist William James looked upon automatic writing as a way of gaining access to levels of the unconscious. In the late nineteenth century, psychologists and psychiatrists who shared the same view began using automatic writing to explore mental disturbances in the unconscious mind. Since then, automatic writing has helped children reveal internal conflicts they cannot verbalize, has helped therapists establish communication with the insane, and sometimes has prompted disturbed criminals to reveal information that is helpful in solving crimes.

Automatic writing continues to be used in modern times in attempts to reach the dead or discarnate beings. It was used in the early twentieth century in the famous "psychic excavations" of Glastonbury, England. Automatic writing has periodic upswings of popularity, influenced to a great extent by popular authors on the occult.

Critics warn of dangers in automatic writing. According to some, the writer is vulnerable to harassment or possession by demonic spirits and the evil-minded dead. Some psychologists say the real danger is in dredging up material from the unconscious that is difficult to handle. See **Cross correspondences; Glastonbury; Montgomery, Ruth; Roberts, Jane; Smith, Hélène; Super-ESP.**

Sources: Slater Brown. *The Heyday of Spiritualism.* New York: Hawthorn Books, 1970; Alfred Douglas. *Extrasensory Powers: A Century of Psychical Research.* London: Victor Gollancz Ltd., 1976; Ivor Grattan-Guinness. *Psychical Research: A Guide to Its History, Principles and Practices.* Wellingborough, Northamptonshire, England: The Aquarian Press, 1982; Stoker Hunt. *Ouija: The Most Dangerous Game.* New York: Harper & Row, 1985; James H. Hyslop. *Contact with the Other World.* New York: The Century Co., 1919; William James. "Notes on Automatic Writing." 1889. In Frederick Burkhardt, gen. ed., and Fredson Bowers, text ed. *The Works of William James: Essays in Psychical Research.* Cambridge, MA: Harvard University Press, 1986; Anita Muhl. *Automatic Writing.* New York: Helix Press, 1963; Frederic W. H. Myers. *Human Personality and Its Survival of Bodily Death.* Vols. 1 and 2. 1903. New York: Longmans, Green & Co., 1954; J. B. Rhine and Robert Brier, eds. *Parapsychology Today.* New York: The Citadel Press, 1968; J. B. Rhine and J. G. Pratt. *Parapsychology: Frontier Science of the Mind.* Springfield, IL: Charles C. Thomas, 1957; Ian Stevenson. "Some Comments on Automatic Writing." *The Journal of the American Society for Psychical Research* 72, no. 4 (October 1978): 315–32.

Automatisms

Automatisms fall into two categories: motor and sensory. Motor automatisms are unconscious muscular movements such as writing or painting, which seem to be directed by another personality or intelligence, usually believed to be discarnate, or by extrasensory guidance. Sensory automatisms are the products of spontaneous inner visions and hearing. Automatisms were the focus of much study in the late nineteenth and early twentieth centuries, as psychical researchers searched for evidence of survival after death.

In motor automatisms the medium is in a dissociated state of consciousness or trance. In automatic writing the medium may be aware of writing, but not of the words being written. Various automatisms have been used to communicate with the spirit world since ancient times. Automatic speech, in which a medium surrenders the vocal chords to an entity or deity, has been used by oracles, prophets, and modern-day channelers.

During the height of Spiritualism, motor automatisms were often seen as spirit-directed. In more recent times, researchers have been more skeptical. Many psychical researchers now believe that the majority of automatisms are the products of secondary personalities who produce knowledge or information the person has learned unconsciously, or information obtained paranormally through a super-ESP. A rare few cases seem to be explainable only as spirit communications.

The most common motor automatism is automatic writing. Many people try automatic writing in an effort to make contact with entities, or to communicate with friends and relatives who are dead. See **Automatic writing.**

The second most common motor automatism is automatic painting. Numerous cases have been documented of people with little or no artistic training suddenly being overcome by the desire to draw or paint in distinctive, professional styles. They feel guided by a spirit, and may actually feel an invisible hand pushing theirs. In some cases the style is recognizable as that of a deceased artist.

One of the most famous automatic painting cases is the Thomas-Gifford oils of the early twentieth century. Robert Swain Gifford was an American artist who died suddenly on January 15, 1905. Six months later Frederic Thompson, a New York City engraver, was seized with the urge to sketch and paint pictures. He experienced visions of gnarled trees and misty landscapes, favorite subjects of Gifford.

Thompson had previously met Gifford, but was not well acquainted with him. When Thompson painted he felt he was Gifford, though he did not know Gifford was dead. Thompson would tell his wife, "Gifford wants to sketch." Sometimes he heard Gifford's voice telling him to finish the artist's work.

Thompson produced numerous works, which reminded buyers of Gifford's style and sold at good prices. After about two years, haunted by a recurring vision of gnarled oak trees, he began to worry that he was going insane. He met Dr. James H. Hyslop, philosopher and psychical researcher, who arranged a series of sittings with different mediums to identify the personality responsible for the art. The mediums, in trance, picked up information about Gifford that was coming through Thompson. Thompson, reassured of his sanity, resumed his artistic work, locating the actual scenes he saw in his visions and executing them on canvas. Hyslop was convinced the source of his inspiration was Gifford, and that he had found a true case of spirit obsession.

Automatic music composition has also been claimed. An unusual case is that of Rosemary Brown, a London woman with limited musical ability, who in 1970 began to compose sophisticated works, which she said came from the deceased composers Liszt, Beethoven, Brahms, Debussy, Schubert, Chopin, and Stravinsky.

Some works have been recorded. Music critics acknowledge that the channeled works follow the various styles of the composers, but are not as good as should be expected of such musical geniuses.

Dowsing is a type of motor automatism. An extrasensory guidance influences the movements of the rod held by a dowser. See **Dowsing.**

Problems associated with motor automatisms include compulsion, obsession, and a feeling of possession. The automatism may go out of control until a person feels taken over by it. Some people who experiment with automatic writing, inviting communication from any entity who cares to answer, say they feel possessed by demons who torment them mentally and physically, even rape them. Such possession has not been proved conclusively; some psychologists say the effects are created by paranoia, not demons. The effects usually disappear in time, or after an exorcism.

Other types of motor automatisms include impulsive behavior, such as deciding to do or not to do something at the last minute without knowing why. Inhibitions and sudden physical incapacities are also automatisms.

Sensory automatisms include apparitions, inspirations, hallucinations, and dreams. Until English psychical researcher Edmund Gurney began research in this area in 1882, hallucinations were assumed to be due to physical disorders. Gurney's research established that paranormal visions and sounds are often unrelated to disorders. Inspirations of genius appear in hallucinations to writers, artists, scientists, and others. Apparitions include those of the living, in which a person is seen in two places at the same time. Inner voices issue instructions, sometimes in conjunction with motor automatisms. See **Channeling; Cryptomnesia; Super-ESP.**

Sources: Alfred Douglas. *Extrasensory Powers: A Century of Psychical Research.* London: Victor Gollancz Ltd., 1976; Ivor Grattan-Guinness. *Psychical Research: A Guide to Its History, Principles and Practices.* Wellingborough, Northamptonshire, England: The Aquarian Press, 1982; Stoker Hunt. *Ouija: The Most Dangerous Game.* New York: Harper & Row, 1985; James H. Hyslop. *Contact with the Other World.* New York: The Century Co., 1919; F. W. H. Myers. *Human Personality and Its Survival of Bodily Death.* Abridged ed. Edited by Susy Smith. New Hyde Park, NY: University Books, 1961; J. B. Rhine and J. G. Pratt. *Parapsychology: Frontier Science of the Mind.* Springfield, IL: Charles C. Thomas, 1957. J. B. Rhine and Robert Brier, eds. *Parapsychology Today.* New York: The Citadel Press, 1968; Ian Stevenson. "Some Comments on Automatic Writing." *Journal of the American Society for Psychical Research* 72, no. 4 (October 1978): 315–32.

Avatar

In Hinduism a human incarnation of the Divine who functions as a mediator between people and God. *Avatar* is a Sanskrit term literally meaning "descent." The concept is expressed in the sacred writings of the *Ramayana* and *Mahabharata* (the latter of which includes the *Bhagavad-Gita*), but is not present in the Vedas or the Upanishads.

The avatars who appear in the epics of the *Ramayana* and *Mahabharata* are Rama and Krishna, incarnations of Vishnu, the sky god and protector of the universe. Vishnu is said to have had anywhere from ten to thirty-nine incarnations, all of whom appeared to save the world in times of crisis. Rama and Krishna are the most beloved and worshiped; Krishna is considered the most perfect expression of the Divine. The potential number of avatars is countless. Vishnu's final avatar will be Kali, who will appear at the end of Kali Yuga, the present era, and destroy the wicked and usher in the new era of Maha Yuga. See **Kali Yuga.**

Hindus accept Gautama Buddha as an avatar.

The bhakti (devotional) movements of Hinduism have often centered around avatars, who are supposed to possess *siddhis*, psychic abilities and paranormal powers, such as the ability to materialize apports, levitate, bilocate, and the like. Exceptional holy men in India are called avatars. Ramakrishna was displeased by the appellation, professing himself to be a scholar. Sai Baba is called an avatar. See **Sai Baba**. Compare to **Bodhisattva**.

The term "Avatar" also has been made a registered trademark for a pricey, self-described "proprietary technology" consisting of training in consciousness development. The Avatar program was conceived around 1986 by Harry Palmer of Elmira, New York, a Scientologist for thirteen years who had become disillusioned with Scientology's teachings. Palmer built the training around the concept that people experience and are what they believe. The program is intended to be an experiential re-engineering of consciousness to free people from their own self-imposed limitations. Centers are located around the world.

Sources: Erlendur Haraldsson. *Modern Miracles: An Investigative Report on Psychic Phenomena Associated with Sathya Sai Baba.* New York: Fawcett Columbine, 1987; Solange Lemaitre. *Ramakrishna and the Vitality of Hinduism.* 1959. Woodstock, NY: The Overlook Press, 1984; K. M. Sen. *Hinduism.* Harmondsworth, Middlesex, England: Penguin Books, 1961.

Avebury

The oldest megalithic site in Britain, and perhaps the largest megalithic site in the world. Avebury covers 28 1/2 acres six miles west of Marlborough in Wiltshire, southern England; its site includes the modern village of Avebury. Larger and more extensive than Stonehenge, it is said that more than a quarter of a million people could stand within the boundaries of its circle. The henge was in active use between 2600 B.C. and 1600 B.C., thus predating the Druids.

It is believed by some that the Avebury stones are repositories of Earth and psychic energy, which may be detected by clairvoyance and dowsing. See **Leys**. Such energy may be responsible for paranormal phenomena that has long been reported at the site, including eerie small figures seen flitting about the stones at night and strange lights drifting and bobbing over the ground. See **Earth lights**. Around World War I, a scene suggesting retrocognition (seeing into the past) was reported by a woman who saw the sounds and lights of a fair in progress among the stones. It had been at least fifty years since a fair had taken place there. See **Retrocognition**. In the late 1980s, Avebury became a major site of the mysterious crop circles, geometric indentations made in fields, which defy explanation. See **Crop circles**.

The henge comprises a large, circular ditch 1,200 feet wide and surrounded by a fifteen-foot-high bank. Inside are two or three smaller circles. The henge is intersected by four avenues, possibly causeways to give ancient users access to the interior. The layout resembles a Celtic cross.

Ringing the inner edge of the ditch are the remains of the Great Stone Circle, which once contained some one hundred sandstone sarsens. Only twenty-seven remain, due to destruction in the sixteenth and seventeenth centuries by Puritans, who smashed and burned the stones, and by farmers, who wanted to clear the land. The largest remaining stone is about twenty-five feet tall and weighs about sixty tons. The stones alternate in shape from pillars to diamonds.

No records survive attesting to the original purpose and uses of the henge, and excavations have yielded little insight. The antiquarians John Aubrey and William Stukeley took great interest in Avebury in the seventeenth and eighteenth centuries, respectively. Stukeley saw the henge as part of a larger sacred pattern laid out over the entire landscape, and theorized both Avebury and Stonehenge were sites of serpent worship. According to the most widely held modern theory, Avebury was a settlement of the Bronze Age Beaker Folk and most likely was a burial site. The charter of King Athelstan, dated in the tenth century, does say burials were made there, and burial remains have been found at the base of four stones. The West Kennet long barrow, located near the henge, is said to be England's largest prehistoric tomb.

Another nearby landmark, Windmill Hill, bears an earthwork on top and may have predated Avebury. This site may have been a cattle market, trading post, or ritual site, judging from the animal bones excavated there. The purpose of Silbury Hill, yet another nearby landmark and Europe's tallest artificial mound, is unknown.

According to other theories, Avebury was used for religious festivals in honor of Goddess. The alternating shapes of the stones suggest fertility rites. Tradition has it that on Beltane (May Eve), a pagan fertility festival, village girls would sit on the Devil's Chair, one of the huge stones, and make a wish. It is also theorized that Avebury may have had astronomical purposes, as the avenues, stones, and other features were aligned to the May Day sunrise and the morning rise of Alpha Centauri in November. An occult theory holds that Avebury was a psychic power center, and that tapping the stones enabled communication with other megalithic sites. See **Megaliths.**

Sources: Janet and Colin Bord. *Mysterious Britain.* Garden City, NY: Doubleday, 1978; Peter Lancaster Brown. *Megaliths, Myths, and Men.* New York: Taplinger Publishing Company, 1976; Aubrey Burl. *Rings of Stone.* New York: Ticknor & Fields, 1979; Michael Dames. *The Avebury Cycle.* London: Thames and Hudson, 1977; Paul Devereux. *Places of Power.* London: Blandford, 1990; Rosemary Ellen Guiley. *The Encyclopedia of Witches and Witchcraft.* New York: Facts On File, 1989; Francis Hitching. *Earth Magic.* New York: William Morrow, 1977; John Michell. *The New View Over Atlantis.* Rev. ed. San Francisco: Harper & Row, 1983; Jennifer Westwood, ed. *The Atlas of Mysterious Places.* New York: Weidenfeld & Nicholson, 1987.

Ayurveda

See **Behavioral medicine.**

B

Bacon, Francis

See **Saint Germain**.

Barbanell, Maurice

See **Spiritualism**.

Barrett, William

See **Parapsychology; Society for Psychical Research (SPR)**.

Behavioral medicine

Approaches to healing that are holistic in nature and take into account the interrelations between mind, body, and spirit, and between the human organism and the environment. Non-Western healing systems, such as Ayurveda and Chinese medicine, have been based on a holistic foundation since ancient times; but Western medicine has since the seventeenth century been based on the Cartesian philosophy of dualism, the separation of mind and body. Beginning in the 1960s, however, the broad humanistic movement and various scientific researches have provided impetus for the integration of so-called alternative and conventional medicines.

The term "behavioral medicine" is preferred to "holism" and "holistic medicine." The term "holism" was coined from the Greek *holos,* "whole," in 1926 by Jan Smuts, a student of biology and the first prime minister of South Africa, in his book, *Holism and Evolution.* Several decades later Smuts's holistic perspective on biological evolution was expanded by psychologist Abraham H. Maslow and others in defining human nature and developing psychologies of health and transcendence that treat the human being as a whole organism and not a collection of parts. See **Psychology**. Maslow also recognized that suppression, frustration, or denial of the "essential core," or inner nature of a person, could result in illness.

The humanistic movement, coupled with a revival of interest in Eastern philosophy, brought renewed interest to holistic health in the 1960s. At about the same time, scientific research began providing evidence of the mind-body link. One product of that research, psychoneuroimmunology (PNI), explores the collaboration between the mind, the brain, the body's self-protection mechanisms, and the immune system.

Among the significant research findings was the work of psychiatrist George Solomon. In the 1960s he observed that women with certain personality traits— passivity, long-suffering—succumbed to rheumatoid arthritis more quickly; and that rats with tumor cell implants that were put under stress died more quickly than implanted rats not subjected to stress. Solomon called the new field "psychoimmunology."

In the 1970s another breakthrough occurred. Psychologist Robert Ader discovered that rats could be conditioned to depress their immune systems. Ader tested his theory with immunologist Nicholas Cohen and changed the term psychoimmunology to "psychoneuroimmunology," to reflect the suspected role of the nervous system in immunity.

In the late 1970s, neuroscientist Karen Bulloch traced direct neurological paths between the brain and the immune system. Later research demonstrated that the immune system produces chemicals that feed information back to the brain.

PNI demonstrates empirically the role that emotions have on physical health; the body essentially is a mirror of the mind. One well-known example of the enormous power of the mind is the experience of Norman Cousins, former editor of the *Saturday Review*. Cousins suffered from ankylosing spondylitis, a degenerative condition in which the connective tissue of the spine disintegrates. Doctors put his chances of recovery at 1 in 500. Cousins said he took himself off conventional medication and substituted massive doses of vitamin C and an emotional therapy of humor. He made a full recovery.

Attitude modification, relaxation, and imagery have been used increasingly in the treatment of catastrophic illness such as cancer. Research has shown that imaging can increase the number of circulating white blood cells, and can also increase the level of thymosin-alpha-1, a hormone that benefits auxiliary white blood cells (the so-called T helper cells), which produces feelings of well-being. Cancer patients who have used imagery have shown dramatic improvements, from significant shrinking of tumors to complete disappearance of the disease. Imagery is used to treat a wide variety of health problems, from minor complaints

such as headaches and stomach aches to serious diseases and disorders such as heart disease, cancer, arthritis, and neurological illnesses. See **Creative visualization; Imagery.**

Research also has shown how emotions make a person more susceptible to illness, especially cancer and heart disease. Most damaging are chronic or suppressed anger, fear, guilt, a lack of love of life, and a deep inner conviction of being unloved, unloving, or unlovable. Surgeon Bernie S. Siegel, renowned for his alternative therapy with cancer patients, theorizes that all disease is ultimately related to lack of love or to love that is only conditional. Herbert Benson, a cardiologist and pioneer in research into the effects of relaxation, believes the "Faith Factor," a deep personal religious or philosophical faith, can play a significant role in health. See **Aura; Biofeedback; Bodywork; Healing, faith and psychic; Music; Relaxation; Universal life force.**

Sources: Herbert Benson with William Proctor. *Beyond the Relaxation Response.* New York: Times Books, 1984; Fritjof Capra. *Uncommon Wisdom: Conversations with Remarkable People.* New York: Simon & Schuster, 1988; David Gelman with Mary Hager, *et al.* "Body & Soul." *Newsweek* (November 7, 1988): 88–97; Daniel Goleman. "The Mind Over the Body." *New Realities* 8, no. 4 (March/April 1988): 14–19; Richard Grossman. *The Other Medicines.* Garden City, NY: Doubleday, 1985; Dora Kunz, comp. *Spiritual Aspects of the Healing Arts.* Wheaton, IL: The Theosophical Publishing House, 1985; Steven E. Locke and Douglas Colligan. *The Healer Within.* New York: E. P. Dutton, 1986; Abraham H. Maslow. *Toward a Psychology of Being.* Princeton: Van Nostrand, 1962; George W. Meek, ed. *Healers and the Healing Process.* Wheaton, IL: The Theosophical Publishing House, 1977; Robert Ornstein and David Sobel. *The Healing Brain.* New York: Simon & Schuster, 1987; Martin L. Rossman. *Healing Yourself: A Step-by-Step Program for*

Better Health through Imagery. New York: Pocket Books, 1987; Bernie S. Siegel. *Love, Medicine & Miracles.* New York: Harper & Row, 1986; Rob Wechsler. "A New Prescription: Mind Over Malady." *Discover* (February 1987): 51–61.

Benedict, St. (also St. Benedict of Nursia) (c. 480–c. 547)

Father of Western monasticism and founder of the Benedictines, the oldest Christian religious order in the West, which greatly influenced the spread of civilization in the Middle Ages. The only source for documenting Benedict's life is *The Dialogues* by Gregory the Great (Gregory I), pope from 590–604.

Benedict was born c. 480 in the Sabine town of Nursia. He was sent to Rome to be educated, but was so revolted by the licentiousness of the city that he and his nurse fled to Enfide, a village about thirty miles away. After a time Benedict then went to a remote place now called Subiaco, where he encountered a monk, Romanus, who led him to a cave. Here, at about age fourteen, Benedict became a hermit, and spent three years living in the cave. His sanctity and alleged miraculous powers began to attract followers. Benedict organized them into twelve monasteries of twelve monks each, and each under a prior. Benedict exercised supreme rule over all. The Subiaco monastic community became a permanent settlement, but Benedict at some point left abruptly, allegedly because another priest, Florentius, attempted to undermine him.

In about 525 Benedict went to Monte Cassino and destroyed the temple to Apollo at its top. In its place he established (c. 530) the first structures of a monastery that would become the most famous in the world, the birthplace of Western monasticism. The monastery attracted a large following of disciples, as well as church officials from Rome and Capua, who came to consult Benedict for his wisdom and prophetic powers.

At about this time, he probably wrote his famous *Regula Monachorum,* called the Rule, a monastic rule that became the standard for monastic living throughout the Western world. The Rule basically calls for a year of probation, a vow of obedience to a single abbot or abbess, moderate asceticism, and prayer and work (*"Ora et labora"* became a motto of the Benedictines). Scholarship in the twentieth century has discovered that Benedict's rule was influenced by, and passages were accommodated from, the *Rule of the Master,* a monastic document also dating from the sixth century but which was not as spiritual, personal, and broad as Benedict's Rule.

Benedict expanded his activities beyond the monastery to the surrounding population, curing the sick, distributing alms and food, and providing aid and counseling. It is alleged that he raised the dead on at least several occasions.

Benedict foretold his own death six days in advance, and instructed his monks to dig a grave. As soon as the task was accomplished, he fell ill with fever and deteriorated. In his final moments, he stood, supported by monks, and died with his hands raised in prayer.

Gregory the Great, in *The Dialogues, Book Two,* offers the following description of one of Benedict's mystical experiences:

In speaking of their hopes and longings, they [Benedict and the deacon Servandus] were able to taste in advance the heavenly food that was not yet fully theirs to enjoy. . . . In the dead of night he [Benedict] suddenly beheld a flood of light shining down from above more brilliant than the sun, and with it every trace of darkness cleared away. Another remarkable sight followed. According to his own description, the whole world was gathered up before his eyes in what ap-

peared to be a single ray of light. As he gazed at all this dazzling display, he saw the soul of Germanus, the bishop of Capua, being carried by angels up to heaven in a ball of fire.

In the same text, Gregory comments,

The light of holy contemplation enlarges and expands the mind in God until it stands above the world. In fact, the soul that sees Him rises even above itself, and as it is drawn upward in His light, all its inner powers unfold. Then when it looks downward from above, it sees how small everything really is that was beyond its grasp before.

The Order of Saint Benedict (OSB) is the oldest order of monks in the West; for over five centuries it was the only monastic order in the West. During the Middle Ages Benedictines were called the Black Monks, referring to the color of their habit. There are Benedictine monasteries worldwide today in the Roman Catholic and Anglican churches. In the late 1980s there were 535 houses and over 14,000 members of the Benedictines, including Carthusians, Cistercians, Trappists, and other related orders.

Benedict's feast day is July 11 in the Western church and March 14 in the Eastern church.

Sources: John J. Delaney. *Dictionary of Saints.* Garden City, NY: Doubleday, 1980; Vergilius Ferm, ed. *The Encyclopedia of Religion.* Secaucus, NJ: Poplar Books, 1955; Gregory the Great. *The Dialogues, Book Two.* Indianapolis: Bobbs-Merrill, 1967; F. C. Happold. *Mysticism: A Study and an Anthology.* Rev. ed. Harmondsworth, Middlesex, England: Penguin Books, 1970; Robert Maynard Hutchins, ed. *Great Books of the Western World.* Chicago: Encyclopaedia Britannica, 1952; Louis Kronenberger, ed. *Atlantic Brief Lives.* Boston: Little, Brown, 1971; Michael Walsh, ed. *Butler's Lives of the Saints.* Concise ed. San Francisco: Harper & Row, 1985.

Bermuda Triangle

A mysterious area in the Atlantic Ocean where paranormal events are alleged to occur. The Bermuda Triangle is bounded by Florida, Bermuda, and Puerto Rico. It is also called the Devil's Triangle, Limbo of the Lost, Hoodoo Sea, Twilight Zone, and Port of Missing Ships. Numerous planes and ships have vanished there without a trace. Most incidents reportedly have occurred in good weather or near a landing site or port. Just before disappearing crews have made radio contact indicating that nothing was amiss. In rare instances missing ships have been found, but without their crew or passengers.

The Bermuda Triangle was named in 1945, after the disappearance of six Navy planes and their crews on December 5, a sunny, calm day with ideal flying conditions. Prior to that scores of ships of all sizes reportedly had vanished in the area. Strange phenomena have been reported since Christopher Columbus's voyage to America. Columbus wrote in his logs that his compass acted strangely, and that an unexplained light emanated from the sea.

Other phenomena witnessed in the area include bright lights or balls of fire; a calm yet unnatural look to the ocean; sudden red flares in the sky that appear to be explosions; the turning of the sky yellow, hazy, and foggy; and objects that appear to be UFOs. Airplane crew members report sudden power failures, compass-spinning, strong magnetic pulls on planes toward the sea, and their inability to control the plane's altitude.

In the lore of fishermen, the Bermuda Triangle is inhabited by devils, demons, and monsters that kidnap ships. Some scientists say unusual weather conditions are responsible. Other theories propose that phenomena are caused by alignments of the planets, time warps that trap ships and planes, forces emanating from the unknown ruins of Atlantis, or

Benedict, St. (also St. Benedict of Nursia) (c. 480–c. 547)

cosmic tractor beams sent from UFOs or hidden sea beings to kidnap ships and people.

Skeptics claim misleading information and contrived reporting have created a false mystery, adding that most disappearances can be attributed to bad weather, abandonment, or explainable accidents. They say that incidents that occur in the Triangle are automatically considered mysteries because of the legends.

A similar ocean area said to be the site of mysterious disappearances is the Devil's Sea off the southeast coast of Japan. Some cases have been blamed on the activity of an underwater volcano.

Sources: Charles Berlitz. *The Bermuda Triangle.* New York: Avon Books, 1974; Charles Berlitz. *Without a Trace.* New York: Ballantine Books, 1977; Edgar Cayce. *Edgar Cayce on Atlantis.* New York: Warner Books, 1968; Adi-Kent Thomas Jeffrey. *They Dared the Devil's Triangle.* New York: Warner Books, 1975; Lawrence David Kusche. *The Bermuda Triangle Mystery Solved.* New York: Warner Books, 1975.

Bernard of Clairvaux (1090–1153)

Christian saint, mystic, and doctor of the Western church, known as Doctor Mellifluous, "The Honey-Mouthed Doctor," for the spiritual sweetness of his teachings. Bernard was born in Fontaines, France, near Dijon, to a leading family of the nobility. He excelled in his early studies, especially in literature, while at the same time giving evidence of great piety. At about the age of twenty-three he entered the reformed Benedictine community at Citeaux, to which he was eventually followed by his father and five brothers. In 1115 the abbot, St. Stephen Harding, sent Bernard to found a new daughter house that was to become famous as the Cistercian Abbey of Clairvaux.

Though Bernard sought quiet and solitude to contemplate, the needs of the church, the orders of his superiors, and the urgent pleas of rulers caused him to spend much time in travels and controversies. Early in his career, when denounced to Rome for "meddling" in high ecclesiastical affairs, he won over his accusers by explaining that he would like nothing better than to retire to his monastery, but had been ordered to assist at the synod of Troyes. He likewise found himself called upon to judge the rival claims of Innocent II and Anacletus II to the papacy, and traveled widely to bring others over to the side of Innocent. His other activities included assisting at the Second Lateran Council (1139), preaching the Second Crusade (1146), and countering the theological errors of Abelard (1139) and of Gilbert, bishop of Poitiers (1147–1148). Worn out by his labors, and distressed by the failure of the Crusade, he died at Clairvaux on August 20, 1153. He was canonized by the Roman church in 1174, and formally declared a doctor of the church in 1830 by Pope Pius VIII.

Despite his many activities, the real center of Bernard's life was prayer and contemplation: from them he drew strength for his labors and journeys and inspiration for his writings. Bernard, like all Christians, believed that the vision of God and union with him was the end for which humankind was created. This can only be fully attained in the afterlife, but Bernard and many others throughout the ages have claimed an experience, even in this life, of that vision and union. This mystical experience, like the beatific vision of which it is a foretaste, is, in the Christian view, a free gift of God; the most that we can do is desire it and strive to remove obstacles to it. The methods of removing obstacles are the subject of ascetical and mystical theology. Many Christians before Bernard had described this mystical experience, but he was one of the first to address himself to the theological understanding of it, though not in any systematic way.

Ascetical theology deals with groundwork of the spiritual life: the eradication of vices, the cultivation of virtue, the attainment of detachment, by which one learns to give up one's own will and accept God's will for oneself. Bernard's works in this field include *De Gratia et Libero Arbitrio* (Of Grace and Free Will) and *De Gradibus Humilitatus et Superbiae* (Of the Steps of Humility and Pride). Bernard's teaching is typical of the paradoxical Christian view of humankind, simultaneously affirming our dignity as made in the image and likeness of God (which image, for Bernard, consisted primarily in free will) and our need for humility as a creature—a fallen creature, in whom the likeness to God is obscured by sin.

But for Bernard, as for the author of the Johannine books (Fourth Gospel) of the New Testament, the beginning, end, and driving force of the whole mystery of creation and redemption is love: God's love for humankind enabling humankind to love God in return. In *De Dilgendo Deo* (Of Loving God), Bernard presents motives for loving God, both those that all may acknowledge (the gifts of creation) and those that compel Christians, who believe that God became incarnate and died to save them (the goods of redemption). Here, as elsewhere in his writings, the humanity of Christ has the central role.

Love is nurtured by conversation; and so in the four books *De Consideratione* (Of Meditation), written for his pupil who had become pope as Eugene III, Bernard discusses meditation, or mental prayer, by which one converses with God and may perhaps attain a vision of God and union with him even in this life. It is in the eighty-six *Sermones super Cantica Canticorum* (Sermons on the Song of Songs) that Bernard eloquently

expounds on this vision and union, and the desire for it. As many would do after him, he sees these ancient Hebrew poems as describing the union of God and the soul as a mystical marriage. Bernard stresses that the mystical experience is, precisely, an experience, and thus strictly incommunicable, only to be known by one who has experienced it. Yet he is far from any shallow emotionalism, and the work manifests a profound and precise knowledge of doctrinal subtleties. See **Mysticism; Prayer.**

Sources: Bernard of Clairvaux. *Opera Omnia.* Joannis Mabillon, ed. In Migne's *Patrologia Latina.* Paris, 1854; Etienne Gilson. *The Mystical Theology of Saint Bernard.* Translated by A. H. C. Downes. New York: Sheed & Ward, 1940; Bruno Scott James. *Saint Bernard of Clairvaux: An Essay in Biography.* London: Hodder & Stoughton, 1957; Ailbe J. Liddy, O.Cist. *Life and Teaching of Saint Bernard.* Dublin: M. H. Gill & Son Ltd., 1950; *St. Bernard's Sermon on the Canticle of Canticles.* Translated by a priest of Mount Mellary. Dublin: Browne and Nolan, Ltd., 1920; Watkin Williams. *The Mysticism of Saint Bernard of Clairvaux.* London: Burns Oates & Washbourne, 1931.

Berry, Thomas

See **Planetary consciousness.**

Besant, Annie

See **Theosophy.**

Betty Books

See **White, Stewart Edward.**

Bhagavad-Gita

See **Hinduism; Yoga.**

Bhagwan Shree Rajneesh

See **Alternative religious movements.**

Bilocation

The appearance of an individual in two distant places at once. It is not known precisely what occurs in a bilocation, but prevailing theory suggests that it is the projection of a double. The double may be perceived by others as a solid physical form, or may appear ghostly. Typically, the double acts strangely or mechanically, and often does not speak or acknowledge when others speak to it.

Bilocation is an uncommon but ancient phenomenon. It is said to be experienced, and even practiced by will, by mystics, ecstatics, saints, monks and holy persons, and magical adepts. Many Christian saints and monks were famous for bilocation, such as St. Anthony of Padua, St. Ambrose of Milan, St. Severus of Ravenna, and Padre Pio of Italy. In 1774 St. Alphonsus Maria de'Ligouri was seen at the bedside of the dying Pope Clement XIV, when in fact the saint was confined to his cell in a location four days' journey away.

Early psychical researchers, such as Frederic W. H. Myers, one of the founders of the Society for Psychical Research in England, collected and studied reports of bilocation, but the phenomenon receives scant scientific attention in modern times.

Spontaneous and involuntary bilocation sometimes presages or heralds the death of the individual seen.

See **Apparition; Out-of-body experience (OBE).**

Sources: John Ferguson. *An Illustrated Encyclopedia of Mysticism and the Mystery Religions.* New York: Seabury Press, 1976; Hornell Hart and Ella B. Hart. "Visions and Apparitions Collectively and Reciprocally Perceived." *Proceedings of the Society for Psychical Research* 41, part 130 (1932–1933): 205–49; Vivian Worthington. *A History of Yoga.* London: Routledge & Kegan Paul, 1982.

Bioenergetics

See **Bodywork.**

Biofeedback

The electronic measurement and presentation of information concerning physiological processes, such as brain-wave rhythms, heart rate, blood pressure, skin temperature, and muscle tension. The information then is used to control those processes. Since the 1960s biofeedback has been used in parapsychology in psi testing, and in health care as an alternative treatment for various physical, behavior, and psychological disorders and conditions. Biofeedback also helps one achieve altered and mystical states of consciousness; it is sometimes called "electronic yoga."

Biofeedback is based on the principles that behavior can be changed by making changes in environment, and that by mentally recognizing a biological function, control may be gained over it. Initially, biofeedback was applied to brain waves. Brain waves were discovered and measured in 1924 by Hans Berger, but it was not until the 1950s that Western attention was turned to the possibility of producing certain brain waves at will. In 1958 researcher Joe Kamiya hypothesized that subjects continuously fed data on their brain waves might be able to regulate them. In experiments with college students, Kamiya added a relay circuit to an EEG machine so that a tone sounded whenever alpha brain waves (corresponding to a state of relaxation) were generated. Students quickly learned to control the tone. Kamiya went on to study the brain waves of Zen meditators. By the end of the 1960s, considerable research was being done on states of consciousness and their corresponding brain waves (see Table of Brain-wave Patterns, below).

Early biofeedback experiments also were done with laboratory animals in conjunction with a system of rewards and punishment. Notable is the work of Dr. Neil E. Miller, who trained rats to alter various involuntary internal processes. Dr. Herbert Benson trained monkeys to lower their blood pressure. Benson and other researchers then turned their attention to human subjects, studying and electronically monitoring practitioners of Transcendental Meditation, who demonstrated how they could change their body processes through meditation.

Table of Brain-wave Patterns

Brain waves are measured in hertz, or cycles per second. There are four major stages of brain-wave activity, ranging from beta, the shortest and fastest, to delta, the longest and slowest. At the borderlines between states, brain waves usually show a mixture of two patterns.

Pattern	Hertz	Characteristics
Beta	13–26	Active, waking consciousness, eyes open
Alpha	8–13	Eyes closed, body relaxed; also daydreaming with eyes open. Average person can maintain awareness.
Theta	4–8	Deep relaxation, drowsiness; the hypnagogic state before sleep. Average person cannot maintain awareness; meditators can, and show smoothest waves with quiet mind, body, and emotions.
Delta	0.5–4	Sleep or unconsciousness

The Process of Biofeedback

To monitor various physiological processes, the body is attached by electrodes to the appropriate device: electroencephalograph (EEG) for brain waves, the most common device used; electromyograph (EMG) for muscular tension; plethysmograph for blood volume; electrocardiograph (EKG) for heart functions; galvanic skin response (GSR) for skin temperature. One process is monitored at a time. Feedback is given immediately by tones, beeps, lights, digits, needles moving on graphs, or light patterns on a screen. The subject is taught relaxation exercises with breathing and visualization, similar to yoga techniques, and observes the changes in the feedback. The subject learns how to achieve desired results, such as lowered blood pressure or an alpha-level state of consciousness. As training progresses the subject learns how to control physiological processes through thoughts and moods, or by shifting body position. Eventually, the subject does not need electronic equipment to achieve results.

Early biofeedback training required going to a clinic, where monitoring equipment was available. Technology advances have produced hand-held biofeedback units for home use, which monitor skin moisture.

Biofeedback and Psi

Biofeedback can teach individuals how to increase their alpha brain waves. This is the altered state of consciousness just below waking consciousness that is attained in meditation and relaxation and is associated with right-brain activities such as creativity and intuition. The alpha state is not necessary to achieve successful results in laboratory tests for psi, but studies have shown that it is conducive to psi. Subjects who are trained in biofeedback or meditation, and thus slip easily into an alpha state, tend to score high in psi tests. Biofeedback is one of the common induction methods used in tests in which subjects are first put into altered states. See **Altered states of consciousness; Inspiration; Intuition; Meditation.**

Biofeedback and Mystical States

Biofeedback has been shown to help induce mystical states of awareness similar to those found in the practice of Sufism, Zen, yoga, and other spiritual disciplines. It leads to a mind-body unity and "expanded self-unfolding," and enables the practitioner to exert control over the states of awareness achieved. Experienced meditators generate long trains of alpha waves, followed by deeper states of theta waves, a brain-wave level at which the average person becomes drowsy and begins to drop into sleep. In meditators, however, consciousness does not diminish in the theta state. In Zen this state is said to be "knowing" rather than "thinking." At the lower end of theta, just before delta waves, the state of sleep, meditators become "conscious of the unconscious."

In meditation experiments using biofeedback with college students in England, C. Maxwell Cade discovered a hierarchy of states of consciousness, each with physiological correlations. State Four is comparable to traditional meditation and the "relaxation response"; State Five and beyond are mystical levels. At these stages Cade's subjects sounded like mystics in their speech. Some wept with joy; others, who had no demonstrable artistic talent, produced beautiful drawings and ecstatic poetry.

Cade and others devised a "Mind Mirror" device, which monitors muscle tone, brain-wave cycles, and right- and left-brain activity. The Mind Mirror showed that in mystical states, the subjects experience new patterns of neural activity that affect both hemispheres of the brain, as well as both parts of the limbic system and brain stem, thus indicating that mystical states of awareness can be induced by balancing right and left sides of the brain. Biofeedback may be promising as a means to achieve that balance. See **Mystical experiences.**

Biofeedback and Health

Biofeedback demonstrates the connection between mind and body in health, by teaching subjects to use relaxation and thought to control body processes. It is used to affect both the voluntary and involuntary nervous systems. Biofeedback treats stress-related disorders, alcoholism, drug addiction, asthma, neuromuscular disorders, chronic and migraine headaches, insomnia, poor circulation, back pain, and arthritis. In some cases it can reduce the awareness of pain, thus cutting or eliminating the need for drugs. Children learn to use it as well as adults. See **Relaxation.**

Biofeedback is used in "theta training," a means in psychotherapy to induce a reverie state that will produce hypnagogic imagery. Induced imagery helps a patient sort through "unfinished business" and is used in the treatment of psychosomatic illness, neuroses, anxiety, amnesia, and in emotional disturbances of youths.

Perhaps one of the most important applications of biofeedback lies in "body consciousness," as part of humanistic and transpersonal psychologies and behavioral medicine. Body consciousness strengthens the mind-body link, which in turn influences the total psychophysiological well-being. See **Behavioral medicine.**

Sources: Herbert Benson, M.D. *The Relaxation Response.* New York: Avon Books, 1976; Herbert Benson, M.D. *Your Maximum Mind.* New York: Random House, 1987; Nona Coxhead. *The Relevance of Bliss: A Contemporary Exploration of*

Mystic Experience. London: Wildwood House, 1985; Hoyt L. Edge, Robert L. Morris, John Palmer, and Joseph H. Rush. *Foundations of Parapsychology.* Boston: Routledge & Kegan Paul, 1986; Mark Golin. "The Biofeedback Way to Starve Stress." *Prevention* (June 1987): 30–32; Elmer and Alice Green. *Beyond Biofeedback.* New York: Delacourt Press, 1977; Richard Grossman. *The Other Medicines.* Garden City, NY: Doubleday, 1985; Frederick J. Heide. "Relaxation: The Storm Before the Calm." *Psychology Today* (April 1985): 18–19; Charles Honorton, R. Davidson, and P. Bindler. "Feedback-augmented EEG Alpha, Shifts in Subjective State, and ESP Card-Guessing Performance." *The Journal of the American Society for Psychical Research* 65 (1971): 308–23; William G. Roll, Robert L. Morris, and J. D. Morris. *Research in Parapsychology 1972.* Metuchen, NJ: Scarecrow Press, 1973; Charles T. Tart. *States of Consciousness.* New York: E. P. Dutton, 1975; "Warm Hands and Children's Migraines." *Psychology Today* (December 1984): 71; John White and James Fadiman, eds. *Relax.* New York: The Confucian Press, 1976; John White, ed. *Frontiers of Consciousness.* New York: Avon Books, 1975; Benjamin B. Wolman, ed. *Handbook of Parapsychology.* New York: Van Nostrand Reinhold, 1977.

Bird

A nearly universal symbol of the soul. Birds are messengers to the gods and carriers of souls to heaven. The ancient Egyptians equated birds with the *ba,* or soul; a hawk represented the soul of Horus and the pharaoh. The Hindus associate birds with higher states of being. The Aztecs believed that the dead were reborn as colibris, the birds of their patron god, Huitzilopochtli. In trance shamans assume the shape of birds in order to leave the body and soar through the universe. Among some Native Americans, birds personify the wind and rain.

In folklore, myth, and fairy tales around the world, birds possess the ability to talk and offer guidance or collaboration to humans. Birds bring news and are the omens of death, especially black birds such as crows and nocturnal birds such as owls.

Psychiatrist Carl G. Jung said birds represent spirit, angels, supernatural aid, and thoughts and flights of fancy. In alchemy the bird represents forces in the process of activation. Madame Helena P. Blavatsky, cofounder of the Theosophical Society, said birds are on an evolutionary track to become devas, a type of exalted beings. See **Deva.**

See **Symbols**; Compare to **Horse.**

Sources: H. P. Blavatsky. *The Secret Doctrine.* 1888. Pasadena, CA: Theosophical University Press, 1977; J. E. Cirlot. *A Dictionary of Symbols.* New York: Philosophical Library, 1971; Mircea Eliade. *Shamanism.* Princeton, NJ: Princeton University Press, 1964; Ake Hultkrantz. *The Religions of the American Indians.* 1967. Berkeley: University of California Press, 1979; Carl G. Jung, ed. *Man and His Symbols.* 1964. New York: Anchor Press/Doubleday, 1988; Barbara G. Walker. *The Woman's Encyclopedia of Myths and Secrets.* San Francisco: Harper & Row, 1983.

Black Elk, Nicholas (1863–1950)

Oglala Sioux mystic and medicine man. Bestowed with great powers of healing and prophecy at an early age, he died without realizing part of his great vision to restore the wholeness and harmony of his people.

Black Elk (Ekhaka Sapa) was born in the Moon of the Popping Trees (December) 1863, on the Little Powder River, to Black Elk, a medicine man, and Sees the White Cow. His second cousin was Crazy Horse.

At about age four, he began to hear voices, which frightened him. At age five he had his first vision, heralded by a kingbird that spoke to him. In the vision he saw two men coming toward him from the clouds. When they drew close, they wheeled about, turned into geese, and vanished.

Black Elk's "great vision," in which he was empowered by the Grandfathers, or Powers of the World, occurred when he was nine. He fell ill and passed into a death-like coma for twelve days. The two men came down from the clouds again, bearing spears that flashed lightning. He went out-of-body and was taken away by them into the clouds. There he was greeted by formations of horses at the four quarters, and by the Grandfathers, representing the four quarters, the sky, and the earth. The Grandfathers took him to the center of the world, showed him the universe, and bestowed upon him the tools that would give him the power to heal and the power to destroy. He was named Eagle Wing Stretches. The Grandfathers showed him the sacred hoop of his people (representing their collective soul or spiritual unity); in the center bloomed a holy stick that was a tree. The tree stood at a crossroads; one road, red, was the sacred path and the other, black, was the path of materialism and hardship.

The Power of the Earth revealed himself to Black Elk as an old man, and said that Black Elk would need great power, for times of great trouble were ahead. He was shown his people, starving and in distress, their sacred hoop broken. A voice told Black Elk that he had been given the sacred stick and his nation's hoop, and in the center of the hoop he should set the stick and make it bloom into a flowering tree. (The stick is the equivalent of the World Tree.) Toward the end of the vision, he stood on the highest mountain—he later identified it as Harney Peak in the Black Hills—and saw the whole hoop of the world. "And while I stood there I saw more than I can tell and I understood more than I saw; for I was seeing in a sacred manner the shapes of all things in the spirit, and the shape of all shapes as they must live together like one being," he later related (*Black Elk Speaks,* 1932). He saw the sacred hoop mended, and many sacred hoops of all peoples joined together in one circle, and one great flowering tree sheltering all.

Black Elk told no one of his vision, but his personality changed markedly; he became like a withdrawn old man. He continued to have visions, especially of the two messenger-like men from the clouds. He found he could understand birds and animals. Whenever he had a prophetic vision, he felt lifted out of himself.

In 1876 he had a vision of the Battle of Little Big Horn a day before it occurred. His family joined Crazy Horse in resisting the efforts of the United States government to place them on a reservation. After Crazy Horse was killed by soldiers, Black Elk, his family, and others retreated to Canada, where they joined Sitting Bull. The harsh winters and lack of food eventually drove them back to the United States.

According to tradition medicine men cannot use their power until they reenact their vision for others to see. In Black Elk's eighteenth summer, he began reenacting parts of his great vision. He became an effective healer. He described the process as being a hole through which "the power from the outer world" came through.

In 1886 he joined Buffalo Bill Cody's Wild West Show, thinking that if he could see and understand the world of the *Wasichu* (white man), he could fulfill his great vision and help his people. He spent three years in the show, and performed for Queen Victoria in London during her Diamond Jubilee in 1897.

Back in the United States in 1889, Black Elk found many of his people involved in the messianic Ghost Dance religion, which prophesied the demise of

---

the white race and the restoration of a pristine world for Native Americans. See **Ghost Dance religion**. He discovered that the Ghost Dance fit his great vision and he became an adherent. He performed and then led the dance, went into trances, and experienced visions out-of-body; in one vision he was given instruction for making the sacred shirts of the ghost dancers.

The movement ended with the massacre at Wounded Knee Creek on December 29, 1890. Black Elk participated in and advocated the fighting that followed; but the leaders, seeing their people starving and facing great odds, surrendered. Black Elk was among those sent to live on the Pine Ridge Reservation in South Dakota.

In 1930 American writer John G. Neihardt sought to find an Indian who had lived through the messianic period who could retell the days firsthand. He was sent to Black Elk in Manderson, South Dakota. There the writer found a dispirited old man who thought he could salvage his great vision through Neihardt. Black Elk gave his recollections in Sioux (he spoke no English), and they were translated by his son, Ben. The story, augmented with the recollections of others whom Black Elk knew, were published as *Black Elk Speaks: Being the Life Story of a Holy Man of the Oglala Sioux* (1932).

Neihardt was among those who witnessed Black Elk's last trip to Harney Peak to address the Six Grandfathers and apologize for his failure to mend the sacred hoop. He said that if he had any of his power left, the Thunder Beings of the west would answer him with thunder and rain. The trip took place during a drought season under a clear blue sky. Black Elk painted and dressed himself as he had been in his great vision. In his address to the Grandfathers and the Great Spirit, Black Elk expressed hope that some little root of the central tree still

lived, and asked the Powers to nurture it. Clouds gathered and a thin rain fell for a few minutes.

Black Elk bestowed a sacred pipe on Neihardt, who apparently failed to grasp its mysteries. These Black Elk relayed in 1947 to Joseph Epes Brown, who published them in *The Sacred Pipe: Black Elk's Account of the Seven Rites of the Oglala Sioux* (1953). Black Elk died on August 17, 1950, at Manderson.

Later observers have felt that Black Elk did fulfill his great vision, manifested in the renewal of Native American interest in traditional ways.

Wallace Black Elk (b. 1921) is a Lakota Sioux medicine man who was acquainted with Black Elk and refers to him as "grandfather," a term customarily applied to respectful relationships with an older and wiser person. Wallace Black Elk was instrumental in lobbying for passage of the American Indian Religious Freedom Act of 1977. He lectures and teaches on the sacred pipe and other Lakota medicine ways. See **Mysticism; Sacred pipe; Shamanism**.

Sources: Frederick J. Dockstader. *Great North American Indians: Profiles in Life and Leadership.* New York: Van Nostrand Reinhold, 1977; Paula Gunn Allen. "American Indian Mysticism." *Shaman's Drum* no. 14 (Mid-Fall 1988): 39–46; Joseph Epes Brown. *The Sacred Pipe: Black Elk's Account of the Seven Rites of the Oglala Sioux.* Norman, OK: University of Oklahoma Press, 1953; John G. Neihardt. *Black Elk Speaks: Being the Life Story of a Holy Man of the Oglala Sioux.* 1932. New York: Pocket Books, 1972; Shirley Nicholson, comp. *Shamanism.* Wheaton, IL: The Theosophical Publishing House, 1987.

Blake, William (1757–1827)

English mystic, poet, artist, and engraver whose visionary art finds a contemporary audience, but who was much misunderstood in his day. He experienced much disappointment, which left him increasingly embittered and caused him to isolate himself from others.

William Blake was born in London on November 28, 1757, where he lived most of his life. From his early years, he experienced remarkable visions of angels and ghostly monks. As his spiritual awareness developed, he saw and conversed with the angel Gabriel, the Virgin Mary, and various historical figures.

As a teenager Blake read philosophy and religion and wrote poems, but had no formal schooling until his father sent him to the Royal Academy to study art. In 1772 he was apprenticed to an engraver, and began to make his living in the trade at age twenty-two. At twenty-three he had his first exhibit of original paintings at the Royal Academy.

Blake was shaped by the prevailing influences of his day, including the religious symbolism in Gothic art and architecture, and the writings of eighteenth-century Swedish mystic Emanuel Swedenborg. He joined for a time the Swedenborgian Church of the New Jerusalem in London. He considered Newtonian science to be superstitious nonsense, and distinguished it from science in general.

In 1788 he developed a method of engraving that enabled him to design illustrations and print words at the same time. Blake called it "Illumined Printing" and thought it would earn him enough money to become an independent publisher, but he underestimated its expense. Nevertheless, he employed it for nearly all of his poetry over a twenty-year period.

Blake believed that the only reality was imagination, and that imagination turns nature inside out. In imagination the external world changes perspective and becomes part of the imagining human being. In this respect Blake led the life of a contemplative, who turned inward to the deep center of his soul in order to find God.

The first of his poems to be published appeared when he was twenty-six. About six years later (1789), he printed *Songs of Innocence,* the first of his many own works which he also engraved and illustrated. His most famous poem, "The Tyger," was part of his *Songs of Experience* (1794). His longer and even more symbolic poems were written when he was in his forties, including *Milton* (1804–1808) and *Jerusalem* (1804–1820).

During his final four years of life, Blake created two of his best known and most mystical sets of illustrations, of the biblical Book of Job, and of Dante's *Divine Comedy.* But even after a brilliant and very prolific life, he was regarded by his contemporaries primarily as an engraver of other people's designs; few appreciated or even knew of his original works, and of those who praised his engravings, even fewer knew also of his poems.

Blake lived and died in poverty, in large part due to his inability to compete in the highly competitive field of engraving, and due to a general lack of appreciation of his vision. Recognition of his genius grows each decade. His art communicates his vision universally, even if his illustrations often do not conform to popular images. Blake expressed his unique and personal mystic vision, no matter how "unreal" it seemed to others. His inner vision used the senses but went beyond them, and he found this vision to be essential to personal integrity.

Sources: S. Foster Damon. *A Blake Dictionary: The Ideas and Symbols of William Blake.* Boulder, CO: Shambhala Publications, 1979; Northrop Frye, ed. and intro. *Selected Poetry and Prose of William Blake.* New York: Modern Library, 1953; F. C. Happold. *Mysticism: A Study and an Anthology.* Rev. ed. Harmondsworth, Middlesex, England: Penguin Books, 1970;

Maung Ba Han. *William Blake: His Mysticism.* 1924. Darby, PA: Folcroft, 1974; Robert Maynard Hutchins, ed. *Great Books of the Western World.* Chicago: Encyclopaedia Britannica, 1952; Louis Kronenberger, ed. *Atlantic Brief Lives.* Boston: Little, Brown, 1971.

Blavatsky, Madame Helena Petrovna (1831–1891)

Russian-born mystic and cofounder of the Theosophical Society. An outspoken and controversial figure, Madame Helena Petrovna Blavatsky—known as HPB—helped to spread Eastern religious, philosophical, and occult ideas throughout the West. She endeavored to give the study of occultism an accepted, scientific, and philosophical foundation.

HPB exhibited psychic gifts as a small child, claiming an awareness of the consciousness and voice of all objects, organic and inorganic, and the existence of nonphysical beings.

Her father, Peter von Hahn, was in the army. Her mother, Helena Andreyevna, wrote novels about socially

Madame Helena P. Blavatsky

constricted Russian heroines, and was called the George Sand of Russia. When Helena Andreyevna died at age twenty-eight, the eleven-year-old HPB and her sister and brother went to live with their maternal grandparents. Their grandmother, Helena Pavlovna de Fadeev, was a princess of the Dolgorukurov family and a famous botanist. Both women provided strong role models for HPB, attributes she amplified with stubbornness, a fiery temper, and unwillingness to conform to society's expectations. At age seventeen, to spite her governess, Helena married Nikifor (also Nicephor) V. Blavatsky, forty, but never consummated the marriage and abandoned him a few months later.

From 1848 to 1858, HPB traveled the world. She claimed to have entered Tibet to study with the Masters for two years. She returned to Russia in 1858, only to leave again with Agardi Metrovich, an Italian opera singer. In 1871 Metrovich was killed in an explosion on board a boat bound for Cairo. HPB went on to Cairo, where she founded the Société Spirite for occult phenomena along with Emma Cutting (later Emma Coulomb). Dissatisfied customers, charging fraud, closed the society.

HPB emigrated to New York in 1873, where she impressed others with psychic feats. Throughout her career she claimed to perform physical and mental mediumship, levitation, out-of-body projection, telepathy, clairvoyance, clairaudience, and clairsentience. These powers were never proved or disproved, as she never submitted to scientific tests—nor, apparently, was she ever asked to do so. Her own interests, however, were not in the psychic powers themselves, but in the laws and principles of nature that governed them.

In 1875 HPB received word that her husband was dead. She married a Russian peasant, Michael C. Betanelly, but later learned that Blavatsky was still alive and her legal spouse. Betanelly divorced her for desertion in 1878. She never returned to Blavatsky.

In 1874 HPB had met Colonel Henry Steel Olcott, a lawyer, agricultural expert, and journalist who covered Spiritualist phenomena. They formed a lifelong friendship. In September 1875 HPB and Olcott founded the Theosophical Society along with William Q. Judge, an American attorney, and others. See **Theosophy.**

HPB's first book, *Isis Unveiled,* appeared in 1877. In the preface she stated that the book was "a plea for the recognition of the Hermetic philosophy, the ancient universal wisdom." *Isis Unveiled* outlines the basic precepts of the Masters and the secret knowledge they were said to protect. Its success outshone that of the society, which by 1878 had nearly folded.

In July 1878 HPB became the first Russian woman to acquire US citizenship, a move she took to keep the English in India from thinking she was a Russian spy. HPB and Olcott left for India in December of that year to revive the society and study Hindu and Buddhist religions.

In India HPB quickly gained supporters, including English journalist A. P. Sinnett, statesman Allen O. Hume, and various high-caste Indians and English officials. She helped Sinnett and Hume begin corresponding with the Masters Koot Hoomi and Morya. Although the Masters' handwriting was different from HPB's, critics asserted she wrote the letters herself, but the charges were never proved conclusively.

In 1882 HPB moved the society's international headquarters to an estate in Adyar, near Madras, where she had a shrine room constructed to allow the Masters to manifest their communications. Her former colleague, Emma Cutting Coulomb, moved to Adyar to manage the household. Later Coulomb and her husband were fired on charges of dishonest practices.

In 1884 HPB toured Europe with Olcott. While they were there the Coulombs published letters, which they said were written by HPB, that gave instructions for the Masters' manifestations and for operation of the shrine through secret back panels. The panels apparently had been built by Coulomb in HPB's absence in order to ruin her reputation. In December 1884, Richard Hodgson of the Society of Psychical Research (SPR) in London arrived at Adyar to investigate the phenomena there; by spring he had released a scathing report alleging fraud and trickery by HPB and her associates. The report remained controversial for more than one hundred years. In 1986 the SPR published an article in its *Journal* stating that the report was prejudiced, that Hodgson had ignored all evidence favorable to HPB and had not proved his case, and that an apology was due.

Because of the controversy, Olcott sent HPB to Europe in 1885. She eventually settled in Germany and continued to work despite deteriorating health. By 1885 the French-born Swedish countess Constance Wachtmeister had moved in with HPB and remained with her while she wrote her second book, *The Secret Doctrine* (1888), her greatest work. It outlines a scheme of evolution relating to the universe (cosmogenesis) and humankind (anthropogenesis), and is based on three premises: (1) Ultimate Reality as an omnipresent, transcendent principle beyond the reach of thought; (2) the universality of the law of cycles throughout nature; and (3) the identity of all souls with the Universal Oversoul and their journey through many degrees of intelligence by means of reincarnation, in accordance with "Cyclic and Karmic law."

The Secret Doctrine is said to be largely based on an archaic manuscript, *The Book of Dyzan,* which HPB interpreted. Parts of *The Secret Doctrine* purportedly were communicated to her by the Mahatmas, who, she said, impressed thoughts in her head, which she wrote down. Critics, however, said she drew on existing works.

By the end of 1889, HPB had written two more books: *The Key to Theosophy*, an introduction to theosophical thought and philosophy; and *The Voice of the Silence*, a mystical and poetic work on the path to enlightenment.

One of the reviewers of *The Secret Doctrine*, activist Annie Wood Besant, had converted to Theosophy, and her home became the headquarters of the Theosophical Society in London. Besant, known for her support of progressive causes, brought another generation of liberal intellectuals into the society and became its president after Olcott's death in 1907.

By the end of 1890, HPB's health had declined to the point where she could not walk, and so traveled in what looked like a giant perambulator. She suffered from heart disease, Bright's disease of the kidneys, and rheumatism, complicated by influenza. She died at her home on May 8, 1891. Her body was cremated. One-third of her ashes remained in Europe, one-third went to America with William Judge, and one-third went to India, where Besant later scattered them in the Ganges River. Theosophists commemorate her death on May 8, called White Lotus Day.

Sources: Bruce F. Campbell. *Ancient Wisdom Revived: A History of the Theosophical Movement.* Berkeley: University of California Press, 1980; Robert S. Ellwood. *Eastern Spirituality in America.* New York: Paulist Press, 1987; Krysta Gibson. "The Theosophical Society." *The New Times* (November 1987): 1+; Marion Meade. *Madame Blavatsky: The Woman Behind the Myth.* New York: G. P. Putnam's Sons, 1980; J. Gordon Melton. *Encyclopedic Handbook of Cults in America.* New York and London: Garland Publishing, 1986; Howard Murphet. *When Daylight Comes: A Biography of Helena Petrovna Blavatsky.* Wheaton, IL: The Theosophical Publishing House, 1975; A. P. Sinnet. *Incidents in the Life of Mme. Blavatsky.* London: Redway, 1886; Lewis Spence. *The Encyclopedia of the Occult.* 1920. Reprint. London: Bracken Books, 1988; *H. Blavatsky and Her Writings.* Pamphlet. Wheaton, IL: The Theosophical Society in America, n.d.; Gertrude Marvin Williams. *Priestess of the Occult: Madame Blavatsky.* New York: Alfred A. Knopf, 1946; Colin Wilson, ed. *Dark Dimensions: A Celebration of the Occult.* New York: Everest House, 1977.

Bodhisattva

In Buddhism an enlightened being who postpones or renounces nirvana in order to remain in the universe to give spiritual guidance to all beings still caught in the wheel of rebirth. Bodhisattvas (a Sanskrit term for "enlightened being") generally are less advanced than buddhas, but buddhas are sometimes referred to as bodhisattvas.

Bodhisattvas were an early concept of the Mahayana school of Buddhism, which recognizes two types of bodhisattvas: earthly and transcendent. The other major Buddhist school, Theravada, teaches self-enlightenment, and maintains that once nirvana is reached, there remains no ego or karma to warrant rebirth as a bodhisattva.

The earthly bodhisattva seeks buddhahood through attaining enlightenment and service to others. Six *paramitas* (virtues or perfections) must be acquired and practiced: (1) generosity, or total self-surrender; (2) morality; (3) patience; (4) zeal, effort to overcome obstacles; (5) meditation, constantly perfected; and (6) wisdom, which cannot be obtained without first getting rid of attachment and repulsion. Practicing the *paramitas* helps one to see the illusory nature of the self. Many rebirths may be required to accomplish these.

Transcendent bodhisattvas have attained perfect wisdom and are free of rebirth. They manifest to lead others to enlightenment, and are the objects of great devotion. The most popular transcendent bodhisattva of Mahayanists is Avalokitesvara, the spiritual son of Amitabha, the Buddha of Meditation of infinite light. Avalokitesvara was born from a tear shed by Lord Buddha at sight of the suffering in the world. Called "the compassionate," he is represented in female form as Kuan-yin in China, the goddess of mercy and protector of women, and Kwannon in Japan, also goddess of mercy.

Bodhisattvas also are part of the Pure Land school of Buddhism, which teaches that salvation is possible by faith and good works. Bodhisattvas also are recognized in Zen Buddhism.

The concept of the bodhisattva cuts across all religious lines to include all "spiritual warriors" and heroic beings who are dedicated to compassion and service to others. Bodhisattva nature exists in everyone. See **Buddhism; Karma; Reincarnation.** Compare to **Avatar.**

Sources: Robert Aitken. *Taking the Path of Zen.* San Francisco: North Point Press, 1982; John Blofeld. *The Tantric Mysticism of Tibet.* Boston: Shambhala Publications, 1987; *The Encyclopedia of Eastern Philosophy and Religion.* Boston: Shambhala, 1989. Dainin Katagiri. *Returning to Silence: Zen Practice in Daily Life.* Boston: Shambhala Publications, 1988; Yong Choon Kim. *Oriental Thought.* Totowa, NJ: Rowman and Littlefield, 1973; Maria Leach, ed., and Jerome Fried, assoc. ed. *Funk & Wagnalls Standard Dictionary of Folklore, Mythology, and Legend.* San Francisco: Harper & Row, 1979; Maurice Percheron. *Buddha and Buddhism.* 1956. Woodstock, NY: The Overlook Press, 1982; Alan W. Watts. *The Way of Zen.* New York: Vintage Books, 1957.

Bodywork

Health therapies that involve manipulation of the body and its bioelectrical energy field. There are numerous types of bodywork, involving massage, physical manipulation, movement, breathing, realignment of the energy field, and energy transfer. These therapies assume the existence of a universal life force that affects health, and the existence of a self-healing capacity within everyone, which can be stimulated by the therapy. See **Universal life force.** Bodywork is often combined with other therapies, including allopathic (science-based) medicine.

Bodywork takes into account the role of the mind and emotions in physical health, and the organism's overall interaction with the environment and the universal life energies. Some therapies are based on the belief that form influences consciousness, and that the body can be redesigned or refined to improve psychological and spiritual growth.

Although many bodywork methods are ancient, bodywork as a movement began around the late nineteenth to early twentieth centuries, due in part to the work of psychiatrist Sigmund Freud. In 1886 Freud published a paper on male hysteria, a physical disorder, which Freud demonstrated is largely psychological in origin. The paper had a great impact on one of Freud's followers, Wilhelm Reich, who developed a therapy combining bodywork with psychoanalysis that bears his name (see Reichian massage on page 69).

Bodywork therapy involves a high level of intuitive awareness on the part of the therapist; psychic abilities sometimes develop over the course of time. Patients sometimes report psychological insights and breakthroughs, as well as experiences such as apparent past-life recall, clairvoyance, clairaudience, and so on.

Major Types of Bodywork

Acupuncture
This ancient Chinese therapy, dating to c. 3000 B.C., is based on the principle that there is a nervous connection be-

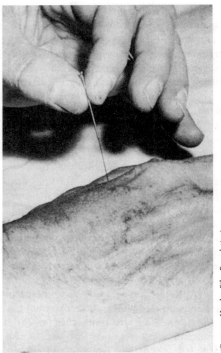

Acupuncture

(Courtesy Hartley Film Foundation)

tween the body's organs and the body's surface. Needles are inserted under the skin at various points to treat various conditions by manipulating *ch'i,* the universal life force, which flows through the body along energy pathways called meridians. Acupuncture is good for pain relief, and is also used to treat addictions. In China it is used as an analgesic for surgery, and to treat conditions that normally require surgery in the West, such as appendicitis.

Acupressure

Stimulation of the acupuncture points by finger and hand pressure instead of with needles. Acupressure can be self-administered and can provide relief when acupuncture is not immediately available, or where pain medication is not desirable.

Alexander Technique

A therapy of massage and manipulation combined with verbal instruction, developed in the late nineteenth century by F. Mathias Alexander, Australian Shakespearean actor and monologist. Massage of the neck enables energy to flow up the spine to the head, which controls body movement. The "reconditioned" individual moves, thinks, works, and speaks much better than before.

Bioenergetics

An outgrowth of the theories of Wilhelm Reich developed by Alexander Lowen, a psychiatrist and student of Reich. According to Lowen repressed emotions and desires affect physiology by creating chronic muscular tension and a loss of vibrancy. Lowen developed a bodywork therapy of difficult postures, muscle manipulations, and breathing techniques, some of which can be painful. The patient releases emotions by screaming, crying, and kicking. The bodywork is combined with psychoanalysis of childhood experiences and dream imagery.

Chiropractic

The manipulation of the spine and joints by hand to rebalance or repair the body's neurological functions and restore the body's energies. Its premise is that poor posture, stress, accidents, and traumas produce abnormalities in the joints and muscles, which may be corrected by realigning the spine. Dr. George J. Goodheart developed chiropractic into applied kinesiology, "the science of muscle activation," in which hurt muscles are treated by work on their opposing, weak muscles.

Feldenkrais Technique

Modern movement and posture therapy developed by the Russian-born Israeli, Moshe Feldenkrais, and based on the ancient premise that the body is a mirror of the mind. The Feldenkrais technique aims to improve posture through self-awareness of stance, gesture, and movement, which in turn improves self-image, vitality, and creativity.

Polarity
A therapy developed by Dr. Randolph Stone to balance the energy flow within the body. Polarity therapy uses gentle manipulations, exercise, diet (usually vegetarian), positive thoughts and attitudes, and love.

Reflexology
Ancient therapy of finger and thumb pressure applied to the feet, the surfaces of which correspond to various organs of the body. The pressure stimulates the flow of the universal life force. The origins of reflexology are not known, but it was in use in ancient China, India, and Egypt.

Reichian Massage
Wilhelm Reich's technique holds that neuroses and most physical disorders are caused by blockages in the flow of emotional and sexual energy (orgone). The blockages manifest as "body armor," defensive contractions of muscles that run in horizontal bands across the eyes, mouth and jaw, diaphragm, abdomen, and pelvis. The therapist intuitively senses where the greatest body armor is, and uses forceful massage and other techniques—such as eye movements, the gag reflex, facial expressions, screaming, kicking, and crying—to dissolve it. After the physical therapy comes psychoanalysis.

Reiki
An Oriental energy transfer therapy in which the universal life force is channeled through a healer to the patient. Reiki was developed in the late nineteenth century by Dr. Mikao Usui, Japa-nese scholar and minister, allegedly upon ancient Sanskrit texts. Different schools presently exist.

Energy is transferred by touching parts of the body and "brushing" the aura in downward, fluttering movements. Therapists may also employ visualization of secret symbols.

Rolfing (also called Structural Integration)
Modern physical therapy developed by Swiss biochemist Ida Rolf. Rolfing seeks to realign the human body in a straight line. Misalignment causes thickened fascia, the connective tissue between muscles and the sheaths of muscles, which impair movement and posture. The fascia is stretched in deep massage, which at times can be quite painful.

Seiki-jutsu
A Japanese therapy of transferring seiki, universal healing energy, to the patient through a healer. Seiki enters through the crown at the point of the hair whorl, where it travels down the spine to the sacrum and fills the body. The therapist sometimes places the hands on top of the head and the knee against the sacrum.

Shiatsu
A Japanese therapy of finger pressure, similar to acupressure, and massage, which further stimulates and balances the universal life force.

Therapeutic Touch
Modern energy transfer therapy developed by Dora van Gelder Kunz, a clairvoyant and meditation teacher, and Dolores Krieger, a nurse. The universal life force is transmitted through touch, holding the hands over the affected area of the body, or brushing the patient's energy field with strokes of the hand. Scientific studies of Therapeutic Touch show that it increases the oxygen-

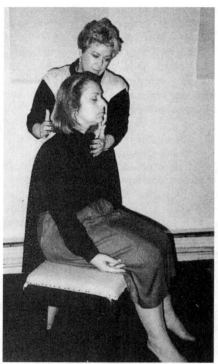

(Author's Collection)

Kathleen Fanslow-Brunjes, R.N., scans woman's aura to sense areas that need treatment with Therapeutic Touch.

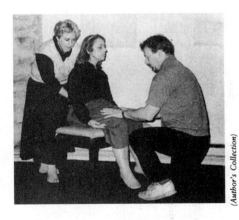

(Author's Collection)

In Therapeutic Touch the practitioner channels energy to the patient through the hands.

carrying capacity of red blood cells, lowers high temperatures, and reduces restlessness. It is used in hospitals and hospices, and is particularly effective with autonomic nervous system, circulatory, lymphatic and musculoskeletal disorders, and some mental disorders.

Touch for Health

A system developed by Dr. John F. Thie, which combines applied kinesiology for diagnosis and "acupressure touch," a form of light acupressure, for treatment of the musculoskeletal system.

See **Aura; Behavioral medicine; Chakras; Healing, faith and psychic; Yoga.**

Sources: Sherry Suib Cohen. *The Magic of Touch.* New York: Harper & Row, 1987; Kathleen A. Fanslow. "Therapeutic Touch: A Healing Modality throughout Life." *Topics in Clinical Nursing* (July 1983): 72–79; Moshe Feldenkrais. *Awareness through Movement.* New York: Harper & Row, 1977; Winifred Gallagher. "The Healing Touch." *American Health* (October 1988): 45–53; Richard Grossman. *The Other Medicines.* Garden City, NY: Doubleday, 1985; Dolores Krieger. *The Therapeutic Touch.* New York: Prentice-Hall Press, 1979; Mirka Knaster. "Dolores Krieger's Therapeutic Touch." *East/West* 19, no. 8 (August 1989): 54–59+; Lucinda Lidell with Sara Thomas, Carola Beresford Cooke, and Anthony Porter. *Massage: The Complete Step-by-Step Guide to Eastern and Western Techniques.* New York: Fireside Books, 1984; Janet Macrae. *Therapeutic Touch: A Practical Guide.* New York: Alfred A. Knopf, 1988; Robert Neubert. "Reiki: The Radiance Technique." *New Realities* 7, no. 4 (March/April 1987): 18–22; Maruti Seidman. *A Guide to Polarity Therapy.* Rev. ed. North Hollywood, CA: Newcastle Publications, 1986; Dr. Andrew Stanway. *Alternative Medicines: A Guide to Natural Therapies.* Rev. ed. Harmondsworth, Middlesex, England: Penguin Books, 1986.

Book test

A test for evidence of survival after death that was originated in the early twentieth century by English medium Gladys Osborne Leonard, and her spirit control, Feda. It is possible that the test was suggested by Feda herself as proof of communication from the dead.

In the book test, a communicating spirit, called a "communicator," delivers a message to a living person through a medium, specifying a book in a location to which the medium has not had access. The communicator gives the book's exact location on a shelf, such as third from the left on the top shelf, and specifies a page number. The text on that page is to contain the message.

Leonard was very successful with book tests, sometimes naming books that were unknown to her sitters, but which bore out personal messages as the communicating spirits claimed.

Book tests were common immediately before World War I and after, when interest in communication with the dead was at a high. The rate of success of the tests was not high; in one analysis of 532 tests (1921), 17 percent were successful and 19 percent approximately successful. Slightly more than 38 percent were total failures, with the remainder dubious or nearly total failures. Nevertheless, many successful book tests could not be explained in terms of telepathy between medium and sitter, but seemed to be paranormal. They are not, however, considered proof of survival after death.

Nina Kulagina, Russian physical medium, demonstrated extraordinary success with book tests, by naming the first letters of each paragraph of given pages in a book chosen by random but not opened. See **Leonard, Gladys Osborne; Mediumship; Newspaper test.**

Sources: Alan Gauld. *Mediumship and Survival.* London: William Heinemann Ltd., 1982; Susy Smith. *The Mediumship of Mrs.* *Leonard.* New Hyde Park, NY: University Books, 1964; Russell Targ and Keith Harary. *The Mind Race.* New York: Villard Books, 1984.

Buckland, Raymond

See **Witchcraft.**

Buddhism

Religion of the "awakened one," based on the teachings of the historical Buddha, Shakyamuni ("Sage of the Sakyas"), born Siddhartha Gautama (c. 566 B.C.–486 B.C.). Buddhism is one of the world's great religions, although some argue that it is a philosophy and not a religion. It originated in India, where it died out after the twelfth and thirteenth centuries, and spread through Asia and eventually to the West.

In Asia Buddhism is known as the *Buddha-Dhamma,* or the "eternal truth of the Awakened One," referring to both

Buddha sculpture

(Courtesy Office of Tibet)

the truth concerning Buddha and the truth espoused by Buddha. In the view of Buddhism, life is full of suffering and is impermanent and without essence. Because of earthly cravings and ignorance, the individual is caught on the wheel of *samsara,* or rebirth. Only by overcoming those conditions can the individual break the cycle and attain nirvana, the merging with Brahman, the Absolute.

There is no concept of an eternal, individual soul in Buddhism. The karmic attributes that make up a personality, called *skandas,* or "aggregates," scatter upon death and recollect in rebirth to form a new but transitory personality.

Buddhas, or "awakened ones," have appeared throughout human history and will continue to appear. According to Buddhist tradition, at least twenty-four Buddhas preceded Siddhartha Gautama over a 120,000-year period. However, there is no historical documentation of their existence.

The Birth of Siddhartha Gautama

Siddhartha ("He who accomplishes") Gautama (also spelled Gotama) was born to the leaders of the noble Sakya clan, who lived in a basin of the Ganges River in India. He became known as the Buddha ("the Awakened or Enlightened One"), the Savior of Humankind.

The legend surrounding the Buddha's birth, life, and teachings has a number of variations, and different dates of his life are given. In China, for example, he is believed to have been born in 947 B.C., and in Ceylon and Southeast Asia his birth date is 543 B.C. Several centuries after his death at the age of eighty, legends accorded him a miraculous birth parallel to the immaculate conception of Christ.

According to legend Siddhartha Gautama incarnated on earth because the bodhisattva (compassionate one and future Buddha) Avalokitesvara looked down from heaven and was moved by the suffering of humans and even the plight of the gods and demons. Intending to save them all, he decided to send his earthly reflection into the womb of Maya, queen of King Shuddhodana, a member of the *kshatriya* (warrior) class. The king and queen had been married for thirty-two months but had not consummated their marriage (in another version they had abstained from intercourse for months prior to the immaculate conception).

One night Maya experienced a dream in which she was taken up into heaven on a cloud and deposited at a palace. Avalokitesvara, in the form of a white elephant with six tusks, approached her and painlessly pierced her side with a tusk. In this fashion his earthly reflection entered her womb. The fetus was not nourished by the mother, but fed by a drop of elixir taken from an open lotus at the moment of his conception. Thus Gautama was not polluted by human flesh.

Ten lunar months later, he was born in the Lumbini gardens outside Kapilavatsu, the capital where the king and queen resided. Maya took hold of a tree branch and delivered the infant painlessly from her right side. The birth was attended by the gods Brahma and Indra.

Maya placed the child on a white lotus. Gautama rose up and surveyed space by glancing in the Ten Directions, then took seven steps toward each of the four cardinal points. He claimed rank as first in the world and vowed to end birth, old age, suffering, and death. He declared this to be his final birth.

Seven days after his birth, Maya died and rose into heaven. (Sudden death or separation from mother is part of the myth of the hero.) Gautama was raised by Maya's sister, Mahaprajapati Gautami, who married the king.

Shuddhodana was soon visited by an ascetic, who advised him of thirty-two primary marks and eighty secondary marks that would appear on the body of the Buddha to identify him. These were duly found upon the body of Gautama.

The Buddha's Enlightenment

As a youth Siddhartha excelled in martial arts and in his studies, surpassing the knowledge of his teachers. At age sixteen he married reluctantly but in accordance with custom. His father was relieved; for, according to prophecy, if his son became an ascetic he would not take the throne and continue the family rule.

The married life bored Gautama, however, and four times he left his palace. The Four Meetings, as they are called, marked the first stage in his spiritual development. Gautama encountered an old man, a sick man, a dead man, and a monk. From them he realized that old age, suffering, and death are inescapable, and salvation lies in religion. He resolved to pursue religion and shortly went into "the Great Retirement."

Fortunately, his son, Rahula, had just been born, thus ensuring the continuation of his family line, so Gautama felt free to leave. One night he slipped out of the palace and went to a forest, where he cut his hair, abandoned his royal clothing, and renounced all comforts. He was twenty-nine.

His search for truth and knowledge led him to hermits, yogis, and Brahmins, with whom he studied. None, however, provided the enlightenment he sought. He acquired five disciples.

His awakening finally came when he sat himself under a bodhi-tree (a fig tree, also called bo-tree, and popularly called pipal) and meditated. Mara, the god of death and personification of evil (the approximate equivalent of the Devil), worried that if Gautama succeeded in liberating humanity there would be no one left to tempt; he attacked Gautama with an army of demons and the furies of the elements. Failing to break his meditation, Mara sent his three daughters, Lust, Restlessness, and Greed, but Gautama dismissed them with a glance.

After four weeks Gautama had his awakening with his realization of the Four Noble Truths: (1) Existence is suffering, and suffering is unavoidable; (2) suffering is caused by desire; (3) the elimination of desire will bring suffering to an end; and (4) there is a means to eliminate desire and thus suffering. The latter is called the Eightfold Path, also the Middle Way, for Gautama the Buddha envisioned it as a middle road between the extremes of asceticism and worldly life. The Eightfold Path consists of right speech, right conduct, right livelihood, right effort, right mindfulness, right concentration, right views, and right intentions.

The Buddha spent seven days on this awakening, then continued meditating for another five weeks. In the sixth week, he went to Lake Muchalinda, where Mara hurled a furled rainstorm at him, but he was protected by the snake spirit of the lake, which spread its cobra hood over him. His meditation was ended by two monks who offered him food, which he took in a bowl (now the begging bowl of monks).

The Buddha never intended to enlighten the masses, whom he saw as steeped in superstition and magic and suppressed by the Brahmins. Instead he sought to address the warrior class. In his first sermon, called the "Sutra of Setting in Motion the Wheel of Doctrine," he expounded upon the Four Noble Truths, the law of karma, and the concept of *anatta* (no-self), which holds that there is no permanent essence of any one human being, but a constantly changing collection of aggregates that come together each time there is a rebirth. See **Reincarnation.**

The Buddha then spent forty-five years evangelizing throughout northeastern India, to the displeasure of the Brahmins. His five disciples formed a growing community of monks. At first the Buddha refused to admit women to the community, saying that a religion of men will last one thousand years, but a religion that admits women will last only five hundred years. He relented and allowed his aunt (his stepmother) to join. (He returned home after an absence of thirty-five years and reconciled with his family.)

Despite his desire to teach only the elite, his teachings spread throughout the masses and many sought to follow him. The Buddha elaborated on the Four Truths by giving five rules for everyday life: (1) Be compassionate and respect the lowliest form of life; (2) give and receive freely, but never take anything that is not given; (3) never, without exception, lie; (4) avoid drugs and drink; and (5) respect woman and commit no illicit and unnatural carnal act.

At age eighty the Buddha took a meal with a lowly blacksmith, who inadvertently served him poisonous mushrooms, or, by some disputed accounts, spoiled pork. The Buddha became ill and knew he was about to die. Seated in a lotus position, he gave his final instructions to his choice disciples, including Ananda, his favorite, and Maitreya, whom he said would be the next supreme Buddha come to earth thousands of years hence. The Buddha summarized his teachings. When he was done, he lay down on his right side and entered into meditation; a heavenly music wafted down from the sky. At some indeterminate moment, he passed into nirvana (later some Buddhists disagreed that he entered nirvana, but instead vowed not to until all beings had achieved it). The Buddha was later deified, first as a semidivine being and then as a divine being.

The Spread of Buddhism

By the time of Christ, Buddhism was declining in India. By the fifth century it was being absorbed into Hinduism, and by the twelfth century it no longer existed as a viable force in India. It spread throughout Asia, however, where it took firm hold in the ensuing centuries, coexisting with or merging with indigenous religions and philosophies, among them the Confucianism and Taoism of China, the Shintoism of Japan, and the Bon of Tibet.

Various schools and sects have emerged; the two major ones are Mahayana and Theravada Buddhism. Mahayana Buddhism holds that all have the potential for enlightenment and emphasizes faith in the Buddha, love of humankind, compassion, charity, and altruism. The Buddha is considered to be an eternal being, an embodiment of absolute truth, who occasionally takes human form. Theravada Buddhism holds out salvation to the monks and nuns who join the community, and prescribes a discipline for individual undertaking. The Buddha is regarded as a human teacher.

In Tibet Tantric Buddhism is called Vajrayana, "the indestructible vehicle." In mythology the *vajra* is the weapon of Indra, the king of gods, and is made from the bones of a *rishi,* an exalted yogi. As the *vajra* has a magical nature, so does Vajrayana. If practiced correctly Vajrayana is a Short Path to destruction of the ego and to enlightenment. Incorrect practice imperils the practitioner. See **David-Neel, Alexandra.**

The teachings of Vajrayana are supposed to be secret, passed orally from guru to *chela,* or student. The emphasis is on transmutation of the three poisons— passion, aggression, and ignorance—into wisdom, rather than on destruction of them to clear the path to enlightenment. This emphasis lends comparison to Western alchemy. See **Alchemy.** There is also much use of complex symbology in meditation. See **Mandala; Symbols.** Empowerment comes with initiation. See **Ritual.**

Buddhism made few inroads in the West until the nineteenth century, when the Transcendentalists, the Theosophical Society, and others disseminated information about Eastern philosophies and religions. Following the World Parliament of Religions in Chicago in 1893, authentic Buddhist teachers began coming to the West.

The growth of Buddhism in the West has necessitated adaptations to the Western culture. Asian Buddhism traditionally is masculine, hierarchical, and authoritarian, practiced by monks who have withdrawn from the world and who are supported by followers. Western Buddhism, particularly in the United States, has grown more democratic and open to the full participation of women. Western practitioners seldom desire to withdraw from the world, and so Buddhism is integrated into daily life. See **Meditation; Milarepa; Mysticism; Yoga; Zen.**

Sources: The Encyclopedia of Eastern Philosophy and Religion. Boston: Shambhala, 1989; Rick Fields. *How the Swans Came to the Lake: A Narrative History of Buddhism in America.* Boulder, CO: Shambhala Publications, 1981; Richard A. Gard, ed. *Buddhism.* New York: George Braziller, 1962; Don Morreale, ed. *Buddhist America: Centers, Retreats, Practices.* Santa Fe, NM: John Muir Publications, 1988; Geoffrey Parrinder, ed. *World Religions: From Ancient History to the Present.* New York: Facts On File, 1983; Maurice Percheron. *Buddha and Buddhism.* 1956. Woodstock, NY: The Overlook Press, 1982; Nancy Wilson Ross. *Buddhism: A Way of Life and Thought.* New York: Alfred A. Knopf, 1980.

C

Caddy, Eileen

See **Findhorn**.

Caddy, Peter

See **Findhorn**.

Caduceus

An esoteric symbol of spiritual enlightenment and higher wisdom. The caduceus is a wand entwined by two snakes and topped by wings or a winged helmet. It also is associated with healing, and has been the emblem of physicians for centuries. The T shape of the caduceus is derived from the *tau* cross, a T-shaped cross used in the ancient Egyptian and Mithraic mysteries initiations.

In Greco-Roman mythology, the caduceus belongs to Hermes (Mercury), the shrewd and swift messenger god who flies as fleet as thought. Hermes carries his magical wand when escorting souls to the underworld. Originally, the wand was a symbol of reconciliation of arguments. According to legend, Hermes came upon two snakes fighting and thrust his wand between them. The snakes became entwined on the wand and remained attached to it.

The wand is made of olive wood, symbolic of peace and the continuity of life. Its shaft represents power; the serpent represents wisdom or prudence; the wings are diligence; and the helmet symbolizes high thoughts. Overall, the caduceus symbolizes immortality. With a touch of his caduceus, Hermes could put mortals to sleep or raise the dead. The Romans viewed the caduceus as a symbol of moral conduct and equilibrium.

The caduceus actually predates Greco-Roman mythology, appearing in Mesopotamian cultures around 2600 B.C., where its serpents signified a god who cured illness. The association of the caduceus with medicine and health was passed from the Middle East to the Greek culture. In ancient India the caduceus appeared in temples as a symbol of the four elements: the wand (earth), the serpents (fire and water), and the wings (air).

In Hindu and Buddhist esoteric teachings, the caduceus represents the transformation of spiritual consciousness through the vehicles of the body's pranic energy system. The wand is the spine, or *Bramadanda* ("stick of Brahma"), and the serpents are the *kundalini* force, or serpent-power, which resides in the earth. The *kundalini* rises up through the *ida* and *pingla* nervous channels along the spine, entwines around the six major chakras of the body, and flowers with wings at the crown chakra. The wings signify the rise of the consciousness through higher planes of awareness, the result of the flow of *kundalini*.

In Freemasonry the caduceus represents the harmony and balance between negative and positive forces, the fixed and the volatile, the continuity of life and the decay of life. See **Chakra; Kundalini.**

Sources: J. E. Cirlot. *A Dictionary of Symbols.* New York: Philosophical Library, 1971; Manly P. Hall. *The Secret Teachings of All Ages.* 1928. Reprint. Los Angeles: The Philosophic Research Society, 1977; Edith Hamilton. *Mythology.* New York: New American Library, 1940; C. W. Leadbeater. *The Chakras.* Wheaton, IL: Theosophical Publishing House, 1927; *New Larousse Encyclopedia of Mythology.* New ed. New York: Crescent Books, 1968; Anthony S. Mercatante. *Encyclopedia of World Mythology and Legend.* French's Forest, Australia: Child & Associates, 1988; Samuel H. Sandweiss. *Sai Baba: The Holy Man and the Psychiatrist.* San Diego, CA: Birth Day Publishing, 1975; Arthur Edward Waite. *A New Encyclopedia of Freemasonry.* Combined ed. New York: Weathervane Books, 1970.

Cagliostro, Count Alessandro (1743–1795)

A friend and successor of Comte de Saint Germain, Cagliostro was a glamorous figure in the royal courts of Europe, where he reputedly practiced magic, psychic healing, alchemy, scrying, and occult arts. Some historians label him a fraud and fake, while others say his psychic and occult gifts were genuine, and that he was a generous man who tried to help the poor.

His real name is often given as Guiseppe Balsamo, born in 1743 in Palermo to a poor Sicilian family. Balsamo was a real person, but his identity as Cagliostro is disputed. According to legend the young Cagliostro was a street-smart child, and learned early how to turn his natural psychic talent for precognition into a lucrative fortune-telling business.

Cagliostro

At twenty-three he went to Malta, determined to make a name and fortune for himself, and was initiated into the Order of the Knights of Malta, where he studied alchemy, the Kabbalah, and other occult secrets. He changed his name to Count Alessandro Cagliostro, borrowing the surname from his godmother. Later he joined the Freemasons in England, which had a great influence on his beliefs. See **Freemasonry.**

Cagliostro spent most of his adult life as a nomad among royalty in Europe, England, and Russia. In Rome he met and married Lorenza Feliciani, who became his partner in various occult ventures, such as crystal-gazing, healing by laying on of hands, conjuring spirits, and predicting winning lottery numbers. They also sold magic potions, the elixir of life, and the philosopher's stone. They held seances, transmuted metals, practiced necromancy, cast out demons, and hypnotized people. Cagliostro's accurate fortune-telling gifts led to a new name: "The Divine Cagliostro."

Spectacular success invariably breeds resentment, and Cagliostro fell out of favor with the medical community and the Catholic church. In 1875 he and his wife were victimized in an infamous fraud, the

"Queen's Necklace Affair." The two were set up by Countess de Lamotte, who swindled 1.6 million francs for a diamond necklace—ostensibly for Marie Antoinette—and accused them of stealing the necklace.

Cagliostro and Lorenza were among those jailed and tried for the fraud. According to legend Cagliostro won freedom for himself and his wife by telling a fantastic story of his life. He had been raised in Medina, Arabia, by a man, Althotas, who taught him his occult knowledge. He explained his wealth as coming from the Cherif of Mecca, who mysteriously set up open bank accounts for him wherever he went. He denied being a three-hundred-year-old Roscrucian, and said he had prophesied that the Countess de Lamotte was a dangerous woman.

Cagliostro and Lorenza went to England, where he predicted the French Revolution. But a London newspaper published an exposé of Cagliostro's true personal history, which destroyed his glittering reputation.

Humiliated, he and his wife went to Rome, where Cagliostro attempted to create an "Egyptian Freemasonry" order. The church had him arrested and thrown in jail for eighteen months of questioning at the hands of the Inquisition. He was found guilty of "impiety, heresy, and crimes against the church" and was sentenced to death on April 7, 1791. Lorenza was sentenced to life imprisonment in a convent in Rome, where she is believed to have died in 1794.

Pope Pius VI commuted Cagliostro's sentence to life imprisonment. He was sent to San Leo, where he spent four years in solitary confinement in a subterranean cell. Shortly after being moved to a cell above ground, he died, allegedly of apoplexy, on March 6, 1795. Rumors that he lived and miraculously escaped persisted for years in Europe, Russia, and America. See **Saint Germain; Smith, Hélène.**

Sources: David Carroll. *The Magic Makers.* New York: Arbor House, 1974; Manly P. Hall. *The Secret Teachings of All Ages.* 1928. Los Angeles: The Philosophical Research Society, 1977; Charles Mackay, L.L.D. *Extraordinary Popular Delusions and the Madness of Crowds.* 1852. Reprint. New York: L. C. Page, 1932; Kurt Seligmann. *The History of Magic and the Occult.* New York: Pantheon Books, 1948; Colin Wilson. *The Occult.* New York: Vintage Books, 1971.

Calumet

See **Sacred pipe.**

Campbell, Joseph (1904–1987)

Mythologist, scholar, writer, editor, and teacher. Born March 26, 1904, in New York City, the young Campbell was fascinated with Native American legends, whetting his unending appetite for understanding myths and humankind. He traveled in Europe before attending Columbia University, where he earned a bachelor's degree in 1925 and a master's degree in English and comparative literature in 1927. As a member of the track team, he was one of the fastest runners of the half-mile in the world. He also was a jazz musician, playing the saxophone, guitar, and ukulele.

In 1927 he returned to Europe for postgraduate study in Arthurian romances at the universities of Paris and Munich. He was influenced greatly by the contemporary European art of the day, and continued his appreciation of contemporary art for the rest of his life. While in Europe Campbell began his unending study of author Thomas Mann, and psychiatrists Sigmund Freud and Carl Jung. He was especially caught up in the writings of James Joyce (1882–1941) because of Joyce's use of mythological themes to express modern visions.

In 1934, after returning to the United States, Campbell rented a house in

Joseph Campbell

(Courtesy Sarah Lawrence College)

Woodstock, New York, for $20 a year. There he spent the next four years reading the classics of many world cultures. During this time he became convinced of the universal parallels between myth, dreams, and art. He thereafter often drew upon Jung's archetypes of the collective unconscious, as well as ethnologist Adolf Bastian's concept of "elementary ideas." Campbell believed that Bastian was the first scientist to show that the world's mythologies, ritual practices, folk traditions, and major religions share certain symbolic themes, motifs, and patterns of behavior. Campbell spent much of his life documenting and explaining these key notions.

The same year he moved to Woodstock, Campbell began teaching at Sarah Lawrence College in Bronxville, New York, where he remained for thirty-eight years. He was Professor Emeritus until his death in 1987.

In 1938 Campbell married one of his former students, Jean Erdman, who graduated from Sarah Lawrence that same year. Erdman danced with Martha Graham and later became a distinguished choreographer and artist.

The importance of Joyce in Campbell's early life is illustrated by Jean Erdman's recollection that during the early years of their marriage she would be on one of Joseph's arms, and a copy of Joyce's *Finnegans Wake* (1939) would be under his other arm. Campbell's first book, coauthored with Henry Morton Robinson, was *A Skeleton Key to Finnegans Wake* (1944). References to *Finnegans Wake* appear thereafter throughout Campbell's work.

In 1942 Campbell signed a contract with Simon and Schuster for $750 to write a "self-help book." The publisher envisioned merely an updated *Bullfinch's Mythology*, but Campbell wrote instead *The Hero with a Thousand Faces* (1948), a truly original masterpiece, which broke new ground for scholars in many disciplines. The book established him as a world authority in mythology. The work presents a definitive study of the archetype of all myth: a single hero and a single journey-pattern, which emerges from behind many different versions. After describing various examples of myth-telling in this book, Campbell observes, "It will be always the one, shape-shifting yet marvelously constant story that we find, together with a challengingly persistent suggestion of more remaining to be experienced than will ever be known or told." The work quickly won Campbell exceptional praise and soon became a classic in the field. His fame and reputation could be justified by this work alone.

In the four-volume series *The Masks of God* (1959–1968), Campbell presents his study of mythologies. He groups them as either Primitive, Oriental, Occidental, or Creative.

In 1969 Campbell wrote the script for a film, *Stairways to the Mayan Gods*. In it he anticipates the concepts concerning the ascent and decline of Mayan Indians of Mexico and Central America, which he was to develop in his magnum opus, *The Way of the Animal Powers: Historical Atlas of World Mythology* (1983).

He probes the connections between myths and human behavior in *Myths to Live By* (1973), and presents the imagery of dreams in *The Mythical Image* (1974). In *The Inner Reaches of Outer Space* (1984), Campbell presents a concise statement of the basic premises of his mythology and approach to comparative religions. Finally, the most comprehensive of Campbell's work is the elegant publication of *The Way of the Animal Powers*.

Campbell's writings often seek and find patterns amid the details of a specialized topic, such as in *Erotic Irony and Mythic Forms in the Art of Thomas Mann* (1973). But he also illustrates broad truths with many specifics, such as in *The Inner Reaches of Outer Space*. Always, however, his consistent theme is the saying he often quoted from the Vedas: "Truth is one, the sages speak of it by many names." This concept even motivated him in his other major contributions to scholarship, such as completing and editing four posthumously published works of Heinrich Zimmer (1890–1943), the great Indologist and Sanskrit scholar, whom Campbell referred to as "my guru." The Zimmer works included *The Art of Indian Asia*, in two volumes, and *Myths and Symbols in Indian Art and Civilization. The King and the Corpse— Tales of the Soul's Conquest of Evil,* also by Zimmer, was edited by Campbell and published in 1948.

Campbell also edited anthologies, including one of basic Jung writings entitled *A Portable Jung* (1971), in which he presents a concise biographical sketch on Jung and an authoritative outline of Jung's life and works. Even more significant were the six volumes of *Papers from the Eranos Yearbooks*. These important papers were originally published in thirty-five volumes in several languages from 1934 to 1966. Many of the world's most notable scholars participated in the series, among them Erich Neumann, Gilles Quispel, Mircea Eliade, and Carl G. Jung. The volumes are entitled by their thematic subjects: Spirit and Nature, The Mysteries, Man and Time, Spiritual Disciplines, Man and Transformation, and The Mystic Vision.

The film *A Hero's Journey: The World of Joseph Campbell* included biographical material on Campbell as well as an introduction to his main themes. But Campbell's leitmotifs (especially "Truth is one" and "Follow your bliss") came across even more effectively in the popular PBS television program *The Power of Myth,* a series of interviews with Campbell by journalist Bill Moyers during 1985 and 1986. The main topic is myth, but religion in general and Christianity in particular are also thematic. Only six of the twenty-four hours of interviews were included in the PBS series. The PBS series was published as a book by the same title, which quickly became a bestseller.

The TV series and book contributed much to the popularization of Campbell and his works. The Moyers interviews were done mostly at the ranch of Campbell's friend, filmmaker George Lucas. Campbell's concept of the Hero's Journey was the inspiration for the very successful *Star Wars* film trilogy by Lucas, as well as many other significant artifacts in contemporary popular culture.

Along with Campbell's obvious sources, such as Jung, Joyce, and Zimmer, he also called frequently upon more obscure influences, such as the Gnostic Gospel of Thomas, to which he referred often, starting soon after its discovery in 1948. No matter what source he called upon, at least one of his leitmotifs would usually emerge.

When asked by Moyers to comment on his idea of following one's bliss, Campbell explained how he came to it while considering three terms for the transcendent in Sanskrit: one means "being," a second means "full consciousness," and the third means "rapture." He recalled, "I don't know whether my consciousness is full consciousness or not, I don't know whether my being is proper being or not, but I do know where my rapture is. Let me hang on to rapture, and that will bring me both being and full consciousness, and it works."

During the last twelve years of Campbell's life he had several dialogues with friend and radio talk show host Michael Toms, which Campbell referred to as "religious experiences." Nine of them were published in 1988 as the book *An Open Life: Joseph Campbell in Conversation with Michael Toms*, with a foreword by Jean Erdman. Toms wrote a brief life of Campbell as the introduction to the book, in which he especially notes how Campbell's own life was "rich with examples of the mythic lore he so dearly loved to recount, especially in its seemingly small synchronicities," which Toms appropriately inventories. These included "chance" meetings with J. Krishnamurti, Adelle Davis, John Steinbeck, and biologist Ed Ricketts.

Campbell received the Hofstra Distinguished Scholar Award, and the National Institute of Arts and Letters Award for Contribution to Creative Literature; was a president of the American Society for the Study of Religion; and was a director of the Society for the Arts, Religion, and Contemporary Culture. In 1985 he was granted the medal of honor of the National Arts Club; and in 1986 he received the Honorary Doctorate of Humane Letters from Sarah Lawrence.

The Joseph Campbell Chair in Comparative Mythology was established at Sarah Lawrence in 1988. At the ceremony honoring him, a colleague, John Grim, observed that "in Joseph Campbell's final work, time appears to spiral, to interweave with space revealing a new perspective for seeing the diverse faces of the universe."

Campbell called upon anthropology, archaeology, biology, literature, ecumenical theology, philology, philosophy, comparative religions, art history, Jungian psychology, and popular culture to evolve his unique mythology. He evolved new insights in mythology by bringing humanistic values and universal spiritual experiences to the best of modern science and art. He died at age eighty-three on October 31, 1987, at his home in Honolulu, Hawaii, after a brief illness. See **Mythology.**

Sources: Joseph Campbell. *The Inner Reaches of Outer Space: Metaphor as Myth and as Religion.* New York: Harper & Row, 1988; Joseph Campbell, ed. *Papers from the Eranos Yearbooks.* Bollingen Series 30. Princeton: Princeton University Press, 1968; Joseph Campbell. *The Hero with a Thousand Faces.* 1949. New York: World Publishing Company, 1970; Joseph Campbell. *The Way of the Animal Powers: Historical Atlas of World Mythology.* 1983. London: Times Books, 1988; Joseph Campbell, ed. *Myth, Dreams, and Religion.* Dallas: Spring Publications, 1970; Joseph Campbell. *Erotic Irony and Mythic Forms in the Art of Thomas Mann.* San Francisco: Robert Briggs Associates, 1973; Joseph Campbell with Bill Moyers. *The Power of Myth.* New York: Doubleday, 1988; Jo (sic) Campbell. *Stairways to the Mayan Gods.* Film script. Cos Cob, CT: The Hartley Film Foundation, 1969–70; John M. Maher and Dennis Briggs, eds. *An Open Life: Joseph Campbell in Conversation with Michael Toms.* Burdett, NY: Larson Publications, 1988; Robert A. Segal. *Joseph Campbell: An Introduction.* New York: Garland Publishing, 1987; "Joseph Campbell: Making the Bones of Folklore Sing." *Sarah Lawrence* (Spring-Summer 1988): 13–15; "Thus Spake Zoroaster: An Interview with Joseph Campbell." *Omni* (December 1988): 143–44.

Castaneda, Carlos (b. 1925?)

Anthropologist and author of a number of books purported to be his true experiences learning lessons about the *nagual* (ordinary) and *tonal* (extraordinary) worlds from a Yaqui sorcerer. Little is known about Carlos Castaneda, who keeps himself out of the public eye. Critics have charged his accounts of his experiences are fictitious, or at best "faction."

In interviews Castaneda has given deliberately false information about himself, warning interviewers he would do so. According to immigration and other records, he was born Carlos Cesar Arana Castaneda on December 25, 1925, in Cajamarca, Peru. He came to the United States in 1951. From 1955 to 1959, he was a prepsychology student at Los Angeles City College. He enrolled at the University of California at Los Angeles and switched to anthropology. His intent, he has said, was to enter graduate school and become an academic, and he thought his success would be guaranteed if he published a paper first. He decided to research ethnobotany, or psychotropic plants used by sorcerers.

In 1960, on his research trip to Mexico, he was directed to don Juan Matus, an elderly Yaqui said to possess the knowledge Castaneda sought. He met don Juan in an Arizona bus depot near the border. After numerous visits over a year, don Juan then announced that he was in fact a *brujo,* or sorcerer, who had learned his art from a *diablero,* a sorcerer with evil powers and the ability to shapeshift. In 1961 don Juan took Castaneda on as an apprentice, and introduced him to another sorcerer, don Genaro Flores, a Mazatec Indian, who also would serve as his tutor. Castaneda first had to learn how to see nonordinary reality—"stopping the world"—which he did with the help of peyote (called "Mescalito" by don Juan), datura (Jimson weed), and *Psilo-cybe mexicana* mushrooms. His apprenticeship lasted from 1961 to 1965, when he decided to terminate it.

Castaneda's experiences became the subject of his first book, *The Teachings of Don Juan: A Yaqui Way of Knowledge* (1968), the forward of which says, "This book is both ethnography and allegory." The book was accepted as his master's thesis, and became an underground bestseller. In 1968 Castaneda returned to Mexico to show the book to don Juan, and began a second apprenticeship, which lasted until 1971. His second book, *A Separate Reality: Further Conversations with Don Juan,* appeared in 1971. His third book, *Journey to Ixtlan: The Lessons of Don Juan* (1972), in which Castaneda acquires a coyote sorcerer's companion, was accepted as his doctoral dissertation. In *Tales of Power* (1974), Castaneda parted ways with dons Juan and Genaro. Together they jump off a cliff into an abyss, and Castaneda experiences the "two inherent realms of all creation, the tonal and the nagual." Forces compel Castaneda to return to Mexico, however, and in *The Second Ring of Power* (1974), he discovers he has been drawn by nine other apprentices of don Juan, five women and four men, who expect him to take don Juan's place as teacher. One of the women, doña Soledad, turns her powers against Castaneda and engages in a fierce battle of sorcery. Castaneda's adventures continued for at least another four books.

Many reviews of his books have been favorable, yet there has been much debate as to whether or not the books are documented fact, are embellished fact, or are entirely fiction. Whether or not don Juan exists is unknown, as there is no evidence of him outside of Castaneda's writing. The name may be a pseudonym. Critics have pointed to the absence of Yaqui terms and evidence of culture in don Juan's conversation and habits. According to Castaneda don Juan was born in 1891 and was part of the diaspora of Yaquis all over Mexico, becoming a nomad. Critics also have pointed to *The Third Eye* (1956), an alleged autobiographical account of a Tibetan lama, T. Lobsang Rampa, who proved to be an Englishman. Castaneda has stated that it is "inconceivable" that he could concoct such a person as don Juan, and that he was only a reporter.

Castaneda criticized Timothy Leary for having naive views that psychedelic drugs alone have the power to alter the world. Castaneda said that to alter the world something else, such as sorcery, is required. Drugs comprised only the initial phase of his apprenticeship; don Juan later taught him to achieve the same results without drugs. See **Drugs in mystical and psychic experiences.** Compare to **Andrews, Lynn V.**

Sources: Carlos Castaneda. *The Teachings of Don Juan: A Yaqui Way of Knowledge.* New York: Simon & Schuster, 1968; Carlos Castaneda. *A Separate Reality: Further Conversations with Don Juan.* New York: Simon & Schuster, 1971; Carlos Castaneda. *Journey to Ixtlan: The Lessons of Don Juan.* New York: Simon & Schuster, 1972; Carlos Castaneda. *Tales of Power.* New York: Simon & Schuster, 1974; Carlos Castaneda. *The Second Ring of Power.* New York: Simon & Schuster, 1977; Timothy Leary. *Flashbacks: An Autobiography.* Los Angeles: Jeremy P. Tarcher, 1983; Daniel Noel, ed. *Seeing Castaneda: Reactions to the "Don Juan" Writing of Carlos Castaneda.* New York: G. P. Putnam's Sons, 1976; Leslie A. Shepard, ed. *Encyclopedia of Occultism and Parapsychology.* 2d ed. Detroit: Gale Research Co., 1984.

Cayce, Edgar (1877–1945)

American psychic renowned for his trance readings in which he diagnosed illness and prescribed remedies. Called "the sleeping prophet," Edgar Cayce practiced absent healing for forty-three years, help-

(Courtesy Edgar Cayce Foundation Archives)

Edgar Cayce

ing to cure people from all over the world. He never went beyond grammar school and never studied medicine, but from an unconscious state he could prescribe drugs and treatments that were said to be accurate in more than 90 percent of his cases.

Cayce was born on March 18, 1877, in Hopkinsville, Kentucky. He had psychic powers from an early age, including the ability to see nonphysical beings (who were his childhood companions) and the auras of others.

His curative powers came to light in 1898 when he was twenty-one and working as a salesman. He suffered a persistent hoarse throat and intermittent laryngitis, which resisted medical treatment and forced him to give up his job. As a last resort, he enlisted the aid of a hypnotist, who provided temporary relief. He was then hypnotized by Al Layne, who asked him to describe, while in trance, the cause of his affliction and a cure. Cayce did so, and at the end of the session had his voice back. Layne suggested diagnosing others in the same way. Cayce was dubious but agreed to try. He began giving readings on March 31, 1901.

On June 17, 1903, he married Gertrude Evans. They had two sons, Edgar Evans and Hugh Lynn.

Cayce's success with readings was so great that thousands began to seek him out for help. Though he knew nothing of medicine, he was able accurately to diagnose conditions and prescribe remedies. He could read for anyone anywhere in the world—he needed only a name and address. Cayce was able to put himself into a self-induced hypnotic trance, during which he would give the person a "reading" of his or her condition. Cayce's prescribed treatments involved aspects of physiology, biology, chemistry, and anatomy. His ability to name parts of the body astounded practitioners.

In 1911 he made his first reference in a reading to karma as a cause of physical ailment, and from then on many of his readings concerned karma. He attributed various ailments and conditions to harmful deeds or passions in past lives. In readings he sometimes spoke about the fabled civilizations of Lemuria and Atlantis, and how the latter's inhabitants had misused their technological power. See **Atlantis; Lemuria.** He came to believe in reincarnation. According to information given in his readings, some of his own past lives included one as one of the first celestial beings to descend to earth prior to Adam and Eve; as an Atlantean; as Ra-Ta, a high priest in Egypt 10,600 years ago; as a Persian ruler; as a Trojan warrior; as Lucius of Cyrene, mentioned in the New Testament as a minor disciple of Jesus; and various other lives. He believed he had acquired his scientific knowledge from a former life as a chemist in Grecian Troy. See **Reincarnation.**

Cayce's readings were dismissed by the medical community at large because of his lack of formal training. Neverthe-

less, he did gain the support of hundreds of medical practitioners. Over the course of his life, he gave approximately 30,000 readings, which continue to be studied and interpreted.

Cayce and his family moved to Virginia Beach, Virginia, where in 1928 he established the beginnings of the Association for Research and Enlightenment (ARE), founded in 1931. See **Association for Research and Enlightenment.** He worked quietly throughout the 1930s, giving an average of two readings a day. He had vivid dreams that seemed to contain past-life and prophetic information. He prophesied the Second Coming of Christ in 1998, accompanied by cataclysmic earth changes.

In 1943 Thomas Sugrue's biography of Cayce, *There Is a River,* was published, which greatly increased the demand for his help. In response he increased his readings to four to six a day, giving 1,385 readings between June 1943 and June 1944. Even at that pace, his mail was backlogged three to four years. In August 1944 he collapsed from exhaustion. His own readings had warned him that if he attempted more than two readings per day, he would disintegrate, yet Cayce was too moved by the suffering of others to cut back. Following his collapse he went into the mountains near Roanoke, Virginia, to recuperate, returning home in November 1944. On January 1, 1945, he told friends he would be "healed" on January 5, and they took it to mean his death. He died peacefully on January 3, 1945, at the age of sixty-seven. Gertrude died the following April 1.

The ARE now is under the direction of Hugh Lynn's son, Charles Thomas Cayce.

Methods and Philosophy

When Cayce gave a reading, he simply lay down and relaxed; his objective mind became inactive and his unconscious took over. He believed that each cell had a consciousness of its own, and during a reading he was able to see every gland, organ, blood vessel, nerve, and tissue inside a body. The cells communicated with his unconscious and told him what was troubling them.

His diagnosis would then be based upon a variety of causative factors. Glandular conditions could cause many problems; so could childhood bumps and bruises, which produced lesions that later caused disturbances. Karmic conditions (spiritual heredity) also could predispose a body to certain weaknesses.

Cayce viewed the body as one interconnected network of organs and tissues; when something was wrong with one part, the whole network became disturbed. This disturbance was due to the body not properly assimilating what it needed to maintain its natural equilibrium.

Healing could take place only through natural channels in order to restore the natural equilibrium. Cayce's prescribed treatments were a unique combination of osteopathy, chiropractic therapy, electrical procedures, vibrations, massage, therapeutic baths, manipulation, foods and diet, medicinal compounds, drugs, herbs, tonics, exercises, and rest. Most treatments were intended to be implemented under the professional guidance of a medical practitioner.

The chief difference between Cayce's suggested treatments and those of the medical community was that Cayce sought to heal the whole body by treating the causes rather than the symptoms of a patient's problem.

The individual patient, however, played a key role in healing because it was first necessary to have faith in a higher power's ability to heal. Cayce believed that as a Christian, God gave him the power to cure as a gift to help other people. But it would not be he, Cayce, who would affect the change in an individual's condition; the patient would use his or her own positive attitudes to influence the outcome. The patient had to view the reading with hope and prayer rather than perceive it as a freak event or last resort. The reading had to be a spiritual event, with results that were not only physical, but mental and spiritual as well. "Mind is the builder," Cayce was fond of saying.

The right attitude also was necessary in order to successfully follow treatment procedures. The body, with its delicate chemistry and nervous impulses, responded to commands from the mind, and what the mind chose and held before itself either quickened the body or let it go slack to psychic impulses.

Cayce believed that everyone has a natural psychic ability, and such phenomena as dreams and premonitions are expressions of that ability. He said that psychic ability is merely an extension of faith and love, and that psychic perception and psychokinesis (PK) are higher forms of creativity. Everything has its fields with complex patterns of vibration. When fields of the human psyche are set into motion within a given field, psychic perception or PK takes place.

Cayce said that if the mind and will are directed toward shared creativity, then resources will be drawn from the soul to yield helpful psychic impulses needed for those tasks. A person who has purity of heart and enduring love toward others will always have a ready supply of psychic energy available.

Cayce Organizations

In addition to the ARE, three organizations have grown up around Cayce's work. The oldest, chartered in 1930, is Atlantic University in Virginia Beach, a formal educational program offering a master's degree in transpersonal studies. The Edgar Cayce Foundation, also at Virginia Beach, was chartered in 1948 to provide permanent custodial ownership for the Cayce readings and their supporting documentation. The foundation's primary roles are publishing, information management, and applied research. The Harold J. Reilly School of Massotherapy, under the auspices of Atlantic University, opened in 1986, offering a diploma program certified by the Commonwealth of Virginia in massage, hydrotherapy, diet, and preventive health care practices based on the Cayce readings. See **Altered states of consciousness; Healing, faith and psychic; Psi.**

Sources: Mary Ellen Carter. *My Years with Edgar Cayce.* New York: Warner, 1974; W. H. Church. *Many Happy Returns: The Lives of Edgar Cayce.* San Francisco: Harper & Row, 1984; Rosemary Ellen Guiley. *Tales of Reincarnation.* New York: Pocket Books, 1989; Nicholas Regush. *The Human Aura.* New York: Berkely, 1974; Jess Stearn. *Edgar Cayce—The Sleeping Prophet.* New York: Bantam Books, 1968; Thomas Sugrue. *There Is a River.* Rev. ed. Virginia Beach, VA: ARE Press, 1973; Edgar Cayce Foundation, Virginia Beach, VA.

Chakras

In yoga vortices that penetrate the body and the body's aura, through which various energies, including the universal life force, are received, transformed, and distributed. Chakras are believed to play a vital role in physical, mental, and emotional health and in spiritual development. They are invisible to ordinary sight but may be perceived clairvoyantly. Some people say they can activate the chakras to whirl faster and can direct the flow of energy through them.

Chakra is Sanskrit for "wheel." Chakras are said to be shaped like multicolored lotus petals or spoked wheels that whirl at various speeds as they process energy. Chakras are described in Hindu and Buddhist yogic literature. There are differences between the two

systems, and in various Western descriptions of the chakras.

There is no accepted scientific evidence that the chakras exist; until recently, they were dismissed by Western medicine. They have been increasingly acknowledged, along with the acupuncture meridians and other Eastern systems, in alternative treatments. Evidence for the existence of chakras, albeit controversial, has been presented by Hiroshi Motoyama of Japan, who hypothesized that if an enlightened person could influence the chakras, the energy output would be measurable. Using a lead-lined recording booth, Motoyama measured the energy field opposite various chakras which subjects claimed to have awakened, usually through years of meditation. He found that the energy levels at those areas were significantly greater than over the same areas of control subjects.

The health of chakras is diagnosed by clairvoyance, by energy scans with the hands, and by dowsing with a pendulum. Clairvoyants say that health disturbances often manifest in the aura, and thus in the chakras, months and sometimes years before they manifest in the physical body.

There are seven major chakras and hundreds of minor ones. In the aura the etheric, astral, and mental bodies are said to each have seven major chakras. The seven major etheric centers, which are most directly concerned with physical health, lie along the spinal column. Each is associated with a major endocrine gland, a major nerve plexus, a physiological function, and a psychic function. The higher the position along the spinal column, the more complex the chakra and the higher its functions.

The chakras are connected to each other and to the body through the *nadis,* channels of subtle energy. There are thousands of nadis, of which three are the most important. The *sushumna,* the central channel, originates at the base of the spine and rises to the medulla oblongata at the base of the brain; it processes en-

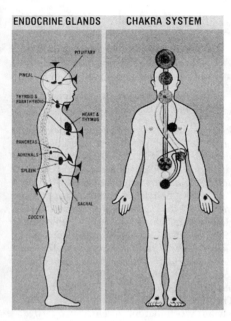

ENDOCRINE GLANDS   CHAKRA SYSTEM

PITUITARY

PINEAL

THYROID &
PARATHYROID

HEART &
THYMUS

PANCREAS

ADRENALS

SPLEEN

SACRAL

COCCYX

The chakra system

ergy coming in from the etheric field. The *ida* and *pingala* also extend from the base of the spine to the brow and end at the left and right nostrils. They crisscross the sushumna in a spiral that resembles the shape of a caduceus. See **Caduceus.** They wrap around, but do not penetrate, the chakras, and are concerned with the outflow of energy.

The universal life force is said to enter the aura through the chakra at the top of the head, and is filtered down to the other chakras, each of which transforms the energy into usable form for the functions it governs. When *kundalini* is aroused, it rises up the chakra system through the sushumna. See **Kundalini; Universal life force.**

Each chakra has its own coloration, number of petal "spokes," and speed of vibration. When the chakras are balanced and healthy, their colors are clear and luminous and their rotation is smooth. In

poor health they become cloudy and irregular or sluggish in rotation. Chakras that are blocked are believed to adversely influence the body functions they govern. In alternative healing there are techniques for clearing chakra blockages and stimulating rotation.

In Laya Yoga, the yoga of concentration upon the chakras and the nadis, each chakra has its own dominant and subdominant mantra sounds and complex symbologies of geometric shapes, sexual symbols of lingam and yoni, and letters of the Sanskrit alphabet. Combinations of mantras (chants), *pranayama* (breath control), and visualizations are employed in Laya Yoga to cleanse and balance the chakras, and to raise the kundalini. See **Yoga.**

The seven major etheric chakras are the root, the sacral, the solar plexus, the heart, the throat, the brow, and the crown:

1. The root (*muladhara*) is located at the base of the spine and is the seat of *kundalini*. It is concerned with self-preservation, one's animal nature, taste, and smell. It is the least complex of the seven centers, divided by only four spokes. It is orange-red in color.

2. The sacral (*svadhisthana*) lies near the genitals and governs sexuality and reproduction. It has six spokes and is primarily red. In some systems the root chakra is ascribed reproductive functions, and the sacral chakra is overlooked in favor of the spleen chakra, a rosy pink and yellow sun with six spokes located halfway between the pubis and navel. It influences overall health and in particular governs digestion and functions of the liver, pancreas, and spleen. The spleen chakra is seen as minor in other systems.

3. The solar plexus (*manipurna*) rests just above the navel. It has ten

spokes and is predominantly green and light red. It is associated with the emotions, and is the point where astral energy enters the etheric field. The solar plexus affects the adrenals, pancreas, liver, and stomach. Most trance mediums work through this chakra.

4. The heart (anahata) has twelve glowing golden petals and is located midway between the shoulder blades, in the center of the chest. It governs the thymus gland and influences immunity to disease. It is linked to higher consciousness and unconditional love.

5. The throat (visuddha) is a sixteen-spoke wheel of silvery blue that is associated with creativity and self-expression and the search for truth. It is prominent in musicians, singers, composers, and public speakers. This chakra also influences the thyroid and parathyroid glands and metabolism, and is associated with certain states of expanded consciousness.

6. The brow (ajna), located between the eyebrows, is called the third eye for its influence over psychic sense and spiritual enlightenment. It has ninety-six spokes, half of which radiate a yellow-rose color and half of which radiate blue and purple. This chakra is associated with the pituitary gland, the pineal gland, intelligence, intuition, and psychic powers, called siddhis in Hindu yoga.

7. The crown (sahasrara) whirls just above the top of the head. Its 972 spokes radiate a glowing purple, the most spiritual of colors. It is not associated with any glands, but reveals the individual's level of conscious evolution. The crown cannot be activated until all the other chakras are refined and balanced; when activated it brings supreme enlightenment and cosmic consciousness. While other chakras rotate in slight depressions, the crown chakra whirls in a dome. In religious art deities, saints, and mystics are portrayed with radiant crown chakras in the form of halos or domed headdresses.

See **Aura; Bodywork; Healing, faith and psychic.**

Sources: Barbara Ann Brennan. *Hands of Light: A Guide to Healing through the Human Energy Field.* 1987. New York: Bantam Books, 1988; Richard Gerber. *Vibrational Medicine.* Santa Fe, NM: Bear & Co., 1988; Bernard Gunther. *Energy Ecstasy and Your Seven Vital Chakras.* North Hollywood, CA: Newcastle Publishing, 1983; Shafica Karagulla and Dora van Gelder Kunz. *The Chakras and the Human Energy Fields.* Wheaton, IL: The Theosophical Publishing Co., 1989; C. W. Leadbeater. *The Chakras.* 1927. Wheaton, IL: The Theosophical Publishing Co., 1980; Vivian Worthington. *A History of Yoga.* London: Routledge & Kegan Paul, 1982.

Channeling

A form of mediumship in which information is communicated from a source perceived to be different from the conscious self. Sources are identified variously as nonphysical beings, angels, nature spirits, totem or guardian spirits, deities, demons, extraterrestrials, spirits of the dead, and the Higher Self. Channeling is done in a dissociated or altered state of consciousness. As mediumship it has existed in virtually all cultures throughout history and has gone through cycles of acceptance and rejection. As a New Age phenomenon, channeling has almost exclusively focused on the delivery of religious or spiritual information allegedly obtained from spiritual sources, such as highly evolved and nonphysical entities (who usually have exotic names), angels, Jesus, God, and the Virgin Mary.

Historical Overview

The desire to communicate with nonworldly beings is perhaps as old as humanity itself. In prehistoric and primitive cultures, designated individuals—a priest, shaman, oracle, or person of similar function—had the privilege and responsibility of seeking out the wisdom of these beings and delivering it to the masses. See **Shamanism.**

Communicating with gods in trance was a highly developed art among the priestly class of the ancient Egyptians. The ancient Greeks had their oracles. The early Chinese, Tibetans, Japanese, Indians, Babylonians, Assyrians, and Celts channeled discarnate spirits or deities. The prophets, saints, and holy men and women of Judaism, Christianity, and Islam received divine guidance that took the form of channeling. See **Oracle; Prophecy.**

Other forms of channeling have included divination and healing, performed by wizards, wise women, witches, soothsayers, and the like; and possession, in which an entity seizes control of an individual. Such cases usually are seen as demonic, and were prevalent during the Middle Ages. It is argued by some that possession is not true channeling because it is involuntary.

In the nineteenth and twentieth centuries, Spiritualism gained a large following with its emphasis on survival of death and the purported abilities of mediums to contact the spirits of the dead. See **Mediumship; Seance; Spiritualism.** During the same era, Madame Helena P. Blavatsky, cofounder of the Theosophical Society, claimed to channel the wisdom of various Tibetan adepts. See **Blavatsky, Madame Helena P.; Theosophy.**

In the wake of the decline of Spiritualism, channeled works were produced, but channeling itself did not regain widespread attention in the West until the late 1960s and early 1970s, when Jane Roberts began publishing her Seth books. See **Roberts, Jane.** Roberts inaugurated a resurgence of channeling of higher entities, rather than spirits of the dead, whose lu-

minaries have included Jach Pursel (Lazaris), JZ Knight (Ramtha), Pat Rodegast (Emmanuel), Elizabeth Clare Prophet (Saint Germain), and others. Popular interest in channeling was further fueled in the 1980s by actress Shirley MacLaine, whose spiritual odyssey was aided by California channeler Kevin Ryerson. Undoubtedly, many frauds filled the field, as they had done during the peak of Spiritualism. By the late 1980s, the channeling explosion was over, though popular interest remained.

The Process of Channeling

Channeling can be spontaneous or induced. The channeler has no control over spontaneous channeling, which may involve falling into sudden trance states or lapses of consciousness. Many channelers begin with spontaneous episodes, then learn to control the process and to induce it. Induction methods vary, and include meditation, prayer, self-hypnosis, fasting, chanting, dancing, sleep deprivation, breathing techniques, smoking herbs, or taking hallucinogenic drugs. See **Altered states of consciousness.**

Mental channeling is the mediation of thoughts, words, images, and emotions, and is accomplished in a variety of ways. In full trance the channeler's personality becomes displaced, and another entity or personality takes temporary possession, using a voice and gestures different from those of the channeler. See **Direct-voice mediumship.** The channeler is unaware of what is said or done and may have no recollection upon regaining normal consciousness. Jane Roberts's channeling of Seth was of this type. Mental channeling also is done in a light trance or dissociated state, in which the channeler is partially or fully aware of the process. The channeler's voice may or may not change; or he or she may communicate via automatic writing, a planchette, Ouija board, or similar device.

Mental channeling is also accomplished through sleep and dreams.

Physical channeling involves physical effects, such as psychic or spiritual healing, psychokinesis, and materializations. Physical mediumship was popular in the early days of Spiritualism for producing such effects as apports, ectoplasm, levitation, and so on.

In its most liberal interpretation, channeling also includes the processes of imagination, intuition, inspiration, and premonition. See **Inspiration; Intuition; Premonition; Spirit guide.**

Channelers receive channeled information in a variety of ways. In addition to the direct use of vocal chords mentioned above, information comes clairaudiently, in visions, or in the form of thoughts in words or images, or in feelings.

In cases where individuals have not exhibited mediumistic ability since childhood, channeling usually occurs as a breakthrough during the process of spiritual development or psychic experimentation. Jane Roberts's interaction with Seth began with a Ouija board, for example, while Jach Pursel, Pat Rodegast, Kevin Ryerson, and others had their breakthroughs after meditation experience.

Rodegast, who lives in Connecticut, began practicing Transcendental Meditation twice a day in 1972. She began to experience inner visions, which she feared were hallucinations. Like many others who are initially frightened by the phenomena of spiritual unfoldment, Rodegast sought therapy and also joined a spiritual community in her effort to understand what was happening to her. After about two years of alternately resisting and accepting the inner visions, she then clairvoyantly perceived a being of golden light who identified himself as Emmanuel.

Ryerson's channeling spontaneously began in the 1970s, six months after he joined a meditation group organized around the study of Edgar Cayce teachings. It took him another six months to learn how to control the process. Various entities speak through him, including an Essene named John; an Irish pickpocket named McPherson, and a West Indian named Obadiah. When Shirley MacLaine filmed the television miniseries based on her book *Out on a Limb,* Ryerson not only played himself, but so did his entities, who recreated a channeling session he had done with MacLaine during her spiritual search.

Theories on Channeled Sources

Various theories have been put forward to explain the channeling phenomenon. The simplest and most basic explanation is that the channeled sources are who—or what—they say they are. Ancient channelers believed they were indeed invoking specific spirits of the dead, deities, or nature or animal spirits. This view also is held by Spiritualist mediums, who believe they communicate with the dead, and remains prevalent in societies where channeled information is routinely sought for prophecy, healing, divination, and advice. New Age opinions on the sources are more divided, with some individuals taking channeled sources at their face value and others believing in theories advanced by psychologists.

Psychiatrist Sigmund Freud was highly skeptical of channeling. He believed it to be wish fulfillment, the emergence of material that had been repressed in the conscious mind. Psychiatrist Carl G. Jung offered two possible explanations: (1) the channeled entities came from complexes that had become repressed and separated from waking consciousness, including the Shadow, the least evolved aspect of a person; or (2) they represented archetypes accessed in the collective unconscious, the shared racial memories residing deep within all human beings. In keeping with Jung's view, American psychologist Jean Houston calls channeled entities "goddings," or personae of the Self. Some channelers believe they are calling upon their own Higher Self, a level of wisdom not normally accessed in waking consciousness. The Higher Self also has been called the "oversoul" and "superconscious."

There is evidence to support the notion that channeled entities are part of the channeler. Studies of mediums undertaken in the first part of the twentieth century show that many spirit controls had characteristics remarkably similar to the mediums themselves. Eileen J. Garrett believed her controls were part of her own self, but most mediums believe controls to be separate, external entities. They have contended that the process of channeling forces the entities to filter through their human hosts in order to communicate.

Some psychologists believe channeling is pathological in origin, and is symptomatic of multiple personality disorder. In multiple personality cases, individuals are host to two or more personalities, each of which has its own identity, memories, beliefs, and history. However, the individual usually has little or no control over the personalities. Mediums and channels, on the other hand, control the access of the channeled entities and generally lead otherwise normal lives.

Still other theories related to the channeled-entity-as-self idea hold that human consciousness is far more complex than believed. Thus each individual may actually have multiple consciousnesses of varying levels of sophistication; only a few individuals, however, become aware of these and gain access to them. Or channeling may be but one part of a universal Mind to which all consciousnesses in creation are connected.

The Future of Channeling

Champions of channeling see practical applications, such as spiritual and personal counseling, divination, forecasting the future, and delving into the past. These "applied psi" functions have all been undertaken at various times by psychics with mixed results. Generally, psychically obtained information is too fragmentary or inaccurate to be useful or reliable, though many success stories exist. However, William H. Kautz, founder and director of the Center for Applied Intuition in California, claims that in more than five hundred channelings examined, few inaccuracies occurred; the key is the posing and motivation of the questions asked of the channeled source. See **Applied psi; Psychic archaeology; Psychic criminology.**

One pitfall of the New Age wave of higher entity channeling is the tendency among many individuals to have blind faith in the channeled material, simply because it reportedly comes from a more highly evolved being. Various guidelines have emerged for evaluating channels.

One positive outgrowth of the channeling phenomenon is the encouragement for individuals to develop their own connections to a source of higher wisdom, especially through intuition. In that regard channeling moves from the theatrical arena of an anointed few to the everyday routine of all people. See **Findhorn; Knight, JZ; Montgomery, Ruth; Pursel, Jach.**

Sources: Roger Anderson. "Channeling." Parapsychology Review 19, no. 5 (September/October 1988): 6–9; William E. Geist. "Spiritual Chic: Gaining Success with Channeling." The New York Times (May 30, 1987): B1; William H. Kautz. "Channeling: Mediumship Comes of Age." Applied Psi (January/February 1987): 3–8; William H. Kautz and Melanie Branon. Channeling: The Intuitive Connection. San Francisco: Harper & Row, 1987; Jon Klimo. Channeling: Investigations on Re-

ceiving Information from Paranormal Sources. Los Angeles: Jeremy P. Tarcher, 1987; Katharine Lowry. "Channelers." *Omni* (October 1987): 47–50+; Suzanne Kluss Malkin. "Confessions of a Former Channeler." *New Realities* 10, no. 1 (September/October 1989): 25–31; Corrinne McLaughlin. "Evaluating Psychic Guidance and Channeling." *Venture Inward* 4, no. 1 (January/February 1988): 36–39+; Pat Rodegast and Judith Stanton, comp. *Emmanuel's Book: A Manual for Living Comfortably in the Cosmos.* 1985. New York: Bantam Books, 1987; David Spangler. *Channeling in the New Age.* Booklet. Issaquah, WA: Morningtown Press, 1988; Alan Vaughan. "Channeling." *New Realities* (January/February 1987): 43–47.

Chanting

The continuous recitation of a mantra, sutra, word, or phrase as part of meditation or a religious or magical rite, which helps one achieve an altered state of consciousness, ecstasy, communion with the Divine, or summon psychical power for magical, exorcism, or healing purposes.

Chanting is done in rhythm, sometimes in cantillation (musical modulations), which creates a pattern of energy and power. Yogis emphasize developing a beautiful voice and cadence in chanting. In some schools of Zen Buddhism, sutras are chanted in a monotone, with the voice trailing off at the end of the chant.

Chanting is an ancient, universal practice, and is often done in conjunction with drumming, hand-clapping, dancing, or the fingering of beads on a rosary. Rosaries are widely used in chanting in Buddhism, Islam, Hinduism, and Christianity. Group chanting, accompanied by dancing, hand-clapping, or drumming, is considered more effective in raising consciousness because the energies and movement of many people are united, which facilitates achievement of the objective. Group chanting is sometimes done to the point of exhaustion.

In all of the major religions, the most powerful chants are the names of God, which are limitless. According to the Vedic scriptures, the chanting of the name of God creates a transcendental sound that awakens spiritual consciousness, and liberates one from ego and the material plane. The Vedas say that chanting the name of the Lord is the only means to spiritual progress in the Kali Yuga age of quarrel and hypocrisy, which began five thousand years ago and will last 432,000 years. The Krishnas incorporate the name of the Lord in a sixteen-word *maha*-mantra, which they also believe will help liberate them from reincarnation: "Hare Krishna Hare Krishna/Krishna Krishna/Hare Hare/ Hare Rama Hare Rama/Rama Rama/ Hare Hare." The mantra is chanted in *kirtana,* a group activity accompanied by hand-clapping and musical instruments, or in *japa,* private meditation with a rosary.

Various Hindu and Buddha chants use Om, which represents Brahman, the Absolute Followers of the Pure Land sect, the largest Buddhist order in Japan, chant the name Buddha to help liberate them from reincarnation, thus enabling them to join Buddha in the Pure Land of spirit.

Followers of Islam chant the ninety-nine names of Allah, called "the Beautiful Names." In Christianity the chanting of the name of Jesus in prayer was recommended by Diadochus of Photice in the middle of the fifth century, and by John Climacus in the early seventh century. This became the "Jesus Prayer," or "Lord Jesus Christ, Son of God, have mercy on me." Christian chants include four Western forms, Gregorian, Gallican, Mozarabic, and Ambrosian; three Eastern forms, Byzantine, Syrian, and Armenian; and Coptic and Ethiopian chants of northern Africa. Jewish cantillation consists of biblical texts.

Chanting is part of tribal society rituals to raise psychic power, pay tribute to deities, appease supernatural powers, exorcise demons, control the weather, ensure success in hunt and war, bring blessings of prosperity and fecundity, and accompany funeral and initiation rites. In Vodoun thousands of chants exist to accompany rites, composed in various African dialects and Haitian Creole, a blend of French, English, and Spanish. Shamans chant "power songs" as they dance. Words vary according to individuals, but melodies and rhythms are handed down in tribes through generations. The Navajo chant elaborate myths as part of curing rituals, which also include sand painting. The long texts must be chanted perfectly, or they are rendered invalid or result in the disease they are intended to cure.

Witches and Pagans combine chanting and dancing to raise a group psychic energy field called a "cone of power," which is released to effect magic. The chants may be names of Goddess or the Horned God, or phrases relative to spells. See Cone of power.

In magic the success of a conjuration or spell depends heavily upon the sound vibrations created by chanting, a belief that dates back thousands of years. The ancient Egyptians were aware of the power of sound upon people, and reasoned that the same power could be applied to tap into the occult forces of the universe. The magician believes that the rhythmic chanting of magic words and names of God sends out waves of energy, which helps the magician reach a state of frenzy and summon his or her inner power. See Mantra.

Sources: Margot Adler. Drawing Down the Moon. Rev. ed. Boston: Beacon Press, 1986; Richard Cavendish. The Black Arts. New York: Perigee Books, 1967; Chant and Be Happy: The Power of Mantra Meditation. Based on the teachings of A. C. Bhaktivedanta Swami Prabhupada. Los An-geles: The Bhaktivedanta Book Trust, 1983; John Ferguson. An Illustrated Encyclopedia of Mysticism and the Mystery Religions. New York: Seabury Press, 1976; Michael Harner. The Way of the Shaman. New York: Bantam Books, 1986; Bruce Kapferer. A Celebration of Demons. Bloomington, IN: Indiana University Press, 1983; Maria Leach, ed., and Jerome Fried, assoc. ed. Funk & Wagnalls Standard Dictionary of Folklore, Mythology, and Legend. San Francisco: Harper & Row, 1979; Ormond McGill. The Mysticism and Magic of India. Cranbury, NJ: A. S. Barnes & Co., 1977; Milo Rigaud. Secrets of Voodoo. San Francisco: City Lights Books, 1985; Starhawk. The Spiral Dance. San Francisco: Harper & Row, 1979.

Chantways

Curing ceremonies of Native Americans of the Southwest, especially the Navajo, who practice the art in its highest form. Chantways last from one to nine days and invoke supernatural powers to cure physical and psychical ailments. They involve lengthy and precise chants or songs, prayers, dancing, purifications, rattling, medicinal herbs, and sand paintings, which are colored paintings on dry ground of religious and mythical symbols pertaining to the cure. Chantways have largely retained their importance. Some Navajo will not accept conventional medical treatment without an accompanying chantway.

The principle behind chantways is the belief that disease or bad luck result from an imbalance in the delicate harmony of the cosmos. Imbalances can be caused only by human beings. The chantway restores the harmony. According to Navajo mythology, the ceremonial instructions for chantways were given to the Dinneh ("the People," as the Navajo call themselves) by the Holy Ones, who were never seen by human eyes, through intermediary spirits such as the Wind People. The very first apprentices spent seven days and seven nights in purification and instruction. They were told that the sand paintings had to be done on Mother Earth, so that the sacred knowledge could be had by all who needed it. The first chantway to be witnessed by a Caucasian was reported in 1891.

In a nine-day chantway, the first four days involve cleansing and invitations to the Supernaturals to appear, followed by four days during which they arrive, and a final day of curing. The chant is a lengthy reenactment from mythology concerning the mortal hero or god who first received the ceremony. The text must be chanted precisely and without error, otherwise it is invalidated. Serious errors in the chant may cause the *hatathli*, or chanter, to fall ill with the same affliction he is trying to cure. The chanter usually is a man who volunteers for the job, and spends years learning chants before he is allowed to practice. Typically, he learns one great rite and a few lesser ones, plus the Blessing Way, which concludes every ceremony.

The arrival of the Supernaturals is marked by the sand painting, which also must be done with great precision within a single day's time. Each chantway has perhaps a hundred or more illustrations, of which the chanter or patient chooses four. They are drawn in the five sacred colors of white, red, black, yellow, and blue. The Supernaturals are depicted by figures that are elongated, perhaps to indicate their power and nonworldly origin. The figures may be arranged at the cardinal points of the painting, and may be accompanied by sacred animals or plants. Some paintings include the sun or moon, or Father Sky and Mother Earth representations.

The sand painting is empowered with a sprinkling of pollen and the placement of sacred feathers and items from a medicine bundle. The patient then sits on the painting and the painted earth is pressed against his or her body, especially the ailing parts, thus making the patient one with the Supernaturals and sharing their power. The sickness falls from the patient as the earth falls back to the ground. At the conclusion of the ceremony, before the sun sets, the painting is erased with a sacred feather staff and the sand is carried away and disposed of.

There are no permanent copies of sand paintings. Reproductions sold for the tourist trade are executed with deliberate errors so that the power is preserved for the actual ceremonies. The designs have been woven in rugs—which are not used in the ceremonies—and painted on boards.

The Navajo are believed to have learned the art of sand painting from the Pueblo, who went to live with the Navajo after the Great Pueblo Revolt against the Spanish in 1680. The Pueblo's sand-painting rituals are on a smaller scale; paintings remain several days after the cure before they are destroyed. Sand painting ceremonies also are done by the Cheyenne, Arapaho, and Gros Ventre of the Plains.

Sources: Eugene Baatoslanii Joe and Mark Bahti. *Navajo Sandpainting Art.* Tucson, AZ: Treasure Chest Publications, 1978; Maria Leach, ed., and Jerome Fried, assoc. ed. *Funk & Wagnalls Standard Dictionary of Folklore, Mythology, and Legend.* San Francisco: Harper & Row, 1979; Franc J. Newcomb and Gladys Reichard. *Sandpaintings of the Navajo Shooting Chant.* New York: Dover Publications, 1975; Ruth M. Underhill. *Red Man's Religion.* Chicago: University of Chicago Press, 1965.

Charismatic renewal

Charismatic renewal, also called "neo-Pentecostalism," refers to the movement in the 1960s and 1970s to reestablish a personal, more joyously expressive communion with God and emphasize the gifts of the Holy Spirit.

In contrast to so-called classic Pentecostalism, which is sectarian in nature, the charismatic movement emphasized renewal of faith in the established denominations, including Catholicism. While Pentecostalism appealed mainly to lower-class whites and African-Americans from the South, charismatic renewal spread through the mainly white middle- and upper-middle-class churches, giving the movement greater respectability and acceptance by church authorities. Predominantly African-American denominations did not experience the same wave of renewal, as their worship services had always included joyous singing, dancing, spontaneity, and evidence of the Holy Spirit.

The word "charismatic" comes from the Greek words *charismata* or *charisms,* meaning "spiritual gifts." Speaking in unknown tongues was only one of the gifts bestowed by the Holy Spirit on the early Christians; others included wisdom, knowledge, faith, healing, the ability to work miracles, prophecy, the ability to discern spirits, speaking in tongues, and the interpretation of tongues. Classic Pentecostals believe that tongues signify the reception of the Holy Spirit, although many charismatic leaders came to regard tongues as only one possible sign. Above all else charismatic renewal represented an immediate, life-transforming experience.

Until the 1950s Pentecostalism actively isolated itself from other Christian denominations, believing it had the correct approach and decrying the liberal, ecumenical position of the World Council of Churches (WCC). By the end of that decade, however, South African Pentecostal leader David J. du Plessis began bridging the gap, approaching the WCC and working to integrate the various denominations. Du Plessis was "disfellowshiped" from the Assemblies of God in 1962 for his work with the WCC. Other efforts at ecumenical accommodation were put forth by the Full Gospel Business Men's Fellowship International (FG-BMFI), a Pentecostal worship group founded by Armenian-American Demos Shakarian, a California dairyman and millionaire.

Since speaking in tongues and healing gifts were looked upon by many people as sideshow events, not Christian worship, those in the mainline churches who had received the Holy Spirit kept it to themselves. The first traditional minister to declare his experience was Dennis Bennett, a successful pastor of St. Marks Episcopal church in Van Nuys, California. His quiet revolution in 1960 split the congregation, and Bennett was removed to an inner-city parish in Seattle, Washington, where he continued to preach charismatic renewal.

In 1963 divinity students and faculty at Yale University began speaking in tongues, and the first Catholic Pentecostal prayer meeting was held in Pittsburgh, Pennsylvania, at Duquesne University in 1966. Many Catholics embraced charismatic renewal as a breath of fresh air in what some viewed as out-of-date orthodoxy, as the movement spread to the University of Michigan and the University of Notre Dame. The Michigan group at Ann Arbor founded an ecumenical group called the "Word of God" and published a periodical entitled *New Covenant,* which served as a clearinghouse for renewal information. Little by little the movement grew into a cause: a revolt against entrenched theology.

In his book *The New Charismatics II,* Richard Quebedeaux attributes the success of the movement with Western society's rediscovery of the supernatural and the occult. He notes that in an age fascinated by psychics, astrology, near-death experiences, and prophecy, Pentecostal phenomena such as healing, tongues, and exorcism would have great appeal. To psychical researcher James H. Hyslop, such Christian events *were* occult; to him healing miracles, casting out devils, and Christ's divination skills and resurrection proved the survival of the soul and the psychic nature of Christianity.

In 1969 Roman Catholic bishops in the United States moved cautiously to incorporate charismatic renewal. Noting that charismatics showed greater zeal for prayer, praise, worship, and scripture, Pope Paul VI blessed the movement in 1973 and presided over a charismatic mass in 1975. Not every cleric was won over, however; Episcopalian bishop James A. Pike denounced charismatic renewal as a new heresy. See **Glossolalia; Pentecostals.**

Sources: Keith Crim, general ed. *Abingdon Dictionary of Living Religions.* Nashville: Abingdon Press, 1981; W. J. Hollenweger. *The Pentecostals: The Charismatic Movement in the Churches.* Minneapolis: Augsburg Publishing House, 1972; James H. Hyslop. "Christianity and Psychic Research." *The Journal of the American Society for Psychical Research* 10, no. 5 (May 1916): 253–74; Richard Quebedeaux. *The New Charismatics II.* San Francisco: Harper & Row, 1983; John Sherrill. *They Speak with Other Tongues.* New York: McGraw-Hill Book Co., 1964.

Ch'i

See **Universal life force.**

Ch'i Kung

See **Qi Gong.**

Chinmoy, Sri (b. 1931)

Hindu mystic with a significant following in the West, especially the United States.

He was born Chinmoy Kumar Ghose ("Sri" is an honorific he acquired later) on August 27, 1931, in Chittagong, India. He displayed a talent for music and poetry as a child. When he was about twelve years old, his parents died. He was taken in by relatives at the Sri Aurobindo ashram in Pondicherry, India. See **Aurobindo, Sri.**

About two years later at Pondicherry, Chinmoy had an intense spiritual awakening in which he attained *nirvikalpa samadhi* (Sanskrit for "changeless samadhi"), the highest, transcendent state of consciousness in Hindu mysticism. *Nirvikalpa samadhi* is the realization of "I am Brahman" and is a union with Brahman, the Absolute, in which there is no subject-object. Chinmoy's experience included a past-life memory of having had the same awakening in a previous life.

For the next twenty years, Chinmoy pursued a spiritual study at Pondicherry. In 1964 he felt summoned to teach in the West and went to live in New York. He soon spread his teachings elsewhere in the world.

Chinmoy has taught Raja Yoga, in which consciousness is controlled through meditation. He has conducted meditation sessions at the United Nations. He plays a number of musical instruments, and performs at some of his public appearances.

Chinmoy has published more than forty books, many of them collections of his numerous lectures, as well as volumes of poetry. See **Meditation; Yoga.**

Sources: J. Gordon Melton, Jerome Clark, and Aidan A. Kelly. *New Age Almanac.* Detroit: Visible Ink Press, 1991; Leslie Shepard, ed. *Encyclopedia of Occultism and Parapsychology.* 2d ed. Detroit: Gale Research Co., 1984.

Chiropractic

See **Bodywork.**

Christianity

See **Christology; Jesus of Nazareth; Mysticism, Christian.**

Christian Science

See **Church of Christ, Scientist.**

Christology

Doctrines and theories of the meaning of the belief in Christ (Jesus of Nazareth). The various Christological debates are often about subtle theological distinctions of academic interest, but sometimes also address issues with significant consequences. Typically, how a religious group thinks of Christ will greatly influence its psychology, anthropology, mythology, liturgy, and philosophy.

Most Christologies are based on the New Testament, and in particular the Gospel books of Matthew, Mark, and Luke, though some look to the Old Testament in the promises and prophecies that anticipated the coming of the Messiah. A number of Christologies also call upon extra-theological and secular sources.

The first Christology was developed by Paul, one of Jesus' twelve apostles. Paul conceived of Jesus as the Christ, a preexistent divine being who had descended into man to save humankind from the powers of law, sin, and death. The resurrected Christ was raised up to sit at the right hand of God, and would return at some point in the future to judge humankind.

Since the time of Paul, innumerable Christologies have been conceived. They are complex and their history has been fraught with controversy. Early Christologies focused on Jesus as the incarnation of Logos (God or the Ultimate Reality) and not as the historical man. Christological controversies of the Patristic Age (which concerns the lives, writings, and doctrines of the Fathers of Christianity) usually focus on the questioning of the (full) humanity and/or (full) divinity of Jesus. These included Gnosticism as the

The crucifixion of Jesus

major Christian deviation in the second century, from which evolved Docetism, which held that Christ only appeared to be human. Arianism denied that the divinity of Jesus preexisted as the Son of God. Apollinarianism held that preexisting divinity replaced the human spirit of the human Jesus. The church denounced such teachings as heresies, usually by statements from formal councils. In reaction to such misunderstanding of Jesus' humanity, Nestorianism nearly denied the unity of God and humanity within his person. The Council of Chalcedon in 451 established Christ as one person with two unified natures; the concept held sway until the Enlightenment.

Christologies of the Middle Ages, Renaissance, and Reformation placed great emphasis on the meaning of Christ's passion and crucifixion. During the Enlightenment in the eighteenth century, Jesus came to be regarded as a moral teacher; and in the nineteenth century interest returned to the historical Jesus.

More modern Christologies examine both the historical Jesus and Jesus as the absolute bringer of salvation and, in his death, the definitive Word of God. Some modern Christologies start "from below" rather than "from above," finding Jesus first to be truly human, and then discovering his divinity in and through his humanity.

Seminal works in contemporary Christology include those of Karl Barth, Oscar Cullman, Karl Rahner, Edward Schillebeeckx, George H. Tavard, and Paul Tilich. Rahner's *A New Christology* (1980) is seen by some as an indispensable reference for all modern Christologies in progress.

Lively debates center on the "dilution" of Christian orthodoxy by liberal theologians in America. Michael Dummet at Oxford points to an apparent consensus among teachers of Catholic theology in American seminaries that Jesus died without believing that he was Christ of the Son of God; that he knew nothing of the Trinity; that he knew from his mother who his natural father was; that he taught the imminent arrival of a messianic figure called the Son of Man but never claimed that this was himself. They are teaching, Dummet observes, that when Jesus died, his body remained in the tomb and decomposed there.

Newer Christologies indicate less emphasis on biblical sources and more importance being given to scientific, psychological, and social considerations. Modern Christologies undoubtedly will respond to the renewed interest in mythology, such as developed by Joseph Campbell. See **Campbell, Joseph; Mythology.**

Unorthodox Christologies include ecumenical efforts that attempt to place Jesus in a context with other religions, especially concerning the question of the dual natures of divinity and humanity. A unique approach to Christology that is the most compatible with New Age ecumenism is that in *The Coming of the Cosmic Christ* (1988) by the prolific Dominican priest, Matthew Fox. The author argues for focus on the "Cosmic Christ," a living Christ who can bring about a living cosmology. See **Creation spirituality.**

Sources: Glenn F. Chestnut. *Images of Christ: An Introduction to Christology.* San Francisco: Harper & Row, 1984; Ian Davie. *Jesus Purusha.* West Stockbridge, MA: Inner Traditions/Lindisfarne Press, 1985; Stephen T. Davis, ed. *Encountering Jesus: A Debate on Christology.* Philadelphia: Westminster John Knox, 1988; Matthew Fox. *The Coming of the Cosmic Christ.* San Francisco: Harper & Row, 1988; Geddes MacGregor. *Gnosis: A Renaissance in Christian Thought.* Wheaton, IL: Theosophical Publishing House, 1979; David L. Miller. *Christs.* New York: Seabury Press, 1981; Karl Rahner and Wilhelm Thusing. *A New Christology.* New York: Crossroad/Seabury Press, 1980.

Church of All Worlds

Neo-Pagan church, which aided the growth of neo-Pagan and Witchcraft religions throughout America and influenced the inclusion of environmental consciousness as part of neo-Paganism.

The Church of All Worlds (CAW) was founded by Tim Zell (who later changed his name to Otter G'Zell and then Otter Zell) and a group of friends who were students at Westminster College in Fulton, Missouri. The group had taken its inspiration from psychologist Abraham Maslow's concepts of self-actualization; the ideas of author Ayn Rand; and, chiefly, Robert A. Heinlein's bestselling novel, *Stranger in a Strange Land* (1961), about a human being raised by Martians who returns to Earth and establishes the Church of All Worlds and preaches "grokking" (deeply understanding) the divinity in others.

Zell's CAW filed for incorporation in 1967 and was formally chartered on

March 4, 1968, thus becoming the first neo-Pagan church to be federally recognized. The state of Missouri, however, refused to recognize it until 1971 because of its lack of dogma concerning God, the hereafter, the fate of souls, heaven and hell, sin and punishment, and other questions of concern to mainstream religion.

The early CAW followed Heinlein's fictional model and organized itself into nests. There were nine circles of advancement, each named after a planet. One progressed by passing study courses and undertaking psychic training. The process was intended to be ongoing. CAW's dogma was that it had no dogma; its basic belief was lack of belief. The only sin in the eyes of the church was hypocrisy, and the only crime was interfering with another. The unofficial goal of CAW was to achieve union with all consciousness. Zell expressed impatience with religions that emphasized personal salvation, which he considered insignificant.

By 1970 CAW's focus had shifted to ecology and environmentalism. Inspired by Teilhard de Chardin and his own visions, Zell conceived of a Gaia hypothesis independently of British scientist James Lovelock. Zell initially used the term "Terrebia" and later changed it to "Gaea," an alternate spelling of Gaia. See **Planetary consciousness.**

Zell's emphasis on environmental activism created dissension in the church, and some of the original founders split off. The CAW formed alliances with other neo-Pagan groups, aimed at achieving "eco-psychic potential," but these were short-lived.

By 1974 nests were established in more than a dozen states throughout the United States. The same year Zell married his second wife, Morning Glory (born Diana Moore). In 1976 continued dissension in the mother nest led the Zells to leave CAW and St. Louis. After a period of traveling and various residences, they settled in Ukiah, California, in 1985.

Zell's departure effectively shattered the CAW, which declined significantly by 1978. The mother nest eventually disbanded. A few nests remained in other cities, including Chicago and Atlanta. By 1988 CAW had all but ceased to exist outside of Ukiah.

In 1988 the Zells announced a revamped church structure and plans to restore CAW as a national church. The nine circles of advancement were redefined. The highest level is held by Otter Zell, who has achieved the Eighth Circle; no one has ever achieved the Ninth Circle.

The CAW views itself as a spiritual and physical eclectic mother for the celebration of life and Nature. According to Zell, its purpose is to weave evolutionary theologies into daily life so that people can both understand and assist worldwide changes, such as a greater ecological consciousness.

CAW recognizes the Earth Mother Goddess and the Horned God, who represent the plant and animal kingdoms, respectively. It is dedicated to celebrating life and maximizing human potential. It celebrates the eight seasonal festivals recognized throughout neo-Paganism and Witchcraft.

CAW administers several subsidiaries: The Ecosophical Research Association (ERA) was founded in 1977 by Morning Glory Zell to research arcane lore and legends. For the ERA's first project, the Zells created unicorns from baby goats by surgically manipulating the budding horn tissue to grow together as a single central horn. In 1984 they leased four unicorns to Ringling Brothers/Barnum and Bailey Circus. Another ERA project was to research mermaid legends off the coast of New Guinea.

Nemeton, a neo-Pagan networking organization founded by Gwydion Penderwen and Alison Harlow, merged with the CAW in 1978. Nemeton includes Forever Forests, an organization devoted to tree-planting and reforestation, and Annwfn, a fifty-five-acre tract in Mendocino County, California, which CAW operates as a wilderness retreat.

Lifeways is a teaching order founded and directed by Anodea Judith, president of CAW since 1986. It provides instruction on healing, bodywork, magic, psychic development, dance, ritual, music and, religion.

The Holy Order of Mother Earth (HOME) is a group of individuals dedicated to magical living and working with the land. See **Neo-Paganism; Witchcraft.**

Sources: Margot Adler. *Drawing Down the Moon.* Rev. ed. Boston: Beacon Press, 1986; Rosemary Ellen Guiley. *The Encyclopedia of Witches and Witchcraft.* New York: Facts On File, 1989; Anodea Judith. "Church of All Worlds: Who Are We; Where Are We Going; and How Will We Get There?" *Green Egg* 21, no. 81 (Beltane 1988): 15; Otter G'Zell. "'It was 20 Years Ago Today . . .'" *Green Egg* 21, no. 81 (Beltane 1988): 2; Church of All Worlds, Ukiah, CA.

Church of Christ, Scientist (Christian Science)

The second-largest Christian denomination founded in the United States, Christian Science stresses the healing aspects of Christian ministry. Central to this process is the idea that the human being is a spiritual image of God, and as such does not suffer sin, disease, or death. Through prayer and the realization that evil is not real, people can be healed through the power of God.

Christian Science was founded by Mary Baker Glover Patterson Eddy (1821–1910). She was raised in a Calvinist home in Bow, New Hampshire, and spent much of her early life as an invalid. She married George Washington Glover in 1843; he died in 1844. She delivered George Washington Glover, Jr., after his

father's death. Her invalidism prevented her from caring for the baby, and she allowed his doting nurse to adopt him. She married Dr. Daniel Patterson, a dentist, in 1853, but divorced him twenty years later.

Eddy pursued various cures and treatments. In 1862 she obtained relief from magnetic mental healer Phineas Parkhurst Quimby, and spent several months studying his techniques. She left Quimby after suffering a relapse, convinced that the only true healing comes from God.

In 1866 she experienced a miraculous healing. Near death with severe internal injuries due to a fall on icy pavement, Eddy turned to the Bible and read Matthew 9:1–8, in which Jesus tells a paralytic man to "take up your bed and go home." Eddy realized that disease was an illusion that could be overcome, and suddenly recovered.

She spent the next three years studying the Bible and discovering she could heal others. Beginning in 1870 she attempted to impart her newfound wisdom to anyone who would listen, which immediately brought her ridicule and persecution. Students gathered, however, and Eddy began teaching the principles of what she called Christian Science: that there is no death of the spiritual human being, that God is the healer, that there is no such person as the Devil, that heaven and hell are not places, and that there is no life in matter. She officially dropped Quimby's practice of head manipulation from Christian Science practice in May 1872; she said that there was no healing agent, either of mind or magnetic force, but only the unity with God, which left no room for disease. To Eddy Jesus was not a deity; he was a man who had expressed the idea of Christian healing.

Resistance by traditional churches to integrate her ideas into orthodox Christian worship forced Eddy to establish her own religion, and the first services were held June 6, 1875. On October 30 of the same year, she published *Science and Health with Key to the Scriptures* to clarify the spiritual meanings of scripture as they relate to healing and Christian Science. The book went through various publishers and revisions, as Eddy was never satisfied with the final result. At her death the texts were frozen as authoritative, along with the later *Manual of the Mother Church.*

In 1876 she formed the Christian Science Association for students residing in Massachusetts. On January 1, 1877, she married her third husband, Asa Gilbert Eddy, who became the first person to use "Christian Science practitioner" as his profession.

On August 23, 1879, the Commonwealth of Massachusetts granted a charter to incorporate the First Church of Christ, Scientist, in Boston; and the Massachusetts Metaphysical College for the instruction of Christian Science practitioners opened in 1881. Eddy became the church's first pastor, although she later renounced the ministry, saying Christian Science was to follow the Bible and *Science and Health,* not a person. The first issue of the *Journal of Christian Science* appeared in 1883, and the National Christian Scientists Association for non-Massachusetts residents organized in 1886.

No sooner had the structure been crafted than Eddy began tearing it down amid controversy and recrimination. In 1889 she dissolved the church, college, and Christian Science Association; the church did not reorganize until 1892.

Eddy endured intense criticism, with some reporters branding her a witch and occultist. Julius Dresser, who had introduced her to Quimby, began teaching mental healing, called the New Thought Movement, with his wife, Annetta, in 1883. He accused Eddy of stealing and debasing Quimby's procedures, which she vehemently denied. Followers of the

Mary Baker Eddy

(Courtesy First Church Christ Scientist)

New Thought Movement still mark Eddy as a plagiarist, although Quimby's son, George, gave her credit for Christian Science, saying he wouldn't want his father connected with the religion.

Former students sued her for fraud, while she countersued by claiming these students had practiced "malicious animal magnetism" against her and her organization. Asa Eddy had died in 1882, the victim, Eddy believed, of "mental malpractice," or psychic attack. See **Psychic attack.**

Eddy's reported obsession with mental malpractice fueled speculation about Christian Science as occultism. Eddy apparently did not believe that even her *Science and Health with Key to the Scriptures* fully explained the spiritual meanings she wished to impart. Such wisdom was gained through often-secret lessons taught by a trained instructor. Eddy explicitly claimed that the end result of Christian Science knowledge was the power to heal, and she feared those people who would use the power to impart evil instead. Such ideas of secrecy, supersensory knowledge, and healing power form traditional definitions of occult practice. Eddy's philosophy corresponded closely to that of eighteenth-century Swedish mystic Emanuel Swedenborg, who postulated that a spiritual imbalance causes a material imbalance, or disease, which the mind can cure.

Despite controversy Christian Science continued to attract believers, and Eddy reestablished the First Church of Christ, Scientist, on September 23, 1892. She served as the first pastor, but later declared that Christian Science churches would have no pastor, only the Bible and *Science and Health*. Eddy remained controversial for the remainder of her life. She founded the *Christian Science Monitor* newspaper in 1908. At the time of her death on December 3, 1910, in Chestnut Hill, Massachusetts, she had approximately 100,000 followers.

Following her death Adam H. Dickey, her private secretary and a chairman of the board of directors of the Mother Church, charged that she had been killed by "mental murder," psychic attack, and malicious thoughts directed against her by her enemies. Aware of these attacks, she had attempted to ward them off by instructing her staff in protective mental exercises. She reportedly claimed to be working in a level of consciousness that would mean instant death to any who crossed her. Dickey's claims greatly embarrassed church officials.

Eddy's simple organization, with no ordained clergy or hierarchy, remains in place as Christian Science in modern times. Services are led by the First Reader, who reads from the King James Version of the Bible, and by the Second Reader, who reads the explanatory passages from Eddy's book.

As the Mother Church, the Boston church grants charters to branch churches worldwide under the authority of the board of directors. Each branch is responsible for operating a reading room to make Christian Science literature available to the public. The board of directors has complete authority over theological matters and church governance, based upon *The Manual of the Mother Church*, written by Eddy.

Christian Science, along with Pentecostalism and the charismatic renewal movement, has brought new interest in the idea of Christian healing, the most attractive concept of Mary Baker Eddy's philosophy. Except for childbirth Christian Scientists do not use traditional medical services or medicines. Court decisions have put Christian Science practitioners on a par with conventional medical professionals, allowing patients to deduct costs of consultations as they would medical expenses. Debate still arises over whether Christian Science parents can withhold medical care from children, but the testimonials of complete cures further the church's strength.

Christian Science involves much more than faith healing. It emphasizes a total spiritual discipline of Bible study and prayer.

Some critics call Christian Science a cult, citing use of an extra-biblical source of authority, veneration of a human teacher to the point of infallibility, devaluation of Jesus Christ as Lord, and a denial of the doctrine of salvation by grace alone. Eddy, a devout Christian, would have been the first to refute that label. Her intention, as stated in the *Manual*, was a return to "primitive Christianity and its lost element of healing." See **Healing, faith and psychic.**

Sources: Norman Beasley. *The Cross and the Crown: The History of Christian Science.* New York: Duell, Sloan and Pearce, 1952; Keith Crim, general ed. *Abingdon Dictionary of Living Religions.* Nashville: Abingdon Press, 1981; John Godwin, ed. *The Occult in America.* New York: Doubleday, 1982; Anthony A. Hoekema. *The Four Major Cults.* Grand Rapids: William B. Eerdmans Publishing Co., 1963; J. Gordon Melton. *Encyclopedic Handbook of Cults in America.* New York: Garland Publishing Inc., 1986.

Church of Jesus Christ of Latter-day Saints, the (Mormonism)

Largest and most successful Christian denomination founded in the United States. Based in Salt Lake City, Utah, the Church of Jesus Christ of Latter-day Saints claims a worldwide membership of over 4 million believers. In the United States it is strongest in the Rocky Mountain states.

The church began with the divine revelations of Joseph Smith, Jr. (1805–1844), the son of poor Vermont farmers and laborers, Joseph Smith and Lucy Mack Smith. Smith was a youth when his family moved to Manchester, Oneida County (now Ontario County), western New York. During the nineteenth century, Oneida County was inflamed by one religious movement after another—from Presbyterians, Methodists, and Baptists; from great revival preachers like Charles Grandison Finney; and from groups like the Oneida Perfectionists, Millerites, and Spiritualists. So many ideas caught fire in the area that locals called it the Burned-Over District.

By 1820 to 1821, another revival was in progress among the Presbyterians, Methodists, and Baptists, with fire-and-brimstone preachers of each sect exhorting sinners to confess and avoid the religious lies of the other two groups. Most of the Smith family had become Presbyterian, but young Smith could not make up his mind. He prayed for divine guidance to select the one church that was right.

According to Smith's own account in *The Pearl of Great Price*, a pillar of light descended from the heavens, bringing two Personages, ostensibly God the Father and one whom he called "my Beloved Son." These Personages told Smith to choose no existing denomination, for they were all wrong, and he would be shown the true church.

Smith was reviled and persecuted for

Angel Moroni delivering the plates of the Book of Mormon to Joseph Smith, Jr.

his visions, but they did not stop. On the night of September 21 to 22, 1823, Smith's room was filled with a brilliant white light revealing an angel, Moroni, who appeared as a messenger from God. Moroni told Smith that he had helped write, then bury, a history written on gold plates by his father Mormon of an ancient people descended from Israel who had lived and died in America. He told Smith that Christ had appeared to these people after the resurrection, establishing the church, but knowledge of the gospel had been lost in a great fratricidal war. God had chosen Smith to retrieve these plates, translate their stories with the accompanying seer stones, and resurrect the church to prepare for the latter days (before the Second Coming).

Moroni appeared to Smith three times that night and again the next day.

Drawing of one of the gold plates, which Smith said was written in Egyptian, Chaldiac (Chaldaic), and Assyric (Assyrian)

The angel revealed the plates' hiding place—a hill outside Manchester called Cumorah—but forbade Smith to dig up the plates until four years from that date. Smith did as he was told, and on September 22, 1827, retrieved the golden plates, the seer stones (called the Urim and Thummim), and the breastplate upon which they were fastened.

Smith created a sensation when he brought home the plates, which were covered with Egyptian-like hieroglyphics. To avoid harassment Smith and his new wife, Emma, went to Harmony, Pennsylvania, to translate the plates. He was assisted first by Martin Harris, a farmer, who lost the first 116 pages, and then by Oliver Cowdery, an itinerant schoolteacher. Smith would put the stones in his hat and pull the hat around his face to simulate darkness. Then a character would appear, as if on parchment, accompanied by the English translation.

Smith would read the translation to Cowdery, who wrote it down, then another character would appear in the hat. *The Book of Mormon* was published in March 1830. Moroni supposedly reclaimed the plates and stones, with many of the plates still sealed.

By December 1830 Smith had translated the *Book of Moses* from divine revelation and he later added the *Book of Abraham,* reportedly from an ancient papyrus Smith found with a mummy in 1835. These two books, along with Smith's recollections of his revelations and the Saints' Articles of Faith, appeared in *The Pearl of Great Price* around 1842.

On May 15, 1829, Smith and Cowdery prayed in the woods for guidance about the sacrament of baptism. Suddenly, a holy messenger, whom they later determined was John the Baptist, appeared and conferred upon them the Priesthood of Aaron: an ordination, lost for centuries, which gave the men authority to preach the gospel of repentance and baptize by immersion. Smith would be First Elder and Cowdery Second Elder, and each was commanded to baptize and ordain the other. Not long after the apostles Peter, James, and John appeared, conferring the higher Melchizedek Priesthood, allowing them to lay on hands and perform healing miracles. These revelations established a well-defined apostolic priesthood similar to that of the Catholic church.

Smith organized the Church of Christ on April 6, 1830. The name changed to Church of the Latter-day Saints in 1834, finally becoming the Church of Jesus Christ of Latter-day Saints in 1838. In October 1830 Mormon missionaries went to Kirtland, Ohio, to establish the first Zion and site of the first temple.

One of the Saints' earliest thorny theological problems was the salvation of those already dead. If the true power to ordain and perform sacraments had been lost since the days of the apostles until conferred upon Smith and Cowdery, earlier generations were damned through no fault of their own. To guarantee the dead's salvation, the Saints baptized them in secret temple ceremonies, leaving the dead free to choose salvation for themselves. Mormons keep extensive genealogical records to document the existence of past relatives so that they may be baptized.

Opposition from Kirtland residents forced the Mormons to move on in 1837 and 1838 to Independence, Missouri—the "true Zion," according to Smith. A temple was begun there also, but the Missouri group suffered terrible persecution. During the winter of 1839 to 1840, the Mormons moved again, this time to Commerce, Illinois.

Within a very short time, Commerce, renamed Nauvoo by Smith, was the biggest city in Illinois. (Although Smith alleged that nauvoo means "beautiful plantation" in Hebrew, no such word exists in that language.) Smith had the support and backing of the state's biggest financiers and politicians, and the Mormons began their third temple. Smith solidified his power as the Saints' prophet and leader, receiving revelations that he gathered in the *Doctrines and Covenants*. One of these was the Order of Enoch, which called for all Saints to consecrate their wealth for the common good and redistribution. But the most important doctrine was the Order of Abraham, revealed by Smith on July 12, 1843.

This new order would establish marriage as a "new and everlasting covenant." Smith conceived of heaven as three states of glory: the celestial, for those who kept Gospel laws and ordinances, eventually returning to God the Father; the terrestrial, for those who did not accept Christ but were nonetheless good and honorable; and the telestial, for the rest of the sinners who still would be received by the Holy Ghost. Within these states of glory were an infinite number of new worlds to be governed by godly Mormon men. Like Christ—designated the one who had fulfilled all of God's ordinances—any man could eventually attain godhood. But these heavenly prizes would be awarded only to those who were married—sealed for all eternity—on earth by a properly ordained Mormon priest. And in order to populate the spirit world, Mormon men must populate the earthly one—and that necessitated more than one wife. Such was the birth of polygamy among the Saints.

Not everyone in the church or Nauvoo knew about Smith's polygamist revelations, but they did know that his ego thirsted after power and women. In 1844 Smith declared his candidacy for President of the United States, meanwhile selecting a secret Council of Fifty within the church as his erstwhile cabinet. News of the moves leaked to an opposition newspaper, and Smith reacted by destroying the press. Smith and his brother Hyrum were arrested for treason and held in jail in Carthage, where an angry mob assassinated them both on June 27, 1844. Even after his death, several Mormon women entered into "celestial marriage" with Joseph Smith's spirit.

Mormonism after Smith

After much turmoil and efforts by former Campbellite Sidney Rigdon to assume control of the church, the members selected Smith's confidante Brigham Young. Forced to move yet again, Young led the Saints to a "Zion in the Wilderness" in the Utah Territory, which he called the State of Deseret. Quoted as saying, "This is the place," when the Mormons reached Salt Lake in 1848, Young rebuilt the church into a thriving and powerful organization, serving as its leader for thirty years.

Young officially announced the Mormon practice of polygamy to a shocked world in 1852 (Young himself had twenty-eight wives), immediately encountering government harassment and persecution. By 1862 Congress passed the first antipolygamy laws, giving them real teeth in 1882 with the passage of the Edmunds Act disenfranchising all polygamists. In the face of such pressure, First President Wilford Woodruff announced the church's official discouragement of polygamy in 1890. In 1904 a revelation told members that anyone practicing plural marriage would be excommunicated.

Mormon men dominate the authoritarian church organization, patterned after the Old Testament. Any man who lives according to God's laws can be ordained into the Aaronic priesthood, although the church is officially run by the General Authorities, headed by the first president. Smith said that God appointed him to receive all revelations for the church until God appoints a successor; with the selection of Brigham Young, the office of first president has been designated as the official receiver of church revelations, although any Mormon may receive divine messages. Revelations contradicting church authority are seen as diabolically inspired.

The temple ceremonies of eternal marriage and baptism of the dead are extremely secret, and no Gentile (non-Mormon) may enter the temple. The rituals are believed to resemble Masonic rites, for Smith was a member of the Nauvoo Masons and incorporated Masonic symbols—the square and compass, the beehive, and the all-seeing eye—into Mormon practice. See **Freemasonry.**

The original church has splintered into many other groups. The largest is the Reorganized Church of Jesus Christ of Latter-day Saints, organized in 1853. Members, who do not call themselves Mormons, assert that Joseph Smith never taught polygamy (a position unsupported by the facts). Joseph Smith III accepted the presidency of the Reorganized Church in 1860, and later presidents have all been Smith descendants.

Sources: Daniel Cohen. *The Spirit of the Lord: Revivalism in America.* New York: Four Winds Press, 1975; Keith Crim, general ed. *Abingdon Dictionary of Living Religions.* Nashville: Abingdon Press, 1981; John Godwin, ed. *The Occult in America.* New York: Doubleday, 1982; Klaus J. Hansen. *Mormonism and the American Experience.* Chicago: The University of Chicago Press, 1981; J. Gordon Melton. *Encyclopedic Handbook of Cults in America.* New York: Garland Publishing, 1986; Jan Shipps. *Mormonism: The Story of a New Religious Tradition.* Urbana, IL: University of Illinois Press, 1985; Joseph Smith, Jr., trans. *The Book of Mormon.* Salt Lake City: The Church of Jesus Christ of Latter-day Saints, 1986; Joseph Smith, Jr. *The Pearl of Great Price.* Salt Lake City: The Church of Jesus Christ of Latter-day Saints, 1972.

Church of Scientology

Religious organization founded by L. (Lafayette) Ron Hubbard in 1953, an expansion of his earlier concept of Dianetics. Scientology offers a number of techniques and disciplines to help the individual overcome negative effects of the present and previous lives, a process called "auditing" in order to become "clear." According to Scientology if all people were "clear," the world would be free from drugs, war, pollution, crime, mental illness, and other ills. Scientology has been the focus of numerous controversies and disputes with various governments, and vigorously defends itself against critics.

Hubbard (1911–1986) was born in Tilden, Nebraska. He studied civil engineering at George Washington University in 1931 and 1932, and shortly thereafter began a successful career as a writer. He received the most notice for his works of science fiction.

During World War II, Hubbard served in the Navy and was wounded in the South Pacific. After the war he formulated what he called Dianetics, from the Greek for "thought," a new approach to mental health with psychoanalytic elements. He founded the Hubbard Dianetic Research Foundation in Elizabeth, New Jersey. His first writings on Dianetics, published in 1948, attracted some support, perhaps most important of which came from John Campbell, writer and editor of *Astounding Science Fiction* magazine. Hubbard's book *Dianetics: The Modern Science of Mental Health,* published in 1950, attracted a wide audience, and helped spur the formation of Dianetics branches around the United States.

Central to Dianetics is the theory of "engrams," which are traumatic shocks or psychic scars suffered in the womb or early childhood; they are said to be the cause of all psychosomatic and mental illnesses, for they create programmed responses in a "reactive" mind. They have been compared to psychiatrist Sigmund Freud's theory of repressed desires and psychiatrist Carl G. Jung's theory of complexes. Engrams are eliminated by auditing, a sort of psychoanalytic process in which the individual, with the help of an auditor, recalls minute details of his or her life. The auditor helps the individual erase the engram. Progress is assessed in stages, from "release" to "preclear" to "clear." Those who attain the latter are said to experience such benefits as improved IQ and eyesight, more energy, greater immunity to illness, and faster recovery from injuries.

After an initial fast start, Dianetics soon began to lose momentum. Hubbard, however, was already evolving it into Scientology, which has a much greater and cosmic scope, and which proved to be more enduring and popular. Scientology, a therapeutic system with a spiritual dimension that acknowledges reincarnation and extraterrestrial life, seeks to raise humankind to a higher level of consciousness. Engrams from past lives must also be erased in order to achieve an even higher level of clear, "Operating Thetan." Thetans are the eternal essences of immortal celestial beings who existed long ago, who through the course of experimenting with life in the flesh became trapped as human beings. To become an Operating Thetan, one must clear the engrams of the present life and the past lives of the Thetan, and recover awareness of the celestial origin. Hubbard augmented the auditing process with a device called the "electropsychometer," or "E-meter," a kind of polygraph that would tell an auditor when an individual might not be honest.

In 1952 Hubbard founded the Hubbard Association of Scientologists, which was renamed the Hubbard Association of Scientologists International. In 1953 he incorporated the Church of Scientology; and in 1955 he established the Founding Church of Scientology as an unincorporated, independent church. Scientology has since spread throughout the world.

In 1958 the Internal Revenue Service revoked the church's tax-exempt status. Over thirty years later, the church remains in litigation to reinstate it. In 1963 the Food and Drug Administration seized some E-meters, claiming they had been used in the diagnosis of disease. In 1969 Hubbard won a victory from the US Court of Appeals that auditing was a central practice to the church, akin to confession in the Catholic church. The E-meters were returned.

During the 1960s and 1970s, Scientology faced more criticisms and government problems in the United States, Great Britain, and Australia. It was denounced by some as a cult, and began to undertake vigorous legal defenses. In the late 1970s, the FBI began an investigation concerning allegations that Scientologists were stealing government documents that portrayed Scientology in an unflattering light—a project called Operation Snow White.

On July 8, 1977, FBI agents raided Church of Scientology offices in Washington, DC, and Los Angeles and seized 48,149 documents. On August 15, 1978 nine Scientologists, including Hubbard's wife, Mary Sue, were indicted on twenty-eight counts of conspiring to steal government documents, theft of government documents, burglarizing government offices, intercepting government communications, harboring a fugitive, making false declarations before a grand jury, and conspiring to obstruct justice. All nine pleaded not guilty and went to trial. On October 26, 1979, the nine were found guilty on one count each of the indictment, and sentenced to fines and prison terms of one to five years. The defendants said they would appeal on the grounds that the evidence used against them had been obtained illegally. About one month later, the appellate court released to the media the Scientology documents that had been seized by the FBI.

Early in 1980 Hubbard dropped out of public view, but continued to issue communications to his organization. He died on January 24, 1986. The official cause of death was a cerebral hemorrhage, though no autopsy was performed for religious reasons. His body was cremated and his ashes scattered in the Pacific Ocean.

After the trial, Scientology began softening its image with an emphasis on its message and Hubbard's prolific writings. While the primary focus of Scientology is on helping individuals become "clear," worship services are held at all churches and missions, and a number of religious holidays are observed. The International headquarters are in Los Angeles.

Sources: David G. Bromley and Anson D. Schupe, Jr. Strange Gods: The Great American Cult Scare. Boston: Beacon Press, 1981; John Godwin. Occult America. New York: Doubleday, 1972; L. Ron Hubbard. Dianetics: The Modern Science of Mental Health. 1950. Los Angeles: Bridge Publications, 1984; J. Gordon Melton. Encyclopedic Handbook of Cults in America. New York: Garland Publishing Inc., 1986; Russell Miller. Bare-Faced Messiah: The True Story of L. Ron Hubbard. New York: Henry Holt, and Co., 1987.

Church Universal and Triumphant, the (Summit Lighthouse)

See Alternative religious movements.

Circle

Symbol of oneness, completion, perfection, the cosmos, eternity, and the sun. In psychology the circle symbolizes the Self, the totality of the psyche. A feminine symbol, the circle appears in sacred art and architecture and plays an important role in various religious and magical rites. Many sacred dances are performed in circles. In Islam listeners gather in mosques around teachers in circles called halqahs.

In ritual a circle demarcates a holy space that protects one from negative forces on the outside and facilitates communion with spirits and deities. Within the circle one may ritually achieve transcendent levels of consciousness. Among Native North Americans, circles are known to have great medicine power. See Medicine wheels.

In folk medicine lore, circles drawn around the beds of the sick and of new mothers protect them against demons.

Seances customarily are conducted around a circular table; participants often hold hands. See Seance.

In ceremonial magic magicians draw a magic circle around themselves to protect them from the demons and spirits they conjure. See Magic. To step outside the circle during a ritual, or even to cross the boundary with an arm or leg, is to invite magical disaster. See **Crowley, Aleister.**

In neo-Pagan Witchcraft, or Wicca, all worship and magical rites are conducted within a circle, which provides a sacred and purified space and acts as a gateway to the gods. The Witches' circle symbolizes wholeness, the creation of the cosmos, the womb of Mother Earth, and the Wheel of Rebirth, which is the continuing cycle of the seasons in birth-death-rebirth. See **Witchcraft.**

Sacred circles are constructed or drawn according to ritual, and are purified and consecrated. If the circles are temporary, they are ritually disassembled. If they are permanent, their sacred power is periodically ritually renewed. See **Lotus; Mandala; Megaliths; Stonehenge.**

Sources: J. E. Cirlot. *A Dictionary of Symbols.* New York: Philosophical Library, 1971; Cyril Glasse. *The Concise Encyclopedia of Islam.* San Francisco: Harper & Row, 1989; Rosemary Ellen Guiley. *The Encyclopedia of Witches and Witchcraft.* New York: Facts On File, 1989; Carl G. Jung, ed. *Man and His Symbols.* 1964. New York: Anchor Press/Doubleday, 1988; Barbara G. Walker. *The Woman's Dictionary of Symbols and Sacred Objects.* San Francisco: Harper & Row, 1988.

Clairaudience

The hearing of sounds, music, and voices not audible to normal hearing. The term comes from French for "clear hearing." Clairaudience often is intermingled with other basic psychic perceptions of clairvoyance, "clear seeing," and clairsentience, or "clear sensing." In yoga it is a *siddhi,* and is experienced when the fifth chakra, located at the throat, is activated. See Siddhis.

Clairaudience often is experienced in the dream state and related stages of consciousness. A clairvoyant dream may feature a message whispered by an unknown voice. It is common to hear clairaudient voices and sounds in the hypnagogic and hypnapompic states, which border sleep. It also occurs in past-life recalls of all types, including spontaneous, meditational, waking, and hypnotic regression. The sounds and voices seem like voice-overs to the imaged memories.

Clairaudience is a phenomenon of mystical and trance experiences. Oracles, shamans, priests, prophets, mystics, adepts, saints, and other holy persons throughout history have been guided by clairaudient voices. The voices have been perceived as those of angels, God, spirits of the dead, spirit guides, and the formless Divine Force, the All That Is, sometimes called "The Voice of the Eternal Silence."

Clairaudience often manifests as an inner sound, or an inner voice that is clearly distinguishable from one's own inner voice. A person may recognize it as the voice of a dead relative. The voice may be unknown, but interpreted as coming from a certain spiritual source. Many people who have a sense of their spirit guides identify the inner voices belonging to them. In a more highly developed sense of clairaudience, a person experiences sound as external. Those who travel to the astral plane claim to hear many sounds, not all of them pleasant, due to some of the unfriendly elemental spirits that populate the plane.

The ancient Greeks believed that daimons, intermediate spirits between human beings and the gods, whispered advice in the ears of men. Good daimons acted like guardian spirits, while evil daimons led people astray. Socrates claimed to be guided by a daimon throughout his life, speaking up at times of crisis. When Socrates was sentenced to death in Athens, he chose to stay and accept the sentence because his daimon did not advise him to flee the city.

The Bible tells of numerous clairaudient experiences in which God sends messages to prophets and kings. For example, King Solomon is described hearing the voice of the Lord telling him he has been given a wise and discerning mind, and none like him shall ever come after him. The boy Samuel hears his name called and thinks it is the priest Eli; later he realizes it is the Lord.

Clairaudience has occurred regularly to great men and women in history, and to highly creative individuals. See **Inspiration.** At age thirteen Joan of Arc began to see visions and hear the voices of the angels Michael, Margaret, and Catherine, her spirit guides. In the eighteenth century, English poet William Cowper heard voices giving him advance notice of all important events in his life. In the late seventeenth and early eighteenth centuries, the mesmerists observed that magnetized subjects experienced clairaudience, particularly the voices of the dead, along with other psychic phenomena. Messages from the dead, received by a medium clairaudiently, became an integral part of many Spiritualist seances.

Clairaudience frequently occurs in psychic readings. A psychic may hear voices, music, or sounds relating to a person's past or present. It manifests in times of crisis, as when one sees and hears a loved one in trouble. Shamans use clairaudience in a trance state to communicate with spirit helpers and guardian spirits.

Not all clairaudient experiences are meaningful and to be taken seriously. The inner voice may be cultivated through diligent meditation and awareness of dreams.

Clairaudient voices differ from the disembodied voices sometimes heard at seances and in poltergeist cases, which are considered collective apparitional phenomena. See **Hypnagogic/hypnapompic states; Possession.**

Sources: Slater Brown. *The Heyday of Spiritualism.* New York: Hawthorn Books, 1970; W. E. Butler. *How to Develop Clairvoyance.* 2d ed. New York: Samuel Weiser, 1979; Arthur Ford in collaboration with Marguerite Harmon Bro. *Nothing So Strange: The Autobiography of Arthur Ford.* New York: Harper & Brothers, 1958; Michael Harner. *The Way of the Shaman.* New York: Bantam, 1986; Craig Junjulas. *Psychic Tarot.* Dobbs Ferry, NY: Morgan & Morgan, 1985; C. W. Leadbeater. *The Chakras.* Wheaton, IL: Theosophical Publishing House, 1927; Ormond McGill. *The Mysticism and Magic of India.* Cranbury, NJ: A. S. Barnes & Co., 1977; Ian Stevenson. "Are Poltergeists Living or Are They Dead?" *The Journal of the American Society for Psychical Research* 66, no. 3 (July 1972): 233–52; Joan Windsor. *The Inner Eye: Your Dreams Can Make You Psychic.* Englewood Cliffs, NJ: Prentice-Hall, 1985.

Clairsentience

A superphysical sense perception that is one of the primary tools of a psychic. "Clairsentience" is derived from French for "clear sensing," and was brought into popular usage during the late eighteenth century by the followers of Franz Anton Mesmer, who developed the practice of animal magnetism. See **Mesmer, Franz Anton.**

Clairsentience involves the psychic perception of smell, taste, touch, emotions, and physical sensations that contribute to an overall psychic and intuitive impression. Depending on the psychic's individual techniques, the perceptions may register internally or externally.

Clairsentience is used in conjunction with clairvoyance, or "clear vision," and clairaudience, or "clear hearing." Many people experience clairsentience without being aware of it. They may discuss the fleeting impressions and flashes as imagination. Like other psychic perceptions, clairsentience is tied closely to the intuition and gut feelings.

One of the earliest and most important laboratory experiments involving clairsentience took place between 1920 and 1922 at the University of Groningen, the Netherlands. A psychically gifted student named van Dam was tested in psi guessing games. The experimenters also attempted to telepathically transmit colors, tastes, feelings, and moods. Van Dam participated in a total of 589 trials and scored impressive results.

Some parapsychologists and psychical researchers consider "clairsentience" an archaic term, but it continues to be used by practicing psychics. See **Empathy.**

Sources: W. E. Butler. *How to Develop Clairvoyance.* 2d ed. New York: Samuel Weiser, 1979; Craig Junjulas. *Psychic Tarot.* Dobbs Ferry, NY: Morgan & Morgan, 1985; Edgar D. Mitchell. *Psychic Exploration: A Challenge for Science.* Edited by John White. New York: Paragon Books, 1974; Sybo A. Schouten and Edward F. Kelly. "On the Experiments of Brugmans, Heymans, and Weinberg." *European Journal of Parapsychology* 2, no. 3 (November 1978): 247–90; Joan Windsor. *The Inner Eye: Your Dreams Can Make You Psychic.* Englewood Cliffs, NJ: Prentice-Hall, 1985.

Clairvoyance

The perception of current objects, events, or people that may not be discerned through the normal senses. Clairvoyance, from the French for "clear seeing," is a common psychic experience. The seeing may manifest in internal or external visions, or a sensing of images. Clairvoyance overlaps with other psychic faculties and phenomena, such as clairaudience, clairsentience, telepathy, precognition, retrocognition, psychometry, and remote viewing.

Clairvoyance appears to be a general ability among humans, and it also appears to exist in animals. Research in this area, which is largely limited to anecdotal case studies, has been highly controversial. See **Animal psi.**

Clairvoyance has been acknowledged, used, and cultivated since ancient times. Prophets, fortune-tellers, shamans, wizards, witches, cunning men and women, and seers of all kinds through all ages have employed clairvoyance. Many have been born with clairvoyance as a natural gift; others have consciously developed it through training. Egyptian and Greek priests used herbal mixtures to induce temporary clairvoyance, especially in training and initiating novices. The Pythia oracle at Delphi in ancient Greece also induced clairvoyance for prophetic visions, using smoke inhaled from burning laurel leaves. Other ancients discovered clairvoyance-inducing properties from certain natural springs and wells. Shamans induce clairvoyance through ecstatic dancing, chanting, and drumming, and sometimes with the help of hallucinogens. The ecstatic ritual dance to achieve clear vision has been used by many cultures throughout history, including the ancient Egyptians, Hindus, and Sufis. In yoga clairvoyance results from the opening of the sixth chakra, located between the brows, which is called the "third eye." Clairvoyance is one of many psychic by-products, called *siddhis,* of yogic spiritual development.

Clairvoyance is experienced in different ways and degrees. In its simplest form, clairvoyance is the internal seeing of symbolic images, which must be interpreted according to a person's own system of meanings. In its highest form, clairvoyance is the viewing of nonphysical planes, the astral, etheric, and spiritual worlds and the beings that inhabit them, and the auric fields surrounding all things in nature. Most clairvoyant experiences fall between the two.

Lawrence LeShan, American psychologist, defines reality as being divided into two kinds, "sensory reality" and "clairvoyant reality." Sensory reality is normal, everyday life, flowing in real-time, perceived with the five senses. Clairvoyant reality is lifted out of this track to a place where time is illusory, judgments impossible, and all things are perceived as interconnected.

Various terms have been put forth to describe different states of clairvoyance:

- X-ray clairvoyance: The ability to see through opaque objects such as envelopes, containers, and walls to perceive what lies within or beyond.

- Medical clairvoyance: The ability to see disease and illness in the human body, either by reading the aura or seeing the body as transparent. Edgar Cayce, one of the most famous of all medical clairvoyants, viewed the Akashic Records on the astral plane to obtain information, including remedies and cures.

- Traveling clairvoyance: The ability to see current events, people, and objects that are far away. See **Remote viewing.**

- Spatial clairvoyance: Vision that transcends space and time. Another term for this is traveling clairvoyance, but it also relates to precognitive clairvoyance, or visions of the future, and retrocognitive clairvoyance, or visions of the past. This type of clairvoyance is employed by shamans, diviners, and psychics who work in applied psi fields such as psychic archaeology and psychic crime detection.

- Dream clairvoyance: The dreaming of an event that is happening simultaneously. Dream clairvoyance may be combined with precognition, which is especially helpful and instructive in all matters in personal life, as an early warning system.

- Astral clairvoyance: Perception of the astral and etheric planes, and the elementals, demons, devas, and other beings that inhabit them. It is also the perception of the aura and auric colors, thought-forms, and other partial manifestations of thought.

This is another level of vision used by shamans, yogis, and adepts.

- Spiritual clairvoyance: Vision of the higher planes and angelic beings; a mystical state of being and knowing.

Clairvoyance and Western Science

Although adepts and nature-oriented societies have taken clairvoyance for granted for thousands of years, Western science has not. The first scientific efforts to study clairvoyance came during the days of mesmerism in the early nineteenth century, when magnetized subjects displayed clairvoyance and other psychic phenomena. In the 1830s Alphonse Cahagnet, a French magnetist and follower of eighteenth-century Swedish mystic Emanuel Swedenborg, a great clairvoyant who could peer into the spiritual realm, systematically studied a young woman named Adele Magnot. In magnetic trance Magnot experienced clairvoyant visions of the spirit world, seeing and conversing with the dead. She was able to describe their features, characteristics, and the clothing they wore at the end of their lives. She heard them clairaudiently, and relayed their messages to the living. At first Magnot saw her own relatives, then was able to see the dead relatives of strangers who provided only names. The accuracy of her readings was verified by many and recorded by Cahagnet.

In the 1870s another Frenchman, Professor Charles Richet, began testing for clairvoyance by asking subjects to guess cards concealed in envelopes. In 1889 some of his outstanding work was done with a medium known as Leonie B., whom he hypnotized. Richet's work was taken a great deal further in the 1930s by American parapsychologist J. B. Rhine, who used a special deck of symbol cards to conduct thousands of tests for both clairvoyance and telepathy. See **ESP cards.**

In the decades since, impressive evidence, has been accumulated to support the existence of clairvoyance. In parapsychology it is considered one of three classes of psychic perception, along with telepathy and precognition; there is much overlap among the three. While many scientists acknowledge that the capacity for clairvoyance seems to exist through the general human population and in animals, others disagree, contending clairvoyance does not exist or is merely a form of telepathy.

Development and Direction of Clairvoyance

Psychics and occultists say virtually anyone can develop the clairvoyant faculty with the proper training, such as through scrying exercises of gazing into mirrors, specula, crystal balls, flame, and shiny objects; yoga exercises to stimulate the third-eye chakra; and auric sight exercises of gazing at magnets in the dark. This assertion has not been borne out in the laboratory, however. Most likely, the clairvoyant faculty may be enhanced through development of one's spiritual consciousness, which facilitates use of the sixth sense. See **Clairaudience; Clairsentience.**

Sources: Slater Brown. *The Heyday of Spiritualism.* New York: Hawthorn Books, 1970; W. E. Butler. *How to Develop Clairvoyance.* 2d ed. New York: Samuel Weiser, 1979; Alfred Douglas. *Extrasensory Powers: A Century of Psychical Research.* London: Victor Gollancz Ltd., 1976; Arthur Ford in collaboration with Marguerite Harmon Bro. *Nothing So Strange: The Autobiography of Arthur Ford.* New York: Harper & Brothers, 1958; Manly P. Hall. 1928. Reprint. *The Secret Teachings of All Ages.* Los Angeles: The Philosophic Research Society, 1977; Michael Harner. *The Way of the Shaman.* New York: Bantam, 1986; Craig Junjulas. *Psychic Tarot.* Dobbs Ferry, NY: Morgan & Morgan, 1985; C.

W. Leadbeater. *The Chakras.* Wheaton, IL: Theosophical Publishing House, 1927; Robert R. Leichtman, M.D., and Carl Japikse. *Active Meditation: The Western Tradition.* Columbus, OH: Ariel Press, 1982; Lawrence LeShan. *The Medium, the Mystic, and the Physicist: Toward a General Theory of the Paranormal.* New York: Viking Press, 1974; Ormond McGill. *The Mysticism and Magic of India.* Cranbury, NJ: A. S. Barnes & Co., 1977; Edgar D. Mitchell. *Psychic Exploration: A Challenge for Science.* Edited by John White. New York: Paragon Books, 1974; Russell Targ and Keith Harary. *The Mind Race.* New York: Villard Books, 1984; Joan Windsor. *The Inner Eye: Your Dreams Can Make You Psychic.* Englewood Cliffs, NJ: Prentice-Hall, 1985.

Cloud dissolving (also cloud busting)

An alleged feat of psychokinesis (PK) in which clouds are made to disappear by concentration of thought and will. Tests and observations of cloud dissolving have never been conclusive. It is most likely that the clouds dissipate of their own accord.

Skeptics point out that fair-weather cumulus clouds, once formed, usually disappear on their own within fifteen to twenty minutes, and are replaced by similar-looking clouds off to one side. Hence an untrained observer could "dissolve" a cloud and then assume, because the rest of the sky appeared the same, that the cloud was actually gone.

This explanation, however, does not explain the ancient phenomenon of weather control—bringing the sun or making it rain—as performed by shamans in various cultures around the world. The shaman enters an ecstatic trance, through dancing, chanting, drumming, rattling, and sometimes ingestion of hallucinogenic drugs, and takes a magical flight to the sky or spirit world to communicate with spirits and deities and bring about the desired changes in weather. Similarly, various Indian tribes have rain dance ceremonies. In such cultures human beings are viewed as but one part of the complex, living whole of Nature, connected to all other living things and to Nature itself (see **Planetary consciousness**). It is possible that a subtle psychokinetic process may take place, enabling human beings to influence the elements. How effective this process is remains unknown. See **Psychokinesis; Shamanism.**

Sources: Mircea Eliade. *Shamanism.* Princeton, NJ: Princeton University Press, 1964; *Into the Unknown.* Pleasantville, NY: Reader's Digest, 1981; Denys Parsons. "Cloud Busting: A Claim Investigated." *The Journal of the Society for Psychical Research* 38, no. 690 (December 1956): 352–64; Ruth Montgomery. *Strangers Among Us.* New York: Fawcett Crest, 1979; Susy Smith. *Today's Witches.* Englewood Cliffs, NJ: Prentice-Hall, 1970.

Collective unconscious

Concept of psychiatrist Carl G. Jung that refers to the memories of mental patterns that are experienced and shared by a large number, if not all, humans. Likewise, most members of a single culture may have a more specific collective unconscious, while sharing also in the more universal patterns. "Collective unconscious" is synonymous with "universal consciousness."

In developing the concept of the collective unconscious, Jung broke away from psychiatrist Sigmund Freud's view that the unconscious was exclusively personal and formed of repressed childhood traumas. Jung affirmed a personal unconscious, and said that underneath it lies a much deeper layer, the collective unconscious, which is separate. The collective unconscious does not derive from personal experience, nor is it acquired, he said. Rather, it is inborn. He chose the descriptive term "collective" because this part of the unconscious is universal.

While the contents of the personal unconscious consist of repressed and forgotten material, the contents of the collective unconscious consist essentially of archetypes, or primordial images or patterns of instinctual behavior. These contents have never been in consciousness, but they can appear in consciousness in the form of images and instincts. For the archetypes to manifest, involvement is required from the personal consciousness in the form of complexes, images, and ideas that form a core derived from one or more archetypes and having an emotional tone.

Jung said his hypothesis of the collective unconscious was no more daring than to assume the existence of instincts. Nor was the hypothesis philosophical or speculative; it was empirical, demonstrable by the identification of archetypes. See **Archetypes.**

The collective unconscious is supported by extensive research, such as by Joseph Campbell in his studies of the world's mythologies. Scholars have found Jung's understandings of symbols of the collective unconscious compatible with symbols in the writings of the great Spanish mystics, John of the Cross and Teresa of Avila. See **Jung, Carl Gustav; Symbols.**

Sources: Frieda Fordham. *An Introduction to Jung's Psychology.* 3d ed. Harmondsworth, England: Penguin Books, 1966; Calvin S. Hall and Vernon A. Nordby. *A Primer on Jungian Psychology.* New York: New American Library, 1973; C. G. Jung. *The Archetypes and the Collective Unconscious.* 2d ed. Bollingen Series 20. Princeton: Princeton University Press, 1968; Andrew Samuels, and Bani Shorter and Fred Plaut. *A Critical Dictionary of Jungian Analysis.* London: Routledge & Kegan Paul, 1986.

College of Psychic Studies

See **Spiritualism**.

Colors

Seven primary wavelengths, or vibrations, of light visible to the human eye—red, orange, yellow, green, blue, indigo, and violet—which have had occult, religious, philosophical, and healing significance since ancient times. Colors are believed to have specific effects upon body, mind, and spirit.

Color lore is ancient and is part of the mystical, magical, and healing systems developed by the ancient Indians, Chinese, Tibetans, Egyptians, Greeks, Persians, Babylonians, and others. Modern scientific evidence supports some of the ancient claims made about colors.

Red, the longest wavelength of visible colors, is associated with physical and material forces, while violet, the shortest wavelength, is associated with spirituality and enlightenment. Black, the absence of color, is virtually universally associated with evil; while white, the combination of all colors, is associated with the Godhead and purity. In terms of the three aspects of human beings, the body is associated with red, the mind with yellow, and the spirit with blue. Some Hindu gods, usually attributes of Vishnu, are portrayed with blue skin to denote their divine nature.

The Pythagoreans said that white light—the Godhead—contains all sound and color, and that the seven colors of the spectrum correspond to the seven known planets and the eight notes of the scale. Both the first and eighth notes of the scale correspond to red, the eighth note having a higher vibration of red.

The Old Testament tells that the seven colors of the spectrum were given by God as a rainbow, a token of a covenant between God and humankind. The symbolisms and uses of color in religious art were strictly regulated in the early church, a practice that began to decline in the Middle Ages. According to early standards, the colors of robes and ornaments indicated whether or not a saint had been martyred, and for what acts or work.

Healing with colors has been in use for thousands of years in China and in Indian Ayurvedic medicine. The ancient Egyptians and Greeks also made use of colors.

In the modern West, color healing received little attention until the late nineteenth century. Edwin Babbitt's *The Principles of Light and Color* (1878) reaffirmed the Pythagorean correspondences of music and color, and the power of light to "vitalize." In 1933 Dinshah Ghadiali published his three-volume *Spectro Chrometry Encyclopedia* (1933), proposing that colors denote chemical potencies in higher vibrations. Ghadiali said that white light contains all colors in a harmonious balance, and imbalances in the body are created by deficiencies or excesses of particular colors. He said balance could be restored by subjecting the patient's whole body, or a part of it, to colored lamp light.

Modern color therapy, also called "light therapy," "chromatherapy," and "colorology," is controversial and is considered an alternative or supplemental treatment. Patients are exposed to colored lights, prescribed certain colored foods to eat, or given water steeped in sunlight in colored containers. Color breathing is an exercise of visualizing the inhalation and exhalation of colored breath during meditation.

The Effects of Color

Scientific research in the 1970s and 1980s showed that colored light does have an effect upon the body. The perception of color by the eye triggers biochemical reactions; there is no difference if the person is color-blind.

Blue, by far the favorite color named in surveys, has been demonstrated to be one of the most beneficial colors, helping to lower blood pressure, perspiration, respiration, and brain-wave activity. Green also is soothing. Warm colors, such as yellow (the least favorite color named in surveys), red, and orange, raise blood pressure and metabolic rates; orange stimulates the appetite. Pink is beneficial in small doses; it relaxes and neutralizes aggressive behavior. Some jails have "pink rooms" for violent inmates, which replace the need for handcuffs and tranquilizers. However, prolonged exposure to pink produces the opposite effect: irritability, aggression, and emotional distress.

Some psychologists and color consultants employ colors to produce various effects in hospitals and workplaces. Seriously ill patients, for example, are placed in rooms with subdued colors, and short-term patients are placed in rooms with bright, warm colors. Color visualization therapies are used in psychotherapy, in which patients visualize themselves showered by or filled with particular colors. In the workplace pastel shades of blue and green seem to enhance employees' productivity and sense of well-being. Color experts recommend that no room should be a single color, but reflect a variety of light wavelengths.

Sources: Jane E. Brody. "From Fertility to Mood, Sunlight Found to Affect Human Biology." *The New York Times* (June 23, 1981): C1+; Jane E. Brody. "Surprising Health Impact Discovered for Light." *The New York Times* (November 13, 1984): C1–3; Linda Clark and Yvonne Martine. *Health, Youth, and Beauty through Color Breathing.* New York: Berkely, 1976; Richard Gerber. *Vibrational Medicine.* Santa Fe: Bear & Co., 1988; Manly P. Hall. *The Secret Teachings of All Ages.* 1928. Los Angeles: The Philosophic Research Society, 1977; Roland Hunt. *The Seven Keys to Color Healing.* San Francisco: Harper & Row, 1971; *Individual Reference File of Extracts from the Edgar Cayce Readings.* Virginia Beach, VA: Edgar Cayce Foundation, 1976; C. W. Leadbeater. *The Science of the Sacraments.* 1920. Madras, India: The Theosophical Publishing House, 1980; S. G. J. Ouseley. *The Science of the Aura.* 1949. Romford, Essex: L. N. Fowler & Co. Ltd., 1982; John N. Ott. *Health and Light.* New York: Pocket Books, 1983; S. Andrew Stanway. *Alternative Medicines: A Guide to Natural Therapies.* Rev. ed. Harmondsworth, England: Penguin Books, 1986.

Committee for the Scientific Investigation of Claims of the Paranormal (CSICOP)

Organization devoted to debunking all claims of the paranormal. CSICOP is the champion of skeptics and the scourge of believers. Some observers feel the organization goes to excessive lengths to discredit the paranormal. CSICOP has been described by critics as not a scientific group, but an advocacy group with a strong and hidden religious agenda.

CSICOP, based in Buffalo, New York, began as an offshoot of the American Humanist Association. The impetus was a manifesto against astrology, published in the September-October 1975 issue of the *Humanist* and signed by 182 scientists, including eighteen Nobel prize winners. The manifesto, "Objections to Astrology," was the idea of the editor of the *Humanist* at the time, Paul Kurtz, professor of philosophy at the State University of New York in Buffalo.

The manifesto protested what they alleged was growing newspaper exploitation of the public's interest in astrology, and asserted that the public did not realize the distinction between astrology and astronomy. The manifesto was published in conjunction with an article attacking Michel Gauquelin, a French researcher who set out to discredit astrology, but whose statistics instead supported some astrological phenomena, most notably the Mars Effect. According to the Mars Effect, physicians and sports champions tend to be born within two hours of the rise and culmination of Mars, Jupiter, and Saturn. See **Astrology.** Gauquelin threatened legal action over the article, and the entire issue received national publicity. Kurtz and several others founded CSICOP, first informally, and then formally in the spring of 1976, when it incorporated separately from the American Humanist Association.

Dennis Rawlins, a cofounder who was skeptical of the occult, later began to question the integrity of the debunkers. Writing in *Fate* magazine, Rawlins said he observed "underhanded" efforts to try to discredit Gauquelin. CSICOP members could not disprove Gauquelin with his own data; instead, they reconfirmed his findings. They then attempted to arrange new data that would disprove his Mars Effect hypothesis, Rawlins said. Rawlins subsequently left CSICOP.

CSICOP's stated objectives are "to establish a network of people interested in examining claims of the paranormal; to prepare bibliographies of published materials that carefully examine such claims; to encourage and commission research by objective and impartial inquirers in areas where it is needed; to convene conferences and meetings; to publish articles, monographs, and books that examine claims of the paranormal; to not reject on *a priori* grounds, antecedent to inquiry, any or all of such claims, but rather to examine them openly, completely, objectively, and carefully."

CSICOP's journal, originally named *The Zetetic* and renamed *The Skeptical Inquirer* after three issues, pursues scientific concerns about the perceived public credulity about the paranormal. The first two issues of *The Zetetic* (the name derives from an ancient Greek school of skeptical inquiry) were edited by Dr.

Marcello Truzzi, sociologist at Eastern Michigan University, Ypsilanti. Truzzi left after two issues and founded his own organization, which continues to publish *The Zetetic Scholar,* an independent skeptical inquiry journal.

CSICOP has successfully debunked numerous paranormal claims. The organization views itself as unbiased, but tends to take a hostile attitude toward anything paranormal, which supposedly is a danger to society. This stridency alienates many moderate skeptics.

One of the celebrated members of CSICOP is James Randi, known as the Amazing Randi, a stage magician who debunks the paranormal. Randi attempted to discredit Uri Geller, renowned for his psychokinetic metal bending, by duplicating Geller's feats through sleight of hand. See **Uri Geller.** He has exposed as frauds a number of evangelical faith healers, psychic dentists, and healers who used a variety of stage magic tricks to appear to be gifted with clairvoyance and divine healing.

In the summer of 1988, *Nature,* a prestigious British journal that had surprised scientists by publishing an article in support of homeopathy, sent Randi to investigate the French lab where the research for the article had been done. Randi's team failed to duplicate the research results, touching off a controversy. Jacques Benveniste, a French government scientist whose work was the first to yield scientific evidence in support of homeopathy, claimed Randi's team was not thorough and ignored corroborating evidence. Furthermore, Randi was said to have distracted the French researchers with sleight-of-hand spoon-bending tricks. Randi countered the stage tricks were done during breaks for entertainment and to diffuse tension. *Nature* published another article retracting the first article.

Sources: "CSICOP Defined." Parapsychology Review 19, no. 1 (January/February

1988): 5; Michel Gauquelin. *Birth-Times.* New York: Hill and Wang, 1983; Richard L. Hudson. "Nature Debunks Piece It Just Published That Supported Homeopaths' Claims." *The Wall Street Journal* (July 27, 1988): 30; James Randi. *The Faith Healers.* Buffalo, NY: Prometheus Books, 1987; Dennis Rawlins. "sTARBABY." *Fate* 34, no. 10, issue 379 (October 1981): 67–98; Leslie A. Shepard, ed. *Encyclopedia of Occultism and Parapsychology.* 2d ed. Detroit: Gale Research Co., 1984.

Cone of power

In modern Witchcraft a force field of psychic energy raised by a coven of Witches for magic purposes. The Witches join hands and begin dancing in a ring and chanting to raise the power, which is visualized as a cone, the base of which comprises the circle, and the apex of which either extends into infinity or is pictured as a person or symbolic image. When the energy peaks in intensity, the group releases it toward accomplishment of a goal, such as a spell or healing.

Cones of power also are raised through cord magic. The Witches sit inside a magic circle and hold ends of overlapping or interwoven cords. As the Witches chant, either aloud or silently, knots are tied in the cords. Power is released when the knots are untied.

The energy projected by the cone of power is similar to that raised in a group prayer meeting. Witches who have developed their psychic abilities can sometimes see the cone of power as a luminous, pulsating cloud flooded with changing colors, or as a silvery-blue light.

In 1940 many covens of Witches gathered in the New Forest in England to raise a cone of power to prevent Hitler from invading the country. The energy was directed against the men in the German High Command, either to convince them the invasion would not be successful, or to confuse their minds so that the plans never reached fruition. The ritual was performed on Lammas Day (also called Lughnasadh), August 1, a Pagan agrarian holiday that is an important sabbat in Witchcraft. Thirty-one years later, in 1971, Witches in California came together on Lammas Day to raise a cone of power directed at ending the war in Vietnam. See **Witchcraft.**

Sources: Margot Adler. *Drawing Down the Moon.* Rev. ed. Boston: Beacon Press, 1986; Patricia Crowther. *Witch Blood!* New York: House of Collectibles, 1974; Stewart Farrar. *What Witches Do: A Modern Coven Revealed.* Rev. ed. Custer, WA: Phoenix Publishing, 1983; Gerald B. Gardner. *Witchcraft Today.* New York: Magickal Childe, 1982; Starhawk. *The Spiral Dance.* San Francisco: Harper & Row, 1979; Doreen Valiente. *An ABC of Witchcraft Past and Present.* Custer, WA: Phoenix Publishing, 1973; Doreeen Valiente. *Witchcraft for Tomorrow.* Custer, WA: Phoenix Publishing, 1978.

Consciousness

See **Altered states of consciousness; Kundalini; Meditation; Mystical experiences; Mysticism; Psi.**

Contemplation

See **Prayer; Mystical experiences.**

Control

In mediumship a spirit or entity that acts as the primary intermediary between the medium and other discarnates who wish to communicate to the living through the medium. The control literally controls which entities will communicate, and when, how, and in what order. A control usually stays with a medium permanently.

A control manifests during a trance or dissociated state of consciousness, such as during automatic writing. The medium may not be aware of the control until told by a sitter who has witnessed the spirit's manifestation. In 1924 Arthur Ford was in trance when a spirit came through and announced, "Tell Ford that I am to be his control and that I go by the name of Fletcher." Fletcher later communicated that he was able to work well with Ford because he had the right pitch, or vibration, for maintaining contact. See **Ford, Arthur Augustus.**

Gladys Osborne Leonard's control was Feda, an Indian girl who died around 1800. Feda helped Leonard become a professional medium. Leonard could send Feda anywhere to retrieve information. Through her Leonard could describe locations she had never before seen, and recite information from pages in books in distant rooms. See **Book test; Leonard, Gladys Osborne.**

There is evidence that controls may be secondary personalities of a medium. Similarities exist between certain mediums and their controls. The controls of Leonora Piper, celebrated American mental medium, were extensively studied by Eleanor Sidgwick of the Society for Psychical Research, London. Although the controls claimed to be autonomous, discarnate beings, Sidgwick was of the opinion that they were probably extensions of Piper or fabrications. Their knowledge of various subjects matched Piper's own knowledge. The controls said they possessed subtle bodies, and that in order to communicate through the medium, they had to "enter the light," a sort of energy or power. Piper vacated her body but remained attached via the astral cord, while the controls occupied her form and operated it. Occasionally, Piper recalled being in the spirit state and seeing spirits of the dead there. If confronted with mistakes, the spirits seldom owned up to them, but explained them away by saying that entering the light created confusion, or that they could not manipulate Piper's body in ways unaccustomed to her.

Eileen J. Garrett, another famous medium, allowed herself to be extensively tested by psychiatrists, including Ira Progoff. Progoff concluded that Garrett's spirit guides came from her own personality, and that two of them, Tehotah, a symbol of creation, and Rama, a symbol of the life force, were Jungian archetypes. See **Garrett, Eileen J.; Mediumship.** Contrast with **Channeling.**

Sources: Arthur Ford in collaboration with Marguerite Harmon Bro. *Nothing So Strange: The Autobiography of Arthur Ford.* New York: Harper & Brothers, 1968; Alan Gauld. *Mediumship and Survival.* London: William Heinemann Ltd., 1982; Ivor Grattan-Guinness. *Psychical Research: A Guide to Its History, Principles and Practices.* Wellingborough, Northamptonshire, England: The Aquarian Press, 1982; Ruth Montgomery. *A Search for the Truth.* New York: Bantam Books, 1968.

Cook, Florence (1856–1904)

British medium who became famous for spirit materializations, but was exposed as a fraud. She began giving seances as a teenager, at a time when mediumship was sweeping like wildfire through England. She said she had first realized her psychic gifts as a child, when she heard angelic voices.

Cook's control spirit was Katie King, who claimed to be the daughter of a buccaneer. King, when materialized, bore a suspiciously strong resemblance to Cook. Cook gained widespread fame for materializing King with lights on at a time when virtually all seances were conducted in the dark. Her seances gradually became more and more theatrical, and the materializations more dramatic, from hands to faces to the entire form.

In her seances Cook retired behind a curtain or was shut up in a cabinet, and was tied to a chair with a rope, the knots of which were sealed with wax. The sitters prepared themselves by singing Spiritualism songs. After a few minutes, King, pale and white with fixed eyes, emerged from behind the curtain or the back of the cabinet. Meanwhile, Cook moaned and sobbed out of sight. Katie would not speak, but only smiled and nodded. After the sitters had been awed and entertained, the spirit disappeared behind the curtain or back of the cabinet. The sitters, following Cook's instructions, waited and then looked for Cook, whom they always found still clothed and tied, and profoundly exhausted from the experience.

Cook attracted the attention of Spiritualist investigators, including the eminent British scientist William Crookes. Investigators were amazed at King's flesh-like appearance; more than one concluded the "spirit" was Cook herself. She was caught at least twice in fraud. Once, a sitter grabbed a "spirit hand" that was sprinkling him with water, and found he had grabbed Cook, who was seated at the seance table. The medium protested that she was only reaching to retrieve a flower the spirits had taken from her dress. In 1873 a sitter grabbed King first by the hand and then the waist. The spirit struggled and was pulled away by two of Cook's friends. The lights went out. The sitters waited five minutes, then opened the cabinet and found Cook dressed and tied. Nevertheless, the sitter was convinced he had touched a living person, probably Cook.

On another occasion, in 1880, Sir George Sitwell noticed that King's spirit robes covered corset stays, an unusual requirement for a spirit. He seized her. The curtain was pulled aside to reveal Cook's chair empty and the ropes slipped.

Crookes subjected Cook to numerous tests. He photographed King and walked arm in arm with the spirit, convinced of her validity. For the photographs, taken in 1874, Cook lay down on a sofa behind a curtain and wrapped a shawl around her head. Katie appeared in front of the curtain. Crookes looked behind the curtain to see that a female form still lay on the sofa, but never lifted the shawl to verify that the form was that of Cook. In another experiment he attached Cook to a galvanometer, which passed a mild electrical current through her. Crookes reasoned that the slightest movement on Cook's part would register on the meter. Katie appeared though the meter's needle never moved.

Crookes and other supporters of Cook were undaunted by exposures of her fraud, claiming she was somnambulistic and never intended deliberately to deceive sitters. See **Mediumship; Materialization.**

Sources: Alfred Douglas. *Extrasensory Powers: A Century of Psychical Research.* London: Victor Gollancz Ltd., 1976; Alan Gauld. *Mediumship and Survival.* London: William Heinemann Ltd., 1982; Alan Gauld. *The Founders of Psychical Research.* London: Routledge & Kegan Paul, 1968; Trevor H. Hall. *The Spiritualists.* London: Gerald Duckworth & Co. Ltd., 1962; R. G. Medhurst and K. M. Goldney. "William Crookes and the Physical Phenomena of Mediumship." *Proceedings of the Society for Psychical Research* 54, part 195 (March 1964): 25–156; Janet Oppenheim. *The Other World: Spiritualism and Psychical Research in England, 1850–1914.* Cambridge: Cambridge University Press, 1985.

Cooke, Grace (1892–1979)

Popular British Spiritualist who founded the White Eagle Lodge, a Spiritualist organization, and wrote numerous books on spiritual growth and healing with the help of her spirit guide, White Eagle, who had incarnated as a Native American chief.

Cooke was born in London on June 9, 1892. As a child she had her first psychic vision of White Eagle and other Native American spirits one night as they appeared in a circle around her bed. The visions came just before she fell asleep, probably as she drifted into the hypnagogic state. Most of the natives wore bright colors, but the tallest, a stately, elder chief, was dressed in white. In the dream state, the chief took her to the astral plane to a place of great beauty, where she saw elemental spirits. He revealed himself as White Eagle, one of the Great White Brotherhood, the Brotherhood of the Cross of Light within the Circle of Light. He explained the spiritual work he and Cooke were to accomplish together during Cooke's life.

Cooke became a Spiritualist medium in 1913. While popular attention was focused on communicating with the dead, Cooke preferred to emphasize spiritual development and esoteric teachings, which she felt were desperately needed in the world.

Her first church was a small one in Middlesex, but she eventually left it because of the congregation's preoccupation with proof of survival.

In 1936 White Eagle and other spirits in the Great White Brotherhood instructed Cooke to form an organization for those people ready to practice brotherhood among men and be channels of light, or light-bearers. Cooke established the White Eagle Brotherhood at Burstow Manor in Surrey, later moving headquarters to Pembroke Hall in Kensington, London. The hall was destroyed by bombs in World War II, and the Brotherhood moved to new premises in Kensington, and to Edinburgh, Scotland. In 1945 the White Eagle Lodge was further established at the present headquarters at New Lands in Liss, Hampshire. The organization has been administered by a trust since 1953. Throughout her ministry Cooke was aided by her husband, Ivan, and their two daughters. The White Eagle Lodge grew to an international or-

(Photo by Leon Isaacs. Courtesy The White Eagle Lodge.)

Grace Cooke

ganization, including a publishing trust of spiritual books and tapes.

Cooke was a teacher of meditation, and published two books on the subject, *Meditation* (1955) and *The Jewel in the Lotus* (1973). In her later years, she experienced vivid reincarnational memories of previous lives as a Mayan and Egyptian priestess, both under the tutelage of White Eagle. Using a meditational technique learned from an Eastern adept, Cooke would rise through her crown chakra and read the Akashic Records. The stories of these two past lives are recorded in Cooke's book *The Illumined Ones*.

Cooke said the Mayan civilization in which she lived as Minesta flourished at least ten thousand years ago in the foothills of the Andes, an advanced culture established by an extraterrestrial race by way of Atlantis. Though archaeologists date the earliest Mayans to about A.D. 350 in Central America, Cooke was confident that archaeological remains would be found in South America to confirm her visions. In 1965 some remains were found in Peru that indicated a Mesoamerican influence, or vice versa.

As a Mayan Cooke was guided in her spiritual development by Hah-Wah-

Tah, an incarnation of White Eagle. She was initiated into the Plumed Serpent, the Brotherhood of the White Magic, the circle of adepts. She married her brother, To-waan.

In the afterlife White Eagle as Hah-Wah-Tah continued to be Cooke's spiritual guide, and eventually informed her she would reincarnate in Egypt. She was born as Ra-min-ati, guided by the high priest, Is-Ra, or White Eagle. She followed a spiritual path, was initiated into the mysteries of Osiris, and, together with her husband, Ra-hotep, was crowned pharaoh of the Two-Lands.

Cooke believed White Eagle was the legendary Hiawatha. This was never confirmed by White Eagle, who told her only that his most recent incarnation had been as White Eagle, Mohawk chief of the League of Six Nations of the Iroquois. Cooke was struck by the resemblance between renderings of Hiawatha and her visions of White Eagle.

In her work Cooke emphasized the discovery of deep, spiritual truths; the spreading of and living by the light of love; and healing. She died on September 3, 1979, in Liss, Hampshire, at the age of eighty-seven. See **White Eagle Lodge**.

Sources: Grace Cooke. *The Illumined Ones.* New Lands, England: White Eagle Publishing Trust, 1966; Grace Cooke. *Sun Men of the Americas.* New Lands, England: White Eagle Publishing Trust, 1975; Ingrid Lind. *The White Eagle Inheritance.* London: Turnstone Press, 1984; *The Story of the White Eagle Lodge.* New Lands, England: White Eagle Publishing Trust, 1986; The White Eagle Lodge.

Crandon, Mina

See **American Society for Psychical Research (ASPR)**.

Creation spirituality

A movement to redefine and revitalize Christianity by restoring an element of sensual, playful, and creative mysticism that is accessible to all people, not merely an elite of ascetics. The predominant spokesperson for creation spirituality is Matthew Fox, a Dominican priest who in 1988 was silenced temporarily by the Vatican for his unorthodox views. Fox is founder of the Institute in Culture and Creation Spirituality (ICCS), an avant-garde master's degree program at Holy Names College in Oakland, California.

It is Fox's contention that Christianity is moribund and cannot survive into the third millennium in its present form. The original, cosmic mysticism of Christ has been suppressed by a patristic, moralistic, and anthropocentric framework that has wreaked severe psychic damage by alienating human beings from the cosmos, the planet, and each other. This alienation has manifested in misogyny; child and sexual abuse; drug, alcohol, and entertainment addiction; materialism; and perhaps most important of all, the matricide of Mother Earth.

Creation spirituality celebrates the blessings of God's creation and not the original sin doctrine of the church. It holds that everyone is a mystic, but humanity has lost touch with this transformative power due to the Newtonian-Cartesian mechanistic, dualistic thought of the Enlightenment. According to Fox creation spirituality is the oldest tradition in the Bible, espoused by the prophets and by Jesus. It was at the center of the teachings of the Greek church fathers of the fourth and fifth centuries, and of various medieval mystics, most notably Meister Eckhart, Hildegard of Bingen, Julian of Norwich, Francis of Assisi, and Mechtild of Magneburg. Creation spirituality also is at the core of mystical traditions both East and West.

Fox's philosophy began to take shape in the 1960s, when he went to Paris to earn a doctorate in spirituality at the Institut Catholique. There he studied under Father M. D. Chenu, who acquainted him with creation spirituality and with the Liberation spirituality developing in Latin America. Upon his return to the United States, Fox taught at Aquinas Institute and Barat College. At the latter, a women's college, his own feminism was born. In 1977 he founded the ICCS at Mundelein College in Chicago, and in 1983 moved the program to Oakland. Fox's numerous papers, articles, and books have addressed creation spirituality and the question of the relationship between mysticism and social justice. His 1983 book, *Original Blessing: A Primer in Creation Spirituality*, brought him to public attention.

Creation spirituality advocates the rebirth of an earthy, ecstatic mysticism that reveres the feminine principle, sexuality, passion, play, prophecy, creativity, and the divine child within, all of which is diametric to the orthodox Christian mystical tradition of mortification of the senses. Creation spirituality embraces panentheism, which holds that God is in everything and everything is in God. (Panentheism is often confused with pantheism, deemed a heresy by the church, which holds that God is everything and everything is God.) It advocates a return of body consciousness in worship, that is, movement and dance; if worship is not playful, it loses its transformative power.

In *The Coming of the Cosmic Christ* (1988), Fox articulates his concept of a Cosmic Christ, as opposed to a historical Jesus, who embodies the aforementioned qualities. The appropriate symbol of the Cosmic Christ is Jesus as Mother Earth, who is crucified yet risen daily. Fox says that in order for Christianity to survive, the church must turn from its preoccupation with the historical Jesus and begin a quest for the Cosmic Christ. However, it cannot be undertaken without a living cosmology that embraces a "holy trinity of science (knowledge of creation), mysticism (experiential union with creation and its unnameable mysteries), and art

(expression of our awe at creation)," Fox says. Such a cosmology—which also lies at the heart of the planetary consciousness movement—must teach that the universe is not a machine, but an awesome mystery.

Fox says that Western religion has not nourished people in the mystical tradition, but has piled on one moral law after another. The primary influence in this development of the church was St. Augustine of Hippo, a fourth-century theologian and one of the most important church fathers, whose views were dualistic and patristic, and who was preoccupied with human guilt and personal salvation. Fox observes that in a world of interdependence of all things, there can be no such thing as personal salvation.

The Cosmic Christ is an archetype, and must be reincarnated repeatedly in the mind and imagination before it takes hold as a force. When it does a paradigm shift will occur in Christianity. Creativity will become the most important moral virtue; there will be a return of folk art as divine creativity is rediscovered within all people. Fox believes it also will bring an age of deep ecumenism.

Fox was brought to the attention of the Vatican in 1984 by the Seattle chapter of a conservative, ad hoc group, Catholics United for the Faith (CUFF). The CUFF chapter termed Fox a "danger" to the Catholic faith. Cardinal Joseph Ratzinger, prefect of the Sacred Congregation for the Doctrine of Faith—formerly the Holy Office of the Inquisition—ordered an investigation of Fox's writings and statements. Fox was supported by his Dominican superiors, who examined his work and found nothing heretical.

Ratzinger, however, found otherwise. In 1987 he termed Fox's ideas "dangerous and deviant," and said *Original Blessing* was a personal and subjective interpretation of Christian spirituality. In 1988 Ratzinger formally accused Fox of: (1) denying the existence of original sin and the doctrine of the church in its regard; (2) referring to God as "Mother" and "Child"; (3) hiring a self-described Witch, Starhawk, to teach at ICCS; (4) having liberal views on homosexuality; and (5) being a fervent feminist. Fox was requested to observe a year of silence commencing December 15, 1988.

Fox was never accorded the opportunity to face his Vatican inquisitors. He agreed to the silencing, believing it only served to call more attention to his work. In his formal response to the charges, Fox said that (1) he did not deny original sin, but objected to its importance and its use as a starting point in religion. God's creation should be celebrated as an original blessing. (2) God has been called "Mother" by Pope John Paul I and medieval mystics, and in the Scriptures, and referred to as child by medieval mystics. (3) In the 1960s the Second Vatican Council formally declared in its Declaration on Non-Christian Religions that it is "foreign to the mind of Christ to discriminate or harass persons because of their religion," and no exception was made of Wicca (Witchcraft). (4 and 5) The church's oppression of homosexuals and women is tantamount to fascism. "The Vatican's obsession with sex is a worldwide scandal which demonstrates a serious psychic imbalance," Fox said in an open letter to Ratzinger.

Fox has been called a "New Age priest" by the media, though that is not a label he chooses. He sees many flaws in New Age thought, some of which he terms "pseudo-mysticism." Practices that have become distorted, he says, are excessive preoccupation with states of consciousness, enlightenment, and past lives, without any attention paid to social responsibility and conscience. See **Eckhart, Johannes; Goddess; Hildegard of Bingen, St.; Julian of Norwich; Mysticism; Mysticism, Christian; Planetary consciousness.**

Sources: Matthew Fox. *Original Blessing: A Primer in Creation Spirituality.* Santa Fe, NM: Bear & Co., 1983; Matthew Fox. *The Coming of the Cosmic Christ.* San Francisco: Harper & Row, 1988; Matthew Fox. "Is the Catholic Church Today a Dysfunctional Family? A Pastoral Letter to Cardinal Ratzinger and the Whole Church." *Creation* (November/December 1988): 23–37; Jane Gross. "Vatican Silences 'New Age' Priest." *The New York Times* (October 21, 1988); Laura Hagar. "The Sounds of Silence." *New Age Journal* (March/April 1989): 52–56+; Sam Keen. "Original Blessing, Not Original Sin." *Psychology Today* (June 1989): 55–58; "Priest Barred from Public Speech or Writing for Liberal Teachings." *The New York Times* (October 19, 1988).

Creative visualization

The use of positive, affirming mental pictures to obtain goals. A vivid mental picture of a desired goal is held in the mind as though it already were accomplished. Creative visualization is widely employed in the creative arts, sports, business, alternative medicine, religious practices, psychotherapy, the mystical and occult arts, psychical research, and in personal self-improvement. Other terms for it are "positive thinking," "positive imaging," "dynamic imaging," "creative imaging," "imaging," and so on.

The power of thought, imagination, and will to effect changes in circumstance is ancient knowledge. See **Imagery.** Creative visualization is an aid in helping the individual marshal the resources necessary to accomplish what is desired. It also is believed to help establish a harmony that facilitates fortuitous synchronicities, that is, opportunities and "lucky breaks." See **Synchronicity.**

Creative visualization seems to be most effective when practiced in a relaxed or altered state of consciousness, such as in a daily prayer or meditation session. Some individuals call on a higher power, such as the Divine, the Higher Self, or a spirit guide or guardian angel to help realize the goal.

The concept of creative visualization has been popularized in the West through various writings, such as the many books by Norman Vincent Peale, a Methodist minister. Peale's initial book on the subject, *The Power of Positive Thinking* (1952), advises a combination of prayer, a faith in God, a positive frame of mind, and affirmations, words or phrases that trigger positive forces. For example, "I am beautiful and loved" and "I am successful" are affirmations. When repeated, written down, and contemplated, affirmations become part of consciousness.

Psycho-Cybernetics (1960), by plastic surgeon Maxwell Maltz, discusses the tremendous influence of the imagination upon self-image. Maltz observed that patients with poor self-image had no boost in self-esteem from plastic surgery, while those whose self-image was good or was improved experienced positive transformations after surgery.

In *Creative Visualization* (1979), author Shakti Gawain likens creative visualization to "magic" in the highest sense of the word. Positive energy attracts more positive energy. See also **Meditation; Prayer.**

Sources: Shakti Gawain. *Creative Visualization.* New York: Bantam Books, 1982; Vernon Howard. *The Mystic Path to Cosmic Power.* Reward ed. West Nyack, NY: Parker Publishing, 1973; Vernon Howard. *Psycho-Pictography: The New Way to Use the Miracle Power of Your Mind.* Reward ed. West Nyack, NY: Parker Publishing, 1973; Maxwell Maltz. *The Magic Power of Self-Image Psychology.* New York: Pocket Books, 1970; Maxwell Maltz. *Psycho-Cybernetics.* New York: Pocket Books, 1969; Edgar D. Mitchell. *Psychic Exploration: A Challenge for Science.* Edited by John White. New York: Paragon Books, 1974; Norman Vincent Peale. *Positive Imaging: The Powerful Way to Change Your Life.* FCL ed. Pawling, NY: Foundation for Christian Living, 1982; Norman Vincent Peale. *The Power of Positive Thinking.* New York: Prentice-Hall, 1952; Jane Roberts. *The Seth Material.* First published as *How to Develop Your ESP Power,* 1966. Englewood Cliffs, NJ: Prentice-Hall, 1970; D. Scott Rogo. *Psychic Breakthroughs Today.* Wellingborough, Northamptonshire, England: The Aquarian Press, 1987.

Creativity

See **Inspiration.**

Croiset, Gerard (1909–80)

Dutch clairvoyant with healing powers, who gained international fame for his ability to find missing persons, animals, and objects.

Croiset was born March 10, 1909, in Enschede, the Netherlands, to Jewish parents in the theater profession. His clairvoyance manifested by age six. He suffered an unhappy childhood. He was neglected by his parents, who divorced when he was eight, and was neglected or abused in a series of orphanages and foster homes. He was frequently punished for talking about his visions. At age thirteen he dropped out of school and drifted through a series of low-level, unskilled jobs.

In 1934 Croiset married Gerda ter Morsche, the uneducated daughter of a carpenter. The first of their four children, a son, was born in 1935. Croiset opened his own grocery store but was a poor business manager. The turning point in his life came in 1935, when a former customer introduced him to local Spiritualists, who helped him develop his psychic ability. He experienced visions in symbols, and he had to learn how to interpret them.

From 1937 to 1940, Croiset's psychic reputation in Enschede grew quickly. He worked as a psychometrist, finding people, objects, and animals. An ability to heal by touch also manifested, and he treated soldiers wounded in World War II.

The second turning point in Croiset's life occurred in December 1945, when he attended a lecture on parapsychology given in Enschede by Willem Tenhaeff of the University of Utrecht. Croiset was so inspired that he volunteered to be one of Tenhaeff's test subjects.

After several months of tests in Utrecht, Tenhaeff concluded that Croiset was one of the most remarkable psychics he had ever encountered; his ability remained fairly constant.

Tenhaeff became Croiset's mentor, introducing him to police work and bringing him to the international public eye. Croiset was tested by parapsychologists all over the world. He solved crimes in at least half a dozen countries, found lost documents for public officials, and helped scholars identify artifacts and historical manuscripts. His passion was finding missing children. He did many readings over the telephone, which he said helped keep confusing mental images to a minimum.

Croiset screened requests for his services by intuition. He said that a vibration would begin and make him feel filled inside. A serious problem would cause him to see many colors, which would begin to spin around him until they formed pictures, which appeared to shoot out at him like an image in a 3-D movie.

Croiset accepted no payment for his psychic readings, but accepted donations at his healing clinic, where he treated over one hundred patients a day. He knew instantly upon seeing a patient whether or not he could help the person, and how. He sometimes saw the conditions or diseases were psychic in origin and connected to experiences. Occasionally, he treated sick animals.

In 1953 the Parapsychology Institute was created at the University of Utrecht, and Tenhaeff was named director. In 1956 Croiset and his family moved from Enschede to Utrecht so that he could be near Tenhaeff.

One of Croiset's most significant contributions to parapsychology was to popularize the "chair test," first performed in the 1920s by Pascal Forthuny. In the test a distant meeting place and time were scheduled. The chairs at the site were numbered, and one chair was selected at random to be the test chair. From one hour to twenty-six days in advance, Croiset predicted who would sit in the chair. A tape of his prediction would be played at the meeting, and the information verified by the person occupying the chair. The first chair test took place in 1947 in Amsterdam, before a meeting of the Dutch Society for Psychical Research.

Croiset died on July 20, 1980. His healing clinic continued under the direction of his son. See **Psychic criminology**.

Sources: Jack Harrison Pollack. *Croiset the Clairvoyant.* Garden City, NY: Doubleday, 1964; W. H. C. Tenhaeff. *Telepathy and Clairvoyance.* Springfield, IL: Charles C. Thomas, 1972; Benjamin B. Wolman, ed. *Handbook of Parapsychology.* New York: Van Nostrand Reinhold, 1977.

Crookes, William

See **Cook, Florence; Parapsychology; Society for Psychical Research (SPR)**.

Crop circles

Large circles and other patterns that appear inexplicably in the middle of grain fields when the crop is several feet high. Most crop circles have been found in Southeast England since the early 1980s. But other countries—including the United States—have reported them as well. Some have been exposed as hoaxes but others remain unexplained.

Crop circles measure from as small as ten feet in diameter to as large as three hundred feet. They appear overnight, sometimes preceded by amber lights reportedly hovering above the Earth. The grain inside the circles usually has been found lying horizontally, seemingly knocked down or crushed by some tremendous force, yet unbroken and still growing. No tracks leading up to them have been found, giving additional credence to theories suggesting some external force from above was responsible.

In the years between 1980 and 1987, between 100 and 120 crop circles were found in England. Over the following years the numbers increased dramatically: 112 in 1988; 305 in 1989; and 400 in 1990.

With the increase in numbers of circles also came significant changes in their appearances. Where the phenomenon once was limited to circles of varying sizes, new formations began taking shape that ranged from large circles surrounded by smaller ones to elaborate patterns that resembled some form of ancient hieroglyphs, featuring rectangles, rings, spurs, and pathways linking circles to one another.

Theories as to the origins and causes of these crop circles are as multiple as the shapes themselves. Some theories blame natural forces, such as violent weather patterns or the effects of irrigation. Others claim the shapes were left by UFOs, because of the appearances of anomalous lights prior to some circle formations. Still other theories suggest the circles are communications from other intelligent life forces, perhaps a planetary intelligence of Earth itself.

In 1988, before the sudden proliferation and variation of crop circles, Terrence Meaden (a British physicist with the Tornado Storm Research Organization, who had studied some fifty crop circles) dismissed them as the result of rare meteorological events, which he called stationary whirlwinds, or sudden vortices of wind. Meaden said these bursts of air sink to the ground and flatten crops in a spiral, but because they last only a few seconds cause relatively minor damage.

Similar circles began appearing in grain fields in the United States outside of Kansas City, Missouri, in September 1990. US scientists also were quick to point to freak weather patterns, stating that vortices could be caused by temperature imbalances in the upper and lower portions of the atmosphere.

Other researchers have argued that the crop circles were due to excess circular irrigation, which alters the salts and silts in the soil, leaving anything growing vulnerable to powerful winds.

While these theories of natural causes might explain the singular circle formations, they fall far short of answering questions about those shapes that resemble pictograms.

In a 1990 challenge to Meaden's "whirlwinds," British psychical researcher Ralph Noyes wrote in a paper presented at a conference in Bournemouth, England, to the Society for Psychical Research: "The impression can no longer be resisted that a factor is at work that exhibits a capacity for invention and design, in short, some degree of intelligence."

That view was also shared by another British researcher and electrical engineer, Colin Andrews. He maintained that the circles seem to be elaborate pictograms created by some sort of intelligent life force as an attempt to communicate with humankind.

Charles D'Orban of London University's School of Oriental and African studies went one step further, likening the pictorial shapes in one crop field in Wiltshire, England, to ancient Sumerian text. D'Orban deciphered the symbols in the field to be a warning to increase the number of water wells—a suggestion that drought was on the way. His finding, in July 1990, was made during one of the country's hottest and driest spells in recent years.

Another British researcher, John Haddington, described dramatic 1990 configurations as a Buddhist ritual tool known as *vajra,* a representation of the unbreakable absolute in the universe. He concluded that something of a divine nature may have a message to convey to humans about their existence.

During the proliferation of crop circles during the summer of 1990 in England, researchers and television crews staked out several locations, hoping to answer the mystery behind the formations. During one such vigil, crews armed with special infrared cameras and recording devices failed to pick up any photographic evidence or record any sounds, even through noises could be heard above them near one field, where a spiral-shaped formation was discovered the next morning.

Sources: Richard Beaumont. "More Circular Evidence." *Kindred Spirit* 1, no. 8: 25–28; "Bumper Crop of Cropfield Circles." *Strange Magazine* no. 6 (1990): 33; John Haddington. "The Year of the VAJRA." *Global Link Up* issue 44 (Autumn 1990): 4–9; "Hoaxes and Phenomena." *Global Link Up* issue 44 (Autumn 1990): 10–11; Pat Delgado and Colin Andrews. *Crop Circles, The Latest Evidence.* London: Bloomsbury Publishing, 1990; Donna McGuire and Eric Adler. "More Puzzling Circles Found in Fields." *The Kansas City Star* (September 21, 1990): A1+; Ralph Noyes. "Crop Circles: Further Indications of a Paranormal Factor." Paper presented to Conference of the Society for Psychical Research, Bournemouth, England, July 1990; Michael Poynder. "Cairns and Crop Circles." *Kindred Spirit* 2, no. 1: 24–26; Michael T. Shoemaker. "Measuring the Circles." *Strange Magazine* no. 6 (1990): 34–35+; Robert Smith. "The Crop Circle Mystery." *Venture Inward* 7, no. 1 (January/February 1990): 12–16.

Cross correspondence

A cross correspondence occurs when the information communicated through one medium corresponds with information communicated through another, independent medium. There is no normal explanation for the occurrence. Some psychical researchers believe cross correspondences provide strong evidence in support of life after death. Others say they are produced by the mediums in an unconscious telepathic network.

Psychical researchers have defined three types of cross correspondences: simple, complex, and ideal. In simple cross correspondences, two or more mediums produce the same word, words, or phrases, or similar phrases that are clearly interconnected. In complex cross correspondences, topics are mentioned only indirectly. Ideal cross correspondences involve messages that are incomplete until put together.

The Society for Psychical Research (SPR) in England studied cross correspondences intently between 1901 and 1932. The principal communicators appeared to be three of the founders of the SPR, all of whom had been interested in the question of survival after death: Edmund Gurney, who died in 1888, Henry Sidgwick, who died in 1900, and Frederic W. H. Myers, who died in 1901. Of the three men, Myers was most interested in proving survival after death, and had stated while living that he would attempt to communicate posthumously. Sidgwick had been open to the possibility of survival, while Gurney had been skeptical. These three were joined by other deceased communicators.

Leonora Piper, a prominent American medium, claimed to establish contact with the spirits of the three men through automatic writing. Her impressive results generated much publicity, and inspired about twelve other women to try the same thing, all independently. One of the principals was Margaret Verrall of Cambridge, England, who shared Myers's interest in classicism. After some time of automatic writing, the scripts of which were collated and examined by members of the SPR, the cross correspondences were noticed. For example, "Myers" would give Verrall one part of a message, and the rest to another automatist in India (Alice Fleming, the sister of Rudyard Kipling). Over a period of years, other mediums had similar results. Most of the communications of "Myers" contained references to classical literature.

SPR member Frank Podmore believed that cross correspondences were the result of telepathic communication among the living. He suggested that one automatist telepathically broadcast material, which was picked up by other automatists. Psychical researchers have not found any clear evidence for that sort of phenomena, however. Also, the idea for cross correspondences did not originate with anyone living. The plan seems to have been devised on the "other side" by "Myers." Myers, when living, knew full well that researchers would attempt to explain communications of entire messages through one medium in terms of telepathy and clairvoyance on the part of the medium. But if pieces of messages were disseminated with apparent deliberation, it would strengthen the case for survival.

Some of "Myers's" communications support that notion. In automatic writing through Piper, he purportedly stated, "I am trying with all forces . . . together to prove that I am Myers." And in automatic writing through Fleming: "Oh, I am feeble with eagerness—how can I best be identified?"

The principal investigators of the SPR concluded that the cross correspondences were the products of the deceased SPR leaders and others. Though the style and content of their messages conformed with their living personalities, they were not conclusive proof of survival after death.

One of the last mediums to participate in the SPR's research was Gladys Osborne Leonard. In subsequent years cross correspondences have appeared in other psychical research experiments, but have not been the subject of great attention. See **Automatisms.**

Sources: Richard Cavendish, ed. *The Encyclopedia of the Unexplained.* New York: McGraw-Hill, 1974; Alfred Douglas. *Extrasensory Powers: A Century of Psychical Research.* London: Victor Gollancz Ltd., 1976; Alan Gauld. *Mediumship and Survival.* London: William Heinemann Ltd., 1982; Ivor Grattan-Guinness. *Psychical Research: A Guide to Its History, Principles and Practices.* Wellingborough, Northamptonshire, England: The Aquarian Press, 1982; J. B. Rhine and Robert Brier, eds. *Parapsychology Today.* New York: The Citadel Press, 1968; H. F. Saltmarsh. *Evidence of Personal Survival from Cross Correspondences.* London: G. Bell & Sons, Ltd., 1938.

Crowley, Aleister (1875–1947)

English magician and occultist, self-described as the "Beast of the Apocalypse" and called by the media "The Wickedest Man in the World." Crowley, a man of no small ego, both enraged and fascinated others with his rites of sex magic and blood sacrifice. Despite his excesses some consider him one of the most brilliant magicians of modern times.

He was born Edward Alexander Crowley on October 12, 1875, in Leamington Spa, Warwickshire. His parents, members of a fundamentalist sect, the Plymouth Brethren, raised him in an atmosphere of repression and religious bigotry. He rebelled to such an extent that his mother christened him "the Beast" after the Antichrist.

Crowley was drawn to the occult at a young age and was fascinated by blood, torture, and sexual degradation. He studied at Trinity College at Cambridge but never earned a degree, instead devoting his time to writing poetry and studying occultism.

On November 18, 1898, he joined the London chapter of the Hermetic Order of the Golden Dawn (HOGD) and was christened "Frater Perdurabo" (another of several magical names he used was "the Master Therion"). He quickly advanced to the highest grade in the Order. Through yoga he recalled alleged past lives as Pope Alexander VI, renowned for his love of physical pleasures; Edward Kelly, the notorious magical assistant to John Dee, the astrologer of Queen Elizabeth I; Cagliostro; and Eliphas Levi, who died on the day Crowley was born. Crowley also believed he had been Ankh-f-n-Khonsu, an Egyptian priest of the Twenty-Sixth Dynasty.

After leaving Trinity he named himself Count Vladimir and pursued his occult activities full time in London. Stories of bizarre incidents circulated, perhaps fueled in part by Crowley's mesmerizing eyes and aura of supernatural power. Some individuals professed to see a ghostly light surrounding him, which he said was his astral spirit. His flat was said to be pervaded by an evil presence, and people who crossed him were said to suffer accidents.

Samuel Liddell MacGregor Mathers, one of the founders of the HOGD, taught Crowley the Sacred Magic of Abra-Melin the Mage from an old manuscript Mathers claimed to have translated. The manuscript supposedly was inhabited by a nonphysical intelligence that provided Crowley's source of magical power. Mathers and Crowley quarreled and reportedly attacked each other psychically with astral vampires and demons. Following his expulsion from the HOGD, Crowley traveled and delved into Eastern mysticism. He lived for a time at Boleskin Manor on the southern shore of Loch Ness in Scotland.

He had an enormous sexual appetite, and his animal vitality and raw behavior attracted an unending stream of willing women. In 1903 he married Rose Kelly, the first of two wives, who bore him one child. He had a steady string of mistresses, whom he called "Scarlet Women"—the most famous was Leah Hirsig, whom he called "the Ape of Thoth"—and sired illegitimate children. He was fond of giving his women "Serpent Kisses," using his sharpened teeth to draw blood. He tried unsuccessfully to beget a child by magic, the efforts of which he fictionalized in a novel, *Moonchild* (1929).

On March 18, 1904, Kelly received communications from the astral plane to contact the Egyptian god Horus. Crowley performed a ritual and contacted Horus's spirit messenger, Aiwass, whom Crowley took to be his "True Self." Over three days Kelly took dictation from Aiwass in trance. The result was *Liber Legis,* better known as *The Book of the Law,* one of Crowley's most important works. Central to it is the Law of Thelema: "Do what thou wilt shall be the whole of the law," which Crowley said means doing what one must and nothing else.

Aiwass also said that Crowley had been selected by the "Secret Chiefs," the master adepts, to be the prophet for the coming new Aeon of Horus, the third great age of humanity.

In 1909 Crowley began a homosexual relationship with the poet Victor Neuberg, who became his assistant in magic. By 1912 he was involved with the Ordo Templi Orientis occult order, and became its leader by 1922.

From 1915 to 1919, Crowley lived in the United States. In 1920, while driving through Italy, he had a vision of a hillside villa. He found the place on Sicily, took it over, and renamed it the Sacred Abbey of the Thelemic Mysteries. Envisioned as a magical colony, the villa served as the site for numerous sexual orgies and magical rites, many attended by his illegitimate children. The behavior led Benito Mussolini to expel Crowley from Italy in May 1923.

In 1929 Crowley married his second wife, Maria Ferrari de Miramar, in Leipzig, Germany.

Crowley's later years were plagued with poor health, drug addiction, and financial trouble. He earned a meager living by publishing his writings. Much of his nonfiction is rambling and muddled, but continues to have an audience. Besides *The Book of the Law,* his other most notable work is *Magick in Theory and Practice* (1929), considered by many occultists to be a superb work on ceremonial magic. He spelled "magic" as "magick" to distinguish true magic from stage magic.

In 1934, desperate for money, Crowley sued sculptress Nina Hammett for libel in her biography of him, *Laughing Torso* (1932), in which she stated that Crowley practiced black magic and indulged in human sacrifice. The testimony given at the trial so repulsed the judge and jury that the trial was stopped and the jury found in favor of Hammett.

In 1945 Crowley moved to a boarding house in Hastings, where he lived the last two years of his life, dissipated and bored. During these last years, he met Gerald B. Gardner, called the father of modern Witchcraft, and shared ritual material with him. Crowley died on December 1, 1947. He was cremated in Brighton and his ashes were sent to followers in the United States.

Crowley's other published books include *The Diary of a Drug Fiend* (1922); *The Stratagem,* a collection of fiction stories; *The Equinox of the Gods* (1937), which sets forth *The Book of the Law* as humankind's new religion; and *The Book of Thoth* (1944), his interpretation of the Tarot. Two volumes of his autobiography were published. See **Hermetic Order of the Golden Dawn; Magic.**

Sources: Richard Cavendish, ed. *The Encyclopedia of the Unexplained.* New York: McGraw-Hill, 1974; Rosemary Ellen Guiley. *The Encyclopedia of Witches and Witchcraft.* New York: Facts On File, 1989; Perrott Phillips, ed. *Out of This World.* London: Reader's Digest Assn., 1976; John Symonds and Kenneth Grant, eds. *The Confessions of Aleister Crowley, an Autobiography.* London: Routledge & Kegan Paul, 1979; Colin Wilson. *The Occult.* New York: Vintage Books, 1973.

Cryptomnesia

The unconscious memory of information learned through normal channels. Cryptomnesia is one possible explanation for memories of past lives and communications with the dead. Information that is consciously "forgotten" may be stored deep within the unconscious indefinitely. According to psychiatrist Carl G. Jung, this forgetting is not only normal but necessary. Otherwise, the mind would become unbearably cluttered. Hypnosis, an altered state of consciousness, automatic writing, or inspiration can stimulate recall of the buried information, which seems "new."

Psychical researchers consider the possibility of cryptomnesia when investigating cases of reincarnation, or a medium's communication with the dead. The possibility of cryptomnesia is strong if research shows that the information apparently obtained paranormally can be found in existing sources, and that the person may have had access to those sources; and that the information does not go beyond those sources.

The earliest case of cryptomnesia recorded in psychical research occurred in 1874, when the English medium William Stainton Moses purported to contact the spirits of two young brothers who had died in India. The deaths were verified by a check of records. Further research disclosed that six days prior to the seance,

The Times had run an obituary of the boys. The information given at the seance included all the information that was in the obituary, and nothing more.

The case for cryptomnesia is especially strong if the paranormal information contains the same errors as the existing sources. In 1977 a twenty-three-year-old woman named Jan was hypnotized on British television by a past-life regressionist. She recalled a life as Joan Waterhouse, a famous witch in Chelmsford, who was tried for witchcraft and set free in 1566. Jan gave the date as 1556. Experts discounted the regression as cryptomnesia, because the error in date was published in a Victorian reprint of a rare pamphlet on the trial. Only two copies of this reprint are in existence; one of them is on display at the British Museum. It is possible that Jan saw the pamphlet, though she did not recall doing so. She had only a grammar school education, yet gave accurate details of the trial and the major figures in it.

Cryptomnesia is also considered the explanation for some cases of recitative xenoglossy. This occurs in instances of past-life memories in which a person speaks a few words and phrases of foreign languages he or she has not learned. See Xenoglossy.

When cryptomnesia occurs the individual usually is not aware of it. Two mediums investigated by psychologist Ian Stevenson claimed not to have read the obituaries of people they contacted through their Ouija board. Yet Stevenson discovered that one of them was in the habit of working on crossword puzzles in the Daily Telegraph, which appeared on the same page as the obituaries. Stevenson concluded that the obituary information fell within range of the eye and was absorbed unconsciously.

It is difficult for researchers to eliminate the possibility of cryptomnesia in many afterlife and reincarnation cases, because no one knows the limits of how much the brain can store for how long. In one of the most famous cryptomnesia cases, information obtained by a girl at age twelve was dredged up years later as "contact with the dead." Under hypnosis the woman, identified only as "Miss C.," communicated with a Blanche Poynings, who said she had been a minor person in the court of Richard II. The period details provided were remarkably accurate. Asked what books she had read about Richard II, Miss C., using a Ouija under hypnosis, acknowledged that as a girl she had read the novel Countess Maud, by Emily Holt. The details in the novel corresponded to the material provided by Blanche Poynings, though Miss C. altered the portrayal of the Blanche personality.

In the 1960s Finnish psychiatrist Reima Kampman obtained similar results with secondary school students hypnotized to recall past lives. Kampman suggested to his subjects that they were back in past lives, then asked them (under hypnosis) for the original source of their memories. Some cited books they had seen or read as a small child.

Cryptomnesia is ruled out in cases where the information goes beyond accessible records to facts that can be verified only by other people or in personal diaries. It is also eliminated in cases where the individual is extremely unlikely to have had access to any sources, such as very young children who remember previous lives. The famous Bridey Murphy reincarnation case of 1952 is possible but unproven cryptomnesia, according to Stevenson, because the enormous knowledge of period detail went far beyond what can be explained in normal circumstances. See Past-life recall.

Sources: Alan Gauld. Mediumship and Survival. London: William Heinemann Ltd., 1982; Carl G. Jung, ed. Man and His Symbols. 1964. New York: Anchor Press/Doubleday, 1988; Ian Stevenson. "Cryptomnesia and Parapsychology." The Journal of the Society for Psychical Research 52, no. 793 (February 1983): 1–30; Ian Wilson. *All in the Mind*. Garden City, NY: Doubleday, 1982; Benjamin B. Wolman, ed. *Handbook of Parapsychology*. New York: Van Nostrand Reinhold, 1977.

Crystals

Clear and colored quartz, as well as semi-precious and precious stones—all generally referred to in modern usage as "crystals"—have, more than any concept or object, become synonymous with the New Age. From the 1980s crystals were widely used as amulets and talismans with reputed healing, psychic, or magical properties. There is no scientific evidence that crystals have paranormal properties, but adherents believe that the stones emit vibrations undetectable by ordinary means.

The modern popularity of crystals is a new twist on ancient and universal lore. Early civilizations valued crystals for their alleged protective properties against disease, bad luck, evil, and sorcery, and for their physical and mental healing properties. Ancient peoples most commonly wore crystals as amulets in jewelry and breastplates. This practice continued throughout the Middle Ages, when European nobility wore them to ward off the plague. Crystals also were ground into a powdered form and administered as medicines for a variety of disorders.

As in ancient times, crystals are worn in pendants, rings, and other jewelry, carried in small pouches, placed about

Large chunks of quartz are believed to energize rooms.

Variety of crystals and semiprecious stones fashioned into objects for decoration or crystalwork

(Photo by Bonnie Sue)

Left: Herkimer diamonds. Right: Crystal jewelry.

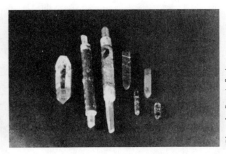

Crystal wands

(Photo by Bonnie Sue)

homes and offices, and crushed or soaked in water for gem elixirs. They are said to alleviate stress, stimulate creativity, enhance dreams, and awaken the psychic senses and higher consciousness. In some forms of healing therapy, they are laid in patterns on the body's chakra points and energy meridians. They also are used in divination, in which they are cast in lots or selected from piles, and in meditation. They are used in alternative medical treatment of animals as well as humans. Crystals are often fashioned in wands and other magical tools.

Some crystal enthusiasts believe they can "program" certain stones, such as clear quartz, for certain functions. The stones are first "cleared" by immersing them in salt, exposing them to sunlight, or some other technique, and then they are "programmed" through meditation or concentration. Stones that are "double terminated," or have points on both ends, are said to have greater powers.

Individuals who claim to channel entities say the purpose of the crystal renaissance is to teach spiritual awareness and help heal. See **Amulet; Colors; Talismans.**

Sources: Randall N. Baer and Vicki Vittitow Baer. *The Crystal Connection: A Guidebook for Personal and Planetary Ascension.* San Francisco: Harper & Row, 1987; E. A. Wallis Budge. *Amulets and Superstitions.* 1930. New York: Dover Publications, 1978; Edmund Harold. *Focus on Crystals.* New York: Ballantine Books, 1986; Ursula Markham. *Fortune-Telling by Crystals and Semiprecious Stones.* Wellingborough, Northamptonshire, England: The Aquarian Press, 1987; Jake Page. "Supreme Quartz." *Omni* (October 1987): 95–100; Katrina Raphaell. *Crystal Enlightenment.* New York: Aurora Press, 1985; Uma Silbey. *The Complete Crystal Guidebook.* New York: Bantam Books, 1987.

Cults

See **Alternative religious movements.**

Culture hero

See **Mythology.**

Curse

See **Psychic attack.**

D

Dalai Lama

The religious and temporal leader of Tibet. *Dalai Lama* means "ocean of wisdom." Tibetans usually refer to His Holiness as Yeshe Norbu, "the Wish-fulfilling Gem," or Kundun, "the Presence." According to Tibetan belief, the Dalai Lama is an emanation of Chenresi, the Buddha of Compassion, the national deity of Tibet who vows to help and protect all living things. Chenresi is often depicted as a herdsman with four arms, or as a being with eleven heads, one thousand arms, and an eye in the palm of his hand.

The Dalai Lamaship is not a hereditary succession, but a succession of reincarnations. Prior to his death, the Dalai Lama selects the circumstances of his next incarnation. He may give clues as to where he may be found, or the clues may manifest after his death. Oracles, high lamas, and astrologers are consulted, and the search goes out for an infant born near the time of the Dalai Lama's death who is his reincarnation. Candidates, who include peasant children, are tested for past-life recall by lamas and must identify personal objects owned by the Dalai Lama. The child also may recognize high lamas, or recite scriptures he has not been taught. Once certified the new Dalai Lama is taken to the Potala Palace in Llasa to be enthroned and schooled. A

regent rules in his name until he is old enough to assume his duties.

The Dalai Lamaship was instituted in the fourteenth century by Tsongkhapa (b. 1357), the founder of the Yellow Hat branch of Tibetan Buddhism, the church of most Tibetans and Mongols. Khapa went to Lhasa, the capital of Tibet, where he instituted religious reforms, created a monastic hierarchy, and discouraged the magical practices of the Red Hat branch, which had evolved out of the native Bön religion and early Buddhism. The First Dalai Lama, Gendün Drub, was born in 1391 as an incarnation of Chenresi.

Of the early Dalai Lamas, two became famous: the fifth and the sixth. The Great Fifth seized secular power in 1642 with the help of Mongol troops. He defined the powers of the Dalai Lamaship. He traveled to Peking, where the Manchu emperor received him as King of Tibet and named him "Universal Ruler of the Buddhist Faith." Until the end of the nineteenth century, there existed a reciprocal relationship between the Dalai Lama and the Emperor of China, who wielded some secular power in Tibet.

The Great Fifth enlarged the Potala—originally constructed as a meditation pavilion in about the seventh century by a Tibetan king—by turning it into a thirteen-story palace. He was afraid that if he died before it was completed, work would come to a halt. He died dur-

His Holiness the Fourteenth Dalai Lama, Tenzin Gyatso

ing construction of the second story. The news of his death was concealed for thirteen years so that the palace could be completed; a monk who resembled him was substituted in his place for public appearances, and a regent actually ruled. In 1697 the Sixth Dalai Lama, already in his teens, was revealed.

Melodious Purity, as the Sixth Dalai Lama was called, was renowned for his drinking and his consorting with numerous women in Tantric sexual rites. He wrote love songs that continue to be sung in the present day. The Manchu emperor, plotting against him, invited him to Peking and had him poisoned along the way. The murder of Melodious Purity encouraged the later murders of the young ninth, tenth, eleventh, and twelfth Dalai Lamas by the Chinese, all with the tacit approval of the ruling regents.

The Thirteenth Dalai Lama, Thupten Gyatso, managed to avoid this fate; he ruled during the latter nineteenth

and early twentieth centuries. Thupten Gyatso improved living standards, reorganized the army, and opened the isolated country to the technological advances of the industrialized world. In 1912, the year following the revolt against the Manchu dynasty in China, the Chinese were driven out of Tibet and the country was independent until 1950.

Thupten Gyatso died in 1933. Several days after his death, the face of his corpse, which had been ceremonially enthroned prior to burial, turned to the east, giving a sign for the whereabouts of his successor. The Fourteenth Dalai Lama, His Holiness Tenzin Gyatso, was born to a large peasant family in the northeastern village of Takster on July 6, 1935. He was taken by procession to Lhasa in 1939 and was enthroned on the Lion Throne in 1940.

In 1950, at age sixteen, Tenzin Gyatso assumed full political power as the head of the Tibetan state due to the invasion and occupation of Chinese Communist troops. For nearly nine years he led a policy of nonviolence against the occupation, during which he worked to reassert independence. In 1959 a revolt in eastern Tibet was crushed, and Chinese troops marched on Lhasa. The Dalai Lama, his family, and others fled to India.

Since 1960 Tenzin Gyatso has resided in exile in Dharmsala, India, called "Little Lhasa." He has been active on behalf of Tibet, traveling throughout the world to meet with religious and political leaders, among them the late Pope Paul VI, and Pope John Paul II. He has established educational, cultural, and religious organizations to preserve Tibetan culture and religion. He has been instrumental in the passage of three United Nations resolutions reaffirming the fundamental human rights of Tibetans (1959, 1961, and 1965), which have been ignored by the Chinese. Tenzin Gyatso has stated that his incarnation is the Dalai Lama's most difficult, and that the lineage may end with him. See **Lama.**

Sources: Barbara and Michael Foster. *Forbidden Journey: The Life of Alexandra David-Neel.* San Francisco: Harper & Row, 1987; His Holiness the Dalai Lama of Tibet. *My Land and My People: Memoirs of the Dalai Lama of Tibet.* 1962. New York: Potala Corp., 1983; The Office of Tibet, New York City.

Da Love-Ananda (formerly Da Free John) (b. 1939)

American mystic and founder of the Free Daist Communion, a body of five institutes that disseminate Da Love-Ananda's teachings.

Da Love-Ananda was born Franklin Jones on November 3, 1939, in Jamaica, Long Island, New York. By his own account, he was "Illumined" from birth (he capitalizes numerous words to emphasize their importance), and he spent his early years in a condition he called "Bright," in which he was "a radiant form, a source of energy, bliss, and light." However, he was moved by the unhappiness of others and their lack of awareness that "Divine Happiness" was innate within them. At age two-and-a-half, he says, he renounced the Bright to develop and teach a "God-Realizing Way" of life for ordinary people.

In 1957, at age seventeen, he entered Columbia University, where he studied philosophy. In 1961 he did graduate work in English at Stanford University, where he also volunteered for experiments with psychedelic drugs, including LSD, mescaline, and psilocybin. In the mid-1960s he studied yoga and reportedly achieved the arousal of the *kundalini* force. He also became involved for a time in Scientology, where in 1968 he met Nina, whom he married. In the same year he visited India, where he met Swami Muktananda Paramahansa (1908–1982)

and became his *chela,* or student, for two years. In 1969 Muktananda bestowed upon him the name "Love-Ananda," meaning "the Divine Love-Bliss," but he continued to use his given name.

On September 10, 1970, while in a temple of the Vedanta Society in Hollywood, California, Da Love-Ananda had what he described as a permanent awakening to "the Transcendental Divine Self, or Consciousness Itself." He established the Dawn Horse Communion ashram, based upon Bhakti (devotional) Yoga, and taught four stages of development: the way of Divine Communion; the way of Relational Enquiry; the way of Recognition; and the way of Radical Intuition. In 1973 he assumed the name "Bubba Free John." Bubba was a childhood nickname, and Free John a rendering of Franklin Jones, meaning "a free man through whom God is Gracious."

By 1979 he had dropped Bubba in favor of "Da" ("Giver of Life"), which had been revealed to him in a vision. It is interpreted as an honorific meaning "one who Gives or Transmits the Divine Influence and Awakening to living beings." His organization was known as the Johannine Daist Communion, comprising the Laughing Man Institute, the Free Communion Church, the Advaitayana Buddhist Order, and the Crazy Wisdom Fellowship.

By 1986 Da Love-Ananda had written more than thirty works and had established three meditation centers: the Mountain of Attention in northern California, Tumomama in Hawaii, and Translation Island Hermitage in Fiji. However, he was greatly discouraged by the inability or refusal of the average person to "Realize the Truth," and knew his teachings were doomed to failure. On January 11, 1986, he reportedly died at the Translation Island Hermitage. Then, in the presence of his physician and several witnesses, he reportedly reentered his body in an act of love for humanity. It is claimed that he actually died and resurrected himself and did not merely have a near-death experience.

His alleged physical death freed him from his teaching and his need to interact with ordinary people. He resides at the Hermitage, where he merely "Stands Free" and is "Boundlessly Radiant" in all directions, ready to "Offer the direct Realization of Truth" to all who will receive "His Gift." He lives almost as a recluse, cared for by a small number of attendants and granting audiences to a few practitioners. He adopted new titles, and is known informally as "Da Love-Ananda" or "Heart-Master Da Love-Ananda," and formally as "Avadhoota Da Love-Ananda Hridayam." "Avadhoota" refers to one who has passed beyond worldly attachments and desires; "Hridayam" is Sanskrit for "heart."

The Free Daist Communion, the present name of Da Love-Ananda's religious organization, dedicates itself to spreading his teachings. It includes five fellowships for different levels of practice: the Laughing Man Institute, based in San Rafael, California; the Dawn Horse Fellowship; the Ajna Dharma Fellowship; the Advaitayana Buddhist Fellowship; and the Crazy Wisdom Fellowship.

Sources: Heart Master Da Love-Ananda. *Compulsory Dancing.* First published as *Conversion.* 1979. San Rafael, CA: The Dawn Horse Press, 1987; Heart Master Da Love-Ananda. *The Knee of Listening: The Early Life and Radical Spiritual Teachings of Heart-Master Da Love-Ananda (Da Free John).* 1972. San Rafael, CA: The Dawn Horse Press, 1987; Leslie A. Shepard, ed. *Encyclopedia of Occultism and Parapsychology.* 2d ed. Detroit: Gale Research Co., 1984; John White, ed. *What Is Enlightenment? Exploring the Goal of the Spiritual Path.* Los Angeles: Jeremy P. Tarcher, 1984.

David-Neel, Alexandra (1868–1969)

French explorer, author, and scholar of Tibet, the first Western woman to enter Llasa, the forbidden capital of Tibet. Alexandra David-Neel spent fourteen years in Tibet as one of the first Westerners to probe that nation's mysticism and magic. She claimed to be descended from Genghis Khan on her mother's side. She was the consummate adventurer, and stated once that the surest elixir to youth is travel and intellectual activity.

She was born Louise Eugenie Alexandrine Marie David on October 24, 1868, in Paris, and was raised in Brussels from age five. Her father, Louis David, was a Huguenot activist and friend of novelist Victor Hugo. Her introduction to occultism came at age fifteen, when she read a journal published by the Supreme Gnosis, an occult society in London. In 1888, at age twenty, she went to London to study for a year and boarded at the Supreme Gnosis quarters. There she was exposed to Theosophy, Rosicrucianism, and Spiritualism.

In 1889 she went to Paris to study at the Sorbonne, and lived with Theosophists in the Latin Quarter. She became interested in Buddhism, and wrote articles on religion and occultism for various intellectual journals.

In 1891 she inherited money, which enabled her to travel to India and Ceylon to the edge of the Himalayas. After her return to Paris, she worked as a singer under the pseudonym Mademoiselle Myrial, after one of Hugo's characters. In 1900, at age thirty-two, she met Philip Neel, a bachelor and engineer seven years her senior, and became one of his mistresses. They were married in 1904 in Tunis. After two years of a stormy union, David-Neel left. They remained married, however, and Philip supported her financially during most of her years of travel.

Da Love-Ananda (formerly Da Free John) (b. 1939)

Potala Palace in Lhasa, Tibet

By 1904 David-Neel had termed herself a "rational Buddhist," and wrote her articles from this perspective. She lectured to Theosophical audiences in London and Paris in 1910. In 1911 she returned to India to study Oriental languages. There she met Sri Aurobindo Ghose.

In 1912 she met the Maharaj Kumar (Crown Prince) of Sikkim, Sidkeong Tulku, who invited her to Gangtok, the capital of Sikkim, which lies at the border between India and Tibet. She and the prince, younger than she, formed a romantic friendship. David-Neel was entranced by the Tibetan culture and took quickly to its customs. Sidkeong introduced her to lamas of both the Red Hat (traditional) and Yellow Hat (reformed) branches of Tibetan Buddhism. The populace treated her as an emanation of Queen Victoria, who was regarded as Palden Llamo, the patron goddess of Tibet.

On April 15, 1912, David-Neel had the first of two audiences with the Thirteenth Dalai Lama, held in Kalimpong, India. He advised her to learn Tibetan. Later, a *naljorpa*, a wizard, advised her to enter Tibet—despite the fact that travel there was forbidden to foreigners—and be initiated by a master. Instead she returned to Sikkim to resume her study of Sanskrit, believing that her destiny lay in writing a major work on comparative branches of Buddhism. Her circumstances changed radically in 1914, when the early death of Sidkeong cut off her access to royal courts and World War I prevented her return to Europe.

She became a disciple of the Gomchen (Great Hermit) of Lachen, whom she had met in 1912. The Gomchen lived as a hermit in the Sikkim Himalayas at De-Chen in the Cave of Clear Light, located at 12,000 feet. In exchange for instruction in Tibetan and Tantra, she pledged complete obedience and taught him English. The Gomchen gave her the name "Lamp of Wisdom." She took up residence as a hermit in a cave one mile below his. One of her servants was a minor *tulku,* a boy of fifteen named Aphur Yongden, who later became her adopted son and a lama in his own right.

David-Neel developed a telepathic rapport with the Gomchen, considered the highest form of teaching but rarely attained due to the insufficient psychic development on the part of the pupils. She also learned various psychic arts, such as *tumo* breathing, by which Tibetan yogis keep themselves warm in the frigid winters, and which prepares one for spiritual emancipation. See **Milarepa.** She had sensations of having been a nomad of Central Asia in a previous life. The Gomchen is most likely the one who initiated David-Neel into the Short Path of Tibetan mysticism and gave her permission to reveal her knowledge. The Short Path, preferred by Tibetan sorcerers and magicians, requires no long-term monastic discipline, and the initiate may undertake whatever experiments are desired for advancement.

In 1916 David-Neel illegally entered Tibet at the invitation of the Panchen Lama, second in rank to the Dalai Lama, and spent time at his monastery at Shigatse. As a result the British expelled her from her Sikkimese hermit's cave. All her servants save Yongden, who had a British passport, deserted her. She and Yongden departed for Japan. From there they went into China and secretly penetrated Tibet again in a dangerous journey, reaching their goal of Kumbum, the monastery that probably served as the model for the Shangri-La in James Hilton's novel *Shangri-La.* David-Neel spent two-and-a-half years at Kumbum, during which she translated rare manuscripts into French and English, and observed the magical and psychic feats of Tibetan adepts.

In 1921 she set out with Yongden and a new party of servants for Lhasa. She had no money—presumably funds from Philip were stolen by Chinese officials—and dressed in tattered clothing. She was beset by bandits but was never harmed, and frequently took hospitality from them. Yongden passed her off as a sorceress and as the wife of a deceased sorcerer to cajole offerings of food from peasants. She also masqueraded as a *kamdora,* a female spirit or fairy whose blessings are sought.

The journey to Lhasa took three years due to detours caused by local fighting, bandits, wild animals, and avoidance of government officials. The last stage of the journey was made across the uncharted and treacherous Po country, whose wild inhabitants were rumored to be cannibals. David-Neel walked through deep snow, slept in icy caves, and was often ill. She had to resort to *tumo* to stay alive, and to *lung-gom* traveling, a type of entranced movement that enables rapid progress without food, water, or rest. Accomplished *lung-gom-pas* bound along as though their bodies are very light; they are reputed to fly at times. It is believed that when in trance, they cannot be disturbed, for to do so prompts the god within them to depart prematurely, causing their death.

Reaching Lhasa in February 1924 was anticlimactic for David-Neel, and by April she was anxious to leave. Her beggar's disguise prevented her from accessing the intellectual and educational opportunities there.

By 1925 she and Yongden were back in Paris, and David-Neel was famous for the publicity of her exploits. She lectured and began a demanding schedule of writing books and articles.

In 1928 she purchased a small villa outside of Digne in southern France and named it Samten Dzong, the Fortress of Meditation. There she and Yongden toiled over their manuscripts.

After Philip's death in 1941, David-Neel acknowledged having participated in and observed Tantric sexual rites during her travels. She had also learned a mild version of the *chöd* ("to cut up") ritual, a grim rite designed to harness occult forces and liberate one from all at-tachments. In the *chöd* the participant sacrifices himself or herself to dismem-berment and devouring by a hungry horde of ghouls, then renounces the sac-rifice as illusion because he or she is noth-ing, and therefore has nothing to give. David-Neel may have continued to prac-tice the *chöd* during her later years in France.

Yongden was expected to manage David-Neel's estate, but the lama, an al-coholic, died of uremic poisoning in 1955. David-Neel hired a secretary, Jeanne Denys, in 1958. Denys came to despise the ill-tempered David-Neel, and devoted ten years to an unsuccessful at-tempt to prove her works as fiction.

In 1959 David-Neel hired Marie-Madeleine Peyronnet, who looked after her until she died just short of age 101 on September 6, 1969. Twenty years later Peyronnet was still working at Samten Dzong, which is now a conference center and museum. Most of David-Neel's books and artifacts went to various other museums.

David-Neel's works include more than thirty titles, and contain descriptions of Tibetan practices, rituals, and ceremo-nies that Westerners are unlikely ever to see performed again. Her best-known books are *My Journey to Lhasa* (1927), an account of her penetration to the cap-ital; *Magic and Mystery in Tibet* (1929), anecdotal accounts of magical and mys-tical practices; *Initiations and Initiates of Tibet* (1930), a more serious discussion of Tantric lore and mystical rites; and *Bud-dhism: Its Doctrines and Its Methods* (1936), a recapitulation of an earlier work on Buddhist doctrines. During her life she received many honors, including the French Legion of Honor, the gold medal of the Geographical Society of Paris, the silver medal of the Royal Bel-gian Geographical Society, and the In-signe of the Chinese Order of the Brilliant Star.

Of all her adventures, David-Neel considered her stay at the hermit's cave in the Sikkimese Himalayas to be the sum-mit of her dream. She inspired many, in-cluding Lama Anagarika Govinda, who tutored under the same Gomchen. See **Dalai Lama; Shambhala; Thought-form.**

Sources: Alexandra David-Neel. 1929. *Magic and Mystery in Tibet.* New York: Dover Publications, 1971; Alexandra David-Neel. *My Journey to Lhasa.* 1927. Boston: Beacon Press, 1986; Barbara and Michael Foster. *Forbidden Journey: The Life of Alexandra David-Neel.* San Fran-cisco: Harper & Row, 1987; Leslie A. Shepard, ed. *Encyclopedia of Occultism and Parapsychology.* 2d ed. Detroit: Gale Research Co., 1984.

Dead Sea Scrolls

See **Essenes; Gnosticism.**

Deathbed visions

Paranormal experiences of the dying. Most deathbed visions are apparitions of the dead or mythical or religious figures, and visions of an afterworld. Deathbed visions are significant because they pro-vide evidence, albeit not scientific, in sup-port of survival of consciousness after death. The visions share certain traits with mystical experiences, such as a marked sense of the sacred, profound peace, and elation.

Deathbed visions have been recorded since ancient times. Early psychical re-searchers, among them James H. Hyslop and E. Bozzano, collected and studied cases around the turn of the twentieth century. The first systematic study was done by William Barrett, English profes-sor of physics and psychical researcher. Barrett became interested in 1924 when his wife, a physician specializing in ob-stetrical surgery, told him about a woman patient whose deathbed visions transformed her into a state of peace and radiance just before she died.

Several decades later other significant research was conducted by Karlis Osis under the auspices of first the Parapsychology Foundation and then the American Society for Psychical Research. Between 1959 and 1973, Osis collected data on tens of thousands of deathbed and near-death experiences in the United States and, in a joint effort with Erlendur Haraldsson, in India. Their findings confirmed Barrett's research, the experiences of Elisabeth Kübler-Ross and others who work with the terminally ill and dying, and research of the near-death experience (NDE). See **Near-death experience (NDE)**.

Deathbed visions share common characteristics not influenced by racial, cultural, religious, educational, age, and socioeconomic lines, such as radiant lights, scenes of great beauty, beings of light, and feelings of great peace. Most deathbed visions are of glowing beings of light: apparitions of the dead known to the dying, or great religious or mythical figures, such as the Virgin Mary, Jesus, or other deities, angels, and so on. These figures are called "take-away apparitions" because their apparent purpose is to summon or escort the dying to the afterworld. Their appearance usually elicits a response of joy, peace, happiness, and cessation of pain, though a small number of individuals react with fear or denial.

People who attend the dying may see the take-away apparitions, albeit rarely, or perceive an unusual light or energy in the room. They may also witness an energy cloud form over the dying, which in a few cases has been reported to assume the shape and appearance of the dying, connected to the body by a silvery cord. When the person dies, the cord is severed, and the astral shape dissipates. See **Out-of-body experience (OBE)**.

Total visions, in which the dying behold (or are transported out-of-body to see) a preview of the afterworld, occur in about one-third of deathbed visions. Such visions usually are of endless and exquisitely beautiful gardens. Other visions are of great architectural structures and symbols of transition such as gates, bridges, rivers, and boats. These afterworld scenes may be populated with angels or spirits of the dead and, in a small number of cases, may be permeated with celestial music. Typically, colors are vivid, and the dying one feels uplifted. Seldom do afterworld visions conform to the religious expectations of the dying.

About half of all deathbed visions studied by Osis and Haraldsson lasted five minutes or less. Another 17 percent lasted between six and fifteen minutes, and 17 percent lasted more than one hour. Approximately 76 percent of the patients died within ten minutes of their vision, and almost all died within one or several hours.

Theories discounting deathbed visions propose that they are hallucinations induced by drugs, fever, disease, oxygen deprivation, wish-fulfillment, and depersonalization. However, such hallucinations arising from these factors usually concern the present and not the afterworld. Furthermore, Osis and Haraldsson found that deathbed visions are most likely to occur to patients who are fully conscious.

Deathbed visions are significant to thanatology, the scientific study of death, for they show death not as extinction but as a wondrous transition, a rite of passage that should be undergone consciously and with dignity. There are various arts to "right dying," as exemplified in the ancient Western mystery traditions and in the Tibetan Book of the Dead. In the modern West, however, this passage is undermined by fear of death and high technology that enables vegetative husks to cling to pointless life as long as possible. See **Apparition; Encounter phenomenon.**

Sources: William Barrett. *Death-Bed Visions: The Psychical Experiences of the Dying.* 1926. Wellingborough, Northamptonshire, England: The Aquarian Press, 1986; W. Y. Evans-Wentz, comp. and ed. *The Tibetan Book of the Dead.* 3d ed. London: Oxford University Press, 1960; Michael Grosso. *The Final Choice: Playing the Survival Game.* Walpole, NH: Stillpoint Publishing, 1985; Edmund Gurney, Frederic W. H. Myers, and Frank Podmore. *Phantasms of the Living.* London: Kegan Paul, Trench, Trubner & Co. Ltd., 1918; Karlis Osis. *Deathbed Observations by Physicians and Nurses.* Monograph no. 3. New York: Parapsychology Foundation, 1961; Karlis Osis and Erlendur Haraldsson, *At the Hour of Death.* Rev. ed. New York: Hastings House, 1986.

Decline/incline effects

Two phenomena associated with psi testing in the laboratory. The decline effect occurs when a high-scoring subject's performance begins to decline, either within a run (a fixed group of successive trials) or a session (all trials completed within one sitting). The term also applies to the diminishing of one's psi talent in general. The incline effect is the opposite: a subject's scores increase in runs and sessions.

The decline effect is said to be the most consistent finding in parapsychology: The more a subject is tested, no matter how gifted, the progressively lower his or her scores. Scores that are above chance in the beginning slide to chance or below. Many gifted subjects lose their talent after only a few runs, while others can endure through thousands of trials. Pavel Stepanek, a gifted Czech subject, managed to last ten years before his ability declined. Some subjects regain their ability after a hiatus. Many test subjects have reported a loss of spontaneity and attention and a drop in enthusiasm during tests of twenty runs.

Less gifted subjects are not tested as extensively as gifted ones, yet they do suffer the decline effect, usually between sessions. Declines within a single session are rare. The attitude of the experimenter also is a factor; if the subject senses a waning interest, scores tend to drop.

Charles T. Tart, American parapsychologist, hypothesized in the 1960s that the reason for the decline effect is the lack of immediate feedback for the test subject. The perception of psi is a subtle process. Proficiency in recognizing it depends on being able to distinguish subtle internal cues and feelings. Without immediate feedback a subject has no way of judging which cues are correct and which are not. The result is confusion and a decline in scores.

Another major factor is boredom. Many tests involve numerous repetitions of tasks, such as guessing cards and dice throws. Not surprisingly, the subjects psychically burn out.

The incline effect, in which scores become progressively higher, may reflect learning and skill improvements on the part of the subject. Some parapsychologists believe scores can be improved by giving subjects immediate feedback on results. The incline effect occurs far less frequently than the decline effect. See **Experimenter effect.**

Sources: Hoyt L. Edge, Robert L. Morris, John Palmer, and Joseph H. Rush. *Foundations of Parapsychology.* Boston: Routledge & Kegan Paul, 1986; Stanley Krippner, ed. *Advances in Parapsychological Research 2: Extrasensory Perception.* New York: Plenum Press, 1978; J. B. Rhine and Robert Brier, eds. *Parapsychology Today.* New York: The Citadel Press, 1968; Charles T. Tart. *Psi: Scientific Studies in the Psychic Realm.* New York: E. P. Dutton, 1977.

Déjà vu

A disorientation of time in which one feels that one has been to an unknown place before, or has experienced a situation before. Déjà vu is an impression of familiarity that is unexpected, and applies to events, experiences, sensory impressions, dreams, thoughts, statements, desires, emotions, meetings, visits, the act of reading, the state of knowing, and, in general, living. The term, French for "already seen," was first used to describe such experiences in 1876 by E. Letter Boirac, who called it *"la sensation du déjà vu."* It was introduced to science in 1896 by F. L. Arnaud. There is no adequate English equivalent for the term "déjà vu."

Déjà vu is a common psychological experience. In a 1986 poll conducted by the University of Chicago's National Opinion Research Council, 67 percent of adult Americans reported instances of déjà vu, up from 58 percent in 1973. In other studies déjà vu is experienced more frequently among women than men, and among younger people than older.

Theories explaining déjà vu differ widely. Some psychologists call it "double cerebration." As early as 1884, theories were advanced suggesting that one hemisphere of the brain receives information a split second earlier than the other half. In 1895 English psychical researcher Frederic W. H. Myers theorized that the subconscious mind registered information sooner than the conscious mind. The biological process of déjà vu, if there is one, has not been proved.

Reincarnationists say déjà vu is caused by fragments of past-life memories jarred to the surface of the mind by familiar surroundings or people. Others say it may be the product of out-of-body travel during sleep, or other extrasensory phenomena such as clairvoyance or telepathy. Still others, using psychiatrist Carl G. Jung's theory of the collective unconscious, say déjà vu happens when one draws on the collective memories of humankind.

Jung had a profound déjà vu experience on his first trip to Africa. Looking out the train window, he felt he was returning to the land of his youth of five thousand years earlier. He explained it in *Memories, Dreams, Reflections* (1961) as "recognition of the immemorially known." See **Collective unconscious.**

Sources: Andrew Greeley. "Mysticism Goes Mainstream." *American Health* (January/February 1987): 47–56; Joseph Head and S. L. Cranston. *Reincarnation: The Phoenix Fire Mystery.* New York: Julian Press/Crown, 1977; Gardner Murphy. "Direct Contacts with Past and Future: Retrocognition and Precognition." *The Journal of the American Society for Psychical Research* 61, no. 1 (January 1967): 3–23; Vernon M. Neppe. *The Psychology of Déjà Vu.* Johannesburg, South Africa: Witwatersrand University Press, 1983; Benjamin B. Wolman, ed. *Handbook of Parapsychology.* New York: Van Nostrand Reinhold, 1977.

Demon

A low-level spirit that interacts in the affairs of the physical world. Demons are universally believed to exist in numerous varieties, and may be either entirely good, entirely evil, or capable of both. They may offer advice and assistance or be responsible for bad luck, disease, illness, and death. Demons may be summoned, controlled, or expelled by qualified adepts, such as a priest, magician, sorcerer, or shaman.

"Demon" means "replete with wisdom," and is derived from the Greek *daimon,* "divine power," "fate," or "god." To the Greeks daimons were intermediary spirits—including those of deified heroes—between humankind and the gods. A daimon acted as an advisory spirit. See **Inspiration.**

(From Historiarum Veteris Testamenti icones, 1543)

Demons, by Hans Holbein the Younger

Demons in Western religion and lore have been classified into various systems since at least A.D. 100–400. The *Testament of Solomon,* which dates to this period, describes Solomon's magic ring for commanding demons called the djinn, and gives the names and functions of various Hebrew, Greek, Assyrian, Babylonian, Egyptian, and perhaps Persian demons. During the sixteenth and seventeenth centuries, Christian demonologists catalogued demons into various hierarchies of hell and ascribed to them attributes and duties, including ambassadorships to earthly nations. The most complex hierarchy was devised by Johann Weyer, who estimated that there were 7,405,926 demons serving under seventy-two princes.

Much demon lore concerns sexual intercourse between demons and humans. Demons with such sexual appetites are in the demonologies of the ancient Hebrews, Egyptians, Greeks, Romans, Assyrians, Persians, and other cultures.

Judaic demonology is complex and is derived from Hebrew, Christian, Arabic, Germanic, and Slavic sources. Kabbalistic works contain contradictory conceptions. The *Zohar* follows a Talmudic legend of the origin of certain demons as the products of sexual intercourse between humans and demonic powers: Every pollution of semen results in demons. Other demons, such as Lilith, were created as disembodied spirits during the six days of Creation, especially at twilight on the Sabbath eve; they too are associated with sexual intercourse with humans—the "night terrors." Other Kabbalistic writings speak of demons created out of fire and air, demons that fill the air between the Earth and the moon, and good demons that help people. There are demons who, with angels, are in charge of the night hours, and interpretations of diseases, and those who have seals that must be used to summon them.

In Christianity demons are associated only with evil. They include the angels who cast their lot with Lucifer and were thrown along with him out of heaven, as well as pagan deities turned into demons by the church. As agents of the Devil, demons devote themselves to leading humans astray, tormenting them, assaulting them sexually, and in some cases possessing them. Prior to the twelfth century, sex with demons was not considered possible, but the belief became dogma by the fourteenth century. Demons in the shape of human males (incubi) were said to prey on women, while demons in female shapes (succubi) preyed on men. During the Inquisition heretics, who eventually included witches, were accused of engaging in sexual orgies with demons. The sex usually was portrayed as unpleasant and painful, although according to the church, which had a low view of women as weak and inclined toward immorality, some women enjoyed copulation with demons. Monstrous births were explained away as the products of human-demon intercourse. See **Witchcraft.**

In other cultures, such as Shinto-Buddhist Japan, demons are associated with ghosts of the dead.

Demons that plague humans with problems and illness are exorcised according to rituals. It is universally believed that demons may be kept at bay through various preventive rituals, such as certain prayers or charms, or by certain amulets worn on the body or kept on the premises. See **Amulet; Exorcism; Possession.**

In ritual magic demons are summoned by elaborate ritual and dispatched on tasks. They are considered to be tricky and rather dangerous to work with. See **Crowley, Aleister; Hermetic Order of the Golden Dawn; Psychic attack.** Compare to **Angel.**

Sources: Richard Cavendish. *The Black Arts.* New York: Perigee Books, 1967; Rosemary Ellen Guiley. *The Encyclopedia of Witches and Witchcraft.* New York:

Facts On File, 1989; Jeffrey Burton Russell. *Lucifer: The Devil in the Middle Ages.* Ithaca and London: Cornell University Press, 1984; Gershom Scholem. *Kabbalah.* New York: New American Library, 1974.

Depossession (also releasement)

The exorcism of attached discarnate human spirits and nonhuman spirits allegedly attached to living people, causing a host of physical, mental, and emotional ills. Types of depossession are practiced around the world.

"Depossession" as such is an outgrowth of past-life therapy, largely as a result of the research of American psychologist Edith Fiore. The term "depossession" is preferred to "exorcism," which connotes demonic possession.

Fiore and other past-life therapists attest that in regressing patients to past lives, they observe interference from attached spirits. Among about 30,000 cases, Fiore estimated that 70 percent of all patients have at least one spirit attached to them, but are not aware of it. The spirits allegedly create problems such as unexplained mood swings and behavior, chronic pains and illnesses, mental illness, suicidal urges, and drug and alcohol abuse.

Most spirits are believed to be deceased humans who have not left the earth plane. They are said to attach themselves to a member of their family or find an individual who is weakened by substance abuse, hostility, or severe illness. Nonhuman spirits include elementals and evil-natured entities.

Depossession usually is accomplished merely by persuading the spirits to depart. Patients subsequently say they feel lighter and better, though this may be due at least in part to expectations of relief.

According to Fiore many possessions are karmic, caused by spirit possession in past lives on the part of the patients.

Some therapists say that past-life recalls may concern not the patients, but their attached spirits. See **Past-life therapy (PLT)**.

Depossession has precedence in the West. During the height of Spiritualism, people suffering from unusual mental symptoms often attended seances in hopes of having "low" spirits exorcised. The first medically trained person to approach mental illness as due to spirit possession was Carl Wickland, an American physician and psychologist who had attended numerous Spiritualist seances. Wickland and his wife, Anna, attributed all manner of mental conditions and illnesses to confused, benign spirits who were trapped in the auras of living people. The Wicklands depossessed patients in the late nineteenth and early twentieth centuries. Wickland invented a static electricity machine that transmitted low-voltage electric shock to the patient, causing the possessing spirit great discomfort. The device was a forerunner of low-voltage electric shock treatment used in psychotherapy.

Wickland then forced the spirit to leave its victim, enter Anna's body, and then finally depart forever. If the spirit resisted, Wickland called on "helper spirits" to keep the possessing spirit in a so-called "dungeon," out of the aura of the victim or Anna, until the spirit gave up its selfish attitude and departed.

Titus Bull, a New York physician and neurologist, used a medium in the early twentieth century to persuade obsessing entities to depart. See **Exorcism; Possession; Thought-form**.

Sources: Dr. Edith Fiore. *The Unquiet Dead: A Psychologist Treats Spirit Possession*. Garden City, NY: Dolphin/Doubleday & Co., 1987; Edith Fiore, Ph.D. "Freeing Stalemates in Relationships by the Resolution of Entity Attachments." *The Journal of Regression Therapy* 3, no. 1 (Spring 1988): 22–25; Louise Ireland-Frey. "Clinical Depossession: Releasement of At-

tached Entities from Unsuspecting Hosts." *The Journal of Regression Therapy* 1, no. 2 (Fall 1986): 90–101; Hiroshi Motoyama, Ph.D. "Bodily Healing through Releasement." *The Journal of Regression Therapy* 2, no. 2 (Fall 1987): 108–9; D. Scott Rogo. *The Infinite Boundary*. New York: Dodd, Mead & Co., 1987; Carl Wickland. *Thirty Years Among the Dead*. 1924. North Hollywood, CA: Newcastle Publishing Co., 1974.

Depth psychology

See **Psychology**.

Dervish

See **Sufism**.

Deva

In Hinduism and Buddhism, an exalted being of various kinds. The term *deva* is Sanskrit for "shining one."

Hinduism distinguishes three kinds of devas: mortals who live in a higher realm than other mortals, enlightened people who have realized God, and Brahman in the form of a personal God.

In Buddhism devas are gods who live in various realms of heaven as a reward for their previous good deeds; however, they are still subject to rebirth.

Madame Helena P. Blavatsky, co-founder of the Theosophical Society, introduced the concept of devas to the West, defining them as types of angels or gods who were progressed entities from a previous planetary period. They arrived on earth before elementals or human beings, and would remain dormant until a certain stage of human evolution was reached. At that time the devas would integrate with elementals and help further the spiritual development of humankind, Blavatsky said.

In modern times devas are popularly thought of more as nature spirits, who may elect to help people. They usually are invisible, but may be seen by clairvoyance. They are said to communicate through clairaudience and meditation.

The amazing produce of Findhorn in Scotland, and of Perelandra in Washington, DC, has been attributed to cooperation between people and devas. Devas manifest as "architects" of nature; one is assigned to every living thing, even the soil. The deva designs blueprints for all living things, and orchestrates the energies necessary for growth and health. At Findhorn and Perelandra, devas dispense advice on planting, fertilizing, watering, and general plant care. Despite human destruction of the environment, which dismays and perplexes the devas, the devas remain willing to work with those human beings who make an effort to understand the intricacies and harmonies of nature. See **Nature spirits; Findhorn.**

Sources: H. P. Blavatsky. 1888. *The Secret Doctrine.* Pasadena, CA: Theosophical University Press, 1977; Findhorn Community. *The Findhorn Garden.* New York: Harper & Row Perennial Library, 1975; Paul Hawken. *The Magic of Findhorn.* New York: Bantam Books, 1976; *The Encyclopedia of Eastern Philosophy and Religion.* Boston: Shambhala, 1989; *The New Age Catalogue.* New York: Doubleday/Dolphin, 1988.

Dharma

In Hinduism and Buddhism, law, truth, or doctrine that defines the cosmos; also, duty, truth, righteousness, virtue, ideal, phenomena, and so on. Dharma has many-shaded meanings, depending on context. "Dharma" is Sanskrit from the Aryan root *dhar,* to uphold, sustain, or support. Its Pali form is *dhamma,* which is generally used in Theravada Buddhism.

In Hinduism dharma is the supreme operating law of the universe, governing earth and all beings upon it and all gods in the cosmos, existing with neither beginning nor end in time. The major aspects of dharma that govern human beings and the world are *samsara,* or reincarnation; karma, the law of cause and effect; and *moksha,* the spiritual liberation from the bondage of reincarnation. Dharma also refers to the continuous effort to eliminate karma by surrendering to divine will. Dharma is duty; it relates to moral nature and behavior rather than religious beliefs. Each individual has his or her own dharma to follow in the quest for spiritual development. Communities have collective dharmas to provide educational and social supports to their members.

Within the context of reincarnation, dharma is the purpose to which an individual is born, created by a need in a particular time and place. Karma is the conditioning that makes fulfillment of dharma possible.

In Buddhism dharma comprises teachings about the universe and a discipline, a means by which to attain awakening. It arises from humankind's attempts to understand the world. The essence of dharma is expressed in the Four Noble Truths:

1. Suffering exists. There are three general types of suffering: suffering of pain, which is physical and mental; suffering of change, which superficially appears to be pleasure but actually is suffering; and pervasive compositional suffering, which is part of karma and rebirth. (Rebirth and reincarnation are not equivalent; see **Reincarnation.**)
2. Suffering is caused by karma and "afflictive emotions" such as desire, hatred, ignorance, lack of self-control, jealousy, and anger.
3. Suffering is ended by the extinction or cessation of its causes.
4. Causes are overcome through the

Noble Eightfold Path, which consists of Right View, Right Determination, Right Effort, Right Speech, Right Conduct, Right Livelihood, Right Mindfulness, and Right Concentration.

Dharma is the second of the Three Treasures; the first is the Buddha and the third is the *Sangha,* or the kinship and harmony of all things. Dharma, the second Treasure, is the "truth of Buddhism" or "the way." The three poisons to Dharma are hatred, ignorance, and greed.

Buddhists do not follow Buddha; they follow dharma, the way of Buddha. The dharma is the universe, which is both empty and void and full and complete. Karma is the action of dharma, and freedom from karma is freedom from blind response to it. The enlightened soul sees karmic hindrances as fundamentally empty and does not become burdened by them. A *gatha* (verse stating major points of Buddha dharma) intended to free one from blind response to karma is the Purification Gatha:

> All the evil karma ever created by
> me since of old,
> on account of my beginningless
> greed, hatred, and ignorance,
> born of my body, mouth, and
> thought,
> I now confess, openly and fully.

The term "dharma" also refers to attributes or phenomena called "elements of being," which are minute impulses of energy. Dharmas comprise the *skandas,* the karmic aggregates of form, feelings, perceptions, impulses, and consciousness, which in turn comprise the illusory nature of all sentient beings. See **Karma.**

Sources: Robert Aitken. *Taking the Path of Zen.* San Francisco: North Point Press, 1982; John Blofeld. *The Tantric Mysticism of Tibet.* Boston: Shambhala Publications, 1987; Tenzin Gyatso, His Holiness the Fourteenth Dalai Lama. *Kindness, Clarity,*

and Insight. Ithaca, NY: Snow Lion Publications, 1984; Virginia Hanson and Rosemarie Stewart, eds. *Karma: The Universal Law of Harmony.* 2d ed. Wheaton, IL: Theosophical Publishing House, 1981; Yong Choon Kim. *Oriental Thought.* Totowa, NJ: Rowman and Littlefield, 1973; Solange Lemaitre. *Ramakrishna and the Vitality of Hinduism.* 1959. Woodstock, NY: The Overlook Press, 1984; Maurice Percheron. *Buddha and Buddhism.* 1956. Woodstock, NY: The Overlook Press, 1982; K. M. Sen. *Hinduism.* Harmondsworth, Middlesex, England: Penguin Books, 1961.

Dianetics

See **Church of Scientology.**

Direct-voice mediumship

A method of spirit communication, in which a spirit speaks directly to an audience without using a medium's vocal apparatus. In early Spiritualism direct-voice mediumship took the form of the dead communicating to the living by speaking through trumpets and megaphones, which amplified their voices. Sometimes a spirit voice seemed to emanate from a point in space near the medium. According to some Spiritualists, the vocalization was made possible by an artificial larynx constructed by the spirits and activated by ectoplasm. The spirits were said to use ectoplasmic rods to manipulate the trumpets and megaphones, which floated around the rooms.

Most early Spiritualist mediums employed direct-voice communication at one time or another, though some specialized in it more than others. In the 1850s the Spirit Room of Jonathan Koons, an Ohio farmer, was famous for spirits that talked and played musical instruments. After attending several seances, Koons claimed he was directed by a band of spirits to build the room and procure fiddles, guitar, drums, a horn, tambourine, triangle, and other instruments. He and his wife acted as mediums. Audiences were impressed by the cacophony of sound while the instruments flew about the room. Voices described as "unearthly" sang songs in an undistinguishable language, while the chief spirit, King Number One, spoke through a tin horn from different corners of the room.

Direct-voice mediumship was often suspected of ventriloquist fraud. However, records of some seances conducted in the nineteenth century attest to the authenticity of the spirit voices, which talked at the same time as the medium, or several of which talked at once from different locations. As of the late twentieth century, direct-voice mediumship was a rarity.

One of the best-known modern direct-voice mediums is Leslie Flint of England. Flint, a Spiritualist, retired from giving public seances in 1976, after more than thirty-five years of direct-voice mediumship. The spirits seemed to speak from a point above and slightly to the left of Flint's head. Psychical researchers thought Flint might actually receive messages clairvoyantly and then surreptitiously substitute his own voice. Flint was extensively tested—he called himself "the most tested medium in England"—but no evidence of fraud was ever found. The most dramatic test was done in London and New York in 1970. Flint's lips were sealed with plaster, and a throat microphone showed no evidence of use of his vocal chords, despite the manifestation of ghostly voices. See **Ectoplasm; Spiritualism**. Contrast with **Channeling**.

Sources: Slater Brown. *The Heyday of Spiritualism*. New York: Hawthorn Books, 1970; Richard Cavendish. *Encyclopedia of the Unexplained*. New York: McGraw-Hill, 1974. John Godwin. *Occult America*. New York: Doubleday, 1972. Edgar D. Mitchell. *Psychic Exploration: A Challenge for Science*. Edited by John White. New York: Paragon Books, 1974.

Displacement

In psi testing, perception of information other than the "target," either in time or context. In laboratory tests for psi, displacement was first documented in 1939 by Whately Carrington, a psychical researcher at Cambridge University in England. Since then it has been observed as a common occurrence in psi testing, usually affecting time and sequences. For example, a person being tested to give the order of face-down ESP cards may experience a displacement of one or two cards either forward or backward. Similarly, the receiver in a telepathy or clairvoyance test of a series of photographs or images may see them correctly, but one or more images forward or behind the target.

In the ganzfeld stimulation test, in which a receiver attempts to identify one of several images transmitted telepathically, more than one image may be received, sometimes so vividly that a decoy is chosen over the target image.

Parapsychologists call displacement a type of "psychic noise." It is caused by two main factors: the absence of linear time in the higher planes, where psychic awareness functions; and the psychic association of a group of potential targets, when they become difficult to tell apart.

Displacement also occurs in psychic readings and precognitive dreams, when unpleasant news or conditions are suppressed or buried in nonthreatening information or symbols. See **Psi hitting and psi missing; Stained-glass window effect**.

Sources: June G. Bletzer. *The Donning International Encyclopedic Psychic Dictionary*. Norfolk, VA: The Donning Co., 1986; Mary Ellen Carter. *Edgar Cayce on Prophecy*. New York: Warner, 1968; Edgar D. Mitchell. *Psychic Exploration: A Challenge for Science*. Edited by John

White. New York: Paragon Books, 1974; Russell Targ and Keith Harary. *The Mind Race.* New York: Villard Books, 1984; Joan Windsor. *The Inner Eye: Your Dreams Can Make You Psychic.* Englewood Cliffs, NJ: Prentice-Hall, 1985; Benjamin B. Wolman, ed. *Handbook of Parapsychology.* New York: Van Nostrand Reinhold, 1977.

Divination

The art of foretelling the future, finding the lost, and identifying the guilty by a host of techniques. Divination has existed and has served a social function in all civilizations throughout history, by providing a means for solving problems and resolving disputes. The responsibility for divination customarily falls to a priest, prophet, oracle, witch, shaman, witch doctor, medicine man, psychic, or other person reputed to have supernatural powers.

Innumerable divinatory, or mantic, methods exist, and diviners use the ones sanctioned by their cultures. Techniques fall into two broad categories: the interpretation of natural or artificial signs, omens, portents, and lots; and the direct communication with gods and spirits through visions, trance, dreams, and possession. All divination is an attempt to communicate with the divine or supernatural in order to learn the will of the gods; and even in the interpretation of signs and lots it is assumed that the gods interfere to provide answers to questions. A skilled diviner also employs a keen sense of intuition and an innate understanding of human psychology. A typical divination consists of advice as well as prediction—sometimes more of the former than the latter.

In early civilizations divination was primarily a royal or holy function, used for guidance in matters of state and war, and to forecast—and therefore avoid or

(US Library of Congress)

Diviner

mitigate—natural disasters. Most courts employed royal diviners, whose very lives often depended upon the accuracy of their forecasts. The Chaldeans and Babylonians had elaborate divinatory systems under the auspices of priests, who saw portents in virtually everything in nature around them. The ancient Chinese had court astrologers and other diviners who interpreted cast lots of yarrow sticks (the *I Ching*), bones, and other objects. Early Egyptian priests slept in temples in hopes of receiving divinatory information from the gods in a dream. In ancient Rome a special caste of priests called augurs interpreted signs in nature, believed to be messages sent by the gods. Augurs interpreted such natural phenomena as the flights of birds, the patterns of clouds and smoke, and the markings on the livers of sacrificed animals (livers, rather than hearts, were believed the central organ of the body). The Greeks divined dreams and consulted special oracles, who went into trance to allow the gods to speak through them. The most famous oracle resided at Delphi, near the base of Mount Parnassus. The Greeks helped spread divination among the masses by popularizing astrological horoscopes. See **Astrology.**

In tribal cultures divination remains

largely a royal or sacred function. In shamanic cultures divination is performed by shamans, who go into trance to communicate with spirit helpers. In parts of Africa, the king's diviner has the force of law. The royal oracles of the African Zande employ numerous methods of divination. The simplest is to place two sticks in an anthill and see which stick has been eaten by the following day. Another method is use of a "rubbing board," an object made of two pieces of wood. The pieces are rubbed together, and yield an answer when they stick together. Most common is the *benge* oracle. The benge poison, obtained from a plant and similar to strychnine, is fed to a chicken. Answers are divined from the length and nature of the fowl's death throes. The chicken's survival also yields an answer.

All cultures employ divinatory methods that consist of interpreting artificial signs. The most common involve sortilege, or the casting of stones, bones, shells, and other objects, which yield answers from the patterns of their fall. Two popular divination methods, Tarot cards and the *I Ching,* are of this type. In western Uganda the Lugbara fill small pots with medicines, which represent the suspects of a crime. The pots are set on the fire; whichever one does not boil over fingers the guilty one. In other methods suspects are required to consume awful potions or stews; the guilty one will suffer indigestion.

In the East divination is more an accepted part of daily life than it is in the West. In India some parents publish ads of the horoscopes of their newborn children and the horoscopes of their marriageable children, which include the astrological lineage of the entire family. In parts of the Middle East, royalty still confer with astrologers in making decisions. In China palmistry is used in some forms of holistic health therapies. The female matchmakers of Korea analyze horoscopes when pairing marriageable young men and women.

In Western society divination has been associated with sorcery. The Old Testament contains many proscriptions against consulting diviners; some of the Hebrew terms for "diviner" have been translated as "witch." As early as 785, the Catholic church forbade the use of sorcery as a means of settling disputes, but that did not prevent consultation of village wizards and wise men and women. During the Middle Ages and Renaissance, diviners who invoked demonic forces were punished by fines, humiliation in a pillory, or loss of property; some who were also convicted of witchcraft were put to death. Despite disapproval from the church and the scientific community, and the many laws against fortune-telling (widely considered a fraud), divination has never been eradicated; the average person has too great a desire to attempt to see into the future. See **Dreams; Dowsing; Omen; Oracle; Prophecy.**

Sources: Hachiro Asano. *Hands: The Complete Book of Palmistry.* New York: Japan Publications, 1985; Mircea Eliade. *Shamanism.* 1951. Princeton: Princeton University Press, 1964; James G. Frazer. *The Golden Bough: The Roots of Religion and Folklore.* New York: Avenel Books, 1981; Michel Gauquelin. *Dreams and Illusions of Astrology.* Buffalo, NY: Prometheus Books, 1979; Emile Grillot de Givry. *Witchcraft, Magic and Alchemy.* New York: Houghton Mifflin, 1931; Michael Loewe and Carmen Blacker. *Oracles and Divination.* Boulder: Shambhala, 1981; Lucy Mair. *Witchcraft.* New York: McGraw-Hill, 1969; Max Marwick, ed. *Witchcraft and Sorcery.* 2d ed. Harmondsworth, Middlesex, England: Penguin Books, 1982; Keith Thomas. *Religion and the Decline of Magic.* New York: Scribner, 1971.

Divine Light Mission

See **Alternative religious movements.**

Dixon, Jeane (b. 1918)

American psychic most famous for her prediction of President John F. Kennedy's assassination in 1963. Jeane Dixon has successfully predicted world and personal events since the 1940s. She also foresaw the assassinations of US Senator Robert Kennedy in 1968, American civil rights activist Martin Luther King in 1964, and Indian civil rights leader Mahatma Gandhi in 1948, and the attempted assassination of Alabama Governor George Wallace in 1972. She predicted such historical events as the launching of *Sputnik* by Russia, Nikita Khrushchev's rise and fall in power, and Richard M. Nixon's destiny as US president some twenty years before his election victory.

Dixon was born Jeane Pinckert in Wisconsin in 1918 and grew up in California. She married James Dixon at the age of twenty-one. After a brief time spent in Detroit, the couple established a real estate business in Washington, DC.

Dixon's gifts for prophecy were evident from her earliest years. As a toddler she would ask for things that had not yet arrived in the mail, or talk about events that had not yet occurred. When Dixon was eight, a Gypsy predicted she would become a great psychic.

Dixon believes her powers are a gift from God for the purpose of serving humanity. Thus she established a policy of not charging fees and directing income from books, a syndicated horoscope column, and other sources into a foundation she created in 1964, Children to Children.

Dixon says she receives her information through meditation, prayer, telepathy, psychometry, visions, and dreams. For example, she received telepathic messages from unspecified sources concerning the impending assassinations of Martin Luther King and Robert Kennedy. She foresaw the deaths of President Franklin D. Roosevelt and actress Carole Lombard

after touching their hands. Dixon warned Lombard not to fly for several weeks, but the actress, who was promoting war bonds during World War II, disregarded the warning and was killed the same night in a plane crash. Dixon's precognition of John F. Kennedy's assassination came to her in a vision years beforehand, and was published in 1956 in *Parade* magazine. She warned Kennedy not to go to Dallas, where he was assassinated on November 22, 1963.

Of all her methods of receiving information psychically, visions are the most dramatic. Dixon says she can sense the arrival of a vision three days before receiving it. During the entire four days, she says she feels uplifted and inspired. The visions—which always deal with great events of international significance—are sometimes in color and sometimes in black and white. They may be accompanied by music and voices.

Sources: Denis Brian. *Jeane Dixon: The Witnesses.* New York: Warner, 1976; Jeane Dixon and Rene Noorbergen. *My Life and Prophecies.* New York: Bantam Books, 1970; Edgar D. Mitchell. *Psychic Exploration: A Challenge for Science.* Edited by John White. New York: Paragon Books, 1974; Ruth Montgomery. *A Gift of Prophecy.* New York: Bantam Books, 1966.

Dolmen

See **Megaliths.**

Donne, John (1572–1631)

English preacher, prose writer, and poet of mystical experiences, considered one of the greatest poets of his day. John Donne was hailed as a theologian; his contemporaries called him "our English Tertullian," after the great Carthaginian theologian (c. 180–c. 230). He carried on the tradition of Augustine, Jerome,

Thomas Aquinas, and other Christian church fathers in his brilliant and inspired "metaphysical" poetry, very little of which was published during his life.

Donne was born in London to a Roman Catholic family. He studied law and theology at Oxford, and perhaps Cambridge, but he took no degree because his Catholicism prevented him from swearing allegiance to a Protestant queen. Gradually, he leaned more and more toward Protestantism.

In 1598 he was made secretary to Sir Thomas Edgerton. He fell in love with Ann More, the daughter of Sir George More, and married her secretly. In anger Sir George had Donne fired from his post, which ruined any future in public service.

After ten years of extreme poverty, Donne was ordained a minister of the Church of England in 1615. He was enormously successful, and in 1621 was named Dean of St. Paul's Cathedral, a position he held until his death ten years later. During this last phase of his life, Donne wrote more than 160 sermons and much religious poetry containing erotic imagery.

In 1623 Donne nearly died from illness. When his health was restored, he wrote *Devotions,* an account of his illness and recovery. *Devotions* is comprised of twenty-three units, each of which offers a Meditation, Expostulation, and Prayer.

Shortly before his death, Donne preached his own funeral sermon and went to bed. He ordered his portrait to be painted on his shroud; he contemplated it for several days before passing away on March 31, 1631.

Donne's language and imagery concerning the ecstatic state are remarkably similar to the writings of the great Spanish mystics, St. John of the Cross and St. Teresa of Avila. Like them, Donne expresses the ecstatic union of the human soul with God, often comparing it to love between humans. His best-known work is *The Extasie.*

Sources: F. C. Happold. *Mysticism: A Study and an Anthology.* Rev. ed. New York: Penguin, 1970; Elizabeth T. Howe. "Donne and the Spanish Mystics on Ecstasy." *Notre Dame English Journal* (Spring 1981): 29–44; Louis Kronenberger, ed. *Atlantic Brief Lives.* Boston: Little, Brown, 1971; Peter A. Piore, ed. *Just So Much Honor: Essays Commemorating the Four-Hundredth Anniversary of the Birth of John Donne.* University Park, PA: Pennsylvania State University Press, 1972; A. J. Smith. *John Donne.* New York: Methuen, 1985.

Double

An apparition of a living person. Doubles are exact replicas of persons, including clothing, and often deceive witnesses with their solid appearance. They usually are seen in a location distant from the real person. Some doubles act strangely or mechanically.

The true nature and cause of the double are not known. Popular occult theory holds that doubles are projections of an astral body. The projections may happen involuntarily or, in the case of certain adepts, be accomplished at will. See **Bilocation.** The appearance of doubles often is associated with the imminent death of the person.

The double is known by various names, including "Beta body," "subtle body," "fluidic body," and "pre-physical body." It is called a "fetch" in Irish and English folklore. In Irish lore a fetch seen in the morning is a portent of long life for the individual, while a fetch seen in the evening is an omen of impending death. A German term for the double is *doppleganger,* which comes from an expression meaning "double walker." In Sweden it is called the *vardøger.*

Beliefs about doubles exist in tribal cultures. One widespread belief is that the double is the soul, which is the reflection of the body.

The ancient Egyptians said the soul itself had a double called the *ka*. Upon death the ka resided in the tomb along with the corpse, while the soul departed for the underworld. A special part of the tomb, called "the house of ka," was reserved for the double, and a priest was appointed to minister to it with food, drink, and offerings.

It is possible to see one's own double. Shortly before his death by drowning, poet Percy Bysshe Shelley saw his double. The English antiquarian John Aubrey records the case of Lady Diana Rich, daughter of the Earl of Holland, who saw her mirror-image double while walking in the garden one morning. A month later she died of smallpox.

English medium Eileen J. Garrett theorized that the double is a means of telepathic and clairvoyant projection, and can be manipulated to expand one's consciousness. See **Apparition; Out-of-body experience (OBE)**.

Sources: Katherine Briggs. *An Encyclopedia of Fairies: Hobgoblins, Brownies, Bogies, and Other Supernatural Creatures.* New York: Pantheon Books, 1976; E. A. Wallis Budge. *Egyptian Magic.* 1901. New York: Dover Publications, 1971; Maria Leach, ed., and Jerome Fried, assoc. ed. *Funk & Wagnalls Standard Dictionary of Folklore, Mythology, and Legend.* San Francisco: Harper & Row, 1979; Sheila Ostrander and Lynn Schroeder. *Psychic Discoveries Behind the Iron Curtain.* Englewood Cliffs, NJ: Prentice-Hall, 1970; Lewis Spence. *An Encyclopedia of the Occult.* Reprint. London: Bracken Books, 1988.

Dowsing

Divination by using a forked rod, bent wire, or pendulum to locate people, animals, objects, and substances. The method has numerous applications, including finding underground water, oil, coal, minerals, cables, and pipes; locating missing people, murder victims, and murderers; locating lost objects and animals; and mapping archaeological sites before digging begins. Dowsing also is used to diagnose illness.

Dowsing is ancient, dating back some seven thousand years; its exact origins are unknown. Ancient Egyptian art portrays dowsers with forked rods and headdresses with antennae. Ancient Chinese kings used dowsing rods. During the Middle Ages, dowsing was used widely in Europe and Great Britain to locate coal deposits. It was associated with the supernatural, which gave rise to the terms "water witching" and "wizard's rod." Reformation leader Martin Luther said dowsing was the work of the Devil. To counteract evil influences, medieval dowsers baptized their rods with Christian names. In the United States, dowsing has been used since pre-Republican times, primarily to find water well sites.

It is not known how or why dowsing works. Psychic ability is thought to play a key role. The dowser may have an innate psychic ability to tune in to the person, substance, object, or whatever is being sought. As the dowser approaches the right location, the rod begins to twitch and jerk up and down, sometimes violently. German scientist Baron Karl von Reichenbach believed the jerking of the rod was due to earth force fields, which sent out vibrations and radiations. Supposedly, the dowser psychically picked up the vibrations and translated them by subtle muscle movements to the rod. More recent experiments have shown that dowsing rods are sensitive to electrostatic and electromagnetic fields.

The force field theories, however, do not explain why many dowsers work strictly off maps in their homes, far away from the actual field sites. Nor do they explain why many dowsers, like clairvoyants, are able to get images of the past and future.

Many dowsers believe that one must be born with the innate ability to dowse, but experiments have shown that almost anyone can learn how to do it. Experiments in Russia have demonstrated that dowsers can transmit their sensitivity to others by touching them as they dowse. Russian tests also have demonstrated that women are twice as successful at dowsing as men. Scientists there theorized that unknown force fields responded better to the polarity in women's bodies. In 1986, however, a study of the astrological charts of a small group of American dowsers revealed some common characteristics, thus buttressing the innate ability theory. The majority of charts had fire as the dominant element, strong ties to the planet Pluto, and a higher frequency of lunar and solar eclipses, among other characteristics.

Dowsing Tools

Forked dowsing sticks usually are made of hazel, ash, rowan, or willow, and occasionally metal, whalebone, and plastic. Wands or bobbers are stripped tree branches, stiff wires, or the ends of fishing rods, which have been weighted on one end. Angle rods are made of metal. Ordinary coathangers suffice, though copper and aluminum wires are said to be more responsive. In Europe the rod has given way to the pendulum, which is suspended on a string and rotates in response to questions or as a dowser scans a map. The dowser usually "tunes" the instrument by concentration and visual images. Dowsers who locate missing persons may first hold their instrument over a personal item belonging to the person.

Some exceptionally skilled dowsers have learned how to dowse without a tool. Uri Geller, the Israeli renowned for his psychokinetic mental bending, learned to dowse with his bare hands, holding them outstretched with palms down. When he locates hidden objects, he feels a resisting force on his palms, similar to the effect created by putting two similar poles of a magnet together.

Dowsing as a Science

Dowsing was widely used until the nineteenth century, when scientists rejected it as superstition. In the twentieth century, dowsing made a comeback, especially in Europe and Great Britain, where it has been used successfully in archaeological digs, the search for minerals, and in medicine. During World War I, dowsers helped locate mines, unexploded shells, and buried mortars for the military.

The Abbé Alexis Mermet of France believed in dowsing as a science as early as 1906, an activity he documented in his classic book, *How I Proceed in the Discovery of Near or Distant Water, Metals, Hidden Objects, and Illnesses*. Mermet dowsed archaeological sites at the request of the pope and found dozens of murderers and missing persons. After 1930 dowsing became known as radiesthesia in Europe. The term was coined by the Abbé Alex Bouly, a French priest and dowser, who hoped it would rid dowsing of its occult taint and make it acceptable as a science. "Radiesthesia" comes from the Latin root for "radiation" and the Greek root for "perception." The term is widely used throughout Europe, but less so in the United States and Great Britain. Bouly also founded *L'Association des Amis de la Radiesthesie* in 1930. In 1933 the British Society of Dowsers was formed. International radiesthesia congresses are held regularly in Europe.

In the United States dowsing is used by some oil, gas, and minerals companies, some of whom say they have found dowsers to be more accurate than geologists using "scientific" techniques. Many water and pipe companies use dowsing to locate buried cables and pipes, and to find damaged spots. During the Vietnam War, the Marines used dowsing rods to locate mines, booby traps, and sunken mortar shells. Dowsers also have contributed research toward the understanding of mysterious earth energies, such as leys. Despite the advances dowsing still struggles to be recognized as a "legitimate" field. The American Society of Dowsers estimates that there are more than 25,000 dowsers in the United States.

Dowsers were persecuted during the Stalinist era in the Soviet Union, as were psychics and occultists in general. After Stalin's death in 1953, serious research in dowsing was resumed. Dowsing is called BPE, for "Biophysical Effects Method." It is heavily used in geological and archaeological work.

Dowsing in Medicine

In Europe, Great Britain, and elsewhere, dowsing is sometimes used as a diagnostic tool in alternative medicine. A pendulum is suspended over the patient's body and "attuned" to healthy parts. As it is moved over unhealthy parts, the pendulum's movements change. The dowser also may ask questions and divine answers according to the rotation of the pendulum; clockwise for "yes," counterclockwise for "no."

Medical dowsing was pioneered largely by three French priests, Mermet, Bouly, and Father Jean Jurion. In experiments with doctors, Bouly was able to identify cultures of microbes in test tubes by dowsing. Mermet developed dowsing techniques to help missionaries identify medicinal plants in foreign countries. Jurion accurately diagnosed disease and illness. Though harassed by the French Order of Physicians, he treated more than 30,000 patients over twenty-five years.

Medical dowsing is prohibited in the United States under the 1976 Pure Food,

Drug, and Cosmetic Act, which prohibits diagnosis or attempted healing by using a device, except under very stringent conditions. See **Geller, Uri; Psychic archaeology.**

Sources: American Society of Dowsers. "How Can I Tell If I Am a Dowser?" *The New Age Catalogue.* New York: Doubleday/Dolphin, 1988; Christopher Bird. "Dowsing: The Medical Potential." *New Realities* 3, no. 2 (October 1979): 57–61; John P. Boyle. *The Psionic Generator Pattern Book.* Englewood Cliffs, NJ: Prentice-Hall, 1975; Uri Geller and Guy Lyon Playfair. *The Geller Effect.* New York: Henry Holt, 1986; George P. Hansen. "Dowsing: A Review of Experimental Research." *The Journal of the Society for Psychical Research* 51, no. 792 (October 1982): 343–67; James R. Morgan, M.S., F.R.C. "Dowsing." *The American Dowser* 27, no. 2 (May 1987): 16–18; Sheila Ostrander and Lynn Schroeder. *Psychic Discoveries Behind the Iron Curtain.* Englewood Cliffs, NJ: Prentice-Hall, 1970; Sarah Wooster. "A Statistical Look at Natal Aspects of Dowsers." *The American Dowser* 26, no. 2 (May 1986): 40–44; Richard D. Wright. "Towards a Definition of Dowsing." *The American Dowser* 26, no. 1 (February 1986): 7–11.

Doyle, Sir Arthur Conan

See **Fairies.**

Dragon Project Trust

See **Megaliths; Power point.**

Dreams

The meaning of dreams has puzzled humankind since antiquity. Everyone dreams, regardless of whether or not dreams are recalled upon awakening. The overwhelming majority of dreams deal metaphorically with issues, events, and people in the life of the dreamer, and every element in a dream has significance to the dreamer.

Some dreams are paranormal, involving clairvoyance, precognition, and telepathy (shared dreams) between two or more people. Others are interpreted as having past-life content. A still different type is the lucid dream, in which the dreamer is aware of the dream and in some cases can direct its outcome.

Historical Beliefs about Dreams

In ancient times dreams were seen as supernatural events, bearing prophecies, predictions, divinations, and messages from the gods. All primitive religions, including those of the present, view dreams as a way for spirits to speak to human beings. One of the earliest extant works on dream concepts and interpretations is the Chester Beatty papyrus of Egypt, which dates to 2000 B.C. It discusses good and bad dreams, dream associations and plays on words, and the concept of "contraries," that is, to dream of one thing is to realize the opposite in real life. Dream interpretation also was important to the ancient Babylonians and Greeks, although Aristotle dismissed gods as the sources of dreams. The Greeks attempted to incubate healing dreams by spending a ritual night in the temple of Aesculapius, the god of healing. The "right" dream meant a cure.

In the second century A.D., the Roman Artemidorus of Ephesus developed the most comprehensive system of dream interpretation until the time of Sigmund Freud. Artemidorus believed that dreams were continuations of the activities of the day, and were influenced by the dreamer's sex, age, occupation, and station in life.

The Old and New Testaments make numerous references to the interpretations of dreams. The early Hebrews used dream interpretation to influence behavior and thought.

The importance of dreams and their meanings was prominent in the writings of the church fathers, including St. Augustine, up to the time of Thomas Aquinas (1226–1274), who, following the lead of Aristotle, decided to ignore dreams. Early Christianity reinforced the belief in the divinatory power of dreams, especially the significance of vivid and repetitive dreams. The ancient Greek custom of dream incubation was for a time kept alive in the practice of nocturnal vigils at the shrines of Christian saints. But during the Middle Ages, the church, in establishing itself as the ultimate authority, taught that dreams should be ignored.

The Reformation of the sixteenth century heralded the end of widespread belief in miracles and supernatural events, though dreams still retained their importance. At the popular level, dream interpretation continued to be an important service offered by wizards and astrologers, and was the subject of magical formulae and various handbooks. Dream dictionaries, based largely on the work of Artemidorus, proliferated.

Before the late nineteenth century, psychological explanations were not given to dreams. Psychiatrist Sigmund Freud, in his pioneering work, *The Interpretation of Dreams* (1900), considered dreams the "royal road" to the unconscious, and believed they were wish fulfillments of repressed infantile desires. Events during the day, which Freud called "day residues," triggered nocturnal releases of these repressed elements in the form of dreams. To interpret dreams Freud used free association, in which the dreamer says whatever comes to mind in relation to the various elements in a dream. Because of the sexual nature of Freud's psychology, dream elements invariably are seen as phallic or vaginal symbols.

Angel appearing to Joseph in a dream (Matthew 1:20)

(The New Testament, Dover Publications)

Psychiatrist Carl G. Jung considered dreams the expression of contents of the personal unconscious and the collective unconscious. He said the purpose of dreams is compensatory, to provide information about the self, achieve psychic equilibrium, and offer guidance. Jung believed that dream symbols from the collective unconscious have universal, or archetypal meanings (see **Archetypes**), but those from the personal unconscious do not, and take on meaning from the individual's experiences, beliefs, and cultural, racial, ethnic, and religious heritage. Only the dreamer, not an outsider, can interpret a dream's true meaning.

Jung considered dream interpretation of utmost importance in the process of individuation, or becoming whole. Dream symbols are the raw language of the unconscious, brought to the attention of the conscious without censor. Dreams tell us the frank state of our inner lives, showing us where we are in terms of individuation and showing us what needs to be dealt with consciously. For example, symbols of the shadow, the repressed aspects of the self, often appear in dreams to demand our attention.

According to Jung, our psyche seeks to have a dialogue with us, and brings us information in three successive ways: first, psychically, as in dreams; second, through "fate" such as accidents, illness, and so on; and third, through physical disorder and illness. To ignore our dreams is to court more drastic events.

Since Freud and Jung, other theories have been put forward on the nature, function, and meaning of dreams. For the most part, however, they are elaborations on the work of these two giants.

The Nature of Dreams

In the early 1950s, it was discovered in research at the University of Chicago that dreams occur during the rapid eye movement (REM) stages of sleep. Typical seven-hour periods of sleep by healthy adults are divided into sixty- to ninety-minute cycles, each of which has a REM period, during which dreams occur. Each dream period is longer than the previous one; they range from five to ten minutes for the initial one, which occurs about ninety minutes after the onset of sleep, to up to forty minutes for the final period prior to awakening. REM sleep has been found to be crucial to the process of learning new skills.

Infants spend most of their sleep in cycles associated with dreaming. Animals also appear to dream.

Robert W. McCarley and J. Allan Hobson, psychiatrists at Harvard Medical School, have theorized that dreams are born in the brain stem when neurons, using the chemical acetylcholine, fire bursts of electrical signals to the cortex, where higher thought and vision originate. The cortex attempts to make sense of the signals by rearranging them, along with real memories, into a story, which accounts in part for the bizarre nature of most dreams.

Dreams usually occur in color and seldom with smells or tastes. The reason for the lack of the latter may be due to the fact that only visual neurons fire during REM. Most people are likely to remember the last dream prior to awakening. However, lab studies have shown that if dreamers are awakened during earlier dream periods, they will recall those dreams as well. Unless written down, however, the details of most dreams fade within five to ten minutes.

Dreams, Creativity, Health, and Death

Dreams have provided inspiration since time immemorial. Solutions to problems, ideas for inventions, and artistic expressions have found their way to the conscious mind through dreams. For example, artist and poet William Blake found dreams to be a continuing source of inspiration and artistic subjects, as did Salvador Dali and other artists of the sur-

realistic schools. The idea for *Dr. Jekyll and Mr. Hyde* came to author Robert Louis Stevenson in a dream, and inventor Elias Howe conceived of the sewing machine from a dream.

There is some evidence that dreams are harbingers or barometers of health problems. Jung noted that when some patients dreamed of destruction of or injury to horses—an archetypal symbol of the animal life within the human body—they subsequently were shown to be in the early stages of serious illness, such as cancer. A 1987 study by Dr. Robert Smith of Michigan State University showed that cardiac patients who dreamed of destruction, mutilation, and death had worse heart disease than those who did not. The dreams worsened as did the conditions, despite the fact that the patients did not know the severity of their disease.

Dreams also sometimes serve as a way to prepare an individual for death. Terminally ill patients sometimes have transitional dreams, such as entering beautiful gardens, crossing bridges, or walking through doorways, which occur shortly before death and which often bring peace of mind.

Paranormal Dreams

Dreams universally have been seen as sometimes having prophetic content. Seeing into the future through dreams customarily has been the province of the priest, shaman, or diviner. Various folklore techniques also exist for inducing precognitive dreams, though most are of dubious value. Precognitive dreams may occur once or twice during an individual's life, or not at all; some people, especially those who exhibit other psychic talents, seem to have frequent precognitive dreams. See **Precognition**. Precognitive dreams, which the dreamer eventually learns to discern from ordinary dreams, may be accompanied by certain symbols or emotions.

Some dreams appear to be spontaneously telepathic. Freud observed that "sleep creates favorable conditions for telepathy," and referred often to dream telepathy in his clinical work with patients. Dream telepathy has been of interest to psychical researchers and parapsychologists since the late nineteenth century. The founders of the Society for Psychical Research (SPR) in London collected 149 dream telepathy cases in their study of spontaneous paranormal experiences, published in *Phantasms of the Living* (1886). More than half of the dream cases involved death, and most of the remainder concerned crises or distress.

The first known experimental effort to induce telepathic dreams was conducted during the same time period by an Italian psychical researcher, G. B. Ermacora. He used a medium whose control spirit allegedly sent telepathic dreams to the medium's four-year-old cousin.

Various other dream studies have been conducted in the twentieth century, some by the SPR and the American Society for Psychical Research, as well as by others.

There are about half a dozen scientific demonstrations of telepathy in dreams, the most famous of which was research conducted from 1962–74 by Montague Ullman, Stanley Krippner, and others at the Dream Laboratory of the Maimonides Medical Center in Brooklyn, New York. When subjects were in REM stages, a person in another room attempted to telepathically transmit a target art image, usually depicting people and archetypal in character. The subjects were then awakened and asked to describe their dreams. The next day they were shown several possible targets and asked to rank them in terms of matching the content and emotions of their dreams. In some cases the dream correspondences would occur one to two days after the target had been transmitted. Overall, the correlation of dream images to target im-

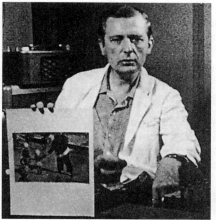

Dr. Stanley Krippner and artwork used in dream telepathy experiments at the Dream Laboratory of the Maimonides Medical Center, Brooklyn, New York

ages was significantly above chance. The rapport between agent and subject was an important factor in success. Characteristics that indicated an ESP influence included unusual vividness, colors, and detail, and a somewhat puzzling nature to the dreamer.

Studies of ESP experiences in general show that dreams are involved in 33 percent to 68 percent of all cases. In telepathic cases dreams are involved in 25 percent; and in precognitive cases dreams are involved in approximately 60 percent. About 10 percent of ESP experiences occur when an individual is at the borders of sleep. See **Hypnagogic/hypnapompic states**. Individuals who undergo ESP tests in laboratories sometimes have precognitive dreams about elements in the tests.

Lucid Dreams

In a lucid dream, the dreamer is aware of the fact that he or she is dreaming. Lucid dreams occur during REM stages. Nearly everyone has at least one lucid dream, and a very few people dream lucidly often. Aristotle, in the fourth century B.C., mentioned the existence of lucid dreaming. The earliest extant written account of a lucid dream (in Western history) is contained in a letter written in 415 by St. Augustine, who described the lucid dream of a Carthaginian physician, Gennadius. Lucid dreams have been ignored by many dream researchers, or dismissed as impossible. Some researchers, however, feel lucid dreams hold great potential as creativity and healing tools.

There are varying degrees of lucidity in dreams. At the lowest level, one awakes from a realistic dream and realizes it was a dream, not reality. At the highest level, one is aware of the dream as it takes place, and can influence its course and outcome. The form taken by a lucid dream seems to mirror the dreamer's mental state. The initiation of awareness of dreaming can be triggered by various factors, such as the stress of a nightmare, incongruous elements, or a spontaneous recognition that the reality is different from waking reality. Generally, lucid dreams are characterized by light (sometimes very bright), intense emotions, heightened colors and images, flying or levitation, and a sense of liberation or exhilaration. Some are almost mystical in nature. Sex plays a prominent role in lucid dreams, especially for women.

Interest in lucid dream research was piqued in the late 1960s by the now classic study by British researcher Celia E. Green. Subsequent work in the 1970s and 1980s by British parapsychologist Keith Hearne, and by the American researchers Ann Faraday, Patricia Garfield, and Stephen LaBerge, among others, sustained this interest.

Lucid dream studies, however, have been inconsistent. Some have demonstrated that, with practice—using autosuggestion and other techniques—individuals can cause themselves to dream lucidly or exert greater control over their lucid dreams, such as dreaming about certain topics. The art of controlling dreams certainly is not new; the earliest recorded mention of lucid dreaming as a learnable skill dates to eighth-century Tibetan yoga practices. Philosopher P. D. Ouspensky taught himself how to enter lucid dreams from a waking state; he called them "half-dream" states.

The applicability of lucid dreams is controversial. Advocates believe that controlled lucid dreaming can be applied to creativity, problem solving, relationships, health, and the riddance of nightmares. It is estimated that 10 percent of the population may be able to learn dream control with some proficiency. Such individuals typically are at peace with their lives.

LaBerge and some other researchers relate lucid dreams to out-of-body experiences, most of which occur during sleep or while a person is in bed. See **Imagery; Out-of-body experience (OBE); Prophecy; Symbol; Telepathy.**

Sources: Sharon Begley. "The Stuff That Dreams Are Made Of." *Newsweek* (August 14, 1989): 41–44; Sigmund Freud. 1900. *The Interpretation of Dreams.* New York: The Modern Library, 1950; Patricia L. Garfield. *Creative Dreaming.* New York: Ballantine Books, 1974; C. E. Green. *Lucid Dreams.* London: Hamish Hamilton, 1968; Robert A. Johnson. *Inner Work.* New York: Harper & Row, 1986; C. G. Jung. *Dreams.* From *The Collected Works of C. G. Jung.* Vols. 4, 8, 12, and 16. Princeton: Princeton University Press, 1974; Morton Kelsey. *Dreams: A Way to Listen to God.* New York: Paulist Press, 1978; Stanley Krippner and Joseph Dillard. *Dreamworking: How to Use Your Dreams for Creative Problem-Solving.* Buffalo, NY: Bearly Limited, 1988; Stephen LaBerge. *Lucid Dreaming.* New York: Ballantine Books, 1985; John A. Sanford. *Dreams and Healing: A Succinct and Lively Interpretation of Dreams.* New York: Paulist Press, 1978; John A. Sanford. *Dreams: God's Forgotten Language.* 1968. San Francisco: Harper & Row, 1989; Keith Thomas. *Religion and* the *Decline of Magic*. New York: Charles Scribner's Sons, 1971; Montague Ullman and Claire Limmer, eds. *The Variety of Dream Experience*. New York: Continuum, 1987; Montague Ullman and Stanley Krippner with Alan Vaughan. *Dream Telepathy: Experiments in Nocturnal ESP*. Baltimore: Penguin, 1973; Montague Ullman and Nan Zimmerman. *Working With Dreams*. Los Angeles: Jeremy P. Tarcher, 1979; Benjamin B. Wolman, ed. *Handbook of Parapsychology*. New York: Van Nostrand Reinhold, 1977.

Drop-in communicator

A strange entity, unknown to both medium and sitters, who manifests unexpectedly at a seance. Drop-in communicators have been studied by some psychical researchers since the late nineteenth century as possible evidence that seance spirits are real and not constructs from the medium's subconscious, and that the information they provide does not come from telepathy or super-ESP on the part of the medium. The ideal drop-in provides information that has never been in print in a public source, and which is known to (and can be verified by) only a small number of people.

Most drop-in cases, however, are inconclusive, with drop-ins manifesting only once or twice and giving insufficient information to verify their identities. Nonetheless, the majority of drop-ins seem to have motives for manifesting — sometimes nothing more than to talk about themselves, as though they were lonely.

One famous drop-in with a mission was the case of Runolfur Runolfsson, who dropped in on medium Hafstein Bjornsson in 1937 and identified himself as a rough, hard-drinking Icelander who had died in 1879 at age fifty-two. Over the course of several sittings, Runolfsson said he wanted to find his missing leg bone. He said he had gotten drunk,

passed out at the shore, and drowned, and that his corpse had been picked apart by birds. The thigh bone was still missing.

The identity and details of Runolfsson's life were verified. His thigh bone was discovered interred between the walls of a house, apparently left by a carpenter. The bone was buried, and Runolfsson expressed his thanks. He stayed in contact with Bjornsson and became one of his controls.

Drop-ins are on rare occasions accompanied by physical phenomena such as table-tilting, mysterious lights, apports, scents, and strange noises.

It may be argued that some of the alleged highly evolved entities that are channeled also are drop-in communicators, for they manifest without warning. However, these entities provide little, if any, concrete historical data that may be checked by researchers; some of them claim never to have lived on earth. The entity Seth, who first appeared at a Ouija session to Jane Roberts and her husband, gave information about the previous lives of himself and Roberts and her husband in nineteenth-century Boston. This information was examined by psychiatrist Ian Stevenson, a leading expert on reincarnation. Stevenson felt the material was derived from Roberts's own subconscious. See **Super-ESP; Worth, Patience; Xenoglossy.**

Sources: Alan Gauld. "A Series of Drop-in Communicators." *Proceedings of the Society for Psychical Research 55* (July 1971): 1966–72; Alan Gauld. *Mediumship and Survival*. London: William Heinemann Ltd., 1982; Erlendur Haraldsson and Ian Stevenson. "An Experiment with the Icelandic Medium Hafstein Bjornsson." *The Journal of the American Society for Psychical Research 68*, no. 2 (April 1974): 192–202; Erlendur Haraldsson and Ian Stevenson. "A Communicator of the 'Drop In' Type in Iceland: The Case of Runolfur Runolfsson." *The Journal of the American*

Society for Psychical Research 69, no. 1 (January 1975): 33–59; Jane Roberts. The Seth Material. First published as How to Develop Your ESP Power. 1966. Englewood Cliffs, NJ: Prentice-Hall, 1970; D. Scott Rogo. Psychic Breakthroughs Today. Wellingborough, Northamptonshire, England: The Aquarian Press, 1987; Ian Stevenson. "A Communicator Unknown to Medium and Sitters." The Journal of the American Society for Psychical Research 64, no. 1 (January 1970): 53–65; Ian Stevenson and John Beloff. "An Analysis of Some Suspect Drop-in Communicators." The Journal of the Society for Psychical Research 50, no. 785 (September 1980): 427–47.

Drugs in mystical and psychic experiences

Consciousness-altering agents that induce, enhance, or inhibit experiences of a psychical, transpersonal, or mystical nature. Laboratory research with drugs has yielded disparate results. Opinions concerning the validity of psychedelic drug-induced experiences vary. Some take the position that drugs do not cause mystical experiences, only pseudomystical experiences that have no transcending, lasting impact; others feel that psychedelic drugs duplicate mystical experiences and are of value in psychotherapy.

The use of drugs as religious sacraments is an ancient custom found in every part of the world. The visions that occur during the experiences have spiritual purposes and are interpreted accordingly. The purpose may be to commune with the Divine, to seek life's purpose, or to undergo a spiritual initiation. In some shamanic traditions, novices ingest a psychotropic drug that enables them, so they claim, to take their souls out-of-body and contact mythical and spirit beings, deities, animals, and objects. They are transformed and empowered when they return to ordinary consciousness. See Shamanism.

The shamanic flight is evocative of the reports of flying in some of the European witchcraft trials during the Middle Ages and Renaissance. The accused witches were said to ride broomsticks, animals, and demons through the air to mountainous places, where they indulged in vile orgies of copulation with monsters and demons, dancing, and feasting, which was sometimes said to include the flesh of roasted infants. These flights allegedly were made possible with magical flying ointments, rubbed on the body, which contained toxic and hallucinogenic ingredients.

Drugs as a means of achieving mystical experiences generally are eschewed in Eastern disciplines, although some yogis take them. Drugs are held to interfere with the natural evolution of the psyche that occurs during yoga. The attainment of nirvikalpa samadhi, the highest mystical state, cannot occur without sufficient integration of the intellect, emotions and intuition, which drugs cannot provide. Nor can drugs artificially duplicate this state. It is held that most elevated drug experiences still occur within the realms of maya, or illusion, and do not completely transcend the ego or the empirical self. In Tantra hallucinogens play a minor role; alcohol is featured in rites of sensual pleasure.

In the Western high magic tradition, mind-altering drugs also are discouraged. The magician works from an altered state of consciousness that ideally is created from within, so that he or she remains in command of the consciousness. Moderate use of alcohol is considered acceptable for raising power in some magical rites.

Experiments with a variety of drugs on the effects of psi ability have been conducted since the 1920s. Results have been largely meaningless, due to the impossibility of controlling subjective variables. No two people react to the same amount of a drug in exactly the same way. Caffeine has been shown on at least one occason to have a positive influence on psi ability, while alcohol has been shown to both improve and depress test results. Marijuana, and particularly the strong psychedelic drugs like LSD (lsyergic acid diethylamide), mescaline, and psilocybin, trigger too much disorientation and instability to yield meaningful results. The most effective means of inducing an altered state of consciousness that is conducive to psi appears to be relaxation. See **Ganzfeld stimulation.**

Some research has been devoted to exploring the potential mystical nature and benefits of psychedelic drugs, especially mescaline, psilocybin, and LSD. The psychedelic state generally is characterized by a loosening of the ego boundary and the distinction between self and object; heightened emotions and sensory stimuli; and an opening to the unconscious, collective unconscious, and superconscious realms. The experience goes through various stages, beginning with patterns and images from personal memory and heightened sensory phenomena, and progressing to distortions in time and space, visionary landscapes, transcendence of time and space, cosmic archetypes, beings and symbols, and participation of or observation in mythical and archetypal dramas. Not all experiences reach the same levels.

The physical mechanism at play is the inhibition of the production of serotonin caused by psychedelics. Serotonin helps the brain regulate stimuli. It can also be depressed by fasting, meditation, exhaustion, concentration, and extreme temperatures.

Mescaline was first classified in the 1880s by Louis Lewin, a German pharmacologist, and was synthesized in 1918. By the 1950s, when novelist and critic Aldous Huxley was introduced to it, mescaline had been the subject of moderate experimentation, including by psychologists who thought it would provide insight into their patients' mental processes.

Mescaline takers feel they can remember and "think straight," but visual images are intensified, particularly colors, which appear to be supernaturally brilliant. Interest in space and time drop dramatically, and the taker loses interest in doing much of anything save drinking in the Being and "is-ness" of everything. The high lasts eight to ten hours. Mescaline apparently creates no physical dependency. "Bad trips," or negative experiences, are most likely to happen to individuals who are prone to depression or anxiety, or who suffer from jaundice.

Huxley, who later took LSD, became an advocate of drugs as a doorway to visionary or perhaps even mystical experiences. He said hallucinogenic drugs served to enlarge the "reducing valve" in the brain and nervous system, which prevents the mind from being overloaded by constant cosmic awareness, the Mind at Large. See **Huxley, Aldous.**

LSD was discovered in 1943. Albert Hoffman, a Swiss chemist, was working with a derivative of lysergic acid, an active ingredient in the ergot fungus of rye, and began to hallucinate after absorbing it through his skin. By 1947 LSD was receiving worldwide publicity. In the late 1950s, it came to the attention of Timothy Leary, a psychologist on the faculty of Harvard University who was experimenting with psilocybin. Working with Richard Alpert (later Ram Dass) and others, Leary became one of the foremost advocates of LSD, viewing it as a cure for society's ills. See **Leary, Timothy; Ram Dass.**

Publicity about bad trips and uncontrollable flashbacks led the Food and Drug Administration to severely restrict access to LSD to only selected researchers in 1963.

In the 1960s Robert Masters and Jean Houston conducted LSD experiments. In *Varieties of Psychedelic Experiences* (1966), they identified four levels in the unconscious reached during LSD trips: (1) The sensory level comprises vivid eidetic images, usually of animals, landscapes, mythical contents, architecture, and so on, all of which have been previously recorded by the brain. (2) The recollective analytic level brings in emotions of repressed or forgotten events; the subject may clearly see solutions to problems. (3) The symbolic level comprises images that are historical, legendary, mythical, ritualistic, and archetypal in nature. The subject may act out myths, perform rituals, or undergo initiations. (4) The integral level is self-transformation, religious enlightenment, and possibly mystical union. Of their 206 subjects, only forty attained level three and only eleven attained level four.

In psychotherapy LSD initially was thought to have promise as a model for schizophrenia, but it proved to be too unpredictable to be useful for that purpose.

The most extensive research into LSD and its uses in psychotherapy has been conducted by psychiatrist Stanislav Grof, who believes LSD can be a powerful catalyst in the healing process by activating and intensifying symptoms so that they can be dealt with, integrated, and resolved. Grof began his clinical work in 1956 in Prague and came to the United States in 1967, working first in humanistic psychology and then transpersonal psychology. See **Psychology**. From 1967 to 1973, he worked at the Maryland Psychiatric Research Center, where he conducted more than three thousand LSD sessions and had access to more than two thousand other sessions conducted in the United States and Czechoslovakia.

According to Grof LSD experiences cannot be explained in terms of traditional psychotherapy, nor are any two trips the same. The value of the drug lies in mapping uncharted realms of human consciousness, of which Grof identifies three domains: (1) psychodynamic, which involves emotionally relevant memories; (2) perinatal, which relates to either real-istic or symbolic experiences of birth (and therefore, also to death, which is closely related); and (3) transpersonal, in which the consciousness transcends time and space. This domain includes embryonic and fetal experiences; past lives; psychic abilities; out-of-body experiences; organ, tissue, and cellular experiences; the arousal of *kundalini* energy; and encounters with suprahuman spiritual beings, extraterrestrials, deities, other universes, the universal Mind, and the supracosmic and metacosmic Void (primordial emptiness). Experiences of death-rebirth in the perinatal state are said to force a reexamination of one's life and help bring about change and growth. Grof's later work concerned nonchemically induced altered states of consciousness, with which he said he obtained the same results as with LSD. See **Altered states of consciousness; Kundalini; Peak experiences; Spiritual emergence; Tobacco.**

Sources: Sybille Bedford. *Aldous Huxley: A Biography*. New York: Alfred A. Knopf/Harper & Row, 1973; Emma Bragdon. *The Call of Spiritual Emergency: Crisis of Spiritual Awakening*. San Francisco: Harper & Row, 1990; W. V. Caldwell. *LSD Psychotherapy: An Exploration of Psychedelic and Psycholytic Therapy*. New York: Grove Press, 1968; Fritjof Capra. *Uncommon Wisdom: Conversations with Remarkable People*. New York: Simon & Schuster, 1988; Nona Coxhead. *The Relevance of Bliss: A Contemporary Exploration of Mystic Experience*. London: Wildwood House, 1985; Ram Dass. *The Only Dance There Is*. Garden City, NY: Anchor Books/Doubleday, 1974; Stanislav Grof. *Realms of the Unconscious*. New York: The Viking Press, 1975; Stanislav Grof. *Beyond the Brain: Birth, Death, and Transcendence in Psychotherapy*. Albany, NY: State University of New York, Albany, 1985; Rosemary Ellen Guiley. *The Encyclopedia of Witches and Witchcraft*. New York: Facts On File, 1989; Michael Harner. *The Way of the Shaman*. New York: Bantam, 1986; Aldous Huxley. *The*

Drugs in mystical and psychic experiences

Doors of Perception. New York: Harper & Row, 1954; Timothy Leary. *Changing My Mind, Among Others.* Englewood Cliffs, NJ: Prentice-Hall, 1982; Holger Kalweit. *Dreamtime & Inner Space: The World of the Shaman.* Boston: Shambhala Publications, 1984; Serge King. *Kahuna Healing.* Wheaton, IL: The Theosophical Publishing House, 1983; Charles T. Tart. *States of Consciousness.* New York: E. P. Dutton, 1975; Charles T. Tart, ed. *Transpersonal Psychologies.* New York: Harper & Row, 1975; Roger N. Walsh and Frances Vaughan, eds. *Beyond Ego: Transpersonal Dimensions in Psychology.* Los Angeles: Jeremy P. Tarcher, 1980; Andrew Weil. *The Natural Mind: A New Way of Looking at Drugs and the Higher Consciousness.* Boston: Houghton Mifflin, 1972; Benjamin B. Wolman, ed. *Handbook of Parapsychology.* New York: Van Nostrand Reinhold, 1977.

Druids

The priestly caste of the Celts, a Germanic tribe that spread out over much of Europe, the British Isles, and parts of Asia Minor in the sixth and fifth centuries B.C. Not much is known about the Druids, who have been romanticized in modern times. Their traditions were oral and were largely lost when the Romans crushed the Celts in the first century A.D. The Romans and Greeks wrote a little about the Druids from about the second century B.C. to the fourth century A.D.— the Romans, including Julius Caesar, perhaps from a biased point of view. Other knowledge has come from archaeological digs.

Druid means "knowing the oak tree" in Gaelic; the robur oak was sacred to the Celts. The exact role and purpose of the Druids in Celtic society is uncertain, and many theories have been advanced over the centuries. They have been equated with the Persian Magi and the Hindu Brahmins. Some controversial modern theories hold that they were a shamanic possession cult, as evidenced by their human sacrifice, chanting, drumming, night fires, and apparent ecstatic dancing.

By most classical accounts, the Druids were a noble caste of both men and women who were responsible for passing on theological and philosophical wisdom, knowledge and skills in science (including astronomy and construction of a calendar), augury, composition, sacrificial procedures, and herbal medicine. They conducted religious rites and sacrifices, and also acted as jurists. They may have been magical bards, especially in Wales. Their duties apparently varied according to geographic region.

According to classical texts, the Druids had a set of magical beliefs, but little is known beyond a few charms. The mistletoe, which was sacred because it grows parasitically on the oak, was used in various formulae. Pliny provides the only extant account of a Druidic ritual, the harvesting of mistletoe, which was done on the sixth day of the new moon. A Druid dressed in a white robe climbed an oak tree. Using his left hand, he cut the mistletoe with a sickle, probably made of gilded bronze. The mistletoe was caught in a white cloth before it touched the ground. It was used in rituals, which also included the sacrifice of two white bulls. A feast followed.

The Druids made prophecies from dreams, the movements of the crow, eagle, and hare, and the death throes and characteristics of the entrails of sacrificed animals and humans. They conducted their religious rites in sacred oak groves, and near rivers and lakes where Celtic water deities were thought to dwell. They sacrificed victims by shooting them with arrows, impaling them on stakes, stabbing them, slitting their throats over cauldrons (and then drinking the blood), or, according to Strabo, burning them alive in huge wickerwork cages. An archaeological find in 1984 of the remains of a remarkably preserved young Celt man, buried in a bog near Manchester, England, supports the Roman reports. The Lindow Man, as the remains are called, appears to have been a Druid priest chosen by lot to be sacrificed. After a meal of scorched cake that may have been burned bannock (a ground barley griddle cake used in Druidic rituals), the young man had his throat cut, his windpipe crushed, his head bludgeoned, and his face held under water. The serene expression on his face indicates he went to his death willingly.

The Romans feared the Celts and found their human sacrifice customs revolting and barbaric; they began a systematic destruction of Celtic culture in the first century A.D. Emperor Claudius banned Druidism in A.D. 43. In battle the Romans found the Celts to be fierce and fearless, which the Romans attributed to the Celts' belief in immortality, a second life after death (not the same as reincarnation). In 60 Roman troops assaulted the Celts' holy stronghold on the island of Mona (Mon or Anglesey). According to Tacitus wild Druid women dressed in black dashed about "like the Furies," screaming and howling curses at the Roman soldiers. The Romans prevailed, killing everyone, including the Druids. The sacred oak groves were demolished. The shattering defeat plunged the Celts and Druidism into decline.

Interest in the Druids was renewed in the sixteenth and seventeenth centuries, with their romanticization in literature. In the seventeenth century, British antiquarian John Aubrey theorized that the Druids had built Stonehenge, a view that has since been disproved but has remained a popular belief into modern times. In the early eighteenth century, antiquarian William Stukeley, who agreed with Aubrey, organized a revivalist Druid Order, which had no association with the ancient Druids. In 1781 a British carpenter, Henry Hurle, formed the Ancient Order of Druids, a benefit society whose principles were drawn heavily from Freemasonry. In 1833 the group split in two. The Ancient Order of Druids retained its mystical underpinnings, while the United Ancient Order of Druids became a charitable organization. The Ancient Order of Druids attracted many occultists, including Freemasons, Order of the Golden Dawn initiates, and Rosicrucians. The organization split again in 1963 with the formation of the Order of Bards, Ovates, and Druids, which drew off much of the original group's membership. Other Druid groups flourished in Britain in the early twentieth century.

In the United States, modern Druidism has had a small following, beginning in 1963 with the founding of the Reformed Druids of North America. The order was conceived by a group of students at Carleton College, Northfield, Minnesota, as a facetious protest against a school requirement that students attend religious services. Though the requirement was dropped in 1963, the reformed Druids caught on. The order expanded in a collection of autonomous "groves." Rituals were written from anthropological literature, such as Fraser's *The Golden Bough*. P. E. I. (Isaac) Bonewits emerged as a Druidic leader in the mid-1970s and added much to the modern writings. Some groves eventually split off to form the New Reformed Druids of America, and Bonewits left to form his own organization, Ár nDraíocht Féin ("Our Own Druidism") in 1983. By the late 1980s, Ár nDraíocht Féin was the only active, national Druid organization, with headquarters in Nyack, New York. Bonewits's goal was to pursue scholarly study of the Druids and their Indo-European contemporaries, and reconstruct a liturgy and rituals adapted to modern times. Like the British Druid organizations, the American groups claim no connection with the ancient Druids.

Modern Druids celebrate eight seasonal pagan festivals in outdoor henges and groves. The most prominent festival is the summer solstice. In England the neo-Druids were allowed to gather for eighty years at Stonehenge, until they were prohibited from doing so in 1985, due to vandalism by spectators during the public gatherings. A Stonehenge replica in eastern Washington State is used by many American Druids. See **Stonehenge.**

Sources: Margot Adler. *Drawing Down the Moon.* Rev. ed. Boston: Beacon Press, 1986; Malcolm W. Browne. "'Bog Man' Reveals Story of a Brutal Ritual." *The New York Times* (January 26, 1988): C-1, C-11; Georges Dottin. *The Civilization of the Celts.* New York: Crescent Books, 1981; Robert Graves. *The White Goddess.* Amended and enlarged ed. New York: Farrar, Straus and Giroux, 1966; Stuart Piggott. *The Druids.* New York: Thames and Hudson, 1986; Ward Rutherford. *The Druids: Magicians of the West.* Rev. ed. Wellingborough, Northamptonshire, England: The Aquarian Press, 1983; Jennifer Westwood, ed. *The Atlas of Mysterious Places.* New York: Weidenfeld & Nicholson, 1987.

E

Earth lights (also ghost lights, spook lights)

Mysterious luminous phenomena seen around the world, including more than one hundred sites throughout the United States and others in Britain, Japan, and elsewhere. Earth lights are inexplicable balls or patches of light reported to have been seen in remote areas, often near power lines, transmitter towers, mountain peaks, isolated buildings, roads, and railway lines. Neither marsh gas nor artificial lights, most earth lights are yellow or white, while others are red, orange, or blue. The lights may change color as they are observed. They appear randomly or regularly at particular sites, varying in size and configuration, and may be "active" for years. Some appear and become "inactive" after short periods of time.

Researchers have identified several common characteristics of earth lights: (1) The lights appear only in remote areas; (2) the lights are elusive, and the viewer must be at the proper distance and angle to see them; (3) the lights react to noise and light, such as from flashlights or car headlights, by receding into the distance or disappearing altogether; (4) the lights are often accompanied by outbreaks of gaseous materials; (5) observers frequently report a buzzing or humming sound in the vicinity of the sightings.

Perhaps the most famous earth lights are the Marfa lights, named after Marfa, Texas, about two hundred miles south of El Paso. These lights, first reported in 1883 by Robert Ellison, a settler, are often seen to the southwest of the Chinati Mountains. The Marfa lights frequently bounce up and down. One resident described them as running across the mountain like grass fire. Investigators who have chased the lights say they seem to possess intelligence and play games with humans.

Another active site is near Joplin, Missouri, where yellow and orange lights are visible every night from dusk until dawn. The lights have defied attempts to explain them and appear to be true anomalies. When viewed through binoculars, they appear to be diamond-shaped with hollow and transparent centers. They leave behind luminous pinpoints of light dancing in the air, as though they have their own intrinsic luminosities.

Since 1913 intense, multicolored lights also have been reported in the Brown Mountains of North Carolina. In 1916 a researcher from the United States Geological Survey dismissed the phenomenon as nothing more than train lights. Yet the lights continued to appear even after a flood later that year disrupted train service to that region for several weeks.

Not all reported earth lights are anomalies. Some have been shown to have natural explanations, most commonly car headlights. The anomalies have produced numerous theories as to their origins, causes, and meaning.

Some researchers theorize that earth lights are produced by seismic stresses beneath the earth. These stresses are said to generate high voltage that creates small masses of ionized gas, which are then released into the air near the fault line. Support for this theory can be found at several locations where earth lights have been reported. These include: seven of eight lochs in Scotland—sites of earth light activity—which are on a major fault line; the remote valley of Hessdalen, near Norway's Swedish border, which is in a fault region that has been subjected to earth tremors; and the Brown Mountain lights of North Carolina, which could be linked to the nearby Grandfather Mountain fault.

While study of earth lights is a modern phenomenon, early societies were apparently aware of them and incorporated them into their beliefs and practices. For example, the Native American Snohomish of Washington State regarded them as doors to the worlds beyond; while the Yakima, another Washington tribe, believed they could help them divine the future. The Australian Aborigines claim the spirits of the dead or evil beings manifest themselves as what they call *min-min* lights.

Earth lights also have been linked to locations where sacred shrines and monuments were erected by early societies. They have been seen around Viking burial sites, Himalayan temples, and other mystical or holy places, such as at England's Glastonbury Tor, the Castlerigg Stone Circle, and other Megalith sites.

Not surprisingly, the earth lights phenomena have sparked debate among those who claim they are terrestrial in origin and others who feel they are convincing evidence of UFOs. Researcher Paul Devereux's theory that earth lights represent an unfamiliar, but terrestrial form of electromagnetic energy has played a prominent role in at least one controversial study that suggests energy given off by the lights could spark changes in the brain that might lead some individuals to imagine they've had an encounter with a UFO. In laboratory experiments electromagnetism has been shown to affect the brain's hippocampus region, causing a subject to undergo an altered state of consciousness. Researchers have been able to duplicate the same kinds of visions and bodily sensations experienced by people who claim to have come in contact with extraterrestrials.

Sources: Paul Devereux. *Earth Lights Revelation.* London: Blandford Press, 1990; Paul Devereux. *Earthmind.* New York: Harper & Row, 1989; Sharon Jarvis, ed. *True Tales of the Uninvited.* New York: Bantam Doubleday Dell, 1989.

Earth mysteries

See **Dowsing; Earth lights; Leys; Megaliths; Planetary consciousness; Power point.**

ECKANKAR*

Religious movement founded in 1965 by the late Paul Twitchell, dedicated to presenting the teachings of ECK. ECK is the Holy Spirit, the life force, the "Audible Life Current" that sustains all life, and which manifests in light and sound. ECKANKAR headquarters are in Minneapolis, Minnesota, with followers in approximately one hundred countries.

ECKANKAR involves the study of Spirit in the lower worlds of matter, energy, space, and time. According to Twitchell, the 971st Living ECK Master, it is older than all religions on Earth, and traces of it can be found in most spiritual teachings. It was formerly a secret path to

*The terms ECKANKAR, ECK, Mahanta, and Soul Travel are trademarks of ECKANKAR.

Sri Paul Twitchell

his real name was Peddar Zaskq, that he never knew his real parents, and was raised by foster parents named Twitchell. His authorized biography, *In My Soul I Am Free* (1968), by Brad Steiger, says that he was an illegitimate child born on a Mississippi riverboat, and was raised by his father and stepmother in China Point, a southern town.

Twitchell said his father, a businessman who traveled widely, learned the art of Soul Travel, an expansion of consciousness, from an Indian holy man, Sudar Singh, of Allahabad. The elder Twitchell taught it to his older son and daughter. The daughter, Kay Dee, taught Paul Twitchell, the youngest, how to leave his body when he was three.

As a youth Twitchell met Singh in Paris, and with his sister went to Singh's ashram in Allahabad to study for a year. During World War II, he joined the Navy as a gunner. Small and wiry at five-foot-six, he was nicknamed "little toughie." He said he took numerous out-of-body trips during the war to save others in trouble and heal the sick.

In 1944, while Twitchell was serving aboard a Navy ship in the Pacific, a Tibetan master named Rebazar Tarzs appeared to him in his soul body. Tarzs, who claimed to be about five hundred years old, introduced Twitchell to a spiritual and mystical mystery called ECKANKAR.

Following the war Twitchell returned to the United States and settled in Seattle. He worked as a newspaper reporter and freelance writer for pulp magazines. He visited India again, and had intensive encounters in Soul Travel with Tarzs.

His spiritual beliefs were further influenced by his exposure to the Self-Realization Church of Absolute Monism, in Washington, DC; Scientology, in which he advanced to "clear"; and the Ruhani Satsang Sikh movement. Twitchell and his first wife joined the Self-

God. Central to ECKANKAR is mastery of "the Ancient Science of Soul Travel," which is the expansion of inner consciousness through the physical, astral, causal, mental, and etheric planes. Soul Travel provides the direct path to realization of SUGMAD (a sacred name of God).

According to ECKANKAR one may attain spiritual illumination without the asceticism required of adepts in other religions. ECKANKAR, a blend of Western and Eastern esoteric philosophies, espouses high moral values and a detachment from materialism. Initiates advance through various levels. The sacred scriptures of ECK are the *Shariyat-Ki-SUGMAD,* twelve volumes on the inner planes, the first two of which were transcribed by Twitchell.

Little is known about Twitchell's early life. He declined to give a birth date, and said not long before his death that

Living ECK Master Sri Harold Klemp

adoration among his followers, who called him the Mahanta, the embodiment of the highest state of God Consciousness on Earth. By 1988 ECKANKAR had established 284 centers in twenty-three countries.

In his later years, Twitchell said enemies were trying to assassinate him because of his spiritual beliefs, and he quit traveling alone. He died in 1971 and the ECK Rod of Power was handed to Darwin Gross. Gross's authority was challenged in 1980, and on October 22, 1981, he was succeeded by Harold Klemp, who had been named by Twitchell in 1970 as the third American Living ECK Master. Gross was later expelled from the Order of ECK Masters on charges of spiritual insubordination.

ECKANKAR headquarters were moved from Las Vegas, Nevada, to Menlo Park, California, in 1975, and then to Minneapolis, Minnesota, in 1986.

Realization Church, associated with the Self-Realization Fellowship of Paramahansa Yogananda, and lived on the grounds for more than five years. In 1955 they separated and left the church. They were divorced in 1960.

In 1964 Twitchell married Gail Atkinson, a University of Washington student. They moved to San Diego upon Tarzs's instructions to prepare for their life's work in ECKANKAR. Twitchell was to become the first American to be a Living ECK Master, or human representative of God, charged with the mission to spread the secret teachings of ECKANKAR.

In 1965 Twitchell began to write and lecture on ECKANKAR. Interest grew rapidly. Twitchell lectured around the world, and claimed to use Soul Travel to heal, exorcise ghosts from haunted houses, find missing persons and criminals, and help others in their spiritual quests. He inspired great admiration and

Soul Travel

Soul Travel, according to ECKANKAR, is the soul's journey home to God, an upliftment into ecstatic states of consciousness. The ability to leave the physical body at will and travel into the spiritual realms is taught to all ECKists. Twitchell preferred the term "Soul Travel" over "bilocation," which he felt sounded too much like astral projection (deemed harmful) and did not express the breadth and depth of ECKANKAR.

According to ECKANKAR the soul is sheathed in protective bodies. The ECKist travels in the Atma Sarup, the soul body. The travel is done in the four spirito-materialistic planes below the soul plane: physical, astral, causal, and mental. Soul Travel may be done alone, but it is preferable to be accompanied by a spiritual master who has attained the soul plane and is living—that is, the Living ECK Master.

Soul Travel may be accomplished through several basic methods, including dreaming, contemplation, and chanting "SUGMAD," "HU," or other holy words.

Sources: ECKANKAR: An Introduction. Booklet. Minneapolis: ECKANKAR, n.d.; John Godwin. Occult America. Garden City, NY: Doubleday, 1972; Harold Klemp. Soul Travelers of the Far Country. Minneapolis: ECKANKAR, 1987; Leslie A. Shepard, ed. Encyclopedia of Occultism and Parapsychology. 2d ed. Detroit: Gale Research Co., 1984; Brad Steiger. In My Soul I Am Free. Minneapolis: ECKANKAR, 1968; Paul Twitchell. ECKANKAR: The Key to Secret Worlds. San Diego: Illuminated Way Press, 1969; Paul Twitchell. The Spiritual Notebook. Menlo Park, CA: IWP Publishing, 1971; Paul Twitchell. The Tiger's Fang. New York: Lancet Books, 1967.

Eckhart, Johannes
(c. 1260–1327)

Dominican theologian and mystic, founder of "German mysticism." Johannes Eckhart is known generally as "Meister Eckhart" or simply "Meister" (Master). He is considered the most important medieval German mystic, and one of the most important figures in Christian mysticism.

Eckhart is said to have been born in Hockheim in Thuringia; no exact records of his date and place of birth exist. At about age fifteen, he joined the Dominican Order at Erfurt, where his exceptional abilities were recognized, and he was eventually sent to the Dominican Higher School in Cologne to study theology. There it is likely that he heard Thomas Aquinas and Albertus Magnus, who had a profound influence on the development of his mystical philosophy. Eckhart also was greatly influenced by Plotinus, Dionysius the Areopagite, Au-

gustine, and Erigena. He returned to Erfurt, and sometime between 1290 and 1298 was named prior.

He attended the University of Paris in 1300, and in 1302 received the title of Meister of Theology. The following year he was elected the first Provincial-Prior of the Dominican Order for Saxony (most of northern Germany and Holland). In 1307 he also became Vicar-General of Bohemia and was given the task of ridding the area of its notoriously lax ways and heretical views. The problems were compounded by the animosity between the Dominican and Franciscan orders.

In 1311 Eckhart returned to Paris, and in 1314 went to Strasbourg, where he launched his brilliant career as a preacher and teacher. He was enormously popular and drew large audiences, to whom he preached in their own language, not in Latin. He coined many philosophical and theological words. He was a prolific writer, composing in Latin. At around 1322 he went to Cologne.

On September 26, 1326, Eckhart was formally accused of heresy, in part because he was one of many victims of the political turmoil between Louis IV of Bavaria and Pope John XXII, and the difficulties between the Dominicans and Franciscans. The king disputed the election of the pope, who in turn excommunicated him. The dispute provided on opportunity for the Archbishop of Cologne, a Franciscan, to drive out Dominicans and bring them up before the Inquisition.

Eckhart was found guilty of nearly one hundred counts of heresy; his teachings were said to be dangerous to the common people in their own tongue. Though technically not answerable to the Archbishop of Cologne, Eckhart felt obliged to defend himself and his order and submitted to a trial. The ill-informed judges were no match for him, but the trial dragged on for nearly a year. Eckhart appealed to Pope John XXII, who ordered the documents in question to be sent to Avignon for hearings by a papal commission. Soon after his arrival there, Eckhart fell ill and died sometime before April 30, 1328. The exact circumstances of his death are not known: he may have died in Avignon, or on the road back to Cologne, or in Cologne.

Following Eckhart's death the commission dismissed seventy-one of the charges but found that seventeen works, of which Eckhart admitted preaching fifteen, were heretical. Another eleven were questionable. In 1329 Pope John XXII issued a bull condemning the seventeen works. The bull also said that prior to his death, Eckhart had revoked and deplored the twenty-six articles he admitted preaching that might be considered heretical. Therefore the pope would not excommunicate him posthumously. Modern theologians see Eckhart's renunciation not as a denial of the truth of his teachings, but only as an acknowledgment that some of his teachings might generate heretical opinions.

The condemnation hurt the spread of Eckhart's teachings, but pupils kept them alive. His work had a great influence on German and Flemish mystics of the fourteenth and fifteenth centuries, then nearly disappeared, but was preserved by the Dominican Order. Beginning in the nineteenth century, Eckhart was rediscovered, especially by the existential philosophers such as Georg Wilhelm Frederich Hegel, Johann Gottlieb Fichte, and Martin Heidegger, who were influenced by him. Later Zen Buddhist scholar D. T. Suzuki compared him to Zen masters, and the theologian Rudolph Otto analyzed his philosophy alongside that of the great Indian mystic and philosopher Sankara (788–820).

Eckhart's philosophy, which presumes a living cosmology, has found (along with the works of other medieval mystics) new meaning in the creation spirituality pioneered by Dominican Matthew Fox. See **Creation spirituality.**

Eckhart's Theology

Eckhart's theology is complex. The type of mysticism Eckhart taught is called "speculative" or "essential." He affirmed God as the "I am that I am" of the Old Testament, and distinguished between the Godhead and God. Godhead is "beingness," and God is creation, the "becoming" of all things. God can be born in and fill the soul, which in turn reflects the divine back to God while retaining its own identity. Mystical union between the God and the soul is achieved in the soul's depths, from where emanates a spark that unites the two while leaving them separate. The spark, said Eckhart, is indestructible, transcends time and space, and is the seat of conscience.

Eckhart saw the underlying, unbroken unity of all things existing in an ever-present Now, concepts found in Eastern mysticism and more recently in quantum physics. He said the soul is troubled by perceiving created things as separate. Instead, one must awaken to "Absolute Seeing," in which all things are appreciated simply for their "beingness" and not projected upon with our own thoughts. He emphasized the need to become one with whatever occurs at the moment.

Eckhart was not impressed with good works. What matters, he said, is the inner attitude. Detachment was a fundamental theme of Eckhart's preaching, appearing everywhere in his works. "You must know that to be empty of all created things is to be full of God, and to be full of created things is to be empty of God," he wrote in a short treatise, *On Detachment.* Thus the soul can only receive God when it is emptied. Eckhart emphasized an inner detachment, even from external religious exercises. Those who are "attached to their penances and external exercises" cannot understand Divine truth, he said in *Sermon 52.*

Another of his fundamental concepts, and among the most controversial, was the birth of the Son in the soul. The Father gives birth to the Son in eternity, and so is always giving birth to the Son. God's ground is the same as the soul's ground, so the Father then gives birth to the Son in the soul. The just man, therefore, takes part in the inner life of the Trinity. This concept formed the basis for Eckhart's teachings about the identity of sonship between the just man and the Son of God. In the condemnation of Eckhart, it was considered "suspect of heresy."

One of his heresies was his refutation of the prevailing view that humankind is God's greatest creation. He argued that all things are equal; they are all the same in God, and are God himself.

Sources: Anne Bancroft. *The Luminous Vision: Six Medieval Mystics and Their Teachings.* London: George Allen & Unwin, 1982; John Ferguson. *An Illustrated Encyclopedia of Mysticism and the Mystery Religions.* New York: Seabury Press, 1976; F. C. Happold. *Mysticism: A Study and an Anthology.* Rev. ed. Harmondsworth, Middlesex, England: Penguin Books, 1970; Robert Maynard Hutchins, ed. *Great Books of the Western World.* Chicago: Encyclopaedia Britannica, 1952; C. F. Kelley. *Meister Eckhart on Divine Knowledge.* New Haven: Yale University Press, 1977; Louis Kronenberger, ed. *Atlantic Brief Lives.* Boston: Little, Brown, 1971; Bernard McGinn et al. *Meister Eckhart: Teacher Preacher.* Ramsey, NJ: Paulist Press, 1986; *Meister Eckhart: The Essential Sermons, Commentaries, Treatises, and Defense.* Translated and introduction by Edmund Colledge, OSA and Bernard McGinn. New York: Paulist Press, 1981; Cyprian Smith. *The Way of Paradox: Spiritual Life As Taught by Meister Eckhart.* Ramsey, NJ: Paulist Press, 1988; Joseph R. Strayer, ed. in chief. *Dictionary of the Middle Ages.* New York: Charles Scribner's Sons, 1984; Frank Tobin. *Meister Eckhart: Thought, Language.* Middle Ages Series. Philadelphia: University of Pennsylvania Press, 1986; Michael Walsh, ed. *Butler's Lives of the Saints.* Concise ed. San Francisco: Harper & Row, 1985.

Ecstasy

The psycho-physical condition that accompanies the apprehension of what one experiences as the ultimate reality. The ultimate reality may differ, as for Indian mystics and Christian saints, for example. Yet, as psychical researcher Frederic W. H. Myers observed, "the evidence for ecstasy is stronger than the evidence for any other religious belief" (*Human Personality and Its Survival of Bodily Death,* 1903).

Religious ecstasy, such as discussed by the mystic-theologians, including Augustine, Thomas Aquinas, and Meister Eckhart, may be the experience of that which is presumed by faith to be an anticipating of the beatific vision—the ultimate and everlasting experience of being in the presence of God. Typically, there is a sudden, heightened inner consciousness of stillness and peace, a loss of sense of self, and an identification with God and all things. Such ultimate religious experience may be best described by the mystic poets, exemplified by William Blake. See **Blake, William.** Related also is the "quietness of the soul" described by the great Spanish mystics John of the Cross and Teresa de Avila, and Italian mystic Catherine of Siena, although they often experienced also the "dark night of the soul." See **John of the Cross, St.**

The state of ecstasy feels timeless. One may believe the state endures a long time, though usually it lasts less than half an hour; some recorded ecstasies allegedly have lasted several days. The longest on record is an astonishing thirty-five years, claimed by a Tyrolean woman, Maria von Moerl (1812–1868).

In her book *Mysticism* (1955), Evelyn Underhill describes three distinct aspects under which the ecstatic state may be studied: the physical, the psychological, and the mystical. She comments that many of the misunderstandings that surround the topic come from the refusal of experts in one of these areas to consider the results arrived at by the other two.

Physically, ecstasy is a trance, accompanied by a lowered breathing and circulation, rigidity of limbs, and even total anesthesia. The onset of ecstasy usually is gradual, following a period of contemplation of the Divine. It can occur suddenly and seem to seize a person, a condition some mystics call rapture. Psychologically, all ecstasy is a complete unification of consciousness or what Underhill termed "complete mono-ideism," that is, the deliberate focus on one idea. The latter, when an exalted form of contemplation, is related to the "centering" advocated by Zen meditation masters. Mystically, ecstasy is an exalted act of perception—"the last term of contemplation," as described by Underhill: "The word has become a synonym for joyous exaltation, for the inebriation of the Infinite."

The study of ecstasy has been called "the psychology of joy" by Jungian analyst Robert A. Johnson, who, in *Ecstasy: Understanding the Psychology of Joy* (1987), approaches the topic in relation to the myth of Dionysus. The unique Greek god, being half-mortal and half-god, is described by Johnson as "the personification of divine ecstasy, who can bring transcendent joy or madness." But in the myth of this god we can find also "the capricious, unpredictable thrill of joy" as well as the "personification of wine and its ability to bring either spiritual transcendence or physical addiction."

Such revival of interest in the topic of ecstasy may be influenced at least partly by the American humanistic psychologist Abraham H. Maslow (1908–1978). In fact, ecstasy may be similar to what Maslow called "peak experiences," or sudden moments during which a person experiences a feeling of unity and joy that surrenders to serenity.

In his classic, *Toward A Psychology of Being* (1962), Maslow observed that it is the nature of a desire to be replaced by another desire as soon as the first desire is satisfied. Moreover, he found the drive for self-actualization (realizing one's fullest potential) can be observed in exceptional individuals in whom all lower needs are satisfied. He proposed that self-actualizing people (people who are unusually healthy psychologically) have had, or appear to have, intense insight, joy, or awareness, which he termed "peak experiences." See **Peak experiences.**

In popular culture visions of ecstasy may be "heaven on earth." However, not all visions are ecstatic, as seen in visions described in the biblical writings of Isaiah, Ezekiel, Hosea, Micah, Daniel, and John. Such visions are often vehicles through a prophet of revelations intended for the faithful humankind, rather than primarily personal ecstatic experiences. In fact, some visions are denounced in the Bible, such as by Jeremiah (14:14) and Ezekiel (13:7). See **Prophecy.**

Ecstasy is also distinct from fantasy, which may also be a generally pleasant experience, but is more imagined than real. These can be experienced while asleep or while awake, as in daydreams. They can take on an extreme form, such as in hallucination, in terms of being a false perception that may have the character of a true sense perception, but without the appropriate physical stimulation.

Ecstasy in the form of rapture is often accompanied by a "carrying-away" sensation (related in its concrete form to levitation of the body), as recorded in detail by John of the Cross, Teresa of Avila, Bernard of Clairvaux, Marie de l'Incarnation, and other great mystics. This is distinct from out-of-body experiences.

Popular use of the word "ecstasy" usually is reserved for peak experiences, including those artificially induced by a super-tranquilizer called Ecstasy (MDMA), which became illegal in 1985 and then became the model for powerful "designer drugs" similarly nicknamed. See **Mystical experiences; Mysticism; Psychology; Synchronicity.**

Sources: John Ferguson. *An Illustrated Encyclopedia of Mysticism and the Mystery Religions.* New York: Seabury Press, 1976; Fred H. Johnson. *The Anatomy of Hallucinations.* Chicago: Nelson Hall, 1978; Robert A. Johnson. *Ecstasy: Understanding the Psychology of Joy.* San Francisco: Harper & Row, 1987; Abraham H. Maslow. *Toward A Psychology of Being.* Princeton, NJ: Van Nostrand, 1962; Frederic W. H. Myers. *Human Personality and Its Survival of Bodily Death.* Vols. 1 and 2. 1903. New ed. New York: Longmans, Green & Co., 1954; J. D. Page. *Psychopathology: The Science of Understanding Deviance.* 2d ed. New York: Oxford University Press, 1975; Evelyn Underhill. *Mysticism.* 1955. New York: New American Library, 1974; Donald Wigal. *A Sense of Life.* New York: Herder & Herder, 1969.

Ectoplasm

A white, fluidic substance said to emanate from the bodily orifices of a medium that is molded by spirits to assume phantom physical shapes. Substances purported to be ectoplasm have been photographed, but the existence of the substance has never been proven. It once was a frequent characteristic of Spiritualist seances.

According to some mediums, ectoplasm is exuded only under certain conditions, such as in trance states during a seance. It is damaged by exposure to light, a reason given why seances are held in dark or dimly lit rooms.

Ectoplasm supposedly manifests as a solidified white mist and has a peculiar smell. In some cases the smell may be due to chemical trickery. "Ectoplasm" can be created from a mixture of soap, gelatin, and egg white, which, when blown into the air, shimmers and glows in bubble-

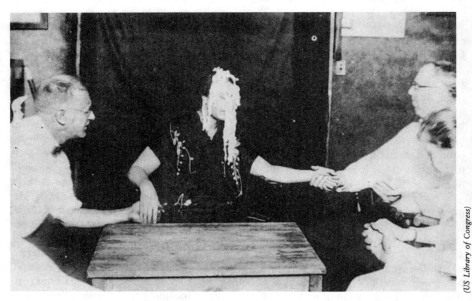

(US Library of Congress)

Medium Mina Crandon, known as "Margery," allegedly producing ectoplasm at seance

like forms. Another recipe calls for tooth-paste and peroxide. A common trick among fraudulent mediums in the late nineteenth century was to use muslin.

Nevertheless, many witnesses have testified to the actuality of ectoplasm. The most common manifestation of ectoplasm at early Spiritualist seances was phantom hands, called pseudopods, which shook the hands of sitters and felt icy to the touch. Ectoplasm was the subject of extensive studies by psychical researchers well into the twentieth century. It is not a phenomenon of channeling. See **Home, Daniel Dunglas; Materialization.**

Sources: Richard Cavendish, ed. *The Encyclopedia of the Unexplained.* New York: McGraw-Hill, 1974; I. G. Edmonds. *D. D. Home: The Man Who Talked with Ghosts.* Nashville: Thomas Nelson, 1978; John Godwin. *Occult America.* Garden City, NY: Doubleday, 1972; Janet Oppenheim. *The Other World: Spiritualism and Psychical Research in England, 1850–1914.* Cambridge, England: Cambridge University Press, 1985.

Eddy, Mary Baker

See **Church of Christ, Scientist.**

Electronic voice phenomenon

The recording on magnetic tape of what seem to be supernatural voices, some of which are audible. Some of the voices identify themselves as the spirits of the dead. Other theories to explain them propose that they are extraterrestrials, impressions from the Akashic Records, or an unknown phenomenon of the subconscious mind. Many psychical researchers believe the voices, at least in some cases, are merely intercepted radio transmissions or static, or distorted mechanical noises.

Electronic voices are also called "Raudive voices," named after a Latvian psychologist, Konstantin Raudive, a lead-ing researcher into the phenomenon in the 1960s and 1970s. Raudive was inspired by the experimentation of Friedrich Jurgenson, Swedish opera singer, painter, and film producer. In 1959 Jurgenson tape recorded bird songs in the Swedish countryside near his villa. On playback he heard a male voice discuss "nocturnal bird songs" in Norwegian. At first Jurgenson thought he had picked up a radio broadcast, but thought it strange that such an accident would be a discussion of bird songs. He made other bird song recordings. He heard no voices during taping, but playback yielded many voices, which seemed to have personal information for him, plus instructions on how to record more voices.

Jurgenson experimented with the voices for several years. In 1964 he published a book in Sweden, *Voices from the Universe,* along with a record. Jurgenson and Raudive met in 1965.

Raudive recorded over 100,000 electronic voice phrases. The voices speak in different languages, some very clearly, others sounding like bad long-distance telephone connections. Some of the words and phrases are clear, while other messages seem to be delivered in code. Sometimes one or two voices are heard, at other times a multitude of them. The voices are identifiable as men, women, and children. Raudive published his research in German in *The Inaudible Made Audible,* translated into English in 1971 under the title *Breakthrough.*

The phenomenon has been studied by numerous psychical researchers around the world and has generated a great deal of controversy. Some researchers agree the voices are paranormal, while others believe they are natural sounds, such as someone rubbing the case of a tape recorder, or the white noise that occurs on tape.

Between 1970 and 1972, the Society for Psychical Research in London commissioned D. J. Ellis to investigate the phenomenon. Ellis concluded that the voices most likely were a natural phenomenon. He said the interpretation of the sounds was highly subjective and was susceptible to imagination.

Raudive, who died on September 2, 1974, expressed no particular theory. At the time of his death, he was studying a parakeet that apparently had begun uttering meaningful sentences in German, in a manner characteristic of the Raudive voices.

Research into the electronic voice phenomenon continues by various individuals and groups. The American Association-Electronic Voice Phenomena, founded in 1982 by Sarah Estep, has more than two hundred members in thirty-four states in the United States and eleven foreign countries. The association calls itself "a metaphysical organization interested in spiritual evolvement as well as all genuine evidence for postmortem survival," and focuses on "objective contact with those in other dimensions through tape recorders, televisions, and computers." See also **Phone calls from the dead.**

Sources: Peter Bander. *Carry On Talking: How Dead Are the Voices?* Gerrards Cross, England: Colin Smythe Ltd., 1972; Peter Bander. *Voices from the Tapes: Recording from the Other World.* New York: Drake Publishers, 1973; Raymond Bayless. "Correspondence." *The Journal of the American Society for Psychical Research* 53, no. 1 (January 1959): 35–38; D. J. Ellis. *The Mediumship of the Tape Recorder.* Pulborough, England: Self-published, 1978; Alan Gauld. *Mediumship and Survival.* London: William Heinemann Ltd., 1982; Edgar D. Mitchell. *Psychic Exploration: A Challenge for Science.* Edited by John White. New York: Paragon Books, 1974; Sheila Ostrander and Lynn Schroeder. *Handbook of Psi Discoveries.* New York: Berkley, 1974; Konstantin Raudive. *Breakthrough: An Amazing Experiment in Electronic Communication with the Dead.* New York: Taplinger, 1971.

Elementals

See **Nature spirits.**

Emmanuel

See **Channeling.**

Empathy

Tuning in on an intuitive or psychic level to the emotions, moods, and attitudes of a person, group of people, or animals. Empathy is neither entirely conscious nor entirely unconscious, but falls in between. It apparently involves psi phenomena such as the telepathic transmission of feelings and thoughts, sometimes over long distances. Empathy in face-to-face situations may be derived in part from an unconscious reading of muscular movements and tension.

Empaths are particularly susceptible to feelings of suffering and distress. The physical ills of another may manifest in the empath's own body in the same place, while emotional disturbances may manifest as depression. These conditions are picked up from places as well as people. For example, an empath may walk into a church and sense the suffering of all the people who have come to the church for solace: the church itself may seem to cry. Some empaths can sense illness and disease in another before the other person is aware of the problem, as in cases of cancer. These empathetic experiences are not the same as psychometry, which requires touching objects to gain impressions, or with Therapeutic Touch, a type of medical diagnosis done by scanning one's aura with the hands.

Empaths may sense death at a distance, sometimes before it occurs. The sensations may involve the afflicted part of the body; an empath may feel chest pain concerning a person who is about to die of a heart attack. Empathy at a distance is most likely to occur between people who have close emotional ties. Twins are particularly noted for empathetic or sympathetic links, and mothers often are empathetic with their children.

Some empaths find that in addition to sensing emotions, they absorb them like sponges. The impact can be devastating in the encounter of distress and depression, sometimes leaving an empath drained of energy.

Cases have been documented of animals exhibiting empathy at a distance. Pets sense when their owners are in trouble or have been injured or killed, and become agitated or depressed. Pets also sense when something happens at a distance to another animal in the household. Research indicates that animals retain an empathetic link to their offspring, parents, and litter mates. See **Animal psi; Clairsentience; Psychic attack.**

Sources: Isaac Bonewits. *Real Magic.* Rev. ed. York Beach, ME: Samuel Weiser, 1989; Craig Junjulas. *Psychic Tarot.* Dobbs Ferry, NY: Morgan & Morgan, 1985; Sheila Ostrander and Lynn Schroeder. *The ESP Papers: Scientists Speak Out from Behind the Iron Curtain.* New York: Bantam Books, 1976; D. Scott Rogo. *Psychic Breakthroughs Today.* Wellingborough, Northamptonshire, England: The Aquarian Press, 1987; Benjamin B. Wolman, ed. *Handbook of Parapsychology.* New York: Van Nostrand Reinhold, 1977.

Encounter phenomenon

Any one of a wide range of experiences involving alternate realities and nonphysical beings, as found in folklore, mythology, mysticism, shamanism, parapsychology, and psychology. Seemingly disparate encounters—such as visions of angels, possession, channeling of entities, religious conversions, shamanic journeys, near-death experiences (NDEs), and UFO abductions—share some common characteristics. Various theories have been put forward to explain encounters, though the nature and purpose of such experiences perhaps cannot be accounted for by any single explanation.

Encounters with alternate realities may seem arbitrary and accidental, thrust upon the ordinary consciousness without warning. Most encounters, however, are motivated and have intention. For example, some come in response to crises such as life-threatening situations, or are brought about deliberately through pursuit of a spiritual path, or are mechanisms by which to escape stressful situations. Whether the motivation comes from an external source or from within is a matter of debate.

Despite a great variety in the types of encounters with alternate realities, records through the ages show a marked similarity in characteristics: (1) feelings of friendliness, love, wonder, awe, fearlessness; (2) being anointed as a messenger to humanity; (3) instruction, initiation, rite of passage, or enlightenment; (4) psychokinetic feats such as levitation, flying, passing through material objects; (5) the appearance of unusual or overpowering light, or of beings of light; (6) transportation to a nonordinary realm; (7) passage across a threshold or border; (8) an inkling of the ineffable; (9) revelations; and (10) extrasensory perception (ESP). Not all encounters necessarily have all characteristics.

Theories to explain encounters fall into three general categories: (1) literal; (2) projections from the unconscious; (3) interaction with a higher realm of consciousness.

Literal

The simplest explanation of encounters is that they are what they appear to be and must be taken at face value. Probably the majority of people who have encounters interpret them accordingly (assuming the experiences are not denied).

Therefore, a meeting with a fairy is just that, as is a vision of the Virgin Mary, or an encounter with a flying saucer full of extraterrestrials.

However, cultural and personal beliefs play a powerful role in shaping the nature of an encounter and one's interpretation of it. Thus the Devil of the Middle Ages perhaps becomes the UFO-related Man in Black of modern times. See **Men in Black**. The NDE, with its characteristics of tunnels, overpowering light, the feeling of a divine presence, and clairaudient voices, closely resembles many mystical experiences and religious conversions, such as that of St. Paul. See **Paul, St.** Even extraterrestrials, many of whom purport to come as helpers to humankind, resemble the helping angels of earlier ages. UFO abductee Betty Andreasson, under hypnosis, drew pictures of her alien kidnappers that resembled other pictures drawn by other abductees; pear-shaped heads, cat's eyes, nostril holes, and a slash for a mouth. Yet Andreasson's own religious orientation led her to interpret them as "angels."

As culture and personal belief shape the nature of encounters, so do encounters reinforce culture and personal belief. A repetition of a type of encounter makes it more likely that other individuals in the same culture who find themselves open to alternate realities will have the same type of experience.

Projections from the Subconscious

The influence of culture and personal belief lends some credence to the second group of theories that hold that encounters involve no literal external agents such as aliens or angels, but are exteriorizations of the unconscious. The encounter is said to happen when the unconscious deems a flight from reality necessary to relieve stress. The individual experiences a depersonalization and identifies with a culturally acceptable role model. The unconscious decides what kind of encounter will take place. Some encounters are so powerful that the person's life is permanently changed. Such experiences may be the result of a long-term germination deep within the unconscious. Collective encounters, such as mass visions of the Virgin Mary, may then be viewed as projections from the collective unconscious symptomatic of a racial struggle for spiritual development. Psychiatrist Carl G. Jung thought UFOs might be collective archetypal expressions of a great transformation in human consciousness.

Reliance upon this type of escape from reality can lead to chronic altered states of consciousness and mental illness, as seen in schizophrenia and multiple personality, in which encounters are of a negative nature.

Interaction with a Higher Realm of Consciousness

From this viewpoint at least some encounters are genuine interactions with the Mind at Large, a divine creative power permeating the universe, and are intended to further the spiritual development of human consciousness. Thus they are archetypes of enlightenment, preparing the way for a new psychophysical adaptation to the environment, as described in Teilhard de Chardin's "noosphere," or for postmortem survival in a new form of consciousness.

Encounters with alternate realities involve psi in various forms, as well as (on occasion) supernormal physical abilities. Some parapsychologists state that psi shows the presence of an alternate and deep level of psychic functioning, one that has little value and presence in the ordinary world, but which seems more appropriate for alternate realities toward which humankind might be evolving.

The matter of survival after death has vexed psychical researchers for more than a century. No scientific proof of survival has been found, leaving belief in immortality of the soul to religion and personal conviction. NDEs provide convincing evidence of survival to many, yet still are not considered scientifically evidential.

The "Encounter-Prone Personality"

Research shows that some individuals are more likely to have encounters with alternate realities than are others, raising more questions as to the source of the phenomenon. The most significant factor seems to be excessive stress and trauma in childhood, including physical, sexual, and psychological abuse, neglect, a negative home atmosphere, and serious illness. These findings do not necessarily mean that these stresses cause encounters, only that individuals who report encounters are more likely to have these factors in their backgrounds. Such stresses can result in dissociation, in which part of the psyche splits off from itself as a means of self-defense. Children under these conditions seem more likely to have early alternate realities encounters, such as seeing nonphysical beings while awake.

Some studies, but not all, have shown that childhood tendencies toward fantasy and imagination also are factors.

Some researchers believe that encounters with alternative realities are all or predominantly fantasy, while others disagree. See **Extraterrestrial encounters; Mystical experiences; Near-death experience (NDE); Planetary consciousness; Shamanism.**

Sources: Hilary Evans. *Alternate States of Consciousness: Unself, Otherself, and Superself.* Wellingborough, England: The Aquarian Press, 1989. Michael Grosso. *The Final Choice: Playing the Survival Game.* Walpole, NH: Stillpoint Publishing, 1985; Kenneth Ring and Christopher J. Rosing. "The Omega Project: An Empirical Study of the NDE-Prone Personality." *Journal of Near-Death Studies* 8, no. 4 (Summer 1990): 211–39; Peter M. Rocjewicz. "The Extraordinary Encounter Continuum Hypothesis and Its Implications for the Study of Belief Materials." *Folklore Forum* 19, no. 2 (1986): n.p.

Enlightenment

See **Mystical experiences; Mysticism.**

Enneagram

See **Gurdjieff, Georgei Ivanovitch.**

Erhard, Werner

See **est.**

Erlendur, Haraldsson

See **Deathbed visions; Sai Baba.**

ESP (extrasensory perception)

A so-called "sixth sense," in which sensory information is perceived through means beyond the five senses of sight, hearing, smell, touch, and taste. ESP brings a person information about the present, past, or future. It seems to originate in a second, or alternate, reality.

The term "ESP" was used as early as 1870 by Sir Richard Burton. In 1892 Dr. Paul Joire, a French researcher, observed people who were hypnotized or in trance, and used ESP to describe the ability to externally sense without using the known senses. In the 1920s Dr. Rudolph Tischner, a Munich ophthalmologist, used ESP to describe "externalization of sensibility." The term was popularized in the 1930s by American parapsychologist J. B. Rhine to cover psychic phenomena analogous to sensory functions. Rhine was one of the first parapsychologists to test for ESP in the laboratory.

The term ESP is sometimes applied in popular usage loosely, and sometimes inaccurately, to any psychic or paranormal phenomena. ESP may be divided into two broad categories: telepathy and clairvoyance, both of which may be directed forward (precognition) and backward (retrocognition). ESP does not include psychokinesis (PK) or out-of-body experiences.

In *New Frontiers of the Mind* (1937), Rhine notes that historically learned people long held a common assumption that nothing enters the human mind except through the five senses, and that therefore the mind is subject to the laws of the mechanical world. Since the birth of psychical research in the late nineteenth century, researchers have devoted a great deal of effort to trying to prove in the laboratory that ESP exists, and to discover the physical mechanism by which it operates. The mind has been equated with the brain, and scientists have searched to discover how ESP registers in the brain/mind.

However, mounting evidence has demonstrated that ESP exists, but that it cannot be explained or quantified by physical laws; and, furthermore, that mind (consciousness) and brain are two distinct entities. At the same time, research in quantum physics points to the existence of a second, nonmaterial universe. Thus the Western scientist increasingly must come to terms with an Eastern mystical concept: that an extrasensory force exists in another reality, and intersects and integrates with the physical world.

ESP does not function like a sense. There is no localization, which governs other senses that receive information through various parts of the body; and it does not depend on any of the other five senses. Nor does ESP depend upon such factors as geography, time, intelligence, age, or education.

Explanations of ESP

Prior to Rhine's research at Duke University in North Carolina, other psychical researchers had attempted to name and define the "hidden sense." In the nineteenth century, Professor Charles Richet coined the term "cryptesthesia." Frederic W. H. Myers, one of the founders of the Society for Psychical Research, used "telesthesia" for what later came to be called "clairvoyance" or "seeing at a distance." At one time researchers generally believed that any psychic transfer of information required two people, one to send and one to receive. This premise was subsequently disproved, for clairvoyance involves the perception of information that doesn't seem to be in anyone's mind. Rhine coined the term "general extrasensory perception" (GESP) to include both telepathy and clairvoyance. Later the term "psi" was designated to cover ESP, or GESP, and PK. See **Psi.** Some Russian scientists call ESP "bioinformation."

Researcher Louisa E. Rhine proposed that ESP begins in the deep unconscious, the storehouse of memories, hopes, fears, and so on. Here contact is made between the objective world and the center of the mind. The individual is unaware of the contact until and unless information filters up to the conscious mind. Similarly, psychiatrist Carl G. Jung proposed that the conscious mind has subliminal psychic access to the collective unconscious, a vast repository of accumulated wisdom and experience of the human race. See **Collective unconscious.**

In a theory published in 1960, Dr. Hilda Gertrud Heine of the University of New Zealand proposed that macrophages, a type of cell present in connective tissue, lymph nodes, and bone marrow and tied to nerve endings, are the body's ESP organs, sending and receiving impressions below the level of normal perception. Such cells are more sensitive and active in childhood, and deteriorate without proper diet.

More recently, other theories have focused on the existence of a second consciousness that integrates with both physical and second realities. This second consciousness may be called soul, subliminal self, superconsciousness, transcendent ego, dream self, or a host of similar names. Subliminal barriers exist between the two consciousnesses, otherwise the waking conscious would be bombarded with information rising up out of the second reality. (A further discussion of metaphysical and physical theories of ESP is incorporated with PK under **Psi.**)

Forms of ESP

How information from the second reality reaches the conscious mind depends upon the following: the conditions that exist at the moment the information becomes available; the natural proclivities for ESP in the individual; and the colorations and distortions created by prejudices, thoughts, and conditionings. In a study of 10,000 cases involving ESP, the findings of which were published in 1963, Louisa E. Rhine divided ESP into four basic forms: realistic dreams (39 percent); intuition (30 percent); unrealistic dreams (18 percent); and hallucinations (13 percent). Realistic dreams contain vivid, detailed imagery of the information conveyed. Intuition includes "gut feelings," forebodings, and premonitions. Unrealistic dreams contain fantastical imagery and symbols. Hallucinations include visual and auditory sensations that relay information. Rhine suggested that dreams may be the most efficient carriers of ESP messages, because in sleep the barriers to the conscious mind appear to be thinnest.

Rhine also said the ESP that proves to be inaccurate may be the result of distortions and blockages of the conscious mind. Most ESP incidents occur spontaneously, and a high percent concern crises, accidents and deaths of loved ones, and major disasters. Perhaps trauma and shock enable negative information to break through the subliminal barriers more easily than positive, happy information.

Who Has ESP?

In all types of paranormal gifts, the evidence is strong that the exceptional ability is inherited. Certainly in ages past, those who were renowned as seers, prophets, and diviners appeared to have been born with exceptional ESP gifts, and often to have other family members who were similarly gifted. That does not mean, however, that only selected individuals possess ESP and the rest of the population does not. One theory holds that ESP is a primordial sense that has become less accessible as civilization and technology have advanced; another theory holds that it is a supersense that is evolving in the nervous system.

Psychical research supports the theory that all people have the capacity for ESP, though some are born more talented than others. Most people have at least one ESP experience in their lives. According to a survey published in 1987 by the University of Chicago's National Opinion Research Council, 67 percent of all adult Americans believe they have experienced ESP. Eleven years earlier the figure was 58 percent. The increase may be indicative of an increasing acceptance of the possibility of ESP among the general public.

Studies have shown that certain environmental, emotional, and attitudinal factors affect ESP performance in the laboratory. People who are relaxed, believe in the possibility of ESP, and are intuitive by nature tend to perform better than those who are tense, skeptical, and analytical. See **Sheep/goat effect.** ESP ability can be developed and strengthened with training, although talented subjects who are repeatedly tested in the laboratory begin to decline in performance, perhaps due to boredom. See **Decline/incline effects.** Some individuals say they discover or are able to enhance their ESP through meditation, yoga, and the use of mind-altering drugs. See **Clairvoyance; Drugs in mystical and psychic experiences; Intuition; Meditation; Precognition; Super-ESP; Telepathy; Yoga.**

Sources: Hugh Lynn Cayce. *Venture Inward.* New York: Harper & Row, 1964; Hoyt L. Edge, Robert L. Morris, John Palmer, and Joseph H. Rush. *Foundations of Parapsychology.* Boston: Routledge & Kegan Paul, 1986; Andrew Greeley. "Mysticism Goes Mainstream." *American Health* (January/February 1987): 47–49; Hilda Gertrud Heine. *The Vital Sense: The Implication and Explanation of the Sixth Sense.* London: Cassell & Co., 1960; Lawrence LeShan. *Alternate Realities.* New York: M. Evans & Co., 1967; Gardner Murphy. "Direct Contacts with Past and Future: Retrocognition and Precognition." *The Journal of the American Society for Psychical Research* 61, no. 1 (January 1967): 3–23; J. B. Rhine. *New Frontiers of the Mind.* New York: Farrar & Rinehart, 1937; Louisa Rhine. *ESP in Life and Lab: Tracing Hidden Channels.* New York: Collier Books, 1967; Ingo Swann. *Natural ESP.* New York: Bantam Books, 1987; Benjamin B. Wolman, ed. *Handbook of Parapsychology.* New York: Van Nostrand Reinhold, 1977.

ESP cards

A deck of twenty-five cards of five symbols: a star, a cross, a square, a circle, and a set of three wavy lines. Formerly called Zener cards, ESP cards once were a standard tool in laboratory psychical research for testing telepathy, clairvoyance,

(Photo by Bonnie Sue courtesy FRNM.)

ESP cards

and precognition. The cards are occasionally used in the lab, but they have virtually been replaced by the computer.

Before an experiment the cards are thoroughly shuffled. In a telepathy test, a tester goes through the deck, concentrating on each symbol one at a time; the subject, or percipient, writes down the symbols as they are perceived. In clairvoyance a tester picks cards out of the pack face down and places them down; the percipient records the hidden symbols as they are perceived. In precognition the percipient attempts to name the cards in order before they are shuffled by the sender.

Going through the entire deck constitutes a "run." The score is measured against mean chance expectation (MCE); a percipient may be expected to hit one out of five correctly. Precautions are taken to guard against fraud and accidental invalidation by sealing the cards in opaque containers or envelopes and placing the tester and percipient in separate rooms, sometimes separate buildings.

ESP cards were first used in 1930 at Duke University in North Carolina. They were created by two Duke faculty members, J. B. Rhine and Karl Zener, as a simplification of psi tests using regular playing cards. As early as 1884, such tests had been conducted by Dr. Charles Richet of France, and others.

By 1932, after exhaustive testing, Rhine found eight subjects who consistently scored better than chance. Out of a total of 85,724 tests, the eight had scored 24,364 hits, or 7,219 more than could be expected by chance. From 1933 to 1934, Rhine conducted long-distance tests involving his highest scorer, Hubert Pearce, a Duke divinity student, and J. Gaither Pratt, a graduate student. With Pratt and Pearce in separate buildings, Rhine conducted 1,850 clairvoyance tests over eight months. Pearce's score was so high that the odds against it were 10 followed by 21 zeros to 1, definitely ruling out chance as an explanation.

In 1934 Rhine published these and other results in a controversial monograph, *Extra-Sensory Perception*. Other researchers tried to replicate the results, with mixed results. Critics claimed the tests were invalid because too much potential for fraud existed in the way the cards were shuffled or handled; under certain light the symbols could be vaguely discerned through the backs of the cards. Critics also said there was a possibility that the subjects could have picked up sensory clues, such as body language, from the testers. To avoid such hazards, test procedures were altered, and sender and receiver were placed in separate rooms or buildings.

In 1936 ESP cards were made available to the public. Rhine continued to use them for decades in psi tests, after changing his procedures to eliminate any possibility of fraud or unconscious influence. Test results using ESP cards have scored consistently high overall. One interesting phenomenon is displacement; some subjects correctly identify the card immediately before or after the target card. In modern psychical research laboratories, ESP card images and random orders are generated by computer. See **Displacement; Ganzfeld stimulation; Remote viewing.**

Sources: Into the Unknown. Pleasantville, NY: Reader's Digest, 1981; Edgar D. Mitchell. *Psychic Exploration: A Challenge*

for Science. Edited by John White. New York: Paragon Books, 1974; J. B. Rhine. *New Frontiers of the Mind.* New York: Farrar & Rinehart, 1937; Carl Sargent and Hans J. Eyseck. *Know Your Own Psi-Q.* New York: World Almanac Publications, 1983; Benjamin B. Wolman, ed. *Handbook of Parapsychology.* New York: Van Nostrand Reinhold, 1977.

Essenes

Members of an ascetic sect, Jewish in heritage, most of whom lived in the Qumran settlement on the western shore of the Dead Sea during the century before and the century after the birth of Jesus. Modern interest in them is due mainly to the discovery in the Qumran caves in the 1940s of the documents popularly called the Dead Sea Scrolls.

Modern research on the Essenes in general and the Qumran community in particular is based not only on the Dead Sea Scrolls, but also on the writings of first-century historians, including Philo of Alexandria. According to these descriptions, the Essenes were a peaceful, primarily religious community of about four thousand members who shared their possessions. Their livelihood centered on agriculture and handicrafts. They rejected slavery and believed in the immortality of the soul. After two to three years of preparation, each person took an oath of piety, justice, and truthfulness.

The community had a regular schedule of solemn meals, prayer, and study, especially on the Sabbath. There was a central teacher and titles for various officeholders. The central group opposed marriage. Transgressors were excluded.

Because of the similarity of these practices and those of the early Christian communities, the assumption often is made that there was some relationship between the two. It has even been proposed that some members followed John the Baptist or even became, or were also,

Christians. However, various contemporary writers, such as Nahum N. Glatzer, hold that other direct connections between the Essenes and the early Christians seems unlikely. Still, connections continue to be made, such as in commentaries on the Edgar Cayce readings.

Cayce's readings depict the Essenes, for example, as playing an important part in the spiritual preparations of the Jews for the birth of the Messiah. Cayce saw them as "the outgrowth of the periods of preparations from the teaching of Melchizedek, as prolonged by Elijah and Elisha and Samuel" (Reading 254).

Recent studies do show the importance of Melchizedek in the Essene faith. But Cayce goes further, to propose that Anne (the mother of Mary) and Mary and Joseph (the parents of Jesus) were members of the Essene community, and that Mary and Joseph were married at the Essene temple on Mount Carmel (Reading 5749-15).

The Essenes and the Dead Sea Scrolls are the subjects of ongoing study in the fields of theology and religion. An appreciation of this community, which existed at the most dynamic era of Judeo-Christian history, is vital to the understanding of Western and Eastern religious lifestyles in general. Also important is its influence on the letter and spirit of many of the most important documents of Western civilization. Among these are the *Rule of the Master*, a sixth-century monastic document, which in turn influenced St. Benedict in his *Regula Monachorum*, a work that set the standard for all monastic life and influenced medieval university teachings. See **Benedict, St.; Dead Sea Scrolls; Gnosticism.**

Sources: **Philip Davies.** *Qumran.* New York: State Mutual, 1982; Glenn Sanderfur. *Lives of the Master: The Rest of the Jesus Story.* Virginia Beach, VA: ARE Press, 1988; Marcel Simon. *Sects at the Time of Jesus.* Translated by James Farley. Minneapolis: Augsburg Fortress, 1980;

Krister Stendahl. *The Scrolls and the New Testament.* Westport, CT: Greenwood, 1975.

est (Erhard Seminars Training)

A human potential system launched in 1971 by Werner Erhard, the pseudonym of John Paul Rosenberg, a Philadelphia-born sales training executive. The core est program consists of a sixty-hour seminar, the purpose of which is to force participants to take responsibility for their lives and to transform their ability to "experience" life. Thus problems in life are supposed to resolve themselves. Est is based on various Eastern and Western philosophy systems and motivational training concepts. It peaked in popularity during the 1970s, when tens of thousands of people, including numerous celebrities, rushed to undertake the program. It continues to have adherents, though no longer enjoys fad interest.

The name "est" (always written in lower case) stands for Erhard Seminars Training; in Latin it means "it is." According to Erhard the est system is neither psychology nor group therapy, but a way to open a new awareness of living. Every person, Erhard says, possesses the power to transform his or her life.

Hallmarks of early est seminars included physical discomfort (infrequent breaks) and verbal abuse, including obscenities, heaped upon the participants by the trainers. Early est sessions provided breaks only about every seven hours; this was later improved to about every four hours. According to Erhard physical discomfort is a valuable part of training. The verbal abuse is intended to challenge and break down participants' defense systems and the psychological games they play. The core program is preceded by "pre-training," which sets the ground rules, and various follow-up programs, including a "graduate" program.

Critics say est is narcissistic and leads to simplistic beliefs and inadequate conceptualizations. However, some individuals who have gone through the program say they became freed of all sorts of emotional and psychological complaints, even physical conditions such as migraine headaches.

Erhard was born John Paul Rosenberg in Philadelphia on September 5, 1935, to a Jewish family. His father owned a restaurant. Following graduation from high school in 1952, he married his school sweetheart, Pat, with whom he had three girls and two boys. He worked in a succession of blue-collar jobs, then became a sales manager for a used auto dealer, and then managed a business that sold industrial equipment.

In 1959, at age twenty-four, he left his wife and children and went to St. Louis with another woman, Ellen. To avoid being traced by his family, he adopted a pseudonym formed from the names of physicist Werner Heisenberg and West German finance minister (and later chancellor) Ludwig Erhard. Ellen became his second wife; they had two girls and one boy.

Erhard eventually moved to California, where he worked in various jobs training and developing executives. He studied Zen, yoga, Scientology, Gestalt, Dale Carnegie, Mind Dynamics, and hypnosis. One day while driving on a freeway, he had a transformational experience and soon thereafter quit his job to start est. The Church of Scientology, which automatically expels any member who becomes involved in other disciplines, expelled him.

Following its launch in 1971, est became an immediate hit; it was soon established in Europe. By 1975 est grossed $9.3 million and had a paid staff of 230 plus over six thousand volunteers. Est claimed to have seventy-five thousand graduates, among them Yoko Ono, John Denver, Valerie Harper, Jerry Rubin,

Cloris Leachman, Joanne Woodward, and other celebrities. Erhard predicted that 40 million Americans would take est, but the numbers have fallen far short of that goal.

In 1973, after a thirteen-year silence with his first family, Erhard resumed contact with them, and his ex-wife took est training. The same year he established The est Foundation to make grants in endeavors concerning consciousness and human potential. The Foundation sponsored Swami Muktananda.

Erhard has established other organizations and devoted his attention to working as a foundation administrator. He established the Hunger Project in 1977; the Breakthrough Foundation in 1980; Werner Erhard and Associates in 1981; the Forum in 1985; and Transformational Technologies in 1985. His offices are located in Sausalito, California.

Erhard is the subject of a 1978 biography, *Werner Erhard: The Transformation of a Man, the Founding of est,* by William Warren Bartley.

Sources: Adelaide Bry. *est: 60 Hours That Transform Your Life.* New York: Harper & Row, 1976; Robert A. Hargrove. *est: making life work.* Garden City, NY: Delacourte Press, 1976; Leslie A. Shepard, ed. *Encyclopedia of Occultism and Parapsychology.* 2d ed. Detroit: Gale Research Co., 1984.

Etheric body

See **Aura; Healing, faith and psychic.**

Evil eye

An ancient and nearly universal belief that certain individuals possess the supernatural power to wreak disaster, calamity, illness, and even death with a glance or lingering look. The evil eye, also called "fascination," "overlooking," *mal occhio,* and *jettatura,* is greatly feared in many parts of the world.

The oldest records of the evil eye date back to about 3000 B.C. in the cuneiform texts of the Sumerians and Assyrians. The Babylonians believed in it, as did the ancient Egyptians and Greeks. The Romans were particularly afraid of it. It is mentioned in the Bible. Most tribal cultures fear it, and it is part of the black magic of Vodoun. Superstitions about the evil eye are still prevalent in Europe, especially in the Mediterranean region, and in Mexico and Central America.

The evil eye falls into two categories. Witches, sorcerers, witch doctors, and medicine men are said to cast deliberate evil eyes. Most cases of evil eye are unintentional, however; a person may be cursed with evil eye from birth and not know it. Pope Pius IX and Pope Leo XIII were both said to possess the evil eye. Consequently, believers must be on constant guard against the inadvertent malevolent glance. It may come from a stranger who admires one's children; children, along with women and animals, are particularly vulnerable to its effects. The evil eye is most likely to strike when one is at the peak of prosperity and happiness.

Numerous amulets exist to ward off the evil eye. The most common are two phallic symbols, the *corno,* a curved horn, and the "fig," a clenched hand with thumb stuck through middle and fourth fingers. The ancient Romans used phallic amulets after their phallic god, Priapus, also called Fascinus, from which comes "fascination" or bewitchment. Other amulets include eyes, bells, brass, red ribbons, garlic, and shamrocks.

If an unprotected person is hit with the evil eye, immediate action must be taken to avoid disaster. In Italy men grab their genitals. Spitting will nullify the evil, as will making the signs of the *corno* or fig with the hand. Some victims rush to a witch, wise woman, or sorcerer for a counter-spell.

The death-dealing evil eye is possessed by various tribal shamans and witch doctors, and appears frequently in Native American folklore. The fatal look may be used in conjunction with the pointing of the shaman's finger, stick, or wand, which sends negative energy streaming toward the victim. See **Eye of Horus; Psychic attack.**

Sources: James Bonwick. *Irish Druids and Old Irish Religions.* 1894. Reprint. Dorset Press, 1986. E. A. Wallis Budge. *Amulets and Superstitions.* 1930. New York: Dover Publications, 1978; Lawrence Di Stasi. *Mal Occhio/The Underside of Vision.* San Francisco: North Point Press, 1981; Martin Ebon. *Psychic Warfare: Threat or Illusion?* New York: McGraw-Hill, 1983; Frederick Thomas Elworthy. *The Evil Eye.* 1895. Secaucus, NJ: University Books/Citadel Press, 1987; Douglas Hill and Pat Williams. *The Supernatural.* London: Aldus Books, 1965; Maria Leach, ed., and Jerome Fried, assoc. ed. *Funk & Wagnalls Standard Dictionary of Folklore, Mythology, and Legend.* San Francisco: Harper & Row, 1979.

Exorcism

The expulsion of troublesome or evil spirits, ghosts, demons, or other nonphysical entities. Exorcism rites exist universally, and their use is common in many societies where spirits are believed to interfere frequently in earthly affairs, causing illness, bad luck, and disasters. Exorcisms are performed by the appropriate, trained individual, usually a religious official or magical or occult adept. Western psychologists and psychiatrists also perform a sort of exorcism in the treatment of patients who feel taken over by alien and external personalities.

"Exorcism" derives from the Greek *exousia,* "oath," and refers to "putting the spirit or demon on oath," or invoking a higher authority to bind the entity and compel it to act in a way contrary to its wishes.

Jesus exorcising unclean spirits (Mark 5:8)

(The New Testament, Dover Publications)

Rites vary from simple invitations to leave, to elaborate ceremonies, some involving dance and trance, in which deities are petitioned for help in forcibly expelling the offending entity. Techniques also include prayer, invective, foul odors, incense, and the use of holy substances, such as sacred herbs, blessed water, or salt.

Christianity associates exorcism with demonic possession, which is believed to be caused by Satan. The exorcism is considered a battle for the victim's soul. Only the Roman Catholics offer a formal rite of exorcism: the *Rituale Romanum*, dating back to 1614. Before the rite can be performed, certain symptoms must manifest, such as levitation, superhuman strength, clairvoyance, the forswearing of all religious words or articles, or speaking in tongues. The rite is characterized by violence: the victim suffers pain, extraordinary contortions, disgusting body noises, diarrhea, spitting, vomiting, and swearing. The room may be plunged alternately into heat or cold, and objects may fly about.

Some Protestants perform exorcisms as well. The Pentecostals and other charismatics practice "deliverance ministry," where gifted people drive out devils and heal through the laying on of hands.

In Judaism rabbinical literature dating to the first century refers to exorcism rituals. Perhaps the best-known rite concerns the dybbuk, an evil spirit or doomed soul that possesses the soul of the victim and causes mental illness and a personality change. The dybbuk is expelled through the victim's small toe, and is either redeemed or sent to hell.

In Hinduism, Buddhism, Islam, Shinto, and many other religions, spirits and ghosts are routinely blamed for a host of ills and are cast out of people and places. Most such afflictions are not considered all-or-nothing battles for souls. Typical Hindu exorcism techniques, for example, include blowing cow-dung smoke, pressing rock salt between the fingers, burning pig excreta, beating the victim or pulling the victim's hair, using copper coins as an offering, reciting prayers or mantras, and offering gifts of candy or other presents.

In some shamanic traditions, it is believed that demons or spirits cause maladies and misfortune by stealing souls. The shaman enters an ecstatic trance to search for and recover the soul and drive the demon out.

See **Depossession; Feng shui; Possession; Shamanism; Watseka possession.**

Sources: Julio Caro Baroja. *The World of the Witches.* Chicago: The University of Chicago Press, 1964; Richard Cavendish, ed. *The Encyclopedia of the Unexplained.* New York: McGraw-Hill, 1974; Adam Crabtree. *Multiple Man: Explorations in Possession and Multiple Personality.* New York: Praeger, 1985; Martin Ebon. *The Devil's Bride: Exorcism, Past and Present.* New York: Harper & Row, 1974; Mircea Eliade. *Shamanism.* 1951. Princeton, NJ: Princeton University Press, 1964; Rosemary Ellen Guiley. *The Encyclopedia of Witches and Witchcraft.* New York: Facts On File, 1989; Douglas Hill and Pat Williams. *The Supernatural.* London: Aldus Books, 1965; Bruce Kapferer. *A Celebration of Demons.* Bloomington: Indiana University Press, 1983; Francis X. King. *Witchcraft and Demonology.* New York: Exeter Books, 1987; Malachi Martin. *Hostage to the Devil.* New York: Harper & Row, 1976; Derk Kinnane Roelofsma. "Exorcism and Rites of Deliverance." *Insight* (September 28, 1987); D. Scott Rogo. *The Infinite Boundary.* New York: Dodd, Mead & Co., 1987; Gershom Scholem. *Kabbalah.* New York: New American Library, 1974.

Experimenter effect

In laboratory tests for psi, the unwitting psychic influence of the experimenter upon the subject, thereby influencing the results to fit the expectations of the experimenter. The experimenter effect may be due to the experimenter's bias toward confirming or disproving a hypothesis, or his or her subconscious attitude toward the subject. The effect may manifest in both parapsychological and psychological ways: in an unconscious telepathic communication to or use of psychokinesis (PK) on the subject; or behavior, body language, or attitudes communicated to the subject. As a result the subject may perform exceptionally well or exceptionally poorly.

The experimenter effect was observed in psychical research as early as the 1930s. Before that it was noticed in psychology, in the tendency of patients and therapists to establish a seemingly telepathic rapport. The experimenter effect has been studied and tested by some parapsychologists.

In a psi test, the experimenter has the potential to be the single determining factor in obtaining any significant results. Ideally, the experimenter should be able to ensure an atmosphere in which psi can freely function. Some experimenters are naturally good at inducing this state and others are not.

The first test of the experimenter effect was done in 1938 by researchers Gaither Pratt and M. M. Price. Both researchers had carried out independent tests of the same subjects under similar conditions, but Pratt's subjects scored at chance, while Price's did much better. The experimenters had significantly different approaches to their work: Price gave her subjects minimal explanations of the tests, let them work at their own pace, and encouraged social conversation as a diversion. Pratt was much more serious. He delivered more explanations than necessary, did not encourage social conversation, and kept his subjects focused on the test. Price's subjects apparently felt little or no pressure to score hits; anxiety did not inhibit their psi. Pratt's subjects apparently felt pressured, and as a result did not achieve high scores.

Subsequent tests by other researchers demonstrated that experimenters who seem negative and unsupportive elicit poorer results than experimenters who are positive and friendly. Subjects also appear to be influenced by their perceptions of how much the experimenter believes in psi, and whether or not they like the experimenter or think the experimenter likes them.

Parapsychologist Gertrude Raffel Schmeidler's first tested the sheep/goat effect in 1943. She gave positive reinforcement to the sheep, with a friendly environment, and negative reinforcement to the skeptics. Later she tested both sheep and goats under similar conditions, and found that while the sheep scored highly, their results were less than when they had been given favorable treatment. Interestingly, the goats scored far worse under the positive conditions.

In 1949 American psychologist and psychical researcher Gardner Murphy suggested that certain brilliant test results were due to the intense feelings of the experimenters. The motivation of the experimenter in carrying out tests has not been tested. Some experimenters routinely get results that others do not. American parapsychologist Rhea White concludes that the expectations of the experimenter may be necessary to induce psi, and the more unconscious they are, the more effective they will be. It has been advised that researchers first test themselves to find out if they can administer tests that get significant results. See **Sheep/goat effect.**

Sources: Gertrude Raffel Schmeidler and R. A. McConnell. *ESP and Personality Patterns.* New Haven: Yale, 1958; Charles T. Tart. *Psi: Scientific Studies in the Psychic Realm.* New York: E. P. Dutton, 1977; Charles T. Tart. "Effects of Electrical Shielding on GESP Performance." *The Journal of the American Society for Psychical Research* 82, no. 2 (April 1988): 129–46; Benjamin B. Wolman, ed. *Handbook of Parapsychology.* New York: Van Nostrand Reinhold, 1977.

Extraterrestrial encounters

Various psychic, paranormal, and mysterious phenomena are reported in conjunction with alleged sightings of, or encounters with, extraterrestrial spacecraft and beings. Extraterrestrial (ET) encounters are a global phenomenon and may have been taking place over millennia. See **Ancient astronauts, theory of.** As a social phenomenon ET encounters are as significant as encounters with the Devil during the witchcraft hysteria of the Middle Ages and Renaissance, and reported sightings of the Virgin Mary. There has been virtually no scientific investigation of ETs, however; most scientists take a highly skeptical stance on the subject, as do government agencies.

The age of modern interest in ETs began in 1947. On June 26 a Boise, Idaho, businessman and pilot, Kenneth Arnold, sighted a chain of nine bright objects while flying over the Cascade Mountains in Washington. He estimated their speed to be at 1,600 miles per hour. Arnold said the objects' motion resembled saucers that had been skipped over water, which gave rise to the popular term "flying saucer" to describe unidentified flying objects (UFOs). The famous "Roswell incident" also occurred in 1947. Three UFOs reportedly crashed near Roswell, New Mexico. The United States government claimed the crash was a weather balloon. Although witnesses years later claimed to have seen the bodies of alien beings, the incident remains inconclusive.

Since these incidents an estimated 70,000 sightings and encounters have been reported—probably but a small fraction of the actual number. Approximately 95 percent of the cases have been explained by natural phenomena, aircraft, weather balloons, or hoaxes. The

US Air Force set up a project in the late 1940s to analyze UFO reports; the project ended in 1969. It was advised by J. Allen Hynek, chairman of the Astronomy Department at Northwestern University. Even though most cases appeared to have natural explanations, the minority which did not eventually led Hynek to conclude that UFOs were a reality.

Much controversy surrounds ETs and UFOs. In America the extraterrestrial hypothesis, or ETH, is dominant, holding that aliens are real and encounters with them and their spacecraft must be accepted at their face value—a meeting with a being from another planet whose culture is superior to that of humans. Governments have been charged with conspiracy to conceal the truth about ETs. Skeptics contend that unexplained UFO sightings, especially those in the years immediately following World War II, most likely were real round and wedge-shaped experimental aircraft that were kept secret during the war. European ufologists are more inclined to view ETs as part of the "encounter theories," which hold that ETs are mythical projections from the collective human unconscious, designed to fill a psychological need, and which take on a framework that can be accepted by modern society. Psychiatrist Carl G. Jung did not believe in the physical reality of UFOs, but was interested in their psychological and parapsychological implications, observing that they are "a modern myth of things seen in the sky," and perhaps portents of changes to a new age.

Types of ET and UFO Experiences

Hynek classified UFOs into two major categories based on the distance of the sighting: those seen at more than five hundred feet away, and those seen at five hundred feet or less. The over-five-hundred-feet sightings are subdivided into three classes: (1) nocturnal lights, the most frequently reported, which include objects that either hover or dart around the sky; (2) discs or saucer-shaped objects seen in daylight and which often give off a fluorescent glow; and (3) radar-visual sightings.

Hynek called the sightings made at less than five hundred feet close encounters, and subdivided them into first, second, and third kinds. A close encounter of the first kind involves simply a sighting of a mysterious object. A close encounter of the second kind has visible evidence, such as scorched earth or huge holes or rings marking the spot where the UFO might have landed; sometimes there is interference with electrical circuitry. Close encounters of the third kind involve two types of eyewitness contact with alien beings: straight encounters, in which ETs are seen and perhaps communicated with; and abductions, in which individuals are kidnapped and then returned.

Abductions fall into two categories, planned and random. People who say their abductions were planned cite their first ET experience in childhood, when mysterious events left them with unaccounted for "missing time" or inconspicuous scars, usually on their legs. Such people feel they have been chosen and programmed for some sort of ET project, and have been implanted with monitoring devices. Random kidnappings occur in lonely spots, usually at night, to people who happen to be there. Reports of abductions have constituted the majority of close encounters of the third kind since the 1960s.

Widely disparate eyewitnesses have given similar descriptions of aliens as small, humanoid beings with enlarged heads, enormous, slanted metallic eyes, and gray and green skin. There are also reports of huge, hairy beings, and angelic-like beings. Strangely, with the tens of thousands of reported sightings, no two cases appear to involve exactly the same ship or crew.

Paranormal Phenomena

Some eyewitnesses assert that prior to their encounter they acquired or enhanced existing psychic abilities that helped to bring about their encounter, or to perceive certain of its aspects, or to communicate telepathically with the ETs. Other eyewitnesses claim that psychic or healing abilities manifested after the encounter. The rays of light that emanate from the spacecraft sometimes have been said to be the source of healing powers. Witnesses have claimed that old or recent wounds healed shortly after an encounter. Many encounters are characterized by a hypnotic-like trance before, during, and after the episode. Some witnesses feel compelled to make the contact by going to a certain location or looking out their window. The compulsion may be a physical sensation, like a tingling or a vibrating, or clairaudient voices, or some sort of telepathic command. There may be accompanying strange noises or poltergeist effects, or unusual behavior among animals.

At contact the witness is often bathed in light from the spacecraft. If the witness sees alien beings, there may be communication, either in the witness's own language or by telepathy.

Witnesses who are abducted typically have no recollection of the details, only missing time. Details are recovered under hypnosis. Witnesses then recall being levitated, some in their cars, aboard spacecraft, or floating or flying into the ship. Some are transported to remote locations in wooded areas. After abduction they are subjected to pulsating lights and a physical examination; some report sexual intercourse with the aliens or surgery for the implantation of devices. The ETs try to soothe the witnesses, who feel uncomfortable but not terrified. Witnesses may be given a weighty message to impart to other human beings, or warned not to remember or speak of their experience. Some witnesses claim to have been taken on a trip aboard the spacecraft to the ETs' home planet, or to have been shown various wonders of the universe. The abduction may last only a few hours, or may last weeks. Witnesses are returned to their original setting, sometimes with clothing disturbed. They may have subsequent telepathic communication with the ETs or additional encounters; witnesses may serve as channels or mediums for messages and warnings.

Aftermath

An encounter or abduction generates real emotional stress that continues to act on the person long after the event. Repercussions may include nightmares, anxieties, or depressions, as well as physiological changes. Many witnesses feel transformed and effect major changes in their life-styles, such as adopting a vegetarian diet or becoming active in environmental concerns. Some begin preaching new versions of the age-old messages of impending doom unless greedy humans change their ways.

The "encounter theories" view of ET encounters as a psychological projection, perhaps in response to a mass yearning to raise the consciousness of humankind, has credence. Many ET encounters fit a pattern of encounters with supernatural and divine beings throughout history. Furthermore, modern research shows that ET encounters tend to fit a psychological profile called the "encounter-prone personality." See **Encounter phenomenon.**

Many descriptions of ETs resemble those of sick and starving children—small beings with enlarged heads, big eyes, and spindly limbs, as portrayed in Steven Spielberg's film, *Close Encounters of the Third Kind*. Philosopher Michael Grosso suggests that ETs are mythical projections of the Child archetype, who in myth is the bearer of extraordinary powers, the harbinger of the future, and always under threat. ETs, then, may be symptoms of a racial self-healing (human beings putting themselves on the operating table) and the emergence of a new mythology.

The encounter theories do not discount the possibility of genuine ET encounters, but may explain why so many have occurred since the middle of the twentieth century and the advent of the threat of nuclear annihilation. However, there may never be satisfactory answers to the question of whether or not ET encounters are objective or subjective. See **Archetypes; Collective unconscious; Marian apparitions; Mystical experiences; Mythology.**

Sources: Thomas E. Bullard. "The American Way: Truth, Justice and Abduction." *Magonia* no. 34 (October 1989): 3–7; Hilary Evans. *Gods, Spirits, Cosmic Guardians: A Comparative Study of the Encounter Experience.* Wellingborough, Northamptonshire, England: The Aquarian Press, 1987; Curtis G. Fuller. *Proceedings of the First International UFO Congress.* New York: Warner Books, 1980; Bruce Goldman. "Something Strange: An Interview with Dr. Peter Sturrock." *New Realities 9,* no. 5 (May/June 1989): 35–41; Michael Grosso. "UFOs and the Myth of the New Age." *ReVision* 11, no. 3 (Winter 1989): 5–13; Budd Hopkins. *Intruders: The Incredible Visitations at Coply Woods.* New York: Random House, 1987; Gary Kinder. *Light Years: An Investigation into the Extraterrestrial Experiences of Eduard Meier.* New York: Atlantic Monthly Press, 1987; John Rimmer. "Abductions: Who's Being Taken for a Ride?" *Magonia* no. 36 (May 1990): 3–5; Whitley Strieber. *Communion.* New York: William Morrow, 1987.

Eyeless vision

The perception of images and colors through the skin, especially in touching with the fingers. Other terms for eyeless vision are "skin reading," "skin vision," and "dermo-optics"; the French call it "para-optic ability" and the Soviets call it "bio-introscopy." Eyeless vision may or may not be accompanied by other psychic abilities, such as clairvoyance or telepathy.

Eyeless vision was reported as a higher phenomenon of mesmerism in the eighteenth century. In 1920 an original study of it was published by French physiologist and novelist Jules Romains, who stated that all skin has the capability for eyeless sight, with hands and face the most sensitive. In the early 1960s, eyeless vision became a wonder and a fad in the Soviet Union, where researchers reportedly trained hundreds of blindfolded and blind people to read colors, images, and words through their skin. Less attention has been paid to it in the West.

Various explanations for eyeless vision have been advanced, but none proven. Some researchers theorize that gifted skin readers possess special but unknown cells. Others suggest the phenomenon acts like sonar, in which infrared or radioactive rays from isotopes in the body bounce off objects and are sensed by the skin. The most plausible theory may be that eyeless vision interacts with electromagnetic energy and the meridian energy points on the body. Eyeless sight works best in bright light and usually not at all in pitch darkness. It also fades if objects or people are grounded.

Sources: Henry Gris and William Dick. *The New Soviet Psychic Discoveries.* Englewood Cliffs, NJ: Prentice-Hall, 1978; Sheila Ostrander and Lynn Schroeder. *The ESP Papers: Scientists Speak Out from Behind the Iron Curtain.* New York: Bantam Books, 1976; Sheila Ostrander and Lynn Schroeder. *Psychic Discoveries Behind the Iron Curtain.* Englewood Cliffs, NJ: Prentice-Hall, 1970; Russell Targ and Keith Harary. *The Mind Race.* New York: Villard Books, 1984; Benjamin B. Wolman, ed. *Handbook of Parapsychology.* New York: Van Nostrand Reinhold, 1977.

Eye of Horus

One of the most common amulets of ancient Egypt. The highly stylized eye of the falcon-headed solar and sky god Horus (the Latin version of Hor) is associated with regeneration, health, and prosperity. It has become commonly associated with esoterica and the occult. It is also called the *udjat* eye or *utchat* eye, which means "sound eye."

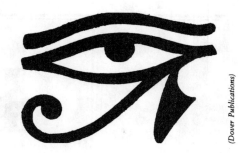

Eye of Horus

(Dover Publications)

Horus, the son of Osiris and Isis, was called "Horus who rules with two eyes." His right eye was white and represented the sun; his left eye was black and represented the moon. According to myth Horus lost his left eye to his evil brother, Seth, whom he fought to avenge Seth's murder of Osiris. Seth tore out the eye but lost the fight. The eye was reassembled by magic by Thoth, the god of writing, the moon, and magic. Horus presented his eye to Osiris, who experienced rebirth in the underworld.

As an amulet the Eye of Horus has three versions: a left eye, a right eye, and two eyes. The eye is constructed in fractional parts, with 1/64 missing, a piece Thoth added by magic. The symbol of modern pharmacies and prescriptions, ℞, is derived from three pieces of the Eye of Horus.

The Egyptians used the eye as a funerary amulet for protection against evil and rebirth in the underworld, and decorated mummies, coffins, and tombs with it. The *Book of the Dead* instructs that funerary eye amulets be made out of lapis lazuli or a stone called *mak*. Some were gold-plated.

Worn as jewelry fashioned of gold, silver, lapis, wood, porcelain, or carnelian, the eye served to ensure safety, protect health, and give the wearer wisdom and prosperity. It was called the "all-seeing Eye." Other attributes associated with it are terror and wrath. According to some myths, the eye took on a personality of its own, swooping down out of the sky to right wrongs.

A variation of the Eye of Horus is the all-seeing eye, or mystical eye, in the Great Seal of the United States. In the mysteries teachings, an open eye symbolizes intellectual power and the pineal gland, the supposed seat of psychic powers. See **Amulet**.

Sources: Sharon Boyd. "The US, Founded on Occultism, Not Christianity." *What Is* 1, no. 2 (1987): 10–14; Bob Brier. *Ancient Egyptian Magic.* New York: Quill, 1981; E. A. Wallis Budge. *Egyptian Magic.* 1901. New York; Dover Publications, 1971; Richard Cavendish, ed. *The Encyclopedia of the Unexplained.* New York: McGraw-Hill, 1974; Manly P. Hall. *The Secret Teachings of All Ages.* 1928. Los Angeles: The Philosophic Research Society, 1977; *New Larousse Encyclopedia of Mythology.* 1959. New ed. New York: Crescent Books, 1968.

F

Fairies

A wide variety of supernatural beings that help or harm humankind. Fairy beliefs are widespread and similar, and are strongest in the Celtic lore of Britain, Ireland, and Europe. Fairy lore may have originated to explain bad luck, natural disasters, epidemics, birth defects, and child illnesses and death.

The word "fairy" derives from the Latin *fata,* or fate, which refers to the mythical Fates, three women who spin and control the threads of life. An archaic English term for fairies is *fays,* which means "enchanted" or "bewitched."

The main theories about the origins of fairies propose that they are: (1) unbaptized, earthbound souls; (2) guardians of the souls of the dead; (3) ghosts of venerated ancestors; (4) Lucifer's fallen angels, condemned to remain on earth; (5) nature spirits; or (6) small human beings.

Medieval romances portrayed fairies as little humans who intermarried with nonfairy people. These stories may refer to diminutive races such as the Lapps or Picts, who were pushed into isolation in woodlands or were pressed into servitude by the Celts and other larger races.

Fairies are said to possess magical powers and consort with witches and other magically empowered humans. They have many names and come in all manner of sizes, descriptions of beauty or ugliness, and demeanor from benevolence to turpitude. Most are small or tiny. Some resemble humans, and some have wings. Some always carry about a magical wand or a pipe. According to lore fairies are invisible, except to humans with second sight or whenever fairies choose to make themselves seen.

Fairies are generally believed to live as a nation in an underground location, similar to the underworld of the dead, where time does not exist. The Land of Fairy, or Elfland, as it is called, is accessed through barrows and mounds. The fairies come out at night to frolic and make mischief. They are fond of kidnapping human women for wives, and human children, who are much more beautiful than the fairy children, or changelings, they leave behind in exchange. They pester humans who keep messy houses, or who do not leave out offerings of food and drink. Grateful fairies reward humans with money and gifts.

Sir Arthur Conan Doyle, the creator of Sherlock Holmes, was a supporter of Spiritualism and a fairy lore enthusiast. In the early 1920s, Doyle was duped by fake photographs of fairies. The photos showed tiny, winged female figures dressed in fashionable gowns, holding tiny pipes and hovering in the air. They allegedly were taken during the summer of 1917 by two young sisters, Elsie and Francis Wright, of Cottingley, Yorkshire. The girls attested the photos were genuine, and said they had the clairvoyant ability to see the fairies.

Doyle wrote about the photos as proof of fairies in a book, *The Coming of the Fairies* (1922). When experts declared the photos were fake, Doyle was ridiculed in the press on both sides of the Atlantic. The Wright sisters did not admit the hoax until the early 1980s. It began as a simple trick on adults, they said, but escalated out of control with the involvement of Doyle. Compare to **Nature spirits.**

Sources: Katherine Briggs. *The Vanishing People.* New York: Pantheon Books, 1978; Katherine Briggs. *An Encyclopedia of Fairies: Hobgoblins, Brownies, Bogies, and Other Supernatural Creatures.* New York: Pantheon Books, 1976; Arthur Conan Doyle. *The Coming of the Fairies.* London: Hodder & Stoughton, 1922; Rosemary Ellen Guiley. *The Encyclopedia of Witches and Witchcraft.* New York: Facts On File, 1989; Charles Higham. *The Adventures of Conan Doyle: The Life of the Creator of Sherlock Holmes.* New York: W. W. Norton & Co., Inc., 1976; Geoffrey Hodson. *Fairies at Work and Play.* 1925. London: Theosophical Publishing House, 1982; Maria Leach, ed., and Jerome Fried, assoc. ed. *Funk & Wagnalls Standard Dictionary of Folklore, Mythology, and Legend.* San Francisco: Harper & Row, 1979; Dora Van Gelder. *The Real World of Fairies.* Wheaton, IL: Theosophical Publishing House, 1977.

Fairy tales

See **Mythology.**

Fakir

In India a type of holy man who allegedly performs magical, miraculous, or paranormal feats. Many fakir tricks are conjurations done with cleverly disguised props and quick sleight of hand. Such tricks include conjuring scalding water into a seemingly empty brass bowl (the sides are double), and making a mango appear to grow from a seed to a plant within minutes (a mango plant is folded, compressed, and concealed). The most famous trick, seldom seen outside of India, is the "rope trick," in which a fakir appears to cause a rope to hang suspended in midair without visible support. The fakir then shimmies up the rope. This is said to be accomplished by a kind of hypnosis the fakirs call maya, a Sanskrit term referring to the illusory nature of the phenomenal world.

Some fakir feats, however, require yogic training involving breath control (*pranayama*), use of mantras, and meditation to induce altered states of consciousness and lower bodily functions. Such feats include lying on a bed of nails or thorns, sometimes for hours or days; immersing feet and limbs in hot ash (see **Firewalking**); and being "buried alive."

Fakirs practice asceticism and live in extreme poverty. The term "fakir" derives from the Arabic term *faqir*, which means "poor person." In Islam a faqir renounces money and the material world, and follows Allah as a beggar. In India fakirs are generally called sadhus. See **Yoga.** Compare to **Avatar.**

Sources: The Illustrated Guide to the Supernatural. Boston: G. K. Hall, 1986. Louis Jacolliot. *Occult Science in India and Among the Ancients.* 1884. New Hyde Park, NY: University Books, 1971; Ormond McGill. *The Mysticism and Magic of India.* Cranbury, NJ: A. S. Barnes & Co., 1977.

False Face Society

An Iroquois medicine society, so named because wooden face masks are used in its healing rituals. The masks are believed to be animated by spirits; as sacred objects they are not to be displayed in public, though some are. The False Face Society is one of the best known of Native American medicine societies.

Members are individuals who have been cured by the society's rituals. Most members are men; women who have been cured of certain ailments may join, though they rarely wear the masks and never perform the healing rituals. Instead the women cook while men do the rituals.

The mythical origins of the False Face Society are explained in the cosmology of the Seneca, an Iroquois tribe. The Great Defender is a giant with a grotesque face, an evil-minded, disease-causing whirlwind who loves to wander the earth. Defender, as he is called, meets Good Mind, the culture hero who is creator of humankind, and bows to the greater power of Good Mind. Good Mind proclaims that henceforth it shall be the duty of Defender to move over the earth and stir things up. Furthermore, Defender shall abandon his evil nature and dedicate himself to benefiting humans, who are about to be created. Defender agrees, saying:

Then shall men-beings offer incense tobacco to me and make a song that is pleasing to me, and they shall carve my likeness from the substance of trees, and my orenda [animating life force or supernatural power] will enter the likeness of my face and it shall be a help to men-beings and they shall use the face as I shall direct. Then shall all the diseases that I may cause them depart [sic] and I shall be satisfied. (Native North American Spirituality of the Eastern Woodlands, 1979)

In the rituals of the False Face Society, the men don grotesque masks to symbolize supernatural beings. Female caricatures usually have ears, while male caricatures do not. Carrying tortoise-shell rattles, the medicine men accept tobacco offerings from villagers, crawl into houses of the sick, and throw ashes to drive out diseases.

If the spirit in a mask dies, the mask loses its healing power. See **Masks; Medicine societies; Tobacco.**

Sources: Ake Hultkrantz. *The Religions of the American Indians.* 1967. Berkeley: University of California Press, 1979; Elisabeth Tooker, ed. *Native North American Spirituality of the Eastern Woodlands.* Mahwah, NJ: Paulist Press, 1979; Ruth M. Underhill. *Red Man's Religion.* Chicago: University of Chicago Press, 1965; The Museum of the American Indian, New York City.

Fatima

See **Marian apparitions.**

Feldenkrais Technique

See **Bodywork.**

Feng shui

An ancient and complex Chinese art that combines mysticism, science, and superstition to determine health, luck, and prosperity according to natural landscapes and the placement of dwellings, buildings, and graves. In the West *feng shui* is sometimes alternately called "geomancy," which is divination by the earth and is not precisely the equivalent of feng shui.

Feng shui translates as "wind" and "water." Its fundamental concept is that in order to be healthy and prosper, one must be in harmony with the earth and receive the benefit of *ch'i,* the universal life principle, which exists in all things and flows through the earth and nature. The yin (female) and yang (male) components of *ch'i* must be in balance. The flow of *ch'i* and the yin-yang balance are affected by contours of the landscape, the presence or absence of water and vegetation, the weather conditions, and the sitings and shapes of buildings and the placement of furnishings in them. Some locations, by their natural virtues, have "good" feng shui, while others have "bad" feng shui. Alterations to the landscape, such as the construction of roads and cities, affect the flow of *ch'i*, and therefore influence the feng shui.

Crucial to good feng shui is the presence of protective mountains of certain shapes, especially those evocative of dragons; the proximity of life-giving water (also associated with money), especially streams or rivers that flow neither too fast nor too slow; and the presence of rich, green trees and vegetation. If *ch'i* flows too fast or in the wrong direction, all a household's fortunes will roll away with it. Straight lines, such as fast-flowing rivers or roads, are detrimental, for they carry a destructive energy called *sha*. The Chinese believe that the best *ch'i* winds and meanders along natural contours; thus there is an aversion to straight roads in modern construction. To live at the end of a straight road is to invite disaster. Ideally, houses, palaces, and tombs should face the south and be located near yang energies of strength, and be protected at the rear by yin energies.

The Origins of Feng Shui

The origins of feng shui date to about the second century B.C., according to surviving evidence. The roots come from (1) Taoism, a philosophy that stresses the holistic nature of the cosmos and is based on patterns in nature. Humanity is a microcosm that reflects Tao, the universe; (2) divination practices based on patterns in nature; and (3) astrology, numerology, and other methods used by the Chinese to determine the correct place of all things. The Chinese have always been concerned with place; the name of the country itself, Chung-guo, means "Middle Kingdom," connoting the heart of the universe.

Many of the early feng shui masters were priests and holy men, whose advice was sought for the siting of all things, including the auspicious location of graves. Problems with money, health, luck, and so on were treated with feng shui cures, the most drastic of which was to abandon the site altogether. The art was taught orally from man to man; in the Confucian tradition, one taught only sons, not daughters.

Around A.D. 300 feng shui split into two main schools, one of which is based on the landscape contours and one of which uses a cosmic compass to chart astrological factors, *I Ching* hexagrams, the Five Phases, and other elements. Around the eleventh century, further metaphysical refinements were added to the art.

Feng Shui Today

Feng shui is still actively practiced in various forms in China and other Pacific countries, such as Hong Kong, Korea, Japan, Singapore, Malaysia, Thailand, Vietnam, and the Philippines. In Tibet it evolved as Tantric Black Hat feng shui, an eclectic form incorporating animism, ancestor worship, and folk cures. Feng shui has been imported to the West but is not widely practiced there, perhaps because it is a closely guarded art. In the East some individuals are professional feng shui masters.

Feng shui requires keen observation, but also is highly intuitive and involves subtle psychic skills. By visiting a site, a feng shui master determines the existing flow and state of *ch'i* and makes recommendations for constructing a home or building that will maximize it; or, if problems exist, he makes recommendations to overcome or minimize them. Mirrors are the most common remedy; strategically placed, they reflect negative *ch'i*. Other common remedies are lighting, wind chimes, hexagrams, and plants, which can divert the flow of *ch'i* to more beneficial channels. Fish tanks repel evil energies. Sometimes problems are solved by moving furniture to face another direction. Associations with the cardinal points are: north—business success; east—good family life; south—fame; and west—children's fame.

Another function of feng shui masters is to cleanse homes and buildings of spirits prior to new occupancy. This is accomplished with an exorcism ceremony called the Tun Fu.

In the East feng shui beliefs have affected modern development. For example, roads have been diverted around locations where residents insist that to tear into the earth would be to cut into their dragon spirit that resides in the land, thus harming their local feng shui.

Western versions of feng shui (which are not equally comparable) are the theory of leys, invisible lines of earth energy said to link sacred sites; the theory of the Hartmann network, a grid of telluric energy lines in accordance to underground streams; sacred architecture, the execution of perfect form through mystical formulae of numbers; and "geobiology," the study of the Earth's influence at a precise point on everything that lives there: people, animals, plants, and so on. Like feng shui these concepts are based on understanding and maximizing the life force that flows through the planet and the cosmos. See **Leys; Power point; Universal life force.**

Sources: Maria Leach, ed., and Jerome Fried, assoc. ed. *Funk and Wagnalls Standard Dictionary of Folklore, Mythology, and Legend.* 1949. San Francisco: Harper & Row, 1972; Michael Loewe and Carmen Blacker. *Oracles and Divination.* Boulder, CO: Shambhala, 1981; Blanche Merz. *Points of Cosmic Energy.* Saffron Walden, England: C. W. Daniel Co. Ltd., 1985; Sarah Rossbach. *Feng Shui: The Chinese Art of Placement.* New York: E. P. Dutton, 1983.

Fetish

An object representing spirits that is used to create a bond between humans and the supernatural. Fetishes are common in animistic societies, and were prevalent in predynastic Egypt. They are often worn on the body to impart their magical powers, such as for protection, luck, love, curing, warding off evil, money, good hunting, gambling, or curses on enemies. Typical fetishes are dolls, carved images, stones, or animal teeth, claws, or bones. They embody specific spirits or are inhabited by them.

The term "fetish" may derive from the Latin *factitius,* made by art, or the Portuguese *feitico,* charm or sorcery. Other terms associated with fetishes are "juju" and "gris-gris," both of which may have derived from a West African term, *grou-grou,* for sacred objects. Early European traders commonly called the grou-grou they encountered juju, meaning dolls or playthings. The gris-gris evolved out of the African American slave culture in the American South, and refers to charm bags filled with magical powders, herbs, spices, roots, bones, stones, feathers, and so on. Gris-gris are used in Vodoun magic. In Santería such charm bags are called *resguardos,* or "protectors." See **Santería; Vodoun.**

Various North American tribes have fetish traditions. Some fetishes are personal, while others are collective, serving a clan, secret society, village, or tribe. See **Medicine societies.** The most elaborate traditions exist among the Zuñi and other Pueblo tribes. Zuñi fetishes are considered to be petrified supernatural beings from the creation myth. According to the story, the first humans came out of four caves in the underworld, called the Lower Regions. The Earth's surface was a frightening place, covered with water, shaken by earthquakes, and filled with beasts of prey. Out of pity for the humans, the Children of the Sun dried and hardened the Earth with lightning arrows, then touched animals to shrink them and turn them to stone. The animals that escaped were the ancestors of today's animals.

Most Zuñi fetishes are animals, reptiles, and birds carved from stone, horn, or shell; small pieces of turquoise, shell, beads, or arrow points tied to the fetish backs increase their power. The most powerful of all are natural stones in animal shapes, which are believed to be the original petrified beings. Some fetishes represent deities, such as the Earth Mother and Creator God, or the Beast Gods, the gods of the most sacred animals. The fetishes are kept either in leather pouches or jars. They require feeding and care, lest ill fortune result.

All Zuñi fetishes are used only for sacred purposes. The ceremonial societies own the most powerful collective fetishes. For example, the fetish of the Rain Priests is the *ettowe,* which represents the nourishment of the Earth Mother and the life-giving breath of Awonawilona, the bisexual Creator God, and which provides the priests' source of rainmaking magical power.

A collector's market for genuine Zuñi fetishes developed during the late nineteenth century. Around 1945 the Zuñi began producing replica fetishes for sale to the public.

Sources: Biren Bonnerjea. *A Dictionary of Superstitions and Mythology.* 1927. Detroit: Singing Tree Press, Book Tower, 1969; E. A. Wallis Budge. *From Fetish to God in Ancient Egypt.* 1934. New York: Dover Publications, 1988; Melita Denning and Osborne Phillips. *Voudoun Fire: The Living Reality of Mystical Religion.* St. Paul: Llewellyn Publishing, 1979; Rod Davis. "Children of Yoruba." *Southern Magazine* (February 1987); Migene Gonzales-Wippler. *Santería: African Magic in Latin America.* New York: Original Products, 1981; Ake Hultkrantz. *Native Religions of North America.* San Francisco: Harper & Row, 1987; Ake Hultkrantz. *The Religions of the American Indians.*

1967. Berkeley: University of California Press, 1979; Hamilton A. Tyler. *Pueblo Gods and Myths.* Norman, OK: University of Oklahoma Press, 1964; Ruth M. Underhill. *Red Man's Religion.* Chicago: University of Chicago Press, 1965.

Findhorn

Experimental spiritual community located in northern Scotland near the Arctic Circle, and the site of a garden seemingly endowed with special powers. At its peak in the late 1960s and early 1970s, Findhorn yielded forty-pound cabbages and other plants and flowers that sometimes grew twice their normal size, despite the fact that the soil was nothing more than sand and gravel and the cold climate of the North Sea made for poor growing conditions. Findhorn residents claimed that they received the directions for planting, cultivating, and managing their gardens from spirits that inhabit the natural world. The Findhorn experiment has come to be viewed as a demonstration of the power and potential of human beings and the natural world living and working together in harmony.

The Findhorn phenomenon began in 1962 when Peter Caddy, an out-of-work hotel manager without prospects for employment, his wife, Eileen, and friend and coworker Dorothy Maclean, moved to the Findhorn Bay Caravan Travel Park. Although the trailer park was a desolate place to live—situated next to a rubbish dump and a rundown building—Caddy felt he had been directed there for a purpose through spiritual guidance his wife had received in meditation. According to Caddy this same voice had been directing every action of their lives up to that point.

Thwarted in all attempts to find work, Caddy started the garden in 1963 to pass the time, even though Findhorn seemed the worst place imaginable to grow anything. Located on a narrow,

Peter and Eileen Caddy, mid-1970s

(Courtesy Hartley Film Foundation)

sandy peninsula jutting into the North Sea, it is exposed to near-constant winds from all sides and its soil is hardly suited for gardening. Still, Caddy went ahead with his planting.

The first sign that they were engaged in a unique undertaking came a few months later. While she was meditating, Maclean made contact with a spirit of the plant kingdom, which she called a "deva," said to hold the archetypal pattern for each individual plant species. The devas provided specific information about every aspect of the garden: how far apart to plant seeds, how often to water, and how to remedy problems. Faced with a question about the garden, Caddy would ask Maclean to seek an answer from the proper deva.

Within a year Findhorn had been transformed. Caddy described the gardens as "overflowing" with life. Cab-

bages, which normally reach four pounds at maturity, weighed over ten times that amount. Broccoli grew so large the plants were too heavy to lift from the ground.

In 1966, when the garden was in full flower, the second major development took place at Findhorn in the person of sixty-six-year-old scholar R. Ogilvie Crombie, a friend of Caddy's. Crombie made his first visit to Findhorn that year. Shortly afterward Crombie was sitting in the Royal Botanic Gardens near his home in Edinburgh, Scotland, when he saw a nature spirit—a three-foot-high, half-man, half-animal—dancing in front of him. Crombie spoke with the creature, who said his name was Kurmos. The spirit explained that he lived in the gardens and helped trees grow. According to Crombie this meeting with Kurmos was preparatory for one that followed with the most important spirit of the entire nature kingdom, Pan. Crombie said that Pan explained that he had been chosen to help renew the lost contact between humankind and the nature spirits. Crombie reportedly passed on to Caddy and the others at Findhorn what he learned from Pan about the elves, gnomes, and fairies like Kurmos who lived and worked in the garden helping things grow. This knowledge was applied to ongoing development at Findhorn.

As word of the garden spread, it became a model community for proponents of the New Age movement. By the early 1970s, more than three hundred people lived, worked, and studied in Findhorn. Residents viewed themselves as the vanguard of a new society based on the principles of cooperation between people and the kingdom of nature.

Of the original members of the Findhorn community, only Eileen remained by the mid-1980s; she and Peter had separated. Peter and some other members moved to Northern California, where they founded a retreat center called Shenoa. Findhorn was left to the care of the next generation. Apparently passing through another phase of development, plants, fruits, and vegetables returned to normal sizes and none of the remaining gardeners reported direct contact with the natural world Maclean and Crombie had experienced in prior years.

Nevertheless, newer members of the community preserve the original spirit and ideas of the founders. Findhorn has a democratic government, a garden school, and a company to help small businesses within the community. A small group of people live in self-sufficiency on the island of Erraid.

Findhorn has spawned at least one imitator—Perelandra, a twenty-two-acre garden and woodland area located sixty miles southwest of Washington, DC. Site of the Center for Nature Research, Perelandra was founded in the mid-1970s by Machaelle Small Wright, who also claims to be in contact with devas and nature spirits. Unlike some of the surrounding farms and gardens, Perelandra appears abundant regardless of season. Roses and vegetables have been grown without any kind of chemicals or organic compounds to repel pests or insects.

Wright's experiences parallel those of Dorothy Maclean's at Findhorn. Wright said she, too, contacted plant devas through meditation. And from the devas she learned everything about her garden—from types of seeds to plant to what fertilizer to use. Wright said that without the devas and nature spirits to guide her work in the garden, she would only be guessing about what to do. See **Deva; Nature spirits; Spangler, David.**

Sources: M. H. Atwater. "Perelandra: Co-operating Co-creatively with Nature." *New Realities* (May/June 1988): 16–20+ ; Findhorn Community. *The Findhorn Garden.* New York: Harper & Row, 1975; Paul Hawken. *The Magic of Findhorn.* New York: Bantam Books, 1976; Leslie A. Shepard, ed. *Encyclopedia of Occultism and Parapsychology.* 2d ed. Detroit: Gale Research Co., 1984.

Firewalking

A centuries-old rite practiced around the world, consisting of walking barefoot across thirty- to sixty-foot-long beds of glowing coals, white-hot stones, or pits of fire. Despite temperatures of 1,200 degrees Fahrenheit to 1,400 degrees Fahrenheit or more, firewalkers are able to traverse this distance without suffering any pain or showing any signs of burns or other bodily damage. Firewalkers prepare for their feat by chanting, praying, or meditating, which brings either a trance-like state or intense beliefs that they will not be burned. In the United States, where it has grown in popularity since the early 1980s, firewalking is promoted as a means for overcoming fear and developing personal power.

Firewalking is universal, occurring in history, legend, folklore, law, and early religion. The tradition, almost always performed within a religious context, belongs primarily to India, Japan, Greece, Fiji, Tahiti, Hawaii, the Phillipines, New Zealand, and the Balkans. The kahuna of Hawaii walk across fiery, hardened lava with nothing but the leaves of the ti plant strapped across the soles of their feet—protected, they believe, by the goddess Pele. See **Huna.** Similarly, firewalking in China tests the protection of devotees by their deities. In Singapore the Tamil "walk on a bed of flowers" by the hundreds on a certain day of the lunar year, to fulfill a vow and express gratitude for blessings from Amman, the Mother Goddess. The rite is preceded by days of fasting and prayer.

Firewalking was known in Rome in the first century A.D., when Pliny the Elder recorded it as part of annual sacrificial rites to Apollo. Jumping over or running through fires was a rite of purification of the Celts, especially in Britain where it was performed at the midsummer solar festivals.

Ordeal by fire—walking over or handling red-hot irons, or walking through fire—is an ancient practice of judging guilt or innocence. The ability to do so without being burned proved one's innocence. The practice was widespread in India from early times, and in Europe during the Middle Ages. Ordeal by fire also was part of the initiation into the ancient mysteries.

The practice of firewalking over hot coals began spreading throughout the West in the 1970s. In the United States, it was practiced for many years by religious/spiritual organizations. In the early 1980s, it was introduced to the lay public primarily by California teacher Tolly Burkan. Burkan, who made his first firewalk years earlier during a personal spiritual odyssey, said that firewalking was a means for individuals to overcome fear and free themselves from its restraints on personal growth, as well as to demonstrate the mind's power over matter.

Firewalking Theories

Firewalkers, as well as scientists, have been unable to explain how people can walk on hot coals or white-hot stones without damage. Doctors say human flesh exposed to 1,200 degrees Fahrenheit should suffer devastating third-degree burns.

Dr. Myrne Reid Coe, Jr., an American scholar, who once walked thirty feet through a fire pit and on another occasion licked red-hot iron bars, has theorized that vaporized moisture from saliva or perspiration forms a protective air cushion that prevents flesh from burning when exposed to extreme temperatures for brief periods. This is called the "Ledenfrost effect," and may be demonstrated by sprinkling water on a hot grill: the droplets dance on the surface.

Dr. Bernard Leikind, an American plasma physicist, has contended that firewalking is not a paranormal experience. The difference between the temperature of the coals and the lesser amounts of actual heat they contain explains why people have not been burned. He compared firewalking to sticking a hand into a hot oven—the air doesn't give off enough energy to cause burns. Touching a cake pan baking in the same oven, however, brings immediate pain and bodily damage. Leikind noted that while both are hot, each contains different heat or thermal energy. He said that coals are like the air in an oven—they do not contain enough heat to burn the soles of a walker's foot.

Both these theories seem to be disproved by the fact that many people have been burned the instant they've set foot onto the hot coals—some so badly that they required skin grafts. Also, some researchers have observed firewalkers standing in place in glowing coal pits for as long as twenty seconds; in Greece firewalkers have been observed kneeling on white-hot coals for several minutes.

Another theory suggests that electrostatic cooling, a phenomenon discovered in the eighteenth century, is involved. The psychokinesis of medium Nina Kulagina of Russia was associated with electrostatic fields; perhaps firewalkers, in their altered states, produce electrostatic fields around their feet and legs that cool the coals.

Firewalkers say the ability to withstand the sizzling temperatures is all internal, a demonstration of the power of the mind over the body. Burkan has suggested that a person's intense beliefs that he or she can walk across hot coals causes the brain to secrete neuropeptides that alter the body's overall chemistry. These chemical changes in the body are what prevent firewalkers from being burned. Andrew Weil suggests that a psychoneurological mechanism is responsible: In a certain state, in which the firewalker is free of fear and in a state of deep relaxation, the body's nervous system absorbs physical energy and electrochemically transmutes it so that the brain experiences it as a euphoric "peak experience."

In a study of ninety-eight first-time firewalkers published in 1985 by Julianne Blake, the majority of successful firewalkers attributed their success to three main factors: group energy and power; charisma of the leader (resulting in a willingness to surrender control to the "powerful other"); and visualization of successful firewalking. Participants used such terms as "alternate reality," "another level," and "energy body" in attempts to explain the process; some compared it to being in a state of hypnosis. Differences in techniques by different leaders did not seem to influence results. The firewalkers ranged in age from four-teen to seventy-three; the median age was thirty-seven.

Blake's results corroborate the theory held by Burkan, Weil, and others that firewalking is similar or the same in process to nonordinary, innate healing. Larissa Vilenskaya, a veteran firewalker who has taken her workshops to Europe, notes several common characteristics in the states of consciousness in both firewalking and mental healing: a feeling of timelessness; a shift in energy during the process; a state of becoming one with the fire or healer; a state of total concentration to the exclusion of all else; a release, letting go, or surrendering to the process; a sense of motivation.

Others compare the state of mind of firewalkers to yogis in a deep trance. In a 1961 electroencephalogram (EEG) study of four yogis, researchers found that neither light, noise, vibration, nor heat stimulation could disrupt their alpha state. Also, hypnotic trances have been known to reduce pain. In such a state, yogis reputedly have immunity to fire.

In Christianity fire immunity is associated with religious miracles. It also was a phenomenon of Spiritualism. See **Healing, faith and psychic; Home, Daniel Dunglas; Peak experiences.**

Sources: Julianne Blake. "Attribution of Power and the Transformation of Fear: An Empirical Study of Firewalking." *Psi Research* 4, no. 5 (June 1985): 62–88; Tolly Burkan with Mark Bruce Rosin. *Dying to Live.* Twain Harte, CA: Reunion Press, 1984; *Facts & Fallacies: Stories of the Strange and Unusual.* Pleasantville, NY: Reader's Digest, 1988; Ruth-Inge Heinze. "'Walking on Flowers' in Singapore." *Psi Research* 4, no. 5 (June 1985): 46–50; Andrew Lang. "The Firewalk." *Proceedings of the Society for Psychical Research* 15, part 36 (1900–1901): 2–15; Max Freedom Long. *The Secret Science Behind Miracles.* Los Angeles: Kosmon Press, 1948; Harry Price. *Perspectives in Psychical Research.* New York: Arno Press, 1975; Dennis Stillings. "Observations on Firewalking." *Psi*

Research 4, no. 5 (June 1985): 51–61; Charles T. Tart. "Firewalk." *Parapsychology Review* 18, no. 3 (May-June 1987): 1–5; Charles T. Tart. *Open Mind, Discriminating Mind: Reflections on Human Possibilities*. San Francisco: Harper & Row, 1989; Larissa Vilenskaya. "Firewalking and Beyond." *Psi Research* 4, no. 5 (June 1985): 89–105; Andrew Weil. *Health and Healing: Understanding Conventional and Alternative Medicine*. Boston: Houghton Mifflin, 1983; John White. "Firewalking." *Venture Inward* (July/August 1986): 36–39.

Firth, Violet Mary

See **Fortune, Dion.**

Flint, Leslie

See **Direct-voice mediumship.**

Flotation

A means of sensory deprivation by floating in a dark, enclosed bathtub-like tank containing heavily salted water. Flotation induces altered and mystical states of consciousness, and causes profound mental and physical transformations. As a therapy it is used in relaxation and stress reduction, and in the treatment of various behavior disorders and physical ailments.

Flotation tanks contain about ten inches of water in which eight hundred to one thousand pounds of Epsom salts have been dissolved; the entire tank weighs about two thousand pounds. The water is heated to between 93 degrees Fahrenheit and 95 degrees Fahrenheit, slightly less than body temperature. The effect of lying in such water in the dark is one of weightlessness; the boundaries of the physical body dissolve. Flotation apparently depresses left-brain activity (logic, language, and analytic thought), while liberating right-brain activity (intuition, creativity, and holistic thought). It also stimulates the secretion of endorphins, the brain's own opiates, neurochemicals that deaden pain and produce euphoria.

John C. Lilly's Experiments

The flotation tank owes its origins to John C. Lilly, American neurophysiologist renowned for his research on the brain and on communication between humans and dolphins. Lilly conceived of flotation experiments in 1954, while researching the neurophysiology of the human brain at the National Institute of Mental Health (NIMH) in Bethesda, Maryland. At the time it was hypothesized that the brain stayed in a waking state because of external stimulation acting upon the end organs of the body. Lilly devised an experiment to remove external stimulation (the term "sensory deprivation" had yet to be invented) to see what happened to consciousness.

Initially, Lilly floated in plain water in a dark tank in a soundproof room, using an underwater head mask in order to breathe. He found that in water of 93 degrees Fahrenheit, the body feels neither hot nor cold while resting.

After a good deal of trial and error to achieve a state of neutral buoyancy, Lilly discovered that the brain does not require external stimulation to stay awake. After tens of hours of experiments, he found he moved through dreamlike, trancelike, and mystical states, all the while remaining conscious. He felt he tuned into networks of communication normally below human levels of awareness, as well as networks of civilizations that were far superior. He learned later that these experiences were similar to those attained through other means to altered and mystical states.

In 1958 Lilly left the NIMH and moved to the Virgin Islands. In the early 1960s, he began experimenting with LSD, using a pure form of the drug, LSD-25, that was at that time legally available.

In an incident not related to LSD, Lilly had a near-death experience (NDE), in which he met two highly evolved entities who said they were his guardians. He perceived them as points of consciousness that radiated love. The beings could approach only so close without the danger of Lilly losing himself as a cognitive being into them. They told him he could perceive them only in a state close to death. See **Near-death experience (NDE); Spirit guide.**

In 1964 Lilly decided to combine LSD and the flotation tank to see if he could contact the beings again without the threat of death. He built his own tank, eight feet deep by eight feet wide, and used sea water, which made him more buoyant and eliminated the need for a breathing mask. At that time there was only one case on record of LSD use by an unattended person, who had become paranoid. Lilly feared psychosis by using LSD in isolation, but prepared himself with mental programming, which he called "metaprogramming," of underlying beliefs and expectations concerning his own safety and what he would encounter, which he then expected to become self-fulfilling during the experiment. From 1964 until 1966, when LSD was outlawed except under certain conditions, he carried out numerous LSD-tank experiments. The sessions lasted twelve hours or more, during which he physically left and reentered the tank numerous times.

In the tank Lilly would leave his body and travel to incredible inner spaces. He returned to his body whenever an experience proved to be overwhelming; he found his tolerance increased over time. Out-of-body he remained centered as a single point of consciousness in a silent black void, which he termed "the absolute zero point." From this vantage he took mystical flight, and found that what he believed to be true did in fact become true. He expected to encounter alien life forms and did, viewing a wide range of beings, some composed of liquids or glowing gases, and some of which resembled Tibetan deities. He entered his own body and went down to the cellular level and then the quantum level.

Lilly was unable to contact the guides until he took three times the normal LSD dosage, three hundred micrograms instead of one hundred. He felt he became a luminous point of consciousness and then perceived them once again as points of consciousness moving toward him through the void, stopping at the threshold of his tolerance to their level of energy. They told him he had the option of staying (and thus dying physically) or returning to his body, but advised him to return and carry out more work. They told him how many more years he would live. His assignment was to achieve this state of awareness on his own, without LSD, and teach others to do the same. They transferred information to him, which would remain "forgotten" until needed. See **Drugs in mystical and psychic experiences.**

After LSD was outlawed, Lilly continued tank experiments without drugs and explored other methods of achieving altered and mystical states.

Therapeutic Uses

Flotation has been shown to achieve dramatic results in stress reduction. Studies using an electromyograph (EMG), which measures muscular tension, show that floaters become more quickly and deeply relaxed than those who use other techniques such as meditation, biofeedback, and progressive relaxation. Flotation also has been shown to increase tolerance for stress by altering the level at which the body releases fight-or-flight biochemicals such as adrenaline, cortisol, and ACTH.

Flotation produces results in creative visualization. Studies show that images held vividly and strongly in the mind are perceived by the subconscious as real, thus making it easier to realize what is imaged. See **Creative visualization.** Visualization in a flotation tank seems more powerful than visualization in altered states induced by other methods. Athletes float while visualizing perfect performance in upcoming competition, which greatly enhances their actual performance. See **Sports, mystical and psychic phenomena in.** Athletes also find that flotation speeds postcompetition recovery and letdown by dilating blood vessels, and by helping the body clear away lactic acid (which causes pain and fatigue) and the fight-or-flight biochemicals (which cause depression, anxiety, and irritability).

Research shows that flotation is effective in reducing or eliminating smoking, drinking, and drug use, and in counteracting drug withdrawal. It also effectively treats high blood pressure, chronic pain, weight reduction, gastrointestinal and cardiovascular ailments, anxiety, headaches, and recovery from cardiac surgery. Tanks are in use in some hospitals.

Flotation tanks reached a fitness fad peak in the early 1980s. See **Altered states of consciousness; Mystical experiences; Relaxation.**

Sources: Michael Hutchison. "One Man, One Float." *Esquire* (November 1984): 29–30; Michael Hutchison. "Isolation Tanks: The State of the Art." *Esquire* (August 1983): 124; John C. Lilly. *The Center of the Cyclone: An Autobiography of Inner Space.* New York: The Julian Press, 1972; John C. Lilly. *Programming and Metaprogramming in the Human Biocomputer.* 1968. New York: Bantam Books, 1974; Barbara M. Ribakove. "Getting Tanked: Sixty Minutes in an Altered State." *Health* (February 1983): 10–12; John White, ed. *Frontiers of Consciousness.* 1974. New York: Avon, 1975.

Ford, Arthur Augustus (1897–1971)

American medium famous for his spirit communications and his advancement of Spiritualism. Ford was engaging and sociable, but his private life was tormented by a battle with alcoholism. His mediumistic talent appeared to be formidable, but posthumous evidence indicates he may have cheated at some seances in his later career.

Ford was born to a Southern Baptist family on January 8, 1897, in Titusville, Florida. He was the second oldest of four children. He had no unusual psychic experiences during childhood. He was excommunicated at age sixteen because of his outspoken skepticism of orthodox church doctrine concerning the nature of heaven and hell.

Ford intended to become a minister, but interrupted studies at Transylvania College in Lexington, Kentucky, to join the Army in 1918 during World War I. He never went overseas. Stationed at Camp Grant in Sheridan, Illinois, he inexplicably began having precognitive dreams of the next day's death list during a severe flu epidemic. Shortly thereafter he began to hear voices whispering the names of soldiers who were about to be killed in action overseas.

After the war Ford returned to Transylvania College, questioning his sanity. A psychology professor, Dr. Elmer Snoddy, convinced him he was merely psychic.

Following graduation Ford was ordained a minister of the Disciples of Christ Church in Barbourville, Kentucky, in 1922. He married Sallie Stewart; the marriage lasted five years.

Ford proved to be an eloquent and popular preacher. His psychic experiences, however, led him to leave mainstream Christianity and join Spiritualism. He moved to New York, where he lectured and gave messages from spirits of the dead, whose voices he could hear by putting himself in a light trance. He met Paramahansa Yogananda, who taught him yoga exercises for controlling his trance and access to the voices.

In 1924 a spirit named "Fletcher" announced himself as Ford's control. See **Control.** Fletcher was the middle name of an otherwise anonymous boyhood friend who was killed in World War I. Fletcher enabled Ford to impress the public with his messages from the dead. Ford traveled the globe and had entrée into high society and royalty. Spiritualists championed him, including Sir Arthur Conan Doyle, who advised him to become a full-time medium.

One of Ford's most famous sittings was conducted in 1929 for Harry Houdini's widow, Beatrice. Prior to his death in 1926, Houdini had agreed to try to communicate posthumously a coded phrase, "Rosabelle, believe." Ford produced the secret message, convincing Beatrice she had contacted Houdini.

In 1930 Ford suffered serious injuries in an auto accident that killed his sister and another woman. Ford's doctor discovered that he apparently went out-of-body when given morphine. He continued to give Ford morphine until he was addicted. Ford freed himself of morphine, but then turned to alcohol to battle insomnia.

Despite these problems Ford enjoyed the peak of his career during the 1930s. He married his second wife, Valerie McKeown, an English widow, in 1938, and settled in Hollywood, California. But his developing alcoholism eventually caused him to miss lectures, suffer blackouts, or appear drunk in public. Fletcher disappeared and Valerie divorced him. His health deteriorated. In 1949 Ford suffered a breakdown. He recovered with the help of Alcoholics Anonymous, but never completely gave up drinking.

Fletcher returned during the 1950s and Ford resumed mediumship. Mainstream churches invited him to speak, but Ford's dream of convincing them to incorporate Spiritualism into their doctrines went unfulfilled.

Beginning in 1964 Ford gave several sittings for the Reverend Sun Myung Moon, whose followers wished Ford to declare Moon the reincarnated Christ and World Savior. Ford refused. See **Alternative religious movements.**

In 1967 Ford conducted his famous and controversial television seance for Bishop James Pike, who sought to communicate with his twenty-year-old son, who had committed suicide in 1966. Pike was convinced he had succeeded, though skeptics denounced the show as a fraud.

Ford spent the last three years of his life in Miami, Florida. He died of a heart attack on January 4, 1971. He was cremated and his ashes were scattered over the Atlantic Ocean. Following his death numerous mediums claimed to receive communication from him. Author Ruth Montgomery, a friend of Ford's, claimed to speak with him via automatic writing, and produced the best-selling *A World Beyond* in 1971.

Also after his death, friends found notes and clippings that indicated that Ford may have cheated in seances with famous people. He may have researched some obscure facts about Pike and others, which were then produced as "evidential" material. Ford, who reportedly had a photographic memory, kept huge files that could have provided this material. The issue has never been proved. Ford often publicly denounced mediumistic fraud.

Ford founded and led several organizations during his life. The most notable is the Spiritual Frontiers Fellowship, formed in 1956, dedicated to exploring spiritual matters. See **Mediumship; Montgomery, Ruth; Spiritualism.**

Sources: Arthur Ford, as told to Jerome Ellison. *The Life Beyond Death.* New York: G. P. Putnam's Sons, 1971; Arthur Ford, in collaboration with Marguerite Harmon Bro. *Nothing So Strange: The Autobiography of Arthur Ford.* New York: Harper & Brothers, 1958; Ruth Montgomery. *A World Beyond.* New York: Fawcett Crest, 1971; Allen Spraggett. *Arthur Ford: The Man Who Talked with the Dead.* New York: New American Library, 1973.

Fortean phenomena (also Forteana)

Any paranormal or anomalous phenomena that defy natural explanation, such as rains of frogs, fish, stones, dead birds, flesh, and snakes; mystifying religious experiences, such as stigmata, the sudden flowing of blood from a person's palms or legs in the same places where Christ bled from being nailed to the cross; weeping statues; floating balls of light in the night sky; spontaneous human combustion; UFOs; ghosts and poltergeists; and monstrous creatures.

Fortean phenomena are named after Charles Fort (1874–1932), an American journalist who is called "the father of modern phenomenalism." After an inheritance enabled him to quit work as a journalist at age forty-two, Fort began collecting and cataloguing thousands of odd phenomena that had no explanation, which he found by poring through scientific and popular journals in the British Museum and New York Public Library. The collecting proved to be so absorbing that he dedicated the remaining twenty-seven years of his life to it. He never attempted to explain these phenomena, but used these examples to point out the limitations of scientific knowledge and the danger of dogmatic acceptance of "natural" laws, which the phenomena seemed to contravene. Fort compiled his research into four books: *The Book of the Damned* (1919); *New Lands* (1923); *Lo!* (1931); and *Wild Talents* (1932).

In *The Book of the Damned,* which lists over one thousand such incidents, Fort challenged the scientific method of accepting a phenomenon as genuine only if it could be proved. To Fort the fact that a phenomenon had occurred and been reported was proof enough; the reason why was less important.

To demonstrate the folly of scientists who were convinced that there must be an explanation for every event—for example, black rains falling on Scotland between 1863 and 1866 were said by scientists to be the result of eruptions of Mt. Vesuvius—Fort advanced his own catch-all theory. He invented the Super-Sargasso Sea, a place above the Earth that contained a collection of matter drawn from the ground below. It was from the Super-Sargasso Sea that the frogs, cannonballs, stones, and countless other objects simply fall to the earth.

Fort's studies of the inexplicable have continued since his death. The more bizarre phenomena continue to be anomalistic rains, including blobs of a jelly-like substance, blood, mussels, Judas tree seeds, and water that smells like sandalwood or bay rum; and spontaneous human combustion (SHC), also called autoincineration. In some cases of SHC, human bodies are burned to ashes by sudden and intense heat with no apparent cause. Surrounding objects, such as furniture, sometimes are not even scorched.

Fortean research is pursued on a scholarly basis by enthusiasts. The International Fortean Organization, founded in 1965 and based in Arlington, Virginia, sponsors investigative teams and provides research and educational programs. Another Fortean organization is the Society for the Investigation of the Unexplained, based in Little Silver, New Jersey. Fort's work has also inspired a science fiction subgenre of "Fortean themes."

Of major interest to modern Forteans are UFOs and related phenomena. Long before the term "UFO" was conceived, Fort uncovered reports of sky oddities dating back to 1779. Modern investigations focus on missing time, close encounters, and a phenomenon known as the "Men in Black," mysterious people dressed in dark clothing who sometimes purport to be government or Air Force representatives, and intimidate UFO witnesses and confiscate UFO photographs taken by private citizens. Forteans link the Men in Black to biblical accounts of angels and wise men, medieval accounts of devils, and, more recently, to phantom photographers and meter readers.

Two other phenomena, possibly related to UFOs, are the "mystery helicopters," black helicopters reported all over the world since 1938, years before the helicopter was invented; and "Mothman," a gray man-sized and man-shaped creature with red eyes, a bill, and wings ten feet in span. More than one hundred reports of Mothman were made in 1966 and 1967 in an Ohio River valley area; a black Mothman-type creature was reported performing aerial stunts over New York and New Jersey in 1887 and 1880. Forteans also investigate reported sightings of the sasquatch, or Big Foot, the Loch Ness Monster, the Yeti, or Abominable Snowman, and other creatures. See **Extraterrestrial encounters; Men in Black.**

Sources: Charles Fort. *The Complete Books of Charles Fort.* New York: Dover Publications, 1974. *Into the Unknown.* Pleasantville, NY: Reader's Digest, 1981; John A. Keel. *The Mothman Prophecies.* New York: Saturday Review Press/E. P. Dutton, 1977; Damon Francis Knight. *Charles Fort: Prophet of the Unexplained.* London: Victor Gollancz, 1971; "Third NYFS Meeting Attracts Overflow Crowd." *The New York Fortean Society Newsletter* no. 3 (March 1988): 1.

Fortune, Dion (1890–1946)

Magical name of Violet Mary Firth, considered one of the leading occultists of her time. An adept in ritual magic, Fortune was perhaps one of the first occult writers to consider occultism as the key to understanding psychology, and vice versa.

Although she called herself a Yorkshirewoman, Fortune was born at Bryn-y-Bia in Llandudno, Wales, on December 6, 1890. Her mother was a Christian Scientist. Her father, a solicitor, was a member of the Firth steel magnate family of Yorkshire, which made its fortune manufacturing guns and cannons for the British government. The family's motto was *Deo, non Fortuna,* "By God, not by chance," which Fortune later used as her magical motto and from which she took her magical name.

Little is known about her childhood. By age four Fortune began having visions of Atlantis; when she was older, she believed she had lived there in a past life as a temple priestess. By her teens she displayed mediumistic abilities.

In 1906 the family moved to London, where she became briefly involved in the Theosophical movement; she left it because she felt much of it was foolish. However, she did believe in the existence of the Masters, not in flesh as Blavatsky had maintained, but on the inner planes.

When she was twenty, Fortune had an experience that set her on the path of magic and occultism. She went to work in an educational institution and was under the supervision of a woman who had studied occultism in India. According to Fortune the woman, who was abusive and had a mean temper, used various combinations of yoga techniques, hypnotism, and projection of negative thoughts to psychically attack Fortune in attempts to force her to do things against her will, or to lower her self-confidence. Fortune managed to rebuff the attacks, but suffered a nervous breakdown.

It took her three years to regain her health, during which time she began studying psychology in order to learn more about mind and will. She preferred Carl G. Jung to Sigmund Freud, but felt neither giant of depth psychology adequately addressed the subtlety and complexities of the mind. She became a lay psychoanalyst at age twenty-three. She believed many of her patients were victims of psychic attack.

Prior to World War I, she experienced a powerful dream in which she met two of the Masters, Jesus and the Comte de St. Germain, and was accepted as a pupil by Jesus. Knowledge of her past lives unfolded before her: an almost unbroken line of priestess work from Atlantis to the present. She also claimed to remember everything she had been taught in those lives.

During the war Fortune served in the Land Army. At some time after the end of the war, she met her first physical master, Theodore Moriarty, an Irishman, Freemason, and occultist of great repute. Moriarty gave Fortune her basic occult training. Her experiences with him are featured in her magical autobiography, *Psychic Self-Defence* (1930), in which he is identified as "Z.," and in her collection of fiction stories, *The Secrets of Dr. Taverner* (1926). He is also described in her novel *The Demon Lover* (1927). Moriarty died in 1923.

In 1919 Fortune was initiated into the London Temple of the Alpha and Omega Lodge of the Stella Matutina, an outer order of the Hermetic Order of the Golden Dawn. The Golden Dawn was the greatest Western magical order of modern times, although it was in decline by the time Fortune joined. She displayed great talent for the magical arts and progressed rapidly. She did not get along with Moina Mathers, the wife of Samuel Liddell MacGregor Mathers, one of the founders of the Golden Dawn, and believed Moina sent psychic attacks upon her. Fortune established her own order, the Fraternity of the Inner Light, devoted to esoteric Christianity. Initially, the order was part of the Golden Dawn, but Moina Mathers expelled Fortune and the order became independent.

In the winter of 1923 to 1924, Fortune went to Glastonbury, where she contacted three more Masters on the inner planes: the Greek philosopher Socrates; Lord Erskine, chancellor of England in the early nineteenth century, whom she believed was the reincarnation of Thomas More; and David Carstairs, who claimed to be a young British officer killed at Ypres in World War I. These Masters directed her magical work during her most productive years. Fortune said Socrates dictated to her *The Cosmic Doctrine,* her essential occult philosophical work. During her life Fortune periodically retreated to Glastonbury, where she immersed herself in the Celtic Otherworld, which she believed lay beneath the Tor, and in Arthurian lore. She also said she came in contact with another inner Master, Merlin, the great magus of British myth and legend. Her experiences are recorded in her book *Glastonbury: Avalon of the Heart.* The house she once lived in is reputedly haunted.

In 1927 Fortune married Thomas Penry Evans, a Welsh physician and occultist. Evans, known as Merlin or "Merl" to Fortune's followers, became her priest in her magical work, injecting a strong pagan element into it. The marriage was stormy and was strained by Fortune's apparent lack of interest in sex. They had no children. In 1939 Evans divorced her and married another woman.

Fortune's years with Evans marked her most fruitful as a magician and writer, however. In addition to the Fraternity of the Inner Light, she ran the Chalice Orchard Club, a pilgrim's center she established at Glastonbury, and founded the Belfry, a temple in West London dedicated to the Mysteries of Isis. She was well known and had a large following. She wrote a number of nonfiction books on the occult and novels with occult themes, many of which remain in print and continue to inspire occultists and neo-Pagans. Of her nonfiction works, she is best-known for *Psychic Self-Defence,* considered the definitive work on psychic attack, and *The Mystical Qabalah* (1936), in which she discusses the Western esoteric tradition and how the Kabbalah is used by modern students of the mysteries. See **Kabbalah.** Her critics predicted that she would lose her magical powers for revealing the secrets of initiates in that book.

Her last two novels, *The Sea Priestess* and *Moon Magic,* are considered by many to be the finest novels on magic. *Moon Magic* was begun around 1939, but reportedly was finished posthumously, with Fortune dictating to a medium.

With Evans's departure Fortune went into decline physically, spiritually, and magically. During World War II, she organized mass magical rites in which participants meditated upon certain symbols with the intent of awakening the mythical King Arthur to come to the country's aid. Her own powers seemed to desert her, however.

Shortly after the end of the war, she was stricken with leukemia, and died on January 8, 1946, at the age of fifty-four. For some years after her death, she continued to run the lodge, allegedly, through mediums. Eventually her presence was deemed unproductive, and a magical banishing ritual was performed.

The Society (formerly Fraternity) of the Inner Light is based in London and continues to offer teachings in the Western occultism. Fortune's work is popular among modern Witches, but the Society stresses that Fortune was not a Witch, and that the Society is not connected with Witchcraft. See **Hermetic Order of the Golden Dawn; Magic.**

Sources: Dion Fortune. *Psychic Self-Defence.* 1930. 6th ed. York Beach, ME: Samuel Weiser, 1957; Rosemary Ellen Guiley. *The Encyclopedia of Witches and Witchcraft.* New York: Facts On File, 1989; Alan Richardson. *Priestess: The Life and Magic of Dion Fortune.* Wellingborough, England: The Aquarian Press, 1987; Leslie A. Shepard, ed. *Encyclopedia of Occultism and Parapsychology,* 2d ed. Detroit: Gale Research Co., 1984; Colin Wilson. *The Occult.* New York: Vintage Books, 1973; Colin Wilson. *Mysteries.* New York: Perigee Books/G. P. Putnam's Sons, 1978.

Fox, George

See **Society of Friends (Quakers).**

Fox, Matthew

See **Creation spirituality.**

Fox sisters

See **Mediumship; Spiritualism.**

Fraternity of the Inner Light

See **Fortune, Dion.**

Freemasonry

The secret and fraternal organizations believed descended from the craft guilds of the stonemasons. These groups, open to membership by men only, represent no single religion or ideology but instead try to foster spiritual development and fraternal charity among all classes and creeds. Also called the Brotherhood or the Craft, the orders provide a network for business, professional, and social success and advancement. The term "Freemasonry" often is shortened to "Masonry."

History and Legend

Architects and builder-craftsmen have always occupied a place of honor in society, dating back to ancient Egypt, Greece, and Rome. Building symbolizes creation, the raising of an edifice in which to glorify and worship gods and humankind, and correlates to the improvement of the body and mind as a temple for the soul.

Perhaps no building in all of history so exemplifies this idea as King Solomon's temple in ancient Israel. The legends of the temple form the cornerstone of Masonry's founding; but in order to remove any direct references to Judaism or Christianity, the story concentrates on Hiram Abiff, the architect and builder assigned to the construction.

In 1 Kings 7:13–45, the Bible tells that Hiram, King of Tyre, sent Solomon a man named Hiram who was highly skilled in bronze work to make all the pillars, vessels, and other decorations necessary for the temple, which he accomplished. The account is repeated in 2 Chronicles 2:13, but Hiram's talents are here expanded to include work in gold, silver, iron, wood, engraving, and fabrics. The biblical references to Hiram end here, but the Freemasons have Hiram murdered at the hands of three of his workmen when he would not reveal the secret Word of God hidden in the temple structure. In ritual Masons "die" as Hiram Abiff died, and are reborn in the spiritual bonds of Freemasonry.

Philosopher Manly P. Hall compared the Hiramic legend to the worship of Isis and Osiris in the ancient Egyptian mystery schools, another reputed source for Freemasonry. Osiris also fell victim to ruffians, and the resurrection of his body minus his phallus—and Isis's search for it—seems symbolically similar to the quest for the Lost Word of God. Followers of the Isis cult were known as "widow's sons," after the murder of her husband/brother Osiris, and Masons also are called "sons of the widow."

Followers of Sufic mysticism believe that the builders of King Solomon's temple were really Sufi architects incorporating the holy words of God in numerical equivalents expressed in temple measurements, making Freemasonry Arabic in origin. According to this view, the Saxon King Aethelstan (A.D. 894–939) introduced Masonry to England after learning of it from the Spanish Moors.

None of these theories or legends can be proven. Most Masonic scholars trace the Craft's history to the development of medieval stonemason craft guilds. The skilled stonemasons, few in number, traveled from town to town and were commissioned by local clergy to build churches and cathedrals. In order to guard their knowledge, the masons organized into guilds, complete with passwords, rules of procedure, payment and advancement, and religious devotion.

How or why the stonemasons' craft guilds attracted unskilled, or speculative members remains a mystery. Speculative members were those men, usually of a higher class than the craftsmen, who were interested in the pursuits of spiritual wisdom, philosophy, and often the occult, with no knowledge of stonemasonry. Perhaps the lodge provided cover for more esoteric activities, but most likely hid the members' radical penchant for political and religious reform.

Most Masonic historians consider Elias Ashmole (1617–1692), astrologer, solicitor, officer of the court of Charles II, and antiquarian, to be the first important nonoperative Freemason in England. For years Ashmole had dabbled in alchemy, Rosicrucian philosophy, and the Kabbalah, and counted as friends Francis Bacon and other founders of what became the Royal Society. Ashmole's diary records his initiation into Masonry in October 1646, by which time the English lodges were so crowded with honorary, or Accepted Masons that few claimed even one skilled craftsman as a member.

By the eighteenth century, nearly every pub in England and Scotland hosted a Masonic lodge. To establish preeminence for the English lodges and standardize ritual, four London lodges merged in 1717 into the Grand Lodge of England, with Anthony Sayer as the first Grand Master. George Payne replaced Sayer the next year, followed by the Rev. John Theophilus Desaguliers as Grand Master in 1719. Desaguliers, a lawyer, Fellow of the Royal Society, and chaplain to Frederick, Prince of Wales, helped not only organize the Grand Lodge but used his considerable influence to spread the Craft worldwide, especially to his French homeland.

Between 1751 and 1753, Scots and Irish Freemasons unaffiliated with the Grand Lodge formed the Antient Grand Lodge, competing directly with the Grand Lodge "Moderns" for participating lodges. Both groups became the United Grand Lodge of England in 1813, which exists today.

Beliefs and Symbols

Speculative Masonry inherited seven fundamental principles from the craft guilds: (1) an organization of three grades, called Entered Apprentice, Fellow Craft, and Master Mason; (2) a unit called a lodge; (3) rules of secrecy; (4) methods of member recognition; (5) histories of the craft contained in approximately one hundred manuscripts called the Old Charges, particularly the *Regis Manuscript* of 1390; (6) a tradition of fraternal and benevolent relations among members; and (7) a thorough Christian grounding.

By 1723 all references to Christianity had been removed with the publication of the Freemasonic *Constitutions,* instead requiring members to believe in God but allowing personal choice of religion. God—or whatever Supreme Being— became known as "The Great Architect of the Universe": T.G.A.O.T.U.

As there are three degrees in Craft Masonry, also known as the Blue Lodge, the number three plays a very important part in all Masonic ritual. Hiram Abiff's three murderers symbolize thought, desire, and action, which each Masonic candidate strives to transmute into spiritual thought, constructive emotion, and labor. Petitioners are called "rough ashlars," or uncut stones, which become the building blocks of the temple.

Speculative Masonry borrowed the tools of the craft as symbols of the order: the square, compass, plumb line, and level. Members wear white leather aprons associated with builders. Ritual colors are blue and gold. The capital letter G appearing in the Masonic compass most likely stands for God. Meetings are held in Lodges or Temples: four-sided rectangular structures decorated with Masonic symbols and black-and-white checkered floors, symbolic of humankind's dual nature.

Another Masonic emblem is the Great Pyramid of Giza, always shown with seventy-two stones representing the seventy-two combinations of the Tetragrammaton, or the four-lettered name of God (YHVH) in Hebrew. The pyramid is flat-topped, unfinished, symbolizing humankind's incomplete nature. Floating above the pyramid is the single All-Seeing Eye of the Great Architect, also associated with Horus, son of Isis and Osiris. Both the pyramid and the All-Seeing Eye appear on the United States dollar bill and the reverse of the Great Seal of the United States. See **Eye of Horus; Pyramids.**

With the formation of the Antient

Grand Lodge, a fourth degree called the Holy Royal Arch was added. After the merger in 1813, the Holy Royal Arch became an extension to the Master Mason's degree, a position to which candidates were "exalted." The Holy Royal Arch signifies complete regeneration from death and the high degree of consciousness possible from an intense, spiritual life and oneness with the Great Architect. Members with the Holy Royal Arch degree no longer belong to the Lodge but to a Chapter, overseen by a Grand Chapter. Only Master Masons may receive this rank.

Throughout the eighteenth and nineteenth centuries, various Masonic groups expanded the rituals of Craft Freemasonry into more esoteric channels, adding degrees and sometimes bizarre ceremonies. The most famous of these were the ancient rituals introduced by the Comte de St. Germain in France, the Egyptian Rites of Count Cagliostro, the German Rite of Strict Observance, and various borrowings from Rosicrucian and Theosophical practices. Universal Co-Masonry, founded in France in 1893, accepted both men and women and attracted prominent Theosophists Annie Besant and Charles Leadbeater.

Many of these rites passed quickly into oblivion, but not all. Thirty higher degrees, representing more spiritual and esoteric understanding, became the Antient and Accepted Rite of the Thirty-Third Degree. Philosopher Manly P. Hall, who himself achieved the Thirty-Third Degree, compares the ascension to the Higher Degrees to "passing beyond the veil" to true mystic union with God.

Only Master Masons may strive for these "perfected" states, and not every Mason even knows of their existence outside the Craft. Higher Degrees are administered by a Supreme Council, made up of members with the Thirty-Third degree, denoted 33°; the most senior Supreme Council is located in Charleston, South Carolina. In the United States, candidates receive each degree individually in an initiation ceremony, whereas in Great Britain 4° through 17° are conferred with 18°; 19° through 29° with 30°, and 31°, 32° and 33° awarded singly.

The Higher Degrees, in order, are: (4) Secret Master; (5) Perfect Master; (6) Intimate Secretary; (7) Provost and Judge; (8) Intendant of the Building; (9) Elect of Nine; (10) Elect of Fifteen; (11) Sublime Elect; (12) Grand Master Architect; (13) Royal Arch of Enoch; (14) Scottish Knight of Perfection; (15) Knight of the Sword, or of the East; (16) Prince of Jerusalem; (17) Knight of the East and West; (18) Knight of the Pelican and Eagle Sovereign Prince Rose Croix of Heredom; (19) Grand Pontiff; (20) Venerable Grand Master; (21) Patriarch Noachite; (22) Prince of Libanus; (23) Chief of the Tabernacle; (24) Prince of the Tabernacle; (25) Knight of the Brazen Serpent; (26) Prince of Mercy; (27) Commander of the Temple; (28) Knight of the Sun; (29) Knight of St. Andrew; (30) Grand Elected Knight Kadosh Knight of the Black and White Eagle; (31) Grand Inspector Inquisitor Commander; (32) Sublime Prince of the Royal Secret; and (33) Grand Inspector General.

Fame and Infamy

Many readers of the above list might liken the Brotherhood to an elaborate fraternity, blessed with an abundance of mystical offices. But the Roman Catholic church and some other Christian faiths take Freemasonry's hermetic side very seriously and outlaw its practice among church members.

The Vatican issued its first papal condemnation of Freemasonry in 1738, and by 1917 decreed that anyone joining a Masonic organization was excommunicated. Many Catholics, including Vatican prelates, had joined Masonic lodges in the beginning. Many church officials continue to look the other way, especially in England, home of most European Masons. The Greek Orthodox church officially condemned Freemasonry in 1933, calling it a system reminiscent of heathen mystery religions.

S. R. Parchment, author of *Operative Masonry* and founder of the Rosicrucian Anthroposophic League, stated in no uncertain terms that Masons believe in the potential of Christ in each man, but not in Jesus as the Son of God. Even the Anglican vicar and Masonic apologist Vindex called Freemasonry the embodiment of all religious systems and ancient mysteries, not the Christian organization inherited from the guilds. Of course, many Masons are not Christians.

Stephen Knight, author of *The Brotherhood*, claims that during ritual ceremonies for the Holy Royal Arch exaltation, candidates learn the Lost Name or Word of God, said to be "Jahbulon." Knight maintains that most Masons do not realize the significance of the name, which he defines as a combination of three names: Jah, for the Hebrew god Yahweh; Bul, the ancient Canaanite fertility god Baal and devil; and On, for Osiris, the Egyptian god of the underworld.

It is impossible, however, to besmirch the characters of so many illustrious Freemasons with devil worship. Wolfgang Amadeus Mozart was a Mason, and probably Christopher Wren, architect of St. Paul's Cathedral in London. Italian nationalist Giuseppe Garibaldi also professed Freemasonry.

Those who believe the United States is a nation destined to rise and prosper ascribe the country's founding as proof of spiritual intervention via the Craft, noting that eight signatories of the Declaration of Independence, including Benjamin Franklin and John Hancock, were Masons. George Washington became a Freemason in 1752, but declined to assume control of all Masonry in the United

(US Library of Congress)

Leaders of the American Revolution who also were Masons

States. As a result each state has a Grand Lodge and Grand Chapter.

The Marquis de Lafayette, who joined Washington during the revolution and ardently supported the American cause, was also a Mason, as were sixteen other presidents: Madison, Monroe, Jackson, Polk, Buchanan, Andrew Johnson, Garfield, McKinley, Theodore Roosevelt, Taft, Harding, Franklin Roosevelt, Truman, Lyndon Johnson, Ford, and Reagan. Vice President Hubert Humphrey and Democrat Adlai Stevenson were also "widow's sons."

In England royalty has joined Freemasonry since the beginning, with the King as Grand Patron, although a woman, Queen Elizabeth II, serves as Grand Patroness. Winston Churchill was a Freemason. British Masonry functions much like old school ties, with the Brotherhood strong in the fields of law, jurisprudence, police, government, and the armed forces. See **Order of the Knights Templar; Rosicrucians; Sufism; Theosophy.**

Sources: Foster Bailey. *The Spirit of Masonry*. London: Lucis Press Ltd., 1957; Keith Crim, general ed. *Abingdon Dictionary of Living Religions*. Nashville: Abingdon Press, 1981; R. A. Gilbert. "Freemasonry & The Hermetic Tradition." *Gnosis* no. 6 (Winter 1988): 24–27; Manly P. Hall. *Freemasonry of the Ancient Egyptians*. 1937. Los Angeles: Philosophical Research Society, 1973; Manly P. Hall. *The Lost Keys of Freemasonry*. 1923. Richmond, VA: MaCoy Publishing and Masonic Supply Company, 1976; Manly P. Hall. *Masonic Orders of Fraternity*. Los Angeles: Philosophical Research Society, 1950; Manly P. Hall. *The Secret Destiny of America*. Los Angeles: Philosophical Research Society, 1944; Stephen Knight. *The Brotherhood: The Secret World of the Freemasons*. New York: Stein & Day, 1984; S. R. Parchment. *Operative Masonry*. San Francisco: Rosicrucian Fellowship, 1930; Henry Sadler. *Masonic Facts and Fictions*. 1887. Wellingborough, Northamptonshire, England: The Aquarian Press, 1985; Idries Shah. *The Sufis*. Garden City, NY: Anchor/Doubleday, 1971; Walter L. Wilmshurst. *The Meaning of Masonry*. 1927. 5th ed. New York: Bell Publishing Co., 1980; Robert Anton Wilson. "The Priory of Sion: Jesus, Freemasons, Extraterrestrials, the Gnomes of Zurich, Black Israelites and Noon Blue Apples." *Gnosis* no. 6 (Winter 1988): 30–39.

Freud, Sigmund (1856–1939)

Physician, founder of psychoanalysis, and one of the major shapers of twentieth-century thought. His psychoanalysis brought him into frequent contact with the occult, a subject which he took interest in privately but rejected publicly. His emphasis on sexual repression and infantile sexual trauma as the roots of all neuroses cost him the support of key colleagues. Nonetheless, Freud was a pioneer in scientific exploration of the human unconscious mind, and his work in the field of psychoanalysis has had a profound influence on modern humankind,

science, culture, and art. He is universally acknowledged to be one of the most influential people of all time.

Freud was born on May 6, 1856, in Moravia (now part of Czechoslovakia). He was the oldest son of eight children by his father's second wife, and was raised in a Jewish household. At age four he was taken to Vienna, where he was an extraordinary student of the art of Leonardo da Vinci, and the classic literature in Hebrew, German, Greek, Latin, French, and English, including the works of Goethe, Dostoevsky, and Shakespeare (some of which he was reading by age eight). At age twenty-five Freud received his M.D. at the University of Vienna and went to work as an assistant physician at Vienna General Hospital and as a demonstrator at a physiological institute. He married at age thirty.

In 1885 Freud went to Paris to work under neurologist J. Martin Charcot. Upon his return to Vienna, he began treating patients with hypnosis. In 1895 he wrote, with Josef Breuer, a work on the treatment of hysteria through hypnosis. As did others, Breuer disassociated himself from Freud when he saw the importance Freud was beginning to give to sexuality. Freud phased out hypnotism and its related authoritarian treatment during the next decade as he made the important discoveries and developments of "free association" and psychoanalysis. The latter now provided methods of treatment that could be added to the previously known biological basis of psychiatry.

His own self-analysis in 1897 led to his seminal work, *The Interpretation of Dreams* (1900). Widespread misunderstanding by critics and even by his colleagues followed this and subsequent works, *The Psychopathology of Everyday Life* (1904) and *Three Contributions to the Theory of Sex* (1905). Freud believed that psychological problems may be traced to repressed childhood experiences, and he developed the theory of the Oedipus complex. Many psychiatrists now refute Freud's belief that the Oedipus complex is common to all cultures.

Most notable of his students who eventually broke with him were Alfred Adler (1870–1937) and Carl G. Jung (1875–1961), both of whom founded their own schools of psychology. While Freud and Jung carried on a lively correspondence, Freud's written references to his former student were often brief and critical.

Freud was a professor at the University of Vienna from 1902 until 1938, when he fled to London to escape the Nazi invasion. He died in London on September 23, 1939. Popular misconceptions about his psychology result partly from poor translations.

Freud and the Occult

In his casework with clients, Freud was confronted with such occult phenomena as premonitions, telepathy between therapist and patient, telepathy in dreams, other occult significances of dreams, "remarkable coincidences," and what he termed "uncanny experiences," such as seeing a double or coming in contact with the evil eye. He wrote a number of papers, lectures, and book chapters on psychoanalysis and the occult, including "A Premonitory Dream Fulfilled" (1899); "Premonitions and Chance" (from *The Psychopathology of Everyday Life*, 1904); "The Uncanny" (1919); "Psychoanalysis and Telepathy" (originally an untitled manuscript dated 1921 and published posthumously); "Dreams and Telepathy" (1922); "A Neurosis of Demonical Possession in the Seventeenth Century" (1923); "The Occult Significance of Dreams" (1925); and "Dreams and the Occult" (1933). He was a member of both the Society for Psychical Research (London) and the American Society for Psychical Research, but made little professional use of the data published by either organization.

Freud was mystified by the occult and kept records of his own personal experiences, which appear to include clairaudience and premonitory dreams. On at least one occasion, he visited a psychic with his associate, Sandor Ferenczi, and was startled by the personal information about him the psychic picked up. He attributed it to the psychic's ability to read Ferenczi's thoughts. He was open to the idea of telepathy in psychoanalytic situations, yet he was ambivalent toward psychical research. Ernest Jones, psychoanalyst and one of his closest associates, discouraged an interest in the occult because Jones thought it would have a bad effect on the emerging psychoanalysis movement. Throughout most of his career, Freud maintained a mechanistic, skeptical view toward occult phenomena.

In his writings Freud equated the occult with superstition, the latter of which he said originates from "repressed hostile and cruel impulses" such as the castration complex. In *The Psychopathology of Everyday Life*, he dismisses outright the possibility of "omens, prophetic dreams, telepathic experiences, manifestations of supernatural forces and the like," stating there are many other explanations for such occurrences. As for himself, he said, "I am sorry to confess that I belong to that class of unworthy individuals before whom the spirits cease their activities and the supernatural disappears, so that I have never been in a position to experience anything personally that would stimulate belief in the miraculous."

Telepathy, however, resisted his attempts at alternate explanations. Although he acknowledged its occurrence, he believed it was a physiological phenomenon and not a psychic one, and involved the transfer of tangible waves of thought. He confessed first that he was mystified by it. Later, by 1921, he said there might be some psychic validity to telepathy. In a manuscript prepared in 1921 for the Conference of the Central Committee of the International Psychoanalytic Association, Freud said, "It no longer seems possible to brush aside the study of so-called occult facts; of things which seem to vouchsafe the real existence of psychic forces other than the known forces of the human and animal psyche, or which reveal mental faculties in which, until now, we did not believe." Despite this admission Freud saw little possibility for collaboration between analysts and occultists in plumbing the depths of the human psyche, because analysts would run a subjective risk of becoming absorbed in occult phenomena. Twelve years later, in "Dreams and the Occult," he acknowledged that there is a core of facts to occultism that is surrounded by a veil of fraud and fantasy, but repudiated any connection between dreams and telepathy: "Telepathy throws no new light on the nature of the dream, nor does the dream bear witness for the reality of telepathy."

In "A Neurosis of Demonical Possession in the Seventeenth Century," Freud analyzed the records of the case of Christopher Haizmann, a Bavarian painter who announced in 1677 that he had signed a pact with the Devil nine years earlier. Haizmann sought protection from the local police, claiming the Devil had offered to help him for nine years in exchange for his soul. The Devil had appeared to him many times in various grotesque shapes, and had sent him terrifying visions of hell. With the end of the contract approaching, Haizmann feared for his soul.

The police sent Haizmann to a holy shrine in Mariazell, where the painter prayed and then claimed that the Blessed Virgin Mary appeared to him and recovered the pact from the Devil. His torments continued, however, and he committed himself to a monastery, where he spent the rest of his life seeing visions of the Devil and his demons. He portrayed his torments in his art. Haizmann died in 1700.

Freud said Haizmann's neurosis was caused by various repressed infantile complexes and homosexual tendencies. He concluded that the Devil represented a father figure to the painter. Haizmann's homosexual leanings were evidenced in his feminine self-portraits, Freud said. Furthermore, he manifested sexual associations with the Devil, as seen in the multiple breasts in his paintings. The number nine, the length of human gestation, represented pregnancy fantasies to Freud; Haizmann, with his nine-year pact, suffered from these, Freud said. This was complicated by Haizmann's painting a penis on every picture of the Devil, which demonstrated that Haizmann "recoiled from a feminine attitude toward his father which has its climax in the fantasy of giving birth to his child. Mourning for the lost father, heightened by yearning for him, [Haizmann's] repressed pregnancy fantasy is reactivated, against which he must defend himself through neurosis and by degrading his father." Freud also said that Haizmann sold himself to the Devil in order to secure peace of mind after the death of his own father.

Jung defended Freud early in Jung's own career, although he had misgivings about Freud's sexual theory and his attitude toward the spirit; any expression of spirituality Freud interpreted as repressed sexuality. Jung was intrigued by the psychic processes he observed in mental patients, which he felt could not be explained away as pathological.

Freud and Jung met for the first time in 1907 in Vienna. Jung was impressed by what Freud had to say about his sexual theory, but retained his reservations about it. Freud urged Jung to make a dogma out of it, as an "unshakable bulwark" against "the black tide of mud of occultism." By "occultism" Jung took Freud to mean everything that psychical research, philosophy, and religion had to say about the human psyche.

In 1909 the two met again in Vienna, and an apparent psychokinesis (PK) incident occurred. As they sat in Freud's study, Jung asked Freud what he thought of precognition and psychical research in general. Freud dismissed them as "nonsensical." As he talked, Jung, who was angered by Freud's attitude, felt a curious sensation overtake him—he felt as though his diaphragm was made of iron and was becoming red-hot, like a glowing vault. At that instant a loud report sounded from the adjacent bookcase and startled them. Jung said, "There, that is an example of a so-called catalytic exteriorization phenomenon." Freud replied that it was "sheer bosh." Jung disagreed and predicted that in a moment another report would sound in the bookcase. As soon as the words were out, another detonation sounded. Freud wrote to Jung that he had been impressed by the incident, until the noises recurred without Jung's presence.

After his break with Freud, Jung was ostracized as a "mystic." In a letter to Jung on May 12, 1911, Freud commented that it was right for Jung to follow his impulses to study the occult, and that undoubtedly Jung would "return home with great riches." In another letter to Jung dated June 15, 1911, Freud said he had been "humbled" in "matters of occultism," and promised to believe "everything that can be made to seem the least bit reasonable," though he would not do so gladly.

In 1921 Freud declined an invitation from English psychical researcher Hereward Carrington to join the Advisory Council of the American Psychical Institute, of which Carrington was director. In a letter dated July 24, 1921, Freud asked Carrington not to use his name in connection with the venture. He said he did not dismiss *a priori* the study of "so-called occult phenomena as unscientific, discreditable, or even as dangerous," and if he were at the beginning of his career rather than at the end of it, he "might possibly choose just this field of research, in spite of all the difficulties." He went on to say that psychoanalysis had nothing to do with the occult and he wanted to keep it separate from "this as yet unexplored sphere of knowledge"; and that he had certain skeptical, materialistic prejudices about the occult, and rejected completely the notion of survival of the personality after death.

Freud told his inner circle of associates that they must prepare for an attack on psychoanalysis by those who believed psychic forces to be real. These "true believers" would be likely to misuse the results of psychoanalysis and thus make the movement look ridiculous to the scientific establishment. See **Dreams; Jung, Carl Gustav; Psychology.**

Sources: George Devereux, ed. *Psychoanalysis and the Occult.* New York: International Universities Press, 1953; Nandor Fodor. *Freud, Jung and the Occult.* Secaucus, NJ: University Books, 1971; Sigmund Freud. *Studies in Parapsychology.* New York: Collier Books, 1963; Stanislav Grof. *Beyond the Brain: Birth, Death, and Transcendence in Psychotherapy.* Albany, NY: State University of New York, Albany, 1985; Rosemary Ellen Guiley. *The Encyclopedia of Witches and Witchcraft.* New York: Facts On File, 1989; C. G. Jung. *Memories, Dreams, Reflections.* Recorded and edited by Aniela Jaffe. New York: Random House, 1961; Robert Maynard Hutchins, ed. *Great Books of the Western World.* Chicago: Encyclopaedia Britannica, 1952; Louis Kronenberger, ed. *Atlantic Brief Lives.* Boston: Little, Brown, 1971; Ernest Jones. *The Life and Works of Sigmund Freud.* Vols. 1, 2, and 3. New York: Basic Books, 1953–1957; Howard A.

Michel with Carol Gruenke. "Did Freud Really Say, 'If I Had My Life to Live Over Again I Should Devote Myself to Psychical Research Rather Than Psychoanalysis'?" The Academy of Religion and Psychical Research *1986 Annual Conference Proceedings: The Relevance of Religion and Psychical Research to Planetary Concerns:* 52–65; Ernest S. Wolf. "Sigmund Freud." *The American Academic Encyclopedia.* Princeton: Arete, 1980.

G

Gaia hypothesis

See **Planetary consciousness.**

Ganzfeld stimulation

In parapsychology an environment of mild sensory deprivation intended to stimulate the receptivity of extrasensory perception. *Ganzfeld* is German for "homogeneous field" or "entire field," and refers to the blank field of vision stared at by a test subject. The ganzfeld originally was used beginning in the 1930s as a test of visual processes; it was first applied to psi testing in 1973.

In a psi ganzfeld test, a receiver attempts to perceive impressions and sensations transmitted by a sender. The perceptions may come through telepathy, clairvoyance, clairaudience, precognition, or combinations of those phenomena. Because it is difficult, if not impossible, to know which form of ESP is involved, ganzfeld experiments usually test for "general extrasensory perception," or GESP.

The Test Procedure

Methodology varies among laboratories, but the following description is a typical procedure. The receiver is settled comfortably in a soundproof room. Visual distractions are eliminated with eye cups (usually halved ping-pong balls) taped over the eyes, which are kept open throughout the experiment. A low red light creates a field of pink blankness. Earphones provide white noise to mask sound distractions. A microphone is clipped to the receiver's clothing or placed nearby. The receiver is relaxed with a short tape of guided imagery.

In a separate, soundproof room, the sender sits in front of a television set and is shown a still picture or a film clip, selected at random by a computer. The sender tries to transmit images and impressions involving all senses to the receiver. The receiver reports what he or she experiences, describing whatever comes to mind, including emotions. This reporting is called a "mentation." It is recorded and monitored by a third person, who has no knowledge of the image being sent, and is outside both soundproof rooms.

The relaxation, white noise, and diffuse light contribute to the receiver's disorientation, with periods of "void" or "blank out," similar to the hypnagogic state or in meditation. Alpha activity in the brain increases. The images that float into the mind are often dream-like or hallucinatory.

The sender transmits for one minute, then rests when the screen goes blank for four minutes. The on-off sequences typically continue for thirty minutes, though the duration seems much shorter to the receiver, who loses sense of time.

When the transmitting is finished, the receiver takes off the eye cups but remains in the room. On a television set, the receiver is shown four possible images and asked to choose which one was the target that was transmitted. All four are ranked from highest to lowest in "hit." The choice is seldom clear-cut; many receivers pick up fragments of more than one of the choices, sometimes all four, even though only one was transmitted. It is uncertain whether this is due to the clairvoyant reception of information directly from files, computers, or videotapes, or to the precognitive viewing of the choices at the last stage of the experiment. Precognition frequently occurs in the beginning of the test, with receivers picking up impressions before the senders know the target. Occasionally, receivers have precognitive dreams of the target the night before the test.

The first scientific use of ganzfeld stimulation in ESP research was done in 1973 by Charles Honorton and S. Harper, who at that time were researching ESP in dreams at Maimonides Medical Center in New York. Honorton and Harper sought psi-conducive conditions common to meditation, hypnosis, and dreams in order to learn how psi is detected. Of thirty people in the first test, nearly half experienced ESP.

In 1979 Honorton became director of the newly established Psychophysical Research Laboratories (PRL) in Princeton, New Jersey, the world's largest facility to pursue ganzfeld testing. The PRL operated until March 1988. Other research centers around the world have studied ganzfeld, using various target materials, such as binary-coded information or music, and sessions of different lengths. The overall success rates are high: 50 percent, compared to an expected chance rate of 5 percent. The "blank-out" periods, when receptivity appears to be sharpest, usually begin to occur about twenty minutes into the experiment.

Sources: Charles Honorton; D. Scott Rogo. *Psychic Breakthroughs Today.* Wellingborough, Northamptonshire, England: The Aquarian Press, 1987; Benjamin B. Wolman, ed. *Handbook of Parapsychology.* New York: Van Nostrand Reinhold, 1977.

Gardner, Gerald B.

See **Witchcraft.**

Garrett, Eileen J. (1893–1970)

Gifted medium who encouraged the scientific investigation of paranormal phenomena, and who founded the Parapsychology Foundation, based in New York City. Garrett was born Eileen Jeanette Vancho Lyttle on March 17, 1893, at Beau Park, County Meath, Ireland, in a culture steeped in Celtic beliefs of spirits and magical powers in mountains and glen. From an early age, she had psychic experiences that included visions of the dead. Because of her clairvoyance, her relatives called her "unbalanced." Later in life she said her Celtic heritage helped prepare her for mediumship.

Garrett never earned an academic degree. Her first husband was Clive Barry, an Englishman twelve years older than she; they lived in London. She bore three sons, all of whom died young, and a daughter. That marriage ended in divorce. During World War I, she ran a hostel for wounded soldiers in need of recuperation before returning to the front. She clairvoyantly saw the deaths of many of them. One of her charges, who had a premonition of his own death, proposed to her. They were married, and one month later he was reported missing and never found. Garrett had a vision of him and two or three others being blown up. Three weeks before the end of the war in

1918, she married another wounded soldier, J. W. Garrett. That marriage also ended in divorce, and Garrett never remarried.

Garrett's trance mediumship began during the rise of interest in Spiritualism following the war. One day she joined a group of women who wanted to contact the dead through table tapping. Unexpectedly, she went into a trance and began speaking of seeing the dead gathered around the table.

The experience was unsettling, and Garrett was referred to a person who hypnotized her and communicated with a so-called control personality, Uvani, who said Garrett would now be a vehicle for communication with spirits. This Garrett resisted, but the door to the other side remained permanently open. She sought help at the British College of Psychic Science in London, where she met James Hewat McKenzie. From 1924 to 1929, McKenzie worked with her to develop her mediumistic talents and trained her to remain aloof from and impartial to the process. She rapidly developed telepathy, clairvoyance, and clairaudience skills, and communicated with poltergeist entities. She worked with leading psychical researchers, including Sir Oliver Lodge and Hereward Carrington and Nandor Fodor. McKenzie died in 1929.

In 1930 the British dirigible R-101 crashed in France on its maiden voyage to India, killing everyone aboard. The incident was among the most famous involving Garrett, for she had experienced premonitions of a disaster involving a dirigible for several years beforehand. In 1926 she had a vision of a phantom dirigible in the sky over London; it appeared normal. In 1928 she saw the airship again, only this time it gave off smoke, was buffeted about, and disappeared. In 1929 she saw a vision of a dirigible in the sky in flames. Also in 1928, during a mediumistic sitting, Garrett gave a message from a deceased Captain Raymond

Eileen J. Garrett

(*Courtesy Parapsychology Foundation, Inc.*)

Hinchcliffe warning his friend, Ernest Johnston, the navigator of the R-101, not to go on the maiden voyage. Johnston did, and Garrett's warnings to officials went unheeded. When the dirigible crashed, Garrett knew about it before the news reached the media.

Three days after the crash, the first of a series of seances were conducted with Garrett in which Uvani delivered information from the dead crew. It was claimed that the R-101 had a gas leak, which was ignored by officials due to a desire to launch on time. Furthermore, the ship had been too heavy for the engines, which backfired and ignited the escaping gas. The information was not considered in the official inquiry to the crash due to the alleged sources, spirits of the dead.

In 1931 the American Society for Psychical Research invited her to the United States. She made visits to Duke University, where she worked with researchers J. B. Rhine and William Mc-

Dougall, the latter of whom she credited with influencing her to continue in psychical research. Rhine termed her experiments as "a turning point in parapsychology."

Garrett took up permanent residency in the United States in 1941, when she moved from France to New York City. Her citizenship was granted by 1947. She launched her own publishing house, Creative Age Press, and *Tomorrow* magazine, a journal on the paranormal. Both are now defunct.

In 1951, at a time when few universities were willing to view parapsychology as a science, Garrett established the Parapsychology Foundation to encourage organized scientific research through grants and international conferences. The foundation sponsors university research around the world. In 1953 Garrett organized the first International Congress of Parapsychology, held at the University of Utrecht, the Netherlands. The PF has continued these annual, thematic conferences, one of its most important functions. A journal, *Parapsychology Review,* has ceased publication.

In the 1960s Garrett worked with American psychologist Lawrence LeShan in his studies of what he termed the "clairvoyant reality": a state of consciousness to which a psychic or medium shifts in order for paranormal abilities to function. The clairvoyant reality is a shift in awareness, and is comparable to mystical states and to the unified whole of quantum physics. LeShan identified four central aspects: (1) There is a central unity to all things, which are part of a larger pattern; (2) time exists in an eternal now; (3) good and evil are illusions, for the harmonious whole of the cosmos is above good and evil; and (4) there is a better way of getting information than through the senses. LeShan's work with Garrett also involved insights into psychic healing. For any kind of psychic healing to be effective, the healer must shift consciousness into the clairvoyant reality. See **Healing, faith and psychic.**

During her career Garrett wrote seven nonfiction books on the paranormal, plus novels under the pseudonym Jean Lyttle. She died on September 15, 1970, in Nice, France, following years of declining health. Her daughter, Eileen Coly, is president of the Parapsychology Foundation.

Views

After World War I, Garrett met Edward Carpenter, whose social and political writings interested her. Carpenter told her she had been born to a state of cosmic consciousness others spent their entire lives searching for in vain. She began to see her perceptions not as hallucinations, but as capacities for inner comprehension, or what Carpenter called cosmic consciousness. She had a profound spiritual experience in which she saw that her need to live in two selves was the result of "positive powers beyond the range of contemporary understanding." Garrett said that the experiences of telepathy, clairvoyance, and trance depended upon a fundamental shift of awareness into a different reality, which she could do by choice by changing her breathing. She learned to control her powers so as not to be exhausted by what she called the "climax of clairvoyance," a state of inspiration in which past, present, and future are perceived simultaneously and one is identified with the unity of the vision.

Garrett remained uncertain of the reality of her controls. Uvani was the dominant one, joined by Abdul Latif, who claimed to be a seventeenth-century Persian physician. Garrett stayed detached from them, viewing them with respect but not being able to explain. Her mediumship encouraged her to study her own deep unconscious. By 1938 she felt her powers were not supernormal in origin, but sprang from her own inner nature. She preferred to think of her controls as "principles of the subconscious" formed by her own spiritual and emotional needs.

Garrett defined psychical research as "the scientific study of the human personality beyond the threshold of what man calls his conscious mind." She championed psychical research because she believed that it held promise for reconciling religion and science, thus restoring spiritual potency to religion. See **Control; Mediumship; Mysticism; Parapsychology.**

Sources: Allan Angoff. *Eileen Garrett and the World Beyond the Senses.* New York: William Morrow, 1974; Eileen Garrett. *Adventures in the Supernormal: A Personal Memoir.* New York: Garrett Publications, 1949; Eileen J. Garrett. *Many Voices: The Autobiography of a Medium.* New York: G. P. Putnam's Sons, 1968; Eileen Garrett. *My Life as a Search for the Meaning of Mediumship.* London: Rider & Co., 1949; "Eileen Garrett Ten Years Later." *Parapsychology Review* 11, no. 5 (September/October 1980): 1–2; Lawrence LeShan. *The Medium, the Mystic, and the Physicist: Toward a General Theory of the Paranormal.* New York: Viking Press, 1974.

Gautama, Siddhartha

See **Buddhism.**

Geller, Uri (b. 1946)

Israeli psychic renowned for his abilities to bend metal objects by stroking or looking at them, and to stop watches or make them run faster. Such psychokinetic (PK) phenomena are called by some the "Geller effect."

During the peak of his public career in the 1970s, Geller worked full time as a professional performer who demonstrated his metal-bending and mind-reading abilities for audiences. By the end of the decade, he was devoting most of his time to private consulting with occasional public appearances. Despite his successful feats, most parapsychologists have not taken him seriously, perhaps because of his entertainment career.

Geller was born on December 20, 1946, in Tel Aviv. He claims he discovered his psychic powers when he was five years old, following an incident involving his mother's sewing machine. He saw a tiny blue spark coming from the machine, and when he tried to touch it, he received a violent shock and was knocked off his feet. He says that his new powers manifested immediately, including an ability to read his mother's mind. A year later he found he could make the hands speed up on a watch his father had given to him. Shortly afterward the spoon bending began. He became a full-time performer in 1969.

In 1971 Andrija Puharich, neurologist and medical electronics expert, brought him to the United States. Geller was tested in 1972 at the Stanford Research Institute (SRI) in California, under the supervision of Edgar D. Mitchell, Russell Targ, Harold Puthoff, and Wilbur Franklin. Geller gave impressive demonstrations of ESP: He correctly identified the numbers on dice eight out of eight times; on twelve out of fourteen occasions, he correctly distinguished empty metal containers from those which contained objects. Tests to prove his metal-bending abilities, however, were inconclusive.

Puharich, who conducted his own study, said that while under hypnosis Geller related a story about a visit from extraterrestrials when he was three years old. A being told Geller it represented "The Nine," aliens who had been watching the world and were afraid of its imminent destruction. Geller was selected as their messenger here on Earth. Puharich published the story in his book *Uri*

(1974), which was widely criticized. Geller later disavowed the story.

In 1974 British mathematician John Taylor conducted another series of experiments that seemed to validate Geller's psychokinetic metal-bending powers. Geller held plastic tubes containing metal rods, which he caused to bend.

As a professional performer, Geller was in constant demand throughout the 1970s. He traveled the world, making frequent television and radio appearances. Following most of these stops, broadcasters were flooded by calls from viewers and listeners who reported their silverware had been bent or watches and clocks began working improperly. His first autobiography, *My Story*, was published in 1975.

Geller's high profile made him an enticing target for debunkers, who attempted to demonstrate how they could perform the same metal-bending feats using stage magic. In the late 1970s, Geller retired from the public limelight, save for occasional appearances, and began private consulting work, including dowsing for minerals and oil. In his second autobiography, *The Geller Effect* (1986), Geller related how he learned to dowse land and maps with his hands. See **Dowsing.** He said others could learn similar abilities through belief, will, and concentration.

Geller lives in Sonning, England, about thirty miles from London. See **Applied psi; Psychokinesis (PK).**

Sources: James Cook. "Closing the Psychic Gap." *Forbes* 133, no. 12 (May 21, 1984): 90–95; Uri Geller. *My Story.* New York: Praeger, 1975; Uri Geller and Guy Lyon Playfair. *The Geller Effect.* New York: Henry Holt & Co., 1986; Jeffrey Mishlove. "Psionics: The Practical Application of Psi." *Applied Psi* (Fall 1984): 10–16; Charles Panati, ed. *The Geller Papers: Scientific Observations on the Paranormal Powers of Uri Geller.* Boston: Houghton Mifflin, 1976; Andrija Puharich. *Uri: A*

Journal of the Mystery of Uri Geller. New York: Bantam Books, 1975; Colin Wilson. *The Geller Phenomenon.* London: Aldus Books, 1976.

Gematria

One of three Kabbalistic systems for discovering the true and hidden meanings of words, using numbers and letters of the alphabet. The numerical values of the letters of words are added together, and then interpreted according to other words with the same numerical values.

Although gematria was developed into a sophisticated system by Kabbalists—predominantly German Kabbalists of the thirteenth century—it was known and used much earlier by other cultures. King Sargon II, who ruled Babylonia in the eighth century B.C., used the numerical value of his name to determine that the wall of Khorsabad should be built to the same equivalent, or 16,283 cubits. The ancient Greeks, Persians, Gnostics, and early Christians used gematria for a variety of purposes. The Greeks applied it to dream interpretation, and the Gnostics to the names of deities. Early Christians arrived at the dove for the symbol of Christ, because the Greek letters of alpha and omega (the Beginning and the End) and the Greek term for dove, *peristera,* add up to the same number, 801.

The Kabbalistic system of gematria is far more complex than merely tallying up numerical values of letters; it involves various methods of analysis by which the mystical purposes of the Scriptures, buildings, and objects may be determined. Not only are the numerical values considered, but also the size and strokes of the letters. The early Kabbalists of the thirteenth century, most notably Eleazar of Worms, applied gematria to the Scriptures, which were believed to have been inspired by God and written in code. Thus, "And lo, three men" from Genesis

18:2, is interpreted as referring to the archangels Michael, Gabriel, and Raphael; for "And lo, three men" and "Elo Michael Gabriel Ve-Raphael" each have the same numerical value of 701.

The early Kabbalists also employed gematria to ascertain the secret, ineffable, and indescribably powerful names of God. These names were incorporated into the incantations of ceremonial magic, used for conjuring and controlling demons.

Not all Kabbalists endorsed the use of gematria. Some believed that it could be manipulated into providing false proof for theories and conclusions.

Lesser known than gematria are notarikon and temurah, two other systems of decoding and analyzing mystical truths. Various methods exist in both systems. In notarikon the first letters of words may be extracted and combined to form new words; or the first, last, and sometimes middle letters of words are combined to create new words or phrases. In temurah letters are organized in tables or mathematical arrangements, which are then substituted for the letters in words; or, letters are rearranged into anagrams. See **Numerology.**

Sources: Richard Cavendish. *The Black Arts.* New York: Perigee Books, 1967; Manly P. Hall. *The Secret Teachings of All Ages.* 1928. Reprint. Los Angeles: The Philosophic Research Society, 1977; Gershom Scholem. *Kabbalah.* New York: New American Library, 1974.

Gem elixirs
See **Crystals.**

General extrasensory perception (GESP)
See **ESP (extrasensory perception).**

Genius
See **Inspiration.**

Geobiology
See **Feng shui.**

Geomancy
See **Feng shui.**

Ghost
See **Apparition; Haunting.**

Ghost Dance religion

Short-lived religious movement among Native American tribes of the Plains and West, which preached the end of white civilization, the creation of a new world inherited by Native Americans, and the return of their dead. The movement ended in 1890 in the tragic massacre at Wounded Knee, South Dakota.

The Ghost Dance religion was named after its hallmark, the Ghost Dance, a shuffling circle dance accompanied by slow chanting, during which dancers experienced mystical visions of the dead and the paradise to come. The movement's roots were in a tradition that existed in Native American culture prior to the arrival of the Europeans. According to that tradition, the Earth would come to an end, be renewed, and the Native American dead would return to coexist in a new world with those living. A dance arose to help the returning dead enter the new world.

As white oppression mounted, however, various Native American prophets emerged in the latter part of the nineteenth century, preaching specifically that the white culture would end in the end of the Earth, and they and their dead ancestors would enjoy a return of the old ways in the new world.

As early as 1850, such prophets at the Columbia River plateau advocated the performance of the traditional dance

Sioux Ghost Dance

that honored the dead, in preparation for the coming new world and the end forever of the whites. The prophecies were a major factor in the Nez Percé war of 1877, which the Native Americans lost.

In 1869 a Paiute mystic named Wodzuwob (also Tavibo), of Nevada, also prophesied the doom of whites and return of their dead ancestors as a result of the traditional dance ceremony. Wodzuwob's son, Wowoka (also Wovoka), expanded his father's teachings. Wowoka, whose anglicized name was Jack Wilson, was thoroughly discouraged about the future of his people. During an eclipse of the sun, he had a vision in which he died twice, was resurrected, and saw God. In the vision Wowoka was told that a flood of water and mud would soon cover the Earth and destroy the white civilization. If they danced the round dance, however, the flood would roll under them. When it receded the Earth would be in an aboriginal state, green and populated with animals and plants. The dead would return, and all Native Americans, living and dead, would enjoy an eternal existence free from suffering.

Wowoka composed songs for the dance, which became known as the Ghost Dance, and began preaching his vision in 1886. He said Native Americans had to earn the right to the new world by living honestly and in harmony, by purifying themselves often, and by avoiding white ways, in particular alcohol. Wowoka also said the dead should no longer be mourned, since they would soon return. He opposed violence against the whites.

The Ghost Dance religion spread quickly through the Western, Southwestern, and Plains tribes, giving hope to shattered and demoralized people. The dance would go on for four or five days. Dancers would become entranced and fall unconscious; they saw visions of their dead ancestors, rolling fields of prairie grass, and huge herds of buffalo.

The movement had the greatest effect among the Sioux, a proud and fierce people who had vigorously resisted the whites, most notably in the spectacular defeat of General Custer at Little Big Horn. After agreeing to live on a reservation, however, they began to suffer hardships. Sioux mystics, Kicking Bear and Short Bull, rejected Wowoka's stance on nonviolence and spoke of eliminating whites.

The Sioux began dancing in the summer of 1890. They performed the dance around a dead cottonwood tree, a Plains symbol of life, hung with ornaments. Dancers wore magical Ghost Dance shirts that supposedly would stop bullets from the white man's guns. The shirts, modeled after one worn by Wowoka, were decorated with eagle feathers at the elbows and red symbols.

Whites perceived the Sioux Ghost Dance as openly hostile, and in November 1890 it was banned on all Sioux reservations. Tensions were exacerbated by splits among Native Americans themselves. Some advocated peaceful coexistence with whites, not resistance.

Despite the ban the Ghost Dance continued. White officials responded by calling in military troops, under the leadership of General Nelson Miles, to the Rosebud and Pine Ridge reservations in South Dakota. Chief Sitting Bull of the Hunkpapas was arrested and, in an ensuing scuffle, was killed along with several of his men.

Miles also arrested Big Foot, leader of the Miniconjou and a Ghost Dance advocate. Big Foot and his followers surrendered without resistance and were ordered to camp at Wounded Knee Creek. On December 29, 1890, cavalry soldiers attempted to gather what few weapons Big Foot's followers had. A gun went off—reports vary as to who fired the shot—and a skirmish broke out. As everyone ran for cover, the cavalry opened fire, as did cannons surrounding the camp, cutting down men, women, and children. Big Foot and approximately three hundred others died; the whites lost almost thirty men, mostly in their own crossfire. The next day, after more fighting between other Sioux and whites, the Sioux surrendered to Miles.

The massacre ended the Ghost Dance religion and brought to an end the Native American wars of the Western frontier.

Sources: Ake Hultkrantz. *Native Religions of North America.* San Francisco: Harper & Row, 1987; Ruth M. Underhill. *Red Man's Religion.* Chicago: University of Chicago Press, 1965; Carl Waldman. *Atlas of the North American Indian.* New York: Facts On File, 1985.

Glastonbury

One of the oldest sacred sites in England, whose history is intertwined with the Holy Grail and Arthurian legends. Glastonbury is believed to rest at the intersection of powerful leys, lines of earth energy. Its mystical lore draws numerous pilgrims and visitors from around the world.

Glastonbury is located in the West Country, on the plains of Somerset Levels, not far from the Bristol Channel. The site includes an abbey, town, and Glastonbury Tor, a terraced volcanic rock 522 feet high and topped with the remains of an old church tower.

Archaeological evidence indicates the area was inhabited from the third or fourth century B.C.; the site may have been sacred to the Druids. The town was nearly on an island, surrounded by marshlands, until the sixteenth century, suggesting it may have been associated with the mysterious island of Avalon in Arthurian lore.

Various legends are associated with the Tor. One holds that King Arthur once had a stronghold atop the Tor, which provided entrance to Annwn, the underworld. Monks built a church there during the Middle Ages; it was destroyed in an earthquake. The present remains are of a later church. Another legend says that the

Abbey ruins, Glastonbury

(Author's collection)

Tor was the home of Gwynn ap Nudd, the lord of Annwn and in later folktales the Fairy King. According to another legend, Chalice Well, located at the base of the Tor, is said to have been built by the Druids. Its reddish, mineral-laden waters are reputed to have magical powers. In recent times the well water was found to be naturally radioactive. Visitors still drink the water for its reputed healing properties, which were known as early as the sixteenth century. The well's flow is 25,000 gallons per day and never fails, even in severe drought. Another legend has it that Joseph of Arimathea, the great-uncle of Jesus, brought the boy Jesus on a trip to Glastonbury, and later built Britain's first above-ground Christian church below the Tor. He threw the chalice used by Jesus at the Last Supper into the Chalice Well. See **Grail, the.**

The abbey was founded in the fifth century. St. Patrick, the legendary founder, is said to have lived and died there and was buried there. Various churches were built at the site over the centuries. The last, dating from the thirteenth or fourteenth century, was destroyed under Henry VIII, who closed down all the abbeys and monasteries in 1539 after his split with the Catholic church. In the ruins the famous Glastonbury Thorn blooms every year, said to be the staff of Joseph of Arimathea, which took root when he leaned upon it.

Arthur and Guinevere are buried in secret graves on the abbey grounds, according to legend. In 1190 monks found remains of a man and the inscription, "Here lies the renowned Arthur in the Isle of Avalon." The bones were reburied in a black marble tomb in 1278, which was destroyed in the dissolution of the abbey in 1539.

The ruins of Glastonbury were purchased by the Church of England in 1907 for excavation under the direction of Frederick Bligh Bond. Bond was extraordinarily successful in locating unknown chapels and parts of the abbey, and concluded that the abbey's construction had involved sacred geometry known by the builders of the Egyptian pyramids and passed down through the stonemasons. Bond's method of excavation was quite unorthodox: He claimed to receive helpful information from the spirits of monks who had lived there and who communicated to him through automatic writing. Bond kept the spirits secret until he revealed them in 1921 in his book, *The Gate of Remembrance,* upon which he was dismissed in scandal by the church. See **Psychic archaeology.**

Bond's belief that Glastonbury is connected to Stonehenge and Avebury by leys has been upheld by modern ley investigators; the entire theory of leys, however, remains controversial. See **Leys.**

In 1929 Katherine Maltwood, a sculptor and illustrator, discovered that natural formations in the Glastonbury area recreate the twelve signs of the zodiac, laid out over a ten-mile-wide circle. John Dee, the royal astrologer to Queen Elizabeth I, is said to have been the first to discover the zodiac in the sixteenth century. The origins of the patterns are unknown.

The occultist Dion Fortune spent the second part of her life living in a house at the foot of the Tor, where she practiced her magical rituals in an adjacent chalet. Later, the house and chalet were acquired by Geoffrey Ashe. The chalet was said to be haunted by a ghost that opened and closed doors and was sometimes visible as a shape in the darkness.

Glastonbury is the site of Christian pilgrimages and seasonal rituals practiced by ritual magicians, Witches, and Pagans, and of various occult and spiritual festivals. Bright and fiery lights have been seen hovering over the Tor. They may be some form of unexplained natural energy. UFO watchers believe that they are connected with extraterrestrial spacecraft. See **Earth lights.** Compare with **Avebury; Stonehenge.**

Sources: Geoffrey Ashe, ed. *The Quest for Arthur's Britain.* New York: Frederick A. Praeger, 1969; Frederick Bligh Bond. *The Gate of Remembrance.* Oxford: Basil Blackwell, 1921; Janet and Colin Bord. *Mysterious Britain.* Garden City, NY: Dou-

bleday, 1978; Paul Devereux. *Places of Power.* London: Blandford, 1990; Rosemary Ellen Guiley. *The Encyclopedia of Witches and Witchcraft.* New York: Facts On File, 1989; Francis Hitching. *Earth Magic.* New York: William Morrow, 1977; Jennifer Westwood, ed. *The Atlas of Mysterious Places.* New York: Weidenfeld & Nicholson, 1987; Colin Wilson. *Poltergeist!: A Study in Destructive Haunting.* London: New English Library, 1981.

Glossolalia

The act of speaking or writing in another, unknown tongue. Although the practice of ecstatic speech has been part of religion for centuries, glossolalia usually denotes the baptism of the Holy Spirit in Pentecostal or charismatic Christian worship.

Originating from the Greek *glossa,* "tongue," and *lalia,* "a talk," glossolalia signifies a recurring phenomenon and not just one outburst. The ability to speak in unknown tongues first came to the apostles at Pentecost, or the celebration seven weeks after Passover. Acts 2:4 in the New Testament tells that "they were all filled with the Holy Spirit and began to speak in other tongues, as the Spirit gave them utterance."

Perhaps as remarkable as the speech itself was that the apostles' listeners recognized their own languages and realized that the apostles should not have been able to speak them. Whatever the apostles said was heard in each one's native tongue.

Not every tongue is intelligible, however; some sound more like gibberish.

The early Christians at Corinth used tongues extensively in their worship services, although few could tell what they were saying or what the tongues meant. St. Paul cautioned the Corinthians about tongues, saying that unless they could be interpreted, they were useless. Paul outlined the uses of tongues thus: as an aid to the worshiper in his private prayer and praise; as a means to prayer when the supplicant is unsure what to ask for; and as a direct communication between God and his followers in public worship—but only when accompanied by interpretation. Such interpretation gives the contents of the tongue as a divine message and not a direct translation. The gift of interpretation ranks on a par with the ability to speak in tongues.

The gift of tongues has been divided into three categories: pure glossolalia, or speaking in a language unknown to the speaker or the hearer; xenoglossolalia or xenoglossy, speaking in a language unknown to the speaker but recognized by the hearer; and heteroglossolalia, speaking in a language known by the speaker but received by the hearer in his native tongue.

By the medieval period, however, church authorities deemed speaking in tongues a miracle associated with the days of the apostles and no longer possible. Various groups—such as French Camisards, Montanists, Jansenists, and Waldensians—tried to revive interest in the practice and found themselves branded as heretics for their beliefs. Later, speaking in a tongue unknown to the speaker became a sure sign of demonic possession. The modern Catholic church considers the ability to speak a recognizable language of which the speaker should have no knowledge as an indicator of diabolic intervention.

Classic Pentecostal Christians see speaking in tongues as a definite sign of baptism by the Holy Spirit. Other groups that advocate glossolalia are the Shakers, Quakers, and Latter-day Saints, or Mormons. Early Methodists spoke in tongues, as did some Presbyterians during the 1830s. During the Shakers's wave of spiritual manifestations (1837–1847), worshipers composed hymns and prayers in tongues delivered by the spirits. Since these languages were unintelligible to mortals, the songs were learned phonetically.

Modern charismatics maintain that the worshiper may or may not speak in tongues following the conversion experience. Like the gifts of healing, wisdom, prophecy, miracles, and spirit divination, the ability to speak in tongues is not given to everyone. See **Charismatic renewal; Church of Jesus Christ of Latter-day Saints, the (Mormonism); Pentecostals; Shakers; Society of Friends (Quakers); Xenoglossy.**

Sources: Keith Crim, general ed. *Abingdon Dictionary of Living Religions.* Nashville: Abingdon Press, 1981; Felicitas D. Goodman. *Speaking in Tongues: A Cross-Cultural Study of Glossolalia.* Chicago: University of Chicago Press, 1972; James H. Hyslop. "Psychic Phenomena and Christianity." *The Journal of the American Society for Psychical Research* 16, no. 1 (January 1922): 59–71; Richard Quebedeaux. *The New Charismatics II.* San Francisco: Harper & Row, 1983; John Sherrill. *They Speak with Other Tongues.* New York: McGraw-Hill Book Co., 1964; Lewis Spence. *The Encyclopedia of the Occult.* Reprint. London: Bracken Books, 1988.

Gnosticism

Dualistic, mystical Christian religion, which flourished in the Mediterranean region during the second century A.D. "Gnostic" comes from the Greek *gnosis,* meaning "knowledge." Gnostics believed that redemption, or liberation of the soul, was possible only through knowledge, gnosis, not faith, *pistis.*

At its origin Gnosticism—the "religion of knowledge" or "the religion of insight"—was a philosophically dualistic religion consisting of at least sixty sects. In orthodox Christian circles, Gnosticism has been dismissed as heretical and pseudo-religious. However, modern scholarship has questioned this view and has considered that the Gnostics may have been the descendants of the original Christians who inherited Christ's esoteric teachings.

Gnostic elements can be found in all religions; in a broad sense, Gnosticism is the creative element in any religion. Gnostic ideas were widespread before the time of Christ, in the Egyptian and Greek mystery cults, Zoroastrianism, Judaism, Buddhism, and Taoism.

The Gnostic terms gnosis and *sophia,* wisdom, appear in the Old Testament. In Paul's first letter to the Corinthians, he uses gnosis to refer to practical knowledge and sophia to refer to speculative questions. As Gnostic sects developed, sophia came to be associated with the highest wisdom attainable, which gives insights into the secrets of God.

The founding of Gnosticism often is credited to Simon Magus, a reputed miracle-worker who was thrown out of the church and whose rise and fall are recorded in Acts. It is more likely that Gnosticism simply arose under various leaders in the ferment of early Christianity and coexisted for a time with the orthodox church. Most Gnostics, in fact, probably would have called themselves Christians, not Gnostics.

Gnosticism was taught in certain Roman and Alexandrian schools, which reached a developmental peak in the second century. The great sect leaders, including Basilides, Valentine, and Marcion, were mystics who saw that the truths of the universe are found in its spiritual or psychic dimensions. At the heart of Gnosticism is the belief that agape, mystical love, is the way to knowledge of God; agape can be attained only after a long and arduous process.

Gnosticism developed a dualism of good (the spiritual) and evil (physical matter). In every person the divine seed—the soul (spirit-good)—was imprisoned in the body (matter-evil), as a result of a cosmic fall. Furthermore, they taught that spiritual salvation is achieved only by

(Dover Publications)

Gnostic talisman

freeing the intrinsically good soul from the intrinsically evil body. Carrying out this dualism to its extreme, radical Gnostics practiced excessive asceticism in their effort to purge themselves of evil.

While Gnostics believed every person possessed the divine seed, they categorized people primarily as either Gnostics—those who were motivated by the spirit and therefore will be saved—or as those who are motivated by matter and therefore will not to be saved. However, they also allowed a third category—those who have the potential to be Gnostics through knowledge, but who are not fully Gnostics. (The word "agnostic," from the Greek *agnost* for "not known" or "not knowable," relates to Gnosticism in that it refers to a person who holds that the uncaused cause [God] and the essential nature of reality are not only unknown, but also unknowable.)

Some Gnostics questioned the suffering and crucifixion of Christ, asking how God could contaminate himself with matter. It was postulated by some that Jesus had escaped physical death by trading places with a surrogate prior to crucifixion. Some Gnostic sects made liberal interpretations of the scriptures and others injected magical formulae into their teachings.

The spread of Gnostic ideas was perceived as threatening by early church officials, who hardened against it. Early Christian scholars who wrote against Gnosticism included Irenaeus, Hippolytus, and Tertullian (c. 160–230). However, Clement of Alexandria (c. 150–215) tried to justify a Gnosticism that would be acceptable to orthodox Christianity. The resulting formulation, along with aspects of Buddhism, Zoroastrianism, and other religious elements, gradually merged with Manichaeism, which adhered to a simplistic and dualistic religious system in which matter is regarded as evil and spirit is good.

Gnostics were persecuted and executed as heretics. By the late Middle Ages, the sects were all but wiped out; the last great persecution occurred in 1244 in France. Gnostic ideas were kept alive, however, by the Freemasons, Rosicrucians, Kabbalists, and various other esoteric orders. A remnant of a Gnostic sect exists today as the Mandeans in Iraq and Iran.

Despite the persecutions Gnosticism had a great influence on Christian liturgy, most notably the sacraments of the Catholic church. Early Christian liturgies, in turn, had an influence on the development of synagogue services.

Interest in the Gnostics was revived in the twentieth century with the discovery of Gnostic manuscripts, previously thought to be lost, in Turkestan between 1902 and 1914 and near Nag Hammadi in upper Egypt in 1945 and 1946 and in 1948. The latter are usually called the Dead Sea Scrolls and have provided the basis for new interpretations of Gnostic beliefs and influence. See **Dead Sea Scrolls.**

Another major factor in the reexamination of Gnosticism is the work of psychiatrist Carl G. Jung, who may be described as a "neo-Gnostic." Between 1912 and 1926, Jung delved into a study of Gnosticism and early Christianity. He found in Gnosticism an early, prototypical depth psychology. He believed that Christianity, and as a result Western culture, had suffered because of the repression of Gnostic concepts. In looking for ways to reintroduce Gnostic ideas to modern culture, Jung found them in alchemy. See **Alchemy.**

The first codex of the Nag Hammadi library found in 1945 was purchased and given to Jung on his eightieth birthday. It is called the Codex Jung.

Others influential in the Gnostic revival are Hans Jonas, a student of the existentialist Martin Heidegger, and religion historian Kurt Rudolph. Jonas, who was influenced greatly by the New Testament scholar Rudolph Bultmann, published his pioneering work, *Gnostic Religion,* in 1934. It introduced many readers to a historical perspective that leads to a better understanding of the early church in general, and the Dead Sea Scrolls in particular.

In 1977 Kurt Rudolph published *Gnosis: The Nature and History of Gnosticism,* a chronological history of many elements leading to ancient Gnosticism, from the beginning of Alexander the Great's campaigns in Asia (334 B.C.) to the most significant elements that led to the Catholicizing of the last Paulicians in Bulgaria in the seventh century. The Paulicians, founded c. 657, followed the teachings of the apostle Paul as interpreted by Marcion, and represented Gnosticism in the extreme, in that they believed in two supreme gods, one of good and one of evil. Rudolph's historical survey of the consequences of Gnosticism, while expertly documented, considers only the European Christian side. He observes that a similar investigation deserves to be made of the effects of Gnosticism in Eastern thought. See **Jung, Carl Gustav; Mysteries.**

Sources: Joseph Campbell, ed. *The Mystic Vision: Papers from the Eranos Yearbooks.* Princeton, NJ: Princeton University Press, 1968; John Dart. *The Jesus of Heresy and History: The Discovery and Meaning of the Nag Hammadi Gnostic Library.* Rev. and expanded edition of *The Laughing Savior: The Discovery and Meaning of the Nag Hammadi Gnostic Library.* San Francisco: Harper & Row, 1988; John Ferguson. *An Illustrated Encyclopedia of Mysticism and the Mystery Religions.* New York: Seabury Press, 1976; Robert McQueen Grant. *Gnosticism and Early Christianity.* New York: Columbia University Press, 1966; Stephan A. Hoeller. *The Gnostic Jung and the Seven Sermons to the Dead.* Wheaton, IL: Theosophical Publishing House, 1982; Hans Jonas. *Gnostic Religion.* Boston: Beacon Press, 1958; Geddes MacGregor. *Gnosis: A Renaissance in Christian Thought.* Wheaton, IL: Theosophical Publishing House, 1979; Kurt Rudolph. *Gnosis: The Nature and History of Gnosticism.* San Francisco: Harper & Row, 1987; "The Gnostic Jung: An Interview With Stephan Hoeller." *The Quest* 2, no. 2 (Summer 1989): 82–86.

(Photo by Bonnie Sue)

Goddess symbol jewelry in silver. Left: crescent moon sits atop double-headed ax of wisdom. Right: Diana dances on crescent moon.

Goddess

The feminine principle of the Divine Force. Widely venerated in earlier times, Goddess is no longer a primary power in the mainstream religions: For the past three millennia she has been subordinated or ignored in favor of the masculine principle. The Supreme Being of Judaism, Christianity, and Islam is male; the Holy Trinity of Christianity, the Father, the Son, and the Holy Ghost, is an all-male triumvirate. Hinduism, though it recognizes female deities, gives priority to the masculine element. Buddhism, which recognizes no Supreme Being, nonetheless holds the male Buddha as the highest and most sacred figure. Since the 1960s, however, Goddess has reawakened in Western consciousness.

Goddess worship extends at least back to the Neolithic era of approximately 10,000 years ago, and may even be as old as the Stone Age of 25,000 to 30,000 years ago. Goddess may have preceded God, creating the universe by fertilizing herself.

The earliest known cult works and works of art are Stone Age sculptures of female figures, some with exaggerated sexual characteristics, believed to represent Goddess as Great Mother. The so-called "Venus figures" date to the time of the Cro-Magnons, between 35,000 B.C. and 10,000 B.C.

Goddess appears universally, primarily as a symbol of fertility, but in multiple facets as the ruler of wisdom, truth, magical powers, nature, fate, the home, healing, justice, love, birth, death, time, and eternity. She is the guardian of the human interior, of emotion, intuition, psychic forces, and mysteries. She is Creator, Nurturer, and Destroyer, and almost always is more powerful than gods. From her all else springs, and without her blessings and good will none may prosper either in heaven or on earth. In various cosmologies she is most often represented as Goddess of the Earth, whose masculine divine counterpart is God of the Sky. In her celestial aspects, she is often Goddess of the Moon, whose rays have been associated with fertilizing power since ancient times. In ancient Chinese myth, there was once a time when Goddess reigned supreme: the *Tao Teh Ching* tells of a time when yin, the female principle, was not ruled by yang, the male principle. The wisdom of Taoism is based on traits that are labeled feminine: intuition, the flow of the forces of nature and harmony with nature. See **Taoism.**

The facets of Goddess are represented by her many aspects, goddesses of various names and attributes; Goddess is said to be She of a Thousand Names. Her multiplicity indicates that multiplicity is natural to woman in her many roles in life.

The beginning of the end of the Golden Age of Goddess commenced circa 1800 B.C. to 1500 B.C., during the time of Abraham, the first prophet of the Hebrew God, Yahweh, who proclaimed that humankind would have no other gods before Yahweh. During the spread of Christianity, worship of Goddess, along with all pagan deities, was routed or suppressed, and the deities were demonized. But the need for veneration of a female figure persisted, and in Christianity that need was transferred to the much-disputed adoration of the Blessed Virgin Mary. At times the cult of Mary has approached that of Goddess worship, but any similarities drawn between Mary and Goddess are discouraged by the Catholic church. The proper place of Mary in Christianity was one of the major disputes in the Protestant Reformation—the Protestants felt she had been given too much emphasis. Mary, as Queen of Heaven, officially occupies a status below that of deity yet more exalted than the saints; through her one may reach Christ and God. Psychiatrist Carl G. Jung said Mary was not quite the fourth Trinity, but was necessary to the understanding of the Trinity, for she represented the anima, the female attributes that reside in all human beings. See **Mary.**

Goddess has existed as a powerful archetype since the Stone Age. Her symbol is the vessel, the inexhaustible container of all wisdom and life forces, and appears in different forms in mythologies—the cauldron, the cup, the bowl—and in the Christian mysteries as the Grail. Christ himself evinced Goddess traits in his ministry of love, peace, and healing, and in his death and resurrection.

Analytical psychologist Erich Neumann observed that the revitalization of the Feminine archetype was essential to correct the "one-sided patriarchal development of the male intellectual consciousness," largely responsible for the "peril of the present-day." Neumann said that "Western mankind must arrive at a synthesis that includes the feminine world—which is also one-sided in its isolation. Only then will the individual human being be able to develop the psychic wholeness that is urgently needed if Western man is to face the dangers that threaten his existences from within and without" (*The Great Mother: An Analysis of the Archetype*, 1955; 1963).

The rediscovery of Goddess in the West in the late 1960s coincided with the women's movement, the ecology movement, and the beginnings of the so-called New Age movement. It was influenced by archaeological discoveries, especially those at Catal Huyuk in Anatolia, the largest Neolithic site (c. 7000 B.C.– 10,000 B.C.), and other Neolithic Anatolian sites of Mersin and Hacilar. The dig at Catal Huyuk commenced in 1961, and detailed reports on all three sites were published in 1966. They indicated a predominant cult of Goddess that extended into the Bronze Age. Archaeologist James Mellaart, who directed the early digs at Catal Huyuk, said the civilization there was "woman dominated." The society appeared to have been peaceful, ordered, and vegetarian. There was no evidence of animal sacrifice, violent death, or of war for a thousand years. The remains of women had been buried with reverence, while the remains of men had been thrown in a charnel house.

The rising consciousness of Goddess led modern women to challenge the subordinate role dealt them by mainstream religions, and the contentions that male superiority is both divinely ordained because of the Fall and naturally ordained because of genes. The Fall has been recast by some women as a scapegoat for men to shove the burden of the question of evil onto women, which has had profound and damaging effects on the perceptions of the "nature" of women, now deeply embedded in the Western psyche, and on the balance of male-female relationships.

Attempts have been made to find a new term for the Supreme Being to incorporate the aspects of Goddess, but without success. Most, such as "God/ess," are awkward. Mary Daly, feminist philosopher and theologian, has suggested changing the conception/perception of god (sic) from "supreme being" to Be-ing, as verb.

Nonetheless, the reawakening of Goddess, like the many facets she has herself, has taken numerous forms: in the celebration of female strength, power, and dynamism; in the continuing rediscovery of female divinity; in the recognition that the Earth is sacred and must be cared for; and in the renewed acceptance and cultivation of "female" traits such as nurturing, peacefulness, intuition, and emotion. Goddess is not surrounded by a hierarchy—every woman, every person, has direct access to her.

New interpretations have been offered of Jung's concepts of anima and animus. Jung ascribed feminine characteristics to the anima and male characteristics to the animus; men and women have both within them. The animus plays a central role in Jung's writings on the psychology of women. Some feminists deplore the anima/animus concept because it pigeonholes characteristics according to sex. Jung's views, of course, reflect the different attitudes toward women of his time. Alternatives have been proposed, such as the psychology of Jean Shinoda Bolen, which is based on female Goddess representations of archetypes: "masculine" traits are associated with the goddesses who evince them, such as Artemis and Atalanta.

Perhaps one of the most visible arenas for the revival of Goddess is in the neo-Paganism and neo-Pagan Witchcraft nature religions. These are largely reconstructions of earlier pagan religions. Most sects recognize both female and male aspects of the Divine Force—Goddess and Horned God respectively—but Goddess is given primacy (some feminist covens worship Goddess exclusively). Goddess embodies the very essence of modern Witchcraft: she is the Great Mother, Mother Nature, Creator, Destroyer, the Queen of Heaven, the Moon (the source of magical power), and the innermost self. Goddess frequently is recognized in a trinity, the Triple Goddess, a personification of her three faces as Virgin, Mother, and Crone, respectively called Diana, Selene, and Hecate. See **Archetypes; Creation spirituality; Moon; Neo-Paganism; Psychology; Witchcraft.**

Sources: Mary Daly. *Beyond God the Father: Toward a Philosophy of Women's Liberation.* Rev. ed. Boston: Beacon Press, 1985; Elizabeth Gould Davis. *The First Sex.* New York: G. P. Putnam's Sons, 1971; Riane Eisler. *The Chalice and the Blade: Our History, Our Future.* San Francisco: Harper & Row, 1987; Rosemary Ellen Guiley. *The Encyclopedia of Witches* and Witchcraft. New York: Facts On File, 1989; Erich Neumann. *The Great Mother: An Analysis of the Archetype.* 2d ed. Princeton, NJ: Princeton University Press, 1963; Shirley Nicholson, ed. *The Goddess Reawakening: The Feminine Principle Today.* Wheaton, IL: The Theosophical Publishing House, 1989; Carl Olson, ed. *The Book of the Goddess Past and Present.* New York: Crossroad, 1989; Starhawk. *The Spiral Dance.* San Francisco: Harper & Row, 1979; Merlin Stone. *When God Was a Woman.* San Diego: Harcourt Brace Jovanovich, 1976; Edward C. Whitmont. *Return of the Goddess.* New York: Crossroad, 1988.

Grail, the

Spiritual mystery in the Western, and especially British, esoteric tradition. It is a pagan story that became Christianized and merged with Arthurian legend, but retained much of its pagan imagery and symbolism. The Grail is a gateway to Paradise, a point of contact with a supernatural and spiritual realm. It possesses unlimited healing power and makes possible a direct apprehension of the Divine.

As a pagan image, the Grail is the Graal, a cup of plenty and regeneration, the vessel in which the life of the world is preserved, and which symbolizes the body of Goddess or the Great Mother. In its Christianized form, the Grail is the chalice used by Christ at the Last Supper, and which held his blood following the crucifixion. It is not known whether such an object truly existed or exists, and there is no definitive image of it. As a spiritual mystery, the Grail represents regeneration through Christ's teachings; in medieval belief blood embodied the soul, and in Christ's case even his divinity.

Various versions of the Grail legend exist. The first written texts appeared toward the end of the twelfth century and flowered through the fourteenth century, though it is likely that the story existed earlier in oral tradition. Originally, the story was pagan. An account attributed to the sixth-century bard Taliesin, but appearing four hundred years later, tells of a magic cauldron in Annwn, the otherworld, in the keeping of nine maidens, which is sought by King Arthur's men. As versions proliferated the story incorporated elements of classical and Celtic mythology, Christian iconography, Arabic poetry, and Sufi teachings. It was first identified with the Last Supper in about 1190.

The Grail was never fully accepted in Catholic apocrypha, but neither was it denied nor labeled as heretical. It was perhaps never fully accepted because it could not be identified with a relic. It was perhaps never suppressed because of its tremendous popularity. Grail symbolisms were absorbed into Rosicrucianism.

A Christian version of the story of the Grail is this: Joseph of Arimathea is charged with preparing Christ's body for the tomb. He has obtained the cup used by Christ at the Last Supper; and while he washes the body, he uses the cup to catch blood that flows from the wounds. When the body of Christ disappears from the tomb, Joseph is accused of stealing it and is jailed without food. Christ appears to him, puts the cup in his care, and teaches him various mysteries, including the Mass. Joseph remains alive in prison by the acts of a mysterious dove, which appears every day and leaves a wafer in the cup. After his release in A.D. 70, according to one version, Joseph traveled to Britain, where he founded the first Christian church at Glastonbury, dedicated to Mary, mother of Christ, and enshrined in it the Grail.

In another version Joseph passes the Grail to Bron, his sister's husband, who becomes the Rich Fisher when he feeds many from the cup with a single fish. The company goes to Avaron (perhaps Avalon, the otherworld of Arthurian lore) and waits for a new Grail keeper.

The Grail is housed in a temple on

Muntsalvach, the Mountain of Salvation. It is guarded by an Order of Grail Knights. The Grail keeper, who is king, is wounded in the thighs or genitals by a spear (associated with the spear wounds of Christ). The causes of the wound are varied, but the result is that the kingdom withers and becomes the Waste Land; it can only be restored when the king is restored to health (a motif common in folktales and fairy tales).

Thus begin the Arthurian quests for the Grail. At Pentecost the Grail appears floating in a sunbeam to the Knights of the Round Table, who pledge to find it. The quests essentially are initiations. Galahad the pure, Perceval the fool, and Bors the humble are the only knights to find the Grail. Perceval finds the wounded king and is asked the ritual question that can heal him: "Whom does the Grail serve?" The answer is not given, but it is the king. Perceval answers correctly, the king heals and is permitted to die, and the Waste Land is restored.

The three knights then travel east to Sarras, the Heavenly City, where they celebrate the mysteries of the Grail, and a mass is said using the Grail. Galahad dies in sanctity and the Grail ascends to heaven. Perceval takes the king's place and Bors returns to Camelot.

Early origins of the Grail legend may be found in the ancient and universal motif of sacred vessel as symbol of power and the source of miracles. Such vessels, feminine symbols, are in Vedic, Egyptian, classical, and Celtic mythology and in various mystery traditions as cups or cauldrons of inspiration, rebirth, and regeneration. The Grail is paralleled in alchemy as the philosopher's stone, which represents the unification with God. In Tibetan Buddhism a corollary is found in the human skulls that represent vessels of transformation.

The Grail also is represented by other feminine symbols, as a dish, womb, or other stone. One version of the legend, *Parzival*, finished in 1207 by Wolfram von Eschenbach, said the Grail was an emerald that fell from Lucifer's crown during his battle with God, and was brought to earth by angels.

Psychiatrist Carl G. Jung said the story of the Grail is very much psychically alive in modern times. The Grail quest is a search for truth and the real Self, and may be seen as a paradigm of the modern spiritual journey to restore the Waste Land and become whole again. There are many paths to the Grail. According to lore the Grail may be seen only by those who have attained a certain spiritual consciousness, who have raised themselves above the limitations of the senses. See **Alchemy; Glastonbury; Goddess; Merlin; Mysteries; Planetary consciousness; Symbol.**

Sources: Manly P. Hall. *The Secret Teachings of All Ages.* 1928. Los Angeles: The Philosophic Research Society, 1977; Emma Jung and Marie-Louise von Franz. *The Grail Legend.* 1960. Boston: Sigo Press, 1986; Caitlin and John Matthews. "The Grailless Lands." *Gnosis* no. 9 (Fall 1988): 8–13; John Matthews. *The Grail: Quest for the Eternal.* New York: Crossroad, 1981; John Matthews, ed. *At the Table of the Grail: Magic and the Use of Imagination.* 1984. London: Arkana, 1987; Lewis Spence. *The Encyclopedia of the Occult.* Reprint. London: Bracken Books, 1988.

Grant, Joan (b. 1907)

Psychically gifted British writer whose technique of past-life recall, "far memory," enabled her to tap into apparent past lives, the biographies of which were published as best-selling novels. In later years she turned her far memory skill to psychotherapy.

She was born Joan Marshall on April 12, 1907, in London, and enjoyed a comfortable upbringing with nannies and governesses, one of whom professed to be a Welsh witch. She said that even as a toddler, she experienced bits and pieces of past lives. Seven previous lives, four as a male and three as a female, emerged during childhood, and Grant assumed that all people had such memories.

She also possessed unusual psychic gifts, which manifested in premonitions of death, precognitive dreams, and a strange type of dream that seemed to involve out-of-body travel to another reality. In these latter dreams, she was older, and was in situations in which she assisted the newly dead to cross over. During World War I, she dreamed of being a nurse on a battlefield, telling soldiers they were dead, and helping them meet loved ones who also were dead. She also helped accident victims who did not realize they had died. These dreams invariably preceded news stories that verified the details of her dreams. Grant was uneasy about her dreams, but could do nothing to prevent them from occurring.

Grant was sensitive to the presence of ghosts. As a child she matter-of-factly accepted piano lessons from the spirit of a dead pianist. As she grew older, she increased her contact with the spirit realm through automatic writing and the planchette.

On November 30, 1927, she married Leslie Grant, a barrister, who was mindful of social appearances and the opinions of his peers and fellow club members. A daughter, Gillian, was born on April 2, 1930.

Once, after a stay in haunted Cluny Castle, Grant vowed that she would understand her unusual abilities, and started a dream journal. She learned that her "true dreams," as she called them, fell into two categories: one in which time proceeded in a linear fashion; and one that transcended time and space so that the "I" that was herself alternated with another personality, such as a newly dead soul.

Grant learned to psychometrize objects. See **Psychometry.** By pressing them to her forehead, she would see moving visual images as though she were seeing them through her third eye. She would pour out incredible details related to the owner of the object, and events that had occurred in his or her life.

The psychometry proved to be the key to unlocking her past lives. Leslie decided to pursue archaeology, and in 1935 the Grants went to Iran to a Sumerian dig. Grant psychometrized the artifacts. In 1936 a longtime friend, Daisy Sartorius, asked Grant to psychometrize five Egyptian scarabs. One of them revealed a young Egyptian girl named Sekeeta. Grant's identification with Sekeeta was so strong that she felt compelled to explore her in more depth. Rubbing the scarab on her forehead, she viewed more episodes from the girl's life. Sekeeta had been the daughter of a pharaoh, and had spent ten years undergoing a rigorous temple training to become a Winged Pharaoh, a ruler and healer. Part of that training involved learning far memory, and viewing at least ten of her previous deaths, so that she would be able to comfort the dying.

Grant believed that she had been Sekeeta, and Sartorius had been Sekeeta's mother. Over the ensuing months, she devoted about two hundred recall sessions to that life, unearthing two or three episodes, not in chronological order, in each session. She learned how to employ far memory herself, an altered state of consciousness in which she shifted the major portion of her consciousness to the past personality, while remaining aware enough to dictate what she saw and felt. She was able to describe daily life in great detail. She discovered that past-life memories were distinguished from imagination because they were active and moving, while fantasies remained passive. Past-life details could not be changed, while fantasies could. The sessions were often physically draining, especially if they concerned traumatic events in the past life.

Grant wrote her biography of Sekeeta, never intending to publish it. She gave it to an acquaintance who in turn gave it to a publisher. The book was published as *Winged Pharaoh* in 1937. The public exposure of her unorthodox experiences contributed to the eventual disintegration of her marriage.

Using far memory Grant tuned in to many past lives, including numerous ones in ancient Egypt. Six more lives were published as biography-novels: *Life as Carola*, about Carola di Ludovici, a sixteenth-century Italian lute player; *Eyes of Horus* and *Lord of the Horizon*, about Ra-ab Hotep, the Nomarch (similar to a lord lieutenant) of the Oryx, who lived one thousand years after Sekeeta in the last reign of the Eleventh Dynasty; *Scarlet Feather*, about a North American female Indian warrior of the second millennium B.C.; *Return to Elysium*, about Lucina, a Greek girl of the second century B.C. who was the ward of a philosopher and a priestess of a mystery cult; and *So Moses Was Born*, about a male contemporary of Ramses II.

In 1958 Grant met Denys Kelsey, a psychiatrist and hypnotherapist who became her second husband. In London they established a practice together. Kelsey recognized potential benefits of past-life recall in treating many neuroses, guilt, and phobias. Grant attended hypnosis sessions, tuning into the past lives seen by the patients, validating their experiences as real or discerning them as fantasies.

Grant believes that human beings go through four phases of evolution: molecules of energy, the mineral kingdom, the plant kingdom, the animal kingdom, and the human realm. Many lifetimes are spent in each phase until consciousness has expanded enough to "graduate" to the next level. During human lives the consciousness eventually becomes too

large for a single personality. An incarnation includes both a soul, or personality, and a component of his total self. The sum total of all the souls is the spirit. After death the soul joins the spirit. In far memory Grant said she was accessing a particular component of her spirit.

According to the Kelsey-Grant practice, if a soul fails to integrate itself into the spirit, fragments split off and form a "ghost," which traps energy. The ghost lingers through subsequent incarnations, until its energy is released, such as in psychotherapy. See **Past-life recall; Past-life therapy (PLT); Reincarnation.**

Sources: Joan Grant. *Far Memory.* New York: Harper & Row, 1956; Denys Kelsey, MB, MRCP and Joan Grant. *Many Lifetimes.* Garden City, NY: Doubleday & Co., 1967.

Guadelupe

See **Marian apparitions.**

Guardian spirit

In tribal cultures a spirit, usually in animal form, that protects individuals, tribes, and clans, or provides magical shamanic power. The animal represents the collective power of an entire species or genus, and customarily has magical powers that enable it to perform extraordinary feats, such as a wolf with the power of flight. Guardian spirits almost always appear in animal form, but may in some cases take on human shape on various occasions. In animal form they can converse with humans. The animal form is rooted in the deep belief that humans and animals are related to one another.

Beliefs about guardian spirits vary. In many tribes it is assumed that males have guardian spirits from birth, otherwise they would not live to adulthood. Some tribes believe that not all males successfully acquire guardian spirits; those who do not suffer weakness and failure in their lives. It is less important, or not important at all, for women to have guardian spirits because women do not become hunters and warriors. Some tribes, however, have minor rites for women to connect with their guardian spirits.

Some tribal societies, such as among Native North Americans, especially those of the Northwest Coast, have totem guardian spirits, which protect entire tribes or clans on both a collective and individual basis. The totem animal is sacred. For example, a clan protected by Bear cannot hunt bear, but is permitted to consume the flesh of a bear killed by another clan.

In shamanic cultures shamans acquire guardian spirits who empower them with their magical powers; one cannot be a shaman without one. The guardian spirit also serves as the shaman's "power animal," or his alter ego. When the shaman enters the altered state of consciousness in which he works, he assumes the form and power of his guardian spirit, seeing it, conversing with it, and using it to help him. It accompanies him on his shamanic journey to the underworld, or on his mystical ascents to the sky. The guardian spirit never is threatening or dangerous to the shaman himself.

The shaman maintains contact with his guardian spirit by regularly "dancing the animal." Guardian spirits do not remain with a shaman throughout life, but have temporary stays and are replaced by new spirits.

The shamanic guardian spirit is not to be confused with "spirit helpers," who are minor powers with specialized functions, such as in healing specific illnesses or diseases. The spirit helpers are used collectively by a shaman. Nor is the guardian spirit the same as the *tonal* (from the Nahuatl or Aztec term *tonalli*), which is one's vital soul and the sign of one's birth date, as represented in spirit animal form. Likewise, guardian spirits are not the equivalent of a "familiar," a spirit in animal form that is dispatched on errands by a magician, sorcerer, or witch.

The most customary means of acquiring a guardian spirit is to undertake a solitary spirit quest or vision quest in the wilderness. For some people guardian spirits first come in dreams. Others acquire them by taking hallucinogenic drugs, which may be part of a vision quest. Contact with one's guardian spirit is part of many initiatory rites into manhood. See **Drugs in mystical and psychic experiences.**

Communication with the guardian spirit most frequently is made through ecstatic dancing, in which the dancer enters a trance state and assumes the form of the animal. The Zuñi, for example, call their dance "Calling the Beasts."

Numerous other names are applied to guardian spirits, among them "tutelary spirit" in Siberian shamanism; "assistant totem" among Australian Aborigines; "spirit of the head," used by the Vasyugán of Siberia; and *nagual,* used among Mexican and Guatemalan shamans (from the Aztec term *nahualli*).

From a tribal perspective, modern Westerners also have guardian spirits, but generally remain unaware of them throughout their lives, thus robbing themselves of an enriching source of greater power. See **Shamanism;** compare to **Spirit guide.**

Sources: Mircea Eliade. *Shamanism.* 1951. Princeton, NJ: Princeton University Press, 1964; Michael Harner. *The Way of the Shaman.* New York: Bantam, 1986; Ake Hultkrantz. *The Religions of the American Indians.* 1967. Berkeley: University of California Press, 1979.

Guided imagery

See **Creative visualization.**

Gurdjieff, Georgei Ivanovitch (1866?–1949)

As much an enigma as his homeland of Russia, G. I. Gurdjieff was considered by some to be the greatest mystical teacher of all time, and by others to be a fraud. His liberation philosophy, commonly called "the Work," set occultism on its ear in the 1920s and paved the way for now-conventional techniques of group and encounter therapy.

His birth date is unknown. Gurdjieff gave it as 1866, but it has been variously given as 1877 by his sister and 1872 by his biographer, J. G. Bennett. All agree, however, that Gurdjieff was born in Alexandropol, in the Russo-Turkish frontier, to Greek and Armenian parents. He spent his early years in the village of Kars. Gurdjieff absorbed the varied cultural influences of the area, which later surfaced in his teachings.

After several, mostly undocumented, years of travel, some of which may have been devoted to spying against England on behalf of Russia, Gurdjieff turned his attention to finding out the "whys" of life. He was familiar with Madame H. P. Blavatsky's Theosophical Society and the occult-Orthodox philosophies of priest Pavel Alexandrovitch Florensky. But instead of embracing any organized occult teaching, Gurdjieff devised his own. He postulated that people are no more than machines run by forces outside their control. Human beings in such a state are essentially asleep. In order to wake up, they must work hard to penetrate their normal state of unconsciousness to reach the true consciousness inside.

Gurdjieff turned increasingly to hypnotism to accomplish this goal. He had acquired extensive, albeit unorthodox medical knowledge on his travels, and believed that the tempo of the blood altered at adolescence to accommodate humankind's normal "asleep" state. He claimed that he possessed new hypnotic techniques that would alter the blood's tempo to break through these so-called "buffers" and evoke the subconscious.

Gurdjieff also held that people must study under those who have escaped their own robotic existences: a teacher, a Man Who Knows. They must form groups or schools; and they must obey all the rules, including the obligation to tell the teacher everything, to keep silent in front of others, and to be prepared for the teacher to lie for the "good" of the students. Students must achieve self-realization through work on themselves, self-observation, and "self-remembering" — conscious awareness of surroundings *and* the self in the situation.

The first Gurdjieffian school opened in Moscow at about the start of World War I. His reputation spread to St. Petersburg, where he attracted Pyotr Demianovitch Ouspensky, who believed in eternal recurrence (endless repetition, not improvement, through reincarnation) and Nietzsche's idea of Superman. He saw Gurdjieff's way as the means of breaking the cycle and eventually attaining perfection.

Ouspensky began teaching the Gurdjieffian "system" to students in St. Petersburg in 1915. In 1917 Gurdjieff moved both groups to Essentuki in the Caucasus to escape the Russian Revolution. There he established the formal procedures, drawn in part from his previous studies with Sufi dervishes of Central Asia, that characterized his later work: hard, physical labor; tasks beneath one's social or cultural station; intense emotionalism; exercise; and complicated dance movements. Gurdjieff called such methods "shocks," designed to change one's preconceived notions of self and further the process of self-awareness. The student begins to lose all preconceived notions and to unify his or her various selves—the "I"s—in harmony. By working on oneself, one can rise above one's mechanical existence, make a soul, and attain immortality.

The intellectual and upper-class students participated in strenuous manual labor and complicated dance exercises. They attended lectures on science, languages, hypnotism, and music. They learned Sufi breathing and dance techniques. They were awakened at all hours to work or just to "be alert." They might be asked to stop whatever they were doing and remain like statues for minutes at a time. They lived frugally and communally, yet were forced to join Gurdjieff in his Rabelaisian feasts and drinking parties.

Gurdjieff's knowledge of occult literature and tradition gave rise to a detailed cosmology. He stated that the universe is governed by two cosmic laws: the Law of Three and the Law of Seven or the Octave. The Law of Three controls the workings of the universe, based on three forces: active, passive, and neutral. Human beings have three bodies: carnal, emotional, and spiritual; and feed on three sorts of food: edible, air, and impressions. By working on themselves, people can rise from the carnal to the spiritual, and manufacture higher substances from the foods they consume: the alchemist's process of transmutation.

The Law of Seven corresponds to Pythagorean theories of harmonics. Gurdjieff saw life's processes as governed by the repetition of seven stages of development, which only proceed if given a boost, or shock, much as music continues along the octave over slower and faster intervals.

Gurdjieff's ultimate symbol for his worldview was the enneagram: a circle whose circumference is divided by nine points, yielding an uneven six-sided figure and a triangle. The enneagram shows the whole universe, the laws of three and seven, and how people cross the intervals of development via shocks administered by a Man Who Knows. Gurdjieff claimed the enneagram was his alone, but it prob-

ably dates to a very similar figure drawn by Jesuit arithmologist Athanasius Kircher in 1665. The enneagram also resembles the Kabbalah's Tree of Life and the medieval symbolic art of Ramon Lull.

Gurdjieff called his system the Fourth Way, or the Way of the Sly or Cunning Man. He explained that traditionally, there were three paths to immortality: those of the fakir, the monk, and the yogi. The fakir undergoes tremendous physical torture and reconditioning to suppress his body to his will, but has no outlet for the emotional or intellectual. The monk possesses great faith and gives himself to his emotional commitment to God, but suffers pains of the body and intellectual starvation. The yogi studies and ponders the mysteries of life, but has no emotional or physical expression. But in the Fourth Way, people do not need to suffer physical, emotional, or intellectual tortures, but merely start from their own life experiences. They work on themselves as they are, trying to harmonize all paths and using every cunning trick they know to keep themselves "awake."

This was not an immutable system, however. Gurdjieff's ideas changed as circumstances warranted, so he forbade his students to write them down and disseminate them.

Gurdjieff left Russia in 1922 and attempted to emigrate to England via Berlin, but was rebuffed over his spy past. Instead he settled with his students in France, buying a large chateau forty miles outside Paris in the Forest of Fontainebleau near Avon. The Prieuré des Basses Loges, shortened to the Prieuré, became the home of The Institute for the Harmonious Development of Man, which operated as a communal school and philosophy center from 1922 to 1924, and was eventually sold in 1933.

Most of his closest students eventually rejected Gurdjieff the man for Gurdjieffian teachings. Ouspensky formally separated from Gurdjieff in 1923 and rejected his theories outright in 1931. Another famous student, A. R. Orage, editor of the British journal *The New Age,* took Gurdjieff's ideas to New York and developed what was called "the Oragean version." He also formally rejected Gurdjieff in 1931.

After 1924 Gurdjieff no longer taught but began writing down his theories and worldview; his style was strange language and tiresome anecdotal detail. He practiced some hypnotic healing, relied on the largesse of rich widows, and otherwise lived on the fringes through World War II until his death in October 1949.

His students then broke silence and began publishing his life and works. The first was Ouspensky's *In Search of the Miraculous,* the best explanation of Gurdjieff's theories. This was followed by Gurdjieff's masterwork, *All and Everything: First Series,* better known as *Beelzebub's Tales to His Grandson* (1950). The book had circulated among his pupils for years, known as THE BOOK. The only one of his books published in his lifetime, *The Herald of Coming Good* (1934), was removed from circulation in 1935. *Meetings with Remarkable Men,* designed to be the second in the series, came out in 1960. The third volume, *Life Is Real Only Then, When "I Am,"* which appeared in the early 1970s, consisted of fragments of writings and diary entries.

Sources: J. G. Bennett. *Gurdjieff: A Very Great Enigma.* New York: Samuel Weiser, 1973; J. G. Bennett. *Gurdjieff: Making a New World.* New York: Harper & Row, 1973; O. M. Burke. "Notes on the Dervishes." *Critique: A Journal of Conspiracies & Metaphysics* no. 25: 37–42; P. D. Ouspensky. *In Search of the Miraculous.* New York: Harcourt, Brace and Co., 1949; James Webb. *The Harmonious Circle: The Lives and Work of G. I. Gurdjieff, P. D. Ouspensky, and Their Followers.* New York: G. P. Putnam's Sons, 1980; Colin Wilson, ed. *Dark Dimensions: A Celebration of the Occult.* New York: Everest House, 1977.

Gurney, Edmund

See Society for Psychical Research (SPR).

Guru

A spiritual master, religious teacher, divine preceptor, or learned Brahmin. *Guru* is a Sanskrit term meaning "teacher." In ancient India the Vedas, Vedanta, and other sacred lore were handed down orally through generations from gurus to disciples.

Traditionally, a Hindu male is initiated into the religion at age twelve, at which time he becomes a student, or *chela,* of a guru to learn the Vedas and other teachings. The student must show great deference to his guru, who confers immortality through his wisdom. The guru holds a more exalted status than the student's family, including his parents. In some Hindu sects, the guru instructs the initiate in a secret mantra, prayers, rituals, and meditations, a practice also followed in Transcendental Meditation.

In some sects of Sikhism, the guru is not a person, but the Word of God, obtained directly from scripture. In other Sikh sects, the human guru is responsible for helping people recognize the way to divine salvation. The Bauls of Bengal sometimes use the term "guru" as a metaphor for whatever makes them understand or think of God.

Yoga systems have been handed down and taught through the ages by gurus. Finding a guru is of paramount importance to yoga disciples.

In Tibetan Buddhism Padma Sambhava, "The Lotus Born" (755–97), was the Great Human Guru of the Bardo Thodöl, the Book of the Dead. He was an incarnation of the essence of the Buddha

Shakyamuni, the historical Buddha, and was the first teacher in Tibet to expound the Bardo Thodöl. According to the Bardo Thodöl, the greatest guru known to humankind in the present cycle of time is the historical Buddha. A *rinpoche,* or "precious guru," is one born under pure, holy conditions.

Tibetan yogis and followers of Tantria define three lines of gurus: superhuman or divine, over which the Supreme Guru sits on the Thousand-petaled Lotus; highly developed humans who possess *siddhis,* or psychic powers; and ordinary religious teachers. Women as well as men may become gurus. The *chela* studies with a guru for a year, and is then evaluated. Upon passing the *chela* receives psychical training. The guru must always be obeyed; it is not possible to change gurus unless the student can demonstrate he or she has advanced beyond the capability of the teacher. For initiation of a student, the guru prepares with ritual exercises for several days, then invokes the divine gurus by communicating with them on the spiritual plane.

In the West the term "guru" is used to describe many types of spiritual teachers. See **Yoga.**

Sources: W. Y. Evans-Wentz, ed. 3rd ed. *The Tibetan Book of the Dead.* London: Oxford University Press, 1960; Geoffrey Parrinder, ed. *World Religions from Ancient History to Present.* New York: Facts On File, 1971; K. M. Sen. *Hinduism.* Harmondsworth, Middlesex, England: Penguin Books, 1961; Vivian Worthington. *A History of Yoga.* London: Routledge & Kegan Paul, 1982.

H

Hag syndrome

See **Psychic attack.**

Hallucinogens

See **Drugs in mystical and psychic experiences.**

Halo

A circle of radiant light, which in art crowns the head of deities, holy beings, and saints. It represents the aura or a crown chakra, which is prominent in a person of high spiritual development. Ancient Egyptians, Greeks, Indians, and Romans used the halo in art to depict supernatural force, mystical states, and superior intellect. In ancient Egypt and Greece, the halo was associated with the sun and resurrection. In the Eleusinian Mysteries, it was bestowed upon the sacrificed and reborn god, usually Dionysus. In Christian art the halo graces saints, angels, Christ, Mary, and other holy persons. Eastern deities usually are depicted with crowns or headdresses rather than halos. In clairvoyance the aura appears as a halo or nimbus around the body, and is most easily visible around the head. See **Aura; Chakras.**

Sources: J. E. Cirlot. *A Dictionary of Symbols.* New York: Philosophical Library, 1971; Stanley Krippner and Daniel Rubin, eds. *The Kirlian Aura: Photographing the Galaxies of Life.* Garden City, NY: Anchor Books, 1974; C. W. Leadbeater. *The Chakras.* 1927. Wheaton, IL: Theosophical Publishing House, 1980; Sheila Ostrander and Lynn Schroeder. *Psychic Discoveries Behind the Iron Curtain.* Englewood Cliffs, NJ: Prentice-Hall, 1970; Barbara Walker. *The Woman's Encyclopedia of Myths and Secrets.* San Francisco: Harper & Row, 1983.

Hare Krishnas

See **Alternative religious movements.**

Harmonic Convergence

The supposed end of the materialistic world, which occurred on August 16 and 17, 1987, according to interpretations of astrological configurations, Native American myth, and Mesoamerican calendars and prophecies. The event, called the Harmonic Convergence, was observed around the world in celebrations of dancing, chanting, meditation, and yoga intended to foster peace and help usher in the next phase in humankind's spiritual evolution.

The Harmonic Convergence was largely the idea of Jose Argüelles, an American art historian who in 1983 connected astrological configurations to chronological forecasts and to his research of Mayan cosmology and calendar. According to Argüelles the Maya, whose classic period peaked between A.D. 435 and A.D. 800, were "galactically informed" beings whose civilization was founded on the principle of harmonic resonance. The Maya were connected to the collective planetary mind and the Hunab Ku, the galactic core, which broadcasts beams of energy. The connection was made via the Kuxan Suum, a vibratory pathway of etheric fibers that extends from the solar plexus to other levels of the universe and to other dimensions.

Argüelles, who published his conclusions in *The Mayan Factor* in 1987, observed that August 16 and 17, 1987, marked a turning point in the Mayan calendar's great cycle, which lasts from 3113 B.C. to A.D. 2012, the year when the Earth will enter a "galactic synchronization phase" and a new era of evolution. At the turning point, if the Earth's spiritual energy did not make a positive shift, a twenty-five-year period of disasters and catastrophes would ensue, and the Earth instead would come to an end in 2012. Argüelles said the Maya left clues as to how the Earth could synchronize with the galaxy, and that these clues would manifest during the Harmonic Convergence in UFO sightings and channeling.

In apparent corroboration of the Maya timetable, the astrological configuration, the Grand Trine, an alignment of nine planets in the solar system, occurred August 16 and 17, 1987, for the first time in 23,412 years. At the same time, the Aztec calendar of thirteen cycles of Heaven and nine cycles of Hell came to an end August 16. According to Aztec prophecies, the end of the ninth cycle of Hell would be followed by the second coming of Quetzalcoatl. The Hopi prophesied that on August 16, 1987, 144,000 Sun Dance mystical teachers would help awaken the rest of humankind to a spiritual awareness. The same date marked the end of a 28,600-year cycle in the Cherokee calendar; the age that follows is called the Age of Flowers, a time when essence of flowers will be recognized and used more as healing and spiritual agents.

To achieve the turning point, a minimum of 144,000 people had to convene August 16 and 17 to foster positive, harmonic energy, Argüelles said. Events were loosely organized at major power points, such as Mt. Shasta, California, where one of the largest gatherings took place; the Black Hills in South Dakota; Machu Picchu, Peru; Sedona, Arizona; the Great Pyramids in Egypt; Mt. Fuji, Japan, and other sacred sites. Those who could not go to a power point headed for the nearest mountain, shore or park. Many took crystals to expose to the sunrise for a recharging of energy.

No exact numbers were recorded of participants at major events, but Harmonic Convergence coordinators estimated they easily surpassed the 144,000 required for success. Argüelles estimated that between 100 million and 200 million people worldwide were made aware of the event through the media. The post-conference slogan, "When the Light hits, the Dark gets tough," referred to a five-year period that was to follow the Harmonic Convergence, during which were predicted major Earth changes and social, economic, and political upheaval as industrial civilization collapsed. According to Argüelles the plunge of the US stock market on October 19, 1987, was a fulfillment of that prophecy. Also during the five years, visits from extraterrestrials, so-called "galactic ambassadors," were to increase.

The message of the Harmonic Convergence was the need to "return to the Earth," and to recognize that the Earth is a sentient, planetary entity. The Convergence was to release positive energy to facilitate the creation of a human power grid, which Argüelles termed the "Earth-light network."

A smaller event, World Cooperation Day, took place on December 31, 1987.

Argüelles recommended that people continue to raise collective energy by gathering in groups of thirteen at the solstices and equinoxes and conducting rituals to tune into the Earth. Thirteen is a significant number in Maya cosmology; Argüelles states that the entire Mayan story of science, myth, galactic measure, and divine strategy can be told in a matrix of thirteen numbers and twenty symbols. The solstices and equinoxes are ancient pagan holidays tied to agrarian cycles. See **New Age; Planetary consciousness.**

Sources: Jose Argüelles. *The Mayan Factor.* Santa Fe, NM: Bear & Co., 1987; Steven S. H. McFadden. "The Great Harmonic Convergence of 1987: Blossoms Unfold in an Age of Flowers." *Earth Star Whole Life New England* 8, no. 58 (October/November 1987): 12–15; Jim Young. "The Stock Market: After the Fall." *Body, Mind & Spirit* (March/April 1988); "A New Age Dawning." *Time* (August 31, 1987): 63; "The End of the World (Again)." *Newsweek* (August 17, 1987): 70–71.

Haunting

The manifestation of inexplicable phenomena attributed to the presence of ghosts or spirits. Phenomena include apparitions, noises, smells, tactile sensations, extremes in temperature, movement of objects, and the like. Despite much scientific inquiry over the last one hundred years or so, very little is known about the nature of hauntings and why they happen.

The term "haunt" comes from the same root as "home," and refers to the occupation of homes by the spirits of deceased people and animals who lived there. Other haunted sites seem to be places merely frequented or liked by the deceased, or places where violent death has occurred. Most hauntings have no apparent reason or purpose. Some are continual and others are active only on certain dates that correspond to the deaths or major events in the lives of the deceased. For example, at Hampton Court in England, the ghost of Sir Christopher Wren is said to be heard walking hurriedly up and down the stairs every February 26, the date of his death in 1723. Some hauntings are brief, lasting only a few weeks, months, or years, while others continue for centuries. Haunted places often are pervaded by an oppressive atmosphere.

Not everyone who goes to a haunted place experiences paranormal phenomena. It is theorized that only individuals with certain psychic attunements or emotional states are receptive.

Few hauntings involve seeing apparitions. In those that do, a ghost may be seen by a single individual or collectively by several people present at the same time. Ghosts vary in appearance—some seem to be real people (or animals), while others appear filmy, fuzzy, nearly transparent, or mostly white. Typically, they are dressed in period costume popular when the person was alive. Most ghosts seen over a period of time by many usually wear the same outfit. Some change their appearances and even their ages. Some are horrific, missing their heads or other body parts.

The most dramatic ghosts are those which reenact dramas, such as a murder or a battle. See **Retrocognition.**

Theories

Thousands of hauntings have been investigated by psychical researchers and parapsychologists since the late nineteenth century. Numerous theories have been advanced, all inconclusive.

Frederic W. H. Myers, one of the founders of the Society for Psychical Research (SPR), defined a ghost as *"a manifestation of persistent personal energy,* or as an indication that some kind of force is being exercised after death which is in some way connected with a person previously known on earth" (*Human Personality and Its Survival of Bodily Death*, 1903). Myers believed that ghosts have no intrinsic intelligence or consciousness, and are meaningless fragments of energy left behind in death.

Eleanor Sidgwick, former secretary of the SPR, theorized that hauntings are a form of psychometry, vibrations of events and emotions imbued into a house, site, or object. Variations of Sidgwick's theory propose that hauntings are impressed upon a "psychic ether" or upon a psi force field, which certain people access under the right conditions. See **Psychometry.**

One popular Spiritualist theory holds that hauntings occur when the spirit of the dead person or animal is trapped on the earth plane for various reasons, doesn't know it is dead, or is reluctant to leave. Gentle exorcisms will send the spirit on to the afterworld.

Ghost Investigations

Researchers employ three basic techniques to investigate a haunting: description, experimentation, and detection. Description involves taking eyewitness accounts. Experimentation involves bringing a psychic to the site to corroborate the eyewitness accounts or provide new information. Psychic readings are unreliable, as telepathy and ESP cannot be ruled out, and often information is given which cannot be historically verified. Detection involves the observation or recording of phenomena. English psychical researcher Harry Price was among the first to use modern technology in his ghost investigations. His most celebrated case was Borley Rectory, which he investigated between 1929 and 1938. Price put together a ghost-hunter's kit that included felt overshoes, steel tape measures, a thermometer, a still camera, a remote-control movie camera, fingerprinting equipment, a telescope, and a portable

telephone. Price believed a poltergeist was present, but his findings were controversial and allegations of fraud were made after his death in 1948. The case remains unsolved.

More recent investigators have witnesses and psychics mark a floor plan of the house or building to show spots where they believe hauntings have occurred. They shoot photographs with regular and infrared film to try to capture ghostly images, and use recorders to try to capture noises and whispers. Various electronic devices, such as heat sensors and Geiger counters, may be used to measure changes in the atmosphere. Such methods are at best imprecise and interpretation of results is often subjective. Critics say ghost investigation is imprecise and not a true science because it is heavily reliant upon eyewitness testimony. See **Apparition; Poltergeist.**

Sources: Loyd Auerbach. *ESP, Hauntings and Poltergeists: A Parapsychologist's Handbook.* New York: Warner Books, 1986; Richard Cavendish. *The Encyclopedia of the Unexplained.* New York: McGraw-Hill, 1967; Tracy Cochran. "The Real Ghost Busters." *Omni* 10, no. 11 (August 1988): 35–36+; Alan Gauld and A. D. Cornell. *Poltergeists.* London: Routledge & Kegan Paul, 1979; Andrew Greeley. "Mysticism Goes Mainstream." *American Health* (January/February 1987): 47–55; *Into the Unknown.* Pleasantville, NY: Reader's Digest, 1981; J. G. Lockhart. *Curses, Lucks and Talismans.* Detroit: Singing Tree Press, 1971; Andrew MacKenzie. *Hauntings and Apparitions.* London: William Heinemann Ltd., 1982; Elizabeth E. McAdams and Raymond Bayless. *The Case for Life after Death.* Chicago: Nelson-Hall, 1981; Edgar D. Mitchell. *Psychic Exploration: A Challenge for Science.* Edited by John White. New York: G. P. Putnam's Sons, 1974; Frederic W. H. Myers. *Human Personality and Its Survival of Bodily Death.* Vols. 1 and 2. 1903. New ed. New York: Longmans, Green & Co., 1954; George Owen and Victor Sims. *Sci-*

ence and the Spook: Eight Strange Cases of Haunting. New York: Garrett Publications, 1971; Peter Underwood. *The Ghost Hunter's Guide.* Poole, Dorset, England: Blandford Press, 1986.

Healing, faith and psychic

The treatment of illness without a known physical curative agent, usually done by an individual who acts as a conduit for healing energy from a higher source of power. Healings of this sort are called by various other names, such as absent healing, paranormal healing, spiritual healing, magnetic healing, New Thought healing, mental healing, and so on, terms which are not necessarily interchangeable.

A wide range of techniques is used, including prayer; invoking the help of God, deities, spirits, or deceased ancestors; the administration of magical or blessed medicines; the projection of will (even long distance); and the laying on of hands. These methods have been used nearly universally at various times since the earliest recorded human history, and continue to coexist with the allopathic (science-based) medicine of industrialized countries. In recent years so-called alternative healing therapies have become more popular, but have become accepted only to a limited extent by the medical establishment.

Religious faith is not a primary characteristic in psychic healing. All living things are held to be permeated and sustained by the universal life force. A depletion in this energy, or an imbalance in it, causes illness and disease. The depletion can be caused by poor diet or lifestyle habits and even "negative thinking." True healers of all types know that they themselves do not heal, but merely are transformers, restoring or rebalancing the life-giving vital force. The absence of required religious faith does not mean psy-

chic healers are nonreligious or atheistic. Most have strong personal religious or spiritual convictions, but do not require religious beliefs on the part of the patient to effect the healing process. See **Universal life force.**

In faith or spiritual healing, the healing is believed to come from God. Renowned healers Ambrose and Olga Worrall believed they were conduits for powers usually attributed to the Supreme Being and various saints. Ambrose Worrall said spiritual healing is a natural phenomenon that works in accordance with natural laws, and can be accomplished long-distance.

There are various forms of psychic and spiritual healing. One is the transfer of the universal life force through touch or passes of the hand. The energy transfer often is accompanied by such sensations as heat, tingling, electrical shock, or impressions of colors. The healer, who becomes a passive conduit for the healing energies, may feel something of the consistency of heavy air leaving him or her, usually through the hands. Worrall felt energy leave him through the solar plexus in long-distance healings. See **Mesmer, Franz Anton.** The patient often feels an infusion of energy. In faith healing the healer usually lays hands on the patient while praying to God for healing. Again, energy exchanges may be felt by both participants.

Another form, characteristic of shamanic healing, is to suck the disease out of the patient. The shaman produces, by sleight of hand, an object purported to be sucked from the patient's body and responsible for the illness. The tangible evidence seems to be mostly for the benefit of the patient and onlooker. Shamans say they can heal without such stage effects, and it is likely that hand passes and the sucking transmit healing forces. See **Shamanism.** Similarly, psychic surgery, which is highly controversial, involves the apparent extraction of objects and tissue alleged to be the cause of illness. See **Psychic surgery.**

Exorcism is also used in healing. The illness is blamed on a possessing spirit, which is ritually driven from the body of the patient. See **Depossession; Exorcism; Macumba; Spiritism.**

Special diets, intended to act holistically on the body, spirit, and mind, are sometimes prescribed as part of a healing.

Gifted healers characteristically are born with their ability, though it has been demonstrated that virtually anyone can learn to tap into healing energies to some extent. Gifted healing ability manifests early in life along with psychic abilities. Typically, they see spirits of the dead and experience clairvoyance, clairaudience, precognition, and perhaps also out-of-body travel. Their clairvoyance may enable them to see the body's energy field and detect disturbances in the field that are related to the disease or illness. See **Aura.** They learn their touch brings relief and healing. They are irrevocably drawn into healing. They refine their techniques through practice and, in many cases, tutelage by another healer. Many of them feel assisted by various spirit beings. Shamanic healers usually are called to healing through visionary experiences or severe illnesses from which they heal themselves. They apprentice themselves to shamans to learn the art.

Healing powers also come with high spiritual attainment, as found among the saints, yogis, and adepts of religions around the world.

Some healings are instantaneous, even the disappearance of tumors and swellings. Many more, however, require numerous treatments, some over a period of years.

How Does Psychic or Spiritual Healing Work?

The mechanisms by which psychic or spiritual healing takes place are unknown. Certainly the consciousness plays a key role, which means that theories explaining psychic healing must be multidimensional, and not limited to the cause-and-effect theory of Newtonian science. Quantum physics has demonstrated that matter is energy and is not static but exists in a dynamic field; it cannot be separated from its activity. The indivisibility of matter and energy forms the basis of the ancient healing practices based on Taoist, Buddhist, and Hindu philosophies.

The will also is a likely factor, as evidenced by laboratory experiments in psychokinesis (PK), in which healers, through prayer or mental projection, have altered the properties of water, caused seeds to germinate and plants to grow more quickly than control groups, and have slowed cancerous tumor growth or speeded wound healing in mice. See **Prayer; Psychokinesis (PK); Worrall, Olga.** It has been suggested that the process of healing may not be a matter of "how" but of "why": the need for a healing exists, and the consciousness selects a path to effect it.

The traditional Western scientific view holds that the universe is dead, and that life is but an infinitesimal and insignificant part of it. Healers reflect the non-Western philosophic view that the universe is a living entity created by a higher consciousness or deity, and that all things within the universe are interconnected. Dora van Gelder Kunz, one of the creators of Therapeutic Touch, a modern version of laying on of hands, states that both healer and healee are "expressions of a unified therapeutic interaction" in which both are healed and made whole.

At least five factors are said to influence the effectiveness of a healing. Their presence, however, does not guarantee that a healing will take place. The factors are:

1. The presence of high levels of the universal life force: Geographic locations, such as certain mountains, sea

locations, wells, or springs are believed to have high amounts of the life force. The springs at Lourdes in France, where apparitions of the Virgin Mary were seen, draw millions of pilgrims every year who hope to be healed by the waters. See **Marian apparitions**. Even certain rooms in a house, or spots in a room, are perceived to have healing energies (compare the presence of *ch'i* in **Feng shui**).

2. The attitude of the patient: Skeptics can be spiritually healed, but fear and distrust can form insurmountable barriers. Likewise, guilt due to feelings that the illness is punishment for a sin inhibits the process. A positive attitude on the part of the patient is believed to facilitate the process and makes it easier for the healer to "tune in" and transmit the energy. A healing demonstration done in the presence of a group of highly skeptical or critical people is likely to fail. Some healers say children are the easiest to treat because they are open and trusting. See **Behavioral medicine**.

3. Relaxation: Both patient and healer must be able to relax. The healing occurs when they tune in to each other, becoming one in a transference of energy. A healer who tries too hard may not be successful. Healing undertaken in the hysterical pitch of evangelism does not always last, even if the patient expects to be cured. The "instant" results in an emotionally charged atmosphere may be psychological and disappear after a time. It must be noted that many evangelistic healings are successful. See **Relaxation**.

4. Love and compassion: The healer must be filled with love and compassion for the patient, and a desire to see the patient returned to wholeness and health. The healer remains detached, however, and does not let the feelings become personal.

5. Petition to higher powers: Healers ask for the help of a deity or spirit, and give recognition to and thanks for it.

Many healers work in an altered state of consciousness. In the 1960s psychologist Lawrence LeShan, in research with psychic healers, found that they could not adequately describe the process of healing, but did describe shifting into a different reality, a state of consciousness he termed the "clairvoyant reality," a shift in one's metaphysical understanding of the world. It is similar but not identical to mystical states, which occur in all cultures around the world, and to the shamanic state of consciousness.

For about eighteen months, LeShan experimented with various meditation techniques until he began to experience this shift of consciousness. He discovered that attaining the clairvoyant reality improves with practice and can be controlled to some extent, but remains largely unpredictable and unreliable. He also discovered that while in this state himself, others with whom he worked reported physical or psychological changes that seemed to benefit them. Furthermore, he could teach others how to reach the clairvoyant reality and awaken their healing powers. See **Garrett, Eileen J.**

Most orthodox medical authorities are skeptical of psychic healing and ascribe its benefits to short-term psychological effects. In the United Kingdom, the General Medical Council allows a physician to prescribe this sort of healing, provided the doctor remains in charge of the case. Healers follow a code of conduct drawn up between the General Medical Council, the Royal Colleges of Medicine, and the Confederation of Healing Organisations. The code prohibits healers from promising results or claiming cures. Many healers belong to the National Federation of Spiritual Healers, which is, along with fifteen other associations, affiliated with the Confederation of Healing Organisations.

Faith Healing

Belief in faith healing has existed in all types of societies throughout history. It is fundamental to Christianity, although it is not universally emphasized in all denominations. Healing was central to the ministry of Jesus, and the New Testament stresses that healing is natural and is the work of God's grace, not human skill. Early Christians considered sickness as caused by Satan; and, like sin, it would yield to prayers of faith. By the end of the fourth century, St. Augustine rejected the validity of the healing gift, but by 424 he had changed his mind. As Christianity developed healing increasingly became a specialized function of the priesthood, and was associated with sacraments, holy shrines, and the relics of saints. The scientific revolution of the seventeenth century negated miraculous healings, and the cures of Jesus came to be regarded as a phenomenon that could no longer happen.

Interest in faith healing began to revive in the late nineteenth and early twentieth centuries with such movements as Christian Science and Pentecostalism. The greatest boost in interest came following World War II, with the rise of evangelistic healers such as Oral Roberts, Jack Coe, and Kathryn Kuhlman.

Faith healings typically take place in a revivalist atmosphere and involve fervent prayer and a laying on of hands. Some recipients say they can feel a transfer of energy. There are numerous cases of cures that cannot be explained medically, but the high degree of expectation and the desperation of many of the sick have been known to effect false and temporary cures, with devastating emotional and physical aftereffects. Some evangelists say they do not know how or why some people are cured and others are not, while others say that failures are due to the patient's inability to understand or receive healing from God.

Some faith healers insist on working in collaboration with doctors, while others who are extremists consider doctors the enemy. Christian Science strikes a different approach, emphasizing nonreliance on traditional medicine. See **Church of Christ, Scientist.**

Faith healing, like psychic healing, has had much opposition from the medical establishment. It predominates in the Pentecostal and charismatic groups, and to some extent in the Methodist denomination. Prayer groups and circles for healing, however, are universal throughout Christianity. See **Cayce, Edgar; Chantways; Worrall, Ambrose.**

Sources: Richard Grossman. *The Other Medicines.* Garden City, NY: Doubleday, 1985; Hans Holzer. *Beyond Medicine: The Facts About Unorthodox Treatments and Psychic Healing.* Rev. ed. New York: Ballantine Books, 1987; Stanley Krippner, ed. *Advances in Parapsychology 4.* Jefferson, NC: McFarland & Co., 1984; Stanley Krippner and Alberto Villoldo. *The Realms of Healing.* 3d ed. Berkeley: Celestial Arts, 1986; Dora Kunz, comp. *Spiritual Aspects of the Healing Arts.* Wheaton, IL: The Theosophical Publishing House, 1985; Lawrence LeShan. *The Medium, the Mystic, and the Physicist: Toward a General Theory of the Paranormal.* New York: Viking Press, 1974; George W. Meek, ed. *Healers and the Healing Process.* Wheaton, IL: The Theosophical Publishing House, 1977; William A. Nolen. *Healing: A Doctor in Search of a Miracle.* New York: Fawcett Crest, 1974; Robert Peel. *Spiritual Healing in a Scientific Age.* San Francisco: Harper & Row, 1987; *Reader's Digest Family Guide to Alternative Medicine.* London: Reader's Digest Assn. Ltd., 1991; Eve Simson. *The Faith Healer.* St. Louis: Concordia Publishing House, 1977; Charles T. Tart, ed. *Transpersonal Psychologies.* New York: Harper & Row, 1975; Andrew Weil. *Health and Healing: Under-*

standing *Conventional and Alternative Medicine.* Boston: Houghton Mifflin, 1983; Ambrose Alexander Worrall. "The Philosophy and Methodology of Spiritual Healing." Booklet. Self-published, 1961; Ambrose A. Worrall with Olga N. Worrall. *The Gift of Healing: A Personal Story of Spiritual Therapy.* New York: Harper & Row, 1965.

Hermetica

Mystical wisdom that, along with the Kabbalah, formed the foundation of the Western occult tradition. According to legend, the wisdom is contained in forty-two books allegedly written by Hermes Trismegistus, or "thrice-greatest Hermes," a mythical composite of the Egyptian and Greek gods Thoth and Hermes, respectively. The alleged surviving fragments of these books are known collectively as the Hermetica. The writings probably are of anonymous Christian authorship, a synthesis of Neo-Platonic, Kabbalistic, and Christian elements passed off as ancient Egyptian wisdom.

The composite of Hermes Trismegistus was created by the Greeks who settled in Egypt, and who identified Thoth and Hermes with one another. Thoth ruled mystical wisdom, magic, writing, and other disciplines, and was associated with healing. Hermes was the personification of universal wisdom and patron of magic; a swift, wing-footed messenger, he carried a magic wand, the caduceus. See **Caduceus.** Both were associated with the spirits of the dead: Thoth weighed their souls in the Judgment Hall of Osiris; Hermes escorted shades to Hades. Both were credited with writing the sacred books of science, healing, philosophy, magic, and law, and revealing the wisdom to humankind.

"Thrice-greatest" refers to Hermes Trismegistus as the greatest of all philosophers, the greatest of all kings, and the greatest of all priests. The story that developed around him held him to be a mythical king who reigned for 3,226 years. He carried an emerald, upon which was recorded all of philosophy, and the caduceus, the symbol of mystical illumination. He vanquished Typhon, the dragon of ignorance and mental, moral, and physical perversion. He is credited with writing 36,525 books on the Principles of Nature. Iamblichus reported the number at 20,000, and Clement of Alexandria at forty-two books.

According to legend, the Hermetic books were written on papyrus and stored in one of the great libraries in Alexandria. Most were lost when the library burned. Surviving fragments supposedly were buried in a secret desert location known only to select initiates.

Extant works, which have been translated into many languages, include *The Divine Pymander* and *The Vision.* *The Divine Pymander* sets forth how divine wisdom was revealed to Hermes, and how he established his ministry to spread the wisdom throughout the world. *The Vision* tells of Hermes' mystical vision and cosmogony, the Egyptians' esoteric wisdom, and the spiritual development of the soul. Passages bear resemblance to the writings of Plato and Philo and to the Gospel of St. John.

The legendary Emerald Tablet (or Emerald Table), which Hermes Trismegistus holds in art, is said to be inscribed with the whole of the Egyptians' philosophy, including the magical secrets of the universe. According to legend it was found clutched in the hand of the body of Hermes Trismegistus in his cave tomb (another version has it that Hermes Trismegistus's mummy was interred in the Great Pyramid of Gizeh). No two translations of the Tablet are the same (a Latin translation dates to c. 1200).

The Emerald Tablet is cited as the credo of adepts, particularly the alchemists, who believed that mystical secrets were hidden in Hermetic allegories. The inscription reads:

'Tis true, without falsehood, and most real: that which is above is like that which is below, to perpetrate the miracles of One thing. And as all things have been derived from one, by the thought of one, so all things are born from this thing, by adoption. The Sun is its Father, the Moon is its Mother. Wind has carried it in its belly, the Earth is its Nurse. Here is the father of every perfection in the world. His strength and power are absolute when changed into earth; thou wilt separate the earth from fire, the subtle from the gross, gently and with care. It ascends from earth to heaven, and descends again to receive the power of the superior and the inferior things. By this means, thou wilt have the glory of the world. And because of this, all obscurity will flee from thee. Within this power, most powerful of all powers. For it will overcome all subtle things, and penetrate every solid thing. Thus the world was created. From this will be, and will emerge, admirable adaptations of which the means are here. And for this reason, I am called Hermes Trismegistus, having the three parts of the philosophy of the world. What I have said of the Sun's operations is accomplished.

In this the alchemists interpreted the transmutation process.

Controversy over the age and authorship of the Hermetica has existed since at least the Renaissance. Isaac Casaubon (1559–1614), French classical scholar and theologian, claimed that the works were not of Egyptian origin but were written by early Christians or semi-Christians. Casaubon's claim helped to bring about a decline in the Renaissance interest in magic. In all likelihood, the Hermetic works were written even later than Casaubon believed, by multiple anonymous authors who used the pseudonym "Hermes Trismegistus." See Al-

chemy; Hermetic Order of the Golden Dawn; Kabbalah.

Sources: Rosemary Ellen Guiley. *The Encyclopedia of Witches and Witchcraft.* New York: Facts On File, 1989; Manly P. Hall. *The Secret Teachings of All Ages.* 1928. Los Angeles: The Philosophic Research Society, 1977; Kurt Seligmann. *The Mirror of Magic.* New York: Pantheon Books, 1948.

Hermetic Order of the Golden Dawn

Short-lived but influential Western occult order. The Hermetic Order of the Golden Dawn arose in England out of Rosicrucianism and attracted such luminaries as Samuel Liddell MacGregor Mathers, one of the founders, occultist Arthur Edward Waite, poet William Butler Yeats, and magician Aleister Crowley. During its height the order possessed perhaps the greatest repository of Western magical and occult knowledge. Rituals developed by the Golden Dawn continue in use by some practitioners of high magic, though others consider them outdated.

The founding of the Golden Dawn is based on a manuscript of alleged antiquity, but which may have been a forgery. In 1884 Rev. A. F. A. Woodford, a Mason and member of an occult study group called the Hermetic Society, claimed to find an old manuscript in a London bookstall. It was handwritten in cipher in brown ink. In 1887 he sent parts of the manuscript to Dr. William Wynn Westcott and Dr. William Robert Woodman, officers in the Rosicrucian Society of England. Wescott in turn consulted Mathers, an occultist, who, with the help of his clairvoyant wife, said the manuscript dealt with the Kabbalah and the Tarot.

A letter attached to the manuscript instructed that anyone deciphering it should contact "Sapiens Dominabitur Astris," in care of a Fräulein Ann Sprengel in Hanover, Germany. Westcott did so, and was advised that he and his associates could establish "an elementary Branch of the Rosicrucian Order in England."

The Isis-Urania Temple of the Hermetic Order of the Golden Dawn was established on March 1, 1888, with Westcott, Mathers, and Woodman, the Supreme Magus of the Rosicrucian Society of Anglia, as the three Chiefs. The secret society quickly attracted a following, initiating 315 people between its peak years of 1888 and 1896.

Its central purpose was "to prosecute the Great Work: which is to obtain control of the nature and power of my own being." To that end it offered teachings on ritual magic, the Kabbalah, the Tarot, astral travel, scrying, alchemy, geomancy, and astrology.

The Golden Dawn offered a hierarchy of eleven degrees—ten corresponding to the *sephirot* of the Kabbalistic Tree of Life plus one degree for neophytes—which were divided into three orders.

Almost from its inception, the Golden Dawn was plagued by internal dissension. Mathers, an eccentric man, sought to have sole control of the organization; he claimed to be in contact with three Secret Chiefs in Paris who had designated him as "Visible Head of the Order." His supporters believed him to be a reincarnation of Michael Scot, a medieval Scottish wizard of great powers, according to legend. By 1891 Mathers and his wife were financially destitute and were supported by a wealthy member, Annie Horniman. They moved to Paris, where Mathers set up his own lodge and bombarded London members with his written materials. Woodman died the same year and was not replaced in the organization.

Westcott resigned in 1897, in the wake of member inquiries into the veracity of Woodford's manuscript. He was succeeded by Florence Farr, who could not hold the order together.

Aleister Crowley was initiated in 1898, and quickly clashed with Mathers. When Crowley was expelled from the Golden Dawn, he retaliated by publishing some of the secret rituals in his magazine, *The Equinox.*

The Golden Dawn began to splinter. Followers of Mathers left to form the Alpha et Omega Temple, followed in 1903 by Waite and others, who formed a group named Golden Dawn that gave greater emphasis to mysticism than magic. Waite departed in 1915, and the group declined.

In 1905 another group was formed, the Stella Matutina, or "Order of the Companions of the Rising Light in the Morning," thus dealing the death-blow to the Isis-Urania Temple. The Stella Matutina attracted occultists Dion Fortune in 1919 and Israel Regardie, Crowley's secretary for a time, in 1934. The Isis-Urania Temple was resurrected as the Merlin Temple of the Stella Matutina in 1917. The Stella Matutina declined in the 1940s after Regardie resigned and published its secret rituals. Some offshoots of the Golden Dawn continue in existence.

The Golden Dawn exerted a powerful influence upon Yeats, its greatest artist member, who was initiated into the Isis-Urania Temple on March 7, 1890, and took the magical name *Daemon est Deus Inversus* (The Devil Is God Reversed). "The mystical life is the centre of all that I do and all that I think and all that I write," Yeats stated in 1892 (*Yeats's Golden Dawn,* 1974). Yeats said that were it not for his study of magic, he would not have been able to produce *The Countess Kathleen* or his book on William Blake. See **Blake, William; Crowley, Aleister; Hermetica; Magic.**

Sources: Richard Cavendish. *The Black Arts.* New York: Perigee Books, 1967; Rosemary Ellen Guiley. *The Encyclopedia of Witches and Witchcraft.* New York:

Facts On File, 1989; George Mills Harper. *Yeats's Golden Dawn.* 1974. Wellingborough, England: The Aquarian Press, 1987; Francis King. *Ritual Magic in England 1887 to the Present Day.* London: Neville Spearman, 1970; Alan Richardson. *Priestess: The Life and Magic of Dion Fortune.* Wellingborough, England: The Aquarian Press, 1987; Colin Wilson. *Mysteries.* New York: Perigee Books/G. P. Putnam's Sons, 1978.

Hildegard of Bingen, St. (1098–1179)

Benedictine abbess and acclaimed prophet, mystic, theologian, writer, poet, composer, and early feminist. The first major German mystic, she is best known for a series of mystical illuminations, or visions, which she experienced and chronicled in mid-life, and which were far advanced of the religious outlooks of her day. Her power and influence made her one of the most important women of her time. Her work has enjoyed renewed, serious interest in modern times.

Hildegard was born to parents of high nobility in the summer of 1098 in the German village of Bickelheim (also given as Bockelheim), located on the Nahe River, a tributary of the Rhine. The village was near Bingen, an important river town about fifty miles southwest of Frankfurt. Hildegard's father was a knight of the Castle Bickelheim. The area was heavily settled by Celts, and Celtic mystical beliefs strongly influenced her religious development.

The youngest of ten children, Hildegard had religious visions from the earliest she could remember. Because of this she was drawn to the church, and began her education in a Benedictine cloister in Disibodenberg at the age of eight. She became a nun at eighteen, and advanced to prioress at age thirty-eight.

In modern times Hildegard would have been called a feminist. She believed in the equality of men and women, but sometimes doubted herself because of criticism from men and their oppression of women. She was often ill, and she blamed it on her frustrated passivity.

Though she had had visions since childhood, Hildegard's great spiritual awakening came in her early forties, when she began to experience particularly intense illuminations and clairaudient messages about the nature of God, the human soul, and all being, and the interconnectedness among all things in the universe. She also experienced visions on sin, redemption, and the nature of the cosmos.

In her second vision, a voice instructed her to write and speak of her supernormal insights. The experience galvanized her to shake off her doubts about her "proper place" as a woman. Still, she had to work within the system. She consulted her confessor, who in turn consulted the archbishop of Mainz. A committee of theologians validated her visions. In collaboration with a monk, Hildegard began writing her first book, *Scivias* ("Know the Ways of the Lord"), a record of twenty-six illuminations. *Scivias,* written in Latin, is highly intellectual and symbolic. Some of the visions deal with prophecy, denunciation of vice, and the universe as egg or sphere. Central to the work is the idea of God as the Living Light: "All living creatures are, so to speak, sparks from the radiance of God's brilliance, and these sparks emerge from God like rays of the sun." *Scivias* was finished in about 1152, and Pope Eugenius III approved of it.

With the publication of *Scivias* Hildegard's fame spread, and she became known as "the Sybil of the Rhine." Eugenius encouraged her to keep writing. She appreciated his approval, but that didn't stop her from scolding the pope to work harder for reform in the church.

Around 1147 Hildegard and her sister nuns left Disibodenberg for another monastery in Rupertsberg, Germany, where they could have more room to live and work. She was consecrated an abbess. In 1165 she founded another monastery in Eibingen, across the river from Bingen, and commuted between there and Rupertsberg every week.

Hildegard kept up an active, work-filled life right up to her death in her early eighties on September 17, 1179. She traveled widely throughout Europe, preaching to clergy, nobility, scholars, and the lay public. Her views influenced many of her powerful contemporaries, such as St. Bernard of Clairvaux and Frederick I Barbarossa.

She denounced corruption in the church, and criticized the Christian, Jewish, and Muslim faiths for being "dried up" and lacking care and compassion.

Hildegard challenged the church time and time again. She downplayed the role of Eve in the fall of Adam, saying Eve was not at fault. Instead, she said, the Devil had used Eve as an instrument to influence Adam. She celebrated human sexuality as the beautiful, spiritual union of two human beings, not just the means for procreation.

Hildegard had a tremendous interest in science and medicine, and between 1150 and 1157 wrote two medical books far advanced for her time. Her approach to medicine was holistic: she integrated the four-element, four-humor natural healing system (which dates back at least to the ancient Greeks) with spiritual wisdom. She prescribed numerous herbal and dietary remedies, all inspired by her spiritual visions.

Hildegard considered music to be the ultimate celebration of God. She composed seventy-seven songs, perhaps divinely inspired, that were more complex than most twelfth-century songs. She considered music to be a better medium than words for the expression of wisdom; wisdom, she said, dwells in the heart of God, is part of all creative effort, and is

the "elusive treasure" sought by the strong and virtuous soul.

She also was a prolific poet and writer, composing a morality play set to music, more than seventy poems, three hundred letters, and nine books. Besides *Scivias,* two other books are major works on theology: *De Operatione Dei* and *Liber Vitae Meritorium.* Hildegard also wrote two biographies of saints and a commentary on the Gospels. She even invented her own language, which she used to describe scientific terms. She said all of her writings were dictated by the Holy Ghost.

Hildegard is included in Roman Catholic martyrology, though she never was formally canonized as a saint. Three attempts were made to canonize her, under Pope Gregory IX, Pope Innocent IV, and Pope John XXII. After 1317 she gradually slipped into obscurity, though Benedictine sisters carefully preserved and copied her texts. Since World War II, her works have been rediscovered, published, and analyzed. In 1979, on the eight hundredth anniversary of her death, Pope John Paul II called her an "outstanding saint." Her feast day is September 17. See **Mysticism.**

Sources: Hildegard of Bingen's Scivias. Translated by Bruce Hozeski. Santa Fe, NM: Bear & Co., 1986; *Illuminations of Hildegard of Bingen.* Commentary by Matthew Fox. Santa Fe, NM: Bear & Co., 1985; Dr. Wighard Strehlow and Gottfried Hertzka, M.D. *Hildegard of Bingen's Medicine.* Santa Fe, NM: Bear & Co., 1988.

Hinduism

Religion indigenous to India, practiced by those who are not Muslim, Buddhist, Jain, or Sikh. Hinduism has no founder, no defining creed, and no centralized hierarchy. It is vast, complex, and subtle, and is both world-affirming and world-denying. The major concepts of the mystical philosophy of Hinduism will be given here.

The oldest documents of Hinduism are the Vedas ("sacred teaching"), which are still held by many to contain the essential truths of Hinduism. Orthodox Hindus ascribe them to divine origin. They are the literature of the Aryans who invaded India in the second millennium before Christ and settled in Punjab. The Aryans compiled the Vedas between about 1000 B.C. and 500 B.C., making them the oldest extant religious literature in the world and the oldest work of literature in an Indo-European language. The Vedas are divided into four books, the oldest of which is the *Rig Veda*. The books essentially served as manuals for the priests in the use of hymns, prayers, magical rites and spells, and meditational practices in the Aryan sacrificial cult. The Vedas recognized gods who were the great supernatural forces of nature and the phenomena in which the powers manifested. These gods did not have the power to aid humankind in its spiritual striving.

The Upanishads, composed beginning c. 900 B.C., comprise the last part of the Vedas, called the Vedanta, or "end of the Vedas." They are the earliest systematic Hindu works of mystical and essentially monistic (only one truly existent being) content. By the time of their appearance, there were numerous ascetics who sought spiritual ecstasy and enlightenment by withdrawing from the world. Many practiced forms of self-mortification, such as gazing at the sun, holding their arms out until they withered, lying on beds of spikes, and hanging upside down from trees. Others were less extreme, retiring from time to time to isolated areas and traveling about the villages spreading their teachings. All these practices continue in modern times, and from a popular perspective, the only true mystic is one who practices self-mortification.

The Upanishads put forth the concept of the One, Brahman, successor to the thousands of Vedic gods, the ineffable cosmic All that holds all things together and unifies all life. Brahman is the one reality and the eternal absolute. Brahman brings all things into existence, supports them, and reabsorbs them in the endless cycle of birth, death, and rebirth, called samsara. Brahman also is identified with the Atman, the immortal part of the self that is the soul in Western thought, and which is eternal, absolute being, absolute bliss, and absolute consciousness. This absolute is within all things, not as an emanation, but as a whole principle. The mystical unity of Brahman with Atman is expressed in the "great word," *tat tvam asi,* or "that thou art" or in "I am Brahman."

The Upanishads also explain the unifying principles in the universe in elemental terms, such as power, breath, and food, thus uniting matter and spirit.

The concept of maya ("deception" or "illusion") forms the foundation of mind and matter and is inseparable from Brahman. Maya has two aspects, one of which is ignorance that prevents one from realizing Brahman, and one of which is knowledge that leads one to Brahman.

Because Brahman is beyond comprehension, in worship the transcendent divine principle is manifest as Ishvara ("lord of the universe"). Ishvara has three aspects: Brahma (not to be confused with Brahman), creator of the universe and belonging to the realm of maya; Shiva, the sustainer and guardian of dharma (the lawful order of the universe, especially pertaining to morality and ethics); and Vishnu, destroyer. Originally, all three were equal in stature, but Brahmanism has declined in favor of the Shaivism and Vaishnavism, as well as the Shaktism of Tantra.

The Hindu mystic strives to escape from selfhood. All individuals are bound to samsara, a bondage which is viewed as characterized by misery and suffering. Samsara is determined by karma, the cause and effect of desire. As long as one remains in bondage to samsara, one cannot know Brahman. The only way to obtain liberation from this cycle is to attain union with Brahman and be emptied of all sense of realization.

To attain this the mystic pursues a spiritual path of world-denying asceticism. In Tantra one follows the worship centered on the Great Mother, especially as personified by Shakti, wife of Shiva, the feminine divine creative power. Tantric rites involving meditation, yoga, and sexual intercourse are intended to awaken the *kundalini* force (the "serpent power" of illumination), attain the *siddhis* ("miraculous powers"), and attain union with the Absolute. There are two forms of Tantra: a left-hand path devoted to debauched rites, and a right-hand path devoted to strict spiritual discipline. Other ascetic paths lie in yoga, which is divided into various schools, each of which has a different emphasis, such as devotion or control of the mind. See **Yoga.**

Other important sacred texts in Hinduism are the Puranas and the *Bhagavad-Gita.* The Puranas ("ancient narratives") concern the legends of the gods and are the primary scriptures for the worshipers of Brahma, Shiva, and Vishnu. The *Bhagavad-Gita* ("song of the exalted one") is the sixth book of the *Mahabharata,* the Indian national epic poem. The *Bhagavad-Gita* is a dialogue between Krishna, the eighth avatar (incarnation) of Vishnu, and Prince Arjuna on the eve of the battle of Kurukshetra. Arjuna is dismayed to see friends and kinsmen in the opposing army and knows many will be killed. Krishna expounds the doctrine of karma and the way to attain union with the Absolute through devotion, knowledge, and selfless action. The *Gita* is related to the Upanishads in content,

but has more emphasis on monotheism (only one God) and theism (the existence of a god or gods, especially a personal creator god and ruler of the world).

The earliest great Hindu figure to espouse monism was the eighth-century mystic Sankara, called the "mystic of the soul" because of his emphasis on right knowledge of the soul. Sankara considered the individual and universal souls as fundamentally identical. His teaching influenced many subsequent teachers for centuries, including nineteenth-century mystic Sri Ramakrishna, who also was a devotee of Kali, the Divine Mother and destructive consort of Shiva.

Ramakrishna (1836–1886) grew up worshiping Kali but later formally taught the Vedanta. He experienced ecstatic visions and trances and the highest states of *samadhi,* and allegedly performed miracles. When he died of cancer on August 16, 1886, he was said to have passed into *mahasamadhi,* the "great sleep." Ramakrishna's teachings were exported to the West by his disciple, Swami Vivekananda, beginning in 1893. Vivekananda believed that in order for religion and philosophy to be effective, they must become socialized. He founded the Ramakrishna Movement, which includes the Ramakrishna Mission, devoted to philanthropic, educational, medical, and social activities; and the Math of Belur, the sanctuary of the Ramakrishna Order, the largest monastic order in India, which oversees the Mission. See **Dharma; Karma; Kundalini; Meditation; Mysticism; Reincarnation; Siddhis; Universal life force.**

Sources: The Encyclopedia of Eastern Philosophy and Religion. Boston: Shambhala, 1989; Solange Lemaitre. *Ramakrishna and the Vitality of Hinduism.* 1959. Woodstock, NY: The Overlook Press, 1984; Jacques de Marquette. *Introduction to Comparative Mysticism.* New York: Philosophical Library, 1949; Geoffrey Parrinder, ed. *World Religions from Ancient History* to *Present*. New York: Facts On File, 1971; Geoffrey Parrinder. *Mysticism in the World's Religions*. New York: Oxford University Press, 1976; Samuel Umen. *The World of the Mystic*. New York: Philosophical Library, 1988.

Holistic healing

See **Behavioral medicine.**

Holy Grail

See **Grail, the.**

Home, Daniel Dunglas (1833–1886)

Scottish physical medium credited with numerous remarkable feats and phenomena, and who was never shown to be a fraud. Daniel Dunglas Home was said to move objects, levitate, change the dimensions of his body, materialize ghostly forms, and be impervious to fire and intense heat. His feats enabled him to travel among the royal and wealthy, who provided him his financial support. He was sickly from childhood.

Home was born in Edinburgh, Scotland, on March 20, 1833. His father was a carpenter. His mother was clairvoyant and claimed descent from a seventeenth-century clairvoyant, Kenneth MacKenzie, known as the "Brahan Seer." Home's own psychic gifts manifested early—at age four he accurately predicted the death of a cousin.

When he was nine, his family moved to Connecticut, where his visions continued. In 1850 his mother predicted her own imminent death. Home saw her in a vision at the time she died; she continued to appear to him through his life to exhort him to use his paranormal powers for good.

At age nineteen Home experienced his first spontaneous levitation in the home of a Connecticut silk manufacturer.

He eventually learned to control his levitation, and witnesses said that on occasion he seemed to fly. In 1853, after entering the Theological Institute in Newburgh, New York, to study religion, he experienced an eleven-hour out-of-body trip during which a spirit guide showed him the afterworld.

For most of his life, Home lived as a guest in various households. He attended seances, but felt most mediums were frauds and avoided contact with them. When he began to conduct his own seances, he did so with the lights on, producing spectral lights, rappings, ghostly hands that shook hands with the sitters, and ghostly guitars that played music. He moved tables, chairs, and objects and tipped tables. He spelled out messages from the dead by pointing at letters of the alphabet written on cards. On occasion he acted possessed, playing the piano or accordion in great frenzy. He also was seen to stretch or shrink his body, once increasing his height by eleven inches to six feet, six inches, and once shrinking to five feet. To prove that he was not secretly manipulating hidden devices, he often asked his guests to hold his hands and feet.

Home credited the phenomena to spirits over whom he had no control. The most reliable was named "Bryan." When in trance Home referred to himself in the third person as "Dan."

In 1855 he traveled to England and Europe, where he was controversial but welcomed in elite circles. His supporters included author Sir Arthur Conan Doyle and poet Elizabeth Barrett Browning. Foes included David Brewster, a noted scientist, and poet Robert Browning, who so disliked Home that he wrote a two-thousand-line poem called *Mr. Sludge the Medium*.

In February 1856 Home announced his spirits required him to withdraw from public life for a year. After giving an audience to Pope Pius IX, he converted to

Catholicism and said he would enter a monastery. He resumed public appearances in exactly a year, giving a convincing audience to Napoleon III and Empress Eugenie.

On August 1, 1858, Home married Alexandrina, the wealthy sister-in-law of Count Gregoire de Koucheleff of Russia. Their son, Gregoire, was born in 1859. Alexandrina died of illness in 1862, and her estate remained tied up in Russia for years, forcing Home to depend once again on patrons.

In 1868 Home produced his most famous levitation, in the London home of Lord Adare. He went into a trance and reportedly floated out a window on the third floor, then floated back in another window. The same year he handled red-hot coals and stuck his head into a fire without being burned.

Home toured England and Scotland, reading poetry for money. He worked briefly as a war correspondent in the Franco-Prussian war of 1870. Returning to Russia he met Julie de Gloumeline, a wealthy woman, and married her in 1871.

From 1871 to 1873, Home allowed himself to be tested by Sir William Crookes in England. The scientist found no evidence of fraud, and his conclusions that Home possessed an independent psychic force earned him severe criticism from fellow scientists. See **Cook, Florence.**

Following the tests Home retired from mediumship and traveled about with his wife and son from his first marriage. Julie bore a baby girl, who died in infancy. Home died of tuberculosis on June 21, 1886, in Auteuil, France, and was buried at St. Germain-en-Laye.

Julie returned to Russia with Home's son. She wrote two books about her husband, *D. D. Home: His Life and Mission* (1888) and *The Gift of D. D. Home* (1890). Home's published works include two autobiographies, *Incidents in My Life* (1862) and *Incidents in My Life, 2d Series* (1872), and an expose of fraudulent mediumistic techniques, *Light and Shadows of Spiritualism* (1877).

Prominent stage magicians such as Harry Houdini, John Nevil Mackelyne, and John Mulholland claimed they could duplicate Home's feats but never did. Houdini announced he would duplicate Home's levitation at Lord Adare's home, but canceled the event, ostensibly due to illness, and never rescheduled it. See **Mediumship; Spiritualism.**

Sources: Slater Brown. *The Heyday of Spiritualism.* New York: Hawthorn Books, 1970; Earl of Dunraven. *Experiences in Spiritualism with D. D. Home.* Glasgow: University Press, 1924; I. G. Edmonds. *D. D. Home: The Man Who Talked with Ghosts.* Nashville: Thomas Nelson, 1978; Trevor H. Hall. *The Enigma of Daniel Home.* Buffalo, NY: Prometheus Books, 1984.

Homeopathy

See **Behavioral medicine.**

Honorton, Charles

See **Ganzfeld stimulation.**

Horse

The horse has had mystical, spiritual, and paranormal associations throught history. The horse, said psychiatrist Carl G. Jung, represents "the mother within us," the intuitive understanding and magic side of humankind. Sacred and revered around the world since ancient times, the horse has been associated with fertility, the forces of nature, and clairvoyance. In India the royal Vedic "Horse Sacrifice" of a consecrated stallion ensured fecundity to the queen and health and prosperity of the kingdom and royal family. The Greek fertility goddess, Demeter, was associated with the horse, as were Aphrodite, goddess of love, and Artemis, goddess of the hunt. In the Hindu *Brihadaranyaka Upanishad*, the horse is a symbol of the cosmos. The ancient Greeks and Romans related the horse to thunder, water, wind, and war. The Celts believed horses carried souls to the land of the dead. Epona, a Celtic mother goddess, was patroness of horses, and also was associated with death and graves, healing spirits, the dog, and birds.

In dreams the horse is often an archetypal symbol of the human body in terms of its animal instincts and drives.

In various shamanic cultures, the horse is an important mystical symbol. It is both a funerary animal, the mythical image of death and the carrier of the souls of the dead, and the means by which the shaman takes magical flights of ecstasy to forbidden realms. In some ecstatic dances, the shaman mounts or carries on his shoulders a symbolic horse made of sticks, leaves, or bamboo. The funerary and ecstatic horse may be eight-legged, headless, or phantom. Among the Yakut and Buryat of Siberia, the drum is called the "shaman's horse." Some shamanic rituals involve horse sacrifice, which enables the shaman to make a mystical ascent to the sky. See **Shamanism.**

In witchcraft lore horses are said to be vulnerable to bewitchment and the evil eye. Witches supposedly borrowed horses at night to ride to sabbats, returning them exhausted in the morning. Brass bells on harnesses and iron horseshoes hung in stables are amulets against witches and the evil eye.

Of all animals the horse is believed to be one of the most psychic. Stories of horses precognitive of unseen danger and thus saving their riders from disaster are legion throughout history.

In the 1920s an American filly named Lady typed out precognitive messages by tapping typewriter keys with her muzzle. Parapsychologists J. B. and Louisa Rhine investigated Lady in 1927, suspecting that she was not clairvoyant, but was picking up telepathic instructions from her owner. The Rhines could not prove their theory. Lady was again investigated in 1946 by Dr. Thomas Garrett, a skeptical New York psychologist, who became convinced of the veracity of her skill. Lady predicted the outcome of horse races, the entry of the Unites States and the Soviet Union into World War II, and the victory of Harry Truman. In 1951 she directed police to the location of a missing boy in Quincy, Massachusetts.

Clever Hans was a Russian stallion who achieved fame in Berlin around 1904 for similar feats. He spelled out answers to questions by shaking his head and nuzzling alphabet blocks, and stomped answers to mathematical questions. An investigator was able to demonstrate that Hans was reading the body language of his owners, which cued him in his responses. In Elberfeld, Germany, a stable of "wizard horses" performed mathematical feats such as extracting cube roots by tapping out answers with right and left front hooves. To demonstrate that no physical signals were given to the horses, Karl Krall, the trainer, had them perform with sacks tied over their heads. See **Animal psi.**

Sources: J. E. Cirlot. *A Dictionary of Symbols.* New York: Philosophical Library, 1971; Mircea Eliade. *Shamanism.* 1951. Princeton, NJ: Princeton University Press, 1964; Miranda Green. *The Gods of the Celts.* Totowa, NJ: Barnes and Noble Books, 1986; *Into the Unknown.* Pleasantville, NY: Reader's Digest, 1981; Geoffrey Parrinder, ed. *World Religions from Ancient History to the Present.* New York: Facts On File, 1971; Doreen Valiente. *An ABC of Witchcraft Past and Present.* Amended ed. Custer, WA: Phoenix Publishing, 1986; Joseph Wydler. *Psychic Pets: The Secret World of Animals.* New York: Stonehill Publishing, 1978.

Hubbard, L. Ron

See **Church of Scientology.**

Humanistic psychology

See **Psychology.**

Huna

Ancient esoteric tradition of the Hawaiian Islands. Huna nearly died out as a result of Christianization following the arrival of Westerners in the eighteenth century, but has been revived in the twentieth century, especially following the modification of laws that outlawed its practice.

Huna is not a religion but rather a philosophy. Its present-day emphasis is on healing and psychic arts; traditionally, it also addressed science, the arts, professions, and magic. *Huna* means "that which is hidden, or not obvious." It is sometimes called Hidden Knowledge. Huna has no hierarchy, but is comparable to a guild. Its initiated practitioners, *kahunas,* meaning "priests, ministers, sorcerers, experts in a profession," function in various specializations.

The origins of Huna are found in mythology and concern the mythical civilizations of Mu (Lemuria) and Atlantis. Long before those places existed, a race of small-statured star people from the Pleiades came to Earth and a sister planet that no longer exists. The Earth visitors settled on the continent of Mu, and became known as the People of Mu, or the Manahuna or Menehune, "the people of the secret power." Their philosophy was Huna, which became divided into three orders: the Intuitionists, who included mystics, philosophers, psychologists, and so on; the Intellectuals, the scientists and engineers; and the Emotionals, the politicians, economists, and athletes. All had psychic powers and practiced forms of

psychic healing. The sister planet self-destructed in much the same fashion as Atlantis did later, which caused cataclysms on Earth, and Mu sank. The Menehune dispersed throughout the Pacific Ocean. In the Hawaiian Islands they intermarried with the natives, and then decided to leave so as not to lose their racial identity. Their legacy was Huna, which was passed on through families, who initiated and trained the kahunas.

At some point the three orders became associated with Hawaiian deities. The Intuitionists became the Order of Kane, the highest and most spiritual god; the Intellectuals became the Order of Lono, god of medicine, meteorology, and agriculture; and the Emotionals became the Order of Ku, the god of the unconscious, sorcery, war, fertility, and rain.

By the time Captain Cook arrived in 1779, Huna had degenerated into little more than a ceremonial priesthood. With the arrival of Europeans in the eighteenth century, conversion to Christianity was rapid. Huna was outlawed by the missionaries.

In the early twentieth century, Max Freedom Long, a schoolteacher and businessman, spent fourteen years in the Hawaiian Islands, during which he recovered much Huna knowledge. He devoted about thirty-six years to decoding the language and further research, and published six books on Huna, which continue to be the major sources. By the latter twentieth century, it was estimated that true kahunas numbered only about 2,500. The Order of Huna International was formed in 1973 by Serge King, a non-Polynesian kahuna.

A true kahuna is one who has been initiated into the tradition by a natural or adoptive parent and trained from childhood. The term is often misused by others who have kahuna abilities but technically are not one, such as psychics, psychic healers, magicians, and so on. Kahunas have counterparts elsewhere in the Pacific. For example, in Tahiti the term is *tahuna* and among the Maori of New Zealand it is *tohunga*.

Healing

Huna takes a holistic approach to healing that takes into consideration attitudes, thoughts, and emotions as well as physical causative factors. The body is held to be an energized thought-form and has an *aka,* an etheric body, which is the pattern on which the physical body is organized. Illness results when the conscious mind conflicts with the patterns of the aka. Healing involves working with the *ku,* the subconscious, or "body-mind."

Like other psychic and spiritual healers, kahuna healers are conduits for the healing properties of *mana,* the effective energy or power that is the Huna concept of the Universal Life Force. See **Universal life force.** Healing comes from the God-head, *Kumulipo.* A healing always begins with prayer and attunement of mind, body, and spirit to the All, followed by spiritual counseling, *Ho'oponopono,* which means "to make right." Traditional treatments include massage and energy field manipulation (see **Bodywork**), blood cleansing, colon cleansing, herbal remedies, special diets, rituals, and amulets, such as charged natural objects (stones, for example) which are determined to be good sources of mana—or which the kahuna charges himself or herself. See **Healing, faith and psychic; Shamanism.**

Psychic Powers

Kahunas consider psychic abilities natural to all people. They cultivate all psi abilities, including telepathy, clairvoyance, precognition, and psychokinesis, the latter of which includes such feats as weather control and firewalking. See **Firewalking; Psi.** The manipulation of mana is integral to the psychic arts. Kahunas also make extensive use of metaphorical symbols and tools from the natural world.

Magic

Magical skills are gained from mental disciplines and use of mana. Evil sorcery is not part of the Huna tradition, though kahunas are sometimes confused with *ano-anos,* evil sorcerers. Traditionally, the sorcerer is feared for his ability to cast a "death prayer" spell in which he kills at a distance. Kahunas possess counter-sorcery magical skills of protection, sending-back, and a sort of exorcism that is not expulsion of an entity, but a ridding of negative influences. See **Magic.**

Sources: Steve Bogardus. "Kahuna: Ancient Hawaiian Healers." *Venture Inward* 4, no. 2 (March/April 1988): 16–19; Enid Hoffman. *Huna: A Beginner's Guide.* Gloucester, MA: Para Research, 1976; Serge King. *Kahuna Healing.* Wheaton, IL: The Theosophical Publishing House, 1983; Max Freedom Long. *The Secret Science Behind Miracles.* Los Angeles: Kosman Press, 1948; Shirley Nicholson, comp. *Shamanism.* Wheaton, IL: The Theosophical Publishing Co., 1987.

Hurkos, Peter (1911–1988)

Professional psychic who gained fame for his work with police in crime cases and for his alleged feats of ESP. Hurkos is best known for his involvement in the celebrated Boston Strangler case in 1964 and the Charles Manson murders in 1969, though he was not successful in the first case and did not complete work in the second.

Hurkos was born Peter Van Der Hurk in Dordrecht, the Netherlands, on

May 21, 1911, to a poor family. He exhibited no psychic talent as a child. At age fourteen he ran away from home to become a merchant seaman. He said he adopted the pseudonym "Hurkos" during the Nazi occupation of Holland in World War II when he worked in the underground resistance. However, this claim later proved to be false.

He worked as a house painter. On July 10, 1941, he and his father were ordered to paint Nazi barracks at the Hague. Hurkos fell off a ladder, broke his shoulder, and suffered a severe concussion. He lapsed into a coma for four days, and his life was saved by a brain operation. When Hurkos regained consciousness, he was psychic. He shocked others by telling them personal information and by predicting deaths. His fingertips were sensitive; through them he could psychometrize objects.

He later said that he had had a near-death experience while comatose. He experienced a life review and was sucked up by a pyramid of light. He found himself facing a celestial jury of nine bearded men dressed in long, filmy robes, surrounded by celestial music. The jury told him he was there by mistake and had to return to earth to finish work. They shot energy into his hands and a "Voice" said he now had great power in them and must use it only for good. The Voice told him said he would hear music from the otherworld in his head, and be able to sit down and play it on the piano. See **Near-death experience (NDE)**.

After his recovery Hurkos was troubled by his psychic gifts. He heard noises in his head and was unable to concentrate. He became extremely sensitive to noise around him and lost his ability to paint. However, he discovered a new gift for music and the ability to heal himself.

One day in 1946 he went to a psychic demonstration and upstaged the psychic with his own ability. The theater offered him his own engagement. In 1947 he took on his first detective case. His fame spread and he began traveling around Europe.

Hurkos's primary crime-solving method was psychometry. He said he got the strongest vibrations from underclothing, but he also worked with locks of hair and fingernails taken from the victims' bodies, and from photographs. As he touched the items, he would see mental pictures and hear the "Voice," either a single voice or the collective voice of the celestial jury. The Voice sometimes gave him actual names of the perpetrators. Touch was not always necessary to get images and the Voice, but whenever possible he touched and slept with objects, awakening with information. Sometimes he received information through automatic writing.

In 1956 Dr. Andrija Puharich, a neurologist and parapsychologist, brought him to the United States and spent two years testing his telepathic ability. Afterward, Hurkos remained in the United States and gained celebrity fame. His career, however, was plagued with failures. In the Boston Strangler case, in which thirteen women in Boston were raped and strangled between 1962 and 1964, he failed to identify Albert DeSalvo, who confessed to the killings. In the Charles Manson case, Hurkos saw an image of Manson and got the name "Charlie." He also said the murders were a ritualistic killing by a gang preoccupied with sex and drugs. But two weeks after beginning work on the case, he was dismissed by police for undisclosed reasons.

William Belk, who financially backed Puharich's experiments, did not fare well with Hurkos. Belk lost money in uranium searches based on Hurkos's advice. Hurkos also told him that his department stores would be profitable, but instead they suffered losses.

Charles T. Tart and Jeffrey Smith, parapsychology researchers, tested Hurkos and found no evidence of ESP in his readings of hair samples in sealed envelopes.

Hurkos predicted he would die on November 17, 1961. He suffered a heart attack and died on May 25, 1988, at the age of seventy-seven in Los Angeles. See **Psychic criminology; Psychometry.**

Sources: Norma Lee Browning. *The Psychic World of Peter Hurkos.* Garden City, NY: Doubleday & Co., 1970; Norma Lee Browning. *Peter Hurkos: I Have Many Lives.* Garden City, NY: Doubleday & Co., 1976; Milbourne Christopher. *Mediums, Mystics & the Occult.* New York: Thomas Y. Crowell, 1975; Arthur Lyons and Marcello Truzzi, Ph.D. *The Blue Sense.* New York: Mysterious Press/Warner Books, 1991; Andrija Puharich. *Beyond Telepathy.* New York: Bantam Books, 1975; Charles T. Tart and Jeffrey Smith. "Two Token Object Studies with Peter Hurkos." *The Journal of the American Society for Psychical Research* 62, no. 2 (April 1968): 143–57; Colin Wilson. *The Psychic Detectives.* 1984. San Francisco: Mercury House, 1985.

Huxley, Aldous (Leonard) (1894–1963)

Author of intellectual and utopian novels and of nonfiction works concerning mysticism, transcendental philosophy, futurism, and the evolution of intelligence. Huxley's experimentation with mescaline and LSD had an impact on the psychedelic drug movement of the 1960s.

Aldous Huxley was born on July 26, 1894, in Godalming, England. He was the third son of Leonard Huxley, a biographer and man of letters, and the grandson of biologist Thomas Henry Huxley. His older brother, Julian, was famous as a biologist and humanist.

Huxley attended Eton, intending to become a biologist, but was forced to drop out when keratitis rendered him blind. After three years he regained enough vision in one eye to read with a magnifying glass. He graduated from Balliol College in 1915. His first book was a volume of poetry, *The Burning Wheel,* published in 1916. He rose to literary prominence during the 1920s and 1930s with novels satirizing the European intellectual "lost generation."

He married Maria Nys in 1919, with whom he had one child, Matthew. They emigrated to the United States in 1937, and settled in California in 1940. There Huxley received treatments that improved his vision.

In the 1940s he became increasingly interested in mysticism, and in the use of drugs to experience nonordinary reality. His views on mysticism, especially Eastern mysticism, as a route to personal psychological freedom are expressed in *The Perennial Philosophy* (1945).

In 1953 he had his first psychedelic experience when he volunteered to take mescaline, the active agent in peyote, in an experiment for a psychologist. In many ways the trip was a disappointment, for Huxley was a poor visualizer and was not treated to grand dramas and visions. See **Imagery.** He saw only colored shapes and the ordinary world around him, though slightly askew and infused with new meaning. He was impressed, however, with his awareness of the wonderful, awesome "is-ness" of all things, and his complete indifference to space and time.

As a result of the experience, Huxley wrote *The Doors of Perception* (1954), after the William Blake quote, "When the doors of perception are cleansed, everything would appear to man as it is, infinite." In it he described his experience and its philosophical, religious, and aesthetic implications. He lamented the absence of sacramental drugs in Christianity. He said the mescaline experience "is what Catholic theologians call 'a gratuitous grace,' not necessary to salvation but potentially helpful and to be accepted thankfully, if made available." The essay had a profound impact on the emerging psychedelic drug culture, and served as inspiration for the rock group, the Doors, which took its name from the title.

Maria was diagnosed with cancer in 1952 and died on February 12, 1955. In her last days, she was not conscious, but Huxley talked to her constantly about going into the light. He believed in the Eastern tradition, as espoused in the Bardo Thodöl, the Tibetan Book of the Dead, that dying is a ritual that should be done with as much consciousness as possible, and that the final thoughts in life greatly determine the circumstances of the next incarnation.

Two months after her death, Huxley was a speaker at the Wainwright House in Rye, New York, where he met the renowned healers Olga and Ambrose Worrall. Olga Worrall, a clairvoyant, told Huxley she perceived a spirit standing by his side who identified herself as his wife. The spirit wished to give Huxley the message that she had heard every word he had spoken to her during her unconsciousness, and that she was grateful for all he had done for her. Huxley wept.

In 1956 he married Laura Archera, an Italian violinist. The same year he took his first dose of LSD. For the remaining years of his life, he took mescaline or LSD but a few more times. He also published *Heaven and Hell*, also the product of mescaline, which concerned visionary experience and its relation to art and the traditional concepts of the otherworld.

In 1960, while lecturing as a visiting professor at the Massachusetts Institute of Technology, Huxley was invited by Timothy Leary to participate in the psilocybin research being conducted at Harvard University by Leary and Richard Alpert (later Ram Dass). Huxley enthusiastically agreed. Leary described him as "a serene Buddha with an encyclopedic mind." Huxley's elitist approach to psychedelics—that they should be filtered down to the masses through the artists, the intelligentsia, and the rich—did not sit well with Leary, who felt the masses should be initiated directly. According to Leary, in his autobiography, *Flashbacks* (1983), during one psilocybin trip, Huxley told him that psychedelics promised to bring about vast changes in society; that the only opposition to them was the Bible; and that Leary's role was to be a "cheerleader for evolution." Huxley professed a great fondness for Leary, but deplored his antics and said on occasion that he "talked such nonsense" about LSD.

Huxley suffered numerous health problems throughout his life. In 1960 he was diagnosed with a malignant tumor at the back of his tongue. Radical surgery was recommended, which would have left him without speech, but Huxley rejected it in favor of radiation. While he remained outwardly optimistic about his prognosis, privately he realized that he was going to die while he was working on his final novel, *Island* (1962), about a society that, unlike the dark utopian one he portrayed in *Brave New World* (1932), does not sacrifice its freedom for perfection. *Island* concerns the society on a fictitious island between Ceylon and Sumatra, where East meets West, and is laced with much Eastern mystical thought. Huxley borrowed from *The Doors of Perception* and his experience with the dying Maria. The islanders have a "moksha-medicine," a drug from mushrooms that prepares one for the gratuitous graces of pre-mystical and full mystical experiences. At one point a dying woman is guided through the Bardo Thodöl. The death ritual apparently was Huxley's realization of his own impending death.

During his final two months in the fall of 1963, Laura read with Huxley Timothy Leary's psychedelic version of the Tibetan Book of the Dead and offered to give him LSD, which he refused; his last trip with acid had been in 1961. On November 22, 1963, in his last hours, Huxley requested LSD when he realized he might not be conscious at the end. Laura administered two doses. She read from the psychedelic Book of the Dead and urged him toward the light. He seemed to be in a state of bliss and peace when he quit breathing. His death was overshadowed by the assassination of President John F. Kennedy the same day.

Controversy remains over Huxley's role in the psychedelic drug movement, as to whether he was an advocate or a bystander. He did write favorably of psychedelics, and his writings were influential. He did not say that drugs led to mystical experiences, however, only that they opened a person to a nonordinary reality. He said that drugs had helped him to understand the writings of mystics; had given him a sense of solidarity with the world and its spiritual principle; and had given him an understanding, not intellectual, of the affirmation that God is Love.

In hindsight Huxley's enthusiasm for psychedelic drugs seems naive. He believed that mescaline was harmless to most people. He said that temporary escape from selfhood is inevitable, so it is better to escape through something that is harmless, morally desirable, and socially nondisruptive, rather than through something detrimental like alcohol or tobacco. He did not anticipate, and perhaps could not have anticipated, the problems psychedelics would cause, or the backlash reaction to them. See **Drugs in mystical and psychic experiences; Leary, Timothy.**

Sources: Sybille Bedford. *Aldous Huxley: A Biography.* New York: Alfred A. Knopf/ Harper & Row, 1973; Aldous Huxley. *The Doors of Perception.* New York: Harper & Row, 1954; Laura Archera Huxley. *This Timeless Moment: A Personal View of Aldous Huxley.* New York: Farrar, Straus, Giroux, 1968; Timothy Leary. *Flashbacks: An Autobiography.* Los Angeles: Jeremy P.

Tarcher, 1983; Guinevera A. Nance. *Aldous Huxley.* New York: Continuum, 1988; Ambrose Worrall with Olga N. Worrall. *The Gift of Healing: A Personal Story of Spiritual Therapy.* New York: Harper & Row, 1965.

Hypnagogic/hypnapompic states (also hypnogogic/hypnopompic states)

Intermediate stages between waking and sleep, during which the mind is receptive to sounds, images, ideas, feelings, and intuitions. Most likely the material rises up from the unconscious, but some of it may be psychic in nature. If dreams provide, as Edgar Cayce said, contact with spiritual and psychic forces, then the hypnagogic and hypnapompic states are the gateways to those forces.

As one descends into the first stage of sleep, one enters the hypnagogic state, a semiconscious twilight during which the conscious mind quiets and transfers dominance to the subconscious mind. During this state one experiences a spontaneously generated reverie of sketchy and fleeting images, impressions, and, quite often, clairaudient voices. The reverie ends as one enters sleep.

The hypnapompic state is similar to the hypnagogic state, occurring at the end of the sleep cycle as one emerges from sleep into wakefulness.

The imagery that occurs in the hypnagogic and hypnapompic states is not the same as dream imagery, but can be equally instructive to the individual in terms of self-understanding. The hypnagogic/hypnapompic reveries are the equivalent of visual thinking, often expressed in the individual's own system of symbols. Interpreted, these symbols can provide answers to questions and problems, and even alert one to future circumstances and events. Rousing oneself from a hypnagogic reverie to record the images, feelings, and sounds is as beneficial as recording dreams upon awakening. See **Dreams**.

Sources: Harmon H. Bro. *Edgar Cayce on Dreams*. New York: Warner, 1968; Patricia Garfield. *Creative Dreaming*. New York: Ballantine, 1974; Craig Junjulas. *Psychic Tarot*. Dobbs Ferry, NY: Morgan & Morgan, 1985; D. Scott Rogo. *Psychic Breakthroughs Today*. Wellingborough, Northamptonshire, England: The Aquarian Press, 1987; Joan Windsor. *The Inner Eye: Your Dreams Can Make You Psychic*. Englewood Cliffs, NJ: Prentice-Hall, 1985; Benjamin B. Wolman, ed. *Handbook of Parapsychology*. New York: Van Nostrand Reinhold, 1977.

Hypnosis

An induced altered state of consciousness in which the subject becomes passive and is responsive to suggestion, and may also exhibit heightened psychic awareness.The term "hypnosis" comes from Hypnos, the Greek god of sleep, and was coined in 1842 by James Braid, a celebrated English surgeon.

The altered state is induced through a variety of methods, such as a fixed gaze; monotonous rhythm of color, movement, or sound; and suggestion. States of hypnosis are (1) light, in which the subject is lethargic and is aware of what is taking place around him or her; (2) cataleptic, in which the muscles become rigid; and (3) somnambulistic, a deep trance in which the subject can be manipulated by the hypnotist's suggestions and experiences hallucinations, anesthesia, and psi phenomena. Contrary to popular belief, hypnosis cannot be used to force a person to act against his or her will.

It is estimated that 90 percent of the population can be hypnotized, although only a small percentage can attain a deep trance. Left-brain dominant people are more susceptible to hypnosis than right-brain people.

The precursor of hypnosis was animal magnetism, developed in the 1770s by Franz Anton Mesmer as a means of healing and eradicating pain. "Animal magnetism" was Mesmer's term for the universal life force, which he sought to restore to balance in sick persons with the application of appropriate magnetic forces. Mesmer's methods included laying on of hands, staring fixedly into the eyes of the patient, and making slow passes in front of the patient with hands or a wand. See **Mesmer, Franz Anton**.

Animal magnetism spread throughout Europe and to a lesser extent America, with spectacular successes reported at healing clinics and temples. Furthermore, magnetized patients, or "somnambules," as they were called, felt no pain during surgery. Side· effects of the deep magnetized trance, called "higher phenomena," included clairvoyance, clairaudience, telepathy, mediumistic ability, hallucinations, remote viewing, and eyeless vision. One of the first early documented cases of the higher phenomena occurred on May 4, 1784, in a healing session conducted by one of Mesmer's students, the Marquis de Puysegur, on a peasant named Victor, who was suffering from toothaches. Puysegur was astonished when Victor began talking volubly while in trance, then acted out instructions from Puysegur, including marking time to a tune which Puysegur sang mentally.

Mesmer had little interest in the higher phenomena, preferring to focus on healing, but other magnetists began to explore them and then exploit them in stage shows. Fraud was not uncommon.

In the 1840s James Braid set out to expose animal magnetism as a fraud; but after attending some demonstrations, became convinced of its validity. He used animal magnetism on his own patients with great success, despite disapproval by the medical establishment. Braid's original term was "neurypnology" or "neuro-hypnosis," which later was shortened to hypnosis.

Braid also was first to discover that old methods of inducing trances—the waving of hands, fixed gazes, and suggestions—were not necessary. Patients could be hypnotized merely by staring at a bright light or by suggestion alone. Hypnosis became a frequently used medical tool to relieve discomfort and pain and to perform surgery without anesthetic.

When chloroform was discovered as an anesthetic in 1848, medical interest in hypnosis dropped sharply in America and England, but less so in Europe, where animal magnetism was more prevalent among doctors. Serious research resumed in the late nineteenth century, when it became recognized as a therapeutic tool in medicine, and when societies for psychical research were established in England and America for the purpose of investigating the paranormal phenomena associated with hypnotism.

Beginning in the 1940s, scientific studies established that hypnosis can enhance performance in psi games, especially if positive suggestions are made that the subject will demonstrate psi ability. Conversely, negative suggestions can adversely affect performance. Studies in the 1960s and 1970s moved away from guessing games to free-response tasks in hypnotically-induced meditation, dreaming, and remote viewing.

Hypnosis also has been demonstrated to be effective in enhancing memory and learning, in treatments for physical and psychological disorders, and in self-improvement. Hypnosis is the most popular means of past-life recall. Self-hypnosis is used in behavior modification, and by mediums and channelers to communicate with spirits.

In the Soviet Union the potential of hypnotism was recognized as early as 1818, when D. Valenski, a surgeon and professor of physiology at the Imperial Academy of St. Petersburg, termed animal magnetism the most important physical discovery in several centuries. The first public demonstration of hypnotism in the Soviet Union took place in 1924, conducted by Dr. L. L. Vasiliev in a demonstration of telepathic hypnosis. During Stalin's oppressive regime, hypnotism fell into disrepute along with all psychic phenomena. Research resumed after Stalin's death in 1953. See **Gurdjieff, Georgei Ivanovitch; Past-life recall; Telepathic hypnosis.**

Sources: Slater Brown. *The Heyday of Spiritualism.* New York: Hawthorn Books, 1970; Eric Cuddon. *The Meaning and Practice of Hypnosis.* New York: Citadel Press, 1965; Alfred Douglas. *Extrasensory Powers: A Century of Psychical Research.* London: Victor Gollancz Ltd., 1976; Martin Ebon. *Psychic Warfare: Threat or Illusion?* New York: McGraw-Hill, 1983; Henry Gris and William Dick. *The New Soviet Psychic Discoveries.* Englewood Cliffs, NJ: Prentice-Hall, 1978; Thomas Jay Hudson. *The Evolution of the Soul.* Chicago: A. C. McClurg & Co., 1904; Ron McRae. *Mind Wars.* New York: St. Martin's Press, 1984; Janet Oppenheim. *The Other World: Spiritualism and Psychical Research in England, 1850–1914.* Cambridge, England: Cambridge University Press, 1985; Robert E. Ornstein, ed. *The Nature of Human Consciousness.* New York: Viking Press, 1974; Sheila Ostrander and Lynn Schroeder. *Psychic Discoveries Behind the Iron Curtain.* Englewood Cliffs, NJ: Prentice-Hall, 1970; Sheila Ostrander and Lynn Schroeder with Nancy Schroeder. *Super-Learning.* New York: Avon Books, 1979; D. Scott Rogo. *Psychic Breakthroughs Today.* Wellingborough, Northamptonshire, England: The Aquarian Press, 1987; Michael Talbot. *Your Past Lives: A Reincarnation Handbook.* New York: Harmony Books, 1987; Charles T. Tart. *Altered States of Consciousness: A Book of Readings.* New York: John Wiley & Sons, 1969; Benjamin B. Wolman, ed. *Handbook of Parapsychology.* New York: Van Nostrand Reinhold, 1977.

I

"I AM" Religious Activity, the

Religious movement founded in 1931 by Americans Guy W. and Edna Ballard. The "I AM" Religious Activity offers believers the opportunity to communicate with the Ascended Masters, particularly Jesus and Saint Germain, and through them to realize the divinity of the Mighty "I AM" Presence in all people.

The group takes its name from Exodus 3:14–15, in which God tells Moses from the burning bush, "I AM who I AM." The Mighty "I AM" Presence represents the individualized existence of God in all people: the light, love, and power of God; God in Action. "I AM" itself comes from YHVH, the Israelite name for God, usually pronounced "Yahweh." The letters are a third-person verb form possibly meaning "He causes to be."

Founder Guy W. Ballard (1878–1939), a Spiritualist and occultist, had been seeking proof of the Ascended Masters for years when he allegedly encountered Saint Germain in 1930 on a trip to Mt. Shasta in California. Ballard was investigating reports that a group of "Divine Men" called "the Brotherhood of Mt. Shasta" had been sighted walking in the mountains. While hiking he met a stranger who looked like another young walker but instead revealed himself as the Ascended Master Saint Germain. He offered Ballard a creamy liquid to slake his thirst, claiming it came from the "Universal Supply." Ballard wrote that the draught had a vivifying effect on him. Saint Germain explained that he had been seeking a person in Europe and America worthy to receive the instructions of the "Great Laws of Life," and had decided that Guy, his wife, Edna, and their son, Donald, should be his "Accredited Messengers." Through a series of meetings, Ballard received Saint Germain's wisdom and plans for implementing the Seventh Golden Age: the "I AM" age of earthly perfection. Ballard also witnessed his own past lives, learning that he had been George Washington.

As a result of the experiences, the Ballards founded the "I AM" Religious Activity, the Saint Germain Press, and the Saint Germain Foundation in Chicago in 1932. Ballard wrote of his enlightenment under the pseudonym "Godfre Ray King" in *Unveiled Mysteries* (1934) and *The Magic Presence* (1935). The Ballards began holding classes and seminars around the country, selecting devoted students, or *chelas,* as "appointed messengers" to carry on the work.

By 1936 the Ballards had published the *"I AM" Adorations and Affirmations* (1935), outlining the decrees, affirmations, and invocations used by students of the "I AM"; *"I AM" Discourses,* a series of lectures by Saint Germain; the *"I AM" Songs,* a hymnal; and the Foundation's magazine, *The Voice of the "I AM."*

Their channeling of Saint Germain and their teachings drew from 1 million to 3 million followers by 1938. The Ballards established a second base in Los Angeles and opened reading rooms and schools.

But pressure and scrutiny from the press, as well as too many mentally unstable people in the audiences, led the Ballards to close their open classes in 1939 and require all chelas to obtain an admission card. One former student, Gerald B. Bryan, published *Psychic Dictatorship in America*, charging the "I AM" activity as fraudulent and a rehash of old occult practices.

Guy Ballard died on December 29, 1939. Edna announced on January 1, 1940, that he had ascended, causing many disbelieving followers to quit. The Ballards had taught that ascension meant victory over physical death and reincarnation, but Guy seemed to leave in the usual manner. Edna carried on and began channeling for Guy as well as Saint Germain.

Disgruntled students filed suit for fraud, and in 1940 Edna and her son, Donald, were indicted for using the mails to obtain money for a religion they allegedly knew was false. The case came to trial in 1942, and the Ballards were convicted, subsequently losing the right to use the mails. After a lengthy appeals process, the verdict was overturned in 1954, and the movement's tax-exempt status as a formal religion was granted in 1957.

In 1941 Edna moved to Santa Fe, New Mexico, and quietly rebuilt the movement. In 1951 the movement bought the famous Shasta Springs Water Company and resort. Donald quit the foundation in 1957 but continued to handle recording activity. Edna died in 1971. Administration passed to a board of directors. The Santa Fe properties were sold and all operations were consolidated in a new world headquarters in Schaumburg, Illinois, by 1978. The movement still runs one school in Denver.

The beliefs of students of the "I AM" Presence center around the reality of one God, all-powerful and all-seeing. God permeates all things as the life and light of the universe, represented by the sun. As God's presence radiates outward, creation occurs, making each person a divine spark of the Mighty "I AM" Presence. God is individualized in each person, and the mission of each person is to realize that presence, the Christ Self, within. The truth of the "I AM" revealed by Saint Germain also explained the power of the Violet Consuming Flame of Divine Love (Saint Germain served as high priest of the Violet Flame) and how to use it to eliminate hatred and discord in the world.

Contact with the Ascended Masters and cooperation with their work is a main goal of the students' lives. The Master Jesus—separate from the Christ—figures as prominently as Saint Germain in "I AM" teachings, leading members to affirm themselves as Christians. The realization of the "I AM" power and its development will enable students to enter the light of divine love and eliminate evil, injustice, and tyranny.

Worship is accomplished through quiet contemplation and study and the repetition of affirmations and decrees. The affirmations are sentences that affirm the person's harmony with God and the blessings due the person as a result of that coexistence. Decrees are fiats from the Mighty "I AM" Presence that may be peaceful or powerful, depending on the occasion. They are repeated daily to release the Violet Flame and to dissipate discord and uncertainty.

Students of the "I AM" place great emphasis on freedom and America's destiny in the plan for the Seventh Golden Age. Consequently, they are quite patriotic and always fly the American flag at teaching centers and meetings. See **Alter-**

native religious movements; Saint Germain.

Sources: Bruce F. Campbell. *Ancient Wisdom Revived: A History of the Theosophical Movement.* Berkeley: University of California Press, 1980; J. Gordon Melton. *Encyclopedic Handbook of Cults in America.* New York and London: Garland Publishing Inc., 1986; Rudolf Steiner. *Rosicrucian Esotericism.* 1961. New York: The Anthroposophic Press, 1978.

I Ching

An ancient system of Chinese wisdom, often consulted in oracular divination. The *I Ching,* or *Book of Changes,* consists of sixty-four hexagrams of solid and broken lines. A hexagram is determined by the results of tossing three coins three times, or tossing fifty yarrow sticks. Each hexagram has a meaning, which must be interpreted by the inquirer.

The *I Ching* represents an entire philosophy based on the concept of a unified and cyclical universe, in which the future develops according to fixed laws and numbers. There is no "coincidence" or "chance," but causality. The *I Ching* shows what is possible when the mature "superior man" is in harmony with the flow of yin and yang energy. Its symbols reveal a high moral, social, and political code.

The *I Ching* does not give definitive answers, but forces the inquirer to look within for answers. It reflects a moment in time, and shows probable outcomes if various alternatives are undertaken. As a teacher it instructs the pupil in how the superior man would respond to situations. Like the Tarot the *I Ching* requires intuitive thought, and an awareness of the flow and flux of energy throughout the universe.

Psychiatrist Carl G. Jung appreciated the *I Ching* for its demonstration of the principle of synchronicity, or "meaningful coincidences": the random tossing of the coins or sticks and their meaningful association with events.

The foundation of the *I Ching* probably dates back thousands of years in Chinese history, the evolutionary product of thought that pondered humankind's relationship to the Universal Principle. The hexagrams are composed of two trigrams, which, according to tradition, were developed by Emperor Fu-hsi around 2852 B.C. The solid lines represent the yang, or male/active/creative energy, and the broken lines represent the yin, or female/passive/receptive energy. Initially, Fu-hsi developed eight trigrams, which represented the eight components of the universe: heaven, earth, thunder, water, mountain, wood and wind, fire, and marsh and lake.

The trigrams were doubled into sixty-four hexagrams by King Wen, a founder of the Chou dynasty, around 1143 B.C. Wen organized the hexagrams, and gave a name and a summary text of attributes and advice to each one. A commentary on the symbolism and meaning of the lines was added by the king's son, the duke of Chou.

The *I Ching* inspired Lao-tzu (604 B.C.–531 B.C.), who drew upon it in the writing of *Tao Teh Ching,* the central text of Taoism. Confucius (c. 551 B.C.–479? B.C.) also was inspired by it in his later years, and added ten commentaries, now called the "Ten Wings" appendices. Confucius is credited with saying, "If some years were added to my life, I would give fifty to the study of the *I,* and might then escape falling into great errors."

For several centuries after the death of Confucius, scholars reinterpreted and commented upon the *I Ching.* In 213 B.C. Emperor Chin ordered the burning of numerous books, among them the Confucian commentaries to the *I Ching.* Some copies survived. In 136 B.C. imperial authorities sponsored a special study of the work. By A.D. 1715 one edition of the book included commentaries from 218 scholars dating back to the second century B.C.

The work did not reach the West until the nineteenth century, when it was translated by James Legge and Richard Wilhelm. Wilhelm's translation—first into German and then into English—includes a foreword by Jung, who saw the *I Ching* as a way to tap into the collective unconscious through meditation upon the symbols.

The methods of consulting the oracle may be simple or elaborate ritual, depending on the individual. Some people toss Chinese coins, others use copper pennies. Yarrow sticks are more complex. In a formal ritual, the inquirer faces south, prostrates himself or herself on the ground, then passes the yarrow sticks through incense smoke while mentally pondering his question. One stick is set aside, and the forty-nine remaining ones are tossed. The language of the text is obscure to the Western mind, and requires patience and a reverent attitude toward the oracle itself in order to be properly understood. See **Synchronicity; Tarot.**

Sources: Judy Fox, Karen Hughes, and John Tampion. *An Illuminated I Ching.* New York: Arco Publications, 1984; Joseph L. Henderson, M.D. "A Commentary on the *I Ching.*" *New Realities* 6, no. 4 (January/February 1985): 31+; James Legge, trans. *The I Ching.* New York: Dover Publications, 1963; Michael Loewe and Carmen Blacker. *Oracles and Divination.* Boulder, CO: Shambhala, 1981; Larry Schoenholtz. *New Directions in the I Ching.* Secaucus, NJ: University Books, 1975. Raymond Van Over. *I Ching.* New York: New American Library, 1972; Richard Wilhelm and Cary F. Baynes, trans. *The I Ching.* Princeton, NJ: Princeton University Press, Bollingen series 19, 1969.

Iddhis.

See **Siddhis.**

Illuminati

Term first used in fifteenth-century Europe to signify adepts, specifically those who were quite learned or who possessed "light" from direct communication with a higher source. It was associated with various occult sects and secret orders, including the Rosicrucians and the Freemasons.

The most highly organized sect, the Order of Illuminati, was founded in Bavaria on May 1, 1776, by Adam Weishaupt, a twenty-eight-year-old professor of law. There were five initial members. Weishaupt may have created the order because he aspired to join the Masons, which he did in 1777. In 1780 he was joined by Baron von Knigge, a respected and high-level Mason, which enabled him to incorporate Masonic elements into his organizational structure and rites. The Order failed to obtain official Masonic recognition, however, at a Masonic conference in 1782.

Illuminism was antimonarchial, and its identification with republicanism gained it many members throughout Germany. In 1784 Masonry was denounced to the Bavarian government as politically dangerous, which led to the suppression of all secret orders, including the Masons and Illuminati. Later the name "Illuminati" was given to followers of Louis Claude de St. Martin (1743–1803), French mystic, author, and founder of the Martinist sect in 1754. See **Cagliostro, Count Alessandro.**

The Order of Illuminati included such distinguished figures as Goethe, Cagliostro, and Franz Anton Mesmer. Cagliostro was initiated in 1781 at Frankfurt to the Grand Masters of the Templars, the name used by the order there. Cagliostro supposedly received money from Weishaupt to be used on behalf of Masonry in France. Cagliostro later connected with the Martinists.

Following its suppression in Bavaria, the Order was revived in 1880 in Dresden under the aegis of Leopold Engel. In 1895 Engel's order was taken over by Dr. Karl Kellner and renamed the *Ordo Templi Orientis* (Order of the Temple of the Orient), officially abbreviated O∴T∴O. Kellner brought in elements of Tantric mysticism and magic. Famous members included the adept Aleister Crowley and Franz Hartmann, a Theosophist who had studied with a secret sect of Rosicrucians in his Bavarian home town, and who was an occultist with a shady reputation.

In 1906 Rudolf Steiner, philosopher, one-time Theosophist, and founder of Anthroposophy, accepted a charter from the O∴T∴O to establish a lodge named Mysteria Mystica Aeterna. It is unlikely that Steiner ever practiced the O∴T∴O's magic; nevertheless, his involvement in the O∴T∴O brought Anthroposophy much criticism. In his autobiography Steiner refers to the O∴T∴O only as the Order, and describes it as "an institution of Freemasonry of the so-called higher degrees." He said he had "no intention whatever of working in the spirit of such a society," but had always respected what had arisen throughout history. "Therefore I was in favor of linking whenever possible, the new with what exists historically . . . I took over nothing, absolutely nothing from this society except the merely formal right to carry on in historical succession my symbolic-ritualistic activity," he said.

Upon Kellner's death in 1947, the O∴T∴O separated. There are now two organizations, one based in England and one based in Berkeley, California.

In Western ritual magic, "Illuminati" refers to any number of secret masters or adepts called upon by magicians to aid their work. Such masters include holy figures such as Jesus, mythical figures such as the mage Merlin, and great reputed adepts from history. The Illuminati may exist only on the inner planes; however, Madame Helena P. Blavatsky, cofounder of the Theosophical Society, maintained that her Eastern Masters had a physical reality.

The idea of a secret brotherhood of adepts called the "Illuminati" has been popularized in the fictional writings of novelist Robert Anton Wilson. See **Crowley, Aleister; Freemasonry; Steiner, Rudolf.**

Sources: Richard Cavendish, ed. *The Encyclopedia of the Unexplained.* New York: McGraw-Hill, 1974; Manly P. Hall. *Masonic Orders of Fraternity.* Los Angeles: The Philosophical Research Society, 1950; Leslie A. Shepard, ed. *Encyclopedia of Occultism and Parapsychology.* 2d ed. Detroit: Gale Research Co., 1984; Rudolf Steiner. *An Autobiography.* New trans. First English translation published as *The Story of My Life.* 1928. Blauvelt, NY: Rudolf Steiner Publications, 1977; Arthur Edward Waite. *A New Encyclopedia of Freemasonry.* Combined ed. New York: Weathervane Books, 1970.

Imagery

Mental phenomena that play significant roles in psi activity, creative and physical performance, behavioral medicine and healing, meditation, mystical experiences, and magic. Imagery includes visual pictures of colors, shapes, patterns, inanimate and animate objects; auditory sensations of words, music, and sound; and thoughts and feelings associated with various stimuli. Imagery is a way to contact the unconscious mind and harness its powers. As such it has been employed since ancient times in the East and among preindustrial societies.

Imagery occurs spontaneously during waking fantasies, dreams, and in hallucinations (apparitions). With training it can be employed deliberately in goal-oriented tasks. Studies have shown imagery to be enhanced in the hypnotic state.

Imagery is subjective. Studies have shown that some people naturally are "high-imagers," while others are "lowimagers." High-imagers tend to develop their own systems of imagery use and associations, employed frequently in everyday situations.

In parapsychology research has been devoted to the relationship between psi and imagery since the late nineteenth century. While spontaneous psi cases indicate that the vividness of imagery is important to the manifestation of psi, laboratory research has been inconsistent, with many tests showing inconclusive or insignificant results. Tests with positive results have indicated, for example, that high-imagers can score significantly above chance in forced-choice clairvoyance tests, and that psi-gifted subjects attribute at least some of their success to their daily practice of imagery exercises. Test results have varied concerning process-oriented imagery (visualizing the performance of a task) versus goal-oriented imagery (visualizing the task as already completed). Imagery training has been shown to enhance scores in psychokinesis (PK) tests. While it is generally concluded that imagery training does benefit psi, there is little agreement on the nature of the training itself. Controversy also exists whether to regard imagery as a trait, skill, state, way of speaking, and so on.

Imagery is a function of the right brain, which synthesizes spatial relationships, pictures, sounds, and emotions. Little is known as to whether subjective imagery is processed by the brain the same way as external sensations. If it is it would pass through three stages: (1) sense data, or impressions without order; (2) gestalt organization into meaningful and recognizable patterns; and (3) associations with memories, thoughts, ideas, and so on, which are activated.

Experiments have shown that psi imagery generally falls into five categories that reflect various stages of mental processing: (1) the target image is presented to conscious awareness unchanged; (2)

the target image is reorganized in a recognizable pattern, but different from the original; (3) part of the target image is embedded in additional and new material, and missing elements are filled in by imagination, memory, and so on (this is often a "near-hit" or "near-miss" in tests); (4) the target image is transformed into a different but similar image; and (5) the target image is not perceived, but does simulate associations on the part of the percipient.

Gifted psychics may receive their psi information in one or two dominant ways, or may experience all five. Gerard Croiset, for example, received both unchanged images and associations. In some cases, a vibration would begin and make him feel filled inside. A serious problem caused him to see many colors, which would begin to spin around him until they formed three-dimensional pictures. In diagnosing illness, for example, an image of peaches meant cancer to him. The association was formed because the night his mother had died of cancer, she had left half-eaten peaches by her bedside. See **Croiset, Gerard.**

Russian psychic Wolf Messing said the thoughts of others became colorful images in his mind; he saw pictures rather than heard words. The thoughts of the deaf and dumb were clearer than those of others. See **Messing, Wolf Grigorievich.**

Some of the most promising research in the manifestation and processing of psi imagery has been done in the Ganzfeld stimulation test. See **Ganzfeld stimulation.**

Both the process-oriented and goal-oriented imagery are used in various techniques for creative visualization, which are intended to yield a host of benefits, including improved health, relationships, career and financial success, spiritual growth and happiness. See **Creative visualization.** Imagery is integral to the martial arts disciplines of the East, and to the moving meditation of Tai Ji Chuan. See **Martial arts; Tai Ji Chuan.** Individuals in the creative arts and in sports use imagery to boost their performance. Studies of athletes show that physiological changes, such as increased heart rate, occur during visualization of performance. The internal imagery is more effective than watching films or videotapes of one's own performance. The imagery is effective, however, only in situations with which the individual has had experience. A baseball player, for example, would not necessarily demonstrate skill as an archer simply by visualizing shooting an arrow. See **Sports, mystical and psychic phenomena in.**

Imagery has played an essential role in many forms of healing. Sick organs and parts of the body are manipulated by vivid images on the part of the patient and the healer. The ancient Greeks recognized the importance of imagery to emotional health, and also used dreams and visions to aid in diagnosis. Paracelsus, one of the leading physicians of the Renaissance, said the imagination had the power to cause and cure illness. The Cartesian split between science and religion in the seventeenth century, however, led medicine down the path of empiricism and the external treatment of symptoms.

Western medicine has only recently begun to reconsider the potential of mental imagery in health care. Since the 1970s imagery has been used increasingly as an alternative or supplemental treatment for a variety of illnesses and disorders, in particular cancer.

According to surgeon Bernie S. Siegel, imagery is one of the most successful psychological techniques that can be applied to physical illness. It is unknown why imagery helps some patients and not others, but Siegel theorizes that in order to be beneficial, imagery must be created by the patient, must be clear, and must be comfortable to the patient. See **Behavioral medicine.**

Imagery is employed in Eastern meditation techniques as a means to transcend thought and reach a unitive consciousness. Images are either geometric shapes, such as a lotus or *yantra,* or divinities. Tantric Buddhism in particular makes extensive use of vivid and complex imagery. Through yoga concentration exercises, the adept trains himself or herself to visualize shapes and colors, then progresses to more complex imagery of Tibetan letters, deities, and mandalas. Ritual dramas are projected through imagery that attains a dream-like state, which the adept controls at will. The visualization demonstrates the illusory nature of the material plane, and that the physical body is created by the mind. See **Lotus; Mandala; Meditation; Yoga.**

While imagery is employed to reach supreme illumination, the state itself is characterized by an absence of all thought, and thus no imagery—one of the reasons why mystics have such a difficult time describing their experiences. See **Mystical experiences; Peak experiences.**

Meditating upon geometric shapes has been shown to enhance intuitive faculties. See **Intuition.**

In magic imagery is used to effect spells and transcend ordinary consciousness. It is both process- and goal-oriented, and employs various symbols and sigils, which are ritually imbued with power. By visualizing the symbol or sigil, the magician accesses the power, spirit, or deity represented by it. Poet William Butler Yeats, a member of the Hermetic Order of the Golden Dawn, recognized the great power of symbols, not only in magic but in art as well. The artist, he believed, could access metaphysical truths through magic (the use of imagery) and translate the truths into the concrete imagery and symbolism of art. See **Magic.** See also **Altered states of consciousness; Drugs in mystical and psychic experiences; ESP (extrasensory perception); Hypnagogic/hypnapompic states; Psychic; Shamanism; Symbol.**

Sources: Jeanne Achterberg. *Imagery in Healing: Shamanism and Modern Medicine.* Boston: Shambhala Publications, 1985; Edwin Bernbaum. "The Way of Symbols: The Use of Symbols in Tibetan Mysticism." *The Journal of Transpersonal Psychology* no. 2 (1974): 93–110; Mircea Eliade. *Yoga: Immortality and Freedom.* Princeton, NJ: Princeton University Press, 1958; Henry Gris and William Dick. *The New Soviet Psychic Discoveries.* Englewood Cliffs, NJ: Prentice-Hall, 1978; Rosemary Ellen Guiley. *The Encyclopedia of Witches and Witchcraft.* New York: Facts On File, 1989; George Mills Harper. *Yeats's Golden Dawn.* 1974. Wellingborough, Northamptonshire, England: The Aquarian Press, 1987; Serge King. *Imagineering for Health.* Wheaton, IL: The Theosophical Publishing House, 1981; Stanley Krippner, ed. *Advances in Parapsychology 4.* Jefferson, NC: McFarland & Co., 1984; Jack Harrison Pollack. *Croiset the Clairvoyant.* Garden City, NY: Doubleday, 1964; Martin L. Rossman. *Healing Yourself: A Step-by-Step Program for Better Health through Imagery.* New York: Pocket Books, 1987; Bernie S. Siegel. *Love, Medicine & Miracles.* New York: Harper & Row, 1986; Will Stapp. "Imagine That!" *New Realities* 9, no. 4 (March/April 1989): 43–47; Frances Vaughan. *Awakening Intuition.* Garden City, NY: Anchor/Doubleday, 1979; "Effectiveness of Sports Imagery Linked to Physiological Changes." *Brain Mind Bulletin* 14, no. 9 (June 1989): 1–2; *Research in Parapsychology 1975: Abstracts and Papers from the Eighteenth Annual Convention of the Parapsychology Association, 1975.* Metuchen, NJ: The Scarecrow Press, 1976.

Incline effect

See **Decline/incline effects.**

Inspiration

A right-brain phenomenon in which profound insights, information, intuitions, and creativity burst through to the waking consciousness in startling clarity. Inspiration enables the great leaps of thought behind the genius, innovation, and invention in all manner of scientific and artistic disciplines. Virtually everyone experiences inspiration; individuals who work in creative or problem-solving occupations seem blessed with frequent inspiration. Some attribute it to divine sources, others to supernormal, spirit, or psychic sources.

Research by the American Society for Psychical Research (ASPR) in the relationship between creativity and extrasensory perception (ESP) shows three shared principles: positive motivation, relaxation, and dissociation. Positive motivation is the need to make contact with material distant in time and space. Relaxation of mind and body is a factor in the richest experiences of both psi and inspiration. In a dissociated state, the mind is passive and receptive. The same factors may be said to apply to many mystical experiences as well.

Inspiration usually occurs suddenly and often with overwhelming intensity, the proverbial bolt out of the blue. However, it is the product of a long period of incubation of processes beyond the waking consciousness. English psychical researcher Frederic W. H. Myers likened inspiration and genius to an expression of "subliminal uprush," in which the unconscious self integrates and reorganizes information into new patterns, which are then pushed into the consciousness in a rush.

Like a mystical or psychic experience, inspiration is fleeting, lasting only a few moments or minutes. Ideas must quickly be written down or acted upon in order to be preserved, for inspiration left solely to memory will fade. Inspiration can fuel prolonged periods of heightened creativity. Poet Henry Wadsworth Longfellow often was inspired as he drifted off to sleep, and would leap from his bed to write down his ideas. Mozart experienced inspiration when he was alone and in "good cheer," such as walking after a good meal, or traveling in a carriage, or during sleepless nights. At those times the ideas flowed best and most abundantly, he said, and he heard his compositions all at once and not as successive parts. The music poured into his thoughts in finished form, needing only to be committed to paper. Albert Einstein's breakthrough to the theory of relativity came with what he called "the happiest thought of my life," when he was inspired by the vision of a person falling off a roof, and the realization that the person was both at rest and in motion simultaneously.

The onset of inspiration sometimes is accompanied by physical sensations, such as chills, burning, tingling, "electric glows," and "fuzzy" feelings that something profound is about to happen. Beethoven said his whole body shivered and his hair stood on end when inspiration struck. He felt plunged into a mysterious state of oneness with the world, in which all the forces of nature were his instruments.

Inspiration can be triggered by meditation, deep prayer, fasting, psychedelic drugs, and even the onset of acute psychosis. Individuals who are skilled in meditation, and thus spend more time in an alpha state, are likely to experience a higher frequency of inspiration. See **Altered states of consciousness; Intuition; Mystical experiences.**

Sources: Nandor Fodor. *An Encyclopedia of Psychic Science.* 1933. Secaucus, NJ: Citadel Press, 1966; Philip Goldberg. *The Intuitive Edge.* Wellingborough, Northamptonshire, England: Turnstone, 1985; Gardner Murphy. "Creativity and Its Relation to Extrasensory Perception." *The Journal of the American Society for Psychical Research* 57, no. 4 (October 1963): 203–14; Gardner Murphy. "Research in Creativeness: What Can It Tell Us about Extrasensory Perception?" *The Journal of the American Society for Psychical Research*

60, no. 1 (January 1966): 8–22; Frederic W. H. Myers. *Human Personality and Its Survival of Bodily Death.* Vols. 1 and 2. 1903. New ed. New York: Longmans, Green & Co., 1954; Edmund Shaftesbury. *Operations of the Other Mind.* Meridien, CT: Ralston University Press, 1924; Lyall Watson. *Beyond Supernature.* New York: Bantam Books, 1987.

Institut für Parapsychologie
See **Paraspsychology.**

Institut Metaphysique International
See **Parapsychology.**

International Society for Krishna Consciousness (ISKON)
See **Alternative religious movements.**

Intuition
A clear and direct knowing from within, also referred to as a hunch, a gut feeling, a gut response, and even luck. Intuition is a knowingness that comes without explanation as to how or why. It is a right-brain function involving extrasensory perception (ESP), but much broader; it functions on physical, emotional, mental, and spiritual levels. Each individual experiences intuition differently. There may be physical sensations, such as tingling of the skin or a feeling of leaden weights in the stomach; clairaudient or inner voices; seemingly inexplicable attractions or aversions to newly met people; inspirational solutions to problems; feelings of closeness to God or the Divine Force; mental imagery; or cues from the environment, such as circumstances that alter plans.

Some definitions of intuition include visions, as well as the transmission of information from spirit guides or entities, though these broad definitions may be disputed by some.

In her studies of ESP, American parapsychologist Louisa Rhine identified intuition as one of four forms in which ESP messages enter the consciousness; the other three are hallucinations (apparitions), realistic dreams, and unrealistic (highly symbolic) dreams. See **ESP (extrasensory perception)**. An estimated 30 percent of ESP messages come through intuition, and concern both events happening at the moment as well as impressions about the future. See **Precognition; Premonition**. Rhine specifically excluded hallucinations from intuition, but said that hallucinations can accompany intuition.

Intuition is highly active in children and adolescents, but by adulthood often becomes repressed in favor of left-brain, analytic thinking. Yet it invariably proves to be right. ESP studies of business executives have shown that highly successful executives have a stronger sense of intuition and rely upon it more than others who are less successful. Individuals in the creative arts, who give freer rein to fantasy and imagination, also tend to be highly intuitive. Intuition is integral to all forms of divination and psychic consultation. See **Divination; Psychic reading.**

All individuals possess intuition, though some are more highly developed intuitively than others; in Western culture women have been conditioned to permit its manifestation more than men. The more a person recognizes and acts upon intuition, the stronger it becomes. An individual may cultivate and strengthen intuition by paying closer attention to whole-body responses to information, people, and situations; by relaxing both body and mind through diet, exercise, yoga, meditation, and prayer; by working with dreams; and by becoming attuned to spiritual forces. Intuition also develops in close personal relationships. Edgar Cayce, who lived in a constant flow of intuition, said one must "know thyself," be close to the Maker, and trust what comes from within. Cayce said that impressions obtained from the physical/mental self, rather than the spiritual self, were not intuition.

According to William Kautz, founder (1979) and director of the Center for Applied Intuition in San Francisco, intuitive information comes from the superconscious mind. To reach the conscious mind, it must travel through the subconscious, where it may be distorted by fears, memories, and impressions stored there. By cultivating intuitive growth through processes previously mentioned, the subconscious obstacles can be reduced or eliminated.

Environmental factors can enhance or inhibit intuition. An ideal intuition-stimulating room is painted light green, aqua, or chartreuse, lit with natural sunlight, and warmed to between 70 degrees or 73 degrees Fahrenheit with a humidity between 60 percent and 70 percent. See **Colors.** Music aids receptivity to intuition by stimulating a relaxed state, triggering memories, and causing right- and left-brain hemispheres to work in greater unity. See **Music.** The presence of plants helps to keep air clean of irritating pollutants.

Intuition, along with other psychic skills, has been applied on an increasing basis since the early 1970s to a wide range of scientific and business endeavors. Kautz developed a technique called "intuitive consensus," in which highly skilled channelers and psychics are given questions related to problems or situations; the information is validated as much as possible by empirical methods. The process has been shown to be effective and save time and money over traditional methods of validating hypotheses. Similar programs have been employed in California by the Stanford Research Institute of San Francisco (SRI) and the Mobius Group of Los Angeles. The importance of intuition in the business world also has received greater recognition since the 1970s, as a vital tool to compete and to assess an ever-increasing flood of data. See **Applied psi.**

Intuition and Psychology and Mysticism

Psychiatrist Carl G. Jung described intuition in *Psychological Types* (1923) as "a perception of realities which are not known to the consciousness, and which goes via the unconscious." Intuition, he said, is not merely a perception, but a creative process with the capacity to inspire. See **Inspiration.** Intellect requires intuition for maximum performance, and dream symbols cannot be interpreted without intuition and imagination.

Jung said human beings orient themselves to the world with four functions: sensation, feeling, thinking, and intuition, the latter of which gives information about both future possibilities and the atmosphere surrounding all experiences; archetypes are inborn forms of intuition. See **Collective unconscious.** Jung used these four types to classify the psychological types. He described extraverted intuitive types as natural risk-takers who tend to have little respect for custom, law, or the feelings of others; they squander their energies and live in the world of reality. Introverted intuitive types tend to be artists, mystics, seers, and prophets, and live with the collective unconscious; they may seem strange and odd to others.

Psychiatrist Roberto Assagioli, founder of Psychosynthesis, a transpersonal psychology, said only intuition gives a true psychological understanding of oneself and others, in an immediate and holistic sort of way. Assagioli distinguished between day-to-day intuition and spiritual intuition. He said intuition may be activated by using the will to quiet the mind.

In mysticism intuition is considered the means by which to achieve direct and immediate truth, and knowledge of the most intimate secrets of life. In deep meditation or contemplation, mystics experience intuitive flashes in which they perceive the ineffable nature of the cosmos, the Divine Force, the soul, and the unity of all things. P. D. Ouspensky, who popularized the Gurdjieff Work, gave the name "Tertium Organum" to what he called "intuitive logic" or "higher logic," defined as the "logic of infinity, the logic of ecstasy," which he said has existed since time immemorial in great philosophical systems and holds the key to the mysteries. The formula of this intuitive logic may be expressed as "A is both A and not A," or "A is All." Ouspensky said Plotinus's treatise, *On Intelligible Beauty,* embodies the fullest expression of this logic. Plotinus said that "every thing contains all things in itself . . . so that all things are everywhere, and all is all. . . . And the splendour there is infinite." See **Imagery; Mystical experiences.**

Sources: Roberto Assagioli. *Psychosynthesis: A Manual of Principles and Techniques.* 1965. New York: Penguin Books, 1976; Harmon Bro. *Edgar Cayce on Religion and Psychic Experience.* 1970. New York: Warner Books, 1988; Litany Burns. *Develop Your Psychic Abilities.* 1985. New York: Pocket Books, 1987; Douglas Dean and John Mihalasky, and Sheila Ostrander and Lynn Schroeder. *Executive ESP.* Englewood Cliffs, NJ: Prentice-Hall, 1974; Marcia Rose Emery. "Intuitive Awareness." *1987 Annual Conference Proceedings: Psychical Research and Spirit.* Bloomfield, CT: The Academy of Religion and Psychical Research (1988): 73–89; Frieda Fordham. *An Introduction to Jung's Psychology.* 1953. Harmondsworth, England: Penguin Books, 1985; Shakti Gawain. *Living in the Light.* San Raphael, CA: Whatever Publishing, 1986; Robert J. Holder. "Intuition Begins in the Home." *New Realities* 8, no. 3 (January/February 1988): 32–33; Carl G. Jung, ed. *Man and His Symbols.* First published in the United States 1964. New York: Anchor Press/Doubleday, 1988; William H. Kautz and Melanie Branon. *Chan-*

neling: *The Intuitive Connection*. San Francisco: Harper & Row, 1987; William H. Kautz, Sc.D., and Melanie Branon. "The Intuitive Connection." *New Realities* 8, no. 4 (March/April 1988): 28–39; Jacques de Marquette. *Introduction to Comparative Mysticism*. New York: Philosophical Library, 1949; P. D. Ouspensky. *Tertium Organum*. 1916. Rev. ed. New York: Alfred A. Knopf, 1981; Louisa Rhine. *ESP in Life and Lab*. New York: Collier Books, 1967; Louisa Rhine. *Hidden Channels of the Mind*. New York: William Sloane Assoc., 1961; Edmund Shaftesbury. *Operations of the Other Mind*. Meridien, CT: Ralston University Press, 1924; Samuel Umen. *The World of the Mystic*. New York: Philosophical Library, 1988; Alan Vaughan. "Intuition, Precognition, and the Art of Prediction." *The Futurist* (June 1982): 5–10; Frances Vaughan. *Awakening Intuition*. Garden City, NY: Anchor/Doubleday, 1979; Lyall Watson. *Beyond Supernature*. New York: Bantam Books, 1987.

J

Jainism

See **Mysticism**.

James, William (1842–1910)

American philosopher and psychologist, a founding member of the American Society for Psychical Research (ASPR), and president and vice president of the Society for Psychical Research (SPR), London.

James was born in New York City, the oldest of four children in a prestigious, wealthy family. His father, Henry James, was a renowned philosopher who eventually followed the religious teachings of Emanuel Swedenborg, but only after intense spiritual struggles. One of William James's three brothers, also named Henry James, was a great novelist.

William James received a privileged education in London, Paris, Boulogne, Geneva, and Bonn. He studied art, science, and medicine, and explored the Amazon before graduating with a medical degree from Harvard at age twenty-seven. Two years later he began a brilliant thirty-five-year career at Harvard teaching physiology, psychology, and philosophy. He was especially interested in Charles Darwin's theory of evolution, and in the works of English philosopher Herbert Spencer, who aided the acceptance of Darwin's theory. During this period James became recognized as America's foremost living philosopher, as well as an exceptional writer. He was controversial, however, in his opposition to American imperialism and the Spanish-American War.

His first book, *The Principles of Psychology* (1890), written over a twelve-year period, developed the pragmatism founded by Charles Peirce and established James's international reputation. In this initial work James also documented his hypothesis that the human mind and body are basically inseparable. In his writing about "the symptoms of the trance" near the end of this book he discusses mystical experience, but only in the context of "hyperaesthesia of the senses." He mentions specifically the "changes in the nutrition of the tissues [which] may be produced by suggestion." He describes the "reported noninflammatory character of the wounds made on themselves by dervishes in their pious orgies." He also mentions "the accounts handed down to us of the stigmata of the cross appearing on the hands, feet, sides and forehead of certain Catholic mystics." He attacks discrimination against Spiritualism and Christian Scientists. After the publication of the book, James lost interest in psychology, calling it a "nasty little subject," adding that "all one cares to know lies outside it."

As a young man, William James suffered severe mental depression in relation to his career indecision, and, like his father, he experienced a "dark night of the soul." But, at age fifty-seven, he had a variety of religious experiences while climbing the Adirondacks, which he described as a meeting in his breast between the gods of all the nature-mythologies and moral gods of the inner life. It has been said that he helped organize the ASPR because of these Adirondack experiences, but in fact they occurred thirteen years after the founding of the society.

In 1886 James began his Gifford Lectures on Natural Religion at the University of Edinburgh. The lectures were interrupted by his Adirondack experiences and two years of illness that followed. Once completed in 1902, the lectures were published in book form as *The Varieties of Religious Experience: A Study in Human Nature* (1902). In these milestone writings, James matured the work he had explored as a "radical empiricist" in the collection of essays he published previously under the title *The Will to Believe* (1897). In his mature writings he saw personal religious faith as a pragmatic solution for people in whom such willingness to believe makes a positive contribution, and proposed that personal faith need not be in conflict with science.

As early as 1896, James had described his philosophical method as "pragmatism," which he said concerned the practical and the concrete; in a choice between the two, it is better to be concrete than practical. His process and its context were more revolutionary than his conclusions, as reflected in the subtitle of his work, *Pragmatism: New Name for Some Old Ways of Thinking* (1907), which he completed during his last year at Harvard. Two years later he wrote a sequel: *Pragmatism: The Meaning of Truth* (1909). The same year his *A Pluralistic Universe* was published. Because of ill health, he was unable to complete writing his philosophical system in *Some Problems of Philosophy* (1911), which

was published posthumously, as were other writings collected as *Essays in Radical Empiricism* (1912).

Throughout his metaphysical writings, James envisioned a universe that an individual can order only through his or her own experience, through an ongoing and never-ending evolutionary process. His leadership of the pragmatist movement was continued by John Dewey (1850–1952). James never constructed a system of either philosophy or psychology, but instead wrote on philosophies and psychologies.

James and Parapsychology

As early as 1869, James was interested in paranormal phenomena, and remained so for the rest of his life. His approach to the paranormal was cautious, and he was adamant about obtaining facts. While in London in 1882, James met the key founders of the SPR—Henry and Eleanor Sidgwick, Frederic W. H. Myers, Edmund Gurney, Frank Podmore, and Richard Hodgson—and joined in collaborative research and investigations. Like the Sidgwicks he set high standards. He profoundly admired Myers, who became one of his close friends. At Harvard James joined with William Barrett and others to found the ASPR in 1885. James also founded the Lawrence Scientific School, a part of Harvard, where psychical research was conducted.

The same year James discovered Boston trance medium Leonora E. Piper through his mother-in-law, Elizabeth Gibbens, who had been to see Piper and was impressed with her abilities. James was so impressed himself that he began sittings with Piper, and continued sittings with mediums throughout the rest of his life. In 1890 he delivered his famous "white crow" lecture, stating that "to upset the conclusion that all crows are black, there is no need to seek demonstration that no crows are black; it is sufficient to produce one white crow; a single one is sufficient." Piper possessed "supernormal knowledge," he said, and thus was a white crow. While James remained committed to empiricism, as he stated in a lecture in 1896, he also was concerned with enlarging the scope of science to include phenomena that cannot be replicated and occur according to no known physical laws. See **Piper, Leonora E.**

James served as vice president of the SPR from 1890 to 1910, and from 1894 to 1895 served as president of the society as well. Around 1898 to 1899, an incident of clairvoyance piqued his curiosity, and he investigated it. The case concerned a Mrs. Titus of Lebanon, New Hampshire, who dreamed where the missing body of a drowned girl could be found. James approached it with skepticism, but concluded in a 1907 article in the ASPR's *Proceedings,* that the case "is a *decidedly solid document in favor of the admission of a supernormal faculty of seership"* (italics are James's).

With the deaths of Myers in 1901 and Hodgson in 1905, James hoped they would provide proof of survival after death. He believed that Hodgson, who allegedly became one of Piper's controls, provided information that could have come only from him, but the proof positive was lacking, and James was disappointed. Nonetheless, he spent time editing Hodgson's alleged communications through Piper.

James had little interest in physical mediumship such as table-tipping, apports, and slate writing, believing there were too many possibilities for fraud. His views of the paranormal were intertwined with his religious philosophy. He was far ahead of the scientists of his day in not accepting the separation of mind and body.

James lauded Myers's theory of the subliminal self, a secondary consciousness or psychic region in which higher mental processes occur. His own theory of a "hidden self" was developed prior to Myers's theory of the subliminal self, and Freud's theory of the unconscious. In *Varieties* James describes the subliminal self as "the most important step forward that has occurred in psychology."

Psychical research convinced James of the validity of telepathy, but not of survival after death. He did, however, consider the possibility of survival.

James died on August 26, 1910, in his summer home in Chocurua, New Hampshire. Various people since have claimed to make contact with him through mediumship or automatic writing. See **American Society for Psychical Research (ASPR); Mysticism; Parapsychology; Psychology; Society for Psychical Research (SPR).**

Sources: Frederic Burkhardt, gen. ed. and Fredson Bowers, text ed. *The Works of William James: Essays in Psychical Research.* Cambridge, MA: Harvard University Press, 1986; Howard M. Feinstein. *Becoming William James.* Ithaca, NY: Cornell University Press, 1984; William James. *The Varieties of Religious Experience: A Study in Human Nature.* 1902. London: Longmans, Green & Co., 1911; William James. *The Principles of Psychology. Great Books of the Western World.* Vol. 53. Edited by Robert Maynard Hutchins. Chicago: Encyclopaedia Britannica, 1952; William James. "A Case of Clairvoyance." *Proceedings of the American Society for Psychical Research* 1, part 2 (1907): 221–31; Louis Kronenberger, ed. *Atlantic Brief Lives.* Boston: Little, Brown, 1971; Gardner Murphy and Robert O. Ballou, eds. *William James on Psychical Research.* New York: Viking Press, 1960; Gerald E. Myers. *William James: His Life and Thought.* New Haven, CT: Yale University Press, 1986; J. White. "William James." In *Webster's New Word Companion to English and American Literature.* New York: Popular Library, 1976; Benjamin B. Wolman, ed. *Handbook of Parapsychology.* New York: Van Nostrand Reinhold, 1977.

Jesus saving Peter (Matthew 14:30–31)

(The New Testament, Dover Publications)

Jesus

In Christianity the son of God, son of man, Messiah, and redeemer of humankind. Mainstream Christianity believes the crucifixion and death of Jesus, c. A.D. 33, to be the central reality of humankind's spiritual salvation. By his death and resurrection from the dead, Jesus restored the relationship between God and humankind, which had been broken by original sin: the fall of Adam and Eve as described in Genesis, the first book of the Bible. Various modern theories dispute the divinity and even the sex of Jesus.

The Historical Jesus

Jesus was a historical person who was documented by several contemporary scribes and historians. The former include the writers of the New Testament Gospels, Matthew, Mark, Luke, and John, and the epistles. The Gospels are primarily testimonies of faith from the early Christian community rather than objective historical records, and thus are admittedly biased as evidence of the historical Jesus. Nonetheless, the use of critical methods of review has led scholars to at least a few generally accepted views.

The Dead Sea Scrolls, Hebrew manuscripts discovered in 1947 on the West bank of the Dead Sea, also include valuable documentation on Jesus and early Christianity. Most significant of the scrolls are the Codex Jung, once the disputed property of the C. G. Jung Institute, and the Gospel of Thomas, a favorite reference of mythologist Joseph Campbell. The Dead Sea Scrolls are important because they are unaltered by scribes or translators, and are closest to the oral tradition that preceded the New Testament Gospels. The subject of ongoing scrutiny by scholars, the scrolls offer no major contradictions to the Gospels. See **Essenes; Gnosticism.**

Jesus was born a Jew in Galilee, probably Nazareth, to parents Mary and Joseph, who were poor (orthodox Christianity presents the birth as virgin). His actual birth date is calculated to be sometime between 8 B.C. and 4 B.C. Little is known about his family life, including the other children of Mary and Joseph. As a youth Jesus worked in his father's trade of carpentry. There is no documentation of what happened to Jesus between the ages of thirteen and twenty-nine; these so-called "missing years" are the subject of continuing speculation and theories.

At about age thirty, he was drawn to John the Baptist, who prophesied repentance and the coming of the Kingdom of God. Jesus was baptized by John and probably became one of his followers, considering himself also a prophet of the coming Kingdom. For at least a year, and perhaps three, he preached, healed the sick by a laying on of his hands, exorcised demons, and allegedly performed various miracles, including producing apports.

He was known as Jeshua ben Joseph, and was addressed respectfully as "my Lord," as rabbis were in his day. He refused to be called Messiah, both because of its political implications and also because he apparently did not consider himself as such. Yet the Palm Sunday crowds called him "King of the Jews," a phrase commonly used by revolutionaries of the day.

Jesus' growing popularity, and that of John the Baptist, aroused the ire of King Herod Antipas and the Romans. John the Baptist was beheaded. Jesus then left Galilee for Jerusalem, where he quickly became popular with the masses. Fearing that the proclaimed Kingdom of God would threaten the Roman Empire, Pontius Pilate, the Roman military governor, arrested Jesus. His crime was his alleged claim to be "King of the Jews." He was condemned and crucified.

Jesus' followers believed that on the third day, he rose from dead and left his tomb, which was discovered empty, and after forty days he ascended to heaven. Furthermore, they believed he would return as the Messiah to save humankind. A movement started by his followers within Judaism became the basis of Christianity. The religion gained a firm foothold in the fourth century under Emperor Constantine, who in 312 was converted after he saw a vision of the Greek letters *chi* and *ro* appear in the sky, followed by a dream in which Christ appeared to him bearing those letters as a symbol.

Judaism does not accept the alleged divinity of Jesus, or that he was the Messiah.

Non-Christian Historical Sources

Historians contemporary with Jesus who wrote about him include Flavius Josephus, a first-century Jewish historian whose work includes the earliest non-Christian references to Jesus. Josephus's references to Jesus in *Antiquities of the Jews,* written in the last decade of the first century, raise problems and serious challenges. In his first mention of Jesus, Josephus simply refers to James, "the brother of Jesus, the so-called Christ." His second reference is more controversial; some scholars think it was Christianized after its original writing. In its present form it declares that Jesus "led many Jews and many of the Greeks [who said that] this was the Christ."

Among Roman historians Tacitus, Suetonius, and Pliny the Younger refer directly or indirectly to Christ. Later, anti-Christian propaganda refers to a false prophet (Jeshu ha-Nocri) who was hanged on the eve of the Passover for sorcery and false teaching.

Modern Theories

Various recent studies of Jesus throw new light on previously unconsidered possibilities. These are often not developed Christologies, but single-concept theories presented somewhat out of any theological context. Most theories that depart from orthodox Christianity are routinely rejected by the ecclesiastical community, sometimes with a great deal of hostility.

Many academic discussions concerning Jesus are comparatively harmless, and even uncontroversial, such as Richard A. Batey's hypothesis that Jesus was an actor, or at least was familiar with contemporary theater. More radical theories include the opinion that Jesus never existed, or that he did not die on the cross, or even the extreme notion that he was an Anti-Christ.

The idea that Jesus was one of the many Levantine magicians is presented by renowned Columbia University scholar Morton Smith in his *Jesus the Magi* cian (1978). The Smith study includes detailed comparisons between Jesus and other prophets, pointing out many unique aspects of Jesus (such as his exorcisms, cures, and eschatological sermons), which are shown to relate more to contemporary magicians than to traditional prophets. Smith carefully documents what "magic" and "magician" meant at the time of Jesus, and he documents what contemporary non-Christians said of Jesus. Smith also shows how a subsequent stylized image of Jesus has been formed and perpetuated.

Other recent and unique commentaries on the life of Christ include that of the psychic Edgar Cayce in *Edgar Cayce's Story of Jesus* (1968), based on Cayce's trance readings. Among the more unorthodox revelations is the premise that Jesus had lived prior lives. This theme in Cayce's readings is developed by Glenn Sanderfur in *Lives of the Master* (1988), in which incarnations of the "Jesus soul" are said to have included Adam, Enoch, Hermes, Melchizedek, Joseph (son of Jacob), Joshua, Zend (father of Zoroaster), and Jesus the Christ.

The Church of Jesus Christ of Latter-day Saints' The Book of Mormon, subtitled "Another Testament of Jesus Christ," refers to appearances of Jesus Christ in ancient America following his resurrection.

Elizabeth Clare Prophet, a channeler who leads the Church Universal and Triumphant, has written and preached extensively about the "hidden years" of Jesus before his resurrection, especially in her book *The Lost Years of Jesus* (1984). The controversial book cites Buddhist manuscripts that state Jesus had spent his "missing years" in India. The manuscripts were discovered in 1887 by Nicolas Notovitch, a Russian journalist. With several collaborators Prophet also analyzes "eyewitness accounts" of travelers who recreated the alleged trek of Jesus to the Himalayas, where he is said to be known as Saint Issa. See **Alternative religious movements.**

Similarly, Kersten Holger, in the popular book, *Jesus Lived in India* (1986), asserts that at age thirteen Jesus traveled the Silk Route toward India, where he studied Buddhism. Holger advances the claims of Ahmadiya Muslims that Jesus survived the crucifixion, after which he went to the Near East and then to India, where he lived to a very old age, perhaps 120. His tomb allegedly exists in Kashmir. Holger hinges part of his theories on the controversial Shroud of Turin as proof that Jesus survived. However, carbon tests in 1988 proved that the Shroud was woven around 1350 and is therefore a fake. See **Shroud of Turin.**

The question of whether or not Jesus actually rose from the dead has given rise to numerous theories. Gospel accounts of the discovery of the empty tomb are inconsistent. Theories propose that the wrong tomb was visited; that the body was stolen; that Jesus' disciples invented the story of the resurrection; that they saw hallucinations and not the real Jesus; and that he survived and somehow escaped. The latter has some modern popular appeal.

Others who claim Jesus survived are Michael Baigent, Richard Leigh, and Henry Lincoln, authors of *Holy Blood, Holy Grail* (1982). They theorize that Jesus was married—as was expected of all rabbis—either to the Magdalen or to Mary of Bethany, the sister of Martha and Lazarus, and sired children. According to their scenario, Jesus was alive when he was removed from the cross, though he was pronounced dead (presumably Pontius Pilate agreed to this subterfuge). Jesus and his family then were smuggled to Marseilles by Joseph of Arimathea. There they established a bloodline that intermarried with the Merovingians, a dynasty of Frankish kings that reached its height from the fifth century to mid-eighth century.

Divinity of Jesus

Various theories question whether Jesus was truly divine or was merely a great adept. The Gospels do not refer to Jesus as God, but present him as the Messiah, the anointed of the Lord. The divinity of Jesus was confirmed at the Council of Nicaea in 325, although the affirmation perhaps was influenced more by politics than theology. The Alexandrians at the council stressed the divinity of Jesus, and Emperor Constantine, perhaps not wanting to alienate Alexandria because of its strategic and commercial values, agreed. The deification of mortals was not an extraordinary matter in those times. Emperors routinely were made gods following their deaths, and Constantine anticipated this for himself.

Fundamental to nearly every Christian tradition that has evolved since Constantine is the tenet that Jesus is God incarnate who rose from the dead; to most Christians he is the one and only God-Man. Traditional Christians believe they share in this union of God and Man "through, with, and in" Christ. To most of those who believe in the Trinity (God the Father, God the Son, and God the Holy Spirit), Christ is the incarnated second person of the Trinity (God the Son). The Trinity is rejected as a doctrine by, for example, the Unitarian Church, a Christian denomination that stresses tolerance of difference in religious opinions.

Sex of Jesus

Theories demonstrating the possibility that Jesus was female ("Christa") have been made by various serious scholars since the Inquisition. *The Sacred Virgin and the Holy Whore* (1988), by Anthony Harris, calls upon both traditional and original sources. The former include new interpretations of the reference by Josephus to Jesus being only five feet tall, and the reference in the Gospel of physician-evangelist Luke to Jesus' "sweating of blood" in Gethsemane. Harris builds a case for Jesus having Turner's syndrome, a form of degeneration of the gonads. The less traditional clues considered by Harris include the study of a female's relics presently in Villeneuve, France, said to be those of Jesus. Critics have pointed to the image of a six-foot man on the Shroud of Turin to discredit the height theory. That argument, however, has been discredited along with the Shroud itself.

Liturgical Presence of Jesus

All the known events in Jesus' life are commemorated in the Christian liturgical year. The most important are his birth (on Christmas), his revelation to the world (on Epiphany), his death (on Good Friday), his Resurrection (on Easter), and his return to heaven (the Ascension). Similarly, Pentecost celebrates the coming of the Holy Spirit to the first Christian communities. The latter phenomenon is of special interest to the contemporary Pentecostal movement.

While the Christology of the post-Pentecost Christian community recalled and commemorated the earthly life of Jesus, it mainly looked forward to his Second Coming (Acts 3:21).

In Catholic and a few Protestant churches, the recreation of the essential mysteries is performed by ordained priests (representing Christ) in the celebration of the Eucharist (called the Mass by Roman Catholics), which is inspired by the historic Last Supper of Christ with his apostles.

Christology and the New Age

The term "New Age" is used by many modern theologians and clergy to refer broadly to all time since the first Pentecost, that is the "new creation" inaugurated through the death and resurrection of Christ. In this sense an emphasis is given to the theological virtue of hope—the stress on the teaching of Jesus that the future realm of Jewish hope was now becoming a reality and would (soon) be consummated. However, the term in ecumenical theology more recently has been used to refer to a new understanding of the church's conciliation (representative government) and catholicity (universality). See **Christology**.

Sources: Michael Baigent, Richard Leigh, and Henry Lincoln. *Holy Blood, Holy Grail.* New York: Delacourte, 1982; John Dart. *The Jesus of Heresy and History: The Discovery and Meaning of the Nag Hammadi Gnostic Library.* Rev. and expanded edition of *The Laughing Savior: The Discovery and Significance of the Nag Hammadi Library.* San Francisco: Harper & Row, 1988; Vergilius Ferm, ed. *The Encyclopedia of Religion.* Secaucus, NJ: Poplar Books, 1955; Jeffrey Furst, ed. *Edgar Cayce's Story of Jesus.* 1968. New York: Berkley Books, 1976; Flavius Josephus. *Antiquities of the Jews.* Grand Rapids, MI: Kregel, 1960; Kersten Holger. *Jesus Lived in India.* Longmead, Dorset, England: Element Books Ltd., 1986; Elizabeth Clare Prophet. *The Lost Years of Jesus.* Livingston, MT: Summit University Press, 1984; James M. Robinson. *The New Quest of the Historical Jesus.* Minneapolis: Augsburg Fortress, 1959; Glenn Sanderfur. *Lives of the Master: The Rest of the Jesus Story.* Virginia Beach, VA: ARE Press, 1988; Morton Smith. *Jesus the Magician.* San Francisco: Harper & Row, 1978; Ian Wilson. *Jesus: The Evidence.* San Francisco: Harper & Row, 1984.

Jin Shin Do

See **Bodywork**.

Jin Shin Jyutsu

See **Bodywork**.

Joan of Arc (1412–1431)

French peasant girl who took up arms against the English on the counsel of disembodied saints, and secured the crown of France for the dauphin Charles. Called the Maid of Orléans, she was executed by the English on charges of relapsed heresy.

Joan, the daughter of a plowman, was born in Domremy, a village between the Champagne and Lorraine districts. She was thirteen when she began to experience visions and voices. At first the voices were accompanied by a light. They instructed her to be a good girl, and go often to church. The voices then began to intervene often in her life, and to be accompanied by forms that Joan identified as the saints Michael, Catherine, and Margaret. The voices usually came during a waking state, but sometimes roused Joan from sleep. Sometimes they were unintelligible.

The saints began to give Joan more instructions and predictions, the latter of which included her taking up of arms like a man; her raising of the English siege of Orléans; the crowning of the dauphin Charles as King of France; her wounding in battle; and that a great victory would be won over the English within seven years. At the time the dauphin, the son of Charles VI, was being challenged as successor to the throne by the English, who controlled portions of France.

On the guidance of the voices, Joan gained an audience with the dauphin in 1429 and impressed him by telling him his daily personal prayer to God.

Charles gave her troops, which she led into battle against the English. She raised the siege of Orléans in May 1429, and Charles was crowned Charles VII on July 17. In gratitude he ennobled Joan and her family. Among the people she was hailed as the savior of France. Her success and popularity were short-lived, however.

Despite Charles's victory, the English retained a firm hold on Paris and parts of Normandy and Burgundy. Joan attempted to wrest control of Paris, but she was ordered to retreat before the battle was decided.

Joan then attempted to raise the English siege of Compeigne on May 23, 1430, but was wounded, unhorsed, and captured. The Duke of Burgundy, an ally of the English, imprisoned her in the tower of Beaurevoir castle. Joan attempted to escape by jumping out of the tower—against the instructions of her saints—and was apprehended. The duke then in effect sold her—for 10,000 francs—to the Bishop of Beauvais, also an English ally, who intended to have her executed.

Joan, interrogated in her cell, honestly described her communication with the saints, and said she could see, hear, kiss, and embrace them. She was charged with seventy counts of sorcery, witchcraft, divining, pseudo-prophecy, invoking of evil spirits, conjuring, being given to the arts of magic, and heresy. She was tried by thirty-seven ecclesiastical judges.

The charges of sorcery and witchcraft could not be substantiated and were dropped. The remaining charges were reduced to twelve, chief among them heresy, the wearing of men's clothing, and the ability to see apparitions. In answering questions Joan demurred until permitted to do so by her voices. She admitted to hearing them daily. She remained unrepentant and was turned over to the English secular arm for punishment.

On May 24, 1431, Joan was publicly condemned as a heretic, but saved herself from execution by recanting at the last moment. She renounced her voices and promised to obey the church. She was sentenced to life in prison.

There, however, she was found once again in men's clothing, and was accused of dressing so on the instructions of her saints. More likely, the guards stole her

Joan of Arc

(US Library of Congress)

own clothing and left her nothing but men's clothing to wear. She was condemned as a relapsed heretic on May 28, 1431. On May 30 Joan recanted her confession and was excommunicated. She was burned at the stake the same day in Rouen. Charles VII never once attempted to help her.

According to legend Joan's heart refused to burn, and the executioner discovered it whole in the ashes.

Pope Calixtus III annulled her sentence in 1450. She was canonized in 1920 by Pope Benedict XV. A national festival in her honor is held in France on the second Sunday in May. Her feast day is May 30.

English psychical researcher Frederic W. H. Myers hypothesized that Joan's visions and voices were externalizations of her own inner voice coming from her subconscious, which Myers called "the subliminal self." He compared her saint guides to the daimon of Socrates, an inner voice Socrates credited to a guiding spirit from childhood. Joan's case, Myers said, exhibited characteristics of motor automatism, in which voices are accompanied by an overwhelming impulse to act in obedience to them. See **Automatisms; Spirit guide.**

In the early twentieth century, English anthropologist Margaret A. Murray put forth the theory that Joan of Arc had been a witch, a member of the "Dianic cult" of paganism, which Murray maintained had survived intact from classical times into the Middle Ages and beyond. Murray said Joan had served as the leader and "Incarnate God" of her group of witches. Murray's theories, published in *The Witch-cult in Western Europe* (1921), were severely criticized by scholars and subsequently discredited. See **Apparition; Witchcraft.**

Sources: Rosemary Ellen Guiley. *The Encyclopedia of Witches and Witchcraft.* New York: Facts On File, 1989; Frederic W. H. Myers. *Human Personality and Its Survival of Bodily Death.* Vols. 1 and 2. 1903. New ed. New York: Longmans, Green & Co., 1954; Regine Pernoud. *Joan of Arc: By Herself and Her Witnesses.* 1962. New York: Dorset, 1964; Montague Summers. *The Geography of Witchcraft.* 1927. London: Routledge & Kegan Paul, 1978; Colin Wilson. *Mysteries.* New York: Perigee Books/G. P. Putnam's Sons, 1978.

John of the Cross, St. (also San Juan de la Cruz) (1542–1591)

Spanish mystic, critically acclaimed as one of the greatest poets of the Spanish Renaissance, as well as one of the greatest Western authorities on mysticism. Born Juan de Yepes y Alvarez, he was at a young age attracted to the Carmelites, a Roman Catholic order founded in the twelfth century by a group of hermits on Mount Carmel, Israel, and devoted to the ancient prophets Elijah and Elisha, who once lived on the mount. St. John of the Cross became a Carmelite monk at age twenty-one and was ordained a priest at age twenty-five.

He became unhappy with the laxity he saw in the order, and worked toward reform with his confidant and friend, St. Teresa of Avila. Together they founded Carmelite monasteries and advocated disciplinary reforms. The intensely mystical correspondence between the two expresses in terms of human love the ecstasy and the agony of their extraordinary struggles for personal spiritual perfection, and specifically the mystical experience of the union of the human soul with God.

At age thirty-five St. John of the Cross was kidnapped and imprisoned by unreformed Carmelites. He escaped after two years in prison, and founded the Discalced Carmelites at age thirty-seven. (The term "discalced" literally refers to being barefoot; however, discalced monks in modern times may wear sandals, rather than shoes, as symbolic of their stricter observance.) He was appointed rector of a new Carmelite college at Baeza.

During his two years in prison St. John of the Cross wrote *The Spiritual Canticle.* Shortly after his escape, he wrote *The Ascent of Mount Carmel, The Living Flame of Love,* and his most famous work, *The Dark Night of the Soul,* which is a continuation of *The Ascent of Mount Carmel.*

These works describe the soul's mystical journey toward God, and detail three stages of mystical union: purgation, illumination, and union. Detachment and suffering are presented as requirements for the purification and illumination of the soul. St. John of the Cross describes the "dark night of the soul" as "an inflowing of God into the soul, which purges it from its ignorances and imperfections, habitual, natural, and spiritual, and which is called by contemplatives infused contemplation, or mystical theology." The phrase "dark night of the soul" has since become a reference to the state of intense personal spiritual struggle, including the experience of utter hopelessness and isolation.

Trained by Jesuits and thoroughly familiar with the teaching of St. Thomas Aquinas, St. John of the Cross brought scholastic theology and philosophy to his poetic genius.

His poems and prose commentaries are classic documents of profound mystical and spiritual theology. He avoided stylist ornamentations found in the baroque poetry of his day, but did use mystical metaphors typical of the period. To appreciate the original and progressive quality of his works as art, they can be compared to those of his contemporaries, such as Luis Ponce de León (1527–1591), also a Spanish monk (Augustinian) and religious poet, but whose typical style is significantly dated when compared to the more universal and timeless work of St. John of the Cross.

His theology flows from and leads to his poetry. In *The Spiritual Canticle*, he describes the "Spiritual Marriage" of God and the human soul: "In this tranquillity the understanding sees itself raised upon a new and strange way, above all natural understanding, to the Divine light, much as one who, after a long sleep, opens his eyes to the light which he was not expecting."

In 1582 St. John of the Cross was sent to Granada. He became Vicar Provincial of Andalusia. He did not get along with the Vicar General, who removed him from authority and had him disgraced. He died on December 14, 1591, in Ubeda.

St. John of the Cross was canonized in 1726. Two hundred years later he was given the extremely rare title Doctor of the Church, that is, an ecclesiastic of extraordinary learning and saintliness. His feast day is December 14. See **Mysticism, Christian; Teresa of Avila, St.**

Sources: Bede Frost. *Saint John of the Cross: Doctor of Divine Love, an Introduction to His Philosophy, Theology, and Spir-*

ituality. New York: Vantage, 1980; F. C. Happold. *Mysticism: A Study and an Anthology.* Rev. ed. New York: Penguin, 1970; Robert Maynard Hutchins, ed. *Great Books of the Western World.* Chicago: Encyclopaedia Britannica, 1952; Louis Kronenberger, ed. *Atlantic Brief Lives.* Boston: Little, Brown, 1971; St. John of the Cross. *Dark Night of the Soul.* 3d rev. ed. Translated by E. Allison Peers from the critical ed. of P. Silverio de Santa Teresa, C.D. Garden City, NY: Doubleday/ Image Books, 1959.

Judge, William

See **Theosophy.**

Judo

See **Martial arts.**

Julian of Norwich (also Juliana of Norwich) (1342–after 1416)

Medieval English mystic, known as "Dame" or "Lady Julian." Apart from mention of her in wills, and an account of a visit to her by Margery Kempe, the sole source of information about Julian is her own work, *The Revelation of Divine Love.* This exists in two manuscript versions: a longer version, found in the British Library in London and the Bibliothèque Nationale in Paris; and a shorter version, found in the British Library. The shorter version is also referred to as *Showings.* Some scholars have assumed that the shorter version is simply an abridgement of the longer, but most scholars consider it an earlier one, written shortly after the original revelations. The longer version appears to be the fruit of Julian's "twenty years, all but three months" of meditation on the first revelation, as she says in chapter 51.

By her own account, she was thirty-one-and-a-half years old in May 1373 when she received the revelations during the crisis of a severe illness. She is mentioned in wills dated 1404, 1415, and 1416, where she is further designated as a "recluse atte Norwyche," being enclosed in an anchorhold at the Church of St. Julian and St. Edward, Conisford. This church belonged to the Benedictines of Carrow, and so it is possible that she had spent some time as a Benedictine nun before embarking on the solitary life of an anchoress, but the evidence is insufficient. Evidence also is lacking of the date of her reclusion, whether before or after the revelations, and of the exact date of her death. Though she is mentioned in various Benedictine martyrologies, the same lack of biographical data has prevented the institution of a formal cause of her beatification.

Julian's book shows certain similarities with the works of fourteenth-century English mystic Walter Hilton, but either might have influenced the other—or the similarities may simply be the result of a similar experience of the divine. Julian quotes the Bible with the freedom and familiarity of one who is intimate with it. There are also traces of the concepts derived from the Neoplatonic works of the early Christian writer Pseudo-Dionysius, but those were part of the whole medieval mystical tradition. When all allowances for influences and sources have been made, *The Revelations of Divine Love* remains a unique and singular but on the whole orthodox work.

According to Julian's account of the original revelations, she had at one time in her youth asked God, if it was his will, that she be given a severe illness so that she might be purged of worldly desires and live the rest of her life more worthily. She had also asked, again subject to the divine will, to have a vision or other experience of the Passion of Christ, that she might truly understand it. She had forgotten these requests when, halfway through her thirty-first year, she fell

gravely ill, received the last rites, and believed herself to be dying. At that point she began to see visions of the suffering of Christ, of the role of the Blessed Virgin, and of the whole plan of salvation, accompanied by spiritual understanding of these matters. The entire experience happened quickly; Julian writes that she saw God "in the twinkling of an eye." It was accompanied by such extreme pain that she later said that had she known it would be so bad, she never would have asked for it, nor would counsel anyone else to ask for the same.

Julian reportedly felt the lower part of her body die away (she may have suffered a heart attack or experienced a *kundalini* awakening). She asked to be propped up so that she could fix her gaze on a crucifix. She felt death take over as her chamber constricted to a dark and narrow space around her bed. Then the visions began: She saw the crown of thorns upon the head of the crucified Jesus, and a shower of dark red pellets of blood running down from it like a summer rain, until the entire chamber was filled with blood. The sixteen visions and their teachings sprang from Jesus crowned by thorns, his skin ripped by flagellation. They occurred as she followed the blood, which first rushed to hell, where she felt the Devil clutching her throat, smelled his breath, and saw his face and claws. The realm of the damned was dark with devils all around. Then the blood rushed upward to a high mountain cathedral (the heart), where Christ sat on a throne (coming to live in the heart). This cosmos was filled with light.

Julian spent the next twenty years contemplating these visions. In her writings she does not present her revelations systematically; images and ideas recur and lead to one another in a way that has its own inner order. She interprets all her images in terms of the scriptures and Christian theology. Certain themes are typically hers: Though she acknowledges the insignificance of everything else compared to God ("all that is made" is shown to her like "a little thing, the size of a hazel-nut"), yet she also maintains, with Genesis, the goodness of all he has made: His works "are wholly good," and all that is made "exists . . . because God loves it."

Julian is deeply aware of God as the Trinity in Unity of orthodox Catholic Christianity, and of Jesus as the Second Person of that Trinity incarnate. More unusual, but far from unique, is her reference to Jesus as "Mother": St. Anselm had used the same image, and there are scriptural precedents (Isaiah 49:15 and 66:13; Matthew 23:37; and also the passages in the Deuterocanonical books, accepted by the Roman church as inspired, where Wisdom is personified as female, Wisdom 7:22–8:1 and Sirach 24:1–22, 30–34). God is also described as both "homely" and "courteous" in his dealings with the soul, which is his royal city, where he delights to dwell.

But first and last it is love that is Julian's message: God's love for his elect (Julian is puzzled by sin and damnation, and her solutions are not quite in accord with correct Catholic doctrine, to which, nevertheless, she submits and clings fast), and the soul's need to return that love: "Wouldst thou witten thy Lord's meaning? Wit it well: Love was his meaning" (chapter 86).

It has been suggested that Julian's revelations are shamanic in nature, involving such hallmarks as the "initiatory" illness, descent to the underworld, exposure to horror and suffering, and spiritual rebirth. After her experience people from all over were drawn to her, though she confined herself to a cell. She had a great reputation as a healer and counselor. Margery Kempe, who was born in 1373, the year of the revelations, recorded her visit to Julian in about 1403 for spiritual counsel. See **Mysticism; Mysticism, Christian.**

Sources: P. Franklin Chambers. *Juliana of Norwich: An Introductory Appreciation and an Interpretive Anthology.* London: Victor Gollancz, 1955; Julian of Norwich. *Revelations of Divine Love.* Translated into modern English and with an introduction by Clifton Wolters. Harmondsworth, England: Penguin Books, 1966; Julian of Norwich. *Revelations of Divine Love.* Translated by James Walsh. New York: Harper & Row, 1961; Julian of Norwich. *Showing of God's Love: The Shorter Version of "Sixteen Revelations of Divine Love."* Edited and partially modernized by Sr. Anna Maria Reynolds. London: Longmans, 1958; Julian of Norwich. *Showings.* New York: Paulist Press, 1978; Paul Molinari, S.J. *Julian of Norwich: The Teaching of a 14th Century English Mystic.* New York: Longmans, Green & Co., 1958.

Jung, Carl Gustav (1875–1961)

Swiss psychiatrist who founded analytical psychology. Carl G. Jung's introspection of humankind's inner realms was fueled to a large extent by his own personal experiences involving dreams, visions, mythological and religious symbolism, and, to some extent, paranormal phenomena. Essentially, he took Sigmund Freud's knowledge of the unconscious and brought it into spiritual realms.

Jung was born on July 26, 1875, in Kesswil, Switzerland. Four years later the Jung family moved to Klein-Huningen near Basel. Jung's entry into mystical and mysterious realms began early in childhood in dreams. As a boy he began to feel he had two personalities; one, a wise old man, stayed with him and had increasing influence on his thought throughout his entire life. See **Archetypes.** He experienced precognition, clairvoyance, psychokinesis, and hauntings. Perhaps his psychic sensitivity was a hereditary gift: His mother and maternal grandmother both were known as "ghost seers." His grandmother, Augusta Preiswerk, once fell into a three-day trance at age twenty, during which she communicated with spirits of the dead and gave prophecies. Jung's mother, Emilie, was as a child ordered by her father, a minister, to sit behind him while he wrote his sermons so that he would not be disturbed by ghosts. She kept a personal journal of paranormal occurrences that took place in the house in which Jung grew up.

In 1898 Jung began to take serious interest in occult phenomena. He decided to become a psychiatrist in 1900 and did his medical training at Basel, Switzerland. When he discovered that his sixteen-year-old cousin had become a practicing medium, he invited her to perform spiritualistic experiments for study. His notes later became the basis for his doctoral thesis and first published paper, "On the Psychology and Pathology of So-Called Occult Phenomena" (1902).

He married Emma Rauschenbach, heiress to a wealthy manufacturing family fortune, in 1903. In 1906 he published one of his most significant early works, *The Psychology of Dementia Praecox.*

Jung became interested in mythology around 1909, the year he resigned a post at Burgholzki Mental Clinic, where he had been practicing for nine years. During that year he traveled to the United States with Freud and received an honorary degree from Clark University in Worcester, Massachusetts. (Jung also received an honorary doctorate from Harvard in 1936, from Oxford in 1938, and from the University of Geneva in 1945.)

In 1910 he was appointed permanent president of the International Congress of Psycho-Analysis. Jung resigned this position in 1914, one year after he also resigned a professorship at the University of Zurich. After these breaks with the establishment, Jung experienced what mythologist Joseph Campbell described as "intense preoccupation" with images of the unconscious and with mythology in relation to dreams.

In May 1910 the Society for Psychical Research in London published Jung's paper "The Psychological Foundations of Belief in Spirits." In it he identified three main sources for the belief in spirits: the seeing of apparitions, mental disease, and dreams, the most common of the three. He said spirits of the dead are created psychologically upon death: Images and ideas remain attached to relatives and are activated to form spirits by intensity of emotion.

From 1907 to 1913, Jung was greatly influenced by Sigmund Freud. Jung once appeared to demonstrate psychokinetic powers in the presence of Freud during a heated discussion. See **Freud, Sigmund.** After several years of close contact, Jung parted company with Freud. A breaking point came when Freud asked Jung to interpret a dream he had, but refused to divulge a key association because it would damage Freud's authority. Jung had significant disagreements with Freud, chiefly over Freud's emphasis on sexuality as the basic, driving urge for people; his dismissal of spiritual aspects of the psyche and of the paranormal; and concerning the meaning of "symbol."

The break with Freud had a profoundly disturbing effect on Jung, and he suffered a six-year-long breakdown during which he had psychotic fantasies. He was called a "mystic"—a pejorative label at the time—and was shunned by his peers. Freud had accused Jung of death wishes against him, after he had "fainted" twice in Jung's presence; Jung denied the charge, but after his break with Freud he developed a "Judas complex" about their relationship. He had highly symbolic and Wagnerian-like dreams in which he killed Freud.

During this psychotic phase of Jung's life, he experienced numerous paranormal phenomena. He became immersed in the world of the dead, which led to his *Seven Sermons to the Dead,* written under the name of the second-century Gnostic writer, Basilides, and published in 1916. He described the spirits of the dead as "the voices of the Unanswered, Unresolved and Unredeemed." Also during this phase, the distinction between his dreams and visions eventually faded out for Jung, and he later recorded them in detail, especially in his autobiographical account, *Memories, Dreams, Reflections* (published posthumously in 1963).

Following his emergence from this period, Jung pursued work on his own theories. One of the most important was his general theory of psychological types, first published in 1921. He distinguished two basic psychological types, extroverts and introverts, who could be grouped according to four basic functions: thinking, feeling, sensation, and intuition. Other significant theories include the anima (feminine principle) and animus (masculine principle), psychic images that exist in everyone as feminine and masculine aspects; the collective unconscious; and archetypes. See **Collective unconscious.**

Jung took issue with Freud's definition of symbols as conscious contents that provide clues to the unconscious background. Such are signs or symptoms, Jung said, while symbols are much different and should be understood as an intuitive idea. See **Symbol.**

He also took issue with Freud on the topic of dreams. Freud saw dream symbolism as universal and said therapists could interpret them. Jung maintained that dreams are the private property of the dreamer and speak a private language that only the dreamer can interpret; some dreams, however, come from the collective unconscious and belong to all humankind. See **Dreams.**

Mythology became especially important to Jung around the time of his writing one of his major works, *Symbols of Transformation* (1911–12). See **Mythology.**

Jung was intensely interested in Gnosticism, particularly its *sophia,* or wisdom, the desirable elements once rejected by the church along with its heretical elements. His explorations of Gnosticism, joined with his interest in alchemy, paved the way for a modern revival of interest in the spiritual dimensions of both subjects. See **Alchemy; Gnosticism.**

In 1927 Jung's interest in mandala symbolism developed. See **Mandala.** In 1928 Jung collaborated with Sinologist Richard Wilhelm on studies of the Chinese Taoist alchemical text, *The Secret of the Golden Flower.* His commentary on this text, published in 1929, is another of his major works.

Jung became president of the General Medical Society for Psychotherapy in 1933, after three years as vice president. His major writing that year was "A Study in the Process of Individuation," his paper for the first Eranos Meeting, an annual gathering of great thinkers held at the lecture hall built at the residence of Olga Froebe-Kapteyn on the shore of Lago Maggiore in Switzerland. Jung's papers for each of the following three annual Eranos meetings were likewise major works: "Archetypes of the Collective Unconscious" (1934), "Dream Symbols of the Individuation Process" (1935), and "Religious Ideas in Alchemy" (1936). His *Psychology and Alchemy* (1944) was based on the 1935 and 1936 Eranos papers. His last major work in this period was *The Psychology of the Transference* (1946).

In 1944 Jung had a near-death experience (NDE) following a heart attack. As he lay in bed, a nurse observed him surrounded by a bright halo of light, the same phenomenon she had witnessed around other patients who were dying. Jung recovered, and recounted later what happened to him during that time.

He felt he was floating high over the Earth and could see from the Himalayas across the Middle East to a part of the

Mediterranean. He became aware that he was leaving the Earth. Then he saw near him a huge block of stone, which had been hollowed out into a temple. To the right of the temple entrance, a black Hindu was sitting in a lotus position. Jung knew he was expected inside the temple. As he drew closer, he felt his earthly desires and attitudes fall away from him, and he became aware that inside he would understand the meaning of his life. At that moment his earthly doctor appeared in the form of the basileus of Kos, the healer at the temple of Aesculapius, the Roman god of healing (Aesclepius in Greek), telling him he had to return to earth. Jung did so but most unhappily and with great resentment against his doctor. He knew the doctor was going to die, however, because he had manifested in what Jung interpreted as his primal form. The doctor did die soon after. See **Near-death experience (NDE)**.

Following the NDE Jung experienced a remarkable transformation in which he felt he was in the happy state felt by the unborn. He had a vision in which he was Adam and a Jew, and his nurse was his Magna Mater, who proceeded to teach him the mystery of the *hieros gamos,* or sacred marriage with the divine.

After the death of his wife in 1955, Jung began building a castle of stone on his newly acquired property in Bollingen, Switzerland. He carved numerous alchemical and mystical symbols into the stone. The ongoing building and altering of his tower signified for him an extension of consciousness achieved in old age. The tower and its symbolic role in his life is a leitmotif in Jung's writings. During his retirement at Bollingen, Jung reworked many earlier papers and developed further his ideas on many topics that are now of intense interest, including mandala symbolism, the *I Ching,* alchemy, synchronicity, and especially the phenomenology of the self, the latter culminating in the major work *Aion* in 1951. See **Alchemy;** *I Ching;* **Synchronicity.**

In *Aion* Jung summarized the roles of the "archetypes of the unconscious" and commented especially on the Christ image as symbolized in the fish. While there may not be a Jungian Christology per se, Jung's work had a major influence on Christian scholarship. See **Christology.** Religious themes are developed by Jung in another major work of the period, "Answer to Job" (1952) as well as in *Mysterium Coniunctionis* (1955–1956), which concerns alchemy. In the latter, his last masterpiece, he states that he was satisfied that his psychology was at last "given its place in reality and established upon its historical foundations."

Jung believed in reincarnation; he drew many of his beliefs from the Tibetan Book of the Dead. He believed his own incarnation was not due to karma, however, but "a passionate drive for understanding in order to piece together mythic conceptions from the slender hints of the unknowable" (Nandor Fodor, *Freud, Jung and the Occult,* 1971). He feared greatly for the future of humankind, and said the only salvation lay in becoming more conscious. He said he believed his work proved that the pattern of God exists in every person.

Three days before he died, Jung had the last of his visionary dreams, and a portent of his own impending death. In the dream he had become whole. A significant symbol was tree roots interlaced with gold, the alchemical symbol of completion. When he died in his room in Zurich on June 6, 1961, a great storm arose on Lake Geneva and lightning struck his favorite tree.

Jungian principles have been found to be applicable to nearly all academic disciplines from mythology to religion to quantum physics, and to nearly all aspects of modern life. His prolific writings have been collected into twenty volumes plus a supplement. See **Grail, the; Psychology.**

Sources: Joseph Campbell, ed. *The Portable Jung.* New York: Penguin, 1971; Nandor Fodor. *Freud, Jung and the Occult.* Secaucus, NJ: University Books, 1971; Nandor Fodor. *Between Two Worlds.* West Nyack, NY: Parker Publishing, 1964; Frieda Fordham. *An Introduction to Jung's Psychology.* 1953. 3d ed. Harmondsworth, England: Penguin Books, 1966; Calvin S. Hall and Vernon J. Nordby. *A Primer on Jungian Psychology.* New York: New American Library, 1973; C. G. Jung, *Memories, Dreams, Reflections.* Recorded and edited by Aniela Jaffe. New York: Random House, 1961; C. G. Jung, ed. *Man and His Symbols.* First published in the United States 1964. NY: Anchor Press/Doubleday, 1988; Peter O'Connor. *Understanding Jung, Understanding Yourself.* New York/Mahwah, NJ: Paulist Press, 1985; Andrew Samuels, Bani Shorter, and Fred Plaut. *A Critical Dictionary of Jungian Analysis.* London: Routledge & Kegan Paul, 1986; "C. G. Jung—A Mystic? Conversations with Aniela Jaffe." *Psychological Perspectives* 19, no. 1 (Spring-Summer 1988): 80–91.

K

Kabbalah (also Cabala, Kabala, Qabalah)

The mysticism of classical Judaism. *Kabbalah* is Hebrew for "that which is received," and refers to a secret oral tradition handed down from teacher to pupil. The term "Kabbalah" was first applied to secret, mystical teachings in the eleventh century by Ibn Gabirol, a Spanish philosopher, and has since become applied to all Jewish mystical practice. Though the Kabbalah is founded on the Torah (the Jewish scriptures and other sacred literature), it is not an intellectual discipline, nor does it instruct the mystic to withdraw from humanity to pursue enlightenment. The Kabbalist seeks union with God while maintaining a full social, family, and community life within the framework of traditional Judaism.

According to legend God taught Kabbalah to angels. After the Fall they taught it to Adam in order to provide humankind with a way back to God. It was passed to Noah, then to Abraham and Moses, who in turn initiated seventy Elders.

The theosophical and mystical lore that grew into the Kabbalah appears to have been influenced by Gnosticism and Neoplatonism.

The earliest form of mystical literature is found in the tradition of the Merkabah mystics (c. 100 B.C.–A.D. 1000). *Merkabah* means "God's Throne-Chariot" and refers to the chariot of Ezekiel's vision. The goal of the Merkabah mystic was to enter the throne world, which was reached after passing through seven heavenly mansions. Merkabah has been called a shamanistic mysticism because of its characteristics. It required fasting and repetitious recitation of hymns and prayers to achieve a trance state. The Merkabah-rider then sent his soul upward (later mystics said downward) to pierce the veil around the Merkabah throne. The soul was assailed along the way by evil demons and spirits; to protect it the mystic prepared in advance magical talismans and seals and recited incantations.

The historical origin of the true Kabbalah centers on a short book titled *Sefer Yetzirah (Book of Creation)*. Its exact date is unknown; it was in use in the tenth century, but may have been written as early as the third century. It is attributed to Rabbi Akiba, whom the Romans martyred. *Sefer Yetzirah* presents a discussion on cosmology and cosmogony, and sets forth the central structure of the Kabbalah. It says that God created the world by means of thirty-two secret paths of wisdom, which are ten *sephirot* and the twenty-two letters of the Hebrew alphabet. The sephirot apparently originally referred to numbers, and later were interpreted as emanations by which all reality is structured. The first *sephirah* emanated from God, and at least the following three from each other. The rest represent dimensions of space. Together they constitute a unity. The twenty-two letters of the alphabet and their sounds comprise the foundation of all things.

In 917 a form of practical Kabbalism was introduced by Aaron ben Samuel in Italy; it later spread through Germany and became known as German Kabbalism or Early Hasidism. It drew upon the Merkabah practices in that it was ecstatic, had magic rituals, and had as primary techniques prayer, contemplation, and meditation. The magical power of words assumed great importance, and gave rise to the techniques of gematria, notarikon, and temura. See **Gematria.**

The German Kabbalists held that God was too exalted for people to comprehend. However, mystics could perceive God's presence in the form of a divine fire or light, which is the first creation, Shekinah, the Mother, God's female aspect. The mystic sought to unite with this glory. The German Kabbalists also conceived of four worlds: God's glory, angels, the animal soul, and the intellectual soul.

Classical Kabbalah was born in the thirteenth century in Provence, France, and moved into Spain, where it was developed most extensively by medieval Spanish Jews. The primary work from which classical Kabbalah developed is *Sefer ha-Zohar (Book of Splendor)*, attributed to a second-century sage, Rabbi Simeon bar Yohai, but actually written between 1280 and 1286 by the Spanish Kabbalist, Moses de León. According to the story, Rabbi Simeon and his son, Eleazar, persecuted by the Roman emperor Trajan, hid in a cave for thirteen years where the Ben-Gurion Airport now stands in Lod, Israel. After Trajan's death the two emerged, but Rabbi Simeon was so distraught at the lack of spirituality among Jews that he returned to the cave to meditate. After a year a voice told him to let the ordinary people go their own way, but to teach those who were ready. The *Zohar* is said to comprise those teachings, which were recorded by disciples.

The *Zohar* presents God as *Ein-Sof* ("without end"), who is unknowable and beyond representation. God created the world out of himself. The aim of humankind is to realize union with the Divine. All things are reflected in a higher world, and nothing can exist independently of all else. Thus human beings, by elevating their souls to unite with God, also elevate all other entities in the cosmos.

The *sephirot* are attributes of God that are described by the names of God; they are language that substitutes for God. They form the central image of Kabbalistic meditation, the Tree of Life. The Tree shows the descent of the divine into the material world, and the path by which people can ascend to the divine while still in the flesh. Each *sephirah* is a level of attainment in knowledge. The seven lower *sephirot*—Sovereignty, Foundation, Endurance, Majesty, Beauty, Loving-kindness and Judgment—correspond to seven energy centers located along the spine in the human body (compare to **Chakras**), and the top three— Understanding, Wisdom, and Crown (Humility)—are mystical steps to unity with God.

Each *sephirah* is divided into four sections in which operate the Four Worlds, which constitute the cosmos: Atziluth, the world of archetypes, from which are derived all forms of manifestation; Briah, the world of creation, in which archetypal ideas become patterns; Yetzirah, the world of formation, in which the patterns are expressed; and Assiah, the world of the material.

The *sephirot* also comprise the sacred, unknowable, and unspeakable personal name of God: YHVH (Yahweh), the Tetragrammaton. So sacred is the Tetragrammaton that other names, such as Elohim, Adonai, and Jehovah, are substituted in its place in scripture. The letters YHVH correspond to the Four Worlds.

Through contemplation and meditation, the Kabbalist ascends the Tree of Life. Only the most stable and ethical, who have first purified their bodies, minds, and spirits, are permitted to approach. The *sephirot* are contemplated by visualizing them vibrating with color (which represents various qualities), together with images of their corresponding Hebrew letters of the divine names of God, and the planets, angels, metals, parts of the body, and energy centers. Breath and sound also are utilized to raise consciousness. The techniques are similar to those of Eastern yoga disciplines. Like yogis, the early Kabbalists experienced illuminations of light and heat that resemble descriptions of *kundalini* awakenings. See **Kundalini; Spiritual emergence; Yoga.**

The "short path" to enlightenment was developed by another thirteenth-century Spanish Kabbalist, Abraham ben Samuel Abulafia (b. 1240). At age thirty-one Abulafia received a prophetic call, and became a pupil of the mystic Baruch Togarmi. Thus educated, Abulafia set down his own form of *tzeruf,* or letter permutation.

Hebrew letters have corresponding attributes and numerical values which, when meditated upon, unify the mind and body and bring the mystic into contact with higher planes. To meditate on letters is to meditate on all of Creation, and to achieve one with the whole. Abulafia's *tzeruf* enabled mystics to attain meaning beyond meaning.

The ideal time to begin *tzeruf* was midnight. The mystic would begin writing sacred letters, combined with visualizations of the Tree and breathing techniques. A *kundalini*-type of ecstasy reportedly would occur quickly. The ecstasy, called *shefa* ("divine influx"), descended into the mystic (as opposed to

the rise of *kundalini*), warming his heart and bathing him in sensations of air, heat, rushing water or oil. (The Merkabah mystics reported the same phenomena.) Like short paths to yoga, *tzeruf* posed dangers of destruction to those who were insufficiently prepared or attempted too much too soon.

Abulafia's school was not followed by many, yet his teachings did have widespread impact on meditative practices. He ran afoul of his peers, however, by revealing the secret pronunciations of the sacred names of God, including the Tetragrammaton, thus unlocking powerful sounds with which to obtain enlightenment.

By the sixteenth century, *tzeruf* instructions were obscured by metaphor in texts, and by the eighteenth century, the practice among Kabbalists all but stopped. *Tzeruf* is not practiced in modern times.

The Spanish Kabbalah, the teachings of the *Zohar,* spread into Europe in the fourteenth and fifteenth centuries. After the expulsion of Jews from Spain in 1492, Kabbalah study became more public. The most important post-expulsion figure to influence what was to become modern Kabbalah was Isaac Luria Ashkenazi (1534–1572), called the Ari. Luria, a student of the great Kabbalist Moses Cordovero (1522–1570), conceived of bold new theories that gave the Kabbalah a new terminology and complex new symbolism. He emphasized letter combinations as a medium for meditation and mystical prayer.

The Hasidic movement emerged from the Lurianic Kabbalah, and made Kabbalah accessible to the masses. The Hasidim are the only major branch of modern Judaism to follow mystical practices. The principle figure in this emergence was Israel ben Eleazar (1698–1760), called the Baal Shem Tov ("the Master of the Holy Name"), whose teaching centered on *devekuth,* or cleaving to God, but in a more personal and emotional way than before. *Devekuth* centers in the here and now; thus concentrated awareness and prayer were reinterpreted in order to be made part of everyday life. For the Hasidim constant prayer is the vehicle to mystical awareness.

For about three hundred years, from 1500 to 1800, the Kabbalah was considered to be the true Jewish theology. Interest in the Kabbalah among Jews began to decline after the eighteenth century. There has been some renewed interest since the Zionist revival in modern times. The Reconstructionist movement, founded in 1922 by Rabbi Mordecai M. Kaplan, has borrowed from Hasidic traditions in espousing a more mystical Judaism. Reconstructionism has grown very slowly, and as of 1989 accounted for only 1 percent of the 5.8 million Jews in the United States.

Modern historians have acknowledged the Kabbalah's profound impact on the development of Judaism and in Jewish life, especially in the areas of prayer, custom, and ethics. Kabbalistic motifs penetrated prayer from about the mid-seventeenth century onward, and also inspired liturgies and rituals. Jewish folk belief absorbed Kabbalistic concepts such as the transmigration of souls (see **Reincarnation**), demonology, and the Messiah. In particular, the *Zohar* and the Lurianic tradition provided rich sources for folk customs.

Kabbalah and Western Occultism

The Kabbalah has left an indelible stamp on the Western magical tradition. Magical applications grew first out of German Kabbalism and then Lurianic Kabbalism. Christian occultists were attracted to the magical amulets, incantations, demonology, seals, and letter permutations, and used practical Kabbalah

as the basis for ritual magical texts. The Tetragrammaton was held in great awe for its power over all things in the universe, including demons.

Beginning in the late fifteenth century, Kabbalah was harmonized with Christian doctrines to form a Christian, or Western, Kabbalah which supposedly proved the divinity of Christ. Cornelius Agrippa von Nettesheim included the Kabbalah in his *De Occulta Philosophia* (1531). Also in the sixteenth century, alchemical symbols were integrated into the Christian Kabbalah.

Interest in the Kabbalah received renewed attention in the nineteenth century from non-Jewish occultists such as Francis Barrett, Eliphas Levi, and Papus. The Kabbalah influenced the Hermetic Order of the Golden Dawn; Dion Fortune called it the "Yoga of the West." Western occultists have linked the Kabbalah to the Tarot and astrology, but these relationships are spurious and have no place in true Kabbalah.

Sources: Harold Bloom. *Kabbalah and Criticism.* New York: Continuum, 1984; Perle Epstein. *Kabbalah: The Way of the Jewish Mystic.* Boston: Shambhala, 1988; Dion Fortune. *The Mystical Qabalah.* 1935. York Beach, ME: Samuel Weiser, 1984; Pinchas Giller. "Kabbalah & Jewish Mysticism." *Gnosis* no. 3 (Fall/Winter 1986–1987): 10–12; Ari L. Goldman. "Reconstructionist Jews Turn to the Supernatural." *The New York Times* (February 19, 1989): 26; Rosemary Ellen Guiley. *The Encyclopedia of Witches and Witchcraft.* New York: Facts On File, 1989; Charles Ponce. *Kabbalah: An Introduction and Illumination for the World Today.* Wheaton, IL: The Theosophical Publishing House, 1973; Gershom Scholem. *Kabbalah.* New York: New American Library, 1974.

Kachinas

Among the Pueblo supernatural beings or the spirits of the ancestral dead, who bring rain and perform other mostly beneficial functions. "Kachina" comes from the Hopi word *kachi,* which means "spirit father," "life," or "spirit." Spirit fathers are associated with the dead. Scholars have debated whether kachinas originally were ancestral dead or rain spirits—the associations between the two are intertwined. Kachinas are not identified with gods, but are considered the gods' intermediaries.

Kachinas were known in pre-Spanish days throughout what is now New Mexico and Arizona, in every village except Taos. The concept may have been introduced from Mexico. In mythological times the kachinas left their home in the sacred San Francisco Mountains and personally visited the villages, where they danced and interacted with the living. They quit their personal visits because they often had to take back with them the souls of the newly dead. Hence they directed that they should be impersonated, and kachinas became associated with a cult of elaborately costumed and masked male dancers. By donning their masks, they become imbued with the kachinas' supernatural powers. The masks must never be worn outside of ceremony, for to do so invites death. See **Masks.**

Kachina cult beliefs vary among Pueblo tribes. The kachinas' chief function is to bring rain for the crops, but they also discipline and entertain children. Not all kachinas are benign—some are said to attack towns and murder the living.

Among the Zuñi kachinas are called *koko.* They are the spirits of the dead who bring rain when they approach villages as ducks, the form assumed by gods (or emissaries of the gods) when they travel. Some koko supervise hunts. Most reside in a great village at the bottom of the mythical Lake of the Dead, which is identified with a real lake called Listening Spring, located at the junction of the Zuñi and Little Colorado rivers. Some *koko* live in the mountains. The Zuñi of-fer prayers to the *koko* and throw offerings of food into the river, to be carried to the Lake of the Dead.

The Zuñi distinguish three categories of *koko:* (1) people who have recently died, and who may or may not make rain; (2) ancestors who have been dead for quite a while, and who are petitioned for health, rain, and good corn crops; and (3) the original *koko,* who comprise children who died by drowning after the Emergence of people from the Underworld (the Zuñi Creation myth) and those who died and returned to the Underworld.

Not all spirits of the Zuñi dead become *koko.* Those who do were initiated during life into the *koko* society; initiates include most men. Some spirits of the dead become *uwanammi,* or water monsters, which also have the power to cause rain. It is believed that in the *koko* village at the lake bottom, the *koko* live happily and dress in beautiful garments. They visit the living by assuming the form of clouds. It is not clear what happens to the spirits of women and children. Wives apparently may join their husbands in the village, but some say the spirits of children are turned into water monsters.

The Hopi dead do not go to a lake, but to the sacred mountains. The Hopi have numerous and clearly defined kachinas. Upon burial the Hopi address a body, saying it is no longer Hopi but changed into a kachina and has become "cloud." The body is given a food offering and instructed to eat, and told, "When you get yonder, you will tell the chiefs to hasten the rain clouds here."

Kachinas also are represented by dolls, which are made for educational purposes for children; among the Powamu the dolls are given to women who want children. Kachina dolls are not idols and are never worshiped. Production of kachina dolls for sale to the public is an important modern craft among the Hopi, who have kept alive much of their rich ceremonial life, which dates to pre-Columbian times.

Sources: Ake Hultkrantz. *Native Religions of North America.* San Francisco: Harper & Row, 1987; Hamilton A. Tyler. *Pueblo Gods and Myths.* Norman, OK: University of Oklahoma Press, 1964; Ruth M. Underhill. *Red Man's Religion.* Chicago: University of Chicago Press, 1965.

Kahuna

See **Huna.**

Kali Yuga

In Hinduism the present age, lasting 432,000 years and characterized by degeneration, violence, ignorance, sorrow, materialism, waning religion, chaos, and evil. A Hindu verse states that the age of Kali Yuga is so abominable that if a person tells the truth, he will be beaten, but if he lies, cheats, and bluffs, he will be liked and accepted. Kali Yuga also is called the "Dark Age" and "Age of Iron."

According to the *Mahabharata* and other texts of the Puranic period (c. A.D. 400 and later), the material universe has a finite life. Time is measured by the *kalpa,* a day in the life of Brahma, the creator. One *kalpa* equals 4,320,000,000 earth years. The day is divided into a thousand cycles of four ages, or yugas. In the morning of a *kalpa,* Brahma creates the three worlds of Earth, Heaven, and Hell, which then begin to deteriorate through the next three yugas. The last is Kali Yuga, which began about five thousand years ago. By the end of Kali Yuga, the degeneration is so great that Brahma destroys the world, appearing as Kalki, an armed warrior mounted on a white horse, wielding a sword of destruction. In some accounts the destruction is wreaked by Vishnu, the protector of the universe, who appears as Kalki. The wicked die,

the good are saved, and the world is created over again. In still other accounts, Vishnu must incarnate as an avatar of Krishna and save the world from Kali, consort of Shiva and goddess of annihilation and destruction.

This process is repeated until Brahma lives one hundred years (the equivalent of 311 trillion, 40 million earth years) and then dies. His death marks the end of the material universe in a giant cataclysm.

In the age of Kali Yuga, people forget their spiritual aim in life and become captivated by the glitter of material things. Lifespans shorten. In Satya Yuga, the golden age, the average lifespan is 100,000 years. In Treta Yuga, the silver age, it drops to 10,000 years, then to one thousand years in Dvapara Yuga, the bronze age. At the beginning of Kali Yuga, it is one hundred years.

The evil effects of Kali Yuga may be counteracted with yoga, chanting, and spiritual devotion. Madame Helena P. Blavatsky, the cofounder of Theosophy, said Kali represents the fall of humankind, and must be overcome before nirvana can be attained. She said the symbol of Kali Yuga is the reversed pentacle, the sign of human sorcery.

Some Hindus and Buddhists believe that the seven rishis, mythical guardians of the human race and keepers of the sacred knowledge, are watching over the earth through the Dark Age from their places high in the Himalayas. See **Yoga.**

Sources: H. P. Blavatsky. *Isis Unveiled: A Master Key to the Mysteries of Ancient and Modern Science and Theology.* London & Benares: The Theosophical Publishing Society, 1910; H. P. Blavatsky. *The Secret Doctrine.* Abridged ed. by Katherine Hillard. New York: Quarterly Book Dept., 1907; Joseph Campbell. *The Masks of God.* Vol. 4, *Oriental Mythology.* New York: Viking Penguin, 1962; W. Y. Evans-Wentz, ed. *Tibet's Great Yogi Milarepa: A Biography from the Tibetan.* 2d ed. London: Oxford University Press, 1951; Joseph L. Henderson and Maud Oakes. *The Wisdom of the Serpent.* New York: Collier Books, 1963; A. C. Bhaktivedanta Swami Prabhupada. *The Path of Perfection: Yoga for the Modern Age.* Los Angeles: The Bhaktivedanta Book Trust, 1979.

Karate

See **Martial arts.**

Karma

In Hinduism and Buddhism, mental and physical deeds that determine the consequences of one's life and rebirth.

Karma is Sanskrit for "deed." In Hinduism karma includes deeds, the consequences of one's life or one's previous life or lives, and the entire chain of cause and effect. There are three types of karma: *agami-karma,* which concerns present causes and effects and which provides influence over the future through the present; *prarabdha-karma,* which is already caused and is in the process of being effected; and *sanchita-karma,* which is accumulated but yet to be effected. The playing out of karma can take place over many lifetimes.

The individual is solely responsible for his or her karma, reaping joy or sorrow as a result of thoughts and deeds. The karma arises from one's *samskaras,* the thoughts, impressions, and attributes accumulated over lifetimes that make up one's character. Karma can be either good or bad with relative consequences. All karma, good or bad, creates more karma. Only the attainment of enlightenment eliminates new karma and the need to reincarnate.

In Buddhism and Zen Buddhism, karma (or *kamma,* as it is called in Pali) is the universal law of cause and effect that may be played out over a cycle of rebirths. Karma is created by the body (acts), mouth (words), and mind (thoughts), and also arises out of intent, even if intent is not carried out. Karma is overcome by adherence to the Three Pure Precepts: cease evil, do good for others, and keep a pure mind. Only when one is free of delusion, hate, and desire is one free of the cause and effect of karma.

Karma generally is viewed as inescapable, though techniques exist to try to mitigate it through meditation and mantra chanting.

The closest Christian equivalent of karma is the biblical tenet that one reaps what one sows. However, since Christianity rejects rebirth and reincarnation, the consequences of one's life on earth are meted out in the eternal afterlife.

Karma is featured in the trance readings of American medium Edgar Cayce, which include past lives. Cayce said that the effects of karma can be symbolic instead of literal, and that karma could be mitigated by "the law of grace." He said the law of grace was both a state of mind and a gift from God, and involved forgiveness, a cessation of harming others. Cayce attributed the physical deformities, debilities, and illnesses of many of his clients to karma from past lives.

Scientific investigation of cases of alleged spontaneous recall of past lives, particularly among Hindu and Buddhist children, show no significant evidence in support of karma. However, there are cases of birthmarks corresponding to death wounds alleged from previous lives, as well as carry-over phobias and philias.

People who undergo hypnotic past-life regression often feel their present lives are the karma of past lives. This could be the result of cultural expectation concerning reward and punishment for good and bad deeds. See **Bodhisattva; Dharma; Reincarnation; Soul mate.**

Sources: Gina Cerminara. *Many Mansions.* 1950. New York: Signet/New American Library, 1978; Gina Cerminara. *Many Lives,*

Many Loves. New York: William Sloane Assoc., 1963; *The Encyclopedia of Eastern Philosophy and Religion.* Boston: Shambhala, 1989; Rosemary Ellen Guiley. *Tales of Reincarnation.* New York: Pocket Books, 1989; Tenzin Gyatso, His Holiness the Fourteenth Dalai Lama. *Kindness, Clarity, and Insight.* Ithaca, NY: Snow Lion Publications, 1984; Manly Palmer Hall. *Reincarnation: The Cycle of Necessity.* Los Angeles: The Philosophical Research Society, 1956; His Holiness the Dalai Lama of Tibet. *My Land and My People: Memoirs of the Dalai Lama of Tibet.* 1962. New York: Potala Corp., 1977; Lynn Elwell Sparrow. *Reincarnation: Claiming Your Past, Creating Your Future.* San Francisco: Harper & Row, 1988; Ian Stevenson. *Children Who Remember Previous Lives.* Charlottesville, VA: University Press of Virginia, 1987; Ian Stevenson. *Twenty Cases Suggestive of Reincarnation.* 2d ed. Charlottesville, VA: University Press of Virginia, 1974; Mary Ann Woodward. *Edgar Cayce's Story of Karma.* New York: Coward, McCann & Geohegan, 1971.

Ki

See **Universal life force.**

Kilner, Walter

See **Aura.**

King, Bruce (1897–1976)

Best known in the occult world as "Zolar," King established one of the largest distribution firms of occult literature in the world, a business he said he entered into accidentally.

King was born in Chicago. He worked as an actor, clothing model and salesman, stockbroker, and part owner of radio stations.

When a popular astrologer named "Kobar" quit at one of his stations, King took over the daily horoscope program,

even though he knew nothing about astrology. At the same time, he became a partner in a venture to install horoscope-dispensing machines in movie theaters. The machines were so successful that King left the radio business. He expanded by distributing horoscopes through stores, using the pseudonym Zolar, based on the word zodiac and probably influenced by Kobar.

As Zolar King sold hundreds of millions of horoscopes around the world. He also cast personal astrological charts, and marketed astrological records and dream interpretations. He distributed Tarot cards, talismans, incense, stones, scarabs, and other occult merchandise. He wrote books, such as *Zolar's Horoscope & Lucky Number Dream Book* and *Zolar's Encyclopedia of Ancient and Forbidden Knowledge.*

King acknowledged that he did not have the astrological aspects for becoming an astrologer. He liked to point out, however, that he was born on the cusp of Leo and Cancer, an auspicious sign for business management. King died on January 16, 1976. See **Astrology.**

Sources: John Godwin. *Occult America.* New York: Doubleday, 1972; Leslie A. Shepard, ed. *Encyclopedia of Occultism and Parapsychology.* 2d ed. Detroit: Gale Research Co., 1984.

Kirlian photography

A technique for photographing objects in the presence of a high-frequency, high-voltage, low-amperage electrical field, the photographs of which show glowing, multicolored emanations said to be auras or biofields. Kirlian photography is named after Semyon Kirlian, part-time inventor and electrician from Krasnodar, Russia, who pioneered work with the procedure in the early 1940s. The process remains highly controversial.

There is no evidence that Kirlian photography is a paranormal phenome-

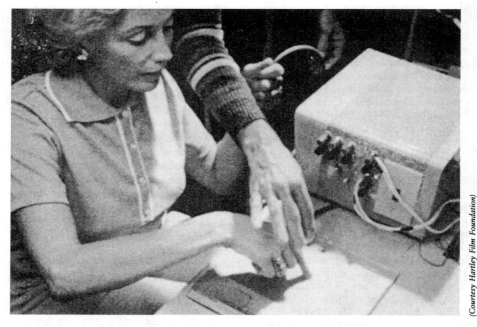

Kirlian photography of fingertips in lab of Dr. Thelma Moss, University of California at Los Angeles

(Courtesy Hartley Film Foundation)

non. Some researchers say it reveals a physical form of psychic energy. Others believe that it reveals the etheric body, one of the layers of the aura believed to permeate all living things, and that an understanding of this energy will lead to greater insights into medicine, psychology, psychic healing, psi, and dowsing. Critics say the technique shows nothing more than a discharge of electricity, which can be produced under certain conditions.

Prior to Kirlian's work, the process of photographing objects in electrical fields was generally known as "electrography" or "electrographic photography." Little value was seen in the process, which received scant attention from researchers. Electrographic photographs date to as early as 1898, when another Russian, Yakov Narkevich Yokdo (also given as Todko), displayed his work at a photographic exhibition. Research

was published by a Czech, B. Navratil, in the early 1900s. In 1939 two Czech researchers, S. Prat and J. Schlemmer, published photographs of leaves showing coronas.

Kirlian used his own-hand for his first experiment, and photographed a strange glow radiating from the fingertips. He and his wife, Valentina, a biologist, experimented with photographing both live and inanimate subjects. In the ensuing years, the couple refined their equipment and graduated from black-and-white to color photography.

The principle of Kirlian photography—and all electrography—is the corona discharge phenomenon, which occurs when an electrically grounded object discharges sparks between itself and an electrode generating the electrical field. The sparks are captured on film, appearing as coronas of light. The discharges can be affected by temperature, moisture, pressure, and other environmental factors. Various Kirlian techniques have been developed, but the most basic uses a Tesla coil connected to a metal plate. The process is similar to one that occurs in nature, when electrical conditions in the atmosphere produce luminescences and auras, such as St. Elmo's fire.

The Kirlians' work was brought to the attention of the West in the 1960s. Response in the scientific community was mixed, but sufficient interest led to a gathering of interested scientists in Alma Ata in 1966. Biophysicist Viktor Adamenko theorized that the energy field was the "cold emission of electrons," and their patterns might suggest new information about the life processes of animate objects. Adamenko and other Soviet scientists discerned that biological energies of humans were brightest at the seven hundred points on the body that coincide with Chinese acupuncture points.

Kirlian photos are said to reveal health and emotion by changes in the brightness, colors, and patterns of the light. Experiments in the 1970s, conducted by Thelma Moss and Kendall Johnson at the University of California's Center for Health Sciences at Los Angeles, showed changes in a plant's glow when approached by a human hand and pricked. When part of a leaf was cut off, a glowing outline of the amputated portion still appeared on film. Moss, Kendall, and other researchers found that the glow around humans similarly reflected changes in emotional state. Psychic healers and the psychokinetic metal-bender Uri Geller were photographed with flares of light streaming from their fingertips when engaged in their respective activities.

Some Kirlian enthusiasts consider the phantom leaf phenomenon evidence for the existence of an etheric body. However, critics say the phenomenon disproves Kirlian photography altogether: If the method truly photographed a bio-field, then the aura should disappear when an organism dies. The effect is produced solely by a high-voltage electric field breakdown of air molecules between two condenser plates.

Supporters nonetheless foresee applications of Kirlian photography in diagnostic medicine. Experiments using Kirlian photographs to detect cancer have been sporadically successful. Some researchers envision diagnostic systems that combine Kirlian photography with computerized tomography (CT) scanners (advanced versions of computerized axial tomography or CAT scanners, which utilize a thin beam of X-rays to photograph an object from 360 degrees) and magnetic resonance imaging (MRI). The latter technique uses no X-rays, but uses magnetic fields to produce images of body cells and water in tissues.

The Soviets have applied Kirlian photography in sports psychology and training as a means of assessing athletes' metabolic processes and fitness. See **Bodywork; Healing, faith and psychic; Plants, psychism of.**

Sources: Robert O. Becker, M.D., and Gary Selden. *The Body Electric: Electromagnetism and the Foundation of Life.* NY: Quill/William Morrow, 1985; Richard Gerber. *Vibrational Medicine.* Santa Fe, NM: Bear & Co., 1988; Stanley Krippner and Daniel Rubin, eds. *The Kirlian Aura: Photographing the Galaxies of Life.* Garden City, NY: Anchor Press/Doubleday, 1974; Edgar D. Mitchell. *Psychic Exploration.* Edited by John White. New York: G. P. Putnam's Sons, 1974; Sheila Ostrander and Lynn Schroeder. *Psychic Discoveries Behind the Iron Curtain.* Englewood Cliffs, NJ: Prentice-Hall, Inc., 1970; Charles Panati, ed. *The Geller Papers: Scientific Observations on the Paranormal Powers of Uri Geller.* Boston: Houghton Mifflin, 1976; Grigori Raiport. "At the Olympics, Soviet Mind Games." *The New York Times* (September 28, 1988); Peter Tompkins. *The Secret Life of Plants.* New York: Harper & Row, 1973.

Knight, JZ (b. 1946)

Channel for "Ramtha, the Enlightened One," said to be an entity who lived on earth 35,000 years ago. Ramtha rose to great popularity in the 1980s with the help of publicity associated with celebrities, including actress Shirley MacLaine.

JZ Knight was born Judith Darlene Hampton on March 16, 1946, in Dexter, New Mexico. One of nine children, she grew up in poverty in New Mexico and Texas. According to her own account, she suffered sexual abuse as a child. She had no early paranormal gifts.

After attending Lubbock Business College in Lubbock, Texas, she married Caris Hensley, a gas station attendant, with whom she had two sons, Brandy and Christopher. The marriage ended in divorce. She then went to work as a cable television salesperson in Roswell, New Mexico, and Tacoma, Washington. During this time she adopted the initials "JZ," J for Judy and Z for her nickname, "Zebra," a reflection of her affinity for black-and-white clothing.

A psychic told her she had "the most awesome power" walking with her, but it did not manifest until 1977. Following her marriage that year to Jeremy Wilder, a dentist, she became interested in the alleged power of pyramids. While she and Jeremy played with pyramids one day, a great, glowing man suddenly appeared in her kitchen and introduced himself as "Ramtha, the Enlightened One."

Ramtha proved to be oddly egotistical and materialistic for an enlightened being, unlike other alleged channeled entities such as Seth, Lazaris, and the unnamed beings who worked with Betty and Stewart Edward White. Ramtha demonstrated a penchant for appearing in kingly raiment and said he had been "the Great Ram" ("the Great God") of the Hindu people, the first conqueror of Earth. Knight was one of his daughters, Ramaya, in his last earthly life. He re-nounced his bloodthirsty ways after becoming so enlightened that he ascended directly from earth to become one with the Unknown God.

Ramtha directed Knight to "become a light unto the world." After a brief study of occultism and mediumship, Knight began channeling Ramtha for family and friends. In November 1978 she gave her first public session, which greatly increased her demand. Ramtha directed her to start charging money.

The channeling strained her marriage, and in 1981 Knight left Wilder for her professed soul mate, Jeff Knight, a trainer of Arabian horses whose picture she had seen in a magazine, and who became her third husband. See **Soul mate.**

Shirley MacLaine became a follower for a while; MacLaine believed that she had been Ramtha's brother in Atlantis. Following the publicity from MacLaine's book *Dancing in the Light* (1985), Knight's following grew enormously. Followers seemed not to mind that Ramtha preached such unoriginal messages as "you are God (God is within)," love yourself, take control of your life, and everyone creates his or her own reality. His messages became increasingly dark. He spoke of impending cataclysms and directed followers to move to the Pacific Northwest, where they would be safe.

Knight built a 13,000-square-foot home with an indoor pool in Yelm, Washington, sixty-five miles south of Seattle. There she established the Messiah Arabian Stud ranch, where forty horses were housed in a stable with chandeliers. Some followers invested in the horses upon Ramtha's advice, but later became unhappy with the advice.

In the late 1980s, Knight encountered financial and legal problems, and in early 1989 she filed for divorce from Jeff. She continued to channel Ramtha. See **Channeling; New Age.**

Sources: Alf Collins. "City Gritty." *The Seattle Times* (March 2, 1989): D3; George

---

Hackett with Pamela Abramson. "Ramtha, a Voice From Beyond." *Newsweek* (December 15, 1986): 42; Jon Klimo. *Channeling: Investigations on Receiving Information from Paranormal Sources.* Los Angeles: Jeremy P. Tarcher, 1987; JZ Knight. *A State of Mind: My Story.* New York: Warner Books, 1987; Katharine Lowry. "Channelers." *Omni* (October 1987): 47–50+; Elizabeth Rhodes. "State of Mind: JZ Knight Preaches Self-love through a 35,000-year-old Spirit." *The Seattle Times* (October 25, 1987): K1+; *Ramtha.* Edited by Steven Lee Weinberg with Randall Weischedel, Sue Ann Frazio, and Carol Wright. Eastsound, WA: Sovereignty, Inc., 1986.

Knights Templar

See Order of the Knights Templar.

Krippner, Stanley

See Dreams; Healing, faith and psychic.

Krishnamurti (1895–1986)

Although he was perhaps one of the most influential spiritual teachers of the twentieth century, Jiddu Krishnamurti (Jiddu is the surname) led no school, nor did he believe in any one path to truth. Instead he denounced all occult theories, organizations, and structured methods as impediments to the search for true reality.

Krishnamurti was born on May 12, 1895, in India, the eighth child of nine in a Brahmin family. His mother sensed his destiny was one of sacred greatness, and gave birth in the home's holy *puja* room, dedicated to the devotion of household gods.

Despite expectations Krishnamurti performed poorly in school, causing teachers and other adults to label him mentally retarded. Nonetheless, at age fourteen he caught the attention of C. W. Leadbeater, who shared with Annie Bes-

(Photo by KARSH Ottawa. Courtesy Krishnamurti Foundation.)

Jiddu Krishnamurti

ant the leadership of the Theosophical Society. Besant, and Madame Helena P. Blavatsky before her, predicted the coming of a bodhisattva, or World Teacher and Lord, Maitreya (the fifth and final Buddha). Leadbeater believed that in Krishnamurti he had found the vehicle.

By early 1909 Krishnamurti and his younger brother, Nityananda, had become wards of the society and were sent to England to enroll at Oxford. Leadbeater and Besant called Krishnamurti "Alcyone" from "Halcyon," the brightest star in the constellation Pleiades. Leadbeater used his clairvoyance to investigate Krishnamurti's past lives and determined that he had been a teacher and healer for generations, and had served as a disciple of Buddha. Krishnamurti joined the society's Esoteric Section, its inner group, in late 1909. In January 1910 he was formally accepted by the Mahatma Master Koot Hoomi (K.H.) and was initiated into the Great White Brotherhood. He was supposedly greeted by the Masters Jesus, Comte de St. Germain, Serapis, Hilarion, Morya, Djwal Kul, K.H., and the Lord Maitreya, who was to incarnate in Krishnamurti's body. Krishnamurti wrote that their acceptance of him was like great sunshine. His notes of the experiences formed the basis of his first book, *At the Feet of the Master,* which most critics ascribe solely to Leadbeater.

Besant and Leadbeater established the Order of the Star of the East in early 1911 as a separate Theosophical organization, with Krishnamurti as its head. In 1922 Besant bought six acres in Ojai, California, where Krishnamurti eventually made his home and which, with the acquisition of more property, became the home of the Krishnamurti Foundation in America.

In August 1922 Krishnamurti began experiencing a profound and extremely painful spiritual awakening. He suffered excruciating headaches, visions, and convulsions, shuddering and moaning, and semiconsciousness, much as a person possessed. These seizures and spiritual manifestations lasted for several years and formed the basis for Krishnamurti's later orientation. He called the ordeal "an inward cleansing." See **Kundalini; Spiritual emergence.**

All this time Nityananda had been gravely ill. Krishnamurti pleaded with the Masters for his brother's life and believed completely in their powers of intercession. When Nityananda died in November 1925, Krishnamurti lost all belief in the incarnated Masters and rarely referred to them. At the 1927 Order of the Star conference, he exhorted his followers to be free of all books, associations, teachers, and authorities.

By 1928 Krishnamurti spoke openly of disbanding the Order of the Star and did so in a public address on August 3, 1929. His speech summed up his philosophy, one that he adhered to throughout his life: Truth cannot be reached by any path, religion, or sect. To find truth the seeker must strive to ascend to it through his or her own discovery. Krishnamurti

did not want followers but sought to set humankind free, which would bring eternal happiness and the total realization of self.

Krishnamurti resigned from the Theosophical Society in 1930. He spent most of his time in Ojai in meditation and observation of nature. By the late 1940s, Krishnamurti had honed the five communications skills that became the hallmarks of his teaching: public talks, dialogues and discussions, personal interviews, casual insights made on walks or at dinner, and silence.

He taught that true understanding was attained only through complete awareness of the mind and its images mirrored in relationships. In order to reach that state, people must come to terms with the following psychological processes in order to free themselves:

1. Awareness: A state of total attention, in which the mind does not struggle or concentrate, does not organize impressions, analyze, or even think. At complete attention thought does not exist, only absorption of observations. Such a state is true meditation.

2. Thought: Accumulated memories, knowledge, and experience, probably arising from conditioning or past response. It is thought that produces each "me." For awareness to function, thought must be silent and still.

3. Imagination: The preconceived images, opinions, ideas, and judgments that distort our perceptions. These images let one compare oneself to others and create psychological and cultural barriers between oneself and others. As with thought, images end with unconditional observation.

4. Conditioning: The shaping of each person by his or her past experiences and thoughts. The only way to break through conditioning is through awareness and acceptance of "what is" without making choices.

5. Knowledge and Learning: Past thoughts and images, which are unable to bring anything new into being, are knowledge. Learning is an active state defined by doing, made possible through awareness without assumptions.
6. Fear, Memory, Attachment, and Dependence: The pleasures, pains, and bonds of past experience. By continually seeking pleasure, the mind is inviting pain and fear of pleasure's end. Only when thought does not interfere can fear be understood.
7. Conflict: The divisive nature of thought, which results in fragmentation and violence. Krishnamurti abhorred all violent response, war, and interpersonal conflict.
8. Relationship: An understanding of the self coming from total unification both physically and psychologically. Thought destroys relationship, salvaged only through awareness.
9. Intelligence: The seeing of what "is." True intelligence has nothing to do with knowledge or thought, but exists only through harmony and the "stillness" of the mind, bringing freedom from thought without conflict and violence.

Krishnamurti also taught that systems do not transform people: people transform systems. He believed real change—revolution—occurred when people moved from sense perceptions to values unencumbered by outside influences.

Seven schools worldwide offer Krishnamurti's approach to learning and personal self-discovery: one in Ojai, one at Brockwood Park, Hampshire, England, and five in India.

Krishnamurti died at Pine Cottage, Ojai, on February 17, 1986. He left orders forbidding any funerary ceremonies or deification of his life. Following cremation his ashes were divided into three parts: one-third for Ojai, one-third for England, and one-third for India, where they were poured into the Ganges River and into the ocean off Adyar. See **Theosophy.**

Sources: Peter Butcher. "The Phenomenological Psychology of J. Krishnamurti." *The Journal of Transpersonal Psychology* 18, no. 1 (1986): 35–50; Bruce F. Campbell. *Ancient Wisdom Revived: A History of the Theosophical Movement.* Berkeley: University of California Press, 1980; Pupul Jayakar. *Krishnamurti: A Biography.* San Francisco: Harper & Row, 1986; Jiddu Krishnamurti. *Krishnamurti's Journal.* San Francisco: Harper & Row, 1982; Krishnamurti Foundation of America, Ojai, California.

Kulagina, Nina

See **Parapsychology; Psychokinesis (PK).**

Kundalini

A psycho-spiritual energy, the very energy of consciousness, said to reside sleeping within the body, and which is aroused either through spiritual discipline or spontaneously to bring new states of consciousness, including mystical illumination. *Kundalini* is Sanskrit for "snake" or "serpent power," so-named because it is said to lie coiled like a serpent in the root chakra at the base of the spine. In Tantra Yoga *kundalini* is an aspect of Shakti, divine female energy and consort of Shiva.

The power of *kundalini* is enormous, and individuals who have experienced it say it is beyond description. The phenomena associated with it vary, and include bizarre physical sensations and movements, pain, clairaudience, visions, brilliant lights, superlucidity, psychical powers, ecstasy, bliss, and transcendence of self. *Kundalini* has been described as liquid fire and liquid light.

Knowledge and cultivation of *kundalini* has been most developed in Indian yoga, which seeks to transmute the energy into higher consciousness. *Kundalini* was considered a rarity in the West prior to the 1970s, when increasing scientific interest was directed to consciousness. In 1932, for example, psychiatrist Carl G. Jung and others observed that the *kundalini* experience was seldom seen in the West.

However, various examinations of mystical literature and traditions show that *kundalini*, known by various names, apparently has been a universal phenomenon in esoteric teachings for perhaps three thousand years. *Kundalini*-type descriptions or experiences are found in the esoteric teachings of the Egyptians, Tibetans, Chinese, some Native Americans, and the !Kung bushmen of Africa. *Kundalini* has been interpreted from the Bible as "the solar principle in man," and is referenced in the Koran, the works of Plato and other Greek philosophers, alchemical tracts (the philosopher's stone), and in Hermetic, Kabbalistic, Rosicrucian, and Masonic writings.

Since the 1970s *kundalini* awakenings have been reported with increasing frequency in the West. There are perhaps two major reasons: More people have been undertaking spiritual disciplines likely to liberate the energy, and more people are aware of what *kundalini* is, and therefore more likely to recognize the symptoms of it.

Not all *kundalini* awakenings follow the classic model set forth in yoga, but seem to vary in intensity and duration. The yogi meditates to arouse the *kundalini* and raise it up through his or her body. (Not all types of yoga are devoted to *kundalini* arousal. See **Yoga.**) First, the yogi feels a sensation of heat at the base of the spine, which may be intensely hot or pleasantly warm. The energy then travels up a psychic pathway parallel to the spinal column. The *sushumna* is the central axis, crisscrossed in a helix by the *ida* and *pingala*. As it rises the *kundalini* activates the *chakras* in succession. See

Chakras. The body becomes cold and corpse-like as the *kundalini* leaves the lower portions and continues its rise. The yogi is likely to shudder, tremble, or rock violently, feel extreme heat and cold, hear strange but not unpleasant sounds, and see various kinds of light, including an inner light. The duration of the *kundalini* may be fleeting, or last several minutes. The goal is to raise the energy to the crown *chakra*, where it joins with Shiva, the male polarity, and brings illumination. The yogi then seeks to lower the energy to another *chakra*, but not below the heart *chakra*; descent to the bottom *chakras* invites ego inflation, rampant sexual desire, and a host of other ills. By repeatedly raising the energy to the crown, the yogi can succeed in having the *kundalini* rest permanently there.

Kundalini is said to open new pathways in the nervous system; the pain associated with it apparently is due to the inability of the nervous system to immediately cope with it. Yogis stress that the body must be properly attuned for *kundalini* through yoga, and that a premature or explosive awakening can cause insanity or death.

Western psychologists and psychiatrists have determined that individuals can experience minor *kundalini* awakenings that may not occur explosively, but gradually over a period of time, thus creating cycles of *kundalini* states in which an individual thinks, acts, and feels markedly different. Symptoms include involuntary, jerky, or spasmodic body movements and postures; pain; unusual breathing patterns; paralysis; tickling, itching, vibrating sensations; hot and cold sensations; inner sounds, such as roaring, whistling, and chirping; insomnia; hypersensitivity to environment; unusual or extremes of emotion; intensified sex drive; distortions of thought processes, from inability to think clearly to superlucidity; detachment; dissociation; sensations of physical expansion; and out-of-body experiences. Symptoms generally can be alleviated by introduction of a heavier diet and temporary cessation of meditation. These lesser-degree experiences indicate that the definition of a *kundalini* awakening may have to be expanded from that of the coiled serpent of yoga.

One of the most dramatic cases of classic *kundalini* awakening occurred to Gopi Krishna (1903–1984), of India, who meditated every morning for three hours for seventeen years. On Christmas Day in 1937, he had an explosive, roaring *kundalini* awakening of liquid light pouring up his spine and into his brain. According to his own account, he rocked and went out of his body enveloped in a halo of light. He felt his consciousness expand in all directions, and a vision of a silvery luster unfolded before him; he was like a small cork bobbing on the vast ocean of consciousness. This extraordinary experience happened once again, and then Krishna was plunged into twelve years of misery, during which he "experienced the indescribable ecstasies of the mystics . . . and the agonies of the mentally afflicted." After twelve years his body apparently adapted to the new energy and he stabilized, but was permanently changed. Everything he saw appeared bathed in a silvery glow. He heard an inner cadence, called the "unstruck melody" in *kundalini* literature. Eventually, he was able to reexperience the bliss just by turning his attention inward. He became, he said, "a pool of consciousness always aglow with light." His creativity soared, and he wrote poetry and nonfiction books.

Krishna devoted much of the remainder of his life to learning everything he could about *kundalini*. He considered it "the most jealously guarded secret in history" and "the guardian of human ev-

olution." He believed it to be the driving force behind genius and inspiration. He also believed that the brain has within it the blueprint for humankind to evolve into a higher level of consciousness, one that will make use of *kundalini*. In educating others about it, Krishna told how it regenerates and restores the body, and thus could be useful in discovering ways to improve health and lengthen life. He also suggested it could be useful in eradicating such conditions as mental retardation.

Krishna was keen to see *kundalini* awakening cultivated, especially in the West. Some researchers following in his footsteps have disagreed with the importance he placed on *kundalini*.

Scientific research of *kundalini* remains embryonic, hampered by the nonphysical nature of the energy and its unpredictability. Another difficulty in identifying cases is the similarity of many symptoms to those caused by mental disturbance and stress. See **Inspiration; Meditation; Mystical experiences; Spiritual emergence.**

Sources: Arthur Avalon (Sir John Woodroffe). *The Serpent Power: The Secrets of Tantric and Shaktic Yoga.* 1964. 7th ed. New York: Dover Publications, 1974; Gene Kieffer, ed. *Kundalini for the New Age: Selected Writings of Gopi Krishna.* New York: Bantam Books, 1988; Gopi Krishna. *Kundalini: The Evolutionary Energy in Man.* Rev. ed. Boston: Shambhala Publications, 1970; C. W. Leadbeater. *The Chakras.* 1927. Wheaton, IL: The Theosophical Publishing Co., 1980; Lee Sannella. *The Kundalini Experience.* Lower Lake, CA: Integral Publishing, 1987; Claire Walker. "How Shall We Approach Kundalini?" *The Journal of Religion and Psychical Research* 12, no. 3 (July 1989): 129–34; Vivian Worthington. *A History of Yoga.* London: Routledge & Kegan Paul, 1982.

L

Lama

In Tibetan Buddhism a senior member of the Tibetan Order, a holy person of advanced rank and great spiritual achievement. Literally, *lama* means "superior" or "none above." Until Communist China invaded Tibet in 1959, lamas served as abbots of the monasteries, and thus had enormous influence over the secular and religious lives of the populace.

(Courtesy Office of Tibet)

Tibetan lama, Kyabje Trijang Lobsang Yeshe Yenzin Gyatso, holding scriptures

The highest of all lamas is the Dalai Lama, the titular head of the Tibetan nation, who has lived in exile since the Chinese occupation. See **Dalai Lama.**

Lamas are not the equivalent of monks (who are students), but are embodiments of Buddha himself. They are of particular importance in the Vajrayana ("Diamond Vehicle") school of Buddhism because they both teach and conduct rituals; one cannot master the teachings without them. Traditionally, before lamas can be called such, they undertake years of Buddhist meditation and philosophy, culminating in a retreat of more than three years. However, in modern times, the term "lama" is often used in addressing any Tibetan monk.

Some lamas are recognized as *tulkus,* that is, the earthly incarnation of a bodhisattva, an emanation of Buddha. See **Bodhisattva.** *Tulkus* (the term refers roughly to a "phantom body") are entitled to be called *rimpoche* (also spelled *rinpoche*), an honorific that means "Precious One."

Tulkus are identified according to tests given by other lamas and *tulkus.* Prior to death a lama may indicate the general area where he will reincarnate. Following his death a search is made for a child born in the specified area at the same time. To pass the test, he must identify objects belonging to the deceased lama. Most lamas are men. See **Trungpa, Chogyam.**

Sources: The Encyclopedia of Eastern Philosophy and Religion. Boston: Shambhala, 1989; Barbara and Michael Foster. Forbidden Journey: The Life of Alexandra David-Neel. San Francisco: Harper & Row, 1987; Christmas Humphreys. A Popular Dictionary of Buddhism. London: Curzon Press, 1984; Maurice Percheron. Buddha and Buddhism. 1956. Woodstock, NY: The Overlook Press, 1982; Leslie A. Shepard, ed. Encyclopedia of Occultism and Parapsychology. 2d ed. Detroit: Gale Research Co., 1984.

Leary, Timothy (b. 1920)

Former college instructor and one of the leading advocates during the 1960s of psychedelic drugs as a means to enlightenment. His involvement with LSD at Harvard University led to his dismissal from the faculty there, and to trouble with the law for a period of years. His signature phrase, "Turn on, tune in, and drop out," became a rallying cry of the 1960s.

Timothy Leary was born on October 22, 1920, in Springfield, Massachusetts. Early on he demonstrated a penchant for challenging authority: He was expelled from high school and Holy Cross College, was silenced at the US Military Academy at West Point, New York, and was expelled from the University of Alabama. He earned his Ph.D in psychology from the University of California at Berkeley in 1950, and taught there as an assistant professor from 1950 to 1955. On October 22, 1955, his wife, Marianne, whom he had married in 1944 and with whom he had two children, committed suicide.

In 1959 Leary became interested in the experimental use of psychedelics in psychology. The same year he accepted a position at Harvard University in the Center for Personality Research. There he met Richard Alpert, an assistant professor who became his colleague in experimental drug research.

In 1960 Leary went to Mexico, where he had his first psychedelic experience after ingesting magic mushrooms; it took him on a trip through evolution, he said. He proposed systematic drug experiments with psilocybin at Harvard, using graduate students and other volunteers.

From its beginning the drug program was both controversial (among the faculty) and popular (among the students). Participants included the beat intelligentsia, such as Jack Kerouac, Arthur Koestler, Allen Ginsberg, Aldous Huxley, and Neal Cassady, as well as Harvard divinity students and Massachusetts prisoners. Leary was profoundly influenced by Ginsberg, who advocated that everyone should take psychedelics. Leary came to see drugs as instant enlightenment for the masses.

In 1962 Leary took LSD for the first time and described it as "the most shattering experience of my life," and one which permanently changed him. He and Alpert then introduced LSD into their drug research program. Leary envisioned that society would be transformed and rid of evils if everyone turned on. He and Alpert discussed the possibilities of dumping LSD in public water supplies. The controversy at Harvard escalated, and when reports began to surface of bad trips and parental objections, Leary and Alpert attempted to find outside funding to carry on their work. They formed the International Foundation for Internal Freedom and planned to move the research to Mexico, but soon were expelled from there, as well as from the Island of Dominica.

Leary and Alpert were dismissed from Harvard in 1963. They established the Castalia Foundation and carried on a communal life-style and research effort in a house in Millbrook, New York. In 1964 Leary married his second wife, Nanette, but the marriage came apart on the honeymoon to Japan and India. Back at Millbrook Leary met and married his third wife, Rosemary Woodruff, in 1965. The Millbrook house was closed down and Leary and Alpert parted ways. Alpert pursued spiritual studies in India, and eventually changed his name to Ram Dass. See **Ram Dass.**

In 1965 Leary's troubles with the law began. In 1970 he was sentenced to a total of twenty years in prison by judges in Houston, Texas, and Santa Ana, California, on separate charges of possession of marijuana. He was incarcerated in the California Men's Colony west in San Luis Obispo, California, but after several months managed to escape with the help of friends in the Weathermen and Black Panthers.

Leary fled to Europe, where he hid in Switzerland and experimented with heroin. He was captured in 1973 and extradited to the United States, where he was incarcerated for thirty-two months on drug and escape charges. During his jail time, he was aided by a friend, Joanna Harcourt-Smith, who legally changed her last name to Leary to help his publicity cause. They parted ways when Leary was released.

In 1978 he married his fourth wife, Barbara. He has lectured widely on the college and New Age conference circuits. He is the author or coauthor of numerous books and monographs on the psychedelic experience. See **Drugs in mystical and psychic experiences.**

Sources: Timothy Leary. *Flashbacks: An Autobiography.* Los Angeles: Jeremy P. Tarcher, 1983; Timothy Leary. *Changing My Mind, Among Others.* Englewood Cliffs, NJ: Prentice-Hall, 1982; Leslie A. Shepard, ed. *Encyclopedia of Occultism and Parapsychology.* 2d ed. Detroit: Gale Research Co., 1984.

Lemniscate

A powerful occult symbol that looks like a figure eight lying on its side. The lem-niscate signifies eternity, infinity, regeneration, the Holy Spirit, infinite wisdom, and higher consciousness. Its serpentine shape has no beginning and no end, and represents the endless spiraling and balancing of opposing forces in the universe. The lemniscate appears in various interpretations of the Tarot, and is used in meditation as a symbol for focusing concentration. In mathematics it represents infinity. See **Symbol.**

Sources: Francis Barrett. *The Magus.* Secaucus, NJ: The Citadel Press, 1967; J. E. Cirlot. *A Dictionary of Symbols.* New York: Philosophical Library, 1971; Eileen Connolly. *Tarot: A New Handbook for the Apprentice.* Van Nuys, CA: Newcastle Publishing, 1979; Craig Junjulas. *Psychic Tarot.* Dobbs Ferry, NY: Morgan & Morgan, 1985; Arthur Edward Waite. *The Pictorial Key to the Tarot.* Secaucus, NJ: Citadel Press, 1959.

Lemuria

Legendary lost continent of the Indian Ocean said to be the original Garden of Eden and the cradle of the human race.

The theory of the existence of Lemuria arose in the nineteenth century, when scientists sought to explain Darwin's theory of evolution of similar species from a common ancestor. Philip Sclater, an English zoologist, suggested that a land bridge once existed during the Eocene Age from the Malay Archipelago to the south coast of Asia and Madagascar, thus connecting India to southern Africa. The theory explained why such animals as the lemur are found primarily on Madagascar and in parts of Africa, but also in India and the Malay Archipelago. Sclater coined the name "Lemuria" after the lemur.

Sclater's hypothesis was supported by other scientists, including Ernst Haeckel, T. H. Huxley, and Alfred Russell Wallace. Haeckel, a German biologist, proposed that the lost continent also had been "the probable cradle of the human race."

Madame Helena P. Blavatsky, cofounder of Theosophy, believed that Lemuria had been inhabited by the Third Root Race of humankind, whom she described as fifteen-feet-tall, brown-skinned hermaphrodites with four arms; some had a third eye in the back of the skull. Their bizarre feet, with protruding heels, enabled them to walk either forward or backward. Their eyes were set far apart in their flat faces so that they could see sideways. They had highly developed psychic powers and communicated by telepathy. Their continent, which covered most of the southern hemisphere, broke up and was destroyed. The Lemurians migrated to Atlantis, where they evolved into the Fourth Root Race. Like the Lemurians, the Atlanteans fled the destruction of their own continent, spreading to other lands and starting the present Fifth Root Race.

W. Scott-Elliott, a Theosophist, claimed to investigate Lemuria with the help of "astral clairvoyance." He said that Lemurians originally laid eggs but evolved to reproduce as do humans. They intermingled with animals to produce apes. Beings from Venus, the "Lords of Flame," came to Lemuria and helped the race achieve reincarnation. At the height of their civilization, the Lemurian continent sank into the ocean.

Philosopher Rudolf Steiner, using information he said came from the Akashic Chronicle (Records), said Lemuria extended from Ceylon to Madagascar, and had included parts of southern Asia and Africa. He also described the Lemurians as the telepathic Third Root Race, who initially had no memory. The goal of Lemurians was to develop will and clairvoyant power of imagination in order to control the forces of nature. Lemuria was destroyed by volcanic activity.

Mu

In 1870 Colonel James Churchward, a former Bengal Lancer and a big game hunter, announced he had learned of a lost continent named Mu, once located in the Pacific Ocean with its center just south of the equator. The continent was six thousand miles long from east to west and three thousand miles wide from north to south. Churchward said he learned this from secret, ancient clay and stone tablets hidden in India, which had been revealed to him by a Hindu priest.

He said human beings first appeared on Mu some 200,000 years ago, evolving into an advanced race of about 60 million people in ten tribes. About 12,000 years ago, a massive volcanic eruption, earthquakes, and tidal waves destroyed the entire continent. Survivors escaped to other lands. Churchward claimed evidence of the existence of Mu may be found in the legends and artifacts of the ancient Greeks, Egyptians, Maya, Cliff Dwellers of North America, Chinese, Burmese, Tibetans, Cambodians, and Pacific Islanders. All the rocky islands now in the Pacific Ocean are remnants of Mu, he said. Churchward never produced the tablets to prove his "discovery." He said his research also included trance visits to previous lives. His four books on Mu generally are regarded as romantic science fiction.

Churchward was supported by Augustus Le Plongeon, a nineteenth-century French physician who was the first to excavate Mayan ruins in the Yucatan. Le Plongeon claimed the Maya and the ancient Egyptians were descendants of the "Muvians." See **Atlantis**.

Sources: H. P. Blavatsky. *The Secret Doctrine*. Abridged ed. by Katherine Hillard. New York: Quarterly Book Dept., 1907; James Churchward. *The Children of Mu*. New York: Ives Washburn, 1931; James Churchward. *The Lost Continent of Mu*. 1926. New York: Paperback Library,

1968; Rudolf Steiner. *Cosmic Memory*. San Francisco: Harper & Row, 1959; *Strange Stories, Amazing Facts*. Pleasantville, NY: Reader's Digest, 1976; Jennifer Westwood, ed. *The Atlas of Mysterious Places*. New York: Weidenfeld & Nicholson, 1987.

Leonard, Gladys Osborne (1882–1968)

Called by some "the greatest of all psychics," Gladys Osborne Leonard worked professionally as a mental medium, passing many tests of leading psychic investigators from Britain and America. Born on May 28, 1882, in Lytham, Lancashire, England, Leonard began to exhibit psychic gifts at an early age, following trauma caused by the unexpected death of a friend of the family. She began to have frequent visions of "Happy Valleys," beautiful places populated by radiantly happy people dressed in flowing, draped clothing. Her family attempted to discourage her and succeeded superficially; Leonard learned to quit talking about them, but her interest in the world of spirit continued.

Although her childhood visions disappeared, in her twenties she became interested in Spiritualism. At the age of twenty-four, when her mother was extremely ill, Leonard awoke to see a shining vision of her in good health, at the apparent moment the woman died.

Leonard pursued her psychic ability, experimenting with table-tipping at seances. At one seance she went into a trance and a spirit control named Feda emerged. Feda claimed to be her great-great-grandmother, a Hindu girl raised by a Scottish family. At age thirteen, around 1800, Feda married Leonard's great-great-grandfather, William Hamilton, and died a year later in childbirth. There was no proof of Feda's existence, though stories of such a girl had been passed down through the generations. Feda remained Leonard's control for more than forty years.

With the advent of World War I, Leonard turned professional. She became famous with her communications with the spirits of the war dead. Sir Oliver Lodge of the British Society for Psychical Research investigated her, and catapulted her into an international spotlight with *Raymond or Life and Death* (1916), an account of her alleged communications with his deceased son, who was killed in World War I in 1915.

Psychical investigators attempted to uncover fraud by having Leonard followed by private detectives; no trickery was ever found. Nor could investigators find conclusive evidence that Leonard used telepathy to obtain personal information from her sitters. Leonard had spectacular successes with proxy sittings, in which a third party, unannounced beforehand, would substitute for a sitter who was requesting information from a deceased person. She also was very successful with "book tests," in which information from books unknown to the medium and sitter would be relayed through spirits. See **Book test.**

In her later years, Leonard's sittings were often characterized by direct voices. Feda, the control, obtained information from other spirits and relayed them through Leonard, using Leonard's vocal chords. But sitters began to hear the direct voices of the other spirits themselves, whispering from a point in empty space in front of Leonard as Feda spoke through her. See **Direct-voice mediumship.**

Like her American counterpart, Leonora E. Piper, Leonard's psychic talents defied explanation by investigators. See **Mediumship; Super-ESP.** Compare to **Piper, Leonora E.**

Sources: Alan Gauld. *Mediumship and Survival*. London: William Heinemann Ltd., 1982; Rosalind Heywood. *The Sixth Sense*. London: Chatto & Windus, 1959; *Into the Unknown*. Pleasantville, NY: Reader's Digest, 1981; Sir Oliver Lodge. *Raymond or*

Life and Death. 12th ed. London: Methuen & Co. Ltd., 1919; Edgar D. Mitchell. *Psychic Exploration: A Challenge for Science.* Edited by John White. New York: Paragon Books, 1974; Susy Smith. *The Mediumship of Mrs. Leonard.* New Hyde Park, NY: University Books, 1964; Benjamin B. Wolman, ed. *Handbook of Parapsychology.* New York: Van Nostrand Reinhold, 1977.

Levitation

A phenomenon of psychokinesis (PK) in which objects, people, animals, and so on lift up into the air without known physical means and float or fly about. Levitations are said to occur in mediumship, shamanistic trance, mystical rapture and trance, magic, bewitchment, hauntings, and possession. Many cases of levitation appear to be spontaneous; some spiritual or magical adepts are said to be able to levitate consciously.

Christianity and Islam record numerous cases of levitation. In the first century, Simon Magus is said to have levitated himself from the top of the Roman Forum in a challenge to St. Peter, as proof of his magical powers. According to legend Peter prayed to God that Simon's deception be stopped, and Simon fell to earth and was killed. Roman Catholic hagiography includes many cases of levitations among saints, the most famous of which is Joseph of Cupertino (1603–1663), who reportedly levitated often and flew through the air, according to eyewitness accounts. He had the peculiar habit of giving a little shriek just before levitating.

St. Teresa of Avila said she levitated spontaneously during states of rapture. According to one eyewitness account by sister Anne of the Incarnation, Teresa levitated a foot and a half off the ground for about half an hour. Teresa wrote of one experience:

"It seemed to me, when I tried to make some resistance, as if a great force beneath my feet lifted me up. I know of nothing with which to compare it; but it was much more violent than the other spiritual visitations, and I was therefore as one ground to pieces" (Evelyn Underhill, *Mysticism,* 1955). The levitation frightened Teresa, but she observed that she could do nothing to stop it, and she did not lose her senses, but saw herself lifted up. See **Teresa of Avila, St.**

At the turn of the twentieth century, Gemma Galgani, a Passionist nun, reportedly levitated during rapture.

Levitation also is recorded in Hinduism and Buddhism. Milarepa, the great yogi of Tibet of the thirteenth century, is said to have possessed numerous occult powers, including the ability to walk, rest, and sleep while levitating—a feat said to be duplicated by Brahmins and fakirs in India. The Ninja of Japan also reportedly have this ability. In Eastern traditions levitation is said to be accomplished through use of secret breathing and visualization techniques involving the universal life force or energy, called by various names, including *prana, ch'i,* and *ki.* Louis Jacolliot, a nineteenth-century French judge who traveled about the East and wrote of his occult experiences, describes the levitation of a fakir in *Occult Science in India and Among the Ancients* (1884, 1971):

Taking an ironwood cane which I had brought from Ceylon, he leaned heavily upon it, resting his right hand upon the handle, with his eyes fixed upon the ground. He then proceeded to utter the appropriate incantations ... [and] rose gradually about two feet from the ground. His legs were crossed beneath him, and he made no change in his position, which was very like that of those bronze statues of Buddha ... For more than twenty minutes I tried to see how [he] could thus fly in the face and eyes of all known laws of gravity ... the stick gave him no visible support, and there was no apparent contact between that and his body, except through his right hand.

Jacolliot was told by Brahmins that the "supreme cause" of all phenomena was the *agasa (akasha)*, the vital fluid, "the moving thought of the universal soul, directing all souls," the force of which the adepts had learned to control. See **Universal life force.**

Levitation also is said to occur in rituals and ceremonies in shamanism and other tribal or non-Western traditions. African witch doctors have been filmed apparently levitating off the ground.

In the Western secular world, levitation sometimes has been viewed as a manifestation of evil. During the Middle Ages and Renaissance, it was common to blame any unusual phenomena upon witchcraft, fairies, ghosts, or demons. Levitation was, and still is, commonly reported in demonic possession cases. Beds, objects, and the possessed are witnessed floating up into the air. In 1906 Clara Germana Cele, a sixteen-year-old schoolgirl from South Africa, suffered demonic possession and was said to rise up to five feet into the air, sometimes vertically and sometimes horizontally. She fell if sprinkled with holy water, which witnesses took as proof of demonic possession. Similarly, poltergeist cases and hauntings are sometimes characterized by levitating objects.

Some physical mediums have been known for their alleged levitations. The most famous was Daniel Dunglas Home, who reportedly did so many times over forty years. In 1868 he was seen levitating out of a third-story window; he floated back indoors through another window. Home was not always in trance during levitations and was aware of what was happening and how he felt. He once described "an electrical fulness (sic)" sensation in his feet. His arms became rigid and were drawn over his head, as though he were grasping the unseen power which

lifted him. Home also levitated furniture and objects. The Catholic church expelled him as a sorcerer. Though Home was never exposed as a fraud, many other mediums were discovered to "levitate" objects with hidden wires and contraptions. See **Home, Daniel Dunglas.**

Italian medium Amedee Zuccarini was photographed levitating with his feet about twenty inches over a table top.

Levitation in controlled experiments is rare. In the 1960s and 1970s, researchers reported some success in levitating tables under controlled circumstances. Soviet PK medium Nina Kulagina was photographed levitating a small object between her hands.

According to skeptics levitations may be explained by hallucination, hypnosis, or fraud. Not all cases may be so dismissed, however. The most likely explanation is the one known by Eastern adepts for thousands of years, of the existence of a force which belongs to another, nonmaterial reality, and which manifests in the material world. See **Psi.**

Advanced practitioners of Transcendental Meditation have received worldwide publicity for achieving "yogic flying," a levitation that consists of low hops while seated in a lotus meditation position. It is said to be accomplished by maximizing coherence (orderliness) in brain-wave activity, which enables the brain to tap into the "unified field" of cosmic energy. Skeptics say yogic flying is accomplished through muscular action. See **Transcendental Meditation (TM).**

Most reported levitations are short, lasting a few seconds or minutes; Joseph of Cupertino once hung in the air for two hours, according to eyewitness accounts. Levitation at will seems to require intense concentration or a trance state; physical mediums who were disturbed during levitation by touch or light suddenly fell back. Saintly levitations often are accompanied by luminosities around the body.

See **Poltergeist; Psychokinesis (PK); Siddhis; Shamanism.**

Sources: Hoyt L. Edge, Robert L. Morris, John Palmer, and Joseph H. Rush. *Foundations of Parapsychology.* Boston: Routledge & Kegan Paul, 1986; Mircea Eliade. *Shamanism.* 1951. Princeton, NJ: Princeton University Press, 1964; John Ferguson. *An Illustrated Encyclopedia of Mysticism and the Mystery Religions.* New York: Seabury Press, 1976; Nandor Fodor. *An Encyclopedia of Psychic Science.* 1933. Secaucus, NJ: Citadel Press, 1966; Rosemary Ellen Guiley. *The Encyclopedia of Witches and Witchcraft.* New York: Facts On File, 1989; Louis Jacolliot. 1884. *Occult Science in India and Among the Ancients.* New Hyde Park, NY: University Books, 1971; *Maharishi's Programme to Create World Peace: Global Inauguration.* Vlodrop, Holland: Maharishi Research University, and Washington, D.C.: Age of Enlightenment Press, 1987; Ormond McGill. *The Mysticism and Magic of India.* Cranbury, NJ: A. S. Barnes & Co., 1977; Evelyn Underhill. *Mysticism.* 1955. New York: New American Library, 1974; Benjamin B. Wolman, ed. *Handbook of Parapsychology.* New York: Van Nostrand Reinhold, 1977.

Leys

Alignments and patterns of powerful, invisible earth energy said to connect various sacred sites, such as churches, temples, stone circles, megaliths, holy wells, burial sites, and other locations of spiritual or magical importance. The existence of leys is controversial. Their study is part of the so-called "earth mysteries," an area of holistic research into ancient sites and their landscapes.

If leys do exist, their true age and purpose remain a mystery. Controversy over them has existed since 1925, when Alfred Watkins, an English beer salesman and amateur antiquarian, published his research and theory in his book, *The Old Straight Track.* Watkins suggested that all holy sites and places of antiquity were connected by a pattern of lines he called "leys" (also called "ley lines," a term some say is inaccurate). Mounds, barrows, tumuli, stones, stone circles, crosses, churches built on pagan sites, legendary trees, castles, mottes and baileys, moats, hillforts, earthworks, and holy wells were all thought to stand in alignment. Using the Ordnance Survey, Watkins claimed that the leys were the "old straight tracks," which crossed the landscape of prehistoric Britain and represented all types of early human activities.

Watkins said that ancient men of the leys, called Dodman surveyors, mapped out the tracks and alignments for trade routes, astronomical sites, and holy sites. Watkins said that the alignments followed natural horizon features such as peaks, or led to other sacred sites. To support his thesis, Watkins noted the inclusion of the word "ley" in many of the villages and farms through which the alignments passed.

After Watkins's theory was published, public fascination with leys remained high until the 1940s, when it began to decline. Interest revived in the 1960s and 1970s, as part of the New Age movement. In the 1960s a magazine, *The Ley Hunter,* was established in Brecon, Wales, to chronicle theories and research. While Britain has been the chief site of investigation, there also is interest in France and the United States. Systems of straight paths also exist in Peru and Bolivia. From the Sun Temple in the center of the city of Cuzco, Peru, forty-one lines called *ceques* spread out into the country, marked by various shrines, hills, bridges, battlefields, graves, springs, and other sites, some of them astronomical sight lines. In Bolivia holy tracks have been shown to converge on Indian shrines at the tops of holy hills.

Many archaeologists and other scientists dispute the existence of leys and say the theory originated by Watkins was contrived because Watkins aligned secular and sacred sites from different periods of history.

Even ley enthusiasts are divided into differing camps. Some hold that the prehistoric alignments can be statistically validated. Others, such as Nigel Pennick of the Institute of Geomantic Research in Cambridge, England, agree but say that alignments continued in historical periods. Still others contend that leys mark paths of some sort of earth energy that can be detected by dowsing, and perhaps was sensed by early humans. The energy is compared to the flow of *ch'i,* the universal life force, found in the art of *feng shui* in China. See **Feng shui.** Points where the ley energy paths intersect are said to be prone to anomalies such as earth lights and poltergeist phenomena and reported sightings of UFOs (one theory suggests that the paths are navigational aids to extraterrestrial spacecraft). These energy leys, however, do not necessarily coincide with physical alignments of sites. See **Dowsing; Earth lights.**

Central to the controversy over leys is the question of what evidence—how many alignments over what distance—validates a ley. Among the most persuasive evidence has been documented in Cornwall, England, where researcher John Michell identified twenty-two alignments between fifty-three megalithic sites over distances up to seven miles. Despite the controversy ley researchers hope to at least come to a better understanding of ancient sacred sites, and of the people who built them. See **Megaliths; Power point.**

Sources: Janet and Colin Bord. *Ancient Mysteries of Britain.* Manchester, NH: Salem House, 1986; Janet and Colin Bord. *Mysterious Britain.* Garden City, NY: Doubleday, 1978; Peter Lancaster Brown. *Megaliths, Myths and Men.* New York: Taplinger Publishing Company, 1976; Aubrey Burl. *Rings of Stone.* New York: Ticknor & Fields, 1979; Paul Devereux and John Steele, David Kubrin. *Earthmind:*

A Modern Adventure in Ancient Wisdom. New York: Harper & Row, 1989; Havelock Fidler. *Earth Energy: A Dowser's Investigation of Ley Lines.* 2d ed. Wellingborough, Northamptonshire, England: The Aquarian Press, 1988; Francis Hitching. *Earth Magic.* New York: William Morrow, 1977; Patrick F. Sheeran. "Place and Power." *ReVision* 13, no. 1 (Summer 1990): 28–32.

Lilly, John

See **Drugs in mystical and psychic experiences; Flotation.**

Lindbergh, Charles (1902–1974)

On his historic solo, nonstop flight across the Atlantic from New York to Paris in 1927, aviator Charles Lindbergh had mystical experiences so profound he was unable to share them with the public for more than twenty years.

The flight was long, thirty-three-and-a-half hours; and at a point over the vast ocean, fatigue and tension began to alter Lindbergh's perception of reality. By the ninth hour, he felt both very detached from and very near to the world below, and it made him think of "the nearness of death" and "the longness of life."

Gradually, as he stared at his instruments, listened to the drone of his engines, and struggled to stay awake, he slipped into an altered state of consciousness that to him seemed to be both wakefulness and sleep. He was conscious of being three elements: body, which was fatigued; mind, which made decisions; and spirit, a driving force, which told him sleep was not needed and that his body would be sustained with relaxation.

He became aware that the fuselage behind him was filled with ghostly presences: vaguely outlined, transparent, weightless forms. Their appearance did not seem sudden; yet one moment they simply were there. Lindbergh, who felt that he was caught in some "unearthly age of time," was neither surprised nor afraid. He could see them without turning his head, as though his skull was "one great eye" with unlimited vision, seeing everything at once in all directions.

The beings spoke with friendly, familiar human voices, discussing the flight and navigation, reassuring Lindbergh, and giving him indescribable "messages of importance unattainable in ordinary life." They moved about freely, passing through the walls of the fuselage, diminishing and increasing in number.

Lindbergh began to lose his sense of his own physical body. He felt weightless and could no longer feel the press of his flesh against the hard stick:

I become independent of physical laws—of food, of shelter, of life. I'm almost one with these vaporlike forms behind me, less tangible than air, universal as aether. I'm still attached to life; they, not at all; but at any moment some thin band may snap and there'll be no difference between us . . .

I'm on the border line of life and a greater realm beyond, as though caught in the field of gravitation between two planets, acted on by forces I can't control, forces too weak to be measured by any means at my command, yet representing powers incomparably stronger than I've ever known . . .

Death no longer seems the final end it used to be, but rather the entrance to a new and free existence which includes all space, all time. (Lindbergh, The Spirit of St. Louis, 1953)

In his reference to "some thin band," Lindbergh may have been aware of the silvery astral cord said to connect the soul to the body, and may have sensed that the severance of the cord meant the transition from earthly life to spirit. His attitude toward death also changed, from that of an end to a beginning.

Lindbergh did not mention his experience in his book about the flight, *We, Pilot and Plane,* published later in 1927. It was not until he wrote *The Spirit of St. Louis,* published twenty-six years later in 1953, that he could bring himself to reveal the experiences. He discussed it more in *Autobiography of Values,* published posthumously in 1977. The reluctance to acknowledge mystical experiences is common; some people spend years coming to terms with them, convincing themselves the experiences were not just dreams or hallucinations. See **Altered states of consciousness; Mystical experiences.**

Sources: Charles Lindbergh. *The Spirit of St. Louis.* New York: Charles Scribner's Sons, 1953; Michael Murphy and Rhea A. White. *The Psychic Side of Sports.* Reading, MA: Addison-Wesley, 1978.—

Lodge, Sir Oliver

See **Piper, Leonora E.; Society for Psychical Research (SPR).**

Lotus

Member of the water lily family, and a sacred symbol in Hinduism, Buddhism, and to ancient Egyptians.

In Hinduism the lotus is a symbol of nonattachment. Just as the lotus floats on water but remains dry, the spiritual seeker should live in the world but not be affected by it. The pink lotus represents yoni, the female reproductive organs. The lingam, or sacred phallus, usually is depicted with the lotus. The fertility goddesses Padma (Lotus), Lakshmi, and Kali are portrayed with lotuses; one myth about Padma holds that she is born from a lotus that springs from the forehead of Vishnu, god of the phallus. The lotus also serves as an important symbol in the Hindu view of creation. The "lotus-naveled" Vishnu puts forth a giant, golden, lotus of a thousand petals, upon which is seated Brahma. The petals expand, and from them grow the mountains and flow the waters of the world. The lotus also is the motif to describe the vital chakras, energy points aligned with the body. See **Chakras.**

In Buddhism the lotus symbolizes the true nature of beings. Buddhists associate it with the birth of Buddha, and it is depicted as his throne or seat.

The seven-petaled lotus appears in Buddhist and Hindu myths, and is sometimes symbolic of the cosmos, with each petal representing a division of the heavens. The Buddhist meditational mantra *"Om mani padme hum"* means, "O, Jewel of the Lotus, Hum." See **Om.**

In the Pure Land school of Chinese and Japanese Buddhism the lotus symbolizes purity and the Buddha's doctrine.

Tibetan Buddhists also associate the lotus with purity. An exalted lama, or *rimpoche* ("The Precious Guru"), or "Lotus-Born," is believed to be born under pure, holy conditions, and is regarded as an incarnation of the essence of Buddha.

In Egypt the blue lotus is associated with the Nile, and thus with fertility. As an emblem of rebirth and immortality, the ancients used it in funeral rites, especially for women and children. Osiris, god of the underworld, was often portrayed wearing lotus headdresses; Horus, the sun god, sat upon a lotus. In Egyptian myth the lotus floating on water represented the newly created Earth.

Sources: The Encyclopedia of Eastern Philosophy and Religion. Boston: Shambhala, 1980; W. Y. Evans-Wentz, ed. *The Tibetan Book of the Dead.* London: Oxford University Press, 1960; Maria Leach, ed., and Jerome Fried, assoc. ed. *Funk & Wagnalls Standard Dictionary of Folklore, Mythology, and Legend.* San Francisco: Harper & Row, 1979; Ormond McGill. *The Mysticism and Magic of India.* Cranbury, NJ: A. S. Barnes & Co., 1977; Barbara G. Walker.

The Woman's Encyclopedia of Myths and Secrets. San Francisco: Harper & Row, 1983.

Lotus seat

The most common sitting posture used in yoga and other forms of meditation. Called *padmasana* in Sanskrit ("perfect posture"), the position requires sitting on the floor or a cushion with legs crossed so that each foot is pressed back into the stomach or is placed on top of the opposite thigh. The hands rest on the knees with palms up, thumbs and forefingers touching. The tongue is placed against the roof of the mouth. The spine and neck are kept straight. In this position the body is in repose, balance, and symmetry, like the lotus blossom. The position facilitates the flow of the universal life force through the top of the head and into the *chakras.* The organs are unobstructed, and breathing may be controlled easily.

In a half lotus posture, one foot rests against the opposite calf rather on top of the thigh or pressed into the stomach.

Both full and half lotus seats are among postures used in *zazen,* the sitting meditation of Zen. The hands, however, shape the "cosmic mudra," an oval formed with left hand overlapping right and thumbs lightly touching, held against the navel.

References to the lotus seat and other *asanas* (postures and exercises) appear in yoga literature dating back to the Upanishads, c. 900 B.C. The yogic lotus seat probably evolved from the most common, comfortable sitting posture of the day. Like other sitting, squatting, and kneeling positions used in prayer, it is considered ideal for relaxation and meditation without the hazard of falling asleep. The full lotus position is natural to Easterners, who practice it from early childhood; but most Westerners, used to sitting in chairs, find it difficult and painful to master. See **Meditation; Relaxation; Yoga.**

Sources: Robert Aitken. *Taking the Path of Zen.* San Francisco: North Point Press, 1982; Alain. *Yoga for Perfect Health.* New York: Pyramid Books, 1957; Herbert Benson, M.D. *The Relaxation Response.* New York: Avon Books, 1976; Bernard Gunther. *Energy Ecstasy and Your Seven Vital Chakras.* North Hollywood, CA: Newcastle Publishing Co., 1983; Willard Johnson. *Riding the Ox Home: A History of Meditation from Shamanism to Science.* 1982. Boston: Beacon Press, 1986; Shunryu Suzuki. *Zen Mind, Beginner's Mind.* New York & Tokyo: John Weatherhill, 1970; Vivian Worthington. *A History of Yoga.* London: Routledge & Kegan Paul, 1982.

LSD

See **Drugs in mystical and psychic experiences; Leary, Timothy; Psychology; Ram Dass.**

Lucid dreaming

See **Dreams.**

M

MacLaine, Shirley

See New Age.

Maclean, Dorothy

See Findhorn.

Macumba

Common term for the Brazilian form of Vodoun and Santería, or the worship of African deities through magic and possession of the spirit. Strictly speaking, there is no "Macumba" religion; the word refers to the two principal forms of African spiritual worship in Brazil: Candomblé and Umbanda. Macumba sometimes refers to black magic, but that cult is actually called Quimbanda.

African slaves brought to Brazil by the Portuguese in the 1550s never relinquished their religion, but syncretized it with Catholicism, keeping its gods and rituals alive in stories and secret ceremonies. The Africans also found much in common with the religious practices of the native Brazilian Indians. By the time the slaves won their independence in 1888, over fifteen generations of Brazilians—black, white, and Indian— had heard the legends of the *orishas* (gods) and how the gods' magical inter-

cession had snared a lover, saved a marriage, healed a sick baby, or eliminated a wicked enemy. Today members of all classes and races of Brazilians privately believe in some sort of ancient spiritual communion with the gods, while publicly professing Catholicism.

Candomblé

Candomblé most closely resembles the ancient Yoruban religions also worshiped in Santería, and retains the Yoruban names of the *orishas*. Spellings are Portuguese, not Spanish, however, so Changó becomes Xangó, Yemayá is Yemanjá or Iemanja, Oggún becomes Ogún, and Olorún is Olorúm. Figures of Catholic saints represent the *orishas,* although Jesus Christ, also called Oxalá, is venerated as a god on his own.

The first Candomblé center was organized in 1830 in the old capital city of Salvador, the current capital of the state of Bahia, by three former female slaves. The women took over the formerly all-male priestly duties when the men had to work in the fields. The women's role as mistresses to white Portuguese masters also elevated their status and solidified their position as spiritual leaders, since the women claimed that the freedom to worship their gods helped maintain their sexual skill and prowess. These three first high priestesses, called the "Mothers of the Saints," trained other women, called "Daughters of the Saints," to follow them, completely cutting men out of the picture. Even today men in Candomblé perform political rather than spiritual duties.

Candomblé ceremonies follow much the same pattern as those for Santería and Vodoun, with invocations to the gods, prayers, offerings, and possession of the faithful by the *orishas*. Afro-Brazilian traditions stress the importance of healing the spirit, and devotees of Candomblé believe the moment of greatest spiritual healing occurs when a person becomes one with his or her *orisha* during initiation into the cult. The stronger the orisha—gods like Xangó or Ogún—the more violent and intense the possession. Often the priest will ask the god to go gently on a new initiate, offering the orisha a sacrificed pigeon or other animal in return for mercy.

Instead of praying to Legba or Elegguá to let the spirits enter, followers of Candomblé call on the Exus, primal forces of all nature who act as divine tricksters and messengers to the gods. Connections exist between Elegguá/Legba and the Exus, however. Some of Elegguá's manifestations in Santería are called Eshus: gods of mischief, the unexpected, life and death.

One of the biggest celebrations to the Yemanjá, "goddess of the waters," takes place every January 1 live on Brazilian television. Over a million celebrants, dressed in white, wade into the ocean at dusk. A priestess, or *mao de santo* (Mother of the Saint), lights candles and then purifies and ordains new priestesses. As the sun sets, worshipers decorate a small wooden boat with candles, flowers, and figurines of the saints. At midnight the boat is launched into the bobbing waves. If the boat sinks, Yemanjá, thought to be the Virgin Mary, accepts her children's offering and promises to help and guide them for another year.

Umbanda

Umbanda was not founded until 1904 and has its origins in Hinduism and Buddhism in addition to African faiths. The teachings of Allan Kardec's Spiritism—that communication with discarnate spirits is not only possible but necessary for spiritual healing and acceptance of one's earlier incarnations—play a large part in the practices of Umbanda.

Umbanda probably derives from the Sanskrit term *aum-gandha,* meaning "divine principle." Umbandistas fear direct contact with the *orishas,* believing that such interaction is too intense for mortals. Instead spirits of divine ancestors act as mediums for communications with the gods, much like the services of a trance channeler or a Native American shaman. The gods go by their Catholic saint names in Umbanda and incorporate many features of their Indian brethren.

Ceremonies start by calling on the Exus for protection against evil. Then the Mothers or Fathers of the Saints become possessed, inviting all who are there to let themselves receive the spirits. The guide mediums are usually Native American or African ancestors, or perhaps a child who died quite young. The most popular Brazilian guides are the Old Black Man (*Preto Velho*) and Old Black Woman (*Preta Velha*), who represent the wise old slaves full of wisdom and healing. As with possession in Vodoun and Santería, those receiving the spirits assume the characteristics of their possessors, performing medicine dances, whirling to drumbeats and chants, smoking cigars and pipes (tobacco is sacred to the Indians), or bending over from advanced age and labor.

Umbandistas believe that healing of the physical body cannot be achieved without healing the spirit; opening the mind to the entrance of a spirit guide via ecstatic trance is key to spiritual growth. Spirits enter the body through the head—

this is also true in Candomblé, Santería, and Vodoun—and are perceived by the physical body through the "third eye," located in the center of the forehead. Spirits never die but travel on an eternal journey through other worlds, sometimes reincarnating in another physical body. Umbandistas believe the most enlightened spirits teach and heal through the mediums of Umbanda, and mediumship forges a link with these highly evolved minds. Each time a medium receives a spirit guide, the medium's mind and spirit are raised to another plane of consciousness.

Quimbanda

Umbandistas generally refer to "lower" or "mischievous" spirits rather than evil ones in the faith that, with education, all spirits eventually evolve to higher consciousness. But for the practitioners of Quimbanda or Cuimbanda, the spirits' evil natures are necessary for their black magic.

Like the followers of Candomblé and Umbanda, Quimbandistas call upon the Exus, but appeal to their identities as tricksters and specialists in witchcraft and sorcery. "King Exu," often identified with Lucifer, works with Beelzebub and Ashtaroth, called Exu Mor and Exu of the Crossroads. Exu of the Closed Paths inspires the most dread in Brazilians, for if prayers to this dark lord succeed, victims could lose job, lover, and family, become ill and eventually die, finding "all paths closed" unless treated by the white magic of the orishas. See Santería; Spiritism; Vodoun.

Sources: Peter Haining. The Anatomy of Witchcraft. New York: Taplinger, 1972; Francis X. King. Witchcraft and Demonology. New York: Exeter Books, 1987; A. J. Laugguth. Macumba: White and Black Magic in Brazil. New York: Harper & Row, 1975; H. John Maier, Jr. "Brazil's Black Magic." Travel Holiday (March 1987); Guy Lyon Playfair. The Unknown Power. New York: Pocket Books, 1975; D. Scott Rogo. The Infinite Boundary. New York: Dodd, Mead & Co., 1987; Alberto Villoldo and Stanley Krippner. Healing States. New York: Fireside/Simon & Schuster, 1987.

Magic

The ability to effect change in accordance with one's will and by invoking the supernatural. The change is accomplished through ritual, in which cosmic powers, supernatural forces, deities or other nonphysical beings, or the forces of nature are invoked and made subservient to the will of the magician. Magic has existed universally since ancient times. The forms of magic range from low sorcery, or spell casting, to high or ceremonial magic, which is a Western mystical path to God. All forms of magic traditionally are secret arts taught only to initiates.

The term "magic" derives from the Greek megus, meaning "great." Magic is often called "white," "black," or "gray," for good, evil, or neutral; yet magic itself is amoral—it is the magician's intent that is good or evil. Some Western practitioners of magic debate the morality of good versus evil magic; but most cultures regard magic that destroys as an acceptable means of self-defense or revenge. See Psychic attack.

According to anthropologist Bronislaw Malinowski (1884–1942), magic has three functions and three elements. The functions are to produce, protect, and destroy. The elements are spells or incantations; rites or procedures; and the consciousness of the practitioner, who undergoes a purification process that alters his or her state of consciousness. This is accomplished through various means, such as fasting, meditating, chanting, visualizing symbols, sleep deprivation, dancing, staring into flames, inhaling fumes, and taking drugs.

The simplest (and earliest) form of magic is mechanical sorcery, in which an

R.Holata Outina.

(New York Public Library)

Sorcery consultation in the New World

act is performed to achieve a result. Paleolithic cave paintings at Trois Frères, France, for example, depict images suggesting magical rituals for successful hunts. Other sorceries include tying or untying knots, blood sacrifices, sticking pins in or melting waxen images or poppets, and the like. Sorcery is also called sympathetic magic or imitative magic: By properly imitating the desired result, it will come to pass in reality. Personal items of the victim are usually essential for this type of magic, such as bits of clothing, excrement, urine, or hair or nail clippings. Another key factor is knowledge of the spell by the victim; expectation can contribute to achieving the desired result. However, some sorcerers do not disclose curses to the victims because the victims would likely hire another sorcerer to break the curse.

Every society has different strata of practitioners of magical arts, known by various names, such as witch doctor, wizard, diviner, wise woman, witch, and so on, as well as sorcerer and magician. Magic also may be the province of a priest or religious leader. Some specialize, such as in healing, divining, prophesying, and cursing. The aptitude or ability to practice such magic is usually considered to be innate and hereditary, passed down through family lines. Such individuals are likely to possess psychic skills.

In the West systems of low magic and high magic were developed by the ancient Greeks. Low magic, the sorcery of spells and potions provided for a fee, acquired an unsavory reputation for fraud by the fifth century B.C. High magic, which involved working with spirits, was akin to religion. The Neoplatonists practiced high magic.

In the ensuing centuries, as Christianity made its way throughout Europe, low magic became the sorceries, witchcraft, and folk magic of rural populations, while high magic became an intellectual and spiritual pursuit of elaborate ceremony. High magic flourished in the late Middle Ages and Renaissance as a reaction to the growing power of the church-state, which proscribed or denied all magic outside the bounds of religious miracles. It was drawn from the Hermetica, Neoplatonism, the Kabbalah, and from Oriental lore brought back to Europe by the Crusaders, and was nurtured by various secret societies, temples, and lodges. See **Freemasonry; Hermetica; Order of the Knights Templar; Rosicrucians.**

Magic was discredited by the scientific revolution of the seventeenth and eighteenth centuries, but interest was revived in the nineteenth century by occultists such as Francis Barrett and Eliphas Levi, whose respective works, *The Magus* (1801) and *Dogma and Ritual of High Magic* (1856), were influential. Magical fraternities reached a peak with the Hermetic Order of the Golden Dawn in the late nineteenth century. See **Hermetic Order of the Golden Dawn.** Golden Dawn rituals and derivative rituals continue to be practiced.

In ceremonial magic the purpose of all rituals is to unite the microcosm with the macrocosm—to call forth God or a god and join the human consciousness with its essence. The supreme purpose of ceremonial magic is union with God, in which object and subject cease to exist. It is a path of self-realization, conducted under the aegis of the Higher Self.

The initiate first learns to achieve *samadhi*, a state of one-pointed concentration, with lower forces personified as elementals and astral beings. These are akin to the primal archetypal forces residing within the magician's own collective unconscious; and through these the magician begins to understand his or her own nature. Gods and goddesses are then invoked as the magician refines the consciousness and comes to terms with the aspects of the Self that are the weakest. In Jungian terms these would comprise the Shadow. A male magician, for example, would seek to develop his anima, his female essence, by invoking a goddess.

The foundation of ceremonial magic is the Hermetic Qabalah (the spelling favored by magicians), an amalgam of the Hermetica and Jewish Kabbalah, as used by the Golden Dawn. The Tree of Life, which contains the essence of the Qabalah, provides the symbols by which a spiritual language can be communicated between beings in different states of existence, that is, God, angels, and humankind.

Ceremonial magic rituals have three basic elements: (1) love and devotion; (2) invocation; and (3) drama. While all rituals must be dramatic to be effective, drama in particular involves enactment of a deity's story, in which the magician identifies with and becomes the deity. Ritual clothing, magical tools, symbols, and colors are of utmost importance, for they attract desired magical forces to the magician. See **Ritual.**

Aleister Crowley, one of the greatest and most controversial magicians to emerge from the Golden Dawn, said that every intentional act is essentially a magical act. He believed that if more people became magicians, they would learn their true selves and purposes in life, and there would be less conflict and confusion in humanity.

Magic in the modern religion of neo-Pagan Witchcraft includes both ceremonial and low magic. Officially, there are proscriptions against using magic for anything other than benefit, and against blood sacrifice. Some traditions of modern Witchcraft have incorporated elements of other magical systems into their rites and beliefs, such as Tantra, Vodoun, Santería, and various tribal societies. See **Alchemy; Crowley, Aleister; Fortune, Dion; Grail, the; Kabbalah; Mysticism; Witchcraft.**

Sources: Isaac Bonewits. *Real Magic.* Rev. ed. York Beach, ME: Samuel Weiser, 1989;

Richard Cavendish. *The Black Arts*. New York: Perigee Books, 1967; Aleister Crowley. *Magick in Theory and Practice*. 1929. New York: Dover Publications, 1976; Dion Fortune. *The Mystical Qabalah*. 1935. York Beach, ME: Samuel Weiser, 1984; William G. Gray. *Inner Traditions of Magic*. 1970. York Beach, ME: Samuel Weiser, 1978; Rosemary Ellen Guiley. *The Encyclopedia of Witches and Witchcraft*. New York: Facts On File, 1989; Israel Regardie. *Ceremonial Magic: A Guide to the Mechanisms of Ritual*. Wellingborough, England: The Aquarian Press, 1980; Jeffrey B. Russell. *A History of Witchcraft*. London: Thames and Hudson, 1980; Charles T. Tart, ed. *Transpersonal Psychologies*. San Francisco: Harper & Row, 1975; Robert Wang. *The Qabalistic Tarot: A Textbook of Mystical Philosophy*. York Beach, ME: Samuel Weiser, 1983.

Maharaj Ji

See **Alternative religious movements**.

Maharishi Mahesh Yogi

See **Transcendental Meditation (TM)**.

Mahatmas

See **Theosophy**.

Maimonides Dream Laboratory

See **Dreams**.

Mana

See **Universal life force**.

Mandala

A design, usually circular, which appears in religion and art. The term *mandala* is Sanskrit for "circle." In Hinduism and Buddhism, the mandala has religious ritual purposes and serves as a *yantra*, a geometric-design emblem or instrument of contemplation. The mandala form also appears in Christianity, Gnosticism, and other religions, as well as in mythology, alchemy, healing practices, art, and architecture. It is used in modern psychotherapies as a therapeutic tool. In essence the mandala represents the point at which macrocosm and microcosm meet; it symbolizes the mystic's journey through various layers of consciousness to the center, which is the ultimate, supreme union with the Divine.

Mandalas may be drawn, painted, constructed in three-dimensional figures, and danced. They may also be images constructed in the mind, especially among the lamas of Tibet.

The circular shape of a mandala represents a natural and ultimate wholeness, and appears in symbols dating back to the Paleolithic Age, notably as spirals and sun wheels. Plato described the psyche in terms of a sphere. In Zen the circle signifies enlightenment.

Mandalas have three basic properties of construction: (1) a center, which signifies the Godhead, the Beginning, and the Eternal Now, or, in psychotherapy, the Self, which is the total psyche; (2) symmetry; and (3) cardinal points. The center is universal to all mandalas, while symmetry and cardinal points vary according to purposes and designs. Symmetry is comprised of concentric and counterbalanced geometric figures. The polarities often are expressed in terms of sexual tension. It is the mandala's purpose to harmonize polarities, to make order out of chaos.

Typically, the circle is oriented to four points. Sometimes this is done by squaring, in which a square is drawn around the outside of the circle; other times it is done by geometric designs, such as interpenetrating triangles, or other designs drawn within the circle.

This orientation hearkens back to Hindu and Buddhist creation myths. Before the Hindu god Brahma began creation, he stood on a thousand-petaled lotus (a mandala in itself) and looked to the four points of the compass. Similarly, Buddha, after being born, stepped onto an eight-rayed lotus flower that rose up from the earth, and looked into ten directions of space, one for each ray of the lotus, plus up and down. See Lotus. In Jungian psychology the cardinal points of the mandala are associated with thought, feeling, intuition, and sensation, which people need for psychic orientation.

Virtually anything round can be viewed as a mandala: the sun, the moon, the Earth, a clock, an equilateral cross, the zodiac, the wheel, a rotunda, a halo, a flower, a maze, a labyrinth, a rose window of a cathedral. King Arthur's Round Table is a mandala, completed by the legendary vision of the Holy Grail, which appeared in its center before a gathering of the king and his knights. Octagons also are mandala shapes. Squares and triangles suggest mandalas, since circles may be drawn within squares and vice versa. Triangles appear often in circular mandalas.

The fullest development of the mandala in ritual has occurred in Tibet, where it is believed that the mandala was introduced in the eighth century by the Tantric guru Padma Sambhava, who left a profound impact upon Tibetan Buddhism. Tibetan mandalas are elaborate, intricate, and full of concepts; the smallest details have precise symbolic meanings. The design is built up around a core structure of four circles grouped at cardinal points around a fifth circle in the center.

While the mandala is itself a symbol with form and meaning, what it symbolizes is formless: It expresses and communicates with the ineffable, a consciousness deeper than conceptual thought. It also prepares minds at ordinary levels of consciousness for what will be perceived at deeper levels in meditation. In a mandala reside innumerable deities, who are the approximate equivalents of the archetypes of the collective unconscious in Jungian thought, and the beings that are sometimes encountered on hallucinogenic mystical trips. See Drugs in mystical and psychic experiences; Flotation. The deities exist simultaneously in the mind and body of the devotee, and are related to forces existing throughout the mentally created universe. They may occasionally take on an external life force of their own. See Thought-form.

Western interest in the mandala is largely due to psychiatrist Carl G. Jung, who observed it in the works of alchemy and in medieval Christian art, notably depictions of Christ (the center) surrounded by his four evangelists at the cardinal points. (The depiction of Christ has long been associated with similar ancient Egyptian portrayals of Horus and his four sons.) Jung also studied Eastern mandalas. He found that the integrative properties of the mandala had benefit in psychotherapy; by drawing mandalas patients could begin to make order out of their inner chaos.

Mandalas are part of Navajo sand painting, a drawing made upon the Earth for the purpose of healing, and in which the patient sits at the center. See Medicine wheels; Meditation; Music; Symbol.

Sources: Jose and Miriam Argüelles. Mandala. Boston: Shambhala Publications, 1985; John Blofeld. The Tantric Mysticism of Tibet. Boston: Shambhala Publications, 1987; J. E. Cirlot. A Dictionary of Symbols. New York: Philosophical Library, 1971; C. G. Jung. Mandala Symbolism. 1959. Princeton: Bollingen/Princeton University Press, 1972; Carl G. Jung, ed. Man and His Symbols. 1964. New York: Anchor Press/Doubleday, 1988; C. G. Jung. "Commentary." The Secret of the Golden Flower. Translated and explained by Richard Wilhelm. Rev. ed. San Diego: Harcourt

Brace Jovanovich, 1962; Ajit Mookerjee and Madhu Khanna. *The Tantric Way: Art, Science, Ritual.* Boston: New York Graphic Society, 1977.

Mantra (also Mantram)

Certain sacred names and syllables used in Hindu and Buddhist spiritual practices. "Mantra" is derived from the Sanskrit *man,* "mind," and *tra,* "to deliver."

In Hinduism a mantra is a name for God or of an avatar of the deity chosen for devotion by a *chela,* or pupil. The *chela* is initiated into a spiritual path with the mantra, which holds the essence of the guru's teachings. The mantra is kept secret. Meditating upon it clarifies the mind and leads to enlightenment.

In Buddhism a mantra is a syllable or syllables that represent cosmic forces, aspects of buddhas, or the name of Buddha. the mantra is repeated in meditation, which in Vajrayana Buddhism is accomplished by visualizations and body postures.

While most common in Hinduism and Buddhism, mantras are used in other religions, including Judaism, Christianity, and Islam. The names of God or gods are powerful mantras, and any formalized prayer (such as "Hail Mary" or "Our Father who art in heaven") is in essence a mantra. The Old Testament gives the most powerful personal name of God as Yahweh, called the Tetragrammaton (represented by the Hebrew letters YHVH), so awesome that it was spoken in ancient times only by high priests on Yom Kippur, the Day of Atonement, the most sacred Jewish religious holiday. "Adonai" and "Elohim" were substitutions for Yahweh.

Mantras are charged with vibrational power. Chanting a mantra or meditating silently upon it helps one attain an altered state of consciousness in which the true nature of the mind may be perceived; the unity of mind with Mind.

Lama Anagarika Govinda defined a mantra as a "tool for thinking," a "thing which creates a mental picture" (*Foundations of Tibetan Mysticism,* 1969). The mantra, Govinda said, is knowledge, the truth of being beyond right and wrong, real being beyond thinking and reflecting. What the mantra expresses in sound exists and comes to pass.

There are three ways to use mantras: verbal, semiverbal, and silent. The verbal, in which anyone can hear the mantra, is considered by some as the lowest form, while the silent repetition is the highest. Others, such as the Krishna sect, feel verbal chants are more powerful. In the semiverbal form, the vocal chords vibrate but no sound is heard.

The correct pronunciation and intonement of the mantra is of utmost importance, creating powerful vibrations, which in turn affect the vibrations of all things in the universe, including deities and lower spirit beings. The mantra is considered a manifestation of *shabda,* or sacred sound, which can be harnessed to create or destroy. This concept also is found in the ancient Greek theory of music, in which the keynote of a particular organism, body, or substance can be used to cause it to disintegrate. Mantric power reputedly is used by yogis and fakirs for such psychokinetic feats as weather control, teleportation, apports, and levitation. The Tibetan yogi Milarepa was said to have used mantras to create a hailstorm that destroyed enemies of his family. For using sacred power for evil purpose, Milarepa served years of penance.

Some Buddhist sects consider pronunciation less important than intent and proper mantric training. This may be because many Buddhist mantras are unintelligible, being comprised of old, rough translations of Sanskrit sounds.

The most sacred Hindu mantra is Om, the Supreme Reality, the sound from which the universe was created. Among the variations of Om mantras are the

Hindu "Om, Tat, Sat Om," meaning "O Thou Self-existent One," and the Buddhist "Om mani padme hum," meaning "O, Jewel of the Lotus, Hum," or "The Supreme Reality (is the) lotus jewel of Oneness." "Om mani padme hum," also called the "Mani" mantra, is used by many Buddhists daily for a variety of purposes: as an amulet against evil and bad luck; to facilitate ablutions and bodily eliminations; to heal; and, in the Pure Land sect, to seek entry to the Pure Land upon death. The repetition of Om in meditation creates spiritual light and power, which cleanses the subtle body and helps eliminate disharmony.

In Tibetan Buddhism the six syllables of "Om mani padme hum" mean that one may transform one's impure body, mind, and speech into the exalted body, mind, and speech of a Buddha by following a path of an indivisible union of method and wisdom. Om signifies body, speech, and mind (see Om); mani means jewel and symbolizes a method for enlightenment; padme means "lotus" and symbolizes wisdom (see Lotus); and hum symbolizes indivisibility. The mantra "Hum" also is comparable to "Om," and plays an important role in Tantric rituals. It is associated with the chakras of the lower body, particularly the root chakra where the kundalini resides, ready to be awakened with the correct mantra. See Kundalini.

The most sacred mantra to Krishna devotees is the sixteen-word "Hare Krishna Hare Krishna/Krishna Krishna/Hare Hare/Hare Rama Hare Rama/Rama Rama/Hare Hare."

Magical Uses of Mantras

Since the time of the ancient Egyptians and Assyrians, magicians have used mantras for conjuring and casting spells. The mantras are "names of power," which have been passed down from the Egyptians, Gnostics, and Hebrews. Many names of power are the true and secret names of God, such as Yahweh or Adonai, or nonsensical syllables drawn from the first letters of various biblical passages. These are used to summon spirits and to serve as amulets against misfortune.

The general Hindu and Buddhist populations use mantras as amulets for protection against illness, evil, and bad luck. In Sri Lanka exorcists use secret mantras, along with songs, drumming, dance, and curative oils, to expel demons and ghosts responsible for possession, sickness, and misfortune.

The twentieth-century English magician Aleister Crowley created the mantra AUMGN, an expansion of Om which he said was the magical formula of the universe. Crowley believed the sound vibrations of AUMGN were so powerful that a magician using them would be able to control the forces of the universe.

See **Meditation; Transcendental Meditation (TM).**

Sources: John Blofeld. *Mantras: Sacred Words of Power.* New York: E. P. Dutton, 1977; Richard Cavendish. *The Black Arts.* New York: Perigee Books, 1967. *Chant and Be Happy: The Power of Mantra Meditation.* Based on the teachings of A. C. Bhaktivedanta Swami Prabhupada. Los Angeles: The Bhaktivedanta Book Trust, 1983; *The Encyclopedia of Eastern Religion and Philosophy.* Boston: Shambhala, 1989; W. Y. Evans-Wentz, ed. *The Tibetan Book of the Dead.* 3d ed. London: Oxford University Press, 1960; W. Y. Evans-Wentz, ed. *The Tibetan Book of the Great Liberation.* London: Oxford University Press, 1954; W. Y. Evans-Wentz. *Tibet's Great Yogi Milarepa: A Biography from the Tibetan.* 2d ed. London: Oxford University Press, 1951; Jack Forem. *Transcendental Meditation.* New York: E. P. Dutton, 1973; Lama Anagarika Govinda. *Foundations of Tibetan Mysticism.* First American ed. York Beach, ME: Samuel Weiser, 1969; Tenzin Gyatso, His Holiness the Fourteenth Dalai Lama. *Kindness, Clar-*

ity and Insight. Translated and edited by Jeffrey Hopkins, coedited by Elizabeth Napper. Ithaca, NY: Snow Lion Publications, 1984; Bruce Kapferer. *A Celebration of Demons.* Bloomington, IN: Indiana University Press, 1983; Maria Leach, ed. and Jerome Fried, assoc. ed. *Funk & Wagnalls Standard Dictionary of Folklore, Mythology, and Legend.* San Francisco: Harper & Row, 1979; Robert R. Leichtman and Carl Japikse. *Active Meditation: The Western Tradition.* Columbus, OH: Ariel Press, 1982; Ormond McGill. *The Mysticism and Magic of India.* Cranbury, NJ: A. S. Barnes & Co., 1977; Evelyn Underhill. *Mysticism.* New York: New American Library, 1974.

Margery

See **American Society for Psychical Research (ASPR).**

Marian apparitions

The appearance or manifestation of the Blessed Virgin Mary. Countless Marian apparitions have been reported over the centuries, but the Catholic church, which investigates the most promising in lengthy procedures that can take years to complete, has decreed only a few of them to be genuine.

Most Marian apparitions consist of the appearance of a luminous woman who is identified as Mary. She may or may not speak. If she does she identifies herself and delivers a message urging people to pray more and lead a more devout life. She also asks for churches and shrines to be built to her. Miraculous healings often are reported in the wake of sightings. Other paranormal phenomena associated with the apparitions are brilliant lights, spinning and unusual lights, burning bushes, spinning crosses, celestial music, sweet, incense-like smells, apports, and so on. Some witnesses experience ecstatic trances.

Catholic dogma states that religious apparitions are not ghosts, but are mystical phenomena permitted by God. The Marian apparitions that have been deemed authentic occurred in Guadalupe, Mexico, in 1531; in Paris in 1830; at La Salette, France, on September 19, 1846; at Lourdes, France, between February 11 and July 16, 1858; at Knock, Ireland, on August 21, 1879; at Fatima, Portugal, between May 13 and October 13, 1917; at Beauraing, Belgium, between November 29, 1932 and January 3, 1933; and Banneaux, Belgium, in 1933. The apparitions at Guadalupe, Lourdes, and Fatima are the most celebrated. All sites of authenticated apparitions are visited each by pilgrimages in hopes of miraculous cures.

Unauthenticated apparitions also draw the faithful. Two of the most famous sites are Zeitoun, Egypt, and Medjugorje, Yugoslavia.

At Zeitoun, a suburb of Cairo, more than seventy Marian apparitions and other unusual phenomena were reported in the vicinity of the St. Mary's Coptic church over a fourteen-month period beginning on April 2, 1968. The longest apparition, on June 8, 1968, lasted for more than seven hours. The phenomena were witnessed by hundreds of thousands of people and were captured on film. Miraculous cures were reported.

At the remote village of Medjugorje, Marian apparitions began appearing to six adolescent villagers on June 24, 1981. For the next eighteen months, apparitions appeared daily to at least one of the six, totalling nearly two thousand by 1985. Miraculous healings and other phenomena have been reported. The six "seers," as they are called, say Mary has appeared to bring a message from Christ: Atheists must convert and return to the ways of God, and change their lives to peace with God and with their fellow man. Returning to God can be achieved through peace, conversion, fasting, penance, and prayer.

Pilgrims who visit the church and rectory say Mary appears to them during prayer. Photographs taken appear to show images of Jesus and Mary.

Marian apparitions have been reported elsewhere, such as at Lubbock, Texas, in 1988 to parishioners of the St. John Neumann Roman Catholic church.

Marian apparitions might be explained in terms of the "encounter phenomenon," in that they are archetypal projections from the human unconscious to answer a need, such as spiritual hunger. Mary's authority cannot be denied, and she brings about transformations in those who profess to see her. See **Archetypes; Encounter phenomenon; Mythology.**

Sources: Juan Arintero. *Mystical Evolution in the Development and Vitality of the Church.* Vol. 1. St. Louis: B. Herder, 1949; Donald Attwater. *A Dictionary of Mary.* New York: P. J. Kennedy, 1960; Robert Broderick, ed. *The Catholic Encyclopedia.* Nashville: Thomas Nelson, 1976; Victor DeVincenzo. "The Apparitions at Zeitoun, Egypt: An Historical Overview." *The Journal of Religion and Psychical Research* 11, no. 1 (January 1988): 3–13; Ann Marie Hancock. "Signs and Wonders of Her Love." *Venture Inward* (September/October 1988): 12–15; Louis Kronenberger, ed. *Atlantic Brief Lives.* Boston: Little, Brown, 1971; Coley Taylor. *Our Lady of Guadelupe: Marian Library Studies No. 85.* Dayton, OH: University of Dayton, 1961; Paul Weingarten. "Weeping Pilgrims Claim to See Faces of Jesus, Mary in Clouds." *The Seattle Times* (August 16, 1988).

Martial arts

Various styles of Oriental combat, either empty hand or with weapons. Thousands of styles of martial arts exist.

Martial arts originally were developed to achieve victory in battle. Over the centuries, however, they became philosophical and spiritual disciplines for cul-tivating a deeper meaning in life, and became steeped in Buddhism, Taoism, Shintoism, and Zen. They remained shrouded in secrecy until the Korean War, and since then have been exported increasingly to the West. Empty hand martial arts are the most popular in the West.

Regardless of style the key to all martial arts is skillful use of the universal life force (*ch'i* in Chinese and *ki* in Japanese), which permeates all things and can be directed throughout the body. The universal life force exists in the opposites of yang and yin, active/masculine and passive/feminine, which are in constant interplay. The force is controlled by uniting it with mind and body in physical movement, breathing techniques, and meditation. See **Universal life force.**

The grandfather of martial arts in China is Kung Fu, Chinese boxing, which dates to about A.D. 520 in northern China. Its development is credited to a wandering Indian monk named Bodhidharma, also called Ta-Mo. According to legend Bodhidharma was the son of King Sugandha of India and was skilled in martial arts. In mid-life he became a monk and crossed the Himalayas on foot. At the Shaolin monastery in China, he found monks in terrible physical condition, and taught them a set of exercises for conditioning body and mind. He also taught them Buddhism, and it is believed that the Zen philosophy was born there.

Over time the Shaolin exercises were expanded and adapted to animal movements. Stressing power strikes, kicking, and use of muscle, they became the "hard" school of Kung Fu. Various styles have evolved since.

Kung Fu practitioners widely believe in a traditional death touch called *dim mak.* If a body is struck at a certain point in a certain manner at a certain time of day, a delayed death inevitably follows. At first the victim feels unharmed, then later becomes ill and dies. It is said that the art of dim mak is possessed by only a handful of old masters.

A "soft," or internal form of Kung Fu was developed in the thirteenth century by a Taoist monk, Chang Sang-fen. Instead of meeting force with equal force as in the hard school, the soft school stresses a maximization of internal energy through tranquility. Yielding becomes strength and strength becomes yielding—the interplay of yin and yang, which the artist works to his advantage. Self-defense rests more on avoidance of blows rather than strikes and counterstrikes. See **Tai Ji Chuan.**

Karate, which means "empty hand," originated on Okinawa and was used against the Japanese when they invaded the island in 1609. It was introduced formally to Japan in the early twentieth century, and combines the indigenous methods with Kung Fu. It is based on blows delivered with the hand, head, feet, and knees.

In Japan the grandfather of martial arts is Jiu Jitsu ("gentle or soft skill"). According to legend Jiu Jitsu is about two thousand years old, but scholars date it to the ancient sumo fighting c. 23 B.C. Jiu Jitsu was formalized during the Tokugawa shogunate (1603–1868), when the samurai were idled by nearly three hundred years of relative peace, and the need for empty hand fighting grew. Swords were outlawed in 1876. A theoretical basis for the art of swordsmanship was developed in order to keep the art from degenerating. Jiu Jitsu was heavily influenced by Zen, which had a great appeal to the samurai. It emphasized the striking of vital points, kicking, strangling, and joint locking. It has evolved into Judo, a sports version, which emphasizes joint dislocation. It also was the precursor of Aikido ("the way of harmony with the spirit of the universe"), a modern Japanese martial art founded in 1922 by Morihei Ueshiba, a Jiu Jitsu instructor. The main objective of Aikido is the uni-

Aikido

(Courtesy Hartley Film Foundation)

fication of mind, body, and *ki*—self-realization through discipline—and the manifestation of love and harmony in all actions. Techniques stress harmonization with the moves of one's opponent.

Ueshiba early in his life embarked on a spiritual quest for *budo,* the inner essence of martial arts. He had a mystical experience in mid-life one day while sitting under a persimmon tree. The universe quaked and a golden spirit sprang up from the ground and veiled his body and changed it into one of gold. His mind and body became light. He understood the birds and became aware of "the mind of God." At that moment he understood that the source of budo is God's love for all beings, and the training of budo is to assimilate and utilize that love in the mind and body.

Ninjitsu is a stealth art, and was originated in the fourth century by the Chinese General Sun Tsu. The ninja are skilled at silent killing. They learn how to dislocate their own joints, and how to use breathing and meditation to stay underwater for prolonged periods and control their heartbeats to avoid detection.

Most martial arts have feats of incredible power, such as powerbreaking, which is the breaking of thick pieces of wood, layers of tile or bricks, and so on with the hand, foot, elbow, head, or even fingertips. In Kung Fu the "iron palm" is a single blow with the hand that kills.

Other amazing feats are immunity to fire, cuts, severe blows, and the like. The purpose of these feats is to make the student aware of the power within. The feats are accomplished by directing the *ch'i* or *ki* to various parts of the body. When the body is full of *ch'i*, it is exceptionally strong. See **Psychokinesis (PK)**.

Ueshiba often demonstrated his command of *ki*. He was five feet tall and weighed only 120 pounds, yet by directing his *ki* down to the ground could remain rooted to the spot and resist the efforts of several men to pick him up. Likewise, he used *ki* to send several assailants flying, while barely moving himself. He used *ki* to make himself lighter, so that he could walk on top of teacups without breaking them.

Ch'i cannot be accumulated in the body quickly, but must be built slowly through regular and unhurried practice of form. Humor and joyfulness are part of the discipline. Westerners, who are always in a hurry for instant results, often make the mistake of undertaking martial arts training too rapidly and too seriously.

Ch'i is regulated through breathing, which is used to center it in the solar plexus area, the seat of vital energy. Various martial arts movements call for specific techniques of inhaling or exhaling. Exhaling is accompanied by sound, often a scream or shriek, which helps to release the *ch'i* at the opponent and throw him or her off balance. Sound also is used to dissipate the force of *ch'i* contained in a punch or kick.

By harmonizing with his or her opponent, the martial artist learns to anticipate hostile moves and avoid or preempt them. This requires a state of "no mind" or "not fighting," in which the mind is disengaged and the body reacts instinctively, going with the flow of *ch'i* energy. In Japanese this state is called *nen*, which connotes a concentration or one-pointedness. Nen is not concerned with winning or losing or with strategy. With the proper connection to *ki*, it becomes a supernatural power that sees all things clearly; one absorbs the opponent's moves into one's own. One must not think with the mind, for to do so makes one vulnerable by freezing or interfering with nen.

Ueshiba said this supernatural power enabled him literally to dodge bullets. In 1924, while on a trip to Inner Mongolia, Ueshiba and his party were attacked several times by bandits and soldiers of the Chinese Nationalist Army. His martial arts training enabled him to intuitively sense from which direction the bullets would come. He could see small pebbles of white light flashing just before the bullets, and said he dodged them by twisting and turning. On another occasion, in 1925, he was challenged by a sword-wielding opponent. Ueshiba had no weapon, and again anticipated the sword thrusts by seeing little pebbles of white light that flashed first. His opponent exhausted himself and gave up.

Other, lesser-known Oriental martial arts have gained a following in the West. Tae Kwon-Do is a thirteen-hundred-year-old style from Korea. *Tae* means "to kick or smash with the feet"; *kwon* means "to punch or destroy with the hand or fist"; and *do* means "method." Hwarang-Do, also from Korea, was exported to the United States in 1972. It stresses external power, internal power, weapon power, and mental power. The latter includes training in controlling the mind and developing psychic powers, especially clairvoyance and telepathy. It also teaches meditation and healing.

Zen is a major influence in two Japanese martial arts with weapons: Kyudo, "the way of the bow," and Kendo, "the way of the sword." In Kyudo the importance is placed not on hitting the bull's eye, but on how the shooting is done and one's state of mind when the arrow is released. In modern Kendo the emphasis is on improving one's spiritual development and moral conduct.

See **Buddhism; Meditation; Qi Gong; Taoism; Zen.** Compare to **Sports, mystical and psychic phenomena in.**

Sources: Bob Klein. *Movements of Magic: The Spirit of T'ai-Chi-Ch'uan.* North Hollywood, CA: Newcastle Publishing, 1984; Peter Lewis. *Martial Arts of the Orient.* New York: Gallery Books, 1985; Dai Liu. *T'ai Chi Ch'uan and Meditation.* New York: Schocken Books, 1986; Charles T. Tart. *Open Mind, Discriminating Mind.* San Francisco: Harper & Row, 1989; Kisshomaru Ueshiba. *The Spirit of Aikido.* Tokyo: Kodansha International, 1984.

Mary

The mother of Jesus referred to in the Christian Gospels, also called "Blessed Virgin," "Virgin Mary," or in some contexts by Christians simply "Our Lady." Early church councils, including those at Ephesus in 431 and at Chalcedon in 451, gave her the title *Theotokos* ("God-bearer"); thus the title "Mother of God" is widely used, especially among Catholics.

According to Catholic doctrine, Mary is the single exception to the state of Original Sin due to her Immaculate Conception. Original Sin, a teaching of most Christian theologians, holds that the condition of Adam and Eve after their fall from grace is the spiritual state in which all humankind is conceived. Mary, however, was destined to be the mother of Christ; thus God infused her soul with grace at the moment of her conception in the womb of her mother, St. Anne, which freed her from lust, slavery to the Devil, depraved nature, darkness of intellect, and other consequences of Original Sin. The idea of the Immaculate Conception was rejected by Thomas Aquinas in the thirteenth century.

Mary and her proper place in Christian theology have been a subject of much controversy over the centuries. It is evident that she absorbed characteristics of previous pagan goddesses, thus fulfilling the need for worship of a Mother-figure. Early church fathers attempted to discourage worship of her by saying that God would never be born of a woman. For the first five centuries after Christ, she was depicted as lower in status than even the Magi, who were graced by halos in sacred art; the Marianite sect, which considered her divine, was persecuted for heresy. In the early fourth century, Constantine I ordered all goddess temples destroyed and forbade the worship of Mary, so that she would not overshadow her Son. The people, however, refused to accept Christianity without worship of Mary; they substituted her for the Great Goddess. She was prayed to as a Mother who intercedes for her children. By the sixth century she was shown in art with a halo, and by the ninth century she was named Queen of Heaven. By the eleventh century, she had eclipsed Jesus in popularity and as the savior of humankind. The great Gothic cathedrals were built to her, not to her Son.

In accepting Mary the church had to grapple with her sexuality. Though the Bible refers to Jesus' brothers and sisters, Mary became "the Virgin," who never defiled her body with sexual intercourse during her entire life. Furthermore, she had not died as a mere mortal, but had been raised from the dead by Jesus, and assumed into heaven as a live woman. The Assumption became an article of faith in 1950.

Devotion to Mary is a vital part of the Catholic liturgical life, especially in the Eastern Orthodox churches. However, the latter churches are averse to abstract theologizing about Mary. The theological, philosophical, and other academic studies of Mary are collectively called "Mariology," a distinct discipline that includes biblical references to her, doctrines and devotions associated with her, and her role in religious history and thought. There is a Mariological Society of America and several centers of Mariological research, including the Marianum, the theological faculty directed in Rome by the Servite Fathers. There is also the Marian Library at the University of Dayton, Ohio, one of several schools owned and operated by the Society of Mary (Marianists), a Roman Catholic religious order devoted especially to "filial piety," a devotion to Mary similar to that which they believe is accorded Christ.

Catholics observe several feast days in Mary's honor, including the Immaculate Conception, her Nativity, Purification, Annunciation, and Assumption. Several popular religious practices focus on devotion to Mary, most notably the rosary, which is the saying of fifty "Hail Marys," five "Our Fathers," and five doxologies ("Glory be to the Father . . .") while meditating on specific traditional mysteries. This association with the rosary stems from apparitions of Mary seen at Fatima, Portugal, in 1917. The apparition identified herself as the Lady of the Rosary, and asked that believers say the rosary every day. See **Marian apparitions.**

Several Marian devotional prayers (such as "little offices") and traditions (such as various novenas, which are nine days' devotions) have their origins in medieval times, when Marian devotion was especially intense throughout Europe, as evidenced by the number of artifacts and cathedrals built for Mary. The religious order Servants of Mary, or Servites, dates from these times. While most Catholic religious orders include Marian devotions in their tradition, several religious orders—particularly of nuns—are devoted specifically to Mary.

Many mystical experiences and miraculous healings throughout history have centered on devotion to Mary, in particular her alleged appearances in apparitions. See **Goddess; Jesus.**

Sources: Juan Arintero. *Mystical Evolution in the Development and Vitality of the Church.* Vol. 1. St. Louis: B. Herder, 1949; Donald Attwater. *A Dictionary of Mary.* New York: P. J. Kennedy, 1960; Robert Broderick, ed. *The Catholic Encyclopedia.* Nashville: Thomas Nelson, 1976; Elizabeth Gould Davis. *The First Sex.* New York: G. P. Putnam's Sons, 1971; Robert Graves. *The White Goddess.* Amended and enlarged ed. New York: Farrar, Straus and Giroux, 1966; Barbara G. Walker. *The Woman's Encyclopedia of Myths and Secrets.* San Francisco: Harper & Row, 1983.

Masks

Coverings for the face that are used in ritual, liturgies, theater, and folk art, the purpose of which is to transform the wearer—and possibly the viewer by association—into something other than what he or she is, such as an animal, an ancestor, or a presumed image of a supernatural being.

The mask is a sacred object of power. It does not conceal, but liberates. By donning it wearers allow themselves to become possessed by the spirit in the mask or represented by the mask, which enables them to invoke the powers of that spirit. It is a lightning rod of spiritual and psychic energy. In Jungian terms a mask connects its wearer to archetypal powers residing within the collective unconscious. The mask is a mediator between the ego and archetype, the mundane and the supernatural, the comic and the sacred. It connects the present to the past.

In prehistoric societies masks succeeded disguises that covered all or part of the body and magically transformed the wearer. Perhaps the first prehistoric masked dancer is the "Sorcerer," a Neolithic-Age cave painting at Trois Frères in France. The masked figure is half human and half animal, wearing stag antlers, and poised in dance-step.

Although the symbolisms of masks vary from culture to culture, commonal-

(Courtesy Hartley Film Foundation)

Bali master mask maker

(Courtesy Hartley Film Foundation)

Mask maker wearing the Mask of Rangda

ities between mask symbols and myths have been found in different societies, such as African, Native North American, and Oceanic tribes. A standard motif to explain the origin of masked dance concerns a wandering tribesman who comes upon masked, dancing animals, steals their masks, and takes them back to his own village, where he teaches others what he saw. Masks and their dances also are bestowed by culture heroes.

Masks play an important role in religious, healing, exorcism, and funerary rituals. Sri Lankan exorcism masks, for example, are hideous, in order to frighten possessing demons out of bodies. Among Native North Americans, bear masks invoke the healing powers of the bear, considered the great doctor of all ills. Masks in shamanism, however, are uncommon, except among the Inuit; the shaman's costume itself may be considered a mask. In funerary rites masks incarnate the souls of the dead, protect wearers from recognition by the souls of the dead, or trap the souls of the dead.

In most cultures masks symbolize beneficent spirits, of nature, deities, the dead, and the animal kingdom. Native North Americans have used masks to represent evil spirits, over which the medicine men are believed to have power. Similar attribution is made in Ceylon.

The making of a mask is a sacred ritual in itself; there are many rules and taboos. It may be done in secret or to chanting. Masks must be made of certain materials and only at certain times of the year by certain people. The Awa mask society of the Dogon of Mali feed their masks ritual blood sacrifices, an appeasement to the spirits within the masks. Mask-making is part of initiation into many ancestor cults and male secret societies; in the latter, according to one theory, the object of the masks is to frighten women by portraying demons and ancestral spirits.

Prior to donning masks, it is universally customary for wearers to prepare by contemplating the mask features and the supernatural energy bound up within them. After use masks are carefully stored or ritually burned or buried. Vestiges of such rituals may be seen in various liturgical vesting ceremonies, though not in the Christian liturgical tradition.

In the West masks have lost much of their sacred and deep symbolic meaning. They were integral to Greek drama, both secular and liturgical medieval ceremonies, the Renaissance court masque, and nineteenth-century mime and pantomime. However, in the modern day, the West has nothing comparable to the use of masks in Japanese No drama, for example. Westerners tend to focus on the superficiality of masks rather than on the essence of what masks represent.

In transpersonal psychology masks are used to help people identify with archetypes and liberate suppressed parts of the Self, thus seeing themselves in new ways. See **Archetypes**.

Sources: Joseph Campbell. *The Masks of God.* Vol. 1, *Primitive Mythology.* New York: Viking, 1959; Joseph Campbell. *The Way of the Animal Powers: Historical Atlas of World Mythology.* Parts 1 and 2. London: Times Books, 1983, 1988; Mircea Eliade. *Rites and Symbols of Initiation.* New York: Harper & Row, 1958; Mircea Eliade. *Shamanism.* 1951. Princeton, NJ: Princeton University Press, 1964; Ron Jenkins. "Two Way Mirrors." *Parabola* 6, no. 3 (August 1981): 17–21; Carl G. Jung. *Man and His Symbols.* First published in the United States 1964. New York: Anchor Press/Doubleday, 1988; Stephen and Robin Larsen. "The Healing Mask." *Parabola* 6, no. 3 (August 1981): 78–84; Claude Levi-Strauss. *The Way of the Masks.* Seattle: University of Washington Press, 1988; Steven Lonsdale. *Animals and the Origins of Dance.* New York: Thames and Hudson, 1982; Meredith B. McGuire. "Healing Rituals in the Suburbs." *Psychology Today* 23, no. 1/2 (January/February 1989): 57–64.

Masonry

See **Freemasonry**.

Materialization

The appearance of seemingly solid objects and spirit forms out of thin air. Eastern adepts who have mastered the *siddhis* ("miraculous powers") are said to be able to materialize objects. Sai Baba of India is renowned for materializations of food, precious gems, jewelry, *vibuti* (holy ash), religious objects, and so on. See **Milarepa; Sai Baba; Siddhis; Yoga**.

A phenomenon of physical mediumship, materializations were particularly popular during the peak of Spiritualist seances during the nineteenth and early twentieth centuries, then became less common as other forms of mediumship came into prominence.

Objects, or apports, commonly materialized at Spiritualist seances included vases, coins, flowers, and musical instruments. Luminous and phantom-like objects, animals, and human spirits also appeared. Often, human hands were the only body parts to materialize at a seance; they were called "pseudopods." D. D. Home and Eusapia Palladino were among numerous mediums famous for causing ghostly forms to appear, which felt solid and cold to the touch. More sensational was the materialization of the entire form of a spirit. Florence Cook, a British medium who became famous while in her teens, was the first medium to materialize full spirit forms in good light. She allegedly produced her control spirit, Katie King, who resembled Cook in appearance and was garbed in flowing white clothing. However, she was exposed for fraud.

Some mediums exhibited a skill in dematerialization, making themselves, or parts of themselves, disappear. On December 11, 1895, Mademoiselle d'Esperance, a medium, dematerialized her lower body at a seance in Helsinki, Finland. For about fifteen minutes, d'Esperance's skirt lay flat on the chair. She was fully conscious, but felt as though she were dreaming.

It was not uncommon for mediums to fake materializations with the help of stage magic trickery. Seances usually took place in a darkened room, which made it easy to conceal wires, trap doors, and other apparatus, as well as provide a cover for surreptitious movement. The dark also stimulates the imagination; if one expects to see spirits, one undoubtedly will. Furthermore, Victorian etiquette usually prevented thorough searches of a medium's personage, and required observance of the medium's rules. Typically, the medium retired behind a curtain and requested no peeking until several minutes after the spirit had disappeared.

Materializations of spirits usually proved to be the medium in disguise. Cook was exposed more than once. See **Cook, Florence.** In 1875 Frank Herne, a young, professional English medium, was exposed at a seance in Liverpool. Herne, who specialized in materializing spirit faces and bodies, was seized by an impolite sitter, who had the nerve to grab him and turn up the gaslight to take a closer look at the "spirit head." Herne had about two yards of stiff muslin wrapped around his head and hanging down to his thighs. Another British medium of the same period, Mary Showers, also was caught red-handed. After Showers retired behind a curtain, the spirit face of her control, Florence Maples, appeared to the sitters. When the spirit bid good-bye and disappeared behind the curtain, a sitter leaped up and yanked the curtain open prematurely. The "spirit" struggled to close the curtain, but her headgear fell off, revealing Showers beneath.

Home exposed a letter written from one medium to another, which he had obtained, and which explained how the materialization trick could be done. The medium was to take a very thin, muslin "spirit robe," fold it into a small piece, and secret it in her drawers, where no polite sitter would dare inspect. Once she was behind curtains or in a cabinet, she undressed down to a double layer of shifts, donned the robe, and emerged as the "spirit."

Some materializations, however, remain unexplained. Home, for example, was never exposed as a fraud. See **Apport; Ectoplasm.**

Sources: Alfred Douglas. *Extrasensory Powers: A Century of Psychical Research.* London: Victor Gollancz Ltd., 1976; Alan Gauld. *Mediumship and Survival.* London: William Heinemann Ltd., 1982; *Into the Unknown.* Pleasantville, NY: Reader's Digest, 1981; Janet Oppenheim. *The Other World: Spiritualism and Psychical Research in England, 1850–1914.* Cambridge, England: Cambridge University Press, 1985; Benjamin B. Wolman, ed. *Handbook of Parapsychology.* New York: Van Nostrand Reinhold, 1977.

Mathers, Samuel Liddell MacGregor

See **Hermetic Order of the Golden Dawn.**

Medicine bundle

A bag made of leather or an animal pelt in which Native Americans keep an assortment of objects with healing, magical, and supernatural powers. Medicine bundles are known to almost all tribes. They are the equivalent of a church reliquary and held with the same reverence. Some are small and simple, while others contain more than one hundred items. Such objects include fetishes and charms, ritual items, herbs and healing paraphernalia, magical objects, scalps, hooves, feathers, claws, stones, arrow points, remains of ancestors, symbolic miniatures, and the like. The importance of medicine bundles in the religions of Native North Americans varies considerably.

The instructions for composing medicine bundles are given to clans, societies, and individuals by the Supernaturals, or guardian spirits, in dreams or visions. The bundles are concrete tokens of medicine power that the spirits have bestowed

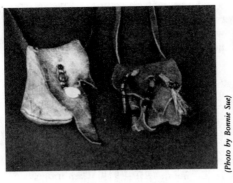

Contemporary pouches fashioned after medicine bags

(Photo by Bonnie Sue)

upon the recipients, such as for healing—which may be general or limited to one illness—or hunting. Entire medicine societies have sprung up around bundles, such as the Midewiwin of the Ojibwa. The Buffalo Medicine Society had a medicine bundle containing deer hooves, feathers, bells (for keeping time to chants and songs), wands of buff tails, sweet grass incense, and medicinal herbs and roots. It was carried into battle, where its contents were used to treat the injured.

On special occasions, such as prior to war, communal hunts, long trips, and the moving of village sites, the bundles are opened according to rituals of song, dance, and recitation. Thus the bundle's supernatural power is invoked to ensure success of the venture. Not all items are necessarily removed for a specific purpose. To dream of a medicine bundle—such as before a hunt—is considered propitious.

Individual medicine bundles are either buried with their owners or passed to relatives. Collective bundles are kept and passed down by medicine men, designated custodians, or descendants of the original visionary. Some collective bundles of earlier days reputedly had great power, which was ritually renewed as required.

Christian missionaries caused many medicine bundles to be buried or destroyed, turning them into a rarity. Their use has revived with the renewal of interest in native culture.

Medicine bundles are not limited to North American tribes; the Aztecs, for example, carried medicine bundles that contained images of various gods. See Fetish; Medicine societies.

Sources: Ake Hultkrantz. *Native Religions of North America.* San Francisco: Harper & Row, 1987; Ake Hultkrantz. *The Religions of the American Indians.* 1967. Berkeley: University of California Press, 1979; Elisabeth Tooker, ed. *Native North American Spirituality of the Eastern Woodlands.* Mahwah, NJ: Paulist Press, 1979; Ruth M. Underhill. *Red Man's Religion.* Chicago: University of Chicago Press, 1965.

Medicine societies

In the traditions of Native North Americans, closed cults of people who have been endowed with supernatural powers, especially curative. Medicine societies predominate among hunter-gatherers, especially around the Great Lakes region, and among some planters, such as the Pueblo of the Southwest. They are shamanic in structure.

The name "medicine society" was given to these groups by the French; the French term *médecin* means "doctor," and also is the basis of the Western terms "medicine man" and "medicine woman" for individual practitioners. (It is argued that such terms as "medicine man" are obsolete, yet they continue to be used by many Native Americans. "Shaman" is often substituted.)

Perhaps the greatest and most organized medicine society is the Midewiwin, also called the Grand Medicine Society, of the Ojibwa, Menomini, and Winnebago. More recently, it has been called the Mide Society. The term Midewiwin is derived from *mide,* meaning "sound of the drum," and *wiwin,* meaning "doings."

The Mide Society has the structure and practice of a mystery school. According to myth the society has ancient origins and was founded by Nanabozho, the Great Hare culture hero, on instructions from the Great Spirit. Moved by the sickness and weakness of humanity, Nanabozho revealed sacred secrets to the otter and inserted white clam shells in its body to make it immortal. Historical evidence suggests the Mide Society originated in the late seventeenth century. The first white reports of it date to the 1880s. It is still active in present times.

Membership is not limited to shamans, but is open to others who are interested in spiritual pursuits and who have experienced a vision in which supernaturals directed them to join the society. See **Vision quest.** Members are required to pay initiation fees.

The novice undertakes a lengthy and rigorous training under the guidance of an older society member. Training includes instruction in the sacred primordial myth, the traditions of the society, magical songs, and various occult and healing practices. The novice advances through four degrees: The first is associated with aquatic animals in the creation myths, including the mink, otter, muskrat and beaver; the second is associated with creatures of the air (owl or hawk); the third is associated with the more powerful land creatures, such as wildcat or serpent; and the fourth is associated with the bear, the most powerful land animal (the bear has widespread associations with healing in Native American traditions).

Each degree confers greater power and requires an initiation. The candidate is "shot" in the chest with the society's fetish, the white clam shell; the shells are kept in a medicine bundle made of a whole otter skin. Upon being "shot," the candidate falls "dead" and is "resurrected" with a touch of the shell or medicine bundle. The higher he progresses, the more shells—and the greater the power—is acquired by the candidate.

The hierarchy includes four levels each of earth and sky, which teach the initiate the powers of magical flight, metamorphosis, divination, prophecy, love charms, handling fire without harm, sucking out disease, and prescribing herbal remedies. The Mide Society includes the ancient shamanic vocations of *tcisaki,* male diviners who communicate with the manitou (manifestations of supernatural powers) in a shaking tent; *nanandawi,* the tribal doctor who uses shamanic healing techniques; *wabeno,* or "men of the sky," who handle fire and hot coals in order to interpret dreams, heal, and assist in novice spirit contacts; and *meda,* family healers who also use shamanic techniques.

One of the Mide Society's most significant functions is its *Dzibai,* or "Ghost midewiwin," a ceremony to help the ghosts of the newly dead journey to the ghost world as quickly as possible.

The Omaha have a shell society that resembles the Mide Society.

The Zuñi have twelve medicine societies, which specialize in various diseases and illnesses. Membership requires no vision, but sickness—men and women who have become ill and been treated by a member of a medicine society are required to join, lest they put themselves at risk again. Some societies also require individuals to belong to certain clans. Though women may join, they do not hold office.

Tutelage in the secret traditions and rituals is given by the one who performed the cure. Healing is usually done by sucking, but is not performed in trance, as is characteristic of shamanistic healing. Each society has its own fetish and beast god patrons. Rituals involve fetishes, both society and personal, which are placed on altars.

Some Zuñi medicine societies are part medicine and part hunting; in addition to taking part in communal hunts, the members specialize in illnesses believed to be caused by certain animals. See **False Face Society; Fetish; Shamanism.**

Sources: Joseph Epes Brown. *The Spiritual Legacy of the American Indian.* New York: Crossroad, 1987; Mircea Eliade. *Shamanism.* Princeton, NJ: Princeton University Press, 1964; John A. Grim. *The Shaman: Patterns of Religious Healing Among the Ojibway Indians.* Norman, OK: University of Oklahoma Press, 1983; Ake Hultkrantz. *Native Religions of North America.* San Francisco: Harper & Row, 1987; Ruth M. Underhill. *Red Man's Religion.* Chicago: University of Chicago Press, 1965.

Medicine wheels

Large circles of stone laid out in the North American Plains by historic Native North American tribes. The appellation of "medicine wheel" is modern, due to the association of the circles with supernatural forces. Little archaeological or cultural lore exists to shed light on medicine wheels' uses, although recent evidence suggests they were astronomical and calendrical.

Little is known about the early Plains tribes, who led a nomadic life and built no lasting habitats or structures. They lived only a few seasons in any one spot. When they moved to new locations, they left behind small stone circles, which apparently were used for anchoring tipis, and mysterious large circles now called medicine wheels. The remains of approximately fifty known medicine wheels are scattered across the Plains, mostly in Canada and some in the United States.

Sizes and patterns of medicine wheels vary, ranging from a few feet to sixty yards in diameter. They are comprised of loaf-sized stones laid out in circles, with a central cairn of rocks. Some cairns measure three to four yards high by ten yards wide, requiring tons of rocks. Some medicine wheels have additional cairns built along the perimeter, or smaller rock circles built outside the main circle. Some wheels have spokes connecting the rim to the central cairn.

The most spectacular is the Bighorn Medicine Wheel, located at the 10,000-foot summit of Medicine Mountain in the Bighorn Mountains of Wyoming. The central cairn itself is ten feet wide and is attached to the perimeter by twenty-eight spokes of stones. The wheel has six peripheral cairns, five outside the perimeter and one inside. The estimated age of the wheel is between one hundred and two hundred years old, based on an analysis of a tree limb found placed in one of the cairns. At the turn of the twentieth century, local Native Americans interviewed professed to know nothing of the wheel's builders, except that it was "made by people who had no iron," meaning that it was very old. The wheel was recognized as a holy site, however, and it is possible that Native Americans did not want to reveal information related to sacred activities. The circle is a shape considered to have great power. In the 1920s anthropologist George Grinnell was told by Cheyenne that the wheel was the ground plan of a medicine lodge. See **Sun Dance.**

In 1972 astronomer John Eddy began an investigation of medicine wheels, beginning with Bighorn. He determined that the wheel had been laid out on lines related to the summer solstice (at winter solstice, the wheel is buried under snow and is useless). It may have been used to sight the rise of stars such as Sirius, Aldebaran, and Rigel. It had no apparent uses for lunar or planetary alignments. The twenty-eight spokes, however, may have served as day counters in a lunar cycle.

Eddy investigated other medicine wheels and found only a few that seemed to have astronomical alignments. Many were too disturbed for measurements; ones that were intact seemed to have been built for other, unknown purposes. The Moose Mountain Medicine Wheel in southern Saskatchewan, Canada, displays dramatic summer solstice alignments like Bighorn. Eddy calculated that it may have been in use at about the time of Christ. An archaeological investigation of the central cairn yielded small chunks of charcoal which were radiocarbon-dated to c. 440 B.C. These findings indicate that early Native North Americans may have had a far more advanced culture than previously thought.

In modern usage the medicine wheel has been adopted by some as a vehicle for medicine power, protection, and spiritual growth. The wheel is constructed according to ritual, marked with the cardinal points, and consecrated to the spirits. It is used for ceremonial purposes. Some medicine wheels are constructed around ceremonial tipis, sweat lodges, and even homes. Compare to **Circle; Mandala.**

Sources: Joseph Epes Brown, ed. *The Sacred Pipe: Black Elk's Account of the Seven Rites of the Oglala Sioux.* 1953. New York: Penguin Books, 1971; John Redtail Freesoul. *Breath of the Invisible: The Way of the Pipe.* Wheaton, IL: Theosophical Publishing House, 1986; Ray A. Williamson. *Living the Sky: The Cosmos of the American Indian.* Norman, OK: University of Oklahoma Press, 1984.

Meditation

Any of various disciplines of mind and body that enable one to achieve higher states of consciousness. Meditation has no intrinsic goal, but the goal toward which it is applied is the transformation of consciousness; it is a tool for self-improvement or spiritual growth.

Alan Watts meditating in Zen garden at Hammond Museum, New York, early 1950s

(Courtesy Hartley Film Foundation)

The ultimate goal of mystical meditation is union with the Absolute. Mystical meditation is practiced usually by the nonsecular world in concert with withdrawal, asceticism, strict diet, and other regimens. Secular meditators use meditation as part of daily life in order to improve health, creativity, self-esteem, success, and relationships; cultivate psychic powers; and gain self-knowledge. Meditation in itself will not accomplish these goals, but may help people develop their own powers and abilities to do so. Scientific research of meditation has shown that regular practice has health benefits.

Meditation is practiced universally, but has become more formalized as a spiritual discipline in the East. There are numerous techniques of meditation, which may be grouped under general types. Contemplation, found more in the Western tradition, includes all practices of thinking about meaning, such as prayer, concepts, and questions. Contemplation does not quiet the mind or effect bodily rest. Concentration is found more in the Eastern tradition, especially in yoga, and involves attempts to transform consciousness by mental control, to go beyond thought to absence of thought.

The goal of concentration meditation is to achieve mystical states of consciousness. Posture is important. The mind is concentrated on a single object, such as breath control, a mantra (sounds, words, or phrases), a *yantra* (geometric shape), candle flames, a koan (Zen puzzle), and so on. Detached awareness meditation also is more characteristic of Eastern methods, especially in the many schools of Buddhism. The best-known of these methods in the West is the *zazen,* or sitting meditation, of Zen. See **Zen.**

The priesthoods, adepts, and other practitioners of mystical meditation spend long periods in meditative states. Secular meditators, especially in the West, generally meditate once or twice a day for twenty minutes or so. Popular Western interest in meditation arose in the 1960s, and most meditation techniques that have been adopted are derived from Hinduism and Buddhism. Despite the greater sophistication of meditation in the East, few modern Easterners meditate.

The earliest meditators probably were the shamans of the Stone Age hunting and gathering societies, who used ecstatic states to heal, divine, and prophesy. The *Rig Veda,* the earliest recorded literature of northern India, composed c. 1000 B.C., mentions meditative ecstasy (apart from the soma cult, which was practiced until about 700 B.C.), but offers no formal techniques. Siddhartha Gautauma (c. 566 B.C.–486 B.C.), the founder of Buddhism, awakened to enlightenment while meditating under a bodhi tree. Thus in Buddhism salvation, or awakening, is achieved through the meditation of self-transformation. The supreme goal is nirvana, or release from the limitations of existence. See **Buddhism.**

The first extant written evidence of formalized meditation in India or China did not appear until about the fourth or fifth century B.C. in the Taoist work the *Tao Teh Ching.* The Taoists placed great emphasis on breath control and considered meditation to be a skill acquired in stages. In the most advanced stages, one achieved "fetal breathing," in which one breathed without inhaling or exhaling. At this point the pulse ceased, and the meditator transcended conscious thought to a state of Great Quiescence, the highest form of enlightenment and the final goal of Taoist meditation. See **Taoism.** In India the Upanishads discuss the psychology of meditation, as a way to control the senses and actions and free one from the bondage of the external world (nirvana). Formal meditation techniques developed during a highly creative period from about 200 B.C. to A.D. 200 or 400, most likely as a response to Buddhism. See **Yoga.**

The most detailed classical Buddhist treatise on meditation is the *Visuddhimagga* ("Path of Purification"), part of the *Abhidhamma.* The *Visuddhimagga,* summarized in the fifth century by the monk Buddhaghosa, sets forth advice on the preparations and surroundings for meditation, and describes various meditative states and the consequences of attaining nirvana.

Buddhist meditation is approached through purification (*sila*), concentration (*samadhi*), and insight (*punna*), all of which work together. The student begins with purification, following a strict ascetic and moral code, and learning mindfulness (*sati*), a minimal awareness of sensory perceptions without allowing them to stimulate thoughts. Mindfulness then leads to "seeing things as they are" (*vipassana*).

The path of concentration involves fixing the mind upon a single object. The *Visuddhimagga* recommends forty such objects, such as colored wheels, corpses, reflections (as on the attributes of Buddha), sublime states, formless contemplations, and the four elements of nature. Each object has its own distinct results, but all are on the route to nirvana.

With practice the concentration leads to states of full absorption (*jhanas*). There are eight *jhanas,* the lowest of which produces a cessation of bodily awareness, and rapture or bliss. At the highest level, there is neither perception nor nonperception.

Once the *jhanas* have been mastered, the student embarks on the path of insight, which begins with four kinds of mindfulness, of the body, feelings, mind, and mind objects. The mindfulness then leads to higher and higher states of insight. Part way up is a state of pseudo-nirvana, characterized by luminosities, rapturous feelings, happiness, lucidity, and so on, which fool the meditator into thinking he or she has achieved nirvana. If this state is successfully passed, the meditator becomes increasingly aware of each moment as it arises and passes, and of the unsatisfactory nature of all phenomena. The meditator experiences tremendous physical pain as he or she seeks a cessation of all mental processes. The pain ceases in a state of effortless insight, and nirvana is attained when consciousness ceases to have an object.

The first experience of nirvana lasts less than a second, but it permanently transforms the meditator by burning away aspects of his or her ego and desires. The master meditator learns to attain nirvana at will for longer and longer periods. Each experience brings additional transformations, which result in significant changes in personality: the meditator loses attachments to the material world, and loses undesirable traits such as selfishness, hatred, anger, and so on. Ultimately, the meditator seeks to become an awakened being (*arahant*), who is completely freed from the wheel of becoming, and cannot accumulate any more karma that will necessitate a rebirth to the physical world.

Beyond nirvana is *nirodh* (cessation), which is the absolute cessation of consciousness and the quiescence of bodily processes. It is extremely difficult to obtain. The body's metabolism drops to the minimal level necessary to maintain physical life, a state that can be maintained no longer than seven days. The meditator must decide beforehand exactly how long he or she will stay in *nirodh.*

Tibetan Buddhist meditation draws on classical Buddhist methods, as well as elements from the native Bön religion and from Vajrayana, the "Diamond Vehicle" School of Buddhism. Meditation comprises one of three parts of the Tibetan approach to spiritual training. The other two are hearing, which includes reading, study, and listening to lectures; and contemplation. Meditation is the third successive step. After study one contemplates what has been learned, then absorbs it through meditation. The mind meditates in two ways: one, through observation and investigation; and two, through focus and absorption. Furthermore, one can approach the objective of meditation in two ways. In one way the objective shares a quality with the mind, and through meditation exerts a profound effect upon one and how one lives. For example, meditating upon love or compassion makes one more loving or more compassionate. In the second way, the objective creates an opposite effect: Meditating upon death or emptiness makes one more alive and full.

In the Western tradition, the first Christian monks of the fourth century, hermits who lived on the Egyptian desert, practiced a discipline of purification and meditation as a way to unite with God. Their techniques either were borrowed from the East or were spontaneous rediscoveries of the same. The Desert Fathers had the Christian equivalent of mantras, phrases from the Scriptures repeated either silently or verbally. In the Catholic tradition, the path to God is characterized by purification, asceticism, prayer, and contemplation. Contemplation includes recollection, which is concentration and the elimination of all thoughts and sensory phenomena; and introversion, which is concentrating the mind on its deepest part, the prelude to union with God. See Ecstasy; Prayer.

Meditation also is part of the mystical practices of Judaism and Islam, the Kabbalah and Sufism, respectively. See Kabbalah; Sufism.

In the 1950s scientists in India and Japan began studying yogis and Zen monks in meditation. In the 1960s Western scientists began to study Transcendental Meditation (TM) practitioners, at the invitation of TM founder Maharishi Mahesh Yogi. Studies have been uneven, but generally show that meditation lowers the body's metabolism, slows brain waves, and induces relaxation. Individuals who meditate regularly show greater resistance to stress and illness, and say they feel better psychologically. Meditation has been shown to be effective in treating addiction. See Altered states of consciousness; Biofeedback; Drugs in mystical and psychic experiences; Mystical experiences; Mysticism; Relaxation; Transcendental Meditation (TM).

Sources: Daniel Goleman. *The Meditative Mind: The Varieties of Meditative Experience.* Los Angeles: Jeremy P. Tarcher, 1988; Willard Johnson. *Riding the Ox Home: A History of Meditation from Shamanism to Science.* 1982. Boston: Beacon Press, 1986; Da Liu. *T'ai Chi Ch'uan and Meditation.* New York: Schocken Books, 1986; Charles T. Tart, ed. *Transpersonal Psychologies.* San Francisco: Harper & Row, 1975; John White, ed. *Frontiers of Consciousness.* 1974. New York: Avon, 1975.

Mediumship

Entranced communication with alleged nonphysical entities, sometimes accompanied by paranormal physical phenomena. Mediumship is an ancient and universal practice, undertaken to commune with the divine, prophesy, communicate with spirits of the dead, perform paranormal feats, and channel the universal life force for healing. Mediums have been known by various names, such as oracle, soothsayer, wizard, cunning woman, wise woman, witch, medicine man, sorcerer, shaman, fortune-teller, witch doctor, mystic, priest, prophet, and channeler.

Mediumship falls into two main categories: mental and physical. In mental mediumship the medium communicates through inner vision, clairaudience, automatic writing, and automatic speech. Physical mediumship is characterized by rappings, apports, levitation, or movement of objects and other paranormal phenomena. Mediums of both types communicate with spirits through one or more entities called "controls" (or spirit guides), which usually remain permanently with the medium. Prevailing theory among parapsychologists holds that controls are not external spirits but secondary aspects of the medium's own personality that become externalized. Believers, however, accept the spirits at face value. See Control.

The gift of mediumship manifests early, when a child is witness to an unseen world. This ability may be repressed by disapproving adults, especially in the West. Mediumship also can begin at any later age as the result of a trauma, such as a blow to the head, a near-death experience, extreme emotional shock, or profound grief.

In the modern West, mediumship is a hallmark of Spiritualism and concerns communication with the dead. Prior to the development of Spiritualism around the middle of the nineteenth century, mesmerists discovered that some subjects who were "magnetized," or hypnotized, seemed to fall under the control of spirits and deliver messages from the "other side."

As Spiritualism spread it attracted primarily housebound women into mediumship—not because women necessarily are predisposed to it, but because it provided relief from a narrow existence. Mediumship gave these women attention and, most important, freedom: freedom of movement and travel and freedom for outrageous behavior "caused" by the spirits.

From the 1850s through the 1870s, the period of greatest growth for Spiritualism, housewives began holding tea parlor seances for their friends. Those who attended in turn discovered their own alleged mediumistic talent. In fact mediumship seemed to run along bloodlines, with all the women in a family sharing the gift. Because the press criticized female mediums for being corrupted of their femininity, many avoided publicity and were content with small-scale social diversions. Others became professional, advertised, and charged money for their performances.

Women comprised most of the mediums who took to the lecture circuit and delighted in shocking their audiences with deep trance voices and theatrics. Cora Richmond, famous on both sides of the Atlantic, gave "trance lectures." The audience selected a jury (usually all male), which chose a topic of discourse that was usually science or some "masculine" subject. Richmond entered a trance and gave an instant "spirit" lecture on it. Her audiences invariably were impressed, though skeptics contended that the talks were bland, monotonous, and predictable.

Other female mediums were more dramatic. Some reveled in being possessed by male spirits, who "forced" them to swear and drink whiskey from a bottle. In America two female mediums engaged in a fist fight on stage because their spirit controls hated each other. Such theatrics both shocked and fascinated onlookers of both sexes.

A sexual liberation side existed to Spiritualism mediumship as well. Both mediums and their clients enjoyed the physical contact of holding the hands, knees, legs, and feet of a medium, and caressing and kissing "spirit" materializations. Some mediums engaged in affairs under the direction of their spirits. Those who bore illegitimate babies sometimes claimed the infants were "spirit babies" produced by consorting with their controls. Others said their controls ordered them to leave their husbands and to counsel other women to divorce their spouses as well.

Despite fame, notoriety, and freedom, mediumship seldom led to riches. The lucky mediums, such as Daniel Dunglas Home, attracted wealthy benefactors. In America the average medium earned five dollars for a night's performance away from home, and one dollar per hour at home. Female mediums complained bitterly about their low incomes. Another hazard was ostracization. Despite the adulation of clients, many women-turned-mediums found themselves spurned by family and friends who disapproved of their behavior.

Mediumship, and in particular physical mediumship, suffered from exposés of fraud during early Spiritualism. Competition drove some mediums to stage magic to create their special effects. Many mediums who claimed to materialize spirits were caught impersonating the spirits themselves by walking around in the darkened seance rooms dressed in gauze. See **Materialization.** William Crookes, British physicist and chemist who investigated mediums, said of more than one hundred mediums he knew, all resorted to tricks at times. Mediums who were caught, such as Eusapia Palladino, complained that public expectations for a performance pressured her into cheating. Most Spiritualist mediumship today is mental rather than physical. Fraud, however, does not explain all phenomena associated with mediumship. It is possible, for example, that genuine psychokinesis

(PK) occurs in mediumship—but whether it is caused by the medium or alleged spirits is a matter of controversy.

Theories have been put forward that mediumship is a form of mental disorder, for similar phenomena occur in schizophrenia: altered states of consciousness, visions, disembodied voices, and the temporary possession of a medium by a spirit entity or personality. Many prominent mediums have been extensively interviewed and observed by psychiatrists and psychologists. However, mediums carry on normal lives and learn to control their trance states, while schizophrenics have no control over the voices, visions, and personalities that assault them without warning.

Beginning in the late nineteenth century, psychical researchers investigated mediums for evidence of survival after death. While some mediums produced impressive results, such research remains inconclusive. Scientific interest in mediums declined in the second half of the twentieth century as researchers turned to other areas. See **Channeling; Oracle; Spiritualism.**

Sources: Alfred Douglas. *Extrasensory Powers: A Century of Psychical Research.* London: Victor Gollancz Ltd., 1976; Alan Gauld. *Mediumship and Survival.* London: William Heinemann Ltd., 1982; Jon Klimo. "The Psychology of Channeling." *New Age Journal* 3, no. 6 (November/December 1987): 32–40+; R. Laurence Moore. *In Search of White Crows.* New York: Oxford University Press, 1977; Janet Oppenheim. *The Other World: Spiritualism and Psychical Research in England, 1850–1914.* Cambridge: Cambridge University Press, 1985; Alberto Villoldo and Stanley Krippner. *Healing States.* New York: Fireside/Simon & Schuster, 1986; Benjamin B. Wolman, ed. *Handbook of Parapsychology.* New York: Van Nostrand Reinhold, 1977.

Medjugorje

See **Marian apparitions.**

Megaliths

Groups of standing stones or large stone structures dating to the Neolithic or Bronze Age. Megalith ruins exist around the world. They are believed to have had sacred, astronomical, or burial purposes. Many are said to possess healing and magical powers, or to be repositories of great electromagnetic energy that causes or contributes to paranormal phenomena in proximity to the stones.

"Megalith," meaning "great stones," comes from the Greek *megas,* "great," and *lithos,* "stone." Generally, any large structure of stone may be termed a "megalith," but the term usually is applied to ancient stone circles and tombs.

Megaliths are divided into two classifications: dolmens and menhirs. Dolmens are tombs of one or more chambers. Some are long in shape, while others are round with passages connecting the chambers. Long tombs are common in parts of Wales, Scotland, and England, while round dolmens with passages are most common to Ireland and western parts of Britain. Some dolmens are covered with earth, forming mounds or tumuli.

Human remains have not been found in all dolmens, indicating that some may have served simply as temples for rites of the dead. Bone shards found at some sites suggest that sacrificial rites, perhaps even cannibalism, may have occurred.

Menhirs are single standing stones or groups of standing stones that are arranged in circles, also called either cromlechs or henges. Of the two, henges are more complex, containing one or more entrances and being surrounded by a ditch or earthwork bank; England's Stonehenge is perhaps the best known of these. Thousands of stone circles exist around the world; there are some three thousand of them throughout the British Isles alone.

Many menhirs, especially holed

ones, are attributed with healing and fertility powers. A holed stone is a female symbol, associated with the Great Goddess, bringer of fertility, healer and protector. See **Goddess**. Typically, rites involved hugging the stone or passing through the hole in order to benefit from its magical powers.

Menhirs usually are associated with local supernatural lore. They are the gathering places of fairies and other spirits, and witches and those who practice the occult arts. Some are said to move and dance at night, or on certain holy nights. Others are reputed to be the petrified remains of people who were punished. The Rollright Stones in the Cotswolds of England, for example, are said to be an invading king and his knights, petrified by a witch to prevent their invasion of England.

Photographs of some menhirs show radiations of light emanating from them, leading some researchers to theorize that the creators of the stones imbued them with "earth energy" for sacred or psychic purposes. Individuals have reported discomfort near some menhirs at night, saying the stones radiate disturbing energy forces, which produce electric shock sensations when touched. See **Dowsing; Leys.**

Carnac, in Brittany, is the site of the greatest and oldest of all megalithic remains, comprising approximately three thousand standing stones arranged into avenues, dolmens, mounds, and cromlechs. The original number of stones is estimated at 11,000 or more. One mound-covered dolmen dates to c. 4700 B.C., older than Stonehenge or the Pyramids of Egypt.

The Dragon Project Trust (DPT), established in Britain in 1977, has conducted research of the energies and paranormal phenomena associated with megalithic sites throughout Britain. As of 1990 no site had been fully checked, though many had been dowsed and measured for one or more of the following: radioactivity, ultrasound and audible sound anomalies, magnetism, radio propagation, and light phenomena. The DPT also initiated a dreams project, in which volunteers sleep at certain megalithic sites. Early results showed the emergence of curious dream patterns. See **Avebury; Earth lights; Glastonbury; Power point; Stonehenge.**

Sources: Janet and Colin Bord. *Mysterious Britain.* Garden City, NY: Doubleday, 1978; Peter Lancaster Brown. *Megaliths and Men.* New York: Taplinger, 1976; Paul Devereux. *Places of Power.* London: Blandford, 1990; Rosemary Ellen Guiley. *The Encyclopedia of Witches and Witchcraft.* New York: Facts On File, 1989; Francis Hitching. *Earth Magic.* New York: William Morrow, 1977; Jennifer Westwood, ed. *The Atlas of Mysterious Places.* New York: Weidenfeld & Nicholson, 1987.

Meister Eckhart

See **Eckhart, Johannes.**

Men in Black

Mysterious phenomenon associated with unidentified flying object (UFO) sightings and encounters. Various individuals who claim to have sighted UFOs, been abducted by extraterrestrials, or experienced unaccounted-for "missing time" are sometimes later visited by Men in Black (MIB)—men literally dressed all in black—who discourage the individuals from persisting in their claims. MIB also allegedly have threatened and harassed individuals and their families; one person's death has been attributed to MIB.

MIB apparently have been active in America since 1947, when the first "flying saucer" reports were made. They have been especially active during periods of great UFO activity. MIB seem predominant in America, but have been reported elsewhere, including Europe, Scandinavia, Australia, New Zealand, and South Africa.

One of the earliest reports of an MIB visit, a classic case, occurred in 1953 to Albert K. Bender, a Bridgeport, Connecticut, factory clerk and enthusiast of UFOs, the occult, black magic, monsters, and science fiction and horror films. Bender organized an international flying saucer bureau, and through his research believed he discovered where extraterrestrials come from and why they visit Earth. He wrote a letter about this to a friend. After he mailed the letter, three men dressed in black suits visited him; one had his letter. After the visit Bender became ill. He acted "lobotomized," in the words of one friend, and suffered severe headaches, which he said were controlled by "them." If he thought about revealing his information, he was hit with a debilitating headache. He dropped all of his UFO-related pursuits.

Reports of MIB show some common characteristics. The facial features and complexions of MIB lead others to think they are of Oriental or Italian extraction. They have a penchant for dressing in dark or black clothing, which is either amazingly wrinkle-free or very wrinkled. They drive about in large, dark or black cars. Some have unusual hair growth, as though their head has been shaved and the hair has grown back unevenly. MIB sometimes have odd ways of walking, either as though intoxicated, or with a gliding or rocking motion as though their hips were on swivel joints. Some have been seen wearing the Great Seal of the United States in their lapels. The voices of MIB also are unusual in extremes: monotones, singsongs, and whines, and sometimes eloquent in timbre.

MIB visit UFO witnesses unannounced at home or work, usually coming in threes. Sometimes they appear after a sighting, but before the individual has contacted authorities or a UFO-related organization. They often pass themselves off as representatives of the federal government or military intelligence. Curiously, they seem to know quite a bit of personal data concerning those they visit. Some people report that MIB have resorted to intimidation, threats, and harassment to stop their interest in UFOs or their UFO research. Witnesses of UFOs have been told by MIB that they did not see what they thought they did. At least one UFO researcher has been threatened with death by a Man in Black; the MIB claimed that a UFO abductee who died had done so because he "knew too much."

While most MIB incidents concern UFOs, they also have been reported in connection with sightings of monsters and other nonhuman entities.

Folklorists link the MIB to legends of the Devil, who in earlier times was often said to appear in the form of a tall black man or a man in black. One theory holds that the Devil, MIB, Trickster, and other similar supernatural beings are part of the same phenomenon, a projection of the unconscious in order to meet a psychological need on the part of the percipient. It also has been suggested that the MIB are thought-forms created by collective fear residing in the unconscious. In Eastern mysticism the MIB have a parallel in the "Brothers of the Shadow," evil beings who try to prevent occult students from learning the great truth. See **Collective unconscious; Encounter phenomenon; Extraterrestrial encounters; Fortean phenomena; Thought-form.**

Sources: John A. Keel. *The Mothman Prophecies.* New York: Saturday Review Press/E. P. Dutton, 1975; Peter M. Rojcewicz. "The 'Men in Black' Experience and Tradition: Analogues with the Traditional Devil Hypothesis." *Journal of American Folklore* 100 (396) (April-June 1987): 148–60; Brad Steiger. *Mysteries of Time* and Space. New York: Dell/Confucian Books, 1976.

Menhir

See Megaliths.

Merlin

Legendary Arthurian wizard who has been interpreted in modern times as a Celtic mystic and shaman, and as an archetype of the Trickster and the Magician. In the Western mystery tradition, he and his consort, Viviane, the Lady of the Lake, represent Jachin and Boaz, the male and female principles of the cosmos, force and form.

Merlin, whose name is a Latinized version of the Welsh "Myrddin," may be a composite of real and mythical characters. He may be in part a deity, perhaps derived from Mabon, or Maponos, the British Apollo who served as the divine ruler of Britain. He may have been a real prophet or bard, or several bards.

The first written references to Merlin are in the Latin works of Geoffrey of Monmouth, a twelfth-century Welsh cleric. In the early 1130s, Monmouth wrote The Prophecies of Merlin, verses of prophecies going beyond the twelfth century, attributed to a Merlin who lived in the fifth century. It is likely that Monmouth made up much of the book himself. Monmouth mentioned Merlin again in the History of the Kings of Britain, completed around 1135 to 1136, which provided the basis for the Arthurian legends. Monmouth described Merlin as a magical boy whose parents were a mortal woman and a daimon, a Greek-derivative term that means "spirit," but which later Christians interpreted as a Devil's demon. According to Christianized legend, Merlin's father was the Devil himself, sent to earth to obstruct the works of Jesus. The Devil assumed the shape of a dragon or serpent (the symbol of wisdom and, in Christianity, of evil) and seduced Merlin's mother. However, the boy decided to devote himself to the light, and discarded all of the Devil's powers that he inherited save two: prophecy and miracle-making.

Merlin possessed great powers of prophecy and magic because of his half-supernatural nature. He arranged for the birth of Arthur through the seduction of Ygerna (Igraine) by King Uther Pendragon. After Arthur was born, Merlin dropped from Monmouth's story. Monmouth also confused matters by placing Merlin in both the fifth and sixth centuries.

Monmouth wrote of Merlin the prophet in a third poetic work, The Life of Merlin, and composed Merlin's adult biography in Vita Merlini, written c. 1150. Vita Merlini has been interpreted as much more than a biography, but as a text of Celtic mysticism. R. J. Stewart, British authority on Merlin, calls the Vita Merlini "one of our oldest and most profound texts of western magical and spiritual enlightenment." The Vita presents a series of questions, such as why is there suffering, death, love, and so on, which are answered in the form of cosmic visions that lead to greater questions, and reveal the small part humans play in a much greater cosmic landscape.

Merlin appears in other medieval works, and in later chivalric tales and romantic poems. A French poetical version of History of the Kings of Britain, written around 1150, tells of Merlin directing Arthur on the establishment of his Round Table. Sir Thomas Malory's Le Morte d'Arthur, published in 1485, tells how Merlin raised Arthur, secured him the throne by having him pull the sword of Branstock from the stone, and served as his magical adviser. Merlin appeared and disappeared at will, possessed omniscient awareness, and cast the most powerful of spells. Malory's work provides the modern popular conception of Merlin, despite the fact that Merlin disappeared from the story early in Arthur's reign, after the Round Table was formed. According to one legend, Merlin allowed himself to be tricked by Viviane (also called Nimue), for whom he had great passion. Viviane persuaded Merlin to teach her all his magical arts, which she then used to trap him in a tower of hawthorn, a spiny shrub or tree associated with fairies and witches, which she weaved around him nine times while he slept in the Forest of Broceliande, a magical place where no one who entered came out quite the same. When Arthur missed Merlin from his court, he dispatched Sir Gawain to find him. In the Forest of Broceliande, Merlin spoke to the knight from a cloud of smoke and told him he will never more be seen, and instructed him to tell Arthur to undertake without delay the quest of the Holy Grail.

In other versions (1) Viviane trapped Merlin in a tower of air; (2) Merlin simply disappeared into thin air, where he continued to exist as a shadow who had the power to communicate with humans; (3) he retired to a stone vault and sealed himself inside; (4) he was buried alive under a stone in the Forest of Broceliande.

Merlin usually is portrayed as a wise, old man, tall and gaunt with a long white beard. He has in fact three aspects: youth, mature prophet, and elder. As an archetype of the magician, one who uses the powers of both earth and sky (the microcosm and macrocosm) to transform, he serves as the model for many fictional characters, including Mr. Spock of "Star Trek" and Obi Wan Kenobe of *Star Wars*.

The deeper meanings of Merlin are the subject of ongoing research by Arthurian experts. See **Archetypes; Grail, the; Magic.**

Sources: Bulfinch's Mythology. Reprint. New York: Avenel Books, 1984; Henry Gilbert. *King Arthur's Knights.* 1911. London: Bracken Books, 1986; Manly P. Hall. *The Secret Teachings of All Ages.* 1928. Los Angeles: The Philosophic Research Society, 1977; Rosemary Ellen Guiley. *The Encyclopedia of Witches and Witchcraft.* New York: Facts On File, 1989; John Matthews, ed. *At the Table of the Grail: Magic and the Uses of Imagination.* 1984. London: Arkana, 1987; R. J. Stewart, ed. *The Book of Merlin.* Poole, Dorset, England: Blanford Press, 1987; R. J. Stewart. *The Mystic Life of Merlin.* London: Arkana, 1986; R. J. Stewart. *Living Magical Arts.* Poole, Dorset, England: Blanford Press, 1987.

Merton, Thomas (1915–1968)

Trappist monk, peace activist, and one of the most important Catholic writers of the twentieth century. Thomas Merton was influenced by mysticism, Asian religions (Zen Buddhism in particular), monastic life, and the social concerns of his times.

Merton was born on January 31, 1915, in Prades, France, of an American Quaker mother. His father was a New Zealand landscape artist. He was orphaned at fifteen. He studied briefly at Cambridge University, but later received his bachelor's and master's degrees from Columbia University in New York City. After graduation he worked in Harlem at a Catholic center for the poor and taught English at Columbia (1938 to 1939).

While at Columbia Merton became briefly interested in communism. A much greater influence on him was Daniel Clark Walsh, one of Merton's mentors at Columbia. Walsh's teachings influenced Merton's distinctions between person, nature, and individual, which he developed in his writing.

In 1941 Merton entered the Order of Cistercians of the Strict Observance (Trappists) at their monastery in Gethsemani, Kentucky. He was ordained a priest in 1949, taking the religious name Father M. Louis, and later served as master of novices. (Gethsemani has since become one of the country's acclaimed personal renewal centers.)

Merton wrote several novels during his youth, one of which, *My Agreement with the Gestapo,* was published posthumously in 1969. Three books of poetry were published between 1941 and 1947 with little notice. Then his autobiography, *The Seven Story Mountain* (1948), became a best-seller and catapulted him to fame. In the book Merton tells of his gradual conversion from agnosticism to Catholicism in 1938, and his reasons for becoming a Trappist.

The autobiography and subsequent works of spiritual meditations and reflections, which contain much autobiographical material, have been compared to the spiritual journals of St. Augustine and John Bunyan, and in terms of social reflection have been compared to other modern religious journals, including those by Black Elk, Richard Rubenstein, Albert Schweitzer, and Harvey Cox.

Merton's books can be grouped by subject matter into three stages. Those published between 1948 and 1960 deal mainly with ascetic practices for relating to the materialist world. Those between 1960 and 1965 are mainly concerned with social issues and social criticism, while those from 1965 to 1968 show his interest in Eastern mysticism. Merton scandalized many Catholics with his study of the parallels between Eastern (especially Zen Buddhism) and Western religious traditions. With exceptional insights comparable to his contemporary, Alan Watts, Merton produced *The Way of Chuang Tzu* (1965), *Zen and the Birds of Appetite* (1968), and *Mystics and Zen Masters* (1967).

Merton viewed conversion as a continuing process, and his mystical journey has been compared to those of the great Spanish mystics and other contemplatives. The integrating principle of his art and life was his concept of God incarnating with humankind. He believed that being a mystic was to some extent necessary for a poet.

In his later years, he became an outspoken opponent of the Vietnam War. He wrote the words for several freedom songs for the Civil Rights movement, and edited *Gandhi on Non-Violence* (1965). Merton and his writings have influenced peace activists of many faiths. He and Dorothy Day were among the writers for *The Catholic Worker* who greatly influenced the brothers Daniel and Philip Berrigan and other charismatic leaders of the antiwar resistance in the late 1960s and early 1970s, and later such notable social reform activists as actor Martin Sheen.

In 1965 he was allowed to live as a hermit at Gethsemani, and spent most of the last three years of his life in solitude.

On December 10, 1968, Merton died while attending an ecumenical conference of monks in Bangkok. The cause of death was electrocution from contact with an electrical fan that had faulty wiring. His body was returned to the United States in an airplane that, ironically, also brought back bodies of American soldiers who fought in the Vietnam War.

Sources: Monica Furlong. *Merton: A Biography.* San Francisco: Harper & Row, 1980; Michael Mott. *The Seven Mountains of Thomas Merton.* Boston: Houghton Mifflin, 1984; M. Basil Pennington. *Thomas Merton, Brother Monk.* San Francisco: Harper & Row, 1987; Paul Wilkes, ed. *Merton by Those Who Knew Him Best.* San Francisco: Harper & Row, 1984; George Woodcock. *Thomas Merton— Monk and Poet: A Critical Study.* New York: Farrar, Straus and Giroux, 1978.

Mescaline

See **Drugs in mystical and psychic experiences; Huxley, Aldous.**

Mesmer, Franz (or Friedrich) Anton (1734–1815)

Flamboyant German healer, whose method of laying on of hands and giving suggestions to patients led to the development of therapeutic hypnotism.

Born at Iznang on Lake Constance, Germany, around 1734, Mesmer initially intended to enter the church. He discovered a gift for mathematics and science, and decided to study medicine at the University of Vienna. There he interpreted the prevailing theory of the times that a magnetic fluid permeates and links all things and beings, including human beings, on earth and in the heavens.

The idea of such a fluid or force was not new, but dated from ancient times in both East and West. It is the approximate equivalent of the Hindu *prana,* the Chinese *ch'i,* and the Japanese *ki.* Paracelsus believed in such a force. J. B. van Helmont, a late-sixteenth-century scientist, put forth the theory that all humans radiate a magnetic fluid, which can be used to influence the minds and bodies of others through will. In particular Mesmer borrowed from the ideas of Richard Mead, an English physician, who in 1704 published a treatise on the power of the sun and moon on the human body.

Mesmer's thesis, *De Planetarum Influxu* ("On the Influence of the Planets"), caught the attention of Father Maximilian Hehl, a Jesuit priest, court astrologer to Empress Maria Theresa, and a professor of astronomy at Vienna University. Hehl also believed in a planetary magnetism that influenced physical health, and used magnets made in the shape of body organs to correct magnetic imbalances. He gave magnets to Mesmer, who qualified as a physician in 1765 and used the magnets in some spectacular healings. He would lay the magnets on patients and pain would cease. Mesmer surmised his own body was a magnet, for he noticed that, when once bleeding a patient, the flow of blood increased when he approached and decreased when he left. He published his theory in 1775; the public reacted enthusiastically and patients began to seek him out.

A few years later, Mesmer observed the work of an exorcist, Father Johann Gassner, who maintained that all illness was caused by demonic possession and could be cured only by exorcism. This led Mesmer to the discovery that he could cure without the help of Hehl's magnets. The vital force or healing energy could be transmitted directly from healer to patient through touch or with the help of iron rods or wands. He called this force "animal magnetism."

Mesmer fell out of favor with Hehl and the Viennese medical profession, but his esteem increased with patients, who flocked to him for cures. In 1778 he moved to Paris to set up a fashionable hospital that was more like a seance parlor than a medical facility. The rooms were lit with low light, perfumed, and decorated with mirrors, crystal objects, beautiful paintings, and handsome clocks. Mesmer himself seemed more like a wizard than a physician, dressed in purple robes and carrying an iron wand. While a chamber orchestra played soft music, he and his assistants would move among the patients, waving hands and wands, stroking them and magnetizing them. Many phenomenal cures were effected, made all the more mysterious and awesome by the hysterics and convulsions of his patients as they were cured. Rich and poor alike descended upon the clinic. Mesmer entertained well, hosting coffee socials and carrying on lively conversations with his clients.

So many patients came to his clinic that Mesmer began treating them en masse. He created a device called the *baquet,* a round wooden bathtub that he filled with "magnetized water" and iron filings. Up to thirty iron rods protruded from the lid of the tub, which were placed on as many patients on whatever part of the body required healing. The patients were then tied to each other with moistened rope, forming a magnetic chain.

Mesmer's success resulted in the inevitable animosity of the Medical Academy. Louis XVI was a supporter of Mesmer, but agreed under pressure to establish two commissions to investigate Mesmer and animal magnetism. The first, which published its findings in 1784, found no evidence to support the existence of animal magnetism and recommended that members of the Faculty of Medicine who practiced it be expelled. The second commission supported the first.

Mesmer's fortunes soon declined. A doctor consulted him with a phony illness, allowed Mesmer to heal him, then accused him of fraud.

Mesmer fell into further discredit when one of his staunchest supporters, Antoine Court de Gebelin, an Egyptologist known for his writings on the Tarot, died while sitting at a baquet. But the populace continued to patronize him, and Mesmer maintained his clinic until 1789, when the French Revolution forced him to flee the country. He went to Karlsruhe, then to Vienna in 1793. He was accused of being a French spy and thrown in jail for two months. Upon his release Mesmer returned to Lake Constance, where he died in 1815. See **Hypnosis.**

Sources: Slater Brown. *The Heyday of Spiritualism.* New York: Hawthorn Books, 1970; Eric Cuddon. *The Meaning and Practice of Hypnosis.* New York: Citadel Press, 1965; Alfred Douglas. *Extrasensory Powers: A Century of Psychical Research.* London: Victor Gollancz Ltd., 1976; Janet Oppenheim. *The Other World: Spiritualism and Psychical Research in England, 1850–1914.* Cambridge: Cambridge University Press, 1985; Kurt Seligmann. *The History of Magic and the Occult.* New York: Pantheon Books, 1948; Colin Wilson. *The Occult.* New York: Vintage Books, 1973.

Messing, Wolf Grigorievich (1899–1972)

One of Russia's most famous psychics. Wolf Messing dazzled Josef Stalin, accurately predicted the end of World War II, and impressed audiences all over the Soviet Union with his clairvoyant powers. He was a small, trim man with piercing eyes and a mane of wiry hair, which he combed straight back. He never married, and spent much of his life in isolation and loneliness.

Messing was born on September 10, 1899, in Gora Kalwaria, near Warsaw, Poland. His psychic abilities manifested early, and he was performing for the public by his teens. In Vienna in 1915, Albert Einstein invited him to his apartment, where Messing met Sigmund Freud. Freud tested his psychic ability, with impressive results. Messing toured the world as a celebrity.

In 1937 he incurred Adolph Hitler's wrath by publicly predicting that Hitler would die if he "turned toward the East," to Russia. Hitler put a 200,000-mark price on his head. In 1939 Messing fled to Russia, only to land under the terrifying repression of Josef Stalin. Russian psychics were forced to go underground or risk being shot, but Messing managed to impress Stalin.

Stalin assigned Messing to psychically rob a bank. Messing took an empty attaché into a Moscow bank, handed the clerk a blank piece of paper, and mentally ordered him to fill it with 100,000 rubles. The clerk did so. When the test was concluded, Messing handed back the money; the clerk suffered a heart attack when he realized what he'd done. Messing said he used telepathic hypnosis to influence others in this fashion. He claimed to have eluded the Gestapo and Stalin's police.

Stalin allowed Messing to perform around the country. In Novosibirsk, on March 7, 1944, he forecast the death of Hitler and the exact date that the Nazis would surrender.

After the war Messing worked as an entertainer under the direction of Goskonsert, which lumped him with thousands of musicians, dancers, and circus performers. He was officially billed as a "concert artist." In reward for his popularity and success, he was given a three-room apartment with no telephone in Moscow, where he liked to retreat and read books. He was often recognized on the streets.

In explaining his secrets of clairvoyance, Messing said that others' thoughts became colorful images in his mind; he saw pictures rather than heard words. He always attempted to touch his subjects by the hand, which he said helped clear his own mind of distractions. He denied reading facial muscles, and said it was easier for him to read blindfolded. The thoughts of the deaf and dumb were clearer than those of others, he said.

Messing was not a faith healer, but could diagnose illnesses, and could relieve headaches by placing his fingertips lightly on the temples of the sufferer.

Russian scientists sought to find a physiological reason for his clairvoyance, but Messing rarely let himself be examined. A neurologist discovered that portions of his head and chest generated more heat than other parts of his body, but never discovered why. Some scientists believed that when Messing took a subject by the hand, he subconsciously received muscle movements that aided him in his reading.

In his later years, Messing's psychic talents declined, but Goskonsert refused to let him retire because of his enormous popularity. He was never allowed outside to the West, perhaps out of fear that he would defect. Following a period of illness, Messing died on November 8, 1972.

Sources: Henry Gris and William Dick. The New Soviet Psychic Discoveries. Englewood Cliffs, NJ: Prentice-Hall, 1978; Tatiana Lungin. Wolf Messing: The True Story of Russia's Greatest Psychic. New York: Paragon House, 1989; Sheila Ostrander and Lynn Schroeder. The ESP Papers: Scientists Speak Out from Behind the Iron Curtain. New York: Bantam Books, 1976; Sheila Ostrander and Lynn Schroeder. Psychic Discoveries Behind the Iron Curtain. Englewood Cliffs, NJ: Prentice-Hall, 1970.

Milarepa (c. 1052–1135)

Great yogi of Tibet, revered as a national hero and venerated as a Fully Enlightened One in other Asian countries. Once a sorcerer of formidable power who worked the Left-Hand Path of magic, Milarepa repented and devoted himself to the pursuit of dharma. His name means "cotton-clad Mila" (Mila is given as "O man!"), and he was renowned for his power to generate tumo, or psychic heat, in order to stay warm in Tibet's harsh environment wearing nothing more than a cotton robe. More than any other Buddhist yogi, Milarepa experimented with the elements of consciousness. His biography, written in the fifteenth century, is a source of inspiration to modern Buddhists.

Milarepa was born in 1052 (or, by some accounts, in 1038 or 1025) in Tibet, near the edge of Nepal. His father was a merchant who was away at the time of his birth. When the news reached him, he named the infant Thopaga, "Delightful to Hear." Interestingly, Milarepa possessed a beautiful voice, and throughout his life would spontaneously burst into song.

Milarepa's father died when he was seven, and his family fell victim to his rapacious paternal aunt and uncle, who took the inheritance and turned them out. For years Milarepa, his mother, and sister endured great hardship, which gave birth to festering resentment on the part of Milarepa and his mother. One day when he was seventeen, he came home drunk, and apologized to his mother by promising to do whatever she wanted. She ordered him to find a magician who would teach him the sorcery necessary to take revenge on the cousins.

Milarepa found a black magician named Lama Yungtun-Trogyal, "Wrathful and Victorious Teacher of Evil," who reputedly could kill at a distance and send tempests to ruin crops. When he had learned the black arts, Milarepa destroyed a house in which one of his cousins was celebrating a wedding feast. A witness saw it filled with vermin, and a giant scorpion the size of a yak pulling down its central pillar. Thirty-five people were killed, but Milarepa spared the lives of his aunt and uncle in order that they should endure more pain and misery. The destruction of the house was not enough to satisfy his mother, who asked him to rain hailstorms on the crops. This Milarepa did, conjuring a fierce storm of hail, heavy rain, and strong wind.

Milarepa regretted these actions, but remained in the service of the sorcerer and gained a formidable reputation himself. At age thirty-eight he at last repented, and with his teacher's blessings, devoted himself to pursuing dharma. He became a pupil of Marpa, founder of the Kargyut-pa school of Tibetan Buddhism, who introduced the Short Path of enlightenment, including intense yoga and development of the *siddhis,* or psychic powers. See **Siddhis.**

Milarepa remained with Marpa for six years. During that time he underwent intense spiritual disciplines, beginning with the breaking of the will, which is the total surrender of oneself, body and soul, to an ideal. Marpa relentlessly eradicated Milarepa's self-will and subjected his pupil to frequent beatings. He had Milarepa build a house of stone, only to order him

several times to tear it down and start over again. The house, in Lhobrag, southern Tibet, still stood at the time of Alexandra David-Neel's explorations of Tibet in the early twentieth century. Marpa and Milarepa painstakingly saved numerous Buddhist scriptures from the sacking and burning of Moslems who invaded northern India. As a result Tibetan Buddhist literature is the most extensive in all Buddhism.

By the age of forty-four, Milarepa had atoned for his sorcery and was then initiated by Marpa. One night Milarepa dreamed his home was in ruins and his mother was dead. He returned home and found conditions as in his dream. He gathered her bones and, by one account, placed them in a sack, which he used for a pillow for the rest of his life. By another account he followed tradition and had them fashioned into *tsha-tshas,* miniature reliquaries, which he placed in a *stupa,* a burial mound. Milarepa then vowed to live the life of an ascetic and devote himself to meditation. However, he vowed not to enter nirvana, the final liberation from physical existence, until all other sentient beings had obtained salvation. His own sanctity would redeem both his parents.

He retired to a cave, the "White Cave of the Horse's Tooth," so high up in the hills and difficult to reach that few bothered to seek him out. This was just as well, for Milarepa did not want to be distracted from his meditation. He was visited by his chief disciple, Rechung-Dorje-Tagpa, and by Dzze-se, a girl to whom he had been betrothed in childhood but had never married.

Milarepa ate only nettle broth, and became extremely thin. His body and hair took on the green color of the nettles. He endured the bitter cold in his thin cotton robe with the help of *tumo.* He eventually attained a state of pure intellectual light, and was then able to subsist on *amritsa,* the ambrosia of the gods.

During his hermit years, he allegedly developed even more incredible psychic powers: He was witnessed flying, and he traveled out-of-body at will not only anywhere on earth, but also to other planes and worlds, where he would hold discussions with spiritual masters; he could transform himself into a flame, bird, or running stream. These powers gained him unfavorable attention from others, who were interested in using them for material gain, so Milarepa left his cave and traveled to the area near Mount Everest, where he stopped at a place called Between the Rivers at Lap-chi.

A jealous lama, Tsaphuwa, sent a concubine to Milarepa to offer him poisoned curds. By clairvoyance Milarepa knew the plot, but ate the poisoned curds anyway. He explained to the concubine that the poison could not hurt him, but he was ready to depart his life. He summoned his disciples and for many days preached on the law of karma and the Real Truth. The earth and the skies filled with gods who gathered to listen, and a most heavenly music played. Milarepa sang numerous hymns.

He at last fell ill and sank into *samadhi,* a prelude to nirvana. He was eighty-four. On his funeral pyre, he reanimated his corpse, and then was resurrected in the Indestructible Body, which is both the spiritual body and the phenomenal body. Flames rose up around the funeral pyre. He sang a final hymn and then sank in a trance into the Clear Light, part of the first stage of the Bardo Thodöl ("Between Two"), the after-death state. The cremation was accompanied by all manner of unearthly and glorious sights and sounds. The sky reportedly became a mandala. Comets blazed across it, and flowers fell.

When the fire was spent, the disciples were keenly disappointed to find that *dakinis* ("sky-walkers," female embodiments of the complete wisdom of Buddha) had taken away all the bones and ashes. To mollify them the dakinis gave them one last grand vision of a great *chaitya* (reliquary), projecting the image of Milarepa, before bearing it away to the east, to the accompaniment of celestial music and sights.

Milarepa's songs and hymns, composed through his life, continue to be sung in modern Tibet. Places where he is said to have walked are venerated. See **Yoga.**

Sources: Bernard Bromage. *Tibetan Yoga.* 1952. Wellingborough, Northamptonshire, England: The Aquarian Press, 1979; Alexandra David-Neel. *Magic and Mystery in Tibet.* 1929. New York: Dover Books, 1979; W. Y. Evans-Wentz. *Tibet's Great Yogi Milarepa: A Biography from the Tibetan.* 2d ed. London: Oxford University Press, 1951; Christmas Humphreys. *A Popular Dictionary of Buddhism.* London: Curzon Press, 1984; Vivian Worthington. *A History of Yoga.* London: Routledge & Kegan Paul, 1982.

Miracle

An occurrence that is perceptible to the senses, transcends the natural course of events, and takes place within a religious context. More precise definitions, and criteria for distinguishing miracles from other paranormal events, depend on the various definitions of "nature" and "religious." Nineteenth-century cultural anthropologists tended to classify all claims of miraculous events under the heading of magic; more modern schools tend to classify any extraordinary way of interacting with the cosmos as a religious occurrence and therefore as a "miracle," regardless of whether or not it is considered valid by religious authorities.

One's concept of nature affects whether or not one considers miracles possible, and what one considers to be miracles. Modern scientific views of nature, and therefore of the definition and possibility of miracles, fall roughly into two schools. The rational materialist view, dominant in the nineteenth century, eventually came to explain everything that is or can be in terms of matter and energy, governed by rigid laws that determine all events. In this view the supernatural is an illusion—but so are a great many other things, rather harder to explain away.

In the twentieth century, Albert Einstein's general theory of relativity and the uncertainty principle of Werner Heisenberg, a founder of the quantum theory, has led to a less rigidly deterministic scientific model of the universe: If science must acknowledge randomness on the part of the smallest particles, or waves, of matter, it seems less improbable that other actions also transcend the laws of matter and energy. In addition, psychology seems to indicate that the mind— even the unconscious mind—has a greater control of the body than mechanistic theories allow (see **Behavioral medicine**). Many scientists thus have been more willing to admit that "there are more things in heaven and earth" than were dreamed of in nineteenth-century science. This is not, however, so much an acceptance of the supernatural as it is a willingness to include in nature what may seem supernatural in the present state of human knowledge.

From the point of view of religion, the immanent god of pantheistic religions is neither distinct from nature nor its creator, and thus is not supernatural and cannot work miracles. Polytheistic religions abound in stories of what modern Western people would call the miraculous. However, it is not always clear from the outside which events are considered miracles and which (especially in shamanistic religions) are considered "natural."

Religions and philosophies, such as Christian Science and Buddhism, that consider the material world an illusion would not be expected to admit the possibility of miracles as such: If matter does not exist or is normally subject to direct manipulation by mind, there would be nothing extraordinary, or miraculous, in such manipulation. Buddhism, however, shows some ambivalence. Though the enlightened can perform what would be considered miracles by the unenlightened, and though Gautama Buddha himself is said to have done so to assist his followers to conversion, the stricter Buddhist schools have maintained that they should not be performed. On the other hand, Mahayana Buddhism, especially in China, has many stories of miraculous occurrences.

Islam theoretically admits the possibility of miracles, but Muhammad refused to perform them, reminding his followers that all things, being made by Allah, are signs of His power and goodness. Nonetheless, miracle stories are recounted of Sufi holy men, and some of the orders are known for preternatural achievements, such as swallowing coals and the like.

Miracles have a more important role in Judaism and Christianity. Both trace their origin to events viewed as both historical and miraculous: the Exodus of the Jews from Egypt in Judaism, and the Resurrection of Jesus in Christianity. It is Christianity, especially in the Catholic tradition, that has developed the most systematic account of miracles. On the one hand, it accepts the idea of a natural order of things and laws of nature, which are considered the work of God. On the other hand, it maintains that God can suspend or otherwise intervene in the natural order, and has done so at least on certain occasions in the past. The Roman church has in one document declared both that miracles can occur and can be known to have occurred, and that "there can never be a real opposition between faith and reason" (and, presumably, between faith and science). The God who reveals himself is the same God who made the natural world and the human mind, and "He cannot contradict Himself" (Vatican I, Constitution *De Filius*).

In this view miracles are considered an intervention in nature or a suspension of its laws, not a violation of them, and always have a religious purpose. The New Testament miracles are presented as providing a divine sanction of the person and message of Christ. This stress on the meaning of the miracle sets the Judeo-Christian concept of miracle apart from miracle stories in other religious traditions. It has also enabled certain schools of modern theology to downplay the historical authenticity of the miracle stories as less important than their purpose and meaning. See **Magic**.

Sources: R. G. Collingwood. *The Idea of Nature.* New York: Oxford University Press, 1945; Heinrich Denziger. *Enchiridion Symbolorum.* 33d ed. Expanded and enlarged by Adolf Schonmetzer, S.J. Freiburg-im-Breisgau: Herder, 1965; David Hume. *Of Miracles.* La Salle, IL: Open Court, 1985; Peter Kreeft. "Apologetics: Why Miracles Make Sense." *National Catholic Register* (May 11, 1986): 1+; C. S. Lewis. *Miracles: A Preliminary Study.* New York: Macmillan, 1947.

Mirror

A gateway to magic, the supernatural, the soul, and the mysteries of the universe. Since ancient times, mirrors—as well as all smooth, reflective surfaces—have been used for divination, magic, and repelling evil; they also have been greatly feared for their power to steal the soul. In recent times mirrors have been used as tools in psychic development to increase clairvoyance and gain knowledge of so-called past lives.

The precursor to the mirror is the body of still water in a lake, pond, pool, or bowl. The ancient Romans believed mirrors originated in Persia, where they were used by the magi for divination. The Romans, Greeks, and Egyptians used mirrors made of bronze or silver; the Chinese and Hindu also used metals. Glass mirrors were introduced in the thirteenth century in Venice, but metal mirrors and polished surfaces have continued to be used throughout the centuries.

Divination with mirrors is called crystallomancy, catoptromancy, and scrying. The ancient witches of Thessaly are said to have written their oracles upon mirrors with human blood. They also taught Pythagoras to divine by holding a mirror up to the moon. In Rome, a culture of enthusiastic diviners, a special class of mirror-readers emerged called *specularii*. In the fourth century, Emperor Julianus religiously consulted his specularii, blindfolded boys who stood before mirrors and chanted charms to see the future.

In the West magic mirrors were particularly popular from the Middle Ages to the nineteenth century. They were used by all classes of society, but especially by magicians, witches, sorcerers, and cunning men and women. Catherine de Medici and Henry IV often consulted their magic mirrors. Albertus Magnus and Agrippa divined with one, as did Cagliostro. John Dee, the royal magician to Queen Elizabeth I, used a crystal egg and a black obsidian mirror.

In more recent times, mirrors as magic tools have fallen out of widespread popular fashion, but are still used by diviners, psychics, and students of psychism.

Mirrors are more commonly used for divination in the East than in the West. In parts of India, preparation for mirror divination involves rituals of fasting, prayer, and perfuming of the mirrors. In Tibet mirrors are used for *tra*, divination by the reading of signs and visions, an esteemed skill which requires a natural gift and instruction from a *trapa*, or practitioner. The trapa uses a mirror made of polished metal or stone, or gazes into a clear lake or the clear sky. He recites mantras and empties his mind, eventually seeing visions.

Fear of mirrors is universal. In many tribal societies, the reflection is believed to be the soul. Exposing the soul in a mirror or reflecting surface makes it vulnerable to danger and death. The Zulus believe dark pools of water harbor beasts that will drag away their reflections; Basutos believe crocodiles will do the same. A common belief in many cultures holds that a person who sees his or her reflection will soon die. This is the basis for the Greek myth of Narcissus, who looked upon his reflection in the water and pined and died. The ancient Greeks also believed that dreaming of seeing one's reflection was an omen of death. A worldwide folklore custom is the removal of mirrors from sick rooms, lest the mirror draw out the soul of weakened persons, and the turning or removal of mirrors upon a death in the house. According to superstition whoever looks into a mirror following a death will also die. An old custom in some parts of Germany called for the covering up of all shiny, reflective surfaces after a death.

Mirrors are associated with evil. In Russian folklore they are the invention of the Devil and will draw souls out of bodies. In other superstitions, if one looks into the mirror long enough at night or by candlelight, one will see the Devil; thus it is advisable to cover up mirrors in the bedroom at night. The candlelight is not advisable because fire is the element of spirit, and attracts the unseen. Witches and vampires cast no reflections in mirrors. The look of the evil eye will shatter a mirror or poison its surface. Conversely, mirrors may be used to protect against evil. They can reflect the evil eye; in the seventeenth century, it was fashionable in Europe to wear small mirrors in hats. The ancient Aztecs protected their homes from witches at night by leaving a knife in a bowl of water at the threshold. A witch would see her reflection, or soul, pierced by the knife and would flee.

Numerous superstitions surround mirrors. Breaking one means bad luck for seven years, or disaster or death; a mirror that falls and breaks of its own accord is an omen of impending death in the house. A girl who gazes at the moon's reflection in a mirror will learn her wedding day; if performed on Halloween, the ritual will reveal a vision of her future husband. In Ozark lore to see an absent friend appear in a mirror means he will soon die; babies under a year in age should not see their reflections, or they will be cross-eyed or die before their second birthday.

Students of the occult use mirrors to look into the world of spirit. Gazing into one supposedly reveals visions of spirit guides and helps one gain auric sight, the ability to see the aura. Some believe that the face changes seen by staring into a mirror are images of past lives. Mirrors painted black on the convex side are considered an excellent tool for developing clairvoyance. See **Scrying**.

Sources: W. E. Butler. *How to Develop Clairvoyance.* 2d ed. New York: Samuel Weiser, 1979; Frederick Thomas Elworthy. 1895. Reprint. *The Evil Eye.* Secaucus, NJ: University Books/Citadel Press, n.d.; *The Encyclopedia of Occult Sciences.* New York: Robert McBride & Co., 1939; James G. Frazer. *The Golden Bough: The Roots of Religion and Folklore.* 1890. Reprint. New York: Avenel Books, 1981; Craig Junjulas. Lecture on "Psychic Awareness." Vahalla, NY, October 5, 1987; Michael Loewe and Carmen Blacker. *Oracles and Divination.* Boulder, CO: Shambhala, 1981; Elizabeth Pepper and John Wilcock. *Magical and Mystical Sites.* New York: Harper & Row, 1977; Vance Randolph. *Ozark Magic and Folklore.* New York: Columbia University Press, 1947; Jane Sarnoff and Reynold Ruffins. *Take Warning! A Book of Superstitions.* New York: Charles Scribner's Sons, 1978; Harry E. Wedeck. *A*

Treasury of Witchcraft. Secaucus, NJ: Citadel Press, 1961.

Montgomery, Ruth (b. 1912)

Author who says she communicates with spirit guides via automatic writing. Montgomery's subjects have included reincarnation, magnetic healing, Atlantis, Lemuria, Earth changes, and visits from aliens and advanced spiritual beings.

She was born Ruth Schick in Princeton, Indiana, on June 11, 1912. Her early ambition was to be a missionary, but she pursued journalism instead. Montgomery attended both Baylor and Purdue universities, but never graduated with a degree. She had several reporting jobs, culminating in her most important post with the International News Service (INS) in Washington, DC, which later merged with United Press International. She met her husband, Robert H. Montgomery, a management consultant, in Detroit.

Montgomery was introduced to the occult in 1956 in St. Petersburg, Florida, when she attended seances given by Sr. Malcolm Pantin, whose mediumship included spirit communications through floating trumpets. In Washington Montgomery attended seances given by the Reverend Hugh Gordon Burroughs of the Spiritualist Church of Two Worlds. She began to use a Ouija board, which enabled her to make contact, she believed, with Burroughs's control, Father Murphy, and her dead father. She also attended Burroughs's controversial Spiritualist camp in Ephrata, Pennsylvania, Camp Silver Belle. She wrote articles about her experiences for INS.

In 1958 Montgomery met trance medium Arthur Ford and formed an enduring friendship. Through Ford and her deceased father, she received messages that she should write about life after death. Ford also told her she had the ability for automatic writing. It manifested in 1960,

and an entity announced himself as "Lily," a writer of alleged repute in a past life who would be her control for other spirits who wished to communicate material for books. Critics, such as the Committee for the Investigation of Claims of the Paranormal (CSICOP), have contended Montgomery is not communicating with external beings, but with her own subconscious. See **Automatic writing; Ouija.**

Montgomery's third book, *A Gift of Prophecy* (1965), about Jeane Dixon, was her first of numerous bestsellers. Her fourth book, *A Search for the Truth* (1966), dealt with her spiritual explorations and firmly established her as an occult author.

According to Montgomery she did not believe in reincarnation until she undertook a thorough investigation of it with the help of her guides, which resulted in *Here and Hereafter* (1968). Toward the end of the 1960s, Montgomery left journalism and her husband retired from the Small Business Administration. Her last nonoccult book was *Hail to the Chiefs: My Life and Times with Six Presidents.*

When Ford died in 1971, he allegedly joined Lily's group of guides, and aided Montgomery in writing *A World Beyond* (1971), about life after death. Montgomery believes she and Ford have shared numerous intertwined past lives as part of a group karma, in Atlantis, Moab, Egypt, Persia, Tibet, Greece, France, Italy, and England. In *Companions Along the Way* (1974), Montgomery states that according to her guides, she lived during the lifetime of Jesus, as a girl named Ruth, the alleged sister of Lazarus. Their father, Jeremiah, was Ford.

At the behest of her guides, Montgomery wrote a book about aliens on Earth—*Aliens Among Us* (1985)—who ostensibly were here to train the upcoming leaders of the New Age. Such leaders would be among the survivors of the pole shifts predicted for the turn of the twenty-first century, which Montgomery's guides agreed would usher in an era of peace after a period of great turmoil.

One of her most popular theories concerns walk-ins, the subject of *Strangers Among Us* (1979). Montgomery says a walk-in is a highly developed discarnate entity who takes over the body and personality of an incarnate adult in order to work to raise spiritual consciousness and help prepare the world for the cataclysms. Hundreds of thousands of walk-ins are said to be on Earth, most as ordinary people. Most keep their identities secret, but some have announced themselves publicly with various groups and societies.

According to Montgomery some walk-ins come from other planets, while others come from the "sixth dimension"; they have been visiting Earth for millennia. She says Jesus Christ surrendered to a walk-in upon his baptism by John the Baptist. Other alleged walk-ins include Joseph, Meister Eckhart, Christopher Columbus, Albert Einstein, Emanuel Swedenborg, Gandhi, Moses, Quetzalcoatl, William Penn, Benjamin Franklin, John Greenleaf Whittier, and Abraham Lincoln.

Sources: Florence Graves. "Searching for the Truth: Ruth Montgomery Investigates Life, Death and the Hereafter." *New Age Journal* (January/February 1987): 25–29+ ; Ruth Montgomery. *A Search for the Truth.* New York: Bantam Books, 1968; Ruth Montgomery. *Companions Along the Way.* New York: Popular Library, 1976; Ruth Montgomery. *Aliens Among Us.* New York: Fawcett Crest, 1985; Ruth Montgomery. *Strangers Among Us.* New York: Fawcett Crest, 1979; Ruth Montgomery with Joanne Garland. *Ruth Montgomery: Herald of the New Age.* New York: Doubleday/Dolphin, 1987; Violet M. Shelley. "Extra!! Extra!! All About Ruth Montgomery." *Venture Inward* 3, no. 2 (March/April 1987): 50–52.

Moon

Symbol of the feminine principle, the occult side of nature, the psychic, emotion, intuition, inspiration, imagination, and the deep layers of the subconscious. Its phases correspond to the menstrual cycles of women and the seasons of nature; it is linked to fecundity, moisture, wetness, and the tides. It is a symbol of life, death, and rebirth: it waxes, wanes, vanishes from the heavens for three days, and then reappears to grow again to fullness.

Early humankind noticed that the moon regulated the tides, and came to believe that it regulated all moistures as well, including blood and the moistures within the human body. The moon appeared to regulate all growth and life cycles. It was believed to be responsible for fertilization, and women who desired to become pregnant thus slept under the rays of the moon. In the first century A.D. the Roman naturalist Pliny the Elder catalogued the moon's apparent influence over life in his thirty-seven-volume work, *Natural History.* Pliny put forth many prescriptions for regulating all activities of daily life according to the moon's phases.

Because the moon appeared to die and be reborn each month, it became associated with immortality, rebirth, and the Land of the Dead. Plutarch, the first-century Greek essayist and biographer, conceived of the moon as a way-station for souls following death and prior to rebirth. According to the Upanishads, the moon is where unenlightened souls go to rest and await reincarnation (enlightened souls go to the sun).

The moon was considered a force of nature until about 2600 B.C., when it became personified, first as the Man in the Moon, and then as gods and goddesses of the moon. Lunar goddesses predominate over gods, because of the moon's reflective (passive) nature and because of its associations with the regulation of life.

The moon is associated with witchcraft, magic, and sorcery, and is considered to be the source of witches' power. It is personified by the Triple Goddess—the virgin, mother, and crone—usually represented by the classical deities Diana (Artemis), Selene, and Hecate. The ancient witches of Thessaly were said to have the power to draw the moon down from the sky at their command; a symbolic ritual of drawing down the moon is still performed in modern Witchcraft. Witches hold their meetings, called "circles" or "esbats," and work their magic spells in accordance with lunar phases. The waxing moon is propitious for growth, achievement, good fortune, and healing spells; the waning moon is propitious for banishing spells and the undoing of harm and negative influences.

The moon itself is believed to cast a spell; one may become moonstruck beneath its silvery rays. The term "mania," derived from "moon," means ecstatic revelation; "lunacy" means possessed by the spirit of Luna. Nights of the full moon provide the greatest power for magic and the world of spirit. In folklore those cursed by lycanthropy are said to turn into werewolves under the spell of the full moon.

Moon power is mind power. The moon is Goddess's "wise blood" in women. In ancient times women withdrew to moon huts during menstruation to contemplate and absorb the power of the dark moon.

In astrology the moon exerts a powerful force in horoscopes and in daily affairs. As the moon moves through the zodiac, different creative forces are brought into play. When the moon is between signs, it is "void of course," a time of uncertainty and instability.

Sources: Joseph Campbell. *The Masks of God.* Vol. 4, *Oriental Mythology.* New York: Viking Penguin, 1962; J. E. Cirlot. *A Dictionary of Symbols.* New York: Philosophical Library, 1971; Grace Cooke with White Eagle's teaching. *Sun Men of the Americas.* New Lands, England: White Eagle Publishing Trust, 1975; Rosemary Ellen Guiley. *The Encyclopedia of Witches and Witchcraft.* New York: Facts On File, 1989; Rosemary Ellen Guiley. *Moonscapes: A Celebration of Lunar Astronomy, Magic, Legend and Lore.* New York: Prentice-Hall, 1991; Monica Sjöö and Barbara Mor. *The Great Cosmic Earth Mother: Rediscovering the Religion of the Earth.* San Francisco: Harper & Row, 1987; Starhawk. *The Spiral Dance.* San Francisco: Harper & Row, 1979; Keith Thomas. *Religion and the Decline of Magic.* New York: Charles Scribner's Sons, 1971; Doreen Valiente. *Witchcraft for Tomorrow.* Custer, WA: Phoenix Publishing, 1978; Barbara G. Walker. *The Woman's Encyclopedia of Myths and Secrets.* San Francisco: Harper & Row, 1983.

Moon, Sun Myung

See **Alternative religious movements.**

Mu

See Lemuria.

Muhammad (c. 570 or 571–632)

The Messenger of God and the Prophet of Islam, believed by followers to be the bearer of the last of all Divine revelations before the end of the world. *Muhammad* means "the Praised one" or "he who is glorified"; it was either given at birth or was a nickname. According to tradition there are two hundred names for Muhammad, such as "Joy of Creation," "Beloved of God," and so on. Mention of his name is customarily followed by one of several invocations, such as "God bless him and give him peace."

Muhammad was an inspired prophet and religious reformer in the Semitic and biblical tradition, preaching holy war and the triumph of justice. He was an energetic, attractive man described as having a beautiful face. He is believed to have been illiterate, and to have obtained his wisdom directly from God in revelations. He believed in a God who is both personal and transcendent. He also accepted the Christian beliefs in Jesus as the Messiah, and in the immaculate conception of Mary and the virgin birth. However, he believed that Judaism and Christianity had distorted God's revelations to Moses and Jesus, and that the pagan Arabs lived in ignorance of God's will. As the Prophet, he reformed and revolutionized Arabian religion and life. Islam became not a new religion, but the "original" word of God.

Only two dates are certain in Muhammad's life: the year of his emigration from Mecca to Medina, 622, and the year of his death, 632. Information concerning his earlier life is lacking in detail. The primary source is the Koran (Qu'ran), the holy book of Islam given to him by Allah (God) in a series of revelations.

Muhammad probably was born in Mecca between 567 and 572, most likely in 570 or 571. His lineage was traced back to Ishmael and Abraham. His father died prior to his birth, and he was made a ward of his grandfather, Abd al-Muttalib, the founder of the pagan Hashimite tribe of the Quryash of Mecca, a cult of idols. Muhammad was given to a Bedouin foster mother to raise in the desert. His foster family soon realized they had an unusual child, for many unusual events took place. According to one account, two men dressed in white appeared one day when the boy was four or five. They threw him down, opened his chest, and stirred their hands around. In later years Muhammad said the men were angels who had come to wash a dark spot from his heart with snow; thus was he purified of original sin. Muhammad also had an unusual large mark between his shoulders, ringed by hair, said to be the

"Seal of Prophecy," the sign of the last Divine Messenger to the world.

Muhammad returned to Mecca while still a young child. When he was eight, his grandfather died and he became a ward of an uncle, Abu Talib. As a youth he managed trade caravans belonging to a wealthy widow, Khadijah. During one caravan he met a Christian monk who recognized him as a future prophet.

At age twenty-five he married Khadijah, who was then forty-four. She had either two or three sons, who died in infancy, and four daughters.

In 610, at age forty, Muhammad entered a life of asceticism, withdrawing to the mountains near Mecca to pray and meditate. One night the angel Gabriel appeared in his dreams as the Messenger of Allah and gave him the first revelation of the Koran. The night is called the "Night of Power." The Koran was revealed gradually over the rest of his life, in nearly daily trance states, with the final revelation coming just months before his death in 632. The Koran totals 6,666 verses and forms the doctrine of Islam. Muhammad remained in constant awe of its unfoldment, which came sometimes via angels and sometimes via clairaudience. His trances were torporous; in them he had a red face and breathed heavily.

Three years after the first revelation, he began his calling as Prophet, in which he sought to restore the religion of Abraham. He began preaching to his own clan that if they did not worship God instead of their idols, they would be punished. The followers of the new religion were called Muslims, which is derived from a term that means "they that surrender to God."

Muhammad's success in converting others naturally stirred the animosity of the Quryash, which feared loss of prestige as guardians of the Ka'bah, a cube of masonry (with a Black Stone in one corner) in a large open square in Mecca. The square was founded by Abraham and surrounded by idols, and it drew great numbers of pilgrims, who were one of Mecca's key sources of income.

Muhammad would have no compromise with the Quryash, which then banned commerce with his clan, the Hashimites. Persecutions of the Muslims began, driving some of them to Abyssinia. Muhammad benefited from protection accorded by his uncle, but when Abu Talib died, animosity toward the Muslims escalated.

Khadijah died in 619 at the age of sixty-five. Muhammad married another widow, Sawdah, thirty-five.

The first pledge of fealty to Islam by pilgrims to Mecca took place in 620. Persecutions continued, and Muslims fled to Yathrib. Muhammad himself emigrated to Yathrib in 622, now observed as the year in which the Islamic era began. Yathrib became the first Islamic state, and became known as Medina, "the city of the Prophet."

In Medina Muhammad was joined by his second wife, Sawdah, and a band of seventy followers. He soon married a six-year-old girl, A'ishah, who became his favorite wife; she had an innate ability to stimulate his intuition and sense of spiritual immanence. The marriage was consummated when she came of age. Throughout the course of his life, Muhammad had ten wives and at least two concubines. (Islamic law limits the number of wives to four per man, but a revelation of the Koran allowed the Prophet to have more.)

The growing opposition to Islam eventually led to a Holy War. In the view of the Muslims, all unbelievers and idolaters had no "right" to peace. The Koran exempted from the ranks of unbelievers the followers of divinely revealed religions, including Jews, Christians, Zoroastrians, and Sabians, the latter of whom included a number of smaller religions, and later the Hindus.

Fighting broke out in 624; Muhammad's forces numbered only three hundred. In 630 Muhammad led an army of 10,000 into Mecca, which offered but token resistance. He destroyed the idols at the Ka'bah. Within weeks, the city officially converted to Islam. There followed conversions all over Arabia.

In March 632 Muhammad led 30,000 people (by some accounts, 90,000) in a farewell pilgrimage, during which he delivered the last revelation of the Koran in his sermon on Mount Arafat. The new religion was named Islam ("surrender" or "reconciliation") and the law of Islam was established. Muhammad died on June 8, 632, and was buried in his house. His death was followed by a period of confusion and civil wars.

Islam now has an estimated 800 million to 900 million followers in various sects around the world. It accepts Jesus and the prophets of Judaism as prophets of Islam. It seeks to restore the pre-Fall state of the Garden of Eden, in which humanity in its essence was perfect and capable of perceiving God in the Unseen.

Its fundamentals are the Five Pillars: the profession of faith; the canonical prayer or worship; the fast; the legal tithe; and the pilgrimage. The canonical prayer rituals are elaborate, done five times a day at certain times, with certain attitudes and prostrations, preceded by ablutions. The worshiper must face toward Mecca. In addition there are other types of prayer, done at night or upon certain occasions. The mystical path is practiced by Sufis. See **Sufism**.

Sources: Emile Dermenghem. *Muhammad and the Islamic Tradition.* 1955. Woodstock, NY: The Overlook Press, 1981; John L. Esposito. *Islam: The Straight Path.* New York: Oxford University Press, 1988; Cyril Glasse. *The Concise Encyclopedia of Islam.* San Francisco: Harper & Row, 1989; Lex Hixon. *Heart of the Koran.* Wheaton, IL: The Theosophical Publishing House, 1988; Thomas W. Lippman. *Understanding Islam: An Introduction to the Moslem*

World. New York: New American Library, 1982.

Murphy, Bridey

See **Reincarnation.**

Murphy, Gardner

See **American Society for Psychical Research (ASPR).**

Music

Arrangements of sound, which, aside from creating entertainment, are believed to affect physical, mental, emotional, and spiritual states. The ability of music to positively or negatively influence health, character, morality, and consciousness has been known since ancient times. It is one of the oldest therapies, and in nearly all cultures has been believed to facilitate healing, meditation, and religious experience.

According to Eastern traditions thousands of years old, vibration emanating from a spiritual source creates the physical universe. Sacred sound—*shabda*—has long been applied to healing and spiritual unfoldment, combined with chants, musical instruments, postures, and rhythmic movements. See **Chanting; Mantra; Om.** The ancient Chinese believed music to be the basis of everything: all things, including human beings, were molded according to the music that was performed within them. Confucius stated that if the music of a kingdom changed, then its society would alter itself accordingly. Plato, too, believed that music had the power to bring about the downfall of the state, and said it was the duty of the legislature to suppress "effeminate" and "lascivious" music and promote dignified and pure music. In the sixth century, Boethius associated music with morality.

His work, *De Musica,* was widely used by scholars up until the middle of the nineteenth century.

The ancient Greeks believed in the healing power of music; it was applied to aid digestion, induce sleep, and treat mental disturbance. Plato offered many ideas on music in education and culture, and banned or approved of various instruments, modes, and rhythms. Aristotle placed great power in flute music to rouse emotions and provide catharsis; he said music affects human character. Pythagoras, who is credited with discovering the diatonic scale, found that all music can be reduced to numbers and mathematical ratios, and concluded that all phenomena in the universe could be similarly explained. Pythagoras devised numerous medical medicines "calculated to repress and expel the diseases of both bodies and of souls," according to Iamblichus. See **Pythagoras.**

Shamans and healers have long used music combined with chant and rhythmic movement to induce the altered states of consciousness necessary to carry out their work. See **Shamanism.** The Sufis use music in healing, believing that it, combined with the use of colors, affects the body's endocrine system.

The belief that music influences moral character prevailed until about the start of the twentieth century, when attitudes toward music began to change. Technology made music accessible almost any time via recordings. With advances in media communications, music became an integral part of radio, film, and then television. Presently, society is bombarded with several hours of music a day from these sources, without having the awareness of the effect of the music upon the body and consciousness.

Research has shown that the elements of music that have physiological and psychological effects are (1) rhythm, which has the most immediate and intense effect, especially on the pulse rate and emotions; (2) tone or pitch, which is the specific quality and vibration of a note; (3) interval, the distance between notes, which creates melody and harmony; and (4) timbre, the specific nature of an instrument or voice, which evokes associations.

Music's effects are due largely to entrainment, a principle of physics in which the stronger vibrations of one object will cause the weaker vibrations of another object to begin oscillating at the same rate as the stronger. Entrainment was discovered by Dutch scientist Christopher Huygens in 1665. For example, a room full of grandfather clocks whose pendula are set swinging asynchronously will synchronize with the rhythm of the dominant clock. Also, muscle cells, when brought close together, will begin to pulse in harmony.

Thus the rhythms of music can entrain the mind, body, and spirit by affecting the rhythms of physiological and neurological processes. Music has been shown to affect pulse rate, skin temperature, blood pressure, muscle tension, and brain-wave activity. It can help the release of biochemicals, such as endorphins. It can alleviate pain, reduce the amount of anesthesia required during surgery, help postoperative recovery, aid in head trauma injuries, and bring temporary relief to people suffering from debilitating disease. It relaxes, excites, releases emotions, and helps to induce altered states of consciousness, out-of-body experiences, and peak experiences similar to those which occur in deep meditation or with the help of psychedelic drugs. Music also has been shown to affect the health of plants and the health and behavior of animals.

The power of sound, which is measured in cycles per second (hertz), has been demonstrated in experiments. The eighteenth-century German physicist Ernst Chladni found that playing a violin near a sand-covered disk caused the sand to form geometric shapes. In the 1930s Hans Jenny, a Swiss sound researcher, created a wide range of natural shapes, such as honeycombs and shells, by vibrating sand, liquids, powders, and putty on metal disks at different frequencies. Jenny's work led Peter Guy Manners, a British osteopath, to develop the controversial "cymatic therapy," in which the "correct" sound of a healthy organ or part of the body is applied directly to a diseased counterpart.

Research results vary considerably, and the precise nature of the effects of music remains scientifically inconclusive. Researchers know that states of arousal are affected by music, but don't know much about the hormonal changes caused by music, or what music does electrochemically in the brain. However, music is viewed as a helpful alternative treatment in medicine.

Music therapy, which languished during the nineteenth century and began to revive in the twentieth century, focuses on the areas of pain relief, stress reduction, and occupational therapy. Interest in music as a transpersonal therapeutic tool is due largely to the work of Helen L. Bonny, founder of the Bonny Foundation in Salina, Kansas. Bonny had her first peak experience induced by music in 1948, while playing the violin at a religious ceremony. She later undertook training as a music therapist, and experimented with music combined with prayer and meditation. Bonny concluded that music could induce introspective or ecstatic states without the need for psychedelics. Bonny's book, *Music and Your Mind* (1973), written with Louis M. Savary, paved the way to an explosion of books on the health effects of music.

In therapy music appears to work best when used in conjunction with spoken instructions in the background; Guided Imagery and Music (GIM), as it is called, is used in hospitals and clinics and in psychological counseling and psychiatric treatment. It also has been used successfully in prisons.

Music also has harmful effects, such as pieces that arouse base instincts or passions, or induce melancholy. Some forms of rock music, especially heavy metal, are debilitating, have been shown to adversely affect the health of plants and laboratory mice, and have been associated with depression, aggression, and destructive behavior. Similarly, some types of music pumped into exercise salons for aerobic workouts create confusion in the brain and work to weaken muscles rather than strengthen them. Syncopated rhythms have been shown to have a deteriorating psycho-physiological effect. Certain rhythms have been shown to induce epileptic seizures in unusually sensitive listeners.

New Age music, which dates to the 1970s, is based on the idea that music can expand consciousness and alter awareness. Critics label much of it as simplistic or bodiless, but many New Age composers, like music therapy composers, attempt to create music that will foster physical and psychological well-being and harmony. Many have returned to ancient theories about music as sources of inspiration. In the field of behavioral medicine, music had potential for helping to maintain wellness.

Various individuals report being able to see or sense colors and shapes when listening to music. Clairvoyants report awareness of music thought-forms, created by the vibrations of sound. See **Altered states of consciousness; Behavioral medicine; Creative visualization; Imagery; Out-of-body experience (OBE).**

Sources: Jeanne Achterberg. *Imagery in Healing: Shamanism and Modern Medicine.* Boston: Shambhala Publications, 1985; Roberto Assagioli. *Psychosynthesis: A Manual of Principles and Techniques.* 1965. New York: Penguin Books, 1976; Rosemary Bitzel. "Tripping on Music." *Unicorn Times* (April 1979): 8; Pamela

Bloom. "Soul Music." *New Age Journal* (March/April 1987): 58–63; Helen L. Bonny and Louis M. Savary. *Music and Your Mind.* New York: Harper & Row, 1973; Joscelyn Godwin. *Harmonies of Heaven and Earth: The Spiritual Dimension of Music from Antiquity to the Avant-Garde.* Rochester, VT: Inner Traditions International, Ltd., 1987; Manly P. Hall. *The Secret Teachings of All Ages.* 1928. Los Angeles: The Philosophic Research Society, 1977; Steven Halpern with Louis Savary. *Sound Health: The Music and Sounds That Make Us Whole.* San Francisco: Harper & Row, 1985; Arthur W. Harvey. "Utilizing Music as a Tool for Healing." In *The Fourth International Symposium on Music: Rehabilitation and Human Well Being.* Edited by Rosalie Rebolla Pratt. Lanham, MD: University Press of America, 1987; Arthur W. Harvey. "Music and Health." *International Brain Dominance Review* (Fall 1987): 9–11; Hal A. Lingerman. *The Healing Energies of Music.* Wheaton, IL: The Theosophical Publishing House, 1983; R. J. Stewart. *Music and the Elemental Psyche: A Practical Guide to Music and Changing Consciousness.* Rochester, VT: Destiny Books, 1987; David Tame. *The Secret Power of Music.* Rochester, VT: Destiny Books, 1984; Andrew Watson and Nevill Drury. *Healing Music.* Bridport, Dorset, England: Prism Press, 1987; "Music Facilitates Healing, Bodymind Coordination." *Brain Mind Bulletin* 8, no. 2 (December 13, 1982): 1+. Sources from *Conference Proceedings.* The Second National Music and Health Conference, Eastern Kentucky University, April 7–8, 1988: M. Susan Claeys. "The Role of Music and Music Therapy in the Rehabilitation of Traumatically Injured Clients." 118–139; Kay Gardner. "On Composing Medical Music." 12–20; Jonathan S. Goldman. "Sonic Entrainment and the Brain." 30–59; Arthur W. Harvey. "Moving Music into the Mainstream of Behavioral Medicine." 1–8.

Myers, Frederic W. H.

See **Apparition; Society for Psychical Research (SPR).**

Mysteries

In the strictest sense, secret religious cults that flourished during the Hellenistic period, involving adoration of various deities and rites of spiritual transformation and rebirth. "Mystery" derives from the Greek *myein,* "to close," and refers to the closing of the lips or the eyes. The *mystes,* or initiate, was required to keep the secrets of the cult. In a broader sense, the term "mysteries" also is applied to esoteric teachings and the rites of secret societies outside of the classical world.

The Hellenistic mystery cults were pre-Indo-European and pre-Semitic in origin, although their advanced elements probably came from the Indo-Europeans. The mysteries involved the worship of deities from Greece, Syria, Anatolia, Egypt, and Persia. Some were limited to either men or women; the Eleusinian mysteries of Greece are probably the best-known of those which admitted both sexes.

Regardless of orientation the mysteries shared some common characteristics: They were centered on a divine female as the vessel of transformation, even if they were cloaked in patriarchal form; their purpose was to secure eternal life in the afterworld, through rebirth or redemption; they contained an erotic-sexual element of union with the primal mother; there was preparation and consumption of special food and drink as part of the transformative process or as reenactment of a holy meal of the gods and goddesses; there were blood sacrifices; there were elements of magic and ecstasy in the rites; the initiate was revealed the secrets and the instructions of the cult.

The rites of the mysteries consisted of religious dramas of the deities, reenactments of the *hieros gamos* (sacred marriage), and/or the death and rebirth of a deity. Psychiatrist Carl G. Jung observed that the ancients learned how to escape spiritual death by submitting themselves to the dramas of the mysteries, which became an original experience for each initiate.

Mystery Cults

The Eleusinian mysteries, the most popular and influential of the Greek cults, centered on the rape, abduction, and marriage or death of Kore (Persephone), and her reunion/resurrection with her mother, Demeter, the grain goddess. The rites were intimately linked to the cycle of fertility of the Earth. The self-sacrifice of Kore was at the heart of the transformation, the fruit of which was the birth of a divine son, spiritually conceived and born, whom she held on her lap.

The Dionysian mysteries, the second most important Hellenistic cult, centered on Dionysus (Bacchus), the Thracian bull-god and ruler of the dead and souls who became the god of the vine and vegetation. Immortality could be obtained through communion with him in ecstatic rites apparently involving consumption of wine and the raw flesh of a sacrificed animal, and sex. Descriptions of the rites ranged from banquets to orgies in which the initiates tore the sacrificial animal to pieces and devoured it. The Villa of Mysteries, discovered in the ruins of Pompeii in 1910, includes a room called the Initiation Chamber, which is painted with Dionysian scenes and features Dionysus and his beloved, Ariadne. According to one interpretation of the mysteries, the rites represented the individuation process of the Self, in the transformation of both Dionysus and Ariadne through their sacred marriage. Both are portrayed in the Villa of Mysteries paintings.

In the mysteries of Isis and Osiris, the Egyptians observed a mystery play of succession, the death of a pharaoh and the succession of another, with a funeral ritual of mummification and burial in which the dead would be mystically joined in the underworld by Osiris. During the Hellenistic period, the mysteries of Isis and Osiris centered on the death of Osiris and his rebirth in the underworld with the help of Isis, and the birth of Isis's divine son, Horus, whom she held on her lap.

The Mithraic mysteries were a male cult of Persian origin centered on the slaying of a bull by Mithra, god of light and beneficence, which guaranteed the fruitfulness of the earth. The initiates consumed bread and water, representing the body and blood of the divine bull. Initiates were believed to be under the divine protection of Mithra, who would protect their souls from darkness.

Evidence for mystery rites concerning the mystical wisdom of Woden (Odin), the patriarch of Teutonic gods, is found in the mythical *Poetic Edda* and *Prose Edda* of the Viking Age (A.D. 800–1100). Woden, whose name derives from the proto-Germanic term for "master of inspired psychic activity," is the god of magic, poetry, wisdom, and war, and once was considered the primal ancestor of the royalty of northern Europe. To obtain wisdom he hung from Yggdrasil, the World Tree, for nine days in a trance, and thus learned the secrets of the runes. Similarly, human initiates into the Wodenic (or Odinic) mysteries hung themselves from a symbolic Yggdrasil. Another rite centered on Woden's winning back the poetic mead, the source of inspiration fermented from the blood of a god, Kvasir, and which was being hoarded by a giant. See **Runes.**

There were also Judaic and Christian mysteries. Rites of circumcision, baptism, and anointing the forehead with oil may be seen to have similarities with the ancient mystery rites of initiation into a select religious community. The Jewish holy meal of Seder reenacts a religious drama, the Exodus from Egypt.

The primary Christian mysteries are the Eucharist, the Cross, and the baptism. The rite of the Eucharist involves the consumption of bread and wine as the body and blood of Christ, a means of seeking salvation through union with Christ. Goddess or Great Mother remains a hidden part of these rites, as the cup which holds the blood and wine, and the womb in which the rebirth of baptism takes place. The Cross represents the scheme of the universe, the entire history of the cosmos before and after the crucifixion of Christ; it foreshadows the coming of the transfigured Christ. The baptism, the fundamental mystery, represents initiation into the divine life of the resurrected Christ.

The cult of Mary, who holds her divine son on her lap, also has associations with Goddess and the ancient mysteries.

The Hellenistic mysteries came to an end with Christianity. The elements and purpose of the ancient mysteries—resurrection to eternal life—have been preserved in the rites of various secret societies such as the Freemasons and Rosicrucians. See **Alchemy; Freemasonry; Goddess; Grail, the; Mary; Rosicrucians.**

Sources: Joseph Campbell, ed. *The Mystic Vision: Papers from the Eranos Yearbooks.* Princeton: Princeton University Press, 1968; Linda Fierz-David. *Women's Dionysian Initiation: The Villa of Mysteries in Pompeii.* Dallas: Spring Publications, 1988; Manly P. Hall. *The Secret Teachings of All Ages.* 1928. Los Angeles: The Philosophic Research Society, 1977; C. W. Leadbeater. *Ancient Mystic Rites.* First published as *Glimpses of Masonic History,* 1926. Wheaton, IL: The Theosophical Publishing House, 1986; Marvin W. Meyer, ed. *The Ancient Mysteries: A Sourcebook.* San Francisco: Harper & Row, 1987; Erich Neumann. *The Great Mother: An Analysis of the Archetype.* 2d ed. Princeton: Princeton University Press, 1963; Lewis Spence. *The Encyclopedia of the Occult.* Reprint. London: Bracken Books, 1988; Edred Thorsson. "The Way of Woden: The Runic Mysteries of the Hidden God of the North." *Gnosis* no. 9 (Fall 1988): 31–35.

Mystical experiences

A wide range of experiences in which one suddenly transcends the bounds of ordinary consciousness to an ineffable awareness beyond time, space, and the physical. Mystical experiences intrinsically defy description, so the effort here will at best hint at their nature.

Mystical experiences are universal, and share some common traits, despite differences in culture and religion. They are invariably spiritual, yet not necessarily religious; one need not be a monk or priest in order to have one. However, all personal religious experiences are rooted in mystical states of consciousness, and mystical experiences are part of all religions.

Though mystical experiences are common as a whole, they occur unbidden to an individual perhaps once or twice in a lifetime, if at all. According to a survey (1987) by the National Opinion Research Center in Chicago, 43 percent of adult Americans say they have had some type of mystical experience. In British polls published in 1978 and 1979 in the *Journal for the Scientific Study of Religion*, 56 percent of churchgoers said they had had such an experience. According to the British polls, mystical experiences were more likely to occur to those who were older, better educated, and regularly attended church.

Psychologist and philosopher William James identified four general characteristics of mystical experiences:

1. Ineffability. Mystical states are more like states of feeling than intellect, subtly shaded and with fine nuances that are difficult to convey in their import and grandeur to another. Consequently, much mystical literature is filled with paradoxes and symbolism.
2. Noetic quality. Mystical experiences are states of knowledge, insight, awareness, revelation, and illumination beyond the grasp of the intellect. There is awareness of unity with the Absolute, of immortality of the soul, of great truths. Time and space are transcended.
3. Transiency. Mystical experiences are fleeting in linear time, though they seem to be eternal. Most last a few seconds, some perhaps up to ten minutes. It is rare to sustain a mystical state for more than a half-hour, or perhaps one to two hours at best. Eastern adepts are able to sustain prolonged periods of *samadhi,* a mystical state of one-pointed concentration; and some reportedly are able to sustain the highest states of nirvana (satori in Zen) and even the rarely attained *nirodh.* See **Meditation.**
4. Passivity. The individual feels swept up and held by a superior power. This may be accompanied by a sensation of separation from bodily consciousness (see **Out-of-body experience [OBE]**); trance; or such phenomena as prophetic speech, automatisms, mediumistic trance, healing powers, visions, and voices. Such phenomena are regarded in Eastern thought as states of pseudo-enlightenment: partway up to the real thing, but not quite there.

James described the simplest form of mystical experience as the deepened sense of significance of a maxim or formula—a sort of aha! that bursts upon a person when something is seen in an entirely new light. Compare to **Inspiration.** He also classed déjà vu as a simple mystical experience. See **Déjà vu.** Higher up on the mystical ladder are the sudden awareness of truths which burst upon one in dreamy states and reveries, and the sudden awareness of the presence of God or the Absolute, and one's unity with it—the *tat tvam asi,* "that thou art," realization described in the Upanishads. R. M. Bucke, a Canadian doctor who studied mystical experiences, called this latter state "cosmic consciousness," or consciousness of the cosmos and of the life and order of the universe.

A minority of mystical experiences occur spontaneously. Typically, they occur when a person is alone and in a relaxed state of mind. Many things can trigger a mystical experience: dreams, words, phrases, music, art, sounds, smells, daydreaming, the play of light upon the land and sea, nature, or a near-death experience. See **Near-death experience (NDE).**

Most mystical experiences are sought through some form of inducement, usually as part of a spiritual or religious regimen. Techniques include hypnosis and autohypnosis, flotation tanks and sensory deprivation, sleep deprivation, fasting, chanting, dancing, breath control, sexual rites, yoga, and meditation. In the Eastern religions, yoga and meditation are the paths to enlightenment. (According to the Vedantists, spontaneous mystical experiences are impure; only through yoga can one obtain pure enlightenment.) See **Meditation; Yoga; Zen.** The Sufis, the mystical sect of Islam, practice meditation, prayer, and ecstatic dance. Ecstatic dance also is used in shamanic cultures. See **Shamanism; Sufism.** In the Christian tradition, mystical disciplines include prayer, contemplation, and meditation. Mysticism in Western orthodoxy reached its peak with the great medieval mystics, and has largely been lost in Protestantism. St. Teresa of Avila wrote of the "orison" (meditation) of union, in which the soul is fully awake as regards to God.

The role of alcohol, anesthesia, and psychoactive drugs as inducers of mystical experiences is controversial. It is argued on one hand that drugs induce true mystical experiences, and argued on the other that they induce pseudo-experiences which have no lasting value.

See **Drugs in mystical and psychic experiences.**

As yet there are no discernible differences between spontaneous and induced mystical experiences, in terms of their characteristics or their effects.

Physical Phenomena

Mystical experiences flood an individual with a sense of well-being, joy, and optimism. The ecstasy can reach such heights as to become almost unbearable torment and pain, as seen in the writings of the great Christian mystics. See **Ecstasy.** A number of physical phenomena are characteristic of various mystical experiences.

Decrease in bodily functions is common especially in sustained mystical states; breathing, pulse, circulation, and brain waves slow, and one loses awareness of the body. In the state of rapture described by Christian mystics, the body seems to be on the verge of extinguishing. St. Teresa of Avila wrote in *The Interior Castle* that in the orison of union, the soul "is utterly dead to the things of the world and lives solely in God. . . . I do not even know whether in this state she has enough life left to breathe. It seems to me she has not; or at least that if she does breathe, she is unaware of it."

The rise of the powerful *kundalini* energy, which in yogic literature resides at the base of the spine and under certain conditions of spiritual discipline rises to the crown *chakra,* is reported cross-culturally. Christian mystics, such as St. Therese (1873–1897, not to be confused with St. Teresa of Avila), sometimes experienced the heat, energy, spontaneous body movements and pain characteristic of a yogic *kundalini* awakening. The same phenomenon is reported among the !Kung bushmen of Africa, and in Sufism, Taoism, Buddhism, and shamanism. In a nonreligious context, *kundalini* awakening is called a "spiritual emergence" or "spiritual emergency." See **Kundalini; Spiritual emergence.**

Various mystical states are characterized by light, either exteriorized or internal, described as "illumination," "radiance," "lightning," "light of grace," and other terms. Within the Christian tradition, the classical mystical experience involving light occurred to St. Paul while on the road to Damascus. A brilliant light from heaven blinded him for three days, and he went without food and water. When his sight was restored, Paul was converted to Christianity. He ceased his persecutions of Christians and worked to spread the new religion. See **Paul, St.** In the Islamic tradition, Muhammad, the founder of Islam, was awakened one night by an overpowering light, marking the first revelation to him of the Koran. See **Muhammad.**

Heat is a by-product of the enormous energy generated by some mystical experiences, especially in *kundalini* awakenings. Taoism and Vajrayana Buddhism have elaborate techniques for manipulating this heat. See **David-Neel, Alexandra; Milarepa.** Richard Rolle, the "father of English mysticism," experienced intense heat that manifested physically; he associated it with a fire of burning love.

R. M. Bucke's initial mystical experience, which came in a moment of dreamy, passive reverie, involved fire imagery, but Bucke did not disclose whether he also felt heat. The experience, a vision that lasted but a few seconds, occurred spontaneously in 1872 when he was thirty-five. It led him to investigate mystical experiences and write his classic book, *Cosmic Consciousness* (1901). Wrote Bucke:

All at once, without warning of any kind, I found myself wrapped in a flame-colored cloud. For an instant I thought of fire, an immense conflagration somewhere close by in that great city; the next, I knew that the fire was within myself.

Directly afterward there came upon me a sense of exultation, of immense joyousness accompanied or immediately followed by an intellectual illumination impossible to describe. Among other things, I did not merely come to believe, but I saw that the universe is not composed of dead matter but is, on the contrary, a living Presence; I became conscious in myself of eternal life. . . .

In the very highest mystical states, however, all physical, mental, and emotional sensations, all imagery, fall away.

A mystical experience often leads to dramatic changes in one's ordinary consciousness and life-style. Most typically, one renounces or loses interest in material pursuits. See **Mysticism.**

As mentioned earlier, the Eastern traditions discount and disregard the physical phenomena associated with mystical experiences; however, they are esteemed within the Christian tradition. Paranormal powers such as levitation, telepathy, clairvoyance, materializations, and so on are called *siddhis* in yoga, and are obstacles that must be overcome in pursuit of true enlightenment. See **Siddhis.** On the other hand, Christian mystics have been revered for their levitations, bilocations, halos, odors of sanctity, stigmata, and so on.

Science and the Mystical Experience

Some scientists believe the mystical experience is a physical phenomenon that arises in the brain, and can be induced with the proper stimulation of the temporal lobes, which lie beneath the brain's major hemispheres. Around the turn of the twentieth century, a British doctor, John Hughlings, noticed that epileptics have different temporal lobes. He identified various temporal lobe traits, such as the epileptics' seizures and dreamy states, as well as déjà vu, dissociation, alienation, and *jamais vu* (in which familiar surroundings seem strange). In 1933 American surgeon Wilder Penfield induced mystical-like phenomena in epileptics by stimulating their brains with electric currents. In the late 1970s and the 1980s, further relationships were established between the temporal lobes and paranormal experiences, using electromagnetic stimulation. However, the temporal lobe model does not explain all mystical experiences, and thus remains controversial.

Mystical Experiences and Psychology

In Freudian psychology mystical experiences generally are dismissed as illusion. Psychiatrist Carl G. Jung saw them as a liberation of the unconscious. Humanistic psychologist Abraham H. Maslow called certain mystical experiences "peak experiences" and believed they are essential to health and to self-actualization, the realization of one's fullest human potential. See **Peak experiences**. Transpersonal psychology explores the mystical experience for its therapeutic potential. See **Psychology**.

Sources: Richard Maurice Bucke. *Cosmic Consciousness.* 1901. New York: E. P. Dutton, 1969; Nona Coxhead. *The Relevance of Bliss: A Contemporary Exploration of Mystic Experience.* London: Wildwood House, 1985; William James. *The Varieties of Religious Experience: A Study in Human Nature.* 1902. London: Longmans, Green & Co., 1911; Lee Sannella. *The Kundalini Experience.* Lower Lake, CA: Integral Publishing, 1987; Dennis Stacy. "Transcending Science." *Omni* 11, no. 3 (December 1988): 54–60+; John White, ed. *The Highest State of Consciousness.* Garden City, NY: Anchor Books/ Doubleday, 1972; Joshua C. Whiting. "Sources of Spontaneous Mystical Experience." *The Journal of Religion and Psychical Research* 10, no. 3 (July 1987): 148–157.

Mysticism

The belief in or pursuit of unification with the One or some other principle; the immediate consciousness of God; or the direct experience of religious truth. Mysticism is nearly universal and unites most religions in the quest for the One. There are different types of mysticism, and different understandings of what constitutes mystical union. Mysticism is not confined to monks and ascetics, but touches most people at least once in life.

The term "mysticism" is derived from the classical Greco-Roman mystery cults. It may have come from *myein,* which means to close the lips and eyes, and refers to the sacred oath of the initiate, the *mystes,* to keep secret about the inner workings of the religion. In Neoplatonism "mysticism" came to be associated with secrecy of any kind. The term *mystica* appeared in the Christian treatise, *Mystica Theologia,* of an anonymous Syrian Neoplatonist monk of the late fifth or early sixth century, known pseudonymously as Dionysius the Areopagite. In this treatise mysticism is seen as a secrecy of the mind.

Despite the various approaches to mysticism, there are some characteristics common to mysticism in general. Philosopher W. T. Stace studied Roman Catholic, Protestant, ancient classical, Hindu, and American agnostic mystical experiences and found seven common themes: (1) a unifying vision and perception of the One by the senses in and through many objects; (2) the apprehension of the One as an inner life; (3) an objective and true sense of reality; (4) feelings of satisfaction, joy, and bliss; (5) a religious element that is a feeling of the holy and sacred; (6) a paradoxical feeling; and (7) inexpressible feelings.

Types of Mysticism

Mystics subscribe to one of two theories of Divine Reality: emanation and immanence. In the emanation view, all things in the universe are outflowing from God. In the immanence view, the universe is not projected from God, but is immersed in God.

Mysticism can be either nonreligious or religious. Nonreligious mysticism derives much of its experience and content from Nature, though many religious mystics have found their way to God or the Absolute through Nature. Nature mysticism sometimes is called pantheistic mysticism, in that God or the divine being is in everything and everything is divine. Not all transcendent experiences with Nature are mystical, however, but may simply be overwhelming joy or ecstasy. In a mystical experience, the boundaries between subject and object disappear: one becomes one with Nature as opposed to having a heightened appreciation for it.

Religious mysticism falls into two major groups: monistic and theistic. Monistic mysticism seeks unity and identity with a universal principle. Theistic mysticism seeks unity, but not identity, with God.

Perhaps the ultimate monistic mysticism is expressed in the Upanishads of India, in the concepts of "I am Brahman" (the all-pervading principle) and *tat tram asi,* "that thou art," meaning that the soul is the eternal and Absolute Being. Monistic mysticism also is found in Taoism, which seeks unity with Tao, the ineffable Way. Theistic mysticism, unity with God, characterizes Christianity, Judaism (in the Kabbalah), and Islam (the Sufi sect) and also is found in Hinduism. See **Hinduism; Kabbalah; Mysticism, Christian; Sufism; Taoism.**

Parallel to both theism and monism is yoga, a mysticism of the soul, which seeks nirvana, a state of ineffable peace characterized by extinction of desires and freedom from reincarnation, and which subsists in God. The mystical goal of Jainism also is nirvana, though Jainism has no concepts of Supreme Being or Absolute. The soul is eternal and so is the universe, which passes through infinite cosmic cycles. See **Yoga.**

There is disagreement as to whether Buddhism is truly mystical. The Buddhist goal of nirvana, described as "become Brahman," is not a union of the soul with the divine or an abstract principle. There is no permanent ego in Buddhism, and the existence of the soul is unclear. In nirvana there is no personal survival, no becoming of any kind; one is extinguished in phenomenal existence. See **Buddhism; Meditation; Zen.**

In Africa mysticism is found in ecstatic possession religions, in which mediums are possessed by, and become the servant or property of, ancestral or divine spirits. Such people become the "wife of the god" and are bound in sacred marriage. They unite with the god in ecstatic trance rituals, in which they assume the behavior of the god or allow the god to speak through them. These practices are world-affirming and cannot be compared to the pathological possession cases of Western society.

Native American religions contain concepts of both monotheism and polytheism. The Supreme Being, who in some cases is unnamed because it is unknowable, is both the Creator and the sum total of all deities, spirits, and creative powers. Native American religions are diverse, and there is no one Native American mystical path. There are, however, common fundamentals that underlie the various approaches to mysticism.

Foremost is the Native American view that the Earth is sacred, and that it is a living, intelligent being with holy powers. "Earth Mother," as the land is often called, is treated with great respect. Also holy are all phenomena associated with the earth—its geographical features and elements—as well as all life forms upon it, and the heavens above it. Everything is animated with Spirit, a view similar to the *kami* of Shinto, and to the outlook of other tribal societies. All of these beings and phenomena, along with the planet and the cosmos, ideally exist in balance and harmony. It is the duty of every creature to look after its daily business in a responsible fashion, which maintains the balance and serves the greater good. Failure to do so brings imbalance, which results in disease, illness, and misfortune, not only to the offending creature but to the Whole.

Native Americans feel a particular kinship with animals, and in many respects regard them as superior peoples because they were placed on Earth before humans.

Native Americans do not draw the distinctions between the sacred and secular as found in Western religion. The sacred is part of everyday life, accessible by all, not a few selected holy persons. At an early age, most Native Americans begin to experience the supernatural, usually through visions and dreams, and integrate it into daily life. What a Westerner would term "psychic" or "paranormal" is part of the Native American's ordinary reality. Thus it is not remarkable to communicate with animals, the natural environment, or Supernatural Beings; see spirits; or have precognitive or prophetic dreams. Medicine men and women, who are endowed with greater than ordinary powers, are able to use the supernatural realms in ways to serve and help others, particularly in healing. See **Shamanism.**

Mystical communion with the sacred varies from group to group, even subgroup to subgroup, and includes dance, song and chant, the sacred pipe, purifying sweats (a preliminary for sacred undertakings), fasts, dreams, vision quests, and occasional use of psychotropic drugs. As in other cultures, the Native American experience of the mystical takes place within a framework of language, traditions, concepts, rituals, and interactions developed over thousands of years, and which reside in the racial collective unconscious. See **Sacred pipe; Sweat; Vision quest.**

The Mystical Path

Theologian Rudolph Otto defined mysticism more by method: the mysticism of introspection and the mysticism of unifying vision. In introspection the mystic turns inward in contemplation and meditation, withdrawing from the external world, and finding within the depths of the soul the One. In the unifying vision, which Otto also called the Way of Unity, the mystic looks outward to the world to find the One.

Evelyn Underhill, in her classic study, *Mysticism* (1955), defined five psychological stages along the mystical path. Not all may be experienced by any one mystic. The path itself is characterized by a vacillation between states of intense pleasure and intense pain. The five stages are:

1. The Awakening of the Self to Consciousness of Divine Reality. Typically, this is a well-defined, often sudden experience and is characterized by great joy.
2. The Purgation of the Self. The mystic, through discipline and/or mortification, attempts to rid himself or herself of imperfections and material desires, which are obstacles to unity.
3. Illumination. A happy state of apprehension of the Divine Presence, experienced in contemplation and meditation. It is not true union. Many mystics never get beyond Illumination. Artists and highly creative people tend to have Illumination experiences.
4. The Purification of the Self. Also called the "Dark Night of the Soul." The mystic attempts total surrender of Self, personal identity, and will to the Divine, and is plunged into a painful and unhappy state of the absence of the Divine Presence.

5. Union with the One. The mystic achieves a permanent and transcendent level of reality.

In Eastern mysticism a still higher stage is reabsorption of the individual soul into the Infinite. The Sufis, too, consider such annihilation the only true attainment of God.

Phenomena of Mysticism

Mysticism invariably is accompanied by phenomena such as visions, voices, oracular dreams, paranormal powers (clairvoyance, telepathy, psychokinesis, bilocation, levitation, and so on), raptures, trances, and hyper-emotionalism. Some argue that such phenomena must be excluded from the mystical experience, while others contend they are preliminary and important to the mystical goal. In the Eastern meditation and yoga disciplines such phenomena, called *siddhis,* are distractions, obstacles, and pseudo-enlightenment, which must be overcome in order to achieve the true objective. See **Siddhis.**

Mysticism and Science

A great deal has been written, especially from a "New Age" perspective, about the apparent parallels and common worldview between modern physics— quantum and relativity—and the Eastern mysticism of Buddhism, Taoism, Hinduism, and Zen. It is argued that physics and mysticism are complementary approaches to the same reality. Much controversy surrounds these assertions within the scientific community. The founders and great theorists of modern physics—who were mystical in their own outlook, were acquainted with Eastern philosophy, and advocated interdisciplinary communication—nonetheless have said modern physics neither support nor refutes mysticism. The debate will continue as new theories are put forward.

Sources: Paula Gunn Allen. "American Indian Mysticism." *Shaman's Drum* no. 14 (Mid-Fall 1988): 39–46; Joseph Epes Brown. *The Spiritual Legacy of the American Indian.* New York: Crossroad, 1987; Fritjof Capra. *The Tao of Physics.* 2d ed. New York: Bantam Books, 1984; Nona Coxhead. *The Relevance of Bliss: A Contemporary Exploration of Mystic Experience.* London: Wildwood House, 1985; F. C. Happold. *Mysticism: A Study and an Anthology.* Rev. ed. Harmondsworth, Middlesex, England: Penguin Books, 1970; Ake Hultkrantz. *Native Religions of North America.* San Francisco: Harper & Row, 1987; William Johnston. *The Inner Eye of Love: Mysticism and Religion.* San Francisco: Harper & Row, 1978; Geoffrey Parrinder. *Mysticism in the World's Religions.* New York: Oxford University Press, 1976; Samuel Umen. *The World of the Mystic.* New York: Philosophical Library, 1988; Evelyn Underhill. *Mysticism.* 1955. New York: New American Library, 1974; Ken Wilber, ed. *Quantum Questions: Mystical Writings of the World's Great Physicists.* Boston & London: New Science Library/ Shambhala, 1985.

Mysticism, Christian

Mysticism for followers of Christ and his teachings is essentially a personal experience of, or at least an approach to, the sacred in general, and to a presence of God in particular, distinctively through, with, and in Christ. Characteristically, it takes the form of a sense of openness to a union with God through Christ, although Christians do not all agree on the nature(s) and person(s) of Christ. It normally includes frequent periods of (if not the state of) intense prayer, meditation, or contemplation.

Christian mysticism is best understood if the Christian person is seen as one who believes, or professes, or is assumed to have active faith in Jesus and the truth taught by him. More precisely, the Christian mystic is ideally seen as one who is fully incorporated into Christ, bears true witness to the spirit of Christ, and accepts the spiritual structure established by Christ, that is, his Mystical Body, the church.

While not all Christian nonsecular mystics lead an austere life, they do practice some degree of asceticism, which is relative to many changing historical, political, or other factors. What was austere for the desert monks of the early centuries, for example, may be very different from the asceticism of cloistered monks of today. Approaches to Christian mysticism have changed along with other theological issues, especially in the sixteenth century, when Martin Luther broke from Catholicism. Luther stressed "justification by grace, through faith," with the Bible alone (and not also papal authority) being the rule of faith. Luther also retained a belief in the Real Presence, not just a symbolic representation, of Jesus in the Sacrament of Communion. Roman Catholic mysticism includes belief in the Eucharist as the true Body and Blood of Christ, under the appearance of bread and wine.

The Christian mystical experience includes visions, such as of a sacred presence, not necessarily of God and/or Christ himself. For example, visions of saints and especially of Mary are documented in the various rites of the Roman Catholic church and Eastern Orthodox church. See **Marian apparitions.**

Catholic mysticism includes worship of the Father, the Son, and the Holy Spirit, as well as formal liturgical and sacramental rites, most notably the Celebration of the Eucharist (the Mass). More uniquely Catholic is a veneration of Mary and many canonized saints, for whose intercession Catholics pray. See **Mary.** Within Catholicism many religious orders of men and women have distinctive approaches to mysticism, such as the strict order of Trappists, who often practice silence. Another order, the Society of Mary (Marianists), advocates a spirituality of "filial piety" to Mary, that is, the son-like love which they believe Christ had (and has) for his mother.

The integration of Christian mysticism into various other expressions of spirituality are as numerous as the cultures to which Christianity has spread over two thousand years. The extremes can be seen in Vodoun practices, where the externals of certain rituals show the direct influence of Christian liturgies and practices, as well as in Santería. Mythologist Joseph Campbell and other scholars found in such universal influences "many songs; one voice."

Scriptural Foundation

Much of the theology of Christian mysticism is rooted in interpretations of the Old and New Testaments. In the Old Testament, "seeing God" is exceptional and can even mean death to the viewer (Exodus 33:20); a person who survives such a mystical experience does so by special privilege, as it was with Jacob (Genesis 32:31). Yet in the Psalms it is the virtuous and upright who contemplate Yahweh's face (Psalm 11:7), such as the Levite in exile, symbolizing the devout who does not yet see Yahweh. He "thirsts for God" and asks "when shall I go to see the face of God?" (Psalm 42:2). But the experience of seeing Yahweh is sometimes kept secret and is not always comprehensible, as with Daniel, the Psalm writer who does not understand what his vision means (Psalm 27:8). In more modern times, it is not unusual for those favored with visions not to understand their purpose or meaning, such as those who have seen visions of the Virgin Mary.

On the other hand, Yahweh promises Hosea that "I will speak to the prophets, I will increase the visions . . ." (Hosea 12:10). Moreover, Yahweh commands Habakkuk to "write the vision down, inscribe it on tablets to be easily read . . ." (Habakkuk 2:2). In the spirit of this same passage from Habakkuk, which says the vision is "eager for its own fulfillment," the Christian liturgical year applies the passage to the expectation of Christ's (second) coming commemorated during the annual Advent (pre-Christmas) season. Concerning Christ's Second Coming, the mysticism of at least one Christian denomination, the Seventh-Day Adventists, includes a belief that it will occur in the very near future. The early Christians thought similarly.

This eagerness to see the face of God is personified in the fundamental Christian mystique—the desire for union in Christ. This envisioning is expressed in John: Speaking of himself as Son of God, Christ says, "It is my Father's will that whoever sees the Son and believes in him shall have eternal life . . ." (6:40).

Essential to the beliefs of Christian mystics is the ultimate goal of the Beatific Vision, in which they will see God "as he is" (1 John 3:2). Even at its most intense, the envisioning is itself already more than a symbol about which Christ speaks (God as a presence and reality), while alluding to the time of the final vision of God: "I shall no longer speak to you in metaphors" (John 16:25). This notion of Christian mysticism is compatible with the metaphors of the Hero's Journey to his ultimate goal; in this sense the archetypical Hero certainly includes Christ and each Christian.

The Book of Revelation (The Apocalypse) speaks of this ultimate mystical state in symbols, such as the "heavenly Jerusalem," which the visionary describes in terms prophetic of planetary consciousness: "Then I saw a new heaven and a new earth; the first heaven and the first earth had disappeared now, and there was no longer any sea" (21:1). The sea here is considered the home of the apocalyptical dragon and symbolizes evil (Job 7 and 12), and will "dry up" and become "a road for the redeemed to cross" (Isaiah 51:9–10) as it did at the Exodus. The misuse of nature seems to cooperate only for a while, but such misuse turns in on its abusers. The "returning waters" overwhelmed the enemies of the Chosen People so that "not a single one of them was left" (Exodus 14:5–31). An awareness of this rebirthing cycle contributes ecumenically to contemporary planetary consciousness as it sees the returning of nature to its pristine state. The mystical process is not only a cleansing, but a rebirthing of creation. For Christians this New Creation is realized through, with, and in Christ as Teilhard de Chardin's Omega Point. See **Planetary consciousness; Teilhard de Chardin, Pierre.**

As in other religions, Christian approaches to mysticism also include meditation, prayer, contemplation, public worship (liturgy), and asceticism. Christianity likewise has also documented saintly and/or heroic (not necessarily martyred) individual mystics, as well as false or even diabolical activity in each of these areas; there are both legitimate and illegitimate documentation of unusual experiences, including miracles, visions, and other mystical phenomena. While some faiths perceive the possibility of achieving exceptional mystical experiences primarily, if not exclusively, through one's human efforts (such as by contemplation or fasting), Christian mysticism involves "good works" with dynamic interfacing of the individual with Christ in the Mystical Body (spiritual Christian community). The latter doctrine, intrinsic to Christian mysticism, is developed by St. Paul throughout his epistles.

In judging the authenticity of Christian mystical experiences, interdisciplinary approaches of science and by many non-Christian faiths are employed, as well as additional criteria such as the discernment of God's action through Christ in individuals, the apparent union of the individuals with Christ, and the reception in Christ of unmerited grace. Alleged mystical experiences, such as apparitions, are scrutinized with intense caution, especially by the Catholic church.

Christian mysticism has played a vital role in both Western and Eastern cultures, most demonstrably in the arts.

Since the nineteenth-century discoveries in psychology and related disciplines, the study of mysticism has usually included scientific scrutiny. The foundation for interdisciplinary study of Christian mysticism in the twentieth century was laid by psychologist and philosopher William James in his milestone study, *The Varieties of Religious Experience* (1902). Here James attempted to show empirically that dimensions of consciousness exist beyond or beside the realm of everyday experience. See **James, William.**

Christian mysticism was also of special interest to psychiatrist Carl G. Jung, who saw it as part of the collective unconscious. It continues to be investigated by Jungian scholars.

Recent Trends

The popularity within Protestant groups of proclaiming one's born-again Christianity has spread within Catholicism. It is often accompanied by dramatic public witnessing or personal Epiphany ("a showing forth" of Jesus to the Gentiles).

Since the Ecumenical Council Vatican II in the 1960s, ecumenism among Christians and with other faiths has revived interest in all aspects of spirituality, especially the mysticism leading to and flowing from the Cosmic Christ about which Teilhard de Chardin, Matthew Fox, and others write.

Women theologians, philosophers, and writers are also redefining the role of women in Christian spirituality and mysticism from perspectives such as women's mysteries (birth-death-rebirth) and the Great Mother/Mary archetype. See

Creation spirituality; Goddess; Mary; Mysteries; Mystical experiences; Mysticism; Prayer.

Sources: Mortimer J. Adler, ed. "Experience." Chapter 25, *The Great Ideas: A Syntopicon of Great Books of the Western World.* Chicago: Encyclopaedia Britannica, 1952; Saint Thomas Aquinas. *Summa Theologica.* Part I, Q 112, A 5; Part III, Q 9, A 2; Part III Suppl., Q 92, A 1; Mary E. Giles, ed. *The Feminist Mystic: And Other Essays on Women and Spirituality.* New York: Crossroad, 1989; F. C. Happold. *Mysticism: A Study and an Anthology.* Rev. ed. Harmondsworth, Middlesex, England: Penguin Books, 1970; William James. *The Varieties of Religious Experience: A Study in Human Nature.* 1902. London: Longmans, Green & Co., 1911; Bernard McGinn and John Meyendorff, eds. *Christian Spirituality I: Origins to the Twelfth Century.* New York: Crossroad, 1985; Robert L. Moore, ed. *Carl Jung and Christian Spirituality.* Mahwah, NJ: Paulist Press, 1988; Evelyn Underhill. *Mysticism.* 1955. New York: New American Library, 1974; Christin Lore Weber. *WomanChrist.* San Francisco: Harper & Row, 1987; Donald Wigal. *A Presence of Love.* New York: Herder & Herder, 1969.

Mythology

Stories that explain the creation of the cosmos; the reasons for the characteristics of the features of the Earth, the animals, plants, and human beings; supernatural traditions; and gods and culture heroes. Myths (and fairy tales, which are degenerated myths) hold the wisdom of a culture. They reflect how the individual relates to his or her culture and to the universe; they are archetypal encounters and comprise a language of the psyche. Without myths, a society decays.

Myths come into consciousness as revelations. The stories are reenacted through ritual, which is a means of accessing the spiritual power of a myth.

An important figure in mythologies is the culture hero, a human, animal, or bird who gives a culture to its people. Typically, the culture hero steals or liberates the sun or fire, masters the elements, and teaches people how to hunt, grow food, make tools, and heal the sick. He also teaches ceremonies and rites. After delivering the culture, the culture hero often goes away into the west, from whence he will return at some time in the future, or when needed by his people. In Native American mythologies, for example, the culture hero often is identified with the Trickster, as well as Transformer or Creator. In Native South American mythologies, the culture hero usually is the Creator.

Mythology has lost much of its importance in modern Western civilization, which has evolved away from an orientation to Earth, spirit, and intuition to a preoccupation with technology and control of nature and emotion. Myth is commonly regarded as a child's fantasy. By losing touch with myth, however, modern society has lost its sense of wonder and awe at the natural world and the universe—perhaps one reason for the exploitation of the resources of the planet, pollution of the environment, and destruction of other living things in the name of "progress." See **Planetary consciousness.**

The great minds of depth psychology, Sigmund Freud, Carl G. Jung, Alfred Adler, and others took interest in mythology. Jung said myths are not invented but are experienced. He said they were "original revelations of the preconscious psyche, involuntary statements about psychic happenings. Pathology is mirrored in myth; mythological motifs in unconscious fantasy are statements of the psyche about itself.

Thanks in large part to the work of Jung and the later contributions of mythologist Joseph Campbell and others, interest in mythology has revived in the West. Campbell's seminal work, *The Hero with a Thousand Faces* (1949), pre-

sents a definitive study of the archetype of all myth: a single hero and a single journey-pattern, which emerges from behind many different versions.

In *The Masks of God: Creative Mythology* (1968), Campbell notes that mythology serves four basic functions: (1) to bridge one's local consciousness with transcendent, universal realms; (2) to provide images with which to interpret the relationship between local and universal consciousnesses; (3) to empower moral order and reconcile one to one's culture or environment; and (4) to "foster the centering and unfolding of the individual in integrity" with oneself, one's environment, and the universe.

Campbell lamented the absence of myth in modern Western culture, and said culture is now changing too quickly for things to become mythologized. He advocated the study of comparative mythology, which would lead to an understanding of the experience and meaning of life.

The effort to reconnect individuals to mythology is called by some "personal mythology," which refers to the inner infrastructure that guides an individual through life on both conscious and unconscious levels. Personal mythology provides a means for organizing experience and opening the individual to the mysterious, transcendent realms of the universe.

The term "personal mythology" was popularized by psychologist David Feinstein, who, with psychologist Stanley Krippner, has since the mid-1970s taught thousands of individuals "to live more mythically." Feinstein built upon the term "personal myth," which was first used in psychiatric literature in 1956 by Ernst Kris to describe elements of the personality that influence whether or not therapy has a lasting effect. According to Krippner and Feinstein, humankind now has greater capacity than at any other time in history to construct personal mythologies, which in turn can be used to influence life patterns in a positive way, by reconnecting the individual to the numinous. In *Personal Mythology: The Psychology of Your Evolving Self* (1988), they define five stages in a person's "evolution of consciousness," that is, one's consciousness and the consciousness of the culture in which one is embedded. The stages are: (1) recognizing and defining a personal myth and knowing when it is no longer an ally; (2) identifying an opposing myth; (3) conceiving a unifying mythic vision from the two opposing myths; (4) moving from vision to commitment by testing insights; and (5) weaving the new mythology into daily life.

When preparing to present the initial steps in this process, the authors call upon two key concepts of Joseph Campbell's from *The Hero with a Thousand Faces*: "Myth is the secret opening through which the inexhaustible energies of the cosmos pour into human cultural manifestations," and "It has always been known the prime functions of mythology and rite supply the symbols that move the human spirit forward."

Other self-help approaches to personal mythology involve becoming acquainted with various archetypes, such as the Magician, Sage, Wanderer, Child, Mother, and so on, to determine what role they play in one's life. The influence of archetypes changes as one goes through different life stages. See **Archetypes; Dreams; Psychology; Ritual.**

Sources: Joseph Campbell. *The Inner Reaches of Outer Space: Metaphor as Myth and as Religion.* San Francisco: Harper & Row, 1988; Joseph Campbell. *The Hero with a Thousand Faces.* 1949. New York: World Publishing, 1970; Joseph Campbell, ed. *Myth, Dreams and Religion.* Dallas: Spring Publications, 1970; Joseph Campbell. *The Masks of God: Creative Mythology.* Vol. 4. New York: Viking, 1969; Joseph Campbell with Bill Moyers. *The Power of Myth.* New York: Doubleday, 1988; "Thus Spake Zoroaster: An Interview with Joseph Campbell." *Omni* (December 1988): 143–44; "The Value and Uses of Mythology." *Sarah Lawrence* (Summer 1986); David Feinstein and Stanley Krippner. *Personal Mythology: The Psychology of Your Evolving Self.* Los Angeles: Jeremy P. Tarcher, 1988; Maria Leach, ed. and Jerome Fried, assoc. ed. *Funk & Wagnalls Standard Dictionary of Folklore, Mythology, and Legend.* San Francisco: Harper & Row, 1979; Carol Pearson. *The Hero Within: Six Archetypes We Live By.* New York: Harper & Row, 1986; Andrew Samuels, Bani Shorter, and Fred Plaut. *A Critical Dictionary of Jungian Analysis.* London: Routledge & Kegan Paul, 1986.

N

Native American mysticism

See Mysticism.

Nature spirits

Various types of beings or spirits said to dwell in the nature kingdom; they possess supernatural powers and are usually invisible to humans, save those with clairvoyant sight. Belief in the existence of nature spirits is ancient and universal and persists in animistic religions. Nature spirits come in countless types, shapes, sizes, and dispositions. Some are regarded as benevolent toward humans, while others are mischievous and enjoy playing tricks on them, or are malevolent and seek to harm them. Some are human-like in appearance, while others assume shapes of animals, half-human half-animals, or fabulous-looking beings.

Nature spirits usually are attached to a thing or place in nature, such as trees, rivers, plants, bogs, mountains, minerals, and so on. For example, in China there are nature spirits that watch over rice, silk, roads, gateways, and the like. The Shinto religion of Japan includes worship of nature, nature forces, and nature spirits. The ancient Greeks and Romans also worshiped nature spirits, who inhabited every glen and pool and even the air.

Elementals, a well-known type of nature spirit, are a lower order of spirit beings that exists as the life force of all things in nature: minerals, plants, and animals; the four elements of earth, air, fire, and water; the planets, stars, and signs of the zodiac; and hours of the day and night. They are ruled by archangels, and are generally viewed as benevolent creatures who maintain the harmony of nature.

The Neoplatonic Greeks (c. third century A.D.) grouped elementals according to the four elements of life. Earth elementals are gnomes, ruled by the angel Ariel; air elementals are sylphs, ruled by Cherub; water elementals are undines, ruled by Tharsis; and fire elementals are salamanders, ruled by Seraph. In the fifth century, Proclus added a fifth group that lives beneath the ground; and in the eleventh century, Psellus added a sixth group, the *lucifugum*, which means "fly-the-light." Interest in elementals in the four cardinal groups was revived in the Middle Ages and Renaissance, when alchemists and magicians sought to control the forces of nature and the universe.

Elementals also include elves, who live in the woods and along the seashore, and household spirits such as brownies, goblins, bogles, and kobolds. Fairies are sometimes included within the elemental category, as are mannikins, which are male fairies who also have attributes of elves, gnomes, and brownies. In the lore of many Native North American tribes, water babies, nature spirits in small human form, inhabit lakes, streams, springs, and other bodies of water. Water babies are not malicious, but are wont to play tricks upon humans and are feared. Other types of "little people," as some are called, inhabit the forests and mountains; some possess powerful medicine, which they may bestow upon humans in times of need.

Elementals appear to clairvoyants in forms that can be recognized easily by humans. Many are said to wear clothing and jewelry. Gnomes appear as dwarfish humans who live in caves and the mountains. Sylphs appear as butterflies, undines as waves, and salamanders as lizard-like creatures who frolic in flames. British Spiritualist Grace Cooke said elementals enjoy human company, can understand human speech, and respond to music. They have their own karmic evolutions, progressing toward higher forms of life.

British medium Geraldine Cummins channeled information about elementals, purportedly from the deceased Frederic W. H. Myers, one of the founders of the Society for Psychical Research in London. In automatic writing "Myers" described elementals as the essence that emanates from forms of life, such as trees and plants, and which coalesces into a form perceived by the human mind as a sprite.

Practitioners of magic purportedly command elementals to perform tasks.

Some elementals are said to be deceitful and hateful of humans, and delight in causing accidents and tragedies. These entities usually are associated with certain kinds of ritual magic, and may be natural or artificial. They may be dispatched on missions of psychic attack. Those who practice magic say that such elementals, when summoned, attach themselves to the human aura, and are extremely difficult to control. Unless they are properly dismissed when no longer needed, they drain energy from the aura. Artificially created elementals are most commonly called thought-forms. See Deva; Fairies; Psychic attack; Thought-form.

Sources: June G. Bletzer. *The Donning International Encyclopedic Psychic Dictionary.* Norfolk, VA: The Donning Co., 1986; Katherine Briggs. *The Vanishing People: Fairy Lore and Legends.* New York: Pantheon Books, 1978; Richard Cavendish. *The Black Arts.* New York: Perigee Books, 1967; Grace Cooke. *The Illumined Ones.* New Lands, England: White Eagle Publishing Trust, 1966; Geraldine Cummins. *Beyond Human Personality.* London: Ivor Nicholson & Watson, 1935; Manly P. Hall. *Paracelsus: His Mystical and Medical Philosophy.* Los Angeles: The Philosophical Research Society, 1964; Geoffrey Hodson. *Fairies at Work and Play.* 1925. Wheaton, IL: Theosophical Publishing House, 1982; Maria Leach, ed., and Jerome Fried, assoc. ed. *Funk & Wagnalls Standard Dictionary of Folklore, Mythology, and Legend.* San Francisco: Harper & Row, 1979; *The New Age Catalogue.* New York: Doubleday/Dolphin, 1988; Kathryn Paulsen. *The Complete Book of Magic and Witchcraft.* New York: New American Library, 1970; Rudolf Steiner. *The Influence of Spiritual Beings Upon Man.* Spring Valley, NY: Anthroposophic Press, 1961; Doreen Valiente. *An ABC of Witchcraft Past and Present.* Amended ed. Custer, WA: Phoenix Publishing, 1986.

Naturopathy

See Behavioral medicine.

Nazca lines

Giant lines, geometric figures, and human and animal drawings on the desert mesa close to the village of Nazca and near the Ingenio Valley, Peru. The purpose of the markings is not known for certain. Theories advanced propose that they had astronomical functions, or once marked an airfield for the landing of ancient extraterrestrials and their spacecraft. Research in the 1980s suggests that the lines were integral to ancient religious ceremonies honoring mountain gods associated with the weather, forces of nature, and fertility, and possibly with out-of-body trips taken by Indian priests who ingested hallucinogens in sacred rites.

The lines are of various lengths and run parallel or intersect over an area of more than forty miles in length and five to ten miles in width. Some are geometric shapes, while others are humans, animals, reptiles, birds, whales, and insects. Some are crisscrossed by straight lines. The figures and lines appear to have been formed by pushing aside the top crust of pampa to expose the lighter yellow soil beneath; they can only be seen clearly from the air. The lines are extremely fragile and have been damaged by road construction and vehicles, and by tourists who began flocking to see them in the 1970s following the popularization of the "ancient astronaut" theory.

The Nazca lines are believed to have been created between 500 B.C. and A.D. 500 during the Nazca culture, which preceded the Incas. Some researchers believe the lines are newer, dating to 1000. It is possible that the Incas may have used or elaborated upon Nazca-built lines. Neither the Nazcas nor the Incas left behind written records to explain the lines, and Spanish conquerors made but a few references to them in their writings. Local inhabitants call them "Inca roads." They first received archaeological attention in 1926.

The theory that the lines were meant for astronomical purposes was first proposed in the 1940s by Paul Kosok, an American archaeologist, who was supported by Maria Reiche, a German mathematician. Both believed that the lines marked the positions of the sun, moon, planets, and stars for agricultural purposes. Many lines radiate from centers located on little hillocks, some of which contain ruins of small stone structures that could have served as observation points or altars. However, the astronomical theory was discredited in 1968 by Gerald S. Hawkins, English astronomer, who used the same computer analysis he had applied to Stonehenge to test the Nazca lines. See **Stonehenge.** Hawkins found too few celestial alignments to support the astronomical theory.

At about the same time, author Erich Von Däniken theorized the lines were created by extraterrestrials to guide the landings of their spacecraft. He suggested the local inhabitants imitated the markings to encourage the "space gods" to return. See **Extraterrestrial encounters.**

In the 1980s researchers such as anthropologist Johan Reinhard, archaeologist Josue Lancho, and science journalist Evan Hadingham saw possible connections between the Nazca lines and underground canals in the area, and similarities with religious pictographs drawn on soil in Chile and Bolivia. They theorize that some of the figures represent animal "sky gods" that were seen in the stars, or served functions in ancient rites to worship the mountain gods who still are believed to control rain, and therefore fertility and prosperity. Rites to petition the mountain gods continue to be performed in Bolivia, for example, by villagers who walk straight-line paths to mountain summits.

The ingestion of powerful hallucinogens such as *datura* and the San Pedro cactus continues to be part of sacred rites in the Andean cultures. It is theorized that the Nazca lines were drawn to represent what ancient shamans saw during their out-of-body, psychedelic trips, and to help them connect with their spirit helpers, who assumed animal shapes. See **Drugs in mystical and psychic experiences; Shamanism.**

Sources: William R. Corliss, ed. *Ancient Man: A Handbook of Puzzling Artifacts.* Glen Arm, MD: The Sourcebook Project, 1978; Erich Von Däniken. 1968. *Gods from Outer Space.* New York: Bantam

Books, 1972; Evan Hadingham. *Lines to the Mountain Gods: Nazca and the Mysteries of Peru.* New York: Random House, 1987; Gerald S. Hawkins. *Beyond Stonehenge.* New York: Harper & Row, 1973; Jennifer Westwood, ed. *The Atlas of Mysterious Places.* New York: Weidenfeld & Nicholson, 1987.

Near-death experience (NDE)

Term coined in the 1970s by the American physician Raymond Moody to describe the mystical-like phenomena experienced by individuals who appear to die and then return to life, or who come close to death. Until the 1975 publication of Moody's landmark book, *Life After Life,* few people would talk openly about an NDE experience. By 1982, however, a Gallup poll revealed that some 8 million adult Americans claimed to have had an NDE.

Moody, along with other NDE researchers, including Kenneth Ring, a psychologist and founding member of the International Association of Near-Death Studies at the University of Connecticut, identified several traits common to NDEs, although the experiences themselves are unique to each individual. In an NDE people generally experience one or more of the following phenomena in this sequence: a sense of being dead, or an out-of-body experience in which they feel themselves floating above their bodies, looking down; cessation of pain and a feeling of bliss or peacefulness; traveling down a dark tunnel toward a light at the end; meeting nonphysical beings who glow, many of whom are dead friends and relatives; coming in contact with a guide or Supreme Being who takes them on a life review, during which their entire lives are put into perspective without rendering any negative judgments about past acts; and finally, a reluctant return to life.

Despite the numbers of people who claim to have had an NDE, the experience has not been scientifically proved.

All that is known about the phenomenon is based on anecdotal material.

Skeptics believe the NDE is a dream, or only a hallucination brought about by a lack of oxygen, the release of endorphins (the body's own pain-killers), or increased levels of carbon dioxide in the blood. Ronald K. Siegel, a researcher at the University of California at Los Angeles school of medicine, reportedly reproduced NDE-type phenomena in laboratory experiments by administering LSD and other drugs. See **Drugs in mystical and psychic experiences.** NDE researchers say there is no evidence supporting drugs as a cause, and say other drug-induced experiences may parallel an NDE but are not the same thing. The researchers have argued that such explanations ignore the fact that many clinically dead individuals are able to give elaborate accounts of their resuscitations or report conversations they heard in other parts of the hospital while apparently out of their bodies. In one recollection—offered as proof against oxygen deprivation as the cause of an NDE vision—psychotherapist Michael Sabom told of a patient who, while out of body, watched his physician perform a blood test that revealed both high oxygen and low carbon dioxide.

Almost all reported NDEs are described as positive experiences. Fewer than 3 percent of the experiences are described as negative or unpleasant. The NDE is not limited to religious or "good" people. Many who have NDEs do become more spiritual or develop a belief in some type of God after their return from death. Most say they lose their fear of death and begin believing in an afterlife. Almost all discover a new and positive purpose for their lives, finding meaning it previously lacked. In some cases the NDE leaves individuals with heightened intuitive or psychic abilities, including precognition, clairvoyance, and telepathy.

Because the NDE is so profound, some individuals have difficulties adjusting after their return to their lives. In her study of the aftereffects of the NDE, *Coming Back to Life* (1988), author P. M. H. Atwater found that near-death survivors identified these as their most common negative reactions: anger, because they had to return to life; guilt, for not being sorry about leaving; disappointment, because once again they were back in their bodies; dumbfoundedness and inability to talk about their experience (or fear of talking about it); and depression at the realization that they had to resume their lives.

On the positive side, survivors offered these reactions: ecstasy at the wonder of their experience; thrill because of what they were able to experience; gratitude for what had happened to them; awe and lack of words to describe what happened; evangelism in wanting to tell others why they shouldn't fear death; and humility at the overwhelming nature of their experience.

According to research by Ring and colleagues, some individuals may be more prone to NDEs than others due to factors in their psychological makeup. Such factors include abuse, neglect, and dissociation experienced in childhood. NDE-prone personalities are not necessarily more likely to come close to death, but if they do they are more likely to experience NDE phenomena than other individuals. See **Encounter phenomenon.**

Ring, philosopher Michael Grosso, and others have theorized that the NDE may be a form of enlightenment or "gateway to a higher consciousness," and could have a transformative effect on the entire planet if enough people have similar experiences. Ring further has suggested that one does not have to die in order to experience similar enlightenment, or at least to assimilate the lessons of an NDE.

In a theological variation on that view, Carol Zaleski, a religion lecturer at Harvard, published a 1987 study, *Other-world Journeys,* that compared stories of "otherworld visions and journeys" found in medieval Christian literature to modern near-death accounts. She argues that the modern NDE stories, like their medieval counterparts, provide a way for individuals to incorporate a "religious sense of the cosmos" into their scientific/secular understanding. Putting aside the question of validity, Zaleski adds that the near-death testimony is "one way in which the religious imagination mediates the search for ultimate truth." Zaleski also notes that the modern NDE has its historical roots in the earliest myths that told of the hero or shaman and even "ordinary mortal" who passes through the gates of death only to return with a lesson for the living. See **Mysticism; Out-of-body experience** (OBE). Compare to **Deathbed visions.**

Sources: P. M. H. Atwater. *Coming Back to Life.* New York: Dodd, Mead, 1988; Amy Sunshine Genova. "The Near-Death Experience." *McCall's* (February 1988): 103–6; Michael Grosso. *The Final Choice: Playing the Survival Game.* Walpole, NH: Stillpoint Publishing, 1985; Raymond A. Moody, Jr., M.D. *Life After Life.* New York: Bantam Books, 1975; Raymond A. Moody, Jr., M.D. *Reflections on Life After Life.* Harrisburg, PA: Stackpole Books, 1977; Raymond A. Moody, Jr., M.D. *The Light Beyond.* New York: Bantam Books, 1988; Kenneth Ring. *Life at Death: A Scientific Investigation of the Near-Death Experience.* New York: Coward, McCann & Geoghegan, 1980; Kenneth Ring. *Heading Toward Omega.* New York: William Morrow, 1984; Kenneth Ring and Christopher J. Rosing. "The Omega Project: An Empirical Study of the NDE-Prone Personality." *Journal of Near-Death Studies* 8, no. 4 (Summer 1990): 211–40; Stephen Sabom. "Otherworld Journeys" (Review). *Journal of Near-Death Studies* 6, no. 4 (Summer 1988): 258–63; Carol Zaleski. *Otherworld Journeys: Accounts of Near-Death Experience in Medieval and Modern Times.* New York: Oxford University Press, 1987.

Neo-Paganism

An eclectic modern movement primarily concerned with revived and reconstructed pre-Christian nature religions and mystery traditions. As a movement it dates from about the 1960s, drawing its base from a wide spectrum of individuals interested in the occult revival, environmentalism, mythology, spiritual awareness, and comparative religions.

Neo-Paganism is loosely organized with no central authority, and is interpreted on a highly individualistic and personal basis; it is a religion, a philosophy, and a way of life. There are various neo-Pagan groups and churches, most of which are in the United States, England, and Canada, and also in Australia and Europe; but it is probable that the majority of neo-Pagans—or Pagans, as some prefer—practice their religion on a solitary basis. For some, being a "solitary" is necessary to protect their privacy and jobs, as neo-Paganism often is falsely associated with Devil-worship cults. Many neo-Pagans also are Witches.

The term "pagan" comes from the Latin *paganus,* which means "country dweller," and was applied in previous centuries to those who still believed in pre-Christian deities. The isolated country dwellers were among the last to be converted to Christianity.

The first neo-Pagan organization in the United States was Fereferia, which began in 1959 as the Fellowship of Hesperides and was incorporated as Fereferia in California in 1967. Its founder was Fred Adams, then a graduate student at Los Angeles State College. Fereferia, which comes from Latin for "wilderness festival," was a Goddess-and-Nature system that preached an abandonment of technology and a return to a peaceful, loosely organized vegetarian society, a utopia as envisioned by Adams. Fereferia is still in existence with a small following.

In the United States, two organizations that most influenced the early development and spread of neo-Paganism were Pagan Way and the Church of All Worlds. See **Church of All Worlds.** Pagan Way emerged in 1970, the product of an international collaboration between persons in America and Britain who also were involved in the reconstruction of Witchcraft as a religion. Pagan Way was organized in groves, which grew quickly and thrived during the 1970s. No central organization was ever established, and by 1980 Pagan Way evolved into new groups. Pagan Way rituals, written largely by Ed Fitch, are in the public domain and continue to be practiced.

Neo-Pagan networking is fulfilled primarily by Circle Sanctuary, established in 1974 near Mt. Horeb, Wisconsin, by Selena Fox, Jim Alan, and others. It is now run by Fox and her husband, Dennis Carpenter. In addition to networking, Circle offers counseling services and neo-Pagan and Wiccan training programs.

In Britain the Pagan Front was established in 1971 by members of the four branches of the Old Religion, or Witchcraft. It later changed its name to Pagan Federation, and remains active out of London headquarters. It espouses three principles: (1) love for and kinship with Nature; (2) adherence to the Pagan Ethic, "Do what you will but harm no thing"; and (3) a belief in reincarnation.

Beliefs, Philosophies, and Rites

Although neo-Paganism takes many forms, it has three general principles: polytheism, pantheism, and animism. However, not all neo-Pagans believe in all three principles. Generally, neo-Pagans view creation as an unbroken and interconnected whole, and hold all life equally sacred. The Divine Force has numerous personifications, but most revered is Goddess in her many aspects. Also recognized and worshiped is the Horned

God (not to be confused with the Devil) in various aspects. The various gods and goddesses are more than deities, they are also archetypes of the collective unconscious. (As Christianity supplanted paganism, pagan deities all came to be associated with the Devil. Neo-Pagans do not worship the Devil, nor do they practice or condone blood sacrifice.)

Most neo-Pagans believe in reincarnation and follow the ethic as stated previously. The development of psychic and magical skills is integral to most faiths.

Religious holidays are eight traditional seasonal holidays, also observed by Witches as sabbats. They include the winter and summer solstices and spring and fall equinoxes, as well as the agrarian/pastoral holidays of Imbolc (also Imbolg), February 2; Beltane (also Bealtaine, Walpurgisnacht), April 30/May 1; Lughnasadh (also Lammas), July 31/August 1; and Samhain, October 31/November 1. The sabbats celebrate the wheel of birth-death-rebirth, made possible by the union of Goddess and Horned God. Great outdoor festivals are organized on private land around the sabbats; some are attended by hundreds of people.

Neo-Pagan rituals are patterned on pre-Christian fertility, ecstatic, and mystery traditions. The mysteries of the Descent of Goddess to the Underworld, from earlier worship of Demeter and Kore, Inanna, and Ishtar, are often reenacted.

Neo-Pagan liturgies are constantly freshened with new material, and neo-Pagans value this creative right to shape their own worship. When possible, rites are conducted outdoors, and involve chanting, drumming, and dancing to achieve an ecstatic state. The use of alcohol or other drugs in rites is an individual matter. Some rites involve a trance channeling of Goddess or the Horned God, who is "drawn down" to speak through a high priestess or high priest or other designate. Many neo-Pagans, like many

Witches, conduct their rituals in the nude ("skyclad") in order to achieve a closer communion with nature.

Some neo-Pagans have looked beyond pre-Christian Western religions and have integrated into their faiths elements of Native American religions, Eastern religions, shamanic practices, and African and Latin religions.

Because of neo-Paganism's emphasis on the fertility cycles of nature, neo-Pagans generally have liberal attitudes toward sex, believing it should be celebrated and enjoyed, not repressed. Actual sexual rites to reenact the Goddess-Horned God union are less common than in the earlier days of neo-Paganism, reflecting the overall trends toward conservative sexual behavior. Most sexual rites now are performed symbolically.

Social Responsibilities

Because of their aversion to centralized authority, and the need for many to remain private about their religion, neo-Pagans have not organized on a great scale for social causes. However, many individuals, and some churches and groups, work for environmentalism and animal welfare, against nuclear weapons and nuclear energy, and for various charitable causes. Of particular interest to some neo-Pagans is child abuse, especially ritual child abuse, practiced by some satanic groups and often blamed on neo-Pagans and Witches.

In the mid-1980s, neo-Pagans began to recognize the need to provide social services for their own. The chief champion of this has been P. E. I. (Isaac) Bonewits, Archdruid of Ár nDraíocht Féin ("Our Own Druidism"), a neo-Pagan group based on reconstructed Druidic rites. See **Mysteries; Witchcraft.**

Sources: Margot Adler. *Drawing Down the Moon.* Rev. ed. Boston: Beacon Press, 1986; Rosemary Ellen Guiley. *The Ency-*

clopedia of Witches and Witchcraft. New York: Facts On File, 1989.

Neo-Pentecostalism

See Charismatic renewal.

New Age

Controversial term applied to a spiritual and social movement encompassing a broad range of interests in religion, philosophy, mysticism, health, psychology, parapsychology, ecology, and the occult. It is virtually impossible to define precisely what constitutes "New Age," as no two opinions agree; and much of what is called "New Age" is not new, but a renewed cycle of interest and rediscovery. The term "New Age" has replaced the "Age of Aquarius" label used in the 1960s.

"New Age" has been used in the past, such as for the names of various periodicals. These include the Freemasons' journal, New Age, christened in 1914; and a London weekly newspaper, The New Age, founded before World War I and which featured articles on social, political, economic, spiritual, and psychological issues.

The New Age has no organization and no central leaders, though there are networks of like-minded individuals, and various people are widely regarded as spokespersons of New Age thought. There is no organized agenda. New Age beliefs and activities are highly individual and eclectic, and essentially are part of a striving to be whole: the individuation process described by psychiatrist Carl G. Jung, or the self-actualization described by humanistic psychologist Abraham H. Maslow. See Psychology. There is a general interest in pursuing a sadhana, a spiritual path, toward self-realization; in transforming the world through spiritual consciousness that unifies all religions; and in looking after planetary concerns.

The New Age is largely a phenomenon of the industrialized West, with the greatest activity taking place in the alchemical crucible of the United States, where it is the latest expression in a mystical and occult tradition that extends back to the founding of the nation. J. Gordon Melton, an American Methodist minister, church historian, and scholar of nonconventional religions, dates the approximate beginning of the New Age to 1971, when it was first articulated. Small groups in the 1960s, outgrowths of the beatnik and hippie movements, had begun to call themselves "new age," but it was not until the 1970s that New Age networks, organizations, periodicals, and publications emerged.

David Spangler, one of the most eloquent observers of the essence of the New Age, sees it as "a metaphor for being in the world in a manner that opens us to the presence of God—the presence of love and possibility—in the midst of our ordinariness."

Spangler's books, Revelation: The Birth of a New Age (1976) and Emergence: The Rebirth of the Sacred (1984), are among the best presentations of New Age ideals. Another is Marilyn Ferguson's The Aquarian Conspiracy (1980; 1988). However, Ferguson's accurate observations that New Age proponents are everywhere in all levels of society, plus her unfortunate choice of the word "conspiracy," have been seized upon by some fundamentalist anti-New Age forces as evidence of a massive, anti-Christian New Age plot to dominate the world.

Among the concepts that stand out in New Age thought are that one creates one's own reality; that divinity exists within; and that there is a need for renewed recognition of the feminine principle and the use of "feminine" traits such as intuition.

New Age thought is not new in and of itself, but new expressions of eternal laws of the universe, mind, and heart. In

The New Religions (1970; 1984), Jacob Needleman observes that the modern spiritual questing has to do with "the formation of something that is authentically one's own *I*, one's own source, the source of the truly human within the self and within the community." The "one's own source," says Needleman,

can never be classified as either ancient or modern, as either thought or feeling, as either psychological, spiritual, or even religious in its customary sense. It is always new, but not necessarily novel or innovative—though it often first appears that way. We are speaking here of the appearance within man and within the life of humanity of something entirely new and which yet, when it appears, is seen to obey fundamental, eternal laws.

The New Age has found the greatest growth in the United States for several reasons. The very essence of America as the melting pot of the world has given it a long tradition of absorbing and syncretizing the diverse elements of other cultures, including their religions. Asian immigrants, some of whom have come to America specifically to spread Eastern religions, have found receptive audiences, especially since the 1960s. The nation's materialism also makes it ripe for transformational change. In the late nineteenth century, French statesman and author Alexis de Tocqueville as much as predicted the New Age with his observations on the coexistence in America of materialism and a strong religious spirit. "If ever the faculties of the great majority of mankind were exclusively bent upon the pursuit of material objects, it might be anticipated that an amazing reaction would take place in the souls of some," de Toqueville said in *Democracy in America*. "I should be surprised if mysticism did not soon make some advance among a people solely engaged in promoting their own worldly welfare."

The New Age has had ample precedents. In fact, as scientist and philosopher Pierre Teilhard de Chardin observed in *The Phenomenon of Man* (1955), humankind has in every age of history declared itself to be at a turning point. While this is in a sense true because we advance in an upward spiral, Teilhard said, "There are moments when this impression of transformation becomes accentuated and is thus particularly justified."

The foundation for the New Age in America was laid in the birth of the nation, many of whose leaders were steeped in Masonic and Rosicrucian mystical thought, and were influenced by Confucian philosophy. "A New Order of the Ages Begins," proclaims the reverse side of the Great Seal of the United States. Democracy and the individual's right to self-direction in the pursuit of life, liberty, and happiness helped to foster a culture more open to innovation and change than any other culture before it. In the early and mid-nineteenth century, the Transcendentalists became acquainted with Eastern religions and philosophies. They espoused a philosophy that emphasized intuition as well as intellect and, contrary to the prevailing scientific views, a living, evolutionary universe. Transcendentalism in turn influenced the subsequent movements of Theosophy, which represented the first broad effort to disseminate Eastern teachings in the West; Spiritualism; mental healing; Christian Science; and New Thought, the latter of which presented a synthesis of unorthodox medicine, religion, and psychology.

Beginning in the late nineteenth century, the number of alternative religious groups began growing in the United States, and accelerated following World War II. In 1965 immigration restrictions on Asians were revised to be comparable to quotas for Europeans, which brought a wave of Asians to the country. The social and political unrest of the 1960s offered a fertile ground for Eastern religions to expand beyond their own ethnic communities—primarily to an audience of single, upwardly mobile urban adults. Other influences were the experimentation with psychedelics as a means to higher states of consciousness, and the development of humanistic psychology. In the mid-1980s, actress Shirley MacLaine was instrumental in bringing the New Age to the mainstream masses with her public accounts of her own spiritual awakening. For many MacLaine's frank confessions about beliefs in reincarnation and extraterrestrials made acceptable the open exploration of many topics.

New Age activity by no means has been limited to America. The environmental consciousness that arose in the 1960s, for example, and which led to the political activism of the Greens in Europe (and to a lesser extent in North America), may be seen as part of the New Age. In Britain one of the leading figures in New Age thought is Sir George Trevelyan, who in 1971 founded the Wrekin Trust in West Malvern, Worcestershire. The Wrekin Trust is an educational charity "concerned with promoting awareness and study of the spiritual principles that operate through us and the universe"; it seeks to combine ageless wisdom with modern science and psychology to present a holistic worldview. The Trust is based on the medieval concept of the university, to find methods and systems of knowledge leading to union with the One.

The present search for the spiritual has continued to focus on the Eastern religions and philosophies. Though the deep, mystical cores of Judaism and Christianity are similar to the religions of the East, their popular practice has lost elements individuals appear to need, and which they find in Eastern thought: for example, the presence of the cosmos, the sacramental universe, in religious life (the Eastern Orthodox church has been the only branch of Christianity to retain this element). The universe of the East is alive and interconnected, not dead and mechanical. Eastern religions offer different concepts of the Absolute (see **Mysticism**). For those individuals who are disillusioned with material pursuits, Eastern thought shows that satisfaction of desire does not bring happiness, and that desire must be transformed through rigorous exercises (yoga and meditation). Such exercises are no longer a part of Western religions, save in the monasteries or in a few religious communities such as the Hasidim.

While interest in Eastern religions has increased, Catholicism, the mainline Protestant denominations of Christianity, and Judaism have lost followers. Many have gone to evangelical Christian sects, while others have drifted away from religion in general or sampled Eastern and so-called "new" religions. However, there is a danger in New Age ecumenism, in that the individual may remain religiously rootless, skipping about and collecting a superficial grab bag of only the most convenient doctrines and practices. As Jacob Needleman has stated, it is not enough to unlock the higher energies within the psyche. Without "a serious and extended inner discipline guided by exact knowledge and the support of a rightly ordered community," such energies are merely channeled to the pursuits of the ego. Initially, Eastern religions as practiced by Westerners are spiritual experiences which pass through the individual. Needleman has raised the question as to how much time and help is required to transform the experiences into a spiritual force within.

Flirtation without commitment is one factor that has led critics to call the New Age superficial, exploitative, narcissistic, fraudulent, cultish, anti-Christian, and a host of other uncomplimentary terms. Certain fundamentalists and other opponents of New Age thought claim the

New Age is indeed organized—by Satan, who leads an army of demonic minions against humankind. Constance Cumbey, one of the most prominent New Age critics and who has seized on the "conspiracy" theory, has attempted to draw parallels between the New Age and Nazism, and contends the Lucifer-led New Age is plotting to destroy Christianity and Western civilization. Other less strident fundamentalists take a more reasoned approach, but still see New Age thought on Christ and Jesus as flawed and misguided.

Such extreme claims must be dismissed. However, the criticisms of narcissism, superficiality, exploitation, and fraud have some legitimacy—but there is not a single field which does not have its abusers. The New Age is not anti-Christian, but part of it does reflect dissatisfaction with the failure of organized Christianity to provide spiritual nourishment. Some cults are identified with the New Age, but cults existed long before the New Age.

Proponents of the New Age call it a "revolution in consciousness" and predict it will permeate mainstream culture and push out new frontiers. To some extent mainstream penetration of New Age thought has already occurred, most notably in the areas of behavioral medicine, physics, psychology, and business, and in the growing cultivation of intuition and the increasing acceptance of psi as a normal function of the human organism. Concerning psi, 67 percent of all American adults say they have experienced extrasensory perception, according to a survey published in 1987 by the University of Chicago's National Opinion Research Council. This reflects a dramatic change from a 1974 Roper poll, which found only 53 percent believed in the reality of psi.

The term "New Age" was quickly imperiled through overuse and misuse. The media did the most damage, equating "New Age" with the more offbeat or questionable pursuits. Those who liked the term and found great power in what it conveyed could find no adequate substitute. By the 1990s, as New Age interests merged into the mainstream, the need for the term as a label began to disappear. Indeed, if New Age thought is to transform, then it must become the norm, not the exception. See **Age of Aquarius; Alternative religious movements; Christology; Planetary consciousness.**

Sources: Gina Cermina. *Insights for the Age of Aquarius.* Englewood Cliffs, NJ: Prentice-Hall, 1973; Constance E. Cumbey. *The Hidden Dangers of the Rainbow: The New Age Movement and Our Coming Age of Barbarism.* Shreveport, LA: Huntington House, 1983; Robert S. Ellwood, ed. *Eastern Spirituality in America.* New York: Paulist Press, 1987; Marilyn Ferguson. *The Aquarian Conspiracy: Personal and Social Transformation in the 1980s.* Rev. ed. Los Angeles: Jeremy P. Tarcher, 1988; Otto Friedrich, *et al.* "New Age Harmonies." *Time* (December 7, 1987): 62–72; Andrew Greeley. "Mysticism Goes Mainstream." *American Health* (January/February 1987): 47–55; William H. Kautz and Melanie Branon. *Intuiting the Future: A New Age Vision of the 1990s.* San Francisco: Harper & Row, 1989; Christopher Lasch. "Soul of a New Age." *Omni* (October 1987): 78–85+; Robert Lindsey. "Spiritual Concepts Drawing a Different Breed of Adherent." *The New York Times* (September 29, 1986): A1+; Texe Marrs. *Dark Secrets of the New Age: Satan's Plan for a One World Religion.* Westchester, IL: Crossway Books, 1987; J. Gordon Melton. *Encyclopedic Handbook of Cults in America.* New York: Garland Publishing, 1986; Jacob Needleman. *The New Religions.* New York: Crossroad, 1984; *The New Age Catalogue.* New York: Dolphin/Doubleday, 1988; Ron Rhodes. "The Christ of the New Age Movement." *Christian Research Journal* (Summer 1989): 9–14; Joanne Sanders. "The New Age in the Media Spotlight: Can It Take the Heat?" *The Common Boundary 5,* issue 3 (May/June 1987):

3–4; Anne A. Simkinson. "The Rise and Fall of New Age Publishing." *Common Boundary* (September/October 1990): 22–23; David Spangler. *The New Age*. Issaquah, WA: Morningtown Press, 1988; Pierre Teilhard de Chardin. *The Phenomenon of Man*. 1955. New York: Harper & Row, 1965; Kenneth L. Woodward with Patricia King, Peter McKillop, and Anne Underwood. "From 'Mainline' to Sideline." *Newsweek* (December 22, 1986): 54–56; The Wrekin Trust.

Newspaper test

An experiment attempting to prove survival after death. The newspaper test, similar to the book test, was prevalent in psychical research in the early twentieth century.

The test was created in 1919 by Feda, the spirit control of British medium Gladys Osborne Leonard, who was successful in book tests. In the newspaper test, a medium, working under controlled circumstances, communicated with her controls to give information about news stories to be published the next day in the London *Times* before it went to press. Such information, including page numbers of stories, could not be known by either medium or sitter.

In sittings with the Reverend Charles Drayton Thomas, a member of the Society for Psychical Research (SPR), Leonard provided words, names, and numbers, and the locations in which they were to appear on certain pages. Thomas acknowledged that most of the names were common enough to be found in virtually every issue of the London *Times*. However, Feda correctly gave page positions to within one-quarter of a column. In twelve sittings in which 104 items were given, Thomas determined seventy-three were accurate, twenty were inconclusive, and nineteen were wrong. The chance odds were eighteen successes, ten inconclusives, and seventy-six failures.

Feda stated that the information was provided to her by Thomas's deceased father, and gave evidential information that convinced Thomas this was true. In *Some New Evidence for Human Survival* (1922), Thomas said his father communicated that he was assisted by higher helping spirits, who took him to the *Times* office where he could see the etheric shadows of type not yet set.

Despite the success of the newspaper tests and other similar tests, no evidence yet is considered conclusive, scientific proof of survival after death. See **Book test; Leonard, Gladys Osborne.**

Sources: Theodore Flournoy. *From India to the Planet Mars: A Study of a Case of Somnambulism*. New York and London: Harper & Brothers, 1900; Rev. Charles Drayton Thomas. *Some New Evidence for Human Survival*. London: W. Collins Sons & Co. Ltd., 1922.

Ninja

See **Martial arts.**

Nirvana

See **Buddhism; Meditation; Mystical experiences; Yoga.**

Nostradamus (1503–1566)

French physician and prophet whose far-reaching prophecies have caused controversy for centuries. Nostradamus, a gifted clairvoyant, made approximately one thousand predictions to the year 3797. Some scholars say more than half the predictions have come true.

Nostradamus was born Michel de Nostredame in St. Remy de Provence, the oldest of five sons in a well-educated Jewish family. His parents converted to Catholicism, which exposed Nostradamus to both the occult wisdom of the Kabbalah and the prophecies of the Bible. As a child he experienced visions, which he believed were a divine gift from God.

At home Nostradamus was educated in Hebrew, Latin, Greek, mathematics, medicine, astronomy, and astrology. In 1522 he was sent to Montpellier University to study medicine. He earned a degree and license, and went to work treating plague victims throughout southern France. He possessed an uncanny gift for healing and quickly became famous, despite opposition from fellow physicians to his unorthodox cures. He refused to bleed patients and he made his own medicines, the recipes of which have not survived.

Around 1534 Nostradamus settled in Agen, married, and fathered two children. He met Julius Cesar Scaliger, a philosopher and student of astrology, who may have introduced Nostradamus to the art of prophecy. A few years later, Nostradamus's life and medical practice fell apart when the plague claimed his entire family and the Inquisition sought him for questioning concerning a friend of Scaliger's. Nostradamus left Agen and apparently drifted around Europe for about six years. According to legend his prophetic vision began to flower during this time, and he delved further into a study of the occult.

He settled down again, in Salon en Craux de Provence, where he married Anne Ponsart Gemelle, a wealthy widow who bore him six children. Sometime after 1550 he began to record his prophetic visions, which came to him by "the subtle spirit of fire," delivered in fragments and accompanied by a voice from limbo, which he believed to be the "Divine Presence." He summoned the visions by scrying every night alone in his study, gazing into a bowl of water set in a brass tripod. He began his sessions with a magic ritual attributed to the ancient oracles of Branchus. He touched the tripod with a wand, then dipped the wand into the water and touched the tip to his robe. He recorded the things he saw and heard, often not understanding them. Mindful of the Inquisition, he phrased the prophecies in rhymed quatrains written in a mixture of Greek, French, Provençal, and Latin; some words were further disguised in anagrams. He arranged the quatrains in groups of hundreds, or "centuries," which were not in chronological order.

The first prophecies were published in 1555 as Les Propheties de M. Michel Nostradamus. They were an immediate success in aristocratic circles, gaining him the favor of Catherine de Medici and cementing his reputation as a prophet. He published a second, larger edition of Propheties in 1558.

He enjoyed fame and success until 1566, when his health declined due to gout and dropsy. He died during the night of July 1 that year, and was buried upright in a wall of the Church of the Cordeliers in Salon. In 1791 superstitious French soldiers opened his grave. His bones were reburied in the Church of St. Laurent, also in Salon.

Nostradamus wrote ten centuries, but inexplicably left the seventh incomplete. At the time of his death, he had been planning to write eleventh and twelfth centuries. Scholars have puzzled over the prophecies for hundreds of years. Some seem clear, while others seem to have various interpretations. Among the many great events of history Nostradamus is credited with having foreseen are the Napoleonic wars; the history of British monarchs from Elizabeth I to Elizabeth II, including the abdication of Edward VIII; the American Revolutionary War and Civil War; the rise and fall of Hitler; the assassinations of Abraham Lincoln, John F. Kennedy, and Robert Kennedy; and the rise of Iran's Ayatollah Khomeini. He also foresaw air and space travel, including manned rockets to the moon, and submarines, which would be used for war. He is also said to have prophesied the development of the atomic bomb.

During World War II, Nostradamus's quatrains were used by both Axis and Allied powers for propaganda purposes. The Germans air-dropped over France selected quatrains, which they claimed foretold victory by the Nazis. The British countered by air-dropping quatrains over Germany and occupied countries that foretold the Nazis' defeat. The US government used quatrains in film shorts shown in movie houses that portrayed America as the torch of freedom for the world.

Nostradamus predicted three reigns of terror created by what he termed three Antichrists. The first two are believed to be Napoleon and Hitler. According to some interpretations, the third is a yet-unnamed Middle Eastern despot who, with the aid of the Soviet Union, will start a nuclear World War III between 1994 and 1999 by destroying New York City. This great war is to be presaged by famines, drought, earthquakes, and volcanic eruptions. The war itself is to last twenty-seven years, when the Antichrist will be defeated and killed. Following that, a one-thousand-year golden age of peace will reign.

In a letter to his infant son, Cesar, Nostradamus notes that his prophecies extend to the year 3797, when the world supposedly will come to an end.

Nostradamus always believed that it is possible to alter the predicted course of the future through awareness and action. If his prophecies have been interpreted accurately in terms of the wars and disasters that have come to pass, humankind has made precious little headway toward mastering its fate. See **Prophecy; Scrying.**

Sources: Richard Cavendish, ed. *The Encyclopedia of the Unexplained.* New York: McGraw-Hill, 1974; Jean-Charles de Fontbrune. *Nostradamus: Countdown to Apocalypse.* New York: Holt, Rinehart and Winston, 1980; Henry C. Roberts. *The Complete Prophecies of Nostradamus.* New York: American Book-Stratford Press, 1969; *The Man Who Saw Tomorrow.* Documentary film, Warner Brothers, 1981.

Notarikon

See **Gematria.**

Numerology

A system of divination and magic based upon the concept that the universe is constructed in a mathematical pattern, and that all things may be expressed in numbers, which correspond to vibrations. By reducing names, words, birth dates, and birthplaces to numbers, a person's personality, destiny, and fortune may be determined.

Pythagoras is credited as the father of numerology, due to his discovery that the musical intervals known in his time could be expressed in ratios between the numbers 1, 2, 3, and 4. He also observed that the numbers 1 through 4 add up to 10, which begins the cycle of numbers over again, for all numbers larger than 9 may be reduced by a single digit by adding the digits together. Pythagoras reasoned that the entire universe could be expressed numerically, creating a mystical system expanded by other early Greek philosophers. He is quoted: "The world is built upon the power of numbers."

Each primary number is ascribed certain characteristics and values, and a male or female aspect. Odd numbers are masculine, active, and creative, while even numbers are feminine and passive.

In the Greek mysteries, the number 888 represented the "Higher Mind." The Greek variation of "Jesus," "Iesous," equals 888. The number 666 represented the "Mortal Mind." In the New Testament, 666 is called the number of "the Beast."

The early Hebrews placed great importance upon numbers, basing the letters of the Hebrew alphabet upon them and relating them to cosmic forces. In the Middle Ages, the teachings of the Merkabah sect of Judaism became intertwined with numerical mysticism. In the thirteenth century, German Kabbalists developed the interpretation of the Scriptures through a system of number mysticism. See **Gematria.**

Both the Greeks and the Hebrews considered 10 the perfect number. Pythagoras said that 10 comprehends all arithmetic and harmonic proportions, and, like God, is tireless. All nations reckon to it because when they arrive at 10 they return to 1, the number of creation. The Pythagoreans believed the heavenly bodies were divided into 10 orders. According to the Kabbalah, there are 10 emanations of numbers out of Nothing. The emanations form the 10 sephiroth of the Tree of Life, which contains all knowledge and shows the path back to God.

In the nineteenth century, when scientific discoveries were made about light, magnetism, and electricity, the theory that numbers were energy patterns of vibrations became popular.

In numerological divination all numbers are reduced to nine roots between 1 and 9. Each number corresponds to a letter of the alphabet:

```
1 2 3 4 5 6 7 8 9
A B C D E F G H I
J K L M N O P Q R
S T U V W X Y Z
```

To find the numerical value of a name, all the numbers of the letters are added together and reduced to a single digit; for example, if a name totals 45, it is reduced to 9 by adding 4 plus 5. Briefly, the numbers represent:

1—unity, creation, independence
2—duality, emergence
3—power, generative force
4—solidity, dullness
5—sensuality, pleasure
6—perfection, harmony, balance
7—mysticism, psychic, magic
8—material success, justice
9—spiritual, mental achievement

The numbers 11, 22, and 33 are master numbers and are not reduced to single digits. People whose names correspond to these numbers are said to be highly developed spiritually. The number 33 is that of avatar.

Numerologists believe that one's full name given at birth is the expression of the vibratory forces of the universe, which determine one's character and destiny. Changing one's name can alter these factors, but several years supposedly are required for the vibrational patterns to readjust.

Various formulae exist for detailed name analysis. Adding up vowels reveals one's "heart's desire" or "soul's urge"; adding up consonants reveals aspects of one's personality. The frequency of various letters determine's the karmic lessons to be faced in life. The sum of the month, day, and year of birth tells the birth path, or the general direction of one's life. The sum of one's full name and birth date equals a power number, which acts as a beacon to guide one through life.

All words may be converted to numbers to see how virtually anything complements or clashes with one's life, including one's career and city of residence. Numerology also is used to determine the propitious days for various activities, as a guide in health matters and selecting business and marriage partners and friends, and to predict the future. It may also be used in the selection of gifts, colors for one's decorating scheme, and names for one's baby. See **Tarot.**

Sources: Francis Barrett. *The Magus.* 1801. Reprint. Secaucus, NJ: The Citadel Press,

1967; Richard Cavendish. *The Black Arts.* New York: Perigee Books, 1967; Eden Gray. *A Complete Guide to the Tarot.* New York: Bantam Books, 1972; Manly P. Hall. *The Secret Teachings of All Ages.* !928. Los Angeles: The Philosophical Research Society, 1977; Helyn Hitchcock. *Helping Yourself with Numerology.* West Nyack, NY: Parker Publishing, 1972; Gershom Scholem. *Kabbalah.* New York: New American Library, 1974; Colin Wilson. *The Occult.* New York: Vintage Books, 1973.

O

Od

See **Universal life force.**

Odic force

See **Universal life force.**

Odyle

See **Universal life force.**

Olcott, Colonel Henry Steel

See **Blavatsky, Madame Helena Petrovna;
Theosophy.**

Om

In Hinduism, the most sacred and comprehensive expression of spiritual knowledge. Om, also represented as Aum, is a mantra, a symbol of form and a manifestation of spiritual power. Om also appears in Buddhism, most notably the Vajrayana, or "Diamond Vehicle" school.

The symbol of Om represents supreme consciousness, which encompasses and reveals the physical, mental, and unconscious; the three states of consciousness (waking, dreaming, and deep sleep, or the unconscious); and the three principles of creation as embodied in Brahma, Vishnu, and Shiva.

In the Mandukya Upanishad, Om, the imperishable Brahman, the Supreme Reality and Truth, transcends past, present, and future. The Self is one with Om, and has three aspects: the universal person who is conscious only of external objects; the universal person who is conscious only of his or her dreams; and the universal person who is in the dreamless sleep of the lord of all, Prajna, a state of bliss. Beyond is a fourth aspect of ineffable peace and supreme good, the Self which *is* the syllable Om. The Taittiriya Upanishad states that, "He who meditates on Om attains to Brahman."

"*Om mani padme hum,*" Sanskrit for "O, Jewel of the Lotus, Hum," is a mantra of enlightenment (jewel) arising within consciousness (lotus). To recite it assists in the transformation from the impure state to the pure. In Tibetan Buddhism the mantra is "*Om Mani Peme Hung,*" and is the oldest and greatest of mantras in that form of Buddhism. The exact meaning of the mantra is complex, and relates to compassion and the desire for the attainment of nirvana of all sentient beings.

In yoga Om is a powerful mantra that pierces the material nature of the body to purify and bring the soul in touch with the Absolute. To meditate upon Om is to connect with the Self. See **Mantra.**

Sources: The Encyclopedia of Eastern Religion and Philosophy. Boston: Shambhala,

1989; Bernard Gunther. *Energy Ecstasy and Your Seven Vital Chakras*. North Hollywood, CA: Newcastle Publishing, 1983; Lama Anagarika Govinda. *Foundations of Tibetan Mysticism*. First American ed. York Beach, ME: Samuel Weiser, 1969; Tenzin Gyatso, His Holiness the Fourteenth Dalai Lama. *Kindness, Clarity and Insight*. Translated and edited by Jeffrey Hopkins, coedited by Elizabeth Napper. Ithaca, NY: Snow Lion Publications, 1984; Ormond McGill. *The Magic and Mysticism of India*. Cranbury, NJ: A. S. Barnes & Co., 1977. *The Upanishads*. Translated by Swami Prabhavananda and Frederick Manchester. New York: Signet, 1957.

Omen

A sign, often of a supernatural or psychic nature, of a future event. Many omens are found in the natural world. The ancients of East and West examined the entrails of animals and observed changes in the elements and the movements or appearances of animals and birds. They also observed the movement of heavenly bodies. Unusual occurrences, such as monstrous births, eclipses, comets, meteors, novae, floods, storms, and earthquakes, were considered to be omens of disasters or of divine unhappiness with humankind.

The ancient Babylonians, Sumerians, and Assyrians were prodigious record-keepers of omens, listing them on tablets and constantly updating them according to experiences. Virtually everything that happened portended something. The Druids produced omens by observing the death struggles of their sacrificial human victims.

Dreams have provided omens for thousands of years. Unlike oracular dreams, in which an explicit divine message is given to the dreamer, omen dreams are symbolic and must be interpreted. Some precognitive dreams are clearer, in which the dreamer previews

plane crashes, car accidents, ship sinkings, fires, and other disasters.

The appearance of apparitions and visions also is considered an omen. Joan of Arc's soldiers were bolstered by heavenly visions of St. Michael and of the Holy Spirit, which appeared as a dove perched on the Maid's shoulder. In the sixteenth and seventeenth centuries in England, it was common for people to report seeing great visions in the sky of galloping horses, dragons, armies in battle, and angels with owls' heads. The English Civil War (1642–1648) was presaged by numerous visions of armies marching through the skies.

Vision and apparition omens are still seen. A vision of a deceased person may be viewed as an omen of the impending death of a member of the family. In Ireland the banshee, or "fairy woman," heralds the death of members of old families and great and holy persons. The appearance of spectral animals, ghostly ships, and spirits is universal and often considered to be an omen. See **Divination; Prophecy.**

Sources: Katherine Briggs. *An Encyclopedia of Fairies: Hobgoblins, Brownies, Bogies, and Other Supernatural Creatures.* New York: Pantheon Books, 1976; E. A. Wallis Budge. *Amulets and Superstitions.* 1930. Reprint. New York: Dover Publications, 1978; Robert Graves. *The White Goddess.* Amended and enlarged ed. New York: Farrar, Straus and Giroux, 1966; Michael Loewe and Carmen Blacker. *Oracles and Divination.* Boulder, CO: Shambhala, 1981; Charles Mackay. *Extraordinary Popular Delusions and the Madness of Crowds.* 1852. Reprint. New York: Farrar, Straus and Giroux, 1932; Keith Thomas. *Religion and the Decline of Magic.* New York: Charles Scribner's Sons, 1971.

Oracle

A method of divination and prophecy in which deities or supernatural beings are consulted, usually through a human medium who, while in a trance possession, allows the entity to speak. Various cultures throughout history have relied heavily upon oracles for advice and wisdom as to the best course of action to take.

In ancient Greece and Rome, oracles were often sought by leaders for important political and military advice. The mediums were sibyls, women priestesses usually past childbearing age, who resided in caves believed to be the thrones of deities. Major sibyls resided in Phrygia, Libya, Persia, Samos, Cumae, Cimmeria, Marpessa, Tibur, and Erythrae; the most famous was at Delphi, in a temple built on limestone in the sixth century B.C. near Mt. Parnassus, about one hundred miles from Athens.

At Delphi a priestess called the Pythia or Pythonness was the oracular medium; she resided with snakes, symbols of prophecy and wisdom. Initially the Pythia served the Earth Goddess, Gaea (Gaia), who eventually gave way to the sun god, Apollo, who, according to myth, slew the sacred python in residence. On certain days inquirers were chosen by lot and paid a fee to ask a question of the oracle. The Pythia retired to an inner chamber and induced a frenzied trance, perhaps by drinking blood, inhaling smoke, or chewing laurel leaves. Her elliptical pronouncements and moanings were interpreted by priests, who translated them into hexameter verse. The Greeks and Romans believed the Pythia inhaled mysterious vapors from cracks in the rocks, though scientists have found no evidence of such. King Croesus of Lydia led his army to disaster on the basis of a Delphic prophecy. Told that if he declared war on the Persians a great army would be destroyed, he assumed the losers would be the enemy; but his own great army was destroyed instead.

Zeus was oracle to the Romans, who believed the god resided in the oak trees at Dodua and spoke through the mouths of the Peleiads (doves). The Peleiads may have been priestesses impersonating doves. The old Prussians believed that gods inhabited oaks and other high trees and whispered answers to inquirers.

The ancient Babylonians consulted priestesses as oracles, and also relied upon the dream visions of deities. Major oracular centers were at Mani and in Sargonid Assyria. The goddess Ishtar was referred to as "She Who Directs the Oracles."

In the Old and Middle Kingdoms of Egypt (2680 B.C.–1786 B.C.), women of important families were known as prophetesses, and had access to the goddesses Hathor and Neith. Other oracular consultation took place in the form of dreams. In the Middle Kingdom (2000 B.C.–1786 B.C.), dreams were believed to be sent by the gods so that humankind might know the future. Oracular dreams were both deliberately sought and spontaneous. In the New Kingdom (1570 B.C.–1342 B.C.), the first fully developed oracular procedure appeared with the use of cult statues. The statues, usually of Amun, god of fertility, agriculture, and the breath of life, were carried in portable shrines on the shoulders of priests during festivals. The statues allegedly could nod and talk, perhaps due to surreptitious manipulation by a priest. Or the priest indicated a "yes" answer by moving toward the inquirer, and "no" by recoiling. The statues were consulted by both commoner and royalty for predictions and dispensations of the law. A papyrus of magical spells from the third century A.D. gives a ritual for transforming a boy into an oracle.

The primary function of ancient Hebrew priests was to divine and give oracles. The priests were consulted at sanctuaries where Yahweh, God, was believed to be present. Their procedure included the use of Urim and Thummim, of which little is known, but apparently were objects the priests consulted. Answers were given by lots, though the oracle could give a "no-answer." Many answers required interpretation by the priests.

In China, where divination is an ancient art, there is no equivalent of the Delphic-type of oracle. Inspired answers to questions have been sought through the production of signs, such as casting the *I Ching,* or in the signs of nature, such as cloud formations.

Trance oracles are traditional in Tibet. Most of the mediums are men who exhibited natural psychic gifts in childhood, though some suddenly develop their ability in adulthood. Typically, they are members of laity, not the priesthood. It is believed that their psychic powers are bestowed by deities, who belong to the phenomenal order of existence at levels ranging from higher than humans to lower. Some deities are destructive and dangerous. The medium enters a trance in a procedure similar to those used by shamans in Siberia and Alaska. Beforehand, the medium is expected to abstain from sex, alcohol, tobacco, and meat.

Various state oracles reside in monasteries throughout Tibet. One of the most important, in Nechung Gumpa, is the mouthpiece of Pe Har, a destructive deity. The Nechung oracle has played a key role in the location and identification of several incarnations of the Dalai Lama, and helped the esteemed thirteenth Dalai Lama thwart a black magic assassination attempt.

In Africa the Azande witch doctors use oracles to determine the perpetrators of bad spells and illness. One method is the *iwa,* a rubbing board; another is *benge,* a strychnine-like poison administered to a fowl, which ideally does not die. The actions of the poisoned fowl are interpreted. The Cape Ngui of South Africa consult diviners who are women possessed by the spirits of their ancestors.

There is evidence that pre-Christian tribes of Germanic and Scandinavian peoples consulted oracles. The wizards and village wise women of the Middle Ages who were consulted for their clairvoyant gifts were a form of oracle. The oracular practice was condemned by the Christian church. However, a Christian priest is treated as an oracle when he is consulted for advice, for he is expected to have a superior communication with God. Spiritualist mediums who consult the spirits of the dead also are a type of oracle.

In the modern West, the term "oracle" is rarely used, though individuals and oracular methods continue to be consulted for divine or inspired guidance. See **Channeling; Divination;** *I Ching;* **Prophecy.**

Sources: Bob Brier. *Ancient Egyptian Magic.* New York: Quill/Morrow, 1981; James G. Frazer. *The Golden Bough: The Roots of Religion and Folklore.* 1890. New York: Avenel Books, 1981; Michael Loewe and Carmen Blacker. *Oracles and Divination.* Boulder, CO: Shambhala, 1981; Max Marwick, ed. *Witchcraft and Sorcery.* 2d ed. Harmondsworth, Middlesex, England: Penguin Books, 1982; Edgar D. Mitchell. *Psychic Explorations: A Challenge for Science.* Edited by John White. New York: Paragon Books, 1974; Monica Sjöö and Barbara Mor. *The Great Cosmic Mother: Rediscovering the Religion of the Earth.* San Francisco: Harper & Row, 1987; Merlin Stone. *When God Was a Woman.* San Diego: Harcourt Brace Jovanovich, 1976; Keith Thomas. *Religion and the Decline of Magic.* New York: Charles Scribner's Sons, 1971; Danah Zohar. *Through the Time Barrier: A Study in Precognition and Modern Physics.* London: William Heinemann Ltd., 1982.

Order of the Knights Templar

Military arm of the church during the Crusades and one of the most powerful monastic societies in Europe. The Order of the Knights Templar symbolized the holy struggle of Christians against the infidels. But their enormous wealth, jealously coveted by kings and popes, and their secret rituals brought about their spectacular downfall and the establishment of sorcery as evidence of heresy.

In A.D. 1118, about twenty years after the founding of the Kingdom of Jerusalem by Godefroy de Bouillon and a group of crusaders, French knight Hugues de Payns ("of the pagans") led a group of nine other French noblemen to the Holy Land, where they encamped next to the alleged site of King Solomon's Temple. Vowing to protect Christians traveling to the holy places, especially between Jerusalem and St. Jean d'Acre, the knights pledged chastity, poverty, and obedience. They called themselves the Order of the Knights of the Temple, or Templars.

Although led by de Payns, the real power behind the Order was St. Bernard of Clairvaux, head of the Cistercian Order of monks and supported by Pope Honorius II. The pope officially recognized the Templars as a separate Order in 1128, giving it unheard-of sovereignty. The Order was exempt from local taxes, could impose its own taxes on the community, was immune from judicial authority, could appoint its own clergy, and answered only to the pope. Membership was restricted to men of noble birth who had to undergo various probationary periods and initiation rituals before acceptance. Attached to these noblemen were various artisans and manual laborers. The head of the Order was the Grand Master, followed by his deputy the Senechal, the Marshal, and the Commander.

The Order's battle standard was a red eight-pointed cross on a background of black and white squares called the Beauceant, with the cross on a plain background of white as the official symbol. Their battle cry was *"Vive Dieu, Saint Amour"* ("God Lives, Saint Love"),

and the motto was *"Non nobis Domine, non nobis, sed Nomini Tuo da gloriam"* ("Not for us, Lord, not for us, but to Thy Name give glory"). The Templar seal showed two knights sharing one horse, a sign of poverty and service.

By the beginning of the fourteenth century, the Templars had become one of the most powerful organizations in Europe and the Middle East, with branches in Scotland, England, Aragon, Castile, Portugal, Germany, and the Kingdom of Naples, all headquartered from the main Temple in Paris. They had amassed huge wealth and, unlike the Order of Hospitalers of St. John, supported no charities. They also lent money, although at rates lower than the Jews or Lombards.

For years stories circulated about the Templars' secret rituals, and whether they were Christians or had become "Mahometans," or followers of Muhammad. The Templars had always maintained close ties with the Sufis, the mystic sect of Moslems, sharing their esoteric knowledge of alchemy and the Jewish Kabbalah. The Templar battle cry, "God Lives, Saint Love," closely parallels the Sufi search for the Beloved as the symbol of God. The father of founder Hugues de Payns was a Moor from southern Spain, and may have been heavily influenced by Sufi thought. Each group admired the other's spiritual dedication and monastic determination.

Others claimed the Templars worshiped a devil named Baphomet, who appeared in various forms, including a huge black cat. These rituals supposedly included kissing the cat's behind, bestiality, sodomy, kissing the Grand Master's genitals, roasting children alive, idol worship, denunciation of Christ and the Virgin Mary, intercourse with demons and succubi, and overall loss of their souls to the Devil. All these rumors had been around since the Order's founding, but no one gave them much currency until 1307.

At that time King Philip IV of France, called the Fair, was in debt to the Templars and increasingly irritated at their protection from secular jurisdiction. He decided that the Templars' wealth was his last source of funds. On October 13 he seized the Temple in Paris and arrested Grand Master Jacques de Molay and 140 Templars, as well as every Templar his soldiers could find throughout France. Charged with heresy and blasphemy, the victims were hideously tortured to extract confessions. Philip needed the church's support. He bullied a weak Clement V, the first Avignon pope, into signing a papal bull authorizing the Templars' trials and seizure of their properties.

The trials and tortures lasted for seven years, while the king and pope bickered over jurisdiction and disbursement of the property. Philip's charges of heresy and witchcraft, supported by the tortured confessions, gave the Inquisition new evidence in its hunt for enemies, especially ones with property worth taking. Such powerful arguments, preying on the deepest fears of the medieval mind, caused the eventual deaths of many supposed heretics and witches by the mid-1700s.

Pope Clement V officially abolished the Order and all its branches in 1312 at the Council of Vienne, transferring the property to the Hospitalers. They, in turn, paid Philip IV money he said the Templars had owed him. A great deal of the assets were seized directly by Philip and King Edward II of England for their own use or as gifts to friends. Resisting papal pressure, the kings of Spain and Portugal transferred the remaining assets into new orders, allowing Templars to obtain membership.

In 1314 Grand Master de Molay was promised life in prison if he confessed his crimes in public. In March soldiers led him and his chief lieutenant onto a scaffold in front of a packed crowd of clergy,

nobility, and commoners. But de Molay, who had been Philip IV's friend and godfather to the king's daughter, frustrated the king's triumph by loudly proclaiming his innocence and that of all the Templars. Enraged, Philip IV sentenced the Grand Master to be burned alive. As the flames took his body, de Molay supposedly cursed Philip's family to the thirteenth generation and called for Philip IV and Clement V to join him before God's throne within a year. Clement died within a month, Philip died in November, and Philip IV's Capetian dynasty withered within one generation, to be replaced by the Valois.

Although the truth probably died with Grand Master de Molay, Temple tradition maintains that the Order did not go with him. One persistent story says that some of the survivors of the persecutions fled to Scotland disguised as stonemasons. As a disguise the Templars borrowed masonic symbols and called themselves Freemasons, giving birth to that secret society. The Templars were always known as builders, going back to the founding of the Order on the site of Solomon's Temple. One of the dearest wishes of their mentor, St. Bernard of Clairvaux, was to build cathedrals that would esoterically transmit the secret teachings he carried from early church fathers. Sufi tradition also uses buildings as permanent repositories of esoteric knowledge.

Another theory says that Geoffroy de Gonneville, a Templar, brought a message from de Molay before his death to a group of Templars meeting in Dalmatia, telling them of a resurgence of their Order in six hundred years. At the end of this meeting, or "convent," as it was called, the Supreme Council of the Order remained in Corfu for three years, then dissolved. But before disbanding the Council supposedly launched the Order of the Rose-Croix, or Rosicrucians.

Later accounts insist that the

eighteenth-century adept, the Comte de St. Germain, was a Templar. The Comte also participated in Rosicrucian and Freemasonic rituals, and some Masonic scholars believe he was attempting to reintroduce Templar secrets into those two organizations. Albert Pike, Masonic historian, has stated that Count de Cagliostro, another eighteenth-century occultist and a student of St. Germain's, was a Templar agent. Cagliostro's introduction of Egyptian rites into Freemasonic ceremonies was, according to Pike, an attempt to revive the worship of Isis.

Regardless of whether the Knights Templar actually founded these organizations, their spiritual power does live on in the traditions of all secret societies and esoteric organizations. See **Cagliostro, Count Alessandro; Freemasonry; Rosicrucians; Saint Germain.**

Sources: Gaetan Delaforge. "The Templar Tradition Yesterday and Today." *Gnosis* no. 6 (Winter 1988): 8–14; Rosemary Ellen Guiley. *The Encyclopedia of Witches and Witchcraft.* New York: Facts On File, 1989; Manly P. Hall. *Masonic Orders of Fraternity.* Los Angeles: The Philosophical Research Society, 1950; Barbara W. Tuchman. *A Distant Mirror: The Calamitous 14th Century.* New York: Ballantine Books, 1978.

Order of the Rosy Cross

See **Rosicrucians.**

Ordo Templi Orientis

See **Crowley, Aleister; Illuminati.**

Orgone

See **Universal life force.**

Osis, Karlis.

See **Deathbed visions.**

Ouija

A board and pointer used for divination and by some as a means to contact spirits or entities. The name comes from the French and German words for "yes," *oui* and *ja* (ja is mispronounced with a hard "j"). Critics of the Ouija, who include authorities in most denominations of Christianity, say it is dangerous and a tool of the Devil. Advocates say that it, like other forms of divination, is a legitimate means to discover insight, wisdom, and self-truths and to communicate with discarnate beings.

The board includes letters of the alphabet, numerals 0 through 9, the words "yes" and "no," and a heart-shaped pointer on three felt-tipped legs. One or two people place their fingertips on the pointer, which moves to answer questions. In most cases answers probably rise up from the subconsciousness of the users, even when "spirits" identify themselves and give messages. However, Ouija pointers have been known to fly off the board and spin out of control, as though being directed by unseen forces, and some users claim to be harassed by external agents contacted through the board.

Precursors to the Ouija date back to ancient times. In China before the birth of Confucius (c. 551 B.C.), similar instruments were used to communicate with the dead. In Greece during the time of Pythagoras (c. 540 B.C.) divination was done with a table that moved on wheels to point to signs, which were interpreted as revelations from the "unseen world." The rolling table was used through the nineteenth century. Other such devices were used by the ancient Romans as early as the third century A.D., and in the thirteenth century by the Mongols. Some Native Americans used "*squdilatc* boards" to find missing objects and persons, and obtain spiritual information. In 1853 the planchette came into use in Europe. It consisted of a triangular or heart-shaped platform on three legs, one of which was a pencil. The medium or user moved the device over paper to draw pictures and spell out messages.

The modern Ouija, which is marketed as a game, was invented by an American, Elijah J. Bond, in 1892. Bond sold his patent to William Fuld, who is considered to be the father of the Ouija. Fuld founded the Southern Novelty Company in Baltimore, Maryland (later known as the Baltimore Talking Board Company), and marketed the board as "Ouija, the Mystifying Oracle."

The Ouija enjoyed enormous popularity during and after World War I, when many people were desperate to communicate with loved ones killed in the war and Spiritualism was in a revival. In 1966 Fuld sold his patent to Parker Brothers game company of Beverly, Massachusetts. Interest in the Ouija picked up again in the 1960s and 1970s, along with renewed interest in the occult and supernatural. Parker Brothers stresses that the Ouija is a game for entertainment purposes.

In parapsychology the Ouija is considered a form of automatism, an unconscious activity that picks up and amplifies information from the subconscious mind. Critics of the Ouija say users have no control over repressed material that might be released, and thus can suffer psychosis.

Nor do users have control if the board is used to contact spirits. Edgar Cayce called it a "dangerous toy." Some demonologists say the Ouija opens the door to possession by evil spirits, perhaps requiring exorcism and psychiatric care.

Ouija advocates use the board to divine the future, find lost objects, obtain daily guidance, and gain spiritual insight. The board has been the beginning step in several famous cases of mediumship and channeling. In 1913 a Ouija put St. Louis housewife Pearl Curran into contact with a seventeenth-century English spirit who called herself Patience Worth. In 1919 Stewart Edward White and his wife, Betty, were introduced to entities called the "Invisibles." In 1963 Jane Roberts and her husband, Robert Butts, began Ouija experiments that led to contact with the entity Seth. In all three cases the Ouija activity began casually, almost as a lark. Once the entities revealed themselves, communication advanced to automatic writing and use of vocal chords. See **Automatisms; Montgomery, Ruth; Planchette; Roberts, Jane; White, Stewart Edward; Worth, Patience.**

Sources: Gina Covina. *The Ouija Book.* New York: Simon & Schuster, 1979; Stoker Hunt. *Ouija: The Most Dangerous Game.* New York: Harper & Row, 1985; Jane Roberts. *The Coming of Seth.* New York: Pocket Books, 1976; Stewart Edward White. *The Betty Book: Excursions into the World of Other-Consciousness.* New York: Berkley Medallion Books, 1969.

Our Lady of Lourdes

See **Marian apparitions.**

Ouspensky, Pyotr Demianovitch

See **Gurdjieff, Georgei Ivanovitch.**

Out-of-body experience (OBE)

A phenomenon in which a person feels separated from his or her physical body and seems to be able to travel to, and perceive, distant locations on Earth or in nonworldly realms. The out-of-body experience (OBE) may be associated with psi, but is not in itself a paranormal experience.

Descriptions of the OBE, which are nearly universal, date to antiquity and contain many similarities. Nonetheless, scientific evidence for the OBE is inconclusive, prompting skeptics to hypothesize that the OBE is not an exteriorization but a mental exercise in an altered state of consciousness. OBEs also are called "astral projection," "astral travel," and "exteriorization." Approximately one-quarter of the adult Western population believe they have had at least one OBE.

Cultural Beliefs

The belief that the consciousness can separate from the body has been held in many civilizations throughout history. The ancient Egyptians described a *ka*, a vehicle of the mind and soul (*ba*). The mysteries of Isis and Osiris had initiation rites that required projection of the *ka*. The initiation rites of the Mithraic mysteries also centered on out-of-body projection. Plato held that the soul could leave the body and travel. Socrates, Pliny, and Plotinus gave descriptions of experiences that resemble OBEs; Plotinus wrote of being "lifted out of the body into myself" on many occasions. Plutarch described an OBE that occurred to Aridanaeus in A.D. 79. The Tibetan Book of the Dead describes a "Bardo-body," an ethereal duplicate of the physical body, in which the deceased find themselves. The existence of an apparitional body is acknowledged in Mahayana Buddhism. The ancient Chinese said they could achieve OBE during meditation. OBEs are a phenomenon of yoga, but not a goal; they, like other phenomena called *siddhis*, can be obstacles to enlightenment. See **Siddhis.**

Shamans in tribal cultures say they project themselves out-of-body at will by achieving an ecstatic state of consciousness.

The belief in doubles, phantom duplicates that appear to be real, is widespread. See **Bilocation; Double.**

Characteristics of the OBE

While accounts of OBEs vary, there are common characteristics. Most often reported is the existence of a second, subtle body that becomes the vehicle for travel. The subtle body is described as a ghostly, semitransparent double of the physical body that is either naked, clothed in duplicate clothing, or clothed in other apparel. To other individuals it is usually invisible, though its presence may be sensed. If seen it appears to be an apparition. Some individuals report having no form at all, or being points of light or presences of energy. The existence of a silvery cord connecting the astral form to the physical body is reported seen or sensed in a minority of cases.

In the astral form, OBE travelers report moving about the earth plane like apparitions, passing through walls and solid objects. They say they travel with the speed of thought. Travel to non-earthly realms called the astral plane are much different, with contact with objects and beings who "feel" solid and real.

The onset of an OBE occurs spontaneously during waking consciousness; before, during, and after sleep; during severe illness; and at times of great stress, trauma, or fear. Some individuals believe that OBEs occur to everyone during sleep. OBEs also can be induced by hypnosis, meditation, and other techniques. The physical body may be lying, sitting, or standing.

The near-death experience (NDE) usually involves some form of OBE. Some people who have clinically died or come close to death report the separation of their consciousnesses from their bodies. They watch efforts to restore their physical forms to life, or travel into an apparent afterlife state. See **Near-death experience (NDE).**

The OBE is often preceded by a perception of strong and high-frequency vibrations. Individuals report leaving through their head or solar plexus, or simply rising up and floating away. Re-entry is accomplished by returning through the head or solar plexus, or by melting back into the body. It is believed that if the silver cord is severed while one is out-of-body, physical death occurs because the body has been cut off from its soul. The cord also is said to snap when the body dies and the consciousness, or soul, is released.

Individuals who are in pain often report an absence of pain during an OBE.

Historical Research

The most systematic, early experimentation in OBEs was conducted by four individuals. Yram, born Marcel Louis Forhan (1884–1917), was a Frenchman who believed everyone was capable of astral travel in a variety of bodies of various densities and dimensions, which he chronicled in his book, *Practical Astral Travel*. Yram paid out-of-body visits to a woman whom he later married; the two traveled astrally together and experienced ecstatic astral sex.

Sylvan Muldoon, an American, researched OBEs from 1915 to 1950, as a result of his spontaneous OBEs beginning at age twelve. Muldoon was a sickly youth who spent a good deal of time in bed. As his health improved, his OBEs became less frequent. Muldoon traveled about in a double the exact duplicate of his physical body. He remained on the earth plane. He sometimes felt pain when out-of-body, which runs contrary to most descriptions. Muldoon believed that dreams of falling and flying corresponded to movements during astral travel. He wrote of his research in *The Projection of the Astral Body* (1929), coauthored with psychical researcher Hereward Carrington.

Englishman Oliver Fox, born Hugh G. Callway in 1885, was also a sickly child. He did not experience OBEs until adulthood, however, when he succeeded in inducing them with lucid dreaming; he experimented between 1902 and 1938. Fox's "Dream of Knowledge" was an ef-fort to remain awake mentally while sleeping physically. He published his account in 1920 in *English Occult Review;* it was later published as a book, *Astral Projection.*

Englishman J. H. M. Whiteman claimed to have more than two thousand OBEs between 1931 and 1953, which he described in *The Mystical Life* (1961). He had his first OBE at age twelve in 1919 without realizing what had happened. Whiteman considered his OBEs to be mystical experiences. He sometimes found himself in the form of a child or a female.

More recently, various surveys have sought to establish the frequency and nature of OBEs. A difficulty in assessing the results, however, is that perceptions of what constitutes an OBE vary. A 1954 survey of 155 Duke University sociology students by Hornell Hart yielded 27.1 percent who said they had had an OBE. Two surveys of undergraduates at two British universities by Celia Green (1967) yielded 19 percent (of 115 persons) and 34 percent (of 380 persons). In 1971 Charles T. Tart reported that 44 percent of 150 marijuana users said they had been out-of-body. The first survey of randomly selected individuals, one thousand residents and students from Charlottesville, Virginia, conducted by John Palmer and M. Dennis (1975), drew a positive response from 25 percent of the students and 14 percent of the residents.

Laboratory experiments have tended to yield disappointing results, even with individuals who claim to be able to project out-of-body at will. Tests for ESP during OBEs have had sporadic results. Typically, individuals asked to travel to distant locations and report back what they observed have been either partially or completely wrong. Subjects, on the other hand, feel they have observed something quite clearly.

Tests conducted with animals have been more promising. For example, experiments conducted in the late 1970s with psychic Keith Harary and kittens showed a measurable change in one kitten's behavior during Harary's out-of-body efforts to calm two of them. However, it is possible the results could have been obtained by psychokinesis, telepathy or clairvoyance. See **Animal psi.**

Other tests done during sleep have showed that the OBE does not correspond to the dream state, which occurs during the REM (rapid eye movement) stage of sleep.

Theories to explain OBEs fall into two camps: (1) that something does leave the body, and (2) that nothing leaves the body. None of the theories in either camp adequately explains OBEs.

Those who believe that something leaves the body ascribe to one of three general explanations: (1) a physical double travels in the physical world; (2) a nonphysical double travels in the physical world; and (3) a nonphysical double travels in a mental astral world. The first theory is problematic because it requires the existence of unknown matter and energy and an unknown (and inaccurate) means of seeing. The second theory presents a great unknown, "nonphysical double," whatever that is; and it assumes that if consciousness is projected from the body, then it must normally be "in the body," which also is unknown. In the third theory, if such a mental astral realm exists, it is not known whether it is created by private thought or is part of a collective unconscious shared by all. Thus do all OBE trips go to the same astral world?

Those who think nothing leaves the body in an OBE look to two main theories: (1) parapsychological, in which the OBE is imagination plus psi; and (2) psychological, in which the OBE is a hallucinatory experience, the manifestation of the Self to the Self, the ego's denial of the inevitable death of the physical body. Both theories assume that nothing survives physical death, a notion many people find difficult to accept.

Psychiatrist Carl G. Jung considered the nature of OBEs in his work with patients, some of whom reported seeing doubles. Jung hypothesized that in some cases the doubles were a projection of archetypes, representing hypothetical contents of the collective unconscious and revealing hidden psychological meanings.

Monroe, Hemi-Sync, and the OBE

Despite the lack of scientific evidence, the work and OBE claims of Robert A. Monroe have attracted a wide audience, including numerous scientists. Monroe, who says he has had thousands of OBEs, does not attempt to prove anything concerning OBEs; the experiences, he says, must simply be accepted for what they are.

A former radio and television executive of Westchester County, New York, Monroe began having spontaneous OBEs during his sleep in 1958. At first he thought he was mentally ill. Then he decided to experiment and investigate. In 1961 he and his family moved to Richmond, Virginia. There, in 1962, he established a research and development operation to pursue his experiments. Monroe published his account of his OBE adventures in *Journeys Out of the Body* in 1971. He described an astonishing range of experiences, both pleasant and unpleasant, in which he encountered other intelligences, some of whom provided assistance; demonic or subhuman entities and thought-forms who attacked him; an energy presence of overwhelming magnitude (he does not say whether or not it was "God"); the astral forms of other humans; sexual experiences on the astral level, which produced intense shocks by a seeming interflow of electrons (comparable to Yram's experience). He occasionally had difficulty reentering his body, and on one occasion entered a corpse by mistake.

Monroe identifies various levels of reality encountered in the OBE state. Locale I is the here-and-now earth plane. Locale II is the astral plane, the place where everyone goes in sleep, and where numberless beings and entities and concepts of heaven and hell exist; it is infinite. Locale III transcends time and space and appears to be a parallel universe. According to Monroe there are yet unidentified, higher realms beyond our ability to comprehend.

Following *Journeys* Monroe pursued research in inducing OBEs through sound by producing brain waves associated with the OBE state. The research was conducted at his own laboratory, renamed the Monroe Institute for Applied Sciences in 1971. In 1975 he obtained a patent for Hemi-Sync, sound that synchronizes the left and right hemispheres of the brain and induces physical sleep while allowing the mind to remain alert and active. With Hemi-Sync he devised a program called the "Gateway Voyage," which takes participants to successively expanded levels of consciousness. Not all participants report having OBEs. Those who do describe Locale I and II experiences, including meeting the spirits of the dead and

nonphysical entities, and experiencing mystical bliss in the presence of what some believe is God. No one other than Monroe, apparently, has reached Locale III.

Sources: Jean-Noel Bassior. "Astral Travel." *New Age Journal* (November/December 1988): 44–49+; David Black. *Ekstasy: Out-of-the-Body Experiences.* Indianapolis: Bobbs-Merrill, 1975; Susan J. Blackmore. *Beyond the Body: An Investigation of Out-of-the-Body Experiences.* London: William Heinemann Ltd., 1982; Susan Blackmore. *Parapsychology and Out-of-the-Body Experiences.* Monograph. London: Transpersonal Books, 1978; Robert Crookall. *Out-of-the-Body Experiences: A Fourth Analysis.* New York: University Books, 1970; Robert Crookall. *The Jung-Jaffe View of Out-of-the-Body Experiences.* Booklet. London: World Fellowship Press, 1970; Oliver Fox. *Astral Projection: A Record of Out-of-the-Body Experiences.* 1920. Secaucus, NJ: The Citadel Press, 1962; Celia Green. *Out-of-the-Body Experiences.* London: Hamish Hamilton, 1968; Janet Lee Mitchell. *Out-of-Body Experiences: A Handbook.* Jefferson, NC: McFarland, 1981; Robert A. Monroe. *Journeys Out of the Body.* Garden City, NY: Doubleday, 1971; Robert A. Monroe. *Far Journeys.* Garden City, NY: Dolphin/Doubleday, 1985.

P

Palmistry

A method of divination by the shape of the hands and the lines and mounds on the palms and fingers. Palmistry is one of the oldest forms of divination, and until modern times was more commonly known as cheiromancy or chiromancy.

The exact age and origin of palmistry are not known. Prehistorical hand prints found on cave walls in France, Spain, and Africa may have had a magical significance connected with the development of palmistry. As a method of divination, it is believed to have started as early as 3000 B.C. in either China or India and then spread westward. One theory places its beginning at about 1100 B.C., when the first written works appeared on physiognomy, the art of judging a person based on facial features.

Palmistry was popular during the Middle Ages. Adherents believed that the lines upon a hand were stamped by occult forces and would reveal character and destiny. They looked for support to such biblical scriptures as Isaiah 49:16, "Behold, I have graven thee on the palms of thy hands; thy walls are continually before me"; Job 27:7, "He sealeth up the hand of every man; that all men may know his work"; and Proverbs 3:16, "Length of days in her right hand, and in her left hand riches and honor."

Most Western medieval hand-readers were village wise women, witches, and Gypsies. Among the Kabbalists rabbis were skilled at it and read palms after Sabbath to foretell the future.

In the fifteenth century, the church forbade palmistry and other forms of divination and ordered all written works on the subjects confiscated, merely driving the practice underground. Intellectual interest waned of its own accord with the advent of the age of science and reason in the seventeenth century. Palmistry became a parlor art, popularized in the nineteenth and twentieth centuries by such figures as "Cheiro," the pseudonym of "Count" Louis Harmon, an Irish fortuneteller.

In India, China, and other parts of the East, palmistry remains part of some esoteric teachings and continues to be used for divination.

A palmist first looks at the shape of the hand, which indicates physical or artistic activities. The left hand is said to reveal destiny at birth; the right is a map of how successfully the destiny has been carried out. Roles of the hands are reversed for left-handed people. The palmist then observes the lines, digits, and fleshy mounds, which have correspondences to the signs of the zodiac, sun, moon, and planets, and indicate such factors as longevity, health, emotions, intellect, love, luck, money, psychic ability, and so on.

In one form of Chinese palmistry, the hand is analyzed based on the five elements of earth, air, fire, water, and ether, which represent the physical, emotional, creative, intellectual, and spiritual aspects of a person. In acupuncture and moxa therapy, the lines of the palm are said to reveal changes in internal organs.

As a means of prediction, palmistry, like other forms of divination, reflects the conditions of the moment. Edgar Cayce once said that a palmistry prediction was about 20 percent absolute and 80 percent chance, depending on free will. Palmists say choices can physically change the hands, within certain limits. In China it is believed that the palm patterns can be improved through Zen and yoga disciplines, especially in young children. See **Divination**.

Sources: Michael Asano. *Hands: The Complete Book of Palmistry.* New York: Japan Publications, 1985; Raymond Buckland. *Buckland's Complete Book of Witchcraft.* St. Paul, MN: Llewellyn Publications, 1986; Emile Grillot de Givry. *Witchcraft, Magic and Alchemy.* New York: Houghton Mifflin, 1931; Shifu Terence Dukes. *Chinese Hand Analysis.* New York: Samuel Weiser, 1987; Charles Emmons. *Chinese Ghosts and ESP.* Metuchen, NJ: Scarecrow Press, 1982; *Individual Reference File of Extracts from the Edgar Cayce Readings.* Virginia Beach, VA: Edgar Cayce Foundation, 1976; Nancy MacKenzie. *Palmistry for Women.* New York: Warner Books, 1973; Gershom Scholem. *Kabbalah.* New York: New American Library, 1974; Keith Thomas. *Religion and the Decline of Magic.* New York: Scribner, 1971; Doreen Valiente. *An ABC of Witchcraft Past and Present.* Custer, WA: Phoenix Publishing, 1973.

Paracelsus (1493–1541)

One of the greatest alchemists and Hermetic philosophers, whose remarkable but unorthodox healing methods endeared him to the public and estranged him from the medical establishment. Paracelsus believed in natural magic, a holistic approach to medicine, and the existence of the aura, which influenced health. His contemporaries called him "the Second Hermes" and "the Trismegistus of Switzerland." Later writers often erroneously labeled him a magician.

He was born on or near November 10, 1493, in Einsiedeln, Switzerland; another birth date given is December 17, 1493. The only son of a poor German physician, he was christened Philippus Aureolus Theophrastus Bombast von Hohenheim. He was known as Theophrastus until he graduated from college, when he renamed himself Paracelsus, or "above Celsus," which reflected his egotistical belief that he was greater than the Roman physician Celsus.

In school Paracelsus excelled in chemistry and medicine, earning a bachelor's degree in the latter from the University of Vienna in 1510. He also earned a doctorate, perhaps from the University of Ferrara.

At age twenty he began a series of long travels that lasted over a twelve-year period. It is thought that he learned the Hermetic secrets from Arabian adepts in Constantinople, and learned about elementals and other spirits from the Brahmins of India. After great success as an army physician, he set himself to reforming medicine. His disdain for physicians was exceeded only by his hatred of women. There is no record of any romantic involvements in his entire life.

As a doctor Paracelsus gained fame for his gift of healing. He believed in a universal, natural magic bestowed upon all things by God, and which manifested in physicians as healing ability. All things in nature served a good purpose, he said, even the midnight dew, which he collected on plates of glass. His natural remedies often worked when the traditional wisdom of the day did not. While other doctors treated wounds by pouring boiling oil on them to cauterize them, or amputating limbs after they became gangrenous, Paracelsus maintained wounds would heal naturally if kept clean and drained. He is credited with successfully treating syphilis, gout, leprosy, and ulcers with mercury.

He practiced an early form of homeopathy by treating plague victims with minute amounts of their own excrement. He practiced holism, believing that mind and body affected the other. Imagination, he said, was the route to self-discovery.

He believed the Hermetic principle that human beings had a vital body (an etheric double created and energized by the vital life force of the universe), and that when the vital body was depleted, physical ailment was the result. Paracelsus said the vital body could be reenergized by bringing it into contact with another vital body that had an overabundance of the vital life force. He is credited with having been the original discoverer of mesmerism, a theory of magnetic healing put forward in the late eighteenth century by Franz Anton Mesmer. See **Mesmer, Franz Anton; Universal life force.**

Like most alchemists and physicians of his time, Paracelsus believed in astrology, the idea that humankind was governed by the movements of heavenly bodies. He used magical astrological talismans that were metal disks inscribed with planetary symbols.

In alchemy Paracelsus led the way in introducing chemical compounds into medicine, and in describing zinc. He believed in the *prima materia,* the essence that is the world soul, and key to the philosopher's stone. See **Alchemy.**

His egotism antagonized his peers. His searing putdowns of colleagues were so offensive that he seldom lasted long in a post, and roamed from city to city, plagued by increasing drinking problems. In his early thirties, Paracelsus was invited to the chair of medicine and philosophy at the University of Basel. At a lecture he burned the books of Galen and Avicenna and proclaimed that his cap had more learning in it than all the heads in the university, and his beard had more experience than all the academies. After less than a year, Paracelsus was forced to flee town.

In his travels around Europe, he borrowed money in taverns to pay for his drink. According to legend he always repaid the loans with handsome interest from some mysterious fund. He wore clothes until they were rags. He worked cures and revised old manuscripts, making a brief comeback with the publication of *Wundartzney* in 1536.

The Arch-Bishop Duke Ernsty of Bavaria invited Paracelsus to Salzburg in 1541. He died there within six months, on September 24. It is said that he was found on a bench at the White Horse tavern in Salzburg. It is believed he was poisoned or else killed in a scuffle by assassins who were hired by his enemies. After he was buried, his bones were dug up several times, moved, and reburied. His memory as a great healer remained alive with the public. As late as 1830, when an epidemic of cholera swept close to Salzburg, people made a pilgrimage to his grave and prayed. The cholera spared the residents of Salzburg, but ravaged other parts of Austria and Germany.

Paracelsus was the first man to write scientific books for the public. His writings—which he dictated to his disciples—comprise most of what is known about the ancient Hermetic system of medicine. During Paracelsus's time the Hermetic wisdom was rediscovered and put to use. It declined again, only to be rediscovered once more in the latter half of the twentieth century. See **Hermetica.**

Sources: Francis Barrett. *The Magus.* 1801. Reprint. Secaucus, NJ: The Citadel Press, 1967; Richard Cavendish. *The Black Arts.* New York: Perigee Books, 1967; Manly P. Hall. *The Secret Teachings of All Ages.* 1928. Reprint. Los Angeles: The Philosophical Research Society, 1977; Kurt Seligmann. *The History of Magic and the Occult*. New York: Pantheon Books, 1948; Colin Wilson. *The Occult*. New York: Vintage Books, 1973.

Paranormal photography

See Spirit photography.

Parapsychology

The scientific study of psi and related subjects. *Para* means "beyond" in Greek, and parapsychology focuses attention on the borders of psychology, essentially the mind-body connection and on the relationship between consciousness and the objects of its awareness.

As a science parapsychology dates back to the late nineteenth century with the formation of the Society for Psychical Research (SPR) in London. In its early days, parapsychology was called "psychical research," a term that is most commonly used in Britain today. Throughout its history parapsychology has been met with a great deal of skepticism and even hostility by the general scientific community.

Before the beginnings of parapsychology, paranormal phenomena in Western culture were either associated with the divine or the demonic or were largely ignored. The ancient Greeks and Romans, for example, believed in clairvoyance and precognitive dreams—usually regarded as messages from the gods—and consulted divine oracles.

The Bible contains many references to paranormal phenomena, including apparitions, clairvoyance, levitation, precognitive dreams and prophetic visions, and communication with spirits of the dead. In the later Middle Ages, the Catholic church called such phenomena "demonic" unless manifested through a saint. But earlier on St. Augustine at-

tempted to form an objective concept of telepathy, as did St. Isidore of Seville; their attitude recurred in Prospero Lambertini, later Pope Benedict XIV, who in the eighteenth century investigated alleged miraculous and paranormal phenomena. Lambertini's conclusions make him a prototypical psychical researcher. He said that paranormal experiences occur to all kinds of people, even animals, and are neither divine nor demonic, but (here echoing St. Thomas Aquinas) are evidence of the innate capabilities of those having the experiences.

The Swedish mystic Emanuel Swedenborg experienced his incredible clairvoyant visions in the eighteenth century, but they were to have a far-reaching effect on later researchers. See **Swedenborg, Emanuel.** In the late eighteenth century, Franz Anton Mesmer developed his "magnetic" healing of patients. Paranormal phenomena were observed in some individuals and became the object of curiosity and study. See **Mesmer, Franz Anton.** The rise of Spiritualism in the nineteenth century kindled a great interest in communication with the dead and in physical mediumship. See **Mediumship; Spiritualism.**

In 1870 and 1871, the London Dialectical Society was among the first to undertake scientific investigations of phenomena associated with Spiritualism; results were poor. In 1872 William Crookes, eminent physicist and member of the Royal Society, conducted experiments with the famous physical medium, Daniel Dunglas Home, and a Mrs. Clayer, a nonprofessional medium. Crookes concluded he had witnessed paranormal phenomena, which brought him much criticism from his contemporaries.

William F. Barrett, another physicist, was impressed, however, and in 1876 undertook experiments with hypnotized subjects and mediumistic subjects. Barrett believed an organization needed to be established to investigate the paranormal, a goal he finally realized in 1882 with the founding of the SPR.

The early years of the SPR were devoted to investigations of spontaneous psychic phenomena, mediumship, and the question of survival after death. The primary goal was to establish evidence for the existence of psychic phenomena. Researchers such as Frederic W. H. Myers, Henry Sidgwick, Frank Podmore, Edmund Gurney, and Richard Hodgson compiled an impressive amount of positive evidence and established the foundations of scientific inquiry. The SPR's work led to the founding of the American Society for Psychical Research (ASPR) in 1885. See **American Society for Psychical Research (ASPR); Society for Psychical Research (SPR)**.

Trends in Research

Before 1930 most psychical research was qualitative and took place outside the laboratory. Mediums were investigated under conditions that were controlled as much as possible. Investigation of spontaneous phenomena, such as apparitions, depended upon reports from individuals, followed by interviews after the fact, and on written documentation.

The 1930s ushered in an era of controlled laboratory experiments that were evaluated statistically. The major pioneer of this era was J. B. Rhine. He and his wife, Louisa E. Rhine, had undertaken psychic investigations and were among those who found evidence of fraud by the celebrated Boston medium, Mina Stinson Crandon, known as "Margery" in seances. John Thomas brought Rhine to Duke University in North Carolina in 1927 for the summer. Rhine stayed on to help William McDougall, the head of the psychology department, in rat experiments for his Lamarckian research. In 1930, at the suggestion of colleagues, Rhine began experimental ESP research

in an effort to replicate work that had recently been published by the SPR. McDougall wanted to establish psychical research as a legitimate university discipline. In devising the research program, McDougall and the Rhines sought to establish standard test procedures and to demonstrate that psychic ability is a natural faculty. Test subjects were not celebrity mediums, but average people, mostly student volunteers. Experiments involved forced-choice tests, such as guessing cards in telepathy and clairvoyance tests, and results were evaluated statistically against chance. See **ESP cards.**

Rhine's impressive reports of consistent and sustained results, released in 1934, were highly controversial, but sparked more interest and led to refinements in testing procedures. Experiments with dice for psychokinesis (PK), the influence of mind over matter, began in 1934. See **Psychokinesis (PK)**. Rhine's findings on PK, first published in 1943, were again controversial.

Rhine trained other researchers, many of whom are still active in parapsychology today; the Rhine era of research in forced-choice tests with cards and dice lasted until about 1965. Rhine is credited with naming the discipline—he adopted "parapsychology" from the German term, *parapsychologie*, which was introduced in the late nineteenth century by philosopher-psychologist Max Dessoir. Rhine also coined the term "extrasensory perception," commonly referred to as ESP. See **ESP (extrasensory perception)**. Much of the terminology used in the field today developed out of Rhine's research at Duke. The early promise of his work—that psi could be shown to be universal and controllable—was not fulfilled, however, and remains elusive.

Between 1930 and 1960, little research was done on spontaneous phenomena, though notable work was done beginning in 1948 by Louisa E. Rhine. Her findings confirmed the major findings of the SPR. Work was also done by G. N. M. Tyrrell in England, who produced a now-classic study on apparitions. See **Apparition.**

By the 1960s the concept of consciousness was rediscovered in psychology, and parapsychological interest began turning to the psychological processes involved in psi, as ESP and PK collectively are known. See **Psi.** This focused increasing attention on "process-oriented" research on psi, that is, on how psi performance is affected by variables such as altered states of consciousness, time, distance, mood, personality, and attitude toward psi. Tests were devised for free-response ESP (instead of forced-choice). Here subjects described whatever images or information came to mind.

One of the best examples of free-response experiments was the dream ESP work conducted at Maimonides Hospital in Brooklyn, New York, under the direction of Montague Ullman and Stanley Krippner, in the 1960s and 1970s. After that program ended, free-response work continued in a sensory-deprivation condition called the "ganzfeld," adapted from mainstream psychology by Maimonides team member Charles Honorton, a Maimonides team member. See **Altered states of consciousness; Dreams; Ganzfeld stimulation.** Still other significant free-response research was in remote viewing, the seeing of distant objects clairvoyantly or by out-of-body travel, conducted beginning in the 1970s by Russell Targ and Harold Puthoff of the Stanford Research Institute in California, and by many others. See **Remote viewing.**

Interest in macro-PK revived in the 1960s, marked by experiments with Ted Serios (see **Thoughtography**), Uri Geller, Nina Kulagina, and others. The term "macro-PK" was applied to observable phenomena that do not require statistical evaluation, such as large-scale movement of objects or metal bending. Micro-PK occurring at a quantum level has attracted the attention of some physicists.

Beginning in the 1970s, some parapsychologists advocated paying less attention to proving the existence of psi and more attention to applying it to other sciences and fields. The future of applied psi is uncertain, due to the unpredictable and unreliable nature of psi itself. See **Applied psi; Dowsing; Psychic archaeology; Psychic criminology.**

Parapsychology Elsewhere

Some of the roots of European psychical research go back to interest in mesmerism. In the late nineteenth century, some attention was devoted to Spiritualist phenomena. Psychical research began to intensify around 1900, especially in relation to psychology and abnormal psychology. In 1914 the Institut Metapsychique International was founded in Paris, and in 1928 the Institut für Parapsychologie was founded in Berlin.

Researchers such as Theodore Flournoy, Pierre Janet, Hans Bender, Charles Richet, and others explored automatisms, telepathic hypnosis, and mediumship. See **Automatic writing; Automatisms; Smith, Hélène; Telepathic hypnosis.** Exposés of fraudulent mediums, however, diminished this emphasis in the 1930s.

Following World War II, the first Chair of Parapsychology was established at Utrecht University in the Netherlands, and was accepted by W. H. C. Tenhaeff. In 1953 the university was host to the First International Conference on Parapsychological Studies, sponsored by the Parapsychology Foundation, an organization established in 1951. See **Garrett, Eileen J.**

Statistical research in the fashion of Rhine has been conducted in Europe, but never to the same extent as in the United States or Britain; most research has concerned spontaneous and individual cases.

However, experimental research on the Anglo-American model has increasingly gained a foothold in Europe, which has produced some of the finest recent research, reported in the *European Journal of Psychology*.

Interest in psi in Soviet-bloc nations has developed independently of the West with its own terminology, such as "psychotronics" or "bio-communication" in place of parapsychology. See **Psychotronics.**

In Russia investigation of psi intensified following the visit of medium Daniel Dunglas Home in 1871. By the late 1870s, Russia had a periodical, *Rebus,* devoted exclusively to the subject. Research was conducted in hypnosis and telepathy, and information was exchanged with European and British researchers.

After the Russian Revolution, psychical research continued. Most notable was the work of L. L. Vasiliev, who investigated hypnosis at a distance. Vasiliev attempted to confirm a hypothesis that hypnosis was produced by the radiation of brain waves, but his efforts failed when neither distance nor electromagnetic influence was shown to have any impact on hypnosis.

During the Stalinist regime, psychical research was discredited and repressed. As late as 1956, telepathy, for example, was officially defined as antisocial and impossible.

Little is known about Soviet research since then. In 1970 Lynn Schroeder and Sheila Ostrander published *Psychic Discoveries Behind the Iron Curtain,* which described their visit to the Soviet Union in 1968. According to the authors, Soviet psychical research was advanced compared with that in the West, and the beneficiary of much more funding and government support. The Soviets were said to be focusing on how to harness psychic power, especially for military purposes. Also in the late 1960s, Nina Kulagina, a Leningrad housewife with alleged PK powers, came to attention, but dropped from the scene within a few years.

Czech researchers have pursued paranormal healing in the form of "bioenergy," a term for the universal life force.

Psychical research societies and organizations also have been established in Mexico, Latin America, Japan, and South Africa. In Latin America much attention is devoted to psychical healing. In Mexico the Catholic church includes education on parapsychology in its seminary training programs for priests.

The Progress and Future of Parapsychology

The Rhine era brought parapsychology some increased academic acceptance, but further progress has been slow. Although the number of parapsychology courses taught has increased, few universities have institutionalized parapsychology. The Parapsychological Association, founded in 1957, was not admitted to the American Association for the Advancement of Science until 1969. The Koestler Chair of Parapsychology was established in 1985 at the University of Edinburgh, funded in part from a bequest from writer Arthur Koestler.

Disagreement exists among parapsychologists as to how much the field has progressed since 1882. The empirical evidence for psi remains inadequate, though some researchers feel psi has been proven. Certainly, the lack of progress can be attributed in part to the lack of research funds and serious support by the scientific and academic communities. Fraudulent research has been exposed over the years, especially in the 1970s; despite the low incidence of it, the integrity of the field sometimes has been seriously damaged. Many scientists, however, remain skeptical about parapsychology, and some of them work actively against it. See

Committee for the Scientific Investigation of Claims of the Paranormal (CSICOP).

Some researchers forecast an increasing emphasis on applied science, including parapsychology, in the twenty-first century. They predict that individuals will be trained in visualization, meditation, and control of physiological processes, and in the development and use of psychic abilities. One of the most promising areas for applied psi is seen in behavioral medicine. It is also speculated that advances in physics will show psi to be some sort of special physical phenomenon. The interaction of psi with consciousness remains largely unexplored.

The interest that spawned psychical research in the late nineteenth century was in part a reaction to the materialistic mode of thought that separated science and religion. It is significant that recent research into consciousness and physics points to the need to reintegrate the two. To that end parapsychology may be able to play a major role. See also **Animal psi; Decline/incline effects; Drugs in mystical and psychic experiences; Experimenter effect; Psi hitting and psi missing; Sheep/goat effect.**

Sources: John Beloff. *The Importance of Psychical Research.* Monograph. London: The Society for Psychical Research, 1988; John Beloff. "The Changing Face of Parapsychology." *ASPR Newsletter* 14, no. 1 (January 1988): 1–3; Susan Blackmore. "Do We Need a New Psychical Research?" *Journal of the Society for Psychical Research* 55, no. 810 (January 1988): 49–59; Martin Ebon, ed. *The Signet Handbook of Parapsychology.* New York: New American Library, 1978; Hoyt L. Edge, Robert L. Morris, John Palmer, and Joseph H. Rush. *Foundations of Parapsychology.* Boston: Routledge & Kegan Paul, 1986; Ivor Grattan-Guinness. *Psychical Research: A Guide to Its History, Principles and Practices.* Wellingborough, Northamptonshire, England: The Aquarian Press, 1982; Edgar D. Mitchell. *Psychic Exploration: A Challenge for Science.* Edited by John White. New York: Paragon Books, 1974; A. R. G. Owen. "Parapsychology: Failure or Success?" *ASPR Newsletter* 15, no. 1 (Winter 1989): 1–3; Betty Shapin and Lisette Coly, eds. *Parapsychology's Second Century: Proceedings of an International Conference Held in London, England, August 13–14, 1982.* New York: Parapsychology Foundation, 1983; Benjamin B. Wolman, ed. *Handbook of Parapsychology.* New York: Van Nostrand Reinhold, 1977.

Parapsychology Foundation

See Garrett, Eileen J.

Past-life recall

The remembering of alleged previous lives. Past-life recall can occur spontaneously or can be induced through various methods such as hypnosis, bodywork, or yoga. Whether the memories actually are of historical past lives or are reconstructions of material from the subconscious is a matter of controversy. Scientific investigations of spontaneous past-life memories have yielded impressive evidence in support of reincarnation, but past-life recall remains scientifically inconclusive.

Eastern mysticism provides for past-life recall. As early as A.D. 400, Patanjali, credited with compiling the *Yoga Sutras,* said that all details of past lives and all impressions of karma exist in the *chitta,* or subconscious mind, and can be awakened through yoga meditation.

Past-life memories also seem to bubble to the surface of consciousness spontaneously, particularly in young children in non-Western cultures. James G. Matlock, American parapsychologist and anthropologist, hypothesizes that children remember past lives more readily than adults because they are physically and psychologically less mature. With maturity past-life memories have more difficulty penetrating the waking state.

One of the earliest documented cases of spontaneous past-life recall is that of Katsugoro, a Japanese son of a farmer born in 1815. At age nine Katsugoro told his sister about his previous life as the son of a farmer in another village. He had died of smallpox at age six in 1810. He said that until he was four, he had remembered everything about his past life, including his death, burial, between-lives state, and rebirth. He described his previous-life family and village, though he had never been to the village. An investigation corroborated his statements.

Modern scientific investigations of past-life recall have focused on the spontaneous memories of children. One of the leading investigators is Ian Stevenson, professor of psychiatry at the University of Virginia, who began investigating claims in the 1960s and collected more than two thousand cases by the late 1980s. Most of them occur in the East, where cultural support for past-life recall exists. Western cases are few and weak because parents tend to ignore or suppress what they think are fantasies. Stevenson considers a case "solved" when a child's statements are accurate in reference to an identifiable deceased person.

Matlock identifies four types of spontaneous past-life memory: (1) verbal—the recall of names, dates, and other facts; (2) imaged—that which enables children to recognize people and places; (3) behavioral—personality traits, interests, skills, and so on; and (4) physical—similarities in appearance to the deceased, including birthmarks. These memories exist in varying strengths, depending upon any number of variables, such as the circumstances of the deceased's life and manner of death, and particular cultural beliefs about how one may be reborn.

Certain universal features do exist. In almost all documented child cases, the subject was between the ages of two and five when he or she first began talking about a past life; the mean age is about two-and-a-half years. Cases beginning at or beyond age eight are rare. A high number involve violent death or sudden natural death. "Unfinished business" figures in many cases, and may account for the recall. Birthmarks may exist where a death wound was made. Or an inexplicable phobia might be related to the manner of death, such as fear of water due to drowning.

Some children make only a few statements about a past life, while others talk incessantly about it and demand to be taken to their previous home. Some may talk about past lives at certain times of the day, such as just after waking from sleep, or when they are stimulated by a person or object. Some children say they remember their past life because they did not eat a "fruit of forgetfulness" given to them by spirit guides before reincarnating.

Other theories hold that so-called past-life memories are instead the products of telepathy, inherited memory, spirit possession, cryptomnesia (forgotten memories), and paramnesia (illusions of memory on the part of the children or adults involved). Stevenson does not reject those theories, but refutes them for the majority of cases.

Many individuals feel they experience spontaneous past-life recall through déjà vu, dreams, intuitive flashes, visions, and resonances (strong likes and dislikes). Information obtained from these experiences usually is sketchy and seldom yields anything that can be verified historically.

Physical traumas—especially head injuries that result in unconsciousness, concussion, or coma, and illnesses involving high fevers and delirium—have been known to stimulate apparent past-life memories. One of the most dramatic cases was that of Dorothy Eady of England. In 1907, at age three, Eady fell down a flight of stairs. She was pronounced dead but revived with no injuries. Soon after she began having strange dreams of a temple and garden, and began complaining to her parents that she was not "home," but did not know where "home" was. As she grew older, she came to believe that she had lived in ancient Egypt as a young and illicit lover of Sety the First (1306 B.C.–1290 B.C.), a pharaoh in the Nineteenth Dynasty. She had been a priestess sworn to virginity, but had become pregnant with Sety's child and had committed suicide.

Eady began experiencing nocturnal out-of-body trips to visit Sety in the afterworld, and in turn was visited by his spirit at night. She moved to Egypt and lived in the primitive village of Arabet Abydos where the ruins of Sety's temple are located. She believed that if she renewed her ancient priestess vows of chastity and fealty, she and Sety would be reunited forever upon her death. Eady died in 1981.

Hypnosis is by far the most common means of induced past-life regression. In hypnotic regression an individual is put into a trance, usually light but sometimes deep, and directed to go back in time and describe what he or she experiences. Some individuals have vivid and moving experiences, others do not. Here again, most memories are not evidential.

The appearance of past-life memories under hypnosis was first observed during the practice of mesmerism in the late eighteenth century. See **Hypnosis**. One of the first systematic researchers of induced past-life recall was Colonel Albert de Rochas, a French psychical investigator who hypnotized nineteen men and women subjects beginning in 1904. He found they regressed easily to past lives, but his efforts to verify their information were largely unsuccessful, due to lack of records and, in some cases, inconsistencies between records and regression testimony.

Hypnotic recall of past lives is not scientifically reliable, as was demonstrated as early as 1906 in the Blanche Poynings case in England. A young woman, identified as Miss C., claimed under hypnosis to have lived as Blanche Poynings at the end of the fourteenth century during the reign of King Richard II. Poynings said she was a close friend of Maud, the Countess of Salisbury, and gave great detail about the Countess's life. An investigation disclosed that the true source of Miss C.'s "past life" was a novel, *Countess Maud or the Changes of the World, A Tale of the Fourteenth Century* (1892), which Miss C. had read but had forgotten.

Some hypnotic past-life regressions have defied explanation, such as the famous Bridey Murphy case, which touched off a storm of controversy. In 1952 Morey Bernstein, a businessman and amateur hypnotist in Pueblo, Colorado, experimented with a twenty-nine-year-old housewife to see if he could regress her past birth. She regressed to the life of Bridget (Bridey) Murphy, who lived in County Cork, Ireland, between 1798 and 1864. Critics attempted to debunk the case as a hoax. Ian Stevenson examined the evidence and considered it to be in support of reincarnation.

Beginning in the late 1960s, Helen Wambach, American psychologist, conducted a ten-year survey of past-life recalls under hypnosis among 1,088 subjects. She regressed them to periods between 2000 B.C. and the 1900s (not all subjects had lives in a specific period) and collected data concerning race, sex, class, clothing and utensils, and the death experience. She concluded that fantasy and genetic memory could not account for the patterns that emerged in the results.

Wambach found that 49.4 percent of past lives were as females and 50.6 percent as males, which matches true biological balance. In all time periods, the great majority of lives were lower class and less than 10 percent were upper class, which also reflected general population conditions. Based upon the number of lives reported in each time period, Wambach extrapolated world population figures, and found they were consistent with historical population growth.

With the exception of eleven subjects, all descriptions of clothing, footwear, and utensils were consistent with historical records. Racial distribution also conformed with history. Of those who reported going through deaths, 49 percent said they experienced acceptance, calm, and peace; 30 percent reported joy and release; 20 percent said they watched the death while floating above the body; and 10 percent said they were upset or saddened by the experience.

Past-life memories can also be induced through meditation and other techniques for achieving altered states. See Cayce, Edgar; Cooke, Grace; Grant, Joan. Rhythmic activity, such as dancing, drumming, chanting, or long-distance running, produces altered or ecstatic states in which apparent past-life memories manifest. Bodywork, such as acupuncture or deep massage, also has been said to stimulate such memories. Past-life recall induced by hallucinatory drugs must be discounted. Some psychics give past-life readings, describing to clients details of the clients' past lives based on impressions received by the psychic. See Past-life therapy (PLT); Reincarnation; Soul mate.

Sources: Morey Bernstein. *The Search for Bridey Murphy*. 1965. Rev. ed. New York: Avon, 1975; Jonathan Cott. *The Search for Om Sety*. Garden City, NY: Doubleday, 1987; Alan Gauld. *Mediumship and Survival*. London: William Heinemann Ltd., 1982; Marshall F. Gilula, M.D. "Past-Life Recall while Running." *Journal of Regression Therapy* 2, no. 2 (1987): 128–30; G. M. Glaskin. *Windows of the Mind*. New York: Delacourt Press, 1974; Bruce Goldberg. *Past Lives, Future Lives*. New York: Ballantine Books, 1982; Rosemary Ellen Guiley. *Tales of Reincarnation*. New York:

Pocket Books, 1989; Lafcadio Hearn. *Gleanings in Buddha Fields*. Boston: Houghton Mifflin, 1897; Frederick Lenz. *Lifetimes: True Accounts of Reincarnation*. New York: Fawcett Crest, 1977; James G. Matlock. "The Decline of Past Life Memory with Subject's Age in Spontaneous Reincarnation Cases." In M. L. Albertson, D. S. Ward, and K. Freeman, eds. *Paranormal Research*. Ft. Collins, CO: Rocky Mountain Research Institute, in press; Shirley MacLaine. *Dancing in the Light*. New York: Bantam Books, 1985; James G. Matlock. "Reincarnation." Lecture to Summer Study Program (FRNM), revised and expanded, July 23, 1987; Ian Stevenson. *Children Who Remember Previous Lives*. Charlottesville, VA: University Press of Virginia, 1987; Ian Stevenson. *Twenty Cases Suggestive of Reincarnation*. 2d ed. Charlottesville, VA: University Press of Virginia, 1974; Ian Stevenson. *India: Cases of the Reincarnation Type*. Vol. 1. Charlottesville, VA: University Press of Virginia, 1975; Ian Stevenson. "Some Questions Related to Cases of the Reincarnation Type." *Journal of the American Society for Psychical Research* 168, no. 4 (October 1974): 395–413; Michael Talbot. *Your Past Lives: A Reincarnation Handbook*. New York: Harmony Books, 1987; Helen Wambach. *Reliving Past Lives*. New York: Harper & Row Perennial Library, 1978; Ian Wilson. *All in the Mind: Reincarnation, hypnotic regression, stigmata, multiple personality, and other little understood powers of the mind*. Garden City, NY: Doubleday, 1982.

Past-life therapy (PLT)

A type of psychotherapy in which the causes of present physical and psychological problems are traced to alleged past-life traumas and death experiences. Past-life therapy (PLT) has been claimed to be effective in treating phobias, fears, aversions, cravings, guilt, sexual dysfunctions, anger, insomnia, depression, insecurity, low energy, chronic headaches and other pains, physical disorders, and weaknesses of parts of the body. PLT sometimes brings relief when other methods of psychotherapy fail; phobias seem to be particularly responsive, sometimes after a single session. "Trait guilt" (such as fears of doom and burning in hell), which is so deep-seated that it seldom responds to traditional psychoanalysis, does reportedly respond to PLT. The relief achieved by PLT is said to be achieved by the release of energy that is trapped in the past life.

PLT presupposes belief in reincarnation, or at least the acceptance of the possibility of it. However, most past-life therapists say positive results can be achieved regardless of belief in reincarnation on the part of the patient; most do not attempt to prove reincarnation or convince their patients of the validity of it. Therapists acknowledge that reincarnation may not be the only explanation; psychoanalysis has long recognized that fantasizing imaginary events can have the same therapeutic benefits as the retrieval of real memories. Nonetheless, many therapists feel the experiences of their patients are not likely to be fantasy, or at least not entirely fantasy, because most past lives reported are dreary and humdrum, not glamorous and exciting. From a Jungian perspective, past lives can be explained as archetypal material, or universal character formations deep within the psyche, which become projected into the conscious as "past life." See **Archetypes.**

PLT began to take form as a therapy in the 1960s, following the sanctioning of hypnosis as a clinical treatment by the British Medical Association in 1955 and by the American Medical Association in 1958. PLT goes beyond traditional psychotherapy. Psychiatrists Carl G. Jung and Sigmund Freud both said that the individual's worst fears, pain, and trauma are buried deep within the unconscious mind. Freud believed the roots of those problems could be uncovered in early childhood experiences. Psychoanalyst

Otto Rank advocated going back further, to the time spent in the womb. With the increase in hypnotherapy, some therapists discovered that many patients automatically regressed to what seemed to be previous lives when asked to identify the source of a problem, thus prompting experimentation with regression.

The use of PLT as an alternative therapy led to the formation of the Association for Past Life Research and Therapy (APRT) in Riverside, California, in 1980. It is estimated that roughly 80 percent of patients who seek PLT do so in order to eliminate a phobia, habit, or negative tendency. The great majority of patients are adults; therapists are divided on whether or not past-life therapy is appropriate for children, but agree it is not appropriate for schizophrenics or those who have difficulty separating reality from fantasy. Therapists stress that PLT does not necessarily replace conventional treatment, especially medical.

In 1982 psychologist and past-life therapist Helen Wambach surveyed APRT therapists concerning their work. She obtained data from twenty-six therapists who had been working in the field for an average of 7.2 years and had regressed a total of 18,463 patients. According to the findings, 94 percent of all patients regressed to one or more apparent previous lives. A majority said that they experienced improvement in a physical symptom. Many felt they discovered past-life karmic ties with individuals in their present life, and were able to release suppressed hostility and guilt, resulting in improvement of present relationships.

Twenty-five therapists reported taking their patients through past-life deaths. Seventy-two percent of those who went through the experience observed it while floating above their bodies; 54 percent perceived a white light and moved toward it; 15 percent reported a tunnel. Of those whose physical problems were connected to death experiences, 60 percent reported relief of symptoms after going through the death.

The apparent ability to relive death experiences may hold the most promise for PLT. Most patients discover that though circumstances leading to death are sometimes traumatic, death itself is pleasant. The past-life death experience is used in alternative treatment of the terminally ill to help them overcome their fears of dying. It also seems to help people who are not terminally ill to overcome fear of death, and in some cases helps patients realize how to better fulfill their soul's purpose. In regression a great deal of pain in past-life death is associated with regret over opportunities not taken.

People who undergo PLT say they come into contact with their own inner wisdom, which continues to guide them long after the therapy. They also often change their view of their life, seeing it as part of a spiritual progression in which the soul constantly strives for perfection. They say they become aware of certain universal laws, such as karma, self-responsibility, and the right of others to progress in their own fashion. They learn there is no "good" or "bad," but that everything is relative, an opportunity to learn and advance.

Although remarkable cures and improvements are claimed for PLT, as of the late 1980s there had been no significant long-term or follow-up studies to determine if results last. Nor had there been any systematic studies using control groups. Past-life material that comes out of PLT usually cannot be proved; but most clients do not require proof to realize improvement in a condition. See **Depossession; Hypnosis; Karma; Past-life recall; Reincarnation.**

Sources: Hazel Denning. "Philosophical Assumptions Underlying Past-Life Therapy." *Journal of Regression Therapy* 1, no. 2 (Fall 1986): 67–72; Edith Fiore. *You Have Been Here Before.* New York: Ballantine Books, 1978; Bruce Goldberg. *Past Lives, Future Lives.* New York: Ballantine Books, 1982; Denys Kelsey and Joan Grant. *Many Lifetimes.* Garden City, NY: Doubleday, 1967; Franklin Loehr, D.D. "Healing the Dying: Contributions to Thanatology." *Journal of Regression Therapy* 2, no. 1 (September 1987): 38–42; Morris Netherton and Nancy Shiffrin. *Past Lives Therapy.* New York: Grosset & Dunlap/Ace Books, 1978; Helen Wambach (adapted by Chet Snow). "Past-Life Therapy: The Experiences of Twenty-Six Therapists."*Journal of Regression Therapy* 1, no. 2 (Fall 1986): 73–80; Helen Wambach. *Life Before Life.* New York: Bantam Books, 1979; Helen Wambach. *Reliving Past Lives.* New York: Harper & Row Perennial Library, 1978; Brian L. Weiss. *Many Lives, Many Masters.* New York: Fireside Books, 1988. Roger Woolger. *Other Lives, Other Selves.* Garden City, NY: Doubleday & Co., 1987.

Patanjali

See **Yoga.**

Paul, St.

Christian apostle and missionary, and one of the most, if not the most, influential figures in the establishment of the Christian religion. Paul's conversion to Christianity resulted from a profound mystical experience.

Paul, called Saul in Hebrew, was born a Jew in Tarsus of Cilicia (Anatolia) between A.D. 1 and A.D. 10. Since major events of his life are recorded in his own letters and in The Acts of The Apostles, more is known about his life than of other principal leaders of the infant church.

In his early career, Paul studied the strict observance of Jewish law. He even participated in the persecution of Christians. However, about A.D. 36, Paul had a mystical encounter with the risen Christ, one of the most dramatic visionary experiences recorded in religious journals (Galatians 1:15–16; Acts 9, 22, 26). En route to Damascus to arrest Christians, he encountered a dazzling light and heard a voice say, "Why do you persecute me?" He saw no figure of Christ, but interpreted the experience as such. See **Encounter phenomenon; Mystical experiences.**

Paul was blinded by the light and was led to Damascus. There his vision was restored by Ananais, and he was baptized. Thereafter Paul considered himself to be one of the apostles, as were those who traveled with Christ before his resurrection.

As the first leader of the early Christian movement beyond the Jewish community, Paul was soon known as the "apostle to the Gentiles." The thirteen letters (epistles) in the New Testament attributed to him are from those written during ten years of missionary journeys to Anatolia (now the Asian part of Turkey), Cyprus, and Greece. During that time he changed his name from Saul to Paul. He advised the new Christian churches concerning proper behavior as Christians, and preached that Jesus was the savior of all nations.

Paul was a pioneer in evolving the revolutionary concepts of Christianity. He accommodated Jewish ideas to Gentile traditions and circumstances. He was also at the heart of controversies within the church, especially unresolved conflicts with Peter over the extent to which Gentile Christians had to observe Jewish law. He argued in favor of protecting Christianity from intrusion by Jewish and Hellenistic ideas and practices.

Acts describes the pattern of his successful but often radical apostolic methods, which often resulted in the conversion of many people but also conflicted with secular authorities. He was beaten and arrested on more than one occasion. In Jerusalem he was arrested and imprisoned for two years, but continued to preach. He appealed his case to Caesar and was sent to Rome to be tried as a Roman citizen. There he was jailed for two more years, but probably was acquitted and was set free. Eventually, Paul was arrested again and was martyred c. 67, when Nero had him executed. His liturgical feast day, shared with Peter, is June 29.

Paul's Teachings

All of Paul's major concepts build on his analogy of the church as the "Body of Christ." It is used throughout his teaching of the relationship between Christ and/as the church; it is also the foundation for his theology of justification, redemption, sacraments, and his understanding of the general dynamic of the entire Christian life. Therefore Paul's frequent use of the phrases "in Christ" and "with Christ" is especially significant. However, modern controversies surround Paul's seemingly contradictory condemnation of the flesh while he used images of the body to praise the soul, most notably throughout his concept of the Mystical Body of Christ.

Paul's concept of justification by faith has influenced the key notions of contrasting philosophies of man, such as existentialist philosopher Jean Paul Sarte's unconditioned human freedom; and psychologies such as Carl G. Jung's individuation, and Abraham H. Maslow's self-actualization, since they each also focus on the necessity of developing resources, creative exercise of freedom, and overcoming self-deception in order to achieve meaningful existence. See **Psychology.**

There has been a significant revival of interest in Paul's theology since the 1960s with the advent of worldwide charismatic movements. Paul first introduced the word "charisma" (from the Greek meaning "grace") into theological terminology and explained the charisma as characteristic of the faithful in general, who use the special gifts of the Holy Spirit to build up the community in a special way and to get charismatic movements started. However, Paul emphasized ethics over miracles, finding the reconciliation of the different social groups within the churches as more "miraculous" than the miracles recorded in the gospels. See Charismatic renewal; Christology; Jesus; Mysticism, Christian.

Sources: "An Introduction to the Letters of Saint Paul." In *The Jerusalem Bible.* New York: Doubleday, 1966; Pat Alexander, ed. *The Lion Encyclopedia of the Bible.* Rev. ed. Tring, England: Lion Publishing, 1986; James L. Breed. "The Church as the 'Body of Christ': A Pauline Analogy." *Theology Review* 6, no. 2 (1985): 9–32; W. D. Davies. *Paul and Rabbinic Judaism: Some Elements in Pauline Theology.* Minneapolis: Augsburg Fortress, 1980; *Experiences in Faith, Book III.* New York: Herder & Herder, 1969; John McManners, ed. *The Oxford Illustrated History of Christianity.* Oxford, England: Oxford University Press, 1990; *Nourished with Peace: Studies in Hellenistic Judaism.* Edited by Frederick Greenspahn, Earle Hilgert, and Burton Mack. Homage Series no. 9. Atlanta: Scholars Press, 1984.

Peak experiences

Psychologist Abraham H. Maslow's term for nonreligious quasi-mystical and mystical experiences. Peak experiences are a sudden flash of intense happiness and feelings of well-being, and perhaps awareness of "ultimate truth" and the unity of all things. They are accompanied by a heightened sense of control over the body and emotions, and a wider sense of awareness, as though one is standing on a mountaintop. Maslow described peak experiences as having a special flavor of wonder and awe. The individual, he said, feels at one with the world and pleased with it; he or she has seen the ultimate truth or the essence of all things.

Maslow's ground-breaking work on peak experiences and the innate spiritual yearnings of all human beings brought a scientific interest to mysticism that had been absent since psychologist and philosopher William James's work at the turn of the twentieth century. See James, William.

Maslow described peak experiences as self-validating, self-justifying moments with their own intrinsic value; never negative, unpleasant or evil; disoriented in time and space; and accompanied by a loss of fear, anxiety, doubts, and inhibitions.

There are two types of peak experiences: relative and absolute. Relative peak experiences are those in which there remains an awareness of subject and object, and which are extensions of the individual's own experiences. They are not true mystical experiences, but rather inspirations, ecstasies, and raptures. Probably the majority of peak experiences fall into this category. Absolute peak experiences are of a mystical nature, and can be comparable to the experiences of the great mystics of history. They are timeless, spaceless, and characterized by unity, in which subject and object become one.

Maslow said all individuals are capable of having peak experiences. Those who are not have somehow repressed or denied them. Individuals most likely to have peak experiences are self-actualized: mature, healthy, and self-fulfilled.

Peak experiences have therapeutic value in that they foster a sense of being lucky or graced; release creative energies; reaffirm the worthiness of life; and change an individual's view of himself or herself. Maslow cautioned against seeking out peak experiences for their own sake, echoing the lessons of mystics who have pointed out that the sacred exists in the ordinary. Maslow believed that domestic and public violence, alcoholism, and drug abuse stem from spiritual emptiness, and that even one peak experience might be able to prevent, or at least abate, such ills.

Peak experiences also have been compared to myth: They fulfill on a personal level what myths historically have fulfilled for whole peoples. Both embody truths that are independent of factual knowledge, and bring about changes of attitude. Symbols, however, have a more minimal role in peak experiences than in myths.

Shortly before his death in 1970, Maslow defined the term "plateau experience" as a sort of continuing peak experience that is more voluntary, noetic, and cognitive. He described it as a witnessing or cognitive blissfulness. The plateau experience can be achieved through long and hard effort over the course of a lifetime, he said.

Critics of humanistic psychology see peak experiences as having a hedonistic philosophy—a morality of heightened pleasure. Psychologist James Hillman observes that peaks and highs say nothing of the worth of the person having them, for they can occur among psychopaths and criminals. Transcendence by means of a high, he says, is a psychopathological state in disguise. See Ecstasy; Inspiration; Mystical experiences; Mythology; Psychology.

Sources: Thomas Armour. "A Note on the Peak Experience and a Transpersonal Psychology." The Journal of Transpersonal Psychology 1, no. 1 (Spring 1969): 47–50; Daniel Goleman. The Meditative Mind: The Varieties of Meditative Experience. Los Angeles: Jeremy P. Tarcher, 1988; James Hillman. Re-Visioning Psychology. New York: Harper & Row, 1975; Edward Hoffman. "Abraham Maslow and Transpersonal Psychology." The Common Boundary 6, issue 3 (May/June 1988): 3–5; Abraham H. Maslow. Religion, Values and Peak Experiences. 1964. New York: Penguin Books, 1976; Abraham H. Maslow. Toward a Psychology of Being. 1962. 2d ed. New York: D. Van Nostrand Co.,

1968; Abraham H. Maslow. "The Farther Reaches of Human Nature." The Journal of Transpersonal Psychology 1, no. 1 (Spring 1969): 1–9; Arthur Warmouth. "A Note on the Peak Experience as a Personal Myth." Journal of Humanistic Psychology 5, no. 1 (Spring 1965): 18–21.

Pendulum

A rod-like instrument with a suspended weight used in divination. The pendulum is alleged to read energy patterns emanating from beings and objects, and communicate the information to the user by swinging back and forth or in circles. The weight is any object—a metal plumb, a button, a coin, for example—that is hung from a rod by a thread, string, or wire.

The precursor of the pendulum is the divining rod or wand, used since ancient times and referred to in the Bible as Jacob's Rod. Like the divining rod, the pendulum is said to work on the principle that every organism has an envelope of positive and negative energies. Each living organism must develop a means by which it can sense these energies, so that it can use the positive energies and avoid the negative. The pendulum serves as a tool that humans apparently can use to amplify the signals. The process by which this takes place is unknown, but users say they "tune in," perhaps through psi, to the energy of whatever is being sought. Most people are able to use a pendulum with some success, but some individuals seem to have an innate gift for it.

Uses of the pendulum have been diverse throughout history, but the most common are the finding of water, minerals, and objects buried in the ground, and the finding of lost objects, thieves, missing persons, and hidden treasure. Modern uses include medical diagnosis and treatment, geological prospecting, and military activities. In medical diagnosis, also called medical radiesthesia, the pendulum appears to pick up energies emanating from every cell, tissue, and organ. Negative energies are associated with disease and positive energies with good health. These claims are unproved scientifically and are not accepted by orthodox medicine. The pendulum has also proved useful in the military. During the Vietnam War, US Marines were trained to use pendula for locating underground mines, ammunition dumps, and tunnels, and to trace enemy movements. During World War II, British intelligence forces reportedly used pendula to try to divine Hitler's next moves. The pendulum also has been used in archaeological digs, and in police work to locate missing persons, bodies, and criminals.

T. C. Lethbridge, British archaeologist who became intrigued by dowsing, conducted considerable research with the pendulum following his retirement to Devon in 1957. A neighbor, an old woman reputed to be a witch, advised him that the pendulum is far more accurate than the forked-stick divining rods also used by dowsers. In his experiments Lethbridge discovered that a pendulum appeared to have precise responses to various substances. The responses were determined by two rate factors: the length of the string suspending the weight, and the number of times the pendulum rotated. For example, he found that the response for silver was twenty-two circular rotations of a pendulum on a twenty-two-inch string.

Lethbridge discovered the pendulum was astonishingly accurate. By working out rate tables, he was able to find a wide range of things, including truffles. He also discovered that the pendulum was sensitive to emotions and thoughts. He put forth theories that the pendulum could sense death, time, and other non-physical dimensions. Lethbridge determined that a pendulum on a forty-inch string registered death. Beyond that length objects seemed to respond at their normal rate plus forty, though the pendulum reacted not over them, but off to one side. Lethbridge proposed that if forty was death, then rates beyond forty indicated a parallel dimension beyond death, in which everything continued to exist but not in the same position. Still another dimension appeared to exist beyond the rate of eighty. Lethbridge also determined that forty was the rate for the concept of time. Between forty and eighty, time seemed to exist in an eternal now, then began to flow again between eighty and one hundred twenty, when it stopped again.

Lethbridge's theories about time and dimensions beyond death remain highly controversial. His widow, Mina, said excessive work with the pendulum depleted his vitality and contributed to his death of a heart attack. See **Dowsing; Psychic archaeology; Psychic criminology.**

Sources: J. Havelock Fidler. *Earth Energy: A Dowser's Investigation of Ley Lines.* 2d ed. Wellingborough, Northamptonshire, England: The Aquarian Press, 1988; Greg Nielsen and Joseph Polansky. *Pendulum Power.* Wellingborough, Northamptonshire, England: Excalibur Books, 1984; T. C. Lethbridge. *The Power of the Pendulum.* London: Routledge & Kegan Paul, 1976; T. C. Lethbridge. *Ghost and Divining-Rod.* London: Routledge & Kegan Paul, 1963; Colin Wilson. *Mysteries.* New York: Perigee Books/G. P. Putnam's Sons, 1978.

Penn, William

See **Society of Friends.**

Pentecostals

Members of various denominational Protestant Christian churches who seek a personal relationship with God through baptism in the Holy Spirit, often characterized by speaking in tongues.

Pentecostalism arose in late-nineteenth- and early twentieth-century

America in reaction to the secularization and rigid traditionalism of the established churches. According to Norwegian religious scholar Nils Bloch-Hoell, the breakdown of the old order occasioned by the Industrial Revolution, the optimism of the nineteenth century, the rise in science, and particularly the diversity and tolerance of American religion made disaffected Protestants prime candidates for a more individual worship characterized by the "proof" of Spirit baptism: speaking in tongues, interpretation of tongues, and the gifts of prophecy and healing.

"Pentecostal" comes from the Jewish celebration of Pentecost, seven weeks after Passover. Since Jesus Christ was crucified and resurrected during Passover, Christians measure Pentecost seven weeks after Easter Sunday. In Acts 2:2–4 of the New Testament, the gathered apostles experienced "a sound [came from heaven] like the rush of a mighty wind, and it filled all the house where they were sitting. And there appeared to them tongues as of fire, distributed and resting on each one of them. And they were all filled with the Holy Spirit and began to speak in other tongues, as the Spirit gave them utterance."

For a Pentecostal true communion with Christ has not been achieved until he or she has received the Holy Spirit and, like the apostles, spoken in tongues to announce that joyous event. After the days of the twelve apostles and St. Paul, however, the rapidly growing church began moving away from the gifts of tongues, prophecy, and healing, believing them miracles of earlier times. Various groups sought to reinstate these practices as evidence of true Christian faith, often to be branded as heretics, such as the Waldensians, Montanists, Jansenists, and French Camisards. By the fifteenth century, anyone speaking in an "other tongue" was believed bewitched and possessed by the Devil.

In the nineteenth century, however, religious revivals sparked by the Great Awakening in Europe and America led to the establishment of new denominations and independent religious thinkers, many of whom wanted proof of the Lord's existence and humankind's relationship to him. Baptists and Methodists, especially, believed that people could be made perfect through God's grace. Some of them—usually the poorer classes and those unschooled in the academics of religion—impatiently sought signs of his favor and broke away from their established churches.

One such dissident was Charles Fox Parham, an ordained Methodist minister who left Methodism in 1894 to become an itinerant Holiness minister. (The Holiness Movement revived interest in Methodist founder John Wesley's ideas of "sanctification"—that once a person had become a converted Christian, he or she must experience a second, distinct act of grace, expressed by receipt of the Holy Spirit, to become truly saved.) Parham emphasized God's gift of healing, and finally collected enough followers to found a Bible college in Topeka, Kansas, to seek the Holy Spirit.

Parham's thirty-six students gathered in an unfinished mansion called Stone's Folly in the summer of 1900. By December the group concluded that no visitations of the Holy Spirit had occurred in the Bible unless accompanied by speaking in tongues. All of the students prayed for such a sign, but with no results. Finally, on either New Year's Eve 1900 or New Year's Day 1901 (both dates are credited), Agnes Ozman asked Rev. Parham to lay his hands upon her, just as the apostles had received Christ. When he did Agnes poured forth strange, wonderful sounds: an unknown tongue. Pentecostals celebrate this date as the birth of the modern Pentecostal movement.

Within days all the students and Parham himself began to speak in unknown tongues, a phenomenon now known as glossolalia. But financial setbacks and accusations of trickery caused Parham to lose the school, his students, and most of his money. He left for greener pastures in Houston, Texas, with only his wife and sister.

Still able to attract crowds, Parham met William Joseph Seymour, a former slave. Pentecostalism appealed to African-Americans, since it emphasized exuberant worship and the chance for anyone to receive God's special blessing. Although Seymour had not yet received the Spirit, he took Parham's teachings with him to Los Angeles, California, where he was to head an African-American storefront church. He told his congregation that unless they had been so baptized, they were not full Christians. Disliking such ideas, the congregation fired him. But Seymour continued preaching anyway, from street corners and private homes.

Seymour's audiences grew, leading him to rent a former African Methodist Episcopal Church at 312 Azusa Street. On September 9, 1906, an eight-year-old boy received "the fire" of the Holy Spirit, and the church's fame spread as more and more people claimed to speak in tongues, prophesy, and either heal or be healed. Revival fever spread like wildfire, and hostility by the established churches and in the newspapers only served to publicize the phenomenon around the world. Meetings were held day and night, attracting gamblers, drunks, prostitutes, mediums, Spiritualists, and mockers, as well as those truly seeking religious renewal.

Besides an emphasis on sanctification and the initial integration of the races, the early Pentecostals also were convinced of "British Israel"—the idea that Anglo-Saxons are descendants of one of the missing ten tribes of Israel. This idea died with the separation of the church into various white and black groups, and is no longer held by Pentecostals today.

Within twenty years of its founding, Pentecostalism split into various sects and denominations, although all Pentecostals share some tenets of belief. Primary among these is the emphasis on the active, visible signs of the Lord's work: speaking in tongues, the laying-on of hands for healing, divination of spirits, miracles, and prophesying. Pentecostal churches now flourish in Europe, Latin America (especially Brazil and Chile), Africa, Asia, Australia, and even the Soviet Union.

Pentecostals also believe that if the Lord is busy, so is the Devil. Pentecostals guard against demons of sickness, fornication, and divorce, although they disagree on whether a Christian may be possessed or simply obsessed. The exorcism of such devils is known as "deliverance ministry," a procedure whereby the minister or healer, often accompanied by the entire congregation, confronts the demons with prayers and laying-on of hands. The demons depart under such pressure, calling themselves by the vice they exhibit: Lust, Envy, Greed, and so forth. Although some Pentecostal pastors reluctantly admit that psychiatric help may be necessary, the power of prayer is paramount.

Ironically, German Evangelists in the early 1900s attempted to defeat the spread of Pentecostalism by branding it satanic. In 1911 an unnamed mentally ill girl claimed to be possessed by a Pentecostal demon, who boasted that Pentecostalism was a plot to put Christianity into confusion. The girl prophesied that when her demon was exorcised, Pentecostalism would end. Doctors and psychiatrists attributed her ravings to dementia, but some Germans still believe Pentecostalism to be diabolically inspired.

The largest American Pentecostal denomination is the Assemblies of God, established about 1914. The most famous members of this denomination are television evangelists Jimmy Swaggart, who left the church in 1988 under the cloud of scandal, and Jim and Tammy Faye Bakker, who were forced out of their ministry in 1987 in scandal. Both Swaggart and Jim Bakker were accused of sexual improprieties, and the Bakkers also were accused of financial mismanagement of their evangelical empire. Jim Bakker was convicted on charges of the latter and was sent to federal prison. Other large Pentecostal sects include the Church of God in Christ; the Pentecostal Holiness Church; the International Church of the Foursquare Gospel, founded by evangelist Aimee Semple McPherson, a former minister of the Assemblies of God; and the Church of God (Cleveland, Tennessee). Oral Roberts, who introduced millions to the Pentecostal message via television and radio, later became a Methodist minister. See **Charismatic renewal; Glossolalia.**

Sources: Richard Cavendish, ed. *The Encyclopedia of the Unexplained.* New York: McGraw-Hill, 1974; Keith Crim, gen. ed. *Abingdon Dictionary of Living Religions.* Nashville, TN: Abingdon Press, 1981; W. J. Hollenweger. *The Pentecostals: The Charismatic Movement in the Churches.* Minneapolis: Augsburg Publishing House, 1972; Richard Quebedeaux. *The New Charismatics II.* San Francisco: Harper & Row, 1983; D. Scott Rogo. *The Infinite Boundary.* New York: Dodd, Mead & Co., 1987; John Sherrill. *They Speak with Other Tongues.* New York: McGraw-Hill Book Co., 1964.

Personal mythology

See **Mythology.**

Peyote

See **Drugs in mystical and psychic experiences.**

"Philip"

An artificial poltergeist created as an experiment by Canadian parapsychologists during the 1970s. Their success demonstrates how "real" spirits can be products of human will, expectation, and imagination.

The experiment was conducted by eight members of the Toronto Society for Psychical Research, under the direction of parapsychologists A. R. G. Owen and Iris M. Owen. None was psychically gifted. Their purpose was to try to create, through intense and prolonged concentration, a collective thought-form.

First, the group fabricated a fictitious identity, physical appearance, and personal history. "Philip Aylesford" was born in 1624 in England and followed an early military career. At age sixteen he was knighted. He had an illustrious role in the Civil War, fighting for the Royalists. He became a personal friend of Prince Charles (later Charles II) and worked for him as a secret agent. But Philip brought about his own undoing by having an affair with a Gypsy girl. When his wife found out, she accused the girl of witchcraft, and the girl was burned at the stake. In despair Philip committed suicide in 1654 at age thirty.

The Owen group began conducting sittings to try to conjure Philip in September 1972. They meditated, visualized him, and discussed the details of his life. No apparition ever appeared, but occasionally some sitters said they felt a presence in the room. Some also experienced vivid mental pictures of "Philip."

After months with no communication, the group tried table-tilting through psychokinesis (PK). This activity, made popular in Spiritualism seances, involves sitting around a table and placing fingertips lightly upon the surface. Spirits allegedly move or tilt the table; but a modern theory, proposed by British psychologist Kenneth J. Batcheldor, holds that the effects are created by the sitters' expectations.

After the Owen group conducted several sessions, the table top began to vibrate, resound with raps and knocks, and move seemingly of its own accord. Philip then began to communicate by rapping in response to questions.

Philip answered questions consistent with his fictitious history, but could provide nothing beyond what the group had conceived. Philip also gave other historically accurate information concerning real events and people. The Owen group theorized this material came from their own collective unconscious.

Sessions with Philip continued for several years. A levitation and movement of the table were recorded on film in 1974. Efforts to capture Philip's voice on tape were inconclusive. Members of the group thought whispers were made in response to questions, especially those made by Iris Owen, who seemed to have a special rapport with Philip. See **Electronic voice phenomenon.**

The Philip results encouraged other groups in Toronto and Quebec to try similar experiments. These groups created "Lilith," a French-Canadian spy during World War II; "Sebastian," a medieval alchemist; and "Axel," a man from the future. All personalities communicated by their own unique raps.

Encouraged by their success in producing poltergeist effects in "PK by committee," as they called it, the Owen group sought to create a visual apparition. But after 1977, with no further progress, interest waned and the experiment eventually was discontinued. See **Poltergeist; Psychokinesis (PK).**

Sources: Iris M. Owen with Margaret Sparrow. *Conjuring Up Philip.* New York: Harper & Row Publishers, 1976; Iris M. Owen. "'Philip's' Story Continued." *New Horizons Journal of the New Horizons Research Fund* 2, no. 1 (April 1975): 14–20; Iris M. Owen. "'Philip's' Fourth Year."

New Horizons Journal of the New Horizons Research Fund 2, no. 3 (June 1977): 11–15; D. Scott Rogo. *Minds and Motion . . . The Riddle of Psychokinesis.* New York: Taplinger Publishing Co., 1978; Colin Wilson. *Poltergeist! A Study in Destructive Haunting.* London: New English Library, 1981.

Phone calls from the dead

Literally, a telephone call from someone who has died, usually one with whom the recipient shared a close emotional relationship.

In such a call, the telephone usually rings normally, but may sound flat and abnormal. The connection usually is bad, and the voice of the dead one fades. The voice is recognizable, however, and the speaker may use pet names and words. The call is terminated abruptly, either by the caller hanging up or the line going dead. If the voice is too faint, the recipient may hang up in frustration.

If the recipient knows the caller is dead, he or she is too shocked to speak, and the call abruptly ends. If the recipient does not know the caller is dead, he or she may chat for up to thirty minutes. Most phone calls from the dead occur within twenty-four hours of the death of the caller, though some have been reported as long as two years from the time of death.

The purpose of these mysterious calls seems to be to leave either a farewell message, a warning of impending danger, or information needed by the living. Actress Ida Lupino received a telephone call from her father six months after his death; he told her the whereabouts of some papers needed to settle his estate.

Some calls are made in apparent observance of holidays, birthdays, and anniversaries. The caller may do nothing more than repeat a phrase, such as, "Hello, Mom, is that you?"

There are cases of phone calls being placed to the dead as well. The caller conducts a normal conversation and discovers later the person was dead at the time of the call.

No satisfactory explanation exists to explain phone calls from the dead, but several theories have been put forward. One holds that the dead do place the calls by supernatural manipulation of the telephone mechanisms and circuitry. Another holds that they are hallucinations caused in part by psychokinesis done subconsciously by the recipient. A similar theory suggests the calls are entirely fantasy. Still another theory holds that they are tricks played on the living by low-level spirits.

Phone calls from the dead are not taken seriously by most modern parapsychologists. In the early twentieth century, investigators modified the telegraph and wireless in hopes of communicating with the dead. Thomas Edison, whose parents were Spiritualists, worked on but did not complete a telephone that he hoped would connect the living and the dead. In the 1940s "psychic telephone" experiments were conducted in England and America to try to reach the dead. Interest rose in the 1960s, when Konstantin Raudive announced that he had captured voices of the dead on electromagnetic tape. See **Electronic voice phenomenon.**

Sources: Stanley R. Dean, ed. *Psychiatry and Mysticism.* Chicago: Nelson-Hall, 1975; S. Ralph Harlow. *A Life after Death.* Garden City, NY: Doubleday, 1961; Elizabeth McAdams and Raymond Bayless. *The Case for Life after Death.* Chicago: Nelson-Hall, 1981; D. Scott Rogo and Raymond Bayless. *Phone Calls from the Dead.* Englewood Cliffs, NJ: Prentice-Hall, 1979; Susy Smith. *The Power of the Mind.* Radnor, PA: Chilton Book Co., 1975.

Piper, Leonora E. (1857–1950)

One of the most important mental mediums in the history of psychical research. Leonora E. Piper, a Boston housewife, unexpectedly became a medium in 1884 when she consulted J. R. Cocke, a blind healing medium, and passed into a trance herself. In trance she wrote an impressive message for one of the other clients present, a judge, which purported to come from his deceased son. A succession of spirit guides began to appear, and Piper set up her own sittings, attracting the attention of prominent psychical researchers. She entered trances with much teeth grinding and spasms. Her voice changed dramatically as different spirits spoke through her.

Her first spirit control was a Native American girl named, improbably, Chlorine, who introduced a cast of discarnate heavyweights that included Johann Sebastian Bach, Henry Wadsworth Longfellow, and Commodore Vanderbilt. Chlorine soon gave way to a French doctor, Dr. Phinuit (pronounced "finney"). He was a colorful character who, oddly, knew little French and only a little about medicine. Nor could he ever give a coherent or verifiable account of his alleged life on earth. Although these controls appeared to be fictitious, they usually managed to produce accurate information for the sitters. Phinuit tended to be unreliable and did not always come through for Piper.

In 1885 Piper attracted the attention of psychologist and philosopher William James. He attended a number of sittings, some with his wife, at which personal information was given. James was impressed with Piper, and felt lucky guesses and previous knowledge on the part of Piper could not explain all of her performances.

For years Piper was investigated by both the Society for Psychical Research (SPR) in England and the American Society for Psychical Research. Richard Hodgson, secretary of the American branch of the SPR in Boston, kept numerous full records and administrated many sittings. The investigators hired private detectives to shadow Piper to make certain she did no research that would enable her to give personal information to her sitters. Hundreds of sitters were introduced to her anonymously. Investigators never uncovered any hint of fraud.

In 1892 Dr. Phinuit was replaced by a new control, George Pellew, known as GP. Pellew said he was a young New York man who had recently died, and who had attended one of Piper's sittings five years before as an anonymous sitter. GP recognized anonymous sitters who had known the living Pellew, and carried on intimate conversations with them.

GP lasted until 1897, when the tenor of Piper's seances began to change. She did more automatic writing. She apparently inherited the controls of English medium William Stainton Moses, who died that year. The spirits that came through identified themselves to Piper only as great historical figures who preferred to remain anonymous with such names as "Doctor" and "Imperator," but their descriptions of themselves and the information they gave corresponded with information recorded about Moses's controls. Messages received through Piper became increasingly more spiritual and much less personal. In 1905 Hodgson died and allegedly became one of her controls.

Piper ended her trance mediumship in 1911 but continued to do automatic writing. One of her more significant messages came on August 8, 1915, when she received a communication from Hodgson for Sir Oliver Lodge, intimating the impending death of his son, Raymond, in World War I.

During her mediumship career, Piper traveled to London on three occasions in order to be tested by psychical researchers while out of her natural setting. Investigators attempted to explain her impressive successes by advancing theories of telepathy and super-ESP, but could not account for many of her sittings. See Control; Cross correspondence; Medium-ship; Super-ESP. Compare to Leonard, Gladys Osborne.

Sources: Alan Gauld. *Mediumship and Survival.* London: William Heinemann Ltd., 1982; Sir Oliver Lodge. *Raymond or Life and Death.* 12th ed. London: Methuen & Co. Ltd., 1919; Edgar D. Mitchell. *Psychic Exploration: A Challenge for Science.* Edited by John White. New York: Paragon Books, 1974; Alta L. Piper. *The Life and Work of Mrs. Piper.* London: Kegan Paul, Trench, Trubner & Co., Ltd., 1929; Benjamin B. Wolman, ed. *Handbook of Parapsychology.* New York: Van Nostrand Reinhold, 1977.

PK

See **Psychokinesis (PK).**

PK party

An informal gathering of people for the purpose of psychokinetic metal bending, or the willing of metal to bend. The party is led by an experienced individual and helpers who teach the participants how to create a "peak emotional experience" by focusing a unified mental energy on silverware, rods, saw blades, drill bits, or other metal objects. A group of fifteen to forty people is said to be the best number for the most effective results.

Interest in psychokinetic metal bending arose from the feats of Uri Geller, who received a great deal of media attention in the 1970s for his alleged ability to psychically bend keys and silverware.

A procedure for psychokinetic metal bending is to create an intense point of concentration in the mind, bring the point down through the arm and hand and into the metal, command the metal to bend, and release the energy. The actual process by which this takes place is not known.

Participants say they initially feel the metal become warm and sticky, then soft enough to bend with little pressure. This state, called "warm forming," typically lasts from five to twenty seconds. The heat seems to come from within the metal. In rare cases both metal and surrounding air drop in temperature, a phenomenon similar to the temperature drops reported in some poltergeist cases. Some researchers believe psychokinesis (PK) is responsible for some poltergeist disturbances.

Participants can try various levels of metal bending, the most advanced of which is getting metal to bend of its own accord without being touched. Silver-plated silverware works best; sometimes the silver plating splits with a popping sound. Copper seems to be resistant to bending, and in some cases becomes so hot that it must be dropped. Metal that is annealed or cast is difficult to warm form.

Participants also may attempt to pop open or sprout seeds held in the hand.

Geller, who allowed himself to be tested under controlled circumstances, performed psychokinetic metal bending for two professional magicians, Artur Zorka and Abb Dickson, in 1975. Zorka gave Geller a forged steel fork with a nylon handle, which was especially resistant to physical stress. Geller took hold of it and within moments the fork exploded into pieces. Geller also bent a key; Zorka reported seeing the bending taking place. The magicians concluded that no trickery was involved. See **Geller, Uri; Psychokinesis (PK)**.

Sources: Jack Houck. "PK Party History." *Psi Research* 3, no. 1 (March 1984): 67–77; Charles Panati, ed. *The Geller Papers: Scientific Observations on the Paranormal Powers of Uri Geller.* Boston: Houghton Mifflin, 1976.

Planchette

A nineteenth-century precursor to the Ouija, designed to open the user to automatic writing and drawing. *Planchette* means "little board" in French, and the invention of the device is generally credited to a French Spiritualist by the same name, M. Planchette. Another account credits the invention to a German milkmaid. The planchette began appearing in Europe in the 1850s, and quickly became popular as part of the Spiritualist movement. Mediums used it to communicate with the dead and with spirit guides, and to divine the future or find lost persons and objects.

The planchette consists of a thin, heart-shaped platform with three legs, two of which are on wheels and one of which is a pencil. The medium or user places fingertips on the platform and invites spirits to communicate by writing out messages or drawing pictures. The medium may be in a state of altered consciousness during the process and unaware of the message. In some cases the medium produces what appears to be an exact replica of the handwriting of a deceased person.

Around the turn of the twentieth century, the planchette was supplanted in popularity by the Ouija. It is still used, and is popular as a toy. See **Automatisms; Ouija**.

Sources: Gina Covina. *The Ouija Book.* New York: Simon & Schuster, 1979; Stoker Hunt. *Ouija: The Most Dangerous Game.* New York: Harper & Row, 1985; *Into the Unknown.* Pleasantville, NY: Reader's Digest, 1981.

Planetary consciousness

An outgrowth of the ecology movement of the 1960s, expanded with the concept of the Earth as a living, self-regulating organism. Planetary consciousness takes on spiritual dimensions with an awareness of the delicately balanced and interconnected relationships between all things and sentient beings on the planet, not only with each other, but with Mother Earth herself, and presages the possible emergence of a global consciousness. However, if present abuses of the planet are not abated, no such evolutionary leap in consciousness will take place; instead, the human race may snuff itself out of existence.

The need to solve ecological problems took on renewed urgency in the 1980s with evidence of the disastrous consequences of the destruction of the rain forests; the contamination of the soil, potable water, and oceans; depletion of energy reserves; global warming through the greenhouse effect; and depletion of the protective ozone layer in the atmosphere.

The pollution of the Earth is the product of the Industrial Revolution, barely two hundred years old, though the roots of an abusive attitude toward the planet are much older. Some scholars blame early Western thought: the simplistic dualism of Platonic philosophy, which separates the ideal from the phenomenal world; and the Christian religion, whose transcendent God exists apart from nature. Furthermore, the redemption theme of Christianity, by emphasizing a salvation into the spiritual realm, turns attention away from the natural world. In contrast, it is pointed out, Eastern religions and philosophies conceive of an interconnected web of life on Earth and throughout the cosmos, in which nature and all sentient beings are sacred. Societies with animistic beliefs also venerate the natural world.

Other scholars, such as Thomas Berry, American historian and Passionist priest and a leading spokesperson for planetary consciousness, observe that a general Christian sensitivity to the natural world and cosmology existed through the Middle Ages. But in the fourteenth century, and especially in the wake of the Black Death that depopulated Europe, redemption became the driving force in the

Christian experience. The rise of science in the secular world focused attention on improving the world by controlling nature.

In the seventeenth century, science and religion split. Science saw the natural world, and the universe, as separate and mechanical, and devoid of an immanent God. German astronomer Johannes Kepler stated in 1605 that his aim was to show that the universe was like a clockwork. English philosopher Francis Bacon stated that one should come to know nature in order to control her. A significant contribution to this split was the almost complete dualism of French philosopher René Descartes, who held the reality of the physical world to be mechanistic and divorced from any inner life principle.

Regardless of religion and philosophy, people are polluting the Earth and using up its resources at a frightening pace. Industrialized nations both East and West are guilty of deplorable environmental records.

An effective presentation to the general population of the consequences of the chemical poisoning of the global environment was the seminal book by Rachel Carson, *Silent Spring* (1962). Carson's book, and other important works that followed, helped fuel the environmental movement. Another milestone was biologist and ecologist Barry Commoner's *The Closing Circle* (1971), which holds that industrialized societies have replaced natural and biodegradable substances with synthetics, which strain the ecosystem.

In 1982 the United Nations General Assembly formulated the document entitled "World Charter for Nature," which Berry has called "one of the most impressive documents of the twentieth century." The charter presents twenty-four "principles of conservation by which it proclaims all human conduct affecting nature is to be guided and judged," and includes these fundamental truths:

Mankind is a part of nature and life depends on the uninterrupted functioning of natural systems which ensure the supply of energy and nutrients.

Civilization is rooted in nature, which has shaped human culture and influenced all artistic and scientific achievement, and living in harmony with nature gives man the best opportunities for the development of his creativity, and for rest and recreation.

Despite such reports, warnings, and proclamations, the decreases in pollution have been insufficient to reverse what is now perceived as the rising cumulative effect of earlier abuses. At the same time, a new awareness of the Earth has developed: one Berry calls the "ecological age" to reflect the interdependence of all living and nonliving systems of the earth.

The Gaia Hypothesis

The "Gaia hypothesis," that the Earth is a self-regulating organism, was put forward in the early 1970s by James E. Lovelock, a British biologist. Lovelock began to conceive the idea in the early 1960s, while working as a consultant for the Jet Propulsion Laboratory of the National Aeronautics and Space Administration in Pasadena, California.

Lovelock made a number of discoveries that indicated the presence of a biological self-regulating mechanism, whereby: (1) the amount of methane and oxygen in the Earth's atmosphere has remained nearly constant for hundreds of millions of years, despite the fact that methane and oxygen interact to destroy each other; (2) the oceans have contained approximately 3.4 percent salt; and (3) the planet has sustained a fairly constant surface temperature, despite the fact that the sun is now radiating 25 percent more heat than it did 3.5 billion years ago when life on the planet first appeared. A homeostasis seemed to be at work.

Lovelock acknowledges he was not the first to conceive the idea of biological regulation: as early as 1958, the hypothesis was put forward by Alfred Redfield that the chemical composition of the atmosphere and oceans was biologically controlled. Other scientists undoubtedly had considered the same hypothesis, Lovelock said, but the idea never gained much audience.

The name Gaia, after the Greek Earth Mother goddess, was proposed to Lovelock by novelist William Golding. Lovelock and evolutionary biologist Lynn Margulis's coauthored papers on the hypothesis, published in scientific journals, went largely unnoticed, but Lovelock's 1979 book, *Gaia: A New Look at Life on Earth,* caught attention.

According to the hypothesis, humankind is part of an overall complex biosphere organism. People, along with all other life forms on the planet, make an integral contribution to Gaia's homeostasis, which in turn makes life possible.

Critics of the Gaia hypothesis contend that life on the planet was created by and is maintained through a series of fortuitous events. Proponents of the hypothesis see it as much more: evidence of the Earth as a living, conscious entity, an idea with profound spiritual implications. Lovelock maintains that his hypothesis does not suppose the existence of a purposeful planetary self-regulation.

Even supposing an automatic self-regulation has serious ramifications for pollution. Human abuse of the planet is throwing the homeostasis out of kilter and seriously jeopardizing the organism as a whole, as though the human race is a cancer. There are three solutions hypothesized: (1) the organism of Gaia will die, taking the cancer and everything else with it; (2) Gaia will restore balance by ridding itself of the cancer, and humankind will become extinct; or (3) humankind can instead begin to function as a planetary nervous system for Gaia, working in harmony with the organism.

The latter possibility lies at the heart of the Gaia hypothesis. Technology already has turned the world into a global village. Lovelock says that Gaia, through human technology, has awakened and is aware of herself, and has seen herself through the eyes of space cameras. He suggests that the collective intelligence of humans constitutes a Gaian brain and nervous system that can anticipate environmental changes. The result may be that in the future, nationalism will disappear in the face of the need "to belong to the commonwealth of all creatures which constitute Gaia."

The evolutionary leap into a unified human consciousness was envisioned by the French priest and philosopher, Pierre Teilhard de Chardin. Teilhard coined the term "noosphere" (from the Greek *noos,* or "mind"), to describe this "planetization of the Mind." Noogenesis, the evolutionary genesis of the mind, will culminate in the Omega Point, when the noosphere will be created. Similarly, the Indian mystic and philosopher, Sri Aurobindo, saw the next stage of evolution as the "Supermind," a product of the increasing spiritual development of individual consciousness, which would manifest on both an individual and collective level.

Still another possibility is put forward by British physicist Peter Russell, who hypothesizes the evolution of a completely new and planetary level of consciousness, "Gaiafield," a self-reflective consciousness that emerges from the interactions of all the minds within the social superorganism. Gaiafield, says Russell, would have new characteristics unimaginable to present human consciousness.

Whether or not any evolutionary leap of consciousness happens will depend on changes in human behavior. Teilhard saw the Omega Point from a cosmic perspective, perhaps thousands or even millions of years away, while Aurobindo projected the Supermind within a century; neither, however, was living in a time of ecological crisis. Russell and others collapse the timeframe to decades.

The changes deemed necessary to prevent disaster and instead make the leap require fundamental shifts away from self-centered consumer life-styles and commerce. Lovelock also advocates the establishment of a new planetary science, geophysiology, to bring all natural sciences together in a Gaian perspective. Berry says we must realign ourselves with bioregions, identifiable geographical areas that are self-sustaining. Berry also states that the European culture could learn about the Earth from Native Americans, whose culture has retained within its collective unconscious intimate psychic bonds with the Earth.

From a spiritual perspective, Berry says that what is needed is a "New Story," a creation myth for the universe and the planet Earth in all their unfolding levels of expression. The American mythologist, Joseph Campbell, also saw the need for a planetary mythology of the world as a whole, with no national boundaries.

Russell says the individual raising of consciousness through meditation may have a collective effect of unifying and raising the consciousness of humanity as a whole. Studies of Transcendental Meditation groups have shown a synchronization of brain activity during meditation. If an increasing number of people meditate, the effect may be felt on the human race as a whole.

Sources: Elias V. Amidon and Elizabeth J. Roberts. "Gaian Consciousness." *ReVision* 9, no. 2 (Winter/Spring 1987): 3–5; Thomas Berry. *The Dream of the Earth.* San Francisco: Sierra Club Nature and Natural Philosophy Library, 1988; Thomas Berry. "The Viable Human." *ReVision* 9, no. 2 (Winter/Spring, 1987): 75–82; Peter Borrelli, ed. *Crossroads: Environmental*

Priorities for the Future. Washington, DC: Island Press, 1988; Lester R. Brown. *State of the World: A Worldwide Institute Report on Progress Towards a Sustainable Society*. New York: W. W. Norton, 1988; Rachel Carson. *Silent Spring*. Boston: Houghton Mifflin, 1962; Jean Hardy. *A Psychology with a Soul: Psychosynthesis in Evolutionary Context*. London: Routledge & Kegan Paul, 1987; James E. Lovelock. *The Ages of Gaia: A Biography of Our Living Earth*. New York: W. W. Norton, 1988; J. E. Lovelock. *Gaia: A New Look at Life on Earth*. Oxford: Oxford University Press, 1979; Philip Novak. "Tao How? Asian Religions and the Problem of Environmental Degradation." *ReVision* 9, no. 2 (Winter/Spring, 1987): 33–40; Peter Russell. *The Global Brain: Speculations on the Evolutionary Leap to Planetary Consciousness*. Los Angeles: J. P. Tarcher, 1983; Pierre Teilhard de Chardin. *The Phenomenon of Man*. 1955. New York: Harper & Row, 1965; Anne Lonergan and Caroline Richards, eds. *Thomas Berry and the New Cosmology*. Mystic, CT: Twenty-third Publications, 1987; George Trevelyan. *A Vision of the Aquarian Age: The Emerging Spiritual World View*. Walpole, NH: Stillpoint, 1984; Ross Evan West. "Gaia: The New Mother Earth." *New Realities* 10, no. 1 (September/October 1989): 16–23.

Plants, psychism of

The theory that plants are sensitive to the thoughts and emotions of people around them, and have themselves emotions, memory, and powers that enable them to communicate with people. This notion harks back to ancient times, when plants were perceived to possess magical powers. Modern researchers have experimented with plant psi since the 1960s, but results have been largely inconclusive. Nonetheless, many people who have cared for plants attest to their sensitivity to their environment and caretakers.

George Washington Carver, the agricultural chemist who developed the peanut and sweet potato into scores of independent products, attributed his success with plants to love. Botanist Luther Burbank once stated that he could make a plant grow according to his own design simply by willing his thoughts and love. Burbank said he developed the spineless cactus in this way.

Studies have shown that plants are surrounded by energy fields that may be dowsed and which respond to radionics treatments. Plants also seem to be influenced by human thought, emotion, and intent; the well-being or demise of other living things around them; and to music. Many scientists, however, reject the idea of plant sensitivity and attribute unusual growth to carbon dioxide exhaled in human breath and inhaled by plants. Nevertheless, some cases of plant growth have defied scientific explanation. At Findhorn, a small community of people living on the harsh North Sea coast of Scotland, the flourishing plants have baffled agronomists. The community attributes its success to its communication with spirits called devas and to members who meditate and talk directly to the plants about their beauty and the community's gratitude and love for them. See **Deva; Findhorn.**

Intriguing but inconclusive research on the possible psychic properties of plants was conducted during the 1960s by polygraph expert Cleve Backster. After attaching lie detector electrodes to the leaf of a dracaena, Backster observed that the plant seemed to respond emotionally to care, such as watering, and to threats, such as attempts to burn it and even to think about burning it. He concluded that plants would go into defensive faint in the presence of human hostility, but would respond positively to the heartbeat of a loving person.

Backster attempted to determine whether plants have their own extrasensory perception and are capable of communicating with other living things. He measured the electrical resistance on leaf surfaces in response to the killing of distant brine shrimp by random dumping into boiling water. Backster achieved significant results, but other researchers were unable to replicate them, leading some to conclude that the "experimenter effect" played a role in Backster's outcome. See **Experimenter effect.**

Other of Backster's experiments — the reactions of plants to human emotions — were replicated in the early 1970s by Marcel Vogel, a research chemist for International Business Machines. Vogel said that plants sent out their own energy in response to loving thoughts; he could feel this energy on his palms. He also said plants seemed to respond to thoughts from a distance, and theorized that plants stored energy from thoughts in some form of memory.

Russian scientists also found evidence for a plant memory. A geranium attached to electrodes reacted negatively to the mere presence of a person who had previously pinched and burned it for several days, but reacted positively to the presence of a person who had previously cared for the plant.

Experiments with prayer have shown that praying over seeds and plants seems to influence faster and more luxuriant growth than control seeds and plants that do not receive prayer.

Psychic healers also have been shown to have a positive effect on plants. Ambrose and Olga Worrall, for example, directed their healing energy to rye seedlings six hundred miles distant, resulting in a spectacular growth rate 84 percent faster than normal. The healer Oskar Estebany seemed to impart beneficial energies to water he held in a flask in his hand, and which then was poured on barley seeds.

Experiments with music have demonstrated that plants thrive in a background of classical music but suffer when rock and heavy metal are played.

In the 1950s researchers discovered that plants responded to radionics treatments for the elimination of pests. The US Department of Agriculture, however, considered the evidence insufficient. Radionics remains illegal in most states in the United States.

Although the psi properties of plants remain scientifically inconclusive, researchers have discovered that plants do have ordinary ways of communicating with humans. Plants that do not get enough water emit a high frequency noise as their cell structure breaks down. Monitoring plant noise might benefit farming by telling farmers precisely when to water crops, and could be used by researchers in the development of more hardy strains of crop plants. Compare to **Animal Psi.**

Sources: Edgar D. Mitchell. *Psychic Exploration: A Challenge for Science.* Edited by John White. New York: G. P. Putnam's Sons, 1974; Sheila Ostrander and Lynn Schroeder. *Psychic Discoveries Behind the Iron Curtain.* Englewood Cliffs, NJ: Prentice-Hall, Inc., 1970; "Scientists Listen to Noises of Plants in Droughts." *The New York Times* (September 4, 1988): 29; Peter Tompkins. *The Secret Life of Plants.* New York: Harper & Row Publishers, 1973; Benjamin B. Wolman, ed. *Handbook of Parapsychology.* New York: Van Nostrand Reinhold, 1977.

Plateau experience

See **Peak experiences.**

Plato (c. 428 B.C.–347 B.C.)

Greek philosopher and one of the most important thinkers in Western history. Plato's work has had a huge impact on the development of Western philosophical, religious, and mystical thought. He lived during a time of great transition in classical Greece, when the city states were failing. Although many of his writings dealt with politics, they were based on a spiritual philosophy concerned with the nature of the truly Real. He believed that philosophy was the greatest good given to humankind by God.

Plato was born in Athens c. 428 B.C. to an established and prestigious family. He harbored political ambitions, but dropped them following the trial and suicide of his friend Socrates in 399 B.C. Plato left Athens and traveled widely through Greece, Italy, and Egypt. He began to write dialogues in defense of Socrates. The elder philosopher had not actually been his tutor, but Plato admired him greatly. It is debated how much of Plato's work reflects Socrates and how much was Plato's own infusion. Plato also was influenced by Pythagoreanism.

After leaving Athens Plato met Archytas of Tarentum, a Pythagorean mathematician, and was influenced by his views on the value of mathematics as a research tool in science. According to occult lore, in Egypt he was initiated into the mysteries in a rite in a subterranean hall of the Great Pyramid.

Plato returned to Athens and founded the Academy, the first university, in 387 B.C., which he intended would explore all fields of knowledge and their interrelation. His greatest pupil was Aristotle.

Plato wrote in the form of dialogues, for he felt discussion was the best way to learn. The key figure in the dialogues is Socrates. The dialogues form three major groups: (1) inquiry, a presentation and defense of Socrates' views; (2) speculation, the development of a systematic philosophy that apparently derives from both Socrates and Plato; and (3) criticism, appraisal, and application, in which the philosophy is tested.

Meno, from the early group, and *Phaedo, Symposium, Phaedrus,* and *Republic,* from the middle group, outline Plato's philosophy, central to which is the Theory of Forms (or Theory of Ideas) and

(New York Public Library)

Plato

a belief in the immortality of the soul as existing separately from the body and the mind before and after death. These works also offer discussions on the nature of love, the dialectic method, the form of the Good, and the ideal society. *Phaedo* has been called "the Magna Carta of Western mysticism." *Republic* contains the fullest exposition.

According to the Theory of Forms, given in *Phaedo,* the material world is an imperfect copy of the real and true perfect world. Forms are like original blueprints—the ideas or concepts behind the material world. We see an object for what it is, but its essence, its "is-ness," is the idea of the object, which holds the perfect vision of Beauty, Goodness, and Love, which together constitute the One. Form constitutes real identity, and can be applied to concepts as well as objects. Forms do not change and are the same for every observer.

The ultimate reality and the source of reality of everything else is the Form of the Good, which Plato likened to the illuminating sun. The Form of the Good is ineffable, yet explains all else. To become aware of it is to have a mystical experience in which one understands why all other forms are what they are.

According to Aristotle in *Metaphysics,* the Theory of Forms is derived from the Pythagorean theory of numbers: the forms are the same as numbers. Aristotle said that Plato differed from the Pythagoreans on two points. The Pythagoreans held that numbers have as constituents the unlimited and the limit, while Plato said forms have as constituents the one and the great and the small. The Pythagoreans said things are numbers, but Plato placed mathematics between forms and things.

Plato regarded the world of forms as the highest reality, which subsequently has been named the Self or Higher Self. The Theory of Forms anticipated psychiatrist Carl G. Jung's concept of archetypes. See **Archetypes.** Many of Plato's followers derogated the physical world in favor of the world of forms.

In *Republic* Plato advanced the idea that most people go through life asleep and in a dream; it is the job of the philosopher to waken them. Plato illustrated this with his famous metaphor of the cave:

Imagine mankind as dwelling in an underground cave with a long entrance open to the light across the whole width of the cave; in this they have been since childhood, with necks and legs fettered, and they can only look forward, but light comes to them from a fire burning behind them higher up at a distance. Between the fire and the prisoners is a road above their level, and along it imagine a low wall has been built, as puppet showmen have screens in front of them over which they work their puppets . . .

Plato went on to say that the prisoners would name the shadows they saw as things, and that someone brought into the brilliant sunlight would not be able to see the things that were truly real, and would avert his eyes back to the shadows. The cave image made a profound impression on psychiatrist Roberto Assagioli, who made it a fundamental of Psychosynthesis. See **Psychology.** The theme of being asleep through life has been echoed by others, such as Theosophist Rudolf Steiner and mystic G. I. Gurdjieff.

Plato was influenced by the Pythagorean teaching that humans, separate from God (the Monad), must work to purify themselves in preparation for the return to God. To free the soul for this task, Plato advocated repression of bodily desires.

Plato died in Athens at about age eighty. His disciples split into two camps: the Academics, who continued to meet at the Academy, and the Peripatetics, who followed Aristotle. The Academy remained in operation until A.D. 529, when the Emperor Justinian closed the schools of Athens.

During the first centuries A.D., Neoplatonism developed out of Platonic thought, most notably under the Hellenic philosopher Plotinus (204/205–270), and later under Porphyry and Iamblichus. It absorbed Christian, Jewish, and Eastern religious elements, as well as Pythagorean, Aristotelian, and Stoic philosophy elements, and placed more emphasis on mystical vision. Neoplatonism was at a peak from about 250 to 550, then died out under pressure from orthodox Christianity.

In the Neoplatonic view, the cosmology was seen as ordered and based on One, or Unity. The soul could become more unified with Unity through purification and simplification. Every doctrine was considered to be only a shell for a spiritual truth that could only be discovered through meditation and mystical exercises. The corporeal bodies of religion and philosophy had little value, and material science was not emphasized at all.

Plotinus established that the goal of humankind is the vision of and union with God, which is achieved through the withdrawal from everything that is external and finite, in order to concentrate on immutable and perfect Reality. He also firmly established that the ultimate nature of the universe is spiritual, and from it flows a material world. From a World Soul, individual souls descend to the material world and forget their divine origins, thus becoming caught in the bondage of rebirth. Souls can liberate themselves only by turning away from the material toward God in a transcendent ecstasy.

Plotinus disagreed with the dualism of the Gnostics that matter is inherently evil; rather, he said, matter is base, but the universe is inherently good. Later Neoplatonic thought absorbed Gnostic elements.

In one form or another, Platonic thought dominated philosophy, science, and theology until the thirteenth century. It influenced the development of Christian mystical thought, to a limited extent through Clement of Alexandria and Origen, and to a great extent through Augustine, who was influenced by Plotinus (see **Augustine, St.**) and Dionysius the Areopagite, the latter of whom developed the foundation of medieval mystical theology and angelology. In the thirteenth century, Aristotle was rediscovered and given predominance, especially in the works of St. Thomas Aquinas. Platonic thought has had revivals periodically throughout history. See **Mysticism.**

Sources: Manly P. Hall. *The Secret Teachings of All Ages.* 1928. Los Angeles: The Philosophical Research Society, 1977; F. C. Happold. *Mysticism: A Study and an Anthology.* Rev. ed. Harmondsworth, Middlesex, England: Penguin Books, 1970; Jean Hardy. *A Psychology with a Soul: Psychosynthesis in Evolutionary Context.* London: Routledge & Kegan Paul, 1987; Edouard Schure. *The Great Initiates: A Study of the Secret Religions of History.* San Francisco: Harper & Row, 1961; Samuel Umen. *The World of the Mystic.* New York: Philosophical Library, 1988; *The Republic of Plato.* Translated with introduction and notes by Francis MacDonald Cornford. London: Oxford University Press, 1941; *The Works of Plato.* Selected and edited by Irwin Edman. 1928. New York: Tudor Publishing Co., 1934.

Plotinus

See **Plato.**

Podmore, Frank

See **Apparition; Society for Psychical Research (SPR).**

Polarity

See **Bodywork.**

Poltergeist

A spirit, usually mischievous and sometimes malevolent, which manifests by making noises, moving objects, and assaulting people and animals. "Poltergeist" comes from the German *poltern,* "to knock," and *geist,* "spirit." Some cases of poltergeists are unexplained and may involve actual spirits. In other cases the phenomena seem to be caused by subconscious psychokinesis (PK) on the part of one individual.

The most common poltergeist phenomena are rains of stones, dirt, and other small objects; throwing and moving of objects, including large pieces of furniture; loud noises and shrieks; strange lights; apparitions; and vile smells. With the development of technology, poltergeists have adapted to interfering with telephones and electronic equipment, and turning lights and appliances on and off. Some poltergeists are said to pinch, bite, hit, and sexually assault the living.

Poltergeist activity usually begins and stops abruptly. A typical occurrence lasts several hours to several months; some have been reported to last several years. Activity almost always occurs at night when someone is present—typically an "agent," an individual who seems to act as a focus or magnet for the activity. The agent is a factor in most cases, both those that seem paranormal or that may be caused by human PK. Agents usually are females under age twenty.

Poltergeist disturbances have been reported around the world since ancient times. A computer analysis of five hundred cases from 1800 to the present, collected from around the world, was done in the late 1970s by parapsychologists Alan Gauld and A. D. Cornell. They identified sixty-three general characteristics, including the following: 64 percent involved the movement of small objects; 58 percent were most active at night; 48 percent featured raps; 36 percent involved the movement of large objects; 24 percent lasted longer than one year; 16 percent featured communication between poltergeist and agent; 12 percent involved the opening and shutting of doors and windows.

Prior to the nineteenth century, poltergeist occurrences were blamed on the Devil, demons, witches, and the ghosts of the dead. The Gauld-Cornell analysis found only 9 percent of cases attributed to demons, 7 percent to witches, and 2 percent to spirits of the dead. Most of the demonic and witch attributions occur in non-Western cases. Poltergeist activity at seances is attributed to spirits of the dead.

The development of psychical research in the late nineteenth century brought scientific scrutiny to the phenomenon. Among early investigators were two founders of the Society for Psychical Research, Sir William Barrett and Frederic W. H. Myers. Myers believed that some poltergeist cases were genuine, and observed that poltergeist phenomena were distinct from ghost hauntings.

In the 1930s psychologist and psychical researcher Nandor Fodor advanced the theory that some poltergeist disturbances were caused not by spirits but by human agents who were suffering from intense repressed anger, hostility, and sexual tension. Fodor successfully demonstrated his theory in a number of cases, including the famous "Thornton Heath Poltergeist" in England, which he investigated in 1938. The case involved a woman whose repressions caused a poltergeist outbreak and apparent vampire attack. Fodor was severely criticized by Spiritualists, and in turn won a libel suit against a Spiritualist newspaper.

The research of William Roll, project director of the Psychical Research Foundation in Durham, North Carolina, has supported the psychological dysfunction theory. Beginning in the 1960s, Roll studied written reports of 116 poltergeist cases spanning four centuries and more than one hundred countries. Roll identified patterns of what he called "recurrent spontaneous psychokinesis" (RSPK), which are inexplicable, spontaneous physical effects. He found that the most common agent was a child or teenager whose unwitting PK was a way of expressing hostility without fear of punishment. The individual usually was unaware of being the cause of the disturbances, but was secretly or openly pleased with their occurrence.

Other investigators have found that agents often are in poor mental or physical health and thus are vulnerable to stress. Patients with unresolved emotional tensions have been associated with houses where poltergeist activity took place. In studying the personalities of agents, psychologists have found anxiety reactions, conversion hysteria, phobias, mania, obsessions, dissociative reactions, and schizophrenia. In some cases psycho-therapy eliminates the poltergeist phenomena.

The psychological dysfunction theory has been disputed by other researchers, including Gauld and Cornell, who said that the psychological tests used were invalid. Psychiatrist Ian Stevenson has proposed that spirits of the dead may account for more poltergeist cases than realized. In studying a number of cases attributed to living agents and to spirits of the dead, Stevenson noted significant differences. The phenomena in living agent cases was without purpose and often violent, while cases involving spirits of the dead featured intelligent communication, purposeful movement of objects, and little violence.

See **Apparition; Haunting; Mediumship; "Philip."**

Sources: Loyd Auerbach. *ESP, Hauntings and Poltergeists: A Parapsychologist's Handbook.* New York: Warner Books, 1986; Alan Gauld and A. D. Cornell. *Poltergeists.* London: Routledge & Kegan Paul, 1979; Elizabeth E. McAdams and Raymond Bayless. *The Case for Life after Death.* Chicago: Nelson-Hall, 1981; Edgar D. Mitchell. *Psychic Exploration: A Challenge for Science.* Edited by John White. New York: G. P. Putnam's Sons, 1974; Frederic W. H. Myers. *Human Personality and Its Survival of Bodily Death.* Vols. 1 and 2. 1903. New ed. New York: Longmans, Green & Co., 1954; A. R. G. Owen. *Can We Explain the Poltergeist?* New York: Garrett Publications/A Helix Press Book, 1964; D. Scott Rogo. *On the Track of the Poltergeist.* Englewood Cliffs, NJ: Prentice-Hall, 1986; William Roll. *The Poltergeist.* Garden City, NY: Nelson Doubleday, Inc., 1972; Ian Stevenson. "Are Poltergeists Living or Are They Dead?" *The Journal of the American Society for Psychical Research* 66, no. 3 (July 1972): 233–52; Keith Thomas. *Religion and the Decline of Magic.* New York: Charles Scribner's Sons, 1971; Peter Underwood. *The Ghost Hunter's Guide.* Poole, Dorset, England: Blandford Press, 1986; Lyall Watson. *Beyond Supernature.* New York: Bantam Books, 1987; Colin Wilson. *Poltergeist! A Study in Destructive Haunting.* London: New English Library, 1981.

Positive imaging

See **Creative visualization.**

Positive thinking

See **Creative visualization.**

Positive visualization

See **Creative visualization.**

Possession

The taking over of a person's mind, body, and soul by an external force perceived to be a deity, spirit, demon, entity, or separate personality.

Possession generally is unwanted and troublesome. It has been recognized since antiquity, and has been blamed for virtually every conceivable problem of luck, health, wealth, love, and sanity. Some types of possession, such as by gods or the Holy Spirit, are desirable and voluntary. Some types of mediumship, such as direct voice and channeling, are forms of temporary possession by spirits of the dead or nonphysical entities. The cure for unwanted possession is exorcism, performed according to a specified ritual. Voluntary possession, on the other hand, terminates at the end of a religious ceremony, healing ritual, or sitting.

Except for possession by the Holy Spirit, Christianity regards possession as the work of Satan. Medieval theologians devoted considerable attention to demonic possession. The Devil was said to possess a person by entering the mind and soul or by using an intermediary, such as a witch or wizard, to send a demon into the victim. Bewitched food was a favored explanation. Possession caused the victim to behave in a vile manner and renounce God. The only way to rid the person of the demon or Devil was to perform ritual exorcism. Cases of demonic possession continue to be reported in modern times, and formal exorcisms sometimes are performed by priests.

In Judaism the most feared and evil possession is by a dybbuk, a doomed soul that enters a person's body and causes abominable behavior and great mental and spiritual anguish. The dybbuk is exorcised by a *ba'al shem,* a miracle-working rabbi.

In many societies possession is a fact of daily life that ranges from a nuisance to a serious problem. The victim is most often a woman from the lower classes who believes her personal problems (such as illness, menstrual pain, barrenness, the death of children, miscarriage, abuse by husbands or fathers, or her husband's infidelities) are caused by the intervention of evil spirits. She seeks out an exorcist as one might seek out a psychotherapist. The exorcism provides a way to gain social stature as well as to relieve the problems.

In the West possession is not always viewed as demonic but also as an encounter with confused spirits. It is held that some possessing spirits may be souls of the dead who do not realize they are dead and try to return to a body; these spirits may depart willingly upon being told or invited to leave. In other cases possession may be caused by spirits who are attempting to communicate specific messages or warnings. In either case the victim may experience severe headaches, sleep disorders, strange noises or lights, voices, poltergeist phenomena, and perhaps temporary insanity.

Possession and Mental Illness

The idea that mental illness may be caused by possessing spirits is ancient. It has modern adherents but is not endorsed by the medical establishment.

Early in the twentieth century, Dr. James H. Hyslop, an early president of the American Society for Psychical Research, wrote in his book *Contact with the Other World* (1919) that if people believe in telepathy, then long-distance invasion of a personality, possibly of a low or malevolent nature, is possible. Hyslop also believed that many people suffering from hysteria, multiple personality, dementia praecox, or other mental disturbances showed signs of invasion by discarnate entities. His call to the medical establishment to take such situations into account went largely unheeded. His views were shared by some, most notably Dr. Titus Bull and Carl A. and Anna Wicklund. See **Depossession.**

More recently, M. Scott Peck, a self-described "hardheaded scientist," graduate of Harvard University, and practicing psychiatrist in Connecticut, has said that two of his multiple personality patients also suffered from possession by evil spirits that were intent on destroying their victims' minds. The spirits were exorcised. Peck wrote about the cases in his book *The People of the Lie* (1983).

California psychiatrist Ralph Allison has stated that many cases of multiple personality are the result of spirit possession, both nonthreatening and demonic. His controversial book, *Minds in Many Pieces* (1980), discusses some of these patients and the paranormal occurrences surrounding them.

Other psychiatrists have found that only exorcism, such as invoking the Lord's name, eliminates one or more of the multiple personalities. The efficacy of a religious exorcism probably is due to the patient's own religious beliefs.

In parts of Latin America where Spiritism beliefs are strong, disorders such as epilepsy, schizophrenia, and multiple personality may be treated as possession cases. Allen Kardec, the pseudonymous, French nineteenth-century founder of Spiritism, believed certain illnesses caused by spirits or by fragments of a person's past lives could be treated with the help of spirit guides.

Kardec's theories were fashionable in France for a while, but did not catch on in the rest of Europe. They took root in Latin America, particularly Brazil, where they were compatible with existing traditions.

Brazilians still practice healing according to "Kardecismo," as Spiritism is called, or similar practices such as Umbanda or Candomblé. Many physicians and psychiatrists are Spiritists. See **Spiritism.**

Voluntary Possession

In many non-Western cultures, communication with spirits and deities is central to religious worship. Possession by a god shows the possessed to be worthy of the god's notice and protection. In such ceremonies, worshipers chant and dance until they are "mounted" by a god, becoming the god's "horse," and take on that god's personal characteristics. For as long as possession lasts—perhaps several hours—the worshiper exhibits the speech, habits, and behavior of the god. He or she becomes oblivious to pain or extremes in temperature, and may issue prophecies. See **Macumba; Santería; Vodoun.**

The most similar counterpart in Christianity is voluntary possession by the Holy Spirit. The origin is the possession experienced by the apostles of Christ on the first day of Pentecost. The Book of Acts describes how flames appeared above their heads, and that they spoke in tongues unknown to them. Speaking in unknown tongues and other ecstatic communion with God characterized early Christian worship, but was replaced by more austere practices. See **Glossolalia.**

Ecstatic communion has been revived in modern times by the Pentecostal movement, founded in 1901 when a group of Kansas worshipers were filled with the Holy Spirit. Pentecostals may speak in tongues, perform faith healing, and writhe on the floor. The largest group of Pentecostals in the United States is the Assemblies of God, with thousands of members worldwide. See **Charismatic renewal; Exorcism; Pentecostals.**

Sources: Martin Ebon. *The Devil's Bride, Exorcism: Past and Present.* New York: Harper & Row, 1974; Adam Crabtree. *Multiple Man: Explorations in Possession and Multiple Personality.* New York: Praeger, 1985; Richard Cavendish, ed. *Mysteries of the Unexplained.* New York: McGraw-Hill, 1974; D. Scott Rogo. *The Infinite Boundary.* New York: Dodd, Mead & Co., 1987; Bruce Kapferer. *A Celebration of Demons.* Bloomington: Indiana University Press, 1983; Melita Denning and Osborne Phillips. *Voudoun Fire: The Living Reality of Mystical Religion.* St. Paul, MN: Llewellyn Publications, 1979; J. Gordon Melton. *Encyclopedic Handbook of Cults in America.* New York and London: Garland Publishing Inc., 1986; Malachi Martin. *Hostage to the Devil.* New York: Harper & Row, 1976; Guy Lyon Playfair. *The Unknown Power.* New York: Pocket Books, 1975.

Postcognition

See **Retrocognition.**

Power point (also power place, power center)

A location, site, object, or edifice believed to be sacred, or to possess magical or supernatural energies, or to be the dwelling place of spirits of the dead, nature spirits, or gods. The "power" at power points emanates from an ineffable spiritual source, identified as cosmic in origin or part of the living Earth. Coming in contact with it instills feelings of wonder, awe, fear, fascination, and mystery.

Thousands of power points exist all over the Earth, dating to antiquity. Many are natural, such as mountains, streams, rivers, lakes, springs, forests, and caves, which are places where the universal life force, the force that sustains all things in the cosmos, is believed to be concentrated.

Mountains in particular are holy places; their elevations take them nearer to the heavens and make them ideal abodes of gods and centers of the cosmos. For example, the Himalayas are the embodiment of the Hindu god, Himalaya; the most sacred peak, Mt. Kailas, is occupied by Shiva, god of destruction, who sits on the summit in meditation. The summit of Mt. Fuji is the divine mandala of the Buddha Sengen Dainichi. The Greek pantheon lived on Mt. Olympus. The Hopi venerate the San Francisco Peaks as the abodes of ancestral spirits and kachinas. Accordingly, to be closer to the life force and to the gods, the human race throughout history has erected shrines, temples, monasteries, churches, and other holy places on or near sacred peaks.

Water is associated with life-giving and healing, and numerous water sources are venerated for their healing powers, such as the Ganges River in India and the spring at Our Lady of the Lourdes in France, which attract thousands of pilgrims every year. See **Marian apparitions.** Water sources, including wells, are widely believed to be gates to the underworld, occupied and guarded by nature spirits who may bestow good fortune if propitiated or addressed with a charm.

Many of the greatest power points have had some kind of structure erected over them, such as the pyramids of Egypt and Central America, megalithic sites, burial mounds, temples, astronomical sites, and Gothic cathedrals. Early builders perhaps either intuited the *genius loci* (the spirit of a place) where they felt energized, or determined it through observation and measurement of forces. According to the theory of leys, various ancient sacred sites are connected by lines of earth energy, and certain sites are vortices that radiate multiple lines. According to another theory, developed after World War II by a German doctor, Ernst Hartmann, the Earth has a grid pattern of telluric energy lines influenced by underground streams. See **Dowsing; Feng shui; Leys.**

Many manmade edifices at power points are believed to have been constructed according to sacred geometry (also called sacred architecture), thus adding to their power. In sacred geometry perfect forms may be made visible through mathematical formulae. Pythagoras is known for articulating sacred geometry, though he was not the first to use it. The pyramids of Egypt, the Greek Parthenon, and nearly all the Romanesque and Gothic cathedrals throughout Europe were designed according to this mystical philosophy of numbers. See **Pyramids; Pythagoras.**

Dowsers get reactions at power points, including the indication that sacred sanctuaries may be built over blind springs. Scientific instruments placed at sites have recorded anomalous levels of electromagnetic or radioactive energies. It is not known whether such energies occur naturally, or whether they were created (at least in part) by the erection of monuments such as megaliths and temples.

Paranormal phenomena are frequently reported at power points, including apparitions, earth lights, and poltergeist disturbances. Some sites are believed to emit noises and ultrasound signals; one of the Colossi of Memnon, Egypt, once was said to issue a musical note at dawn

Power point (also power place, power center)

each day. In addition, individuals have reported psi phenomena such as clairvoyance and retrocognition, as well as out-of-body experiences. Statistical evidence indicates a possible link between geomagnetic field activity and some psi activity in humans, thus suggesting that the phenomena are caused by the energies at the sites.

Mystical experiences often occur at power points, thus drawing spiritual pilgrims. For example, the Lakota undertake vision quests at the sacred Bear Butte in the Black Hills of South Dakota, where they spend three days fasting and praying. Sometimes ecstasies come unexpectedly: John Muir, the founder of the Sierra Club, and Henry David Thoreau recorded some of their experiences while out in the wilderness.

In 1977 the Dragon Project Trust was founded in Britain to research energetic and paranormal phenomena at ancient sites. Research involves psychic archaeology using psychics, sensitives, and dowsers, and individuals with scientific, technical, and geomantic skills. Paul Devereux, founding director of the Dragon Project Trust, has theorized that understanding these phenomena may lead to an understanding of, and possibly communication with, a planetary intelligence or spirit, which he calls "Earthmind." See **Avebury; Earth lights; Glastonbury; Medicine wheels; Megaliths; Planetary consciousness; Psychic archaeology; Sedona, Arizona; Stonehenge; Universal life force.**

Sources: Edwin Bernbaum. "Sacred Mountains." *Parabola* 13, no. 4 (Winter 1988): 12–18; Paul Devereux. *Places of Power.* London: Blandford, 1990; Paul Devereux and John Steele, David Kubrin. *Earthmind: A Modern Adventure in Ancient Wisdom.* New York: Harper & Row, 1989; Jamake Highwater. "Spirit Dwellings." *Omni* (May 1988): 64–75; Blanche Merz. *Points of Cosmic Energy.* Saffron Walden, England: C. W. Daniel Co., Ltd., 1985; Patrick F.

Sheeran. "Place and Power." *New Realities* 13, no. 1 (Summer 1990): 28–32; Jim Swan. "Magical Places of Power." *New Realities* 7, no. 1 (September/October 1986): 56–62.

Prayer

An act of communing with the Divine or the supernatural. There are numerous types of public and private prayers, which are universal in religions. Prayer, said philosopher and psychologist William James, "is the very soul and essence of religion" (*Varieties of Religious Experience,* 1902). Depending on the religion, prayers may acknowledge a supreme deity; a pantheon of deities, saints, and divine personages; ancestral spirits; or the spirits and forces of nature.

The simplest forms of prayer are petitions for oneself or for others, thanksgivings, and intercessions. These are directions of psychic energy toward accomplishment of a goal, and involve words, symbols, and images. Petitions and intercessions are enormous sources of power and energy, and have been credited with great accomplishments and miraculous healings. Their driving force is love; prayers that are selfish or offered by unbelievers are ineffective. Norman Vincent Peale is one of the best-known Christian advocates of the power of prayer.

Healer Ambrose Worrall said all thoughts are prayers. The accepted idea of prayers—memorized phrases and verse learned in church—are good mind cleansers, he said, but lack the dynamism to be effective. An effective prayer concentrates not on the elimination of an existing condition, but on the creation of a desired condition.

The highest forms of prayer are mystical in nature and are contemplative and meditative; these constitute higher states of awareness and being, the highest of which is union with the Divine. In such states words, symbols, and images fall away. Mystical prayer opens up aspects of reality beyond rational thought; it is a movement of mind and soul into the Source of all being. As Christian mystic Julian of Norwich observed, "Prayer oneth the soul with God." See **Mystical experiences.**

Various definitions of the types of prayer have been made. St. Teresa of Avila described four stages of prayer: (1) recollection, a process of concentration and withdrawal; (2) quiet, the first stage of union with God, in which the mind is open to the Divine and the desire for material things falls away; (3) tumescence, a state of wisdom arising from inspiration; and (4) union with the Divine.

Prayer and Psi

Psychic phenomena and powers are associated with both prayer and meditation. The literature of Western mystics describes clairvoyance, clairaudience, levitation, precognition, prophecy, and so on as unsought by-products of mystical prayer. St. Anthony clairvoyantly saw one man dead and his brother dying a day's walk away; he directed monks to the spot to save the dying man. St. Francis, the thirteenth-century founder of the Franciscan Order, reportedly levitated many times while in rapture, as did the seventeenth-century Franciscan St. Joseph of Cupertino, who could "fly" short distances and stay aloft for a considerable time. Such phenomena may be compared to the *siddhis* of Eastern meditation and yoga. See **Levitation; Siddhis; Transcendental Meditation (TM); Yoga.**

Early in the history of parapsychology, attention was directed to the relationship between psi and prayer. Frank Laubach's popular book, *Prayer: The Mightiest Force in the World* (1946), advocated ceaseless prayer, which Laubach believed had the power to change the world. In the 1950s Reverend Franklin Loehr, a chemical engineer who founded the Religious Research foundation in Los Angeles, conducted experiments on the power of prayer on seeds and seedlings. He found that the prayed-for seeds and seedlings usually sprouted faster and grew more quickly than those which had no prayer. Similar studies were conducted by others with healers who prayed over seeds, plants and water for plants. See **Plants, psychism of.**

In the late 1960s, Karlis Osis, then director of research for the American Society for Psychical Research, conducted an informal research of religious practices and psi with small groups of meditators. Participants often were in apparent telepathic communication and shared the same visions.

Prayer done in a group is attested to be far more powerful than prayer done by an individual, for a synergy takes place in group dynamics. The Osis participants, for example, shared a buoyancy of mood, feelings of openness and meaningfulness, and intense love. The synergy may be due to the synchronization of brain waves, as shown in some studies of meditators. See **Healing, faith and psychic; Meditation.**

Sources: John Ferguson. *An Illustrated Encyclopedia of Mysticism and the Mystery Religions.* New York: Seabury Press, 1976; F. C. Happold. *Mysticism: A Study and an Anthology.* Rev. ed. Harmondsworth, Middlesex, England: Penguin Books, 1970; F. C. Happold. *Prayer and Meditation: Their Nature and Practice.* Harmondsworth, Middlesex, England: Penguin Books, 1971; William James. *The Varieties of Religious Experience.* 1902. New York: Modern Library, 1936; Geddes MacGregor. *Gnosis: A Renaissance in Christian Thought.* Wheaton, IL: The Theosophical Publishing House, 1979; Thomas Merton. *Contemplative Prayer.* Garden City, NY: Image Books, 1971; Norman Vincent Peale. "Your Prayers Will Get Results." *Plus: The Magazine of Positive Thinking* 38, no. 2, part 1 (March 1987): 1–10; Ry Redd. "Can Prayer or Meditation Invoke Benefits of Psi?" *Journal of Religion and Psychical Research* 10, no. 1 (January 1987): 1–12; D. Scott Rogo. "Researching the Power of Prayer." *Science of Mind* (June 1988): 30–34+; Ambrose Alexander Worrall. "Essay on Prayer." Self-published, 1952.

Precognition

The direct knowledge or perception of the future, obtained through extraordinary means. Precognition is the most frequently reported of all extrasensory perception (ESP) experiences, occurring most often (60 percent to 70 percent) in dreams. It also happens spontaneously in waking visions, auditory hallucinations, thoughts that flash into the mind, and a sense of "knowing." Precognitive knowledge also may be induced through trance, channeling, mediumship, and divination.

The majority of spontaneous precognitive experiences happen within forty-eight hours of the future event, particularly within twenty-four hours. A rare few happen months or even years before the actual event takes place. Severe emotional shock seems to be a major factor in precognition. By a four-to-one ratio, most concern unhappy events, such as death and dying, illness, accidents, and natural disasters. Intimacy also is a key factor; 80 to 85 percent of such experiences involve a spouse, family member or friend with whom one has close emotional ties. The remainder involve casual acquaintances and strangers, most of whom are victims in major disasters such as airplane crashes or earthquakes.

The difference between precognition and premonition is rather blurry. In general precognition involves knowledge of a specific event, while premonition is a sense or feeling that some unknown event is about to happen. See **Premonition.**

While all prophecy is precognition, not all precognition is prophecy; the latter involves an element of divine inspiration. See **Prophecy.**

Precognition has been known and valued since ancient times, when prophets and oracles were sought for their access to the future. The Greeks considered the future immutable. Free will, however, changes the perceived future, as seen in the many cases of people saving their lives and avoiding disasters by changing their plans based upon precognitive information. Psychical researchers estimate that one-third to one-half of all precognitive experiences may provide useful information to avert disasters.

This apparent ability to alter the perceived future makes precognition difficult to understand. If precognition is a glimpse of the true future, then the effects are witnessed before the causes. Such conditions do occur in quantum physics. The most popular theory holds that precognition is a glimpse of a possible future that is based on present conditions and existing information, and which may be altered depending upon acts of free will. That theory implies that the future can cause the past, a phenomenon called "backward causality" or "retrocausality."

Another and controversial theory contends that the precognitive experience itself unleashes a powerful psychokinetic (PK) energy, which then brings the envisioned future to pass. Such self-fulfilling prophecies were examined in the 1960s by London psychiatrist J. A. Barker, who contended in his book, *Scared to Death,* that people who died in the manner and at the time predicted by fortune-tellers were literally "scared to death" and contributed somehow to their own demise. Barker studied more precognitions concerning the Aberfan, Wales, coal slide disaster in 1966, which killed 144 people. He established the British Premonitions Bureau, which collected precognitive data in an attempt to avert disasters. Barker succeeded in finding a number of "human seismographs" who tuned in regularly to disasters but could not accurately pinpoint times.

Despite the difficulty in understanding precognition, it is the easiest form of extrasensory perception to test in the laboratory. The first systematic study of precognition was undertaken in the early twentieth century by J. W. Dunne, a British aeronautics engineer, who published his findings and theories in 1927 in the classic, *An Experiment with Time.* Dunne based his study on his own precognitive dreams, which involved both trivial incidents in his own life and major news events that appeared in the press the day after a dream. When he first realized he was seeing the future in his dreams, Dunne worried that he was "a freak." His worries eased when he discovered that precognitive dreams are common; so common, he concluded, that many people have them without realizing it, perhaps because they do not recall details or fail to properly interpret dream symbols.

Dunne's Theory of Serial Time proposes that time exists in layers of dimensions, each of which may be viewed in different perspectives from different layers. The origin of all the layers is Absolute Time, created by God. Dunne's theory later was rejected by the scientific community.

The next significant systematic research of precognition was begun in the 1930s by J. B. Rhine and Louisa Rhine at the Parapsychological Laboratory at Duke University. J. B. Rhine's original goal was to prove telepathy, but his experiments with ESP cards also revealed precognition and PK. See **ESP cards.** Following Rhine's work other researchers have conducted a variety of experiments for precognition in ongoing research.

One peculiarity of precognition is that one seldom foresees one's own death, perhaps because the trauma is too great for the ego to accept. Some notable exceptions exist: Abraham Lincoln dreamed of his own death six weeks before he was assassinated. His dream was not of being shot and dying, but of being an observer after the fact. He saw a long procession of mourners entering the White House. Going inside, he saw the mourners file past a coffin, and was shocked to see that the coffin contained his own body. American presidents John Garfield and William McKinley also experienced foreknowledge of their violent deaths. See **Dreams; Prediction.**

Sources: J. W. Dunne. *An Experiment with Time.* 1927. London: Faber & Faber Ltd., 1973; Herbert B. Greenhouse. *Premonitions: A Leap into the Future.* New York: Bernard Geis Assoc., 1971; Edgar D. Mitchell. *Psychic Exploration: A Challenge for Science.* Edited by John White. New York: Paragon Books, 1974; Gardner Murphy. "Direct Contacts with Past and Future: Retrocognition and Precognition." *Journal of the American Society for Psychical Research* 61, no. 1 (January 1967): 3–23; Sheila Ostrander and Lynn Schroeder. *Psychic Discoveries Behind the Iron Curtain.* Englewood Cliffs, NJ: Prentice-Hall, 1970; Louisa Rhine. *ESP in Life and Lab.* New York: Collier Books, 1967; Louisa Rhine. *Hidden Channels of the Mind.* New York: William Sloane Assoc., 1961; Russell Targ and Keith Harary. *The Mind Race.* New York: Villard Books, 1984; Russell Targ and Harold Puthoff. *Mind-Reach: Scientists Look at Psychic Ability.* New York: Delacorte Press, 1977; Lyall Watson. *Beyond Supernature.* New York: Bantam Books, 1987; Joan Windsor. *The Inner Eye: Your Dreams Can Make You Psychic.* Englewood Cliffs, NJ: Prentice-Hall, 1985; Benjamin B. Wolman, ed. *Handbook of Parapsychology.* New York: Van Nostrand Reinhold, 1977; Danah Zohar. *Through the Time Barrier: A Study in Precognition and Modern Physics.* London: William Heinemann Ltd., 1982.

Prediction

A type of prophecy in which information about future events is obtained through psychic gifts, divine inspiration, the reading of signs, or the altering of conscious-ness. While prophecy is of a grand scale, relating to large groups or nations of peo-ple, predictions concern the individual. The majority of psychic readings are de-voted to questions about probable events in an individual's future.

Predictions are based on precogni-tion, or direct knowledge of the future. This knowledge is sought through many ways: intuition, dreams, or visions in scrying; or through the reading of signs, such as in astrology, the Tarot, palmistry, numerology, and other methods of divi-nation. In shamanic and oracular cul-tures, mind-altering drugs sometimes are taken to induce prophecy from a divine or supernatural source.

Predictions may be colored by the perceptions and prejudices of the individ-ual. They often are difficult to pinpoint in time, because time is not linear but exists in an ever-present now. See **Displace-ment; Precognition; Psychic reading; Stained-glass window effect.**

Sources: June G. Bletzer. *The Donning In-ternational Encyclopedic Psychic Dictio-nary.* Norfolk, VA: The Donning Co., 1986; Mary Ellen Carter. *Edgar Cayce on Prophecy.* New York: Warner, 1968; Jane Roberts. *Adventures in Consciousness.* New York: Bantam Books, 1979; *Myster-ies of the Unexplained.* Pleasantville, NY: Reader's Digest, 1982.

Premonition

A type of prophecy that is a sense of fore-warning or foreboding of a probable fu-ture event, characterized by a state of anxiety, unease, and a gut-level feeling. Premonitions tend to occur before disas-ters, accidents, deaths, and other trau-matic and emotionally charged events.

There is no clear-cut line between premonition and precognition, which is direct knowledge of the future. In general premonition is sense-oriented, dominated by a syndrome of physical unease, depres-sion, or distress that has no discernible source or reason. "I feel like something bad is going to happen" is a typical ex-pression of a premonition. Precognition, on the other hand, is more precise, in-volving visions or dreams of the event that is yet to take place.

For example, in 1948 the prominent Soviet psychic Wolf Messing traveled to Ashkhabad to give several public perfor-mances of his abilities. As he walked along the streets of the city, he was seized with a terrible dread and an intense desire to get out as soon as possible. The feel-ings were so strong that he canceled his shows—the only time in his entire life that he did so—and left the city. Three days later a massive earthquake leveled Ashkhabad and killed 50,000 people. Messing's premonition saved his life; however, he had no specific forewarning of an earthquake.

On October 21, 1966, twenty-eight adults and 116 children were killed when a landslide of coal waste tumbled down a mountain in Aberfan, Wales, and buried a school. Up to two weeks beforehand, at least two hundred people experienced both premonitions and precognitions about the disaster, according to three sur-veys taken afterward. Premonitions in-cluded depression, a feeling that "some-thing bad" was about to happen (some people accurately pinpointed the day), sensations of choking and gasping for breath, uneasiness, and impressions of coal dust, billowing black clouds, and children running and screaming.

While most premonitions occur in a waking state, some occur in dreams. Since the language of dreams is symbols, the premonition may go unnoticed. If premonitions occur often enough in dreams, the individual may learn to rec-ognize distinguishing symbols or emo-tional tone.

Premonitions are an intuitive early warning system, probably occurring frequently but too subtly to be noticed by the conscious mind. Some premonitions apparently register on the subconscious and cause people to act, without knowing why. In the 1960s W. E. Cox examined rail passenger loads on American trains that had accidents between 1950 and 1955. He compared passenger loads on the same runs on the day of the accident, each of the preceding seven days, the preceding fourteenth day and twenty-eighth day. He found a remarkable drop-off in passenger counts on some but not all accident days. One, the Chicago & East Illinois *Georgian,* was carrying only nine passengers on the day of its accident on June 15, 1952; five days beforehand it had carried a more typical sixty-two passengers. Cox concluded that many people who had intended to travel on disaster-bound trains had unconsciously altered their plans or missed the trains by being late.

The same factor may prevent many people from sailing on doomed ships. The *Titanic* carried only 58 percent of its passenger load on its disastrous maiden voyage in April 1912, in which 1,502 of 2,207 passengers perished when the ship sank after colliding with an iceberg. A group of twenty-two stokers may have been saved by collective subconscious premonition. They arrived late at the Southampton dock, and Captain Smith declared the *Titanic* would sail without them. When the *Empress of Ireland* sank in the Lawrence River in 1914, its first-class was two-thirds empty and its second-class half-empty.

Psychiatrist Ian Stevenson recorded more than nineteen cases of premonitions and precognitions about the *Titanic* in England, America, Canada, and Brazil, which occurred during the two weeks prior to the ship's sailing date of April 10. Between April 3 and 10, several people, including J. Pierpont Morgan, abruptly canceled their passage. Some people canceled after dreaming the ship

was doomed; others said it was bad luck to sail on a ship's maiden voyage. Some of the survivors said they experienced uneasy feelings but sailed anyway.

No one knows why some people are alerted to danger through premonitions, while others are not. Premonitions may be affected by an individual's overall psychic openness.

Following the Aberfan disaster, a British Premonitions Bureau was established in January 1967 to collect and screen early warnings in an effort to avert disasters. A year later the Central Premonitions Bureau was established in New York City for the same purpose. Though called "premonitions" bureaus, they sought specific precognitive information, not vague feelings of unease. Both bureaus struggled along for years on low budgets and with public relations obstacles. Most of the tips they received did not come to pass; those that did often were inaccurate in terms of time, rendering them equally useless. See **Clairsentience; Precognition.**

Sources: Rustie Brown. *The Titanic, the Psychic & the Sea.* Lomita, CA: Blue Harbor Press, 1981; W. E. Cox. "Precognition: An Analysis, II." *Journal of the American Society for Psychical Research* 50, no. 1 (January 1956): 99–109; Herbert B. Greenhouse. *Premonitions: A Leap into the Future.* New York: Bernard Geis Assoc., 1971; Henry Gris and William Dick. *The New Soviet Psychic Discoveries.* Englewood Cliffs, NJ: Prentice-Hall, 1978; Edgar D. Mitchell. *Psychic Exploration.* Edited by John White. New York: G. P. Putnam's Sons, 1974; *Mysteries of the Unexplained.* Pleasantville, NY: Reader's Digest Assn., 1982; Jane Roberts. *The Nature of Personal Reality.* Englewood Cliffs, NJ: Prentice-Hall, 1974; Benjamin B. Wolman, ed. *Handbook of Parapsychology.* New York: Van Nostrand Reinhold, 1977; Danah Zohar. *Through the Time Barrier.* London: William Heinemann Ltd., 1982.

Prophecy

A divinely inspired vision or revelation of great events to come, which are of such magnitude as to affect races, groups of people, and countries. All prophecies come from precognition, or knowledge of the future, but not all precognitive experiences are prophecies; the key difference is the divine spark or inspired element. Sometimes, however, little or no distinction is made between a prophecy and a prediction. In religions prophecies are made by prophets, great men and women divinely chosen to preach the divine message, such as Jesus, Muhammad, and Siddhartha Gautama (Buddha). In another sense prophecies are psychic readings of the collective unconscious, the anticipation of the manifestations of the collective will.

In ancient times prophecies were made by oracles, prophets and prophetesses who went into ecstatic trances and allowed deities to speak through them. The ecstasy was induced through various methods, such as by inhaling the smoke of sacred wood or drinking the blood of a sacrificed animal. The ancient Egyptians used cult statues that spoke. The Greeks placed great store in oracles, and considered their prophecies unchangeable.

The ancient Hebrews had many prophets, or *navi*, a term which comes from the root for "to well up, to gush forth." The Old Testament contains numerous prophets and prophecies; eighteen of the thirty-nine books are ascribed to prophets. The origin and nature of prophecy is not clear, but it is evident from the Old Testament that men appointed by God to become prophets could not resist doing so, sometimes becoming transformed in the process, as was Saul, who became St. Paul. Moses, who initially resisted his calling, was described as a prophet unequaled for his acts and mighty deeds in Deuteronomy 34:10–12. Some prophets had priestly functions (Samuel and Ezekiel), and Isaiah was a member of the nobility; but many prophets were removed from the functions of church and state, and challenged both whenever the need arose.

The Hebrew prophets formed a professional class. Their primary concern was adherence to the path of righteousness by both individual and nation, though some were often sought for menial divination matters such as the location of a farmer's lost asses. Elijah established the Sons of the Prophets, an order which lived to prepare for the birth of the Messiah.

The Hebrews sometimes used divination methods to prophesy, usually the observation of natural phenomena and patterns. Many prophesied in ecstatic states, in which the spirit of Yahweh was believed to possess them. Some used alcohol and music to induce states of ecstasy when important prophetic visions were required.

The *Didache,* an early Christian manual written in the first century A.D., uses the terms "apostle" and "prophet" interchangeably, and gives instructions for telling the difference between true and false prophets.

In Islam the prophet Muhammad received divine inspiration so that he could renew the guidance given prophets before him, including those in Judaism and Christianity. Muslims believe that all peoples throughout history have had prophets to guide them; the number of prophets throughout history is as high as 240,000 by some estimations.

Muhammad was chosen as the Seal of the Prophets, the last of all prophets for the rest of time. The Koran is the product of divine revelations given him by an angel over a twenty-year period.

Mormonism got its start in 1823 when Joseph Smith, Jr., became the prophet of a new religious order during a mystical experience in which he learned of an ancient book recorded by prophets and written on plates of gold by the prophet-historian Mormon. Smith was led to the plates after a series of revelations; the book, known as The Book of Mormon, is the gospel for the Church of Jesus Christ of Latter-day Saints. See **Church of Jesus Christ of Latter-day Saints, the.**

Throughout history psychically gifted laypeople also have been called prophets. Nostradamus (1503–1566) believed his visions were inspired by God. Thomas the Rhymer, a thirteenth-century Scot, said he was given his gift of prophecy by the Queen of Elfland. Another Scottish prophet, Odhar Coinneach of the sixteenth century, also said he obtained his gift from the fairies, who gave him a magic holed stone. Edgar Cayce (1877–1945) is often called the "prophets' prophet." Cayce left a legacy of more than 14,000 trance readings. Jeane Dixon, American psychic, prophesied the death of President John F. Kennedy. See **Cayce, Edgar; Dixon, Jeane; Nostradamus; Oracle; Prediction.**

Sources: Mary Ellen Carter. *Edgar Cayce on Prophecy.* New York: Warner Books, 1968; Jean-Charles de Fontbrune. *Nostradamus: Countdown to Apocalypse.* New York: Holt, Rinehart and Winston, 1980; James G. Frazer. *The Golden Bough: The Roots of Religion and Folklore.* New York: Avenel Books, 1981; Michael Loewe and Carmen Blacker. *Oracles and Divination.* Boulder, CO: Shambhala, 1981; Edgar D. Mitchell. *Psychic Exploration: A Challenge for Science.* Edited by John White. New York: G. P. Putnam's Sons, 1974; Geoffrey Parrinder, ed. *World Religions from Ancient History to Present.* New York: Facts On File, 1971; Merlin Stone. *When God Was a Woman.* San Diego: Harcourt Brace Jovanovich, 1976.

Prophet, Elizabeth Clare

See **Alternative religious movements.**

Prophet, Mark

See **Alternative religious movements.**

Psi

The twenty-third letter of the Greek alphabet, generally used in parapsychology to include extrasensory perception (ESP) and psychokinesis (PK). In 1946 English psychologist Dr. Robert Thouless and his colleague, Dr. W. P. Weisner, suggested "psi" as a designation for ESP and PK because both are so closely related. The term has since inaccurately expanded in popular usage to include almost any paranormal experience or phenomenon.

Theories of Psi

Despite decades of research, psi continues to elude physical and quasi-physical theories of how it functions; it operates outside the bounds of time and space. No physical variable influences psi test results in the laboratory. Various theories that psi is some type of wave, particle, force, or field have been proposed and discarded. Psi is not, nor is it affected by, the four forces of physics: strong nuclear force, weak nuclear force, gravitational force, or electromagnetic force. Psi is not subject to the laws of thermodynamics or the law of gravity. It requires no exchange of energy, which is particularly remarkable in the case of apparent PK: for example, according to the mechanical laws of physics, the dematerialization of a copper penny would require the energy of a small nuclear bomb. Nor is psi governed by the theory of relativity, which holds that no particle or object can move faster than the speed of light, or 186,000 miles a second.

Failure to explain psi in physical terms has forced researchers to look for alternative explanations. Some occultists believe psi is a "vibration" that manifests throughout the universe, but scientists regard that view with great skepticism.

Physiological Characteristics Associated with Psi

Since psi is intangible, one way scientists have attempted to identify it is through measurements of involuntary physiological processes in the autonomic nervous system of laboratory test subjects. The most common measures are the galvanic skin response (GSR), which records sweat gland activity, and the plethysmograph, which measures changes in blood volume in the finger that are caused by dilation or constriction of blood vessels. Less frequently used is the electroencephalograph (EEG), which measures brain-wave activity. The GSR and plethysmograph indicate emotional arousal, and are used in psi tests of emotionally charged versus emotionally neutral targets. Autonomic activity increases when information that is emotionally charged for the percipient appears to be conveyed psychically.

Studies with ganzfeld stimulation show that an alpha state of brain-wave activity appears to be conducive to psi. Psi performance also improves with positive mood and expectation and a friendly atmosphere provided by the experimenter. It decreases with anxiety, negative mood and expectation, boredom, and a hostile environment provided by the experimenter. See **Altered states of consciousness; Animal psi; Decline/incline effects; Dreams; Experimenter effect; ESP (extrasensory perception); Ganzfeld stimulation; Mysticism; Parapsychology; Plants, psychism of; Psychic; Psychokinesis (PK); Sheep/goat effect.**

Sources: Alfred Douglas. *Extrasensory Powers: A Century of Psychical Research.* London: Victor Gollancz Ltd., 1976; Hoyt L. Edge, Robert L. Morris, John Palmer, and Joseph H. Rush. *Foundations of Parapsychology.* Boston: Routledge & Kegan Paul, 1986; Lawrence LeShan. *The Medium, the Mystic, and the Physicist: Toward a General Theory of the Paranormal.* New York: Viking Press, 1974; Lawrence LeShan. *Alternate Realities.* New York: M. Evans & Co., 1967; Edgar D. Mitchell. *Psychic Exploration: A Challenge for Science.* Edited by John White. New York: Paragon Books, 1974; J. B. Rhine. *The Reach of the Mind.* New York: William Sloane Assoc., 1947; Benjamin B. Wolman, ed. *Handbook of Parapsychology.* New York: Van Nostrand Reinhold, 1977.

Psi hitting and psi missing

Terms characterizing responses on laboratory tests of psi guessing games. An accurate response is called a "psi hit" and an inaccurate response a "psi miss." Results of hits and misses are figured against chance. The performance of a test subject may be affected his or her overall attitude toward psi (see **Sheep/goat effect**), the comfort or discomfort established by the experimenter, or by distortions in psi reception (see **Displacement**). Boredom with repetitive testing increases psi missing. In some experiments the subject is directed to deliberately miss the targets, called "low aiming." In that respect the "miss" becomes a "hit." See **Psi.**

Sources: Gertrude Schmeidler, ed. *Extrasensory Perception.* New York: Atherton Press, 1969; Benjamin B. Wolman, ed. *Handbook of Parapsychology.* New York: Van Nostrand Reinhold, 1977.

Psilocybin

See **Drugs in mystical and psychic experiences; Leary, Timothy; Ram Dass.**

Psionics

See **Applied psi.**

Psychic

A person with exceptional ability to acquire information through extrasensory perception (ESP) and/or affect objects with psychokinesis (PK) on demand. Some psychics use their talent in a professional capacity. Psychics are not necessarily the same as mediums, who obtain their information from spirits of the dead through temporary trance possession. A psychic may have mediumistic abilities, and vice versa. Some psychics also possess healing ability.

Many people claim to be "psychic" because they have occasional ESP or PK experiences, or because they are highly intuitive (see Intuition). Most such experiences are spontaneous. However, even professional psychics are not 100 percent accurate, nor can they always perform on demand.

Psychics generally acquire their talent in one of two ways: They are born with it and manifest their abilities in childhood; or they suffer a severe or life-threatening emotional or physical trauma that triggers the ability. The subsequent experiences can be unsettling, even frightening, especially when they are precognitive dreams or visions of death and disaster. Some psychics who fall into the second category at first fear they are suffering insanity. Most, however, find that they cannot rid themselves of their gifts and thus learn to live with them and use them. Every psychic develops a unique method of accessing and controlling his or her power.

Throughout history psychics have filled various roles: priest or priestess, prophet, soothsayer, seer, diviner, fortuneteller, healer, shaman, wizard, and witch. In some societies psychics have occupied high positions in state or religion. In the modern West, in the latter part of the twentieth century, some efforts have been made to apply psychics to a host of professional fields. See Applied psi.

Any person can develop at least some psychic ability with training and practice. Success varies, however, and seldom reaches the level of extraordinary psychics whose gifts are innate or acquired through trauma.

Fears of Psychic Abilities

The opening of psychic powers often brings fears about the consequences of possessing or using them. Psychics must learn to overcome fears and adjust to psychic ability as a normal part of life.

According to studies of psychics, common fears include: the unknown; loss of control of the process, resulting in possession; loss of control of life direction; sickness and depression resulting from empathy to others; forced and unalterable self-changes; isolation from ordinary people; confusion over "reality"; inability to communicate experiences; frightening others; temptations to misuse powers; and being defined and validated by powers. Parapsychologists who have an unconscious fear of psi may unwittingly skew their experimentation results through the "experimenter effect." See ESP (extrasensory perception); Experimenter effect; Psi; Psychic reading.

Sources: Hugh Lynn Cayce. *Venture Inward.* New York: Harper & Row, 1964; J. B. Rhine. *New Frontiers of the Mind.* New York: Farrar & Rinehart, 1937; "You Can Be Your Own Psychic." Virginia Beach, VA: ARE Press, 1987; Charles T. Tart. "Psychic's Fears of Psychic Powers." *The Journal of the American Society for Psychical Research* 80, no. 3 (July 1986): 279–92; U. S. Williams. "Laurie McQuary: From Coma to Psychic Aid for Business." *Northwest Women in Business* (March/April 1987): 16–18.

Psychic archaeology

The application of clairvoyance and other psychic skills to the field of archaeology, especially in the location of dig sites and the identification of artifacts. Sometimes called "intuitive archaeology," psychic archaeology is controversial despite some impressive successes.

The primary psychic skill employed is psychometry, in which a psychic handles objects or photographs to receive clairvoyant impressions related to an object, its history, and its uses and users. See **Psychometry.** Other psychic skills employed are dowsing, used for locating optimum dig sites; retrocognition, or seeing into the past; and automatic writing, in which information is channeled from entities or the dead. See **Automatic writing; Dowsing; Retrocognition.** Psychics who are experienced in remote viewing—clairvoyance of remote sites based upon geographic coordinates—have been shown to be well-suited to psychic archaeology. See **Remote viewing.**

In the broadest sense, psychic archaeology is employed by virtually all archaeologists and anthropologists who use their intuition, and even dreams, to guide them. One of the more dramatic cases of the latter is that of Herman V. Hilprecht, who in 1893 was able to decipher a cuneiform inscription following a dream in which an ancient temple priest gave him key information.

Perhaps the first, best-known case of deliberate psychic archaeology was Frederick Bligh Bond's use of automatic writing in the excavations of the ruins of Glastonbury Abbey in England. Bond, an architect, was appointed by the Church of England in 1907 to find the remains of two chapels. According to records the chapels had once existed but had been destroyed after Henry VIII closed all monasteries following his break with the Catholic church.

Unbeknownst to the Church of England, Bond was an occultist. He sought the services of his friend John Allen Bartlett, who was an automatic writer, and with him petitioned spirits associated with the abbey to help him locate the chapels' ruins. Bond received information in Latin and Old English, as well as drawings, from an entity who identified himself as "Gulielmus Monachus," or "William the Monk." The monk, plus other spirits who collectively called themselves the "Watchers from the Other Side" and the "Company of Glastonbury," provided details of the Edgar and Loretto Chapels. The spirits said they obtained their information from a "Universal Memory." They said Henry VIII had brought about the downfall of the abbey out of his greed, and it was their desire to see Glastonbury rise once again to spiritual prominence. Bond did not assume the Watchers were the spirits of the dead, but thought they might have been part of his own deep unconscious.

In the ensuing excavations, Bond found everything exactly as the spirits had indicated. He kept the source of his success secret until 1917, when he published his full account in *The Gate of Remembrance.* The Church of England was angered and embarrassed, and forced Bond out by 1922, when excavations were stopped. Bond went to America, where he continued to receive information from spirits about Glastonbury, King Arthur (who reportedly was buried there), and the Holy Grail. All of Bond's books continue to be banned from the Glastonbury Abbey bookshop. See **Glastonbury.**

In the 1930s the psychometry feats of Stefan Ossowiecki, a Polish chemical engineer who received psychic training from a Jewish mystic, led to psychic archaeology experiments by Polish scholars. Until his death in 1945 at the hands of the Nazis, Ossowiecki participated in various experiments with artifacts. Some of his information was not verified for years; for example, he stated that the Magdalenian people, who existed about 15,000 years ago, had possessed the bow and arrow, which archaeologists at the time disputed. It has since been proved that the bow and arrow date much earlier, to the Neanderthals.

Ossowiecki believed he got his information from the Akashic Records. Edgar

Cayce believed likewise; in his many trance readings, he provided information about ancient Egypt, the Sphinx, and the Great Pyramid, some of which has been verified. Cayce also spoke a great deal about the legendary Atlantis, the existence of which remains unproven. See **Atlantis**.

Since the 1970s psychic archaeology has been used to find dig sites in North America, Egypt, and elsewhere. One academic supporter has been Canadian archaeologist J. Norman Emerson, who has worked with psychic George McMullen. McMullen has said he sees movie-like images while holding artifacts, and is aided in his work by beings of light. In the late 1970s, McMullen was part of a team put together by the Mobius Group, a consulting service in Los Angeles, which went to Egypt to test the viability of psychic archaeology. McMullen and psychic Hella Hammid provided information that helped locate the buried city of Marea, the ruins of Marc Antony's palace, and the probable sites of the library of Alexandria, Cleopatra's palace, and Marc Antony's tomb. The team also found the underwater ruins of a temple and the lighthouse of Pharos in the eastern harbor of Alexandria.

Although some researchers claim high and reliable success rates with psychics, others have conducted experiments with wrapped and unwrapped artifacts that show psychic archaeology is not reliable. One seemingly insurmountable drawback to psychic archaeology is the reliability of psychically obtained information about past cultures that cannot be verified through other sources. Nonetheless, it may continue to be valuable as an aid to locating dig sites. See **Applied psi; Intuition**.

Sources: Frederick Bligh Bond. *The Gate of Remembrance.* Oxford: Basil Blackwell, 1921; Hoyt L. Edge, Robert L. Morris, John Palmer, and Joseph H. Rush. *Foundations of Parapsychology.* Boston: Rout-

ledge & Kegan Paul, 1986; Jeffrey Goodman. *Psychic Archaeology: Time Machine to the Past.* New York: G. P. Putnam's Sons, 1977; David Jones. *Visions of Time: Experiments in Psychic Archaeology.* Wheaton, IL: The Theosophical Publishing House, 1979; Stephan A. Schwartz. *The Secret Vaults of Time.* New York: Grosset & Dunlap, 1978; Stephan A. Schwartz. *The Alexandria Project.* New York: Delacorte Press, 1983; Alan Vaughn. "Intuition, Precognition, and the Art of Prediction." *The Futurist* (June 1982): 5–10; Colin Wilson. *The Psychic Detectives.* San Francisco: Mercury House, 1985.

Psychic attack

An allegedly paranormal assault upon humans or animals that causes physical or mental distress, injury, illness, or even death. Psychic attack is said to happen by two means: (1) the human direction, such as by a sorcerer, of nonphysical agents such as malevolent spirits, demons, or thought-forms; and (2) a human assault accomplished by out-of-body projection of a double or astral form.

In sorcery the equivalent of psychic attack is a curse. Some tribal sorcerers are renowned for their alleged ability to magically kill others with a wasting disease that seems to resist medical help and reportedly leaves some victims virtually bloodless by the time of death. Some magical rituals involve "sending," in which the curse is fatally delivered to the victim by an animal familiar in the form of a snake or scorpion or other fearsome creature. In other rituals a substitute for the victim, such as a doll or snip of the victim's hair, serves as a sympathetic magical link that transmits the attacks.

The occultist Dion Fortune wrote extensively on psychic attack, and said it is much more common than believed. In her classic work on the subject, *Psychic Self-Defence* (1930), Fortune described her own experiences combating psychic attack. The first occurred when she was twenty and was nearly psychologically destroyed by an employer whom she believed was adept in occultism. Fortune suffered a nervous breakdown and believed her aura had been depleted in much the same way that a battery can be drained.

The most common symptom of psychic attack is the "hag syndrome," in which the victim awakens feeling a crushing weight on the chest accompanied by paralysis. In some attacks the victim may see a form, hear noises, or smell vile odors. Nightmares occur in some cases.

The hag syndrome has been documented since ancient times and occurs presently in an estimated 15 percent of the adult population worldwide. There are no definitive explanations for it. The second-century Roman physician Galen attributed it to indigestion. In the Middle Ages, incubi and succubi were blamed. The modern Freudian psychoanalyst Ernest Jones said sexual repression was the cause. Another modern theory suggests sleep disorders are responsible. Various folklore traditions attribute hag attacks to witchcraft and sorcery.

The hag syndrome also resembles some cases of alleged vampirism recorded in Eastern Europe dating to about the fifteenth century. Nocturnal attacks upon the living were blamed upon the restless spirits of certain dead. The attacks stopped when the suspected corpses were disinterred (they were reportedly found to be incorrupt) and were staked, dismembered, or burned.

Other symptoms of psychic attack, according to Fortune, include feelings of overwhelming dread and fear, which deteriorate to nervous exhaustion, mental breakdown, and a physical wasting away of body tissue; the presence of bruises on the body after nighttime astral attacks; odd footprints about the area; inexplicable outbreaks of fire; poltergeist phenomena; and the precipitation of slime, as though armies of slugs had crawled

across the floor. Philosopher William James, writing in *The Varieties of Religious Experience* (1902), records a man's description of an apparent hag attack characterized by an invisible presence evoking a feeling of horror, a sensation of pressure on the chest, and "a large tearing vital pain."

To be most effective, psychic attacks are supposed to be launched during the waning moon and especially at the new moon. The moon is said to govern psychic forces, and these phases rule the so-called left-hand path, or evil path, of magic. See **Moon.**

According to Fortune psychic vampirism, another form of psychic attack, is rare. She defines a psychic vampire as a person with sharp canine teeth who travels astrally at night to bite victims and suck the life force out of them. The term has degenerated in more recent occult use to mean any person whose presence is tiring and seems to sap the energy of others.

The prescribed defenses against psychic attack are: (1) to sever all contact with the suspected people, places, or paths of study; (2) to avoid going to the sea, for water is the element of psychic forces; (3) to keep the stomach full, which shuts down the psychic centers, which serve as ports of entry; (4) to get plenty of sunshine; (5) to avoid being alone; and (6) for those trained in occultism, to undertake certain protective and banishing rituals. See **Church of Christ, Scientist; Fortune, Dion; Hermetic Order of the Golden Dawn; Thought-form.**

Sources: Dion Fortune. *Psychic Self-Defence.* 1930. 6th ed. York Beach, ME: Samuel Weiser, 1957; Rosemary Ellen Guiley. *The Encyclopedia of Witches and Witchcraft.* New York: Facts On File, 1989; Rosemary Ellen Guiley. *Vampires Among Us.* New York: Pocket Books, 1991; David J. Hufford. *The Terror that Comes in the Night: An Experience-Centered Study of Supernatural Assault Traditions.* Philadelphia: University of

Pennsylvania Press, 1982; William James. *The Varieties of Religious Experience.* 1902. New York: The Modern Library, 1936; Janet and Stewart Farrar. *A Witches' Bible-Compleat.* New York: Magickal Childe, 1984.

Psychic criminology

The use of psychics in the investigation and jury selection of civil and criminal cases. A controversial field, psychic criminology nonetheless has grown in the decades following World War II due to the publicized successes of various celebrity psychics.

Since antiquity seers and dowsers have been sought out to help locate missing persons and solve crimes. The field of modern psychic criminology began taking shape in the mid-nineteenth century, when Joseph R. Buchanan, an American physiologist, coined the term "psychometry" and said it could be used to measure the "soul" of all things. Buchanan further said that the past is entombed in the present. Researchers who followed Buchanan theorized that objects retain imprints of the past and their owners— variously called "vibrations," "psychic ether," "aura," and "odic force"—that could be picked up by sensitives. Psychics who handled objects belonging to crime victims were found to provide information that often could help solve the crime. See **Psychometry**.

Psychic detection was used in Europe during and after World War I. Professor Antal Hermann, a Hungarian sociologist, argued for a wider acceptance of metaphysics and of "suggestive powers" and their use in modern criminology. In the early 1930s, the matter was taken up by the Viennese Criminological Association but was not decided.

In 1925 Sir Arthur Conan Doyle, creator of Sherlock Holmes, predicted that the detectives of the future would be clairvoyants or, if they were not, they would all use clairvoyants. By the latter part of the twentieth century, hundreds of psychics were working regularly with police in North America, Britain, and Europe, though their success was erratic.

Many professional psychics who work in the field prefer to be called "intuitives" or "viewers" to avoid a perceived taint on the term "psychic." Most work *pro bono* for law enforcement, although some accept donations from, or charge fees to, private parties involved in a case.

Law enforcement agencies remain divided over the effectiveness of psychics. Some departments make regular use of selected individuals and have established written procedures for doing so; others feel psychics make no difference in solving cases. Departments that do use psychics often are reluctant to admit it publicly. When sensational cases break, police are overwhelmed with tips from people claiming to be psychic. In the 1980 to 1981 investigation of child murders in Atlanta, Georgia, police received more than 19,000 letters from alleged psychics. All tips were analyzed, but police said none was instrumental in solving the case.

Techniques

Most psychic detection involves psychometry of personal items belonging to the victim—undergarments often are preferred because they seem to yield the strongest "vibrations"—or items found at the crime scene. By handling these psychics say they see images or receive information pertaining to the crime. For example, they may see a reenactment of the crime, or the location of a body or murder weapon, or the location of a suspect's whereabouts. Some feel as though they have entered the perpetrator's mind. Some also receive information through intuitive flashes, dreams, auras, automatic writing, channeling, hypnosis, dowsing, and graphology. Psychics often visit crime scenes to pick up additional information.

Sometimes the information is cryptic—numbers, letters, and vague descriptions—and cannot immediately be deciphered. Psychically obtained information is not always reliable and does not always lead to a solution of a case. Most psychics who work in this field have not been tested scientifically; thus no baseline exists by which to measure the effectiveness of psychic detection work. At the least, however, it provides psychological solace to individuals and can provide law enforcement agencies with more latitude in pursuing leads.

Psychics in the Courtroom

Lawyers sometimes use psychics in selecting juries and in preparing their cases. Psychics predict which prospective jurors will be beneficial for a lawyer's client, and which witnesses for the opposition will prove most damaging to a case. They also advise lawyers when clients or prospective witnesses are lying, and when settlement offers will be made by the other side. Results are mixed, but many lawyers remain open-minded about future use of psychics; some feel the presence of a psychic during selection keeps potential jurors honest in their answers to questions. Defense lawyers for Jean Harris, convicted in 1981 of murdering Dr. Herman Tarnower of Scarsdale, New York, used a psychic in the jury selection. The psychic accurately predicted Harris would be convicted if she testified. Attorney Melvin M. Belli of San Francisco said he has used psychics in jury selection.

The testimony of psychics is inadmissible in court.

Psychic criminology has raised the issue of violation of constitutional rights. It is argued that psychics who pick up information from a suspect's mind might conceivably violate constitutional privacy guaranteed by the Fourth Amendment. As long as psychics stay off the witness stand, that contention may never be tested; rather, psychics may continue to play behind-the-scenes roles. In 1986 lawyers interviewed by *The National Law Journal* foresaw continued and increasing use of psychics in law enforcement. See **Applied psi; Croiset, Gerard; Hurkos, Peter; Remote viewing.**

Sources: Joseph P. Blank. "The Woman Who Sees through Psychic Eyes." *The Reader's Digest* (December 1978): 107–12; Norma Lee Browning. *Peter Hurkos: I Have Many Lives.* Garden City, NY: Doubleday & Co., 1976; Geraldine Cummins. *Unseen Adventures.* London: Rider & Co., 1951; Mary Ann Galante. "Psychics: Lawyers Using Seers to Help Select Juries, Find Missing Children." *The National Law Journal* 8, no. 20 (January 27, 1986): 1+; Whitney S. Hibbard and Raymond W. Worring. *Psychic Criminology: An Operations Manual for Using Psychics in Criminal Investigations.* Springfield, IL: Charles C Thomas, 1982; Jeffrey Mishlove and William H. Kautz. "An Emerging New Discipline!" *Applied Psi* 1, no. 1 (March/April 1982): 1; Arthur Lyons and Marcello Truzzi, Ph.D. *The Blue Sense.* New York: Mysterious Press/Warner Books, 1991; Paul Tabori. *Crime and the Occult.* New York: Taplinger, 1974; Colin Wilson. *The Psychic Detectives.* 1984. San Francisco: Mercury House, 1985; Richard and Joyce Wolkomir. "Clairvoyant Crime Busters." *McCall's* (October 1987): 162–64; Kenneth L. Woodward. "The Strange Visions of Dorothy Allison." *McCall's* (September 1978): 28–38; "Visions of the Dead." *Newsweek* (April 17, 1978): 52; Dixie Yeterian. *Casebook of a Psychic Detective.* New York: Stein and Day, 1982.

Psychic reading

A sitting with a psychic or medium in which psychic ability is used to answer a client's questions. Most people seek psychic readings for information about the future, advice on how to handle problems and relationships, communication with departed loved ones, and divination for finding missing persons and objects. Such services have been rendered by psychically gifted people since ancient times.

A typical reading lasts for thirty to sixty minutes. Fees vary from voluntary contributions of a few dollars—typical of psychic fairs—to hundreds of dollars charged by famous psychics.

Methods vary according to the individual psychic. The most popular in the present day are astrology, Tarot, numerology, psychometry, palmistry, aura reading, access to the so-called Akashic Records, and trance channeling. Another widely used method is scrying, in which the psychic gazes into a crystal, mirror, other reflective surface, or flame.

Characteristics of psychic reading also vary according to the psychic. The session may begin with an overview provided by the psychic, followed by questions and answers, or may be entirely question and answer. In Tarot readings it is customary for the client to come with a single question, which is thought or written down prior to the reading.

The settings for readings also vary. Mediumistic seances typically take place in dimly lit or darkened rooms. Many psychics prefer comfortable rooms with low light or candle light and incense, which they say enhances their "attunement." Some channelers lie down. Some give readings over the telephone.

Responsible psychics do not encourage their clients to seek frequent readings. They believe clients should not become dependent upon readings to make decisions; instead, readings should be used as one of many tools for inner growth and self-reliance. See **Channeling; Divination; Mediumship; Prophecy.**

Psychic surgery

The alleged performing of paranormal surgery with bare hands, in which the body is opened and closed without use or benefit of surgical instruments; or paranormal surgery done with simple objects such as kitchen knives. Patients remain fully conscious and allegedly experience no pain. The surgeon reputedly uses paranormal powers or is guided by spirit helpers. While some observed surgeries remain unexplained, many have been exposed as fraud, accomplished by sleight-of-hand tricks known to most stage magicians.

Psychic surgery received much Western media attention in the 1960s and 1970s, prompting thousands of people suffering from chronic, debilitating, or terminal illnesses to seek treatment in the Philippines and Brazil, where psychic surgery largely is practiced by Spiritists. Some patients have reported cures that are supported by medical diagnosis, but many have not been cured. Most psychic surgeons resist scientific and medical investigation, thus raising suspicion about their purported paranormal abilities. Some practitioners have allowed themselves to be photographed and filmed.

Psychic surgery is performed under septic conditions, yet patients claim not to suffer postoperative infections. Some psychic surgeons say they operate only on the etheric body, or "perispirit" of the patient; they do not touch the flesh, but make hand passes and motions in the air just above the body. Others claim to penetrate the body with kitchen knives, scissors, or their fingers in order to remove tumors and growths. Such operations are accompanied by spurting blood and the production of stringy or lumpy masses said to be tumors; the incisions are closed without stitches and leave faint or no marks. The patient walks out and resumes normal activity.

Psychic surgeons also give "spiritual injections," in which the surgeon points his finger at the patient and "injects" medicine. Patients report feeling tingling or jabbing sensations. Drops of blood appear on the flesh as though it has been pricked with a needle. In some cases the blood has been shown to be animal blood.

Some of the "tumors" removed from patients have been found to be chicken or pig organs, other lumps of animal flesh, or balls of cotton wool palmed by the surgeon. Kidney stones have been exposed as ordinary pebbles. Animal blood is concealed in little cellophane bags in the palm or in false thumbs; in some cases the blood is already congealed when it allegedly spurts out of the patient. Using the blood, wads of cotton, and sheets for diversion, the appearance of penetration can be created by folding the knuckles against the skin. Many psychic surgeons demonstrate on obese patients, whose fatty skin is easy to manipulate.

If patients complain of pain, no cures, or other postoperative problems, psychic surgeons often blame them on the spirits, past-life karma, or a lack of harmony between the patient, healer, and magnetic vibrations in the room.

One of the most famous psychic surgeons was "Ze Arigo," the pseudonym of Jose Pedro de Feitas of Brazil. A peasant with a third-grade education, Arigo allegedly treated up to three hundred patients a day for nearly two decades, correctly diagnosing their ailments and writing out medically correct prescriptions. He reputedly could stop blood flow with verbal command. His trademark was his rusty jackknife, which he used in operations. He said he was guided by a "Dr. Fritz," the spirit of a long-dead German doctor whom he had never met in life. Arigo was sued by the Brazilian Medical Association and Catholic church for illegal practice of medicine and witchcraft; he was jailed in 1958 and 1964.

In 1968 Andrija (Henry K.) Puharich, an American doctor, led a team of doctors to Brazil to investigate Arigo. Electroencephalograph tests showed he had no yogi-like ability to control his own blood flow, body temperature, or brain waves. Nonetheless, Puharich believed that Arigo controlled an unknown form of life energy.

Arigo was killed in an auto accident on January 11, 1971. "Dr. Fritz" reappeared in 1980 as the spirit guide to a Brazilian obstetrician and gynecologist, Edson de Quieroz.

The fraud and controversy of psychic surgery precludes its serious investigation by many parapsychologists. Nonetheless, it is possible that paranormal processes occur among some psychic surgeons, who typically have strong mediumistic ability, a deep religious belief, a vivid imagination, a weak ego, and an undeveloped intellect. They may be adept at stimulating the natural self-healing processes of the patient. See **Healing, faith and psychic; Spiritism.**

Sources: Milbourne Christopher. *Mediums, Mystics, and the Occult.* New York: Thomas Y. Crowell, 1975; Martin Ebon, ed. *The Psychic Reader.* New York: The World Publishing Co., 1969; John G. Fuller. *Arigo: Surgeon of the Rusty Knife.* New York: Thomas Y. Crowell Co., 1974; Stanley Krippner and Alberto Villoldo. *The Realms of Healing.* 3d ed. Berkeley, CA: Celestial Arts, 1986; George W. Meek, ed. *Healers and the Healing Process.* Wheaton, IL: The Theosophical Publishing House, 1977; Guy Lyon Playfair. *The Unknown Power.* New York: Pocket Books, 1975; James Randi. *Flim-Flam!* Buffalo, NY: Prometheus Books, 1982; Harold Sherman. *"Wonder" Healers of the Philippines.* Los Angeles: DeVorss & Co., 1967; D. Scott Rogo and Raymond Bayless. "Psychic Surgery." Correspondence. *The Journal of the Society for Psychical Research* 44, no. 738 (December 1968): 426–28; Ian Stevenson. "Tests Prove This 'Psychic Surgery' Was Fraudulent." *Psychic News* (July 18,

1970): 3; Tom Valentine. *Psychic Surgery.* 1973. New York: Pocket Books, 1975.

Psychic vampirism

See **Psychic attack.**

Psychokinesis (PK)

A form of psi that is the apparent influence of mind over matter through invisible means, such as the movement of objects, bending of metal, and the outcome of events. The term "psychokinesis" comes from the Greek words *psyche,* meaning "breath," "life," or "soul," and *kinein,* meaning "to move." PK occurs spontaneously and deliberately, indicating that it is both an unconscious and conscious process.

What PK is and how it operates remain an enigma, though many theories have been put forward. It cannot be explained in terms of physics, nor is it affected by any of the forces or laws of physics. It has been held to be a supernatural ability, a human ability possessed only by extraordinary individuals, and a human ability possessed by all people. If one assumes the existence of extrasensory perception (ESP), then PK is a necessary consequence. In physics, if information is obtained from a system (as with ESP), then that system is disturbed (resulting in PK).

PK has been observed since ancient times. Levitations, miraculous healings, invisibility, luminosities, apports, and other physical phenomena have been attributed to adepts and holy people around the world. Many of the remarkable phenomena reported in the Bible may be viewed in terms of PK. The New Testament, particularly Acts, contains many possible psi events, including PK. For example, Paul and Silas, imprisoned in Ephesus, prayed and sang hymns; at midnight their shackles fell off and the prison doors swang open (Acts 16:19–40).

Magic spells, curses, and rituals to control the weather also may involve PK. For example, the evil eye, a universal belief that certain individuals possess the power to harm or kill with a look, could involve the psychic projection, consciously or unconsciously, of ill will. See **Evil eye.**

PK manifests in mediumship in alleged materializations and dematerializations, apports, levitations, table-tipping, raps, and the manifestations of ectoplasm and pseudopods. The nineteenth-century medium Daniel Dunglas Home was renowned for his ability to handle hot coals without being burned, and to levitate. See **Home, Daniel Dunglas.** During Home's time there were also "electric people" who experienced a "high-voltage syndrome": They could make knives and forks cling to their skin, and could by their touch send furniture flying across a room.

Another medium renowned for PK was Rudi Schneider, whose materializations and telekinetic movement of objects was intently studied by psychical researchers during the first part of the twentieth century.

Since the 1930s PK has been of major research interest, and it has become the fastest-growing field of parapsychology, particularly in the United States and the Soviet Union. Statistical findings from controlled laboratory studies, however, have resulted in contradictory findings. Some experiments have been attacked for their methodologies, or tainted with accusations of fraud.

In the final analysis, PK can be said to occur, but it is not known under what conditions or by what requirements. Patterns have been identified according to experimenters and subjects, but these patterns cannot be applied to all circumstances. There is evidence that PK is adversely affected by a subject's boredom or anxiety. See **Experimenter effect; Sheep/goat effect.**

Psychokinesis experiment at University of California at Los Angeles: Subject attempts to affect spin of silver dollar and make it land heads.

American parapsychologist J. B. Rhine began studying PK in 1934 with dice tests done under controlled laboratory conditions at Duke University in North Carolina. Rhine was by no means the first to study PK; but his work, which followed on the heels of his ground-breaking research in ESP, yielded significant findings. Rhine conducted an experiment with a gambler who claimed that he had the power to influence falling dice to turn to specific numbers or number combinations. Early results were beyond the probabilities of chance, which startled Rhine, but subsequent experiments yielded uneven results. Rhine did not immediately publish his findings for several reasons: PK suffered from a dubious reputation at the time; he had used himself as an occasional subject; and the studies were too insufficiently controlled.

Rhine finally agreed to publish when an assistant, Betty Humphrey, noted that subjects scored significantly better with the dice early in the experimental sequence rather than toward the end. This effect was attributed to lessening interest on the part of the subjects, similar to what was found in studies with ESP subjects. (Further studies by other Duke researchers sought to have subjects land the dice in a specified place, but these tests also were criticized for lack of rigorous methods of control.)

Rhine observed that PK does not seem to be connected to any physical processes of the brain, or to be subject to any of the mechanical laws of physics. Rather, it seems to be a nonphysical force of the mind that can act upon matter in statistically measurable ways. It produces results that cannot be explained by physics.

Rhine also found that PK is similar to ESP in its independence of space and time. He concluded further that ESP is a necessary part of the PK process, and one implies the other. In order to exert an influence upon matter, such as the outcome of tossed dice, ESP must come into play at precisely the right point of space and moment of time, Rhine said. He also observed that both ESP and PK were adversely affected by drugs and were influenced by hypnosis and the mental state of the subject. See ESP (extrasensory perception); Psi.

Rhine was of the opinion that faith healing and folk magic healing were PK phenomena, in which a psychogenic effect, sometimes at a distance, was exerted upon the body. See Healing, faith and psychic.

Rhine's research marked the beginning of a significant new phase in PK research. Before 1940, research of observable PK was largely limited to physical mediumship, which usually was performed in the dark during seances. Thus scientific controls were difficult and the possibility of fraud was high. After Rhine's exploratory work, PK research fell into two classes: macro-PK, or observable events; and micro-PK, weak or slight effects usually not visible to the naked eye and requiring statistical evaluation. Emphasis was given to micro-PK.

In the late 1960s, a new method for testing micro-PK was devised by American physicist Helmut Schmidt. His apparatus was the "electronic coin flipper," which operates on the random decay of radioactive particles. As decay occurs particles or rays are emitted at rates that are unaffected by temperature, pressure, electricity, magnetism, or chemical change. The rate of emission is completely unpredictable and cannot be manipulated by fraud. Subjects were asked to exert their mental energy on flipping the coin to heads or tails so that bulbs on the device would light up in one direction or another; some did successfully influence the coins. The electronic coin flipper was the prototype for random event generators, computerized techniques that have since played a major role in tests for both ESP and PK, and have yielded significant PK test results.

Schmidt also was interested in learning if animals had powers of PK. In experiments where animals produced positive results, Schmidt found the interpretation difficult. He theorized that the researcher could play a role in influencing findings by using his own PK on the experimental subjects. This has proved to be a major obstacle in all psi tests with animals, because it is virtually impossible to tell if it is the animals or the researchers who are using PK abilities. Since Schmidt's work there has been very little research conducted in animal PK, but most studies follow the guidelines he developed. See Animal psi.

Macro-PK began to make a comeback in research in the 1960s, with individuals who performed PK feats not in the dark but in the light, and under controlled laboratory conditions. Israeli psychic Uri Geller dazzled television audiences with his alleged powers to bend or break metal with a few taps of his fingers and mental concentration. Geller's powers were said to be so intense that while performing on television, some viewers noted their own household objects undergoing similar changes. Efforts to test Geller in laboratory conditions largely were not successful. Critics, most notably professional magicians, claimed that Geller used sleight-of-hand, though these charges were never proved. See Geller, Uri.

The most famous Soviet PK subject was Nina Kulagina, a housewife from Leningrad, born in the mid-1920s, whose abilities were revealed to the West in 1968. Kulagina was observed by Western scientists, who witnessed such phenomena as the movement of many different sizes and types of stationary objects; the altering of the course of objects already in motion; and impressions upon photographic film. Kulagina also reportedly exerted PK upon a frog's heart that had been removed from the animal, first by changing its rate of beating and then stopping it altogether. She also was photographed apparently levitating objects.

During the 1970s PK was the focus of more research, with increasingly sophisticated methods applied to both micro-PK and macro-PK. Some researchers turned their attention to the use of psychics, mediums, and others who apparently could influence static objects and materials. One subject was Ingo Swann, a New York artist and psychic who could change the temperature of nearby objects by one degree, and could also affect the magnetic field of a magnetometer. Others have pursued PK healing experiments with animals and plants. Tests in which healers handled wounded mice, and water to be applied to barley seeds, showed impressive results. PK effects also have been observed on microorganisms and enzymes. In some cases results are marginal or have not been successfully replicated; yet researchers believe the area holds promise for discoveries that can shed further light on the healing process.

Researchers have noticed a "linger effect" in many experiments. For example, temperatures influenced by an agent continue to rise or fall for a period of time after the agent leaves the premises. Water that has been held by healers and seems to influence the growth of plants continues to exert the influence even after being boiled.

Among other areas of research interest are the role of meditation and other altered states of consciousness in PK, and the existence of retroactive PK, or "retro-PK," in which the subject attempts to influence the event—such as a sequence of numbers produced by a random event generator—after it has already happened. However, it is not possible to rule out conclusively that either the subject or the experimenter unconsciously exerted PK on the generator at the time the numbers were selected.

Beyond the laboratory some researchers have studied spontaneous or unconscious PK, such as hauntings, apparitions, poltergeists, and physical phenomena associated with death and dying. See **Apparition; Apport; Deathbed visions; Electronic voice phenomenon; Haunting; Levitation; Materialization; Plants, psychism of; Poltergeist; Thoughtography.**

Sources: "Body and Soul." *Newsweek* (November 7, 1988): 88–97; Hoyt L. Edge, Robert L. Morris, John Palmer, and Joseph H. Rush. *Foundations of Parapsychology.* Boston: Routledge & Kegan Paul, 1986; Renee Haynes. *The Society for Psychical Research: 1882–1982, A History.* London: Macdonald & Co., 1982; H. H. J. Keil, Benson Herbert, J. G. Pratt, and Montague Ullman. "Directly Observable Voluntary PK Effects: A Survey and Tentative Interpretation of Available Findings from Nina Kulagina and Other Known Related Cases of Recent Date." *Proceedings of the Society for Psychical Research 56,* part 210 (January 1976): 197–235; Elizabeth E. McAdams and Raymond Bayless. *The Case for Life after Death.* Chicago: Nelson-Hall, 1981; Edgar D. Mitchell. *Psychic Exploration: A Challenge for Science.* Edited by John White. New York: Paragon Books, 1974; Sheila Ostrander and Lynn Schroeder. *Psychic Discoveries Behind the Iron Curtain.* Englewood Cliffs, NJ: Prentice-Hall, 1970; J. B. Rhine. *The Reach of the Mind.* New York: William Sloane Assoc., 1947; Louisa E. Rhine. *Mind Over Matter: Psychokinesis.* New York: Collier Books, 1970; D. Scott Rogo. *Psychic Breakthroughs Today.* Wellingborough, Northamptonshire, England: The Aquarian

Press, 1987; Russell Targ and Harold E. Puthoff. *Mind Reach: Scientists Look at Psychic Ability*. New York: Delacorte Press, 1977; Lyall Watson. *Beyond Supernature*. New York: Bantam Books, 1987; Robert Winterhalter. "Is There a Relationship Between God and Psi?" *The Journal of Religion and Psychical Research* 10, no 3 (July 1987): 158–68; Benjamin B. Wolman, ed. *Handbook of Parapsychology*. New York: Van Nostrand Reinhold, 1977.

Psychology

The science of human behavior. "Psychology" is derived from the Greek *psyche*, for "breath," "spirit," or "soul." Psychotherapy is therefore the nurturing of the spirit or soul. The discussion here shall focus on the emergence of humanistic and transpersonal psychologies, which emphasize human potential and transcendence of self, and seek to blend traditional Western therapies with Eastern philosophy, behavioral medicine, and the experience of altered states.

Psychology did not emerge from philosophy as a separate, experimental science until the late nineteenth century. It had been shaped by the mechanistic, dualistic ideas of René Descartes in the seventeenth century, that mind exists separate from body but interacts with it at a point in the brain. The classical psychoanalysis of Sigmund Freud became established around the turn of the twentieth century. Freud focused on pathology — his works contain more than four hundred references to neuroses but none to health — and emphasized the need for a strong ego. He also presumed that humans are forever in mental conflict that can be reduced but never resolved. See **Freud, Sigmund.**

Behaviorism, another school that arose in the early twentieth century, emphasized measurement of observable behavior without consideration of consciousness. The chief exponent of Behaviorism was psychologist B. F. Skinner, whose experiments with animals led to his principles of programmed learning via reinforcement and reward.

Carl G. Jung, who broke away from Freud, was the first Western psychiatrist to see the importance of transpersonal experience in mental health. He stated that the approach to the numinous, not the treatment of neuroses, was the real therapy, and that by experiencing the numinous one is "released from the curse of pathology." He termed the process of becoming whole as "individuation." To that end Jung explored the inner psychic landscape of the contents of the unconscious, both personal and collective. See **Archetypes; Collective unconscious; Jung, Carl Gustav.**

At about the middle of the twentieth century, there was growing evidence that psychology needed to address behavior associated with health and well-being rather than only pathology, and that psychology had underestimated the human potential for psychological growth and well-being. A major breakthrough developed to make psychology "the study of man" by regarding the human being as a whole organism and not a synthesis of parts. This shift brought together science, medicine, the humanities, and religion.

Humanistic Psychology

The "third force" of psychology, as humanistic psychology is called, is an orientation toward the whole of psychology rather than a school or area. It is most identified with Abraham H. Maslow (1908–1970). Trained as an experimental psychologist at the University of Wisconsin, Maslow decided after the start of World War II that he would transform psychology into an instrument for world peace and improvement of the human condition.

Maslow believed that all human beings have innate spiritual yearnings to experience the sacred and fulfill themselves to their maximum potential of goodness. Maslow called these yearnings "B-values," the B standing for cognition of Being, or a fully integrated and holistic state. B-values include truth, goodness, beauty, wholeness, dichotomy-transcendence, aliveness, uniqueness, perfection, necessity, completion, justice, order, simplicity, richness, effortlessness, playfulness, self-sufficiency, and so on.

Maslow was disturbed by what he observed as the total collapse of societal values throughout the modern world. He deplored the devaluation of spiritual experiences, tender emotions, marriage, parenthood, and friendships. He said the collapse of values has created a spiritual emptiness that breeds increasing violence, alcoholism, and drug abuse.

The root of this collapse is dichotomy, the Cartesian view that subject and object are forever separate, which prevents a holistic outlook. Religion and science have been dichotomized since the seventeenth century. The result, Maslow said, is that both have become too narrowly defined, literally crippled. Science could not deal with the transcendent and the sacred, with values and ethics. Religion, cut away from knowledge and further discovery, was forced to take the stance that it had nothing more to learn: that its founding revelations were complete and eternal truths. As the exclusive jurisdiction of a priesthood, religion has become removed from both human nature and the world of nature; that is, it has been taken out of the ordinary, which is where all the great mystics attest that the sacred lies.

Maslow said that phenomenology and existentialism had much to offer psychology by providing it the underlying foundation of philosophy it lacked. Existentialism, he said, would lead to the establishment of another branch of psychology of the fully evolved and authentic Self and its way of being.

While human beings do possess inherently pathological natures, which are dealt with in Freud's psychology, they also possess inherently good inner natures, Maslow said. This good inner nature manifests as a natural striving for healthy living, honesty, creativity, compassion, unselfishness, and so on. A truly fulfilled and "self-actualized" individual (a term Maslow coined), who was mature, healthy, and filled with a zest for living, is one who has successfully integrated his or her lower, animalistic, "instinctoid" self with his or her higher, godlike self. Neither self is denied, repudiated, or "overcome."

The self-actualized individual is happier, healthier, and more creative. (Maslow did not equate creativity with great talent—which he said is independent of goodness and health of character—but merely with an ability to do anything, even routine things, creatively.) Self-actualization is not a transcendence of problems, for all people suffer tragedies, pain, and problems in addition to joy and health. Self-actualization, rather, makes more possible the transcendence of the self.

Maslow found that self-actualized people, who cut across the spectrum of society, are more likely to experience B-cognition. They are also more likely to have "peak experiences," the nonreligious equivalent of a mystical experience of sorts. Peak experiences reinforce the holistic outlook and enhance creativity. See **Peak experiences.**

Maslow said that self-knowledge is the major but not the only path to self-improvement. He said the new force in psychology did not deny behaviorism and Freudianism but supplemented and expanded them.

Maslow advanced his alternative theories during the 1940s. In 1954 the publication of his book *Motivation and Personality* had a major impact. This was followed in 1956 by *The Self*, edited by

Clark Moustakas. In 1957 Maslow, Moustakas, and others organized the first formal meetings to discuss the launching of the new psychology, which was called by a variety of names: holistic-dynamic psychology, positive psychology, self-psychology, organismic psychology, orthopsychology, ontopsychology, axiopsychology, metapsychology, autonomous psychology, self-directive psychology, and person psychology. More meetings were held in 1958. The American Association for Humanistic Psychology and the *Journal of Humanistic Psychology* came into being in 1961. Later "American" was dropped from the name in order to reflect an international scope. (Originally, the organization's name was the American Association of Orthopsychology, but the Association of Orthopsychiatry protested that the name was too similar to its own. "Humanistic psychology" was proposed by Maslow's son-in-law, Stephen Cohen.)

Interest in human potential was further fueled by Maslow's books *Religion, Values and Peak-Experiences* (1964) and *Toward a Psychology of Being* (1968). Humanistic psychology is now recognized as a division of psychology by the American Psychological Association.

Transpersonal psychology

Humanistic psychology barely had been organized when Maslow recognized yet a "fourth force" emerging from it, which overlapped with humanistic psychology but went beyond it. In 1967 he called this force "transhumanistic psychology," borrowing a term coined in 1957 by English biologist Sir Julian Huxley. It concerns transcendent experiences and values, called variously ultimate purpose, ultimate meaning, point Omega, unitive consciousness, and so on. Its emphasis, Maslow said, is on the experiencing individual, and it recognizes the sacredness of all things. In 1968 he said that humanistic psychology was transitional, paving the way for a higher fourth psychology.

The new area was officially named "transpersonal psychology." *The Journal of Transpersonal Psychology* was launched in 1969, and was then made part of the newly formed Transpersonal Institute. A Transpersonal Center was formed as a second division of the Institute in 1970. In 1971 the Institute's board of directors decided to form a new membership association, the Association for Transpersonal Psychology.

Essentially, transpersonal psychology is an empirical investigation of consciousness, the groundwork for which was laid at the turn of the twentieth century by psychologist and philosopher William James, but which was not developed for some fifty years. In transpersonal psychotherapy ego is illusion, something to be transcended so that the individual can identify with the total Self. Body and mind are not separate, but subsystems of each other. Transpersonal psychology assumes everyone has the capacity for self-healing.

The distinctions between humanistic and transpersonal psychologies are often blurry, but there are significant differences. For example, humanistic psychology addresses development of personality and achievement of ego goals, which are considered obstacles to transpersonal realization in transpersonal psychology.

Transpersonal psychotherapy, which requires an experiential foundation on the part of the therapist, includes both Eastern and Western methods of working with the consciousness, including traditional Western methods such as dream analysis and imagery; Eastern meditation and yoga; behavioral medicine; bodywork; and the transpersonal experience of altered states of consciousness as a means of achieving higher states.

In a transpersonal experience, the consciousness is expanded to overcome space and/or time to identify with other consciousnesses, phenomena, or states. Various phenomena, including telepathy, out-of-body experiences, clairvoyance, precognition, clairaudience, and space and time travel, are transpersonal experiences.

Psychiatrist Stanislav Grof, who has conducted extensive research with LSD, divides transpersonal experiences into two major categories. The first includes phenomena related to the material world, such as people, animals, plants, inanimate objects, and processes. It is further divided into subgroups characterized by either separateness or the limitations of linear time. The second category goes beyond Western objective reality to include experiences of "archetypal visions, mythological sequences, experiences of divine and demonic influences, encounters with discarnate or suprahuman beings, and experiential identification with the Universal Mind or Supracosmic Void." The latter is described by Grof as "the ultimate of all experiences . . . the mysterious primordial emptiness and nothingness that is conscious of itself and contains all existence in germinal form." (*Beyond the Brain*, 1987) See **Drugs in mystical and psychic experiences.**

Experiences that traditional psychiatry would label pathological are being explored in transpersonal psychology for their therapeutic value. Transpersonal psychology is still in its infancy and is still controversial. Critics say it is not sufficiently defined, has too few practitioners, and infringes too much upon religion.

Jung's work plays a prominent role in transpersonal psychology, especially his concept of archetypes. Jung's work has a lesser role in humanistic psychology, which emphasizes the empirical rather than the spiritual.

Psychosynthesis

Psychosynthesis, a humanistic/transpersonal psychology, actually preceded Maslow; and as it developed parallel to humanistic and transpersonal psychologies, it absorbed elements of both. Psychosynthesis is perhaps the most mystical of modern psychologies, but is not as well known, perhaps because its founder, Italian psychiatrist Roberto Assagioli (1888–1974), did not like to write.

Assagioli, a contemporary of Freud and Jung, was raised in an intellectual household. His father was Jewish and his mother was a Catholic with strong mystical interests; she was the first Italian Theosophist. Whereas Freud found an interest in Greek myths and Jung in alchemy, Assagioli gravitated to Eastern philosophy and religion. He studied Hindu and Buddhist mysticism, as well as Christian mysticism. He also was particularly influenced by Plato, especially Plato's image of the soul awakening in a dark cave and discovering that the world that had been taken for granted is but a shadow or illusion. See **Plato.**

Assagioli brought the work of both Freud and Jung into Italy, but saw limitations in both. He felt Freud neglected the higher consciousness, while Jung was too preoccupied with the unconscious, where, Assagioli said, one could get lost. In developing Psychosynthesis Assagioli placed emphasis on strengthening the consciousness and putting the repressed parts of the psyche back together. He viewed himself as playing a role similar to that of Gautama Buddha, dedicating himself to helping others achieve enlightenment.

Assagioli drew on various philosophies and mystical traditions, and on his own mystical experiences, as well as on the psychologies that preceded him. He was vague about the exact origins of Psychosynthesis, and presented no systematic framework of it in his two books, *Psychosynthesis: A Manual of Principles and Techniques* (1965) and *The Act of Will* (1973), and numerous articles and booklets. (*The Act of Will* resulted from spiritual guidance he received while seriously ill with a high fever. After his fever broke, he informed his secretary that "'They' want me to write a book.")

Assagioli believed the conscious personality is but a small part of the whole being. The unconscious exists in four levels, including the superconscious, a reflection from the Higher Self and containing potential. As one becomes more aware of the superconscious, one becomes more attuned to spiritual forces. Elements and functions coming from the superconscious, such as intuition, inspiration, and aesthetic, ethical, religious, and mystical experiences, are effective in changing both inner and outer worlds.

Assagioli also placed great emphasis on the importance of values, and on the strengthening and use of the will.

Psychosynthesis is a conscious and planned reconstruction of the personality. It makes use of a wide range of techniques, including those borrowed from other psychologies. Critics contend that Psychosynthesis is superficially optimistic and not sufficiently grounded in intellectual discipline.

Sacred Psychology

This experiential psychology was developed by Jean Houston, psychologist and past president of the Association for Humanistic Psychology. It is based on exercises steeped in myth, the mysteries, and archetypes, with the goal of realizing one's full potential and knowing the High Self.

Houston defines three realms of experience: the THIS IS ME, which is ordinary reality; the WE ARE, the realm of the collective unconscious; and the I AM, the realm of God, which is immanent in the High Self. By learning to access the WE ARE through "ritual theater," the THIS IS ME becomes placed in the service of the I AM. According to Houston training in sacred psychology reorganizes one's neurological circuitry so that one is receptive to powerful forces from the deep psyche and the universe.

Toward a Western Yoga

All of these modern psychologies comprise the overall "human potential movement," which may provide the means for the development of a truly Western yoga. In the 1960s and 1970s, attention was turned toward the philosophies and religions of the East; in the 1980s some attention began to shift back to the Western tradition. While cross-fertilization is both beneficial and essential to spiritual growth, the Western tradition cannot be ignored, but must be explored and revitalized. See **Mysticism.**

Sources: Roberto Assagioli. *Psychosynthesis: A Manual of Principles and Techniques.* 1965. New York: Penguin Books, 1976; Roberto Assagioli. *The Act of Will.* New York: Penguin Books, 1973; J. F. T. Bugental. "The Third Force in Psychology." *Journal of Humanistic Psychology* 4, no. 1 (Spring 1964): 19–26; Piero Ferrucci. *What We May Be: Techniques for Psychological and Spiritual Growth Through Psychosynthesis.* Los Angeles: Jeremy P. Tarcher, 1982; Tom Greening. "The Origins of the *Journal of Humanistic Psychology* and the Association of Humanistic Psychology." *Journal of Humanistic Psychology* 25, no. 2 (Spring 1985): 7–11; Stanislav Grof. *Beyond the Brain: Birth, Death and Transcendence in Psychotherapy.* Albany, NY: State University of New York Press, 1985; Jean Hardy. *A Psychology with a Soul: Psychosynthesis in Evolutionary Context.* London: Routledge & Kegan Paul, 1987; James Hillman. *Re-Visioning Psychology.* New York: Harper & Row, 1975; Edward Hoffman. *The Right to Be Human: A Biography of Abra* ham Maslow. Los Angeles: Jeremy P. Tarcher, 1988; Jean Houston. *The Search for the Beloved: Journeys in Sacred Psychology.* Los Angeles: Jeremy P. Tarcher, 1987; Geraint ap Iorwerth. "Humanistic Psychology and the Judeo-Christian Heritage." *Journal of Humanistic Psychology* 25, no. 2 (Spring 1985): 13–34; Abraham H. Maslow. *Religion, Values and Peak Experiences.* 1964. New York: Penguin Books, 1976; Abraham H. Maslow. *Toward a Psychology of Being.* 1962. 2d ed. New York: D. Van Nostrand Co., 1968; Abraham H. Maslow. *The Farther Reaches of Human Nature.* New York: The Viking Press, 1971; Anthony J. Sutich. "Some Considerations Regarding Transpersonal Psychology." *The Journal of Transpersonal Psychology* 1, no. 1 (Spring 1969): 11–20; Anthony J. Sutich. "Association for Transpersonal Psychology." *The Journal of Transpersonal Psychology* 4, no. 1 (1972): 93–97; Charles T. Tart, ed. *Transpersonal Psychologies.* New York: Harper & Row, 1975; Frances Vaughan. *The Inward Arc: Healing & Wholeness in Psychotherapy & Spirituality.* Boston: New Science Library/ Shambhala, 1986; Miles Vich and Rollo May. "Debating the Legitimacy of Transpersonal Psychology." *The Common Boundary* 4, issue 4 (July/August 1986): 5+; Roger N. Walsh and Frances Vaughan, eds. *Beyond Ego: Transpersonal Dimensions in Psychology.* Los Angeles: Jeremy P. Tarcher, 1980.

Psychometry

A psychic skill in which information about people, places, and events is obtained by handling objects associated with them. The percipient receives impressions through clairvoyance, telepathy, retrocognition, and precognition. The act of reading an object in this manner is called "psychometrizing." Psychics say the information is conveyed to them through vibrations imbued into the objects by emotions and actions in the past.

The term "psychometry" comes from the Greek words *psyche,* "soul," and *metron,* "measure." It was coined in 1840 by Joseph R. Buchanan, an American professor of physiology who saw psychometry as a means to measure the "soul" of objects. Buchanan conducted experiments in which students could identify drugs in vials by holding the vials. He kept his research quiet out of fear of ridicule, and did not publish his findings until 1849 in his book, *Journal of Man.*

Buchanan's work interested a contemporary, Professor William F. Denton, an American professor of geology, who conducted his own experiments in 1854 with his sister, Ann Denton Cridge. When Cridge placed wrapped geological specimens to her forehead, she experienced vivid mental images of their appearances. Denton, who did not consider the possibility of telepathy between himself and his sister, recorded his experiments in a book, *The Soul of Things.* He defined psychometry as a "mysterious faculty which belongs to the soul and is not dependent upon the body for its exercise."

Early Spiritualist mediums used psychometry at seances. One popular psychometry feat was billet-reading, also called "cryptoscopy," in which the medium handled a sealed envelope and revealed the contents of the letter inside.

British medium Geraldine Cummins called psychometry "memory divining," and coupled it with automatic writing in a dissociated state. Cummins would hold an object and concentrate upon the word "stillness," or visualize a dark pool, until an inner voice or images prompted her to begin writing. She said she was not aware of what she wrote; she described the process as taking dictation. Sometimes the images made her feel as though she were in a theater watching a play.

Gustav Pagenstecher, psychical researcher, conducted more than one hundred psychometry experiments from 1919 to 1922 with a medium identified as Sr. Maria Reyes de Z. Given an object,

Maria would fall into a cataleptic trance and produce information from the present and past that involved all physical senses. Pagenstecher did not believe telepathy was at work, but only the medium's ability to pick up vibrations that were condensed in the objects. The vibrations, he said, were imbued by the thoughts of the objects' owners.

Supposedly the best "psychically conductive" materials are metals. If an object has been owned by more than one person, such as an antique, a percipient may pick up information about different people.

People as well as objects may be psychometrized. The percipient focuses on an individual and attempts to pick up images and sensations. In flower psychometry a person picks a flower and holds it while meditating upon a problem. A psychic or percipient then holds the flower and receives impressions from the flower's aura. See **Psychic archaeology; Psychic criminology.**

Sources: W. E. Butler. *How to Develop Psychometry.* London: The Aquarian Press, 1971; Geraldine Cummins. *Unseen Adventures.* London: Rider & Co., 1951; Sheila Ostrander and Lynn Schroeder. *The ESP Papers: Scientists Speak Out from Behind the Iron Curtain.* New York: Bantam Books, 1976; Sheila Ostrander and Lynn Schroeder. *Handbook of Psi Discoveries.* New York: Berkley, 1974; Gustav Pagenstecher. "Past Events Seership: A Study in Psychometry." Edited by Walter Franklin Prince. *Proceedings of the American Society for Psychical Research* 16, part 1 (January 1922): 1–107; Benjamin B. Wolman, ed. *Handbook of Parapsychology.* New York: Van Nostrand Reinhold, 1977.

Psychotronics

The interdisciplinary study of the interactions of matter, energy, and consciousness. Psychotronics was developed in Eastern Europe, but has a following elsewhere in Europe and in the United States. The International Association for Psychotronic Research held its first international congress in Prague in 1973.

The term "psychotronics" was coined by Czechoslovakian researchers in the 1960s as a replacement for "parapsychology." A Czech manifesto presented at a parapsychology conference in Moscow in 1968 described psychotronics as "the bionics of man." Psychotronics assumes that the universe is triadic, not dualistic, and is comprised of humankind, universe, and psychotronic energy, which is claimed to be the aura or vital force that emanates from all living things. This energy may be the basis for all psychic phenomena. See **Universal life force.**

Psychotronics includes research for ways to apply this energy to other fields, such as medicine, physics, biophysics, biology, psychophysiology, anthropology, and psychology. See **Applied psi.** Particular attention has been devoted to finding ways to harass cosmic energies in devices.

Psychotronic Generators and Other Devices

The belief that psychic energy can be transferred from humans to objects dates back to the ancient Polynesian Huna. In the eighteenth century, Baron Karl von Reichenbach, a German chemist, believed the energy could be stored. In 1921 Charles Russ, a British doctor, demonstrated a device that, when gazed upon, apparently caused a solenoid to move. At about the same time in France, Paul Joire designed a device with a needle that turned when a person stood near or stared at it.

In the late 1960s Robert Pavlita, a Czech inventor and design director for a textile plant, produced small devices which he said were psychotronic generators. Pavlita, who claimed to have spent more than thirty years in private research to develop the devices, said he had been inspired by certain "ancient manuscripts," which he declined to name. A few Western researchers were shown the devices and films of them in operation. The nature of their operation was kept secret.

Pavlita's generators resembled small machine parts, humanoid figures, fat writing utensils, and Easter Island monoliths. They allegedly collected energy from any biological source. This energy was then used to enhance plant growth, purify polluted water, kill insects, and cause lower life forms such as snails to go into a state of hibernation.

In the United States, a psychotronic generator allegedly activated by visual energy was developed by Woodrow W. Ward of Houston in 1970. Ward's device, called a psionic generator, was activated directly by energy streaming from the eyes. It responded more quickly to children, and during certain planetary configurations and full phases of the moon.

The United States Psychotronics Association, founded in 1975 in Chicago, sells an array of psychotronics devices.

Sources: John P. Boyle. *The Psionic Generator Pattern Book.* Englewood Cliffs, NJ: Prentice-Hall, 1975; Martin Ebon. *Psychic Warfare: Threat or Illusion?* New York: McGraw-Hill, 1983; Ron McRae. *Mind Wars.* New York: St. Martin's Press, 1984; Sheila Ostrander and Lynn Schroeder. *Psychic Discoveries Behind the Iron Curtain.* Englewood Cliffs, NJ: Prentice-Hall, 1970; "Second International Congress on Psychotronic Research." Monte Carlo, June 30–July 4, 1975, proceedings; US Psychotronics Association.

Pursel, Jach

The channel since 1974 of Lazaris, said to be a highly evolved consciousness who has never incarnated in physical form. Lazaris is known for wit, warmth, and practical guidance on a wide range of emotional and spiritual topics. He has an international following, including many celebrities.

(Photo by Norman Seeff. Courtesy Concept: Synergy.)

Jach Pursel

Pursel was raised in Lansing, Michigan, and met his future wife, Peny, in a ninth-grade class. Both attended the University of Michigan and graduated with degrees in international relations and political science. They planned to go to law school and start their own law firm, but instead Pursel went to work for State Farm Insurance and entered its executive program. By age twenty-seven Pursel was a regional supervisor in Florida.

Pursel had little interest in metaphysics, but had learned to meditate with Peny's encouragement. Usually, he fell asleep. One night during a business trip in early 1974, Pursel meditated and found himself in a dense forest with a brook and a thatch-roofed log cabin. He entered the cabin and saw a man dressed in a white robe standing next to a counter. Behind the man there was a blackboard, and there was a fire lit in the fireplace. The man introduced himself as "Lazaris" and began talking about the universe and reality.

Jach Pursel channeling Lazaris

After the first encounter, Pursel tried to contact Lazaris again but could not. On the night of October 3, 1974, Peny had an intuitive feeling that Pursel should meditate; she would ask questions of him in his meditative state. Pursel thought he fell asleep. When he awoke he was told that Lazaris had made his first official appearance, and for two hours had answered Peny's questions in a voice and speech that sounded faintly Chaucerian Middle English.

Pursel channeled Lazaris daily for the next two weeks, during which the entity made "adjustments" to make the transmission of information the clearest possible. Peny was fascinated, but Pursel was frightened. After hearing Lazaris on tape, however, he began to get comfortable.

Lazaris, who speaks in the first person plural of "we," explained that he had appeared in order to talk to Peny; if he talked only with her he would be satisfied that he had accomplished his purpose. He had observed her through many lifetimes and wanted to help this "gem of energy," as he called her. He had prepared for the channeling by giving Pursel a "nudge" in several of his lifetimes to follow certain evolutionary developments.

For months the Pursels said nothing about Lazaris, then confided in a friend, Michaell Prestini, who joined them in Florida. Peny decided she wanted to make Lazaris available to others. Word spread and Lazaris was sought for consultations. In 1975 Peny began to teach a course with Lazaris in psychic development.

By 1976 the work with Lazaris had grown to the point where Pursel left his insurance job and, with Peny and Prestini, established Concept: Synergy, an organization to handle seminars and tape production. In 1978 Peny and Prestini realized they were in love. The Pursels divorced; Peny and Prestini married and later changed their last name to North. Despite the divorce and marriage, the three remained good friends.

Shortly after they moved the business to California, first to San Francisco for a number of years and then to Beverly Hills. Word about Lazaris continued to spread. In 1987 Lazaris published his first book, *The Sacred Journey: You and Your Higher Self,* followed in 1988 by *Lazaris Interviews, Book I* and *Lazaris Interviews, Book II.* Pursel and the Norths established Isis Rising, a chain of art galleries in California and Florida, and Visionary Publishing, an art publishing company.

In 1988 Pursel and the Norths moved Concept: Synergy to Palm Beach, Florida. Pursel travels widely, channeling Lazaris for workshops and seminars throughout the United States. Lazaris counsels clients all over the world, mostly by telephone. "Friends of Lazaris" have included celebrities Michael and Pat York, Shirley MacLaine, Lesley Anne Warren, Sharon Gless (who thanked Lazaris in her 1986 and 1987 Emmy Award acceptance speeches), Ted and Casey Danson, Barry Manilow, and New Age luminaries Barbara Marx Hubbard and Marilyn Ferguson.

Lazaris

According to Lazaris he has never been in physical form, nor will he ever be so. He says that every consciousness, early in its development, makes a choice to grow physically or nonphysically, and he chose to remain nonphysical. He is a multileveled consciousness who is aware of his own various selves in multiple dimensions (the reason for referring to himself as "we"). He says that all consciousnesses, physical or not, have this multidimensional quality; humans are not yet aware of their multiple selves, but someday will be. Lazaris is neither male nor female, explaining that gender is transcended at the level on which he functions.

As a nonphysical being, Lazaris is outside the space-time continuum, giving him a perspective not limited by past, present, and future and the predispositions natural to those who are physical. He states he is not communicating to be a guru or master, but to be a friend, to help empower people to solve their own problems, to create better realities, and to reach the highest aspects of their own Self. He seeks to remind people that pain and fear are not the only methods of growth, but that one may grow more elegantly through joy and love; one does create one's own reality with no exceptions; there is a God/Goddess/All That Is who loves us and knows our names; and that "You love—you love 'good enough.'"

Lazaris describes his channeling process:

When you turn on your television set and watch the evening news, you don't for a moment suspect that the anchor person is sitting inside that little box ... We would liken our communication to that process. We do not enter the physical form of the Channel [Pursel]. We don't get anywhere near that Physical Plane of Reality, but rather, we connect energies that are thoughts into a system of vibration that we then transmit through the cosmos and the various levels. The system of vibration then enters your reality through the Mental Plane, then drifts down, in its way, to the Physical Plane— much as a television signal to the antenna—and then is amplified and comes out of the vocal chords, the mouth, and the speaking structure of that which is the Channel.

Lazaris's seminars include lectures, guided meditations, and "Blendings," times when he blends his energy with that of the participants. In longer workshops he personally greets the participants and gives them crystals he has charged with energy. See **Channeling**.

Sources: Philip H. Friedman. "The Magic, Mystery, and Muses of Love." *New Realities* 7, no. 6 (July/August 1987): 34–35; William H. Kautz and Melanie Branon. *Channeling: The Intuitive Connection.* San Francisco: Harper & Row, 1987; Jon Klimo. "The Psychology of Channeling." *New Age Journal* (December 1987): 32–40+; *Lazaris: Lazaris Interviews, Book I.* Beverly Hills, CA: Concept: Synergy Publishing, 1988; *Lazaris, The Sacred Journey: You and Your Higher Self.* Beverly Hills, CA: Concept: Synergy Publishing, 1987; Katherine Lowry. "Channelers." *Omni* (October 1987): 47–50+; Katherine Martin. "The Voice of Lazaris." *New Realities* 7, no. 6 (July/August 1987): 26–33; "New Age Harmonies." *Time* (December 7, 1987): 62–72; "The Sacred Journey: You and Your Higher Self." *Body Mind Spirit* 7, no. 1 (January/February 1988): 23; Paul Zuromski. "A Conversation with Jach Pursel and Lazaris." *Body Mind Spirit* 7, no. 1 (January/February 1988): 17–22; Jach Pursel/Lazaris on *The Merv Griffin Show.* July 25, 1986.

Puthoff, Harold

See **Remote viewing**.

Pyramids

Four-sided conical structures, the ancient remains of which are found throughout the world. According to prevailing scientific theories, ancient peoples used pyramids either as ceremonial structures or burial chambers. Various occult theories suggest they were used for initiations into the mysteries, as repositories or transformers of cosmic energy, or as records of the history of the Earth, including messianic prophecies.

The greatest popular attention has been focused on the Great Pyramid (Cheops) of Gizeh in Egypt. Pyramid building took place primarily from the Third to Sixth Dynasties of the Old Kingdom (3100 B.C.–2181 B.C.). Approximately eighty known major pyramids were constructed, most of which are now rubble. By the end of the Sixth Dynasty, all arts and crafts were in decline. A resurgence of pyramid building occurred in the Twelfth and Thirteenth Dynasties. There is no evidence of any original burial in any pyramid, indicating that burials were incidental to a primary purpose.

The Great Pyramid is believed to have been constructed c. 2700 B.C. by Pharaoh Khufu (Cheops in Greek). It covers 13.1 acres, has a base of 756 square feet, and rises 450 feet in height. It is estimated to have originally been 481.4 feet high. It is missing its capstone, if it ever had one.

One of the most perplexing mysteries of the pyramids is how they were constructed. The blocks of the Great Pyramid's quarried stone average 2.5 tons. Eighteenth-Dynasty tomb paintings show construction by manual labor, hauling the stones with ropes along wooden planks. According to the historian Herodotus (484 B.C.–425 B.C.), 100,000 men labored for twenty years to build the pyramid, which was a monument to Cheops. The pyramid contains an interior room called the King's Chamber, which has a lidless box and an empty box that could have been a sarcophagus. No mummy of Cheops has been found. Later Arabic historians said the pyramid was built by Hermes to preserve scientific knowledge during the Flood. See **Hermetica**.

Some modern speculative theories propose that the stones were levitated into place by Atlanteans or extraterrestrials. Edgar Cayce, during his trance readings, said the Great Pyramid is 10,000 years old and was built by a consortium of Egyptians, Atlanteans, and itinerant Caucasians from southwest Russia. The consortium was led by Hermes, an Egyptian high priest named Ra Ta (a past incarnation of Cayce), and an adviser named Isis. The pyramid served as a storage place for all of human history and prophecies up to the year 1998 (the time of the Second Coming of Christ, according to Cayce), recorded in the languages of mathematics, geometry, and astronomy. Cayce said it also was an initiation temple where, thousands of years later, Jesus was initiated during his "missing years" as preparation for his public career.

According to philosopher Manly P. Hall, the Great Pyramid was built by survivors of Atlantis as the first temple of the mysteries, where initiates entered as humans and left as gods. The initiation of the "second death" took place in the King's Chamber, where the initiate was symbolically crucified upon the cross of the solstices and equinoxes and buried in the coffer. The initiate's soul, the *ka*, left the body as a human-headed hawk and traveled through celestial realms to learn cosmic truths. There is no known evidence of such rites.

The geometry of the pyramid is alleged to generate supernatural powers. According to the Egyptian Book of the Dead, the power of the pyramid awakens the god who sleeps in the soul. In 1959 Karl Drbal, a Czech radio engineer, claimed that razor blades placed in the cavity of a pyramid modeled on the Great Pyramid would be sharpened by some sort of energy within twenty-four hours. This eventually created a fad in which pyramids were credited with reviving ailing plants, speeding the healing of wounds and burns, curing headaches, providing restful sleep, and enhancing meditation. Pyramid meditators said their psychic faculties opened, and some claimed to communicate with extraterrestrials.

Similar theories are put forth concerning the step pyramids of Meso-America, which are believed to have served ceremonial, calendric, and astronomical purposes; the Aztecs performed human sacrifices atop them. Some occultists propose that the pyramids were foci for cosmic or telluric forces. Cayce attributed Mayan pyramids to Atlanteans and Lemurians, who used them for rites to cleanse away undesirable behaviors. See **Ancient astronauts, theory of; Atlantis; Cayce, Edgar; Lemuria; Mysteries.**

Sources: William R. Fix. *Pyramid Odyssey.* Urbanna, VA: Mercury Media, 1978; Manly P. Hall. *The Secret Teachings of All Ages.* 1928. Los Angeles: The Philosophical Research Society, 1977; John Michell. *The New View Over Atlantis.* San Francisco: Harper & Row, 1983; Peter Tompkins. *Secrets of the Great Pyramid.* New York: Harper & Row, 1978; Peter Tompkins. *Mysteries of the Mexican Pyramids.* 1976. New York: Harper & Row, 1987; Max Toth and Greg Nielsen. *Pyramid Power.* New York: Warner Books, 1976.

Pythagoras (c. sixth century B.C.)

Greek philosopher and mathematician, best known for major contributions to astronomy, geometry, and music theory. His teachings influenced Socrates, Plato, Euclid, Aristotle, and thinkers in many disciplines down to the present day. Iamblichus listed 218 men and seventeen

(New York Public Library)

Pythagoras, by Gafurius, Theorica Musica, 1492

women among the most famous of Pythagorean philosophers of ancient times. Pythagoras achieved such stature during and after his life that he was virtually deified, and numerous legends sprang up around him: for example, that he was the son of God, and that he had a gold shin bone. It is said that he was the first person to call himself a philosopher.

Pythagoras was born on the island of Samos. According to legend he was named after the Pythia, the oracle at Delphi, who prophesied his birth and said that he would be a great contributor to the wisdom of humankind. Little is known about his early life. Pythagoras left Samos about 530 B.C. to escape Polycrates' tyrannical rule. It is said that he traveled widely throughout the ancient world, and was initiated into the mysteries of Isis in Thebes, and to the mysteries of Babylonia, Chaldea, Adonis, and probably Eleusis. He may even have gone to India and studied with the Brahmins.

He settled in the Dorian city of Croton, southern Italy, where he attracted a community of men and women followers, some of whom became organized as an order. He initiated followers with a sacred formula based on the letters of his name. Disciples were ranked by degrees, and only those of the higher degrees were allowed into the inner court of his temple, where Pythagoras revealed the most secret teachings. He was fond of lecturing at night.

At age sixty he married one of his disciples, a young girl named Theano, and fathered either three or seven children; accounts vary. He wielded great influence over local politics. He believed in a scientific government similar to the priesthood of Egypt. Croton had an aristocratic constitution and was governed by a Council of One Thousand, comprised of representatives of the wealthy families. Over this body Pythagoras organized the Council of Three Hundred, recruited from initiates who recognized Pythagoras as their leader. It was the goal of the Pythagorean Order to become the head of state throughout southern Italy. But around 450 B.C. an anti-aristocracy, anti-Pythagorean revolt forced out most of the Pythagoreans, including Pythagoras himself. He went to Metapontium, where he died, allegedly at the age of nearly one hundred.

The Pythagorean Order lasted for about another two hundred and fifty years, with the founding of centers on the Greek mainland, and the influence of Pythagorean teachings has lasted to the present. Since individual Pythagoreans contributed to the order's philosophy and contemporary records were not reliable, it is not possible to identify which of the order's concepts are specifically those of Pythagoras himself.

Neopythagoreanism, a Hellenistic school of philosophy, was founded in the first century B.C. by Publius Nigidius Figulus and was espoused by Apollonius of Tyana. Neopythagoreanism professed unbroken lineage from the Pythagorean Order, and was absorbed into Neoplatonism in the third century A.D. See **Plato**.

Major Teachings

Pythagoras is best known for the fundamental geometric theorem named for him, which states the square of the hypotenuse of a right triangle is equal to the sum of the squares of the sides containing the right angle. The theorem's corollary states that the diagonal of a square is incommensurable with its side.

Pythagoras conceived of the universe as a living being, animated by a great Soul and permeated by Intelligence. He called God the Monad, the Supreme Mind. Humankind was separate, save for the soul, which was a spark of the Monad that was imprisoned in a mortal body. The task of human beings was to purify themselves in preparation for return to the Monad.

Pythagoras said all sidereal bodies were alive and had souls; the planets were deities. According to Aristotle Pythagoras also believed that the Earth had a dual rotation and circled the sun; but this potentially sacrilegious teaching was saved for only the most trusted disciples.

Furthermore, Pythagoras saw the cosmos as a mathematically ordered whole. Everything in the universe and in nature was divided into threes. The universe had three worlds: (1) the Supreme World, a subtle essence that was the true plane of the Monad; (2) the Superior World, the home of the immortals; and (3) the Inferior World, the home of mortal gods, daimons, humans, animals, and all material things. Living beings had a triune nature: body, soul (which Pythagoras related to mind), and spirit. He also said that all arts and sciences are based on three elements: music, mathematics, and astronomy.

Pythagoras described numbers as an intrinsic and living virtue of the Monad. He ascribed to each a principle, law, and active force of the universe. The first four numbers contain the basic principles of the universe, since adding or multiplying them produces all other numbers. Besides three, Pythagoras gave special meaning to the numbers seven and ten. Seven, comprised of the numbers three and four, represents the union of human and divinity. It is the number of adepts and great initiates. Ten is a perfect number (1 + 2 + 3 + 4) and represents all the principles of the Monad. Pythagorean number theories survive in modern-day numerology. See **Numerology.**

In the area of music, Pythagoras is credited with discovery of the diatonic scale. He discovered that all music can be reduced to mathematical ratios. These ratios also could be applied to the universe, he said, which gave rise to his curious theory of the Harmony (or Music) of the Spheres. The theory was based on harmonic relationships drawn between all heavenly bodies, which produced music as the bodies rushed through space. This divine music could not be heard by human beings, however (except perhaps by the enlightened, such as Pythagoras), as long as humankind was in its fallen, material state.

Pythagoras believed in the healing power of music, and composed "musical medicine." He favored stringed instruments, especially the lute; he said songs sung to the lute purified the soul. He advocated avoidance of flutes and cymbals. See **Music.**

Pythagoras also taught herbal and medicinal plant lore. He opposed surgery. In other teachings he said friendship was the truest and nearest to perfection of all relationships. Anarchy was the greatest crime. He told his disciples that once they were initiated, they had to allow the truth to descend into their beings and apply it in daily life. To accomplish this they had to bring together three perfections: (1) to realize truth in intellect; (2) to realize virtue in the soul; and (3) to realize purity in the body. Regarding the latter he advocated not eating beans, and said meat-eating clouded the reason. He himself ate meat occasionally, but said judges in particular should not eat meat before sitting at trial.

The Pythagoreans believed in the immortality of the soul, in the soul's ability to separate from the body, and in reincarnation. See **Reincarnation.**

Sources: Andre Dacier. *The Life of Pythagoras.* York Beach, ME: Samuel Weiser, 1981; Peter Gorman. *Pythagoras: A Life.* Boston: Routledge & Kegan Paul, 1978; Manly P. Hall. *The Secret Teachings of All Ages.* 1928. Los Angeles: The Philosophical Research Society, 1977; Edouard Schure. *The Great Initiates: A Study of the Secret Religions of History.* San Francisco: Harper & Row, 1961; Ward Rutherford. *Pythagoras: Lover of Wisdom.* York Beach, ME: Samuel Weiser, 1984.

Q

Qabala (also Qabalah)

See **Kabbalah; Magic.**

Qi

See **Universal life force.**

Qi Gong (also Ch'i Kung)

An ancient Chinese art and science of breath, posture, motion, sound, intention, and visualization to cultivate *qi,* the vital force, throughout the body. Its origins date to the oracle bones of ancient China, and it is mentioned in the *Tao Teh Ching* text of Taoist mysticism.

Qi gong literally means "work on the ch'i," and involves the forceful expelling of toxins. The breath is heard, unlike the often silent breath control of Tai Ji Chuan and some forms of yoga. "Healing Sounds" Qi Gong involves the coordination of mantra-like syllables with breath, movement, vibration, and awareness in order to purify the major organs of the body.

There are three main types of Qi Gong. Medical Qi Gong is often referred to as "acupuncture without needles." It is used to strengthen the immune system and treat various diseases. Qi Gong doctors reportedly possess extraordinary abilities, such as the manipulation of patients' limbs at a distance, and the ability to effect physical and chemical changes by projecting intention on acupuncture points.

Buddhist and Taoist Qi Gong expand into a discipline of mental and spiritual development with martial art and meditational practices. Compare to **Tai Ji Chuan.**

Sources: Kenneth S. Cohen. "Exercises for Youth and Vitality." *East/West Journal* (January 1982): 52–55; Roger Jahnke. "Qigong: Awakening and Mastering the Profound Medicine That Lies Within." *Newsletter of the International Society for the Study of Subtle Energies and Energy Medicine* 1, no. 2 (Fall 1990): 3–7.

Quakers

See **Society of Friends.**

R

Radiesthesia

See Dowsing.

Rainmaking

See Cloud dissolving.

Rajneesh Foundation International

See Alternative religious movements.

Ramakrishna, Sri

See Hinduism.

Ram Dass (b. 1931)

Psychologist, humanist, and popular spokesperson on enlightenment. Ram Dass was born Richard Alpert on April 6, 1931, in Boston, Massachusetts, to a Jewish family. His father, George Alpert, was a lawyer who helped found Brandeis University and was president of the New York, New Haven, and Hartford Railroad. Richard Alpert pursued a career in psychology, specializing in human motivation and personality development. He earned his master's degree at Wesleyan University and his doctorate at Stanford University in 1957. He taught at Stanford and the University of California at Berke-

ley. In 1958 he joined the faculty in the Department of Social Relations and the Graduate School of Education at Harvard University.

At Harvard he met Timothy Leary, who in 1961 introduced him to the hallucinogen psilocybin. He later described the experience as a turning point in his life. He said he discovered that "I" existed beyond his social and physical identity, and entire realms of possibility opened up. From 1961 to 1963 Alpert, Leary, and others pursued a program of research with psilocybin and LSD-25, administering the drugs to volunteer graduate students, prison inmates, ministers, scientists, and others. Although the research was not to include undergraduates, some were given the drugs anyway. See Leary, Timothy.

The drug research was controversial, and in 1963 Alpert and Leary were fired from Harvard—the first professors to be dismissed from the university in the twentieth century. For the next four years, Alpert and Leary continued their association and research through the Castalia Foundation, a private foundation they established, and through the community they formed at Millbrook, New York.

By 1967 Alpert had become aware of the limitations of psychedelics as a spiritual practice, and traveled to India on a search for Eastern methods of enlightenment. He met his guru, Neem Karoli Baba (known to his Western devotees as

Ram Dass

"Maharaji"), and settled in a small temple in the Himalayas to study yoga, meditation, and bhakti (devotional) practices. Maharaji gave him the Hindu name "Ram Dass," meaning "servant of God." The following year Ram Dass returned to the United States and continued to pursue a variety of spiritual practices, including Bhakti Yoga, focused on his guru and on the Hindu deity Hanuman; Karma Yoga; Sufism; and meditation in the Theravada, Mahayana, and Zen traditions of Buddhism.

Soon after his return, he began sharing his spiritual insights with increasingly large audiences. He continues to teach widely, now emphasizing compassionate service as a spiritual path. He trains AIDS volunteers and works with the dying, and is a member of the board of directors of the Seva Foundation, a nonprofit organization that supports health, ecology, and service projects around the world, especially in developing countries.

Although the focus of his practice shifted away from psychedelics after he met his guru, Ram Dass believes that they fulfilled an important role in opening up Western culture to the wisdom of the East. In lectures given in 1970 and 1972, he observed that he honors LSD for being "one of the major breakthroughs in this culture," because it enabled people to experience other planes of reality, and by temporarily dissolving the ego, prepared them to face physical death with greater awareness and equanimity. He has acknowledged that there were mistakes of excesses in the Harvard research, including giving LSD to undergraduates and in underestimating the speed at which the whole of society could be enlightened. He said he continues to take psychedelics.

In 1974 Ram Dass created the Hanuman Foundation, based in Santa Fe, New Mexico. Programs initiated by the Foundation include the Prison-Ashram Project to foster the spiritual growth of prisoners, and the Living-Dying Project to assist terminally ill people who wish to approach death as a conscious, spiritual unfolding. These programs continue today under other auspices.

His books as Ram Dass include *Be Here Now* (1971), considered a landmark spiritual guide of the early 1970s; *The Only Dance There Is* (1974), taken from lectures given at the Menninger Foundation and elsewhere; *Miracle of Love: Stories about Neem Karoli Baba* (1979); *Journey of Awakening: A Meditator's Guidebook* (1982; 2d ed. 1990); *How Can I Help?* (1985) with Paul Gorman, which concerns service to others and is used in medical, nursing, and social service schools, volunteer agencies, hospices, and other service organizations; and *Grist for the Mill* (1987), with Stephen Levine.

Sources: Edgar D. Mitchell. *Psychic Exploration: A Challenge for Science.* Edited by John White. New York: Paragon Books, 1974; Ram Dass. *The Only Dance There Is.* Garden City, NY: Anchor Books/ Doubleday, 1974; Ram Dass. *Journey of*

Awakening: A Meditator's Guidebook. New York: Bantam Books, 1982; Leslie A. Shepard, ed. *Encyclopedia of Occultism and Parapsychology.* 2d ed. Detroit: Gale Research Co., 1984; Seva Foundation.

Ramtha

See Knight, JZ.

Randi, James "The Amazing"

See Committee for the Scientific Investigation of Claims of the Paranormal (CSICOP).

Rapture

See Ecstasy; Mystical experiences.

Rasputin, Grigory Yefimovich (1872?–1916)

Russian mystic, healer, and prophet who predicted his own death, the deaths of Tsar Nicholas II and his family, and the downfall of the nobility in Russia.

Rasputin was born in Pokrovskoye to Siberian peasant parents; he may have been the distant descendant of Siberian shamans. As a youth he worked as a carter and acquired an early reputation for fighting, drinking, and womanizing. He also was attracted to religion.

At age twenty he married a woman four years older than he and became a farmer. They had a son, who died as an infant. Soon after, Rasputin experienced a vision of the Virgin Mary calling to him, and he set out on a two-year religious pilgrimage to Mt. Athos in Greece. When he returned home, he was changed, possessing the ability to heal and cure by prayer. He set himself up as a *starets,* an unordained holy man. When his popularity threatened the village priest, Rasputin left town.

He was drawn to St. Petersburg, Russia's capital, where the nobility and high society were intensely interested in the occult and Spiritualism, due in large part to the 1871 visit by the famed English medium Daniel Dunglas Home. The atmosphere was ripe for someone like Rasputin to be noticed.

Despite his scruffy appearance and odd ways, Rasputin gained quick fame with his healing ability. He attracted the attention of the royal family, Nicholas and Alexandra, whose sole male heir, Alexis, had hemophilia. Rasputin was able to alleviate the boy's suffering. Alexandra became devoted to him, which aroused jealousy and enmity among others in court.

Rasputin's licentious behavior exacerbated his lack of popularity. He boasted of his early days of womanizing, and preached that one must sin before one can be redeemed. He acquired numerous mistresses. By 1911 his behavior was considered a scandal and disgrace. Opposition to him grew, and in 1916 a group of nobles plotted to kill him.

Rasputin presaged his own death, which he wrote down in a letter. He predicted he would be dead by January 1, 1917. If peasants killed him, the monarchy would continue and prosper; but if the nobles killed him, the royal family would die within two years, and the aristocracy would be plunged into trouble for twenty-five years, after which it would be eliminated from the country.

The circumstances of Rasputin's death are bizarre. On the night of December 29 to 30, 1916, Rasputin attended a midnight tea to which he had been invited in the home of Prince Feliks Yusupov, one of his enemies. There he allegedly was fed cakes and wine laced with cyanide, which, incredibly, did not kill him. Yusupov then shot him. Rasputin collapsed, then jumped up and dashed into the courtyard. Yusupov shot him again and beat him with an iron bar. Still he remained alive. The desperate conspirators dragged him to the frozen Neva River, bound him, and pushed him through a hole in the ice. When his body was recovered, the cause of death was determined as drowning; no traces of poison were detected.

True to Rasputin's prophecy, the royal family was murdered within two years. The Russian Revolution and World War I plunged the country into chaos and threatened the old aristocratic order. The nobility finally came to an end twenty-five years later, in World War II, at the hands of Josef Stalin.

Sources: Alex de Jonge. *Life and Times of Grigorii Rasputin.* New York: Dorset, 1982; Colin Wilson. *The Occult.* New York: Vintage Books, 1973.

Recurrent spontaneous psychokinesis

See **Poltergeist.**

Reflexology

See **Bodywork.**

Reich, Wilhelm

See **Bodywork; Universal life force.**

Reichenbach, Karl von

See **Universal life force.**

Reichian massage

See **Bodywork.**

Reiki

See **Bodywork.**

Reincarnation

The return of the soul or essence after death to inhabit a new physical form. Belief in reincarnation has existed for thousands of years, and the concept has flourished at one time or another in virtually every part of the world. Roughly two-thirds of the world's modern population accepts some form of reincarnation or rebirth as a fundamental belief—most notably Hindus and Buddhists, as well as many tribal societies. Western belief in reincarnation is low but has slowly increased since the late nineteenth century, due largely to the influence of Theosophy, the American medium Edgar Cayce, and the introduction of Eastern religions.

Reincarnation beliefs have varied considerably from culture to culture. The ancient Egyptians believed in the reincarnation of great souls whose purpose is to lead humankind. The Egyptians modified that belief over the years to apply reincarnation to the masses. The Egyptian Book of the Dead includes incantations for reincarnation.

In ancient Greece Pythagoras (c. 572 B.C.–479 B.C.) taught reincarnation. Plato (c. 427 B.C.–347 B.C.) said that without successive lives, life in the universe would disappear.

In Africa deeply rooted reincarnation beliefs are held by many tribes. Among those tribes who believe humans reincarnate as humans, childlessness is considered a curse because it blocks souls from being reborn.

In Australia the belief is strongest among the central aboriginal tribes, but is found elsewhere on the continent. With the dying of their ancient culture, some Aborigines believe they will reincarnate as "Whitefellows" in the continuing evolution of their souls.

Throughout the Pacific Island cultures, reincarnation also holds strong. It is found among the Balinese, Okinawans, Ainu (northern Japan), Tasmanians,

Maoris (New Zealand), Fijians, and the inhabitants of New Caledonia, Solomon Islands, and Melanesia.

In North America many Native American tribes believe in reincarnation. The Tlingits of Alaska, for example, attach great importance to it as a glorious continuation of personal identity. Prior to the birth of an infant, a soul announces its intent to reincarnate through dreams to the pregnant woman or her close relatives. At birth the infant must be correctly identified according to previous lives, and given the tribal name of the person he or she was before. In this way the child can take credit for all the good deeds done by his or her previous incarnations. An infant who is not identified correctly is denied his or her right to accumulated glory.

Reincarnation beliefs also exist among Native Central and South Americans, and perhaps were one reason why the Spanish conquistadors took over with such relative ease. The Spaniards were hailed as reborn gods, Quetzalcoatl in Mexico and Virochas in Peru, and the natives were anxious to submit to their whims—with disastrous results.

With rare exception past lives are not recalled spontaneously; most of those who do remember past lives naturally are children. According to various traditions, forgetfulness of past lives is necessary to the process of reincarnation.

Reincarnation in Islam

The concept of reincarnation was known to ancient Persians prior to the arrival of Islam. The teachings of the prophet Zarathustra allude to it, and it is explicitly taught in *The Desatir*, a mystical work written c. 500 B.C. In the sixth century A.D., the prophet Muhammad received the Koran, the Bible of Islam, from Allah. The Koran makes no direct reference to reincarnation, but some of its passages are interpreted as referring to it;

one example is chapter 25—Sura Zakhraf—Meccan Verses 5-10-6: "And He sent down rain from above in proper quantity and He brings back to life the dead earth, similarly ye shall be reborn."

After Muhammad reincarnation passed into esoteric teachings. Three aspects of rebirth are generally accepted by various esoteric schools: (1) the periodical incarnation of the Perfect Man or Deity; (2) the return of the Imam (a divinity formerly manifest in Muhammad) or other spiritual leader after death; and (3) the return of ordinary souls. Some of the Ism'ilis say that Krishna reincarnated as Buddha and then Muhammad. See also **Sufism.**

Reincarnation in Hinduism

Samsara, the "wheel of rebirth," is taken for granted by Hindus from earliest childhood. Hindus believe reincarnation is caused by the imperfections of the soul when it first comes into the world. Ignorance and desire perpetuate the need to reincarnate. The soul perfects itself by purifying and realizing itself, and shedding earthly desires. It is able to quit samsara when it is reunited with Brahman, the Absolute.

Samsara is influenced by karma, the law of cause and effect. Good is rewarded and evil is punished. Humans may reincarnate in lower life forms. The number of incarnations is limitless. Successive lives are separated by a period of rest in which the soul contemplates its progress. See **Karma.**

It is not certain exactly how old the concept of reincarnation is in Hinduism; there are inferences to rebirth or reincarnation in the oldest sacred writings, the Vedas, some dating to c. 1000 B.C. The Upanishads, which elaborate upon the Vedas, refer to reincarnation. Reincarnation is explained more fully in the *Bhagavad-Gita* ("The Lord's Song" or "Song of Krishna"), part of the *Mahab-*

harata, composed c. 400 B.C. to A.D. 200. In the Gita Krishna, the eighth avatar (incarnation) of Vishnu, explains that the self is eternal. "Both I and thou have passed through many births!" Krishna says to Arjuna. "Mine are known to me, but thou knowest not of thine." Krishna explains that through continual striving through many lives, the soul can at last attain a state of supreme happiness and grace.

Hinduism regards reincarnation as misery and a sorrowful burden, a bondage from which to escape. At times in India's history, reincarnation and the law of karma have been abused by the ruling Brahmin caste as a way to manipulate the masses.

Reincarnation in Buddhism

Buddhism, which prevails in parts of India and throughout Asia, derives a doctrine of rebirth (distinct from reincarnation) from Hinduism. According to the Pali Canon, the early scriptures of the Theravada school, Buddha taught that the individual has a lesser self, which dies with the body, and a greater self, which survives. However, Buddhism has evolved with the concept of *anatta,* or "no self" or "non-self," which holds that there is no personality or ego which remains intact from life to life. Instead the personality disintegrates at death into sparks or pieces, which coalesce with other sparks to form a new personality. The life force, or will to live, is what survives, taking with it the good and bad karmic attributes developed during the life. Incarnations are caused by karma and earthly cravings, which must be overcome in the pursuit of spiritual perfection. Prior to rebirth parents are chosen for karmic reasons.

Liberation from rebirth is achieved when one overcomes the "three unwholesome roots" — desire, hatred, and delusion — and attains nirvana ("extinc-

tion"), or enlightenment, a state of ineffable peace.

The wheel of rebirth has six states of existence through which sentient beings revolve as long as there is evil karma to be worked off: gods (devas); *asuras* (elemental forces); humans; animals; *pretas* ("hungry ghosts," who live in a purgatory of unsatisfied desires); and denizens of hell. In Buddhism "hell" is another state of temporary purgatory, the nature and duration of which is determined by karma. It is only in the human state that one has a chance to awaken spiritually; when that is accomplished, there is no longer a need to remain on the wheel, but one may choose to be reborn. See **Bodhisattva.** Like Hinduism, Buddhism views birth as misery and a burden.

Both Hindus and Buddhists believe that the last thought at the moment of death determines the character of the next incarnation. Thus it is of vital importance to die properly, and a yogic art of dying and choosing the next womb is taught to adepts. According to the Tibetan Book of the Dead, the Bardo, or after-death state, lasts for forty-nine days. It is characterized by three stages of deteriorating consciousness: Clear Light, or supreme serenity; visitations from the Peaceful and Wrathful Deities; and a reckoning of karma that ends in rebirth. The transition itself from life to death occurs in a state of unconsciousness over three-and-a-half to four days; the Book of the Dead sets forth procedures for making the transition without losing consciousness.

Reincarnation in Judaism

Gilgul is the Hebrew term for transmigration, the passage of a soul upon death into another body. There is no direct reference to gilgul in the Torah, unless one looks for it in allegories. It is, however, contained in the Kabbalah, the body of mystical works based on early esoteric teachings, compiled beginning in medieval times by rabbis.

According to the Kabbalah, the early Jews believed in the transmigration of great prophets: Adam became David, who was to become the Messiah. The *Zohar* (Book of Splendor), an influential work first published c. 1280 but attributed to teachings in the first century A.D., extends gilgul to everyone: "All souls are subject to the trials of transmigration . . ."

Not all Kabbalists viewed gilgul as a universal law, however, but related it to sins against procreation and sexual taboos. Others said reincarnation was punishment for Cain's slaying of Abel, and would quit only when all the dead were resurrected. A few Kabbalists advanced the view that humans could transmigrate into animals, or even into plants or rocks.

The Kabbalah was prominent in Jewish thought from about the thirteenth to eighteenth centuries. Later Kabbalistic works developed the idea of "main souls" belonging to one root, which was Adam. When Adam fell his soul scattered into sparks, which could only be reassembled through gilgul.

In the nineteenth century, the Kabbalah fell out of fashion with skeptical Jewish scholars, and gilgul lost its place in teachings. As of the twentieth century, gilgul has not been taught in the three main branches of Judaism—Reform, Conservative, and Orthodox—but is taught by the Hasidic sect.

Reincarnation in Christianity

Edgar Cayce once said, "I can read reincarnation into the Bible, and you can read it right out again!" Reincarnation is not taught in any of Christianity's mainstream denominations. Christians who believe in reincarnation feel there is evidence for the concept in the Bible, despite the lack of direct reference to it. In the Book of Matthew, Jesus says John the Baptist was once the prophet Elijah, who was supposed to return to earth before the coming of the Messiah. John the Baptist denied that he was, but reincarnationists explain that in terms of the "forgetfulness" that descends before every new life.

Opponents to reincarnation say there is nothing on the subject in the Gospels or St. Paul, and say only Jesus has the power to be born again on the earth. Proponents say reincarnation is implied in the New Testament, and find it significant that Jesus did not refute the concept. They add that from the perspective of the authors of the Gospels, Jesus' return was imminent and would bring the end of the world, which obviated reincarnation.

The Gnostics, who influenced Christian doctrine, believed in reincarnation, according to ancient Coptic records discovered around 1945 in Egypt. The Gnostic manuscript *Pistis Sophia* ("Knowledge-Wisdom") tells how Jesus explained to Mary Magdalene that he had brought about the rebirth of advanced souls, including Elijah (Elias) as John the Baptist. Early Christians called Pre-Existants, who included such church authorities as Justin Martyr and Origen, believed in the doctrine of the preexistence of the soul, which implies reincarnation. This doctrine apparently was cast out in 553 when the Roman Emperor Justinian, who had made himself head of the church, anathametized (cursed) Origen.

Belief in reincarnation survived, along with other Gnostic views, into the Middle Ages in religious sects such as the Cathars and Albigenses, in groups such as the Knights Templar, Rosicrucians, and Freemasons, and among alchemists, Kabbalists, and others.

Western secular interest in reincarnation was revived in the nineteenth century, when Madame Helena P. Blavatsky introduced Theosophy, Eastern esoteric thought, to the West. In *Isis Unveiled* Blavatsky said reincarnation was caused by "ignorance of the senses."

In the twentieth century, belief in reincarnation has spread fairly evenly throughout the predominantly Christian West, according to the few public opinion polls that have been taken.

In 1969 a George Gallup poll of adults in twelve countries showed that belief in reincarnation ranged from a low of 10 percent (the Netherlands) to a high of 26 percent (Canada). The United States registered 20 percent, while the United Kingdom scored 18 percent.

A 1981 Gallup poll in the United States alone showed a 3 percent increase in reincarnationists, to 23 percent, or a total of about 38 million adults. Slightly more women were believers (25 percent) than men (21 percent). Roughly one-quarter of those in major religious denominations said they were believers: 26 percent of Methodists, 25 percent of Catholics, 22 percent of Lutherans, and 21 percent of Protestants.

None of the mainstream Christian denominations officially recognizes or teaches reincarnation, though various members of the clergies have speculated on or supported it. The Unity Church (sometimes called the New Age Church) recognizes reincarnation, and invites the teaching of it to church members. The church emphasizes "regeneration" rather than reincarnation, stating that regeneration, or the purification of the soul, eventually makes reincarnation no longer necessary.

Scientific Investigation of Reincarnation

Efforts have been made to scientifically investigate reincarnation and validate claims of past lives. Most notable of these is the research of Ian Stevenson, professor of psychiatry at the University of Virginia, who began investigating spontaneous reincarnational memories among children around the world in the 1960s. In India, other researchers have investigated cases since the 1920s. See **Past-life recall.**

Reincarnation has yet to be proven scientifically, but Stevenson acknowledges evidence in support of reincarnation. A major problem in reconciling reincarnation with science is that science does not recognize the existence of the consciousness apart from the brain, as an essence that survives the brain after bodily death. Heredity and environment are said to be the sole agents responsible for the formation of body and personality.

Reincarnation as the Opposite Sex

Beliefs in sex switching vary from culture to culture. In some societies where the status of women is very low, it is considered impossible for a man to reincarnate as a woman (as the Druse of Lebanon believe), or it is considered karmic punishment. Some early Kabbalists maintained that gender change was unnatural, and that a man who reincarnated as a woman would be barren.

Western believers in reincarnation generally accept sex change as part of the soul's development. Stevenson and other researchers have collected cases involving alleged gender change.

Reincarnation of Humans in Nonhuman Form

The belief in transmigration of humans to the lower kingdoms is held by Hindus, Buddhists, and many African tribes, and some Native Americans, such as the Inuit. In Africa beliefs of rebirth of the human soul in nonhuman forms are more commonplace than human-to-human rebirth beliefs. Nonhuman forms include animals, birds, reptiles, insects, plants, and fabulous monsters.

The ancient Egyptians believed that the human soul could occupy animal forms in perfecting itself, and could spend up to three thousand years in animal bodies before returning to a human form. The ancient Greek concept of "metempsychosis," the passage of a human soul into a human or animal body, was learned from the Egyptians. It is uncertain whether metempsychosis was taught literally or figuratively by Pythagoras and Plato. According to some Platonists, a regressed human soul did not actually become the soul of an animal, but took over the body like a daimon or spirit guide. See **Spirit guide.**

Justin Martyr, an early Christian philosopher (c. 100–165), believed that "unworthy" human souls were put into the bodies of wild beasts. That idea was opposed by other early Christians, including Tertullian (c. 160–230), who dismissed it as ridiculous. In the modern West, transmigration of humans to animals is widely rejected, even among those who believe in reincarnation, including the Unity Church. The chief argument advanced against this belief is that the highly developed human consciousness could not possibly operate in a lower form of life. Furthermore, the law of karma would not be served, for an animal could not possibly understand or appreciate what happened.

Stevenson has found no convincing evidence in his research to support transmigration to lower life forms. The Cayce readings contain no such occurrences, although Cayce did state that humankind's attitude toward and treatment of animals produces a karmic reaction from the animal kingdom itself.

Reincarnation in the Subhuman Kingdoms

Hindus and Buddhists believe all forms of life reincarnate as part of their own spiritual evolution. Some Westerners believe in a one-way process in which subhuman entities advance to the human kingdom and beyond. According to Theosophy subhuman species belong to a "group soul," a collective consciousness. When an animal dies, for example, its individuality is absorbed into the pool. New animal souls are reborn from sparks sent off by the group soul—similar to the Buddhist concept of rebirth for humans. Theosophy also holds that several parallel evolutionary streams exist on planet Earth. One stream begins with minerals and works its way up through plants, shrubs, trees, antediluvian reptiles and lower mammals, mammals, and domestic animals to finally reach human beings (three levels of primitive, ordinary, and advanced). Another stream also begins with minerals, but follows a different path through grasses, ants, bees, etheric creatures, fairies, fire spirits, sylphs, astral devas, and higher devas. Birds belong to a stream that ends in nature spirits and devas.

The group soul concept exists in the teachings of Zarathustra, who asked the Creator Ahura-Mazda what happened to the consciousness of a dog when it died. According to the *Vendidad,* a Zoroastrian scripture, Ahura-Mazda answered, "Oh holy Zarathustra! it goes into a stream of water, where, from a thousand male, and a thousand female dogs, a pair—one male and one female—of the Udra [a water dog, perhaps seal or walrus], that reside in the waters, comes into being."

One documented case of alleged animal reincarnation from the 1960s involves a Vietnamese boy who recalled that in his previous life he had a dog, that also had died and gone with him into the afterlife. In the investigation of the case, the boy was taken to the village where he said he had lived, and where still lived the members of his previous family. One of the family members had a dog that had never seen the boy before but acted as though it knew him. The boy believed it was his former pet reincarnated. The boy said that prior to reincarnation, he had been given not fruit, but a "soup of forgetfulness," which he had disposed of by giving it to his dog-spirit. Apparently, the soup did not affect the dog in its next life.

Sources: Theodore Besterman. *Collected Papers on the Paranormal.* New York: Garrett Publications, 1968; John Blofeld. *The Tantric Mysticism of Tibet.* Boston: Shambhala Publications, 1987; Gina Cerminara. *Many Lives, Many Loves.* New York: William Sloane Assoc., 1963; Emily Williams Cook. "Research on Reincarnation-Type Cases: Present Status and Suggestions for Future Research." *Case Studies in Honor of Louisa E. Rhine.* Edited by K. Ramakrishna Rao. Jefferson, NC: McFarland & Co., 1986; Sylvia Cranston and Carey Williams. *Reincarnation: A New Horizon in Science, Religion, and Society.* New York: Julian Press, 1984; W. Y. Evans-Wentz, ed. *The Tibetan Book of the Dead.* 3d ed. London: Oxford University Press, 1960; Joe Fisher. *The Case for Reincarnation.* 1984. New York: Bantam Books, 1985; George Gallup, Jr., with William Proctor. *Adventures in Immortality.* New York: McGraw-Hill Book Co., 1982; Rosemary Ellen Guiley. *Tales of Reincarnation.* New York: Pocket Books, 1989; Tenzin Gyatso, His Holiness the Fourteenth Dalai Lama. *Kindness, Clarity, and Insight.* Ithaca, NY: Snow Lion Publications, 1984; Manly Palmer Hall. *Reincarnation: The Cycle of Necessity.* Los Angeles: The Philosophical Research Society, 1956; Joseph Head and S. L. Cranston, comps. and eds. *Reincarnation in World Thought.* New York: Julian Press, 1967; Joseph Head and S. L. Cranston, comps. and eds. *Reincarnation: The Phoenix Fire Mystery.* New York: Julian Press, 1977; Le-Quang H'u'ong. "Histoires vietnamienes de reincarnation." *Message d'extreme-orient* 2, no. 7 (1972): 535–39; Yong Choon Kim. *Oriental Thought.* Totowa, NJ: Rowman and Littlefield, 1973; His Holiness the Dalai Lama of Tibet. *My Land and My People: Memoirs of the Dalai Lama of Tibet.* 1962. New York: Potala Corp., 1977; Noel Langley. *Edgar Cayce on Reincarnation.* New York: Castle Books, 1967; Frederick Lenz. *Lifetimes: True Accounts of Reincarnation.* New York: Fawcett Crest, 1977; James G. Matlock. "Age and Stimulus in Past-Life Memory Cases: A Study of Published Cases." *The Journal of the American Society for Psychical Research* 83 (October 1989): 303–16; Marcia Moore and Mark Douglas. *Reincarnation, Key to Immortality.* York Cliffs, ME: Arcane Publications, 1968; Marcia Moore. *Hypersentience.* New York: Bantam Books, 1977; Ian Stevenson. *Twenty Cases Suggestive of Reincarnation.* 2d ed. Charlottesville, VA: University Press of Virginia, 1974; Francis Story. *Rebirth as Doctrine and Experience.* Kandy, Sri Lanka: Buddhist Publication Society, 1975.

Relaxation

A state of deep rest in which the metabolism of the body slows; less oxygen is burned, the heart and respiration rates drop, blood pressure drops, and brain waves slow to an alpha state. Relaxation of both mind and body is a key factor in the development of psychic faculties and in the attainment of enlightened states of consciousness. Relaxation is stressed in all Eastern meditation disciplines. It has been demonstrated to be a significant influence on the successful performance of psi in laboratory experiments. Relaxation also has been shown to enhance one's ability to learn new information, perform tasks, and achieve results through creative visualization. In a psychic reading, relaxation is just as important for the client as for the psychic, in order to facilitate the flow of superphysical sense perceptions.

The first systematic study of relaxation in relation to psi was conducted in 1952 by American parapsychologist Gertrude Schmeidler. Schmeidler found that hospitalized concussion patients scored much higher in psi guessing tasks than did patients suffering from other disorders, and concluded it was due to their greater relaxation. Subsequent studies of progressive states of relaxation in psi tests have supported her conclusion.

The importance of relaxation in meditation and mystical disciplines has been known for centuries. Relaxation is paramount to achieving a state of perfect mental solitude and quiet, in which either a union or a communion with the divine becomes attainable. The body must be at ease and the mind stilled to blankness.

Relaxation can be achieved through Eastern yoga and meditation techniques, as well as through progressive muscular relaxation, the loosening of every part of the body from head to toe; chanting; biofeedback; and self-hypnosis. Some people use self-hypnosis tapes, environmental music, and incense. Medium Eileen J. Garrett believed that relaxation is enhanced when one of the five senses is stimulated, such as hearing or smell.

Relaxation is impaired by drugs, including alcohol, tobacco, caffeine, tranquilizers, hallucinogens, and other mind- and mood-altering substances. See **Altered states of consciousness; Biofeedback; Meditation; Yoga.**

Sources: Herbert Benson. *The Relaxation Response.* New York: Avon Books, 1976; Jo An Chase as told to Constance Moon. *You Can Change Your Life through Psychic Power.* New York: Permabooks, 1960; Jack Forem. *Transcendental Meditation.* New York: E. P. Dutton, 1973; Maxwell Maltz. *The Magic Power of Self-Image Psychology.* New York: Pocket Books, 1970; Ormond McGill. *The Mysticism and Magic of India.* Cranbury, NJ: A. S. Barnes & Co., 1977; Sheila Ostrander and Lynn Schroeder. *Handbook of Psi Discoveries.* New York: Berkley, 1974; Sheila Ostrander and Lynn Schroeder. *Super-Learning.* New York: Dell, 1979; D. Scott Rogo. *Psychic Breakthroughs Today.* Wellingborough, Northamptonshire, England: The Aquarian Press, 1987; John White and James Fadiman, eds. *Relax.* New York: The Confucian Press, 1976; Benjamin B. Wolman, ed. *Handbook of Parapsychology.* New York: Van Nostrand Reinhold, 1977; Vivian Worthington. *A History of Yoga.* London: Routledge & Kegan Paul, 1982.

Releasement

See **Depossession.**

Remote viewing

Seeing remote or hidden objects clairvoyantly with the inner eye, or in alleged out-of-body travel. In the past remote viewing was called "traveling clairvoyance" and "telesthesia." The term "remote viewing" was coined in the 1970s by American physicists Russell Targ and Harold Puthoff. Targ suggests a more accurate name is "remote sensing," for it involves psychic impressions of smell, sound, and touch as well as sight.

Remote viewing is one of the oldest and most common forms of psi, and one of the most difficult to explain. As a shamanic skill, it has been used in Tibet, Siberia, Africa, India, and the Americas for centuries. Perhaps the first recorded account of remote viewing was written by Herodotus concerning Croesus, King of Lydia, who in 550 B.C. evaluated seven Greek oracles for accuracy. The oracles were asked by messengers what the king was doing at the moment on the day of inquiry. The Delphic oracle came out the clear winner: The Pythia reported the sight and smell of a tortoise and lamb boiling in a stew in a brass-lid-covered cauldron, which Croesus himself had prepared.

In the eighteenth century, Emanuel Swedenborg was renowned for his clairvoyance, which included remote visions. Philosopher Immanuel Kant, who investigated Swedenborg, recorded one famous incident that took place in 1759.

Swedenborg attended a dinner party in Gothenburg, Sweden. After two hours he excused himself and left the room, returning after some time in a state of anxiety. He announced that a fire had broken out in Stockholm, his hometown, and was spreading rapidly. For several hours he remained agitated, periodically leaving the company, coming back, and reporting on the fire's progress. He was immensely relieved when he saw the fire put out three doors away from his own house. The following day the governor of Gothenburg summoned Swedenborg, who gave a complete description of the fire, its origins, progress, and how it was extinguished. Two days later the governor received a report from Stockholm by courier, describing the fire exactly as Swedenborg had seen it.

In the late eighteenth and early nineteenth centuries, remote viewing, or "traveling clairvoyance" as it was called then, excited much interest among magnetists, who discovered that many of their hypnotized subjects could give detailed accounts of distant locations. Not only could they describe surroundings, people, clothing, and activities, some could "see" into distant stomachs to report their contents, and "see" into brains.

Many experiments in remote viewing were conducted during the nineteenth century. There was no shortage of capable subjects, who worked with eyes closed or blindfolded; some were even blind.

In the late nineteenth century, Frederic W. H. Myers, a founder of the Society for Psychical Research, London, observed that traveling clairvoyance seemed to be a fusion of telepathy, retrocognition, precognition, and clairvoyance. Sometimes the events or activities seen were displaced in time; the subject had the impression of immediacy, when in fact the events had already occurred or had yet to occur. Sometimes they carried on conversations with people seen remotely and "heard" responses. Subjects sent to remote locations to describe them occasionally got lost, and had to find their way by a psychic navigation that resembled the tracking of a hound dog.

In the early to mid-twentieth century, American writer Upton Sinclair and René Warcollier, a French engineer, recorded data relating to remote viewing and other psychic phenomena. In 1972 Targ and Puthoff used this data when they coined the term "remote viewing" and established a research project at SRI International (formerly Stanford Research Institute) in California.

After hundreds of experimental trials over at least ten years, Targ and Puthoff had amassed impressive results. They concluded that remote viewing is a psychic experience that occurs naturally in the lives of many people. They found they could train others to remote view, regardless of innate psychic ability and previous psychic experiences or training. Most viewers can be taught to "go" to a location and accurately describe buildings, geographic features, people, and activities. In many cases the further away the target, the greater the accuracy. They also can be taught to see into opaque containers to describe contents, and to read data and see images on microdot film. Ingo Swann, one of the SRI's leading psychics, used remote viewing to guide a submarine to the previously unknown site of a submerged shipwreck. Swann said he could remotely view sites around the world, given the longitude and latitude.

A related skill developed out of the SRI project is "associative remote viewing," obtaining analytical data through remote viewing. The viewer is asked to describe objects linked with the information desired. Associative remote viewing may have potential for predicting future events, such as election outcomes, stock market trends, and successful ventures, such as determining which of various oil sites should be drilled first.

Associative remote viewing works like this: Simple objects, like a ball or piece of fruit, are assigned to several possible future events. The viewer, who does not know the objects or the possible events, is asked to remote view into the future to see which object is going to be placed in his hands or presented to him on a certain date.

In 1982 Targ and American psychic Keith Harary conducted an associative remote viewing experiment on the silver futures market. A group of anonymous investors bought and sold futures according to the objects perceived by Harary, who did not know what they were. The objects included a vial of perfume, a pair of eyeglass frames, and a plastic bag of washers. The investors made more than $100,000 profit. However, a subsequent experiment to replicate the results failed.

Other major research in remote viewing has been done at Princeton University by the Princeton Engineering Anomalies Research (PEAR) group, established in 1979. PEAR is the first research group to apply modern engineering science techniques to a systematic study of psi phenomena. In experiments of "precognitive remote perception" (PRP), involving men and women of various ages, PEAR determined that it is possible to obtain remote information by means which are not explained by "known physical mechanisms."

Researchers have not been able to explain exactly how remote viewing works. The Soviets put forth the theory that psi is carried on extremely low frequency (ELF) electromagnetic waves, but that does not explain why remote viewing does not get weaker with greater distance. Using the SRI International data, other American and Canadian researchers have found that remote viewing is affected by geomagnetic activity. A higher incidence of geomagnetic activity one or two days before a remote viewing test has an adverse effect; low activity precedes successful tests. In some experiments remote viewers exhibited precognition, by seeing the target site before the target is known or visited by the other participants. See **Out-of-body experience (OBE); Applied psi.**

Sources: Slater Brown. *The Heyday of Spiritualism.* New York: Hawthorn Books, 1970; Alfred Douglas. *Extrasensory Powers: A Century of Psychical Research.* London: Victor Gollancz Ltd., 1976; Robert G. Jahn and Brenda J. Dunne. *Margins of Reality: The Role of Consciousness in the Physical World.* San Diego: Harcourt Brace Jovanovich, 1987; D. Scott Rogo. *Psychic Breakthroughs Today.* Wellingborough, Northamptonshire, England: The Aquarian Press, 1987; Russell Targ and Keith Harary. *The Mind Race.* New York: Villard Books, 1984; Russell Targ and Harold Puthoff. *Mind-Reach: Scientists Look at Psychic Ability.* New York: Delacorte Press, 1977.

Retrocognition (also postcognition)

Seeing into or sensing the past. Retrocognition occurs spontaneously but uncommonly in daily life, dreams, and in parapsychology experiments. It is claimed to be accomplished deliberately by psychics who seek access to past events in order to obtain unknown information useful in the present. Retrocognition is difficult to test scientifically because of the possibility of clairvoyance of existing historical records.

Spontaneous retrocognition usually manifests as a hallucination or vision. The present surroundings are abruptly replaced by a scene out of the past. Although the vision usually is fleeting, some last for minutes and generally feature movement, sounds, and smells.

Retrocognition is a phenomenon of some hauntings and apparitions that seem to be continual replays of events, such as murders or suicides. Psychologist

Gardner Murphy theorized that most ghosts are cases of retrocognition, in which an individual becomes momentarily displaced in time and can perceive scenes from the past.

The most famous and significant case of retrocognition involves apparitions seen at Versailles, dating to the 1770s in tranquil days prior to the French Revolution. Reports of apparitions there were recorded as early as 1870, but Versailles became famous as a case beginning in the summer of 1901. In that year two English academics, Eleanor Jourdain and Annie Moberly, visited the Petit and Grand Trianons. They walked a long route to the Petit Trianon and seemed to lose their way. Upon entering the garden, Moberly suddenly felt depressed. Both felt as though they were walking in a dream. The atmosphere was very still, eerie, and oppressed. The surroundings looked unpleasant and unnatural, almost two-dimensional. They saw and spoke to people in period costume of the 1770s, and saw a kiosk and a bridge that no longer existed.

In subsequent visits to the Petit Trianon, Moberly and Jourdain experienced the recognitive visions again. Their adventure was publicized, and others who visited the garden reported similar experiences. What was unusual about the initial experience of Moberly and Jourdain is the length of their hallucinations, perhaps up to thirty minutes. The haunting appears to be an "aimless haunting," as no extreme emotions are associated with apparitions.

Another well-known case is the Battle of Nechanesmere, which took place on May 20, 685, in Scotland. The Picts, led by King brude mac Beli, staved off an invasion of Northumbrians, led by King Ecgfrith, by killing Ecgfrith, his bodyguards, and most of his army. Survivors fled into the countryside.

On January 2, 1950, 1,265 years later, the aftermath of the battle was witnessed by E. F. Smith, a woman in her fifties. Driving home one snowy evening, Smith suffered a minor car accident about eight miles away from the village of Letham, near Nechanesmere. She began walking toward Letham with her dog.

About a half-mile from the village, Smith observed a mass of torches moving through the dark. She then perceived that they were held by figures who were dressed in period clothes, which she later identified as from the seventh century. The figures were moving through a field, turning over bodies. There was no sound save for the barking of her dog. Investigators theorized she witnessed a scene from the past, the Pictish searching for their dead from the Battle of Nechanesmere.

Yet another famous retrocognition case was all sound and no image. In August 1951 two British women pseudonymously identified as the Norton sisters went to Dieppe, France, for vacation. Dieppe had suffered an air raid during World War II on August 19, 1942, in which Canadian forces sustained heavy casualties. The Norton women heard machine-gun fire, rifle shots, dive-bombing planes, and human shouts and screams. The noise, which sounded like a movie soundtrack, lasted from 4 A.M. to 7 A.M. It was not heard by others.

Retrocognition is used in applied psi fields such as psychic criminology and psychic archaeology, in which past events are reconstructed by psychics to help solve crimes, find dig sites, or identify unknown objects found in digs. The retrocognition usually is done by using psychometry on objects. Some psychics say they enter an altered state of consciousness and consult the Akashic Records, which Edgar Cayce once termed "God's book of remembrance." See **Psychic archaeology; Psychic criminology; Psychometry.** Compare to **Precognition.**

Sources: *Individual Reference File of Extracts from the Edgar Cayce Readings.* Virginia Beach, VA: Edgar Cayce Foundation, 1976; Robert G. Jahn and Brenda J. Dunne. *Margins of Reality: The Role of Consciousness in the Physical World.* San Diego: Harcourt Brace Jovanovich, 1987; Andrew MacKenzie. *Hauntings and Apparitions.* London: William Heinemann Ltd., 1982; Edgar D. Mitchell. *Psychic Exploration: A Challenge for Science.* Edited by John White. New York: Paragon Books, 1974; Gardner Murphy. "Direct Contacts with Past and Future: Retrocognition and Precognition." *Journal of the American Society for Psychical Research* 61, no. 1 (January 1967): 3–23; Sheila Ostrander and Lynn Schroeder. *Psychic Discoveries Behind the Iron Curtain.* Englewood Cliffs, NJ: Prentice-Hall, 1970; Jack Harrison Pollack. *Croiset the Clairvoyant.* Garden City, NY: Doubleday, 1964; Jane Roberts. *Adventures in Consciousness.* New York: Bantam Books, 1979; Joan Windsor. *The Inner Eye: Your Dreams Can Make You Psychic.* Englewood Cliffs, NJ: Prentice-Hall, 1985; Benjamin B. Wolman, ed. *Handbook of Parapsychology.* New York: Van Nostrand Reinhold, 1977; Dixie Yeterian. *Casebook of a Psychic Detective.* New York: Stein and Day, 1982.

Revelation, Book of

The last book of the New Testament, which portrays the Second Coming of Christ, the final triumph of the kingdom of God, and the destruction of all evil; also called the (Book of the) Apocalypse. The opening verse presents the book's title as meaning either "the revelation which Christ possesses and imparts," or "the unveiling of the person of Christ" (1:1). The Book of Revelation is the only book of the New Testament whose character is exclusively prophetic.

The writer of the Apocalypse has traditionally been named as John the Evangelist. Church fathers who identify him as such include Justin, Irenaeus, Tertullian, and Clement of Alexandria. Subsequent scholarship has periodically questioned • the book's authorship. Part of the book

may have been written before the fall of Jerusalem (A.D. 70), and toward the end of the reign of the Emperor Domitian (81–96), who exiled John (the author of Revelation) to the island of Patmos and persecuted Christians. More significantly, there are theological differences (especially concerning the Second Coming) that raise serious doubts as to John the Evangelist being more than the inspiration for the Apocalypse.

The book is written in three parts. Part one features letters addressed to seven of the groups of Christians of the Roman province of Asia. These letters, which may have existed as a separate text, depict Christ's continuing relationship with his followers. Part two features the visions of judgment and the victory of God over the forces of evil. By extensive use of symbols and numbers, especially the number seven, the book foretells (or "reveals") a violent end of the world. Part three features a vision of heaven. The book concludes with a call to all those who listen to "come."

One of the most popular symbols used in Revelation is the Four Horsemen, often called the Four Horsemen of the Apocalypse. These are symbols of the evils to come at the Second Coming: a white horse (conquest), a red horse (war), a black horse (famine), and a pale horse (plague).

There are four main schools of interpretation of the book. The Preterists hold that the book tells the story of the contemporary condition of the state of Rome and the church, told in a sort of mystical code so as to hide the meaning from hostile pagans. Similarly, those of the Historical school hold that the symbolic form tells the story of the church, but the entire historical life of the church, not just its contemporary condition. The Futurists hold that some passages refer to the contemporary scene, and some to the return of Christ at the end of time. The Symbolic school sees the book as a dramatic picture of the war between good and evil, which exists in varying degrees in every historical age. Since part of the book was written during a time of severe persecutions of Christians, its original purpose may have been to assure Christians that they and their faith would be vindicated.

The four great visions presented in Revelation place the seer in a different location. Each paints a distinctive picture of Christ, and each moves the progress of the proceeding condition.

The immediacy of the Last Day has been a belief of many Christian groups. Even the first-century Christians read the New Testament, especially the closing two verses of Revelation, to mean these events were to happen in their lifetime. Ever since, various personal interpretations of Revelation have led religious leaders, usually self-appointed, to foretell a specific time for the final day, usually without the blessing of any major denomination.

Thematic throughout the book is the vision of "a new heaven and a new earth," which will be revealed at the Armageddon (the site and event of the final battle between good and evil), during the Second Coming of Jesus (The Parousia), on Judgment Day. While each major Christian denomination believes in at least aspects of these phenomena, to some degree they are essential to the faith and practice of both the Seventh-Day Adventists and the followers of Charles Taze Russell, who since 1931 have been called the Jehovah's Witnesses. They believe in the nearness of the Second Coming and, moreover, that exactly 144,000 people will go to heaven, and the rest of humanity will live in an earthly paradise.

The Book of the Apocalypse should not be confused with the Apocrypha (from the Greek meaning "hidden things"), which are religious writings that have not been accepted by certain religious groups. For example, Roman Cath-olics and Eastern Orthodox churches accept certain books in their Old Testament that Jews and many Protestants do not consider part of the Bible.

Sources: Pat Alexander, ed. *The Lion Encyclopedia of the Bible.* Rev. ed. Tring, England: Lion Publishing, 1986; T. Alton Bryant. *The New Compact Bible Dictionary.* New York: Pillar Books, 1967; Sherman E. Johnson. "Apocalyptic Literature." In *The Academic American Encyclopedia.* Princeton, NJ: Arete, 1980; *The New Jerusalem Bible.* Garden City, NY: Doubleday, 1966; *The New King James Bible.* Nashville: Nelson Thomas, 1979; *The New Oxford Annotated Bible.* New York: Oxford University Press, 1977.

Ritual

A ceremonial act, especially for religious or sacred purpose. All religions and spiritual, mystical, and magical traditions have their own rituals, which are the means to come into contact with God or gods or supernatural forces. Rituals help one to define oneself in relation to the cosmos, and to mark one's progress through life and one's spiritual unfoldment.

Psychiatrist Carl G. Jung observed that rituals "are an answer and reaction to the action of God upon man, and perhaps they are not only that, but are also intended to be 'activating,' a form of magic coercion" (*Memories, Dreams, Reflections,* 1961). Hsun Tzu, a Chinese philosopher of the third century B.C., said that rituals have three bases: heaven and earth, the source of all life; ancestors, the source of human life; and sovereigns and teachers, the source of government. Rites, said Hsun Tzu, make for harmony in the universe and bring out the best in human beings—they are the culmination of culture.

Rituals have various purposes, which may overlap: placation and propitiation; magical; initiation; invocations; transi-

Siberian shaman performing ritual to alter consciousness

(US Library of Congress)

tion or passage; supplication; fertility; social; sacrifice; healing or cleansing; purification; protection; banishment, and so on. Rituals have various natures. For example, some involve ordeals and physical mortification; others are ecstatic, and still others are contemplative. Some, such as the rites of the mysteries, are reenactments of mythical dramas. See **Mysteries.**

Mircea Eliade, the Romanian-born historian of religion, said rituals of initiation are the most significant spiritual phenomenon in human history, for their purpose is to alter the religious and social status of the individual. They prepare for and parallel the great transitions in body and spirit. Initiation rites are revealed by God or the gods, and to undergo such a rite is to imitate the gods. Eliade defined three broad categories of initiation rituals: puberty or passage into adulthood; entrance into a secret society or order; and entrance into a mystical vocation such as shaman or medicine man. The latter two tend to be ecstatic in nature. Shamanic initiations in particular involve contact with nonordinary reality.

An initiation rite has great depth and complexity. It involves ordeal and sacrifice; one comes face to face with the numinous. It culminates with one's symbolic death and rebirth into a new life, in which one has access to new values. The reborn one is given a new name to reflect his or her new status.

In modern civilization the rite of initiation, where it still exists at all, has lost much of its power. Eliade observed that initiatory themes in the modern West are kept alive largely in the unconscious, expressed through art and literature. Perhaps this is one reason why the subject of mythology, and particularly the hero's journey, has received renewed interest through the works of Joseph Campbell. See **Mythology.**

Jung said that the process of individuation, a person's becoming whole, involves initiatory types of ordeals. However, the only initiation process still alive in the West, he said, is the psychoanalysis of the unconscious process.

The elements of ritual include recitation, chanting, singing, prayer, and invocation; dancing, movement, or postures; costumes or special dress; incense, smoke, candles, or fire; offerings or sacrifices; consumption of food and drink (or, conversely, fasting); purifications; use of sacred objects, relics, tools, images, and symbols. These elements create physical and psychological changes intended to help achieve the goal of the ritual. It is important that all elements of a ritual are observed correctly to ensure success. Failure to do so in some cases is believed to have serious consequences, as in some Navajo healing chants. See **Chantways.**

Rituals are done both individually and collectively. There is greater power in a group, where all energies are focused on the same objective. See **Chanting; Magic; Medicine societies; Sacred pipe; Shamanism; Spiritual emergence; Sweat; Vision quest; Witchcraft.**

Sources: Isaac Bonewits. *Real Magic.* Rev. ed. York Beach, ME: Samuel Weiser, 1989; Mircea Eliade. *Patterns in Comparative Religion.* New York: New American Library, 1958; Mircea Eliade. *From Primitives to Zen: A Thematic Source Book of the History of Religions.* San Francisco: Harper & Row, 1977; Mircea Eliade. *Rites and Symbols of Initiation.* New York: Harper & Row, 1958; Murry Hope. *The Psychology of Ritual.* Longmead, Dorset, England: Element Books Ltd., 1988; C. G. Jung. *Memories, Dreams, Reflections.* Recorded and edited by Aniela Jaffe. New York: Random House, 1961; Andrew Samuels, Bani Shorter, and Fred Plaut. *A Critical Dictionary of Jungian Analysis.* London: Routledge & Kegan Paul, 1986.

Roberts, Jane (1929–1984)

Poet and author, best known for channeling an entity named Seth, the most widely known of all such entities channeled in the twentieth century.

Jane Roberts grew up in Saratoga Springs, New York, and attended Skidmore College. She married Robert Butts, a painter; they lived in Elmira, New York. Prior to the arrival of Seth in 1963, Roberts aspired to a conventional literary career in what she termed "the Establishment"; she published poetry and short stories in various national magazines.

In September 1963 Roberts had her first full-blown paranormal experience one evening as she sat writing poetry. Suddenly, she felt her consciousness lift out of her body, and her mind was flooded with "astonishing and new" ideas. When her consciousness returned to her body, she discovered that, through automatic writing, she had recorded the ideas that had flowed into her mind. The notes were even titled: *The Physical Universe as Idea Construction.*

Intrigued by this episode, Roberts and her husband began experimenting with a Ouija board. (Despite warnings from some that Ouija boards can invite negative spirits, Roberts maintained throughout her life that it was not the Ouija, but one's superstitious fears that produced negative results.) The initial communications through the board were allegedly from Roberts's grandfather, Joseph Adolph Burdo; and then, on December 2, 1963, from a deceased English teacher from Elmira whom Roberts identified pseudonymously as "Frank Withers." A check of local records indicated that such a man had lived and died as the Ouija communications alleged.

After three sessions with Withers, the entity said he preferred to be called Seth, which more aptly expressed "the whole self I am, or am trying to be." Withers, he said, was a part of his much larger personality. On various occasions Seth described Withers as "colorless" and a "fathead."

Seth defined himself as "an energy personality essence" that was no longer focused in physical form. He referred to Roberts as "Ruburt" and Butts as "Joseph," names which he said better expressed their whole, larger personalities. All three had known each other in previous incarnations in seventeenth-century Denmark. In the nineteenth century Roberts had been a medium, and Seth, as a nonphysical being, had communicated through her. Seth suggested twice-weekly communication sessions.

Thus began Roberts's remarkable channeling career. By the fourteenth session with the Ouija, she was able to discard it for clairaudient channeling, done first in light trance and then gradually in deep trance. In deep trance Roberts's features would change and her voice would deepen and take on an odd accent; Seth boomed out to his audience. He said that speaking through her was not comparable to using a telephone, but involved "a psychological extension, a projection of characteristics on both of our parts, and this I use for communication." Other paranormal experiences occurred during work with Seth. Apparitions appeared, including one of Seth; Roberts's facial features changed in the mirror, and her hand changed shape at a seance; both Roberts and Butts had out-of-body experiences. Dreams were important to Seth as gateways to other realities, and he often appeared in dreams or gave others "dream assignments."

Seth said he was a "personality with a message," and that his many lives on earth, male and female, had been to learn with the goal of being a teacher. His central message is that human beings create their own reality through thoughts, actions, and beliefs; in effect they are cocreators of the universe. Furthermore, each individual is a multidimensional being, existing simultaneously in multiple realities. There are no limits to the growth and development of the self.

Human beings reincarnate many times, though not in the fashion in which many believe, Seth said. Lives are not a progression of single incarnations determined by the karma of the preceding life; in fact, there is no karma that punishes or rewards. Rather, progress of the soul depends on the psychic and spiritual focus of the lives. Lives grow out of the inner self; they are forms taken by the con-

sciousness expressing itself. The past, present, and future exist in a simultaneous now, and we experience all of our lives simultaneously.

Seth said that prior to the history of Earth, he had been a "Lumanian." He later was born in Atlantis and subsequently had numerous human lives as man and woman, none of them historical figures of note. He had been a cave man; a Roman man during the time of Christ; a minor pope (probably in the fourth century, according to Roberts's estimate); a spice merchant in seventeenth-century Denmark, when he knew Roberts and Butts; several monks; several black men in Ethiopia and Turkey; a victim of the Spanish Inquisition; a courtesan during the time of David; a Dutch spinster; and several existences as a "humble" wife and mother. His last full incarnation had been in the seventeenth century as the Dutch spice merchant. Frank Withers was a fragment of his personality that would continue to reincarnate on its own.

Seth said that God is neither male nor female, but is "more than the sum of all the probable systems of reality He has created, and yet He is within each one of these, without exception." Human concepts of personality are too limiting to comprehend God's multidimensional existence. God is responsible for All That Is, the inconceivable energy that gives validity to the multidimensional self.

According to Seth there were actually three male individuals whose history blended into that of the one known as Christ. The disciples were fragment personalities formed by the Christ personality. The triune Christ figure represented the inner self, and the disciples represented twelve main characteristics connected with the egotistical self. The crucifixion was not a physical event, but a psychic one. The drama played out by Christ was the manifestation of God in a way comprehensible to individuals at the time. The third personality of Christ will not appear until the event prophesied as the "Second Coming"; this incarnation will be a new gestalt of the three Christs. The individual will be a great psychic and will teach others to use the inner senses that make true spirituality possible. He will not generally be known for who he is. By the time of his birth, Christianity will be in a shambles, Seth said, and he will straighten it out by undermining religious organizations and setting up a new system of thought that will enable each individual to attain intimate contact with his or her own entity, the mediator with All That Is. All of this will be accomplished by the year 2075, Seth said.

Unlike some channelers who followed her, Roberts never sought huge, paying audiences. Seth sessions were done at home before a small circle of friends or students from Roberts's creative writing class. Butts took copious notes by shorthand, which were transcribed. In this way Seth dictated several books of challenging material. Roberts herself wrote two books about the beginnings of her contact with Seth, as well as novels and volumes of poetry inspired by her channeling. She produced another three books attributed to other channeled sources: Seth Two, a group entity that allegedly included Seth, the French impressionist painter Paul Cézanne, and the American psychologist and philosopher William James. She felt that her contact with the latter two involved pieces or constructs of their personalities.

Roberts died in 1984 in Elmira following a period of illness. Other channelers have since claimed to take up communication with Seth. See **Channeling.**

Sources: Jon Klimo. *Channeling: Investigations on Receiving Information from Paranormal Sources.* Los Angeles: Jeremy P. Tarcher, 1987; Jane Roberts. *The Coming of Seth.* First published in 1966 as *How to Develop Your ESP Power.* New York: Pocket Books, 1976; Jane Roberts. *The Seth Material.* Englewood Cliffs, NJ: Prentice-Hall, 1970; Jane Roberts. *Seth Speaks: The Eternal Validity of the Soul.* Englewood Cliffs, NJ: Prentice-Hall, 1972.

Rodegast, Pat

See **Channeling.**

Rolfing

See **Bodywork.**

Roll, William

See **Poltergeist.**

Rolling Thunder (b. 1915)

Intertribal Native American medicine man whose remarkable healings have been witnessed by medical professionals.

Rolling Thunder was born in 1915 into the Cherokee nation. He was recognized at birth as a future medicine man, and at an early age was given special training by tribal leaders. As a teenager he was sent off to live in the woods, and spent long periods in isolation over several years. During this time he learned to communicate with plants and animals. He also experienced profound dreams, one of which contained images and symbols that led to his adoption of the name Rolling Thunder. Dreams have been of great importance to him throughout his healing career.

After his time in the woods, Rolling Thunder served as an apprentice to several medicine men and went through the traditional seven initiatory ceremonies to becoming a medicine man. He did not begin practicing until he was in his thirties following the tradition that practice does not begin until the time is right. His first patient was a seriously ill old woman who was in danger of dying. Following an all-night session singing with Rolling Thunder, she recovered.

Rolling Thunder believes in reincarnation, and that one comes into life with a mission. His healing, like that of other medicine men and shamans, is based on a respect for the Great Spirit and for all life, and on the ability to align himself with and make use of the forces of nature. He says he can hold a strange plant and it will communicate its secrets to him, telling him how to use it in healing. He calls herbs his "helpers." The efficacy of his herbal remedies lies in his knowledge of their spiritual properties, he says. Those who have duplicated the physical mixtures have found they do not work.

Rolling Thunder's totem is an eagle feather; a whole badger skin is his medicine bag. When "doctoring," as he calls it, he assesses the patient's aura and mimics the behavior of a badger, sniffing and growling. He often does not know what "medicine" he will use until after the process has begun; he simply lets the Great Spirit work through him. Often he sucks an illness, and vomits bile, pus, and other foul-looking liquids after doing so. Witnesses have reported seeing a purple glow around his head and hands during healing. At times he finds it necessary to enter the spirit realm to heal, a process he says must be done precisely or else it is dangerous. What scientists call "paranormal phenomena" Native Americans call the "other world," he says.

He undertakes a healing only when directed to do so by the Great Spirit. Illnesses have a purpose, he says, and sometimes illness is a price that must be paid for something else. To cure such an illness will only bring greater suffering to the patient at a later time. He says he is most effective in treating illnesses he himself has suffered first; yet he has performed impressive healings for illnesses and conditions he has not had.

On one occasion he exorcised the spirit of a young woman who had committed suicide, and which was possessing the doctor who attempted to revive her when he discovered her body.

Rolling Thunder's first significant visit with a Western physician occurred in 1970 in California; the two compared their practices. In 1971 he addressed eighty scientists at the Third Interdisciplinary Conference on the Voluntary Control of Internal States, and led them in a morning ritual. Other major appearances include the Association for Research and Enlightenment clinic in Virginia Beach, Virginia.

Rolling Thunder accepts no fees for healing, only small gifts of tobacco. He earned his living as a brakeman for Southern Pacific Railroad—where he was known as John Pope—and worked as a medicine man in his spare time. He served as spiritual adviser to celebrities, including Bob Dylan (who named the Rolling Thunder Revue after him), the Grateful Dead, Joan Baez, and Muhammad Ali. He played a role in the creation of two *Billy Jack* movies.

After thirty-five years at the railroad, Rolling Thunder retired in 1981. Since then he travels extensively, speaking, performing healings, and interpreting dreams for others. Some patients experience dreams of him in advance of healings, which appear to be the initial part of the healing. He lives in Carlin, Nevada. With his wife, Spotted Fawn (Helen Pope), he had two sons, Buffalo Horse and Spotted Eagle. See **Healing, faith and psychic; Shamanism.**

Sources: Doug Boyd. *Rolling Thunder.* New York: Random House, 1974; Stanley Krippner and Alberto Villoldo. *The Realms of Healing.* 3d ed. Berkeley, CA: Celestial Arts, 1986; Shirley Nicholson, comp. *Shamanism.* Wheaton, IL: The Theosophical Publishing House, 1987; Jim Swan. "Rolling Thunder at Work." *Shaman's Drum* no. 3 (Winter 1985): 39–44.

Rosenkreutz, Christian

See **Rosicrucians.**

Rosicrucians

The Order of the Rosy Cross, or Rosicrucianism in its many forms, claims to be the oldest secret society in the Western world, dating back to the ancient Egyptian and Greek mystery schools. Primarily utopian and humanist, its ideals and practices are essentially Christian with strong beliefs in the Great White Brotherhood of Adepts and in reincarnation.

History

According to Harvey Spencer Lewis (1883–1939), first Imperator and founder of the Ancient and Mystical Order Rosae Crucis (AMORC) in the United States, Rosicrucianism dates back to 1489 B.C., when the group of mystic scholars—both men and women—studying under Pharaoh Thutmose III decided to make their order secret, calling it simply the Order or Brotherhood. Succeeding pharaohs continued as Grand Masters through Amenhotep IV, great-great-grandson of Thutmose III.

Amenhotep IV has been called a man born out of his time (1388 B.C.–1350 B.C.). He made enemies of the priests, outlawing the worship of the principal Egyptian god Ammon and establishing one supreme deity. The pharaoh even changed his name to Akhnaton, meaning "glory to Aton," the sun-symbol of the one true God, as Amenhotep meant "Ammon is satisfied." He moved the capital city from Thebes, sacred to Ammon, to a place called Khut-en-Aton, also known as El Amarna, where he supposedly built a temple for the Brotherhood in the shape of the cross. According to Lewis Akhnaton added the cross and rose as symbols of the Brotherhood, adopted the *crux ansata,* or ankh, as the symbol of life, and composed several prayers and chants still used in Rosicrucian ceremonies.

But when Akhnaton died, Ammon-Ra was reinstated as the chief god, and the Brotherhood fled to the temple at El Amarna. Lewis reported that the 296 Fratres living there wore linen surplices tied by a cord and shaved their heads in a round spot on top—the origin of what later became standard attire for Franciscan monks.

For the next several centuries, the Brotherhood concentrated on preserving the sacred truths of Akhnaton and passing the teachings on to worthy students like King Solomon of Israel, Plotinus, Pythagoras, Plato, Solon, and Ammonius Saccas. The legendary Hermes Trismegistus supposedly served as Grand Master after Akhnaton's death, living for 142 years. See **Hermetica.** Lewis traced Freemasonry back to Solomon's use of Rosicrucian teachings to build the temple. This early period culminated in the life of the Master Jesus Christ, whom Lewis claimed had been expected by the Essenes, the Rosicrucians of Palestine.

Following the first few centuries after Christ, the Brotherhood seemed to disappear. Lewis said that the Order decreed each Lodge to determine its year of foundation, and then to operate in cycles of 108 years of activity followed by 108 years of secret inactivity, when operations went underground. In the years immediately preceding "rebirth," members would advertise through symbolic pamphlets, describing what they allegorically called "opening the tomb to find the body of C-R.C." (Christus of the Rosy Cross).

But according to Lewis, the advent of printing in the seventeenth century blew the allegorical rebirth completely out of proportion, giving rise to what most scholars consider the "real" story of Rosicrucianism: the discovery of the long-dead body of Christian Rosenkreutz.

The sources of the legend of Christian Rosenkreutz appeared mysteriously in Kassel, Germany, in 1614 and 1615. Circulated anonymously, the *Fama Fraternitatis dess Loblichen Ordens des Rosenkreutzes (The Fame of the Praiseworthy Order of the Rosy Cross)* and the *Confessio Fraternitatis* told of a mythic young man called Christian Rosenkreutz, born in A.D. 1378. At age five he was placed in a convent to study the humanities, and at age sixteen accompanied one of his teachers to Damcar (Damascus?) in Arabia to continue his education. After three years he went to Fez, Morocco, via Egypt, where he learned even more magic. Upon graduation Rosenkreutz traveled to Spain, where he expected a warm reception from the mystic Moors. He was rebuffed, however, and eventually returned to Germany, where he gathered a small group of men who became the Rosicrucian Fraternity.

The Fraternity built its headquarters, called the Spiritus Sanctum, or House of the Holy Spirit, in 1409, using it to teach an ever-widening circle of occult adepts and to heal the sick. One brother reputedly cured the English Earl of Norfolk of leprosy. Rosenkreutz died in 1484, at 106 years of age, and was entombed in a secret vault in the Spiritus Sanctum. The other brothers continued their missionary work, but in secret.

In 1604, during repairs to the headquarters building, the brothers discovered the vault. Across the door to the tomb was the Latin inscription, "After 120 years I shall open." Inside the seven-sided room were wonderful magical symbols, books, and ritual objects, and the ceiling was illuminated by an artificial sun. But most amazing was the coffin containing Rosenkreutz's body, completely preserved.

These wonders were described in the above-mentioned pamphlets, along with an open invitation to all worthy people interested in the Rosicrucian phenomenon to apply for membership. The brothers did not reveal their whereabouts, but assured all petitioners that printed inquiries would be answered.

In 1616 another anonymous pamphlet appeared, entitled, *Chymische Hochzeit,* or *The Chemical Marriage of Christian Rosenkreutz,* supposedly written by him in 1459. The story tells of a royal wedding ceremony Rosenkreutz attended (not his own marriage); it is full of occult imagery and alchemical propositions, including the creation of homunculi (artificial humans allegedly created by magic).

These revelations created tremendous interest among the growing European occult community, and scores applied to the secret order. But no records exist of anyone hearing from the brothers. Later scholars attribute the authorship of all three pamphlets to Johann Valentin Andreae (1586–1654), a young German Lutheran pastor and reformer. All three documents promoted Protestant ethics and vilified the papacy. Apologies for the works and silence of the Order were written by the German count Michael Maier (1568–1622), counselor to Emperor Rudolf II, and by the English doctor Robert Fludd (1574–1637), both believed to be at least dabblers in Rosicrucian philosophy; yet not one of the three men ever admitted to membership in the Order.

After the flurry of interest subsided, little more was heard from the Fratres of C-R.C. The movement blended into German Pietism, an offshoot of Lutheran doctrine that sought perfection and the expected return of Christ. In 1693 a group of Pietists led by Johannes Kelpius (1673–1708) left for Pennsylvania to accept William Penn's offer of religious sanctuary. They arrived in Philadelphia in 1694, eventually settling farther west on the banks of the Wissahickon River. Staunchly millennialist and communal, the group also practiced occult and healing arts. After Kelpius's death they disbanded, but are remembered as originators of the Pennsylvania hex tradition. Lewis maintained they brought Rosicrucianism to America.

In the early eighteenth century, various authors published several books and manifestos claiming existence of the Brotherhood of the Rosy Cross and outlined the Order's beliefs and practices. In nearly all cases these publications are actually treatises for political and religious reform, championing such causes as the free dissemination of knowledge, universal brotherhood, support of the arts, and the reorganization of the warring countries of Europe into one idealized commonwealth. Others—with guilty consciences, perhaps—took the attacks as the revenge of the martyred Templars, returned to exact punishment on the descendants and institutions that had murdered them. See **Order of the Knights Templar.**

Symbols and Beliefs

Rosicrucian ideals have changed little from those early manifestos. Through study and practice, members still strive for the perfection illustrated by the Masters of the Great White Lodge, with the ultimate goal being admittance into the Lodge and the attainment of true knowledge, or cosmic consciousness. Students progress through twelve degrees of mastery, with the tenth through twelfth degrees conferred psychically, usually in the Order's temples in the East. Worthy members who have mastered nine degrees may choose to enter the Illuminati, a higher organization of the Order. See **Illuminati.**

Similar to the Theosophists, such perfection comes only after various reincarnations, each devoted to achieving a greater oneness with the Supreme Being. Lewis insisted that Rosicrucians do not force members to believe in reincarnation, but that the examples of their daily lives and continual progression to knowledge would prove the point.

Rosicrucians have always been associated with alchemy, concerned on a mundane level with the transmutation of base metals into gold and on a spiritual level with the transmutation of humankind's baser nature into a higher spiritual being. See **Alchemy.** Members stress healthful living, with abstinence from meat, alcohol, and tobacco. Such measures ensure prevention of disease and allow the body to heal itself, aided perhaps by the "Invisible Helpers" of the Rosicrucian Fellowship.

Rosicrucians claim influence on Freemasonry, especially since the eighteenth Masonic degree is the Sovereign Prince Rose Croix of Heredom. Several of the Rosicrucian groups formed in the nineteenth century restrict membership to Masons and incorporate Rosicrucian symbols. See **Freemasonry.**

All Rosicrucian organizations employ the rose and cross, although in various combinations. The Rosicrucian Fellowship places a gold cross with looped ends over a five-pointed star made of rays; the background color is blue. Draped around the cross are seven red roses, sometimes shown climbing the cross and sometimes gathered in a wreath around it.

The symbol of AMORC shows one red rose centered on a gold cross, also with looped ends. Occasionally, the rose has a green stem for decoration. AMORC also uses an equilateral triangle, point down, inscribed with a cross. AMORC registered both these symbols with the United States Patent Office as the only true Rosicrucian symbols.

Symbolically, the cross represents death, suffering, and ultimately resurrection. AMORC employs the crux ansata, or ankh, as representative of reincarnation. The rose has always signified love and secrecy. In Greek mythology Eros, the god of love, gave a rose to the god of silence. Signs for Roman taverns usually showed a rose signifying that anything said "below the rose" (*sub rosa*) in drunkenness would remain confidential. Additionally, Andreae's family crest was a cross of St. Andrew with four roses between the arms, while that of his mentor Martin Luther was a rose with a cross in the center.

Rosicrucian Organizations

AMORC, founded by H. S. Lewis, had its beginnings as the Rosicrucian Research Society or the New York Institute for Psychical Research in 1904. In 1908 Lewis met Mrs. May Banks-Stacey, a reputed Rosicrucian who put him in touch with the Brotherhood in Europe. Lewis traveled to France in 1909, where he claimed he was initiated into the Order and given the authority to "open the tomb of C-R.C." in America for its next 108-year cycle of activity. AMORC was officially chartered in 1915 and held its first national convention in 1917.

At the 1917 convention, Lewis organized the National Rosicrucian Lodge, whereby wisdom-seekers could obtain the elementary teachings through correspondence, with the hope of eventually joining a Lodge. By 1926 Lewis petitioned a Rosicrucian Congress in Belgium to allow students unable to join a Lodge to continue their instruction via correspondence and become part of the Sanctum, or "Lodge at home." Such accommodations allowed AMORC to distribute materials worldwide. Currently, the Order claims approximately 250,000 members in over one hundred countries. Lewis's son, Ralph M. Lewis, succeeded him as Imperator.

In 1927 Lewis moved the Order's headquarters to San Jose, California, where it remains today. The Grand Lodge at Rosicrucian Park has become a tourist attraction, as the headquarters buildings include a planetarium, research facilities, and the Egyptian Museum. Reportedly the only Egyptian museum in the world housed in authentic ancient Egyptian architecture, it contains the largest collection of Egyptian, Babylonian, and Assyrian artifacts on the West Coast.

Max Heindel (1865–1919) founded the Rosicrucian Fellowship in 1909. Born in Denmark as Carl Louis Von Grasshoff, Heindel's spiritual searchings led him first to the Theosophical Society, then to Germany in 1907, where he claimed the Elder Brothers of the Rosicrucian Order appeared to him and initiated him into their mysteries. He studied under an approved Rosicrucian adept, believed to be Rudolf Steiner of the Anthroposophical Society. Returning to the United States, he wrote of his experiences in *The Rosicrucian Cosmo-Conception* and began opening Rosicrucian centers on the West Coast. In 1910, while recuperating from heart disease, he received a vision of the Fellowship's headquarters on Mt. Ecclesia in Oceanside, California, where the group remains. Facilities include a temple for services and a twelve-sided Temple of Healing, built to correspond to the zodiac.

Members of the Fellowship are actively engaged in spiritual healing and astrology, although they do not cast horoscopes for outsiders. They believe in reincarnation and the influence of the planets on life.

Other Rosicrucian organizations include two limited strictly to Freemasons: the Societas Rosicruciana in Anglia, founded in 1866 by Robert Wentworth Little; and the Societas Rosicruciana in Civitatibus Foederatis, originally called the Societas Rosicruciana Republicae Americae, founded in 1878 as an affiliate of the Scottish branch of the Societas Rosicruciana. Members must be Masons of the thirty-second degree. The Societas Rosicruciana in Anglia counted Kenneth MacKenzie, author of the *Royal Masonic Cyclopedia,* and coroner Dr. William Wynn Westcott and Samuel Liddell MacGregor Mathers, founders of the

Hermetic Order of the Golden Dawn, as members.

The Societas Rosicruciana in America, founded in 1907 by Sylvester C. Gould, accepts non-Masons, as does the Fraternitas Rosae Crucis, reputedly the oldest Rosicrucian group in the United States. Founded in 1858 by Pascal Beverly Randolph (1825–1875), the group traces its lineage to the French occultist Eliphas Levi. After Randolph's death, leadership passed to Edward H. Brown, then Reuben Swinburne Clymer, a physician.

Coupling the teachings of Rudolf Steiner and Max Heindel, S. R. Parchment founded the Rosicrucian Anthroposophic League in the 1930s. J. Van Rijckenborgh founded the Lectorium Rosicrucianum in 1971, espousing "transfigurism"—giving up one's life to God in order to escape the cycles of karma and reincarnation. Also starting in the 1970s was the Ausar Auset Society, founded by R. A. Straughn of the Rosicrucian Anthroposophic League. The African-American community is the main audience of Straughn's meditation and health guides.

Sources: Richard Cavendish. *The Encyclopedia of the Unexplained.* New York: McGraw-Hill, 1974; Keith Crim, gen. ed. *Abingdon Dictionary of Living Religions.* Nashville, TN: Abingdon Press, 1981; Manly P. Hall. *Masonic Orders of Fraternity.* Los Angeles: The Philosophical Research Society, 1950; Manly P. Hall. *Orders of Universal Reformation: Utopias.* Los Angeles: The Philosophical Research Society, 1949; Manly P. Hall. *The Secret Destiny of America.* Los Angeles: The Philosophical Research Society, 1944; Max Heindel. *The Rosicrucian Mysteries.* 8th ed. Oceanside, CA: The Rosicrucian Fellowship, 1943; H. Spencer Lewis. *Rosicrucian Manual.* San Jose, CA: Rosicrucian Press, 1918; H. Spencer Lewis. *Rosicrucian Questions and Answers with Complete History of the Order.* 1929. San Jose, CA: Supreme Grand Lodge of AMORC, 1977;

Christopher McIntosh. "The Rosicrucian Dream." *Gnosis* no. 6 (Winter 1988): 14–17; J. Gordon Melton. *Encyclopedic Handbook of Cults in America.* New York and London: Garland Publishing Inc., 1986; *The New Age Catalog.* New York: Dolphin/Doubleday, 1988; S. R. Parchment. *Operative Masonry.* San Francisco: San Francisco Center, Rosicrucian Fellowship, 1930; "The Rosicrucian Emblem." Pamphlet. The Rosicrucian Fellowship, Oceanside, CA; "The Rosicrucians Heal the Sick." Pamphlet. The Rosicrucian Fellowship, Oceanside, CA; Leslie A. Shepard, ed. *Encyclopedia of Occultism and Parapsychology.* 2d ed. Detroit: Gale Research Co., 1984; Lewis Spence. *Encyclopedia of Occultism.* 1920. Secaucus, NJ: Citadel Press, 1960.

Runes

Ancient Norse and Teutonic alphabet sigils, ascribed various magical, mystical, and divinatory properties. Various alphabets have been handed down through the centuries; individual runes have represented letters, deities, qualities, events, and forces of nature. Runic inscriptions surviving from the pagan period always have a religious significance. The term "rune" comes from the Indo-European root *ru,* which means "mystery" or "secret."

Runic symbols have been discovered in rock carvings dating back to the prehistoric Neolithic and Bronze Ages (c. 8000 B.C.–2000 B.C.), carved by tribes that settled in Northern Italy. Rock carvings from the second Bronze Age, c. 1300 B.C., are common throughout Sweden. By A.D. 100 runes were in widespread use in Nordic and Germanic lands. According to myth they were created by Odin (also Woden), god of wisdom, war, and death. Odin sacrificed himself by hanging, pierced by a spear, upon Yggradsil, the World Tree, for nine days and nights, in order to gain secret wisdom. In *Havamal 138,* a mythological poem of the Viking

Age (A.D. 700–1050), Odin took up the runes, lifted them screaming, and fell back again.

The magical powers attributed runes were believed to be released in the etching of names, phrases, memorial inscriptions, and spells upon bone, metal, wood, and stone. Grave markers were inscribed with runes that described the deeds of the dead, and warded off grave robbers. Diviners used runes in the casting of lots. Runes were carved on swords to make them more powerful in battle, and to cause more pain and death to the enemy. Magicians etched them on magical tools, sometimes sprinkling them with blood to make the magic more potent. Runes were etched as amulets on wands, jewelry, personal belongings, chalices, and other items as protection against illness, the evil eye, and sorcery, and to guarantee safety and effect healing. They also were used in weather rites and fertility, birth, and death rites. Lappish *tjetajat,* or wizards, shouted and sang runes. Runes also were used to seal contracts, and in the writing of poetry.

The Viking invaders spread runes throughout Europe, Russia, and Britain; rune usage was at its height during the Dark Ages. In Britain the runic alphabet was called *futhorc,* because the first letters were F, U, TH, O, R, and K. The earliest version of the futhorc alphabet had twenty-four letters divided into three groups of eight. The groups were named after Norse deities: Freya, Hagal, and Tiu. Runes coexisted for centuries with Christian symbols such as the cross. They began to disappear from usage around the fourteenth century, when the church began an earnest campaign against paganism through the Inquisition.

In the late nineteenth century, German occultists revived interest in runes, which became associated with Teutonic superiority and racial supremacy. The "secret chiefs" of the Germanen Order, a runic society founded in 1912, signed their names in runes. Herman Pohl Magdeburg, the order's first chancellor, sold amuletic bronze rune rings to soldiers in World War I as protection in battle. Another occultist, Seigfried Adolf Kunner, reached the extreme of rune mania with the creation of rune exercises, yoga-like postures that mimicked rune shapes. While contorting, the student was supposed to yodel, which would release mysterious, magical forces. Kunner also advocated meditating upon runes to cure illness.

The Nazis perhaps ruined forever two runes: the swastika, originally Thor's hammer and the symbol of the Earth Mother and the sun; and the S sigil, used by the SS.

Runes were popularized as an oracle in the 1980s. Rune tiles are drawn from bags and meditated upon, cast in lots like the *I Ching,* or laid out in crosses or wheels like Tarot cards. Like the *I Ching* and Tarot, runes do not provide answers, but provide the means to answers; they are considered keys to self-transformation. Like Tarot cards runes can be used as meditational tools.

Sources: Ralph Blum. *The Book of Runes.* New York: Oracle Books, St. Martin's Press, 1987; Deon Dolphin. *Rune Magic.* Van Nuys, CA: Newcastle Publishing, 1987; Ralph W. V. Elliott. *Runes: An Introduction.* Manchester, England: Manchester University Press, 1959; Michael Howard. *The Magic of the Runes.* Wellingborough, England: The Aquarian Press, 1980; Michael Loewe and Carmen Blacker. *Oracles and Divination.* Boulder: Shambhala, 1981; *New Larousse Encyclopedia of Mythology.* New ed. New York: Crescent Books, 1968; Dusty Sklar. *Gods and Beasts: The Nazis and the Occult.* New York: Thomas Y. Crowell, 1977; Doreen Valiente. *An ABC of Witchcraft Past and Present.* Amended ed. Custer, WA: Phoenix Publishing, 1986.

Ryerson, Kevin

See **Channeling.**

S

Sacred pipe

A long-stemmed, elaborately decorated pipe sacred to Plains and Woodlands Native Americans. In ritual tobacco smoke from the pipe is the equivalent of visible breath or incense; it is both offering to the spirits and forces of nature, and means of communication with them. Smoking a sacred pipe also is a means to having a spiritual vision.

The sacred pipe also is called a "calumet," from the French *chalumet*, which means "a reed." The name was given by white settlers in North America to ceremonial pipes whose stems were hollow reeds. Early calumets were made of two separate pieces, a bowl carved of clay or stone, sometimes in the effigy of a bird, man, or animal, and a stem of reed, decorated with eagle feathers and symbols. Some calumets were enormous: The bowls were so large they had to be placed on the ground, and the stems reached up to four feet in length. The smoker squatted on the ground to hold the stem. Such calumets eventually gave way to shorter long-stemmed pipes, which were stored in separate pieces but fitted together for smoking. They were held in forked sticks stuck in the ground.

According to myth the sacred pipe originated with the Pawnee and spread to other Plains and Woodlands tribes. The Pawnee and other tribes attribute the original sacred pipe to White Buffalo Calf

Maiden, a representative of the Great Spirit. White Buffalo Calf Maiden appeared one winter long ago and delivered seven gifts, the first of which was the pipe. She said the bowl of the pipe, carved in the likeness of a buffalo calf, represented the Earth and all the four-legged creatures who walked upon her. The wooden stem represented all that grows upon the Earth. The decorative eagle feathers represented all the winged creatures. By smoking the pipe, humankind would join its voice with all these other beings in addressing the Great Spirit.

White Buffalo Calf Maiden's other six gifts were rites in which the sacred pipe was to be used: purifying the souls of the dead; purification in sweat lodges; having visions; dancing the Sun Dance; peacemaking; initiating girls into womanhood; and playing a ball game that symbolizes human life.

Other mythical givers of the first pipe are Duck (Arapahoe), Thunder (Blackfoot), and the prophet Sweet Medicine (Cheyenne).

Sacred pipes are used in a wide variety of clan, society, social, council, and personal affairs; decorations reflect the function. Pipes are used in pipe dances, in which dancers dance with decorated stems, or offer their whole pipes to other dancers or spectators. See **Sun Dance.**

The use of sacred pipes has had a revival among many North American tribes, even those which traditionally did not use them. See **Tobacco**.

Sources: Joseph Epes Brown, ed. *The Sacred Pipe: Black Elk's Account of the Seven Rites of the Oglala Sioux.* Harmondsworth, Middlesex, England: Penguin Books, 1953; John Redtail Freesoul. *Breath of the Invisible: The Way of the Pipe.* Wheaton, IL: The Theosophical Publishing House, 1986; Ruth M. Underhill. *Red Man's Religion.* Chicago: University of Chicago Press, 1965; Museum of the American Indian, New York City.

(Photo by Nandlal Ramdya, United Nations)

Sai Baba

Sacred psychology

See **Psychology**.

Sadhu

See **Fakir**.

Sai Baba (b. 1926)

Hindu avatar whose alleged miraculous and paranormal feats have attracted a large following of devotees, in both East and West. Sai Baba is renowned for his healing; for materializations of an incredible array of apports that include hot foods and liquids; and for bilocation, teleportation, levitation, precognition, and luminous phenomena. He has been the object of limited study by Western psychical researchers, who have been unable to prove the validity of his paranormal feats, but have not uncovered any evidence of fraud.

Sai Baba was born on November 23, 1926, in Puttaparti, a remote village in southern India, north of Bangalore, to the Venkappa Ratnakara family, members of the low Raju caste. His father was a farmer. The boy's full name was Sathyanarayana (Sathya means "truth" and Narayana is a name for God) Ratnakara Raju. His miraculous gifts began mani-

festing during his teens. On March 8, 1940, he allegedly was stung by a black scorpion—although none was ever discovered—and lapsed into unconsciousness for several hours. From then on he exhibited strange behavior and seemed to be a different person. He would fall into trances from which he could not be roused, and would offer spontaneous discourses on ancient Hindu philosophy. He would suddenly sing and recite poetry. On May 23, 1940, he left school. He announced to his family that he was Sai Baba reborn, and presented them with apports of flowers, sugar candy, and rice cooked in milk, which he seemed to materialize with a wave of his hand. Thereafter the boy called himself Sathya Sai Baba.

Sai is a Muslim term for "saint," and *baba* is a Hindi term of respect for "father." The original Sai Baba was a middle-class Brahmin fakir at the turn of the century, who had settled in Shirdi, about 120 miles northeast of Bombay, and had produced astounding miracles.

Sathya Sai Baba quickly attracted followers who were amazed by his miracles and charmed by his personality, but many rejected and criticized him. He was virtually ostracized in Puttaparti. Swamis and avatars traditionally come from the Brahmin caste, and a low-caste Raju boy was thought to have no business attempting to be a man of God. Sai Baba nevertheless predicted that one day he would be surrounded by huge crowds of followers. By the 1970s that prediction had borne out. Thousands of people regularly camp outside his ashram, Prashanti Nilayam ("Abode of Great Peace") in Puttaparti, hoping to get a glimpse of him, receive an apport, obtain an interview, touch him, or listen to a sermon. Sai Baba's Sathya Sai Educational Trust runs five colleges established in India as of 1986, including a boys' college in Brindavan, his second home, an estate near Whitefield, about fifteen miles south of Bangalore (according to legend, Krishna had lived in a "Brindavan").

Sai Baba is best known for his apports; some 75 percent of his devotees claim to have seen or received them. He produces a steady stream of apports with a wave of his hand. They include huge quantities of *vibuti*, holy ash made from burnt cow dung, which is smeared on the body; foods and liquids; religious statues and objects made of gold; precious jewelry; photographs; business cards; even stamps bearing his likeness, which have not been officially issued by the government. He reportedly fills empty bowls with hot, steaming Indian food of most unusual flavors, and produces enough to feed hundreds of people at a time. He opens his fist and drops sticky sweets into the palms of others, yet his own hands are dry. He also produces *amrith,* a honey-like substance. On outings to the nearby Chitravati River, he has reached into sand and pulled out food free of sand. He has plucked apples, pomegranates, mangoes, and other fruits from a tamarind tree. All nonfood objects materialized are bright, fresh, and new. Jewelry includes valuable precious gems. Rings requested by followers fit them perfectly; if a person does not like a particular ring, Sai Baba takes it back and changes it instantly. Business cards bearing his name appear to be freshly printed. Many objects are inscribed with his name.

In his earlier days, he frequently fell into sudden, often convulsive trances, which lasted up to one-and-a-half days, and during which his body would be very cold to the touch. His explanation was that he had been called to another, often distant location to help people in distress or illness. In these other locations, he reportedly appeared as if in the flesh. If he had gone out of body to heal, he sometimes would return showing symptoms of the illness. In one reported instance during a trance, Sai Baba levitated. While in the air, the sole of his right foot split open, and an estimated two kilograms of vibuti poured out. In another trance incident, he opened his mouth and out fell vibuti and golden plates a half-inch in width. One of the plates was inscribed in Telugu, "Sri Rama."

Sai Baba also would appear to teleport himself up a hill, disappearing at its base and appearing at the top of the hill within seconds. From the hilltop he would produce luminosities so brilliant and blinding that others had to shade their eyes. Some witnesses collapsed from the brightness.

Other phenomena attributed to him include the instant changing of the color of his loose robes; his appearance in the dreams of others, seemingly in answer to needs; weather control; unusual smells, often produced at a distance; the appearance of vibuti and amrith on pictures of him and on his apports; psychic surgery; the changing of water into gasoline and into other beverages; mind reading; and clairvoyance. Some of those who touched him experienced a mild electrical shock. Once he was found to have a nest of scorpions living in his bushy hair. During his early days, he forbade photographs and films to be taken of him. Those who attempted to do so surreptitiously found their film to be blank when developed.

From the 1950s to 1970s, Sai Baba had numerous opponents. A government investigation of him was proposed, but never undertaken. By the early 1970s, the criticism abated. At the same time, Sai Baba grew more serious and moody. He began to perform fewer miracles and spend more time preaching about the love of God.

In 1973 Erlendur Haraldsson, a psychologist from the University of Iceland and a psychical researcher, began an investigation of Sai Baba's paranormal phenomena that spanned a ten-year period. He made a number of trips to India to interview Sai Baba, his devotees, and critics. Haraldsson was accompanied on several trips by Karlis Osis, who at that time was with the American Society for Psychical Research; once by Dr. Michael Thalbourne of Washington University; and once by Dr. Joop Houtkooper of the University of Amsterdam.

Sai Baba refused to submit to controlled experiments to test his psi abilities, thus making it impossible to obtain proof. He explained that his powers come from God, and that he produces apports from the superconscious by imagining them first, and transporting them from an unspecified place where they already exist. While observed by the scientists, Sai Baba produced an estimated twenty to forty apports a day, all spontaneously and with great ease. Many of the objects were rare or unusual, such as a double *rudraksha,* an acorn-like nut grown together like Siamese twins, but none were otherwordly. Sleight of hand seemed highly unlikely, for the sleeves of his robes were large and loose. Haraldsson also ruled out hypnosis, and found films of Sai Baba to be inconclusive.

Once Haraldsson and Osis were able to closely observe the materialization of vibuti. Sai Baba spread his hand with the palm down and waved it in quick, small circles. A gray substance appeared in the air just below and close to his palm. He closed his fist around it and then opened it to pour sand-like granules into the open hands of his devotees. The granules turned into fine, delicate ash.

In his research Haraldsson found that Sai Baba's precognitive predictions are not always accurate (one observer estimated a 50 percent "hit" rate), and that not all of his cures work. A number of prominent Indian scientists have observed Sai Baba and feel his miraculous feats are genuine. His followers believe he is God. Sai Baba has predicted he will die in 2020 at the age of ninety-four. See **Avatar.**

Sources: Erlendur Haraldsson. *Modern Miracles: An Investigative Report on Psychic Phenomena Associated with Sathya Sai Baba.* New York: Fawcett Columbine, 1987; N. Kasturi. *Sai Baba.* Bombay, India: Sanathana Sarathi, 1969; Howard Murphet. *Sai Baba: Man of Miracles.* New York: Samuel Weiser, 1976; Samuel H. Sandweiss. *Sai Baba: The Holy Man and the Psychiatrist.* San Diego, CA: Birth Day Publishing, 1975; Arthur Schulman. *Baba.* New York: Viking Press, 1971.

Saint Germain

Ascended Master considered by some the greatest adept since Jesus Christ. As part of the Great White Brotherhood of adepts, Saint Germain protects the wisdom of the ages, only revealing it and himself to those he completely trusts. He administers the Seventh Ray in the theosophical universe, controlling ceremony and ritual.

According to legend Saint Germain's first stay among humankind supposedly occurred more than 50,000 years ago, in a paradise located where the Sahara Desert is today. He led his people in the knowledge that they were part of the great cosmic Source, represented by the Violet Flame Temple, of which Saint Germain was high priest. But some people were tempted by the pleasures of the senses, and he withdrew, leaving them to their fates.

He next appeared in 1050 B.C. as Samuel, prophet of the Lord Jehovah. He anointed Saul as leader of the tribes against the Philistines, but denied Saul when he disobeyed the Lord. Samuel then anointed David king of all the Israelites and the beginning of the Messiah's line. Saint Germain himself allegedly returned as Joseph, Mary's husband and father of the infant Jesus.

In the third century A.D., Saint Germain supposedly returned as St. Alban, the first Christian martyr in Britain. Converted to Christianity by the monk Amphibalus, he hid the holy man during the persecutions of Christians under the Roman Emperor Diocletian. For refusing to give up Amphibalus and renounce his faith, St. Alban was beheaded in 303.

After an incarnation as Proclus (410–485), head of Plato's Academy in Athens, Saint Germain returned to Britain in the late fifth century as Merlin, wizard extraordinaire and counselor to the legendary King Arthur of Camelot. See **Merlin.**

Saint Germain supposedly returned in the thirteenth century as Roger Bacon (1214–1294?), English monk, philosopher, alchemist, and scientist. Years ahead of other medieval thinkers, Bacon believed the world was round and is credited with foreseeing such inventions as hot air balloons, flying machines, spectacles, telescopes, elevators, and machine-driven cars and ships. Many believe he invented gunpowder. Although his three major books, *Opus majus, Opus minor,* and *Opus tertium* were written for Pope Clement I, his fellow Franciscans decided his beliefs were heretical and kept him in solitary confinement for fourteen years, only releasing him shortly before his death.

In 1451 Saint Germain is said to have again walked on Earth as Christopher Columbus, founder of the New World. Roger Bacon, in his *Opus majus,* had earlier predicted that India could be reached by water from the west of Spain, and Columbus wrote that he was merely fulfilling a prophecy when he set sail under the aegis of King Ferdinand and Queen Isabella. After first landing in 1492, Columbus became governor of Hispaniola and eventually discovered Cuba, Puerto Rico, and Venezuela. He died in neglect in 1506, supposedly at the hands of unhappy natives in Central America.

Saint Germain's next life was supposedly that of Sir Francis Bacon (1561–1626), English essayist, philosopher, statesman, and occultist. He is best remembered as the father of scientific inductive reasoning as opposed to the medieval scholastic method. Bacon, reportedly a Freemason and perhaps also a Rosicrucian, dabbled in occultism and alchemy. He served as the guiding inspiration for the Royal Society of London, a group dedicated to the pursuit of science and knowledge. Controversy still exists over whether Bacon wrote the Shakespearean dramas. One theory claims Bacon was the son of Queen Elizabeth I and Robert Dudley, Lord Leicester.

Sir Francis Bacon was supposed to be Saint Germain's last incarnation, and believers claim he ascended as Master on May 1, 1684. But begging one last chance to show humankind the error of its ways, Saint Germain returned as the Comte (Count) de St. Germain to the glittering courts of eighteenth-century France and Germany. Contemporaries called him "the Wonderman of Europe."

The Comte once told a countess that he was a mature man at the turn of the eighteenth century, although many accounts estimate his birth in 1710. He is rumored variously to be the third son of Prince Ferenc Rakoczy II of Hungary, or a Portuguese Jew. Although the Comte cut quite a figure in court, he was not particularly handsome. He dressed well and wore diamonds on every finger. He supposedly spoke (and wrote) Greek,

Latin, Sanskrit, Arabic, Chinese, French, German, English, Italian, Portuguese, and Spanish fluently and without accent. He collected fine art and jewels, played violin and harpsichord, painted, and displayed keen alchemical knowledge, reportedly transmuting base metal into gold. He was a canny statesman, traveling Europe for both Frederick the Great of Prussia and Louis XV of France.

Many critics called the Comte a spy, and there is little doubt that he was working for Frederick at the same time he represented Louis XV. Ministers to Louis finally called the Comte's bluff when he attempted to negotiate a peace between England and France without consulting anyone. Henry Walpole wrote that the Comte lived and worked in London for a few years, and was eventually arrested as a Jacobite in 1743. In 1762 he supposedly helped put Catherine the Great on the Russian throne. Through prophecy the Comte tried to warn Louis XVI and Marie Antoinette of the coming revolution, but his pleadings went unheeded. Even after his death, in 1785 or 1786, the Comte allegedly appeared to members of the French court to warn them of the royal family's death and destruction.

The Comte is not remembered for his political maneuverings as much as his practice of the occult. According to philosopher Manly P. Hall, the Comte was likely a Templar, trying to bring back the Templar tradition through Rosicrucian and Freemasonic societies under cover of his diplomatic missions. The eighteenth-century intelligentsia were fascinated with anything esoteric, and the Comte knew how to play that role with flourish. He lived the latter part of his life at a residence provided him by the Landgrave Karl of Hesse to be dedicated to the study of the occult. See **Order of the Knights Templar.**

The house was the scene of many ritualistic ceremonies, including the initiation of the Count and Countess di Ca-gliostro into the Lodge of Illuminists. According to Cagliostro's memoirs (attributed to someone else), the Comte, resplendent in diamonds, received them at an altar covered with thousands of candles and flanked with acolytes holding bowls of perfume. Cagliostro studied under the Comte and eventually introduced what he called Egyptian rites of Freemasonry to France. See **Cagliostro, Count Alessandro.**

The Comte's last recorded appearance was supposedly in 1822, about forty years after his probable death. He had told friends years earlier that he would retire to the Himalayas, home of many of the Ascended Masters. From there Saint Germain reportedly helped found the Theosophical Society with the Masters Morya and Koot Hoomi and Madame Helena P. Blavatsky in 1875. Blavatsky called Saint Germain the greatest Oriental Adept in Europe. See **Theosophy.**

In 1930 Saint Germain is said to have appeared again to Guy Ballard, a miner and Spiritualist, who, with his wife and son, founded the "I AM" Religious Activity movement. See **"I AM" Religious Activity, the.**

Another group claiming to be in contact with Saint Germain is the Church Universal and Triumphant, founded in the 1960s by Mark L. and Elizabeth Clare Prophet. Both groups strive to achieve spiritual union with the divine I AM Presence and to disseminate Saint Germain's teachings and prophecies about universal wisdom, the world's karma, and what each believer must do to bring about the Seventh Golden Age on earth. See **Alternative religious movements; Freemasonry; Rosicrucians.**

Sources: Bruce F. Campbell. *Ancient Wisdom Revived: A History of the Theosophical Movement.* Berkeley: University of California Press, 1980; Robert Ellwood. *Theosophy: A Modern Expression of the Wisdom of the Ages.* Wheaton, IL: The Theosophical Publishing House, 1986;

Manly P. Hall. *Freemasonry of the Ancient Egyptians*. 1937. Los Angeles: The Philosophical Research Society Inc., 1973; Manly P. Hall. *Masonic Orders of Fraternity*. Los Angeles: The Philosophical Research Society Inc., 1950; J. Gordon Melton. *Encyclopedic Handbook of Cults in America*. New York: Garland Publishing Inc., 1986; *Saint Germain on Alchemy*. Recorded by Mark L. Prophet and Elizabeth Clare Prophet. Livingston, MT: Summit University Press, 1962; *Saint Germain on Prophecy*. Recorded by Elizabeth Clare Prophet. Livingston, MT: Summit University Press, 1986; Kurt Seligmann. *The History of Magic and the Occult*. New York: Pantheon Books, 1948; Lewis Spence. *The Encyclopedia of the Occult*. Reprint. London: Bracken Books, 1988.

Samadhi

See **Meditation; Mystical experiences; Yoga; Zen.**

Sankara

See **Hinduism.**

Santería

Syncretic religion based on ancient African rites and Catholicism. Santería is related in ritual and practice to Vodoun. "Santería" comes from the Spanish word *santo,* meaning "saint." Practitioners are called *santeros* and *santeras.* Yoruba is the liturgical language.

Like Vodoun, Santería came to the Americas with West African slaves, principally from the Yoruban tribes along the Niger River. Forced to convert to Catholicism, the slaves practiced their religion in secret, using Catholic saints as covers for their own gods and blending the two religions. The Spanish and Portuguese masters eventually became fascinated with Yoruban magic and began to practice it themselves. Santería today is practiced predominantly in US cities with large Hispanic populations; in the Caribbean; and in Brazil under the names of Candomblé, Umbanda, and Quimbanda. See **Macumba.**

The Orishas

In the Yoruban language, *orisha* literally means "head-calabash" and is the term for god. The orishas are archetypal forces and are the equivalent of the Vodoun *loa* and the Greek *megaloi theoi.* According to Yoruban wisdom, a person "chooses a head" at birth, that is, one is furnished with a bit of cosmic essence. The essence manifests in the forces and world of nature, which are embodied by the orishas. Like the loa, the orishas exhibit complex human personalities, with strong desires, preferences, temperaments, and various sexual orientations. When the orishas possess their "children," the devotees assume their personalities, performing feats of superhuman strength, eating and drinking huge quantities of food and alcohol, and divining the future with great accuracy.

The oldest ancestor and the first orisha is Obatalá, the father of the gods. Santeros, like Vodounists, believe in a supreme being as creator, but he is incomprehensible and too remote for daily worship. Obatalá is personified as a white man dressed in white and on horseback. He represents peace and purity. Oddudúa, his wife, is a black woman usually depicted breastfeeding an infant and represents maternity. According to myth Obatalá and Oddudúa had two children, a son Aganyú and a daughter Yemayá. Aganyú and Yemayá married and had a son, Orúngan. Orúngan was supposedly so handsome that Aganyú died from envy. When he matured Orúngan forced himself on his mother, who then cursed him and he died. Yemayá, depicted as a beautiful yellow-skinned woman and the goddess of the moon and womanhood, then climbed to the top of a mountain where she died from sorrow. Just before her death, she gave birth to fourteen orishas. The waters released when her abdomen burst caused the flood, and the place where she died became the holy city of Ile Ifé, the same sacred place worshiped in Vodoun.

Second in power to Obatalá is Elegguá, the counterpart of Legba in Vodoun. Elegguá is the god of entryways, doors, and roads, who allows the other orishas to come to earth. All homes keep an image of Elegguá behind the door. Another important orisha is Orúnla, who owns the Table of Ifá, the sacred system of divination.

Each of the orishas appears in many manifestations, and only a priest knows what orisha to invoke. Saints identified with the orishas may or may not be of the same gender. Santeros explain that after the gods' mystical deaths, they were reincarnated in new bodies. A partial list of the saints and their corresponding orishas is as follows: Olorún/Olofi, God the Creator (the Crucified Christ); Obatalá (Our Lady of Mercy); Oddudúa (Saint Claire); Aganyú (Saint Joseph); Yemayá (Our Lady of Regla); Orúngan (the Infant Jesus); Changó (Saint Barbara); Oyá (Our Lady of La Candelaria, also Saint Theresa and Saint Catherine); Oshún (Our Lady of La Caridad del Cobre); Ochosi (Saint Isidro); Dada (Our Lady of Mount Carmel); Ochumare (Our Lady of Hope); Oggún (Saint Peter, Saint Anthony, or Joan of Arc); Babalú-Ayé (Saint Lazarus); Elegguá (the Holy Guardian Angel, Saint Michael, Saint Martin de Porres, and Saint Peter); Orúnla (Saint Francis of Assisi); Ifá (Saint Anthony of Padua); Bacoso (Saint Christopher).

Rites and Practices

Although all worshipers of Santería may be called santeros, the term often refers to the priests or priestesses. The highest order of priest is the omnipotent *babalawo* ("father of secrets"), who has power not only to heal the sick and punish the unjust but to divine the future through the Table of Ifá. All babalawos are male, since Orúnla, the guardian of the Table, is male. Within the order of babalawo are various degrees, ranging from high priest to the one responsible for a particular orisha's sacrifice. Following the babalawos are the priests of orishas who govern the sick or healing; and the priests or priestesses of Orisha-Oko, the god of agriculture. Priests consecrated to lesser orishas or human deities also fall in this third category.

The babalawo's second most important duty is sacrificing the animals as offerings to the orishas. Common sacrificial animals include all types of fowl, goats, pigs, and occasionally a bull. The practice is opposed by animal rights activists in the United States.

Divining the future by reading the seashells (*los caracoles*) of the Table of Ifá is paramount in Santería. Santeros who specialize in Table readings are called *italeros* and are often babalawos dedicated to serving Orúnla. Reading the Table is also called *diloggun* or *mediloggun*. Eighteen shells make up the Table, but the italero only uses sixteen. The smooth shells may be bought in a *botanica* (store where Santería and Vodoun paraphernalia and herbs are sold) by anyone, but uninitiated users, called *aleyos*, may use only twelve. The unbroken sides of the shell are filed until the serrated edges appear, showing what look like tiny mouths filled with teeth. The shells are the "mouthpieces" of the orishas.

During a consultation, called a *registro*, the italero prays to the orishas, rubs the sixteen shells together, then throws them onto a straw mat called an *estera*. The shells are read according to how many of them fall with their "mouths" uppermost. Each pattern of up and down, called an *ordun*, has a corresponding controlling orisha and accompanying proverb. The italero interprets the proverbs to fit the particular situation, since otherwise the oracles sound more like the wisdom found in fortune cookies.

Very often the babalawo finds the questioner has been put under an evil spell, or *bilongo,* by an enemy. Such action requires the victim to place a counteracting spell, called an *ebbo,* on the guilty party. If the ebbo does more damage to the enemy than the original bilongo, it merely enhances the babalawo's *prestige, reputation, and clientele.* Remedies range from herbal baths to complicated spells involving various oils, plants, and intimate waste products of the intended victim. A common prescription is for the questioner to wear a *resguardo,* or protective talisman bag filled with various herbs and dedicated to an orisha.

Another popular divinatory method, normally used to consult Elegguá, is called *"darle coco al santo"* ("give the coconut to the saint"), or reading coconut meat. Coconuts are used in all major Santería ceremonies and form the main ingredient in several spells. To prepare a coconut for divination, the reader must break its shell with a hard object, never cracking the nut on the floor, as that would offend Obi, the coconut's deity. The meat, which is white on one side and brown on the other, is then divided into four equal pieces. The pieces are thrown on the floor, and one of five patterns results. Each pattern has a meaning and must be interpreted for the situation at hand.

Readings of the Table of Ifá by the babalawo help determine all of the important characteristics of a person's life and how he or she should deal with each event in life as it occurs. Upon the birth of a child, the parents consult the babalawo to find the infant's assigned orisha, plant, birthstone, and animal. In Santería stones traditionally associated with birth months have no relation to the birthstone. Good talisman animals include goats, elephants, and turtles; bad ones are many reptiles, venomous insects, some types of frogs, all birds of prey, rats, crocodiles, lizards, and spiders.

Water has great spiritual powers as protection for the santero. Since evil spirits are believed to dissolve in water, all devotees keep a small receptacle of water under the bed to clean away evil influences. The water must be changed every twenty-four hours, and must never be poured on the floor or down the kitchen sink.

Other protective agents against evil are black rag dolls, garlic, and brown sugar. To be especially safe, a santero burns brown sugar and garlic skins in a small pan over hot coals, along with incense and other herbs. The thick smoke, called *sahumerio,* fills the house, seeping into every nook and cranny, even closets and corners where evil spirits can hide.

Healing and Magic

All santeros are accomplished herbalists, since plants, and especially herbs, are sacred to the orishas. Most plants serve dual purposes, as curatives and as magic ingredients, and can be obtained in any good botanica.

The sacred *bombax ceiba* tree, or five-leaf silk-cotton tree, gives the santero curative or magical powers from almost every part of the plant. The tree is worshiped as a female saint, receiving offerings of food, money, and sacrificed animals. Ceibas are very easily offended; a santero won't even cross the tree's shadow without first asking permission. Teas made from the ceiba's roots and leaves help cure venereal disease and urinary tract infections; leaves also work on anemia. Bark teas help cure infertility. The tree trunk and the ground around it facilitate evil spells; if a santero wishes harm upon someone, he must walk naked around the ceiba tree several times at midnight and brush the trunk with his fingertips, softly asking the tree to help him against his enemy. Even the shade of the ceiba attracts spirits, giving strength to spells cast there.

Santerían magic has been described as African magic adapted for Western city life. It is based on the magical principles of sympathy and contagion (see **Magic**), and is used primarily to solve problems and make gains in love, luck, money, business, and health. Santeros who deal exclusively in black magic are known as *palo mayombe* or *brujeria* (a type of witch). The *mayomberos,* who are descendents of Congo tribesmen, are viewed as malignant beings specializing in revenge, necromancy, and the destruction of human life. Ethics do not enter the picture, for evil magic simply serves as a means of survival in a hostile world. Retribution can be avoided by "paying" the demonic forces through offerings of food, liquor, money, and animal sacrifice. Mayomberos operate with impunity, offering death and destruction on behalf of anyone for a price.

Many santeros fear the mayomberos' powers so much that they will not even speak of them except in whispers. Conversely, the mayombero respects the santero's communion with the orishas. Few mayomberos willingly tangle with the orishas directly, much as the lords of darkness avoid the princes of the light. See **Vodoun**.

Sources: Rod Davis. "Children of Yoruba." *Southern Magazine* (February 1987); Migene Gonzales-Wippler. *Santería: African Magic in Latin America.* New York: Original Products, 1981; Judith Gleason. *Oya: In Praise of the Goddess.* Boston: Shambhala, 1987; Mike McLaughlin. "A Voudou Village in the US." *The Seattle Times/ Seattle Post-Intelligencer* (April 5, 1987).

Satori

See **Mystical experiences; Zen.**

Schmeidler, Gertrude

See **Sheep/goat effect.**

Scientology

See **Church of Scientology.**

Scrying

A method of divination done by gazing upon an object such as a crystal ball or mirror until clairvoyant visions are seen on the surface or in the mind's eye. Scrying is an ancient art dating back to the early Egyptians and Arabs. Scryers attempt to look into the future in order to answer questions, solve problems, find lost objects and people, and identify or find criminals.

"Scrying" comes from the English word "descry," which means "to succeed in discerning" or "to make out dimly." The tool of scryers, called a speculum, can be any object that works for an individual, but usually is one with a reflective surface. The oldest and most common speculum is still water in a lake, pond, or dark bowl. Ink, blood, and other dark liquids have been used by Egyptian scryers for centuries. The French physician and astrologer Nostradamus scryed with a bowl of water set upon a brass tripod. His preparatory ritual consisted of dipping a wand into the water and anointing himself with a few drops, then gazing into the bowl until he saw visions. See **Nostradamus.**

Other specula include glass fishing floats, polished metals and stones, and precious gems. Gypsy fortune-tellers made crystal balls the stereotype of the trade. American psychic Jeane Dixon uses a crystal ball. John Dee, the royal magician to Queen Elizabeth I, used a crystal egg and a black obsidian mirror. In Arab countries scryers use their own polished thumbnails. Dr. Morton Prince, a medi-

Glass fishing float used for scrying

cal psychologist of the nineteenth century, used electric lightbulbs in experiments with his patients. Witches use rounded mirrors, the convex side of which is painted black, or small cauldrons, painted black on the inside and filled with water.

Scryers usually have their own individual techniques for inducing their visions. Some who use crystals focus on points of light on the surface. Others enter an altered state of consciousness and allow images to float into their inner awareness. Some images are couched in symbols, which the scryer must learn to interpret. In the Middle Ages, there was a belief that the images formed on a crystal ball or other tool were caused by demons that had been trapped inside by magic.

It is possible to learn the art of scrying with patience and practice. Paramount to success is the ability to relax both mind and body and put the mind in a passive, unfocused state. Some scryers say that when clairvoyance develops the speculum will appear to cloud over with a curtain or mist, which then parts to reveal shapes and colors. With more skill the shapes and colors sharpen to reveal discernible objects, people, and symbols.

For people with natural psychic ability, advancement comes quickly. Exceptional psychic ability tends to manifest in childhood. In Arab countries the best

(Photo by Bonnie Sue)

Sources: W. E. Butler. *How to Develop Clairvoyance.* 2d ed. New York: Samuel Weiser, 1979; Rosemary Ellen Guiley. *The Encyclopedia of Witches and Witchcraft.* New York: Facts On File, 1989; D. H. Rawcliffe. *The Psychology of the Occult.* London: Derricke Ridgway Publishing Co., 1952; Keith Thomas. *Religion and the Decline of Magic.* New York: Charles Scribner's Sons, 1971; Doreen Valiente. *Witchcraft for Tomorrow.* Custer, WA: Phoenix Publishing, 1978.

Seance

Event in which a medium contacts the spirit world. The medium enters an altered state of consciousness and reaches a spirit, called a control by psychical researchers and "spirit friend" or "spirit helper" by many modern mediums. The control, communicating mentally with the medium or speaking directly through his or her vocal cords, conveys information from other spirits for the benefit of the sitters. The spirits may also assist in healing or manifesting physical phenomena such as apports.

Seances from the mid-nineteenth through early twentieth centuries were dominated by physical phenomena, some of which was exposed as fraud. Most modern seances involve mental mediumship, in which the medium relays messages.

In the early days of Spiritualism, seances traditionally took place in darkened rooms. The medium and others—called "sitters"—sat around a table and held hands or placed their hands down on the table. Hands were accounted for in this way to show that any phenomena produced during the seance were not due to sleight of hand. Researchers held or tied down the medium's feet and knees.

The term "seance" has fallen out of fashion, in part due to negative associations caused by earlier fraud. Psychical researchers have long used the term "sitting," which also is used by many modern mediums. Some mediums use "spirit greetings" and others use nothing at all; sessions are billed as "An evening with . . ." Many Spiritualist mediums do not enter a dramatic trance to communicate with the spirit world, nor do they need darkened rooms.

"Seance" sometimes is applied to the trance events of shamans, which customarily take place inside a darkened tent and feature spirit voices, whistlings, shriekings, and manifestations; moving and levitating objects; and rappings and poundings.

There are marked differences between shamanic seances and mediumistic seances, however. The medium usually enters a trance quietly, through self-hypnosis and breathing control, while the shaman achieves an altered state through fasting, ecstatic dancing (which produces hyperventilation), and drumming, and sometimes with the help of drugs. The medium often has little or no control over what takes place at a seance once the trance has been entered; many, in fact, have no recollection of it once they return to a normal state of consciousness. The shaman, on the other hand, retains a high degree of control, remaining lucid enough to command the spirits invoked, go out-of-body, and perform healings, including psychic surgery. See Channeling; Mediumship; Shamanism; Spiritualism.

Sources: Slater Brown. *The Heyday of Spiritualism.* New York: Hawthorn Books, 1970; Alfred Douglas. *Extrasensory Powers: A Century of Psychical Research.* London: Victor Gollancz Ltd., 1976; Alan Gauld. *Mediumship and Survival.* London: William Heinemann Ltd., 1982; R. Laurence Moore. *In Search of White Crows.* New York: Oxford University Press, 1977; Janet Oppenheim. *The Other World: Spir-*

itualism and Psychical Research in England, 1850–1914. Cambridge, England: Cambridge University Press, 1985; D. Scott Rogo. *Psychic Breakthroughs Today.* Wellingborough, Northamptonshire, England: The Aquarian Press, 1987; Alberto Villodo and Stanley Krippner. *Healing States.* New York: Fireside/Simon & Schuster, 1986.

Secret of the Golden Flower, The

See Alchemy; Jung, Carl Gustav.

Sedona, Arizona

Area in central Arizona said to be a power point or "psychic vortex." The site is located in the red rock country near the town of Sedona, about forty miles south of Flagstaff, and is alleged to lie on a ley line. See Leys. The area is sacred to the Yavapai Native Americans, whose myths feature deities who live in the rocks.

Thousands of pilgrims visit the site annually. Experiences reported include visions of spirits (primarily Native American), visions of blue auras over the rocks, clairvoyant dreams, clairaudient bell-like tones, past-life recall, automatic writing, cures, physical changes, and spiritual transformations. Others have visions of what they believe are the remains of an advanced civilization buried far below the rocks. Many of the pilgrims are attracted to Sedona by the seminars of Dick Sutphen, who first visited the area in 1969 and was impressed by the energy he experienced there. See Power point; Sutphen, Richard.

Sources: Robert Lindsey. "'Psychic Energy' and the Pot of Gold." *The New York Times* (February 9, 1988): 9; *Dick Sutphen Presents Sedona: Psychic Energy Vortexes.* Malibu, CA: Valley of the Sun Publishing, 1986; Paul Zuromski. "Dick Sutphen." *Body Mind Spirit* (September/October 1987): 14–18.

Sedona, Arizona

Seiki

See **Universal life force.**

Seiki-jutsu

See **Bodywork.**

Self-actualization

See **Psychology.**

Sensitive

See **Mediumship; Psychic.**

Serios, Ted

See **Thoughtography.**

Seth

See **Roberts, Jane.**

Shah, Idries

See **Sufism.**

Shakers

American religious sect. Also called the United Society of Believers, the Shakers flourished in nineteenth-century America. They lived communally yet stressed complete celibacy to counter sex, the root of all sin.

The Shakers were founded by Ann Lee, a native of Manchester, England. Lee was poor and uneducated. Following her marriage to Abraham Standerin, also called Stanley, she bore four children,

Circle dance of the Shakers of New Lebanon, New York, 1873

three of whom died in infancy and one daughter who did not live past age six. These traumas contributed to her decision to avoid sex.

Lee was deeply religious. In 1758 she joined a splinter group of Quakers headed by Jane and James Wardley, derisively known as the Shaking Quakers because of their shaking dances during worship. Lee became convinced that human carnal nature caused all sin. Tormented, she drew away from her husband and cried out in agony if she gave in to his affections. She preached celibacy to the Wardley group, and eventually took over as its leader. While in Manchester jail in the summer of 1770 for disturbing the peace with noisy religious practices, Ann had a powerful vision of what she believed was the source of all human depravity: the first carnal act committed by Adam and Eve in the Garden of Eden. Ann attributed this act as the cause of humankind's separation from God, confirming her belief that celibacy was the only route to reunification. She then saw Jesus Christ before her, who offered so-lace for her suffering and encouraged her to follow her convictions.

After her release from prison, Ann related her visions to the Wardley group and revealed herself as Ann the Word. They were so impressed they made her head of the sect and began to call her Mother, putting into practice their notions of a dual godhead, both male and female, God the Father and the Mother.

The Shakers were continually harassed in Manchester, and might have disappeared if one of the group, James Whittaker, had not had a vision of a burning tree of life in America. Mother Ann interpreted this vision as a call to take the church to America. She, Abraham, and eight of her followers set sail and arrived in New York City on August 6, 1774.

In 1776 they established their first settlement at Niskayuna near Albany, New York, later called Watervliet, amidst hostility and persecution. Mother Ann moved the church headquarters to Harvard and Shirley, Massachusetts, in 1781, but continued to suffer harassment, often

Shaker women

physical abuse. Although the Shakers did not plan to live together, they chose communal life for protection. Neighbors were hostile toward a group who would not fight in the Revolution, worshiped God in such unorthodox manners, spoke in tongues and received revelations, and followed a woman as church leader. Mother Ann's statements that she was nearly divine, was equal to men, and that women did not have to "be fruitful and multiply" branded her as a witch. Abraham eventually left Ann for another woman, and Ann reverted to her maiden name.

Mother Ann died in 1784, without seeing her church well established. Her spiritual presence apparently remained with the Shakers, however. She had believed in communication with the spirit world and had claimed to talk to Jesus, angels, and Shaker founders who had preceded her. At her death Mother Ann reportedly said that she saw her dead brother William coming for her in a chariot, and follower John Hocknell testified that when she died, he saw her soul float upward into a chariot drawn by four white horses. Shaker literature testifies that she sent messages of moral exhortation and encouragement to her followers for years after her death.

As the first major sect founded by a woman, Shakerism attracted more women than men. The church taught that God had a dual nature, with a masculine spirit embodied in Christ and a female spirit manifested in the presence of Mother Ann. Members of either sex could lead the church. Such early feminist notions appealed to women, who, like Mother Ann, felt subjected to traditional male sexual dominance.

Like Quakers, Shakers took a liberal approach to Bible interpretation, performed no sacraments—not even baptism or communion—refused to take oaths or participate in government, believed in total pacifism, abolition of slavery, and used the more archaic forms "thee" and "thou." Shakers also believed in the free workings of the spirit and communication with the other world. Worship services consisted of singing and dancing, which often evolved into trembling, shouting, leaping, whirling, stomping, rolling on the floor and writhing, speaking in tongues, trances, and other possession phenomena.

Elder Frederick W. Evans, who became a Shaker after a fiery vision showed him surviving unscathed except for the loss of his genitalia, always maintained that Spiritualism had begun with the Shakers. But no extensive spiritual phenomena occurred until August 16, 1837, when a group of young girls at Watervliet began to shake, fall to the ground, and sing songs in unknown languages. The girls claimed to have seen Mother Ann and to have visited heavenly places guided by angels.

The phenomena spread, and spiritual manifestations lasted for about ten years, a period known in Shaker literature as the New Era, Mother Ann's Second Appearing, or Mother's Work. During that time Believers in all the communities became "instruments" for the spirits, exhibiting classic possession phenomena: stiffening bodies, agonizing distortions, screeching, preternatural strength, and the smell of sulfur.

The instruments, or mediums, delivered two types of messages from the spirits: personal words of comfort and concern for individuals, usually received by average Shakers; and moral exhortations and calls for return to Shaker ideals, received by Shaker leaders. Communications in the early years came primarily from Mother Ann and other deceased leaders, but later messages came from Jesus, Mary Magdalene, St. Paul, Columbus, George Washington, Napoleon, Queens Isabella and Elizabeth I, Alexander the Great, William Penn, the Marquis de Lafayette, martyred saints, biblical figures, Indians, Chinese, Arabs, Negroes, and Muhammad. Native American spirit controls were especially popular, causing the mediums to whoop, dance, and smoke the peace pipe. Such controls among the Shakers appear to be the first recorded instances of Native American spirit participation in Spiritualist phenomena.

In 1842 the central ministry at New Lebanon, New York, told the communities to establish a place for outdoor spiritual worship, ostensibly the highest spot in the village. These "Sacred Squares" or "Holy Hills of Zion" were to be visited twice a year, spring and fall, for gatherings with the spirits, called "Mountain Meetings." The crests were fenced or walled, surrounding a Fountain and engraved Fountain Stone. While the stones were tangible, the fountains were visible only to those with spiritual insight. Prior to the meetings, the Shakers fasted and prayed, then dressed themselves in imaginary spiritual garments, often including "spectacles of discernment" to see the spirits, then "bathed" in the fountains. Worshipers carried spiritual musical instruments and plates of spiritual food for a great pantomime feast. The luxurious spiritual garments and delicacies were worlds apart from plain Shaker fare.

By the end of Mother's Work, spiritual messages became cynical and critical of Shaker ideals, especially celibacy. One medium even declared that Mother Ann wanted her followers to abandon celibacy and marry; Elder Evans quashed that idea by saying that if Mother Ann had fallen from the light, good Shakers should not do likewise. The manifestations tapered off and ended about 1847.

Shakerism peaked about 1850, with six thousand members living in twenty communities in New York, Connecticut,

New Hampshire, Maine, Massachusetts, Ohio, Indiana, and Kentucky. They were renowned for their skilled craftsmanship.

Although Shakers believed that after the Millennium marriage would be obsolete, strict celibacy, dependence on conversion alone, and the changes in society after the Civil War brought about the sect's decline and virtual demise. Only two communities remain today: Canterbury, New Hampshire, and Sabbathday Lake, Maine. See **Glossolalia; Mediumship.**

Sources: Edward R. Horgan. *The Shaker Holy Land.* Harvard and Boston: The Harvard Common Press, 1987; Lawrence Foster. *Religion and Sexuality.* New York and Oxford: Oxford University Press, 1981; "Psychic Manifestations Among the Shakers (Part II)." *Journal of the American Society for Psychical Research* 32, no. 11 (November 1938): 339–50; F. E. Leaning. "The Indian 'Control.'" *Journal of the American Society for Psychical Research* 22, no. 6 (June 1927): 346–52; Keith Crim, gen. ed. *Abingdon Dictionary of Living Religions.* Nashville, TN: Abingdon Press, 1981; Slater Brown. *The Heyday of Spiritualism.* New York: Hawthorn Books, 1970.

Shamanism

Magico-spiritual systems in which an adept enters an altered state of consciousness and travels to nonworldly realities in order to heal, divine, communicate with the spirits of the dead, and perform other supernatural feats. The term "shamanism," from the Tungusic term *saman,* originally applied to societies found in Siberia and Central Asia, then was extended to similar systems found elsewhere around the world. It has also been suggested that the term derives from the Sanskrit *saman,* meaning "song," referring to the shaman's magical songs and chants. Shamans belong to the same class of individuals as mystics, in that they are

Java shaman and village chief prepare for ritual

separated from the mainstream of their community by intense spiritual experience. They are predominantly men.

The terms "shaman" and "shamanism" are frequently applied to various kinds of healers, medicine men, witch doctors, mystics, priests, magicians, sorcerers, and diviners, and to societies that had or have shamanic practices but were not or are not shamanic after the Siberian/Central Asian systems. Arguments have been advanced on both sides, to retain narrow definitions of the terms or to loosen them.

Shamanism has been described as "the world's oldest profession"; archaeological evidence suggests shamanic techniques are at least 20,000 years old. Shamans were probably the first storytellers, healers, priests, magicians, dramatists, and so on, who explained the world and related it to the cosmos.

Shamanic systems are complex and diverse, but many share common characteristics. In Siberia and Central Asia, the

Shaman and assistants become horses in trance dance and reenact a battle for onlooking villagers

magico-religious life of the society centers around the shaman, while in other societies shamans share the stage with priests and other adepts. The ecstatic trance sets shamans apart from other religious and magical adepts: shamans cannot become shamans without experiencing ecstatic trances, and they perform all of their functions in trance. They are assisted by tutelary and helping spirits.

Selection and Initiation

Shamans generally are called to their profession in two ways: by heredity, or by spontaneous and involuntary election by the Supernaturals. In some cases shamans can be self-made by seeking out the training; these individuals, however, are considered less powerful. An exception to the latter is found among Native North

Others revive shaman to ordinary consciousness after ritual ends

(Courtesy Hartley Film Foundation)

Shaman in his garb as village chief

cestral spirit, or the spirit of a dead shaman. The candidate is initiated into his power in trance by ritual death, dismemberment, and resurrection. He becomes a new person and takes a new name. In some societies he is considered to be literally dead, and resurrected as a ghost.

The shaman acquires an assortment of helping spirits, which take the form of animals, birds, insects, fish, plants, or spirits of the dead. Each has a specific function and helps him in performing his duties. Shamans also may have a guardian spirit, usually the representative of a genus, such as Bear or Coyote, from which he derives his power. See **Guardian spirit.**

Some shamans, such as among the Australian Aborigines and Native North Americans, receive objects of power, such as crystals, shells, or stones, which are symbolically inserted in their bodies in initiation rituals. See **Medicine societies.**

Powers

The shaman lives in two worlds: ordinary reality and nonordinary reality, also called the "shamanic state of consciousness." Nonordinary reality is a unique altered state of consciousness in which the shaman has access to the three zones of most cosmologies: earth, sky, and underworld, which are connected by a central axis represented by a World Pillar, World Tree, or World Mountain. The shaman remains lucid throughout his altered state, controls it, and recalls afterward what transpired during it. In the shamanic state, the shaman sees other, nonworldly realities, perhaps multiple realities simultaneously. He has access to information that is not accessible in the ordinary reality.

The ability to enter the shamanic state at will is essential to shamanism. Techniques for doing so include drumming, rattling, chanting, dancing, fasting, sexual abstinence, sweat baths, staring

Americans, many of whom undertake a vision quest to ask for healing power or the help of guardian spirits. The shaman becomes distinguished from others by the greater number of his helping spirits, by the intensity of his vision, and by his greater power. See **Vision quest.**

In spontaneous election an individual may suddenly fall seriously ill, and recovers only by healing himself. In other cases he has an involuntary trance or dream in which he is informed by spirits or shades of the dead that he has been chosen to be a shaman. The vision may occur during serious illness.

The candidate then undertakes training by an elder shaman and by a tutelary spirit, usually a semidivine being, an an-

into flames, concentrating on imagery, and isolating oneself in darkness. Some societies employ psychedelic drugs for this purpose, but drugs are not essential to the shamanic process.

The shaman also has the power to see spirits and souls, and to communicate with them. He is able to take magical-mystical flights to the heavens, where he can serve as intermediary between the gods and his people; he can descend to the underworld to the land of the dead. The flights are done by shape-shifting, by riding mythical horses or the spirits of sacrificed horses, by traveling in spirit boats, and the like. He heals, prophesies, shape-shifts, and controls the elements.

Functions

Universally, the shaman's primary function is to heal and restore the individual's connectedness to the universe. Shamans make no distinction between body, mind, and spirit; they are all part of the whole. Shamanism, unlike Western medicine, is not necessarily concerned with the extension of life, but rather is concerned with protecting the soul and preventing it from eternal wandering. Certain life-threatening health hazards of primitive living, such as contaminated water, are accepted as risks of daily life.

The diagnosis of illness generally falls into two categories: the magical "insertion" of a disease-causing object in the body of the patient by a sorcerer or displeased or evil spirit; or "soul loss," in which the patient's soul has wandered off into the land of the dead, been frightened away by a ghost or traumatic experience, or been kidnapped by spirits of the dead. The shaman makes the diagnosis by communicating with his helping spirits.

In the case of "insertion," he "sucks" the offending object from the patient's body. The illness is absorbed by the spirit helpers, who also protect the shaman from becoming ill himself. If the

soul has been lost, he goes out-of-body to the underworld, where he finds the soul, retrieves it, and restores it to the patient. In both cases tangible evidence of the cure is important to both patient and the community. Thus the shaman produces by sleight of hand the disease-causing object—typically a stone, bone, feather, or pottery shard—which he then causes to disappear. If he has retrieved a soul, he tells of his battle with the shades and produces his bloodied weapon as proof. In some societies shamans exorcise disease-causing spirits in seance-like procedures, or by invoking or cajoling them to leave the patient.

The use of sleight of hand does not negate the healing. Shamans who have admitted to sleight of hand say they do not need it to heal, but it is necessary as tangible confirmation that a healing has taken place. The tangible "proof" undoubtedly has a placebo effect of facilitating the patient's own self-healing processes. Some witnessed cases of sucking appear paranormal, as in the healing work of Rolling Thunder. See **Rolling Thunder.**

Dream interpretation is another important function of shamans. They also divine the future, find lost property, identify thieves, control the weather, protect individuals and communities against evil spirits and the evil spells of sorcerers, and perform various religious rites.

Similarities to Other Systems

Overlaps may be found in some shamanism and Eastern religions, meditation, yoga, and alchemy, indicating that the latter perhaps were influenced by the much older shamanism. Dismemberment imagery figures in shamanism and in Tibetan Tantrism. The means of achieving altered and higher states of consciousness are comparable. The psychic powers of shamans are similar to the *siddhis* of yoga. See **Siddhis.** Animal spirits and symbolisms appear in both shamanism and alchemy. See **Alchemy.** Shamans, however, do not seek higher states of consciousness as an end in themselves, but as a medium in which to perform their duties. The similarities do not mean shamanism can be equated with Eastern systems, however, as significant metaphysical differences exist.

Western interest in shamanism has spawned a so-called neo-shamanism, in which shamanic elements are adapted to Western life in an effort to regain a connection to the sacred and an understanding of the interconnectedness of all life, and as a means of personal empowerment. See **Altered states of consciousness; Black Elk, Nicholas; Meditation; Yoga.**

Sources: Jeanne Achterberg. *Imagery in Healing: Shamanism and Modern Medicine.* Boston: Shambhala Publications, 1985; Mircea Eliade. *Shamanism.* 1951. Princeton, NJ: Princeton University Press, 1964; Joan Halifax. *Shaman: The Wounded Healer.* New York: Crossroad, 1982; Michael Harner. *The Way of the Shaman.* New York: Bantam, 1986; Holger Kalweit. *Dreamtime and Inner Space: The World of the Shaman.* Boston: Shambhala Publications, 1984; Shirley Nicholson, comp. *Shamanism.* Wheaton, IL: The Theosophical Publishing House, 1987. Ruth M. Underhill. *Red Man's Religion.* Chicago: University of Chicago Press, 1965; Alberto Villoldo and Stanley Krippner. *Healing States.* New York: Fireside/Simon & Schuster, 1986.

Shambhala

Legendary Tibetan kingdom symbolic of spiritual enlightenment. Tantric texts discuss the kingdom, its spiritual significance, and the path leading to it. Many Tibetans, including both laypeople and lamas, believe Shambhala is a real place, hidden in a secret location deep within the Himalayas. Some Western scholars, however, suggest Shambhala is mythical, and in spiritual teachings represents a desired goal of an enlightened and happy life. Other scholars theorize Shambhala legends may have grown out of one of the ancient and real kingdoms of Central Asia, such as the Zhang-Zhung.

The name "Shambhala" is Sanskrit, and is taken by Tibetans to mean "the Source of Happiness." Laypeople regard the place as a heaven of the gods, while lamas consider it a Pure Land. It is not a heavenly paradise as Westerners might think, but a mystical kingdom that guards the most sacred and secret spiritual teachings of the world, including the Kalacakra ("Wheel of Time"), the highest and most esoteric Tibetan Buddhist wisdom. Part of the Tibetan Canon (the equivalent of the Bible in Christianity), the Kalacakra is a complex system for attaining enlightenment, and its texts form the basis of Tibetan calendars, astrology, astronomy, alchemy, medicine, and human anatomy and physiology. Kalacakra texts are written in obscure symbolism, and lamas say that oral teachings, given only to initiates, are necessary for comprehension.

Little is known about the origins of Shambhala. According to some lamas, it has existed since the beginning of the world. Followers of Bön, the pre-Buddhist religion of Tibet, identify Shambhala with Olmulungring, an invisible kingdom ringed by snow mountains in northwestern Tibet that dates back to 16,017 B.C., when Shenrab, the King of Olmulungring, left his kingdom and crossed a burning desert in order to bring Bön to Tibet. A lineage of kings is said to remain in Olmulungring, where they guard the teachings of Bön.

Buddhists trace Shambhala to Siddhartha Gautama, the founder of Buddhism, c. 500 B.C. Tibetan Buddhists say many of Buddha's teachings were too advanced for the lay public and were not recorded in the Pali Canon, but were passed down orally and written down much later. Much of the oral sermons, which were incorporated into the Tibetan Canon, were given in an invisible spiritual dimension.

Prior to his death, Buddha is said to have assumed the form of the Kalacakra deity and delivered his highest teachings to a group of adepts and gods in southern India. Among those present was eighty-year-old King Suchandra, the first King of Shambhala, who wrote down the sermons and took them back to Shambhala, where he wrote commentaries on them and constructed the Kalacakra mandala. Suchandra is sometimes called the Chief of the Secret Tibetan Brotherhood of Initiates of the Occult Sciences. According to prophecy he shall govern humankind, implying a golden age of divine wisdom on Earth.

The earliest written Tibetan references to Shambhala appear in the Tibetan Canon, the oldest of which were recorded around the eleventh century A.D. The Canon was transcribed from Sanskrit. According to lore the texts were delivered into India in the tenth century, after being kept hidden in Shambhala for more than a thousand years. Kalacakra Tantra is said to have been introduced to India c. A.D. 600, and was a distinctly Buddhist system by the eleventh century.

The earliest written Western references to Shambhala were in 1627, when a group of Catholic missionaries from Europe traveled to Tibet and China and en route heard about a place they called "Xembala," which they believed was another name for Cathay, or China.

Various Buddhist texts give instructions for finding Shambhala, though directions are obscure. It is said that only accomplished yogis may find it, and only with a great deal of difficulty and travail. The kingdom is hidden in the mists of the snow mountains and can be reached only by flying over them with the help of *siddhis,* or spiritual powers. Those who attempt to traverse the peaks by other means will meet their doom.

The kingdom also is described in great detail in the Tibetan Canon and in other texts, such as the *Great Commentary on the Kalacakra,* written by Mipham, a nineteenth-century Buddhist teacher. Different locations are given. According to the early texts, Shambhala is located north of Bodhgaya, a Buddhist shrine in northern India. Hidden by a great ring of snow mountains, the kingdom is shaped like an eight-petaled lotus blossom. Each of the eight regions has twelve principalities. The capital, Kalapa, is at the center, and is surrounded by a second ring of snow mountains. The kingdom is lush and contains gold-roofed pagodas. The palace of the King is ornate and bejeweled, and filled with the scent of sandalwood incense. The residents, who are healthy, wealthy, beautiful, and virtuous, live for hundreds of years. There is no evil, vice, or war. The residents are guaranteed of attaining nirvana in that lifetime or soon after; if they die and are reincarnated, they will not fall to a lower state.

The residents study the Kalacakra, the science of mind, the goal of which is to become enlightened and master time. Kalacakra enabled Shambhala residents to cure themselves of disease and illness. By-products of this spiritual growth included paranormal powers, such as telepathy, precognition, invisibility, and the ability to walk at high speed.

The Kings of Shambhala are enlightened, according to the early texts; each is an incarnated bodhisattva. The texts speak of a prophecy of Shambhala, which foretells a cataclysmic battle between the forces of good and evil. Thirty-two Kings will reign over Shambhala, each for approximately one hundred years, and each reign is characterized by deteriorating conditions around the world: greed, dishonesty, war, and materialism. The "barbarians" will defeat all opposition, until an evil King rises to lead them all in an effort to rule the world. At that point Shambhala will emerge from the mists. The evil King will attack it, only to be defeated by the thirty-second King of Shambhala, Rudra Cakrin, "The Wrathful One with the Wheel." It is estimated that this battle will occur sometime between about 2200 and 2500.

According to Mipham Shambhala lies north of the river Sita in northern Tibet, in a land divided by eight mountain ranges. The palace of the Rigdens, the imperial rulers, is located on top of Kailasa, a mountain in the center of the kingdom. The palace, many square miles in size, looks out over a park and a temple devoted to Kalacakra Tantra. According to another source, Sarat Chandra Das, the kingdom is located in central Asia near the river Oxus.

In some legends of Shambhala, the kingdom vanished from the face of the Earth centuries ago, after its population became enlightened; it now exists on a more celestial plane. The Rigdens continue to watch over the Earth, and will return at some point to save humanity from destruction. Gesar of Ling, a great warrior and king c. the eleventh century in eastern Tibet, is believed to have been guided by the Rigdens. Legend says that he now resides in the celestial kingdom of Shambhala and that he, too, will return to Earth at the time of great crisis and will lead an army to vanquish the forces of darkness. In another version Rigden Pema Karpo, the last successor to King Suchandra, is the one who will return and establish Shambhala as a universal kingdom.

The myth of the return to save humanity has parallels in many religions, including the return of Christ in Christianity, and the final incarnation of Vishnu, Kalki, in Hinduism.

Author James Hilton probably was inspired by Shambhala for his novel about the lost kingdom of Shangri-La,

Lost Horizon. Hilton based his story on the nineteenth-century writings of Abbé Huc, a Catholic missionary who traveled through Tibet and heard a prophecy that resembles that of Shambhala.

Some Theosophist followers of Madame Helena P. Blavatsky believed Shambhala was the residence of the Mahatmas, spiritual adepts, said to live in the mountains of Tibet.

According to Edwin Bernbaum, scholar of Tibetan religion, mythology, and art, Shambhala symbolizes the hidden depths of the mind, the pure region of the superconsciousness, which may be reached through an inner journey. The kingdom's lotus shape is associated with enlightenment and purity, and with the heart chakra, the center of highest wisdom. See **Lotus; Mandala.**

Sources: Edwin Bernbaum. *The Way to Shambhala.* Garden City, NY: Anchor Press/Doubleday, 1980; W. Y. Evans-Wentz, ed. *The Tibetan Book of the Great Liberation.* London: Oxford University Press, 1954; John R. Hinnello, ed. *The Facts On File Dictionary of Religions.* New York: Facts On File, 1984; Chogyam Trungpa. *Shambhala: The Sacred Path of the Warrior.* 1984. New York: Bantam Books, 1986.

Sheep/goat effect

A phenomenon discovered in psychical research that demonstrates that people who believe in psi tend to score positively in psi tests, and people who do not believe in psi tend to score negatively. The phenomenon was discovered in the 1940s by American parapsychologist Gertrude Schmeidler, who named it the "sheep/goat effect." Sheep are believers and goats are nonbelievers.

Schmeidler and other researchers found that "sheep" are more likely to score "hits" in laboratory psi guessing games. "Goats" are more likely to miss targets and thus score below chance. Nonbelievers apparently miss targets through avoidance.

The sheep/goat effect seems to come into play only when positive or negative attitudes about psi are very strong. Sheep who are mild believers and goats who are mild skeptics both tend to score at chance.

Other factors influence hits and misses. People who are outgoing, happy, and relaxed are more likely to score above chance than those who are stiff, reserved, and introverted. Even a sheep who is stiff and reserved will not score as well as a sheep who is eager and relaxed.

Oddly, the sheep/goat effect began to disappear from laboratory tests in the 1970s. Parapsychologists theorize that public attitudes about psi have changed significantly since the 1940s, when psychic experiences were considered more of an anomaly. More people are willing to consider the possible existence of psi, and emotions on the subject are much less charged than they were in the past. Test subjects now are more likely to be influenced by the attitude of the experimenter. See Experimenter effect.

The sheep/goat effect may be applied outside the laboratory in daily life. People who believe in psi and who are relaxed, optimistic, and outgoing are more likely to spontaneously experience a wide range of psi phenomena, and rely more heavily on intuition. Nonbelievers are more likely not to have such experiences; if they do they tend to explain them away as chance, coincidence, or freak occurrences. See Psi hitting and psi missing.

Sources: Alfred Douglas. *Extrasensory Powers: A Century of Psychical Research.* London: Victor Gollancz Ltd., 1976; Martin Ebon. *Psychic Warfare: Threat or Illusion?* New York: McGraw-Hill, 1983; Gertrude Raffel Schmeidler and R. A. McConnell. *ESP and Personality Patterns.* New Haven, CT: Yale, 1958; Gertrude Schmeidler, ed. *Extrasensory Perception.*

New York: Atherton Press, 1969; Benjamin B. Wolman, ed. *Handbook of Parapsychology.* New York: Van Nostrand Reinhold, 1977.

Shiatsu

See Bodywork.

Shinto

Indigenous polytheistic, animistic, and shamanic religion of Japan. Shinto links living Japanese to their ancestral spirits, ancient gods, and elemental energies of the land and nature in a mysterious and shared cosmos. All natural phenomena are considered manifestations of the divine.

Shinto means "the way of the *kami*"; kami usually is translated into English as "gods" or "spirits." "Shinto" derives from the Chinese term "Shen-Tao"; the early, cultured Japanese commonly borrowed Chinese terms, which were considered more distinguished. The Japanese term for Shinto is *Kami-no-michi,* generally translated as "the Way of the gods." The term *kami* is complex and embodies the concept of spirit, deity, or force that is superior, transcendent, other-worldly, sacred, and numinous. Kami are not supernatural beings, but an essence: anything that inspires reverence, awe, mystery, or wonder. Humans, animals, mountains, literally anything in nature can possess kami-nature.

The origins of Shinto are unknown; there is no founder, and no official scriptures exist. There are no doctrine and formal ethics. Some elements of Shinto may have been imported from China. The earliest extant records of Shinto date to the eighth century. In early Japan Shinto existed not as a religion, but as a philosophy of life. Early Shinto took for granted the interwoven nature of the cosmos and all living things in it, without attempting to explain the meaning of it. All things were considered manifestations of the Divine, and believed to possess kami. Eight hundred myriads of kami are mentioned in Japanese myths.

The highest and most venerated kami of all is Amaterasu Omigami, the Sun Goddess and protector of the Japanese nation and people. Amaterasu is one of the children of Izanagi and Izanami, the kami who, according to myth, created Japan as the most beautiful place in the world and sent their offspring to be the kami of nature and the elements, such as the wind, mountains, waterfalls, trees, the ocean, animals, birds, and rocks. These kami, too, are highly venerated.

Also worshiped are the ancestral spirits of clan chieftains and humans who achieved a high degree of spiritual awareness while alive, or who displayed great heroism or even great evil. Such people have their remains enshrined, where the living come to seek favors and intercession. Communication may be established with a kami through a shamanic medium.

Many kami are neither well-defined nor individually named, but are associated with local areas, where they protect villages, clans, and families, and are worshiped at communal shrines. They also are believed to intervene in the lives of humans and are the cause of illness and bad luck. Misfortunes are remedied by exorcisms performed by shamans.

The early Shinto cosmology was divided in three realms: the highest was the High Sky Plain, where superior male and female kami live; the middle was the Manifested World of humans and animate and inanimate beings; the lowest was the Nether World, populated by evil spirits. The early Japanese referred to both the High Sky Plain and the Nether World as the "other world." The three-tiered realm later became condensed into one realm, the Takamagaharam, a heaven in which all kami, superior and evil, and the spirits of the dead coexist.

Early Shinto included many rituals for divination, purification, sorcery, and the seeking of favors from nature. Emphasis was given to thanksgiving to the kami for the bounties of life, and to purification through abstention and exorcism. Sin and evil were not viewed in moral terms, but as a lack of harmony with nature.

Shinto shrines are simple structures, usually a thatched roof supported by pillars. They customarily are located near fresh water which is used for purification. The gateway to the shrine, or *tori,* marks the boundary between the mundane and sacred worlds. Inside the shrine are representations of kami, perhaps rocks or mirrors, but no images. Short sticks with paper strips are symbolic offerings to the kami. Some of the most sacred shrines resemble log cabins, and are entered only by priests; the laity conduct their rituals in worship halls.

A small shrine, or *kamidama* ("god-shelf"), is maintained in Shinto homes, and consists of an altar placed usually in the living room above a closet. Rice, salt, water, and food are left on it daily as offerings to the kami. Purification ceremonies are performed upon rising. Household Shinto is concerned chiefly with rituals for domestic affairs, such as births, deaths, and anniversaries of deaths of ancestors.

Early Shinto absorbed elements of both Confucianism and Buddhism. After the introduction of Buddhism to Japan in the sixth century, Shinto either receded or coexisted in a Dual Shinto, which included Buddhist images and materials. In the eighteenth century, an effort was made to separate Shinto from Buddhism and revive it. In 1868 the Emperor Mutsuhito declared Shinto the state religion, or Daikyo ("great doctrine"), but renounced it in 1884. In the nineteenth century Shrine Shinto and Sect Shinto became distinct from one another. Various forms of both developed.

Tennoism and Post-World War II Shinto

Tennoism, or nationalistic emperor-worship, existed until the end of World War II. Derived from the term *tenno* ("emperor"), Tennoism held that the emperor of Japan was a direct descendant of the creator kami, Izanagi and Izanami, and functioned as ruler and chief priest of the nation. As a living kami himself, he was the primary intermediary between the Japanese people and Amaterasu, the ancestress of the royal house. In Japanese Tennoism is called Kokutai Shinto, or "the Shinto of national structure."

Tennoism took root in Japan's early history, c. the third to fourth centuries A.D. and gained strength as the country was unified by an imperial family. (Although records from the eighth century date the first legendary emperor of Japan much earlier, to the seventh century B.C., historians hold to the later date.) Tennoism went through cycles, reaching a peak between 1868, when Shinto was declared a state religion, and the end of World War II. Schoolchildren were taught that it was the highest morality, and that the emperor was infallible. The laity were forbidden to look directly at the emperor or speak his name. During World War II, Japanese soldiers fought and died in his name. Following Japan's defeat, the nation was forced to adopt a democratic government, and the emperor was forced to renounce his divinity. State Shinto was abolished, but continued as a sectarian religion.

Following the war numerous forms of sectarian Shinto developed, with diverse origins and practices. Some groups emphasize mountain pilgrimages to Mount Fuji or other peaks, where pilgrims hope to have ecstatic experiences. Others practice faith healing, divination, "mystical dancing," and firewalking. In the majority are sects organized around charismatic individuals, church-like in structure and devoted to community work.

Household Shinto continues to be practiced, but is on the decline, especially among the younger population. Shamanic practices also are on the decline, but remain part of the nation's folk religion.

Shinto has been exported to the West and other countries, serving not only transplanted Japanese but other nationalities as well. One such export is the Church of World Messianity (also known as the World Messianity and Johrei Fellowship), founded in 1935 by Mokichi Okada (1882–1955), called Meishu-sama, or "enlightened spiritual leader," by his followers. Meishu-sama received a divine revelation on the summit of Mount Nokogiri on June 15, 1931, in which he saw that a transition to paradise on earth was beginning in the spiritual realm. Because of government persecution in prewar times, Meishu-sama could not establish a religious organization, and so created a foundation dedicated to bringing about the envisioned earthly paradise. Following World War II, the organization began functioning as a church, and established sacred centers in Hakone, Atami, and Kyoto.

Johrei, as the sect is called, incorporates Shinto, Buddhist, and Christian concepts. The kami and ancestral spirits are venerated, as is God; Meishu-sama conceived of a single deity. Johrei centers are located in America, Brazil (where it is the second largest religion after Spiritism), and elsewhere. One of the sect's most important fundamentals is the realization of God's Plan through prototypes; thus the sacred centers serve as prototypes from which spiritual teachings expand into the world. Followers help others by "giving Johrei": the channeling of healing light to the spirit, an energy transfer that radiates out from the palm of the hand, which is extended to, but does not touch, the recipient. Giving Johrei helps purify the body, mind, and spirit, thus facilitating spiritual growth.

Influence of Shinto on Japanese Way of Life

Central to Shinto is the appreciation of the ability of nature to awaken in human beings a sense of the divine in the cosmos. Four elements of Shinto stand out as influential on the Japanese outlook on the world: (1) an exceptional understanding of creativity, and a sense of the interconnectedness of all things in a collective unconscious; (2) a belief in the innate power, beauty, and goodness of life, which fosters cultural attitudes of cooperation and harmony; (3) pragmatism and ability to adapt to change; and (4) universal beliefs, which enable coexistence with other faiths.

Sources: Ichiro Hori. *Folk Religion in Japan.* Chicago: University of Chicago Press, 1968; Yong Choon Kim. *Oriental Thought.* Totowa, NJ: Rowman and Littlefield, 1973; Ikuko Osumi and Malcolm Ritchie. *The Shamanic Healer: The Healing World of Ikuko Osumi and the Traditional Art of Seiki-Jutsu.* London: Century, 1987; Geoffrey Parrinder. *Mysticism in the World's Religions.* New York: Oxford University Press, 1976; Stuart D. B. Picken. *Shinto: Japan's Spiritual Roots.* Tokyo: Kodansha International, 1980; J. Isamu Yamamoto. *Beyond Buddhism.* Downers Grove, IL: Inter-Varsity Press, 1982; Johrei Fellowship.

Shroud of Turin

A yellow strip of linen bearing bloodstains and the brownish image of the body of a bearded man, which for centuries was believed to be the shroud in which Jesus was buried. Measuring about fourteen feet in length and four feet in width, the cloth has been the subject of controversy, debate, and analysis since it came to light in a French church in 1353.

It is considered by the Vatican to be the most important relic in Christendom. The shroud takes its name from St. John's Cathedral in Turin, where it has been held, folded, in a locked silver chest since the fifteenth century, seldom shown to the public. In 1988 the Vatican allowed carbon dating tests of samples of the cloth. According to the test results, the shroud is a medieval forgery.

One of the earliest skeptics of the shroud's authenticity was Bishop Pierre D'Arcis, who in 1389 told Pope Clement VII that the shroud was a forgery and the forger had made a confession. Yet this early dismissal did not deter the development of numerous theories about the shroud's origins and how it got to western Europe.

Nothing is known about the history of the shroud prior to 1353, when it surfaced in the possession of the family of Geoffrey De Charny, Lord of Savoy and Lirey, who built a church at Lirey in that year to honor the Blessed Virgin Mary. The shroud was housed in this church. In 1452 Marguerite de Charny gave it to the Duke of Savoy because she lacked a suitable heir. In 1478 the shroud was taken to Turin, the new capital of Savoy. The relic was willed to the Vatican when King Umberto II, the last Savoy, died in 1983.

Some historians have seen a connection between the shroud, pre-Christian Constantinople, the Crusades, and the de Charny family. The portrait on the shroud is similar to the Mandylion, a Byzantine portrait allegedly made "without hands," and one of the factors said to influence the conversion to Christianity of King Abgar V of Edessa. In 942, the Mandylion portrait was bought by Constantinople.

In 1204 Constantinople was sacked by the Crusader Knights Templar, and the Mandylion, along with many other relics, disappeared. It was speculated that the shroud was among the many relics taken back to Europe by the Knights. In

1307 the Knights were prosecuted for idolatry and heresy. Two of the leading members were exiled and burned at the stake in 1314, one of them being Geoffrey de Charny, a relative of the man who later built the church.

Those who believed the shroud to be authentic argued that a forgery would require skills and knowledge believed to be beyond the medieval capacities. Until 1988 the Vatican allowed only very limited examination of the shroud, and much evidence seemed to favor its authenticity. The church never claimed the shroud to be authentic, but never discouraged the belief, either.

That it is a forgery raises questions as to how the job was done. The shroud bears certain artistic, religious, and civil depictions thought to be known only to those living at the time of Christ. The bloodstained wounds on the image are consistent with the tortures thought to have been inflicted on Christ before death, and indicative of the times in which he lived. In some cases this evidence tallies with mystical visions reported from the fourteenth century to the twentieth century.

Believers maintained that the image was created by some kind of holy fire when Jesus disappeared from the Holy Sepulcher. Computerized enhancement ruled out the idea that the image was painted on or applied with herbs. An analysis of the purported bloodstains compared with the composition of dried blood. There are no linear strokes or change of color from light to dark. In 1898 Secondo Pia photographed the shroud and a negative image was revealed. The shroud was three-dimensional with front and back images, as if it had enveloped a body.

Medieval representational art depicted Jesus clothed rather than naked as he is on the shroud, and paintings of the crucifixion showed nails piercing his hands, not the wrists, as indicated by the shroud. It was not until the 1960s that it was learned that nails were pounded through the wrists because the hands could not support the weight of the body upon the cross.

Furthermore, the cloth is made of linen with a three-to-one twill weave, similar to fabrics dating from first-century Palestine, and not thought to be known in medieval Europe. The shroud contains pollen fossils from plants that grew only in Palestine at the time of Christ.

Early Jewish burial practices included the placement of coin-like objects over the eyelids, which photo enhancement analysis suggested on the image on the shroud. The man depicted on the shroud was hit as many as 125 times with a three-pronged whip, similar to one used by Roman soldiers of the first century, known as a flagra. Other wounds suggest further Roman practices of dealing with prisoners and the act of crucifixion.

In 1988, after years of refusals, the Vatican approved carbon 14 dating testing with a new nuclear device, known as the tandem accelerator mass spectrometer, that allows testing with samples only about the size of a postage stamp. Three samples were dated in independent, blind tests by Oxford University, the University of Arizona, and the Federal Institute of Technology in Zurich, Switzerland, coordinated by the British Museum. All three institutions concluded that the shroud was a medieval forgery dating between 1260 and 1390.

Nevertheless, church officials encouraged the continued veneration of the shroud as a pictorial image of Christ, capable of inspiring religious faith and even miracles. The officials further maintained that more research and evaluation would be needed before the shroud's origins could be conclusively established.

Sources: Malcolm W. Browne. "Tests Show Shroud of Turin to Be Fraud, Scientist Hints." *The New York Times* (September 22, 1988): 28; "Is Shroud of Turin a Fake?" *The Seattle Times* (August 26, 1988): 2; Richard Saltus. "Scientists May Finally Learn Age of Shroud." *Boston Globe* (April 18, 1988): 31–32; H. David Sox. "The Shroud." *New Realities* 1, no. 4 (1977): 42–46; Roberto Suro. "Church Says Shroud of Turin Isn't Authentic." *The New York Times* (October 14, 1988): p. 1+; Frank C. Tribbe. "The Shroud of Turin Confirms Mystical Visions." *Venture Inward* (March/April 1986): 37–40; Ian Wilson. *The Shroud of Turin: The Burial Cloth of Jesus Christ?* Garden City, NY: Doubleday, 1978.

Siddhis

Paranormal and extraordinary powers attained through spiritual development, especially in Tantric and yogic practices. *Siddhis* is Sanskrit for "perfect abilities" or "miraculous powers."

In Hindu yoga siddhis include such abilities as clairvoyance, telepathy, mind-reading, levitation, materialization, rendering one's self and things invisible, projecting out-of-body and entering another body, superhuman strength, and knowing the moment when one will die. These abilities are not to be sought for themselves because they are part of the phenomenal world and thus are obstacles to the realization of the Absolute. Siddhis are inevitable but must be renounced and overcome. If they are not, the yogi becomes merely a magician trapped in the phenomenal world of siddhis, and will not obtain the highest form of *samadhi,* union with the Absolute.

Book III of Patanjali's *Yoga Sutras* is devoted to siddhis, which are attained through the practice of *samyama.* Samyama is a self-control in the final three phases of Raja Yoga, which is the control of the mind through concentration, breath control, posture, meditation, and contemplation. Meditation upon objects or ideas enables the yogi to possess them magically, that is, to understand them by becoming them. According to Patanjali samyama enables a yogi to become invisible because by concentrating on the form of the body, the yogi merges with form and ceases to become an object of perception to others.

In Buddhist yoga *iddhis* (the Pali term for siddhis, which means "Wondrous Gifts") are the eight powers of mastery over the body and nature. The eight powers include invincibility, invisibility, fleetness in running, ability to see the gods, control over spirits and demons, the ability to fly, the preservation of youth, and the ability to make certain pills. Although possession of the iddhis is not viewed as harmful, it is not encouraged because of the danger that they will turn the monk away from the path to enlightenment, nirvana. In fact, the iddhis cannot be avoided, for they are part of the process of dying to the mundane world in order to be reborn in an unconditioned state.

Shakyamuni Buddha, the historical Buddha, forbade the use and display of iddhis, especially to noninitiates. He did this because the same powers could be obtained through magic without spiritual transformation, and such displays would not aid the Buddhist message.

Siddhis also are reported to arise spontaneously in *kundalini* awakenings. In Hindu yoga the kundalini, or "serpent power," is a spiritual force that resides dormant at the base of the spine. When awakened, it rises up through the chakras to the crown. See **Kundalini; Milarepa; Yoga.**

Sources: Mircea Eliade. *Yoga: Immortality and Freedom.* Princeton, NJ: Princeton University Press, 1958; *The Encyclopedia of Eastern Philosophy and Religion.* Boston: Shambhala, 1989; Lee Sanella. *The Kundalini Experience.* Lower Lake, CA: Integral Publishing, 1987.

Sidgwick, Eleanor

See **Society for Psychical Research (SPR).**

Sidgwick, Henry

See Society for Psychical Research (SPR).

Sitting

See Seance.

Smith, Hélène

The pseudonym of Catherine Elise Muller, a late-nineteenth-century medium from Geneva, Switzerland, who aroused considerable controversy over her alleged astral visits to Mars. Smith never worked as a paid medium, but gave seances to friends and admirers for entertainment. She earned a living holding a high position in a large store in Geneva.

Smith's seances were characterized by trances, automatic writing in Arabic, and glossolalia, or speaking in tongues. She hypnotized herself into a trance, and allowed her control, Leopold, to speak and write through her.

Smith claimed she had been a Hindu princess and Marie Antoinette in previous lives. Her present humble life was repayment of a karmic debt for her transgressions as Antoinette. One of the spirits she claimed to channel in trances was a contemporary of Antoinette, the eighteenth-century Italian sorcerer Cagliostro. When the spirit of Cagliostro appeared, Smith's appearance changed markedly to drooping eyelids and a double chin. The spirit used her vocal cords, speaking in a deep bass voice.

Leopold, who controlled a bevy of spirits around Smith, had been transported to Mars, Smith said. The spirits were able to take Smith to Mars while she was in trance. The results of these journeys were crude pictures of Martian landscapes, including plants, houses, and city streets, and automatic writing of a Martian language. Many people believed her.

In the late 1890s, Smith was researched by a number of leading investigators, most notably Theodore Flournoy, a Swiss professor of psychology. Flournoy, using psychoanalytic techniques, spent five years sitting in on seances, researching Smith's personal history, and corroborating historical information she provided at her seances.

Flournoy concluded that Smith had a fantastic imagination, perhaps complemented with telepathy and telekinesis. The Martian language that she produced was a childish imitation of French; a Sanskrit expert declared that 98 percent of the words could be traced to known languages. "Leopold," who was pompous, dignified, and sensible, was probably her most highly developed secondary personality.

Flournoy published his findings in 1900 in *From India to the Planet Mars*. Smith's supporters stood by her, and Flournoy was banished from her life. Ironically, the exposé served to increase her popularity, and Smith enjoyed comfortable wealth and fame. See Super-ESP; Xenoglossy.

Sources: Theodore Flournoy. *From India to the Planet Mars: A Study of a Case of Somnambulism with Glossolalia.* New York: Harper & Bros., 1900; Alan Gauld. *Mediumship and Survival.* London: William Heinemann Ltd., 1982; *Into the Unknown.* Pleasantville, NY: Reader's Digest, 1981; Frederic W. H. Myers. *Human Personality and Its Survival of Bodily Death.* Vols. 1 and 2. 1903. New ed. New York: Longmans, Green & Co., 1954.

Smith, Joseph Jr.

See Church of Jesus Christ of Latter-day Saints, the.

Society for Psychical Research (SPR)

Britain's leading organization for research into the paranormal. The Society for Psychical Research (SPR) was founded in 1882 in London to develop systematic, scientific investigation of certain phenomena which, if genuine, appeared to be inexplicable. Such phenomena included hypnosis and multiple personality, extrasensory perception (ESP), poltergeists, and mediumistic powers, all of which remain topics of debate. In more recent years, other research has been conducted into psychokinesis (PK) effects, anomalous electrical and biophysical effects, out-of-body experiences, and near-death experiences.

The roots of the SPR can be traced to the early investigations of Spiritualist phenomena by Henry Sidgwick, Frederic W. H. Myers, and Edmund Gurney, all Fellows of Trinity College at Cambridge. In 1873 Myers suggested to Sidgwick that they might conduct joint investigations of mediums, following a convincing experience Myers had at a sitting of the medium C. Williams. Williams was known for materializing a spirit named "John King." At the seance the huge, hairy hand of John King seemed to materialize from the ceiling and descend in front of Myers, who grabbed it in his hands. The spirit hand began to dematerialize, shrinking until it disappeared.

Sidgwick was more skeptical about such mediumistic phenomena than Myers, but agreed to conduct investigations. In 1874, at Myers's instigation, an informal group of investigators was set up. The group included Gurney, Walter Leaf, Lord Raleigh, Arthur Balfour and his sisters Eleanor (who married Sidgwick in 1876) and Evelyn (Lady Raleigh), and others, and became known after the formation of the SPR as "the Sidgwick group." The members were wealthy, well educated, and well connected in the high academic, social, and political circles of Britain. They had the money, the time, and the interest to pursue investigations and collect data.

The group's early investigations fell into a predictable pattern. Myers would get excited about a medium and persuade Sidgwick and the others to investigate. More often than not, the medium's feats were exposed as fraudulent or could be explained by normal means, and the group would meet with disappointment. Myers persevered from one medium to another. Despite the disappointments, some evidence was inexplicable in conventional terms.

Meanwhile, the London Dialectical Society, formed in the late 1860s, was conducting scientific, methodical investigations of Spiritualist phenomena. Spiritualist organizations were forming. See **Spiritualism.** In 1875 the Psychological Society was founded by Spiritualist Sergeant Cox with the purpose of investigating psychical phenomena. The idea looked promising to Spiritualists, who desired validation by objective investigators, but Cox's society died with his own death in 1879.

The call for a new society to conduct psychical research was made in 1882 by Sir William Barrett, a prominent physicist who was interested in Spiritualist phenomena, and Edmund Dawson Rogers, a prominent Spiritualist. An organizing conference was held that January. It included Spiritualists and the Sidgwick group. The organization was christened the Society for Psychical Research. Sidgwick was elected president, an office he would hold for nine years, and a steering council was formed.

The council established six research committees to study: (1) thought-transference, later renamed telepathy by Myers; (2) mesmerism, hypnotism, clairvoyance, and related phenomena; (3) German scientist Baron Karl von Reichenbach's research into "sensitives"; (4) apparitions of all types, and hauntings; (5) physical phenomena associated with Spiritualistic mediums; and (6) the collection and collation of data on the history of the above subjects.

The SPR then embarked on a massive amount of research. The Sidgwick group, with its high-level contacts, attracted the interest of numerous eminent people, including researcher William Crookes, Oliver Lodge, author Arthur Conan Doyle, philosopher and psychologist William James, and later psychiatrists Sigmund Freud, Carl G. Jung, and others. By 1886 dissension had broken out between the intellectuals and the Spiritualists, with each camp feeling the other was not doing the proper job for the overall cause. By 1887 a large contingent of Spiritualists had resigned, leaving the intellectuals in full command.

The volume of data collected and published by the SPR by 1900 was staggering: 11,000 pages of reports and articles. In addition, Gurney, Myers, and Frank Podmore, another founding member, produced a 1,416-page book, *Phantasms of the Living* (1886), which included data on hallucinations, both veridical and nonveridical; apparitions; and telepathy; and Myers produced the 1,360-page book, *Human Personality and the Survival of Bodily Death* (1903). Most of this prodigious output was accomplished and analyzed by the Sidgwick group.

In 1885 the American Society for Psychical Research (ASPR) was founded in Boston. In 1887 Richard Hodgson, a university pupil of Sidgwick, left for America to run the affairs of the ASPR. In 1889, due to financial need, the ASPR became an affiliate of the SPR. In 1906 it was reorganized as an independent group. See **American Society for Psychical Research (ASPR)**.

By 1905 the key members of the Sidgwick group were dead: Gurney in 1888; Sidgwick in 1900; Myers in 1901; and Hodgson in 1905. Podmore died in 1910. After death all but Sidgwick, the most skeptical about life after death, reportedly kept working with the SPR through mediumistic communications.

See **Cross correspondence; Piper, Leonora E.** Eleanor Sidgwick became president of the SPR in 1908–1909, and in 1910 became honorary secretary until 1931. She was appointed president d'honneur in 1932.

Since the 1940s the SPR has devoted more attention to mass experiments evaluated by statistical methods, though less so than the American Society for Psychical Research and institutional parapsychology in general.

The SPR defines its current fields of study as:

- Inquiry into the nature of all forms of paranormal cognition, including telepathy, clairvoyance, precognition, retrocognition, remote viewing, psychometry, dowsing, and veridical hallucinations of various kinds.
- Inquiry into the reality and nature of all forms of paranormal action, including PK, poltergeist phenomena, teleportation, and human levitation.
- Inquiry into altered states of consciousness in connection with hypnotic trance, dreaming, out-of-body experiences, near-death experiences, and sensory deprivation, as well as the paranormal effects that appear to be associated with them.
- Investigation of phenomena associated with psychic sensitivity or mediumship, such as automatic writing, alleged spirit communication, and physical manifestations.
- Investigation of evidence suggesting survival after death and evidence suggesting reincarnation.
- Investigation of reports of other relevant phenomena that appear, *prima facie,* to contravene accepted scientific principles.
- Investigation into the social and psychological aspects of such phenomena, within and across cultural boundaries.

- Development of new conceptual models and new ways of thinking concerning the application of accepted scientific theories to the findings of psychical research. The subject of time is of particular interest.

In addition, interest remains high in psi as it relates to medicine, healing, psychiatry, philosophy, anthropology, biology, folklore, and history.

The SPR has no research laboratory and does not express a collective opinion. Findings of researchers are published in the SPR's *Journal* and *Proceedings,* while informal articles appear in the *Newsletter* and *Newsletter Supplement.* Membership is international. See **Psi; Theosophy.**

Sources: The Society for Psychical Research; Slater Brown. *The Heyday of Spiritualism.* New York: Hawthorn Books, 1970; Alfred Douglas. *Extrasensory Powers: A Century of Psychical Research.* London: Victor Gollancz Ltd., 1976; Alan Gauld. *The Founders of Psychical Research.* London: Routledge & Kegan Paul, 1968; Renee Haynes. *The Society for Psychical Research: 1882–1982. A History.* London: Macdonald & Co., 1982.

Society of Friends (Quakers)

Religious order founded about 1650 in England by George Fox. The Religious Society of Friends, or Quakers, as it is commonly called, stresses a personal, almost mystical knowledge of God and the workings of the Lord's "inner light" within all people.

Along with other splinter Puritan groups, such as the Seekers, Baptists, and Ranters, the Quakers arose out of a belief in the empirical existence of Christ. At about age twenty, George Fox, born in 1624 in Fenny Drayton village, Leicestershire, began suffering religious misgivings and spiritual longings. He consulted with various Anglican and Puritan ministers and priests, but they dismissed him as slightly deranged. Fox felt entirely alone until 1647, when at age twenty-three he heard a voice saying, "There is one, even Christ Jesus, that can speak to thy condition."

Immediately after, Fox received the first of four insights: that a Christian is a true believer, revealed through a changed life, not one who follows ceremony or false piety. The second revelation was that a minister is simply one who ministers. Such a calling can happen to anyone, male or female, and requires no theological training or education. Not long afterward Fox received the third insight: that the church is not a place; that there is no holy ground. Corollary to that idea was the belief that ecclesiastical hierarchy was superfluous to the living fellowship. Fox referred to church buildings as "steeple houses," and Quaker places of worship as "meetinghouses."

Fox's fourth insight was that faith is based solely on firsthand knowledge of Christ as a living, personal reality, not on logic, reasoning, historical reporting, or even Scripture. This empirical proof came to be called the Quaker Way: the idea that worshipers need not consult preachers or the Bible to receive knowledge of the Holy Spirit—the so-called "inner light of Christ" present in every human heart.

Although Fox rejoiced in his new faith, it was not until 1652, when he prayed at a place called Pendle Hill, that he received a vision explaining his mission to show Christ in the Present Tense as a personal Being. At that time Fox met with a group of Seekers who, overcome with his message, converted. Fox also converted Judge Fell and his wife, Margaret, who opened her Swarthmore Hall estate for the use of the Quakers, offering them protection from the local authorities. When Judge Fell died, Fox married Margaret in 1669, keeping Swarthmore.

The early Quakers suffered terrible persecution from 1650 to 1690, including prison, beatings, hangings, brandings,

Quaker meeting

and tongue borings. Nonetheless, their influence quickly spread throughout England and to her colonies in America. Quakerism's appeal came from the idea that anyone—no matter whether they were man or woman, black or white, rich or poor, educated or illiterate—could experience Christ and spread his word. Such notions were great class levelers and looked on with abhorrence by many. Quakers practiced "hat honor" and "plain language," refusing to doff their hats except in prayer or use titles acknowledging superiors. The use of "thee" and "thou" flew in the face of seventeenth-century convention. In those days "you" was the plural, polite form of the second-person pronoun, used for superiors, and the others were the familiar, singular forms.

Fox believed that true conversion depended on a changed life, and that by striving for a pure heart, human beings could be perfect. This idea fell under the influence of Pietism and the Holiness

movements of the late eighteenth and early nineteenth centuries and caused a split in the Friends, with Elias Hicks and John Wilbur on the side of Quakerism's uniqueness and J. J. Gurney in the evangelical, even fundamentalist, camp. Although there are three main groups of Friends today—the Friends United Meeting, the Friends General Conference, and the Evangelical Friends Alliance, with beliefs ranging from moderate to liberal to extremely fundamentalist—the schism between the two sides has been partially healed.

The name "Quaker" comes from the idea that worshipers were so overcome with the Holy Spirit that they quaked. Traditional Quaker worship services are silent gatherings without liturgy or ministerial supervision. Such quiet was not enforced but allowed the believers to listen for that "still, small voice" that would lead them. Modern services now include hymns, scripture readings, and even some preaching. Fox felt that while all could be ministers, some were called to help develop "that of God" in all.

Quakers practice pacifism and refuse to take oaths or tithe their incomes to the church. They practice no sacraments, such as marriage, baptism, communion, or blessing of the dead, believing that every minute of life is a sacrament. Marriages are public ceremonies in which the couple declare their vows before God, not a minister. Funerals are simple burials. They stress the Logos doctrine of John, believing that Christ as the Eternal Word and Light shone back as far as all civilization. They do not emphasize the idea of Trinity.

True to their name as Friends, they believe fervently in shouldering each other's burdens and actively working for the good of humankind. During the periods of persecution, Friends never failed to take care of families who had members in prison. Even the children would continue services if all the adults had been incarcerated. Due to the efforts of John Woolman (1719–1792), no Friend could continue in the church and be a slave owner as early as 1785. Quakers operated the famous Underground Railroad before and during the Civil War, helping slaves escape north to freedom in Canada. The American Friends Service Committee, founded in 1917 by Rufus Jones, aids the suffering and destitute worldwide and was instrumental in saving many children from Nazi horrors in World War II. Today Friends are active in the Sanctuary Movement, helping place Central American refugees fleeing terrorist revolutions.

Unlike other religious founders, George Fox did not become a cult leader. By his death in 1691, his fame had been usurped by probably the most famous Quaker, William Penn. Converting to Quakerism against the expectations of his upper-class background, Penn determined to found a "holy experiment" in America. His wishes were granted in 1681, when he received a charter from King Charles II for lands along the Delaware River. Pennsylvania was a haven against religious persecution and one of the first places to govern by consent of the governed. All propertied Christians could vote and hold office.

Penn's efforts as a Quaker also resulted in the affirmation of a jury's right to decide a verdict without fear of retribution. During Penn's trial for inciting a riot in 1670, when he was worshiping with other Friends in Gracechurch Street, London, the jury was continually badgered and eventually jailed for finding him not guilty. Penn begged the jury to remember their rights as Englishmen to pass verdict, and the Court of Common Pleas guaranteed those rights in 1671.

Other famous Quakers include Robert Barclay, ancestor of the Barclay banking family; poet John Greenleaf Whittier; Johns Hopkins, who endowed the now-famous Baltimore hospital and research facility to be open to all regardless of race, creed, or color; feminist Lucretia Mott, who called the first women's rights convention in the United States at Seneca Falls, New York; Elizabeth Fry, who pressured Parliament for women's prison reform and rehabilitation, was instrumental for stopping transportation of women prisoners to Australia, and founded the first school to train nurses; author and Pulitzer-prize winner James A. Michener; President Herbert Hoover; and Rowland Hussey Macy, founder of the department store chain, who made the Quaker practice of selling goods at one established price for all customers standard practice throughout the retail industry.

Sources: Keith Crim, gen. ed. Abingdon Dictionary of Living Religions. Nashville, TN: Abingdon Press, 1981; Daisy Newman. A Procession of Friends. Garden City, NY: Doubleday, 1972; D. Elton Trueblood. The People Called Quakers. Richmond, IN: Friends United Press, 1971.

Soul mate

A soul's ideal counterpart, which must be found for true happiness and fulfillment. The search for the counterpart may consume multiple reincarnations. Soul mates are largely a popular Western phenomenon, especially in the United States. So many definitions of soul mates have been put forth that there is no definitive soul mate and no definitive explanation as to their origins. The notion of searching for one's long-lost soul mate gained great popularity in the 1970s and 1980s—perhaps as a reaction to the sexual freedom of the 1960s—and has become highly romanticized.

A popular theory says soul mates began in a remote time when a cleavage in human spiritual and physical nature occurred, leaving the soul imperfect and in need of searching for its other half. The imperfect halves are reflected in the doctrine of complements of the Platonists, who said that man could find in woman the virtues he lacked. According to the soul mate theory, the two halves may be reincarnated many times before finding each other. At last they join together and fulfill their purpose. The theory assumes that a soul mate is of the opposite sex, and provides a perfect relationship of love and bliss.

Another theory holds that a soul mate is not necessarily a missing half, but a soul with whom one has spent many lives and for whom one has developed a strong affinity. Such soul mates gravitate together again and again to further develop their relationship and help each other reach the highest potential. They are completely in tune with each other and can communicate without words. They love each other unconditionally, cannot bear to be separated from each other, and suffer great misery should their partner die and leave them behind. During the course of many lives together, they may change sex roles.

Still another theory holds that soul mates are not necessarily spouses or lovers, but family members, friends, business partners, and others with whom we have intimate bonds. They may be of either sex, and more than one may be part of our lives.

Elizabeth Clare Prophet, leader of the Church Universal and Triumphant, cites three kinds of soul mates: the twin or counterpart; the companion or lover; and the karmic, who comes into a life to teach hard karmic lessons.

References to three types of soul mates are found in the Edgar Cayce readings: companion souls, who share a spiritual relationship; twin souls, who share a mental relationship and a common purpose or ideal; and soul mates, who share a physical relationship and an affinity built on many incarnations together, and who are in tune with each other's vibrations on physical mental and spiritual levels. Companion souls and twin souls do not necessarily share marriage or a physical relationship. The Cayce readings describe Mary and Jesus as twin souls.

Some people devote a great deal of effort to trying to find their soul mate. Author Richard Bach chronicled his own three-year search for the perfect mate in *The Bridge Across Forever*. He discovered his soul mate was a woman he already knew, actress Leslie Parrish.

Others consult astrologers, psychics, and channelers, attend classes and seminars, undergo past-life regression, and learn visualization and "dream programming" techniques designed to attract soul mates. Some so-called soul mate experts maintain that one must "program" one's self physically, mentally, and visually in order to find the soul mate. Others believe they will instantly recognize their soul mate upon meeting him or her. Opinions differ as to whether soul mates will naturally come together or whether the relationship must be "earned." An obsession with soul mates, however, sets up unrealistic expectations for any relationship.

According to philosopher Manly P. Hall, the doctrine of reincarnation itself negates the need for soul mates. Each soul is complete unto itself and is responsible for its own spiritual development. According to Edgar Cayce, the ultimate soul mate is God or the Christ, the universal consciousness of which every soul is a part. See **Karma; Reincarnation.**

Sources: Richard Bach. *The Bridge Across Forever.* New York: Dell, 1984; Rosemary Ellen Guiley. *Tales of Reincarnation.* New York: Pocket Books, 1989; Manly Palmer Hall. *Reincarnation: The Cycle of Necessity.* Los Angeles: The Philosophical Research Society, 1956; Frederick Lenz. *Lifetimes: True Accounts of Reincarnation.* New York: Fawcett Crest, 1977; Violet M. Shelly and Mark Thurston. "Soul Mates." *Venture Inward* 1, no. 2 (November/December 1984): 13–18; Jess Stearn. *Soul Mates.* New York: Bantam Books, 1984; Dick Sutphen. *You Were Born Again to Be Together.* New York: Pocket Books, 1976; John Van Auken. *Past Lives and Present Relationships.* Virginia Beach, VA: Inner Vision, 1984; Glenn Williston and Judith Johnstone. *Discovering Your Past Lives.* First published as *Soul Search.* 1983. Wellingborough, Northamptonshire, England: The Aquarian Press, 1988.

Spangler, David (b. 1945)

American mystic, writer, and visionary, formerly codirector of the Findhorn Foundation Community.

David Spangler was born on January 7, 1945, in Columbus, Ohio. From an early age Spangler exhibited paranormal gifts, seeing invisible beings and being sensitive to vibrations. In 1951, when he was six, his father, an engineer working for military intelligence, was sent to an air base near Casablanca, Morocco, where the family lived for six years.

A year later, while riding in a car heading toward Casablanca, Spangler had his first mystical experience. It began with an out-of-body experience and shifted through four stages. In the first stage, he had a sense of reawakening as though from sleep, and a sense of identity not as David Spangler but as pure being that was one with creation. In the second stage, he became aware of past and future incarnations, births and deaths, the eternity of the soul, and the continuity of the self. The third stage was ineffable, a powerful feeling of the oneness of all things, and of love, serenity, and power. He had visual impressions of stars and galaxies floating in a sea of spirit, and everything engaging in a rhythmic and joyous dance of life. In the final stage, he perceived the intent behind his incarnation as David Spangler, and felt connected to it and to all other patterns unfolding in creation. He felt great love for all human life. He then returned to his body and normal consciousness. The experience seemed to last hours, but lasted only a few seconds.

Spangler was permanently changed by the experience: He felt that part of him was still seven years old, and another part was now this other, much higher level of consciousness. The sense of double consciousness receded during his childhood, but he could summon it if he wished to enter into it. Later in life he perceived that his mission, his faith journey in this incarnation, was to bring those two levels of consciousness together.

While in Morocco his parents had a profound UFO experience, witnessing a cigar-shaped craft with windows buzz the air base. The craft was tracked for several hundred miles across the Atlantic, over Morocco, and down the coast of Africa. The experience interested his father in researching UFOs.

In 1957 Spangler and his family moved back to the United States; first to Old Deerfield, Massachusetts, where Spangler attended Deerfield Academy, and then in 1959 to Phoenix, Arizona, where he was introduced to the New Age. His parents found groups interested in UFOs and psychic phenomena, and met Neva Dell Hunter, a well-known channeler who gave life readings. In 1964 Hunter invited Spangler to speak at one of her annual conferences on the paranormal. That marked the beginning of his career in public speaking.

At the time Spangler was a student at Arizona State University in Tempe, studying toward a degree in genetics. However, he received a strong inner calling to go in a different direction, and dropped out. From 1965 to 1970, Spangler lived in California, first in Los Angeles and then in the San Francisco area, where he lectured and gave counseling services in partnership with a friend, Myrtle Glines.

Spangler's shifts of consciousness enabled him to perceive the patterns of other beings and qualities. In 1965, during one such shift, a nonphysical "personage" walked into the room and began to converse with him. The being's name was a vibrational, nonverbal feeling. It agreed to be called "John," had a distinct personality, and referred to itself in the first person plural of "we." Spangler began to work with John in a relationship that was not channeling but merely communication; John said that he had manifested to help Spangler bridge the gap between his dual levels of consciousness. John became an amalgam of this being and Spangler.

For about three years, under John's direction, Spangler gave readings for others. John occasionally would bring along other beings or qualities for Spangler to meet.

In 1970 Spangler and Glines traveled to Europe. After visiting Findhorn, they recognized that the community would be the site of their next phase of work. They lived there for nearly three years and became codirectors with founders Eileen and Peter Caddy and Dorothy Maclean.

David Spangler

(Courtesy David Spangler)

At Findhorn another presence manifested. Called Limitless Love and Truth, it was a source of prophetic revelations that had first appeared some years earlier to another man in Britain. Limitless Love and Truth was of great interest to many who were connected with Findhorn, but disagreements over how to define this being and make use of its statements led to splits among followers. The transmissions of Limitless Love and Truth were published in Spangler's first book, *Revelation: The Birth of a New Age* (1976). See **Findhorn.**

Spangler left Findhorn in 1973 and returned to the San Francisco area. He traveled extensively, doing public speaking and consulting. With a group of friends from Findhorn who also returned to the United States, including Glines and his wife-to-be, Julie Manchester (they married in 1981), Spangler set up the Lorian Association, an umbrella organization for projects in publishing, education, and the arts. In 1980 Spangler moved to Madison, Wisconsin, where he helped design courses at the University of Wisconsin in Milwaukee. In 1984 he and Julie and others from the Lorian Association moved to Issaquah, Washington, near Seattle. At about the same time, Spangler retired from public appearances for several years, concentrating on his writing and developing his worldviews and philosophy.

The shift in focus also was accompanied by a change in his relationship with John. Over the years John's nature had changed from a distinct personality to a more mystical quality, until John was more a realm of being or a way of looking at the world. Around 1985 Spangler felt the work with John had reached a point of diminishing return, and the two agreed mutually to stop. He remains in contact with John, though in a much different way.

In his writing and lecturing, Spangler's central message is one of the emergence of what he calls a "planetary sensibility": the birth of a new consciousness that will be a planetary mind and soul, which will bring about an evolutionary leap for humankind. This state of consciousness will reach out to connect with nature as a whole; it will be a true "Gaia mind."

Spangler, a mystic in the Christian tradition, has devoted much of his work to helping individuals reconnect with the sacred, both within themselves and within everyday life. Much of the vitality of Christianity lies outside the church, he says. The institution has lost its ability to provide the individual with the means to have an ecstatic, personal encounter with the numinous. The sacred can be found in the ordinary, Spangler says; individuals can learn to feel in contact with this dimension without having to go to special places or go through special rituals.

Spangler is often identified with the New Age and is considered a leading spokesperson for it; he views part of his work as defining New Age thought and

philosophy. The term "New Age," while controversial to some, holds a great deal of power for Spangler, who says no other term carries quite the meaning of emerging consciousness. He agrees with other observers of the New Age in noting that much of what has been called "New Age" has moved into mainstream culture and thought. He also decries the tendency to see the New Age only in terms of channeling, psychic phenomena, or crystals; to Spangler the New Age is primarily a mythic image of the cocreative power of humanity to shape a future that empowers all life on the planet. See **New Age**.

Spangler's other published titles include *The Laws of Manifestation* (1975); *Towards a Planetary Vision* (1977); *Cooperation with Spirit* (1982); *Emergence: The Rebirth of the Sacred* (1984); and the booklets *The New Age* (1988) and *Channeling in the New Age* (1988). See **Channeling; Planetary consciousness.**

Sources: David Spangler. *Emergence: The Rebirth of the Sacred.* New York: Dell, 1984; David Spangler. *Revelation: The Birth of a New Age.* Elgin, IL: The Lorian Press, 1976; Interview with David Spangler.

Spirit guide

A nonphysical entity, usually perceived as the Higher Self, an angel, a highly evolved being or group mind, or a spirit of the dead. The purpose of a spirit guide is to help and protect an individual, assist in spiritual development, or provide a source of inspiration. Beliefs about spirit guides vary and are widespread in all cultures.

It is widely believed around the world that every individual has one or more spirit guides from birth who remain close during the person's entire life. At death they assist in crossing the threshold to the afterlife. In addition to the primary guides, an individual can be aided by various guides who come and go for certain assignments, such as the work a person must accomplish in life. Some people believe their spirit guides chose their roles for karmic reasons, or that the spirit guides shared past lives with them. Deceased relatives sometimes assume spirit guide roles.

Some individuals are very aware of presences they call their guides. Guides can appear in dreams or speak in an inner voice. Some people receive clairaudient messages or even visions that they attribute to their guides. Artistic individuals sometimes credit their inspiration to guides. Children who have "imaginary playmates" may be cognizant of their spirit guides. A person can attempt to establish communication with guides through meditation and visualization.

Western popular belief in spirit guides comes from the ancient Greeks, who believed in the existence of daimons, intermediary spirits between man and the gods. Daimons could be either good or evil. A good daimon acted as a protector. It was considered lucky to have one, for such a daimon whispered in one's ear advice and ideas. Evil daimons, on the other hand, could lead one astray.

Socrates claimed to be guided by a good daimon throughout his life. The daimon warned him of danger and bad decisions, but never directed him what to do. Socrates said his guardian spirit was more trustworthy than omens from the flights and entrails of birds, two highly respected forms of divination.

British psychical researcher Frederic W. H. Myers hypothesized that Socrates's daimon was his own inner voice, welling up from the "subliminal self," or the unconscious self.

The church turned all daimons into evil demons, the minions of the Devil, but absorbed the concept of a protector spirit in the form of the guardian angel.

Spirit guides generally do not take on animal form, though exceptions exist among individuals who have pursued magical or shamanic training. See **Inspiration.** Compare to **Control; Guardian spirit.**

Sources: Litany Burns. *Develop Your Psychic Abilities.* New York: Pocket Books, 1985; June G. Bletzer. *The Donning International Encyclopedic Psychic Dictionary.* Norfolk, VA: The Donning Co., 1986; Rosemary Ellen Guiley. *The Encyclopedia of Witches and Witchcraft.* New York: Facts On File, 1989; Frederic W. H. Myers. *Human Personality and Its Survival of Bodily Death.* Vols. 1 and 2. 1903. New ed. New York: Longmans, Green & Co., 1954; Alex Tanous and Katherine Fair Donnelly. *Understanding and Developing Your Child's Natural Psychic Abilities.* New York: Fireside Books, 1979.

Spiritism

The philosophy of Allan Kardec, known as Kardecism (Kardecismo in Brazil) in his honor, that originated with the Spiritualist movement that swept Europe in the 1850s.

Writing under the pseudonym of Kardec, the French writer and physician Hippolyte Leon Denizard Rivail (1804–1869) published his seminal work, *Le Livre des Esprits (The Lives of the Spirits),* in 1857. In it Kardec outlined his beliefs that certain illnesses have spiritual causes—especially epilepsy, schizophrenia, and multiple personality—and can be treated psychically through communication with spirit guides. Such ideas were common within the Spiritualist community, wherein mediums appealed to the spirit world to help rid sufferers of obsessing tormentors.

But Kardec took Spiritualist doctrines further, claiming that many of these psychic illnesses were not only the result of spirit interference by others, but were remnants of suffering and turmoil endured by the individual in past lives.

Unlike many Spiritualists he firmly believed in reincarnation; he wrote that each time a soul is reborn, it brings with it "subsystems" of past lives that may even block out the reality of the current life.

According to Kardec each rebirth, however painful, is necessary to enable the soul to improve and eventually attain a higher plane of existence. Kardec taught that a person is composed of three parts: an incarnate soul, a body, and a perispirit, or what Kardec described as a semimaterial substance that unites soul and body and surrounds the soul like an envelope. All souls are created equal, ignorant, and untested, and continue coming back to life until they have nothing more to learn.

At the death of the flesh, the perispirit holds the soul and separates from the body. This process takes longer if the deceased was particularly attached to his or her material existence. Spiritually advanced souls, Kardec believed, receive death with joy as it signifies release and the promise of future enlightenment. On the other hand, the spirits of those unfortunates who died suddenly or violently desperately cling to their bodies, confused and certain they are not dead. Suicides, especially, try to remain with their material existences, and may reincarnate only to commit suicide again. Kardec taught that only when the perispirit has left the flesh does the soul realize it is no longer part of the human world.

Once the perispirit has left the body, the soul returns to the spirit world, where Kardec believed the soul reviews its past lives, its progress to enlightenment, and decides which life-path to pursue next. Each soul has wide latitude in choosing its next life, and often returns to its earthly family. In cases where two spirits desire to occupy the same body, God—described by Kardec as the Supreme Intelligence and First Cause of All Things—breaks the tie.

Kardec believed spirit obsession and possession caused schizophrenia and multiple personality, often through the interference of unhappy past incarnations. Spiritist author Andre Luiz called such obsession "spirit vampirism," in which spirits who suffered greatly on earth devote their energies to persecution of the living instead of progressing through their own spiritual evolution. Kardec did not consider all obsession intentional, however. "Spirit induction" occurs when a confused, recently deceased soul invades a living human on the presumption that death did not happen. Kardec denied the possibility of exorcism by outsiders, whether in the name of the Lord or not. Instead he maintained exorcism must originate from the obsessed through conviction and prayer, noting proverbially that "God helps those who help themselves."

Kardec's theories enjoyed brief popularity in Europe and then gave way to the next intellectual craze. But in Brazil, inured in centuries of African spirits, magic, and superstition, Kardecismo took root and remains a powerful religious force in contemporary society, with centers all over the country. Kardecism also flourishes in the Philippines. It is difficult to estimate how many people who profess to practice the state religion, Catholicism, also call themselves *espiritas*.

Kardecist healing encompasses prayer, counseling, exploration of past lives through a medium, and perhaps psychic surgery. Practitioners of this controversial technique actually claim to open the body without anesthetic or surgical instruments, manipulate vital organs, and use laying-on of hands to heal all kinds of disease and deformity. The mediums may be uneducated and unskilled, but they claim to be guided by the spirits of past physicians.

The Kardecist psychiatric hospitals, staffed by highly trained doctors, operate comfortably alongside their more traditional counterparts in Brazil and have won the admiration of many non-Spiritist physicians. As early as 1912, psychiatrist Dr. Oscar Pittham, saddened with his profession's inability to treat many sufferers successfully, began collecting funds to establish a so-called "spirit hospital." Finally, in 1934, Dr. Pittham's dreams were realized in a new hospital in Porto Allegre. The facility, which doubled in size in 1951, supports more than six hundred beds and a staff of more than two hundred. Other major Kardecist institutions are in Itapira and São Paulo.

Perhaps the hospitals' most remarkable features are their rigorous denial of profit and acceptance of all patients, regardless of race, creed, or ability to pay. Hospital directors do not receive salaries.

All dedicated Spiritist mediums firmly insist that theirs is a God-given talent, not to be used for personal gain. Once a medium begins charging for paranormal services, the gift will disappear. Mediums are doors to the invisible, and the more talented the medium, the more evolved the spirits he or she will be able to contact. One of Brazil's most famous mediums, Chico Xavier, has transcribed well over a hundred books on science, literature, history, Kardecist philosophy, and children's stories, yet lives in poverty. He modestly claims that his spirit guides are the true authors.

Kardec acknowledged that such humility does not characterize every medium. His *Medium's Book* (1861) outlined in detail the function of a medium, and any charlatan who wished to learn the tricks of the trade only had to study Kardec's work. Little research has been done of Spiritist phenomena, since believers consider Kardecismo a religion, not a science. The only major organization collecting and studying Spiritist work is the Instituto Brasileiro de Pesquisas Psicobiofisic (IBPP), or the Brazilian Institute for Psycho-Biophysical Research, founded by Hernani Andrade in 1963.

Spiritists do not proselytize, trying to convince others of the rightness of their faith, but only desire tolerance and the freedom to practice. They accept unquestioningly the existence of spirits and their powers. Proofs, such as table-rapping, voices from beyond, and flying objects, are to believers just so many parlor games. See **Healing, faith and psychic; Macumba; Psychic surgery; Reincarnation; Spiritualism.**

Sources: Guy Lyon Playfair. *The Unknown Power.* New York: Pocket Books, 1975; D. Scott Rogo. *The Infinite Boundary.* New York: Dodd, Mead & Co., 1987; Alberto Villoldo and Stanley Krippner. *Healing States.* New York: Simon & Schuster/Fireside, 1987.

Spirit photography (also paranormal photography)

Photographs of images of unseen people or spirits. Spirit photography had its beginnings in 1861, when Boston jewelry engraver William Mumler took a self-portrait and after developing the photographic plate, noticed the image of a dead person next to his. Since then many individuals have claimed to photograph these "extras." For example, psychic photographer William Hope said he took more than 2,500 pictures of extras in his twenty-year career during the early part of the twentieth century. In most spirit photographs, the extras are seen seated next to or standing alongside the individual whose picture had just been taken.

Spirit photography appeared as Spiritualism was sweeping America, and it quickly became popular with some Spiritualists who took it as proof of survival after death. As Spiritualism moved across the Atlantic to Britain, so did spirit photography.

Spirit photography then sank into disrepute for a number of years because many of the photographs looked fake, a

Spirit photograph

raphy, anymore than for thoughtography, because the spirit, being a pure reality, transcends the physical laws of light and acts directly upon the (film) plate, without going through the camera."

Images of extras found on film not exposed in a camera are actually known as scotographs, another example of spirit photography. Closely related is psychography, messages written on film in the hand of a dead person.

Spirit photography is used by some ghost hunters in their investigations of haunted sites. When the film is developed, the photographer looks for anomalous lights, shadows, and shapes that were not visible to the naked eye. As evidence of paranormal phenomena, spirit photography remains controversial. See **Thoughtography.**

Sources: Hereward Carrington. "Experiences in Psychic Photography." *Journal of the American Society for Psychical Research* 19 (1925): 258–67; T. Fukurai. *Clairvoyance and Thoughtography.* 1931. Reprint. New York: Arno Press, 1975; F. W. Warrick. *Experiments in Psychics.* New York: E. P. Dutton & Co., 1939; Benjamin B. Wolman, ed. *Handbook of Parapsychology.* New York: Van Nostrand Reinhold, 1977.

claim supported by numerous cases involving outright fraud. In some instances photographers exposed negatives of a supposed extra on a film plate to create a double exposure. Other times photographs of individuals said to be extras turned out to be pictures of people who were very much alive. Even so, in some cases these individuals had never been photographed before, making it difficult to explain how these photographs could have been faked if there was no negative.

Debate continues among researchers over whether the images are created by the spirits of the dead themselves, or whether the person sitting for the photograph or the photographer mentally projects the image onto the film, creating a "thoughtograph."

In *Clairvoyance and Thoughtography* (1931), Tomokichi Fukarai, president of the Psychical Institute of Japan, drew links between spirit photography and thoughtography. He noted that the camera "is of no use for spirit-photog-

Spiritual emergence

A range of nonordinary states of consciousness which, though transformative and healing in nature, can be unsettling because of their sudden or dramatic onset. These can include sudden arrivals at new levels of awareness or states of consciousness, transformational energies, and psychic phenomena such as visions of nonphysical beings, clairvoyance, clairaudience, clairsentience, telepathy, and so on.

The term "spiritual emergence" evolved from "spiritual emergency," a term coined in the late 1970s by transpersonal psychiatrist Stanislav Grof and his wife, Christina Grof, after Christina suffered her own psychospiritual crisis. In founding the Spiritual Emergence Network (SEN) in 1980, Christina Grof opted to replace "emergency" with "emergence" so as not to imply that all such experiences are traumatic. Spiritual emergences can involve spiritual emergencies, however. From the standpoint of traditional psychotherapy, such experiences can be interpreted as signs of mental illness (a breakdown), when in fact they are indications of spiritual awakening (a breakthrough).

The seeds of Grof's own spiritual emergence began with the birth of her two children by a previous marriage. During the first birth, in 1968, she experienced a release of tremendous energies and an explosion of white light in her head. Similar phenomena occurred during the second birth. In both cases she was given drugs to counteract the experiences.

Over several years she had a variety of nonordinary experiences of different intensities, including inner visions of birth and death, clairaudience of choral music and chanting, unsettling synchronicities, spontaneous yoga *asanas* (postures associated with meditation), and painful rushes of energy through her body. At the time she did not know that the rushes of energy were the awakening of *kundalini,* or that what she was experiencing was similar to "shamanic illness."

In 1974 she met Swami Muktananda and began a spiritual quest. Mythologist Joseph Campbell urged her to go to Esalen Institute to meet Stanislav Grof, whose research in LSD psychotherapy included phenomena similar to what Christina had experienced.

Shortly after their marriage, Christina experienced her first full spiritual emergency: several days and nights in which she was nearly overwhelmed with energies, emotions, and inner experiences. Rather than trying to quell them, she learned to work through them.

As a result the Grofs and Rita Rohan founded the SEN as an alternative to help others "find their way through unexpected and often unsettling mystical and psychic openings" rather than stop them through traditional psychotherapy. SEN also provides networking, referrals, and information.

The Grofs identified six patterns that are followed in any combination during a spiritual emergence: (1) opening to life myth, an interaction with the archetypal realm of the collective unconscious; (2) shamanic journey; (3) kundalini awakening; (4) emergence of a karmic pattern, such as in past-life recalls; (5) psychic opening, the manifestation of extrasensory abilities; and (6) possession by predatory entities.

Spiritual crises happen both intentionally and unintentionally. They may last seconds, minutes, hours, or weeks. Curiously, the opening to life myth usually lasts forty days, perhaps as a parallel to the forty days Jesus spent in the desert. Spiritual emergence is most likely to occur during times of great physical stress or crisis, such as childbirth, surgery, sex, or near-death; during times of emotional stress and crises; during spiritual practices such as meditation; and during transitional stages of life. Frequently, spiritual emergence temporarily disrupts a person's ability to carry on a normal life.

Spiritual emergences are common in natural human development, and need to be integrated, not suppressed or ignored. Integration, which can go on over a period of years, leads to spiritual growth and enhanced creativity, compassion, relaxation, inner peace, and desire to be of service to others. Failure to integrate them can lead to a deterioration of mental health. See **Archetypes; Kundalini; Psychology; Near-death experience (NDE); Past-life recall; Shamanism.**

Sources: Emma Bragdon. *The Call of Spiritual Emergency: From Personal Crisis to Personal Transformation.* San Francisco: Harper & Row, 1990; Stanislav and Christina Grof. "Spiritual Emergency: The Understanding and Treatment of Transpersonal Crises." *ReVision* 8, no. 2 (1986); Charles T. Tart. *Open Mind, Discriminating Mind.* San Francisco: Harper & Row, 1989; Keith Thompson. "Navigating the Hero's Journey in Tandem: A Profile of Stan and Christina Grof." *The Common Boundary* 6, issue 6 (November/December 1988): 8–11+.

Spiritualism

Religious movement that began in 1848 in the United States and swept both America and Britain, peaking by the early twentieth century but still in existence today. Its original appeal lay in the purported evidence it provided of survival after death, manifested through mediums who communicated with spirits and performed paranormal feats.

Public receptivity to Spiritualism was made possible by the psychism-based movements that preceded it, Swedenborgianism and mesmerism, both of which started in Europe in the late eighteenth century and were exported to the United States.

The concepts of eighteenth-century Swedish philosopher Emanuel Swedenborg, while quite popular in parts of Europe, had a limited following in America. But mesmerism fascinated the masses with its trances in which "somnambules" saw visions of the spirit world, became mediums for spirits of the dead, and exhibited various psychic abilities.

One of the most important figures in America who paved the way for the transition from mesmerism to Spiritualism was Andrew Jackson Davis, a student of Swedenborg who at age seventeen became a successful mesmeric subject in the psychic diagnosis of illness and in prophecy. In 1845 Davis began touring the country giving lectures in trance on what he called "Harmonial Philosophy," his divine revelations on the origin and nature of the universe, what happens to the soul after death, and what is required in the physical life in order to benefit in the spirit life.

As a definable movement, Spiritualism began in 1848, when the Fox sisters of Hydesville, New York, created a press sensation with their communications with spirits by rappings. Margaretta (Maggie) was fourteen and her sister Catherine (Katie) eleven when they and their parents began to hear strange thumping noises at night, which Mrs. Fox believed were caused by a ghost. Maggie and Katie discovered that if they clapped their hands, the raps answered back. By rapping in response to yes-no questions and the spelling out of letters of the alphabet, the spirit allegedly claimed to be a murdered peddler named Charles Rosa, whose throat had been slashed by John Bell, a former occupant of the house, who buried the remains beneath the cellar floorboards. Digging in the cellar yielded some human teeth, hair, and a few bones.

The press had a field day with the story. The girls' older sister, Leah, a shrewd opportunist, took charge of the girls and turned them into a stage act. People flocked to see them. Their seances grew more elaborate, featuring the presence of famous spirits of the dead such as Ben Franklin, and physical phenomena such as levitating and moving objects and tables.

P. T. Barnum brought the girls to New York City, where they impressed William Cullen Bryant, James Fenimore Cooper, George Ripley, Horace Greeley, and others. Skeptics routinely charged them with fraud, claiming the girls had mastered surreptitious joint cracking, ventriloquism, and operation of secret electrical gadgets. However, no trickery was found despite numerous tests.

The success of the Fox sisters inspired others to discover their own mediumistic powers. While many mediums worked for free, many more discovered there was money to be made from a public hungry to witness spirit manifestations. In 1852 Spiritualism was exported to Britain by a Boston medium, Mrs. Hayden, who astonished the British by charging money for her seances. By 1855 Spiritualism claimed 2 million followers and appeared to be a new religion in the making. Spiritualists claimed that the immortality of the soul would at last be proved.

The movement, however, began to suffer. It was condemned by leaders of organized religion, who attempted to get laws passed banning Spiritualism. Many mediums, most of whom were women, found themselves ostracized by family and friends. Investigations of mediums, beginning in the 1850s in Britain and in the 1880s in the United States, exposed numerous frauds, although some gifted mediums remained impressive under the scrutiny. There was increasing internal dissension; and the mediumistic phenomena claimed as proof of survival were never validated by science. By the turn of the century, Spiritualism was virtually finished as a widespread cohesive movement.

The Fox sisters themselves fell victim to their own success. By 1855 both were alcoholics. Maggie became disillusioned with Spiritualism and converted to Catholicism. She attempted to leave the act, but family pressure kept her in until Leah abandoned her younger sisters in 1857 following her marriage to a wealthy businessman.

Katie continued to perform irregularly, achieving new heights with mirror-writing, or backward automatic script, which had to be held up to a mirror to be read. In 1861 she allegedly manifested the spirits of the dead in materializations. In 1871 she went to Britain, where researcher William Crookes declared no one approached her in talent.

In 1888 Maggie and Katie made a public appearance in New York, at which Maggie denounced Spiritualism as a fraud and an evil characterized by sexual licentiousness. She said that she and Katie had created the rappings in Hydesville to play a trick on their mother, and they were able to do so by surreptitious toe cracking. They had learned to use muscles below the knee which are supple in children but stiffen with age; their practice had kept the muscles flexible. Maggie demonstrated on stage how she rapped with her toes. She also stated that Leah had led them around like lambs because she wanted to create a new religion, and that they had rapped at seances in response to body cues from Leah.

Devoted Spiritualists refused to believe Maggie. The sisters then went on tour exposing Spiritualism, although Katie continued to work as a medium. In 1889, for reasons that are unclear, Maggie recanted her confession.

Leah died on November 1, 1890. Katie died of acute alcoholism on July 2, 1892, at age fifty-six. Maggie, ill and destitute, died on March 8, 1893, at age fifty-nine, at a friend's home in Brooklyn.

Spiritualism spread more slowly in Britain than in America, due largely to differences in social conditions and to the great influence of the well-established Church of England. However, it took a firmer and more enduring hold. Efforts to organize groups and churches began as early as 1865. In 1869 The Spiritualist published an article on how to form a home circle for seances, which encouraged interest.

One of the most famous British home circles was that of Hannen Swaffer, a journalist known as the "Pope of Fleet Street," who helped Spiritualism gain respect in the popular press. Swaffer's circle featured the medium Maurice Barbanell, "Mr. Spiritualism," famed for his Native

Photograph of alleged Native American spirit guide at a US Spiritualism camp

American control, Silver Birch. Barbanell, who founded *Psychic News,* still a leading Spiritualist newspaper in London, was a key figure in Spiritualism for more than sixty years.

In 1872 the Marylebone Spiritualist Association was formed to study psychic phenomena and disseminate evidence obtained through mediumship. Now known as the Spiritualist Association of Great Britain and based in London, it is one of the two largest Spiritualist organizations in the world.

The British National Association of Spiritualists was formed in 1884. From that, the London Spiritualist Alliance incorporated in 1896, and later was renamed the College of Psychic Studies. The college is an educational charity that offers programs, mediumship training, consultation services with mediums, and healing services.

In 1890 the National Federation of Spiritualist Churches was formed as a result of the efforts of Emma Hardinge Britten, founder of the Spiritualist journal *Two Worlds,* and others. In 1901 it re-organized as the Spiritualists National Union (SNU) with the purpose of uniting Spiritualist churches and encouraging research into mediumship and healing. Based in Manchester, it is the other of the two largest Spiritualist organizations in the world.

Spiritualism enjoyed a resurgence of popularity during and after World War I, as thousands of bereaved turned to mediums in hopes of contacting loved ones killed in the war. In Britain conversions were helped by the endorsements of respected figures such as Sir Oliver Lodge, who lost a son in the war, and Sir Arthur Conan Doyle, who campaigned tirelessly on behalf of Spiritualism, calling it the basis of all religious beliefs. Unfortunately, the war also opened opportunities for many fraudulent mediums.

The heyday of the great medium was largely over by 1920, but interest in Spiritualism continued on both sides of the Atlantic and elsewhere in the world. Psychical research and Spiritualism began to go separate ways in the 1930s, when American parapsychologist J. B. Rhine was instrumental in taking psychical research into the laboratory.

Modern Spiritualism

Spiritualist churches continue to have followings in America, Britain, Brazil, and other countries. Many of the churches are modeled on Protestant churches, although there is no organized priesthood.

Spiritualist phenomena fall into three main categories: mental mediumship, spiritual healing, and physical mediumship. Mental mediumship includes trance work, automatisms, psychometry, and clairvoyance. (Psychometry generally is not employed in Britain because it is still an offense under the Vagrancy Act as "pretending to tell fortunes.") Spiritual healing takes two forms: contact healing, which is a laying on of hands; and absent healing, in which a medium works with spirit doctors and has no direct contact with the patient, who may not even be aware of the treatment. Absent healing is used when long distances prevent contact, and with skeptical patients. Physical mediumship involves the excrescence of ectoplasm from the medium as an interface with the spirit world, and is characterized by levitations, rappings, apports, telekinesis of objects, psychic lights, music and smells, and other activities. Physical mediumship, very popular in the early days of Spiritualism, is now rare.

Mental mediumistic skills are employed by Spiritualist pastors, who sometimes deliver their sermons in trance. Other main church activities include seances, which usually feature communication with spirits; psychic readings, called "spirit greetings," for members; spiritual healing; and the teaching of psychic and mediumistic skills and meditation techniques. Some Spiritualists discourage communication with the dead in favor of contact with highly evolved entities and spiritual masters.

Healing is of particular importance in Spiritualism. In Britain many Spiritualist healers are members of organizations such as the National Federation of Spiritual Healers and the SNU's Guild of Spiritualist Healers, and are registered with the Confederation of Healing Organizations (CHO). The CHO follows a conduct code set by the General Medical Council. The CHO also requires healers to undergo training, and to work for at least two years under supervision. See **Healing, faith and psychic.**

Modern Spiritualist teachings include concepts from all major world religions and theosophy. Spiritualist tenets hold that a human being is a spirit and is part of God; in worshiping God one strives to understand and comply with the physical, mental, and spiritual laws of nature, which are the laws of God. Spiritualism considers itself a science because it investigates and classifies spirit phenomena. From a philosophical standpoint, Spiritualism studies the laws of nature of both the physical and spirit worlds, and maintains that mediumship and parapsychology have proved that mediums may obtain information through channels besides the five senses.

Spiritualists are divided on reincarnation. Most accept preexistence of the soul and believe in life after death, but consider reincarnation a matter of free will, not a spiritual law. The Spiritists of Allan Kardec, a branch of Spiritualism more popular in Latin America, accept reincarnation as a central doctrine.

The incidence of mediumistic fraud in Spiritualism has declined greatly with stricter controls on mediums, and remedial measures taken in the wake of exposés. Most of the fraud in earlier times involved physical mediumship.

Many Spiritualists attend summer camps for lectures, classes, psychic readings, consultation of mediums, and mediumistic training. The camps began in the United States in the nineteenth century, and were based on the popular Chatauqua camps.

Spiritualism enjoys a larger following in Britain than in the United States, with thousands of churches. The religion had no legal status prior to 1951, when the last Witchcraft Act (of 1735) was repealed. Under the Witchcraft Act it was possible to charge a medium with witchcraft. In the same year, the Fraudulent Mediums Act was passed, which amended the Vagrancy Act of 1824. The Vagrancy Act had been used since 1874 to prosecute mediums. Spiritualists argued that mediumship was essential to their religious worship and practice. Controversy exists over Christian elements in some Spiritualist churches. See **Mediumship; Spiritism.**

Sources: Roger I. Anderson. "Spiritualism Before the Fox Sisters." *Parapsychology Review* 18, no 1 (January/February 1987):

9–13; Jean Bassett. *100 Years of National Spiritualism*. London: The Spiritualists National Union, 1990; Norman Blundson. *A Popular Dictionary of Spiritualism*. New York: The Citadel Press, 1963; Slater Brown. *The Heyday of Spiritualism*. New York: Hawthorn Books, 1970; Alfred Douglas. *Extrasensory Powers: A Century of Psychical Research*. London: Victor Gollancz Ltd., 1976; Alan Gauld. *The Founders of Psychical Research*. London: Routledge & Kegan Paul, 1968; Herbert G. Jackson, Jr. *The Spirit Rappers*. Garden City, NY: Doubleday, 1972; Howard Kerr and Charles L. Crow, eds. *The Occult in America: New Historical Perspectives*. Urbana, IL: University of Illinois Press, 1983; R. Laurence Moore. *In Search of White Crows*. New York, Oxford University Press, 1977; Janet Oppenheim. *The Other World: Spiritualism and Psychical Research in England, 1850–1914*. Cambridge, England: Cambridge University Press, 1985; Tony Ortzen. "Spiritualism in England and America." In *The New Age Catalogue*. New York: Doubleday/Dolphin, 1988.

Spiritualist Association of Great Britain

See **Spiritualism.**

Spiritualists National Union

See **Spiritualism.**

Sports, mystical and psychic phenomena in

Athletes who push themselves to the edge of endurance often experience a wide range of phenomena, from a heightened sense of awareness to paranormal experiences such as clairaudience, to mystical illumination. The experience surprises the person, coming at a moment of intense physical effort and mental concentration. It is almost as though one bursts through time and space into another dimension; athletes refer to this state as "the zone." Mystical and psychic experiences are commonplace among professional athletes; some athletes try to cultivate "the zone" because their performance is greatly enhanced as a result. For some the mystical experience is so wondrous that it far outshines victory.

A study of 4,500 paranormal incidents in professional sports, by Michael Murphy and Rhea A. White, identified at least sixty different sensations that occur in "the zone." At the low end of the scale are bursts of energy, strength, coordination, speed, and endurance; the ability to make the right instinctive move; and a profound sense of well-being. More complex experiences include out-of-body trips, clairaudience, extrasensory perception in terms of knowing what opponents are going to do next, shape changing, a feeling of weightlessness, changes in the perception of time, and willing objects to move (psychokinesis). Transcendent sensations are the awareness of spirits; a sense of unity with all creation; feelings of immortality, ecstasy, and supreme joy; a sense of profound peace and calm; or mystery and awe.

The type of experience varies with the sport. Long-distance runners, for example, often have feelings of floating, flying, and weightlessness. Football players experience changes in shape and size, having the perception that they are suddenly bigger and stronger. This change is sometimes witnessed by other players. John Brodie, former quarterback for the San Francisco 49ers, stated that on five or six occasions, he had seen running backs get larger, then drop in size. Baseball and basketball players and golfers cite changes in time, in which time becomes very compressed or seems to stop. In this compression they are able to accomplish an extraordinary amount of activity. Golfers who are aware of this try to slow time in order to pack more power into their swing. Baseball star Stan Musial said time compression enabled him to accurately gauge the speed of the ball so he could decide whether or not to swing and coordinate his movements to the ball—all in about two/fifths of a second in real time.

Awareness of the presence of ethereal beings is most common in solitary sports, such as mountaineering, flying, and sailing. The being may be nebulous or may take on the appearance of a human being, and may converse with the athlete and offer advice. In his historic flight across the Atlantic in 1927, Charles Lindbergh said that he was accompanied by a host of vaporous spirits who offered guidance. See **Lindbergh, Charles.** Phantoms of ships and crews seen at sea by sailors are legendary. Joshua Slocum, who sailed around the world by himself in the 1890s, claimed the spirit of one of Columbus's crew members took over the helm when he was sick and incapacitated with food poisoning.

Mountaineers who have scaled the Himalayas report the presence of silent "companions." For Frank Smythe, who climbed Everest in 1933, the companion was an invisible presence. In 1975 a British expedition to Everest experienced different paranormal phenomena. Phantom climbers, using telepathic communication, guided Doug Scott and Nick Estcourt through a dangerous area of ice ridges. On another occasion Estcourt, climbing alone, sensed he was being followed and turned around to see a human figure far behind him. He had no idea who it was, but thought it might be one of the Sherpa guides from another of the expedition's camps. Estcourt waited, but the figure never caught up with him, though it kept moving and climbing. Estcourt shouted to it and got no reply. He decided to continue on. At another point he turned around again and looked, but the mysterious climber had vanished. Estcourt could see quite a distance behind

him. Chris Bonington, who led the expedition, offered two theories about the companion: that it may have been the spirit of a Sherpa who had worked closely with Estcourt in 1972, and who was killed in an avalanche in 1973 at a spot near where Estcourt was climbing; or that Estcourt may have had a premonitory extrasensory experience related to the death of a member of the expedition, which happened soon after Estcourt's experience.

The ecstatic experiences in sports—the sense of oneness with the universe, illumination, ecstasy, and joy—are similar to those experienced in yoga and Eastern philosophies and martial arts disciplines. In sports and in martial arts, such experiences make possible superior, peak performances. The attainment of this state of being requires a stillness of mind, relaxation, and a letting go that frees the performer from the anxiety of performing and winning, and allows him or her to "be in the moment"; it is "right-brain" thinking. What often follows is a superior performance that seems effortless, encased in a timeless envelope of space, in which the performer allows the mind and body to do what they have been trained to do. Many describe this moment as trancelike or being on automatic pilot.

"Left-brain" thinking—anxiety, analysis, judgment of performance as good or poor, negative thoughts, fear of mistakes, excessive verbalization during performance—cause a paralysis that leads to inferior results or defeat.

Cultivating "the zone" has become increasingly important in sports psychology, especially in the West, which previously lagged in applying Eastern concepts to training. Athletic training now includes biofeedback, meditation, relaxation, and creative visualization techniques. Athletes who can enter "the zone" most easily tend to be the best in their fields. Research with subjects in problem-solving shows that during intense concentration, there is a marked decrease in the brain's overall metabolic rate, indicating a more efficient brain. It is postulated that the same conditions occur during sports performance: The lower the overall metabolic rate of the brain, and thus the more efficient it is, the better the performance.

Sports psychologists say the same conditions that lead to peak performances in sports can be applied in the business world and any creative endeavor. See Biofeedback; Creative visualization; Martial arts; Relaxation.

Sources: Charles A. Garfield and Hal Z. Bennett. *Peak Performance: Mental Training Techniques of the World's Greatest Athletes.* Los Angeles: Jeremy Tarcher, 1984; Michael Murphy and Rhea A. White. *The Psychic Side of Sports.* Reading, MA: Addison-Wesley, 1978; Lawrence Shainberg. "Finding 'The Zone.'" *The New York Times Magazine* (April 9, 1989): 35–39; Adam Smith. *Powers of Mind.* New York: Random House, 1975.

Stained-glass window effect

A term coined by W. T. Stead (1849–1912), British journalist, psychic investigator, and Spiritualist, to describe how psychic perception is distorted by the subconscious mind. Stead attended numerous mediumistic seances and discovered his own ability for automatic writing. From his experiences and observations, he concluded that the subconscious stains and distorts all information that passes through it to the waking self, just as a stained-glass window imposes patterns and colors upon the white light that passes through it.

The stained-glass window effect appears in psychic perception when information received psychically is distorted by the receiver's subconscious prejudices, attitudes, predispositions, and aversions. Psychically received information, no matter from what alleged source, may be sup-

pressed or altered to fit those factors without the receiver being aware of it. See Channeling; Psychic reading.

Sources: W. E. Butler. *How to Develop Clairvoyance.* 2d ed. New York: Samuel Weiser, 1979; Corinne McLaughlin. "Tuning in to the Best Channel." *New Realities* 7, no. 6 (July/August 1987): 37–42; Janet Oppenheim. *The Other World: Spiritualism and Psychical Research in England, 1850–1914.* Cambridge, England: Cambridge University Press, 1985; Alan Vaughan. "Channeling." *New Realities* 7, no. 3 (January/February 1987): 43–47; Joan Windsor. *The Inner Eye: Your Dreams Can Make You Psychic.* Englewood Cliffs, NJ: Prentice-Hall, 1985.

Starhawk

See Witchcraft.

Steiner, Rudolf (1861–1925)

Philosopher, artist, scientist, and educator, whose "Spiritual Science" movement, called Anthroposophy, is a unique blend of Rosicrucian, Theosophical, and Christian traditions. Rudolf Steiner's teachings address philosophy, social sciences, natural sciences, agriculture, the arts, education, psychology, and religion.

Steiner was born on February 27, 1861, in Kraljevic, then part of Hungary and now in Yugoslavia. His parents were Austrian; his father was a railway clerk and intended for his son to become a railway civil engineer.

By the age of eight, Steiner had clairvoyant awareness of the unseen. His experiences included perception of an apparition of a dead relative and the invisible energies of the plant kingdom. When he discovered geometry in school, he perceived geometric forms as living realities.

At age fifteen he met Felix Kotgutski, an herbalist who taught him the occult lore of plants. When he was nineteen, this individual introduced him to another whom Steiner called "the Master," an adept who gave him his spiritual initiation. Steiner never revealed his identity, in accordance with occult tradition.

From the Master he learned his spiritual mission in life: to develop a knowledge that synthesized science and religion. For the remainder of his life, Steiner dedicated himself to this task, guided by what he called "the occult powers behind me."

In 1879 Steiner went to the Technische Hochschule in Vienna to study mathematics and science, which, as he later acknowledged, gave him a better basis for a spiritual conception of the world than he could have obtained from a study of humanities. He also studied the philosophies of Kant, Fichte, and Hegel and the natural scientific writings of Goethe. At age twenty-two he was invited to edit the definitive edition of Goethe's natural scientific writings.

In 1886 Steiner was hired by the Specht family to tutor four boys, one of whom was autistic. His exceptional tutoring enabled the boy to attend high school, college, and medical school and become a doctor.

Steiner earned his doctorate at the University of Rostock in 1891. His thesis, "Truth and Knowledge" (also entitled "Truth and Science") on the scientific teaching of German philosopher Johann Gottlieb Fichte was followed in 1894 by his major philosophical work, *Die Philosophie der Freiheit* (1894), which has been translated into English as *The Philosophy of Spiritual Activity* and *The Philosophy of Freedom*.

At age forty Steiner felt ready to speak publicly about his spiritual philosophy, his clairvoyant experiences, and what he had learned from them. He explained in an autobiographical sketch that no one under the age of forty was ready to appear publicly as a teacher of occultism, according to the intention of

(Courtesy Anthroposophic Press)

Rudolf Steiner

the Masters; anyone who did so was bound to make mistakes.

By this stage in his life, he had accumulated a great deal of experience in nonphysical realms. Through profound and concentrated meditation, he learned to bridge the physical and nonphysical realms, and to test repeatedly what he experienced in the nonphysical and relate it to the physical. He believed the Hermetic axiom that humankind is the microcosm within the macrocosm of Creation and we have within us the clues to the secrets of the universe. These secrets could be revealed by discovering the true nature of humankind.

Steiner claimed to be able to access the Akashic Records, from which he learned the true history of human evolution. He said that at one time humankind was more spiritual and possessed supersensible capabilities, but lost them in a descent to the material plane. At the nadir of human descent, Christ arrived and provided the opportunity to reascend to higher spiritual levels. For Steiner the life, death, and resurrection of Christ were the most important events in the history of humankind and the cosmos.

In the course of his personal development, Steiner began to perceive countless spiritual beings who exist in higher planes but interact constantly with human beings on the physical plane. He discovered that some beings encourage the advancement of humankind's spiritual consciousness, while others wish people to remain mired in a materialistic, mechanistic world. These latter spirits Steiner called "Ahrimanic" beings, after the Persian personification of evil.

Steiner faced serious inner battles with these forces of evil. His salvation was his immersion in the mysteries of Christ. He warned that the path to higher consciousness, though attainable by anyone who followed an ordered discipline of thought, feeling, and will, required great patience and perseverance, and the preparedness for challenging experiences that had to be faced with great moral courage.

In his lectures Steiner found an enthusiastic audience in the Theosophical Society. His popularity led to his appointment in 1902 as general secretary of the newly founded German Section of the Theosophical Society. Marie von Sievers was named secretary. She became Steiner's second wife in 1914; his first marriage, to Anna Eunicke, a widow, had previously ended in divorce.

Steiner soon became concerned by what he termed the "triviality and dilettantism" he observed in the Theosophical Society. He grew disillusioned with Annie Besant's cultist championship of Jiddu Krishnamurti as the next messiah. He did not believe it possible to build a spiritual science on Eastern mysticism, which he said was not suitable to the spiritual needs of the Western mind. Furthermore, he considered cofounder Madame Helena P. Blavatsky to have distorted occult truths. Within the Society he found an

audience willing to follow his own esoteric research. In 1913 he left the Society and formed the Anthroposophical Society as a vehicle to continue his work. Steiner described Anthroposophy as a path for spiritual growth on four levels of human nature: the senses, imagination, inspiration, and intuition.

The same year that he formed the Anthroposophical Society, Steiner designed and established the Goetheanum, a school for esoteric research, at Dornach near Basel, Switzerland, where he intended to produce Goethe's dramas and his own mystery plays. The Goetheanum opened in 1920 and was burned down in 1922. A new building was designed and constructed, and now serves as the international headquarters for the General Anthroposophical Society, which Steiner reorganized as an international organization with himself as president in 1923.

Steiner died at Dornach on March 30, 1925.

During his last twenty-five years, Steiner traveled around Europe, Scandinavia, and Great Britain to give more than six thousand lectures on spiritual science, the arts, social sciences, religion, education, agriculture, and health. His published works include more than 350 titles, most of which are collections of lectures, as well as books, articles, reviews, and dramas. His key works outlining his occult philosophy are *Knowledge of the Higher Worlds and Its Attainment* (1904–1905); *Theosophy: An Introduction to the Supersensible Knowledge of the World and the Destination of Man* (1904); and *An Outline of Occult Science* (1909). The foundation for his views on Christ and Christianity are in more than a dozen lecture cycles on the Gospels.

One of Steiner's greatest legacies is the Waldorf School Movement, an approach to the education of children, which he developed from his spiritual-scientific research concerning child development. Steiner's social philosophy, which he advanced in 1919 with the phrase, "threefold social order," conceives of ideally consisting of three equal but separate spheres: economic, political, and spiritual-cultural. Education, he said, belonged to the spiritual-cultural sphere. In 1919 he established the first Waldorf School for Boys and Girls in Stuttgart. With five hundred schools, the Waldorf system is now the largest nonsectarian system of education in the world. Steiner also addressed the educational needs of retarded children. Clinics and homes, referred to as Campbell Villages, that teach his methods are highly reputed.

Steiner's agricultural methods for preparing soil inspired chemical-free, biodynamic farming and gardening. With Marie von Sievers he created eurythmy, the art of moving the body, particularly the limbs, to express the inner meanings of music and speech. His guidelines for holistic medicine and pharmacology are widely followed.

The Anthroposophical Society has branches throughout the world; it is strongest in Europe and Britain. See **Illuminati.**

Sources: Robert A. McDermott, ed. and intro. *The Essential Steiner.* San Francisco: Harper & Row, 1984; Robert McDermott. "Anthroposophy" and "Rudolf Steiner." In the *Encyclopedia of Religion.* New York: Macmillan, 1987; A. P. Shepherd. *Rudolf Steiner: Scientist of the Invisible.* 1954. Rochester, VT: Inner Traditions International, 1983; Leslie A. Shepard, ed. *Encyclopedia of Occultism and Parapsychology.* 2d ed. Detroit: Gale Research Co., 1984; Rudolf Steiner. *An Autobiography.* New trans. First English trans. published as *The Story of My Life.* 1928. Blauvelt, NY: Rudolf Steiner Publications, 1977.

Stevenson, Ian

See **Reincarnation; Xenoglossy.**

Stigmata

The spontaneous discharge of blood from wounds on the body, generally replicating those of Christ on the cross. Stigmatics have been measured bleeding as little as a half-pint to as much as a pint and a half a day.

The first recorded stigmatic was Francis of Assisi (who later became St. Francis) in September 1224. He reportedly began to bleed from his palms and feet following an extended fast and contemplation on the crucifixion of Christ.

Although the actual number of stigmatics is not known, Dr. A. Imbert Goubeyre, a French medical professor, catalogued over 320 cases in a two-volume book, *La Stigmatisation, l'ecstase divine, les miracles de Lourdes, réponse aux libres penseurs,* published in 1894. In subsequent years other cases have been reported, including Padre Pio, a well-known Italian monk who died in 1968, and Jane Hunt, an English housewife who began bleeding from her palms in July 1985.

Stigmata do not mirror a single pattern in all manifestations. Instead they seem to match the placement of wounds on the stigmatic's favorite crucifix or other religious object showing Christ on the cross.

In the early stages, the body seems to discharge blood through the skin. When wiped away, there are no wounds or marks beneath the blood. In later stages blisters appear, followed by actual wounds. Some strongly resemble actual puncture wounds, going all the way through the skin. In some cases the skin forms what looks like the head of a nail protruding from the wound.

On some stigmatics the wounds have appeared to close up for a period of time, disappear completely, and then manifest again later, usually around the time of religious holidays.

Most stigmatics have been deeply religious individuals, often associated with religious orders where they lived contemplative lives. Similarly, the appearance of stigmata is generally preceded by lengthy meditations on the crucifixion of Christ, frequently following a deep personal crisis or grave illness. And, in just about every case, the stigmatic had been deeply focused on a favorite religious item, such as a crucifix or statue of Christ on the cross, prior to the onset of spontaneous bleeding.

Ian Wilson, a British researcher who conducted one of the most comprehensive studies of stigmatics, *The Bleeding Mind* (1988), has argued that the bleeding is self-induced by individuals undergoing some form of personal stress. Seeking shelter from their personal suffering, these stigmatics turn to prayer and contemplation. He also drew parallels between the stigmatic and individuals who develop multiple personalities:

What is evident is that stigmata and multiple personality seem to be so closely linked that they could be two different aspects of the same phenomenon. Both seem to be stress induced, seemingly as a response to a metabolism tortured to the end of its tether. In both we find the individual caught up in a flight from reality, providing some sort of release or escape from the constraints on the everyday self, and on the other into an established fantasy world of religious figures and a personal dramatization of the events surrounding the death of Jesus.

Wilson also suggested that the mind, in addition to bringing on the stigmata, can manifest the nail-like formations on a person's flesh. In hypnosis experiments have shown that the body has the ability to make warts and other skin disfigurements disappear.

Other experiments have shown the reverse effect of spontaneous bleeding. Under self-hypnosis hemophiliacs have been able to stop themselves from bleeding uncontrollably.

Sources: Mysteries of the Unexplained. Edited by Caroll C. Calkins. Pleasantville, NY: Reader's Digest, 1982; *Strange Stories, Amazing Facts.* Pleasantville, NY: Reader's Digest, 1977; Ian Wilson. *The Bleeding Mind.* London: George Weidenfeld & Nicolson Ltd., 1988.

Stonehenge

One of the most famous ancient megalithic sites in the world, located on the chalk plain of Salisbury in Wiltshire, England. The remains include a henge and a horseshoe arrangement of standing sandstones and bluestones weighing up to twenty-six tons apiece. Some of the sarsens are topped by lintels, thus suggesting to the Saxons the name "Stonehenge," which means "Hanging Stones."

The original purpose of the site is unknown. It has no associations with the Druids, despite the antiquarian theories of John Aubrey and William Stukeley. Aubrey also believed the site to be a repository of psychic power, a belief which remains popular to the present.

Stonehenge served astronomical purposes and likely had religious, social, and political functions as well. Fifty-six burial pits, named "Aubrey Holes" after their discoverer, contain the remains of cremated human bones, flint and pottery chips, and animal bones. It has been suggested that these holes were associated with entry points to the Underworld.

Stonehenge was built in three major phases from about 3500 B.C. to 1100 B.C. by different peoples. Over the course of construction, portions were left unfinished, were dismantled, and were rebuilt. The arrangement essentially assumed its present shape by about 2000 B.C.

The construction of the trilithons, the lintel-topped sarsens, represents a stupendous engineering feat for primitive

Stonehenge

times. According to one legend, a double circle of giant bluestones was erected with magical help from Merlin, the Celtic wizard of the Arthurian court. Merlin supposedly transported the stones, which were magical healing stones, from Ireland, where they had been delivered by giants. The stones were for a monument to the slain soldiers of Aurelius Ambrosius, who had fought off a Saxon invasion. See **Merlin**. The bluestones, which are believed to come from the Preseli mountains in South Wales, probably were transported over land and sea by a slow process that took up to one hundred years to complete.

In the eighteenth century, Stukeley observed astronomical alignments between four burial stones, the so-called Heel Stone (named by Aubrey because it bears a mark shaped like a heel imprint), and the sun and moon. Sir Norman Lockyear, a British astronomer at the turn of the twentieth century, determined that Stonehenge was constructed to point to the summer solstice. He also theorized that observations of the stars were made

according to stone alignments. In 1965 British astronomer Gerald S. Hawkins stated that "there is no doubt that Stonehenge was an observatory," based on his computer calculations of 165 alignments of the stones with the sun and moon. Hawkins believes Stonehenge was built much more recently and quickly, between 1900 B.C. and 1600 B.C.

Other astronomical theories have been put forward by modern researchers such as John Michell, who concluded that Stonehenge was a solar temple, based upon his gematria and computer calculations. In 1974 Alexander Thom theorized that Stonehenge was an observatory for studying lunar movements, and served as a prototype for observatories elsewhere in Britain.

Until 1985 Stonehenge served as a festival site during the seasonal pagan rites, attended by modern-day Druids, Witches, Pagans, Morris dancers, occultists, and others. In 1900 there was a falling-out between the Druids and the owner of the site (Stonehenge was private property until 1915), when a stone was knocked over during seasonal rites. The owner fenced the site and began charging admission. The Druids responded by ritually cursing him. In 1915 the site was sold to Cecil Chubb, who turned it over to the government, which reopened it to free festivals. The pagan rites were banned in 1985 due to increasing vandalism by hecklers and spectators.

Dowsers say the stones and the site are charged with powerful geomagnetic energies, perhaps deliberately fixed by the ancient builders. However, research conducted in 1987 and 1988 by the Dragon Project Trust, an organization that studies ancient sites in Britain, showed no magnetism registering on a compass, nor any unusual radiation emissions. Subsequent research has revealed no energy anomalies that can be detected by instruments. Anecdotal reports exist of light and sound anomalies associated with the stones. See **Leys; Megaliths; Power point.**

Sources: Peter Lancaster Brown. *Megaliths, Myths and Men.* New York: Taplinger Publishing Company, 1976; Aubrey Burl. *Rings of Stone.* New York: Ticknor & Fields, 1979; Christopher Chippindale. *Stonehenge Complete.* New York: Cornell University Press, 1983; Paul Devereux. *Places of Power.* London: Blandford, 1990; J. Havelock Fidler. *Earth Energy: A Dowser's Investigation of Ley Lines.* 2d ed. Wellingborough, Northamptonshire, England: The Aquarian Press, 1988; Rosemary Ellen Guiley. *The Encyclopedia of Witches and Witchcraft.* New York: Facts On File, 1989; Gerald S. Hawkins. *Beyond Stonehenge.* New York: Harper & Row, 1973; Francis Hitching. *Earth Magic.* New York: William Morrow, 1977; John Michell. *The New View Over Atlantis.* Rev. ed. San Francisco: Harper & Row, 1983; Leon E. Stover and Bruce Kraig. *Stonehenge: The Indo-European Heritage.* Chicago: Nelson-Hall, 1978; Jennifer Westwood, ed. *The Atlas of Mysterious Places.* New York: Weidenfeld & Nicholson, 1987.

Sufism

A branch of Islam that teaches personal, mystical worship and union with Allah, or God. Sufism arose in opposition to the formal, legalistic theology of the early Moslems in the ninth century A.D. It derives its doctrines and methods from the Koran and Islamic revelation.

The Sufi Philosophy

The term "Sufism" comes from the Arabic *suf,* meaning "wool," and refers to the plain wool gowns worn by the early Sufis ("wool-clad"). Rejecting the luxurious excesses of the Caliphs, the Sufis lived simple, communal, ascetic lives, much like the early Christian monks. In fact, Arab conquerors encountering Christian monks or mystics in the Middle East were greatly impressed by them and incorporated many of their habits and beliefs in Sufi tradition. Other influences on Sufi mysticism came from Buddhism, Hinduism, and Persian Zoroastrianism. Mystical love and oneness with God (*tawhid*) form the basic tenets of Sufi faith.

Worshipers observe *faqr,* or "pious poverty," and are therefore known as *faqirs* (fakirs). They follow a Path, or *tariqa,* to divine knowledge (gnosis) through reading, study, prayer, and most especially the *dhikr:* endless repetition of God's holy name or sacred passages from the Koran leading to self-hypnosis, much like recitation of a mantra. Devotees use prayer beads, similar to rosaries.

Following the Sufi Path to enlightened love takes a lifetime, since there is no one moment when true union with God—the vision of God's face described in the Koran—has occurred. Sufis believe that humankind has always been one with God, and the Path merely serves as remembrance of this realization. Death does not stop the faqir's spiritual communications and training but is only another stage of development. According to Grand Sheikh Idries Shah, the Sufi makes four journeys:

1. *Fana,* or annihilation. At this stage the Sufi becomes harmonized with objective reality and seeks unification of his consciousness. He is intoxicated with divine love.
2. *Baqa,* or permanency. Here the Sufi becomes a teacher or *qutub:* the magnet to which all turn for wisdom. He has stabilized his objective knowledge and become the Perfect Man. Rather than uniting with God, the Perfect Man has subordinated his will to God and lives in and through God. (Traditionally, Sufi teachers are male.)
3. Sufis attaining the Third Journey become spiritual guides for all in accordance with their abilities, whereas Stage Two teachers work only in their local areas.
4. In the Fourth Journey, the Perfect Man guides others in the transition at death from physical life to another stage of development invisible to ordinary people. Few attain this plateau of wisdom.

Sufis consider guidance by a wise teacher essential to staying on the Path. These sheikhs—venerated as saints—provide the only access to the secret knowledge of God. Yet Sufi teachers discourage disciples. The goal of Sufism is for each believer to become his own man of wisdom and develop a line of communication with the Beloved.

Such self-awareness takes a long time, however, and most Sufis follow their leader, or sheikh, throughout life. He is the supreme ruler, possessing the greatest knowledge of God, charismatic, and the most disciplined. He is also known as *pir* (Persian for "old man") or *murshid* (Arabic for "one who directs"). Devotees bind themselves to the sheikh by an oath of allegiance and pledge to do

(Courtesy Hartley Film Foundation)

Sufi student meditating near mosque in Isfahan, Iran

his bidding without any sense of their own desires.

Various teachers have established schools, or Orders, which succeeding sheikhs follow or amend. Yet the schools come and go, since their ultimate goal is to prepare Seekers for the Truth. The schools provide the circumstances in which members can attain stabilization of their inner beings comparable to that of the students of Muhammad and are in fact organized similar to Muhammad's early gatherings. One of the most famous is the Order of the Whirling Dervishes, or Mehlevi, founded by Jalaluddin Rumi in the thirteenth century. *Darwish,* or dervish, is another name for faqir. Other Orders include the Rifa'i, or Howling Dervishes; the Qalandari, or Shaven Dervishes; the Chis(h)ti, or Musicians; and the Naqshbandi, or Silent Dervishes, who use no music.

The dervishes' frenzied dancing is but one example of the music, poetry, and dance accompanying Sufi worship. Poets have always been the chief disseminators of Sufi thought, using secret metaphorical language to guard the sanctity of the mystic messages and protect them from heretical examination. The word "troubadour," the medieval songmaster of love, comes from the Arabic root TRB, or "lutanist."

Endless recitation of the dhikr, in concert with chanting songs, swaying, dancing, and rhythmic drum-beating, places the worshiper in trance or a state of possession, much like that seen in Vodoun. Devotees can pierce their bodies with needles or stakes, hold hot coals, and even pull swords across their abdomens with no pain and hardly any blood or wound. At this point the worshiper has become one with the Beloved.

Such ecstatic union with God does not represent the ultimate reward for the Sufi, however. The constant pursuit of the love of God can lead to ecstasy, but it only serves a purpose if the Sufi can take that boundless joy and use it in the temporal world as an experience of love: to live "in the world, but not of it," free from ambition, greed, and intellectual pride, showing love in living and not just knowing it.

Spiritual healing is one love duty practiced by the Sufis, but not before they have studied for at least twelve years. The Sufi healer, like a teacher, acts merely as a guide, leading the patient to diagnose himself or herself under hypnosis brought on by breathing techniques. Healers chant prayers over the patient and pass their hands over the patient's body. Demands for healing cannot come from friends or relatives, and the Sufis cannot impose their will upon the patient. Unlike more orthodox faith-healing methods, patients are not expected to believe they will be cured. Payment may be no more valuable than a handful of barley.

Muhammad decried the worship of the sheikhs as saints, teaching that Allah was the only deity. Yet the Sufis believe that knowledge of the Path to God comes only from the master teachers, who attain saintly blessedness (baraqa). Devotees worship these men openly, making pilgrimages to their tombs and petitioning their intercession. True living saints keep their special powers under wraps, holding them of no account.

The Three Periods of Sufism

There are three main periods of Sufism: classical, medieval, and modern. One of the most important classical Sufis was Junayd (died 920), who turned to the Koran for proof that human struggle in this world was to fulfill God's covenants and become perfect through God.

Taking his ideas further, Junayd's pupil, Husayn ibn Mansur al-Hallaj, taught that humankind was God incarnate. He looked not to the Prophet Muhammad but to Jesus Christ as the supreme example of humankind's glorified humanity. If God is love, then Hallaj reasoned God had created humankind in his image so that people might recognize such divinity within themselves and attain a union with God. Hallaj uttered heretical statements such as "I am the truth," and was crucified in 922 for his beliefs. Like Christ he reportedly cried out, "Father, forgive them, for they know not what they do," as he was nailed to the cross. Hallaj is best remembered as a symbol of the mystic lover.

Establishment of communal brotherhoods and less overt professions of faith characterized the medieval period. The Sufis turned to music and poetry to describe their knowledge of God, hiding their search for the Beloved in beautiful but abstruse verse. Sufic poetry shows many parallels with medieval courtly romance, which also sang of abandoning all for love. The sheikhs consolidated their power during this period.

The most important Sufi of this era, and perhaps the movement's greatest representative, was Abu Hamid al-Ghazzali (1059–1111). A professor at Nizamiyya Madrasa (college) in Baghdad and learned expert on Moslem theology and law at age thirty-three, Ghazzali despaired of finding God in dry study and abandoned his career, wife, and family to seek the truth of his religion. He wandered as a mendicant dervish for twelve years, learning that human beings must rid themselves of evil thoughts, clear their minds, and commune with God through the dhikr. In his books *The Revival of the Religious Sciences* and *The Niche of the Lights,* Ghazzali managed to explain the theology of Islam in connection with humankind's mystical relation to God, bridging the gap between Sufi heresies and Islamic orthodoxy.

Another great medieval Sufi writer was Mohieddin ibn-Arabi (1165–1240), a Spanish Moslem and mystic. Ibn-Arabi described the Prophet Muhammad as the manifestation of the Perfect Man, the man God created to exemplify the divinity of God in man. He also wrote of Muhammad's ascent to Paradise, telling of the Prophet's journey through the infernal regions and purgatory, and his travels through the heavens accompanied by a beautiful guide and serenaded by angelic choirs. Such stories had a powerful influence on Dante Alighieri's *The Divine Comedy.*

Other medieval Christian writers and thinkers influenced by Sufism included Friar Roger Bacon, Cervantes, Averroes, St. Francis of Assisi, Avicebron, and Chaucer. The Knights Templar also took inspiration from the Sufis, sharing esoteric knowledge of alchemy, masonry, and the Jewish Kabbalah. The name of Hugues de Payns, founder of the Knights Templar in 1118, means "of the pagans." His father was known as "the Moor," originating from southern Spain. See **Order of the Knights Templar.**

Sufis claim that Freemasonry actually began in the medieval period with the teachings of Spanish Sufi Ibn Masarra (883–931). Idries Shah sees Masonry as a metaphor for rebuilding, or reedification, of the spiritual human being, and says that the three tools in the Masonic emblem symbolize the three Sufi postures of prayer. He also notes that Freemasons honor Boaz and Solomon, the latter the son of David, as the builders of King Solomon's Temple in Jerusalem, and explains that these two men were actually Sufi architects who built the Temple of the Dome of the Rock on the ruins of King Solomon's temple. The architectural measurements for the temple were allegedly numerical equivalents of Arabic root words that conveyed holy messages, each part relating to every other part in definite proportion. See **Freemasonry.**

Modern Sufism reached its peak under the Mogul and Ottoman empires, in the 1500s to 1800s. Sufis swelled the ranks of Moslem armies during Islamic expansion in the Middle and Far East during the eighteenth and nineteenth centuries, infiltrating local trade unions and marrying royal princesses. Sufis fought fiercely against European expansion on Islamic soil, becoming *mujahidin* ("holy warriors") in the *jihad* ("holy war").

By the twentieth century, however, Sufism had lost much of its influence. Members of the Wahhabi sect, a large puritan revivalist movement in Islam, scorned the Sufis for their mystical excesses and worship of sheikhs and other holy men. Many of today's Muslims continue to practice Sufism, but their brotherhoods are usually secret societies keeping mainly to themselves. Sufism still attracts a wide following in India, and has large groups of devotees in England and the United States. See **Muhammad; Mysticism.**

Sources: Keith Crim, gen. ed. *Abingdon Dictionary of Living Religions.* Nashville, TN: Abingdon Press, 1981; Jacques De Marquette. *Introduction to Comparative Mysticism.* New York: Philosophical Library, 1949; Gaetan Delaforge. "The Templar Tradition Yesterday and Today." *Gnosis* no. 6 (Winter 1988): 8–13; Emile Dermenghem. "Yoga and Sufism: Ecstasy

Techniques in Islam." *Forms and Techniques of Altruistic and Spiritual Growth.* Edited by Pitirum A. Sorokin. Boston: The Beacon Press, 1954; Cyril Glasse. *The Concise Encyclopedia of Islam.* San Francisco: Harper & Row, 1989; Alfred Guillaume. *Islam.* Harmondsworth, England: Penguin Books, 1954; Ja'far Hallaji. "Sufi Hypnotherapy." *Critique: A Journal of Conspiracies and Metaphysics* no. 25; F. C. Happold. *Mysticism: A Study and an Anthology.* Rev. ed. Harmondsworth, Middlesex, England: Penguin Books, 1970; Thomas W. Lippman. *Understanding Islam: An Introduction to the Moslem World.* New York: New American Library, 1982; Geoffrey Parrinder, ed. *World Religions from Ancient History to the Present.* 1971. New York: Facts On File, 1983; John Sabini. *Islam: A Primer.* Washington, DC: Middle East Editorial Association, 1983; Idries Shah. *The Sufis.* Garden City, NY: Anchor/Doubleday, 1971; "What If? The Mantram of the New Age: An Interview with Pir Vilayat Inayat Khan." *The Quest* 2, no. 1 (Spring 1989): 54–59; Peter Lamborn Wilson and Nasrollah Pourjavady. "The Drunken Universe." *The Quest* 1, no. 2 (Winter 1988): 88–91.

Sun Bear (b. 1929)

Chippewa Native American and founder and medicine chief of the Bear Tribe Medicine Society, the purpose of which is to spread Native American spiritual teachings.

Sun Bear was born Gheezis Mokwa in 1929 on the White Earth Reservation in northern Minnesota. He experienced visions as early as age three, and received his spiritual name, Sun Bear, during a vision when he was ill with diphtheria at age four. In the vision he saw a large black bear surrounded by a brilliant rainbow. The bear stood on its hind legs and touched him on the forehead. Since then visions have continued throughout his life, and Sun Bear has felt guided by the spirits.

Sun Bear received his early medicine training from uncles who were medicine men. His formal education stopped at the eighth grade. The Depression forced his family to move around to find work, and at age fifteen he left home to work at various jobs. He eventually went to Hollywood, where he spent ten years as a technical consultant to such programs as "Bonanza," "Broken Arrow," and "Brave Eagle." In 1961 he founded *Many Smokes,* a magazine to promote intertribal communications, Native American writers, and Earth awareness.

After leaving Hollywood Sun Bear worked as an economic development specialist for the Intertribal Council of Nevada, and taught through the Tecumseh Indian Studies Program, which he helped to develop, at the University of California at Davis experimental college.

Until 1970 Sun Bear worked as a medicine man only with Native Americans. A series of powerful visions of cataclysmic Earth changes, such as in the prophecies of Native Americans and others, directed him to expand his audience. The same year he founded the Bear Tribe Medicine Society, named after the Bear Clan, the traditional medicine clan. In Native American mythology the bear inherits the healing powers from the Great Spirit.

The Bear Tribe Medicine Society first settled near Placerville, California, then moved near Reno, Nevada. In 1975 it relocated to its present site near Spokane, Washington, which was named Vision Mountain. No alcohol or drugs are allowed at Vision Mountain. The tribe raises most of its own food. Among its numerous activities are various internship and apprentice programs, medicine wheel gatherings, wilderness retreats, vision quests, and a publishing program. *Many Smokes,* renamed *Wildfire,* is the tribe's magazine.

Most of those who seek out the tribe are non-Native Americans. That, plus

Sun Bear's commercial success in book publishing and on the international lecture-seminar-workshop circuit, has earned him criticism from many more traditional Native Americans, who believe the old ways should not be shared so freely. Sun Bear responds to his critics by saying he is following the directives of the Great Spirit, who says it is time for Natives to share their wisdom with others. Also, one of his medicine man uncles told him that anyone could study and learn the medicine ways. He notes that many non-Native Americans, however, are in too much of a hurry to learn. First, one must be accepted by the spirits, and then begin working with them.

Sun Bear espouses "practical spirituality," which involves connecting with one's own power and learning how to use it, and living in cooperation and peace with others. One of his primary purposes is to teach people how to live in harmony with the Earth without destroying it. Technology is not inherently evil, he says, only the ways it has been misused. He teaches self-sufficiency on the land, and has established a "medicine wheel network" across the United States of wilderness retreat centers established on donated properties.

Sun Bear believes the self-sufficiency and harmony are necessary to prepare for cataclysmic Earth changes, which are forecast in many Native prophecies, as they are in the Christian tradition.

Sun Bear's books include *Sun Bear: The Path of Power* (1984), his autobiography, written with Wabun and Barry Weinstein; *The Medicine Wheel: Earth Astrology*, with Wabun; *At Home in the Wilderness* (rev. ed. 1973); *Buffalo Hearts* (1976); and *The Bear Tribe's Self-Reliance Book* (rev. ed. 1977), with Wabun and Nimimosha. See **Black Elk, Nicholas; Mysticism; Rolling Thunder; Shamanism.**

Sources: Alan Morvay. "An Interview with Sun Bear, Founder and Medicine Chief of

(Courtesy Bear Medicine Tribe)

Sun Bear

the Bear Tribe Medicine Society." *Shaman's Drum* no. 3 (Winter 1985): 20–22; Robert Neubert. "Sun Bear: Walking in Balance on the Earth Mother." *New Realities* 7, no. 5 (May/June 1987): 7–14; Sun Bear. "Native Prophecies: Earth Changes Essential for Cleansing." *Venture Inward* 4, no. 3 (May/June 1988): 12–17+; Sun Bear. *Sun Bear: The Path of Power.* Spokane, WA: The Bear Tribe, 1984.

Sun Dance

Ceremony of Plains Native Americans for health, fertility, and plentiful food. The Sun Dance, one of the most sacred of Native American rites, was at one time outlawed by the US federal government because its elements of self-sacrifice were misunderstood and considered barbaric.

Traditionally, the dance is performed annually during the summer, at a time when the moon is full, by tribes in the North American Plains and prairie west of the Missouri River. The name "Sun Dance" comes from the Dakota; the rite is so-named because fasting dancers gaze at the sun. The dance is called the New Life Lodge by the Cheyenne, the Sacred Dance or Mystery Dance by the Ponca, and the Dance Looking at the Sun (*wiwanyag wachipi*) by the Oglala Sioux. The purpose of the ceremony is to commune with the Earth, sun, spirits, and winds so that a tribe will prosper and have successful hunts.

As a full-fledged ceremony, the Sun Dance dates only to around 1800; the last tribe to adopt it was the Ute in 1890. The dance developed with the coming of the horse, which by the beginning of the nineteenth century enabled Natives, pressed by the spread of white settlers from the east, to migrate throughout the American Plains and hunt large numbers of buffalo. Its development also coincided with the rise of warrior and medicine societies, although the ceremony itself requires no priesthood, permanent lodge, or medicine bundle. The dance incorporates some ancient elements from the Algonkian vision quest and the Omaha reverence of the sacred pole, which is a symbol of the cosmos and the Supreme Being.

Elements of the dance vary among tribes; the following description offers general characteristics. In many cases the dance is sponsored by an individual who has been instructed to do so in a vision or dream. All items used in the Sun Dance are purified in sacred smoke, and the sacred pipe is smoked. A circular Sun Dance Lodge is constructed of poles. The lodge represents the sacred universe with its central pole as the *axis mundi*. The Oglala Sioux, for example, use twenty-eight poles attached to the central pole, for twenty-eight represents various combinations of four and seven, two sacred numbers, as well the number of days in the lunar cycle, the number of feathers in a war bonnet, and the number of ribs

in a buffalo. The lodge is purified by dancing.

Male dancers are chosen and are painted with sacred symbols. Fasting begins prior to the ceremony. The dancers declare which of various sacrifices they will make in the dance. Those who choose to do so have the flesh of their breasts and backs pierced, traditionally with eagle claws or skewers, but in modern times with surgical scalpels. Wooden pegs are inserted under the skin and ropes or leather thongs are fastened to the pegs. The dancers are tied to the center pole, which symbolizes the tying of their spirits to the Great Spirit. They dance, gazing at the sun, until the thongs are ripped free of their flesh. They blow whistles made of eagle bone and decorated with eagle plumes, which represent the sun. By recreating the cry of the eagle, the dancers become the eagle, thus mixing their vital breath with the essence of the sun and life. Sacred pipes are exchanged among the dancers and then with the onlookers.

Traditionally, a dancer was hung from the center pole until his weight caused him to rip free. Also traditionally, buffalo skulls were attached to a dancer's flesh.

The dancers are encouraged by onlookers to persevere. The onlookers wipe the wounds and sweat with bundles of sage leaves. The dancing lasts from two to four days, during which the dancers do not eat or drink. If they do not rip free of all their thongs, they are cut free with a knife. Outside the lodge others fast, sing, and conduct minor ceremonies. At the conclusion there is great feasting and celebration.

The sacrifice of flesh is considered a supreme sacrifice, an indication to the Supreme Being of earnestness and sincerity. The dancer makes this sacrifice on behalf of his people, even all humankind. The flesh represents darkness and ignorance, and its tearing in the Sun Dance represents the breaking free of such bonds.

Without suffering and sacrifice, it is not possible to find identity, freedom, and sacredness. The moment of tearing free is one of ecstasy.

Flesh sacrifices are part of the majority of tribal variations of the Sun Dance, but not by all. The damage to muscle tissue is temporary. Sun gazing is part of a minority of rites. Dancers can blind themselves, usually temporarily.

By the beginning of the early twentieth century, the Sun Dance was outlawed; the sacrifice of living flesh was considered primitive and degenerate. The Sioux petitioned the courts, arguing that the Sun Dance was a sacred rite necessary to the survival not only of the tribes, but of everyone on the Earth. After about fifty years, the Sun Dance was permitted again, but without flesh-piercing. In 1978 the Native American Religious Freedoms Act was passed, and flesh-piercing was allowed once again. See **Altered states of consciousness.**

Sources: Joseph Epes Brown, ed. *The Sacred Pipe: Black Elk's Account of the Seven Rites of the Oglala Sioux.* 1953. New York: Penguin Books, 1971; Joseph Epes Brown. *The Spiritual Legacy of the American Indian.* New York: Crossroad, 1987; Carl A. Hammerschlag. *The Dancing Healers: A Doctor's Journey of Healing with Native Americans.* San Francisco: Harper & Row, 1988; Ake Hultkrantz. *The Religions of the American Indians.* 1967. Berkeley: University of California Press, 1979; John (Fire) Lame Deer and Richard Erdoes. *Lame Deer Seeker of Visions.* New York: Washington Square Press, 1972; Ruth M. Underhill. *Red Man's Religion.* Chicago: University of Chicago Press, 1965.

Super-ESP

A hypothesis that negates survival after death by attempting to explain how apparitions of the dead and communications from the dead are the result of extraordinary ESP of the living. Though it may explain away some cases of alleged life after death, super-ESP must be stretched to ridiculous lengths to explain others.

The term "super-ESP" was coined in the late 1950s by American sociologist and psychical researcher Hornell Hart, and was then popularized by British psychical researcher Alan Gauld. The concept was studied in the nineteenth century by French physiologist Charles Richet, and by the early founders of the Society for Psychical Research (SPR) in England in the late nineteenth and early twentieth centuries. In researching the question of survival after death, the SPR studied mediumistic communications, in which a medium claimed to communicate with the dead, and countless reports of apparitions of the dead. Some researchers believed that mediums could falsify contact with the dead by using telepathy and clairvoyance to glean personal information from the minds of the sitters.

The telepathy hypothesis received a great boost in 1925 with the celebrated Soal case. Psychical researcher S. G. Soal participated in a series of sittings with Blanche Cooper, a London trance medium, who contacted Gordon Davis, a friend of Soal's whom Soal believed was killed in World War I. The discarnate Davis provided personal reminisces, used idiosyncratic speech patterns, and talked about his concern for his wife and "kiddie." Soal was later shocked to find out that Davis was alive and living in London. He theorized that Cooper had picked up information from his own mind or, perhaps even from Davis's mind.

American psychical researcher Gardner Murphy formulated a theory with other researchers that the phenomena of super-ESP (telepathy, clairvoyance, precognition, and retrocognition) may create pseudo-spirit personalities, as well as apparitions of the dead.

But other researchers reject that, and say super-ESP cannot explain numerous other cases in which mediums provide information unknown to the sitters. If super-ESP were responsible, mediums would perform phenomenal feats of mind-reading, scanning the thoughts of perhaps dozens of persons who knew the deceased—and who just happened to be thinking about him or her at the time of the sitting—or clairvoyantly viewing newspaper articles and books for information.

At numerous sittings conducted by British medium Leonora Piper, one of her controls, the deceased George Pellew, recognized and talked with about thirty of Pellew's living friends, who were introduced pseudonymously to Piper. To use ESP to scan the complexities of thirty relationships, and to deliver the information mimicking Pellew, strains believability.

Super-ESP fails to explain the cases of "drop-in communicators," unknown entities who show up unexpectedly at a seance or sitting, and provide verifiable information, or speak through the medium in a foreign language the medium does not know. See **Drop-in communicator.** Nor does super-ESP explain apparitions of the dead. To fit the hypothesis, an apparition is a hallucination projected by a living person who is thinking intensely about the deceased. If more than one person sees the apparition, then, according to super-ESP, it is created by one person and picked up telepathically by the others, who read the thoughts of the creator.

Despite these drawbacks super-ESP maintains a sizable number of adherents, and has been hotly debated over the decades. It cannot be disproven, for there are no known limits to ESP. However, super-ESP requires a degree of ESP functioning that surpasses any feat demonstrated in the laboratory. Support for super-ESP has fallen since the 1970s,

in the wake of research into other areas. See **Mediumship.**

Sources: Alan Gauld. "The 'Super-ESP' Hypothesis." *Proceedings of the Society for Psychical Research* 53, pt. 192 (October 1961): 226–46; Alan Gauld. *Mediumship and Survival.* London: William Heinemann Ltd., 1982; Hornell Hart. *The Enigma of Survival.* Springfield, IL: Charles C. Thomas, 1959; Edgar D. Mitchell. *Psychic Exploration: A Challenge for Science.* Edited by John White. New York: Paragon Books, 1974; Gardner Murphy. "Difficulties Confronting the Survival Problem." *Journal of the American Society for Psychical Research* 39 (1945): 67–94; Karlis Osis. "Linkage Experiments with Mediums." *Journal of the American Society for Psychical Research* 60 (1966): 91–124; D. Scott Rogo. *Psychic Breakthroughs Today.* Wellingborough, Northamptonshire, England: The Aquarian Press, 1987; Benjamin B. Wolman. *Handbook of Parapsychology.* New York: Van Nostrand Reinhold, 1977.

Survival after death

See **Cross correspondence; Deathbed visions; Mediumship; Near-death experience (NDE); Reincarnation.**

Sutphen, Richard (b. 1937)

American author, seminar trainer, and hypnotist who has acquainted a wide popular audience with metaphysics, reincarnation, and "human potential" topics. Richard Sutphen is best known for his work in past-life regression, and was a pioneer in the use of group hypnosis for that purpose.

Sutphen's educational background is in art and advertising. He attended the Art Center in Los Angeles, and later worked for ad agencies in the Midwest for several years. In the late 1960s, after the breakup of his first marriage, he moved to Arizona, living in Prescott and

Scottsdale, where he worked as an advertising freelancer.

Experiences with a Ouija board led him to investigate the paranormal and past-life regression. His own initial past-life memories were of a Mayan life in which he was killed by Christian invaders. He studied hypnosis and self-hypnosis, and began experimenting in hypnotic regression with others. In 1971 he began group regression sessions and research work with various metaphysical organizations in the Scottsdale-Phoenix area. In 1972 he met Trenna, who helped him in his research and later became his second wife. In hypnotic regressions the two discovered they had shared previous past lives, including one as Indians in what is now Mexico, and one in the early 1700s as poor peasants in Marseilles, France.

Sutphen's interest in the power point near Sedona, Arizona, began soon after his move to Arizona, fueled by Lyall Watson's *The Romeo Error*. He visited one of the Sedona vortices and had powerful psychic experiences, leading him to develop programs and materials to bring pilgrims to the area. See **Sedona, Arizona.**

In 1973 Sutphen founded and directed the Hypnosis Center in Scottsdale, which conducted regression research for six months until it was closed in January 1974. He continued to conduct seminars and classes. His first book, *You Were Born Again to Be Together,* appeared in 1976. The same year he conducted the first nationally broadcast past-life regression on Tom Snyder's *Tomorrow* show.

In 1980 Sutphen moved to Malibu, California, where his second marriage ended. His third wife, Tara, helps him run the Sutphen Corporation, which has two divisions: Sutphen Seminars, which conducts seminars in approximately twenty cities every year, and Valley of the Sun Publishing, which publishes books, audio tapes, and videotapes.

(Courtesy the Sutphen Corporation)

Richard Sutphen

In 1984 Sutphen established Reincarnationists, Inc., an organization to conduct and sponsor seminars on reincarnation themes, directed by Tara Sutphen. The "New Age Activists" were formed as the "spiritual action" arm to counteract the activities of various Fundamentalist Christian groups. Plans to establish a Reincarnationists center in Sedona were abandoned by 1987 due to lack of public interest and financial support, and the organization became inactive.

Sutphen has written more than thirty-seven books. Other well-known titles are *Past Lives, Future Loves* (1978), *Unseen Influences* (1982), *Predestined Love* (1988), and *Finding Your Answers Within* (1989).

Sources: Darlene Carter. "A Very Outspoken Interview with Dick and Tara Sutphen." *Self-Help Update* issue 31 (1986); Dick Sutphen. *Past Lives, Future Loves.* New York: Pocket Books, 1978; Dick Sutphen. *You Were Born Again to Be Together.* New York: Pocket Books, 1976; Paul Zuromski. "Dick Sutphen." *Body Mind Spirit* (September/October 1987): 14–18.

Suzuki, D. T.

See **Zen**.

Swaffer, Hannen

See **Spiritualism**.

Sweat

A rite of purification of the body and spirit in the ceremonies of many Native Americans. Sweats take place in a small, circular lodge or tipi in which a central pit has been dug in the earth. Rocks are heated on an outside fire and brought inside to be placed in the pit. Water is thrown on the rocks to create steam, which becomes scented with herbs, such as sagebrush, carried in by the participants. The herbs also serve to protect the face against the intense heat.

There are different kinds of sweats with varying intensities of heat. Baby sweats, the equivalent of a christening, are the mildest, while healing sweats are the hottest. Sweats are undertaken before all sacred ceremonies, rites of passage, and vision quests. In most sweats prayers and petitions are made on behalf of others. There is chanting and self-blessing, in which participants pat themselves. Thanksgiving sweats give thanks to the spirits for the blessings received.

The sweat ceremony is efficiently organized and conducted by a leader. No one may enter or leave the lodge, or drink water, without his permission. Other individuals have specific responsibilities, such as tending the fire and heating the rocks, or singing the chants.

Sweats are conducted in rounds. At the end of a round, the flaps to the lodge are opened and water is brought in for those who desire a drink. More hot rocks are brought in for another round. At the end of the sweat rounds, there is a round of smoking a sacred pipe.

With the intense heat and chanting, it is not uncommon to enter an altered state of consciousness in which one experiences visions or clairaudient phenomena. One also may "see one's spirit," that is, confront one's true nature or fears. See **Sacred pipe; Vision quest.**

Sources: Joseph Epes Brown, ed. *The Sacred Pipe: Black Elk's Account of the Seven Rites of the Oglala Sioux.* Harmondsworth, Middlesex, England: Penguin Books, 1953; Evelyn Eaton. *I Send a Voice.* Wheaton, IL: The Theosophical Publishing House, 1978; Carl Waldman. *Atlas of the North American Indian.* New York: Facts On File, 1985.

Swedenborg, Emanuel (1688–1772)

Swedish scientist and scholar who turned mystic and medium in his later years, communing with spirits to develop a highly detailed description of the structure of the afterlife and universal laws. Swedenborg's views were far ahead of his time, and many of his contemporaries dismissed him as mad. But his works endured, creating a profound impact on Western spiritual beliefs outside the context of religion, the effects of which have lasted to the present. Swedenborg was a major influence upon the secret societies of his time, and on the development of Spiritualism in the nineteenth century. Today's New Age spiritual concepts and philosophies borrow heavily from his work.

For nearly two-thirds of his life, Swedenborg led a creative but unremarkable existence. He was born the second son of the Lutheran bishop of Skara, and exhibited an early talent for science and mathematics. From age eleven to twenty-one, he studied at the University of Uppsala, learning Greek, Latin, several European and Oriental languages, geology, metallurgy, astronomy, anatomy, mathematics, economics, and other subjects. Upon graduation he traveled to Holland, Germany, and England, where he formed a lasting love for the English.

In 1716 King Charles XII of Sweden named him special assessor to the Royal College of Mines. He worked energetically, publishing scientific works, inventing devices such as air-guns and submarines. He attempted twice to marry but was rebuffed both times. He remained single for his entire life, but indulged in mistresses. He was courteous, a gentleman, and gave no clue of the mystical life that was to unfold.

In 1743 the spiritual world burst abruptly upon the fifty-six-year-old Swedenborg in a dream in which he traveled to the spiritual planes. He had paid scant attention to spiritual matters before, although he had argued for the existence of the soul in one of his scientific works, *The Animal Kingdom*. Now he began having dreams, ecstatic visions, trances, and mystical illuminations in which he visited heaven and hell, talked with Jesus and God, communicated with the spirits of the dead (whom he called angels), and saw the order of the universe, which was radically different from the teachings of the Christian church. Swedenborg became convinced that he had been designated by God as a spiritual emissary to explore the higher planes and report his findings back to his fellow men and women, who were woefully ignorant of the truth.

So excited was he by what he saw that Swedenborg resigned his government job and retired on a half-pension so that he could devote all his waking—and sleeping—hours to further spiritual explorations. He began recording the dictations of angels, which he automatically wrote while in light trances. Some of his visionary trances were so deep that he remained in them for up to three days. He nonchalantly explained to his worried housekeeper that he was merely out talking to his friends in the spirit world. The trances were spontaneous at first; then Swedenborg used breathing control to induce them.

He became an ascetic and a semivegetarian, giving up meat and existing primarily on bread, milk, and coffee. Others thought he had gone insane. Immanuel Kant, who studied Swedenborg and found many similarities with his own views, was nonetheless put off, understandably, by Swedenborg's claims of conversations with Plato, Aristotle, and other historical luminaries, and his interplanetary travels.

Swedenborg's first of a prolific outpouring of books, *Worship and the Love of God*, was published in 1745. In 1749 he published the first of the eight volumes of *Arcana Coelestia*, a ponderous exposition of the spirit teachings he received. His most widely read work is *Heaven and Hell*, descriptions of the afterlife. In *Earths in the Universe*, he described his visionary trips to other, inhabited planets. The moon, he said, was peopled by a race which, due to the strange atmosphere, spoke through their stomachs, which sounded like belching.

Swedenborg's ideas, expressed in his stilted and dry writing, were greeted with little enthusiasm by the public at large, and were opposed by the church. He was forced to publish his books at his own expense. His views did not gain a significant following until after his death, when English translations began to circulate in America and England, and laid the groundwork for Spiritualism.

Swedenborg exhibited psychic powers of clairvoyance and remote viewing on numerous occasions. One of the most famous occurred in 1759, when he witnessed a fire in Stockholm from a location three hundred miles away. See **Remote viewing.** He impressed Queen Louisa Ulrica, sister of Frederick the Great, by delivering a private message from her dead brother, Augustus William. In another incident a widow came to him for help in finding the receipt for an expensive silver service, which she believed her husband had paid for prior to his death, though the merchant claimed he had not. Swedenborg directed her to a secret compartment in a bureau, where the receipt was found.

He spent much of his later years in England. He died at the age of eighty-four in London and was buried there.

The Doctrines of Swedenborg

Swedenborg believed that God created humankind to exist simultaneously in the physical, or natural, world and the spiritual world. The spiritual world belonged to an inner domain, along with will. We have lost the ability to recognize and use this inner domain, though we remain in constant contact with it, and are influenced by it. The inner domain has its own memory, which is what survives after death. This memory includes an eternal record of every thought, emotion, and action accumulated over a lifetime—Swedenborg's version of the Akashic Records—and influences whether the soul goes to heaven or hell.

Swedenborg's concepts of heaven and hell are a significant improvement over those offered by Christianity, which feature a bland eternal bliss of adoration and angels singing, or eternal pain and torment under the dominion of Satan. Swedenborg's hell is frightening, but it has no Satan; his heaven is populated by the spirits of the dead who carry on lives and habits much the same as they did on earth. Both have societal structures and governments. Both are the products of state of mind, self-created by each individual during life on earth. According to Swedenborg Jesus' crucifixion did not atone for the sins of humankind; we make our own heaven and hell.

Upon death the spirit enters a transition plane so earth-like that many souls cannot believe they are dead. They are met by dead relatives and friends, then go through a self-evaluation process that leads them to choose their heaven or hell. Regardless of choice, souls continue to wear clothes, eat, sleep, carry on activities, and marry. Some remarry their earthly spouses, while others choose new and more compatible ones.

Selfish, materialistic people naturally choose hell, which is a horrible, dark demiworld of souls with monstrous faces. Souls are free to do anything they did on earth, including murder, rape, torture, lie, and manipulate. The only punishment is incurred when a soul develops vices in excess of his earthly ones; then he is beaten by other souls. The demons who rule hell are human souls, not supernatural beings of another order.

Nor did Swedenborg believe in angels; he used the term to describe certain souls. All angels once were humans.

Souls may choose heaven, which is comprised of city-like communities in which everyone works for the communal good. It is possible for souls to progress in the afterlife, but never to leave heaven or hell, which are permanent states. Swedenborg did not believe in reincarnation.

Swedenborg's visions inspired his followers to establish a religion in his name after his death, and different churches and societies were formed in countries around the world. The first was the Church of the New Jerusalem, founded in England in 1778 and in the United States in 1792. The Swedenborg Society was established in 1810 to publish new translations of his works, create libraries, and sponsor lectures and meetings. As a religion Swedenborgianism has not become a major force.

The Spiritualists of the nineteenth century adopted many of Swedenborg's views, but rejected his hell and divided his heaven into seven spheres through which the soul passes after death. Swedenborg's ideas have survived and been spread throughout the general population largely by intellectuals and writers who have been influenced by them. Blake, Coleridge, Emerson, and Henry James are among writers who have used Swedenborgian themes; James and Emerson were attracted to Swedenborg's ideas even though they were critical of him. Swedenborgianism ran heavily in the James family: theologian Henry James, Sr., father of novelist Henry James, was a Swedenborgian. William James, son of Henry James, Sr., reflected Swedenborg in his philosophical works. In addition to being influenced by his family, William James took his doctrine of pragmatism from Charles Sanders Peirce, a Swedenborgian.

In the eclectic spiritual outlooks that developed in the second half of the twentieth century, Swedenborg's influence is evident in the popular concept of a self-made, self-chosen heaven or hell. See **Spiritualism.**

Sources: Slater Brown. *The Heyday of Spiritualism.* New York: Hawthorn Books, 1970; Alfred Douglas. *Extrasensory Powers: A Century of Psychical Research.* London: Victor Gollancz Ltd., 1976; Edgar D. Mitchell. *Psychic Exploration: A Challenge for Science.* Edited by John White. New York: Paragon Books, 1974; Kurt Seligmann. *The History of Magic and the Occult.* New York: Pantheon Books, 1948; Emanuel Swedenborg. *Divine Providence.* 1764. New York: The Swedenborg Foundation, 1972; Emanuel Swedenborg. *Divine Love and Wisdom.* 1763. New York: American Swedenborg Printing and Publishing Society, 1894; Emanuel Swedenborg. *The Four Doctrines.* 1763. New York: The Swedenborg Foundation, 1976; Colin Wilson. *The Occult.* New York: Vintage Books, 1973.

Symbol

Usually, an object or visual image that expresses a concept or idea beyond the object or image itself. Author J. E. Cirlot defined symbols as "the art of thinking in images" (*A Dictionary of Symbols,* 1971), while psychiatrist Roberto Assagioli defined them as preservers, transformers, and conductors of "a dynamic psychological charge or voltage."

Symbols play a vital role in religions (in archaic societies, all symbolism was religious), but also permeate the whole of society; people respond to symbols both consciously and unconsciously on a daily basis. Historian of religion Mircea Eliade observed that symbols translate the human situation into cosmological terms, and disclose the interdependence of human existence and cosmic structures. The understanding of symbols and the integration of them into the conscious is an important factor in various psychologies.

Psychiatrist Carl G. Jung, who devoted a great deal of his life to studying symbols, said that objects and forms that are transformed into symbols become endowed with a great psychological and redeeming power, and carry messages to the psyche. Symbols are the language of the unconscious, and in particular, the collective unconscious, where reside the accumulated racial memories of humankind. Symbols have a numinous quality that connects them to the archetypes in the collective unconscious.

Jung's break with psychiatrist Sigmund Freud was in part due to a disagreement over what is meant by "symbol." Freud maintained that the contents of the consciousness that provide clues to the unconsciousness are symbols. Jung said these were not symbols but merely signs or symptoms, for the meaning of true symbols is not obvious. To be effective symbols must always be beyond the reach of comprehension. Assagioli, agreeing with Jung, said that those who take symbols literally cannot pass beyond them to arrive at their underlying truth.

While symbols usually are thought of as images, pictures, and designs, anything can become a symbol: natural and manmade objects, numbers, the elements, animals, the Earth, the sky, the heavenly objects, deities, myths, folktales, and even words. Humankind itself is a symbol and, according to Jung, the whole cosmos is a potential symbol. Philosopher Manly P. Hall stated that man is the oldest, most profound and universal symbol, as found in the ancient mysteries, which taught that the macrocosm of the universe was symbolized by man, the microcosm. In fact, symbols comprise the language of the mysteries and of philosophy, mysticism, and all Nature, according to Hall. Symbols both conceal (to the uninitiated) and reveal (to the initiated). See **Mysteries.**

Cirlot stated there are three types of symbols and three components of symbols. The types are (1) conventional, which include constants such as those found in industry and mathematics; (2) accidental, which result from transitory contacts; and (3) universal, which express an intrinsic relationship between the symbol itself and whatever it represents. The components of symbols are (1) the symbol in and of itself; (2) its link to a utilitarian function; and (3) its metaphysical meaning.

Symbols may become degraded over time if original meanings are lost and replaced by lesser values. For example, pearls are now largely regarded as cosmetic objects in jewelry, but once were integral to medicine, magic, religious offerings to gods and the moon, funerary rites, and fertility rituals. Jung said that symbols that are not constantly renewed, and thus lose their dissolubility, lose their redeeming power. Symbols that become too well known also lose their power, becoming mere signs.

Symbolistic thought is believed to have origins in the late Paleolithic Age, when people lived in nomadic hunter/gatherer societies that found shelter in caves and expressed their magico-supernatural beliefs in rock carvings and paintings. Symbols were part of everyday life. Three of the most universal symbols to emerge (in addition to humankind) were stones, animals, and circles. Natural stones were believed to be the dwelling places of deities and spirits. Stones also could be imbued with animation by sculpting. Animals (which include the entire animal kingdom) appear as symbols as early as the Ice Age, c. 60,000 B.C. to 10,000 B.C., and represent humanity's instinctual and primitive nature. This nature was projected onto deities, who bore animalistic attributes or were sometimes represented by animals. The circle is perhaps the most powerful of all symbols, representing the sun, illumination, wholeness, the wheel of life-death-rebirth, the Christ, and the philosopher's stone. In the East the circle often is expressed in the lotus shape and in mandalas. See **Circle; Lotus; Mandala.** In Jungian thought the circle represents the Self, the totality of the psyche.

Symbols are important to all esoteric teachings, for they contain secret wisdom accessible only to the initiated. In Western magic symbols are the keys to raising within the magician the qualities or abilities expressed by the symbols. Poet William Butler Yeats, a member of the Hermetic Order of the Golden Dawn, said of the magical power of symbols, "I cannot now think symbols less than the greatest of all powers whether they are used consciously by the master of magic or half unconsciously by their successors, the poet, the musician, and the artist" (Harper, *Yeats's Golden Dawn*, 1974.) See **Magic.**

While symbols remain integral to daily life in primitive and tribal societies, modern people feel removed from them. Yet symbols continue to permeate our lives in religion, art, literature, folklore, myth, science, and commerce, and act upon us unconsciously. See **Mythology.** Jung said that the human mind has its own history, expressed in symbols, specifically archetypes, or models. Symbols surface in dreams, but some have become completely unfamiliar to us. See **Dreams.**

Jung lamented the deterioration of the symbolic nature of Christianity. Christian symbols, he said, died of the same disease that felled the classical gods: Humankind discovered it had no thoughts on the subject. Jung also lamented Western efforts to adopt symbols from Eastern religions, which he did not think could be assimilated meaningfully into Western culture. He said it was better to admit that Christianity suffered from a poverty of symbols than to attempt to possess foreign symbols to which the West could not be the spiritual heir. See **Alchemy; Archetypes; Collective unconscious; Dreams; Grail, the; Hermetica; Magic; Mythology; Tarot.**

Sources: Roberto Assagioli. *Psychosynthesis: A Manual of Principles and Techniques.* 1965. New York: Penguin Books, 1976; Roberto Assagioli. "Symbols of Transpersonal Experiences." *The Journal of Transpersonal Psychology* (Spring 1969): 33–45; J. E. Cirlot. *A Dictionary of Symbols.* New York: Philosophical Library, 1971; Mircea Eliade. *Patterns in Comparative Religion.* New York: New American Library, 1958; Mircea Eliade. *Symbolism, the Sacred, and the Arts.* Edited by Diane Apostolos-Cappadona. New York: Crossroad, 1988; Manly P. Hall. *The Secret Teachings of All Ages.* 1928. Los Angeles: The Philosophical Research Society, 1977; George Mills Harper. *Yeats's Golden Dawn.* 1974. Wellingborough, Northamptonshire, England: The Aquarian Press, 1987; Carl G. Jung, ed. *Man and His Symbols.* First published in the United States 1964. New York: Anchor Press/Doubleday, 1988; C. G. Jung. *Psychological Reflections.* 1945. Rev. ed. 1949. Bollingen Series 31. New York: Pantheon Books, 1953; Andrew Samuels, Bani Shorter, and Fred Plaut. *A Critical Dictionary of Jungian Analysis.* London: Routledge & Kegan Paul, 1986; Charles T. Tart, ed. *Transpersonal Psychologies.* New York: Harper & Row, 1975.

Synchronicity

The unifying principle behind "meaningful coincidences." Psychiatrist Carl G. Jung termed synchronicity "an acausal connecting principle" that links seemingly unrelated and unconnected events. The concept is integral to Eastern thought, but in Western thought runs contrary to cause and effect. In the West "coincidences" are popularly discounted as chance happenings.

The concept of synchronicity was developed largely by Jung, who credited Albert Einstein as his inspiration. Einstein and Jung met on several occasions during Einstein's professorships in Zurich, Switzerland, in 1909 to 1910 and 1912 to 1913. At that time Einstein was developing his theory of relativity; Jung was inspired to consider a possible relativity of time as well as space.

Later, in the mid-1920s, as Jung was probing the phenomena of the collective unconscious, he encountered numerous synchronicities he could not explain. They were, he said, "'coincidences' which were connected so meaningfully that their 'chance' concurrence would represent a degree of improbability that would have to be expressed by an astronomical figure" (*Synchronicity,* 1952). As an example he cited incidents that happened to the wife of a patient: Upon the deaths of her mother and grandmother, birds gathered outside the windows of the death-chamber. Jung noted the connection of birds to the soul or to messengers of the gods in various mythologies.

In 1930 Jung first used the term "synchronicity," in his memorial address for Richard Wilhelm, who translated the *I Ching* into German. (Jung was fascinated by the patterns found in divination systems such as the *I Ching,* astrology, numerology, and the like.) Years later Jung equated synchronicity with Tao.

In further developing the concept, Jung was greatly aided and influenced by the Viennese physicist Wolfgang Pauli, a Nobel Laureate and associate of Einstein, who proved the existence of non-local causality. Pauli sought out Jung for psychotherapy in 1928. Their ensuing relationship led to a collaborative authorship of *The Interpretation and Nature of the Psyche* (1952), of which Jung's essay, *Synchronicity,* forms the second part.

Jung said synchronicity can be found in events that are meaningfully but not causally related (that is, do not coincide in time and space), as well as in events that do coincide in time and space and have meaningful psychological connections. In addition, synchronicity links the material world to the psychic; synchronistic events, he said, "rest on an archetypal foundation."

Jung applied the term "synchronicity" to various psychological and parapsychological phenomena, such as parapsychologist J. B. Rhine's ESP card guessing experiments at Duke University, which normally would not be considered acausal today. In his own experiment with horoscopes, Jung proposed synchronicity as an explanation for the connection between birth signs and choice of spouses. He drew severe criticism because he relied on subjects biased in favor of astrology.

Synchronicity increasingly is coming to light in the modern research of psychologists, parapsychologists, and scientists on the nature of consciousness. The validities of findings in each discipline are frequently and dramatically underscored by the fact that their complimentary or nearly identical conclusions have been derived independently of each other. Similarities between quantum physics and Eastern mystical thought have been pointed out, as in Fritjof Capra's *The Tao of Physics* (1984), while the parallels between them and the findings of Jungian psychology are verified by mythologists, most notably Joseph Campbell.

In *Synchronicity: The Bridge Between Matter and Mind* (1987), F. David Peat cites the neural research of Eric Kandel, whose studies of the sea slug demonstrate Kandel's theory that the human brain is "structurally unfolding" during each moment of the day. Kandel suggests that this process takes place "from a background of active information which is present both in its own structure and in the external environment." The result, he says, is an "eternally fresh brain." Moreover, the brain is not only receptive in the process, but simultaneously "acts upon the environment to change it and to create a new 'reality.'" Completing the circle, the new reality acts back upon the brain through "a constant process of formation and information." This has profound implications; for the brain's structuring of reality includes not only physical actions but also human relationships, the nature of society, and every person's self-image.

Peat observes that synchronicity appears naturally to a mind that is constantly sensitive to change. As we simultaneously act and react, creativity is energized in our personal synthesis. Synchronicity thus makes integration possible between the analytic and the more heuristic approaches to reality; subjective meaning of phenomena is combined with objective explanations.

Synchronicity also sheds new light on Platonic dualism, which separates body and spirit. This dualism has contributed to many contemporary problems in Western society, as may be seen in materialism, in allopathic medicine's disregard for the influence of the mind in illness and disease, and in the destruction of the environment. An understanding of synchronicity can foster a more holistic viewpoint characteristic of Eastern thought.

Modern interest in syncronicity is appropriate, since even rudimentary awareness of the phenomenon sensitizes a person to the realities and possibilities of universal harmonies and complementariness, even where none was once thought possible. The resulting openness to alternative worldviews could lay a philosophical foundation, if not also a theological framework, for new political, cultural, and even ecumenical unities. See **Jung, Carl Gustav.**

Sources: David Bohm and F. David Peat. *Science, Order and Creativity.* New York: Bantam, 1987; "Beyond Relativity and Quantum Theory." Interview with David Bohm. *Psychological Perspectives* 19, no. 1 (Spring-Summer 1988): 25–43; "Consciousness and the New Quantum Psychologies." *Psychological Perspectives* 19, no. 1 (Spring-Summer 1988): 4–13; Nick Herbert. *Quantum Reality.* New York: Doubleday, 1985; C. G. Jung. *Synchronicity.* From *Collected Works.* Vol. 13. 1952. Princeton, NJ: University of Princeton Press, 1973; *The I Ching or Book of Changes.* German translation by Richard Wilhelm, rendered into English by Carey F. Baynes. Forward by C. G. Jung. 3d ed. Princeton, NJ: University of Princeton Press, 1967; C. A. Meier. "Science and Synchronicity." *Psychological Perspectives* 19, no. 2 (Fall-Winter, 1988): 322; F. David Peat. "Divine Contenders: Wolfgang Pauli and the Symmetry of the World." *Psychological Perspectives* 19, no. 1 (Spring-Summer 1988): 14–24; F. David Peat. *Synchronicity: The Bridge Between Matter and Mind.* New York: Bantam, 1987; Andrew Samuels, Bani Shorter, and Fred Plaut. *A Critical Dictionary of Jungian Analysis.* London: Routledge & Kegan Paul, 1986.

T

T'ai Chi Ch'uan

See **Tai Ji Chuan.**

Tai Ji Chuan (also Tai Chi Ch'uan and T'ai Chi Ch'uan)

A major style of "soft," or internal, Chinese boxing (Kung Fu). *Tai Ji Chuan,* the more recent and more correct phonetic spelling, means "grand or great ultimate fist." It is popular in the West as a form of moving meditation, exercise, and stress reducer. It is steeped in Taoist philosophy and is characterized by slow, fluidic, and continuous movements of the body. Tai Ji stresses harmony with nature and generates physical, psychological, and emotional benefits.

Tai Ji draws on centuries of early Chinese and Taoist philosophies concerning the union of breathing, movement, and meditation as a means to health, longevity, immortality, and, later, as a principle of martial arts. Perhaps the earliest precursor of Tai Ji dates to around 2700 B.C., when Huang Ti, the Yellow Emperor, began to practice a form of exercise called Daoyin (*dao* means "guide" and *yin* means "leading") for longevity. The exercises, also called T'u Na (for "exhale" and "inhale"), combined breathing with movement of the limbs designed to increase oxygen circulation and flush poisons out of the body. Huang Ti was advised by the immortal sage Kuang

Cheng-tze to sit quietly with a peaceful mind. Thus, through exercise and meditation, Huang Ti is said to have reigned for one hundred years, during which he had many wives. He allegedly achieved immortality.

Tai Ji itself was developed in the thirteenth century by Chang San-feng, a Taoist monk, who is said to have been inspired by watching a snake and crane fight. The snake avoided the crane by twisting and turning. According to different versions of the story, Chang San-feng either devised Tai Ji as a method of combat or intended it as a health-promoting discipline complementary to meditation. Tai Ji is still most effective when practiced in conjunction with sitting meditation.

Tai Ji is based on the Taoist philosophy of living in harmony with nature and going with natural flows of energy. The *Tao Teh Ching,* the central text of Taoism, states that soft overcomes hard, and emphasizes the unity of mind and body, which in Chinese alchemy is essential to longevity and immortality. As a "soft" form of Kung Fu, Tai Ji relies on internal power (*qi,* the universal life force), rather than on the external power of muscles, as in the "hard" forms of Kung Fu.

Tai Ji consists of various physical postures and movements called the Form. Some of the movements are adapted from animals and birds—such as "Bring Tiger to the Mountain" and "Snake Creeps Down"—the origins of which date to at least the time of the great Taoist philosopher Chuang Tzu, c. 200 B.C. Some teachers stress formality in movements, while others do not. The body remains soft and springy, and the movements are slow and fluid, as though one is either floating or moving through viscous liquid. As one moves one is aware of slow-motion waves of energy (qi) interacting throughout the body. A high degree of concentration is required, but with practice it becomes effortless.

Tai Ji facilitates the flow of qi through the body. Qi exists as yang, a masculine energy, and yin, a female energy. Both must be in balance in an environment and organism for health and happiness. Yang is pulled down from the heavens and yin is pulled up from the earth through breathing techniques. "Breathing through the feet" is important to Tai Ji, and is based on the works of Chuang Tzu, who said that "The breathing of the true man comes from his heels, while men generally breathe only from their throats."

Qi is circulated throughout the body in eight psychic channels and twelve meridians associated with various organs. Its flow is the basis of internal power, which is controlled through the *dantian,* the central energy center located about two inches below the navel. Through Chu-Gung, the advanced teachings of Tai Ji, one learns to become aware of and use this power instinctively. It is a state of "not doing" or "no mind," in which one lets go of the mind and lets the body react to energy flows.

Push Hands are movements done with a partner, in which one learns balancing and counterbalancing of forces.

The practice of Tai Ji gradually dissolves blockages of qi energy within the body, and between the body and the environment. As a result one maintains better health. There are specific Tai Ji techniques for massage (similar to acupressure, only lacking specific pressure points); the prevention and healing of burns; and energy transfer healing. See **Bodywork.** Tai Ji also is said to enhance lucid dreaming. See **Dreams.**

In Chinese tradition Tai Ji is practiced outdoors at sunrise and sunset.

As a form of combat, Tai Ji relies on using the energy of the opponent to defend oneself. The fighter remains relaxed and still. When the opponent moves, the fighter absorbs the opponent's energy and repulses it. Twists and turns are used to avoid strikes. See **Martial arts; Meditation; Qi Gong; Taoism; Universal life force.**

Sources: Milton Friedman. "Chungliang Al Huang: A Master of Moving Meditation." *New Realities* 9, no. 5 (May/June 1989): 10–20; Bob Klein. *Movements of Magic: The Spirit of T'ai-Chi-Ch'uan.* North Hollywood, CA: Newcastle Publishing, 1984; Peter Lewis. *Martial Arts of the Orient.* New York: Gallery Books, 1985; Da Liu. *T'ai Chi Ch'uan and Meditation.* New York: Schocken Books, 1986.

Talisman

An object, drawing, or symbol believed to be endowed with supernatural or magical power, which then confers its power upon its possessor. In occult lore talismans also attract good luck, success, fortune, health, fecundity, virility, love, and power. The use of talismans has been universal throughout history.

Talismans are active objects—they are transformers and lightning rods. Talismans often are confused with amulets, which protect and ward off, and are passive. An example of a talisman is the magic hat, which renders the wearer invisible, or transports the wearer wherever he or she wishes in the blink of an eye. Magic swords, such as King Arthur's Excalibur and Siegfried's Nothung, are talismans, as are magic wands and magic lamps. In the Middle Ages, holy objects and relics were prized as talismans for their alleged curative powers. During the Renaissance alchemists sought the talisman of the philosopher's stone, the elusive substance or object that would enable them to transmute base metals into silver or gold, or transmute consciousness into a higher state. Precious stones also are considered to be talismans, some amulets as well.

Talismans, like amulets, have provided people with tools in their attempt to control the forces of nature. A talisman can be virtually any object, but generally is endowed with power through one of three ways: from nature (such as a gem); from God, the gods, or supernatural entities (such as Excalibur); and by creation in precise magic ritual (such as a wand). Many rituals exist in the grimoires, or textbooks, of ceremonial magic for the creation of talismans for any purpose, such as acquiring wealth or making good speeches. Such talismans usually are seals or inscriptions made upon metal, stone, parchment, or wax. See **Amulet; Magic.**

Sources: Francis Barrett. *The Magus.* 1801. Reprint. Secaucus, NJ: Citadel Press, 1967; E. A. Wallis Budge. *Amulets and Superstitions.* 1930. New York: Dover Publications, 1978; Richard Cavendish. *The Black Arts.* New York: Perigee Books, 1967; Emile Grillot de Givry. *Witchcraft, Magic and Alchemy.* New York: Houghton Mifflin, 1931; Maria Leach, ed., and Jerome Fried, assoc. ed. *Funk & Wagnalls Standard Dictionary of Folklore, Mythology, and Legend.* San Francisco: Harper & Row, 1979.

Taoism

System of mysticism and philosophy, and the only indigenous religion of China, based on the *Tao Teh Ching,* a slim work attributed to the legendary mystic, Lao

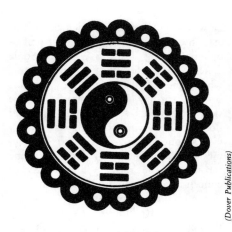

(Dover Publications)

Yin and yang symbol with trigrams

Tzu (born c. 604 B.C.). Scholars, however, date the work to the fourth century B.C. *Tao* means "the Way." Taoism, expanded upon by various sages, provided a metaphysics that was lacking in Confucianism, and facilitated the emergence of neo-Confucianism during the Sung Dynasty from A.D. 960 to 1279. It also helped the entrance of Buddhism into China, and the development of Ch'an (Zen) Buddhism. With Confucianism, Taoism forms the central Chinese thought. It has found popularity in the West.

Little is known about Lao Tzu; there is controversy as to whether or not he existed. According to the biographer Ssuma Ch'ien (145 B.C. –86 B.C.), Lao-tzu came from the southern state of Ch'u, which is now the provinces of Hunan and Hupei. His family name was Li, his personal name was Erh, his courtesy name was Po-yang, and his posthumous name was Tan. He worked as Custodian of the Imperial Archives of the Chou House in the city of Loyang. He reportedly granted an interview to Confucius, who was some fifty years younger, and came to him with questions about rituals.

Lao-tzu's cultivation of Tao allegedly enabled him to live for more than two hundred years, outliving Confucius by 129 years, according to Ssuma Ch'ien. He retired from his job when the Chou House began to decline. As he took the pass westward, Hsin Yi, the warden of the pass, asked him to write a book for his enlightenment. Lao-tzu wrote a two-part book on the meaning of the *Tao* (the Way) and the *Teh* (Virtue or Power), totaling 5,350 words. Initially, the book was called *Lao Tzu*. The name was changed to the *Tao Teh Ching*, or "Classic of the Way of Its Virtue," sometime during the Western Han Dynasty (202 B.C.–A.D. 9). Approximately one thousand commentaries have since been written on the work, the most notable by Han Fei Tzu (d. 233 B.C.), Chuang Tzu (369 B.C.–286 B.C.), Ho Shang Kung (d. 159 B.C.), and Wang Pi (A.D. 226–249). Ho Shang Kung's commentary was the first in detail and comprehensiveness, and was a major influence in the later development of the religion of Taoism.

Taoism is permeated with mysticism. Tao is the Absolute Truth, the Ultimate Reality, the Eternal Ground of Being. It is the origin of all temporal phenomena, including the One, which is the creative principle of Tao and preceded all other things. Unlike Logos, the personal Godhead of Christianity, or Heaven, the remote but purposeful Supreme Being of Confucianism, Tao is impersonal. Tao has a dual nature. The Eternal Tao is unnameable, indescribable, and beyond discussion. It is the mysterious essence of the universe, unborn, nonbeing, above and beyond heaven, above and beyond the universe. Manifest Tao is the named, being.

Within Tao are two complementary principles, the yin, or passive/female/earth principle, and the yang, or active/male/heaven principle. Yin and yang are in constant interaction, ebb and flow, and their balance governs the harmony and well-being of all things.

This key principle of Taoism is expressed in its symbol, the *Tai Ji Tu* ("Diagram of the Supreme Ultimate"): two fishlike figures, one black and one white, contained in a circle. The white figure represents yang and the black figure represents yin. Within each figure is a dot of the opposite color, the lesser yang and lesser yin, demonstrating that each opposing force contains its opposite. The figures are separate yet originate from each other and flow into each other in a perpetual cycle. The Tai Ji Tu shows that these fundamental forces are in continual opposition and interaction, which nourishes all things. The Tai Ji Tu also represents the human being, who is comprised of light and dark.

According to legend, the symbol originated in prehistoric times, though there is no evidence to support that contention. The earliest written description of yin and yang is found in the divinatory book the *I Ching*, which tells of the Great Primal Beginning generating two primary forces, which in turn generate four images, which in turn generate the eight trigrams upon which the *I Ching* is based. See *I Ching*.

Diagrams to express the concept appeared by the Sung Dynasty. An important work was the *Tai Ji Tu Shuo* ("The Diagram of the Supreme Ultimate Explained") of the neo-Confucian philosopher Chou Tun-i (1017-1073), who said the diagram symbolized the production and evolution of all things.

Teh, the virtue or power of Tao, is expressed in *wu wei*, which is nonaction in terms of noninterference. Nature is spontaneous and effortless, and Wu-Wei constitutes going with the flow. Thus in Taoism one avoids aggression and challenges, and instead seeks passivity. Toughness and aggression may be overcome with softness, gentleness, meekness and humility: yang is countered and balanced with yin.

Tao is often identified with Nature, and the same passive principle is applied. One does not seek to control Nature, but to have respect for it and bend to its forces. See **Feng shui.**

Spiritual purification in Taoism comes through purity of heart and avoidance or elimination of desires, which enable the seeker to embrace the One. The best way to accomplish this is through meditation. Taoist meditation is characterized by several features: (1) concentration; (2) breath control; (3) purification of heart and mind; (4) practice of Wu-Wei in daily life; (5) the ability to play the female, or yin, role during mystical union with Heaven, the yang principle.

Breath control is of great importance, as it is in yoga. Lao Tzu favored natural breathing, which induces tenderness, the essential characteristic of life (as opposed to rigidity, the characteristic of death). Lao Tzu considered the infant to be the perfect symbol of Tao, and said it was highly desirable to breathe as an infant does. Later Taoists advocated "fetus breathing," which is so faint that it is nearly extinguished, and which when done precedes the mystical state of *samadhi.*

The return to a newborn state as a way to Tao is expressed in Taoist yoga, which advises (for men) the sublimation of the vital male force at age sixteen, when it is at its apex of strength, into *hsien t'ien,* the prenatal vital force, which leads to spiritual immortality.

Lao Tzu saw immortality in spiritual terms, but some later Taoists looked for physical immortality. From the time of Chuang Tzu to the century following, there was great interest in alchemy and the search for an elixir or yoga of immortality. The elixir specialists, *Fang Shih,* enjoyed great prestige.

Taoism has had a significant influence on Zen Buddhism meditation practices. See **Alchemy; Meditation; Mysticism; Yoga; Zen.**

Sources: Yong Choon Kim. *Oriental Thought.* Totowa, NJ: Rowman and Littlefield, 1973; Da Liu. *T'ai Chi Ch'uan and Meditation.* New York: Schocken Books, 1986; Stephen Mitchell, trans. and intro. *Tao Te Ching.* New York: Harper & Row, 1988; Henry Wei. *The Guiding Light of La Tzu.* Wheaton, IL: The Theosophical Publishing House, 1982; Holmes Welch. *Taoism: The Parting of the Way.* Boston: Beacon Press, 1966.

Tarot

A type of card deck used for divination, self-help, spiritual growth, and the cultivation of intuition and psychic ability. The term "Tarot" is a French derivative of the Italian *tarocchi,* meaning "triumphs" or "trumps."

The Tarot deck consists of seventy-eight cards divided into two parts, the twenty-two-card Major Arcana, or Trumps, and the fifty-six-card Minor Arcana, which has four suits of ten cards each and resembles today's deck of playing cards. The four suits traditionally are wands (which correspond to clubs in playing cards), swords (spades), cups (hearts), and pentacles (diamonds). Each suit has one additional court card not contained in playing cards, the page.

The original purpose and the development of the Tarot are unknown. Numerous theories, many of them fanciful, have been advanced. The earliest surviving records of cards of any type date to the early fourteenth century. Cards that may have been Tarot were created in 1392 for King Charles VI of France by a painter, Jacquemin Gringonneur. The earliest known Tarot cards date to the early fifteenth century in Milan and were designed for the Visconti and Visconti-Sforza families. These early decks were of only the Major Arcana, whose unnumbered images, possibly allegories, represented death, fortune, wisdom, virtues, sciences and arts, and so on. At some

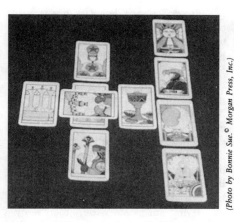

Aquarian Tarot cards in Celtic cross spread

point the Tarot cards probably were merged with playing cards in use throughout Europe, and by the mid-eighteenth century, the seventy-eight-card Tarot deck had become standardized in the "Marseilles" deck, still in use today. The Major Arcana had names and numbers. The cards were used in a game.

At about the mid-eighteenth century, Antoine Court de Gebelin (1725–1784), a French archaeologist and Egyptologist, put forward the theory that the Tarot cards were fragments of ancient Egyptian esoteric wisdom contained in the mythical *Book of Thoth*. This theory had no basis in fact whatsoever—the Rosetta Stone had yet to be discovered—but it caught the popular fancy. The theory was further promoted by a popular fortune-teller, Etteilla, the pseudonym of a Parisian wig-maker named Alliette. Etteilla used the Tarot in fortune-telling. In the nineteenth century, French occultist Eliphas Lévi (1810–1875), the pseudonym of Alphonse Louis Constant, linked the Tarot to the Kabbalah and corresponded the Major Arcana to the letters of the Hebrew alphabet, another spurious interpretation.

In 1910 English occultist Arthur Edward Waite published his interpretation of the Tarot deck, with images designed by fellow occultist Pamela Colman Smith. Waite believed the Tarot cards were no older than the fourteenth century, but their symbols were much older. He said he restored the symbols to their original meanings. He drew in part on the Hermetic Kabbalah, a blend of true Kabbalah and Hermeticism favored by occultists, including the Hermetic Order of the Golden Dawn, of which Waite was a member.

The Rider-Waite deck, as it became known, set the standard for nearly all Tarot decks to follow. Unlike earlier decks the Minor Arcana pip cards were represented pictorially. Since then hundreds of Tarot decks have been designed and published, and many have broken away from traditional symbolism and names.

Tarot cards are read in rituals of shuffling and laying out cards in various spreads. Each position in a spread holds a particular significance. Each card has a different meaning, which is influenced by its position: upright or reversed. In addition, each suit of the Minor Arcana has a meaning. Traditionally, they are: swords—ill fortune or strife; pentacles—financial and material success; cups—good fortune and love; and wands—enterprise and distinction. The Major Arcana have been subject to broad interpretations. Essentially, they are archetypes, and their sequence from 0 to 21 seems to represent the soul's journey to self-realization, the process of individuation or becoming whole, or the alchemical process of spiritual transmutation resulting in the philosopher's stone.

Like the *I Ching*, the Tarot should not be read for definitive "yes" or "no" answers, but for a reflection of existing energies and directions concerning a given situation. Though each card and its position has a unique meaning, the entire layout must be considered synergistically. The Tarot is best used as a tool for seeing one's life from new perspectives. Skillful reading requires good intuition. Tarot cards—particularly the Major Arcana—also are used in meditation and creative visualization exercises as a means of personal growth. The Hermetic Kabbalah as a path of Tarot study continues to draw many students. See **Archetypes; Divination**. Compare to *I Ching*.

Sources: Joseph Campbell and Richard Roberts. *Tarot Revelations.* San Anselmo, CA: Vernal Equinox Press, 1979; Alfred Douglas. *The Tarot: The Origins, Meaning and Use of the Cards.* New York: Taplinger, 1972; Eden Gray. *A Complete Guide to the Tarot.* New York: Bantam Books, 1972; Rosemary Ellen Guiley. *The Mystical Tarot.* New York: New American Library, 1991; Stuart R. Kaplan. *The Encyclopedia of Tarot.* New York: U.S. Games Systems, 1978; Genie Z. Laborde, Ph.D. "Tarot as a Hook to Fishing." *New Realities* 5, no. 2 (1984): 50–54; Sallie Nichols. *Jung and Tarot: An Archetypal Journey.* York Beach, ME: Samuel Weiser, 1980; Carl Sargent. *Personality, Divination, and the Tarot.* Rochester, VT: Destiny Books, 1988; Arthur Edward Waite. *The Pictorial Key to the Tarot.* Secaucus, NJ: Citadel Press, 1959; Jan Woudhuysen. *Tarot Therapy: A New Approach to Self Exploration.* First published as *Tarotmania.* 1979. New ed. Los Angeles: Jeremy P. Tarcher, 1988.

Tart, Charles T.

See **Altered states of consciousness**.

Teilhard de Chardin, Pierre (1881–1955)

Theologian, philosopher, and paleontologist, whose religiously oriented concepts of cosmic evolution are influential in New Age thought. His key concept is that the universe has its own evolutionary history, and that an increasingly complex consciousness is an integral part of the evolution.

Pierre Teilhard de Chardin was born on May 1, 1881, in Sarcenat, France. He was the son of a gentleman farmer; his mother was the great-grandniece of the French novelist known as Voltaire. Early on he had an interest in geology. He began boarding at the Jesuit College of Mongre at age ten, and entered the Society of Jesus in Aix-en-Provence at age eighteen. He was ordained in 1911 and remained a Jesuit for the rest of his life, despite controversy with religious authorities, especially concerning his views related to Darwinism.

From age twenty-four to twenty-seven, Teilhard served as professor at the Jesuit College in Cairo. During World War I he was a stretcher bearer, and was awarded the Legion of Honor and a military medal for his bravery at the front. After the war he taught at the Catholic Institute of Paris. He earned his doctorate in geology in 1922.

In 1923 he took his first trip to China for paleontological and geological research, and returned to his teaching post in Paris in 1924. His teachings on evolution and Original Sin were not well received in the anti-Modernist climate fostered by Pope Pius XI, and he was ordered to repudiate some of his statements. In 1925 he was ordered to remove himself from France.

Teilhard returned to China, where he lived until 1946. He participated in the archaeological excavations at Choukoutien in north China, which led to the discovery of Peking Man. His work in China inspired his examination of evolution, and he began work on one of his best-known books, *The Phenomenon of Man* (1955). The manuscript was completed in 1938, but, like all of his major writings, was not published until after his death.

In 1946 Teilhard returned to France, but was barred from teaching at the College de France. Frustrated, he accepted a research position at the Wenner-Gren Foundation in New York City in December 1951. In 1954 he sought but was denied permission to return to France permanently. He suffered a stroke and died on April 10, 1955.

Among his other major works are *The Divine Milieu* (1957); *The Future of Man* (1959); *Human Energy* (1962); *The Activation of Energy* (1963); *Hymn of the Universe* (1964); and *Christianity and Evolution* (1969).

The church's opposition to his writings continued posthumously, and in 1962 the church issued a monitum (warning) against the uncritical acceptance of his views. Teilhard also has been challenged by scientists and philosophers.

As a young man Teilhard was profoundly influenced by Henri Bergson's *Creative Evolution,* which argued against dualism in favor of an evolving universe. Teilhard was first to perceive of a cosmic evolution in four phases: galactic, Earth, life, and human. Central to his concept of evolution is the integration of the psychic with the physical. Evolution implies the law of *complexification,* which means that as physical matter becomes more complex, so does consciousness, which is intrinsic to all life forms. Thus the human race has arisen from, and is connected to, all other life forms on Earth, both physically and psychically. In its human form, evolution becomes conscious of itself. The convergence of various human groups progressively will shape the ultrahuman, a process now underway. The ultimate goal is a convergence toward Christ, the "Omega point" at which human consciousness finds the ultimate integrity and unity.

Teilhard used such phrases as "cosmogenesis," for the development of a world with humankind at its center; "noosphere," a collective human consciousness within the biosphere of the Earth; "noogenesis," for the growth of the human mind; "hominization" and "ultra-hominization," for the future stages of humankind's transcendent humanization. According to Teilhard the increasing numbers of humans, and the improving communications, are fusing all parts of the noosphere together. As a result humankind will achieve more integrated and intense mental activity. This will facilitate the upward climb to higher stages of hominization. However, Teilhard said, the evolutionary process requires more intense psychic energy than that exerted during most of the twentieth century.

One of Teilhard's greatest contributions was his emphasis on the cosmic Christ, a shift from the dominant redemption orientation of Christianity to a creation orientation. He identified the cosmic Christ as a dimension of the evolving universe. He termed humankind's psychic identity with all forms of life the "cosmic sense," with which human beings see their function in the evolutionary scheme. As a conscious cocreator, people can direct renewed energy to the developmental process.

Teilhard also saw science as an essentially mystical discipline, and perceived the need for science and religion to reconverge.

Despite his great vision, Teilhard did not see beyond the prevailing thought of his day that human exploitation of the planet was essentially a good thing. Rather, he saw the subordination of the Earth to humankind as the fulfillment of the Earth's true meaning, and necessary to the glorious fulfillment of human evolution to ultrahuman. Teilhard showed a certain disdain for those individuals who advocated living in harmony with the Earth. In Teilhard's view the advances of technology, and the growth of the industrial state, provided good energy to be harnessed. He was confident that the industrial sources would find solutions to whatever problems arose with the Earth's shrinking resources.

Nonetheless, Teilhard's thought can be applied to modern ecological concerns. If humankind is psychically connected to all other life forms and has the power to become a cocreator in the evolutionary process and direct further upward development, then it behooves the human race to cease the wanton exploitation of the Earth, its resources, and other life forms—the very basis of humankind's present evolutionary status. To destroy these things is to destroy an intrinsic part of ourselves, and perhaps prevent the attainment of the Omega point. Teilhard did perceive modern humanity to be at a biological turning point, "where it must either lose all belief in the universe or quite resolutely worship it." See **Creation spirituality; Planetary consciousness.**

Sources: Thomas Berry. *Teilhard in the Ecological Age.* Monograph, Teilhard Studies No. 7. Chambersburg, PA: ANIMA Books, 1982; Donald P. Gray. *The One and the Many: Teilhard de Chardin's Vision of Unity.* New York: Herder & Herder, 1969; John and Mary Evelyn Grim. *Teilhard de Chardin: A Short Biography.* Monograph, Teilhard Studies No. 11. Chambersburg, PA: ANIMA Books, 1984; Teilhard de Chardin. *The Divine Milieu.* 1957. Rev. ed. New York: Harper & Row, 1968; Teilhard de Chardin. *The Future of Man.* 1959. New York: Harper & Row, 1969; Teilhard de Chardin. *The Phenomenon of Man.* 1955. New York: Harper & Row, 1965.

Te Kwon Do

See **Martial arts.**

Telekinesis

See **Teleportation.**

Telepathic hypnosis (also hypnosis-at-a-distance)

A combination of telepathy and hypnotism, in which a person may be induced into a hypnotic trance by the projection of thought over any distance. The term was coined in the late nineteenth century by Frederic W. H. Myers, one of the founders of the Society for Psychical Research in London. Telepathic hypnosis has been of particular interest to Russian scientists.

The ability to hypnotize a person at a distance was an early discovery of animal magnetists and mesmerists in Europe. As early as 1818, D. Velinski, a Russian surgeon and professor of physiology at the Imperial Academy in St. Petersburg, documented experiments that demonstrated how a magnetist could act on a patient at a distance simply by concentrating his thought. Velinski considered this a dangerous practice, and urged his colleagues not to use it for anything other than healing.

In 1845 another Russian, a hypnotist named Andrey Ivanovitch Pashkov, documented his telepathic hypnosis of a woman who lived three hundred miles away. At his command she fell into a somnambulistic sleep, which alleviated her rheumatoid arthritis.

In the late 1880s in France, "Leonie B.," a celebrated French medium, was telepathically hypnotized on numerous occasions by psychologists Pierre Janet and M. Gibert. On several occasions in Le Havre in 1886, Gibert demonstrated that he could telepathically hypnotize Leonie from a distance of about two-thirds of a mile. The experiments were observed and documented by Myers.

Beginning in 1924 Russian scientists conducted extensive experiments with telepathic hypnosis, much of it under cover during the repressive Stalinist regime. The experiments have focused on manipulation of behavior and inducement of pain, and have been led by L. L. Vasiliev, who said he successfully hypnotized a subject more than 1,700 kilometers away to fall asleep and awaken on command.

The question remains as to whether a person may be telepathically hypnotized without being aware of it. Russian scientists say they may be, although the phenomenon may be limited to a narrow segment of the population. In general, a subject must give conscious or unconscious approval to being hypnotized. It is estimated that about four in one hundred persons may be put into deep hypnotic trance; it is these, Soviet scientists say, who are most vulnerable to telepathic hypnosis without knowing it. Even so, it would be virtually impossible to command such people to perform acts they would not do when conscious, either for dislike or moral objections. If telepathic hypnosis is feasible, advocates say it may prove useful to the military for espionage and warfare.

In the 1978 world chess championship, held at Baguio, the Philippines, Victor Korchnoi, a Soviet defector who was challenging champion Anatoly Karpov, claimed he was the victim of "telehypnosis." Korchnoi said he was hypnotized to lose the game by a Dr. Vladimir Zoukhar, a Russian hypnotist and parapsychologist, who sat in the fourth row of spectators and stared at him throughout the match. See **Hypnosis; Telepathy.**

Sources: Eric Cuddon. *The Meaning and Practice of Hypnosis.* New York: Citadel Press, 1965; Martin Ebon. *Psychic Warfare: Threat or Illusion?* New York: McGraw-Hill, 1983; Ron McRae. *Mind Wars.* New York: St. Martin's Press, 1984; Frederic W. H. Myers. *Human Personality and Its Survival of Bodily Death.* Vols. 1 and 2. 1903. New ed. New York: Longmans, Green & Co., 1954; Sheila Ostrander and Lynn Schroeder. *Psychic Discoveries Behind the Iron Curtain.* Englewood Cliffs, NJ: Prentice-Hall, 1970; Russell Targ and Keith Harary. *The Mind Race.* New York: Villard Books, 1984.

Telepathy

The mind-to-mind communication of thoughts, ideas, feelings, sensations, and mental images. Telepathy is described in writings and oral lore around the globe. In some tribal societies, such as the Aborigines of Australia, it is an accepted human faculty; in other societies it is considered the province of mystics and psychics. Telepathy has not been proved scientifically, though it has been studied by numerous psychical researchers.

"Telepathy" derives from the Greek terms *tele* ("distant") and *pathe* ("occurrence" or "feeling"). It was coined in 1882 by British psychical researcher Frederic W. H. Myers, a founder of the Society for Psychical Research (SPR). Myers thought "telepathy" expressed the nature of the phenomenon better than other terms, such as the French "*communication de pensées,*" "thought-transference," and "thought-reading."

Research interest in telepathy began with mesmerism in the late eighteenth century. Magnetists discovered that telepathy was among the so-called "higher phenomena" observed in many magnetized subjects, who read the thoughts of the magnetist and carried out unspoken instructions.

Later, psychologists and psychiatrists observed telepathy occurring with their patients. Sigmund Freud experienced it so often that he finally had to address it, terming it a regressive, primitive faculty lost in the course of evolution, but which still had the ability to manifest under certain conditions. Psychiatrist Carl G. Jung took it more seriously, considering it a function of synchronicity. Psychologist and philosopher William James also was interested in telepathy, and tried to encourage more research of it.

With the founding of the SPR in 1884 and the American Society for Psychical Research (ASPR) in 1885, telepathy became the first psychic phenomenon to be studied scientifically. Early tests were simple: A sender in one room tried to transmit a two-digit number, a taste, or a visual image to a receiver in another room. French physiologist Charles Richet introduced mathematical chance to tests, and also discovered that telepathy occurred independent of hypnotism. With the introduction of chance, tests grew more sophisticated. Interest in telepathy increased following World War I, as thousands of bereaved turned to Spiritualism to attempt to communicate with the dead. Telepathic parlor games called "willing" became popular, and mass telepathy experiments were attempted in the United States and Britain.

Research has shown that telepathy most often occurs spontaneously in crisis situations, in which an individual becomes aware of danger to another person at a distance. The information comes in different ways: as fragments of thoughts that "something is wrong"; in dreams, visions, hallucinations, and mental images; in clairaudience; and in words that pop into the mind. The individual may be prompted to action, such as suddenly changing travel plans or contacting the other person. Some cases involve apparent telepathy between humans and animals. See **Animal psi.**

Telepathy appears to be closely tied to emotions, both of the sender and receiver. In cases collected most receivers are women, perhaps because women tend to be more closely linked to their emotions and intuition than men. Geriatric telepathy is fairly common, perhaps because the physical senses become impaired as age advances. Telepathy can be induced in the dream state. It appears to have some biological connections: blood volume changes during telepathic sending, and electroencephalogram monitors show that recipients' brain waves change to match those of senders. Telepathy is adversely affected by dissociative drugs and positively affected by caffeine.

In 1930 American parapsychologist J. B. Rhine began his famous extrasensory perception (ESP) tests at Duke University in North Carolina, using playing cards and special decks with symbols. See

ESP cards. Rhine discovered that it was often difficult to determine whether information was communicated through telepathy, clairvoyance, or precognitive clairvoyance. He concluded that telepathy and clairvoyance are essentially the same psychic function manifested in different ways. Rhine also found that telepathy is not affected by distance or obstacles between sender and receiver.

Other tests have spanned thousands of miles. In 1971 astronaut Edgar D. Mitchell, aboard *Apollo 14,* conducted a telepathy experiment with four recipients on Earth 150,000 miles below. The experiment was not authorized by the National Aeronautics and Space Administration (NASA) and was not revealed until after the *Apollo 14* mission was completed. Mitchell concentrated on sequences of twenty-five random numbers. He completed two hundred sequences. Guessing forty correctly was mean chance. Mitchell said that two recipients had guessed fifty-one correctly, which far exceeded his expectations but nonetheless was only moderately significant.

Theories of Telepathy

Although various theories have been advanced over the centuries to explain how telepathy works, none is adequate. Telepathy, like other psychic phenomena, transcends time and space. The ancient Greek philosopher Democritus advanced wave and corpuscle theories. William Crookes, a nineteenth-century British chemist and physicist, believed telepathy rides on radio-like brain waves. Much later, in the twentieth century, Russian scientist L. L. Vasiliev proposed an electromagnetic theory. American psychologist Lawrence LeShan proposes that every person has his or her own reality, and that psychics and mystics share different realities, which enable them to access information not available to others. See **Ap-**

plied psi; Extraterrestrial encounters; Psi; Telepathic hypnosis.

Sources: J. Allen Boone. *Kinship with All Life.* New York: Harper & Row, 1954; Vincent and Margaret Gaddis. *The Curious World of Twins.* New York: Hawthorn Books, 1972; Eileen Garrett. *Telepathy.* New York: Creative Age Press, 1941; Alan Gauld. *The Founders of Psychical Research.* London: Routledge & Kegan Paul, 1968; Rosemary Ellen Guiley. *Moonscapes: A Celebration of Lunar Astronomy, Magic, Legend, and Lore.* New York: Prentice-Hall, 1991; Edmund Gurney, Frederic W. H. Myers, and Frank Podmore. *Phantasms of the Living.* London: Kegan Paul, Trench, Trubner & Co. Ltd., 1918; Budd Hopkins. *Intruders.* New York: Random House, 1987; Lawrence LeShan. *The Medium, the Mystic, and the Physicist: Toward a General Theory of the Paranormal.* New York: Viking Press, 1974; Edgar D. Mitchell. *Psychic Exploration: A Challenge for Science.* Edited by John White. New York: Paragon Books, 1974; Frederic W. H. Myers. *Human Personality and Its Survival of Bodily Death.* Vols. 1 and 2. 1903. New ed. New York: Longmans, Green & Co., 1954; J. B. Rhine. *New Frontiers of the Mind.* New York: Farrar & Reinhart, 1937; J. B. Rhine. *The Reach of the Mind.* New York: William Sloane Assoc., 1947; Gertrude Raffel Schmeidler and R. A. McConnell. *ESP and Personality Patterns.* New Haven, CT: Yale, 1958; Berthold Eric Schwarz. *Psychic Nexus: Psychic Phenomena in Psychiatry and Everyday Life.* New York: Van Nostrand Reinhold, 1980; Harold Sherman and Sir Hubert Wilkins. *Thoughts through Space.* Rev. ed. Amherst, WI: Amherst Press, 1983; Ian Stevenson. *Telepathic Impressions.* Charlottesville, VA: University Press of Virginia, 1970; Russell Targ and Harold Puthoff. *Mind-Reach: Scientists Look at Psychic Ability.* New York: Delacorte Press, 1977; Russell Targ and Keith Harary. *The Mind Race.* New York: Villard Books, 1984; Lyall Watson. *Beyond Supernature.* New York: Bantam Books, 1987; Debra H. Weiner and Dean I. Rudin, eds. *Research in Parapsychology.* Metuchen, NJ: Scarecrow Press, 1985; Joan Windsor. *The Inner Eye: Your Dreams Can Make You Psychic.* Englewood Cliffs, NJ: Prentice-Hall, 1985; Danah Zohar. *Through the Time Barrier: A Study in Precognition and Modern Physics.* London: William Heinemann Ltd., 1982.

Teleportation (also telekinesis)

The movement of bodies or objects over great distances; a form of psychokinesis (PK). Also, the passage of solid objects through matter by dematerialization and materialization. Teleportation allegedly is accomplished by an adept who combines methodic breathing and intense concentration with manipulation of universal forces of energy. It is ascribed to spiritual adepts during states of ecstasy when the body frees itself from gravity, levitates, and floats through the air, sometimes apparently traveling at great speed. Physical mediums during early Spiritualism featured teleportation of small objects (apports), which seemed to materialize suddenly in front of the sitters.

Apparent teleportation is a common phenomenon of poltergeist cases, where objects seem to materialize from nowhere or distant locations. American parapsychologist William G. Roll has theorized that such manifestations are part of the psychological side to poltergeist outbreaks. A strong neural discharge may combine two distant images so that physical and mental space become synonymous.

Teleportation, or the "apport phenomenon," as it is sometimes called, allegedly has been studied by the United States and Soviet governments for its potential in espionage operations. See **Apport; Materialization; Psychokinesis (PK); Sai Baba; Siddhis.**

Sources: Ormond McGill. *The Mysticism and Magic of India.* Cranbury, NJ: A. S. Barnes & Co., 1977; Ron McRae. *Mind*

Wars. New York: St. Martin's Press, 1984; Edgar D. Mitchell. *Psychic Exploration: A Challenge for Science*. Edited by John White. New York: Paragon Books, 1974; D. Scott Rogo. *Psychic Breakthroughs Today*. Wellingborough, Northamptonshire, England: The Aquarian Press, 1987; Russell Targ and Keith Harary. *The Mind Race*. New York: Villard Books, 1984; Benjamin B. Wolman, ed. *Handbook of Parapsychology*. New York: Van Nostrand Reinhold, 1977.

Tenzin Gyatso, His Holiness the Fourteenth Dalai Lama

See **Dalai Lama**.

Teresa of Avila, St. (1515–1582)

Spanish mystic and Carmelite nun, often known as "Teresa of Jesus" or the "Great St. Teresa," to distinguish her from another Carmelite nun, St. Therese of Lisieux (1873–1897), known as "The Little Flower." Teresa of Avila is one of the best-loved contemplative Christian saints.

She was born Teresa de Cepeda y Ahumada to a noble family on March 28, 1515, in or near Avila in Castile. Her mother died when she was fifteen, which upset her so much that her father sent her to an Augustinian convent in Avila. She stayed for a year and a half, and was brought home by her father when she fell ill. Her exposure to the monastic life convinced her she wanted to become a nun, but her father forbade it as long as he was living. At about age twenty or twenty-one, she left home secretly and entered the Incarnation of the Carmelite nuns in Avila. Her father dropped his opposition.

Teresa was plagued by ill health much of her life, and when serious illness once again befell her in 1538—it appears to have been malaria—her father took her from the convent and put her under the care of doctors. She remained ill, however, and undertook experimental cures given by a woman in the town of Becedas. These measures left her in a death-like coma for three days, and unable to walk for three years. During her illness and convalescence, she took to daily mental prayers, which in turn led to her experiences with mystical prayer. She attributed her recovery to St. Joseph.

In 1555 she experienced visions and revelations. In 1557, after a two-year gap, she experienced her first ecstasy, when she felt carried out of herself. After that she had many extraordinary mystical experiences, including visions of Christ and a sense of his presence at her side. She also had terrifying visions of hell, and once dismissed Satan by calling him "Goose!"

Teresa did not seek out these experiences, but resigned herself to God's will and considered them a divine blessing. She spent long periods in intense meditation, which she called the "prayer of quiet" and the "prayer of union." During these prayers she often fell into a trance, and at times entered upon mystical flights in which she felt as though her soul were lifted out of her body. She likened ecstasy to a "delectable death," saying that the soul becomes awake to God as never before when the faculties and senses are "dead."

In 1562, despite opposition, Teresa founded a convent in Avila with stricter rules than those which prevailed at Carmelite monasteries. She sought to establish a small community that would follow the Carmelite contemplative life, in particular unceasing prayer. In 1567 she was permitted to establish other convents, and went on to found sixteen others. She dedicated herself to reforming the Carmelite order. At age fifty-three she met the twenty-six-year-old John Yepes (later known as St. John of the Cross), who worked to reform the male Carmelite monasteries. After a period of turbulence within the Carmelites, from 1575 to

1580, the Discalced Reform was recognized as separate.

By 1582 Teresa had founded her seventeenth monastery, at Burgos. Her health was broken and she decided to return to Avila. The rough journey proved to be too much, and upon arriving at the convent, Teresa went straight to her deathbed. Three days later, on October 4, 1582, she died. The next day the Gregorian calendar went into effect, dropping ten days and making her death on October 14. Her feast day is October 15. Teresa was canonized in 1662 by Pope Gregory XV and was declared a Doctor of the Church—the first woman so honored—in 1970 by Pope Paul VI.

During Teresa's travels throughout Spain on her reform mission, she wrote a number of books, some of which have become spiritual classics. The first of those was *Life*, her autobiography, written in 1565. On November 18, 1572, Teresa experienced a spiritual marriage with Christ as bridegroom to the soul. One of the fruits of that marriage was a new outflowing from her pen: *The Way of Perfection* (1573), about the life of prayer, and *The Interior Castle* (1577), her best-known work, in which she presents a spiritual doctrine using a castle as the symbol of the interior life. The latter book was revealed to her in a vision on the eve of Trinity Sunday, 1577, in which she saw a crystal globe like a castle that had seven rooms; the seventh, in the center, held the King of Glory. One approached the center, which represents the Union with God, by going through the other rooms of Humility, Practice of Prayer, Meditation, Quiet, Illumination, and Dark Night. She often referred to Christ as the "heavenly bridegroom," but her later visions became less erotic and more religious in character.

Teresa's literary method of linking images has recently been found to be much more intricate and extensive than previously thought. Recent studies have found a timelessness to the writings of Teresa, and elements of feminist spirituality. However, it is also her life and her "centering prayer" that inspire; as she once said to her followers, "I will give you a living book." See **John of the Cross, St.; Levitation; Meditation; Mysticism; Prayer.**

Sources: Carmelite Studies: Centenary of St. Theresa, Catholic University Symposium, 1982, Institute for Carmelite Studies, 1984 IX, 227; John Ferguson. *An Illustrated Encyclopedia of Mysticism and the Mystery Religions*. New York: Seabury Press, 1976; F. C. Happold. *Mysticism: A Study and an Anthology*. Rev. ed. New York: Penguin, 1970; Robert Maynard Hutchins, ed. *Great Books of the Western World*. Chicago: Encyclopaedia Britannica, 1952; Louis Kronenberger, ed. *Atlantic Brief Lives*. Boston: Little, Brown, 1971; Willard Johnson. *Riding the Ox Home: A History of Meditation from Shamanism to Science*. 1982. Boston: Beacon Press, 1986; Irvin Paul. "Santa Teresa de Jesus de Avila." *Journal of Religion and Psychology Research* 4 (July-October, 1981): 179–81; Teresa of Avila. *The Interior Castle*. Translated by Kieran Kavanaugh and Otilio Rodriguez. New York: Paulist Press, 1979; Teresa of Jesus. *Complete Works of Saint Teresa of Jesus*. Translated by E. Allison Peers. New York: Sheed and Ward, 1946.

Thanatology

See **Deathbed visions.**

Theosophy

A philosophical system that teaches that one can gain knowledge of a transcendent reality through revelation or through practice of the occult tradition. The term "theosophy" comes from the Greek words *theos,* "god," and *sophia,* "wisdom." As practiced in modern times, Theosophy claims that all religions stem from the same roots of ancient wisdom, repeating myths and symbols, and that study of these secrets will lead to truth and spiritual oneness.

The primary exponent of Theosophy is the Theosophical Society, an international nonsectarian, nonpolitical, and nondogmatic organization founded in New York City in 1875 by Madame Helena Petrovna Blavatsky (known as HPB), a Russian-born mystic; Colonel Henry Steel Olcott, an American attorney and federal government official; William Q. Judge, an American attorney, and others.

According to HPB the term "theosophy" dates back to the third century A.D. Ammonius Saccas and his disciples in Eclectic Theosophy saw that all religions shared three major ideas: (1) belief in one Supreme, Absolute deity as the Source of all; (2) humankind's immortal nature is a radiation from that deity; and (3) by making oneself as pure as the Source, one could receive the divine secrets. Such efforts are called *theurgy,* or "divine work."

Theosophical Concepts and the Masters

HPB believed that earlier civilizations, such as the Egyptians and Greeks, understood esoteric wisdom better than do modern societies, and that their teachers were proficient in occult arts. These Masters, or "Mahatmas," as they are called in India, live on through the centuries in various incarnations, guarding their knowledge and teaching it to worthy students. Most of the Masters, HPB said, reside in remote regions of Tibet, Mongolia, or India, forming the Brotherhood of Adepts. The concept of such brotherhoods exists in numerous occult traditions.

HPB identified the Masters Koot Hoomi (also Kuthumi), Lal Singh, and Morya as the real founders of the Theosophical Society. She said that the Master Morya, or Master M., had overshadowed her most of her life. Koot Hoomi, or K.H., was the more communicative of the two, sending frequent letters and notes to HPB and her disciples. HPB said he was a Punjabi and had attended the University of Leipzig during the 1870s.

Other Masters important to the Society were Ilarion (also Hilarion), a Greek whom HPB said she had known since the 1860s, and Djwal Kul, who carried messages between Masters. The Maha Chohan, or Supreme Master, also spoke with HPB.

The Masters inspired HPB's writing and are central to understanding her work. Olcott said that he and HPB were visited by the Masters, conversed with them, and were taught by them.

Cycles of Evolution

In *The Secret Doctrine,* HPB conceived of a great cosmic evolutionary plan in which divine potential is unfolded through an orderly progression, moving down from Spirit to matter and back up again. While science sees evolution as the product of external forces and factors, Theosophy views it as the urge to release the potential of consciousness, which becomes more and more defined. Humankind is "the masterpiece of evolution," and all nature tends toward evolving the human potential.

HPB's evolutionary scheme divides stages into Chains, Rounds, and Races, each of which has its own complete cycle. Reincarnation, governed by karma, is a tenet of Theosophy. See **Karma; Reincarnation.**

History of the Theosophical Society

HPB said she first heard from Master Morya in 1851 and was instructed to begin the work that later developed into the Society. Its actual conception occurred after HPB emigrated to the United States in 1873. In the summer of 1874, HPB, who was interested in Spiritualism, read accounts of psychic disturbances and the appearances of spirits at the Eddy farmhouse in Chittenden, Vermont, written for the *New York Graphic* by Colonel Henry Steel Olcott. HPB went to the Eddy homestead; after her arrival the spirits changed from Eddy family members to servants from Russian Georgia, Kurdish tribesmen, and other exotic personalities. She and Olcott became friends, and upon returning to New York, attracted a following of occult enthusiasts.

On March 9, 1875, Olcott received a letter in gold ink on green paper signed "Tuitit Bey, Grand Master of the mystical Brotherhood of Luxor," instructing him to study the occult under HPB. He continued to receive letters and was inspired by them.

In September 1875, at Olcott's suggestion, he, HPB, and others formed the Theosophical Society. The name was proposed by Charles Sotheran, editor of the *American Bibliopolist.* Olcott was named president. The first regular meeting was held on November 11, 1875, with HPB as corresponding secretary and Judge as counsel.

In 1877 HPB's first book, *Isis Unveiled,* was published and well received. But by 1878 the Society was nearly defunct. HPB merged it with the Arya Samaj, a "back to the Vedas" reform movement in India. In February 1879 she and Olcott arrived in India. There HPB made her most important contact in India: the British journalist A. P. Sinnett, who managed an English newspaper in Allahabad and who was interested in the occult. Sinnett invited HPB and the Colonel out to his home in Simla, where HPB captivated the house guests with mysterious tappings, disembodied music, and the materialization of jewelry and dishes.

Sinnett began a correspondence with Master K.H., facilitated by HPB. The Masters were said not to actually write the letters themselves by hand, but to "precipitate" them onto paper through a sort a telepathy and concentration. Koot Hoomi allegedly said that often the agents of the Brotherhood wrote their dictated communications. The letters then would be delivered by apparent paranormal means, such as materializing in a drawer or dropping through a ceiling. Some critics believe HPB wrote the letters herself, but the allegation was never proved. Sinnet received more than one hundred letters from the Masters, which are housed at the British Museum.

HPB and Olcott began a magazine, *The Theosophist,* in July 1879. The Society was thriving among the British in India, and also attracted high-caste Indians. Sections were established all over Europe. In 1882 HPB and Olcott moved the Society's headquarters from Bombay to an old British summer estate in Adyar, near Madras, where it remains today.

In 1884 HPB, Olcott, and a Brahmin, M. M. Chatterji, went to Britain, where they met members of the Society for Psychical Research (SPR) in London. The SPR sent Richard Hodgson to India in December 1884 to investigate the paranormal phenomena said to be happening at Adyar. Hodgson's conclusions of fraud created a great controversy and were never proved. See **Blavatsky, Madame Helena Petrovna.**

In 1889 HPB met Annie Wood Besant, an ardent Freethinker and feminist activist who had reviewed *The Secret Doctrine* and converted to Theosophy. Besant became HPB's last major disciple.

Following HPB's death in 1891, Besant and Judge shared control of the Esoteric Section, but had a falling out in 1894 when Judge sought to take sole control. This divided the Society, and on April 28, 1895, most of the American branches reorganized independently as the Theosophical Society in America.

Judge was appointed lifetime president; he died in 1896. Olcott died in 1907.

Besant teamed with Charles W. Leadbeater, a British clergyman and clairvoyant who became assistant secretary of the European Section. The two expanded the Society's membership but favored an "Esoteric Christianity" over the "Esoteric Buddhism" espoused by HPB. Besant was a gifted writer and orator, and devoted a great deal of her efforts to social and political reforms in India, at one time serving as president of the Congress Party. She founded several schools, among them the present University of Benares.

In 1908 Leadbeater announced that a young Indian, Jiddu Krishnamurti, was to be the next World Teacher and incarnation of the Lord Maitreya. Krishnamurti attracted a large following, but left Theosophy by 1930 to follow his own path. See **Krishnamurti.**

During the 1920s Leadbeater and a few others claimed to continue to receive messages from the Mahatmas through clairvoyant communications on the astral plane.

Besant died at age eighty-six at Adyar on September 20, 1933. Her body was cremated.

Both Besant and Olcott are remembered as fighters on behalf of the rights of native Indians and Sinhalese. Olcott worked to establish civil protection for Buddhists in Ceylon, while Besant was the first woman elected president of the Indian National Congress. Olcott founded many Buddhist schools in Southeast Asia, where he is still highly regarded, as well as the first school in India for the "untouchables," the lowest caste.

After Judge's death in 1896, leadership of the American group passed to Katherine Tingley, a social worker who established the first Theosophical commune at Point Loma, near San Diego, California. In 1919 Tingley founded Theosophical University. The Point Loma property was sold after Tingley's death in 1929. The headquarters moved first to Covina, California, and then in 1951 to its present location in Altadena, California. The publishing program is called the Theosophical University Press.

The American lodges affiliated with the Society in Adyar are based in Wheaton, Illinois, as is the Theosophical Publishing House. The Adyar group sponsors branches of the Society in approximately sixty countries, and there are about 5,300 members in the United States.

Other theosophical organizations include the United Lodge of Theosophists, founded in 1909 and based in Los Angeles, an independent organization of students devoted to the study of and belief in Theosophy.

Sources: H. P. Blavatsky. *The Key to Theosophy.* Pasadena, CA: Theosophical University Press, 1939; H. P. Blavatsky. "Three Basic Truths of Being." *Sunrise* (April/May 1984); Bruce F. Campbell. *Ancient Wisdom Revived: A History of the Theosophical Movement.* Berkeley: University of California Press, 1980; Robert S. Ellwood. *Eastern Spirituality in America.* New York: Paulist Press, 1987; Robert S. Ellwood. *Theosophy: A Modern Expression of the Wisdom of the Ages.* Wheaton, IL: The Theosophical Publishing House, 1986; Michael Gomes. *The Dawning of the Theosophical Movement.* Wheaton, IL: The Theosophical Publishing House, 1987; Marion Meade. *Madame Blavatsky: The Woman Behind the Myth.* New York: G. P. Putnam's Sons, 1980; J. Gordon Melton. *Encyclopedic Handbook of Cults in America.* New York and London: Garland Publishing Inc., 1986; Leslie Price. *Madame Blavatsky Unveiled?* London: Theosophical History Centre, 1986; "Report of the Committee Appointed to Investigate Phenomena Connected with the Theosophical Society." *Proceedings of the Society for Psychical Research* 3 (1885): 201–7; Lewis Spence. *The Encyclopedia of the Occult.* Reprint. London: Bracken Books, 1988; "The Historical Basis of Modern Theosophy" and "Introducing You to the Theosophical Society."

The Theosophical Society in America, Wheaton, IL, n.d.; Gertrude Marvin Williams. *Priestess of the Occult: Madame Blavatsky.* New York: Alfred A. Knopf, 1946.

Therapeutic Touch

See Bodywork.

Third eye

See Chakras.

Thomas à Kempis (1380–1471)

German theologian and compiler or editor of *The Imitation of Christ,* an influential collection of prayers and maxims that seem to be communicated directly from Christ, and which urge readers to model their lives after Christ.

Thomas à Kempis was born in 1380 in Kempen in what is now Germany. His family name was Hermerken; he later took his name from his birthplace. At age thirteen he was sent to a school in Deventer, the Netherlands, run by the Brethren of the Common Life, an order founded by mystic Gerard Groote, the father of the *Devotio Moderna* (New Devotion) religious movement. The Brethren of the Common Life included both Brothers and Sisters, who educated youth and functioned as a social service organization.

In 1399 Thomas à Kempis entered the Augustinian monastery of Mount St. Agnes near Zwolle, Switzerland (near the Zuider Zee), where he spent most of the remainder of his uneventful life. He was ordained in 1414 and later became procurator, subprior, and novice master. He devoted himself to reading, studying, and copying manuscripts. He wrote biographies of Groote and others, sermons, hymns, prayers, and studies of monastic life. He died on August 8, 1471, and was buried at the monastery. His remains were later moved to Zwolle.

Scholars have disagreed over the authorship of *The Imitation of Christ,* and some twenty people have been given the credit. Thomas à Kempis popularly has been assumed to be the author, but it is evident that he edited or compiled the book from the writings of Groote, who was in turn influenced by the Flemish mystic John Ruysbroeck. The complete manuscript was published in Latin in 1427 and was translated into English in the mid-sixteenth century. It was translated into English in 1530 by Richard Whitford, and revised by Harold C. Gardiner in 1955.

Imitation is second only to the Bible in influence and popularity of Christian writings, in part due to its simplicity of language and theology, as well as its practicality; it is a source of brief but pregnant maxims of inspiration and spiritual guidance. While Groote was influenced by Ruysbroeck, his mysticism is much less speculative and much more practical. Typical of the popular spirituality at the time of its origin, *Imitation* reflects often on the Passion of Christ and frequently relates personal mystical experience to the Cross. It espouses a life of meditation and devotion, and a break with worldly lusts.

Imitation is divided into four books. The first concerns breaking the worldly bonds and preparing for the spiritual life; the second concerns advice for leading the devotional life; the third concerns achieving inner peace of mind; the fourth concerns the sacrament of the Eucharist, the union with Christ.

Selections from *Imitation* are read daily by members of several religious orders.

Sources: Robert Broderick, ed. *The Catholic Encyclopedia.* Nashville: Thomas Nelson, 1976; John Ferguson. *An Illustrated Encyclopedia of Mysticism and the Mystery*

Religions. New York: Seabury Press, 1976; Vergilius Ferm, ed. *The Encyclopedia of Religion.* Secaucus, NJ: Poplar Books, 1955; F. C. Happold. *Mysticism: A Study and an Anthology.* Rev. ed. Harmondsworth, Middlesex, England: Penguin Books, 1970; Robert Maynard Hutchins, ed. *Great Books of the Western World.* Chicago: Encyclopaedia Britannica, 1952; Louis Kronenberger, ed. *Atlantic Brief Lives.* Boston: Little, Brown, 1971.

Thought-form

In occultism a nonphysical entity created by thought that exists in either the mental plane or astral plane. Every thought is said to generate vibrations in the aura's mental body, which assume a floating form and colors depending on the nature and intensity of the thought. These thought-forms can be perceived visually by clairvoyants; they may also be sensed on an intuitive level by others. Thought-forms radiate out and attract sympathetic essences.

According to Theosophists and clairvoyants Annie Besant and C. W. Leadbeater, thought-forms fall into three classes: (1) the image of the thinker (see **Bilocation**); (2) an image of a material object associated with the thought; and (3) an independent image expressing the inherent qualities of a thought. Thoughts that are low in nature, such as anger, hate, lust, greed, and so on, create thought-forms that are dense in color and form. Thoughts of a more spiritual nature generate forms that have greater purity, clarity, and refinement.

Thought-forms can be directed at individuals. To have an effect, they must be able to latch on to similar vibrations in the aura of the recipient. If they are unable to do so, according to occult tradition, the thought-forms boomerang back to the sender. Thus one who directs evil thoughts toward another runs the risk of having them return.

The duration of a thought-form, its strength, and the distance it can travel depend on the strength and clarity of the original thought. Thought-forms are said to have the capability to assume their own energy and appear to be intelligent and independent. Equally intense thought can disperse them, or they can simply disintegrate when their purpose is finished. Some may last years. It is believed that some particularly powerful thought-forms can go out of control or turn on their creators.

In magic, thought-forms, also called "artificial elementals," are created by ritual that involves intense concentration, repetition, and visualization. They can be directed at individuals, to protect or heal, or to harm. See **Psychic attack.** In addition, thought-forms may be created to perform low-level tasks and errands. See **Magic.**

Some thought-forms occur spontaneously. "Group minds" are formed whenever a group of people concentrates on the same thoughts, ideas, or goals, such as a team of employees or a crowd of demonstrators. To some extent the group-mind possesses the group, as witnessed in the psychic bonding and power that coalesces in crowds, and in the synergy of a close-knit working group. When the group disperses, the group-mind usually loses power.

In Tibetan occultism thoughts can create a temporary phantom form called a *tulpa.* Tulpas usually assume human shape and are created to be sent out on a mission. In her explorations of Tibetan thought, Alexandra David-Neel successfully created a tulpa, though it was not what she intended and for a time eluded her control.

David-Neel sought to create a lama who would be "short and fat, of an innocent and jolly type." After several months of performing the prescribed ritual, a phantom monk appeared. It assumed a life-like form over a period of

Thomas à Kempis (1380–1471)

time, and existed almost like a guest in David-Neel's apartment.

The tulpa tagged along with her as she went out on a tour. Then, to her distress, the tulpa began to change from a fat, benevolent fellow to a lean and malevolent one. The tulpa went out of her control and became troublesome. He began touching her and rubbing up against her. Others began to see him, but he did not respond to anyone's conversation.

David-Neel decided to dissolve the tulpa, according to certain Tibetan rituals, but the phantom resisted her efforts. It took her six months to eliminate him. The entire episode upset her, and she termed it "very bad luck." See **David-Neel, Alexandra.**

It is theorized that thought-forms may arise spontaneously out of the collective unconscious as archetypes which take on phantom or seemingly real form. This perhaps may explain reports of the Devil, supernatural monsters, other non-human beings, and phenomena associated with UFOs. See **Archetypes; Encounter phenomenon; Men in Black; Music; "Philip"; Psychic attack.**

Sources: Annie Besant and C. W. Leadbeater. *Thought-forms*. 1925. Abridged ed. Wheaton, IL: Theosophical Publishing House, 1969; June G. Bletzer. *The Donning International Encyclopedic Psychic Dictionary*. Norfolk, VA: The Donning Co., 1986; Adam Crabtree. *Multiple Man: Explorations in Possession and Multiple Personality*. New York: Praeger, 1985; Alexandra David-Neel. *Magic and Mystery in Tibet*. 1929. New York: Dover Publications, 1971; Janet and Stewart Farrar. *A Witche's Bible-Compleat*. New York: Magickal Childe, 1984; Barbara and Michael Foster. *Forbidden Journey: The Life of Alexandra David-Neel*. San Francisco: Harper & Row, 1987; Rosemary Ellen Guiley. *The Encyclopedia of Witches and Witchcraft*. New York: Facts On File, 1989; Colin Wilson. *Mysteries*. New York: Perigee Books, 1978.

Thoughtography

A type of paranormal photography in which images are projected psychically onto photographic film, with or without the aid of a camera. The term "thoughtography" was coined by Tomokichi Fukarai, president of the Psychical Institute of Japan, who conducted the first serious study of it during the early 1900s. Previous research had focused on spirit photography, images of dead people and phantom objects captured on film.

Fukarai stumbled onto the phenomenon while conducting a series of experiments with a Japanese medium, Mrs. Nagao. To test her clairvoyance, Fukarai wanted to see if she could discern three Japanese characters that he had photographed on an undeveloped film plate. Although it had been wrapped in paper to seal out any light, Fukarai discovered that the entire surface of the plate had been exposed, not just the area containing the Japanese characters. Fukarai hypothesized that the exposure was caused or influenced by the psychic activity of Nagao. In follow-up experiments with Nagao and other mediums, Fukarai obtained actual images on film, or "thoughtographs."

In recent years research into thoughtography was done under the direction of such leading parapsychologists as psychiatrist Ian Stevenson of the University of Virginia and Denver psychiatrist Jule Eisenbud, who attracted national attention in the 1960s for their work with psychic Ted Serios, who created images on film by staring into the lens of a Polaroid camera.

Serios was a native of Kansas City, Missouri, with a penchant for drama. He realized his psychic ability in 1955, when working as a bellhop in a Chicago hotel. A fellow employee discovered Serios was a good hypnotic subject and possessed remote viewing ability. During one hypnotic trance, Serios said he projected to the astral plane, where he met a spirit who claimed to be the pirate Jean Lafitte, and directed Serios to secret locations of buried treasure in Florida. No big finds were ever located; the publicity apparently enabled another party to beat Serios to it. Serios did turn up a few hundred dollars buried beneath the ground. The spirit Lafitte abandoned Serios, who kept looking for treasure with the help of a syndicate he formed. When Serios had trouble establishing precise locations, an employee handed him a camera and jokingly suggested taking a picture of the image in his mind. Serios did, and the result was a thoughtograph.

Serios never did strike it rich with treasure. Poor health forced him to give up his thoughtography. A psychiatrist told him they were the products of illusion.

Years later Eisenbud met Serios. In 1964, at the invitation of the publisher of *Fate* magazine, Eisenbud began a three-year investigation of the psychic.

In Eisenbud's experiments Serios spontaneously created both identifiable and unidentifiable images of buildings, monuments, and other structures by staring into the lens of a Polaroid camera and snapping the shutter. The film was developed immediately afterward. In addition to spontaneous images, Serios created images of specific objects. Eisenbud would select a target and hold the camera while Serios stared into it. Eisenbud catalogued more than four hundred "normally inexplicable" images on more than one hundred themes during the three-year study period.

Serios also created hundreds of "blackies," prints in which light appeared to be almost or totally excluded, and "whities," prints that were so overexposed they turned white.

Serios frequently held a piece of small black tubing, about one inch in diameter, over the camera lens. He called this his "gismo," which he said helped him focus his mental powers. Eisenbud satisfied himself that the gismo was not a fraudulent device. In 1967 Eisenbud published his results in his book, *The World of Ted Serios,* in which he concluded that the only explanation for Serios's feats was psychokinesis.

Despite the fact that Eisenbud and his team had taken special care to ensure that Serios could not tamper with the film at any time before, during, or after a photo session, critics charged that he was a fake and that his "thoughtographs" could be duplicated by holding a negative over the lens of a camera. Stage magician and debunker James "the Amazing" Randi claimed that Serios palmed a gismo which held a tiny lens with a picture at one end, which would transfer the picture to the film of a camera focused at infinity. Serios never confessed to any fraud, nor was the charge proved.

Both Eisenbud and Stevenson countered that and other charges of fraud by arguing that many of Serios's images contained distortions that could neither be explained nor duplicated. For example, one of his thoughtographs was identified as the Royal Canadian Mounted Police Air Hangar in Ontario. In his version the word "Canadian" on the hangar's sign is inexplicably spelled "Cainadian."

Eisenbud, Stevenson, and other researchers showed interest in the early 1980s in a young Japanese boy, Masuaki Kiyota, who purportedly possessed paranormal abilities to create film images and bend metal objects. During experiments in the United States conducted during 1981, Kiyota was not able to produce any identifiable images on film while under observation. Researchers, however, were convinced that his powers were genuine, a belief they maintained even after Kiyota admitted three years later that he had occasionally cheated during metal bending experiments. He said he had been entrapped into using normal means for bending metal by media efforts to debunk him. See **Psychokinesis (PK); Spirit photography.**

Sources: Jule Eisenbud. "Correspondence on Ted Serios' Alleged 'Confession.'" *Journal of the American Society for Psychical Research* 69, no. 1 (January 1975): 94–96; Jule Eisenbud. "Observations on a Possible New Thoughtographic Talent." *JASPR* 71, no. 3 (July 1977): 299–304; Jule Eisenbud. *The World of Ted Serios.* New York: Pocket Books, 1968; Jule Eisenbud. "Distortions in the Photographs of Ted Serios." *JASPR* 75, no. 2 (April 1981): 143–53; T. Fukurai. *Clairvoyance and Thoughtography.* 1931. Reprint. New York: Arno Press, 1975; Edgar D. Mitchell. *Psychic Exploration: A Challenge for Science.* Edited by John White. New York: Paragon Books, 1974; Ian Stevenson, *et al.* "Correspondence on Masuaki Kiyota." *JASPR* 79, no. 2 (April 1985): 294–95; Colin Wilson. *The Occult.* New York: Vintage Books, 1973; Benjamin B. Wolman, ed. *Handbook of Parapsychology.* New York: Van Nostrand Reinhold, 1977.

Tobacco

Plant sacred to Natives of the Americas. Tobacco is believed to be endowed with supernatural powers to heal, hurt, bring luck, cause ill fortune, and promote affection between husband and wife. It is smoked, snuffed, eaten, mixed in drinks and fermented concoctions, and burned as incense for rituals of harvest, war, puberty, death, initiation, purification, visions, communication with the spirits and gods, and as part of pledges and oaths. Tobacco, along with pipes, is buried with the dead. According to tradition it should be used only for sacred purposes, never for recreation.

The term "tobacco" is a Spanish adaptation from the Arawak term for "cigar." Columbus discovered tobacco among the Arawaks of the West Indies. From archaeological data tobacco was used extensively in Precontact times and was the basis of an elaborate pipe culture. See **Sacred pipe.** It was not used in the Arctic, parts of the Subarctic, and parts of the Columbia Plateau. According to the accounts of early European travelers, some varieties of tobacco were so strong as to be intoxicating. It is not known whether any were hallucinogenic, though some Natives did make use of other hallucinogenic plants.

In Native North American mythologies, tobacco is a gift from the Great Spirit, a tool with which humans can access all manner of Supernaturals. According to tradition tobacco was grown only by men in fields that women were prohibited from entering. When smoked it occasionally was mixed with adulterants, chiefly red willow and osier, in order to stretch the tobacco supplies. When sprinkled in rites, however, tobacco was never adulterated.

In ritual the tobacco smoke is offered to the Great Spirit, the spirits of the wind, moon, sun, water, and thunder, the animistic spirits residing in rocks, trees, and so on, and the spirits of the dead. The smoke, which embodies the breath, carries messages and prayers.

As a medicine tobacco traditionally was mixed with saliva, water, and red sumac as a remedy for head, chest, and stomach ailments. It was blown on affected parts of the body by a medicine man, and was inhaled and exhaled by the patient.

Tribes of South America, the Pacific, the Caribbean, and elsewhere use tobacco in shamanic and other rituals. Among the Jivaro a medicine man squirts tobacco juice from his mouth into the mouth of a novice, thus transferring to the initiate supernatural power in the form of an invisible magic arrow. Other initiatory rites require drinking a hallucinogenic beverage in order to see and meet helping spirits. The Taino of the Greater Antilles inhale a mixture of tobacco and a hallucinogenic mimosa plant in order to commune with ancestors and spirits and produce visions. See **Drugs in mystical and psychic experiences; Shamanism.**

Sources: Ake Hultkrantz. *The Religions of the American Indians.* 1967. Berkeley: University of California Press, 1979; Holger Kalweit. *Dreamtime and Inner Space: The World of the Shaman.* Boston: Shambhala Publications, 1984; Elisabeth Tooker, ed. *Native North American Spirituality of the Eastern Woodlands.* Mahwah, NJ: Paulist Press, 1979; Ruth M. Underhill. *Red Man's Religion.* Chicago: University of Chicago Press, 1965; Carl Waldman. *Atlas of the North American Indian.* New York: Facts On File, 1985; The Museum of the American Indian, New York City; the American Indian Archaeological Institute, Washington, CT.

Totem

See **Guardian spirit.**

Touch for Health

See **Bodywork.**

Trance

See **Altered states of consciousness; Mediumship; Shamanism.**

Transcendental consciousness

See **Transcendental Meditation (TM).**

Transcendental Meditation (TM)

A system of meditation taught by the Maharishi Mahesh Yogi (b. 1918?) in which, through use of a personal mantra, one achieves a fourth state of consciousness: transcendental consciousness. Transcendental Meditation, or TM, as it is called, gained a wide following in the West in the 1960s and 1970s. It does not require

a change in religion, philosophy, or lifestyle. Rather, Maharishi positioned TM as a technique of the "Science of Creative Intelligence." TM is said to bring results more quickly than other methods of meditation, in particular yoga and Zen. It has been shown to decrease drug use, decrease the amount of sleep needed, and increase energy, concentration, and resilience to stress and illness.

According to Maharishi (whose name is Sanskrit for "great seer") TM is rooted in practices thousands of years old, for practices similar to TM can be found in the Vedas. The knowledge has been lost and found many times over the centuries. The yoga teachings, he says, have been distorted from the original teachings.

History

Maharishi learned TM from his guru, Swami Brahmananda Saraswati, Maharaj, Jagat-Guru Bhagwan Shankaracharya of Jyotir-Math, whom Maharishi refers to simply as "Guru Dev" ("Divine Teacher"). After graduating with a degree in physics from Allahabad University in India, Maharishi became a disciple of Guru Dev for twelve years.

After Guru Dev's death, Maharishi retired to a cave in the Himalayas for two years. He then emerged and traveled to South India with no specific plans. In a small town, he was invited to give a few lectures, the popularity of which launched his teaching of TM on a broad scale throughout India. In 1958 he established the Spiritual Regeneration Movement (SRM) in Madras. He conceived of a plan to spread TM throughout the world, and traveled to California in 1959, where he taught the technique and established a national center for the SRM. He then went to New York and Europe.

In 1961 Maharishi began training others as TM teachers in order to meet demand. The same year he founded the International Meditation Society (IMS) as a replacement for the SRM; the neutral name was more appealing to Westerners. In 1965 he founded the Students' International Meditation Society (SIMS) to cater to student demand; it was an immediate success with young people seeking drug-free enlightenment. In 1966 work was completed on a luxurious ashram, the Academy of Meditation, in Rishikesh, India, at the foothills of the Himalayas. TM received a boost in popularity in 1967 when the Beatles became followers for a few months.

In 1971 Maharishi founded the Maharishi International University (MIU), now in Fairfield, Iowa, to integrate TM with other academic disciplines. He also established the Foundation for the Science of Creative Intelligence. In 1972 he unveiled an ambitious world plan to introduce TM into educational programs, social services, prison reform, and psychotherapy.

In the 1980s the growth of TM slowed. This slowdown was due in part to negative publicity concerning Maharishi's income tax problems, which caused him to move his headquarters out of India; and to a controversial TM-*siddhi* program he unveiled based on the *Yoga Sutras* of Patanjali, which involved paranormal feats such as levitation. See **Levitation; Siddhis.**

In 1985 and 1986, Maharishi turned his attention to health and world peace, with the founding of the World Federation of Ayurveda (1985), Maharishi's World Plan for Perfect Health (1986), and Maharishi's Program to Create World Peace (1986). His work in health is directed at spreading the ancient Ayurveda medicine of India and in finding the key to reversing aging (a secret he claims to have discovered, despite his aged appearance).

His world peace program includes teaching the TM-siddhis to advanced meditators. Maharishi states that if seven thousand people collectively practice TM, and especially the TM-siddhis, the coherence of their brain waves will affect others around them, and lead to a reduction in crime, hostility, accidents, and illness. Seven thousand people represent the square root of 1 percent of the world's population, the minimum necessary to cause mass change, according to Maharishi. During 1983 and 1984, Maharishi assembled seven thousand people at MIU to test this hypothesis. TM researchers claimed that for the three weeks of the assembly, global economic indicators improved and crime, accidents, and illness dropped. Critics contend the study was selective to prove the hypothesis.

TM meditators claimed to be responsible for the peaceful unification of Germany in 1988–1989. In April 1990 several thousand TM meditators assembled on four continents. MIU officials claimed that international conflict dropped 44 percent.

After Iraq invaded Kuwait on August 2, 1990, Maharishi called for the US government or a wealthy individual to finance assembling seven thousand people to meditate to prevent war. No assembly was undertaken, and a brief war ensued in January and February 1991. Critics were doubtful that meditation would have prevented it.

Technique

TM is different from other meditation techniques in that it involves neither concentration nor contemplation. According to Maharishi TM can be taught only through personal instruction from a qualified teacher. The student is given a personal mantra and is instructed in how to use it while meditating twice a day for about twenty minutes or so. The mantra has no meaning or associations and, contrary to other Eastern techniques, is not chanted either verbally or mentally;

rather, it is a sound that is thought. TM mantras are not invocations to Hindu deities, as some Christian church officials have charged. People who adopt mantras on their own are said to risk negative effects caused by the improper use of sacred sound.

The meditation does not require special postures. Ideally, it is done in the morning and early evening.

The key principle of TM is that regular use of the mantra enables the practitioner to reach a state of consciousness Maharishi describes as the field of Being, pure creative intelligence, or pure thought. Thoughts rise from the depths of the mind like tiny bubbles rising in a pond, growing in size until they reach the surface level of conscious awareness. Maharishi likens the mind to the ocean: Its surface is active and its depths are still. TM enables the practitioner to experience thought at its origination point, and thus access greater potential for creative intelligence. Here one encounters the True Self, a state of restful alertness in which there is no mental activity. It is a fourth state of consciousness because it is different from the three ordinary states of waking, dreaming, and deep sleep, and from the states of altered consciousness. In this transcendental state, the boundaries between subject and object disappear, and the two become one. At first a seemingly empty state, it is in fact one of silent joy.

Physiological Effects

Like other forms of meditation, TM effects measurable physiological changes, including lowered respiration, heart rate, blood pressure, and lactase (a chemical in the blood associated with strenuous activity and stress), and increased, more synchronized alpha brain waves. Research has shown the changes to be different from those achieved with other techniques of meditation or altering of consciousness. In experiments TM prac-

titioners have shown a decreased need for sleep and increased hand-eye coordination. Practitioners report overall health improvements. Compare **Biofeedback; Meditation; Relaxation.**

Higher States of Consciousness

Three higher states of consciousness can be achieved with practice. The fifth, cosmic consciousness, is defined by Maharishi as transcendental consciousness maintained with the three states of ordinary consciousness in a permanent awareness of the True Self. In this state of Self-Realization, the ego and identity continue to function, but one defines one's self from within rather than from the external world. This state can only be achieved when one is permanently and totally free of stress.

In the sixth state of consciousness, a glorified cosmic consciousness, Maharishi says the individual becomes aware of the finest levels of relative existence, but not the absolute. The more subtle values of all things are perceived, and everything seems composed of and pervaded by pure light.

The seventh state is called by Maharishi unity consciousness, or "Unity," and is characterized by absolute awareness of the external world, or experiencing one's essential unity with all that is. See **Mystical experiences.** Maharishi claims that with TM it is possible to reach these states in a few years, perhaps five to ten, as opposed to many years, if not a lifetime, through yoga or Zen.

Differences

TM differs from Eastern teachings that are considered traditional. There is no espousal of renunciation or withdrawal from the daily world in order to achieve enlightenment. Rather, Maharishi acknowledges the importance of well-being and living in a material world, but without attachment. Nor does he accept the doctrine of maya, which holds that the relative, phenomenological world is illusion and only the absolute is real. Maharishi says the illusion lies in the relationship between absolute and relative. Because of the differences, it is stressed that TM not be mixed with techniques from other systems.

Sources: Harold H. Bloomfield, M.D., Michael Peter Cain, and Dennis T. Jaffe. *TM: Discovering Inner Energy and Overcoming Stress.* New York: Delacorte Press, 1975; Jack Forem. *Transcendental Meditation.* New York: E. P. Dutton, 1973; Richard Gibson. "The Yoga Airborne at Maharishi U. Targets Persian Gulf." *Wall Street Journal* (October 11, 1990): A1; Maharishi Mahesh Yogi. *Transcendental Meditation.* First published as *The Science of Being and Art of Living.* New York: New American Library, 1963; Peter Russell. *The TM Technique: A Skeptic's Guide to the Program.* First published as *The TM Technique.* 1976. Boston: Routledge & Kegan Paul, 1977.

Transpersonal psychology

See **Psychology.**

Tree of Life

See **Kabbalah; Magic.**

Trungpa, Chogyam (1939–1987)

Tibetan Buddhist *tulku,* religious leader, and meditation master in the Kagyu school of Tibetan Buddhism, and one of the most important modern Buddhist teachers for his dissemination of Tibetan teachings in the West.

Chogyam Trungpa was born in a cattle barrow in Geje, a small village in northeastern Tibet, on the day of the full moon during the New Year Festival in February 1939. His family name was Mukpo. According to his mother, on the night of his conception, she had a dream in which a being of light entered her body with a flash. That winter flowers bloomed in the area.

As an infant of less than one year, he was recognized as the eleventh incarnation of Trungpa Tulku, a great Buddhist teacher, and was given the religious name Trungpa Rinpoche. He was raised in monasteries, where he received his schooling and was taught meditation. He rose to supreme abbot of the Surmangt Monasteries, receiving the degree of Khyenpo, the approximate equivalent of a Western doctorate of divinity.

In 1959, at age twenty, he fled to India over the Himalayas when the Chinese invaded and occupied Tibet. His dramatic journey on foot with a party of refugees, including other religious leaders, was fraught with the danger of discovery and death the entire way. To keep warm they practiced the yoga of inner heat, called *tumo.* To help guide them through unfamiliar territory, they used a form of divination called *prasena,* which produces visions.

Trungpa believed he had a duty to preserve and spread the spiritual wisdom he had been taught, and devoted the rest of his life to those ends. In India His Holiness the Dalai Lama appointed him spiritual adviser of the Young Lamas' Home School.

After two years Trungpa went to Britain as a Spaulding Fellow, where he attended Oxford University from 1963 to 1967. In 1966 he published *Born in Tibet,* an autobiographical account of his early life and escape from Tibet, the latter of which he examined within the context of Tibetan Buddhist spiritual teachings. Trungpa was invited to lecture at the Johnstone House Contemplative Community in Scotland, and then was invited to take it over. He did take it over in 1967 with the establishment of the

Samye-Ling Tibetan Centre, named after Samye, the first monastic center in Tibet. Located on a twenty-three-acre wooded estate near the Esk river, Samye-Ling houses lamas who provide training to monks and teach traditional meditation in action.

In May 1969 Trungpa was in an automobile accident in Britain that left him paralyzed on his left side. As a result he could no longer wear his religious robes, which he acknowledged had a devastating effect on him. He continued his teaching "unmasked," as he termed it, which he said eventually brought him more closely in touch with wisdom and "finally cut through the seduction of materialism." He relinquished his monastic vows; and in January 1970, to the displeasure of his Tibetan peers, he married a sixteen-year-old Englishwoman, Diane Judith Pybus.

Within a few months of marriage, he accepted invitations to teach in North America. He and Diane moved to the United States, where Trungpa lectured at the Tail of the Tiger Community in Bernet, Vermont, founded in March 1970 by some of his students from Samye-Ling. Trungpa and Diane then made their home in Boulder, Colorado, where he established Vajrahadtu, an association of more than one hundred meditation communities and centers in the United States, Canada, and Europe; and the Nalanda Foundation, which includes the Naropa Institute, a liberal arts college. Trungpa's arrival in the United States coincided with the movement of interest in Eastern spirituality, and he was well received by a wide range of followers, including poet Allen Ginsburg, novelist William Burroughs, and composer John Cage.

Trungpa wrote eleven books on meditation and Tibetan Buddhism spiritual teachings, and lectured on "enlightened warriorship," emphasizing principles of sacredness and dignity that have inspired great people throughout history.

Over a period of years beginning in 1976, he presented a series of "Shambhala teachings" on that theme, in which he drew upon the mythical and enlightened kingdom of Shambhala. The premise of these teachings is that an enlightened society can be created through the individual discovery of one's inherent goodness and potential for dignity. A Shambhala training program, which teaches meditation and the principles of Shambhala warriorship, is taught through the Vajrahadtu centers. Trungpa also was known for his poetry, calligraphy, floral arrangements, and environmental designs.

Trungpa reportedly drank heavily. He died at age forty-eight on April 4, 1987, in Nova Scotia, leaving behind his widow, Diane, and five children from their marriage. There was no autopsy, but the official cause of death was cardiac arrest and respiratory failure; followers speculated that the true cause of death was cirrhosis of the liver. Trungpa's body was placed in a meditative posture, packed in salt, and flown to Tail of the Tiger in Bernet, Vermont, where students meditated with it until May 26. Some three thousand people gathered to attend the cremation of his body, which was wrapped in gauze, covered with ghee (a clarified butter), and placed atop a twenty-five-foot-high kiln. See **Shambhala.**

Sources: Leslie A. Shepard, ed. *Encyclopedia of Occultism and Parapsychology.* 2d ed. Detroit: Gale Research Co., 1984; Chogyam Trungpa. *Shambhala: The Sacred Path of the Warrior.* 1984. New York: Bantam Books, 1986; Chogyam Trungpa. *Born in Tibet.* 1966. Harmondsworth, Middlesex, England: Penguin Books, 1971; "In Vermont: A Spiritual Leader's Farewell." *Time* (June 22, 1987): 10–13.

Tulku

See **Lama.**

Tulpa

See Thought-form.

Tutelary spirit

See Guardian spirit.

Twitchell, Paul

See ECKANKAR.

Tyrrell, G. N. M.

See Apparition.

U

UFOs (unidentified flying objects)

See **Ancient astronauts, theory of; Encounter phenomenon; Extraterrestrial encounters; Men in Black.**

Ullman, Montague

See **Dreams.**

Unification Church

See **Alternative religious movements.**

Universal consciousness

See **Collective unconscious.**

Universal life force

A vital force or energy that transcends time and space, permeates all things in the universe, and upon which all things depend for health and life. Its existence has been acknowledged universally since ancient times, and it is known by many different names. The Hindus call it *prana,* the Polynesians and Hawaiians mana, the Chinese *qi,* and the Japanese *ki.* Hippocrates called it the *Vis Medicatrix Naturae,* and Galen called it the *Pneuma.* It is referred to as the *Telesma* in the writings attributed to Hermes Trismegistus.

See **Hermetica.** The alchemist Robert Fludd referred to it as *spiritus* and the Kabbalists called it the astral light; hypnotist Franz Anton Mesmer called it magnetic fluid, and psychiatrist Wilhelm Reich termed it orgone energy. More recently, it has been referred to as bioenergy. See **Aura.**

Regardless of what it is called, the characteristics of the universal life force are common. In various systems it can be controlled and manipulated for improved health, longevity, healing, or supernormal physical feats. Following are different concepts of the universal life force.

Prana

Prana, a Sanskrit term, usually is translated as "life force," "vigor," or "vitality." The control of it plays an important role in yoga, Hindu magic, and healing.

According to ancient Hindu teachings, prana is the divine power that acts in the *akasha,* one of the basic elements of the universe. The universe itself is manufactured from the akasha by the power of prana; before existence there was nonexistence, which was not void, but prana. It is the soul of energy, the essence of all motion, force, and power in all things. Prana manifests in the motion of all celestial bodies, and in gravity, electricity, and magnetism. It is part of all forms of life, from the lowest protoplasm to the most complex being. It is part of every inanimate object as a living force. Prana permeates all forms of matter, but is not matter itself; it is often likened to electricity. When a being or material substance reaches the end of its life cycle, it is resolved back into prana.

While prana is all-pervasive, it is more concentrated at the tops of mountains and near running water. It corresponds with concentrations of negative ions.

In yoga the human body maintains a store of prana, which acts as the body's vital "bio-motor." The personal prana is in constant touch with the infinite supply of universal prana. The chakras are focal points for transforming the universal pranic energy into the body's energy system; each chakra funnels a different-colored ray of prana. Orange light is believed to stimulate the spleen chakra, an important center for assimilating and directing prana energy throughout the body. The circulation of prana is highest in the morning, at noon, and in the early evening, and is affected by the movements of the planets and stars. See **Chakras.**

Prana is not breath, but it is manifested in breath, and it is related to *vayu,* the element of air and motion. *Pranayama,* the control of the flow of prana through rhythmic breathing, is central to yoga. The right nostril is positive and represents the sun; the left is negative and represents the moon. Breathing through right and left nostrils must be balanced. The yogi increases prana, thus improving health and vitality, and enabling remarkable physical feats. Pranayama also controls the mind, which in turn controls pranayama. During life the mind keeps prana within the body; at the instant of death, both mind and prana leave the body simultaneously.

In Tantra Yoga prana is used to raise latent psychic powers, called *siddhis.* Yoga adepts who raise the *kundalini*

force see prana as a mystical light of supernormal colors, indescribable in terms of the physical spectrum. See **Kundalini; Siddhis; Yoga.**

In Hindu magic prana is the energy source for all magical feats. Magicians use prana to energize the imagination and will, which are the keys to the Creative Mind Principle, the controlling instrument of genuine magic. See **Fakir.**

Healthy people have an excess of prana, while sick people are depleted in it. Prana is responsible for regeneration and the healing of wounds. It may be transferred from a healthy body to a sick body by a laying on of hands. See **Bodywork.**

Qi

The Chinese term *Qi* literally means "breath," "gas," or "ether"; it has never been clearly defined. Qi was developed as a metaphysical principle, as the source of vitality, harmony, creativity, and moral courage, by various philosophers, including Lao-tzu (c. 604 B.C.–531 B.C.), the legendary author of the *Tao Teh Ching,* Confucius (c. 551 B.C.–479 B.C.?), Mencius (fourth century B.C.), Huainan-tzu, and Kuan-tzu. Lao-tzu conceived of it as a dualistic principle, which evolved into the concept of yin and yang—yang being light, the sun, and the active/dry/masculine principle and yin being dark, the Earth, and the passive/wet/feminine principle. From this dualistic concept arose the Five Elements theory of Chinese medicine, and the basis for the *I Ching.*

Yin and yang are seen as in constant ebb and flow, and must be in balance for optimum health. Yang energy enters the body by flowing downward from the heavens, while the yin flows upward from the earth. They converge at a point in the lower belly called the *hara,* which is located about two inches below the navel and is deep within the body. The hara is likened to a stove or furnace where the life force can, in certain disciplines, be converted into spiritual energy, a process that creates physical heat.

Qi courses through the body in twelve meridians connected to the internal organs. Each meridian has a fixed direction, is associated with one of the Five Elements, and is either yin or yang. The flow of qi can be enhanced by the manipulation of one thousand points, or *tsubos,* along the meridians. The speed of the flow is measured by individuals who are "meridian sensitive."

The earliest extant descriptions of qi in relation to health and healing date to the Han Dynasty (206 B.C.–A.D. 220), in a text entitled *Huang-ti Nei Ching Su Wen* (*The Yellow Emperor's Classic of Internal Medicine*). The text gives the name qi and describes thirty-two forms of it. All living things are in a constant energy exchange with qi; illness results when the exchange is restricted, depleted, or out of balance. If the exchange ceases, the organism dies. Qi is received through food, the breath, and from the environment in general. One's ability to absorb it declines with age.

In martial arts and the "moving meditation" of Tai Ji Chuan, qi is controlled through breathing to bring the mind and body into balance. In addition to the physical meridians, ch'i flows through eight psychic channels in the body, which play a key role in the purification of vital energy. A body filled with qi is strong and resistant to disease and illness, and is likely to live a long life. The term qi is always found in descriptions of Taoist exercises and breathing techniques. See **Feng shui; Martial arts; Meditation; Tai Ji Chuan.** See also **Qi Gong.**

Ki

Ki is the Japanese term for qi. The metaphysical principle of Chinese qi was introduced into Japan in the Nara period (710–794) and Heian period (794–1185). The concept of ki was absorbed into Shinto beliefs about nature, and many compound words were formed relating nature to spirit.

Concepts of ki began to undergo dramatic change with the rise of the samurai class, beginning in the late Heian period and peaking in the mid-nineteenth century. Ki became part of the warrior's discipline of courage, willpower, vigor, conserving energy, and even prolonging breathing as a matter of life and death. Ki was seen as twofold in nature: the unifying principle between the individual and the universe, and the expression of breath-power. Victory depended on ki. These principles of the samurai have carried over into modern-day martial arts.

Mana

"Mana" is a term used in the Huna of Hawaii. Mana has three primary forms, each of which functions in one of the three selves which comprise every person. Mana, the basic life force, operates in the Low Self (*Unihipili*), the subconscious. It has the power to build and maintain forms, including the physical body. *Mana-mana* operates in the Middle Self (*uhane*), the conscious. It is creative willpower and manifests thought and emotion. *Mana-loa* operates in the High Self (*Aumakua*), the superconscious. It is a high-voltage energy that can be harnessed for instantaneous healing and miracles. It contains the power of compassion.

All forms of mana flow through the human body in waves and layers, emanating from the solar plexus and flowing down one leg and back up to the opposite shoulder, with the pattern reversed on the back, so that the flow forms a figure eight. Mana from lower levels can be converted to higher levels. It can be manipulated through breathing and visualization exercises. See **Huna.**

Od

Baron Karl von Reichenbach (1788–1869), a German chemist, metallurgist, and expert on meteorites, used the term "Od" (also "Odic Force," "Odyle") to describe a subtle substance that he said emanates from all things in the universe, including the stars and planets; it streams from crystals. Reichenbach said Od can be observed by clairvoyants as luminous radiations similar to an aurora borealis and can be sensed as hot or cold. He also believed it is affected by the breath and fluctuates during the day and night, and before and after meals.

Goethe anticipated his observations of the luminosities of plants by about twenty-five years, but Reichenbach was the first to make a scientific case for the universal life force by conducting hundreds of experiments with sensitives (but who were not Spiritualist mediums).

In 1845 Reichenbach published his findings in the first part of his *Researches on Magnetism, Electricity, Heat and Light in their relations to Vital Forces*. At the time mesmerism was declining in popularity, and his work was viewed as an attempt to revive it. He was rejected by the scientific establishment, but endorsed by mesmerists, magnetic healers, and Spiritualists. See **Mesmer, Franz Anton**. Reichenbach was a supporter of mesmerism, though he thought the term "animal magnetism" was inappropriate.

The complete edition of *Researches* appeared in 1850. The term "Odyle" was created by a translator who thought it sounded more scientific than "Od."

One of the first tasks of the Society for Psychical Research (SPR) upon its formation in London in 1882 was to study "Reichenbach Phenomena." The SPR's study validated many of Reichenbach's claims. See **Society for Psychical Research (SPR)**. Nevertheless, Reichenbach was shunned by the scientific establishment. He spent his last years in retirement and disappointment at his castle in Reisenberg, Germany.

Orgone

The term "orgone" was coined by Wilhelm Reich (1897–1957), a native of Austria, a student of psychiatrist Sigmund Freud, and a psychoanalyst. In developing the work of Freud between 1936 and 1940, Reich hypothesized on the existence of orgone, a vital force or primordial cosmic energy, as the basis of sex and psychosomatic neuroses. He agreed with Reichenbach that it: permeated all things and existed as a biological energy; was blue in color; and could be demonstrated visually, thermically, and electroscopically in the atmosphere with a Geiger counter. Reich published his theory in 1942 in *The Discovery of the Orgone: The Function of the Orgasm; Sex-Economic Problems of Biological Energy* and in 1948 in *The Cancer Biopathy*.

Reich practiced in the United States and found himself in legal trouble when he developed a device called the "orgone accumulator," a metallic box covered with organic material, which was supposed to concentrate orgone for therapeutic uses. He used the device on cancer patients and reported positive results. The Food and Drug Administration tested the device and deemed it worthless. Reich was enjoined from manufacturing, distributing, and using the device, and from using the term "orgone" in his writings. When he refused he was fined and sent to jail, where he died. The orgone accumulators were destroyed and his books were burned.

Bioenergy

Bioenergy is an Eastern European concept of the universal life force, which is seen to tie all things together, and which may be controlled and directed by will. The energy also is used in Eastern European healing disciplines. The term "bioenergy" was borrowed from Wilhelm Reich, the first to use it to describe the life energy within the body.

Bioenergy is said to radiate from human bodies, and is associated with such psychic phenomena as psychokinesis (PK). It is not certain whether the force originates within the body or is drawn from outside and channeled through the body. Bioenergy and the application of it has been of great interest to researchers in Czechoslovakia and the Soviet Union, who claim to be able to store the energy in generators. See **Psychokinesis (PK)**; **Psychotronics**.

In healing the term "bioenergy" has been applied by Czech researcher Zdenek Rejdak to a touch method that is not related to Reich's bioenergy, but is based on the concept of *prana*. It involves the transmission of vital energy from a healer to a patient whose own energy field is depleted and out of balance. The transmission is done through the "biocurrents" in the aura and can be accomplished at a distance.

Sources: W. Y. Evans-Wentz, ed. *The Tibetan Book of the Great Liberation.* London: Oxford University Press, 1954; Milton Friedman. "From Poland with Prana." *New Realities* 7, no. 6: 10–15; Richard Gerber. *Vibrational Medicine.* Santa Fe, NM: Bear & Co., 1988; Henry Gris and William Dick. *The New Soviet Psychic Discoveries.* Englewood Cliffs, NJ: Prentice-Hall, 1978; Enid Hoffman. *Huna: A Beginner's Guide.* Rockport, MA: Para Research, 1976; Dolores Krieger. *The Therapeutic Touch.* New York: Prentice-Hall Press, 1979; C. W. Leadbeater. *The Chakras.* Wheaton, IL: Theosophical Publishing House, 1927; Solange Lemaitre. *Ramakrishna and the Vitality of Hinduism.* Woodstock, NY: The Overlook Press, 1984; Da Liu. *T'ai Chi Ch'uan and Meditation.* New York: Schocken Books, 1986; Ormond McGill. *The Mysticism and Magic of India.* Cranbury, NJ: A. S. Barnes & Co., 1977; Edgar D. Mitchell. *Psychic Exploration: A Challenge for Science.* Edited by John White. New York: Paragon Books, 1974; Ajit Mookerjee and Madhu Khanna. *The Tantric Way: Art, Science, Ritual.* Boston: New York Graphic Society, 1977; Sheila Ostrander and Lynn Schroeder. *Psychic Discoveries Behind the Iron Curtain.* Englewood Cliffs, NJ: Prentice-Hall, 1970; Ikuko Osumi and Malcolm Ritchie. *The Shamanic Healer: The Healing World of Ikuko Osumi and the Traditional Art of Seiki-Jutsu.* London: Century, 1987; Karl von Reichenbach. *The Odic Force: Letters on Od and Magnetism.* 1926. Secaucus, NJ: University Books, 1968; Kisshomaru Ueshiba. *The Spirit of Aikido.* Tokyo: Kodansha International, 1984; Vivian Worthington. *A History of Yoga.* London: Routledge & Kegan Paul, 1982.

Upanishads

See **Hinduism**; **Yoga**.

Urantia Book, the

A collection of 196 papers of reputed celestial origin, which give a new account of the complex history and structure of the universe; humankind's origin, history, and destiny; and the life and teachings of Jesus. *The Urantia Book* is said to have been written by many superhuman personalities in 1934 and 1935. It is popularly assumed that the work was channeled by human beings who chose to remain anonymous, but according to the Urantia Foundation, which publishes the book and aids the Urantia mission, the technique by which the papers were communicated is unknown to any living person. A group of people who came into possession of the papers formed the foundation in 1950, which published the book in 1955.

The Urantia Book, 2,097 pages in length, presents an integrated picture of the universe that unifies science, philosophy, and religion in a holistic cosmological structure. It seeks to address all religions, but a major section of it is essentially an expansion on the story of Christianity, as seen from a different, cosmic perspective. It contradicts some parts of the Bible, which it says have been distorted, and also presents new information. The book is written in the sexist language of the 1930s and sees the cosmos organized and administered by the male principle: God the Father, Paradise Sons, Planetary Princes, and so on. In content, however, it emphasizes the equality of the sexes. The local universe, Nebadon, is ruled by both Christ Michael and the Universe Mother Spirit celebrated by a "Proclamation of Equality."

Urantia, or Earth, is one of 10 million inhabitable planets (when completed) in the local universe of Nebadon, which, along with other similar universes, makes up the superuniverse of Orvonton. The commission of beings that claims authorship of *The Urantia Book* comes from all sections of the grand universe. The authorization of the book was given by the Ancients of Days, who are the administrators of Orvonton and reside in its capital, Uversa. The book further states that "Orvonton is one of seven evolutionary superuniverses of time and space which circle the never-beginning, never-ending creation of divine perfection—the central universe of Havona. At the heart of this eternal and central universe is the stationary Isle of Paradise, the geographic center of infinity and the dwelling place of the eternal God."

The seven superuniverses, along with the central and divine universe, are called the "grand universe," which is part of the "master universe," the latter of which "embraces the uninhabited but mobilizing universes of outer space."

According to the book, God, the Universal Father, sent out a supreme mandate, "Be you perfect, even as I am perfect," which was carried throughout

the universe by messengers of Paradise, even to "such lowly animal-origin creatures as the human races of Urantia." It is humankind's first duty, highest ambition, and final destiny to strive for perfection of divinity through a search for truth and God.

The history of Urantia began 987 billion years ago when space conditions in a part of Orvonton were deemed favorable for materialization of worlds and life. The planet itself was not formed until 3.5 billion years ago, along with nine other planets; Jupiter and Saturn were formed 4 billion years ago. All inhabitable worlds are registered and numbered, and Urantia was given its number of 606 in the local system of Satania. Urantia obtained its present size about 1 billion years ago, when its formal history began.

The development of Urantia generally followed the plan for inhabited planets in the universe. Once worlds are populated and a Garden of Eden developed, a Material Son and Material Daughter arrive as "biological uplifters" to enhance the racial quality and revelation of God. At an appropriate time in the spiritual and intellectual development, a Paradise Son appears on a bestowal mission to bring the world into a spiritual era in which war, disease, degeneracy, and so on eventually are eliminated.

In the case of Urantia, the first human beings, Andon and Fonta, appeared on the planet 993,473 years ago. Adam and Eve did not appear until 37,904 years ago. Prior to the arrival of Adam and Eve, the planet was beset by the rebellion of Lucifer and Satan, and the deposition of the Planetary Prince, Caligastia, otherwise known to mortals as the "devil." Adam and Eve were over eight feet tall, had glowing bodies, which reflected their higher origins, and were able to communicate by telepathy. They spent 117 years trying to uplift human beings, but were constantly plagued by Lucifer, Satan, and Caligastia. Eventually Eve fell victim to a plot engineered by Caligastia to follow a path of mixing good and evil. The fall of Adam and Eve severely retarded the spiritual development of Urantia, causing it to become a "confused and disordered planet."

Organization of The Urantia Book

The Urantia Book is divided into four sections. Part I describes the nature of the universe. Concepts of deity range from that of a personal Universal Father to impersonal absolutes. The material and gravitational center of the universe, the Isle of Paradise, is referred to as the nuclear source of all energy, matter, life, and personality. An organized hierarchical universe is described, which includes billions of inhabited planets in all stages of physical, mental, and spiritual evolution.

Part II relates to the local galaxy or local universe and its interrelationships, where the ministry of Christ is the central universe reality through which everything else finds meaning and purpose. Personality survival is seen as dependent on the spiritual reality status of the individual. This, in turn, is determined by the free will decisions of the individual toward God, by loyalty to truth, beauty, and goodness as these values are sincerely understood. Nevertheless, evil, sin, and judgment are stern and sober realities in the universe. The central challenge to modern people is to make a well-balanced and sane effort to achieve God-consciousness. Growth toward perfection is seen as the fundamental motivation of life. This growth is evolutionary, culminating, and virtually endless.

Part III narrates the story of the origin and development of Earth, whose universe name is "Urantia." In addition to human biological evolution, it traces the development of civilization, culture, government, religion, the family, and other social institutions, including a view of planetary history, dynamics, and destiny. Papers dealing with the nature and function of religion, the purpose and practice of prayer and worship, and the place of personal and institutional religion in life and society are discussed with both historical and contemporary frames of reference.

Part IV contains a seven-hundred-page version of the life and teachings of Jesus which parallels the New Testament story. This biography includes specific dates, from his birth (August 21, 7 B.C.) to the crucifixion (A.D. April 7, 30), resurrection (April 9, 30), and ascension (May 18, 30). It relates engaging childhood experiences, events in Jesus' struggle to overcome family adversity as a teenage youth, travels, and adventures, through which he gained a thorough knowledge of how life is lived on our world; and vignettes of personal and public ministry.

The Urantia Book *and Christianity*

The Christ who appeared on Urantia in the human form of Jesus of Nazareth was Michael of Nebadon, creator, organizer, and now sovereign of the local universe of Nebadon. There are many Michael Sons, all of whom voluntarily go out from Paradise to oversee portions of the cosmos. Through bestowal incarnations, the Sons mature in their roles as sovereigns as part of their education and training. Michael had seven bestowals on seven different worlds, beginning about 1 billion years ago. His seventh and last bestowal was on Urantia.

Unlike in his previous six bestowals, Michael chose to incarnate on Urantia in the form of mortal flesh and beginning as an infant. Generations of lineages were studied before Joseph and Mary were chosen as parents. The birth of Jesus was not virgin. From an early age, he had a sense of his origin and mission. His so-called "missing years" were spent primarily as the head of a large and poor family following the death of his father. In his twenty-eighth and twenty-ninth years, he undertook a tour of the Mediterranean world, and spent time in Alexandria, where he visited the great library and learned about the world's religions.

Following his crucifixion Jesus was resurrected neither in flesh nor as a spirit, but in the likeness of resurrected ascendant beings of the local Satania system. His corpse remained behind in the tomb and was decayed to dust in a natural but accelerated process by celestial hosts. After a number of appearances to the faithful, Jesus ascended, returning to his status as Michael, now having earned his universe sovereignty as a Paradise Creator Son.

The Urantia Book applauds Christianity for being "one of the greatest powers for good on earth," but laments its descent into politics and commerce. It has become a religion about Jesus rather than the religion of Jesus (the Gospel of the Fatherhood of God and the brotherhood of man). Christianity is handicapped because it has become identified with the local system, industrial life, and moral standards of Western civilization: "thus has Christianity unwittingly seemed to sponsor a society which staggers under the guilt of tolerating science without idealism, politics without principles, wealth without work, pleasure without restraint, knowledge without character, power without conscience, and industry without morality." Furthermore, it is suffering a slow death from "formalism, overorganization, intellectualism, and other nonspiritual trends," especially the mechanistic, materialistic orientation of science. The book urges Christianity to turn away from its material concerns and return to "learn anew from Jesus of Nazareth the greatest truths mortal man can ever hear—the living gospel of the fatherhood of God and the brotherhood of man."

Since its publication *The Urantia Book* has attracted tens of thousands of followers, some of whom are academics, intellectuals, and professionals. The Urantia Brotherhood was formed in 1955 as a religious organization concerned with the spiritual regeneration of humankind; in 1989 it changed its name to the Fifth Epochal Fellowship. The Fellowship works to help members master the teaching of *The Urantia Book,* and to form study groups which in turn can be chartered as Societies. All outreach activity, including sale of the book, is done largely by word-of-mouth.

Sources: Jon Klimo. *Channeling: Investigations on Receiving Information from Paranormal Sources.* Los Angeles: Jeremy P. Tarcher, 1987; *The Urantia Book.* Chicago: Urantia Foundation, 1955; The Urantia Foundation; The Fifth Epochal Fellowship, 529 Wrightwood Ave., Chicago, IL 60614.

V

Vision quest

Ritual common to tribes throughout North America, with the exception of the southwestern United States, for acquiring a guardian spirit or soliciting supernatural guidance. It is most important east of the Rockies and in some parts of western North America. The vision quest provides the average person, not just the medicine man, with access to the spiritual realms for help.

The vision quest, or "crying for a vision," as it is sometimes called, is preceded by sweat-bath purification rites. The individual goes into the wilderness to a sacred place and fasts, thirsts, smokes tobacco, prays, and meditates for a vision. The vigil may last several days and nights. Self-mortification or mutilation, such as cutting off a finger joint, is practiced by some Plains tribes. Some tribes use hallucinogens; small groups in southern California traditionally ingested a drink containing jimson weed, and medicine societies along the Missouri used mescal. See **Medicine societies**. In a successful vision quest, the seeker falls into a trance or experiences a vivid dream in which his guardian spirit manifests, or he receives the sought-after advice from the spirits or Great Spirit.

Vision quests are usually sought by males, sometimes beginning in childhood but usually not until at least puberty. They are a powerful force in the maturation process, providing a focus and sense of purpose, personal strength, and power.

In seeking a guardian spirit, the individual usually asks to receive certain powers, such as for hunting or healing, or for luck in warfare, love, gambling, and so on. The guardian spirit usually appears in animal form, but may change to human form. In bestowing powers, it also may prescribe food taboos; teach a song, which is used to reconnect the individual to the spirit at any given time; and give instructions for ornamentation and the assembly of medicine bundles. All instructions must be followed lest the man lose the spirit. Ideally, the spirit leaves behind a physical token of the vision, such as a feather or claw. If the spirit that appears is undesirable, its power is refused, and at a later time another vision quest is undertaken.

Vision quests also are undertaken at times of war, disease, death, and childbirth (the latter to seek instructions for naming the child). Most Native Americans believe that the vision seeker should abstain from sex for a period beforehand. Some tribes, such as the Algonkians and Salish, have vision quest rites for girls, but the quests are not done after puberty. Plains warriors traditionally undertook numerous vision quests, and thus acquired many guardian spirits, each with a different function.

Most vision quests are solitary affairs, but some are done on a collective basis, such as in the Sun Dance ceremony. See **Guardian spirit; Medicine bundle; Shamanism; Sun Dance; Sweat.**

Sources: Edward S. Curtis. "Medicine Practices of the Lakota Sioux." Excerpted from *The North American Indian*, 1908. *Shaman's Drum* no. 16 (Mid-Spring 1989): 25–31; Michael Harner. *The Way of the Shaman.* New York: Bantam, 1986; Ake Hultkrantz. *The Religions of the American Indians.* 1967. Berkeley: University of California Press, 1979; Ake Hultkrantz. *Native Religions of North America.* San Francisco: Harper & Row, 1987; Lame Deer, John (Fire), and Richard Erdoes. *Lame Deer: Seeker of Visions.* New York: Washington Square Press/Pocket Books, 1972; Ruth M. Underhill. *Red Man's Religion.* Chicago: University of Chicago Press, 1965; Carl Waldman. *Atlas of the North American Indian.* New York: Facts On File, 1985.

Visualization

See **Creative visualization.**

Vivekananda, Swami

See **Hinduism.**

Vodoun (also Voodoo)

Syncretic religion based on ancient African rites and Catholicism. Vodoun has 50 million followers worldwide.

"Vodoun" derives from *vodu,* meaning spirit or deity in the Fon language of Dahomey, now part of Nigeria. Creole slave masters in the New World translated the word into *vaudau.* Creole language derives from French, with definite African patterns of phonetics and grammar. Eventually, the word became *voudou, voudoun, vodoun, voodoo,* and *hoodoo;* the latter two terms are now considered pejorative.

Vodoun is a product of the slave trade, principally in the Spanish and French colonies in the Caribbean such as Jamaica and Saint Domingue, now divided into Santo Domingo and Haiti. Whites forbade their slaves to practice their religion on pain of torture and death. Any slave found possessing a fetish was to be imprisoned, hanged, or flayed alive. See **Fetish.** To save black souls, the masters baptized the slaves as Catholics. Like Santería, Vodoun became a syncretism, with Catholicism superimposed upon secret native rites and beliefs. Tribal deities took on the forms of Catholic saints. Worshipers saw the addition of the saints as an enrichment of their faith, not a profanity. Fetishes were replaced by Catholic statues, candles, and holy relics. See **Santería.**

Serving the Vodoun Loa

The Vodoun pantheon of gods, called *loas* or *mystères,* is enormous, with hundreds of deities. It accommodates additional local deities or ancestral spirits as needs arise. Vodounists acknowledge an original Supreme Being, called *Gran Met,* who made the world, but he is too remote for personal worship. Instead, devotees "serve the loa," seeking to please the gods and receive favors in return. Depending on the rites observed, the loas can be kind, beneficent, wise, violent, sexual, vindictive, generous, or mean.

The oldest of the ancestors is Danbhalah-Wedo, or the Great Serpent (also called Danballah or Damballah). Prior to the days of slavery, Africans worshiped a large python, Danh-gbwe, as the embodiment of the gods. The snake was harmless to humans, and devotees believed that any child touched by the serpent was chosen as a priest or priestess by the god himself. After transportation to the Americas, the slaves substituted a large boa for the python.

Danbhalah-Wedo does not speak, only hisses. *Langage,* the sacred language of Vodoun, which represents long-forgotten African liturgy, descended from Danbhalah's hissing. Those possessed by Danbhalah do not walk but slither, and do not use their limbs.

In the Vodoun creation story, Danbhalah created all the waters of the Earth. The movement of his seven thousand coils formed the hills and valleys of Earth and brought forth the stars and planets of the heavens. Danbhalah forged metals from heat, and sent lightning bolts to form the sacred stones and rocks. When Danbhalah shed his skin in the sun, releasing the waters over the land, the sun shone in the water and created the Rainbow. Danbhalah loved the Rainbow's beauty and made her his wife, Aida-Wedo.

Aida-Wedo is personified as a short coiled snake, much more slender than Danbhalah, which feeds upon bananas and lives mainly in the water. Her bright spectrum decorates Vodoun temples, especially the central support pole, which represents the *axis mundi,* the axis of the world that connects heaven, earth, and the underworld. Aida-Wedo is only one manifestation of the goddess Erzulie, the deity of beauty, love, wealth, and prosperity. Called Maitresse Erzulie, she is the moon and wife of Legba, the sun. As the moon Erzulie is pure and virginal. Contact with her fiery husband burned her skin, so she is depicted as a beautiful, dark-skinned Ethiopian. Her legend compares with the biblical story of the Queen of Sheba and King Solomon. There are many different Erzulies, encompassing not only the virtues of love and good will but also the vices of jealousy, discord, and vengeance.

Although Danbhalah represents the ancestral knowledge of Vodoun, no communion of god and worshiper can take place without the offices of Legba, called "Papa" or Legba Ati-Bon ("Legba of the Good Wood"). He is the Orient, the East, the sun, and the place the sun rises. He governs gates, fences, entryways, and the New Year; no other deity may join a Vodoun ceremony unless Legba has been asked to open the "door." No loa may act without Legba's permission. Depicted both as a man sprinkling water and as an old man walking with a stick or crutch, Legba personifies the ritual waters and the consolidation of Vodoun mysteries; as such he is related to Danbhalah-Wedo. Through syncretization Legba has become identified with St. Peter, the gatekeeper of heaven and the man to whom Christ gave the keys to the Kingdom. Others see Legba as Christ, a mulatto man born of the sun and the moon. Legba also guards crossroads, and as Maître Carrefour ("master of the four roads," or "crossroads") is the patron of sorcery.

A separate classification of loas are the Guedes, the various spirits of death and graveyards, sexual debauchery, and buffoonery, which are worshiped by various cults. The Guedes also govern the preservation and renewal of life and protect the children. Depictions of the Guedes, usually referred to as Guede Nibbho or Nimbo, Baron Samedi, or Baron Cimetière ("cemetery"), show the loa in a dark tailcoat and tall hat like an undertaker. His symbols are coffins and phalluses. Those possessed by Baron Samedi tell lewd jokes, wear dark glasses, and smoke cigarettes or cigars. They eat voraciously and drink copious amounts of alcohol.

Rites and Ceremonies

Each tribe originally had its own customs, rituals, and loas, but many have blended over time. Differentiations exist in music, drums, ceremonies, and even the manifestations of the gods, although the main ones appear in each rite.

Vodoun (also Voodoo)

The two main rites of Vodoun worship are Rada and Petro (also Pethro), both characterized by drumming, dancing, chanting, and ecstatic trance. Rada rites follow more traditional African patterns and emphasize the gentler, more positive attributes of the loas. Devotees wear all-white clothing for the ceremonies. Animals sacrificed—Danbhalah exhorted his followers to partake of sacred blood—include chickens, goats, and bulls.

Petro rites have their origins in Arawak and Carib ceremonies that existed in Haiti during the slavery days. The name "Petro" allegedly comes from Don Juan Felipe Pedro, a Spanish Vodoun priest and former slave who contributed a more violent style of dance. The Carib—from which the word "cannibal" derives—worshiped their gods more violently, emphasizing death and vengeance. Petro ceremonial clothing is red, and the loas are predominantly more menacing, deadly, and ill-tempered; many of their names simply have the appellation *Ge-Rouge* ("red eyes"), after a Rada name to signify the Petro form. Pigs are sacrificed to them.

Guinee, or *lan Guinee* or *Ginen*, symbolizes the homeland of the Africans in diaspora. The sacred city of Guinee is Ifé, the Mecca of Vodoun. An actual Ifé exists in southern Nigeria, but the Ifé of Vodoun is a legendary place where the revelations of the loas descended unto the first faithful. Vodoun devotees refer to themselves as sons or daughters of Guinee: *ti guinin*. Vodounists believe everything in life—administrative, religious, social, political, agricultural, artistic—comes from Ifé, but most especially the art of divination. Since Africa is east of the New World, Ifé represents the celestial position of the sun. All spiritual strength comes from Ifé; when the sacred drums need divine refreshment, they are "sent to Ifé" in a very solemn ceremony signifying death, burial, and resurrection.

A Vodoun temple for either rite is called a *hounfour, humfo,* or *oum'phor.* Within the temple, also known as the "holy of holies," are an altar and perhaps rooms for solitary meditation by initiates. The altar stone, called a *pe,* is covered in candles, food offerings, money, amulets, ceremonial rattles and flags, beads, drums, sacred stones, and other ritual paraphernalia. The snakes symbolizing Danbhalah once lived in the pe's hollow interior, but no longer.

Small jars called *govis* also occupy the pe, containing the souls of loa or revered ancestors (compare to **Fetish**). Vodounists believe a human is made of five components: the *n'âme,* the *z'étoile,* the corps cadavre, the *gros bon ange,* and the *ti bon ange.* The corps cadavre is the mortal flesh. The n'ame is the spirit of the flesh, given by Danbhalah and Aida-Wedo, that allows the body to function while it is alive and passes as energy into the soil after death. The z'étoile is the person's star of destiny and resides in the heavens.

Gros bon ange and ti bon ange refer to a Vodounist's soul; literally translated, they mean the "big good angel" and the "little good angel." The gros bon ange passes into a human being at conception as part of the life force that all living things share. It keeps the body alive and at death returns to the energy reservoir to be used again. But the ti bon ange is one's soul, one's essence, one's aura, the source of one's personality. The ti bon ange travels during sleep to experience dreams, and it leaves the body under possession by the loa. It represents the accumulation of a person's knowledge or experience, and is the most vulnerable to sorcery.

At death the ti bon ange hovers about the body for seven days, where a sorcerer may capture it and make it a *zombi astral,* or zombie of the soul. If the ti bon ange survives such risk, the priest ritually separates the soul from the flesh, releasing it to live in the dark waters for one year and one day. Then the family ritually raises the soul, now called an *esprit,* or spirit, and places it in the govi. The spirits in the govi are clothed, fed, and treated like divine beings, then released to live in the trees and rocks until they are reborn. After sixteen incarnations the spirits return to Danbhalah-Wedo, where they become part of the great cosmic energy.

The walls and floors of the hounfour are covered in *vêves,* elaborate, colored designs symbolizing the gods. These drawings can be permanent or created in cornmeal, flour, powdered brick, gunpowder, or face powder just before a ceremony. They incorporate the symbols and occult signs of the loa being worshiped: a vêve for Legba shows a cross, one for Erzulie a heart, Danbhalah a serpent, and Baron Samedi a coffin. Usually drawn around the center post or the place of sacrifice, the vêve serves as a ritual "magnet" for the loa's entrance, obliging the loa to descend to earth.

Brightly colored ritual flags may hang on the walls or from the ceiling. There are usually pictures of the Catholic saints. Most hounfours even display photographs of government officials, the gods' representatives on Earth. A model boat represents Maîtresse Erzulie and the ritual waters.

Outside the main temple is the *peristyle,* the roofed and sometimes partially enclosed courtyard adjacent to the holy of holies. Since the hounfour probably cannot accommodate all the Vodoun participants and onlookers, most ceremonies and treatment of the sick are held in the open-air peristyle. A low wall encircles the area, allowing those who are not dressed properly or are merely curious to watch less conspicuously. The peristyle's floor is always hard-packed earth without paving or tile.

Holding up the peristyle is the *poteau-mitan,* or center post. The poteau-mitan symbolizes the center of Vodoun,

from the sky to hell, and is the cosmic axis of all Vodoun magic. Usually made of wood and set in a circular masonry base called the *socle,* the post bears colorful decorations and designs representing the Serpent Danbhalah and his wife Aida-Wedo, the Rainbow. The poteau-mitan also symbolizes Legba Ati-Bon ("Legba of the Good Wood"), the way of all Vodoun knowledge and communion with the gods. Geometrically, the placement of the center post forms perfect squares, circles, crosses, and triangles with the socle and the roof of the peristyle, adding to its magical powers. All Vodoun temples have a poteau-mitan, or center, even if the post exists only symbolically.

Outside the peristyle the trees surrounding the courtyard serve as sacred *reposoirs,* or sanctuaries, for the gods. Vodoun devotees believe all things serve the loa and by definition are expressions and extensions of God, especially the trees. They are revered as divinities themselves and receive offerings of food, drink, and money. Like cathedrals, they are places to be in the presence of the holy spirit; banana trees are particularly revered.

Calling the Loas

True communion comes through possession, or "the hand of divine grace." When summoned, the gods may enter a govi or "mount a horse"—assume a person's mind and body. The possessed loses all consciousness, totally becoming the possessing loa with all his or her desires and eccentricities. Young women possessed by the older spirits seem frail and decrepit, while the infirm possessed by young, virile gods dance and cavort with no thought to their disabilities. Even facial expressions change to resemble the god or goddess. The priest or priestess, called *houngan* and *mambo* respectively, acts as intermediary to summon the loa and helps them depart when their business is finished. The houngan and mambo serve as healers, diviners, psychologists, musicians, and spiritual leaders.

The most important symbol of the houngan's or mambo's office is the *asson*, a large ritual rattle made from the calabash, a type of squash with a bulbous end and a long handle. Symbolically, the asson represents the joining of the two most active magic principles: the circle at the round end and the wand at the handle. The handle also symbolizes the poteau-mitan, or vertical post. Inside the dried calabash are sacred stones and snake vertebrae, considered the bones of African ancestors. Eight different stones in eight colors are used to symbolize eight ancestor gods; eight signifies eternity. Chains of colored beads, symbolizing the rainbow of Aida-Wedo, or more snake bones encircle the round end of the calabash. When the vertebrae rattle, making the asson "speak," the spirits come down to the faithful through Danbhalah, the oldest of the ancestors.

Other important members of the worship service include *la place* or *commandant la place*, the master of ceremonies, who orchestrates the flag-waving ceremonies, the choral singing and chanting, and the drum-beating. La place carries a ritual sword made of the finest iron and sometimes decorated with geometric designs and symbols. The sword's name is *ku-bha-sah*, which means "cutting away all that is material." Brandishing his sword from east to west during the ceremonies, la place cuts away the material world, leaving the faithful open for the divine presences. La place's sword also symbolizes the loa Ogou, god of iron and weaponry.

The chorus or *canzo*, composed of fully initiated Vodoun members called *hounsihs* or *hounsis*, performs under the direction of the *hounguenicon* or *hounguenikon*, usually a woman and the second-most powerful member after the houngan or mambo. By sending the chants to the loas in the astral plane, the hounguenicon calls the mystères and demands their presence on earth.

Novices not yet completely in the loas' power are called *hounsih bossales*. The initiate who obtains the sacrificial animals is the *hounsih ventailleur,* and the sacrificial cook is the *hounsih cuisiniere.* The *hounguenicon quartier-maître* oversees distribution of sacrificial food not reserved for the loas.

Two of the most important Vodoun celebrations in Haiti occur July 16 at Sant d'Eau near Ville Bonheur and July 25 in Plaine du Nord. Sant d'Eau is a waterfall, long sacred to Danbhallah and Aida-Wedo. On July 16, 1843, a man named Fortuné was looking for a lost horse, looked up at the palm trees overhead, and reputedly saw a flash of light, which he knew was the Virgin Mary, or Vyej Mirak, the Virgin of Miracles or Our Lady of Mount Carmel. She appeared again in 1881, and local Catholic authorities erected a chapel and shrine in her honor, hoping to usurp the Vodoun worship. But the Vodounists believed the appearance of the Virgin was a visit by Erzulie Freda. The site became holy to both religions, with offerings of food left as frequently as candles. See **Marian apparitions.**

The festival for St. Jacques Majeur, or St. James the Greater, takes place nine days later. Depicted as a warrior on horseback, St. James has become the Catholic version of Ogou Fer, or the god of armor and warfare. For days before the official feast day, Vodoun worshipers travel to Plaine du Nord to wallow in a large mud pond formed by road and building construction begun as early as 1909. In keeping with Ogou's fiery nature, the worshipers bathe frenziedly in the mud, submerging themselves and their children to gain Ogou's favors. Offerings of food and money pour into the mud, and small boys dive for coins. Sacrificing a bull to Ogou climaxes the celebration; as the houngan slices its throat with a machete, the animal's life force becomes part of the loa. Participants collect the bull's blood in a calabash and drink it all around, taking for themselves part of Ogou's divine energy.

Vodoun and Black Magic

Vodoun worshipers may not all practice black magic, but darker aspects of Vodoun do exist. A houngan more involved in sorcery than healing is known as a *bokor* or *boko,* or "one who serves the loa with both hands." The greatest fear of the *bokor* is not a death curse but zombification. See **Zombie.**

Sources: Rod Davis. "Children of Yoruba." *Southern Magazine* (February 1987); Wade Davis, *The Serpent and the Rainbow.* New York: Warner Books, 1985; Melita Denning and Osborne Phillips. *Voudou Fire: The Living Reality of Mystical Religion.* St. Paul, MN: Llewellyn Publishing, 1979; Carole Devillers. "Of Spirits and Saints: Haiti's Voodoo Pilgrimages." *National Geographic* (March 1985); Peter Haining. *The Anatomy of Witchcraft.* New York: Taplinger, 1972; Douglas Hill and Pat Williams. *The Supernatural.* London: Aldus Books, 1965; Mike McLaughlin. "A Voudou Village in the US." *The Seattle Times/Seattle Post-Intelligencer* (April 5, 1987); Milo Rigaud. *Secrets of Voodoo.* San Francisco: City Lights Books, 1969.

W

Walk-in

See **Montgomery, Ruth.**

Watseka possession (also the "Watseka Wonder")

The possession of Mary Lurancy Vennum by Mary Roff ranks as one of the most remarkable examples of spirit control for the victim's benefit instead of harm. It also is considered the best case on record of apparent possession as reincarnation.

In 1864 Mary Roff was a young girl of eighteen in Watseka, Illinois. Since the age of six months, she had suffered fits of depression of increasing violence, and headaches that she attempted to alleviate by bleeding herself. In July 1864 she cut herself with a knife and fainted. Upon regaining consciousness she experienced a raving mania and extrasensory ability, which included clairvoyance and eyeless vision. This state lasted for five days, and then Roff died.

Thirteen years later, in 1877, Mary Lurancy Vennum, a neighbor but near-stranger to the Roffs, and who had been three months old when Roff died, appeared to go insane. For months she suffered fits of trances in which she claimed to see heaven, angels, and the spirits of the dead; occasionally she passed into ecstatic trances in which she claimed to be in heaven herself. The consulting physi-cian, Dr. E. W. Stevens, diagnosed spirit obsession. Under hypnosis Vennum said she was tormented and controlled by evil spirits.

Stevens suggested that one of the spirits might be able to help Vennum control the others, and she answered that "Mary Roff" was willing. Roff's fa-ther, present at the session, agreed, and so Roff took possession of Vennum's body on February 1, 1878. Roff claimed she was doing so in order to help Ven-num heal. Roff remained in control for sixteen weeks, and Vennum behaved only as Roff. She moved back to the Roff home, recognized Roff's old friends, and generally lived as Roff had thirteen years before. She also exhibited clairvoyant powers, had out-of-body experiences, and traveled in astral planes. She said she often saw the dead children of Stevens in heaven, and described going with them in spirit visits to the Stevens household.

On May 21 Roff tearfully told her friends and family that Vennum was coming back. She said good-bye, and within minutes fell into a trance and be-came Vennum again. Vennum was com-pletely healed, both mentally and physi-cally, apparently having been made safe from evil spirit invasion by Roff's long inhabitation.

In 1882 Vennum married a farmer and eventually moved to Rawlins Coun-ty, Kansas. Roff continued to watch over Vennum, taking control from time to time by causing Vennum to go into a trance; during childbirth she protected Vennum from pain. Vennum made numerous references to information she obtained clairvoyantly from Roff, but never fully developed a mediumship due to her family's disapproval and fear. Roff did not manifest independently from Vennum's body, and did not appear to anyone else in Watseka. Vennum died in the late 1940s. See **Possession; Reincarnation.**

Sources: John Curt Ducasse. *A Critical Examination of the Belief in a Life After Death.* Springfield, IL: Charles C Thomas, 1961; Frederic W. H. Myers. *Human Personality and Its Survival of Bodily Death.* Vols. 1 and 2. 1903. New ed. New York: Longmans, Green & Co., 1954; David St. Clair. *Watseka, America's Most Extraordinary Case of Possession and Exorcism.* Chicago: Playboy Press, 1977.

Watts, Alan (1915–1973)

Author of books on the philosophy and psychology of religion; teacher, lecturer, and counterculture leader, especially of the San Francisco renaissance in the 1960s. Though he never formally embraced Zen, he became identified with Zen, which was much in vogue with the intellectuals of the 1950s and 1960s.

Alan Watts was born January 6, 1915, in Chislehurst, Kent, England. At age twelve he read the Fu Manchu novels of Sax Rohmer and became curious about Eastern thought and customs. He wrote his first book, *The Spirit of Zen: A Way of Life, Work, and Art in the Far East,* at age twenty. Two years later he published *The Legacy of Asia and Western Man: A Study of the Middle Way.* Twenty-three other books followed, one every three or four years for the rest of his life, except during the 1950s, when six years separated *The Wisdom of Insecurity* (1951) and *The Way of Zen* (1957).

With a master's degree in theology and a doctorate in divinity, Watts was best known as an interpreter for Westerners of East Indian and Chinese philosophies, and in particular Zen Buddhism. However, he did not consider himself a Zenist, or even a Buddhist, for, as he says in *The Way of Zen,* "this seems . . . to be like trying to wrap up and label the sky." He said also that, in relation to Zen, he was not a scientifically objective academician, "for this seems to me to be like studying birdsong in a collection of stuffed nightingales." During the 1930s he met British Buddhist Christmas Humphreys, who introduced him to Japanese Buddhist scholar D. T. Suzuki.

In 1936 Watts immigrated to the United States and in 1943 became an American citizen. He surreptitiously studied with Zen master Sokei-an Sasaki in Chicago. He attempted an "experiment" of immersing himself back in Christianity, and was ordained an Anglican priest in 1944. He served as the Episcopal chaplain at Northwestern University in Evanston, Illinois, for six years, but became uncomfortable in his role and, in his words, "fled the church." He later observed that the priesthood was "an ill-fitting suit of clothes, not only for a shaman but also for a bohemian—that is, one who loves color and exuberance, keeps irregular hours, would rather be free than rich, dislikes working for a boss, and has his own code of sexual morals."

Watts's bohemian behavior also included extramarital sexual activities, excessive use of tobacco and alcohol, and LSD experiments. The latter drug use he admitted sharing with some of his family and associates who included Timothy Leary, Allen Ginsburg, Jack Kerouac, and Richard Alpert (later Ram Dass.) Watts wrote about his alcoholism and other personal problems, especially in *The Wisdom of Insecurity* (1951).

He earned his master's degree in theology from the Seabury-Western Theological Seminary in 1948 and his doctor of divinity from the University of Vermont in 1958. He then journeyed to California, where he took up residency in Mill Valley and studied Chinese calligraphy. From 1951 to 1957, he was professor of philosophy at American Academy of Asian Studies in San Francisco, and served as dean from 1953 to 1956. From 1951 to 1953, he was a research fellow of the Bollingen Foundation.

But he had not abandoned Buddhism and Taoism. Rather, he wanted to, as he said, bring to Christianity "a form of that mystical and perennial philosophy which has appeared in almost all times and places." To this end, during two-year research fellowships in 1962 through 1964, one at Harvard University in the Department of Social Relations, and a second at the Bollingen Foundation, he traveled in both Europe and the Far East. Watts's ideas on the mystical experience are put forth in *Behold the Spirit: A Study in the Necessity of Mystical Religion* (1947), which was widely praised by reviewers. Critics called it "creeping pantheism," which Watts shrugged off in his preface to the 1972 edition of the book by observing that "all doctrines of God are ultimately false and idolatrous, because doctrines are forms of words which can never be more than pointers to mystical vision . . ." He defined pantheism as "the conception of God as the total energy-field of the universe, including both its positive and negative aspects, and in which every discernible part or process is a sort of microcosm or hologram."

Watts is recognized for his efforts to find a common meeting ground between Western psychotherapy and Eastern schools of thought, including Buddhism, yoga, Taoism, and Vedanta. The fruits of his efforts were published in *Psychotherapy East and West* (1963), in which he observed that the two sides have some parallels, in that they attempt to trans-

Alan Watts

form consciousness and one's inner feelings of one's own existence, and release the individual from conditioning that has been imposed by social institutions. The parallels are not exact, Watts wrote, because Eastern schools do not categorize the mind as a clinical entity, nor separate mind and matter, soul and body, as do Western schools.

In his autobiography, *In My Own Way* (1972), Watts said that his first mother-in-law, Ruth Everett, was very knowledgeable about Zen and influenced him a great deal. Watts married Everett's daughter, Eleanor, in 1936, after she became pregnant with the first of their two daughters. Their baby-sitter, Dorothy De Witt, became Watts's second wife in 1950; the two had five children. Watts was excommunicated upon his second marriage.

In 1963, after moving to California, he married Mary Jane Yates. He once commented, "I have had three wives, seven children, and five grandchildren—and I cannot make up my mind whether

I am confessing or boasting." In his autobiography he described himself as a "terrible father" because of his impatience with the conventional world of childhood that is "an itsy-bitsy, cutie-pied, plastic hoax."

Watts died at age fifty-eight. On the morning of November 16, 1973, "Jano," as Mary Jane Yates was called, attempted to waken him and found him dead. A doctor certified he had died of heart failure. His health had deteriorated for years due to his heavy drinking and smoking, and habits of late-night partying. However, he had also had been experimenting with Zen breathing techniques to reach *samadhi,* a state of enlightenment. Jano believed he had left his body and had been unable to get back into it. Watts often wrote and spoke of his concern about "Zen breathing" throughout his writings, such as in the final pages of *The Way of Zen.*

Stories of strange incidents circulated after his death. According to one, the great gong of Druid Heights in San Francisco, where Watts and Jano had lived, sounded on its own at the time of Watts's death. While alive Watts had predicted he would return to that site after death as a lightning flash. On December 21, the night of the winter solstice, a lightning flash knocked out an underground cable on the lane leading to Druid Heights.

At Watts's Crossing Over ceremony, the abbot of the San Francisco Zen Center gave him the Buddhist name Yu Zen Myo Ko, which means "Profound Mountain, Subtle Light." At the same time, Watts was bestowed the very rare title Dai Yu Jo Mon, which means "Great Founder, Opener of the Great Zen Samadhi Gate." His ashes were interred in a *stupa* on a hillside behind the Zen Center's Green Gulch Farm.

The degree of misunderstanding of Watts is reflected in many of his obituaries. One such obituary simply understated that Watts was a "Zen Buddhist philosopher who became a cult hero to beat and hippie generations." As *East West Journal* observed in 1983, "His iconoclastic positions and theatrical, show-biz streak prevented some scholars and Zen teachers from taking him completely seriously." However, the more objective overview of Watts by George Ingles may be the best final evaluation: "The genius of Alan Watts was in his originality and method—in his ability to remove all obstruction from the mind flow and to simply allow a frolic of words to gush forth in a seemingly magical arrangement of gaiety, wit, and humor with profound meaning and instruction . . ." Gopi Krishna praised Watts as "one of those intellectuals in whom the evolutionary metamorphosis is almost complete . . ." Krishna said that Watts's sexual and sensual appetites were in keeping with the Tantric mystical tradition, though he may have lacked the self-discipline to moderate his behavior. See **Drugs in mystical and psychic experiences; Mysticism; Zen.**

Sources: Robert Ellwood, ed. *Eastern Spirituality in America: Selected Writings.* New York: Paulist Press, 1987; Monica Furlong. *Zen Effects: The Life of Alan Watts.* New York: Houghton Mifflin, 1986; Gene Kiefer, ed. *Kundalini for the New Age: Selected Writings of Gopi Krishna.* New York: Bantam Books, 1988; Alan Watts. "Letting Go: The Art of Playful Living." *East West Journal* 13, no. 4 (April 1983): 306; Alan Watts. *In My Own Way: An Autobiography 1915–1965.* New York: Pantheon Books/Random House, 1972; Alan Watts. *The Essence of Alan Watts.* Millbrae, CA: Celestial Arts, 1974; Alan Watts. *Psychotherapy East and West.* New York: Vintage Books/Random House, 1961; Alan Watts. *Behold the Spirit: A Study in the Necessity of Mystical Religion.* 1947. New York: Vintage Books/Random House, 1972; Alan Watts. *The Way of Zen.* New York: Vintage Books/Random House, 1957.

White Eagle Lodge

Nondenominational Christian church founded in 1936 by British Spiritualist Grace Cooke, in accordance with instructions from her spirit guide, White Eagle. The organization began as the White Eagle Brotherhood at Burstow Manor in Surrey, England, moving in 1945 to New Lands at Liss, Hampshire. The White Eagle Lodge has an international following, and its publishing trust produces books, tapes, and a magazine, *Stella Polaris*. White Eagle's teachings provide the core philosophy, which is centered on a triune Eternal Spirit comprised of the Father, the Mother, and the Son or the Christ. The Father is divine energy; the Mother the creative force and enfolding love; and the Son the Christ-light who descended to earth as the pure light and love, which is in every human being as his or her salvation.

White Eagle's teachings are said to come from the ancient wisdom handed down through the ages by the adepts of the Great White Brotherhood, the Brotherhood of the Cross of Light within the Circle of Light, of which White Eagle is a member.

The teachings include five Cosmic Laws: Reincarnation, Karma, Opportunity, Correspondence, and Equilibrium and Balance. In Opportunity every experience provides a chance to learn and serve. The Law of Correspondence may be expressed as, "As above, so below"; humankind is a microcosm of the universe, governed by the same laws. The Law of Equilibrium and Balance is tied to Karma, in that actions are balanced by reactions.

The White Eagle Lodge places a great emphasis on healing, which is done individually or in groups in meditation, or in laying-on-of-hands ceremonies at a Lodge. Followers believe that the soul must be healed first for any lasting cure to be effected on the physical body,

(Courtesy The White Eagle Lodge)

White Eagle, from the original painting by R. Vicaji

which is the outer shell of the soul. The Lodge preaches living in harmony with the world of nature and with the divine law of love, and using natural remedies, colors, scents, and music in healing therapy. See **Cooke, Grace.**

Sources: Grace Cooke. *Sun Men of the Americas.* New Lands, England: White Eagle Publishing Trust, 1975; Ingrid Lind. *The White Eagle Inheritance.* London: Turnstone Press, 1984; *The Story of the White Eagle Lodge.* New Lands, England: White Eagle Publishing Trust, 1986.

White, Stewart Edward (1873–1946)

American occultist, psychical researcher, and author, whose exploration of alternate realities with his wife, Betty, resulted in the occult nonfiction classic, *The Betty Book,* and several other works.

White was born March 12, 1873, in Grand Rapids, Michigan. He studied at the University of Michigan, where he earned an undergraduate degree in philosophy in 1895 and a master's degree in the same subject in 1903. In 1904 he married Elizabeth Grant.

On March 17, 1919, during a lark with a Ouija board with friends, the Whites had their first encounter with the occult. After a few trials at the Ouija, the pointer, a whiskey glass, repeatedly spelled "Betty." Betty, who was scornful of the Ouija and was not participating, reluctantly took the glass. It went wild in circles. After a few more messages, the glass spelled, "Get a pencil, get a pencil," over and over again.

Betty complied. Thus began nearly a year of automatic writing, in which the communicating entities informed Betty that she would undergo a transformation of consciousness, to be brought in touch with the superconsciousness so that she could relay ideas and realities. The Whites named the spirits "the Invisibles" because of the spirits' desire to remain anonymous.

The Invisibles said their purpose was to prod humankind into devoting more effort to spiritual growth on Earth. Incarnation in the flesh provides certain opportunities for spiritual advancement that are lacking on the other side; the opportunities must be seized, for delays mean greater hardship and struggle later on.

In February 1918 the Invisibles switched from automatic writing to speaking through Betty's vocal cords. During the channeling sessions, Betty did not fall into a trance but remained in a dissociated state. Her waking consciousness seemed merely placed to one side, while another part of her consciousness seemed somewhere else, where the Invisibles showed her scenes to get their concepts and points across. For example, to demonstrate how the spiritual self is the core of being, the Invisibles showed Betty people who looked like X-ray images. Those who had neglected their spiritual development appeared gelatinous with no skeletons, and struck Betty as pathetic

creatures tragically unaware of their sorry state.

The Invisibles underscored the need for balance between the spiritual and the material. The word "God" has been enfeebled, they said. "The world has grown ashamed of the spirit." They also discussed the substance of thought, and how the mind, using thought and attention, magnetizes things, people, and circumstances. To grow spiritually one must fully meet and absorb all experiences. Truth must be more than recognized; it must be absorbed until it is manifested in action. Prayer and relaxation are important in establishing communion with spirit, but one must strive to rise up to spirit, not expect spirit to descend.

After about a year and a half of channeling sessions, the Whites began to organize the material into a book. The sessions lasted from 1919 to 1936; in 1937 *The Betty Book* was published under Stewart's name. The Whites had waited seventeen years to publish because, as White explained, they wanted to make sure the material was true, did work, and would be of general value.

In 1922 the Whites participated in a series of eleven seances with six others, including the medium Ruth Finley, who, with her husband, anonymously wrote *The Unseen Guest*. The seances took place at the home of Margaret Cameron, an automatic writer, and included another nonprofessional medium and her husband, Mr. and Mrs. Gaines. The purpose of the seances was to see, sense, and understand the astral body, which the Invisibles separated from the physical body of Finley. White reported the seances in an appendix to *The Betty Book*. The record was perhaps the first in psychic literature concerning the projection of the astral body witnessed by "reliable people." See **Out-of-body experience (OBE)**.

White wrote a second "Betty book," *Across the Unknown*, published in 1939. The same year, Betty died. Within a half-hour of her death, White sensed her invisible presence, an experience he would have frequently for the rest of his life. Six months after Betty's death, White had a seance with Finley and her husband and received communication from Betty, who wished to describe the afterworld. White published her messages in 1940 in *The Unobstructed Universe,* the first full, first-person account of life after death since the alleged communications of British psychical researcher Frederic W. H. Myers about twenty-five years earlier.

The three "Betty books" elicited such a response that White went on to write other books on the occult. He served as president of the San Francisco chapter of the American Society for Psychical Research. He also was a member of the American Association for the Advancement of Science, and a Fellow of the Royal Geographical Society. He died September 18, 1946, in Hillsborough, California. White's other books include *The Road I Know* (1942), *Anchors to Windward* (1943), *The Stars Are Still There* (1946), and two published posthumously, *With Folded Wings* (1947) and *The Job of Living* (1948). See **Channeling**; compare to **Roberts, Jane.**

Sources: Arthur Ford as told to Jerome Ellison. *The Life Beyond Death.* New York: G. P. Putnam's Sons, 1971; "Excursions into the World of Other Consciousness." *Journal of the American Society for Psychical Research* 31, no. 12 (December 1937): 373–79; Leslie A. Shepard, ed. *Encyclopedia of Occultism and Parapsychology.* 2d ed. Detroit: Gale Research Co., 1984; Stewart Edward White. *Across the Unknown.* Columbus, OH: Ariel Press, 1987; Stewart Edward White. *The Betty Book: Excursions into the World of Other-Consciousness.* New York: Berkley Medallion Books, 1969.

Witchcraft

Magical art and, in the West, both a system of magic and an organized religion. As a magical art, witchcraft usually is regarded with fear and uncertainty, though it provides a social function by enabling the redress of wrongs and grievances, and hope for the end of illness and problems. As a religion Witchcraft often is called "Wicca," an Old English term for "witch," in order to counter the negative stereotypes of Witches as ugly, evil, and Devil-worshipers.

The magical art of witchcraft exists universally. It is a type of sorcery, involving the mechanistic casting of spells and divination. In virtually all cultures, witchcraft is usually considered to be malevolent, though some distinctions exist between "white" and "black" witchcraft. In the lore of the Pennsylvania Dutch, for example, witches, also called *hexenmeisters* and *brauchers,* are consulted for cures and luck as often as for curses. But in most societies, even those where the local sorcerer is a respected individual, perhaps even a religious official, witches and witchcraft are feared as evil. Witches are believed to possess supernormal powers of invisibility, shape-shifting, flying, the ability to kill at a distance, clairvoyance, and astral projection, all of which they use solely to harm others.

Fear of witchcraft has a long history in the West. Witches were renowned in ancient Greece and Rome, especially for their evil eye. Under Roman law "white" witchcraft or sorcery was tolerated, but "black" witchcraft, which resulted in harm or death, was punishable as a civil crime.

As Christianity spread, witchcraft increasingly was associated with Devil-worship; it was practiced by pagans, and all pagan deities were demonized. The Inquisition began in the eleventh century to execute competitors to Christianity as heretics, who eventually included those who were alleged to practice witchcraft and worship the Devil. In the mid-fifteenth century, sorcery, and therefore witchcraft, became a heresy itself by papal decree. Demonologists issued writings describing the abominations of witches: how they worshiped the Devil in obscene rites, ate babies, destroyed crops and herds, raised tempests and hailstorms, and killed their neighbors. Witches invariably were women, for, according to the prevailing ecclesiastical wisdom, women were weak and susceptible to evil corruption.

Over about 250 years, an estimated 150,000 to 200,000 people were executed for witchcraft. Some were burned alive at the stake; others were strangled first and then burned; others were hung. Most of the executions took place in Europe, especially in Germany. In England, which escaped the Inquisition, witchcraft was prosecuted largely as a civil crime rather than as heresy. In America the worst case was the Salem witch trials in 1692 and 1693, in which 141 people were falsely arrested on the basis of accusations by hysterical children; nineteen were hung and one was pressed to death.

Victims of the Inquisition included village wise women and men who had reputed magical, healing, or clairvoyant powers; virtually any person accused of witchcraft; and political figures (a charge of witchcraft was one way to get rid of political enemies). Victims often were tortured into making lurid confessions; those who did not confess often died from the torture.

The persecution of witches largely ended by the 1730s, though cases in Germany continued to be tried for several more decades. The advance of science and industry and the growth of urban centers contributed to a decline in belief in witchcraft and magic. Witchcraft remained active in rural areas, where folk magic artists still were called upon to cure cows, bless crops, ensure love and the like. It retained, however, its associations with evil and the Devil.

In 1951 witchcraft ceased to be a crime in Britain, and in effect came out of the closet, led by Gerald B. Gardner, a British civil servant who spent part of his career in Malaysia. Gardner said that in 1939 he had been initiated into a coven of Witches practicing in the New Forest. It is difficult to say whether Gardner intended to create a new religion, or whether it grew spontaneously from public interest in his writings.

Gardner's coven claimed to be descended from a long line of hereditary Witches, who practiced both a magical craft and a Pagan religion, commonly called "the Craft of the Wise" and "the Old Religion." Other covens scattered about England have claimed the same, and due to their secrecy it is difficult to determine the validity of such claims. There is no evidence that paganism survived as an organized religion of witchcraft through the Middle Ages and beyond, though isolated groups may have existed.

Gardner formed his own coven in 1953. He borrowed ritual material from occult adept Aleister Crowley and added it to the rituals he learned from his first coven. He also apparently added elements of Eastern magic learned during his tenure in Malaysia. With the help of initiate Doreen Valiente, who threw out most of the Crowley material, he fashioned a "book of shadows" of Craft rituals and laws, the secret handbook for initiates.

His public books on the Craft, *Witchcraft Today* (1954) and *The Meaning of Witchcraft* (1959), attracted a large audience and helped to spark a movement of Witchcraft as religion on both sides of the Atlantic and in Australia. The greatest growth occurred in the 1960s and 1970s. The introduction of Witchcraft to America was spearheaded by Raymond and Rosemary Buckland of England (since divorced), who were initiated by Gardner prior to moving to the United States. Most converts to the Craft have been women who feel disenfranchised by Christianity or Judaism and are attracted by the appeal of Goddess worship.

The religion of Witchcraft is highly autonomous. Several dominant traditions, the rough equivalent of denominations, have developed. Gardnerian, named after Gardner, is the largest, followed by Alexandrian, after Alexander Sanders, an Englishman who modeled his tradition on Gardner's. The Dianic tradition mixes religion with feminist politics. There are still hereditary and traditional Witches who claim family lineages of Witches.

In the early years, one joined the Craft only by affiliating with established traditions. A person was initiated only by an initiated Witch, then advanced through three degrees in the coven hierarchy, which qualified one to "hive off" and form a coven. Today the Craft is more open; anyone can self-initiate, form a coven, and even establish a new tradition. Most Witches, however, probably practice as "solitaries."

All who join the Craft become either a priest or priestess. Most covens are run by a high priestess and high priest (the woman holds the superior rank). Most covens are a mix of men and women, but some are all-female or all-male.

Central to most traditions is worship of Goddess and her consort, the Horned God, who are called by the names of various deities. The emphasis on Goddess appears to be post-Gardner, though Valiente says Goddess was always part of the Craft.

Coven meetings and rituals traditionally require nudity (called "skyclad"). This practice may have been emphasized by Gardner because of his own interest and participation in nudist colonies. Some Witches prefer to work and worship robed.

Witches have great reverence for nature and all life forms, and generally believe in some form of reincarnation. The supreme law of the Craft is called the Wiccan Rede: "An' [If] it harm none, do what ye will," an approximation of the Golden Rule. Witches do not worship the Devil and do not perform blood sacrifice rites.

The content and context of rituals is similar to those of neo-Paganism. See **Neo-Paganism.** In addition to what has been handed down and what is created anew, ritual material has been adapted from Western occult societies such as Freemasonry, the Rosicrucians, and the Hermetic Order of the Golden Dawn.

Most initiated Witches undertake magical training. In his book of shadows, Gardner listed eight ways to raise magical power (singly or in combinations): (1) meditation or concentration; (2) chants, spells, and invocations; (3) trance and astral projection; (4) incense, wine, and drugs; (5) dancing; (6) blood control by binding parts of the body with cords; (7) scourging (not enough to draw blood); and (8) ritual sex.

The Wiccan Rede is taken seriously by most Witches, who abjure casting spells to harm others. Magic is to be used to help and to heal; harmful magic rebounds on its perpetrator. There is great debate, however, as to how literally the Rede should be taken. Some Witches believe it is acceptable to cast "binding spells." For example, instead of cursing an enemy, one would bind him, that is, prevent him from doing harm. Other Witches disagree and say binding spells break the Rede. Still other Witches believe in the judicious use of curses, such as against a mass murderer.

Only a small portion of Witches practice their religion openly, due to the danger of harassment from a public that still associates Witchcraft with the Devil. Witchcraft the religion is confused with witchcraft the sorcery and folk magic, and with Satanism, Vodoun, and Santería. Vodoun and Santería also have no connection with Satanism. Some Witches advocate finding another name for their religion; the term "Wicca" is the most popular alternate. See **Circle; Goddess; Planetary consciousness.**

Sources: Margot Adler. *Drawing Down the Moon.* Rev. ed. Boston: Beacon Press, 1986; Rosemary Ellen Guiley. *The Encyclopedia of Witches and Witchcraft.* New York: Facts On File, 1989; Rossell Hope Robbins. *The Encyclopedia of Witchcraft & Demonology.* 1959. New York: Bonanza Books, 1981; Jeffrey B. Russell. *A History of Witchcraft.* London: Thames and Hudson, 1980; Starhawk. *The Spiral Dance.* San Francisco: Harper & Row, 1979; H. R. Trevor-Roper. *The European Witch-Craze.* 1956. New York: Harper & Row, 1969; Barbara G. Walker. *The Woman's Encyclopedia of Myths and Secrets.* San Francisco: Harper & Row, 1983.

Worrall, Ambrose (Alexander) (1899–1972)

Gifted British-born clairvoyant and healer who became famous for healing with his American wife, Olga Ripich Worrall. Ambrose Worrall was born on January 18, 1899, in Barrow-in-Furness, England, on the coast of the Irish Sea. His father was employed for a while in the munitions and military supplies industry, and then ran a stationery store. Worrall was a gifted psychic from early childhood, seeing the glowing forms of spirits of the dead in his bedroom every night. As a youth he discovered that he involuntarily projected himself out-of-body to visit others at night. A customer of the stationery store once complained to his father that she could see him in her room every night when she turned off the light.

Worrall worked in an English munitions plant during World War I. He began to see impending deaths clairvoyantly: a small, thin skeleton floated over someone's head, accompanied by a number that indicated the length of the remaining lifespan. The omen applied either to the person or someone known to him or her. Worrall predicted the death of his sister, Edith, which came to him as an impression that he blurted out to his mother. He eventually suppressed these death visions and they ceased.

Worrall had no early urge to heal with his hands, yet he did find himself compelled to do so on various occasions, as though directed by some mysterious force. When his sister, Barbara, injured her neck, Worrall felt an invisible mass about eight inches in diameter emerge from his solar plexus and protrude about ten inches. A force then literally dragged him to his sister and caused him to place his hands on her neck for about five seconds. The injury was healed instantly. Later, when he began to heal with his wife, Olga, he experienced this solar plexus extrusion again.

After the war Worrall met John E. Cockerill, a Methodist lay preacher who encouraged him to develop his psychic gifts. Worrall joined a group of men and women pursuing psychic studies. He had little success at seances, however, because he tried too hard to achieve results.

In 1922 he emigrated to the United States because of the poor economic conditions in England. He found a sponsoring family in Cleveland, Ohio. He made a pact with friends in England to attempt transatlantic out-of-body contact, and felt he succeeded on at least one occasion.

In Cleveland Worrall went to work for the Glenn L. Martin Company, which later became the Martin Company, a division of Martin Marietta Corporation. Friends began to ask him for "psychic treatments," but Worrall protested that he had no gift for healing. Nonetheless, he followed his impulses to touch and make hand passes, and was astonished to hear that those he treated were cured or experienced significant improvement.

Worrall met Olga Ripich at a Christmas party in 1927. He felt they had known each other before on some other plane. They were married the following June. See **Worrall, Olga.**

In healing Worrall always felt a power build within him and flow from his hands. In his younger years, he clairvoyantly saw a pea-sized ball of light that would direct him where to place his hands; that eventually was replaced by intuitive impressions. He never knew what he was going to do with a patient. He simply relaxed and waited for the impulses to direct him. Sometimes both he and the patient experienced a tingling sensation.

Worrall believed the healing power was drawn from the universal life force. He termed it "paraelectricity" and said it has electrical properties. See **Universal life force.**

He spent his professional career as an engineer for Martin. In December 1928 he was transferred to Baltimore, Maryland, where the Worralls lived for the rest of their lives. He and Olga did occasional healings until 1929, then devoted themselves to a healing ministry. Worrall, however, retained his full-time job and did healing in his spare time. He retired in 1965 and then worked with Olga full time until his sudden death on February 2, 1972.

Like Olga, Worrall was continuously aware of various spirit presences, many of whom were connected with their patients and manifested to give helpful information. Once a spirit of a patient's dead grandmother told him "they" were directing healing energy to the grandson through Worrall, the channel. The Worralls believed that spirits were instrumental in the healing process.

One spirit that manifested to them over the years was an enlightened being who appeared as a seven-foot-tall Native American. He gave his name as "XYZ" and said that was all they needed to know about him. XYZ directed Olga to find a new home in Baltimore, where they established a healing room in one of the bedrooms. After his death Ambrose Worrall began communicating with Olga. He told her that XYZ had assisted him in the crossing over. He also told her that he would work with her from the other side, adding to her healing power, and that many doctors, surgeons, and healers on Earth were similarly aided by helping spirits. See **Healing, faith and psychic; Prayer.**

Sources: Edwina Cerutti. *Olga Worrall: Mystic with the Healing Hands.* New York: Harper & Row, 1975; Ronald S. Miller. "Mystic with the Healing Hands: An Interview with Olga Worrall." *Science of Mind* 56, no. 4 (April 1983): 8–12+; Ambrose A. Worrall with Olga N. Worrall. *The Gift of Healing: A Personal Story of Spiritual Therapy.* New York: Harper & Row, 1965.

Worrall, Olga (1906–1985)

Gifted American clairvoyant and healer who became internationally famous along with her British-born husband, Ambrose Worrall. She was born Olga Nathalie Ripich in 1906 in Cleveland, Ohio, to a Hungarian mother and Russian father. Her father, a theologian in the Russian Orthodox church, had been sent to the United States to organize church activities. Worrall was one of seventeen children.

By the age of three, Olga demonstrated psychic abilities that unsettled her parents. Every night she saw glowing people in her bedroom—spirits of the dead. Some of those she described were people whom the parents knew back in the old country, but did not know were dead. Death notices always arrived after the visions.

By age five Worrall could see her own aura by looking in the mirror, and could see the auras of others. By age eleven she was making precognitive predictions, including the death of her infant brother, which earned her a whipping. After her brother's death, she suppressed clairvoyant vision of auras until later in adulthood.

Worrall's healing ability also manifested early. As a young child, she responded to other people's distress by impulsively placing her hands on them. Her mother discovered that she could banish headaches, and used her frequently for that purpose. As a child Worrall cured her mother of a floating kidney, thus avoiding surgery, and saved the life of a neighbor who miscarried.

In 1925 Worrall went to see a psychic who described her future husband and predicted Worrall would work as a clairvoyant. She met Ambrose Worrall in 1927; they were mutually relieved to discover both had psychic gifts. Ambrose visited her at night out-of-body, and she in turn learned to do the same to him. They were married on June 7, 1928.

In December 1928 Ambrose's company transferred him to Baltimore, Maryland, where they lived the rest of their lives. Their only children, twin boys, were born on June 10, 1929, but became ill and died two months later in August. Some time later the Worralls were visited one night by the spirit of Ambrose's dead sister, Edith, who carried the infants and communicated that they were in her care.

Prior to the twins' deaths, the Worralls had performed healings upon request, as others heard of their remarkable abilities. Their grief prompted them to devote themselves to healing, especially of children. They worked out of a healing room they set up in their home. Ambrose retained his full-time job, and healed in his spare time. They refused payment. They always insisted that their efforts be accompanied by traditional medical help.

In 1950 Olga was invited by a Methodist minister, Albert E. Day, to establish with him a spiritual healing clinic. They operated the New Life Clinic for nine years out of the Mt. Vernon Place Methodist Church in Baltimore. Later the clinic was moved to the Mt. Washington Methodist Church, and Worrall worked with Rev. Robert Kirkley.

In 1956 Worrall's talent came to the attention of parapsychologist J. B. Rhine. Worrall's diagnoses frequently involved communicating with spirits of the dead related to the patient, and Rhine was collecting information on survival of death.

Worrall professed never to understand the true nature of the healing, but could only describe its conditions. Like other gifted healers, she knew the healing came not from herself, but from a higher power. She said gifted healers are biologically constructed to act like battery chargers: They take in the high-voltage energy of God and transform it into energy that can be used by living things. The process is aided by spiritual beings. In addition to people, Worrall healed animals, birds, and plants.

Worrall never studied medicine and said technical knowledge would only confuse her. She was adept at psychic diagnosis, clairvoyantly seeing afflicted parts of the body and knowing intuitively what to do to help them. Prayer was an essential part of the process. Both Worralls said love and compassion, a wholehearted desire to see the patient healed, was of paramount importance.

The Worralls had many spectacular and instantaneous cures, including tumors that shrank to nothing under their touch. Other healings required regular treatment over a period of time, some up to years. A minority of patients were not healed.

Ambrose Worrall died suddenly on February 2, 1972, and almost immediately began communicating with Olga from the other side. She saw him clairvoyantly on a few occasions and heard him clairaudiently. Ambrose confirmed her theory that healers have a certain biological construction by saying that her astral body (and his formerly) were perfect; healing energy flowed through them through the spiritual attunement of the astral body. He said he would stay near her and work with her to give her greater healing powers: When she placed her hands on a patient, he would be placing his as well. Her healings subsequent to his death became more impressive.

Worrall believed strongly that science must support religion, and underwent numerous scientific experiments to demonstrate that a tangible energy source comes through healers. During her life she was tested in the laboratory by physicians, physicists, parapsychologists, and others, including nuclear physicist Elizabeth Rauscher and biophysicist Beverly Rubik. Rubik observed a unique transfer of energy in Worrall's healings. In various tests Worrall energized water, changing its viscosity and electrical properties; sped the growth of rye grass through long-distance prayer; and created wave patterns in cloud chambers. In 1979 she underwent experiments at the University of California at Berkeley.

Tests showed that when Worrall was in her "healing state," or what psychologist Lawrence LeShan refers to as the "clairvoyant reality," her brain waves were at the delta level, the state of deep sleep—yet she was fully conscious and felt at her best. The moment of healing occurred when she and the patient tuned in to each other's wavelength; the patient also registered changes in brain-wave lengths. Other changes observed in Worrall included the extension of her energy field to eighteen feet around her, and increases in energy flowing from her hands during healing.

Worrall died of a heart ailment on January 9, 1985, in Baltimore, where she had worked until just before her death at the New Life Clinic. See **Healing, faith and psychic; Worrall, Ambrose.**

Sources: Edwina Cerutti. *Olga Worrall: Mystic with the Healing Hands.* New York: Harper & Row, 1975; Ronald S. Miller. "Mystic with the Healing Hands: An Interview with Olga Worrall." *Science of Mind* 56, no. 4 (April 1983): 8–12+; Ambrose A. Worrall with Olga N. Worrall. *The Gift of Healing: A Personal Story of Spiritual Therapy.* New York: Harper & Row, 1965; "Olga Worrall 1906–85." *Parapsychology Review* 16, no. 3 (May/June 1985): 9.

Worth, Patience

One of the most famous cases of automatic writing is that of Patience Worth, an alleged discarnate being who manifested through a Ouija board in 1913 to a St. Louis housewife, Pearl Curran. Curran, who had dropped out of school at age fourteen, was persuaded to use the Ouija by a friend, Emily Hutchinson. Curran had little interest, but participated in a number of sessions for more than a year. On July 8, 1913, the pointer spelled out the message, "Many moons ago I lived. Again I come. Patience Worth my name." The announcement marked the beginning of a long friendship and literary partnership between Curran and the mysterious spirit.

During subsequent sessions Patience Worth, speaking in archaic dialogue, revealed herself as an Englishwoman, born to a poor country family in Dorsetshire in 1649. A spinster, she emigrated to the American colonies late in life and was killed in an Indian massacre. She declined to say more about herself.

Hutchinson and Curran discovered that Curran alone could contact Worth through the Ouija, but not Hutchinson alone. Worth began to dictate an enormous volume of 2,500 poems, plus plays, short stories, allegories, epigrams, and six full-length novels, all in diverse historical settings—a total of 4 million words in five years, filling twenty-nine bound volumes. Her works were published and enjoyed great commercial and critical success, especially her first two novels, *The Sorry Tale*, a 300,000-word epic about the life of Jesus, and *Hope Trueblood*, set in Victorian England. *The Sorry Tale* took over two years to dictate through the Ouija. Other novels are *Telka, The Pot Upon the Wheel, Samuel Wheaton,* and *The Merry Tale.* Worth often wrote poetry on demand.

Curran used the Ouija for seven years. After five years she discovered she could anticipate the letters before they were spelled out, then began reciting the letters while the pointer circled the board aimlessly. In 1920 she discontinued use of the Ouija and simply recited the dictation as it came to her in automatic speech.

The relationship began to decline in 1922, when Curran became pregnant with her first child at age thirty-nine, and then suffered the deaths of her husband and mother. By the mid-1920s, public interest in Worth began to diminish, and Curran and Worth communicated less and less frequently. Curran died in 1937.

The writings of Worth have been analyzed by scholars and found to be authentic in detail of various historical periods, and well-constructed in plot and characterization. Controversy remains as to the real identity of Patience Worth. Some experts maintain that Curran, though uneducated, was merely channeling material from the depths of her subconscious or a collective human memory. The vocabulary used by Worth had a very high percentage—up to 90 percent in some stories—of Old English, much higher than that found in any English writing after the thirteenth century. Therefore it is unlikely that a person of rural southern England in the seventeenth century would use such language.

Others agree with Curran and Worth, that Worth indeed was a discarnate spirit with a literary bent, who, centuries after her death, was at last able to express herself creatively. See **Automatisms; Ouija.**

Sources: Gina Covina. *The Ouija Book.* New York: Simon & Schuster, 1979; Stoker Hunt. *Ouija: The Most Dangerous Game.* New York: Harper & Row, 1985; Irving Litvag. *Singer in the Shadows: The Strange Story of Patience Worth.* New York: Macmillan, 1972; Walter Franklin Prince. *The Case of Patience Worth.* Boston: Boston Society for Psychic Research, 1927; Jane Roberts. *The Coming of Seth.* New York: Pocket Books, 1976; Ian Stevenson. *Xenoglossy.* Charlottesville, VA: The University Press of Virginia, 1974.

Wrekin Trust

See **Planetary consciousness.**

X

Xenoglossy

The ability to speak in an unlearned foreign language. Xenoglossy is a phenomenon associated with some cases of past-life recall, and altered states of consciousness such as trance, delirium, sleep, and mediumship.

"Xenoglossy" was coined around the turn of the twentieth century by French physiologist Charles Richet, from the New Latin term *xeno* ("strange, foreign") and the Greek term *glossa* ("tongue"). Documented cases of true xenoglossy are rare. In many instances the "unlearned foreign language" proves to be learned but forgotten phrases dredged up from the subconscious, or pseudo-languages that are partly gibberish. In a few cases, it appears to be the result of telepathy between two people, such as a hypnotist and a subject. Xenoglossy is not to be confused with glossolalia, or "speaking in tongues." See **Glossolalia**.

There are two types of xenoglossy: recitative and responsive. Recitative xenoglossy, in which a person recites words or phrases of a foreign language without understanding their meaning and being able to converse, is more common. Usually, such phrases were learned earlier in life and then forgotten. See **Cryptomnesia**. In responsive xenoglossy the person is able to carry on a conversation in an unlearned language.

A famous case of recitative xenoglossy in past-life recall is that of Swarnlata Mishra, a Hindu girl born in 1948 and researched by Ian Stevenson in 1961. Between the ages of four and five, Swarnlata sang Bengali songs and performed Bengali dances without ever having been exposed to Bengali language or culture. She said she had been a Bengali woman in a previous life, and had learned the songs and dance from a friend.

One of the earliest recorded cases of responsive xenoglossy was reported in 1862 by Prince Galitzin, a mesmerist who magnetized an uneducated German woman. The woman told of a life in eighteenth-century France, and spoke French fluently. In her waking state, she knew no French.

The Jensen case, a hypnotic regression of a thirty-seven-year-old Philadelphia housewife, "T.E.," who was hypnotized by her physician husband, took place in a series of sessions from 1955 to 1956. The personality which emerged was "Jensen," a male peasant farmer who spoke an early form of Swedish in a deep, masculine voice. He was never fluent, but spoke with some effort, sometimes repeating phrases almost automatically. Nevertheless, he conversed in seventeenth-century colloquial Swedish. In deep trance T.E. denied that she ever studied any Scandinavian tongues. No subconscious knowledge of Swedish manifested during hypnosis while T.E. was not in the Jensen personality. Ian Stevenson concluded that T.E.'s ability to speak Swedish was paranormal.

Two other authentic responsive xenoglossy cases are those of Gretchen and Sharada. Gretchen, a German-speaking girl, manifested in 1970 during a hypnotic regression of Dolores Jay, wife of a Methodist minister in Elkton, Virginia. Gretchen understood simple English but responded only in imperfect German. She identified herself as Gretchen Gottlieb, daughter of the mayor of Eberswalde, Germany, who had died at about age sixteen. She apparently lived in the latter half of the nineteenth century. Dolores Jay had never studied German.

Sharada was a Bengali-speaking personality who took over the life of Uttara Huddar, a Marathi-speaking Indian woman, on and off for at least eight years. Huddar, born in 1941, was thirty-three years old when Sharada manifested. In 1974 Huddar was hospitalized for a skin disease. In the hospital she followed the instructions of a visiting yogi who taught patients how to meditate. Huddar then began to suffer extreme mood swings and became a different person, who identified herself as Sharada. Sharada could converse only in Bengali, a language unknown to Huddar and her family.

Sharada apparently had died at age twenty-three during the first half of the nineteenth century, but refused to believe she was dead. She periodically manifested for days or weeks at a time. Huddar and her family learned to coexist with the visiting personality.

Xenography, the writing of unlearned languages, is even more difficult to verify than xenoglossy. Most likely, it is the product of cryptomnesia. Richet reported the case of Madame X, a French medium, who wrote long sentences in Greek while in a state of partial dissociation. He discovered that many of the sentences came from a French-Greek dictionary. However, Gretchen and Sharada wrote in German and Bengali, respectively. See **Smith, Hélène.**

Sources: Rev. Carroll E. Jay. *Gretchen, I Am.* New York: Wyden Books, 1977; Ian Stevenson. *Twenty Cases Suggestive of Reincarnation.* 2d ed. Charlottesville, VA: University Press of Virginia, 1974; Ian Stevenson. *Unlearned Language: New Studies in Xenoglossy.* Charlottesville, VA: University Press of Virginia, 1984; Ian Stevenson. *Xenoglossy.* Charlottesville, VA: University Press of Virginia, 1974; Helen Wambach. *Reliving Past Lives.* New York: Harper & Row Perennial Library, 1978; Benjamin B. Wolman, ed. *Handbook of Parapsychology.* New York: Van Nostrand Reinhold, 1977.

Y

Yantra

See Mandala.

Yeats, William Butler

See Hermetic Order of the Golden Dawn.

Yin and yang

See Bodywork; Martial arts; Taoism; Universal life force.

Yoga

Various systems of spiritual discipline and liberation from the senses. "Yoga" is a Sanskrit term derived from the root *yuj*, "to harness horses to a chariot." In yoga one seeks to become bound to divine reality. Yoga has been developed into a philosophy, but its origins and essence are nonintellectual, even anti-intellectual, and entirely experiential. It is meaningful only if practiced. In yoga the search for the mystery of the universe is undertaken in a search for one's own true self.

Types of Yoga

There are different types of yoga, each of which is based on a specific path of liberation, such as physical action, meditation, concentration, mantras, knowledge, sexual energy, and so on. Some yogas are combinations of other yogas. The goal of all of them is to liberate the spirit from matter and join with the Absolute.

Bhakti Yoga, the path of devotion and love, is centered on a deity, mystic, or saint, or on a task in life. Through bhakti one enters spiritual service.

Hatha Yoga, the purification of the body through physical exercise, consists of thousands òf postures called *asanas*. The purification of the body leads to harmony with, and growth of, mental and spiritual processes. Hatha Yoga is the most popular form in the West, but unfortunately is often practiced strictly for its physical benefits.

Jnana Yoga is the path of knowledge. Wisdom gained through observation, study, and experiment is reflected and meditated upon.

Karma Yoga is the path of selfless service. One performs one's dharma (duty) in everyday acts and business, without attachment to the acts or the fruits of the acts.

Mantra Yoga is the path of prayer and sacred sound through the use of mantras. The most sacred mantra is Om or Aum. See **Om**.

Raja Yoga is the path of mind control through concentration, breath control, posture, meditation, and contemplation. Raja Yoga is the most metaphysical of yogas.

Some yogas combine these yogas. Integral Yoga is a synthesis of yogas emphasizing the whole being, created by Sri Aurobindo. See **Aurobindo, Sri.** Kundalini Yoga utilizes posture and mantra to raise the primal *kundalini* force. See **Kundalini.** Laya Yoga utilizes meditation, breath control, mantras, visualizations, and postures to cleanse the chakra system and raise kundalini. See **Chakras.** Tantric Yoga focuses on the arousal of sexual energy, which is converted to kundalini. Alchemical rites involve the transmutation of kundalini to achieve longevity. See **Alchemy.** Buddhist Tantrism cultivates supernormal powers and the use of magic.

History and Development

Yoga is ancient and predates Brahminism, the early religion forced on the Indus valley by Aryan conquerors between 1500 and 800 B.C. The oldest archaeological evidence for yoga, a faience seal depicting a man in a lotus position, dates to the third millennium B.C. Brahminism, the literature of which was the Vedas, was rigid and materialistic, and yoga existed outside of its bounds as a freelance form of religious thought called Sramanism. Yogis, who espoused austerity, meditation, and nonviolence, were sometimes tolerated and even admired by Brahmins, but often were persecuted and driven out.

Yogis and other Sramanas produced the early Upanishads, which replaced the Vedas and ushered in a new era, Vedanta ("end of the Vedas"), from which modern Hinduism evolved. The Upanishads, which evolved over a period of about one thousand years, present such concepts as Brahman, the Absolute; Atman, the Higher Self; the goal to unite with Brahman; maya, the illusory nature of reality; karma and reincarnation; Aum, the sacred sound representing Brahman and the supreme means to salvation; and the practice of yoga to unite with Brahman.

Yoga is found in Jainism, which in turn influenced yoga, especially concerning the principle of nonviolence and the doctrines of karma and reincarnation. Yoga practices and teachings were introduced to Asia by Gautama Buddha (566 B.C.–486 B.C.), called "the greatest of all yogis." Yoga became part of the various forms of Buddhism that developed, including the Ch'an and Zen meditative schools of China and Japan, respectively.

The *Bhagavad-Gita,* said to have been written by Vyasa between 500 B.C. and 200 B.C., had the greatest influence on the development of yoga; it is the prime literature of both yoga and Hinduism. The *Gita* is a chapter in the *Mahabharata,* an epic poem. It deals with Jnana and Bhakti Yoga, nonviolence, karma, reincarnation and dharma, and introduces the concept of Karma Yoga, thus bringing yoga for the first time out of the realm of the ascetic and into the daily life of all.

Another major influence was the *Yoga Sutras* of Patanjali, essentially a Raja Yoga, and the first systemization and codification of its basic principles, practices, and expected results. There is disagreement as to who was the Patanjali who compiled the Sutras, and when he lived. He has been identified with a Sanskrit grammarian by that name who lived c. 300 B.C., and with another Patanjali who lived c. A.D. 400.

The Sutras are divided into four books: principles, disciplines, miraculous powers (*siddhis*), and illumination. By observing the principles and practicing the disciplines, the yogi attains various states of *samadhi,* contemplation of Reality, the highest of which is a prelude to nirvana, or union with the Absolute. The process takes numerous incarnations, with the yogi resuming in one life where he had left off in the previous life. As part of the process, the yogi attains miraculous powers, such as psychic abilities and the power to fly. They are not end goals, but are considered obstacles to the goal of illumination. See **Siddhis.**

According to Patanjali there are eight steps in yoga for achieving liberation: (1) *yama* (control or restraints); (2) *niyama* (disciplines); (3) *asana* (posture and bodily attitude); (4) *pranayama* (breath control); (5) *pratyahara* (liberation of the senses from exterior objects); (6) *dharana* (concentration); (7) *dhyana* (yogic meditation); and (8) samadhi.

Patanjali's *Sutras* enabled yoga to be understood in a more intellectual and philosophical light. Further systemization continued through the eighteenth century.

In Asia, under the influence of Buddhism, Confucianism, Taoism, and Bön (the early religion of Tibet), yoga evolved into different systems, but still with the same goal of union with the Absolute. Buddhist yoga places more emphasis on the illusion of everything and the negation of ego (Jnana Yoga, on the other hand, acknowledges the existence of ego). The realization of Voidness is the great aim of Theravada Buddhism and Tibetan Buddhism; for to realize it is to attain Dharma-Kaya, the "Divine Body of Truth," the primordial state of uncreatedness.

Tibetan yoga is practiced as a cure to ailments. A higher form of Tibetan yoga is the yoga of dying, as described in the Bardo Thödöl, the Book of the Dead. The Bardo Thödöl, first written down in the eighth century but of ancient origins, places great importance on conscious dying, so that the spirit will be able to truly perceive the forty-nine-day after-death period, culminating, for all but the most enlightened, in another reincarnation. Yoga practiced during life helps prepare one for what to expect after death. There is more emphasis on magic and miraculous powers in Tibetan yoga. Of particular importance are the powers of telepathy; *lung-gom,* a form of effortless and rapid travel by foot; *tumo,* or psychic heat, used to keep warm; and dream recall. See **David-Neel, Alexandra; Milarepa.**

Yoga was exported westward first by the Sufis, during the Moslem invasions of India between 1200 and 1700, but never reached Europe. That was accomplished largely through the colonialism of Britain. Beginning in the nineteenth century, major influences on the spread of yoga west were the Theosophical Society and various Indian mystics, among them Ramakrishna (1836–1886), Aurobindo (1872–1950), Ramana Maharshi (1879–1950), and Yogananda (1893–1952). Yogananda was ordered to the United States by his guru in 1922. He settled in California and remained the rest of his life, spreading yoga teachings. His widely read *Autobiography of a Yogi* (1949) is considered a classic of yoga literature. More recently, yoga teachings and training were spread by Swami Sivananda and Swami Muktananda, the latter of whom became renowned for his reputed siddhi powers.

Yoga does have pitfalls and dangers, as does any occult study. The serious student ideally should work under the supervision of a guru or other teacher. The dangers of yoga are extreme introversion, spiritual hedonism, regression (especially with unprepared novices), and emotional fixation on the guru. See **Drugs in mystical and psychic experiences; Guru; Mandala; Mantra; Meditation; Mystical experiences; Zen.**

Sources: Bernard Bromage. *Tibetan Yoga.* 1952. Wellingborough, Northamptonshire, England: The Aquarian Press, 1979; Mircea Eliade. *Yoga: Immortality and Freedom.* 1958. 2d ed. Princeton, NJ: Princeton University Press, 1969; W. Y. Evans-Wentz, ed. *The Tibetan Book of the Dead.* 3d ed. London: Oxford University Press, 1960; W. Y. Evans-Wentz. *Tibetan Yoga and Secret Doctrines.* 2d ed. London: Oxford University Press, 1958; Willard Johnson. *Riding the Ox Home: A History* of *Meditation from Shamanism to Science.* 1982. Boston: Beacon Press, 1986; M. P. Pandit. *Sri Aurobindo and His Yoga.* Wilmot, WI: Lotus Light Publications, 1987; Bhagwan Shree Patanjali. *Aphorisms of Yoga.* 1928. Translated by Shree Purohit Swami. Introduction by W. B. Yeats. London: Faber and Faber, 1973; Charles T. Tart, ed. *Transpersonal Psychologies.* New York: Harper & Row, 1975; Vivian Worthington. *A History of Yoga.* London: Routledge & Kegan Paul, 1982.

Yogic flying

See **Levitation; Transcendental Meditation.**

Z

Zeitoun

See **Marian apparitions.**

Zen

Sect of Buddhism that developed in China
and Japan, and perhaps the best-known
Buddhist sect in the West because of its
appealing, highly mystical nature. "Zen"
is the Japanese pronunciation of the Chinese term *Ch'an,* an abbreviation of
Ch'an-na, the Chinese approximation of
the Sanskrit term *dhyana,* or meditation.
The Way of Zen is the Way of Meditation.

Like Buddhism in general, Zen has
virtually no theology. It is almost entirely
philosophy, yet it is more than philosophy. It cannot be conceptualized by intellect and logic; it must be experienced.
Enlightenment is the sudden awakening
to the nature of one's own being. It is
the responsibility of the individual and
cannot be obtained through faith in a
deity or savior, through intercession or
through education. Zen stresses the development of an intuitive wisdom that
sees the oneness of all.

Buddhism began penetrating into
China in the first century A.D. Zen developed through the teachings of Bodhidharma, an Indian monk who arrived
in China sometime during the early
sixth century and disseminated teachings,

based on the Mahayana sutras, that were
distinct from other Buddhist schools in
China. Little fact is know about Bodhidharma; legends that sprang up attribute
miraculous features to him. According to
legend he was the Twenty-eighth Patriarch (master) of Buddhism in a line originating with Shakyamuni Buddha, the
Enlightened One, and he went to China
with the intent of establishing Zen there
as its First Patriarch. He became known
as the *pi-kuan* ("wall-contemplating" or
"wall-gazing") Brahman for the nine
years he spent meditating while facing a
wall, until his legs withered away. His
fate is unknown: according to different
legends, he was either poisoned by his ri-
vals, returned eventually to India, or went
on to Japan. He is alleged to have lived to
150 years; he died sometime prior to 534.
The term "pi-kuan" came to be regarded
as the expression for the way to enlightenment in Zen, not in the literal sense of
wall-gazing, but in the steepness and sud-
denness of enlightenment.

Following Bodhidharma the one
who is considered the true founder of
Zen in China was Hui-neng (637–713),
the Sixth Patriarch, who influenced the
adaptation of Buddhism to Chinese
thought. Hui-neng described Zen as "seeing into one's own Nature," a phrase that
crystallizes the essence of Zen enlightenment and is the most significant phrase
ever coined in the development of Zen,
according to Zen philosopher D. T. Su-

Zafus *(cushions)* and zabutons *(mats)* laid out for meditation

Zen meditators

zuki. Hui-neng was posthumously named the "Zen Master of the Great Mirror." The mirror symbolizes in Zen the enlightened mind; the absence of all thoughts is pure mirror-activity in which the mind clings to no object. Hui-neng realized the mirror-nature of the mind in an experience of sudden enlightenment. He taught that "enlightenment is your own nature. Originally it was entirely pure. Only avail yourselves of this mind and you will immediately become a Buddha." In other words, the mind already possesses enlightenment; it merely must be realized.

Following Hui-neng Zen rose to great prominence in China, achieving its peak during the Sung Dynasty (960–1279), a time when other Buddhist sects were declining. Two dominant streams emerged: the Lin-chi sect, which developed the use of paradoxes (called koan in Japanese) as an intense and systematic way to enlightenment, and the Ts'ao-tung sect, which emphasized enlightenment through passive, silent meditation.

In Japan Zen ideas were imported during the Nara period (seventh and eighth centuries), but Zen did not begin to expand and flourish until the monk Eisai (1141–1215) founded the Rinzai (Japanese for "Lin-chi") sect of Zen in 1191. Shortly afterward the Soto (Japanese for "Ts'ao-tung") sect was founded by another monk, Dogen (1200–1253), who remains the most revered of all Japanese Zen masters and is considered a bodhisattva (enlightened one who helps others attain enlightenment). The Rinzai sect adopted the Lin-chi emphasis on koan, while the Soto sect adopted the Ts'ao-tung sect emphasis on silent meditation.

In Japan little of substance was added to the teachings of the Chinese, but Zen nonetheless took on its own unique Japanese character. It flourished and permeated the Japanese culture, remaining a vital force to the present. It has especially influenced the arts and is the basis of the tea ceremony (Dogen imported the first tea from China). See **Martial arts; Sports, mystical and psychic phenomena in.**

Zen, other forms of Buddhism, and Hinduism were introduced to the West in the nineteenth century, and captured the interest of the Trancendentalists. In 1893 Zen was represented at the World Parliament of Religions in Chicago in 1893. Zen teachers and masters were among the Asians who began immigrating to the West, where they taught Zen to an increasing audience. Perhaps the greatest influence on the spread of Zen in the West have been the writings of D. T. Suzuki (1870–1966), Japanese scholar and philosopher; Christmas Humphreys, British journalist and founder of the Buddhist Society; and Alan Watts (1915–1973), British-born theologian and philosopher who, after coming to America, became identified with Zen but never considered himself a Zenist. See **Watts, Alan.**

In Zen enlightenment—satori—can be achieved only by turning the consciousness inward, and meditation is the key means of doing so. The heart of Zen meditation is *zazen,* which literally means "sitting meditation," and traditionally is done in a lotus posture with eyes open and cast slightly downward, and hands forming an oval meditation mudra (gesture) at the abdomen. See **Lotus seat.** As an alternative one may sit in a kneeling posture on a small bench. Breath-counting is employed as one way to empty thoughts and train the mind to achieve *samadhi,* a state of one-pointed concentration. The student must overcome various delusions that are obstacles to samadhi and satori: fantasies, random thoughts, and *makyo,* or "mysterious visions," which are dream-like fantasies, visions, and voices, feelings of bodily distortions, and so on. Makyo constitute a form of pseudo-satori, similar to the pseudo-nirvana described in the Buddhist meditation tract, the *Visuddhimagga.* See **Meditation.** Makyo indicate progress, but must be released as they arise. Other delusions include intense emotions, preoccupation with personal problems, self-doubt, and pain from remaining motionless in posture for long periods of time.

Dogen is considered the greatest master of zazen, for he saw in it the realization of the whole of the Law of Buddha. Dogen said that zazen and enlightenment are one and the same: Enlightenment is already contained in the exercise of meditation. He did not reject the use of koan, but considered them of secondary importance. The unity of all things is the solution to all koan.

The koan are unique to Zen and are a means of achieving a breakthrough in consciousness. They are illogical and cannot be solved intellectually. There are said to be 1,700 koan; perhaps the best-known are, "What is the sound of one hand clapping?" and "What is Mu?" The

student contemplates and meditates upon the koan—perhaps for months—until the answer is seen in a moment of sudden illumination.

In a *zendo* (meditation hall), zazen is interspersed with chanting, bowing, and *kinhin,* a formal walking meditation. The study of Zen is undertaken with a *roshi* (literally, "old teacher"), who is not a guru but a guide.

Sanzen is zazen with consultation—the receipt of a koan and consultation on progress with the roshi.

Suizen is "blowing meditation," an ancient art dating from ninth-century Japan. The instrument used is the *shakuhachi,* the Japanese bamboo flute. The music, which has been handed down orally from master to pupil and is the only music ever used in Zen meditation, recreates the healing and revitalizing qualities of forest breezes and ocean tides.

Satori, the breakthrough of mature Zen consciousness, is, in the words of Suzuki, the "Alpha and Omega" of Zen, and constitutes the beginning of the Zen experience. Satori is the opening of a third eye, a seeing from a new point of view, an awareness of one's own nature. It is beyond duality, a sudden leap to the absolute, timeless nonduality. In meditation it follows (but not always) a period of samadhi. Satori also may come unexpectedly while going about daily activities, the result of years of preparation and practice.

Precious little is written about the experience of satori. Unlike Christian mystics, who have sought to describe the ineffable, couching it often in erotic and highly personal terms, Zen masters simply state that they attain enlightenment. In the Zen experience—and in the Buddhist experience in general—enlightenment is much more impassive and impersonal than in the Christian experience of uniting with a Creator deity. The results, however, are the same for these and all mystical paths: the opening of the heart and the burning away of material attachments and negative attributes.

Suzuki termed satori "an insight into the Unconscious," and described eight characteristics: irrationality, intuitive insight, authoritativeness, affirmation, sense of the beyond, impersonal tone, feeling of exaltation, and momentariness. Psychiatrist Carl G. Jung interpreted satori as the "great liberation" of the unconscious, the totality of the nature of the soul.

Once the initial satori is achieved, it is deepened through meditation until a state of "no-mind" evolves. No-mind, also called "no-thought," is real seeing, beyond the duality of subject-object, and which has no reference to a specific state of consciousness. In no-mind the clarity of satori permeates daily life and manifests in all acts.

Regardless of whether or not satori and no-mind have been attained (processes that consume years if not entire lifetimes), the Zen student seeks in daily life to observe the Ten Grave Precepts and to follow the bodhisattva ideal. The Ten Grave Precepts are: no killing; no stealing; no misuse of sex (that is, perversion or exploitation); no lying; no dealing in intoxicants (originally a reference to alcohol, but includes anything which clouds perception); no speaking of faults of others; no praising of yourself while abusing others; no sparing of Dharma assets (the teachings of the Buddha); no indulgence in anger; and no slandering of the Three Treasures, which are the Buddha, the Dharma, and the Sangha (the way of life of a group of spiritual seekers). The bodhisattva ideal is expressed in the Four Vows:

Sentient beings are numberless, I vow to free them;

Delusions are inexhaustible, I vow to put an end to them;

The Dharma gates are boundless, I vow to open them;

The Enlightened Way is unsurpassable, I vow to embody it.

See **Buddhism; Mystical experiences; Mysticism.**

Sources: Robert Aitken. *Taking the Path of Zen.* San Francisco: North Point Press, 1982; Heinrich Dumoulin. *A History of Zen Buddhism.* London: Faber and Faber, 1963; Rick Fields. *How the Swans Came to the Lake: A Narrative History of Buddhism in America.* Boulder, CO: Shambhala Publications, 1981; Daniel Goleman. *The Meditative Mind: The Varieties of Meditative Experience.* Los Angeles: Jeremy P. Tarcher, 1988; Christmas Humphreys. *A Western Approach to Zen.* Wheaton, IL: The Theosophical Publishing House, 1971; Yong Choon Kim. *Oriental Thought.* Totowa, NJ: Rowman and Littlefield, 1973; D. T. Suzuki. *Zen Buddhism: Selected Writings of D.T. Suzuki.* Edited by William Barrett. Garden City, NY: Anchor Books/Doubleday, 1956; D. T. Suzuki. *The Field of Zen.* New York: Harper & Row, 1970; Alan W. Watts. *The Way of Zen.* New York: Vintage Books, 1957.

Zener cards

See **ESP cards.**

Zombie

A dead person supposedly brought back to a robot-like life through the magical offices of a *bokor,* a Vodoun sorcerer, to perform as a slave. Zombification has been described as the African slave's ultimate nightmare, since not even death releases the slave from unending labor. A natural explanation exists for this seemingly supernatural creature.

The word "zombie," also spelled "zombi," probably comes from the Congo word *nzambi,* which means "the spirit of a dead person." Yet a truly dead person—one who has lost all bodily function, whose brain has ceased operating—cannot be returned to life. In his studies of Haitian Vodoun and zombies, ethnobiologist Wade Davis reasoned that the zombie was a person buried alive, who only seemed dead through extensive drug intoxication. Davis's investigation with various Vodoun priests, or *houngan*, and two people who claimed to be zombies, confirmed that zombies are created by giving the victim a powerful poison, administered topically through an open wound or ingested in the victim's food. The poison, usually a powder, contains various toxic plants and animals and often human remains. The poison puts the victim into a death-like state; the bokor revives the victim with other drugs.

One of the most important ingredients of making a zombie is gland secretions from the bouga toad, bufogenin and bufotoxin, compounds fifty to one hundred times more potent than digitalis, and which cause death by rapid heartbeat and eventual failure. The secretions also contain bufotenine, a hallucinogen.

Other ingredients are ground millipedes and tarantulas; the skins of poisonous white tree frogs; and four types of puffer fish, which contain tetrodotoxin, one of the most poisonous substances in the world—five hundred times more toxic than cyanide, and 150,000 times more potent than cocaine. The powder also contains various plant products: *tcha-tcha* seeds from the albizzia lebbeck tree, a poisonous plant that causes pulmonary edema; *consigne* seeds from a type of mahogany tree with no known toxic properties; leaves from the *pomme cajou*, or common cashew (*Anacardium occidentale*), and the *bresillet* tree (*Comocladia glabra*), which are related to poison ivy and cause severe skin irritations; *maman guepes* (*Urera baccifera*) and *mashasa* (*Dalechampia scandens*), which belong to the stinging nettle family and inject a chemical similar to formic acid into the skin; *Dieffenbachia seguine*, which contains oxalate needles that cause the larynx to swell and make breathing difficult and speaking impossible; and *bwa pine* (*Zanthoxylum matinicense*), which has sharp spines. Ground human remains can be added for effect.

When these drugs are administered, the victim suffers malaise, pallor, dizziness, and a tingling sensation that eventually leads to complete numbness. Next the victim salivates profusely, then sweats, suffering extreme weakness, headache, and subnormal body temperatures, followed by decreased blood pressure and rapid, weak pulse. Next come nausea, vomiting, diarrhea, and gastric pain. The pupils constrict then dilate, then lose all corneal and pupillary reflexes. The lungs suffer severe respiratory distress, then the lips, extremities, and finally the entire body turn blue. First the body twitches crazily, then becomes completely paralyzed. The eyes glaze over, the body cannot move, and the victim may fall into a coma.

Not all survive. Those who do remain conscious and witness their own funeral and burial. The bokor raises the victim from his or her tomb in a day or two, and administers a hallucinogenic concoction of sweet potato, cane sugar, and *Datura stramonium*, commonly called the "zombie's cucumber." Beaten psychologically and sometimes physically, disoriented and desperately frightened, the zombie answers to a new name and follows the bokor into a new "life." Tribal Africans believe that lazy people in life risk being made zombies after death, condemned to work for the bokor into eternity. Traditionally, zombies work the fields, although some believe they are responsible for other work performed at night, like bread baking. A few serve as bookkeepers, and one story tells of a zombie working in a shop. Zombies require little food, but cannot be given salt, which gives them the power of speech and taste and activates a homing instinct that sends the zombies back to their graves away from the bokor's influence.

In Vodoun sorcerers also are said to create zombies by capturing the soul—the *ti bon ange* ("little good angel") of the deceased. The *zombie astral* wanders at the command of the bokor. To guard against such a fate, the deceased's relatives "kill" the body twice, stabbing it in the heart or decapitating it. Without the soul the body is empty, matter without morality. Haitians do not fear being harmed by a zombie as much as becoming one. See **Vodoun.**

Sources: Sharon Begley. "Zombies and Other Mysteries." *Newsweek* (February 22, 1988). Daniel Cohen. *Voodoo, Devils and the New Invisible World.* New York: Dodd, Mead & Co., 1972; Wade Davis. *The Serpent and the Rainbow.* New York: Simon & Schuster/Warner Books, 1985; Mircea Eliade, ed. in chief. *The Encyclopedia of Religion.* New York: Macmillan, 1987; Walter B. Gibson. *Witchcraft.* New York: Grosset & Dunlap, 1973.